China

a Lonely Planet travel survival kit

Chris Taylor
Robert Storey
Nicko Goncharoff
Michael Buckley
Clem Lindenmayer
Alan Samagalski

China

5th edition

Published by
Lonely Planet Publications
Head Office: PO Box 617, Hawthorn, Vic 3122, Australia
Branches: 155 Filbert St, Suite 251, Oakland, CA 94607, USA
10 Barley Mow Passage, Chiswick, London W4 4PH, UK
71 bis rue du Cardinal Lemoine, 75005 Paris, France

Printed by
SNP Printing Pte Ltd, Singapore

Photographs by

Chris Beall (Retna Pictures)	Glenn Beanland	Sonia Berto	Nicko Goncharoff
Clem Lindenmayer	Richard Nebesky	Jo O'Brien	Robert Storey
Chris Taylor	Tony Wheeler		

Photographs for the colour section on Chinese Cuisine were taken by Glenn Beanland

Front cover: Photograph of part of a shop sign on a wall in Hong Kong. This particular character represents 'clock' or 'bell'. (Glenn Beanland)

First Published
October 1984

This Edition
July 1996
Reprinted with December 1996 Update supplement

Although the authors and publisher have tried to make the information as accurate as possible, they accept no responsibility for any loss, injury or inconvenience sustained by any person using this book.

National Library of Australia Cataloguing in Publication Data

Taylor, Chris, 1961 –.
China.

5th ed.
Includes index.
ISBN 0 86442 363 2.

1. China – Guidebooks. I. Goncharoff, Nicko. II. Storey, Robert.
III. Title. (Series: Lonely Planet travel survival kit).

915.10459

text & maps © Lonely Planet 1996
photos © photographers as indicated 1996
climate charts compiled from information supplied by Patrick J Tyson, © Patrick J Tyson, 1996

Chris Taylor

Chris grew up in England and Australia. After completing a degree in English literature and Chinese, he joined the Lonely Planet team to head our phrasebook series. He is currently based in Taiwan as a freelance writer. His work has appeared in *Tokyo Journal*, *The Asia Wall Street Journal*, *The Australian* and various other magazines and newspapers. Chris is also author of Lonely Planet's *Tibet*, *Tokyo city guide* and the *Mandarin phrasebook*; he has coauthored Lonely Planet guides to *Japan* and *Malaysia*, and is presently working on *Cambodia* and *South-East Asia on a shoestring*.

Robert Storey

Robert has had a colourful and chequered past, starting with his first job as a monkey-keeper at a zoo and continuing with a stint as a slot-machine repairman in a Las Vegas casino. After graduating from the University of Nevada in Las Vegas, he went on the road. Shortly after he washed ashore in Taiwan, he got his first respectable job (English teacher). He then diligently applied himself to learning Chinese, studying computer hacking and writing for Lonely Planet. Robert has written or contributed to several Lonely Planet guides, including *Beijing, Seoul, Hong Kong, Macau & Guangzhou* and *Taiwan*.

Nicko Goncharoff

Nicko was born and raised in New York, escaping at age 17 to Colorado, where he hiked, climbed, skied, partied and attended university. Inspired by his globe-trotting father, Nicko bought a one-way ticket to Taiwan immediately upon graduating. He stayed for three years, working as a translator and copy editor, before moving to a job at the Hong Kong bureau of a financial news wire service. Four years later, Nicko joined the Lonely Planet team for this edition of the *China* guide. He has also written Lonely Planet's *Hong Kong city guide*. His home is in Boulder, Colorado.

Michael Buckley

Michael was raised in Australia and has travelled extensively throughout Asia, including trekking and mountain-biking in the Himalayan and Karakoram ranges. He coauthored the first edition of this book and is the author of the travelogue *Cycling to Xian*, which is about bicycling across China and Tibet.

Clem Lindenmayer

Clem developed a love for mountains and languages and for both reasons China caught his attention. Having made the fateful resolution to learn Chinese on a solo trek through Lapland, he studied the language intermittently for several years. He contributed to the fourth edition of *China* and is the author of Lonely Planet's *Trekking in the Patagonian Andes*.

Alan Samagalski

Alan left Melbourne University to work at some legendary Melbourne comedy venues and to travel in Asia. He was the coauthor of the first and second editions of *China* and has worked on Lonely Planet's *Australia*, *Hong Kong, Macau & Canton*, *Bali & Lombok*, *Indonesia* and *Chile*.

From the Authors

See page 990 for authors' acknowledgments.

This Book

The first edition of this book appeared after Michael Buckley and Alan Samagalski spent many months on the road in China in 1983. Alan Samagalski and Robert Strauss researched and wrote the second edition, preparing the way for Joe Cummings and Robert Storey for the third edition. The fourth edition was researched by Robert Storey, Chris Taylor and Clem Lindenmayer. This edition (the fifth) was researched by Chris Taylor, Robert Storey and Nicko Goncharoff. All those involved in producing this book greatly appreciate the contributions of the travellers who put so much effort into writing and telling us of their experiences. Their names appear on page 991.

From the Publisher

This fully revised fifth edition of *China* was produced through the collective effort of a number of people in LP's Melbourne office. Linda Suttie was the editorial coordinator and Louise Keppie was the design coordinator. Editing and proofing were done by Ian Ward, Miriam Cannell, Kristin Odijk, Joanne Horsburgh, Helen Castle, Megan Fraser, Rachel Scully and Christine Niven. Greg Alford provided editorial guidance. Ian proofed the Chinese script and mastered the Chinese software program, as well as helping decipher script.

Louise designed and laid out the book, and was assisted in the mapping by Paul Piaia, Sally Woodward, Chris Lee-Ack, Indra Kilfoyle, Adam McCrow and Chris Klep. Illustrations were drawn by Louise, Trudi Canavan and Michael Signal. Simon Bracken and Adam designed the cover. Valerie Tellini cast a critical eye over the final art pages.

Computer gurus Dan Levin and Rob Flynn set up the soft fonts and instructed in the use of the Chinese software. Miriam Cannell and Kerrie Williams compiled the index. Alex English and Verity Campbell provided additional information on China.

Warning & Request

Things change – prices go up, schedules change, good places go bad and bad places go bankrupt – nothing stays the same. So if you find things better or worse, recently opened or long since closed, please write and tell us and help make the next edition better.

Your letters will be used to help update future editions and, where possible, important changes will also be included in an Update section in reprints.

We greatly appreciate all information that is sent to us by travellers. Back at Lonely Planet we employ a hard-working readers' letters team to sort through the many letters we receive. The best ones will be rewarded with a free copy of the next edition or another Lonely Planet guide if you prefer. We give away lots of books, but, unfortunately, not every letter/postcard receives one.

Contents

Map Legend

BOUNDARIES

————————— International Boundary
————————— Regional Boundary
————————— Disputed Boundary

ROUTES

————————— Freeway
————————— Highway
————————— Major Road
————————— Unsealed Road or Track
————————— City Road
————————— City Street
+‡+‡+‡+‡+‡ Railway
————————— Metro
————————— Walking Track
·················· Walking Tour
————————— Ferry Route
‡+‡+‡+‡+‡+ Cable Car or Chairlift

AREA FEATURES

Parks
Built-Up Area
Pedestrian Mall
Market or Shopping
+ + + + + + Cemetery
Reef
Beach or Desert
Rocks

HYDROGRAPHIC FEATURES

Coastline
River, Creek
Intermittent River or Creek
Rapids, Waterfalls
Lake, Intermittent Lake
Canal
Swamp

SYMBOLS

✪ CAPITAL	National Capital	◔	◨	Embassy, Petrol Station
◉ Capital	Regional Capital	✈	✝	Airport, Airfield
◍ CITY	Major City	◓	✿	Metro Station, Gardens
● City	City	❖	🐘	Shopping Centre, Zoo
● Town	Town	☗	▭	Bike Rental, Gate
● Village	Village	←	A25	One Way Street, Route Number
▪ ▼	Place to Stay, Place to Eat	ﬡ	▲	Stately Home, Monument
⚓ ▼	Cafe, Pub or Bar	◪	▣	Castle, Tomb
✉ ☎	Post Office, Telephone	⌒	⌂	Cave, Hut or Chalet
❶ ❾	Tourist Information, Bank	▲	✳	Mountain or Hill, Lookout
◒ ▣	Transport, Parking	☖	⋎	Lighthouse, Shipwreck
⛪ ⌂	Museum, Youth Hostel	)(	◎	Pass, Spring
⛺ ⛕	Caravan Park, Camping Ground	㇅	⚡	Beach, Surf Beach
✛ ✚	Church, Cathedral	∴		Archaeological Site or Ruins
◖ ❂	Mosque, Synagogue			Ancient or City Wall
▣ ⅶ	Temple, Hindu Temple	⟶ ⟵		Cliff or Escarpment, Tunnel
✛ ★	Hospital, Police Station	++++■++++		Railway Station

Note: not all symbols displayed above appear in this book

Introduction

After almost 30 years of being closed for repairs, the Middle Kingdom finally swung open its big red doors in the late 1970s. Tour groups trickled in, but the prospects for individual travel looked extremely dim. Individuals were welcome to the People's Republic of China (PRC) by invitation only. The first hint that things might be changing was the arrival of solo visitors from Sweden and France (nations favoured by China), who stepped off the Trans-Siberian Railway in 1979.

In 1981, with little fanfare, the Chinese began issuing visas to solo and uninvited travellers through a couple of their embassies overseas, but mainly through various agencies in Hong Kong. News spread slowly by word of mouth, until by 1983 it seemed that just about everyone who landed in Hong Kong was going to China. After all, the world had been waiting over 30 years to travel in the country unfettered by tour guides.

Fifteen years later, the Chinese world has changed immensely. Gone is the socialist paradise of hardy peasants and sturdy workers, uniformly clothed in blue, fashioning a brave new world to the beat of the hammer and anvil. Today a growing middle class shops for Chanel perfume and Lacoste polo shirts. Chinese cinematic productions sweep up awards in the film festivals of Europe. Chinese rockers perform on Asian MTV. China's first sex shop opened recently in Beijing. McDonald's and KFC have spawned a fast-food revolution in Chinese eating habits. And karaoke has invaded the East and set the whole of China singing.

As many commentators like to remark – perhaps a little hopefully – China is becoming more and more like other countries. To be sure, the problems of travel permits, dual currencies, poor transport connections, poor sanitation and lackadaisical service standards have all been vastly improved. But problems remain. China is not always an easy country to travel in. Rampant inflation and a booming local tourist industry have pushed hotel and transportation prices

11

through the roof in many provinces; the increased mobility of local Chinese has put a squeeze on the availability of train and flight tickets; and the authorities are still bent on enforcing double-pricing systems and keeping foreigners out of certain hotels. To top it all off, many foreigners complain that the need to be constantly alert for rip-offs is exhausting.

Nevertheless, somewhere between the push and shove of railway station crowds, the overcharging and the clangour of jack-hammers, China is an experience that stays with you for years after you leave. From the deserts of Xinjiang to the mountains of Tibet, from the Forbidden City of Beijing to the Army of Terracotta Warriors of Xi'an, from relaxing getaways like Yangshuo and Dali to Shanghai's juggernaut assault on the future, China packs more punch than almost anywhere else in the world. What's more, whether we like it or not, something miraculous is happening in China – the latest of many revolutions. The country is reinventing itself.

The sleeping giant stood up in 1949 and, whatever you feel about the place, China is a country that cannot be ignored.

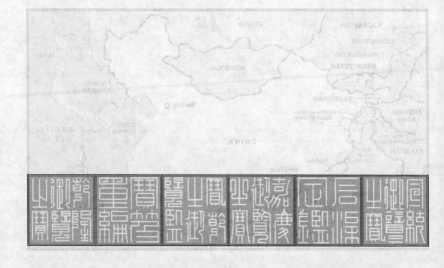

Facts about the Country

HISTORY
Mythological Beginnings
The Chinese claim a history of 5000 years, but early 'records' are of a mythological and legendary nature. The very existence of the Xia Dynasty, documented in early Chinese histories as the first Chinese dynasty, still awaits archaeological verification.

According to legend, the Xia was preceded by a succession of three sovereigns and five emperors. The first of the three sovereigns, Fuxi, is usually depicted alongside his wife and sister, the goddess Nügua. The two are human from the waist up but have dragons' tails. Nügua is credited with

having fashioned human beings from clay and having created the institution of marriage, while Fuxi bestowed the gifts of hunting, fishing and animal husbandry. The ox-headed Shennong, another of the three sovereigns, bestowed agriculture and knowledge of the medicinal properties of plants on the Chinese.

Like the three sovereigns, the five emperors are each credited with having founded certain key elements of the Chinese cultural tradition. For example, the first of them, Huang Di, is said to have brought the agricultural calendar, boats, armour and pottery to the Chinese people. A later emperor, Shun,

---

CHINESE DYNASTIES

Xia	2200 - 1700 BC		**Eastern Wei**	534 - 577
Shang	1700 - 1100 BC		Western Wei	535 - 556
Zhou	1100 - 221 BC		Northern Qi	550 - 577
Western Zhou	1100 - 771 BC		Northern Zhou	557 - 581
Eastern Zhou	770 - 221 BC		**Sui**	589 - 618
Spring & Autumn Period	722 - 481 BC		**Tang**	618 - 907
Warring States Period	453 - 221 BC		**Five Dynasties**	907 - 960
Qin	221 - 207 BC		Later Liang	907 - 923
Han	206 BC - 220 AD		Later Tang	923 - 936
Former Han	206 BC - 24 AD		Later Jin	936 - 946
Later Han	25 - 220 AD		Later Han	947 - 950
Three Kingdoms Period	220 - 280		Later Zhou	951 - 960
Wei	220 - 265		**Liao**	916 - 1125
Shu Han	221 - 263		**Song**	960 - 1279
Wu	222 - 280		Northern Song	960 - 1126
Jin	265 - 420		Southern Song	1127 - 1279
Western Jin	265 - 316		**Western Xia**	1038 - 1227
Eastern Jin	317 - 420		**Jin**	1115 - 1234
Southern & Northern Dynasties			**Yuan (Mongol)**	1271 - 1368
Southern	420 - 589		**Ming**	1368 - 1644
Song	420 - 479		**Qing (Manchu)**	1644 - 1911
Qi	479 - 502			
Liang	502 - 557		**CHINESE REPUBLICS**	
Chen	557 - 589			
Northern	386 - 581		**Republic of China**	1911 - 1949
Northern Wei	386 - 534		**People's Republic of China**	1949 -

devised the writing brush. Dynastic rule commenced when the same Shun abdicated in favour of Yu, the first emperor of the Xia.

Xia & Shang Dynasties

Many historians believe that the Xia Dynasty may actually have existed, though not in the terms depicted in Chinese mythology. The dynasty is claimed to have held power for nearly five centuries from 2200 to 1700 BC, before becoming corrupt and being overthrown by the Shang.

There is more evidence of the existence of the Shang than of the Xia. Archaeological finds have shown for certain that a state existed in the Yellow River plain in the present provinces of Shandong, Shanxi and Shaanxi, and that it held power from 1554 to 1045 BC. It was an agricultural society that practised a form of ancestor worship. It was also marked by the presence of what seems to be a caste of high priests who practised divination using so-called oracle bones. Associated with ancestor worship and divination are the Shang bronze vessels, the surfaces of which are covered with extraordinarily detailed linear designs. Like the Xia

Divination

Divination, as practised by Shang priests, was a procedure that involved applying heat to the bones of cattle or to the shells of turtles. Grooves were carved on one side of the bones and shells, and heated rods were inserted into them. The resulting cracks that appeared on the other side could be 'read' for clues as to everything from the outcome of crops to whether it was wise to put a down payment on that new plough.

For scholars of ancient Chinese, the Shang practice of writing the topic of divination and often the outcome on the bones provide the only surviving record of early Chinese ideographs. Some 50,000 oracle bones and fragments have been unearthed, mainly from storage pits in Xiaotun in Henan. From these, 3000 early Chinese characters have been identified. ■

before it, the Shang fell prey to corruption and degeneracy, and was toppled by the Zhou.

Zhou Dynasty

Like the Shang before it, little is known with any great certainty about the Zhou (1100-221 BC). It is thought that they were a nomadic tribe who came under the influence of the Shang and later displaced it. The Zhou capital was known as Hao and was near Chang'an (present-day Xi'an), the site that was to become the imperial seat of power for many subsequent Chinese dynasties. The Zhou also established another power centre close to present-day Luoyang in Henan, from where they governed the subjugated Shang. The Zhou social structure seems to have been heavily influenced by the Shang, from whom they inherited the practices of divination and ancestor worship.

Historians generally divide the Zhou period into the Western Zhou (1100-771 BC) and the Eastern Zhou (770-221 BC). The demarcation point is the sacking of the traditional Zhou capital of Hao by barbarian tribes, the transfer of power to Luoyang and a loss of effective control by the Zhou over its feudatory states. Nevertheless, Zhou nobles remained symbolic heads of state over a land of warring kingdoms until 221 BC, when they were displaced by the Qin.

The Eastern Zhou, though riven by strife, is thought of as the crucible of Chinese culture. The traditional Chinese division of the period into the Spring and Autumn period (722-481 BC) and the Warring States period (453-221 BC) doesn't follow any historical logic, but rather refers to the periods covered by two historical books of the same names, written during the period, which were to become cornerstones of the classical education system until the Qing collapsed in 1911. The *Spring & Autumn Annals* is traditionally ascribed to Confucius (551-479 BC), a scholar who wandered from state to state during these troubled times in search of a ruler who would put his ideas for the perfect state into practice.

Confucianism wasn't the only important

school of thought to emerge in the Eastern Zhou. The same period saw Laotse pen his *Daode Jing*, or *The Way & its Power* (as it was famously translated by Arthur Waley), the classic text of Taoism. While there were many other competing ideologies in the Eastern Zhou (the Chinese frequently allude to the 'Hundred Schools'), Confucianism and Taoism are two opposing streams that left their mark on all future Chinese thinking, the former pragmatic and socially oriented, the latter personal and mystical.

Mandate of Heaven

The Zhou period is important for the establishment of some of the most enduring Chinese political concepts. Foremost is the 'mandate of heaven', in which heaven gives wise and virtuous leaders a mandate to rule and removes it from those who are evil and corrupt. It was a concept that was later extended to incorporate the Taoist theory that heaven expresses disapproval of bad rulers through natural disasters such as earthquakes, floods and plagues of locusts.

In keeping with this was the idea that heaven also expressed its displeasure with corrupt rulers through rebellion and withdrawal of support by the ruled. This has been referred to as the 'right to rebellion', a slippery concept, since the right to rebellion could only be confirmed by success.

Nevertheless, rebellious expressions of heaven's will were an essential ingredient in China's dynastic cycle, and mark an essential difference with, say, Japan, where the authority of the imperial family derives from a single lineage that, according to legend, can be traced back to the Sun goddess.

Qin Dynasty

The tenuous authority of the Zhou ended in the 3rd century BC, when the state of Qin united the Chinese, for the first time, into a single empire. However, the First Exalted Emperor Qin Shihuang ruled only from 221 to 207 BC. He is remembered above all for his tyranny and cruelty. At the same time, the Qin Dynasty bequeathed administrative institutions that were to remain features of the Chinese state for the following 2000 years.

The state of Qin grew in power during the 5th and 4th centuries BC. In 246 BC the state conquered present-day Sichuan and proceeded to do likewise with the remaining kingdoms that stood in its way. By 221 BC the Qin was victorious, and Qin Shihuang fashioned his conquests into an empire, giving himself the newly coined title *huángdì*, or emperor.

The Qin Dynasty's chief historical legacy was its strong centralised control. It divided its territory into provincial units administered by centrally appointed scholars. Weights and measures and the writing system were standardised. All books inimical to the laws of the state were burnt in accordance with imperial edict. Construction of what much later was to become the Great Wall was undertaken largely by conscripts, of whom countless numbers perished.

Qin Shihuang's heir to the imperial throne proved ineffectual and, shaken by rebellion, the Qin capital near Chang'an fell to an army led by the commoner Liu Bang in 207 BC. Liu lost no time in taking the title of emperor and establishing the Han Dynasty.

Han Dynasty

The Han Dynasty ruled China from 206 BC to 220 AD. While it held the reins of power less tightly than the preceding Qin, it nevertheless maintained many of the institutions of the dynasty that it followed. Its history is complicated by the fact that it is often divided into a Western Han and a Eastern Han, with an interregnum of 14 years (9-23 AD), during which the country was governed by the Xin.

The Western Han was a period of consolidation, notable for the true establishment of the Chinese state and the military extension of the empire's borders. The Eastern Han, after a brief period of stability, fell prey to a process of a weakening and decentralisation of power that in 220 AD saw the abdication of the last of the Han emperors and the beginning of some 400 years of turmoil.

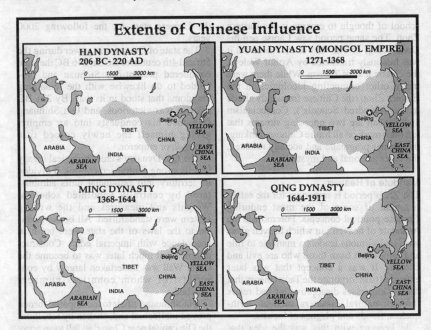

Extents of Chinese Influence

HAN DYNASTY 206 BC- 220 AD

YUAN DYNASTY (MONGOL EMPIRE) 1271-1368

MING DYNASTY 1368-1644

QING DYNASTY 1644-1911

Foreign Contacts

The expansion of the Han brought the Chinese into contact with the 'barbarians' that encircled their world. As a matter of course, this contact brought both military conflict and commercial gains.

To the north, the Xiongnu (a name given to various nomadic tribes of central Asia) posed the greatest threat to China. Military expeditions were sent against these tribes, initially with much success. This in turn provided the Chinese with access to central Asia, opening up the routes that carried Chinese silk as far afield as Rome.

On the diplomatic front, links were formed with central Asian tribes, and the great Chinese explorer Zhang Qian provided the authorities with information on the possibilities of trade and alliances in northern India.

The same period saw the percolation of Chinese influence into areas that were later to become known as Vietnam and Korea.

Decentralisation of Power

From the collapse of the Han Dynasty in 220 AD to the establishment of the Sui in 581 AD, China was riven by more than four centuries of internal conflict that saw some of the most terrible wars in the nation's history. Curiously, however, the turmoil still allowed for a widespread flowering of Buddhism and the arts.

Chinese historians refer to this period as the Wei, Jin and Northern & Southern dynasties. This is a simplification. Altogether 19 kingdoms and fiefdoms competed for power in the period of 316-439 AD alone. Initially the country divided into three large kingdoms; the Wei governing the area roughly north of the Yangzi River while the south was represented by the Wu to the east and the Shu to the west (Sichuan Province is still often referred to as Shu).

The Wei lasted little more than 40 years. Its successor, the Western Jin, fared not much better. By 306 AD its capital, Luoyang, had fallen to Xiongnu horsemen, issuing in 150 years of bloodshed as non-Han tribes fought together for absolute power. In the 5th century the Tuoba tribe eliminated its rivals in the north, and its Sinisised rulers set about consolidating their position through such measures as land reform. But they were to fall too, and the north divided into Eastern and Western Wei.

The Western Wei, though numerically weaker than its rival in the north, set up an efficient administrative system and disbanded Buddhist temples, confiscating much of the faith's accumulated wealth in the process. In 577 AD it defeated the Eastern Wei, and in 581 AD one of its own generals seized power and established the Sui Dynasty. By 589 the Sui had southern China, and the country was once again reunified under a single government.

Sui Dynasty

The Sui Dynasty (589-618 AD) was shortlived but its accomplishments were many. Yang Jian, the Chinese-Tuoba general who established the dynasty, was given the title Wendi, the 'Cultivated Emperor'. He undertook administrative reform, modelling much of it on the earlier Han institutions; the civil service was strengthened at the expense of aristocratic privilege; and land reform was undertaken. All this, along with revisions of the law code, was to serve as the basis for the institutions of the Tang Dynasty that followed fast on the heels of the Sui's collapse.

The Sui went into rapid decline under the rule of Wendi's son, Yangdi. His massive public works in restoring strategically important sections of the Great Wall and establishing the Grand Canal (which did much to achieve the economic cohesion of China) were clearly aimed at strengthening the empire. However, his three unsuccessful incursions onto Korean soil put an enormous burden on the national coffers and fanned the flames of revolt.

Tang Dynasty

Faced with disastrous military setbacks in Korea and revolt on the streets, Yangdi was assassinated by one of his high officials. Meanwhile, another Sui official, posted in the border garrison of Taiyuan, turned his troops back on the capital. His name was Li Yuan (known posthumously as Gaozu) and he was to establish the Tang Dynasty (618-907), commonly regarded by Chinese as the most glorious period in their history.

Gaozu's grab at dynastic succession was not without contest, and it was to take 10 years before the last of his rivals was defeated. Once this was achieved, however, the Tang set about putting the house in order. A pyramidical administration was established, with the emperor at its head, two policy-formulating ministries and a Department of State Affairs below this, followed in turn by nine courts and six boards dealing with specific administrative areas. In a move to discourage the development of regional power bases, the empire was divided into 300 prefectures (zhōu) and 1500 counties (xiàn), a regional breakdown that persists to this day.

The accession of Gaozu's son, Taizong (600-49), to the imperial throne saw a continuation of the early Tang successes. Military conquests re-established Chinese control of the silk routes and contributed to an influx of traders, producing an unprecedented 'internationalisation' of Chinese society. The major cities of Chang'an, Luoyang and Guangzhou (formerly known as Canton), as well as many other trading centres, were home to foreign communities. Mainly from central Asia, these communities brought with them new religions, food, music and artistic traditions. Later in the Tang Dynasty foreign contact was extended to Persia, India, Malaysia, Indonesia and Japan. By the 9th century the city of Guangzhou was said to have a foreign population of 100,000.

The Tang also saw a flourishing of Buddhism. Chinese pilgrims, notably the famous wanderer Xuan Zang, made their way to India, bringing back with them Buddhist scriptures that in their turn brought about a Buddhist renewal. Translation, which until this time had extensively Sinisised difficult

Buddhist concepts, was undertaken with a new rigour, and Chinese Buddhist texts increased vastly in number. One of the consequences of this, however, was a schism in the Buddhist faith. In reaction to the complexity of many Buddhist texts being translated from Sanskrit, the Chan school (more famously known by its Japanese name, Zen) arose. Chan looked to bypass the complexities of scriptural study through discipline and meditation, while another Buddhist phenomenon, the Pure Land school (later to become the most important form of Chinese Buddhism), concerned itself with attaining the 'Western Paradise'.

For Chinese, the apex of Tang dynastic glory was the reign of Xuanzong (685-761), known also by the title Minghuang, or the 'Radiant Emperor'. His capital of Chang'an was one of the greatest cities in the world, with a population of over one million. His court was a magnet to scholars and artists throughout the country, and home for a time to poets such as Du Fu and Li Bai, perhaps China's two most famous rhymers. His reign similarly saw a flourishing of the arts, dance and music, as well as a remarkable religious diversity.

Some might say that all this artistic activity was a sign that the empire was beginning to go a bit soft at the core. Xuanzong's increasing preoccupation with the arts, Tantric Buddhism, Taoism, one of his consorts Yang Guifei and whatever else captured his fancy meant that the affairs of state were largely left to his administrators. An Lushun, a general in the north-east, took this opportunity to build up a huge power base in the region, and before long (755) he made his move on the rest of China. The fighting, which dragged on for nearly 10 years, overran the capital and caused massive dislocations of people and millions of deaths. Although Tang forces regained control of the empire, it was the beginning of the end for the Tang.

More Anarchy & Discord

The 8th and 9th centuries saw a gradual weakening of Tang power. In the north-west

Tibetan warriors overran Tang garrisons, while to the south the Nanzhao kingdom centred in Dali, Yunnan, posed a serious threat to Sichuan. Meanwhile, in the Chinese heartland of the Yangzi region and Zhejiang, heavy taxes and a series of calamities engendered wide-ranging discontent that culminated in Huang Zhao, the head of a loose grouping of bandit groups, ransacking the capital. From 907 to 959, until the establishment of the Song Dynasty, China was once again racked by wars between contenders for the mandate of heaven. It is a period often referred to as the Five Dynasties and Ten Kingdoms period.

Song Dynasty

In 959 Zhao Kuangyin, the leader of the palace corps of one of the so-called Five Dynasties (the Later Zhou), usurped power from a seven-year-old head of state. By 976 he had conquered the dozen or so other kingdoms that stood in the way to reunifying China and established yet another dynasty: the Song (960-1279).

The Song is generally divided into the Northern Song (960-1126) and the Southern Song (1127-1279). The reason behind this division lies with the Jurchen Jin Dynasty, which took control of the north from 1126 and drove the Song from its capital of Kaifeng to the southern capital of Hangzhou.

Despite the continual threat of powerful forces on its borders (the Tibetan/Tangut Xixia kingdom, the Mongol Liao Dynasty and the Jurchen Jin Dynasty), the Song is memorable for its strong centralised government, a renewal of Confucian learning, a restoration of the examination system that fostered a civilian-dominated bureaucracy and what has been referred to as a commercial revolution.

The economic progress of the Song period can be attributed in large part to dramatically increased agricultural production. Land reclamation, new rice strains and improved agricultural techniques and tools all played a role in this development. At the same time improvements in the transport infrastructure, the rise of a merchant class and the introduction of paper money facilitated the growth of wider markets. This commercial revolution allowed for the growth of more urban centres nourished by the influx of goods from around the country. When Marco Polo arrived in China in the 13th century he found prosperous cities on a grander scale than those he was used to at home in Europe. Historians point to the Song Dynasty as the turning point in China's development of an urban culture.

Mongol Reign (Yuan Dynasty)

Beyond the Great Wall lay the Gobi Desert. Beyond that lay only slightly more hospitable grassland stretching all the way from Manchuria to Hungary and inhabited by nomadic Turkic and Mongol tribes who endured a harsh life as shepherds and horse breeders. The Mongols, despised for what was considered their ignorance and poverty, occasionally went to war with the Chinese but had always been defeated.

In 1206 after 20 years of internal war, Genghis Khan united the roaming Mongol tribes into a new national entity: the 'Blue Mongols', under the protection of the 'heavenly sky'. In 1211 he turned his attention on China, penetrated the Great Wall two years later and took Beijing in 1215. Stubborn resistance from the Chinese rulers, conflict within the Mongolian camp and campaigns in Russia delayed the conquest of Song China for many years. Not until 1279 did the grandson of Genghis, Kublai Khan, bring southern China under his sway and establish the Yuan Dynasty (1271-1368). The China ruled by Kublai was the vastest empire the world has ever seen.

The Mongols established two capitals: a summer capital of Shangdu in Inner Mongolia and a winter capital of Dadu, or, as it's now known, Beijing. They made many administrative changes to the Chinese court, the major difference from the Song being the militarisation of administrative organs. Another major feature of the Yuan Dynasty was that the Chinese became 3rd and 4th-class citizens in their own country. Society was split into four categories, with the

The Great Khan, Kublai, ruler of the vast Mongol empire and founder of the Chinese Yuan Dynasty.

Mongols first, their central Asian allies next, northern Chinese third and southern Chinese last.

The Mongols were harsh in administering their rule, but on the economic front at least they were less interfering than the Chinese dynasties that had preceded them. More work was carried out on China's canal system and roads, offering a further stimulus to trade. The commercial revolution that had gathered pace in the Song continued unabated in the Yuan, with inter-regional and even international trade flourishing. Taxes were heavy, however, except for those of Mongol descent, who were exempt.

The grip of the Yuan Dynasty over its vast empire remained strong almost until the very end, despite internal intrigues and widespread Chinese disaffection with their Mongol rulers. By the middle of the 14th century, however, the country had become convulsed by rebellion. Chief among the rebel groups were the Red Turbans, who were guided in their mission by a belief structure which comprised diverse religious sources, ranging from Buddhism to Mani-

Did Marco Polo Go to China?

Anyone would think Marco Polo *discovered* China. Towering over everyone who went before and after him, the Italian merchant occupies a special place in the Western imagination. The stuff of fairy tales, the man who brought spaghetti to Italy (or was it noodles to China?) and invented ice cream, an early pioneer of the travelogue, diligently cataloguing the bizarre wonders of the Far East, Polo has inspired travellers for centuries. Even Christopher Columbus travelled with (and jotted notes in) a copy of *Description of the World*, Polo's account of his wanderings.

It is hardly surprising then that virtually no one has ever thought to ask the question that Frances Wood asks in her recent book, *Did Marco Polo Go to China?*. Ms Wood herself admits to having quoted Marco Polo in her university essays and having drawn on his descriptions of Beijing in her PhD dissertation on the domestic architecture of that city. But this was before her attention was drawn to research into Polo's case by German Mongolists. German Mongolists, she admits, may not 'form a large lobby, but their researches are not to be lightly dismissed'.

Obviously they are not. Polo's travels and observations turn out to be of dubious authenticity. For a start his book – written in 1298 – was 'ghosted' by a popular romance writer of the time with whom Polo shared a Genoese prison cell. The original has not survived and the more than 150 early versions of the book that do are the work of copyists who often 'improved' the tale – there are major discrepancies between them. Moreover, no mention of a Marco Polo can be found in Chinese records, a curious fact when Polo claims variously to have governed Yangzhou, ended a major siege and enjoyed a 17-year special relationship with Kublai Khan as his special emissary to China.

But it is less his extravagant claims than his omissions that go hardest against Polo. Among the many things that Polo fails to have noticed during 17 years wandering around China are Chinese women's bound feet, the popularity of tea, the unique Chinese writing system and, perhaps most damning of all, the Great Wall. No matter how they arrive in China, asserts Frances Wood, 'only someone who is severely visually challenged could fail to notice the Great Wall.' She has a point.

Frances Wood cautiously takes the view that 'Marco Polo himself probably never travelled much further than his family's trading posts on the Black Sea and in Constantinople.' Nevertheless, she concedes, there is much in his account of China that concurs with other contemporary accounts, some of them Persian and Arabic. His book remains a fascinating compendium of medieval knowledge about China – tantalisingly sketchy, wide-eyed and fabulous. And for many centuries it was one of the few references available for travellers setting out to China, even if it was compiled from hearsay and unreliable secondary sources.

Besides, we at Lonely Planet have a grudging respect for Marco, whether he went to China or not. With prices rising by the day and new roads and railway lines springing up everywhere, our guide has barely hit the shelves before travellers are speculating as to whether *we* went to China. It took 700 years for anyone ask the same question of Marco Polo. ∎

---

chaeism, Taoism and Confucianism. By 1367 Zhu Yuanzhang, originally an orphan and Buddhist novice, had climbed to the top of the rebel leadership, and in 1368 he established the Ming Dynasty and restored Chinese rule.

Ming Dynasty

Upon establishing the Ming (1368-1644), Zhu Yuanzhang took the name of Hongwu. He established his capital in Nanjing, but in 1402 Yongle (strictly speaking the third but

effectively the second Ming emperor) set about building a new seat of imperial power on the site of the old Yuan capital in Beijing. In 1420 Beijing was designated the first capital and Nanjing the second (their names mean 'Northern Capital' and 'Southern Capital' respectively).

Hongwu is remembered for his despotism (he had some 10,000 scholars and their families put to death in two particular paranoid purges of his administration), but he was also a strong leader who did much to set China back on its feet in the aftermath of the Yuan collapse. This consolidation was continued by Yongle. He ruled less autocratically, running the court bureaucracy with a steadier hand than Hongwu had, and he carried out effective campaigns in protection of the Great Wall against the Mongols.

Yongle's reign also saw, for the first time, China developing into a strong maritime nation. Zheng He, a eunuch general of Muslim descent, undertook seven great expeditions to South-East Asia, Persia, Arabia and even eastern Africa.

In the final years of Ming rule, official corruption, excessive eunuch power, intellectual conservatism and costly wars in defence of Korea (and ultimately China itself) against the Japanese Toyotomi Hideyoshi brought the nation to virtual bankruptcy. A famine in Shaanxi Province coupled with governmental neglect was the spark for a massive peasant rebellion that brought the Ming to a close.

Qing Dynasty

The Manchus to the north had long been growing in power, and looked with keen interest to the convulsions of rebellion in their huge neighbour. Taking advantage of the turmoil in China, they launched an invasion. Initially held back by the Great Wall, they were allowed to pass by a Ming general, who saw an alliance with the Manchus as the only hope for defeating the peasant rebel armies that now threatened Beijing itself. The Manchus lost no time in inflicting a decisive defeat on the peasant forces, and in June 1644 they marched into the Ming capital and made it their own. They proclaimed their new dynasty the Qing (1644-1911), though it was to be four decades before they finally cleared the south of Ming loyalist forces and pacified the whole country. Today's Chinese 'triads' (the modern secret societies generally thought to be involved in criminal activity, especially drug trafficking), are actually the descendants of secret societies originally set up to resist the Manchus.

Although the Manchus concentrated power in their own hands and alienated the Han Chinese, the reign of the early Qing emperors from 1663 to 1796 was a period of great prosperity. The throne was occupied by three of the most able rulers China has known: Kangxi, Yongcheng and Qianlong. The Qing expanded the empire to its greatest limits since the Han Dynasty, bringing Mongolia and Tibet under Qing suzerainty. Reduced taxation and massive flood control and irrigation projects benefited the peasants.

One problem was that the first three emperors' exceptional competence led to a concentration of power in their hands that none of their successors was a match for. Like the Mongols, the Manchu rulers succumbed to the ways of the Chinese and soon became culturally indistinguishable from them, modelling their government on the

Eunuchs

An interesting feature of the Ming, and one that was principal in its eventual decline, was the ever-increasing power and number of eunuchs in the imperial court. Eunuchs, generally castrated at a young age by their families in the hope that they would attain the imperial court, had been employed by Chinese emperors as early as the Han Dynasty. Traditionally, their role was to serve the needs of the emperor and his harem in parts of the imperial palace that were off limits to all adult males barring the emperor himself.

By the early Ming the number of eunuchs in the service of the emperor was already 10,000, and despite imperial edicts forbidding their access to political power they continued to grow in influence and numbers throughout the Ming. Certain eunuchs (perhaps the most infamous of whom is Wei Zhongxian, who practically ruled all China in the 1620s) assumed dictator-like power and siphoned off massive fortunes while their emperors frollicked with their consorts.

In the late years of Ming rule, eunuchs probably numbered somewhere between 70,000 and 100,000 and exercised enormous control over the nation. ∎

Ming Dynasty. Thus the isolationism and intellectual conservatism of the Ming was passed on to the Qing. China continued to be an inward-looking nation, oblivious to the technological and scientific revolutions taking place in Europe. The coming of Europeans to China hastened the fall of the Qing and helped mould the China we know today.

Coming of the West

The first European ships to anchor off the shores of China were Portuguese in 1516. Although by 1557 they had set up a trade mission in Macau, it was not until 1760 that other European powers – the British, Dutch and Spanish – gained secure access to Chinese markets via a base in Guangzhou. All trade was carried out via a monopolistic guild known as the Cohong; the same guild mediated all non-commercial dealings with the Chinese empire, effectively keeping foreigners at a long arm's length from the political centre in Beijing.

Trade flourished under the auspices of the Cohong – in China's favour. British purchases of tea, silk and porcelain far outweighed Chinese purchases of wool and spices. In 1773, the British decided to balance the books with sales of opium. Despite imperial declarations of wars against

drugs, opium addiction in China skyrocketed and with it so did sales.

After much imperial vacillation and hand wringing, in March 1839 Lin Zexiu, an official of great personal integrity, was dispatched to Guangzhou to put a stop to the illegal traffic once and for all. He acted promptly, demanding and eventually getting some 20,000 chests of opium stored by the British in Guangzhou. This, along with several other minor incidents, was just the pretext that hawkish elements in the British government needed to win support for military action against China. In 1840 a British naval force assembled in Macau and moved up the coast to Beihe, not far from Beijing. The Opium War was on.

For the Chinese, the conflicts centred on the Opium trade were a fiasco from start to finish. While the Qing court managed to fob the first British force off with a treaty that neither side ended up recognising, increasing British frustration soon led to an attack on Chinese positions close to Guangzhou.

The resulting treaty ceded Hong Kong to the British and called for indemnities of six million yuan and the full resumption of trade. The furious Qing emperor refused to recognise the treaty, and in 1841 British forces once again headed up the coast, taking Fujian

Unequal Treaties

The first of the many unequal treaties foisted on the Chinese by the Europeans and later the Japanese was the Treaty of Nanjing. It brought the Opium War to a close with a humiliating slap in the face for the Qing court. According to its terms (there were 12 articles altogether) the ports of Guangzhou, Xiamen, Fuzhou, Ningbo and Shanghai were to be opened to foreign trade; British consuls were to be established in each of the open ports; an indemnity of 21 million Mexican dollars was to be paid to the British; the Cohong was to be disbanded; and, perhaps most humiliating, Hong Kong was to be ceded to the British 'in perpetuity'.

Unequal treaties followed thick and fast once a precedent had been established in Nanjing. The Treaty of Tianjin, originating in a Chinese refusal to apologise for having torn a British flag and culminating in a combined British-French occupation of Tianjin, provided a further 10 treaty ports and more indemnities. Following complications led to the burning of the Summer Palace by the British and the ceding of the Kowloon Peninsula. Further unequal treaties won the French the Chinese vassal state of Vietnam, gave the Japanese Taiwan, the Pescadores and the Liaodong Peninsula, and eventually opened 50 treaty ports from as far south as Simao in Xishuangbanna to Manzhouli on the Russian frontier. In the space of some 50 years or so, a spate of unequal treaties effectively turned China into a colony of the imperial forces of the day. ■

and eastern Zhejiang. They settled in for the winter, and in the spring of 1842, their numbers swollen with reinforcements, they moved up the Yangzi duly dispatching all comers. With British guns trained on Nanjing, the Qing fighting spirit evaporated, and they reluctantly signed the humiliating Treaty of Nanjing.

Decline of the Qing

The Qing was simply the latest inheritor of power in many centuries of dynastic rule. It was administered by Confucian-trained scholars and was headed by Empress Dowager Wu Cixi, a former concubine who saw all attempts to reform the ancient institutions of the empire as a threat to the conservative power base of her government. In short, it was poorly equipped to adapt to the demands of dynamic Western powers who refused to enter into relations with China as mere vassals. Reforming elements within the Qing were perpetually thwarted; rural poverty and Western influence were factors in promoting civil unrest that emerged in four major rebellions in the mid-19th century. The Western powers went on a land-grabbing spree that carved China up into 'spheres of influence'.

The first to go was China's colonial 'possessions'. A war with France from 1883 to 1885 ended Chinese suzerainty in Indo-China and allowed the French to maintain control of Vietnam and eventually gain control of Laos and Cambodia. The British occupied Myanmar (Burma). In 1895 Japan forced the Chinese out of Korea and made them cede Taiwan. By 1898 the European powers were on the verge of carving up China and having her for dinner, a feast that was thwarted only by a US proposal for an 'open-door' policy that would leave China open to trade with any foreign power.

In the face of so much national humiliation it was inevitable that rebellions aiming to overthrow the Qing emerged. The first major rebellion was the Taiping. Led by Hong Xiuquan, a native of Guangdong and a failed scholar whose encounters with Western missionaries had led him to believe

he was the younger brother of Jesus, the rebellion commanded forces of 600,000 men and 500,000 women. The Taipings owed much of their ideology to Christianity. They forbade gambling, opium, tobacco and alcohol; advocated agricultural reform; and outlawed foot-binding for women, prostitution and slavery. Ironically, they were defeated by a coalition of Qing and Western forces – the Europeans preferring to deal with a corrupt and weak Qing government than a powerful, united China governed by the Taipings.

The second major rebellion to rock China was that of the Boxers United in Righteousness, or more simply the Boxer Rebellion. It emerged in Shandong in 1898 out of secret societies who trained in martial arts. The Boxers were fanatically anti-foreign, saw 1900 as the dawn of the new age and believed themselves invincible to the bullets of the foreign forces. Poorly organised, the Boxers roamed in bands attacking Chinese Christians and foreigners. The empress dowager attempted to ride the tide of anti-foreign feeling by declaring war on the foreign powers in 1900. In the event, a combined British, US, French, Japanese and Russian force of 20,000 troops defeated the Boxers, the empress fled to Xi'an and the foreign forces levied yet another massive indemnity on the Qing government.

Fall of the Qing

With the defeat of the Boxers, even the empress dowager realised that China was too weak to survive without reform. But, while the civil service examinations based on irrelevant thousand-year-old Confucian doctrines were abolished, other court-sponsored reforms proved to be a sham.

Furthermore, by now secret societies aimed at bringing down the Qing Dynasty were legion, even existing overseas, where they were set up by disaffected Chinese who had left their homeland. To make matters worse for the Qing, in 1908 the empress dowager died and the two-year-old Emperor Puyi ascended to the throne. The Qing was now rudderless, and quickly collapsed in two events: the Railway Protection Movement and the Wuchang Uprising of 1911.

The railway incident began with the public Chinese sentiment that newly constructed railways should be in Chinese control, not in the hands of the foreigners who had financed and built them. Plans to construct lines to provincial centres using local funds soon collapsed, and the despairing Qing government adopted a policy of nationalisation and foreign loans to do the work. Opposition by vested interests and provincial leaders soon fanned violence that spread and took on an anti-Qing nature. The violence was worst in Sichuan, and troops were taken from the Wuchang garrison in Wuhan to quell the disturbances.

As it happened, revolutionaries in Wuhan, coordinated by Sun Yatsen's Tokyo-based Alliance Society, were already planning an uprising in concert with disaffected Chinese troops. With the garrisons virtually empty, the revolutionaries were quickly able to take control of Wuhan and ride on the back of the large-scale Railway Protection uprisings to victory over all China. Two months later representatives from 17 provinces throughout China gathered in Nanjing to establish the Provisional Republican Government of China. China's long dynastic cycle had come to an end.

Early Days of the Republic

The Provisional Republican Government was set up on 10 October 1911 (a date that is still celebrated in Taiwan as 'Double Tenth') by Sun Yatsen and Li Yuanhong, a military commander in Wuchang. Lacking the power to force a Manchu abdication, they had no choice but to call on the assistance of Yuan Shikai, head of the imperial army and the same man the Manchus had called on to put down the Republican uprisings. The favour cost the Republicans dearly. Yuan Shikai placed himself at the head of the Republican movement and forced Sun Yatsen's resignation.

Yuan lost no time in dissolving the Republican government and amending the constitution to make himself president for

life. When this met with regional opposition, he took the natural next step in 1915 of declaring an imperial restoration and pronouncing himself China's latest emperor. Yunnan seceded, taking Guangxi, Guizhou and much of the rest of the south with it, forces were sent to bring the breakaway provinces back into the imperial ambit, and in the confusion Yuan himself passed away. What followed was a virtual warlord era, with no single power strong enough to hold the country together until the Communists established the People's Republic of China (PRC) in 1949.

Sun Yatsen, revolutionary Republican and hero both to the Communists and to their predecessors, the KMT.

Intellectual Revolution

Chinese intellectuals had been probing the inadequacies of the old Confucian order and looking for a path to steer China into the 20th century ever since early contact with the West, but a sense of lost possibilities with the collapse of the Republican government and the start of a new period of social decay lent an urgency to their worries in the early years of the 1900s. Intellectuals and students were also supported by a sense of nationalism that had been slowly growing in force since the late years of the Qing.

Beijing University became a hotbed of intellectual dissent, attracting scholars from all over China (even Mao was present in his capacity as library assistant). They were merciless in their criticisms of orthodox Chinese society. Some explored ideas of social Darwinism, the Communist Manifesto was translated into Chinese and became the basis for countless discussion groups, others favoured anarchism, and all looked keenly to events unfolding in Russia, where revolutionaries had taken power.

The catalyst for the demonstrations that became known as the May Fourth Movement was the decision of the Allies in Versailles to pass defeated Germany's rights in Shandong over to the Japanese. A huge public outcry ensued and on 4 May 1919 students took to the streets in a protest that combined a sense of nationalist outrage with demands for modernisation. Mass strike action in support of the students took place throughout China. Although the disturbances were quelled and many of the ringleaders temporarily imprisoned, the May Fourth incident is considered a watershed in contemporary Chinese history.

Perhaps most interesting today is the way in which the student protests at Tiananmen in 1989 echoed the slogans and catchcries of the 1919 protests. Students bearing placards marked with 'Mr Science' and 'Mr Democracy' in 1989 were harking back to 1919, when the same slogans were used – perhaps, in fine Chinese tradition, seeking the authority of historical precedent.

Kuomintang & Communists

After initial setbacks, Sun Yatsen and the Kuomintang (the KMT, or Nationalist Party), which had emerged as the dominant political force after the fall of the Qing Dynasty, managed to establish a secure base in southern China, and began training a National Revolutionary Army (NRA) with which to challenge the northern warlords.

Meanwhile, talks between representatives of the Soviet Communist International (Comintern) and prominent Chinese Marxists eventually resulted in several Chinese Marxist groups banding together to form a Chinese Communist Party (which became the CCP) at a meeting in Shanghai in 1921.

The Comintern, from 1922, pushed the CCP to ally with the Kuomintang, probably motivated more by the hope of forming a buttress against Japanese expansionism than by the promise of a Soviet-style revolution in China. The union was short lived. After Sun Yatsen's death in 1925 a power struggle emerged in the Kuomintang between those sympathetic to the Communists and those who – headed by Chiang Kaishek – favoured a capitalist state dominated by a wealthy elite and supported by a military dictatorship.

Shanghai Coup

Chiang Kaishek attempted to put an end to growing Communist influence during the 1926 Northern Expedition, which set out to wrest power from the remaining warlords. With Chiang as commander in chief, NRA forces took the cities of Wuhan and Nanchang, and prepared to move on Shanghai. As NRA troops advanced on the city, Shanghai workers were called upon to strike and take over key installations. Having lured the Communists out of the woodwork, Chiang let loose a reign of terror against the Communists and their sympathisers.

With the help of Shanghai's underworld leaders and with financial backing from Shanghai bankers and foreigners, Chiang armed hundreds of gangsters, dressed them in Kuomintang uniforms and launched a surprise attack overnight on the workers' militia. About 5000 Shanghai Communists were killed. Massacres of Communists and various anti-Chiang factions followed in other Chinese cities. Zhou Enlai managed to escape by a hair's-breadth. Another prominent CCP leader, Li Dazhao, was executed by slow strangulation.

Kuomintang Government

By the middle of 1928 the Northern Expedition had reached Beijing and a national government was established, with Chiang holding both military and political leadership. Nevertheless, only about half the country was under direct Kuomintang control; the rest was ruled by local warlords. China's social problems were legion: children were used as slave labour in factories; domestic slavery and prostitution were rife; the destitute and starving died on the streets; and strikes were ruthlessly suppressed by foreign and Chinese factory owners. In the face of such endemic social malaise, Chiang became obsessed with countering the influence of the Communists.

Civil War

After the massacre of 1927, the Communists were divided between an insurrectionary policy of targeting large urban centres and one of basing its rebellion in the countryside. After costly defeats in Nanchang and Changsha, the tide of opinion started to shift to Mao Zedong, who, along with Zhu De, had established his forces in the Jinggangshan mountains on the border between Jiangxi and Hunan and who advocated rural-based revolt.

Communist-led uprisings in other parts of the country met with some success. However, the Communist armies were still small and hampered by limited resources. They adopted a strategy of guerrilla warfare, emphasising mobility and deployment of forces for short attacks on the enemy, followed by swift separation once the attack was over. Pitched battles were avoided except where their force was overwhelmingly superior. The strategy was summed up in a four-line slogan:

The enemy advances, we retreat;
The enemy camps, we harass;
The enemy tires, we attack;
The enemy retreats, we pursue.

By 1930 the ragged Communist forces had been turned into an army of perhaps 40,000, and presented such a serious challenge to the Kuomintang that Chiang had to wage a number of extermination campaigns against

them. He was defeated each time, and the Communist army expanded its territory.

The Long March

Chiang's fifth extermination campaign began in October 1933, when the Communists suddenly changed their strategy. Mao and Zhu's authority was being undermined by other members of the Party who advocated meeting Chiang's troops in pitched battles; this strategy proved disastrous. By October 1934 the Communists had suffered heavy losses and were hemmed into a small area in Jiangxi.

On the brink of defeat, the Communists decided to retreat from Jiangxi and march north to Shaanxi. In China's northern mountains the Communists controlled an area which spread across Shaanxi, Gansu and Ningxia, held by troops commanded by an ex-Kuomintang officer who had sided with the Communists after the 1927 massacre.

There was not one 'Long March' but several, as various Communist armies in the south made their way to Shaanxi. The most famous was the march from Jiangxi Province which began in October 1934, took a year to complete and covered 8000 km over some of the world's most inhospitable terrain. On the way the Communists confiscated the property of officials, landlords and tax-collectors, redistributed the land to the peasants, armed thousands of peasants with weapons captured from the Kuomintang and left soldiers behind to organise guerrilla groups to harass the enemy. Of the 90,000 people who started out in Jiangxi only 20,000 made it to Shaanxi. Fatigue, sickness, exposure, enemy attacks and desertion all took their toll.

The march proved, however, that the Chinese peasants could fight if they were given a method, an organisation, leadership, hope and weapons. It brought together many people who later held top positions after 1949, including Mao Zedong, Zhou Enlai, Zhu De, Lin Biao, Deng Xiaoping and Liu Shaoqi. It also established Mao as the paramount leader of the Chinese Communist movement; during the march a meeting of the CCP hierarchy recognised Mao's overall

Mao Zedong, the 'Great Helmsman' and paramount leader of the Chinese Communist Party. Mao was a brilliant military strategist, but his radical economic tactics post-WWII ultimately led to the chaos of the Cultural Revolution.

leadership, and he assumed supreme responsibility for strategy.

Japanese Invasion

In September 1931 the Japanese took advantage of the confusion in China to invade and occupy Manchuria, setting up a puppet state with the last Chinese emperor, Puyi, as the symbolic head. Chiang, still obsessed with the threat of the Communists, went ahead with his fifth extermination drive: 'pacification first, resistance later' was his slogan.

The Communists had other plans. In late 1936 in Xi'an they convinced Chiang's own generals to take him hostage, and an anti-Japanese alliance was formed after negotiations with Zhou Enlai. But it did little to halt the advance of the Japanese, who in 1937 launched an all-out invasion; by 1939 they had overrun most of eastern China, forcing the Kuomintang to retreat west to Chongqing.

In 1941 the Japanese assault on Pearl Harbor brought the Americans into the conflict. Hoping to use Chiang's troops to tie down as many Japanese as possible, the Americans instead found Chiang actively avoiding conflict, saving his troops for renewed attacks on the Communists once the Americans had defeated the Japanese. The US general Joseph Stilwell, who was sent to China in 1942 by President Roosevelt to improve the combat effectiveness of the Chinese army, concluded that 'the Chinese government was a structure based on fear and favour in the hands of an ignorant, arbitrary and stubborn man...' and that its military effort since 1938 was 'practically zero'.

Defeat of the Kuomintang

The Kuomintang-Communist alliance had collapsed by 1941 and by the end of WW II China was in the grip of an all-out civil war. The Communist army numbered 900,000 and was backed by the militia and several million active supporters. With the surrender of Japan in 1945, a dramatic power struggle began as the Kuomintang and Communist forces gathered in Manchuria for the final showdown.

By 1948 the Communists had captured so much US-supplied Kuomintang equipment and had recruited so many Kuomintang soldiers that they equalled the Kuomintang in both numbers and supplies. Three great battles were fought in 1948 and 1949 which saw the Kuomintang defeated and hundreds of thousands of Kuomintang troops join the Communists. The Communists moved south and crossed the Yangzi – by October all the major cities in southern China had fallen to them.

In Beijing on 1 October 1949, Mao Zedong proclaimed the foundation of the PRC (*Zhonghua Renmin Gongheguo* in Chinese). Chiang Kaishek fled to the island of Formosa (Taiwan), taking with him the entire gold reserves of the country and what was left of his air force and navy. Some two million refugees and soldiers from the mainland crowded onto the island. President Truman ordered a protective US naval blockade to prevent an attack from the mainland – the USA continued to recognise Chiang's delusion of being the legitimate ruler of all China.

Early Years of the PRC

The PRC began its days as a bankrupt nation. The economy was in chaos following Chiang's flight to Taiwan with the gold reserves. The country had just 19,200 km of railways and 76,800 km of useable roads, all in bad condition. Irrigation works had broken down and livestock and animal populations were greatly reduced. Industrial production fell to half that of the prewar period and agricultural output plummeted.

With the Communist takeover, China seemed to become a different country. Unified by the elation of victory and the immensity of the task before them, and further bonded by the Korean War and the necessity to defend the new regime from possible US invasion, the Communists made the 1950s a dynamic period. The drive to become a great nation quickly was awesome.

By 1953 inflation had been halted, industrial production had been restored to prewar levels and the land had been confiscated from the landlords and redistributed to the peasants. On the basis of earlier Soviet models, the Chinese embarked on a massive five-year plan that was successful in lifting production on most fronts.

At the same time, the Party increased its social control by organising the people according to their work units (*dānwèi*) and dividing the country into 21 provinces, five autonomous regions, two municipalities (Beijing and Shanghai) and around 2200 county governments with jurisdiction over approximately one million Party sub-branches.

Hundred Flowers

While the early years of the PRC saw rapid economic development, immense problems remained in the social sphere, particularly with regard to the question of intellectuals. Many Kuomintang intellectuals had stayed on rather than flee to Taiwan, and still more Overseas Chinese, many of them highly qualified, returned to China soon after Liberation to help in the enormous task of reconstruction. Returning Chinese and those of suspect backgrounds were given extensive re-education courses in special universities put aside for the purpose, and were required to write a self-critical 'autobiography' before graduating. For many it was a traumatic experience.

Meanwhile, writers, artists and filmmakers were subject to strict ideological controls guided by Mao's writings on art during the Yan'an period. The issue came to a head around the figure of a writer, Hu Feng, who, in response to an easing of these controls in the early years of the first five-year plan, spoke out about the use of Marxist values in judging creative work. He soon became the object of nationwide criticism and was accused of being in the employ of the Kuomintang. Before long a witch-hunt was on in artistic circles for evidence of further 'Hu Fengism'.

In the upper echelons of the Party itself opinions were divided as to how to deal with the problem of the intellectuals. But Mao, along with Zhou Enlai and other influential figures, felt that the Party's work had been so successful that it could roll with a little criticism, and in a closed session Mao put forward the idea of 'letting a hundred flowers bloom' in the arts and 'a hundred schools of thought contend' in the sciences.

It was to be a full year before Mao's ideas were officially sanctioned in April 1957, but once they were, intellectuals around the country responded with glee. Complaints poured in on everything from Party corruption to control of artistic expression, from the unavailability of foreign literature to low standards of living; but most of all, criticisms focused on the CCP monopoly on power and the abuses that went with it. The Party quickly had second thoughts about the flowers, and an anti-rightist campaign was launched. Within six months 300,000 intellectuals had been branded rightists, removed from their jobs, and in many cases, incarcerated or sent to labour camps.

The Great Leap Forward

The first five-year plan had produced satisfactory results on the industrial front, but growth of agricultural yields had been a disappointingly low 3.8%. The state was posed with the difficult problem of how to increase agricultural production to meet the needs of urban populations coalescing around industrialised areas. As with the question of dealing with intellectuals, the Party leadership was divided on how to respond. Some, such as Zhou Enlai, favoured an agricultural incentive system. Mao favoured mass mobilisation and inspirational exhortations that he believed would jump-start the economy into first-world standards overnight.

In the end it was Mao who won the day, and the Chinese embarked on a radical programme of creating massive agricultural communes and drawing large numbers of people both from the country and urban areas into enormous water control and irrigation projects. In Mao's view revolutionary zeal and mass cooperative effort could overcome any obstacle and transform the Chinese landscape into a productive paradise. At the same time Mao criticised the earlier emphasis on heavy industry, and pushed for small local industry to be developed in the communes, with profits going back into agricultural development.

Despite the enthusiastic forecasts, at the end of the day inefficient management, little incentive to work in the common field and large numbers of rural workers engaged in industrial projects resulted in a massive slump in agricultural output. With industry in confusion and agriculture at an all-time low, China was struck by two disasters: the floods and droughts which ruined the harvests of 1959 and 1960, and the sudden withdrawal in 1960 of all Soviet aid.

Sino-Soviet Split

Droughts and floods were beyond even Mao's ability to control, but in the Great Leap Forward and the Sino-Soviet dispute that led to the withdrawal of Soviet aid he played no small part. Basically Mao's problems with the Soviet Union stemmed from the latter's policy of peaceful coexistence with the USA, Khrushchev's de-Stalinisation speech and what Mao generally felt to be the increasingly revisionist nature of the Soviet leadership. Sino-Soviet relations became ever frostier, with Khrushchev reneging on a promise to provide China with a prototype atomic bomb and siding with the Indians in a Sino-Indian border dispute.

In 1960 the Soviets removed all their 1390 foreign experts working in China. With the experts went the blueprints for some 600 projects that the two powers had been working on together, including China's nuclear bomb programme.

Mao & the Bomb

Mao took extreme exception to Khrushchev's policy of peaceful coexistence with the capitalist West. In Mao's view confrontation with the forces of imperialism was an inevitability. Khrushchev looked to Lenin and saw the emergence of socialist policies and mass union movements in the West as justifying a more conciliatory line.

As the Soviet press dwelt more and more on the horrors of nuclear war, the Chinese remained remarkably sanguine about its aftermath. Drawing on statements by Mao himself, the Chinese press maintained that while perhaps half of the human race would be wiped out in a nuclear conflagration, imperialism would be annihilated and the remaining victorious socialist peoples would raise a civilisation 'thousands of times higher than the capitalist system' and create 'a truly beautiful future for themselves'.

When the Soviets withdrew their foreign experts in 1960 they took with them scientists working with the Chinese on a Chinese bomb. The soviet scientists shredded all documentation relating to the bomb before leaving, but they had not counted on Chinese ingenuity. Remarkably, piecing the shredded documents together again, the Chinese discovered crucial information that allowed them by 1964 to have successfully built and tested their own bomb. Fortunately, however, Mao never got the opportunity to put his post-holocaust theories to the test. ■

The Cultural Revolution

Although the official scapegoats were the Gang of Four, most non-partisan scholars now agree that the prime mover in the Cultural Revolution was Mao. The Cultural Revolution (1966-70) was another Great Leap Forward, an attempt to create new socialist structures overnight via the process of revolution, which, as the writer Richard Evans in his book *Deng Xiaoping and the Making of Modern China* states, 'Mao saw as having its own redemptive value'.

Mao's extreme views, his recent disastrous policy decisions and his opposition to bureaucratisation, led to his increasing isolation within the Party. In response, he began to cultivate a personality cult with the assistance largely of Lin Biao, the minister of defence and head of the People's Liberation Army (PLA).

In the early 1960s, Lin had a collection of Mao's sayings compiled into a book that was to become known simply as the 'little red book', though its real title was *Quotations from Chairman Mao*. The book became the subject of study sessions for all PLA troops and was extended into the general education system.

Next, Mao launched a purge of the arts with the assistance of his wife, Jiang Qing, an erstwhile Shanghai B-grade movie star. The launching site was a play by Wu Han: *The Dismissal of Hai Rui from Office*. The play's depiction of an upright Song official defying the authorities in defence of the people's rights was felt to be a direct reference to Mao's dismissal of Peng Dehuai, the army marshal who had dared to raise his voice in protest against the Great Leap Forward. The work was attacked on strict Marxist ideological grounds and battle lines were drawn within the Party on how to deal with the problem.

The result was that Mao's opponents were purged and simultaneously wall posters went up at Beijing University attacking the university administration. Mao officially sanctioned the wall posters and criticisms of Party members by university staff and students, and before long students were being issued red armbands and taking to the streets. The Red Guards *(hongweibing)* had been born. By August 1966 Mao was reviewing mass parades of the Red Guards, chanting and waving copies of his little red book.

Nothing was sacred in the brutal onslaught of the Red Guards as they went on the rampage through the country. Universities and secondary schools were shut down; intellectuals, writers and artists were dismissed, killed, persecuted or sent to labour in the countryside; publication of scientific, artistic, literary and cultural periodicals ceased; temples were ransacked and monasteries disbanded; and many physical reminders of China's 'feudal', 'exploitative' or 'capitalist' past (including temples, monuments, and works of art) were destroyed.

By the end of January 1967 the PLA had been ordered to break up all 'counter-revolutionary organisations', an edict that was interpreted by the PLA as all groups with interests contrary to their own. Thousands of Chinese were killed in the ensuing struggles, notably in Sichuan and in Wuhan, where the PLA took on a coalition of 400,000 Red Guards and workers' groups, killing over 1000 people. The struggles continued through to September 1967, and even Mao and Jiang Qing began to feel that enough was enough. 'Ultra-left tendencies' were condemned and the PLA was championed as the sole agent of 'proletarian dictatorship'.

The Cultural Revolution took a new turn as the Red Guards slipped from power and the PLA began its own reign of terror. The so-called Campaign to Purify Class Ranks was carried out by Workers' Mao-Thought Propaganda Teams on anyone with a remotely suspect background – this could mean anything from having a college education to having a distant cousin who lived overseas. Those who needed re-education were sent to schools in the countryside that combined intensive study and self-criticism with hard labour.

Significance & Repercussions Like most of Mao's well-intentioned experiments, the Cultural Revolution was a disaster of vast proportions. One of the few elements to benefit was the PLA, which ended up with a deeper penetration of most government organisations. Vast numbers of Chinese were victims of the revolution.

A major victim of the Cultural Revolution was the man who had done so much to get it started: Lin Biao. In the aftermath of the Cultural Revolution, Mao was troubled by the powers of the PLA, and demanded self-criticisms from senior PLA officers. It is thought that a desperate Lin Biao sought support for an assassination attempt on Mao and, failing to find it, fled with his family to the USSR in a Trident jet. The 'renegade and traitor', as the Chinese press labelled him, died when his plane crashed in Mongolia on 13 September 1971.

The sudden reversal in Lin Biao's fortunes, who until a few days earlier had been Mao's chosen successor and second only to Mao in the people's adoring hearts, was for many Chinese the final straw. The never-ending policy shifts, the mayhem of the Cultural Revolution and countless other mistakes left the majority of Chinese weary and quietly disillusioned.

Post-Cultural Revolution Years

The years immediately following the Cultural Revolution saw a return to some measure of political stability. Zhou Enlai exercised the most influence in the day-to-day governing of China, and among other things, worked towards restoring China's trade and diplomatic contacts with the outside world. In 1972 Nixon visited Beijing and normalised relations between the USA and the PRC. And in 1973, Deng Xiaoping, vilified as China's 'No 2 Capitalist Roader' during the Cultural Revolution, returned to power.

Nevertheless, Beijing politics remained factional and divided. On the one side was Zhou, Deng and a faction of 'moderates' or 'pragmatists'; on the other were the 'radicals', 'leftists' or 'Maoists' led by Jiang Qing. As Zhou's health declined, the radicals gradually gained the upper hand. By the time of Zhou's death in January 1976, Hua Guofeng, Mao's chosen protégé, was made acting premier and Deng disappeared from public view.

Tiananmen Incident

The death of Zhou Enlai and public anger at Jiang Qing and her clique culminated in the Tiananmen Incident of March 1976. Occurring during the Qing Ming Festival, when Chinese traditionally honour the dead, crowds began to gather in Tiananmen Square to lay wreaths for Zhou, recite poems, make speeches and brandish posters. The content of the speeches, poems and banners was as much critical of Jiang as it was eulogistic of Zhou.

The Politburo met in an emergency session and, with the approval of Mao, branded the gathering counter-revolutionary. Through the day of 5 April the crowd fought with police and police vehicles were burnt. The square was occupied by some 30,000 militia during the night and the remaining several hundred protesters were beaten and arrested. The incident was blamed on Deng, who was relieved of all his posts and fled to Guangzhou, before disappearing altogether.

Death of Mao
& Arrest of the Gang of Four

Mao had been a sick man for many years. In 1974 he was diagnosed as having Lou Gehrig's disease, an extremely rare motor-neuron disorder that leads quickly to death. For the last few years of his life he was immobilised and fed through a tube into his nasal passage and his speech was indecipherable. On 8 September 1976 he died.

Mao's chosen successor was Hua Guofeng, who had started his days in relative obscurity as a Party leader in Mao's home county and whom Mao had cultivated and elevated to the giddy heights of premier and Party chairman. At first Hua temporised over dealing with Jiang Qing and the three other leaders of her clique who had come to be known as the Gang of Four. But when the gang announced their opposition to Hua, he acted with the Politburo to have them arrested on 6 October. There were celebrations throughout China when the news was formally announced three weeks later.

The Gang did not to come to trial until 1980, and when it took place it provided a bizarre spectacle, with the blame for the entire Cultural Revolution falling on their shoulders. Jiang Qing remained unrepentant, hurling abuse at her judges and holding famously to the line that she 'was Mao's dog – whoever he told me to bite I bit'. Its meaning was not lost on most Chinese, and privately whispers circulated that the problem had been not a Gang of Four but a 'Gang of Five'. Jiang Qing's death sentence was commuted and she lived on until 1991 under house arrest.

Third Coming of Deng Xiaoping
In the middle of 1977 Deng Xiaoping returned to power for the third time and was appointed to the positions of vice-premier, vice-chairman of the Party and chief of staff of the PLA. His next step was to remove Hua Guofeng. In September 1980 Hua relinquished the post of premier to Zhao Ziyang, a long-standing member of the CCP whose economic reforms in Sichuan in the mid-1970s overcame the province's bankrupt economy and food shortages and won him Deng's favour. In June 1981 Hu Yaobang, a protégé of Deng's for several decades, was named Party chairman in place of Hua.

Final power now passed to the collective leadership of the six-member Standing Committee of the CCP which included Deng, Hu and Zhao. The China they took over was racked with problems, a backward country in desperate need of modernisation. Ways had to be found to rejuvenate and replace an aged leadership (themselves) and to overcome the possibility of a leftist backlash. The wasteful and destructive power struggles that had plagued the CCP since its inception had to be eliminated. The need for order had to be reconciled with the popular desire for more freedom; those with responsibility had to be rewarded but watched over in case of misuse of privilege; the crisis of faith in the Communist ideology had to be overcome;

Deng Xiaoping, twice purged by the Party, survived to become China's leader and to introduce the economic reformation of the 1980s and '90s.

and a regime now dependent on the power of the police and military for its authority had to be legitimised.

Resolution of a Theological Crisis
Deng was able to ward off immediate threats from the leftists by locking them up, but he still had to deal with a major crisis – what to do with Mao Zedong. One step taken was the resolution on the historical role of Mao Zedong issued in 1981 by the Central Committee of the CCP.

Deng had every intention of pulling Mao off his pedestal and making a man out of the god. However, he couldn't denounce Mao as Khrushchev had denounced Stalin, since Mao had too many supporters in the Party and too much respect among the common people. An all-out attack would have provoked those who would otherwise have begrudgingly fallen in line with Deng and his supporters. Instead a compromise stand was taken.

The resolution cited Mao as a great Marxist and a great proletarian revolutionary, strategist and theorist, saying:

CHRIS TAYLOR

CHRIS BEALL

CHRIS TAYLOR

CHRIS TAYLOR

SONIA BERTO

People of China, clockwise from top left:
Tibetan, Uighur, Han, Tibetan, Tibetan

RUSSIA

Karaganda

KAZAKSTAN

MONGOLIA

Almaty

Bishkek

KYRGYZSTAN

Ürümqi

Kashgar

XINJIANG

DUNHUANG
Magao Caves,
the best-preserved
Buddhist cave art
in China

XIAHE
Labrang
Monastery,
'Little Tibet'

Dunhuang   Jiayuguan

Zhangye

Tianzhu

Under
administration
of China

Golmud   Chaka   Xining   Lanzhou

QINGHAI   Linxia

Huashixia   Xiahe

GANSU

TIBET

Xiwu

Songpan

SICHUAN

Delhi

Agra

LHASA
Potala Palace,
Tibetan culture

Shigatse   Lhasa

Chengdu

Lucknow

Zhangmu Tingri Sakya
Kathmandu   ▲ Mt Everest
(8848 m)   Gyantse

Emeishan
Leshan

NEPAL

Thimphu

EMEISHAN
Sacred Buddhist
mountain, trail
to the summit

Varanasi

BHUTAN

Patna

INDIA

Jabalpur

BANGLADESH

LESHAN
The largest
Buddha in the
world

Dali

INDIA

Dhaka

Kunming

YUNNAN

Calcutta

Gejiu

DALI
Old walled
town on edge
of a lake, Bai
minority

Ha Giang

MYANMAR

VIETNAM

XISHUANGBANNA
Dai minority,
subtropical climate

BAY OF
BENGAL

THAILAND   LAOS

Yangon   Vientiane

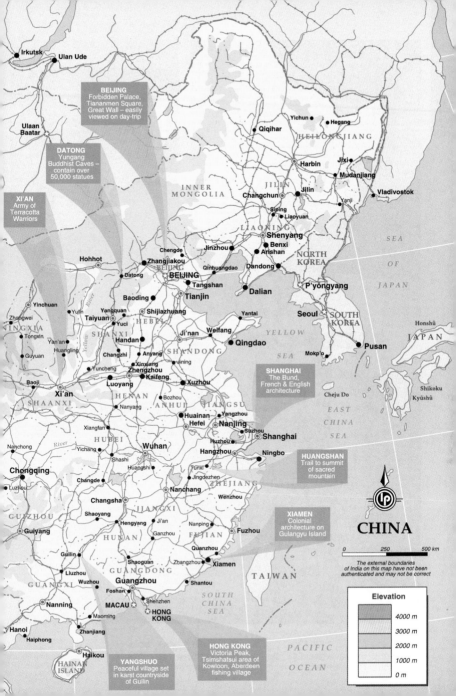

Irkutsk
Ulan Ude
Ulaan
Baatar

BEIJING
Forbidden Palace,
Tiananmen Square,
Great Wall – easily
viewed on day-trip

DATONG
Yungang
Buddhist Caves –
contain over
50,000 statues

XI'AN
Army of
Terracotta
Warriors

Yichun
Qiqihar
Hegang
HEILONGJIANG
Harbin
Jixi
Mudanjiang
JILIN
Vladivostok
Changchun
Jilin
Siping
Yanji
Liaoyuan
LIAONING
Shenyang
Chengde
Jinzhou
Benxi
NORTH
Hohhot
Zhangjiakou
Anshan
KOREA
INNER
MONGOLIA
Datong
BEIJING
Qinhuangdao
Dandong
P'yongyang
Yinchuan
Yangquan
Tangshan
Dalian
Baoding
SEA
Yulin
Shijiazhuang
Tianjin
OF
Zhongwei
Taiyuan
Yuci
HEBEI
Yantai
Seoul
JAPAN
Tongxin
Yan'an
Changzhi
Handan
Ji'nan
Weifang
SOUTH
Honshū
Guyuan
Huangling
Anyang
SHANDONG
Qingdao
KOREA
Yuncheng
Xinxiang
Jining
JAPAN
Baoji
Zhengzhou
Kaifeng
YELLOW
Mokp'o
Pusan
Xi'an
Luoyang
Xuzhou
SEA
Shikoku
SHAANXI
Bozhou
Kyūshū
HENAN
Nanyang
ANHUI
JIANGSU
Cheju Do
Xiangfan
Huainan
Yangzhou
SHANGHAI
Yichang
HUBEI
Hefei
Nanjing
The Bund,
EAST
Shashi
Wuhan
Suzhou
French & English
CHINA
Chongqing
Huangshi
Huzhou
Shanghai
architecture
SEA
Luzhou
Changde
Hangzhou
Ningbo
Tunxi
HUANGSHAN
Changsha
Jingdezhen
Trail to summit
ZHEJIANG
of sacred
Shaoyang
Nanchang
Wenzhou
mountain
Guiyang
Hengyang
JIANGXI
GUIZHOU
Ji'an
Nanping
XIAMEN
Guilin
Ganzhou
FUJIAN
Fuzhou
Colonial
architecture on
Liuzhou
Shaoguan
Quanzhou
Gulangyu Island
GUANGXI
Wuzhou
Zhangzhou
Xiamen
Nanning
Guangzhou
Shantou
TAIWAN
Foshan
MACAU
Shenzhen
SOUTH
Maoming
HONG
CHINA
CHINA
Hanoi
Zhanjiang
KONG
SEA
Haiphong
Haikou
HONG KONG
PACIFIC
HAINAN
YANGSHUO
Victoria Peak,
ISLAND
Peaceful village set
Tsimshatsui area
OCEAN
in karst countryside
of Kowloon, Aberdeen
of Guilin
fishing village

0   250   500 km

The external boundaries
of India on this map have not been
authenticated and may not be correct

Elevation
4000 m
3000 m
2000 m
1000 m
0 m

CHRIS BEALL

CHRIS TAYLOR

GLENN BEANLAND

Top Left: Monks on the roof of Jokhang Temple, Lhasa, Tibet
Top Right: Prayer wheels at Tashilhunpo Monastery, Tibet
Bottom: Pedicab drivers waiting for passengers in Central Beijing

It is true that he made gross mistakes during the Cultural Revolution, but, if we judge his activities as a whole, his contributions to the Chinese Revolution far outweigh his mistakes.

The resolution went on to blame Mao for initiating and leading the Cultural Revolution, which 'was responsible for the most severe setback and the heaviest losses suffered by the Party, the state and the people since the founding of the PRC'.

1980s – Economics in Command

With Deng at the helm, China set a course of pragmatic reforms towards economic reconstruction. In rural China, the so-called 'Responsibility System' allowed agricultural households and factories to sell their quota surpluses on the open market. And in coastal China, Special Economic Zones (SEZs) were established at Zhuhai (next to Macau), Shenzhen (next to Hong Kong) and Shantou and Xiamen (both just across the Taiwan Strait from Taiwan). The results have been nothing short of spectacular: over the last 15 years China has managed average annual growth rates of 9%.

In Communist China, however, the rush of economic reform has generated very little in the way of political reform. In fact, the reforms of the last 15 years might be thought of as a trade-off: increased economic opportunities in return for a continued Communist monopoly on power. The Party – one way or another – controls virtually every facet of public life: it is accountable to nobody but itself; it controls the army; and it controls the government, the courts and industry. In short, very little gets done in China without the approval of the Party. It is hardly surprising that official corruption has become a major problem.

Along with the Communist autocracy and its attendant corruption, the other spectre haunting China is inflation, which has been running at between 20% and 30% over the last five years. Corruption and inflation have between them led to widespread social unrest, and in 1989 resulted in the demonstrations that were put down in the Beijing Massacre.

Beijing Massacre

The immediate catalyst of the protests of 1989 was the death of Hu Yaobang, a reforming element and protégé of Deng's who had been attacked and forced to resign by hardliners in early 1987. Behind the scenes, double-digit inflation, rampant official corruption and a purge of reformist Party members like Hu had given rise to massive social discontent. On 22 April 1989, a week after Hu's death, China's leaders gathered in the Hall of the People for an official mourning service. Outside, approximately 150,000 students and other activists held an unofficial service that soon became a massive pro-democracy protest.

All through April, crowds continued to fill Tiananmen Square so that by the middle of May protesters in and around the square had swelled to nearly one million. Workers and even members of the police force joined in. Protests erupted in at least 20 other cities. Approximately 3000 students staged a hunger strike for democracy in the square. Railway workers assisted students travelling to Beijing by allowing them free rides on the trains. Students enrolled at Beijing's Art Institute constructed the 'Goddess of Democracy' in Tiananmen Square – a statue which bore a striking resemblance to America's Statue of Liberty. The students made speeches demanding a free press and an end to corruption and nepotism. Huge pro-democracy demonstrations in Hong Kong, Macau and Taiwan lent support. The arrival of the foreign press corps turned the 'Beijing Spring' into the media event of 1989.

Through much of May, the CCP was unable to quell the protests, and the imminent arrival of Mikhail Gorbachev for the first Sino-Soviet summit since 1959 precluded the use of arms to dispel the crowds. On 20 May, however, immediately after Gorbachev's departure, martial law was declared, and by 2 June, 350,000 troops had been deployed around Beijing. In the early hours of the morning on 4 June the 27th Army division attacked. Other units loyal to Deng were also employed. Heavy tanks and armoured vehicles made short work of the barricades, crushing anyone who got in their way, while troops with automatic weapons strafed the crowds on the streets.

The number of deaths that resulted from the action is widely disputed. Eyewitness accounts have indicated that hundreds died in the square alone, and it's likely that fighting in the streets around the square and in the suburbs of Beijing may have led to several thousand casualties. Hospitals were filled to overflowing, PLA troops are said to have refused to allow doctors to treat their patients, and rumours circulated of mass graves. The truth will probably never be known. What is certain is that the Party lost whatever remaining moral authority it had in the action, and will no doubt one day have to deal with widespread recriminations.

Hong Kong

In 1984 a Sino-British agreement allowed for the reversion of Hong Kong to China in 1997. The original 'unequal' Treaty of Nanjing (1840) foisted on China by Britain in the Opium War had ceded Hong Kong to the British 'in perpetuity', but the New Territories adjoining Kowloon were 'leased' to the British for 99 years in 1898. In the event, Britain agreed to hand the entire colony lock, stock and skyscrapers back to China when the New Territories' lease expired.

The transition of power looks set to be a bumpy ride. According to the terms of the 1984 agreement, Hong Kong's transfer to Chinese rule is to take place under the concept of 'one country, two systems'. The implementation and administration of this 'system' was laid out in the Basic Law, which promised the former colony a 'high degree of autonomy'. Just how much 'autonomy' though continues to be the subject of acrimonious debate between the UK and China.

It is likely, however, that Beijing's much vaunted 'high degree of autonomy' will amount only to the freedom to make money. In the lead up to the takeover, China has exerted considerable effort to silence Hong Kong voices critical of the Beijing regime; its Hong Kong and Macau Affairs Office has announced the decision to scrap Hong Kong's elected bodies after 1 July 1997; and Beijing has also opposed the establishment of a Court of Final Appeal, an institution that local politicians claim is essential to guaranteeing an independent legal system in Hong Kong.

Taiwan

The people of Taiwan will be watching the Chinese takeover of Hong Kong very closely. The Kuomintang government of Chiang Kaishek fled (or 'withdrew', depending on your politics) to Taiwan in 1949 following the Communist takeover and has been there ever since, getting steadily richer and, in recent years, increasingly democratic. Its foreign currency reserves are among the world's largest; it is arguably the most democratic of the 'Four Little Tigers' (or 'Dragons' as the Chinese refer to them); it has a lively, uncensored press; and it has lifted all travel restrictions for its nationals. However, over this remarkable success story lies the shadow of Communist-Kuomintang politics.

The problem is a simple one. The Nationalists (Kuomintang) occupied Taiwan while still maintaining their right to govern China itself. The Communists, for their part, maintain that Taiwan is a province of the mainland. Reunification is a prickly issue in Taiwan, particularly since many Taiwanese have now had the opportunity to visit mainland China and see for themselves the kind of system they might have to live under if the two countries came together again.

Most Taiwanese are extremely sceptical of the sincerity of China's 'one country, two systems' promises and wonder aloud about the possibility of maintaining the freedoms they have won in their own country when the mainland takes such objection to the limited democratic rights being discussed for Hong Kong.

China, on the other hand, is unwavering in its claims on Taiwan and is not averse to using the threat of invasion to bring the Taiwanese to the table. With Taiwan pushing hard for international recognition (attempts to enter the UN have been vetoed by China), the reality is that invasion is probably the only way China could convince the Taiwanese that it is in their interests to unite.

The Empire, Long United...

Overall, the Deng years have been a period of political stability and rising living standards, but Deng is dying. He is widely thought to have fought a long battle with cancer and to suffer from Parkinson's disease, and reports of heart attacks and strokes frequently find their way into the Hong Kong press.

Officially, Deng is retired. Jiang Zemin heads both the government and the Party as state president and Communist Party general secretary. But Jiang's power is held in place by a fragile web of alliances and compromises between Deng and other ailing Party members whose power operates independently of any official posts. Jiang's mandate after the death of Deng is by no means assured, and in the long run the same might be said of the Party itself.

Faced with a looming inner-Party power struggle and an overall situation of increasingly uneven economic development, both Chinese and foreign experts have begun to voice concerns that China might break up. It has become fashionable to quote the first paragraph of *Romance of the Three Kingdoms*, a classic novel that describes the struggles to reunify the empire during the Three Kingdoms period: 'The empire, long united, must divide; long divided, must unite. Thus it has always been'.

China's empires do indeed have a long tradition of breaking up, and the problems facing the current regime make it ripe for radical change if not total collapse. The problems that led to the protests and bloodshed of 1989 are still present: inflation is thought to be running at around 25% and official corruption permeates the entire system despite occasional widely publicised drives to stamp it out. The central government

meanwhile complains of increasing regional power – in particular the affluent coastal cities of Shanghai and Guangzhou – and has difficulties collecting the taxes it claims as its own. The state is also saddled with some 100,000 state-owned firms, of which at least half are thought to be losing money. Together they employ over 100 million workers; restructuring would result in massive layoffs and social dislocation.

Perhaps most dangerous of all, rural incomes have stagnated in recent years, leading to widespread social unrest: in 1993 alone 830 incidents of rural revolt involving crowds of over 500 were reported in the Chinese press.

If all this were not bad enough, China's looming grain crisis is truly disastrous. Desertification, industrialisation, urbanisation and various energy projects have probably destroyed around a third of China's cropland over the last 40 years. This along with natural disasters, such as frequent flooding in southern China, probably means that China will become increasingly reliant on grain imports.

Ironically, however, if the Western press is not announcing the coming collapse of China (with its attendant consequences for the world economy), it is warning of the dangers of an ascending newly empowered China. Defence spending has been steadily on the rise in recent years and foreign sources currently place figures at anywhere between US$10 billion and US$50 billion annually. Both the USA and China's Asian neighbours are watching the situation closely.

The next few years will be critical for China. A smooth takeover of power in Hong Kong is essential, as is a smooth transition of power in the central government after the death of Deng. Restructuring of the economy has to continue if the government wants to deliver the affluent lifestyle that more and more Chinese are demanding as their right. And the central government will probably find itself under increasing pressure to provide greater freedoms and to undertake a degree of democratic reform. All or any of these could go wrong.

GEOGRAPHY

China is bounded to the north by deserts and to the west by the inhospitable Tibetan Plateau. The Han Chinese, who first built their civilisation around the Yellow River, moved south and east towards the sea. The Han did not develop as a maritime people so expansion was halted at the coast; they found themselves in control of a vast plain cut off from the rest of the world by oceans, mountains and deserts.

China is the third-largest country in the world, after Russia and Canada. Only half of China is occupied by Han Chinese; the rest is inhabited by Mongols, Tibetans, Uighurs, Kazaks and a host of other 'national minorities' who occupy the periphery of Han China, in the strategic border areas. The existence of numerous minority languages is why maps of China often have two spellings for the same place – one spelling being the minority language, the other being Chinese. For example, Kashgar is the same place as Kashi.

From the capital, Beijing, the government rules 22 provinces and the five 'autonomous regions' of Inner Mongolia, Ningxia, Xinjiang, Guangxi and Tibet. Beijing, Tianjin and Shanghai are administered directly by the central government. China also controls about 5000 islands and lumps of rock which occasionally appear above water level.

Taiwan, Hong Kong and Macau are all firmly regarded by the PRC as Chinese territory, and under the 1984 agreement with the UK, Hong Kong will be handed back to China in 1997. Macau will be returned in 1999. There is conflict with Vietnam concerning sovereignty over the Nansha and Xisha island groups in the South China Sea; Vietnam claims both and has occupied some of the Nansha Islands. In 1989 the Chinese took some of these islands from Vietnam by force. Other disputed islands in the Nansha group are also claimed by the Philippines, Taiwan and Malaysia.

China's topography varies from mountainous regions with towering peaks to flat, featureless plains. The land surface is a bit like a staircase descending from west to east.

At the top of the staircase are the plateaus of Tibet and Qinghai in the south-west, averaging 4500 metres above sea level. Tibet is referred to as the 'Roof of the World'. At the southern rim of the plateau is the Himalayan mountain range, with peaks averaging 6000 metres high; 40 peaks rise 7000 metres or more. Mt Everest, known to the Chinese as Qomolangma Feng, lies on the China-Nepal border.

Melting snow from the mountains of western China and the Tibetan Plateau provides the headwaters for many of the country's largest rivers: the Yangzi (Chang Jiang), Yellow (Huang He), Mekong (Lancang Jiang) and Salween (Nu Jiang) rivers. The latter runs from eastern Tibet into Yunnan Province and on into Myanmar.

Across the Kunlunshan and Qilianshan mountains on the northern rim of the Tibetan Plateau and the Hengduanshan mountains on the eastern rim, the terrain drops abruptly to between 1000 and 2000 metres above sea level. The second step down on the staircase is formed by the Inner Mongolia, Loess and Yunnan-Guizhou plateaus, and the Tarim, Sichuan and Junggar basins.

The Inner Mongolia Plateau has open terrain and expansive grasslands. Further south, the Loess Plateau is formed of loose earth 50 to 80 metres deep – in the past the soil erosion which accompanied a torrential rainfall often choked the Yellow River. The Yunnan-Guizhou Plateau in the south-west has a lacerated terrain with numerous gorges, rapids and waterfalls, and is noted for its limestone pinnacles with large underground caverns such as those at Guilin and Yangshuo.

The Tarim Basin is the largest inland basin in the world and is the site of the Xinjiang Autonomous Region. Here you'll find the Taklamakan Desert (the largest in China) as well as China's largest shifting salt lake, Lop Nur (*Luóbù bó*), where nuclear bombs are tested. The Tarim Basin is bordered to the north by the Tianshan mountains. To the east of this range is the low-lying Turpan Depression, known as the 'Oasis of Fire' and the hottest place in China. The Junggar Basin

China & the Spratly Islands

If they were not such a contentious piece of real estate, very few people would have heard of the Spratly Islands. To find them on a map, look for a parcel of dots in the South China Sea hemmed in by Malaysia, Brunei, the Philippines, Vietnam and China way to the north. They all claim the islands as theirs.

It is tempting to ask what all the fuss is about. After all, this is a collection of 53 specks of land, many of which are reefs and shoals rather than islands. The answer is oil. Not that any oil has been discovered in the region, and some experts dispute that any will ever be found. Yet the very possibility that there *might* be oil in the Spratly Islands has set all the countries in the region at loggerheads with each other.

China, the most distant of the claimants, sees its territorial rights to the area as being validated by a historical relationship with the islands that dates back to the Han Dynasty. The ruins of Chinese temples can still be found on some of the islands. Vietnam has for long been a disputant to this claim, and in 1933 the colonial French government of Vietnam annexed the islands. They lost them to Japan in 1939. With Japan's WW II defeat, the question of the Spratly Islands was left unaddressed, and it was not until a Philippine claim in 1956 that the Taiwan Nationalist government reasserted the traditional Chinese claim over the island group by occupying the largest of the islands, Taiping – where they still remain. Vietnam followed by hoisting a flag over the westernmost of the islands. The Chinese struck back in 1988 by sinking two Vietnamese ships.

With all the countries of the region embarking on programmes of updating their military capabilities, exacerbated somewhat by the North Korean nuclear issue, the Spratly Islands remain one of the most potentially destabilising issues in the Asian region. ∎

---

lies in the far north of Xinjiang Province, beyond the Tianshan range.

As you cross the mountains on the eastern edge of this second step of the topographical staircase, the altitude drops to less than 1000 metres above sea level. Here, forming the third step, are the plains of the Yangzi River valley and northern and eastern China. These plains – the homeland of the Han Chinese, their 'Middle Kingdom' – are the most important agricultural areas of the country and the most heavily populated. It should be remembered that two-thirds of China is mountain, desert or otherwise unfit for cultivation. If you exclude the largely barren regions of Inner Mongolia, Xinjiang and the Tibetan Plateau from the remaining third, all that remains for cultivation is a meagre 15% or 20% of land area. Only this to feed a billion people!

In such a vast country, the waterways quickly took on a central role as communication and trading links. Most of China's rivers flow east. At 6300 km long, the Yangzi is the longest river in China and the third longest in the world after the Nile and the Amazon. It originates in the snow-covered Tanggulashan mountains of south-western Qinghai, and passes through Tibet and several Chinese provinces before emptying into the East China Sea.

The Yellow River, about 5460 km long and the second-longest river in China, is the birthplace of Chinese civilisation. It originates in the Bayan Harshan mountains of Qinghai and winds its way through the north of China into the sea east of Beijing. The third great waterway of China, the Grand Canal, is the longest artificial canal in the world. It originally stretched 1800 km from Hangzhou in south China to Beijing in the north, though most of it is no longer navigable.

CLIMATE

China experiences great diversity in climate. Spread over such a vast area, the country is subject to the worst extremes in weather, from the bitterly cold to the unbearably hot. There isn't really an 'ideal' time to visit the country, so use the following information as a rough guide to avoid temperature extremes. The warmest regions in winter are found in the south and south-west in areas such as Xishuangbanna, the south coast and Hainan Island. In summer, high spots like Emeishan are a welcome relief from the heat.

North

Winters in the north fall between December and March and are incredibly cold. Beijing's temperature doesn't rise above 0°C (32°F), although it will generally be dry and sunny. North of the Great Wall, into Inner Mongolia or Heilongjiang, it's much colder with temperatures dropping down to -40°C – you'll see the curious sight of sand dunes covered in snow.

Summer in the north is around May to August. Beijing temperatures can rise to 38°C (100°F) or more. July and August are also the rainy months in this city. In both the north and south most of the rain falls during summer.

Spring and autumn are the best times for visiting the north. Daytime temperatures range from 20°C to 30°C (68°F to 86°F) and there is less rain. Although it can be quite hot during the day, nights can be bitterly cold and bring frost.

Central

In the Yangzi River valley area (including Shanghai) summers are long, hot and humid. Wuhan, Chongqing and Nanjing have been dubbed 'the three furnaces' by the Chinese.

You can expect very high temperatures any time between April and October. Winters are short and cold, with temperatures dipping well below freezing – almost as cold as Beijing. It can also be wet and miserable at any time apart from summer. While it is impossible to pinpoint an ideal time to visit, spring and autumn are probably best.

South

In the far south, around Guangzhou, the hot, humid periods last from around April through September, and temperatures can rise to 38°C (100°F) as in the north. This is also the rainy season. Typhoons are liable to hit the south-east coast between July and September.

There is a short winter from January to March. It's nowhere near as cold as in the north, but temperature statistics don't really indicate just how cold it can get, so bring warm clothes.

Autumn and spring can be good times to visit, with day temperatures in the 20°C to 25°C (68°F to 75°F) range. However, it can be miserably wet and cold, with perpetual rain or drizzle, so be prepared.

North-West

It gets hot in summer, but at least it's dry. The desert regions can be scorching in the daytime. Turpan, which sits in a depression 150 metres below sea level, more than deserves the title of the 'hottest place in China' with maximums of around 47°C (117°F).

In winter this region is as formidably cold as the rest of northern China. In Ürümqi the average temperature in January is around -10°C (14°F), with minimums down to almost -30°C (-22°F). Temperatures in Turpan are only slightly more favourable to human existence.

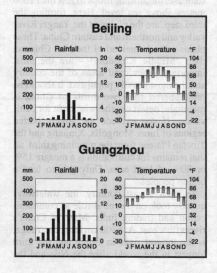

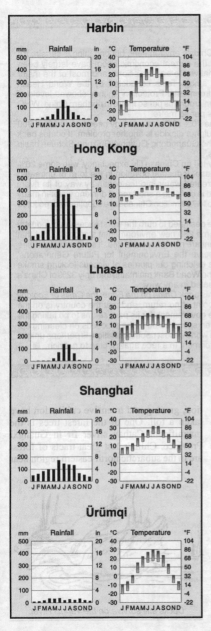

Harbin

Hong Kong

Lhasa

Shanghai

Ürümqi

Tibet

In Tibet it's easy to get the impression that all four seasons have been compressed into one day. Temperatures can vary from below zero during the evening and early morning to a sizzling 38°C at midday, but it always feels remarkably cool in the shade. Winter brings intense cold and fierce winds. Snowfall is far less common in Tibet than the name 'Land of Snows' implies – it's an arid place and the sun is quick to melt off snowfalls. Rainfall is scarcest in the north and west of Tibet. Northern monsoons can sweep across the plains for days on end, often whipping up dust storms, sandstorms, snowstorms, or (rare) rainstorms.

FLORA & FAUNA

Given the fact that China is a large country spanning most of the world's climatic zones, it's not surprising that there is a great diversity in plant and animal life. Unfortunately, human beings have had a considerable impact and much of China's rich natural heritage is rare, endangered or extinct. To the government's credit, more than 300 nature reserves have been established protecting over 1.8% of China's land area. Many animals are officially protected, though illegal hunting and trapping continues. A bigger problem is habitat destruction, caused by agriculture, urbanisation and industrial pollution.

Bird-watching is a possibility, especially in the spring. Some good places for this activity include the Zhalong Nature Reserve in Heilongjiang Province; Qinghai Lake in Qinghai Province; and Poyang Lake in northern Jiangxi Province, China's largest freshwater lake.

Animals are animals – in the wild they wisely avoid humans. Other than some pathetic specimens in zoos, you probably won't get to see many exotic animals in China. Traditionally eaten in China, you can find some of the less exotic varieties – snake, monkey, pangolin, bear, giant salamander and raccoon, as well as dog, cat and rat – on restaurant menus.

Perhaps no animal better represents both

China & the Environment

It is difficult to find reliable facts and figures on China's environment, but one thing is certain: it's in a bad way. China's great leaps forward and the current economic boom have largely been sustained at the expense of controls on industrial waste and emissions, and most of the major cities lie smothered under great canopies of smog. Tests conducted by the World Health Organization (WHO) and China's National Environmental Protection Agency showed levels of airborne suspended particulates to average 526 micrograms per sq metre in northern China. WHO recommends a safe limit of 60 to 90 micrograms per sq metre.

The main problem is coal. It provides for some 70% of China's energy needs and around 900 million tonnes of it go up in smoke every year. Sulphur dioxide is another problem. It comes back to earth in the form of acid rain, and has turned the Guangdong-Guangxi-Guizhou-Sichuan basin area into one of the world's worst affected areas.

Air pollution is thought to be exacting a heavy toll on Chinese life expectancy, with some 26% of all deaths being traceable to respiratory disease. Industrial pollution in the form of untreated waste (China dumps three billion tonnes of untreated water into the ocean by way of its rivers annually) threatens China's coastal wetlands and is creating a shortage of drinking water in many parts of the country. Some reports indicate that up to 700 million Chinese are supplied with polluted water.

The problem is not that China lacks legislature designed to curb the worst excesses of industry (the central government recently established some 230 new environmental standards), but that these laws designed to safeguard the environment are rarely implemented. It's not unusual to see huge billboards proclaiming the need to 'Preserve the Environment for Future Generations' plonked right next to huge industrial complexes belching out plumes of viscous-looking smoke and oozing untreated waste into a nearby river. The World Bank maintains that only 32% of China's annual 25 billion tonnes of industrial waste is treated in any way.

He Bochun, a Chinese intellectual, argues in his book *China on the Edge: the Crisis of Ecology & Development* that China is already past the point of no return, and that the country is on the verge of an ecological catastrophe. The Chinese government, for its part, seems to be taking the attitude that China can get rich and dirty, and then spend some of the proceeds on cleaning up. It's a time-honoured tradition, but then China, the world's most populous nation, is perhaps unique in the grand scale in which it is abusing its environment in a race against time to get rich. ■

the beauty and the struggle of wildlife in China than the panda. These splendid animals are endangered by a combination of hunting, habitat encroachment and natural disasters. Sparsely populated regions of Sichuan, Tibet and Xinjiang provide a habitat for other magnificent creatures, including snow leopards, argali sheep and wild yaks.

The extreme north-eastern part of China is inhabited by some interesting mammals: reindeer, moose, musk deer, bears, sables and tigers. There is also considerable bird life – cranes, ducks, bustards, swans and herons are among the winged creatures found in this region.

Plants have fared somewhat better under the crunch of a billion people, but deforesta-tion, grazing and intensive cultivation have taken a toll. One of the rarest trees is the magnificent Cathay silver fir in Guangxi Province. China's last great tracts of forest are in the subarctic north-eastern region near

Ducks still survive on the Yangzi River.

the Russian border. For sheer diversity of vegetation, the area around Xishuangbanna in the tropical south is the richest part of China. This region also provides habitats for herds of wild elephants; however, both the creatures and the tropical rainforest are under intense pressure from slash-and-burn agriculture.

Hainan Island also has diverse tropical plant and animal life. There are seven nature reserves on the island, though it's fair to say that more than a few endangered species still end up on the dinner plate.

Perhaps the most beautiful cultivated plant is the bamboo. Bamboo – which is actually a grass rather than a tree – comes in many varieties and is cultivated in southeastern China for use as building material and food. Other useful plants include herbs, among them ginseng, golden hairpin, angelica and fritillary.

If you're interested in delving further into China's flora and fauna, two good books on the subject are *Living Treasures* by Tang Xiyang (Bantam Books, 1987) and *The Natural History of China* by Zhao Ji, et al (Collins, 1990).

GOVERNMENT

Precious little is known about the inner workings of the Chinese government, but what is known is that the entire monolithic structure, from grassroots work units to the upper echelons of political power, is controlled by the Communist Party. Although the illusion of democracy is maintained through various means, nobody gets a foot into public life without a lift up from the Party. Theoretically, the government and the Party are distinct, but in practice the Party controls the government through the appointment of thousands of official posts and offices, and through the operation of agencies that parallel and oversee the day-to-day running of all government institutions. Power in China is by no means visible in the form of appointed leaders and designated institutions, as can famously be seen in the case of Deng Xiaoping himself, who has long been regarded the most powerful man

in China while at the same time having no official titles whatsoever.

The highest authority rests with the Standing Committee of the CCP Politburo. The Politburo comprises 25 members. Below it is the 210-member Central Committee, made up of younger Party members and provincial Party leaders. At grassroots level the Party forms a parallel system to the administrations in the army, universities, government and industries. Real authority is exercised by the Party representatives at each level in these organisations. They, in turn, are responsible to the Party officials in the hierarchy above them, thus ensuring strict central control.

The day-to-day running of the country lies with the State Council, which is directly under the control of the CCP. The State Council is headed by the premier. Beneath the premier are four vice-premiers, 10 state councillors, a secretary-general, 45 ministers and various other agencies. The State Council implements the decisions made by the Politburo: it draws up quotas, assesses planning, establishes priorities and organises finances. The ministries include Public Security, Education, Defence, Culture, Forestry, Railways, Tourism, Minority Affairs, Radio & TV, the Bank of China and Family Planning.

Rubber-stamping the decisions of the CCP leadership is the National People's Congress (NPC). It comprises a 'democratic alliance' of both Party members and non-Party members who include intellectuals, technicians and industrial managers. In theory they are empowered to amend the constitution and to choose the premier and members of the State Council. The catch is that all these officeholders must first be recommended by the Central Committee, and thus the NPC is only an approving body.

The Chinese government is also equipped with a massive bureaucracy. The term 'cadre' is usually applied to bureaucrats, and their monopoly on power means that wide-ranging perks are a privilege of rank for all and sundry – from the lowliest clerks to the shadowy puppet masters of Zhongnanhai.

China's bureaucratic tradition is a long one. The assault of the Cultural Revolution had little effect on it and future Chinese revolutions are unlikely to be any more successful. It's chief purpose seems to be to make the life of ordinary Chinese as miserable as possible.

At grassroots level, the basic unit of social organisation outside the family is the work unit *(dānwèi)*. Every Chinese person is theoretically a member of one, whether he or she works in a hospital, school, office, factory or village, though many Chinese nowadays slip through the net by being self-employed or working in a private operation. For those who are members, tight controls are exercised by the leaders of the unit they belong to.

The work unit is a perfect organ of social control and little proceeds without it. It approves marriages and divorces and even childbirth. It assigns housing, sets salaries, handles mail, recruits Party members, keeps files on each unit member, arranges transfers to other jobs or other parts of the country, and gives permission to travel abroad. The work unit's control extends into every part of the individual's life.

The wild card in the system is the army. Comprising land forces, the navy and the air force, it has a total of around 2.9 million members. China is divided into seven military regions, each with its own military leadership, in some cases with strong regional affiliations. A breakdown of central power might see a return to the warlordism of the early 20th century or a unified putsch by the PLA. In any event, the PLA is a force to be reckoned with.

Political Dissidence & Repression

Repressive unelected governments are rarely popular with their constituents and have to come up with ways to deal with dissenting voices. In China's case, the all-pervasive nature of Communist Party control, its intrusion into almost every facet of the individual's life, has made dissidence not only dangerous but also very difficult to carry out. Most Chinese dissidents (at least the well-known ones) have emerged in the few brief moments when the usual tight restraints have been thrown off in protests, such as the Democracy Wall Movement of 1979 and the Tiananmen Square massacre in 1989.

Anyone looking into the history of dissent in Communist China will find no organised movements like Poland's Solidarity or South Africa's African National Congress. The Communist Party has been scrupulously rigorous in nipping any nascent protest movements in the bud. Neither is it possible to find any individuals who, like Aung San Suu Kyi in Myanmar, serve as a focus for the people's democratic aspirations. Many of China's more prominent dissidents, such as Wei Jingshen arrested in the aftermath of the Democracy Wall Movement, emerge from prison years later, exhausted, to a China that moves to a different beat. (After a brief period of freedom, Wei was re-arrested and tried and is now back in prison.)

One of the great problems of Chinese dissenters is that they rarely find much to agree on. The ringleaders of the Tiananmen protests, most of whom fled the country in the wake of the massacre, have failed to organise as a group outside China, and some of them have given up politics entirely – Chen Kaige, famously captured on TV arguing it out with Li Peng, was last seen running a Sizzler-style steak bar in California. Other prominent foreign-based dissidents such as Fang Lizhi and Liu Binyan are considered too old and too removed from current events in China to really matter by many young dissidents.

In recent years, however, the emergence of a free enterprise economy and the flood of new ideas that has come with Deng's open door policies have resulted in high-profile, relatively organised dissent that was previously unthinkable. In spring 1989, for example, a group of 43 intellectuals signed three petitions supporting a call for the release of political prisoners. In mid-1995, a total of 12 petitions had been signed by prominent intellectuals, largely calling for greater freedom of speech and, specifically, a re-evaluation of the Tiananmen Square protests of 1989. The petitions resulted predictably in a round of arrests, but there are signs that the government itself is not of one mind in opposing the calls of the petitions.

More details on this topic can be found in publications such as Amnesty International's China report or *Seeds of Fire – Chinese Voices of Conscience*, edited by Geremie Barmé and John Minford.

ECONOMY

The great achievement of the Deng years – though there is much to complain about – has been a reinvigoration of a moribund economy. Limited economic freedoms have changed the face of China, and the new China is vigorous and forward-looking in a way it never was under the old socialist order. Everywhere the visitor to China looks there are massive construction projects: highways, railway lines, hotels, housing complexes, department stores and airports. Wages and living standards are rising, and Chinese throughout the country are on the move in search of business opportunities. In short a revolution is under way.

What changes have the Deng years seen exactly? Essentially, there has been a move away from central planning towards market forces, a decollectivisation of agriculture, and an abandonment of high-speed 'great leaps' forward for balanced agricultural and industrial growth fuelled by foreign trade, science and technology imports and foreign investment. In short Deng chose a pragmatic approach to achieving the so-called 'Four Modernisations': namely, modernisation of China's industry, agriculture, defence and science and technology. The aim is to transform China into a modern state by the year 2000.

The transition, however, from the centrally controlled, ideologically motivated economy of the Mao years to Deng's vast free-enterprise experiment has not been an entirely smooth one. The hurdle has been the sponsor of change itself: the Party. Never mind the ideological grounds for the centrally controlled economy of the past, the transition has had one overwhelming consequence – guaranteed far-reaching control of the Party's subjects. But economic freedoms have eroded Party power and will continue to do so. Thus the Party has written a catch-22 clause into its mandate to rule: without continued economic freedoms, the Party's days are numbered; with continued economic freedoms Party influence will continue

---

Brand Names

China's socialist market economy is by no means immune to brand consciousness. China's nouveau riche drive to work in Volvos, dress in Lacoste T-shirts, swig back Remy Martin cognac in Japanese-style karaoke parlours and take their kids to McDonald's for dinner. But it's not all imports out there. China has its own brands.

You might look fetching in Pansy underwear (sorry, men only). Horse Head facial tissues are just the ticket in sweaty weather. Wake up to the crow of a Golden Rooster alarm clock, start your breakfast with a glass of Billion Strong Pulpy C orange drink or a cup of Imperial Concubine tea and a Puke cigarette. Long Dong mineral water is refreshing and loaded with health-bestowing minerals and nutrients, though the brand name is probably false advertising. White Elephant batteries are best avoided, but the space-age Moon Rabbit variety gets good press.

White Rabbit candy has been a huge success throughout China and would probably be popular with kids the world over. The best that can be said for Flying Baby toilet paper and Ugly Baby soap, on the other hand, is that they are unusual brand names – though the fatal undertones of the ginseng product called Gensenocide takes the prize in the 'unusual' stakes.

There are no baby themes in condom brand names interestingly enough. Asia Good Oil is an inventive local product name, while Huan Bao Multifunction Condoms gets you thinking – just how many functions *are* there for a condom? ∎

to diminish. The result has been bursts of economic growth followed by panicky austerity drives.

State-Owned Enterprises

State-owned industry is without a doubt the backbone of the socialist economy. In effect, it operates as a vast welfare system providing guaranteed jobs and housing for 100 million Chinese and their dependents (in total perhaps a quarter of the population); it also allows Party control, via the work unit system, of the lives of all employees and their families. The problem is, state-owned industries are a vast drain on the economy. Productivity is low, and anywhere between 40% and 60% (figures vary) of them are losing money. One only has to compare employment figures with productivity figures to see the problem: state-owned industries account for 43% of industrial output but employ around 70% of China's industrial work force.

Reforms of state-owned industry began as early as 1978. Although such reforms have not been without their successes, 17 years later in 1995 the Chinese government was still holding back from thoroughgoing reform. The main problem is the prospect of mass unemployment. Meanwhile, state behemoths soak up public money, creating a credit shortage for more productive private enterprises, and subsidies to state-owned enterprises are thought to be the main driving force behind inflation, which according to some analysts was running at around 25% in 1995 (though official figures are much lower).

Inflation

There is much debate as to the causes of inflation in China, but whatever its causes, the Chinese government doesn't like it. Price hikes of basic consumer items were a fundamental contributing factor in the Tiananmen protests of 1989. The government doesn't want more social unrest.

Unfortunately for the government, the root cause of inflation in China is probably structural. Again those pesky state-owned industries pop up. State-owned industries

borrow vast amounts of money. Most of it ends up as bad debts (approximately US$70 billion in 1994). The standard response of the central government is to cover the shortfall by gunning the printing press of the People's Bank into action and imposing a credit squeeze on private enterprise. Add to this a massive influx of direct foreign investment (over US$30 billion in 1994), and a situation arises in which money-supply growth is far outpacing economic growth.

The Chinese government is currently faced with the dilemma of going about the business of massive reform of its banking system and state-owned enterprises (with all the attendant social implications), or muddling along and hoping that things will gradually improve and that inflation will not lead to widespread social unrest in the meantime.

Meanwhile Down on the Farm

Rural China was the birthplace of Deng's pioneering economic reforms. Having been forcibly collectivised during the Mao era, the 'household responsibility system' of the late 1970s allowed farmers to sell whatever they wanted on the free market after government quotas had been filled. Productivity rose and a new era of plenty was heralded for rural China.

Fifteen years on, rural incomes lag far behind urban incomes. Increased mechanisation and fertiliser use has increased productivity but has also led to a scarcity of work – there are perhaps as many as 100 million farm labourers without regular work. As many as 15 million of them a year flock to the coastal cities, where they generally end up working long hours in poorly paid factory jobs.

As in the industrial sector, partial rural reform has created problems that only very risky thoroughgoing reform can fix. Attempts to free up grain prices and make the growing of basic staples such as rice, wheat and corn more profitable for Chinese farmers has resulted in soaring prices. In 1995 the government reintroduced price caps on grains and has attempted to recentralise the grain trade. As a result many farmers are

Making Money with the PLA

In China's socialist market economy, everything is pay as you go. Even the armed forces have to pay their own way. Not that they're complaining. The People's Liberation Army is doing very well out of China's economic reforms, thank you.

Nobody is quite sure just how many PLA-run business enterprises there are. Even the military itself claims to have no idea, they have proliferated so rapidly. Conservative estimates put the figure at about 20,000. How much money these businesses are raking in is even more of a mystery. But for an idea of the scale of things, the Poly Group – the most successful of China's PLA businesses – recently built the Poly Plaza, a business and hotel complex in Beijing, for US$70 million.

PLA-run businesses by no means restrict their operations to the production of arms. In fact, they'll dabble in almost anything if there's a whiff of hard cash in the air. Cigarette machines, pharmaceuticals, space launchers, TV sets, wallpaper, mountain bikes, hotels, tourist shops, luxury buses and ovens all roll off PLA production lines. In Guangzhou, the military has even been known to conduct war games on TV that allow viewers to bet on the results.

The PLA is successfully paying its own way. The problem now is keeping the whole thing in check. No government or public could sensibly be amenable to the idea of vast money-making corporations backed by their own armies, which is what the various units of the PLA have in effect become. And many units operate beyond the law – who is going to stop them?

The Hainan fiasco of 1993, when US$500 million of Japanese cars were imported duty free and resold on the mainland at enormous profits, was done so in collusion with the PLA. Meanwhile reports of PLA marine units providing armed cover for smuggling outfits proliferate. As PLA businesses extend their interests into Hong Kong, many Hong Kong public figures worry publicly that the former colony will inherit the problem of armed money-making machines that ride rough-shod over all legal processes. ■

switching to more lucrative cash crops that can be sold freely at market prices.

POPULATION

The official figures for 1994 show mainland China (excluding Taiwan, Hong Kong and Macau) with a population of 1,202,900,000 (1.2 billion) people. Only 20% of the total population is classified as urban. The overwhelming majority of Chinese remains rural.

The huge population has to be fed with the produce of around 15-20% of the land they live on, the sum total of China's arable land. The rest is barren wasteland or can only be lightly grazed. Much of the productive land is also vulnerable to flood and drought caused by the vagaries of China's summer monsoons or unruly rivers. Worse still, China's arable land is shrinking at an alarming rate. Industrialisation, urbanisation and erosion are thought to have robbed China of around four million hectares of cropland since 1978. In the same period the population grew by over 130 million.

The Malthusian prospect of an ever-growing population with an ever-shrinking capacity to feed itself, has led the government to vigorously promote a massive nationwide birth-control programme since 1973. Chinese estimates of how many people the country can support range up to 1.4 billion. The current plan is to limit growth to 1.25 billion people by the year 2000, hold that figure steady somehow, and allow birth control and natural mortality to reduce the population to 700 million, which China's leaders estimate would be ideal. Current projections, however, indicate that China's population will be close on 1.5 billion by the year 2010, and that the present population might well double within 50 years.

In recent years the main thrust of the campaign in the cities is to encourage couples to sign a one-child pledge by offering them an extra month's salary per year until the child is 14, plus housing normally reserved for a family of four (a promise often not kept because of the acute housing shortage). If the couple have a second child then the privileges are rescinded, and penalties such as demotion at work or even loss of job are imposed. If a woman has an abortion it entitles her to a vacation with pay.

Birth-control measures appear to be working in the cities, but it's difficult to say what's happening in the villages or if the target of zero growth can ever be reached. The catch is that Chinese agriculture still relies on human muscle and farmers find it desirable to have many children.

On the other hand, families who do abide by the one-child policy will often go to great lengths to make sure their child is male. This

is particularly true in rural China, where the ancient custom of female infanticide continues to this day. In parts of China, this is creating a serious imbalance of the sexes. A recent survey in Shaanxi Province, for example, determined that 145 male infants were being born for every 100 females; the overall average for China is 114 males for every 100 females. Spread over such a huge population, this amounts to a lot of unmarriageable men.

PEOPLE

Han Chinese make up about 93% of the total population; the rest is composed of China's 55 or so minority nationalities, including Mongols and Tibetans. Although minorities account for a bit less than 7% of the population, they are distributed over some 50% of Chinese-controlled territory, mostly in the sensitive border regions.

Some groups, like the Zhuang and the Manchu, have become so assimilated over

Wives for Sale

As China continues to shed the austerities of the hardline Communist years, many of the old ways are returning. Chinese are going back to their temples, burning paper money for their ancestors, playing mahjong and, in time-honoured tradition, the sale of wives in rural China is once again coming back into fashion.

Actual figures are difficult to obtain, but China's Xinhua News Agency admitted that in 1990 courts prosecuted 10,475 cases of women abducted for sale into the rural marriage market. Chinese sources admit that this number probably represents only a small percentage of actual cases.

The central problem seems to be the gangs of Chinese men who abduct young women and take them thousands of km from their home towns and then sell them to rural families as brides. The going price: US$450 to US$550. The women are often drugged and raped by the gangs. It is suspected that the shame prevents many of the women from reporting what has happened to them.

Strong efforts are presently being made in China to stamp out the practice. Men who buy brides are liable to prison sentences of five to 10 years, while the 'traffickers' face a life sentence or execution. More than 30 gang members were publicly shot in July 1992 in Shandong Province for abducting women. ∎

Bai mother and child, from near Dali, Yunnan Province.

the centuries that to the Western eye they look indistinguishable from their Han counterparts; only language and religion separate them. Other minority groups no longer wear their traditional clothing except on market or festival days. Some have little or nothing in common with the Han Chinese, like the Turkic-descended Uighurs of Xinjiang, who are instantly recognisable by their swarthy Caucasian appearance, Turkish-related language, use of Arabic script and adherence to Islam.

Minority separatism has always been a threat to the stability of China, particularly among the Uighurs and the Tibetans, who have poor and often volatile relations with the Han Chinese and whose homelands form the border regions of China. The minority regions provide China with the greater part of its livestock and hold vast untapped deposits of minerals.

Keeping the minorities under control has been a continuous problem for the Han Chinese. Tibet and Xinjiang are heavily garrisoned by Chinese troops, partly to protect China's borders and partly to prevent rebellion among the local population. Chinese migration to minority areas has been encouraged as a means of controlling them by sheer weight of numbers. For example, 50 years ago Inner Mongolia had a population of about four million and Xinjiang had 2.5 million. Today those figures are 20 and 13 million respectively. The Chinese government has also set up special training centres, like the National Minorities Institute in Beijing, to train loyal minority cadres for these regions. Since 1976 the government has tried to diffuse discontent by relaxing some of its grasp on the day-to-day life of the minority peoples, in particular allowing temples and mosques closed during the Cultural Revolution to reopen.

Until very recently, the minorities were exempt from China's one-child family planning guidelines. In the coming decade, government officials hope to extend the one-child family policy to minorities too, but this is sure to provoke further hostility against the Han majority.

ARTS

Many people go to China expecting a profound cultural experience. This has led to a lot of disappointment. While major attractions like the Forbidden City and the

---

China's Dwindling Name Pool

As if a huge money-losing public sector, 1.2 billion mouths to feed, a looming grain crisis, a shortage of marriageable women and Deng Xiaoping's mortality was not enough to worry about, according to *The Economist* China is also running out of names.

Unlike the West, where name-giving got a new lease of life in the 1960s (think of Moon Unit and Bilbo for example), China has got stuck in a bit of a rut on the moniker front. Chinese academics point out that parents have to be more inventive with their kids' names if China is not to slip into a social quagmire of widespread mistaken identities.

The problem does not stop at given names. Although China today has around 3100 surnames, a quarter of the population of China (around 350 million people) share just five surnames: Li, Wang, Zhang, Liu and Chen. The problem is particularly acute in big cities, where thousands of people may share the same surname and given name, written in exactly the same characters. Chinese newspaper reports frequently bemoan wrongful arrests, bank account errors and unwanted surgery performed – all due to instances of mistaken identity.

Researchers are divided as to the solution, but a popular suggestion is to resurrect some of the 8000 surnames that were once in use in China and have now become extinct. Perhaps the authorities might raffle them off like customised license plate numbers. As for given names, one can always hope the next generation will start burning incense, reading Beat poetry and wearing flowers in their hair. ∎

Dunhuang Buddhist caves still stand intact, many of China's other ancient treasures were ransacked or razed to the ground during the Cultural Revolution. Much of China's precious art, including pottery, calligraphy and embroidery, was defaced or destroyed.

Fortunately, since the early 1970s a great deal of work has been done to restore what was destroyed in the Cultural Revolution. Initially, restoration was carried out only on major attractions with foreign tourism in mind, but with local tourism emerging as a major money-spinner in the 1990s tourist attractions all over China are having cash pumped into them. On a less positive note, China's tourist attractions have often been tackily restored and are swarming with pushy souvenir entrepreneurs.

Calligraphy

Calligraphy has traditionally been regarded in China as the highest form of visual art. A fine piece of calligraphy was often valued more highly by a collector of art than a good painting. Children were trained at a very early age to write beautifully, and good calligraphy was a social asset. A scholar, for example, could not pass his examination to become an official if he was a poor calligrapher. A person's character was judged by their handwriting; if it was elegant it revealed great refinement.

The basic tools of calligraphy are paper, ink, ink-stone (on which the ink is mixed) and brush. These are commonly referred to as the 'four treasures of the scholar's study'. A brush stroke must be infused with the creative or vital energy which, according to the Taoists, permeates and animates all phenomena of the universe: mountains, rivers, rocks, trees, insects and animals. Expressive images are drawn from nature to describe the different types of brush strokes – for example, 'rolling waves', 'leaping dragon', 'startled snake slithering off into the grass', 'dewdrop about to fall' or 'playful butterfly'.

A beautiful piece of calligraphy therefore conjures up the majestic movements of a landscape. The qualities of the brush strokes are described in organic terms of 'bone',

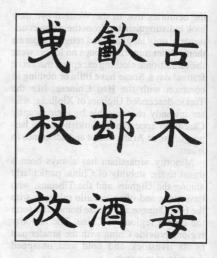

Chinese calligraphy - virtually an art form in itself.

'flesh', 'muscle' and 'blood'. Blood, for example, refers to the quality of the ink and the varied ink tones created by the degree of moisture on the brush.

Calligraphy is regarded as a form of self-cultivation as well as self-expression. It is believed that calligraphy should be able to express and communicate the most ineffable thoughts and feelings, which cannot be conveyed by words. It is often said that in looking at calligraphy 'one can understand the writer fully, as if meeting them face to face'. All over China, decorative calligraphy can be found in temples, adorning the walls of caves and on the sides of mountains and monuments.

Painting

Chinese painting is the art of brush and ink. The basic tools are those of calligraphy, which influenced painting in both technique and theory. The brush line, which varies in thickness and tone, is the important feature of a Chinese painting. Shading is regarded as a foreign technique (introduced to China via

Buddhist art from central Asia between the 3rd and 6th centuries), and colour plays only a minor symbolic and decorative role. As early as the 9th century, ink was recognised as being able to provide all the qualities of colour.

Although you will see artists in China painting or sketching in front of their subject, traditionally the painter works from memory and is not so interested in imitating the outward appearance of the subject as in capturing its lifelike qualities and imbuing the painting with the energy permeating all nature.

From the Han Dynasty until the end of the Tang Dynasty, the human figure occupied the dominant position in Chinese painting, as it did in pre-modern European art. Figure painting flourished against a Confucian background, illustrating moral themes. Landscape painting for its own sake started in the 4th and 5th centuries. The practice of seeking out places of natural beauty and communing with nature first became popular among Taoist poets and painters. By the 9th century the interest of artists began to shift away from figures and, from the 11th century onwards, landscape has dominated Chinese painting.

The function of the landscape painting was to substitute nature, allowing the viewer to wander imaginatively. The painting is meant to surround the viewer, and there is no 'viewing point' as there is in Western painting.

Painting became accepted as one of the activities of a cultured person, along with poetry, music and calligraphy. The scholarly amateur painters were either officials or retired people who did not depend on painting for their income. They painted for pleasure and became their own patrons and critics. They were also collectors and connoisseurs of art, and the arbiters of taste. Their ideas on art were voiced in voluminous writings and in inscriptions on paintings.

Moral qualities appreciated in a virtuous person (in the Confucian frame of things) became the very qualities appreciated in paintings. One of the most important was the 'concealment of brilliance' under an unassuming exterior, since any deliberate display of technical skill was considered vulgar. Creativity and individuality were highly valued, but only within the framework of tradition. Artists created their own style by transforming the styles of the ancient masters, seeing themselves as part of the great continuity of the painting tradition. This art-historical approach became a conscious pursuit in the late Ming and early Qing dynasties.

When the Communists came to power, much of the country's artistic talent was turned to glorifying the revolution and bombarding the masses with political slogans. Colourful billboards of Mao waving to cheering crowds holding up the 'little red book' were once popular, as were giant Mao statues standing above smaller statues of enthusiastic workers and soldiers. Music and opera were also co-opted for political purposes.

Since the late 1970s, the Chinese art scene has gradually recovered. The work of traditionally influenced painters can be seen for sale in shops and galleries all over China, while in the major cities (particularly Beijing) a flourishing avant-garde scene has emerged. The work of Chinese painters has been arguably more innovative and dissident than that of writers, possibly because the results are harder to interpret by the authorities. Art collecting has become a fashionable hobby among China's new rich, and many of China's young artists have been exhibited overseas to critical acclaim – China's New Art Post-1989 included the work of 52 artists and successfully toured Hong Kong, Australia and the USA during 1993 and 1994.

Architecture

Modern China is not exactly an architectural treasure trove, and over the last five years this situation has been exacerbated by the widespread construction of tiled housing blocks and unimaginative office buildings. Nevertheless, somewhere between the imperial structures of Beijing, the lingering colonial buildings of Shanghai, the temples being restored across the country and the occasional rural village that has somehow escaped the ravages of the 20th century, there's still plenty to see.

Traditionally Chinese architecture – from the lowliest village homestead to imperial palace – follows certain principles. A north-south-oriented walled compound (with the main entrance to the south) that houses one or more structures was the basic form. As Chinese lived together in extended-family groups, a walled home would generally house the living quarters for the head of the family in the north, with housing for children and their families on the side.

Chinese Temples Temple architecture in China also tends to follow a certain uniformity. There is little external difference between Buddhist, Confucian and Taoist temples, which again are housed in compounds with a north-south orientation.

Architecturally, the roof is the dominant feature of a Chinese temple. It is usually green or yellow and is decorated with figures of divinities and lucky symbols such as dragons and carp. Stone lions often guard the temple entrance.

Inside is a small courtyard with a large bowl where incense and paper offerings are burnt. Beyond is the main hall with an altar table, often with an intricately carved front. Here you'll find offerings of fruit and drinks. Behind is the altar with its images framed by red brocade embroidered with gold characters. Depending on the size and wealth of the temple there are gongs, drums, side altars and adjoining rooms with shrines to different gods, chapels for prayers to the dead and displays of funerary plaques. There are also living quarters for the temple keepers. There is no set time for prayer and no communal service except for funerals. Worshippers enter the temple whenever they want to make offerings, pray for help or give thanks.

The dominant colours in a Chinese temple are red, gold or yellow, and green. The orange-to-red colour range represents joy and festivity. Green signifies harmony, of fundamental importance to the Chinese. Yellow and gold herald heavenly glory.

White stands for purity and is also the colour of death. Grey and black are the colours of disaster and grief.

The most striking feature of the Buddhist temple is the pagoda. It was probably introduced from India along with Buddhism in the 1st century AD. Because the early pagodas were constructed of wood, they were easily destroyed by fire and subject to corrosion, so materials such as brick, stone, brass and iron were substituted. They were often built to house religious artefacts and documents, to commemorate important events, or as monuments. The Big Goose Pagoda in Xi'an is a monolithic example of pagoda construction.

During the Northern Wei period the construction of cave temples began and was continued during later dynasties. The caves at Longmen near Luoyang, at Mogao near Dunhuang and at Yungang near Datong are some of the finest examples.

In Buddhist art the Buddha is frequently displayed in a basic triad, with a Bodhisattva (a Buddhist saint who has arrived at the gateway to nirvana but has chosen to return to earth to guide lesser mortals along righteous paths) on either side. Their faces tend to express the emotions of joy, serenity or compassion. Sometimes the bodhisattvas are replaced by the figures of Buddha's first two disciples, the youthful Ananda and the older Kasyapa.

Funerary Objects
As early as Neolithic times (9000-6000 BC), offerings of pottery vessels and stone tools or weapons were placed in graves to accompany the departed.

During the Shang Dynasty, precious objects such as bronze ritual vessels, weapons and jade were buried with the dead. Dogs, horses and even human beings were sacrificed for burial in the tombs of great rulers. When this practice was abandoned, replicas (usually in pottery) were made of human beings, animals and precious objects. A whole repertoire of objects was produced especially for burial, making symbolic provision for the dead without wasting wealth or making human sacrifice.

Burial objects made of earthenware were very popular from the 1st to the 8th centuries AD. During the Han Dynasty, pottery figures were cast in moulds and painted in bright colours after firing. Statues of attendants, entertainers, musicians, acrobats and jugglers were made, as well as models of granaries, watchtowers, pigpens, stoves and various other things.

Close trade links with the West were illustrated among these models by the appearance of the two-humped Bactrian camel, which carried merchandise along the Silk Road, among funerary objects. Warriors with west Asian faces and heavy beards appeared as funerary objects during the Northern Wei Dynasty, a foreign dynasty founded by the Turkish-speaking Tobas of central Asia.

The cosmopolitan life of Tang China was illustrated by its funerary wares; western and central Asians flocked to the capital at Chang'an and were portrayed in figurines of merchants, attendants, warriors, grooms, musicians and dancers. Tall Western horses with long legs, introduced to China from central Asia at the beginning of the 1st century BC, were also popular subjects for tomb figurines.

Other funerary objects commonly seen in Chinese museums are fearsome military figures dressed in full armour, often trampling oxen underfoot. The figures may have served as tomb guardians and may represent the four heavenly kings. These kings guard the four quarters of the universe and protect the state; they have been assimilated into Buddhism and you see statues of them in Buddhist temples.

Guardian spirits are some of the strangest funerary objects. A common one has bird wings, elephant ears, a human face, the body of a lion and the legs and hooves of a deer or horse, all rolled into one. One theory is that these figures represent Tubo, the earth-spirit or lord of the underworld who was endowed with the power to ward off demons and evil spirits. He was entrusted with guarding the

tomb of the deceased. Those figures with human faces may have represented the legendary Emperor Yu. He is said to have been the founder of the Xia Dynasty, and was transformed into Tubo after his death.

Ceramics

Earthenware production has a long history in China. As many as 8000 years ago Chinese tribes were making artefacts with clay. The primitive 'Yangshao' culture (so named because the first excavation of an ancient agricultural village was made in the region of Yangshao near the confluence of the Yellow, Fen and Wei rivers) is noted for its distinctive pottery painted with flowers, fish, animals, human faces and geometric designs. Around 3500 BC the 'Lungshanoid' culture (so named because evidence of this ancient culture was first found near the village of Lungshan in Shandong Province) was making white pottery and eggshell-thin black pottery.

Pottery making was well advanced by the Shang period; the most important development occurred around the middle of the dynasty with the manufacture of a greenish glaze applied to stoneware artefacts. During the Han Dynasty the custom of glazing pottery became fairly common. However, the production of terracotta items – made from a mixture of sand and clay, fired to produce a reddish-brown colour and left unglazed – continued.

During the Southern and Northern dynasties, a type of pottery halfway between Han glazed pottery and true porcelain was produced. The proto-porcelain was made by mixing clay with quartz and the mineral feldspar to make a hard, smooth-surfaced vessel. Feldspar was mixed with traces of iron to produce an olive-green glaze. The technique was perfected under the Tang but few examples survive. Three-coloured glazed vessels were also produced during the Tang Dynasty.

By the 8th century, Tang proto-porcelain and other types of pottery had found an international market, and were exported as far afield as Japan and the east coast of Africa. Chinese porcelain did not reach

Europe until the Ming period, and the techniques of making it were not developed there until the 17th century.

Chinese pottery reached its artistic peak under the Song rulers. During this time true porcelain was developed. It was made of fine kaolin clay and was white, thin and transparent or translucent. Porcelain was produced under the Yuan but gradually lost the delicacy and near-perfection of the Song products.

However, it was probably during the Yuan Dynasty that 'blue-and-white' porcelain made its first appearance. This porcelain had blue decorations on a white background; it was made of kaolin clay quarried near Jingdezhen, and mixed with a type of cobalt imported from Persia.

During this period three-coloured and five-coloured porcelain, with floral decorations on a white background, was produced. Another noted invention was mono-coloured porcelain in ferrous red, black or dark blue. A new range of mono-coloured vessels was developed under the Qing.

During the Qing period the production of coloured porcelain continued with the addition of new colours and glazes and more complex decorations. This was the age of true painted porcelain, decorated with delicate landscapes, birds and flowers. Elaborate designs and brilliant colouring became the fashion. Porcelain imitations of other materials, such as gold and silver, mother of pearl, jade, bronze, wood and bamboo, also became popular.

Bronze Vessels

Bronze is an alloy whose chief elements are copper, tin and lead. Tradition ascribes the first casting of bronze to the legendary Xia Dynasty of 5000 years ago. Emperor Yu, the founder of the dynasty, is said to have divided his empire into nine provinces and then cast nine bronze tripods to symbolise the dynasty. However, the discovery in 1928 of the last Shang Dynasty capital at Anyang in Henan Province provided the first solid evidence that the ancient Chinese used bronze.

The Shang ruler and the aristocracy are believed to have used a large number of bronze vessels for sacrificial offerings of food and wine. Through ritual sacrifices the spirits of ancestors were prevailed upon to look after their descendants. The vessels were often buried with the deceased, along with other earthly provisions. Most of the late Shang funeral vessels have short, pictographic inscriptions recording the names of the clan, the ancestor and the vessel's maker, along with important events. Zhou Dynasty bronze vessels tend to have longer messages in ideographic characters; they describe wars, rewards, ceremonial events and the appointment of officials.

The early bronzes were cast in sectional clay moulds, an offshoot of the advanced pottery technology's high-temperature kilns and clay-mould casting. Each section of the mould was impressed, incised or carved with the required designs. By the 5th century BC during the Eastern Zhou period, bronzes with geometric designs and scenes of hunting and feasting were inlaid with precious metals and stones.

Bronze mirrors were used as early as the Shang Dynasty and had already developed into an artistic form by the Warring States period. Ceramics gradually replaced bronze utensils by Han times, but bronze mirrors were not displaced by glass mirrors until the Qing Dynasty.

In China, the mirror is a metaphor for self-inspection in philosophical discussion. The wise person has three mirrors: a mirror of bronze in which to see their physical appearance; a mirror of the people by which to examine inner character and conduct; and a mirror of the past by which to learn to emulate successes and avoid the mistakes of earlier times. The backs of bronze mirrors were inscribed with wishes for good fortune and protection from evil influence. Post-Han writings are full of fantastic stories of the supernatural powers of mirrors. One of them relates the tale of Yin Zhongwen, who held a mirror to look at himself but found that his face was not reflected – soon after, he was executed.

Jade

The jade stone has been revered in China since Neolithic times. While the pure white form is the most highly valued, the stone varies in translucency and colour, including many shades of green, brown and black. To the Chinese, jade symbolises nobility, beauty and purity. Its physical properties have become metaphors for the Confucian ideal of the *jūnzi*, the noble or superior man.

Jade is also thought to be empowered with magical and life-giving properties, and was considered a guardian against disease and evil spirits. Taoist alchemists, hoping to become immortal, ate an elixir of powdered jade. Plugs of jade were placed over the orifices of corpses to prevent the life force from escaping. Opulent jade suits, meant to prevent decomposition, have been found in Han tombs; examples can be seen in the Nanjing Museum and in the Anhui Provincial Museum in Hefei.

Literature

China is home to one of the world's richest literary traditions. Unfortunately, barring many, many years of intensive study, much of it is inaccessible to Western readers. Many of the most important Chinese classics are available in translation, but much of the Chinese literary heritage (in particular its rich corpus of poetry) is untranslatable, though this doesn't stop scholars from trying.

The essential point to bear in mind when discussing Chinese literature is that prior to the 20th century there were two literary traditions: the classical and the vernacular. The classical tradition was the Chinese equivalent of a literary canon, though the principles that informed its structure were vastly different from the principles that are brought to bear when deciding what gets onto an English literature course in a Western university. The classical canon, largely Confucian in nature, consisted of a core of texts written in ancient Chinese that had to be mastered thoroughly by all aspirants to the Chinese civil service, and was the backbone of the Chinese education system. The vernacular tradition arose in the Ming Dynasty and consisted largely of prose epics written for entertainment, and was consequently derided as a lower art form beneath the attention of scholars (though they were widely read all the same).

For Western readers it is the vernacular texts, precursors of the contemporary Chinese novel and short story, that are probably of most interest. Most of them are available in translation and provide a fascinating insight into life in China centuries past. Perhaps the three most famous early 'novels' are: *The Water Margin (shuǐhǔ zhuàn)*, also translated as *Rebels of the Marsh*; *The Dream of the Red Chamber (hónglóu mèng)*, also translated as *The Dream of Red Mansions* and *The Story of the Stone*; and *Journey to the West (xīyóu jì)*.

The Water Margin is the story of a group of rebels in the end of the Northern Song. Early versions of the story are thought to have been around in the 13th and 14th centuries, but it was the version by Jin Shentang dating from 1644 that made the story famous. *Journey to the West* dates back to the 16th century, and the story derives from the true exploits of the Chinese wanderer Xuan Zang, who travelled to India between 629 and 645 AD to collect Buddhist texts. The book is largely comic, and Xuan Zang is accompanied by a pig, a monkey and a feminine spirit. It has been made better known in the West by the Japanese TV series *Monkey*.

For the Chinese, the great classic of vernacular literature is *The Dream of the Red Chamber*. It is the story of domestic life in a scholar family insulated from the greater world, and its documentation of human foibles and family life make the writer, Cao Xueqin, a kind of Chinese Tolstoy. Both *Journey to the West* and *The Dream of the Red Chamber* are published by Penguin classics, the latter coming under the title *The Story of the Stone*.

By the early 19th century, Western novels had begun to appear in Chinese translations in increasing numbers. Chinese intellectuals began to look at their own literary traditions more critically, in particular the classical one, which was markedly different in form from the Chinese that was spoken by modern Chinese. Calls for a national literature based on vernacular Chinese rather than the stultifying classical language grew in intensity.

The first of the major Chinese writers to write in vernacular Chinese was Lu Xun, regarded by many as still the greatest of China's 20th-century writers. Most of his works were short stories that looked critically at the Chinese inability to drag its nation into the 20th century. His most famous work, *The Story of Ah Q*, examines the life of a man who is chronically unable to recognise the setbacks in his life as such, much as China itself seemed unable to accept the desperate urgency of the need to modernise. Lao She, another important early novelist, also produced an allegorical work in *Cat City*, but is famous most of all for *The Rickshaw Boy*, a book that has been translated many times into English. It is a social critique of the living conditions of rickshaw drivers in Beijing.

Literary creativity in post-1949 China was greatly hampered by ideological controls. Mao's 'Yan'an Talks on Art & Literature' edict basically reduced literature to the status of a revolutionary tool, and writers were extolled to seek out ideal forms and to find the 'typical in the individual'. Works that did not show peasants triumphing over huge odds were considered not inspirational enough and condemned as bourgeois.

The years following the Cultural Revolution have seen increased creative freedom in the Chinese literary scene, but it remains an area in which the government maintains careful vigilance. Most writers belong to state-sponsored literary guilds and many write on salary. Naturally they are careful not to bite the hand that feeds them.

One of the most interesting writers in contemporary China is Zhang Xianliang, whose book *Half of Man is Woman* was extremely controversial for its sexual content. Most Western readers find Zhang's sexual politics highly suspect, but his book, now published by Penguin, is worth reading all the same.

The work of another writer, Wang Shuo, still awaits translation into English, but this must only be a matter of time. Much of his work has been adapted for film and he is popular with the younger generation. For the authorities, however, his stories about disaffected urban youth, gambling, prostitution and confidence tricksters are considered a bad influence. Despite this, his works were recently collected in a four-volume set and are widely available in China.

Blood Red Dusk by Lao Gui (literally 'old devil') is available in English by Panda (the Chinese publisher). It's a fascinatingly cynical account of the Cultural Revolution years. Feng Jicai is a writer who has enjoyed great success in China with stories like *The Magic Ponytail* and *A Short Man & His Tall Wife*, which have a satirical magic realist touch to them. His often horrific account of the Cultural Revolution, *Voices From the Whirlwind*, is a collection of anonymous personal accounts of those turbulent years and has recently been published in English by Pantheon Books.

For a recap of some of the latest trends in Chinese literature, look out for a copy of *The Lost Boat: Avant Garde Fiction From China*, edited by Henry YH Zhao (Wellsweep Press, 1994). It has samples from what Zhao identifies as the three main strands in Chinese literature since 1986.

Theatre

Chinese theatre draws on very different traditions to Western theatre. The crucial difference is the importance of music to Chinese theatre, and thus it is usually referred to as opera. Contemporary Chinese theatre, of which the most famous is Beijing opera, has a continuous history of some 900 years, having evolved from a convergence of comic and balladic traditions in the Northern Song period. From this beginning, Chinese opera has been the meeting ground for a disparate range of forms: acrobatics, martial arts, poetic arias and stylised dance. By the 13th century, opera was referred to as *zaju*, or literally a 'dramatic miscellany'. Performances were rarely a single dramatic piece,

Spectacular costumes and (to Western ears) dissonant sounds are features of the Beijing opera.

but rather composed of a number of sequences around set themes.

Operas were usually performed by travelling troupes whose social status was very low in traditional Chinese society. In fact, their status was on a par with prostitutes and slaves and their children barred from social advancement by a government decree that made them ineligible to participate in public-service examinations. Chinese law also forbade mixed-sex performances, forcing actors to act out roles of the opposite sex. Opera troupes were frequently associated with homosexuality in the public imagination, contributing further to their 'untouchable' social status.

Despite this, opera remained a popular form of entertainment, though it was considered unworthy of the attention of the scholar class. Performances were considered an obligatory adjunct to New Year celebrations and marriages, and sometimes to funerals and ancestral ceremonies – a practice that continues to a certain extent in Taiwan.

Opera performances usually take place on a bare stage, with the actors taking on stylised roles that are instantly recognisable to the audience. The four major roles are the female role, the male role, the 'painted-face' role (for gods and warriors) and the clown.

Cinema

While most travellers in China manage to get to at least one opera or acrobatics performance, few get around to seeing any Chinese films. Part of the problem of course is purely linguistic. Films are not much fun if you cannot follow the dialogue. Still, a number of recent Chinese releases have enjoyed success at Western film festivals and in art house cinemas, are subtitled into English and are well worth the effort to track down. Hong Kong often has screenings of China's more offbeat releases.

Much of the early post-1949 film work was ideologically motivated, rich in sentimentality and heroics, and suffered from poor production values. As can be expected, the years of the Cultural Revolution did nothing to improve this state of affairs. The major turning point took place with the graduation of the first intake of students following the end of the Cultural Revolution from the Beijing Film Academy in 1982. This group of adventurous directors, the most well known of whom are Zhang Yimou, Chen Kaige, Wu Ziniu and Tian Zhuangzhuang, became known collectively as the 'Fifth Generation'.

The first film by any of these directors to come to the attention of film buffs in the West was *Yellow Earth (huáng tǔdì)*, a film that depicts the arrival of a PLA officer in a small Shaanxi village to collect peasant folk songs. The story is simple, but the film powerfully employs the visual element to reveal the tenacity of age-old customs in this barren part of China.

A number of other equally powerful and successful films followed hot on the heels of *Yellow Earth*. Zhang Yimou, a director whose films have continued to reap in awards at European film festivals, made *Red Sorghum (hóng gāoliang)*, a film that was adventurous by Chinese standards in portraying an illicit love affair against the backdrop of the Sino-Japanese War.

Huang Jianxin, a director who has recently reappeared after a long absence with *Stand Up, Don't Bend Over*, released *The Black Cannon Incident (hēipào shìjiàn)*, without a doubt the sharpest satire released by any of the Fifth Generation directors. The story revolves around a Chinese interpreter for a German engineer who returns by post a Chinese chess piece (a black cannon) to a friend who left it behind in his house. The telegram he sends to the friend to tell him he has found the piece and sent it on lands him in a quagmire of Kafka-esque bureaucratic suspicions and accusations.

Other films from the mid-1980s in a similar vein were: *Old Well*, a film rich with sexual tension; *Swan Song*, the tragic story of a Cantonese opera composer who dies neglected after his best work is stolen and made famous by a music student; *The Big Parade*, *The One & the Eight*, a unique Chinese depiction of the horrors of China's war with Vietnam; and *The Horse Thief*, a haunting story set in Tibet that sensitively portrays Tibetan lifestyles, and customs completely alien to Chinese sensibilities, such as the sky burial.

After a hiatus following the Tiananmen Square incident, Chinese directors have again resurfaced with some of the best international films of recent years.

The joint winners for the 1993 Berlin Golden Bear award were both Chinese films: one mainland Chinese and one Taiwanese. The mainland Chinese winner, *The Women From the Lake of Scented Souls*, portrays the unhappiness of a woman who runs a sesame-oil mill. Chen Kaige, the director of *Yellow Earth*, released *Farewell My Concubine*, which took joint honours at the Cannes Film Festival.

Meanwhile, Zhang Yimou has emerged as China's foremost director with award-winning releases such as *The Story of Qiuju* and *To Live*.

The good news for Chinese film-goers is that, after many years of such films being deemed unsuitable for local screenings, films like those of Zhang Yimou are being shown in China.

Music

Traditional Chinese musical instruments include the two-stringed fiddle *(èrhú)*, three-stringed flute *(sānxuán)*, four-stringed banjo *(yuèqín)*, two-stringed viola *(húqín)*, vertical flute *(dòngxiāo)*, horizontal flute *(dízi)*, piccolo *(bāngdí)*, four-stringed lute *(pípá)*, zither *(gǔzhēng)*, ceremonial trumpet *(suōnà)* and ceremonial gongs *(dàluó)*.

Popular Music China is beginning to develop a thriving music industry. Much of it is heavily influenced by the already well established music industries in Taiwan and Hong Kong, but these are in turn influenced by Western musical trends, as the recent popularity of Cantonese rap and Taiwanese-language rock experiments have shown. China has generally been slow in developing a market for Western music (much of what is available in the shops is of the Carpenters ilk), but the advent of satellite TV (now widely available) and the popularity of MTV and Channel V, broadcast via Hong Kong's Star TV network, is set to change all this.

China's first concert featuring a foreign rock group was in April 1985, when the British group Wham was allowed to perform. The audience remained sedate – music fans who dared to get up and dance in the aisles were hauled off by the PSB. Since then, things have become more liberal and China has produced some notable local bands. Cui Jian was a pioneer in bringing rock to China. He continues to record, and is occasionally allowed to perform – his politicised vision of a spiritually empty modern China are not popular with the authorities. Recent years have even spawned a number of heavy metal bands that look almost indistinguishable from their Western counterparts. Tang Dynasty is probably the most successful of these. Cobra is an all-woman rock band from Beijing.

On the popular music front, Taiwanese love songs have been enormously successful in China, and Mandarin versions of Hong Kong popular hits produced for the Taiwan and China markets are frequently chart hits.

Two of the Chinese musicians most likely to achieve international success are He Yong and Dou Wei. Dou Wei sang with the very successful metal outfit Hei Bao (Black Panther) before going solo. His solo material is subtle and experimental, in a way it never was with Hei Bao. He Yong's music is classified by many as punk – look out for it, have a listen and decide for yourself.

Taijiquan & Gongfu

Known in the West as 'taichi', *taijiquan* is sometimes referred to as shadow boxing. Strictly speaking it is one of China's martial arts, and the ideas structuring its movements share much with those behind kungfu (*gōngfú*). Taijiquan, however, is only a true martial art in the hands of an exponent who has studied it for decades. For most Chinese, particularly old people, who you might see executing fluid movements in parks at the crack of dawn, taijiquan is a form of exercise. The set patterns of movements are beneficial to muscle tone and the circulatory system, and its exponents claim a host of other pay-offs.

Taijiquan is fascinating to watch. The movements of those skilled in the art are graceful and slow. Taiwan and Hong Kong are better places to study taijiquan than China itself, though in recent years schools have begun to spring up in the West too.

CULTURE

China is real culture-shock territory. Nowadays travellers can wander the length of the South-East Asian trail and rarely be far from familiar comforts, but China is another world – at least outside the major cities like Beijing, Shanghai and Guangzhou. In China, simple things, like buying a railway ticket, can turn into major dramas. Perhaps the occupants of a minibus all collude to make sure you pay double the local fare. Perhaps the deposit you paid for your key at the hotel goes missing and can only be traced through the worker who received it from you and who is now enjoying his day off or is gone for a long

Taijiquan 'workouts' can be witnessed in virtually any Chinese park around dawn.

lunch. China can be frustrating, and often for mysterious reasons.

There are no easy answers to deal with China. Chinese themselves, who leave to live overseas and then return, often find their country as frustrating as we do. Old China hands, who have spent years learning the language, often break down in frustration and wish they'd learnt Italian or French instead. The Chinese will shake their heads and say that life has never been easy in China.

The following are some tips for making life in China a little easier. Bear in mind that the Chinese themselves are generally victims of an ugly system, and deep down many of them are not happy about the way things operate in their country, even if on the surface they go along with it – the woman at the Beijing Railway Station who grabs you and fines you for travelling on a Chinese-price ticket might agree privately that foreigners should pay the same price as Chinese, but it's her job.

Making Contact

Making contact with Chinese when you are travelling is relatively easy. Apart from the language barrier, however, there are some formidable cultural differences that can get in the way of communication. A Chinese travel guide had this to say about encountering foreign guests:

In trains, boats, planes or tourist areas one frequently comes across foreign guests. Do not follow, encircle and stare at them when you meet. Refrain from pointing at their clothing in front of their faces or making frivolous remarks; do not vie with foreign guests, competing for a seat, and do not make requests at will. If foreign guests take the initiative to make contact, be courteous and poised. Do not be flustered into ignoring them by walking off immediately, neither should you be reserved or arrogant. Do your best to answer relying on translation. When chatting with foreign guests be practical and realistic – remember there are differences between foreign and home life.

Don't provide random answers if you yourself don't know or understand the subject matter. Refrain from asking foreign guests questions about age, salary, income, clothing costs and similar private matters. Do not do things discreditable to your country. Do not accept gifts at will from foreign guests. When parting you should peel off your gloves and then proffer your hand. If you are parting from a female foreign guest and she does not proffer her hand first, it is also adequate to nod your head as a farewell greeting.

Educating a billion Chinese to be courteous to foreigners is a formidable task. For many years few foreigners set foot in the country, let alone met the common people. Whether or not most Chinese people actually like foreigners is open to debate – but they are curious about us and sometimes genuinely friendly, and on the whole it is safe to walk the streets at any time.

Making contact with Chinese people can be frustrating. Inevitably it begins with someone striking up a conversation with you on the street, in your hotel or on a train. Unfortunately, many of these conversations have a habit of deteriorating into English lessons. There is also the tendency for every conversation to be a monotonous question-and-answer session, with the questions always being the same.

Conversations with Chinese people usually begin with 'Can I practise my English with you?' followed by 'What country are you from?' and then 'Are you married?', 'How old are you?' and 'Do you have children?'. Then come the questions about money – 'How much do you make?', 'Do you have a car?' and 'How much does a house cost in your country?'. By this time, a crowd will have gathered and everyone will be discussing (in Chinese) your income, material standard of living, and, if the numbers sound good, immigration possibilities.

Chinese have become increasingly forthright in voicing their political opinions in recent years. Disillusionment with the government has become so widespread that very few people seem to worry about being overheard voicing negative opinions. It is still wise, however, to edge around sensitive issues (such as the Tiananmen massacre) initially and sound out the opinion of the person you are talking with before asking any potentially embarrassing questions. Also bear in mind the position of the Chinese – an official tour guide, for example, is unlikely to trot out anything other than the official line during working hours.

Interesting people to talk to are elderly Chinese who learned English back in the 1920s and 1930s when there were large foreign communities in China. Then there are the middle-aged who were learning English just before the Cultural Revolution but were forced to stop and started to pick it up again after a gap of several years. Next comes the younger generation of Chinese who went to school or university after the Cultural Revolution and have been able to take foreign-language courses. Even the level of proficiency attained by self-taught Chinese through English-language programmes on radio or TV is quite remarkable. English is now being taught in high schools, and many young kids have a rudimentary knowledge of the language. Japanese is popular at high school and university levels, and you sometimes come across French, German, Russian and Spanish speakers.

If you want to meet English-speaking Chinese then go to the 'English corners' which have developed in many large Chinese cities. Usually held on a Sunday morning in a convenient park, Chinese who speak or are learning English gather to practise the language. Also seek out the 'English Salons' – evening get-togethers at which the Chinese practise English, listen to lectures or hold debates in English. Don't expect to remain a member of the audience for very long; you may soon find yourself giving the evening lecture and struggling to answer difficult questions about the outside world.

It is unusual for foreigners to be invited to the homes of Chinese, though it is by no means illegal. Many Chinese feel embarrassed by their cramped living conditions and will prefer to invite a foreigner to a restaurant. If a Chinese invites you to a meal, he or she will expect to pay. It is polite to attempt to pay the bill yourself a couple of times – though it is unlikely you will be successful.

Cultural Differences

The cultural gap can be a bigger obstacle to understanding than the language barrier. On the other hand, cultural differences can be fascinating – try to keep a positive attitude. Some of the cultural differences you may encounter in China are noted below.

Face Face can be loosely described as 'status', 'ego' or 'self-respect', and is by no means alien to foreigners. Essentially it's about avoiding being made to look stupid or being forced to back down in front of others. A negotiated settlement of differences that provides benefits to both parties is always preferable to confrontation. Outright confrontation should be reserved as a last resort (Chinese are not shy of using it), and problems should first be tackled with smiling persistence – if one tack fails, try another.

Guānxi In their daily life, Chinese often have to compete for goods or services in short supply and many have been assigned

---

Mind Your Manners

Service standards have been steadily improving in China over the last few years. It's unusual nowadays to be ignored by shop assistants as they read comics and chat over jam jars of tea. Even CAAC flight attendants manage the occasional tight-lipped smile as they toss passengers a packet of biscuits for the in-flight meal. Still, it will be a long time before visitors to China come away praising the politeness of their hosts.

There are signs that the Chinese authorities recognise the problem. In mid-1995, the *Guangming Daily* newspaper compiled a list of '50 Taboo Phrases' to help workers in the service sector avoid offending customers. Taboo phrases include the simple and frequently used *'mei you'*, expressions such as 'I don't know' and rhetorical insults such as 'Didn't you hear me? What are those ears of yours for?'. It is also impolite, the list suggests, for service workers to address their customers as 'country bumpkin' or 'darkie'.

Will it work? It's hard to imagine. At the height of the campaign for politeness I was nabbed in Beijing Railway Station with a Chinese-price ticket (bought from CITS). A hand grabbed my shoulder and a voice bellowed at a hapless Chinese who happened to be walking beside me: 'You! Stay here with the foreigner and translate'. 'But I don't speak English,' said the poor man in terror.

'Well, what are you doing walking next to a foreigner, then?' the voice came back in disgust.

I had to intervene to win the man his freedom and he was shooed off with a 'Get out of here!'. At least they didn't call him a country bumpkin or ask him what his ears were for. Perhaps the Beijing Railway Station staff had memorised the list. ■

jobs for which they have zero interest and often no training. Those who have *guānxi* (connections) usually get what they want because the 'connections' network is, of course, reciprocal. Obtaining goods or services through connections is informally referred to as 'going through the back door' (*zǒu hòu mén*). Cadres are well placed for this activity; foreigners are not.

Speaking Frankly People often don't say what they think, but rather what they think you want to hear or what will save face for them. Thus, the staff at the CAAC office may tell you that your flight will be here 'very soon' even if they know it will be delayed for two days.

Smiling A smile doesn't always mean happiness. Some Chinese people smile when they are embarrassed or worried. This explains the situation where the foreign tourist is ranting and raving at the staff in the hotel lobby, while the person behind the desk stands there grinning from ear to ear.

RELIGION

Chinese religion has been influenced by three great streams of human thought: Taoism, Confucianism and Buddhism. Although each has separate origins, all three have been inextricably entwined in popular Chinese religion along with ancient animist beliefs. The founders of Taoism, Confucianism and Buddhism have been deified. The Chinese worship them and their disciples as fervently as they worship their own ancestors and a pantheon of gods and spirits.

Taoism
(dào jiào)

It is said that Taoism is the only true 'home-grown' Chinese religion – Buddhism was imported from India and Confucianism is mainly a philosophy. According to tradition, the founder of Taoism was a man known as Laotse. He is said to have been born around the year 604 BC, but there is some doubt that he ever lived at all. Almost nothing is known

about him, not even his name. Laotse translates as the 'Old One' or the 'Grand Old Master'.

Legends depict Laotse as having been conceived by a shooting star, carried in his unfortunate mother's womb for 82 years and born as a wise old man with white hair. The most popular story is that Laotse was the keeper of the government archives in a western state of China, and that Confucius consulted with him.

At the end of his life, Laotse is said to have climbed on a water buffalo and ridden west towards what is now Tibet, in search of solitude for his last few years. On the way, he was asked to leave behind a record of his beliefs. The product was a slim volume of only 5000 characters, the *Dao De Jing*, or *The Way and Its Power*. He then rode off on his buffalo.

At the centre of Taoism is the concept of *Dao*. Dao cannot be perceived because it exceeds senses, thoughts and imagination; it can be known only through mystical insight which cannot be expressed with words. Dao is the way of the universe, the driving power in nature, the order behind all life, the spirit which cannot be exhausted. Dao is the way people should order their lives to keep in harmony with the natural order of the universe.

Just as there have been different interpretations of the 'way', there have also been different interpretations of *De* – the power of the universe. This has led to the development of three distinct forms of Taoism in China.

One form held that 'the power' is philosophical. The philosophical Taoist, by reflection and intuition, orders his or her life in harmony with the way of the universe and achieves the understanding or experience of Tao. Philosophical Taoism has many followers in the West.

The second form held that the power of the universe was basically psychic in nature, and by practising yogic exercises and meditation a number of individuals could become receptacles for Tao. They could then radiate a healing, psychic influence over those around them.

The third form is the 'popular Taoism' which took hold in China. The power of the universe is the power of gods, magic and sorcery. Because popular Taoism has been associated with alchemy and the search for immortality, it often attracted the patronage of Chinese rulers before Confucianism gained the upper hand. It's argued that only philosophical Taoism actually takes its inspiration from the *Dao De Jing*, and that the other labels under which 'Taoism' has been practised used Laotse's name to give themselves respectability. As it is commonly practised in China, Hong Kong and Taiwan, popular Taoist worship is still closely bound up with ghosts, exorcisms, faith healing, fortune-telling and magic.

Confucianism
(rújiā sīxiǎng)

More a philosophy than a religion, Confucianism has nevertheless become intertwined with Chinese religious beliefs.

With the exception of Mao, the one name which has become synonymous with China is Confucius *(kǒngzi)*. He was born of a poor family around the year 551 BC, in what is now Shandong Province. His ambition was to hold a high government office and to reorder society through the administrative apparatus. At most he seems to have had several insignificant government posts, a few followers and a permanently blocked career. At the age of 50 he perceived his 'divine mission' and for the next 13 years tramped from state to state offering unsolicited advice to rulers on how to improve their governing, while looking for an opportunity to put his own ideas into practice. That opportunity never came, and he returned to his own state to spend the last five years of his life teaching and editing classical literature. He died in 479 BC, aged about 72.

The glorification of Confucius began after his death, and eventually his ideas permeated every level of Chinese society. To hold government office presupposed a knowledge of the Confucian classics, and spoken proverbs trickled down to the illiterate masses. During the Han Dynasty, Confucianism effectively became the state religion – the teachings were made the basic discipline for training government officials and remained so until almost the end of the Qing Dynasty in 1911. In the 7th and 8th centuries temples and shrines were built in memory of Confucius and his original disciples. During the Song Dynasty, the Confucian bible, *The Analects*, became the basis of all education.

It is not hard to see why Confucianism took hold in China. The perpetual conflict of the Spring and Autumn period had inspired Confucius to seek a way which would allow people to live together peacefully. His solution was tradition. Like others of his time, he believed that there had once been a period of great peace and prosperity in China. This had been brought about because people lived by certain traditions which maintained peace and social order.

Confucius advocated a return to these traditions and also devised values which he thought were necessary for collective wellbeing. He aimed to instil a feeling of humanity towards others and respect for oneself, as well as a sense of the dignity of human life. Courtesy, selflessness, magnanimity, diligence and empathy would naturally follow. His ideal person was competent, poised, fearless, even-tempered and free of violence and vulgarity. The study of 'correct attitudes' became the primary task. Moral ideas had to be driven home to the people by every possible means – at temples, theatres, schools, at home and during festivals, in proverbs and folk stories.

All people rendered homage to the emperor, who was regarded as the embodiment of Confucian wisdom and virtue – the head of the great family-nation. For centuries administration under the emperor lay in the hands of a small Confucian scholar class. In theory anyone who passed the examinations qualified, but in practice the monopoly of power was held by the educated upper classes. There has never been a rigid code of law, because Confucianism rejected the idea that conduct could be enforced by some organisation; taking legal action implied an incapacity to work things out by negotiation.

The result, however, was arbitrary justice and oppression by those who held power. Dynasties rose and fell but the Confucian pattern never changed.

There are several bulwarks of Confucianism, but the one which has probably had the most influence on the day-to-day life of the Chinese is *li*, which has two meanings. The first meaning of li is 'propriety' – a set of manners or a knowledge of how to behave in a given situation – and presumes that the various roles and relationships of life have been clearly defined. The second meaning of li is 'ritual' – when life is detailed to Confucian lengths it becomes completely ordered.

Confucian codes of conduct and clearly defined patterns of obedience became inextricably bound up in Chinese society. Women obey and defer to men, younger brothers to elder brothers and sons to fathers. Respect flows upwards, from young to old, from subject to ruler. Age is venerated since it gives everything (including people, objects and institutions) their dignity and worth; the elderly may be at their weakest physically, but they are at the peak of their wisdom.

The family retains its central place as the basic unit of society; Confucianism reinforced this idea, but did not invent it. The key to family order is filial piety – children's respect for and duty towards their parents. Teaming up with traditional superstition, Confucianism reinforced the practice of ancestor worship. Confucius himself is worshipped and temples are built for him. The strict codes of obedience were held together by these concepts of filial piety and ancestor worship, as well as by the concept of 'face' – to let down the family or group is a great shame for a Chinese.

Buddhism
(fó jiào)
Buddhism was founded in India in the 6th century BC by Siddhartha Gautama of the Sakyas. Siddhartha was his given name, Gautama his surname and Sakya the name of the clan to which his family belonged.

The story goes that though he was a prince brought up in luxury, Siddhartha became discontented with the world when he was confronted with the sights of old age, sickness and death. He despaired of finding fulfilment on the physical level, since the body was inescapably subject to these weaknesses.

Around the age of 30 Siddhartha broke from the material world and sought 'enlightenment' by following various yogic disciplines. After several failed attempts he devoted the final phase of his search to intensive contemplation. One evening as he sat beneath a bo (banyan) tree, he slipped into a deep meditation and emerged having achieved enlightenment. His title 'Buddha' means 'the awakened' or 'the enlightened one'.

Buddha founded an order of monks and preached his ideas for the next four decades until his death around 480 BC. To his followers he was known as Sakyamuni, the 'silent sage of the Sakya clan', because of the unfathomable mystery that surrounded him. It is said that Gautama Buddha was not the only Buddha, but the fourth, and is not expected to be the last.

The cornerstone of Buddhist philosophy is the view that all life is suffering. Everyone is subject to the traumas of birth, sickness, decrepitude and death; to what they most dread (an incurable disease or an ineradicable personal weakness); and to separation from what they love.

The cause of suffering is desire – specifically the desires of the body and the desire for personal fulfilment. Happiness can only be achieved if these desires are overcome, and this requires following the 'eightfold path'. By following this path the Buddhist aims to attain nirvana. Volumes have been written in attempts to define nirvana; the *suttas* (discourses of the Buddha) simply say that it's a state of complete freedom from greed, anger, ignorance and the various other 'fetters' of existence.

The first branch of the eightfold path is 'right understanding': the recognition that life is suffering, that suffering is caused by desire for personal gratification and that suffering can be overcome. The second branch is 'right-mindedness': cultivating a mind free from sensuous desire, ill will and cruelty. The remaining branches of the path require that one refrain from abuse and deceit; that one show kindness and avoid self-seeking in all actions; that one develop virtues and curb passions; and that one practise meditation.

The many varieties of Buddhist meditation use mental exercises to penetrate deep into the psyche, where it is believed the real problems and answers lie, and to achieve a personal experience of the verities of existence.

Buddhism developed in China from the 3rd to 6th centuries AD and was probably introduced by Indian merchants who took Buddhist priests with them on their land and sea journeys to China. Later, an active effort was made to import Buddhism into China. In the middle of the 1st century AD the religion had gained the interest of the Han emperor Ming, who sent a mission to the West; the mission returned in 67 AD with Buddhist scriptures, two Indian monks and images of the Buddha. Centuries later, other Chinese monks like Xuan Zang journeyed to India and returned with Buddhist scriptures which were then translated from the original Sanskrit to Chinese – a massive job involving Chinese and foreign scholars from central Asia, India and Sri Lanka.

Buddhism spread rapidly in the north of China, where it was patronised by various ruling invaders, who in some cases had been acquainted with the religion before they came to China. Others patronised the Buddhist monks because they wanted educated officials who were not Confucians. In the south Buddhism spread more slowly, spreading with Chinese migrations from the north.

There were several periods in which Buddhists were persecuted. Their temples and monasteries were sacked and destroyed, but the religion survived. To a people constantly faced with starvation, war and poverty the appeal of this philosophy probably lay in the doctrines of reincarnation and nirvana borrowed from Indian Hinduism.

Buddhist monasteries and temples sprang up everywhere in China, and played a similar role to the churches and monasteries of medieval Europe. Monasteries were guesthouses, hospitals and orphanages for travellers and refugees. With gifts obtained from the faithful, they were able to amass considerable wealth, which enabled them to set up moneylending enterprises and pawnshops. These pawnshops were the poor man's bank right up to the mid-20th century.

The Buddha wrote nothing; the Buddhist writings that have come down to us date from about 150 years after his death. By the time these texts came out, divisions had already appeared within Buddhism. Some writers tried to emphasise the Buddha's break with Hinduism, while others tried to minimise it. At some stage Buddhism split into two major schools: Theravada and Mahayana.

The Theravada, or 'doctrine of the elders', school (also called Hinayana or 'little vehicle' by non-Theravadins) holds that the path to nirvana is an individual pursuit. It centres on monks and nuns who make the search for nirvana a full-time profession. This school maintains that people are alone in the world and must tread the path to nirvana on their own; Buddhas can only show the way. The Theravada school is the Buddhism of Sri Lanka, Myanmar, Thailand, Laos and Cambodia.

The Mahayana, or 'big vehicle', school holds that since all existence is one, the fate of the individual is linked to the fate of others. The Buddha did not just point the way and float off into his own nirvana, but continues to offer spiritual help to others seeking nirvana. The Mahayana school is the Buddhism of Vietnam, Japan, Tibet, Korea, Mongolia and China.

The outward difference between the two schools is the cosmology of the Mahayana school. Mahayana Buddhism is replete with innumerable heavens, hells and descriptions of nirvana. Prayers are addressed to the Buddha and combined with elaborate ritual. There are deities and bodhisattvas – a rank of supernatural beings in their last incarnation before nirvana. Temples are filled with images such as the future Buddha, Maitreya (often portrayed as fat and happy over his coming promotion) and Amitabha (a saviour who rewards the faithful with admission to a sort of Christian paradise). The ritual, tradition and superstition that Buddha rejected came tumbling back in with a vengeance.

In Tibet and in areas of Gansu, Sichuan and Yunnan, a unique form of the Mahayana school is practised: Tantric or Lamaist Buddhism (*lǎmā jiào* in Mandarin). Tantric Buddhism, often called *Vajrayana* or 'thunderbolt vehicle' by its followers, has been practised since the early 7th century AD and is heavily influenced by Tibet's pre-Buddhist Bon religion, which relied on priests or shamans to placate spirits, gods and demons. Generally speaking, it is much more mystical than other forms of Buddhism, relying heavily on mudras (ritual postures), mantras (sacred speech), yantras (sacred art) and secret initiation rites. Priests called *lamas* are believed to be reincarnations of highly

Buddhism developed in China from the 3rd to 6th centuries AD.

evolved beings; the Dalai Lama is the supreme patriarch of Tibetan Buddhism.

Chinese Religion

Taoism combines with old animistic beliefs to teach people how to maintain harmony with the universe. Confucianism takes care of the political and moral aspects of life. Buddhism takes care of the afterlife. But to say that the Chinese have three religions – Taoism, Buddhism and Confucianism – is too simple a view of their traditional religious life. At the first level, Chinese religion is animistic with a belief in the innate vital energy in rocks, trees, rivers and springs. At the second level, people from the distant past, both real and mythological, are worshipped as gods. Overlaid on these beliefs are popular Taoism, Mahayana Buddhism and Confucianism.

On a day-to-day level, the Chinese are much less concerned with the high-minded philosophies and asceticism of Buddha, Confucius or Laotse than they are with the pursuit of worldly success, the appeasement of the dead and the spirits and the seeking of hidden knowledge about the future. Chinese religion incorporates what the West regards as superstition; if you want your fortune told, for instance, you go to a temple. The other important thing to remember is that Chinese religion is polytheistic. Apart from Buddha, Laotse and Confucius there are many other gods and goddesses, such as hearth gods and divinities for particular professions.

The most important concept in the Chinese popular religious vocabulary is fortune, and the Chinese will go to great lengths to invoke it. Gods have to be appeased, bad spirits blown away and sleeping dragons soothed to keep fortune on one's side. Geomancy (*fēngshuǐ*) is the Chinese art of ensuring that works of human beings complement the hidden 'power lines' of the natural environment. The location of a window, doorway or (most importantly) an ancestor's grave can have a major impact on your fortune. In Hong Kong, many of the largest skyscrapers were only constructed after careful consultation with a geomancer.

Integral parts of Chinese religion are death, the afterlife and ancestor worship. At least as far back as the Shang Dynasty there were lavish funeral ceremonies involving the internment of horses, carriages, wives and slaves. The more important the person, the more possessions and people had to be buried with them to meet the requirements of the next world. The deceased had to be kept happy because their powers to inflict punishments or to grant favours greatly increased after death. Even today a traditional Chinese funeral can still be a lavish event.

Islam
(yīsīlán jiào)

The founder of Islam was the Arab prophet Mohammed. Strictly speaking, Muslims believe it was not Mohammed who shaped the religion but God, and Mohammed merely transmitted it from God to his people. To call the religion 'Mohammedanism' is also incorrect, since it implies that the religion centres around Mohammed and not around God. The proper name of the religion is Islam, derived from the word *salam*, which primarily means 'peace', and in a secondary sense 'surrender'. The full connotation is something like 'the peace which comes by surrendering to God'. The corresponding adjective is 'Muslim'.

The prophet was born around 570 AD and came to be called Mohammed, which means 'highly praised'. His ancestry is traditionally traced back to Abraham, who had two wives, Hagar and Sarah. Hagar gave birth to Ishmael, and Sarah had a son named Isaac. Sarah demanded that Hagar and Ishmael be banished from the tribe. According to Islam's holy book, the Koran, Ishmael went to Mecca, where his line of descendants can be traced down to Mohammed. There have been other true prophets before Mohammed, but he is regarded as the culmination of them and the last.

Mohammed said that there is only one God, Allah. The name derives from joining *al*, which means 'the', with *Illah*, which means 'God'. His uncompromising monotheism conflicted with the pantheism and idolatry of the Arabs. Also, his moral teachings and vision of a universal brotherhood conflicted with what he believed was a corrupt and decadent social order based on class divisions.

The initial reaction to his teachings was hostile. He and his followers were forced to flee from Mecca to Medina in 622, where Mohammed built up a political base and an army which eventually defeated Mecca and brought all of Arabia under his control. He died in 632, two years after taking Mecca. By the time a century had passed the Arab Muslims had built a huge empire which stretched all the way from Persia to Spain. Though the Arabs were eventually supplanted by the Turks, the strength of Islam has continued to the present day.

Unlike in many other countries, Islam was brought to China peacefully. Arab traders who landed on the southern coast of China established their mosques in great maritime cities like Guangzhou and Quanzhou, and Muslim merchants travelling the Silk Road through central Asia to China won converts among the Han Chinese in the north of the country. There are also large populations of Muslim Uighur people (of Turkic descent), whose ancestors first moved into China's Xinjiang region during the Tang Dynasty.

Christianity
(jīdū jiào)

The earliest record of Christianity in China dates back to the Nestorians, a Syrian Christian sect. They first appeared in China in the 7th century when a Syrian named Raban presented Christian scriptures to the imperial court at Chang'an. This event and the construction of a Nestorian monastery in Chang'an are recorded on a large stone stele made in 781 AD, now displayed in the Shaanxi Provincial Museum in Xi'an.

The next major Christian group to arrive in China were the Jesuits. The priests Matteo Ricci and Michael Ruggieri were permitted to set up base at Zhaoqing in Guangdong Province in the 1580s, and eventually made it to the imperial court in Beijing. Large numbers of Catholic and Protestant missionaries established themselves in China following the invasion of China by the Western powers in the 19th century.

Judaism
(yóutài jiào)

Kaifeng in Henan Province has been the home of the largest community of Chinese Jews. Their religious beliefs and almost all the customs associated with them have died out, yet the descendants of the original Jews still consider themselves Jewish. Just how the Jews got to China is unknown. They may have come as traders and merchants along the Silk Road when Kaifeng was the capital of China, or they may have emigrated from India. For more details, see the Kaifeng section in the Henan chapter.

Religion & Communism

Today the Chinese Communist government professes atheism. It considers religion to be base superstition, a remnant of old China used by the ruling classes to keep power. This is in line with the Marxist belief that religion is the 'opiate of the people'. Nevertheless, in an effort to improve relations with the Muslim, Buddhist and Lamaist minorities, the Chinese government is once again permitting open religious activity. However, only atheists are permitted to be members of the CCP. Since almost all of China's 55 minority groups adhere to one religion or another, this rule precludes most of them from becoming Party members.

Traditional Chinese religious beliefs took a battering during the Cultural Revolution when monasteries were disbanded, temples were destroyed and the monks were sometimes killed or sent to the fields to labour. Many temples and monasteries are now derelict or have other functions. Although traditional Chinese religion is strong in places like Macau, Hong Kong and Taiwan, the temples and monasteries have a very minor religious role in mainland China.

Since the death of Mao, the Chinese government has allowed many temples (sometimes with their own contingent of monks and novices) to reopen as active places of worship. All religious activity is firmly under state control and many of the monks are caretakers within renovated shells of monasteries. Pilgrimages to burn incense, throw *shèng bēi* (fortune-telling wooden blocks) and make offerings to the gods by burning fake paper money appear to be common practice in temples once more. There are also stories of peasants rebuilding shrines to local gods, consulting geomancy experts before constructing buildings and graves, and burying deceased relatives with traditional religious ceremonies.

Confucius has often been used as a political symbol, his role 'redefined' to suit the needs of the time. At the end of the 19th century he was upheld as a symbol of reform because he had worked for reform in his own day. After the fall of the Qing Dynasty, Chinese intellectuals vehemently opposed him as a symbol of a conservative and backward China. In the 1930s he was used by Chiang Kaishek and the Kuomintang as a guide to proper, traditional values. Today Confucius is back in favour, with the Chinese government seeing much to be admired in the neo-Confucianist authoritarianism espoused by Lee Kuan Yew of Singapore.

Christianity has also enjoyed a resurgence of popularity in China and it is possible to see recently constructed churches in some towns. It is still officially frowned upon by the government as a form of spiritual pollution, but this is unlikely to do little to stop its spread. What the Chinese government does, however, is make it difficult for Chinese Christians to affiliate with Christians in the West. Churches are placed under the control of the government: the Three-Self Patriotic Movement was set up as an umbrella organisation for the Protestant churches, and the Catholic Patriotic Association was set up to replace Rome as the leader of the Catholic churches.

There is much friction between the government and the Chinese Catholic church because the church refuses to disown the Pope as its leader, and because the Vatican maintains diplomatic relations with Taiwan.

In China today, there are believed to be 14 million Muslims, making them the largest identifiable religious group still active in the PRC. The government has not published official figures of the number of Buddhists, but they must be substantial since most Tibetans, Mongolians and Dai people follow Buddhism. There are around three million Catholics and four million Protestants. It's impossible to determine the number of Taoists, but the number of Taoist priests is very small.

The Cultural Revolution resulted in the closure of Muslim mosques, though many of these have since reopened. Of all people in China, the Tibetan Buddhists most felt the brunt of Mao's mayhem. The Dalai Lama and his entourage fled to India in 1959 when the Tibetan rebellion was put down by Chinese troops. During the Cultural Revolution the monasteries were disbanded (some were levelled to the ground) and the theocracy which had governed Tibet for centuries was wiped out overnight. Some Tibetan temples and monasteries have been reopened and the Tibetan religion is still a very powerful force among the people.

LANGUAGE

The official language of the PRC is the dialect spoken in Beijing. It is usually referred to in the West as 'Mandarin' and is spoken mainly in the north-east and south-west. The official name of Mandarin is *pŭtōnghuà* (common speech), but students of the language will also hear it referred to as *hànyŭ* (Han language), *zhōngwén* and *zhōngguóhuà*. These last two mean simply 'Chinese'. *Huáyŭ* is the word used by South-East Asian Chinese. It is also sometimes used in China. When the Beijing dialect was used as a standard language by the scholarly class in centuries past it was referred to as *guānhuà*. This word has fallen into disuse.

The promulgation of the Beijing dialect as a national language has its origins in the Nationalist period, when Mandarin was called *guóyŭ* (national language). This term is still used in Taiwan and occasionally in China. Putonghua, as promulgated by the

Communists, differs from the Nationalist guoyu in vocabulary and tones but not enough to hamper mutual intelligibility.

Spoken

Dialects Discounting Mandarin, China has six major dialect groups. These subdivide into many more dialects and few of them are mutually intelligible. Around 70% of the population speaks Mandarin. This doesn't mean that it is their first language. In the countryside, people are more likely to speak only a local dialect, though most younger people will at least understand Mandarin.

Chinglish

Initially you might be puzzled by a sign in the bathroom that reads 'Please don't take the odds and ends put into the nightstool'. In fact this is a warning to resist sudden impulses to empty the contents of your pockets or backpack into the toilet. An apparently ambiguous sign with anarchic implications like the one in the Lhasa Bank of China that reads 'Question Authority' is really just an economical way of saying 'Please address your questions to one of the clerks'. On the other hand, just to confuse things, a company name like the 'Risky Investment Co' means just what it says.

If this all sounds confusing, don't worry. It won't be long before you have a small armoury of Chinglish phrases of your own. Before you know it, you'll know without even thinking that 'Be careful not to be stolen' is a warning against thieves; that 'Shoplifters will be fined 10 times' means that shoplifting is not a good idea in China; that 'Do not stroke the works' (generally found in museums) means 'No touching'; and that 'No gang fighting after drinking the liqueurs' is a warning against the cocktail party brawls that have become an increasingly prevalent social problem in the PRC.

The best advice for travellers in China grappling with the complexities of a new language is not to set your sights too high. Bear in mind that it takes a minimum of 15 years of schooling in the Chinese language and a crash course in English to be able to write Chinglish with any fluency. ■

The other major dialect is Cantonese. It is the language most likely to be spoken in your local Chinese takeaway. It is spoken in Guangdong, southern Guangxi and Hong Kong.

All Chinese dialects share the same basic written system.

Written

Chinese is often referred to as a language of pictographs. Many of the basic Chinese characters are in fact highly stylised pictures of what they represent, but most Chinese char-

acters (around 90%) are compounds of a 'meaning' element and a 'sound' element.

Just how many Chinese characters are there? It is possible to verify the existence of some 56,000 characters but the vast majority of these are obsolete. It is commonly felt that a well-educated, contemporary Chinese might know and use between 6000 and 8000 characters. To read a Chinese newspaper you will need to know 2000 to 3000 but 1200 to 1500 would be enough to get the gist.

The question of how many characters you need to know to be able to read certain

---

Chinese & Computers

After long delays, the information revolution has finally arrived in China. Not that long ago the Chinese government frowned on personal ownership of photocopiers and fax machines. Nowadays it's recognised that computer access is a necessity in the drive to modernise.

One catch is that Chinese doesn't lend itself to computer environments very well. A computer keyboard is designed for keying in alphabetic languages, not languages like Chinese with thousands of pictographs. A Chinese 'keyboard' would have to have around 5000 keys. Not surprisingly, Chinese software developers have opted for input methods that use a traditional keyboard.

The easiest input method is to use romanised Chinese, which the computer translates into characters. But when a romanised Chinese word such as yi pulls up over 100 choices, the going can be slow. Moreover, not that many Chinese people are familiar with the romanised version of their language, not to mention the problems faced by dialect speakers such as the Cantonese. Another input method allows the user to find the correct character by the order of the strokes used in normal Chinese writing – this method works but is very slow. Yet another system requires the operator to memorise a code number for each character – thousands of them! Not surprisingly, few people become proficient at this method.

Programmers in China, Hong Kong, Singapore and Taiwan have been looking for solutions. Experiments have been tried with voice input, bypassing the keyboard entirely. Japanese programmers have worked on the same method. After countless hours of effort and billions of dollars in research grants, the results have been poor – no-one has found an adequate substitute for typing.

Input is one side of the equation – the other is output. Mainland China has adopted a standardised format for the storage of Chinese characters on disk. This system works fine for the official 7000 simplified characters, but Taiwan (which uses traditional characters) has an official list of 13,000 characters to deal with and therefore has adopted its own (incompatible) system. Hong Kong uses the traditional writing system but chips in with an additional 150 characters specifically for Cantonese. Chinese programmers have had to work overtime developing fileformat converters and various other tricks to deal with the two (or three?) systems.

In the meantime, the number of computers in China is increasing exponentially. Although many parts are imported, China makes its own personal computers, including such brands as Great Wall and Taiji. Most Chinese companies, as well as many schools and well-to-do individuals, now own PCs. And just what are all these machines being used for? Sometimes for accounting, and sometimes for keeping business records – but mostly for playing video games.

And sometimes for making mischief. Software pirating is ubiquitous in China, and so are computer viruses. In 1989 the dreaded 'Li Peng virus' appeared. The virus asked if you liked Premier Li Peng, and if you answered 'yes' your hard disk was wiped out. ■

Chinese texts is, however, moot. While the building block of the Chinese language is the monosyllabic Chinese character, Chinese words are usually a combination of two or more characters. A student of Chinese, for example, might know the characters for 'look' *(kàn)*, 'home' *(jiā)* and 'dog' *(gǒu)*, but would probably have to look up a dictionary to find out that all three in combination *(kànjiāgǒu)* mean 'watchdog'. A classic example of a less obvious character compound is the combination of *wēi* ('dangerous') and *jī* ('opportunity'), to create the word *wēijī* ('crisis').

Simplification In the interests of promoting universal literacy, the Committee for Reforming the Chinese Language was set up by the Beijing government in 1954. Around 2200 Chinese characters were simplified. Chinese communities outside China (notably Taiwan and Hong Kong), however, continue to use traditional full-form characters. The last few years, probably as a result of large-scale investment by Overseas Chinese and tourism, has seen a return of the full-form characters to China, mainly in advertising, where the traditional characters are considered more attractive, as well as restaurant, hotel and shop signs. There are indications that the two systems are coming into competition in China.

Grammar

Chinese grammar is quite simple. There are no articles ('a'/'the'), no tenses and no plurals. The basic point to bear in mind is that, like English, Chinese word order is subject-verb-object. In other words, a basic English sentence like 'I *(subject)* go *(verb)* to the shop *(object)*' is constructed in exactly the same way in Chinese. The catch is mastering the tones.

Tones

Chinese is a language with a large number of homonyms (words of different meaning but identical pronunciation), and if it were not for its tonal quality, it probably would not work very well as a language. Mandarin has four tones – high, rising, falling-rising and falling. Cantonese has six tones (or nine if you include tonal variations within the six), making it an even more difficult language for foreigners to master than Mandarin. All Chinese words have a tonal value. The word *ma* can mean 'mother', 'hemp', 'horse' or 'scold', depending on the tone:

high	—	*mā*	mother
rising	⁄	*má*	hemp or numb
falling-rising	⌄	*mǎ*	horse
falling	⟍	*mà*	to scold or swear

Actually, as intimidating as this all sounds, English frequently employs all the tones used in Mandarin. The difference is that while we use tonal quality for emphasis or emotion, the tone in Chinese is a basic ingredient in the meaning of a word.

Pinyin

In 1958 the Chinese officially adopted a system of writing their language using the Roman alphabet. It is known as *pīnyīn*. The original idea was to eventually do away with characters. However, tradition dies hard and the idea has been abandoned.

Pinyin is often used on shop fronts, street signs and advertising billboards. Don't expect Chinese people to be able to use Pinyin, however. There are indications that the use of the Pinyin system is diminishing.

In the countryside and the smaller towns you may not see a single Pinyin sign anywhere, so unless you speak Chinese you'll need a phrasebook with Chinese characters.

Since 1979 all translated texts of Chinese diplomatic documents, as well as Chinese magazines published in foreign languages, have used the Pinyin system for spelling names and places. Pinyin replaces the old Wade-Giles and Lessing systems of romanising Chinese script. Thus under Pinyin, 'Mao Tse-tung' becomes *Mao Zedong*; 'Chou En-lai' becomes *Zhou Enlai*; and 'Peking' becomes *Beijing*. The name of the country remains as it has been written most often: 'China' in English and German, and 'Chine' in French – in Pinyin it's *Zhongguo*.

When Hong Kong (a romanisation of Cantonese for 'fragrant harbour') goes over to China in 1997, it *should* become *Xianggang*, an unlikely event.

Pronunciation

Most letters are pronounced as in English, with the exception of the following:

Vowels

a	as in 'father'
ai	as in 'bite'
ao	as in 'cow'
e	as in 'blur'
ei	as in 'weigh'
i	as in 'meet' (after **c, ch, r, s, sh, z** and **zh** it sounds more like the 'e' in 'her')
ian	sounds like 'yen'
ie	as in 'here'
o	as in 'or'
ou	as in 'boat'
u	as in 'flute' when preceded by **q, j, x** or **y**
ü	as the French *'tu'* or German *'ü'* (purse your lips as if to whistle and make the sound 'ee')
ui	as in '**way**'
uo	as in '**war**'

Consonants

c	as in '**bits**'
ch	as in English, but with the tongue curled back
j	as in 'suds'
h	guttural, as in the Scottish 'loch'
q	as in '**bits**'
r	as in 'pleasure'
sh	as in English, but with the tongue curled back
x	as in '**sock**'
z	as in 'su**d**s'
zh	as in 'ju**d**ge', but with the tongue curled back

Note that **c** and **q**, **x** and **s**, and **j** and **z** have roughly the same pronunciation respectively. The pronunciation of the following vowel will change. Thus *ji* is pronounced 'dzee', while *zi* is pronounced 'dzuh'; *xi* is pronounced 'see', while *si* is pronounced 'suh'; and *qi* is pronounced 'tsee', while *ci* is pronounced 'tsuh'. These pronunciations are, however, subject to some dispute and a great deal of regional variation throughout the country.

In Pinyin, apostrophes separate syllables – writing *ping'an* prevents pronunciation of this word as *pin'gan*.

Gestures

Hand signs are frequently used in China. The 'thumbs-up' sign has a long tradition as an indication of excellence. Another way to indicate excellence is to gently pull your earlobe between thumb and index finger.

Finger counting is widely used in China but usually as a confirmation of a spoken number. One of the disadvantages of finger counting is that there are regional differences.

Phrasebooks

Phrasebooks are invaluable – but it's better to copy out the appropriate sentences in Chinese rather than show someone the book; otherwise they'll take it and read every page. Reading place names or street signs is not difficult since the Chinese name is usually accompanied by the Pinyin form; if not you'll soon learn lots of characters just by repeated exposure. A small dictionary with English, Pinyin and Chinese characters is also useful for learning a few words.

Lonely Planet publishes a *Mandarin phrasebook*, a *Cantonese phrasebook* and a *Tibetan phrasebook*.

Pronouns

I	
	wǒ
	我
you	
	nǐ
	你
he/she/it	
	tā
	他/她/它
we/us	
	wǒmen
	我们

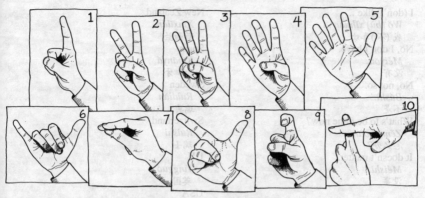

The Chinese system of finger counting

you (plural)
nǐmen
你们
they/them
tāmen
他们

Greetings & Civilities

Hello.
Nǐ hǎo.
你好!
Goodbye.
Zàijiàn.
再见
Thank you.
Xièxie.
谢谢
You're welcome.
Búkèqi.
不客气
I'm sorry.
Duìbùqǐ.
对不起

Small Talk

May I ask your name?
Nín guì xìng?
您贵姓?
My (sur)name is ...
Wǒ xìng ...
我姓 ...

Where are you from?
Nǐ cóng nǎr láide?
你是从哪儿来的?
I am from ...
Wǒ shi ... láide.
我是 ... 来的
I am a foreign student.
Wǒ shi liúxuéshēng.
我是留学生
Are you married?
Nǐ jiéhūnle ma?
你结婚了吗?
Yes.
Yǒu.
有
No.
Méiyǒu.
没有
Wait a moment.
Děng yíxià.
等一下
I want ...
Wǒ yào ...
我要.....
No, I don't want it.
Búyào.
不要.
Do you like ...?
Nǐ xǐhuan ... ma?
你喜欢 ...吗?

I (don't) like ...
Wǒ (bù) xǐhuan ...
我 (不) 喜欢 ...
No, I don't have.
Méiyǒu.
没有
No, not so.
Búshì.
不是
What's to be done now?
Zěnme bàn?
怎么办?
It doesn't matter.
Méishì.
没事

Language Difficulties

I don't understand.
Wǒ tīngbudǒng.
我听不懂.
I understand.
Wǒ tīngdedǒng.
我听得懂.
Do you understand?
Tīngdedǒng ma?
懂吗?
Could you speak more slowly please?
Qǐng nǐ shuō màn yídiǎn hǎo ma?
请你说慢一点好儿?

Countries

Australia
Áodàlìyà
澳大利亚
Canada
Jiānádà
加拿大
Denmark
Dānmài
丹麦
France
Fǎguó
法国
Germany
Déguó
德国
Netherlands
Hélán
荷兰

New Zealand
Xīnxīlán
新西兰
Spain
Xībānyá
西班牙
Sweden
Ruìdiǎn
瑞典
Switzerland
Ruìshì
瑞士
UK
Yīngguó
英国
USA
Měiguó
美国

Shopping

How much is it?
Duōshǎo qián?
多少钱?
Is there anything cheaper?
Yǒu piányì yìdiǎn de ma?
有便宜一点的吗?
That's too expensive.
Tài guìle.
太贵了.
Bank of China
Zhōngguó Yínháng
中国银行
RMB (people's money)
rénmínbì
人民币
to change money
huàn qián
换钱
travellers' cheques
lǚxíng zhīpiào
旅行支票

Post & Telecommunications

post office
yóujú
邮局
letter
xìn
信

envelope
xìnfēng
信封

package
bāoguǒ
包裹

airmail
hángkōng xìn
航空信

surface mail
píngyóu
平邮

stamp
yóupiào
邮票

postcard
míngxìnpiàn
明信片

aerogram
hángkōng xìnjiàn
航空邮件

poste restante
cúnjú hòulǐnglán
存局候领栏

telephone
diànhuà
电话

telephone office
diànxùn dàlóu
电讯大楼

telephone card
diànhuà kǎ
电话卡

international call
guójì diànhuà
国际电话

collect/reverse charges call
duìfāng fùqián diànhuà
对方付钱电话

direct-dial call
zhíbō diànhuà
直通电话

fax
chuánzhēn (or *fax*, as in English)
传真

Places

art gallery
měishùguǎn
美术馆

bank
yínháng
银行

city centre
shì zhōngxīn
市中心

embassy
dàshǐguǎn
大使馆

market
shìchǎng
市场

museum
bówùguǎn
博物馆

university
dàxué
大学

China International Travel Service (CITS)
Zhōngguó Guójì Lǚxíngshè
中国国际旅行社

China Travel Service (CTS)
Zhōngguó Lǚxíngshè
中国旅行社

China Youth Travel Service (CYTS)
Zhōngguó Qīngnián Lǚxíngshè
中国青年旅行社

Foreign Languages Bookstore
Wàiwén Shūdiàn
外文书店

Xinhua Bookstore
Xīnhuá Shūdiàn
新华书店

Directions

Streets and roads are often split up into sections *(duàn)*. Each section is named according to its relative position to the other sections. For example, Zhongshan Lu (Zhongshan Rd) might be split into an east section *(dōng duàn)* and a west section *(xī duàn)*. The east section will be named Zhongshan Donglu and the west will be named Zhongshan Xilu.

Where is the ...?
... *zài nǎlǐ?*
...在 哪里？

I'm lost.
Wǒ mílùle.
我 迷路了

Turn right.
Yòu zhuǎn.
右转
Turn left.
Zuǒ zhuǎn.
左转
Go straight.
Yìzhí zǒu.
一直
Turn around.
Xiàng huí zǒu.
向回走
map
dìtú
地图
north
běi
北
south
nán
南
east
dōng
东
west
xī
西

Accommodation

hotel
lǚguǎn
旅馆
small hotel
lǚshè
旅社
hostel
zhāodàisuǒ
招待所
tourist hotel
bīnguǎn/fàndiàn/ jiǔdiàn
宾馆,饭店,酒店
dormitory
duōrénfáng
多人房
single room
dānrénfáng
单人房
double room
shuāngrénfáng
双人房

bed
chuángwèi
床位
economy room
jīngjìfáng
经济房
standard room (with bath)
biāozhǔn fáng
标准套房
luxury room (with bath)
háohuá tàofáng
豪华套房
hotel name card
lǚguǎn de míngpiàn
旅馆的名片
Can I see the room?
Wǒ néng kànkan fángjiān ma?
我能看看房间?
I don't like this room.
Wǒ bù xǐhuan zhèijiān fángjiān.
我不喜欢这间房间
Could I have these clothes washed, please?
Kěyǐ xǐ zhèixiē yīfu ma?
请把这些衣服洗干净?

Getting Around

I want to go to ...
Wǒ yào qù ...
我要去...
I want to get off.
Wǒ yào xiàchē.
我要下车.
I want to depart at ...
Wǒ yào ... diǎn zǒu.
我要......点开.
Could you buy a ticket for me?
Kěyǐ tì wǒ mǎi yìzhāng piào mā?
可以替我买一张票吗?
What time does it depart?
Jǐdiǎn kāi?
几点开?
What time does it arrive?
Jǐdiǎn dào?
几点到?
How long does the trip take?
Zhèicì lǚxíng yào duōcháng shíjiān?
这次旅行要花多少时间?
one ticket
yìzhāng piào
一张票

to buy a ticket
mǎi piào
买票

to refund a ticket
tuì piào
退票

luggage
xínglǐ
行李

left-luggage room
jìcún chù
寄存处

taxi
chūzū chē/dīshi
出租车

Air

airport
fēijīchǎng
飞机场

CAAC
Zhōngguó Mínháng
中国民航

charter flight
bāojī
包机

one-way ticket
dānchéng piào
单程票

round-trip ticket
láihuí piào
来回票

Bus

bus
gōnggòng qìchē/zhōngbā
公共汽车

minibus
xiǎo gōnggòng qìchē
小公共汽车

long-distance bus station
chángtú qìchē zhàn
长途汽车站

bus map
jiāotōng dìtú
交通地图

When is the first bus?
Tóubān qìchē jǐdiǎn kāi?
头班汽车几点开?

When is the last bus?
Mòbān qìchē jǐdiǎn kāi?
末班汽车几点开?

When is the next bus?
Xià yìbān qìchē jǐdiǎn kāi?
下一班汽车几点开?

Train

train
huǒchē
火车

ticket office
shòupiào chù
售票处

advance rail ticket office
huǒchē piào yùshòu chù
火车票预售处

railway station
huǒchē zhàn
火车站

main railway station
zhǔyào huǒchē zhàn
主要火车站

hard seat
yìngxí/yìngzuò
硬席,硬座

soft seat
ruǎnxí/ruǎnzuò
软席,软座

hard sleeper
yìngwò
硬卧

soft sleeper
ruǎnwò
软卧

middle berth
zhōngpù
中铺

upper berth
shàngpù
上铺

lower berth
xiàpù
下铺

platform ticket
zhàntái piào
站台票

Which platform?
Dìjǐhào zhàntái?
第几号站台?

upgrade ticket (after boarding)
  bǔpiào
  补票

first-class waiting room
  ruǎnwò hòuchēshì
  头等候车楼

subway (underground)
  dìxiàtiě
  地下铁路

subway station
  dìtiě zhàn
  地铁站

Bicycle

bicycle
  zìxíngchē
  自行车

I want to hire a bicycle.
  Wǒ yào zū yíliàng zìxíngchē.
  我要租一辆自行车

How much is it per day?
  Yìtiān duōshǎo qián?
  一天多少钱?

How much is it per hour?
  Yíge xiǎoshí duōshǎo qián?
  一个小时多少钱?

deposit
  yājīn
  押金

Boat

boat
  chuán
  船

hovercraft
  qìdiàn chuán
  汽垫船

pier
  mǎtóu
  码头

Toilets

toilet/restroom
  cèsuǒ
  厕所

toilet paper
  wèishēng zhǐ
  卫生纸

bathroom/washroom
  xǐshǒu jiān
  洗手间

Geographical Terms

road/trail
  lù
  路

street
  jiē/dàjiē
  街, 大街

boulevard
  dàdào
  大道

alley
  xiàng/hútong
  巷, 胡同

cave
  dòng
  洞

hot spring
  wēnquán
  温泉

lake
  hú
  湖

mountain
  shān
  山

river
  hé/jiāng
  河, 江

valley
  gǔ/gōu
  谷, 沟

waterfall
  pùbù
  瀑布

Emergency

police
  jǐngchá
  警察

Fire!
  Huǒzāi!
  火灾

Help!
  Jiùmìng a!
  救命

Thief!
  Xiǎotōu!
  小偷!

Bureaucracy

Public Security Bureau (PSB)
Gōngān Jú
公安局

Foreign Affairs Branch
Wài Shì Kē
外事科

Alien Travel Permit
Wàibīn Tōngxíng Zhèng
外宾通行证

I want to extend my visa ...
Wǒ yào yáncháng wǒde qiānzhèng ...
我要延长我的签证.

... by two weeks.
... liǎngge xīngqī.
两个星期.

... by one month.
... yíge yuè.
一个月.

... by two months.
... liǎngge yuè.
两个月

Health

I'm sick.
Wǒ shēngbìngle.
我生病了.

I'm injured.
Wǒ shòushāngle.
我受伤了

hospital
yīyuàn
医院

pharmacy
yàodiàn
药店

diarrhoea
lādùzi
拉肚子

anti-diarrhoeal drug
huángliǎnsù
黄连素

laxative
xièyào
泻药

fever
fāshāo
发烧

giardia
āmǐbā fùxiè
阿米巴腹泻

hepatitis
gānyán
肝炎

malaria
nüèjì
疟疾

rabies
kuángquǎn bìng
狂犬病

respiratory infection (influenza)
liúxíngxìng gǎnmào
流行性感冒

tetanus
pòshāngfēng
破伤风

Time

What is the time?
Jǐ diǎnle?
几点了?

It is ...
...diǎn ...fēn
(lit: ... hour ... minute)
点...分...

When?
Shénme shíhòu?
什么时候?

now
xiànzài
现在

today
jīntiān
今天

tomorrow
míngtiān
明天

the day after tomorrow
hòutiān
后天

in the morning
zǎochén
早晨

daytime
báitiān
白天

afternoon
  xiàwǔ
  下午
night/evening
  wǎnshàng
  晚上
daylight-saving time
  xiàlìng shíjiān
  夏令时间
Beijing (standard) time
  Běijīng shíjiān
  北京时间

Numbers

0	*líng*	零
1	*yī/yāo*	一
2	*èr/liǎng*	二
3	*sān*	三
4	*sì*	四
5	*wǔ*	五
6	*liù*	六
7	*qī*	七
8	*bā*	八
9	*jiǔ*	九
10	*shí*	十
11	*shíyī*	十一
12	*shí'èr*	十二
20	*èrshí*	二十
21	*èrshíyī*	二十一
100	*yìbǎi*	一百
200	*liǎng*	二百
1000	*yìqiān*	一千
2000	*liǎngqiān*	两千
10,000	*yíwàn*	一万
20,000	*liǎngwàn*	两万
100,000	*shíwàn*	十万
200,000	*èrshíwàn*	二十万

Studying Chinese

Beijing and Taipei are the best places to study Chinese. In Beijing the simplified writing system and Pinyin are used. Living expenses are cheaper in Beijing, though the schools can be expensive for foreigners. Some might find the living conditions uncomfortable, however, and the policy of keeping foreigners separate from Chinese can be frustrating. Foreigners are usually assigned to a separate dormitory and are not permitted to live with Chinese locals. Most foreigners study at the Beijing Language Institute (BLI) *(yǔyán xuéyuán)*, which is east of Qinghua University on the No 331 bus route. There are several other schools in Beijing that accept foreign students.

In Taipei, and elsewhere in Taiwan, living expenses are high but there are many opportunities to find work teaching English. It's not difficult to earn enough money to meet all expenses. Foreigners are permitted to live with the locals in Taiwan, and it's not difficult to find Chinese roommates. Probably the best place to study Chinese is at the National Taiwan Normal University (☎ 363-9123), Mandarin Training Centre *(táiwān shīfàn dàxué)*, 129-1 Hoping E Rd, Section 1, Taipei.

Hong Kong is a good place for studying Cantonese. Although about half the population of Hong Kong speaks Mandarin, the local accent is so radically different from what you hear in Beijing that comprehension can be very difficult. The New Asia Yale in China Language School, at the Chinese University in the New Territories, offers courses in both Mandarin and Cantonese.

Facts for the Visitor

VISAS & EMBASSIES

Visas for individual travel in China are easy to get. China will even issue visas to individuals from countries which do not have diplomatic relations with the People's Republic of China (PRC).

Visas are readily available from Chinese embassies and consulates in most Western and many other countries. In the UK, standard 30-day single-entry visas from the embassy in London take three to five days and cost £25; get an application form in person or by post from there or from the Chinese consulate in Manchester. A visa mailed to you will take three weeks. Your passport must be valid for at least six months after the expiry date of your visa. You might find the embassy discourages independent travellers during the summer. The Chinese embassy and consulates in Australia charge $A30 for the standard single-entry visa and $60 for a double-entry visa for 30 days and can usually process an application within a week. You must apply in person or through a CITS office. In the USA the standard 30-day single-entry visa costs US$30 and takes about one week.

You can easily get a visa in Hong Kong. The standard 30-day visa (which you can use any time within three months) can be obtained from the Visa Office (☎ 2585-1794, 2585-1700) of the Ministry of Foreign Affairs of the PRC, 5th floor, Low Block, China Resources Building, 26 Harbour Rd, Wanchai. They charge HK$100 for 2½-day service and HK$250 for same-day service. The office is open Monday to Friday from 9 am to 12.30 pm and from 2 to 5 pm, and on Saturday from 9 am to 12.30 pm.

If you need more than 30 days or a multiple-entry visa, head to one of the branches of CTS in Hong Kong (see the Tourist Offices section in this chapter). Prices range from HK$160 for a single-entry 90-day visa issued in 2½ days to HK$1500 for a six-month multiple-entry visa issued in four

hours. Some Hong Kong travel agencies can also get you 60 and 90-day and multiple-entry visas. Phoenix Services (☎ 2722-7378), Room B, 6th floor, Milton Mansion, 96 Nathan Rd, Tsimshatsui, Kowloon, is a reliable option. But the 60-day and 90-day visas are valid for only 60 or 90 days *from the day they are issued*.

Visas valid for more than 30 days are usually difficult to obtain anywhere other than in Hong Kong.

Visa applications require one passport-sized photo. Your application must be written in English, and you're advised to have one entire blank page in your passport for the visa.

The visa application form asks you a number of questions – your travel itinerary, means of transport, how long you will stay etc – but you can deviate from this as much as you want. You *don't* have to leave from the place you specify on your visa application form.

Multiple-Entry Visas

Multiple-entry visas allow you to enter and leave the country an unlimited number of times and are available through CTS and some travel agencies in Hong Kong (see above). The cheapest multiple-entry visas cost HK$650 and are valid for 90 days; six-month multiple-entry visas cost HK$900 but allow stays of only 30 days at a time and extensions are close to impossible. The latter are business visas and normally will be issued only if you've been to China at least once before and have a stamp in your passport to prove it.

Border Visas

It is possible to obtain five-day visas at the border at Shenzhen (next to Hong Kong) and Zhuhai (next to Macau). Unfortunately, they are valid for travel only within the Shenzhen Special Economic Zone or the Zhuhai Special Economic Zone respectively.

Visa Types

When you check into a hotel, there is usually a question on the registration form asking what type of visa you have. Most travellers aren't sure how to answer. For most, the type of visa is 'L', from the Chinese word for travel (lǔxíng). This letter is stamped right on the visa. There are seven types of visas, as follows:

L   Travel (lǔxíng)
F   Business (fǎngwèn)
D   Resident (dìngjū)
G   Transit (guòjìng)
X   Student (liúxué)
Z   Working (rènzhí)
C   Stewardess (chéngwù)

Chinese Embassies

Some of the addresses of Chinese embassies and consulates in major cities overseas include:

Australia
    15 Coronation Drive, Yarralumla, ACT 2600
    (☎ (06) 273-4780, 273-4781)
    Consulates: Melbourne, Perth and Sydney
Austria
    Metternichgasse 4, 1030 Vienna
    (☎ (06) 713 67 06)
Belgium
    Boulevare General Jacques 19, 1050 Bruxelles
    (☎ (02) 640 40 06)
Canada
    515 St Patrick St, Ottawa, Ontario KIN 5H3
    (☎ (613) 234-2706, 234-2682)
    Consulates: Toronto and Vancouver
Denmark
    12 Oregards alle, DK 2900 Hellerup, Copenhagen 2900 (☎ 31 61 10 13)
France
    21 Rue de L'amiral Destaing, 75016 Paris
    (☎ (01) 47 20 86 82, 47 20 63 95)
Germany
    Friedrich-Ebert Strasse 59, 53177 Bonn
    (☎ (0228) 35 36 54, 35 36 22)
    Consulate: Hamburg
Italy
    00135 Roma Via Della Camilluccia 613
    (☎ (06) 3630-8534, 3630-3856)
    Consulate: Milan
Japan
    3-4-33 Moto-Azabu, Minato-ku, Tokyo 106
    (☎ (03) 3403-3380, 3403-3065)
    Consulates: Fukuoka, Osaka and Sapporo

Netherlands
    Adriaan Goekooplaan 7, 2517 JX The Hague,
    (☎ (070) 355 15 15, 355 92 09)
New Zealand
    104A Korokoro Rd, Petone, Wellington
    (☎ (04) 587-0407)
    Consulate: Auckland
Spain
    Arturo Soria 111, 28043 Madrid
    (☎ (341) 413-5892, 413-2776)
Sweden
    Ringvagen 56 18134 Lidings
    (☎ (08) 767 87 40, 767 40 83)
Switzerland
    7 JV Widmannstrasse, 3074 Muri Bern
    (☎ (031) 951 14 01, 951 14 02)
UK
    Cleveland Court, 1-3 Leinster Gardens, London
    W2 6DP (☎ (0171) 723-8923, 262-0253)
USA
    2300 Connecticut Ave NW, Washington, DC
    20008 (☎ (202) 328-2500, 328-2517)
    Consulates: Chicago, Houston, Los Angeles, New York and San Francisco

Visa Extensions

Visa extensions are handled by the Foreign Affairs Branch of the local Public Security Bureau (PSB) – the police force. Government travel organisations – like CITS – have nothing to do with extensions, so don't bother asking. Extensions can cost nothing for some, Y25 for most nationalities and Y50 for others.

The situation with visa extensions was very volatile at the time of writing. Extensions of one month no longer seem to be the norm. In most cases, one extension of 15 days is all that is allowed on a standard 30-day visa. At an agreeable PSB you may be able to wangle more, especially with cogent reasons like illness (except AIDS) or transport delays, but don't count on it. Second extensions are rarely granted.

Re-Entry Visas

Most foreign residents of China have multiple-entry visas and don't need a re-entry visa. However, there might be other requirements (tax clearance, vaccinations etc) – if in doubt, check with the PSB before departing.

Other Visas

See the Land section in the Getting There & Away chapter for info on visas for travelling on the Trans-Siberian Railway.

Foreign Embassies in China

In Beijing there are two main embassy compounds – Jianguomenwai and Sanlitun.

The following embassies are in Jianguomenwai:

Austria
   5 Xiushui Nanjie (☎ 532-2061; fax 532-4605)
Bangladesh
   42 Guanghua Lu (☎ 532-2521; fax 532-4346)
Czech & Slovak Republics
   Ritan Lu (☎ 532-1531; fax 532-5653)
India
   1 Ritan Donglu (☎ 532-1908; fax 532-4684)
Ireland
   3 Ritan Donglu (☎ 532-2691; fax 532-2168)
Israel
   Room 405, West Wing, China World Trade Centre, 1 Jianguomenwai Dajie (☎ 505-0328)
Japan
   7 Ritan Lu (☎ 532-2361)
Mongolia
   2 Xiushui Beijie (☎ 532-1203; fax 532-5045)
New Zealand
   1 Ritan Dong 2-Jie (☎ 532-2731; fax 532-4317)
North Korea
   Ritan Beilu (☎ 532-1186)
Philippines
   23 Xiushui Beijie (☎ 532-2794)
Singapore
   1 Xiushui Beijie (☎ 532-3926; fax 532-2215)
Sri Lanka
   3 Jianhua Lu (☎ 532-1861; fax 532-5426)
Thailand
   40 Guanghua Lu (☎ 532-1903; fax 532-1748)
UK
   11 Guanghua Lu (☎ 532-1961; fax 532-1939)
USA
   3 Xiushui Beijie (☎ 532-3831; fax 532-6057)
Vietnam
   32 Guanghua Lu (☎ 532-1155; fax 532-5720)

The Sanlitun Compound in Beijing is home to the following embassies:

Australia
   21 Dongzhimenwai Dajie (☎ 532-2331; fax 532-4605)
Belgium
   6 Sanlitun Lu (☎ 532-1736; fax 532-5097)

Cambodia
   9 Dongzhimenwai Dajie (☎ 532-1889; fax 532-3507)
Canada
   19 Dongzhimenwai Dajie (☎ 532-3536; fax 532-4072)
Denmark
   1 Sanlitun Dong 5-Jie (☎ 532-2431; fax 532-2439)
Finland
   Tayuan Diplomatic Building, 14 Liangmahe Nanlu (☎ 532-1817; fax 532-1884)
France
   3 Sanlitun Dong 3-Jie (☎ 532-1331; fax 532-4841)
Germany
   5 Dongzhimenwai Dajie (☎ 532-2161; fax 532-5336)
Hungary
   10 Dongzhimenwai Dajie (☎ 532-1431; fax 532-5053)
Italy
   2 Sanlitun Dong 2-Jie (☎ 532-2131; fax 532-4676)
Kazakstan
   (☎ 532-6182; fax 532-6183)
Kyrgystan
   Tayuan Diplomatic Building, 14 Liangmahe Nanlu (☎ 532-6458; fax 532-6459)
Malaysia
   13 Dongzhimenwai Dajie (☎ 532-2531; fax 532-5032)
Myanmar (Burma)
   6 Dongzhimenwai Dajie (☎ 532-1584; fax 532-1344)
Nepal
   1 Sanlitun Xi 6-Jie (☎ 532-1795; fax 532-3251)
Netherlands
   1-15-2 Tayuan Building, 14 Liangmahe Nanlu (☎ 532-1131; fax 532-4689)
Norway
   1 Sanlitun Dong 1-Jie (☎ 532-2261; fax 532-2392)
Pakistan
   1 Dongzhimenwai Dajie (☎ 532-2504)
Portugal
   Bangonglou 2-72 (☎ 532-3497; fax 532-4637)
Russia
   4 Dongzhimen Beizhongjie, west of the Sanlitun Compound in a separate compound (☎ 532-2051; fax 532-4853)
Spain
   9 Sanlitun Lu (☎ 532-1986; fax 532-3401)
Sweden
   3 Dongzhimenwai Dajie (☎ 532-3331; fax 532-5008)
Switzerland
   3 Sanlitun Dong 5-Jie (☎ 532-2736; fax 532-4353)

Consulates There are consulates for Australia, Canada, the Czech Republic, France, Germany, Hungary, India, Italy, Japan, New Zealand, Poland, Russia, Singapore, the UK and USA in Shanghai. There are also Australian, French, Japanese, Polish, Thai, US and Vietnamese consulates in Guangzhou and a US consulate in Shenyang. See the relevant chapters on those cities for details.

DOCUMENTS

Given the Chinese preoccupation with impressive bits of paper, it's worth carrying around a few business cards, student cards and anything else that's printed and laminated in plastic.

These additional IDs are useful for leaving with bicycle-renters, who often want a deposit or other security for their bikes – sometimes they ask you to leave your passport, but you should insist on leaving another piece of ID or a deposit. Some hotels also require you to hand over your passport as security, even if you've paid in advance. An old, expired passport is useful for these situations.

If you're travelling with your spouse, a photocopy of your marriage licence just might come in handy should you become involved with the law, hospitals or other bureaucratic authorities. Useful, though not essential, is an International Health Certificate to record your vaccinations.

If you're thinking about working or studying in China or anywhere else along the way, photocopies of university diplomas, transcripts and letters of recommendation could prove helpful.

International Student Identity Cards (ISIC) are not accepted at many places in China. If you do bring one, it helps to back it up with a regular student card and an official-looking letter from your school's registrar. The extra back-up documents are necessary because there's quite a worldwide trade in fake ISIC cards. In addition, there are now maximum age limits (usually 26) for some concessions, and the fake-card dealers have been clamped down on.

Passport

A passport is essential, and if yours is within a few months of expiry, get a new one now – many countries will not issue a visa if your passport has less than six months of validity remaining. Be sure that your passport has at least a few blank pages for visas and entry and exit stamps. It could be awkward to run out of blank pages when you are too far away from an embassy to get a new passport issued or extra pages added.

Losing your passport is very bad news indeed. Getting a new one takes time and money. However, if you will be staying in China or any foreign country for a long time, it helps tremendously to register your passport with your embassy. This will eliminate the need to send telexes back to your home country to confirm that you really exist.

If you lose your passport, you should certainly have some ID card with your photo – many embassies require this before issuing a new passport. Some embassies will accept a driver's licence but others will not – again, an expired passport will often save the day.

Chinese Documents

Foreigners who live, work or study in China will be issued a number of documents, and some of these can be used to obtain substantial discounts on trains, flights, hotels, museums and tourist sites.

Most common and least useful is the so-called 'white card', a simple student ID card with pasted-on photo, usually kept in a red plastic holder (some call it a 'red card' for this reason). Having one of these supposedly allows you to pay for train tickets at local prices. A white card is easily forged – you could reproduce one with a photocopy machine – and the red plastic holders are on sale everywhere. For this reason, you might be approached by touts wanting to sell you a fake one. The fact is that outside major cities like Beijing and Shanghai, railway clerks really have no idea what a white card is supposed to look like – fake ones sometimes work when real ones don't! One French student had a knock-down drag-out battle in Zhengzhou station with a smug booking clerk who threw her absolutely genuine white card into the rubbish bin and told her it was a fake.

The 'green card' is a residence permit, issued to English teachers, foreign experts and students who live in the PRC. It's such a valuable document that you'd better not lose it if you have one or the PSB will be all over you. Foreigners living in China say that if you lose your green card, you might want to leave the country rather than face the music. A green card will permit you to pay Chinese prices in hotels, on flights, on trains and elsewhere. In addition, many hotels offer major discounts to green-card holders (even five-star hotels!). The green card is not really a card but resembles a small passport – it would be very difficult to forge without modern printing equipment and special paper. Green cards are issued for one year and must be renewed annually.

Travel Permit
(tōngxíng zhèng)
In the early 1980s only 130 places in China were officially open to foreign tourists. Then the number swept to 244, and nowadays most of the country is open except for certain remote border areas, especially those inhabited by ethnic minorities.

Most of the places described in this book are open to foreigners, but one incident (like an ethnic riot in Xinjiang) can cause new permit regulations to be issued overnight. To find out about latest restrictions, it's best to check with the PSB in provincial capitals.

To travel to closed places you officially require an Alien Travel Permit (usually just called Travel Permit). The PSB has wide discretion in issuing a permit to a closed place. However, the choice of open places is now so extensive that most travellers won't need to apply. Foreign academics and researchers wanting to poke around remote areas usually need the right credentials or letter of introduction *(jièshào xìn)* before being given a free hand to pursue their lizards, steam trains, yellow-bellied sapsuckers or whatever in remote places.

Travel permits can be demanded from you at hotel registration desks, boat or bus ticket offices and unusual areas during spot checks by police. If you're off the track but heading towards a destination for which you have a permit, the police will either stop you and cancel the destination or let you continue on your way.

The permit also lists the modes of transport you're allowed to take: plane, train, ship or car – and if a particular mode is crossed out then you can't use it. If a mode is cancelled it can be reinstated at the next PSB, but that may be for only a single trip from Point A to Point B. You could try and carry on regardless – or you could lose the permit in the next open city and have to start again.

If you manage to get a permit for an unusual destination, the best strategy is to get to that destination as fast as you can (by plane if possible). Other PSBs do not have to honour the permit and can cancel it and send you back. Take your time getting back – you're less likely to be hassled if you're returning to civilisation. Transit points usually don't require a permit, and you can stay the night.

CUSTOMS
Chinese border crossings have gone from being severely traumatic to exceedingly easy. Although there may seem to be lots of uniformed police around, the third degree at customs seems to be reserved for pornography-smuggling Hong Kongers rather than Western travellers.

Note that there are clearly marked 'green channels' and 'red channels'; take the red channel only if you have something to declare.

You're allowed to import 600 cigarettes or the equivalent in tobacco products, two litres of alcoholic drink and one *pint* (0.5 litre) of perfume. You're allowed to import only 1000 metres of movie film and a maximum of 72 rolls of still film. Importation of fresh fruit is prohibited.

It's illegal to import any printed material, film, tapes etc 'detrimental to China's politics, economy, culture and ethics'. But don't be too concerned about what you take to read. As you leave China, any tapes, manuscripts, books etc 'which contain state secrets or are otherwise prohibited for export' can be seized. Cultural relics, handicrafts, gold and silver ornaments and jewellery purchased in China have to be shown to customs on leaving. You'll also have to show your receipts; otherwise the stuff may be confiscated. Foreigners are rarely searched.

MONEY
Currency

The Chinese currency is known as Renminbi (RMB), or 'People's Money'. Formally the basic unit of RMB is the *yuan*, which is divided into ten *jiao*, which again is divided into ten *fen*. Colloquially the yuan is referred to as *kuai* and jiao as *mao*. The fen has so little value these days that it is rarely used.

The Bank of China issues RMB bills in denominations of two, five, 10, 50 and 100 yuan. Coins are in denominations of one yuan, five jiao and one, two and five fen. There are still a lot of paper versions of the coins floating around, but it is likely that these will gradually disappear in favour of the coins.

Exchange Rates

Exchange rates are as follows:

Australia	A$1	=	Y6.08
Canada	C$1	=	Y6.03
France	FF1	=	Y1.66
Germany	DM1	=	Y5.6
Hong Kong	HK$1	=	Y1.06
Japan	¥100	=	Y7.81
Netherlands	G1	=	Y5.08
New Zealand	NZ$1	=	Y5.43
Switzerland	SFr1	=	Y7.06
UK	UK£1	=	Y12.70
USA	US$1	=	Y8.21

Changing Money

Foreign currency and travellers' cheques can be changed at the main centres of the Bank of China, the tourist hotels, some Friendship Stores and some of the big department stores. Hotels usually give the official rate, but some

will charge a small commission. Top-end hotels will generally change money only for hotel guests. The rates charged at various ports of entry (airports, wharves, the Hong Kong border etc) are usually the official rate, so don't be afraid to change as much as you need on arrival.

Australian, Canadian, US, UK, Hong Kong, Japanese and most West European currencies are acceptable in China. In some of the backwaters, it may be hard to change lesser-known currencies – US dollars are still the easiest to change.

Keep at least a few of your exchange receipts. You will need them if you want to exchange any remaining RMB you have at the end of your trip. Those travelling to Hong Kong can change RMB for Hong Kong dollars there.

Black Market The abolition of Foreign Exchange Certificates (FEC) in 1994 basically knocked China's flourishing black market on its head. Black market moneychangers still attempt to eke out a meagre living in some major cities, but the rates they offer are often less than those offered by the banks – given the risk of rip-offs and the abundance of counterfeit currency floating about, it would be wise to avoid changing money on the streets.

Counterfeit Notes By some accounts China is awash with counterfeit bills. Very few Chinese will accept a Y50 or Y100 bill without first checking to see whether or not it's a fake. Notes that are old and tattered are also sometimes hard to spend. If you are having problems with a note, exchange it for a new one or small change at the Bank of China – counterfeits, however, will be confiscated.

Local Chinese have a variety of methods for checking bills. First of all, they look for the watermark – obviously, if it doesn't have one it's a fake. Many locals maintain that colours tend to be more pronounced in counterfeit notes and the drawn lines less distinct. The texture of a note is also a tell-tale sign –

counterfeits tend to be smoother than authentic bills.

Travellers' Cheques Besides the advantage of safety, travellers' cheques are useful to carry in China because the exchange rate is actually more favourable than what you get for cash. Cheques from most of the world's leading banks and issuing agencies are now acceptable in China – stick to the major companies such as Thomas Cook, American Express and Bank of America and you'll be OK.

Credit Cards Plastic is gaining more acceptance in China for use by foreign visitors in major tourist cities. Useful cards include Visa, MasterCard, American Express, JCB and Diners Club. They can be used in most mid-range to top-end hotels (three-star and up), Friendship Stores and some department stores. Note that it is still impossible to use credit cards to finance your transportation costs; even flights have to be paid for in cash.

Credit card cash advances have become fairly routine at head branches of the Bank of China, even in places as remote as Lhasa. Bear in mind, however, that a 4% commission is generally deducted and usually the minimum advance is Y1200.

It wouldn't be worthwhile to get a credit card especially for your trip to China, but if you already have one you might find it useful. Banks in some of the outlying regions of China can take a long time to debit your account overseas.

American Express American Express has offices in Beijing, Shanghai, Guangzhou and Xiamen. See the entries on these cities for addresses and phone numbers.

Telegraphic Transfers Having money sent to you in China is a time-consuming and frustrating task that is best avoided. On average it takes around five weeks for money to arrive, perhaps even longer in the far-flung provinces. In Beijing and Shanghai, it would be worth checking with the offices of American Express. CITIC also has a reputation for expediting telegraphic transfers more efficiently than the Bank of China.

Bank Accounts Foreigners can indeed open bank accounts in China – both RMB and US dollar accounts (the latter only at special foreign-exchange banks). You do not need to have resident status – a tourist visa is sufficient. Virtually every foreigner working in China will tell you that CITIC is far better to do business with than the Bank of China. Automatic-teller machines have been introduced at the Bank of China and at various other banks, but payment is only in RMB.

Costs

How much will it cost to travel in China? That's largely up to the degree of comfort you need. It also depends on how much travelling you do, and what parts of China you visit. Eastern China, for example, is much more expensive than the west.

Eastern China (basically everywhere between Beijing and Hainan Island) has become very difficult to do on a shoestring. Outside the major cities of Guangzhou and Shanghai, it is very unusual to come across dorm accommodation, and in many cities accommodation rates start at between US$20 and US$30 for a double (singles are rarely available). Food costs remain reasonable throughout China, and if you are careful they can be as little as US$5 per day. Transportation costs can be kept to a minimum by travelling by bus wherever possible (there is no dual-pricing system for the buses) or by travelling hard-seat on the train. Travelling through the booming coastal cities of China for less than US$30 per day, in other words, is quite a challenge.

Western China, however, remains relatively inexpensive (for how long is anyone's guess). Popular backpacker destinations such as Yunnan, Sichuan, Guangxi, Gansu, Xinjiang, Qinghai and Tibet abound in budget accommodation and cheap eats – generally, keeping costs down to US$20 per day is not too difficult. The main drain on the savings will be the long train journeys, on which generally only the hardiest of travellers can face hard-seat.

Mid-range and top-end travellers are much better served in China nowadays than they were several years ago. Top-end hotels have been constructed all over China, and many of the old government guesthouses have been renovated into mid-range hotels. On average, mid-range hotels cost around US$35 to US$50 for a double with air-con, bathroom, TV etc. It is usually possible to eat well in hotel restaurants for around US$5 to US$10. Transport costs are rising rapidly for those who want to move around in a degree of comfort – an eight-hour soft-sleeper train journey, for example, will cost around US$60. It is worth comparing the cost of a flight versus soft-sleeper train travel – often the flights are cheaper or only marginally more expensive.

Top-end travel in China? It's possible to hit the major attractions of the country staying in five-star hotels (US$100 upwards for a double), flying long distances, taking taxis to and from airports, dining on Chinese haute cuisine and enjoying a few drinks in the lobby bar in the evenings for between US$200 and US$250 per day.

Price Gouging Foreigners will inevitably be charged more for most things in China. This situation certainly exists in many other developing countries, but the big difference is that in China, it's official policy. Every business from the airlines and railways to museums and parks are told *by the government* to charge foreigners more. With such official support, many Chinese view ripping off foreigners as their patriotic duty. Sometimes the charge is just a little bit more than a local would pay, but at other times it's 20 times more than the Chinese price. Many foreigners feel that China is the most dishonest country they've ever been to. But just when you reach the end of your tether and you want to hop onto the first flight out of the country, the opposite happens – some total stranger in a restaurant pays for your meal, a passenger you met on the train offers you a free place for the night and lets you

borrow the family bicycle or a young student works as your personal tour guide for the entire day and wants nothing in return. Such moments are especially touching in China, because most Chinese are still poor and can hardly afford to be so generous.

Such individual acts of kindness help to restore your faith in humanity – it's a pity that not everyone is like that. Try not to go around China feeling constantly ripped off, but on the other hand, keep your guard up when necessary. To avoid problems, always ask the price first before you get the goods or services rendered. If you can't speak Chinese, write it down.

Tipping
As some compensation for being constantly ripped off, China is at least one of those wonderful countries where tipping is not done and almost no-one asks for it. When tips are offered in China, they are offered *before* you get the service, not after – that will ensure (hopefully) that you get better service. All things considered, tipping isn't a good idea because it will make it rough for foreigners who follow you.

Bargaining
Since foreigners are so frequently overcharged in China, bargaining becomes essential. You can bargain in shops, hotels, with taxi drivers, with most people – but not everywhere. In large stores where prices are clearly marked, there is usually no latitude for bargaining. In small shops and street stalls, bargaining is expected, but there is one important rule to follow – be polite. There is nothing wrong with asking for a discount, if you do so with a smile. Some foreigners seem to think that bargaining should be an exercise in intimidation. This is not only unpleasant for all concerned, it seldom results in your getting a lower price – indeed, in 'face-conscious' China, intimidation is likely to make the vendor more recalcitrant and you'll be overcharged.

You should keep in mind that entrepreneurs are in business to make money – they aren't going to sell anything to you at a loss.

Your goal should be to pay the Chinese price, as opposed to the foreigners' price – if you can do that, you've done well.

Consumer Taxes

Although big hotels and top-end restaurants may add a tax or 'service charge' of 10% or more, all other consumer taxes are included in the price tag.

WHEN TO GO

See the Climate section of the Facts about the Country chapter for information on seasonal weather variations throughout China.

Local tourism has taken off in a big way in China, and in the summer months, when it hits its peak, getting around and finding accommodation can become quite a headache. Winter is obviously the quietest time of year to get about, but the weather can be miserable and many travellers succumb to killer flus that lay them out for days and leave them with a hacking cough for weeks after. Spring and autumn are the best months to be on the road, particularly in the south-west of China.

Major public holidays are to be avoided if possible. Chinese New Year is a terrible time of year to be travelling.

WHAT TO BRING

As little as possible. It's much better to buy things as you need them than to throw things away because you've got too much to carry. Lightweight and compact are two words that should be etched in your mind when you're deciding what to bring. Drill holes in the handle of your toothbrush if you have to – anything to keep the weight down!

That advice having been given, there are some things you will want to bring from home.

Carrying Bags

Investing in a good backpack is one outlay you will never regret. Look into buying a frameless or internal-frame pack – these are generally easier to store on buses and trains and also more comfortable to walk with. Also consider buying a pack that converts into a carry bag by way of a hood that zips

over the shoulder and waist straps – it is less likely to be damaged on airport carousels and is more presentable if you ever need to discard the backpacker image. Avoid buying carry bags in China unless you really have to – they are generally shoddy.

A day-pack is essential for carrying things around after you've dumped your backpack at the hotel or wherever. A beltpack is OK for maps, extra film and other miscellanea, but don't use it for valuables such as your travellers' cheques and passport – it's an easy target for pickpockets.

If you don't want to use a backpack, a shoulder bag is much easier to carry than a suitcase. Some cleverly designed shoulder bags can also double as backpacks by re-arranging a few straps. Bring suitcases only if you know you won't be carrying your own luggage.

Clothes

In theory, you need only two sets of clothes – one to wear and one to wash. Dark coloured clothing is preferred because it doesn't show the dirt – white clothes will force you to do laundry daily. You can buy any clothing you need in China nowadays.

During the often sweltering summer months, you will really need very little in the way of clothing. The Chinese themselves – men and women – usually dress in shorts, T-shirts and flip-flops (thongs) at this time of the year, so there's no need to worry about offending anyone with your overly casual sartorial standards. It's always a good idea to have a sweater handy if you are planning any high-altitude hikes. Rain gear, fold-up umbrellas and ponchos are all available in China at reasonable prices if you get caught in the summer rains.

If you're travelling in the north of China at the height of winter, prepare yourself for incredible cold. You can buy excellent down or quilt jackets in some of the big cities – the khaki-green PLA models make a functional souvenir. Also very cheap and functional are the fur-lined hats with Snoopy ear covers, but they aren't very fashionable. You might want to bring a stocking (ski) cap – they can be bought in China but are somewhat hard to find and often too small or poorly made. By contrast, good sweaters are a bargain in China. You might want to bring fur-lined boots and mittens – mediocre ones can be bought in China but large (Western) sizes are difficult to find. Western long johns are more comfortable and warmer than the Chinese variety.

Sleeping Bag

Should you, shouldn't you? A sleeping bag is required in China only if you plan to go camping. Hotels provide copious bedding during the winter months, as do the sleeper carriages on trains. Even in Tibet, you can do without a sleeping bag if you are going to be staying in hotels.

Necessities

Absolutely essential is a good pair of sunglasses, particularly in the Xinjiang desert or the high altitudes of Tibet. Ditto for sunscreen (UV) lotion. A water bottle can be a lifesaver in the western deserts.

Outside the major cities, some pharmaceutical items are hard to find, examples being shaving cream, decent razor blades, mosquito repellent, deodorant, dental floss, tampons and contact lens solution. Chinese nail clippers are poor quality.

An alarm clock is essential for getting up on time to catch your flight, bus or train – make sure yours is lightweight and bring extra batteries. Size AA rechargeable batteries can be bought in China but the rechargers are bulky – bring a portable one and plug adaptors if you can't live without your Walkman. A gluestick is convenient for sealing envelopes and pasting on stamps.

The following is a checklist of things you might consider packing:

Passport, visa, documents (vaccination certificate, diplomas, marriage licence photocopy, student ID card), money, money belt or vest, air ticket, address book, reading matter, pen, notepad, gluestick, name cards, visa photos (about 20), Swiss army knife, camera & accessories, extra camera battery, colour slide film, video camera & blank tapes, radio, Walkman & rechargeable batteries, small battery recharger (220 V), padlock, cable lock (to secure luggage on trains), sunglasses, contact lens solution, alarm clock, leakproof water bottle, torch (flashlight) with batteries & bulbs, comb, compass, day-pack, long pants, short pants, long shirt, T-shirt, nylon jacket, sweater, raincover for backpack, umbrella or rain poncho, razor, razor blades, shaving cream, sewing kit, spoon, sunhat, sunscreen (UV lotion), toilet paper, tampons, toothbrush, toothpaste, dental floss, deodorant, shampoo, laundry detergent, underwear, socks, thongs, nail clipper, tweezers, mosquito repellent, vitamins, laxative, Lomotil, condoms, contraceptives, special medications you use and medical kit (see the Health section later in this chapter).

Gifts

Many Chinese people study English and appreciate old English books and magazines. Stamps make good gifts; the Chinese are avid collectors, congregating outside the philatelic sections of the post offices and dealing on the footpath. Odd-looking foreign coins and currency are appreciated. Foreign postcards are sought after, and pictures of you and your family make popular gifts.

A Chinese fan - a practical accessory or decorative gift.

TOURIST OFFICES

Among the many striking Chinese sayings, a particularly applicable one is 'With one monkey in the way, not even 10,000 men can pass'. For the foreign traveller, the three major monkeys in China today are CITS, the PSB and the mass of little bits of paper collectively referred to as 'red tape'.

Local Tourist Offices

CITS The China International Travel Service (CITS) deals with China's foreign tourist hordes, and mainly concerns itself with organising and making travel arrangements for group tours. CITS existed as far back as 1954, when there were few customers; now they're inundated with a couple of hundred thousand foreign tourists a year. Unfortunately, after 40 years of being in business, CITS has still not gotten its act together.

Nowadays, many solo travellers make their way around China without ever having to deal with CITS. In many remote regions, CITS does not offer much in the way of services. In other places, CITS may sell hard-to-get-hold-of train tickets or tickets for the opera or acrobatics or perhaps provide tours of rural villages or factories. It depends on where you are.

All train tickets bought through CITS will be tourist-priced (at least an extra 100% on top of the Chinese price) and there will usually be a small service charge added on to the price of train, boat or plane tickets. CITS has nothing to do with issuing travel permits or visa extensions – for that you must go directly to the PSB.

CITS is a frequent target of ire for all kinds of reasons: rudeness, inefficiency, laziness and even fraud. Bear in mind, however, that service varies enormously from office to office. Expect the worst but be prepared to be pleasantly surprised.

CTS The China Travel Service (CTS) was originally set up to handle tourists from Hong Kong, Macau and Taiwan and foreign nationals of Chinese descent (Overseas Chinese). These days your gene pool and nationality make little difference – CTS has now become a keen competitor with CITS. CITS is trying to cash in on the lucrative Taiwan and Hong Kong markets, while CTS is targeting the Western market, which was previously the exclusive domain of CITS.

Many foreigners use the CTS offices in Hong Kong and Macau to obtain visas and book trains, planes, hovercraft and other transport to China. CTS can sometimes get you a better deal on hotels booked through their office than you could obtain on your own (of course, this doesn't apply to backpackers' dormitories). CTS has 19 branch offices in Hong Kong, and the Kowloon, Mongkok and Wanchai offices are open on Sunday and public holidays. These offices can be crowded – avoid this by arriving at 9 am when the doors open.

CYTS The name China Youth Travel Service (CYTS) implies that this is some sort of student organisation, but these days CYTS performs essentially the same services as CITS and CTS. Being a smaller organisation, CYTS seems to try harder to compete against the big league. This could result in better service, but not necessarily lower prices. CYTS is mostly interested in tour groups, but individual travellers could find it useful for booking air tickets or sleepers on the trains.

Chinese Tourist Offices Abroad

CITS The main office of CITS in Hong Kong (Tsimshatsui East) can book air tickets to China and has a good collection of English-language pamphlets. The main office and Central branch office are open Monday to Friday from 9 am to 5 pm and Saturday from 9 am to 1 pm; the Mongkok branch office keeps longer hours (Saturday from 9 am to 6.30 pm and half a day on Sunday).

Outside China and Hong Kong, CITS is usually known as the China National Tourist Office. Overseas CITS representatives include:

Australia
China National Tourist Office, 11th floor, 55 Clarence St, Sydney NSW 2000 (☎ (02) 9299-4057; fax 9290-1958)

France
China National Tourist Office, 51 Rue Saint-Anne, 75002 Paris (☎ (01) 42 96 95 48; fax 42 61 54 68)

Germany
China National Tourist Office, Eschenheimer Anlage 28, D-6000 Frankfurt (☎ (069) 55 52 92; fax 597 34 12)

Hong Kong
    Main Office, 6th floor, Tower Two, South Seas Centre, 75 Mody Rd, Tsimshatsui East, Kowloon (☎ 732-5888; fax 721-7154)
    Central Branch, Room 1018, Swire House, 11 Chater Rd, Central (☎ 810-4282; fax 868-1657)
    Mongkok Branch, Room 1102-1104, Bank Centre, 636 Nathan Rd, Mongkok, Kowloon (☎ 388-1619; fax 385-6157)
    Causeway Bay Branch, Room 1104, Causeway Bay Plaza, 489 Hennessy Rd, Causeway Bay (☎ 836-3485; fax 591-0849)
Japan
    China National Tourist Office, 6F Hachidai Hamamatsu-cho Building, 1-27-13 Hamamatsu-cho, Minato-ku, Tokyo (☎ (03) 3433-1461; fax 3433-8653)
UK
    China National Tourist Office, 4 Glentworth St, London NW1 (☎ (0171) 935-9427; fax 487-5842)
USA
    China National Tourist Office, Los Angeles Branch, 333 West Broadway, Suite 201, Glendale, CA 91204 (☎ (818) 545-7505; fax 545-7506)
    New York Branch, Lincoln Building, 60E, 42nd St, Suite 3126, New York, NY 10165 (☎ (212) 867-0271; fax 599-2892)

CTS Overseas representatives include the following:

Australia
    Ground floor, 757-759 George St, Sydney, NSW 2000 (☎ (02) 9211-2633; fax 9281-3595)
Canada
    556 West Broadway, Vancouver, BC V5Z 1E9 (☎ (604) 872-8787; fax 873-2823)
France
    10 Rue de Rome, 75008, Paris (☎ (1) 45.22.92.72; fax 45.22.92.79)
Germany
    Düsseldorfer Strasse 14 6000, Frankfurt (☎ (069) 25 05 15; fax 23 23 24)
Hong Kong
    Central Branch, 2nd floor, China Travel Building, 77 Queen's Road, Central (☎ 2521-7163; fax 2525-5525)
    Kowloon Branch, 1st floor, Alpha House, 27-33 Nathan Rd, Tsimshatsui (☎ 2721-4481; fax 721-6251)
    Mongkok Branch, 62-72 Sai Yee St, Mongkok (☎ 2789-5970; fax 2390-5001)
    Wanchai Branch, Ground floor, Southern Centre, 138 Hennessy Rd, Wanchai (☎ 2832-3888)

    China Hong Kong City Branch, 10-12 China Hong Kong City, 33 Canton Rd, Tsimshatsui (☎ 2736-1863)
Indonesia
    PT Cempaka Travelindo, Jalan Hayam Wuruk 97, Jakarta-Barat (☎ (021) 629-4256; fax 629-4836)
Japan
    Nihombashi-Settsu Building, 2-2-4 Nihombashi, Chuo-ku, Tokyo (☎ (03) 3273-5512; fax 3273-2667)
Macau
    Edificio Xinhua, Rua de Nagasaki (☎ 700-888, fax 706-611)
Malaysia
    Yuyi Travel Sdn Bhd, 1st floor, Sun Complex, Jalan Bukit Bintang 55100, Kuala Lumpur (☎ (03) 242-7077; fax 241-2478)
Philippines
    489 San Fernando St, Binondo, Manila (☎ (2) 47-41-87; fax 40-78-34)
Singapore
    Ground floor, SIA Building, 77 Robinson Rd, 0106 (☎ 224-0550; fax 224-5009)
Thailand
    559 Yaowaraj Rd, Bangkok 10500 (☎ (2) 226-0041; fax 226-4712)
UK
    24 Cambridge Circus, London WC2H 8HD (☎ (0171) 836-9911; fax 836-3121)
USA
    2nd floor, 212 Sutter St, San Francisco, CA 94108 (☎ (800) 332-2831, (415) 398-6627; fax 398-6669)
    Los Angeles Branch, Suite 138, 223 East Garvey Ave, Monterey Park, CA 91754 (☎ (818) 288-8222; fax 288-3464)

PSB

The Public Security Bureau (PSB) (*gōngān jú*) is the name given to China's police, both uniformed and plain-clothes. Its responsibilities include suppression of political dissidence, crime detection, preventing foreigners and Chinese from having sex with each other (no joke), mediating family quarrels and directing traffic. A related force is the Chinese People's Armed Police Force (CPAPF), which was formed several years ago to absorb cuts in the People's Liberation Army (PLA). The Foreign Affairs Branch (*wài shì kē*) of the PSB deals with foreigners. This branch (also known as the 'entry-exit' branch) is responsible for issuing visa extensions and Alien Travel Permits.

What sets the Chinese police aside from their counterparts in, say, Mexico and South America, is their amiability towards foreigners (what they're like with their own people may be a different story). They'll sometimes sit you down, give you a cup of tea and practise their English – and the number of competent English speakers is surprisingly high.

The PSB is responsible for introducing and enforcing regulations concerning foreigners. So, for example, they bear responsibility for exclusion of foreigners from certain hotels. If this means you get stuck for a place to stay, they can offer advice. Don't pester them with trivia or try to 'use' them to bully a point with a local street vendor. Do turn to them for mediation in serious disputes with hotels, restaurants, taxi drivers etc. This often works since the PSB wields God-like power – especially in remote areas.

There are a few ways you can inadvertently have an unpleasant run-in with the PSB. The most common way is to overstay your visa. Another risky proposition is to ride your bicycle between cities – in some places, a foreigner riding a bicycle still seems to be a crime. Another possibility is being in a closed area without a permit – fortunately, these days there aren't too many places left in China which require travel permits. Foreign males who are suspected of being 'too friendly' with Chinese women could have trouble with the PSB.

If you do have a run-in with the PSB, you may have to write a confession of your guilt and pay a fine. In more serious cases, you can be expelled from China (at your own expense). But in general, if you aren't doing anything particularly nasty like smuggling suitcases of dope through customs, the PSB will probably not throw you in prison.

BUSINESS HOURS & HOLIDAYS

Banks, offices, government departments and the PSB are open Monday to Saturday. As a rough guide only, they open around 8 to 9 am, close for two hours in the middle of the day (often one hour in winter or three during a heat wave in summer), then reopen until 5 or 6 pm. Sunday is a public holiday, but some businesses are open Sunday morning and make up for this by closing on Wednesday afternoon. CITS offices, Friendship Stores and the foreign-exchange counters in the tourist hotels and some of the local branches of the Bank of China have similar opening hours and are generally open on Sunday as well, at least in the morning.

Many parks, zoos and monuments have similar opening hours and are also open on Sunday and often at night. Shows at cinemas and theatres end around 9.30 to 10 pm.

The restaurant situation has improved drastically in all but the remotest regions of China and nowadays it is always possible to find something to eat at any hour of the day.

Long-distance bus stations and railway stations open their ticket offices around 5 or 5.30 am, before the first trains and buses pull out. Apart from a one or two-hour break in the middle of the day, they often stay open until late at night – say 11 or 11.30 pm.

The PRC has nine national holidays during the year:

New Year's Day
    1 January
Spring Festival
    Usually in February. This is otherwise known as Chinese New Year and starts on the first day of the old lunar calendar. Although officially lasting only three days, many people take a week off from work. Be warned: this is China's only three-day holiday and, unless you have booked a month or two in advance, this is definitely not the time to cross borders (especially the Hong Kong one) or to look for transport or accommodation. Although the demand for accommodation sky-rockets, many hotels close down at this time. Book your room in advance and sit tight until the chaos is over!
International Working Women's Day
    8 March
International Labour Day
    1 May
Youth Day
    4 May – commemorates the student demonstrations in Beijing on 4 May 1919, when the Versailles Conference decided to give Germany's 'rights' in the city of Tianjin to Japan
Children's Day
    1 June

Anniversary of the founding of the Communist Party of China
1 July
Anniversary of the founding of the Chinese PLA
1 August
National Day
1 October – celebrates the founding of the PRC on 1 October 1949

CULTURAL EVENTS

Much of Chinese culture took a beating during the Cultural Revolution and still has not fully revived. Nevertheless, hanging around the appropriate temples at certain times will reward you with special ceremonies and colourful events.

Special prayers are held at Buddhist and Taoist temples on days when the moon is either full or just the thinnest sliver. According to the Chinese lunar calendar, these days fall on the 14th and 15th days of the lunar month and on the last (29th or 30th) day of the month just ending and the 1st day of the new month.

Other notable times when temples are liveliest include the following:

Lantern Festival (yuánxiāo jié)
It's not a public holiday, but it is very colourful. It falls on the 15th day of the 1st moon (approx. mid-February to mid-March). People take the time to make (or buy) paper lanterns and walk around the streets in the evening holding them.
Guanyin's Birthday (guānshìyīn shēngri)
The birthday of Guanyin, the goddess of mercy, is on the 19th day of the 2nd moon (approx. late March to late April) and is a good time to visit Taoist temples.
Mazu's Birthday (māzǔ shēngri)
Mazu, goddess of the sea, is the friend of all fishing crews. She's called Mazu in Fujian Province and Taiwan. The name gets changed to Tianhou in Guangdong Province, and in Hong Kong the spelling is 'Tin Hau'. Her birthday is widely celebrated at Taoist temples in coastal regions as far south as Vietnam. Mazu's birthday is on the 23rd day of the 3rd moon (May or June).
Tomb Sweep Day (qīng míng jié)
A day for worshipping ancestors; people visit the graves of their departed relatives and clean the site. They often place flowers on the tomb and burn ghost money for the departed. Falls on 5 April in the Gregorian calendar in most years, 4 April in leap years.

Water-Splashing Festival (pō shuǐ jié)
In Yunnan Province, this event is held around mid-April (usually 13-15 April). The purpose is to wash away the dirt, sorrow and demons of the old year and bring in the happiness of the new. The event gets staged more often now for tourists.
Ghost Month (guǐ yuè)
The Ghost Month is the 7th lunar month, or really just the first 15 days (approx. late August to late September). The devout believe that during this time the ghosts from hell walk the earth and it is a dangerous time to travel, go swimming, get married or move to a new house. If someone dies during this month, the body will be preserved and the funeral and burial will be performed the following month. The Chinese government officially denounces Ghost Month as a lot of superstitious nonsense.
Mid-Autumn Festival (zhōngqiū jié)
Also known as the Moon Festival, this takes place on the 15th day of the 8th moon (approx. October). Gazing at the moon and lighting fireworks are popular activities at this time. This is the time to eat tasty moon cakes.
Birthday of Confucius (kǒngzi shēngri)
The birthday of the great sage occurs on 28 September of the Gregorian calendar. This is an interesting time to visit Qufu in Shandong Province, the birthplace of Confucius. On the other hand, all hotels in town are likely to be booked out at this time. A ceremony is held at the Confucius Temple starting from around 4 am.

POST & TELECOMMUNICATIONS
Postal Rates

Postal rates in China are as follows:

Letters

Weight	Rate
0-20 grams	Y2.20
20-50 grams	Y4.30
50-100 grams	Y6.70
100-250 grams	Y13.20
250-500 grams	Y26.80
500-1000 grams	Y52.30
1000-2000 grams	Y74.10

Printed Matter

Weight	Rate
0-20 grams	Y1.50
20-50 grams	Y2.20
50-100 grams	Y4.20
100-250 grams	Y7.90
250-500 grams	Y14.80
500-1000 grams	Y23.70
1000-2000 grams	Y39.10

Small Packets

Weight	Rate
0-100 grams	Y5.20
100-250 grams	Y10.50
250-500 grams	Y14.80
500-1000 grams	Y31.30
1000-2000 grams	Y58.50

Theoretically postal rates are uniform throughout China, but in practice you will find that rates differ from post office to post office.

Letters Rates for international surface mail are shown in the table above. Air-mail rates involve an additional Y0.7 for every 10 grams of weight.

Postcards International postcards cost Y1.30 by surface mail and Y1.60 by air mail to anywhere in the world.

Aerogrammes These are Y2.80 to anywhere in the world.

Printed Matter Rates for international surface mail are shown in the table. Each additional kg above 2000 grams costs Y16.50. See Letters entry above for the air-mail surcharge.

Small Packets Rates for international surface mail are shown in the table. See the Letters entry above for the air mail surcharge.

Parcels Rates for parcels vary depending on the country of destination and the post office you send it from. A one-kg parcel should average around Y55 by surface mail and around Y80 by air to most destinations. Rates to Hong Kong are significantly lower.

Post offices are very picky about how you pack things; don't finalise your packing until the thing has got its last customs clearance. Most countries impose a maximum weight limit (10 kg is typical) on packages received – this rate varies from country to country but the Chinese post office should be able to tell you what the limit is. If you have a receipt for the goods, put it in the box when you're

mailing it, since it may be opened again by customs further down the line.

EMS International express mail (EMS) service charges vary according to country, and whether you are sending documents or parcels. It is not available to every country worldwide.

Registration Fees The registration fee for letters, printed matter and packets is Y1. Acknowledgment of receipt is Y0.80 per article.

Domestic Mail Within the same city, mail delivery for a letter (20 grams and below) costs Y0.10, postcards also Y0.10. Out of town, letters are Y0.20, postcards Y0.15. The fee for registration is Y0.30.

Sending Mail

The international postal service seems efficient, and air-mail letters and postcards will probably take around five to 10 days to reach their destinations. If possible, write the country of destination in Chinese, as this should speed up the delivery. Domestic post is amazingly fast – perhaps one or two days from Guangzhou (Canton) to Beijing. Within a city it may be delivered the same day that it's sent.

As well as the local post offices there are branch post offices in just about all the major tourist hotels where you can send letters, packets and parcels (the contents of packets and parcels are checked by the post office staff before mailing). Even at cheap hotels you can usually post letters from the front desk – reliability varies but in general it's OK. In some places, you may only be able to post printed matter from these branch offices. Other parcels may require a customs form attached at the town's main post office, where their contents will be checked.

Large envelopes are a bit hard to come by; try the department stores. If you expect to be sending quite a few packets, stock up when you come across such envelopes. A roll of strong, sticky tape is a useful item to bring along and serves many purposes. String, glue and sometimes cloth bags are supplied at the post offices, but don't count on it. The Friendship Stores will sometimes package and mail purchases for you, but only goods actually bought at the store.

Private Carriers In a joint venture with China's Sinotrans, fast air freight is offered by two foreign carriers: DHL and UPS. Express document and parcel service is offered by two other foreign carriers: Federal Express and TNT Skypak. Such service is offered only in major cities and doesn't come cheap – costs start at around US$50.

Receiving Mail

There are poste restante services in just about every city and town, and they seem to work. The collection system differs from place to place, but one thing all post offices seem to agree on is the Y1 to Y1.5 charge for each item of poste restante mail you collect.

Some major tourist hotels will hold mail for their guests, but this is a less reliable option.

Officially, the PRC forbids certain items from being mailed to it – the regulations specifically prohibit 'reactionary books, magazines and propaganda materials, obscene or immoral articles'. You also cannot mail Chinese currency abroad or receive it by post. As elsewhere, mail-order hashish and other recreational chemicals will not amuse the authorities.

Telephone

China's phone system is undergoing a major overhaul and, given the size of the task, it has so far been remarkably successful. Both international and domestic calls can be made with a minimum of fuss from your hotel room. Even card phones are becoming increasingly widespread.

Most hotel rooms are equipped with phones from which local calls are free. Alternatively, local calls can be made from public pay phones or from privately run phone booths (there's one of these on every corner nowadays); long-distance domestic calls can also be made from the phone booths, but not

usually international calls. In the lobbies of many hotels, the reception desks have a similar system – free calls for guests, Y0.50 for non-guests, and long-distance calls are charged by the minute.

You can place both domestic and international long-distance phone calls from main telecommunications offices. Generally you pay a deposit of Y200 and are given a card with the number of the phone booth you call from. The call is timed by computer, charged by the minute and a receipt will be provided.

Domestic long-distance rates in China vary according to distance but are cheap. International calls are expensive. Rates for station-to-station calls to most countries in the world are around Y20 per minute. There is a minimum charge of three minutes. Reverse-charge calls are often cheaper than calls paid for in China. Time the call yourself – the operator will not break in to tell you that your minimum period of three minutes is approaching. After you hang up, the operator will ring back to tell you how much it cost. There is no call cancellation fee.

If you are expecting a call – either international or domestic – try to advise the caller beforehand of your hotel room number. The operators frequently have difficulty understanding Western names and the hotel receptionist may not be able to locate you. If this can't be done, then try to inform the operator that you are expecting the call and write down your name and room number – this should increase your chances of success.

Card Phones Card phones can be found in hotel lobbies and in most telecommunications buildings. Cards come in denominations of Y20, Y50 and Y100. These cards can only be used in the province you buy them. There are also cards that can be used throughout China, but these cost Y200 – ask for a *quánguókǎ*. Calls made on card phones are charged by the minute.

Direct Dialling Card phones are the cheapest way to make calls in China, but telecommunications centres, hotel business centres and mid-range to top-end hotel rooms also provide domestic (DDD) and international (IDD) direct dialling. Bear in mind that hotels generally levy a 30% surcharge on long-distance calls.

The international access code in China is 00. Add the country code, then the local area code (omitting the 0 before it) and the number you want to reach. Another option is to dial the home country direct dial number (108), which puts you straight through to a local operator there. You can then make a reverse-charge (collect) call or a credit card call with a telephone credit card valid in the destination country.

Dialling codes include:

Country	Direct Dial	Home Country Direct
Australia	00-61	108-61
Canada	00-1	108-1
Hong Kong	00-852	108-852
Japan	00-81	108-81
Netherlands	00-31	108-31
New Zealand	00-64	108-64
UK	00-44	108-44
SA	00-1	108-1*

* For the USA you can dial 108-11 (AT&T), 108-12 (MCI) or 108-13 (Sprint)

The domestic codes for China's provincial capitals and major cities are shown below.

Codes for provincial capitals and major cities

Anhui
  Hefei (0551)
Beijing (010)
  Fujian
  Fuzhou (0591)
  Quanzhou (0595)
  Xiamen (0592)
Gansu
  Lanzhou (0931)
Guangdong
  Foshan (0757)
  Guangzhou (020)
  Shantou (0754)
  Shenzhen (0755)
  Zhanjiang (0759)
  Zhuhai (0756)
Guangxi
  Beihai (0779)
  Guilin (0773)
  Nanning (0771)
Guizhou
  Guiyang (0851)
  Zunyi (0852)
Hainan
  Haikou (0750)
  Sanya (0899)
Hebei
  Chengde (0314)
  Shijiazhuang (0311)
  Qinhuangdao (0335)
Heilongjiang
  Harbin (0451)
  Mudanjiang (0453)

Henan
  Kaifeng (0378)
  Luoyang (0379)
  Zhengzhou (0371)
Hubei
  Wuhan (027)
  Yichang (0717)
Hunan
  Changsha (0731)
  Yueyang (0730)
Inner Mongolia
  Baotou (0472)
  Hohhot (0471)
  Xilinhot (0479)
Jiangsu
  Lianyungang (0518)
  Nanjing (025)
  Suzhou (0512)
  Xuzhou (0516)
Jiangxi
  Jiujiang (0792)
  Lushan (07010)
  Nanchang (0791)
Jilin
  Changchun (0431)
  Jilin (0432)
Liaoning
  Dalian (0411)
  Dandong (0415)
  Shenyang (024)
Ningxia
  Guyuan (0954)
  Yinchuan (0951)

Qinghai
  Golmud (0979)
  Xining (0971)
Shaanxi
  Xi'an (029)
  Yan'an (0911)
Shandong
  Ji'nan (0531)
  Qingdao (0532)
  Qufu (05473)
  Weihai (05451)
  Yantai (0535)
Shanghai (021)
Shanxi
  Datong (0352)
  Taiyuan (0351)
Sichuan
  Chengdu (028)
  Chongqing (0811)
  Leshan (0833)
Tianjin (022)
Tibet
  Lhasa (0891)
Xinjiang
  Ürümqi (0991)
Yunnan
  Kunming (0871)
  Simao (0879)
Zhejiang
  Hangzhou (0571)
  Ningbo (0574)
  Wenzhou(0577)

Essential Numbers There are several telephone numbers which are the same for all major cities. Only international directory assistance is likely to have English speakers:

Local directory assistance	114
Long-distance directory assistance	113, 173
International directory assistance	115
Police hotline	110
Fire hotline	119

Fax, Telex & Telegraph

Major hotels usually operate a business centre complete with telephone, fax and telex service, not to mention photocopying and perhaps the use of typewriters and computers. As a rule, you do not have to be a guest at the hotel to use these services, but you certainly must pay. While it is cheaper to fax from a telecommunications office, hotel business centres are more efficient and provide confirmation receipts – telecommunications centres just provide a bill.

International fax and telexes (other than those to Hong Kong or Macau) cost Y23 per minute with a three-minute minimum charge, making it absurdly expensive to send a one-page fax. International telegram rates are usually around Y3.50 per word, and more for the express service. Rates to Hong Kong and Macau are less.

TIME

Time throughout China is set to Beijing time, which is eight hours ahead of GMT/UTC. When it's noon in Beijing it's also noon in far-off Lhasa, Ürümqi and all other parts of the country. Since the sun doesn't cooperate with Beijing's whims, people in China's far west follow a later work schedule so they don't have to commute two hours' before dawn.

When it's noon in Beijing the time in other cities around the world is:

Frankfurt	5 am
Hong Kong	noon
London	4 am
Los Angeles	8 pm
Melbourne	2 pm
Montreal	11 pm
New York	11 pm
Paris	5 am
Rome	5 am
Wellington	4 pm

ELECTRICITY

Electricity is 220 V, 50 cycles AC. Plugs come in at least four designs – three-pronged angled pins (like in Australia), three-pronged round pins (like in Hong Kong), two flat pins (American-style but without the ground wire) or two narrow round pins (European-style). For the most part, however, you can safely travel with two plugs: American-style and Australian-style.

Conversion plugs are easily purchased in Hong Kong but are difficult to find in China. Battery chargers are widely available, but these are generally the bulky style which are not suitable for travelling – buy a small one in Hong Kong. Chinese cities are experiencing power blackouts more frequently in recent years as the demand for power has grown. This is an especially serious problem in summer because of the increasing use of air-conditioning.

LAUNDRY

Each floor of just about every hotel in China has a service desk, usually near the elevators. The attendant's job is to clean the rooms, make the beds and collect and deliver laundry. Almost all tourist hotels have a laundry service, and if you hand in clothes one day you should get them back a day or two later. If the hotel doesn't have a laundry, they can usually direct you to one. Hotel laundry service tends to be expensive and you might wind up doing what many travellers do – hand-washing your own clothes.

WEIGHTS & MEASURES

The metric system is widely used in China. However, the traditional Chinese measures are often used for domestic transactions and you may come across them. The following equations will help.

Metric	Chinese	Imperial
1 metre (mǐ)	= 3 chi	= 3.28 feet
1 km (gōnglǐ)	= 2 li	= 0.62 miles
1 litre (gōngshēng)	= 1 gongsheng	= 0.22 gallons
1 kg (gōngjīn)	= 2 jin	= 2.2 pounds

BOOKS

Fathoming the enigma of China is such a monumental task that the need for 'China-watchers' and their publications will probably never dry up. Indeed, just keeping up with the never-ending flood of conjecture on the Middle Kingdom would be a full-time job in itself. The following is an abbreviated tour of the highlights.

People & Society

The book that has most captured the Western imagination in recent years is *Wild Swans* (Flamingo, 1991) by Jung Chang. It is a family saga spanning three generations against the backdrop of China's turbulent 20th century history: fascinating both as historical overview and as domestic drama.

Wild Swans is simply the latest (and probably the most ambitious) in what is a long line of I-survived-China (but only just) books. *Life and Death in Shanghai* (Grafton, 1984) by Nien Cheng focuses largely on the Cultural Revolution and is also recommended. *The Dragon's Pearl* (Simon & Schuster, 1994) by Sirin Pathanothai is a fascinating, bizarre account of a childhood

'Wild Swans' or 'Bitter Winds'?

in China by a Thai woman whose politician father sent her to be raised by Zhou Enlai in a gesture of feudal diplomacy. *Son of the Revolution* (Fontana, 1983) by Liang Heng and Judith Shapiro, an early inside-China book, is still well worth reading. Harry Wu, imprisoned by Chinese authorities on charges of espionage in mid-1995, has written eloquently and grimly about his years in prison camps in *Bitter Winds: A Memoir of My Years in China's Gulag* (John Wiley, 1994).

Less riveting, perhaps, *Chinese Lives* (Penguin, 1989) by Zhang Xinxin and Sang Ye is a series of interviews with a broad range of Chinese by two Chinese journalists. A fine account of life in rural China can be found in *Mr China's Son: A Villager's Life* (Westview Press, 1994) by He Liuyi.

State of the nation accounts of contemporary Chinese politics and society by Western scholars and journalists are thick on the ground and tend to become repetitive if you read too many of them. One of the best recent works is *China Wakes* (Times Books, 1994) by Nicholas D Kristof and Sheryl Wudunn. Orville Schell has also been diligently tracking China's awakening in books such as *To Get Rich Is Glorious, Discos and Democracy* and most recently *Mandate of Heaven* (Simon & Schuster, 1994). All three of them make for engaging reading; the latter is concerned mostly with the crisis of faith in the CCP following the Tiananmen Massacre.

Simon Leys was a critic of the Chinese government when it was unfashionable (at least in academic circles) to be so. His account of his visits to China in 1972 and 1973 published in *Chinese Shadows* is well worth tracking down. For a contemporary insight into Chinese society the best book around is Perry Link's *Evening Chats in Beijing* (Norton, 1992). It is everything you could wish of a book about China: intelligent, well written and packed with illuminating insights and observations culled from a long career of writing and thinking about China.

Seeds of Fire: Chinese Voices of Conscience (Far Eastern Economic Review Ltd,

1986) is an anthology of blistering eloquence from authors such as Wei Jingsheng, Liu Qing, Wang Xizhe and Xu Wenli (imprisoned for their roles in the Democracy Movement) and the poet Sun Jingxuan. Wei Jingsheng's description of Q1, China's top prison for political detainees, is utterly horrific.

Biography Biographical appraisals of China's shadowy leaders are immensely popular. Mao, of course, has been the subject of countless biographies (the classic is *Red Star over China* (Penguin, 1972) by Edgar Snow), but it was his personal physician, Zhisui Li, who finally blew the lid on the world's most famous dictator cum pop icon. Li's *The Private Life of Chairman Mao* (Chatto & Windus, 1994) is absolutely compelling in its account of Mao as a domineering manipulator who hypocritically flouted the authoritarian and puritanical rules he foisted on his people – fascinating stuff.

Mao gets similar treatment in *The New Emperors* (Little, Brown, 1992) by Harrison E Salisbury. The book covers the lives of Mao and Deng, but it is Mao who gets the bulk of the book. Deng Xiaoping himself remains elusive. Richard Evans has written an excellent book in *Deng Xiaoping and the Making of Modern China* (Penguin, 1995), but again, after some 230 pages, Deng the man remains a shadowy figure.

Other interesting biographical works include *The White Boned Demon: A Biography of Madame Mao Zedong* (William Morrow, 1984) by Ross Terrill and *Eldest Son: Zhou Enlai and the Making of Modern China, 1898-1976* (Jonathan Cape, 1994) by Han Suyin. Especially worth looking out for is *Claws of the Dragon: Kang Sheng* (Simon & Schuster, 1992) by John Byron and Robert Pack. Subtitled 'The evil genius behind Mao and his legacy of terror in people's China', the book documents Kang Sheng's career as head of the CCP's secret police.

Fiction See the Literature section of the Facts about the Country chapter for recommended readings in translated Chinese literature. Most of it is available inexpensively in major cities in China.

Unfortunately a lot of the fiction written by Westerners involving China tends to be of the potboiler variety, involving dashing Westerners going about their dare-devil business in a romanticised and stereotyped oriental world. If that's your thing, *Peking* (Pan) by Anthony Grey or *Taipan* by James Clavell are good options for long train journeys.

La Condition Humaine, translated as *Man's Estate* (Penguin 1961), by André Malraux is one of the few undisputed classics about China. The novel is set around the ill-fated Communist uprising in Shanghai in 1927.

The work of Jonathan Spence occupies an unusual space somewhere between biography, fiction and history. *The Memory Palace of Matteo Ricci* is a study of the most famous Jesuit to take up residence in China. *The Question of Hu* and *Emperor of China: Self-Portrait of K'ang Hsi* are also highly recommended. *Rose Crossing* (Hamish Hamilton, 1995) by Nicholas Jose is a quirky account of a chance encounter of a 17th-century English naturalist and a eunuch of the deposed Ming court on a deserted island. *Ming: A Novel of 17th Century China* (St Martin's Press, 1995) by Robert Oxnam is another title worth looking out for.

The Chinese-American writers Maxine Hong Kingston and Amy Tan have both written books about the experiences of immigrant Chinese in the USA. Although their novels are not directly about China, they tell a great deal about Chinese relationships and customs. Look out for Kingston's *The Woman Warrior* and *China Men* and Tan's *The Kitchen God*.

History
The most comprehensive history of China available is the *Cambridge History of China*. The series runs to 15 volumes (so far), and traces Chinese history from its earliest beginnings to 1982. A far more practical overview for travellers is *The Walled Kingdom: A*

History of China from 2000 BC to the Present (Flamingo, 1984) by Witold Rodzinsky. It should be available in a handy paperback edition of around 450 pages.

Another wide-ranging history is *A History of Chinese Civilisation* (Cambridge University Press, 1982) by Jacques Gernet. It is far too heavy to travel with but provides comprehensive background reading on the arts and religion in China over the centuries.

The best recent history of modern China is Jonathan Spence's *The Search for Modern China* (Norton, 1991). It fully covers China's history from the late Ming through to the Tiananmen Massacre in lively prose that is a pleasure to read. Spence's *The Gate of Heavenly Peace: The Chinese and Their Revolution, 1895-1980* (Penguin) is also recommended – it is a history of ideas and personalities. *The Great Chinese Revolution 1800-1985* (Chatto & Windus, 1987) by John King Fairbank is another highly rated modern history.

A polemical overview of what Chinese history has been about and where it is all heading is provided in *The Tyranny of History: The Roots of China's Crisis* (Penguin, 1992) by WJF Jenner. The essential argument that China's history has been one of tyranny, and that China's rootedness in history continues to tyrannise it, is a fascinating one, if perhaps a little too clever for its own good. A political history of the Deng years has already appeared in *Burying Mao* (Princeton University Press, 1994) by Richard Baum. For anyone seriously interested in China's stop-go reforms of the last 15 years, this is the book to read. Merle Goldman looks at the tortuous course of democratic reform over recent years in *Sowing the Seeds of Democracy in China: Political Reform in the Deng Xiaoping Era* (Harvard University Press, 1994).

It is worth picking up a copy of *The Soong Dynasty* (Sidgwick & Jackson) by Sterling Seagrave for a racy account of the bad old days under the Kuomintang.

Jonathan Spence again deserves a mention for *To Change China: Western Advisers in China 1600-1960* (Penguin, 1980). It deals with the ongoing and probably misguided

belief in the West that one day, with a little guidance, China will emerge as a place that we all understand.

Finally, all of Peter Hopkirk's books are worth reading. None of them deal with China specifically, but in *The Great Game*, *Foreign Devils on the Silk Road* and *Trespassers on the Roof of the World* (all available in Oxford paperbacks), Hopkirk writes breezily of 19th-century international espionage, exploration, pilfering of lost art treasures and the struggle for territorial domination at the far-flung edges of the Chinese empire in Xinjiang (Chinese Turkestan, as it was then known) and Tibet.

Tiananmen-Inspired The 1989 protests and killings in Tiananmen and the events leading up to them are now covered comprehensively in numerous books, some of them already mentioned above. Richard Evans's *Deng Xiaoping and the Making of Modern China* (see the Biography entry above) in particular has a good synopsis of the events leading up to the killings and a balanced account of what actually happened in the square.

At the time of the massacre, however, many journalists rushed to bring out books on the events. The best of these is *Tiananmen: The Rape of Beijing* (Doubleday, 1990) by Michael Fathers and Andrew Higgins.

Travel Writing
When the wall came tumbling down in the early 1980s, two eminent travel writers got in quick: Colin Thubron with *Behind the Wall* and Paul Theroux with *Riding the Iron Rooster*. Both are published by Penguin and they remain the best recent travel books written about China. Thubron's account is probably the more thoughtful of the two, Theroux's the more provocative; it's worth reading them before you set off or while you are travelling.

Iron and Silk (Vintage, 1986) by Mark Salzman recounts the adventures of a young Chinese-speaking kung fu student in China (filmed as a telemovie). Another good travel book, *From Heaven Lake* (Vintage, 1983) by Vikram Seth of *A Suitable Boy* fame, follows Seth's journey from Xinjiang to Tibet and on to Delhi, back in the days when it was a difficult undertaking. Other possibilities include *Danziger's Travels* (Flamingo, 1992) by Nick Danziger, a good 'Silk Road' book that takes rather a long time to get to China, and *In Xanadu* (Fontana) by William Dalrymple, an epic quest for the pleasure palace of Kublai Khan that fails to turn up a palace.

The Road to Miran: Travels in the Forbidden Zone of Xinjiang (Harper Collins, 1995) follows young archaeologist Christa Paula in search of an ancient lost city in the depths of Xinjiang, while BBC broadcaster Tony Scotland treks around China to find the man who would be emperor (if China's imperial tradition were still in place) in *The Empty Throne: The Quest for an Imperial Heir in the People's Republic of China* (Penguin, 1993).

The Long March: The Untold Story (Macmillan, 1985) by Harrison E Salisbury (difficult to find in paperback) follows the tortuous route of the Long March, which of course provides ample opportunity for reflections on the march itself and on life in rural China.

For some classic travel writing of the old school, turn to Peter Fleming. *One's Company* describes his travels across Siberia and eastern China, meeting such notables as Puyi, the puppet-emperor of Japanese-occupied Manchuria. *News from Tartary* describes his epic six-month trek on the backs of camels and donkeys across southern Xinjiang and into the north of Pakistan.

More classic travel writing can be found in *The Yangtse and Beyond* by Isabella Bird. Originally published in 1899, it has been reissued by Virago.

Business

As Chinese markets open, publishers have been scrambling for books that help investors negotiate the inevitable pitfalls. Two recent publications (and in ever-changing China, the more recent the better) are *China Business: The Portable Encyclopedia for*

Doing Business with China (World Trade Press, 1995) by Edward G Hinkleman and *Doing Business with China* (Kogan Page, 1995) by Jonathan Reuvid. Both books pull together a number of experts to write on legal, taxation and accounting issues, and also include important cultural information.

Invaluable for anyone dealing with China is *The China Phone Book & Business Directory* (Far Eastern Economic Review, bi-annual). Every edition is more comprehensive than the last, and it is packed with essential phone and fax numbers for Beijing and all other major Chinese cities.

Travel Guides

The Hong Kong publisher Odyssey is gradually producing a series of illustrated provincial guides to China. To date there are guides to *Yunnan, Guizhou, Sichuan, Shanghai, Xi'an* and *Beijing*. There is less emphasis on the kind of practical information you find in Lonely Planet guides, but they are attractively packaged and provide good background reading.

It is worth keeping an eye out for reprints of old guidebooks to China. Oxford has re-released *In Search of Old Peking* by LC Arlington and William Lewisohn, a wonderfully detailed guide to a world that is now long gone.

Other Lonely Planet guides to the region include the *Beijing City Guide* and *Hong Kong City Guide* and country guides for *Tibet* and *Hong Kong, Macau & Guangzhou*.

Language

For most travellers the most difficult part of China travel is the language barrier – a phrasebook is essential if you get off the beaten track. Lonely Planet publishes a *Mandarin phrasebook, Cantonese phrasebook* and *Tibetan phrasebook*. Berlitz also publishes a phrasebook, *Chinese for Travellers*.

There are, of course, other phrasebooks on the market. Some people use the *Speechless Translator*, which can be bought in Hong Kong; this has columns of Chinese characters and English translations that you string together to form sentences, with no speaking required. Another useful book is *Instant Chinese* (Round Asia Publishing Company, 1985), which you can find in Hong Kong.

For anyone who finds the normal run of phrasebooks dull and wants something to cuss and swear by, *Outrageous Chinese: A Guide to Chinese Street Slang* (China Books & Periodicals, 1995) by James J Wang is the ticket – use it with care if you want to survive your trip.

Bookshops

The availability of English books is gradually improving in cities such as Guangzhou, Shanghai and Beijing, but in most provincial backwaters there is almost nothing in the way of reading material available. In other words, bring your own.

China's so-called foreign-language bookshops (every city has one) are generally not worth the effort of seeking out, though occasionally they will stock a small selection of moth-eaten classics such as *Vanity Fair* and *Pride and Prejudice*. Stocks in Guangzhou, Shanghai and Beijing are far more comprehensive and include reasonably large selections of Ballantine's publications (mainly American fiction – Gore Vidal, John Cheever, among others). Hotel lobbies are another good place to seek out books and periodicals.

See the Hong Kong & Macau chapter for a listing of bookshops in Hong Kong – it is possibly the best place in Asia to stock up on reading material.

MAPS

One of the big changes to occur in China over the past decade has been the increase in availability of good-quality maps. In the early 1980s, maps were treated as military secrets. The few that were available were great works of fiction – doctored to trick the foreign spies and saboteurs. As China opened up, it slowly dawned on the Chinese leadership that the satellite-based maps published in the West were much better quality than those available in China.

Now the situation has reversed: top-quality maps of almost every Chinese city – even many small towns – are readily available. Some of these show incredible detail – bus routes (including names of bus stops), the locations of hotels, shops and so on. City maps normally only cost Y1 to Y2 – the cost may be partly subsidised by the advertisements.

Maps are most easily purchased from bookstalls or street vendors around railway and bus stations, from branches of the Xinhua Bookstore or from hotel front desks (even cheap Chinese hotels where foreigners can't stay). Unfortunately maps are almost always in Chinese characters. It is only in tourist centres that you will find English maps.

The places to look for English-language editions are the hotel giftshops, Friendship Stores and sometimes the foreign-language bookstores. There are also a few atlases – these cover only major cities and tourist sites, and most are in Chinese characters although there are a few English editions around. English-language editions invariably cost more than the Chinese equivalents.

There seems to be no central place in China where you can go to purchase maps for the entire country. The selection at the Xinhua Bookstore on Wangfujing Dajie in Beijing is decent, but hardly comprehensive.

Some of the most detailed maps of China available in the West are the aerial survey 'Operational Navigation Charts' (Series ONC). These are prepared and published by the Defence Mapping Agency Aerospace Center, St Louis Air Force Station, Missouri 63118, USA. Cyclists and mountaineers have recommended these highly because of their extraordinary detail. In the UK you can obtain these maps from Stanfords Map Centre (☎ (0171) 836-1321), 12-14 Long Acre, London WC2E 9LP, or from The Map Shop (☎ (06) 846-3146), A T Atkinson & Partner, 15 High St, Upton-on-Severn, Worcestershire, WR8 OHJ.

MEDIA
News Agencies

China has two news agencies, the Xinhua News Agency and the China News Service.

The Xinhua (New China) Agency is a national agency with its headquarters in Beijing and branches in each province as well as in the army and many foreign countries. It provides news for the national, provincial and local papers and radio stations, transmits radio broadcasts abroad in foreign languages and is responsible for making contact with and exchanging news with foreign news agencies. In Hong Kong, Xinhua acts as the unofficial embassy.

The main function of the China News Service is to supply news to Overseas Chinese newspapers and journals, including those in Hong Kong and Macau. It also distributes Chinese documentary films abroad.

Chinese-Language Publications

There are over 2000 national and provincial newspapers in China. The main one is *Renmin Ribao* (*People's Daily*), with nationwide circulation. It was founded in 1946 as the official publication of the Central Committee of the Communist Party. Every city worth its salt in China will have its own local version of the *People's Daily,* and like the banner publication they are uniformly boring, concerned more with sloganeering and editorialising than covering the news.

At the other end of the scale is China's version of the gutter press – several hundred 'unhealthy papers' and magazines hawked on street corners and bus stations in major cities with nude or violent photos and stories about sex, crime, witchcraft, miracle cures and UFOs. These have been severely criticised by the government for their obscene and racy content. They are also extremely popular. There are also about 40 newspapers for the minority nationalities.

Almost 2200 periodicals were published at the last count, of which about half were technical or scientific; the rest were concerned with social sciences, literature, culture and education, or were general periodicals, pictorials or children's publications. One of the better-known periodicals is the monthly *Hongqi* (Red Flag), the main Communist philosophical and theoretical journal.

In China the newspapers, radio and TV are the last places to carry the news. Westerners tend to be numbed by endless accounts of heroic factory workers and stalwart peasants and dismiss China's media as a huge propaganda machine. Flipping through journals like *China Today* and *China Pictorial* only serves to confirm this view.

Nevertheless, the Chinese press does warrant serious attention since it provides clues to what is happening in China. When Deng Xiaoping returned to public view after being disposed of in the Cultural Revolution, the first mention was simply the inclusion of his name in a guest list at a reception for Prince Sihanouk of Kampuchea, printed in the *People's Daily* without elaboration or comment. Political struggles between factions are described in articles in the Chinese newspapers as a means of warning off any supporters of the opposing side and undermining its position rather than resorting to an all-out, dangerous conflict. The Letters to the Editor section in the *People's Daily* provides something of a measure of public opinion, and complaints are sometimes followed up by reporters.

Newspapers and journals are useful for following the 'official line' of the Chinese government – though in times of political struggle they tend to follow the line of whoever has control over the media.

Foreign-Language Publications

China publishes various newspapers, books and magazines in a number of European and Asian languages. The *China Daily* is China's official English-language newspaper and is available in most major cities – it even makes its way as far as Lhasa, usually a couple of weeks out of date. The *Shanghai Star* is available in Shanghai.

The *China Daily* has two overseas editions (Hong Kong and USA). Overseas subscriptions can be obtained from the following sources:

Hong Kong
   Wen Wei Po, 197 Wanchai Rd (☎ 2572-2211; fax 2572-0441)

USA
China Daily Distribution Corporation, Suite 401, 15 Mercer St, New York, NY 10013 (☎ (212) 219-0130; fax 210-0108)

China also publishes a large number of very dull magazines in English and other languages. They are seldom seen in China itself but often clutter up periodical racks in university libraries around the world. They have titles like *China Philately* (for stamp collectors), *China's Patents & Trademarks*, *China's Tibet* (the name says it all) and *Women of China*. It's difficult to imagine who reads them.

Imported Publications

In large cities like Beijing, Shanghai and Guangzhou, it's fairly easy to score copies of popular imported English-language magazines like *Time, Newsweek, Far Eastern Economic Review* and *The Economist*. It is also usually possible to find European magazines like *Le Point* and *Der Spiegel*. Foreign newspapers like the *Asian Wall Street Journal, International Herald-Tribune* and Hong Kong's *South China Morning Post* are also available. Imported periodicals are most readily available from the big tourist hotels, though a few Friendship Stores also stock copies.

To China's credit, foreign-language magazines and newspapers are seldom, if ever, censored, even when they contain stories critical of the PRC. Of course, a different set of rules applies to Chinese-language publications from Hong Kong and Taiwan – essentially, these cannot be brought into China without special permission.

Radio & TV

Domestic radio broadcasting is controlled by the Central People's Broadcasting Station (CPBS). Broadcasts are made in *pǔtōnghuà*, the standard Chinese speech, as well as in local Chinese dialects and minority languages. There are also broadcasts to Taiwan in putonghua and Fujianese, and Cantonese broadcasts aimed at residents of Guangdong Province, Hong Kong and Macau. Radio

Beijing is China's overseas radio service and broadcasts in about 40 foreign languages, as well as in putonghua and several local dialects. It also exchanges programmes with radio stations in a number of countries and has correspondents in some.

If you want to keep up with the world news, a short-wave radio receiver would be worth bringing with you. You can buy these in China, but the ones from Hong Kong are usually more compact and better quality.

Chinese Central Television (CCTV) began broadcasting in 1958, and colour transmission began in 1973. Major cities may have a second local channel, like Beijing Television (BTV). Although they've improved in the past few years, Chinese TV shows are designed to guide the public's moral education. Taiwanese and Hong Kong soap operas are, however, more popular.

Notice Boards

Apart from the mass media, the public notice board retains its place as an important means of educating the people or influencing public opinion. Other people who want to get a message across glue up big wall posters (*dàzìbào*, or 'big character posters') in public places. This is a traditional form of communicating ideas in China and if the content catches the attention of even a few people then word-of-mouth can spread it very quickly. Deng Xiaoping personally stripped from China's constitution the right to put up wall posters.

Public notice boards abound in China. Two of the most common subjects are crime and accidents. In China it's no holds barred – before-and-after photos of executed criminals are plugged up on these boards along with a description of their heinous offences. Other memorable photos include people squashed by trucks, blown up by fireworks or fried after smoking cigarettes near open petrol tanks. Other popular themes include industrial safety and family planning. Inspiring slogans such as 'The PLA Protects the People' or 'Follow the Socialist Road to Happiness' are also common.

FILM & PHOTOGRAPHY

China is a mixed bag when it comes to photography. The deserts of Xinjiang and the high plateau of Tibet are among the most photogenic places in the world, as are the minority, subtropical regions of south-west China such as Yunnan Province. The coastal cities and towns of east China, on the other hand, are almost uniformly grey and bleak.

Portraits require some care. If you have befriended a Chinese, he is generally more than happy for you to take his picture. Candid shots of people, however, are viewed with suspicion by many Chinese – why is that foreigner taking my picture? The idea of using photography as a creative outlet is alien to most Chinese, for whom cameras are used to snap friends and family at get-togethers or posed in front of tourist sights. Make contact with people you want to photograph – often a smile and a wave will do the trick.

Buying Film

Imported film is expensive, but major Japanese companies like Fuji and Konica now have factories in China – this has brought prices of colour print film down to what you'd pay in the West, sometimes less. While colour print film is available almost everywhere, it's almost always 100 ASA (21 DIN). Black & white film is virtually unobtainable nowadays.

Imported film is so widely available that there is no need to experiment with local Chinese film – do so at your own risk.

In general, slide film is hard to find – check out major hotels and Friendship Stores if you get caught short. When you do find slide film, it's usually expensive and sometimes out-of-date, though last year's slide film is still better than none. Ektachrome and Fujichrome can be found in Beijing and Shanghai. Kodachrome and Agfachrome are close to nonexistent in China, as is Polaroid film.

Finding the special lithium batteries used by many cameras is generally not a problem, but it would be wise to bring a couple of spares. Some cameras have a manual mode which allows you to continue shooting with a dead battery, though the light meter won't work. Fully-automatic cameras totally drop dead when the battery goes.

Video cameras were once subject to shaky regulations but there seems to be no problem now. The biggest problem is recharging your batteries off the strange mutations of plugs in China – bring all the adaptors you can, and remember that it's 220 V.

You're allowed to bring in 8 mm movie cameras; 16 mm or professional equipment may raise eyebrows with customs. Motion picture film is hard enough to find in the West these days, and next to impossible in China.

Processing

Fast processing is available all over China nowadays. The results shouldn't be any worse than anywhere else – though the occasional mishaps occur, particularly in the colouring.

It is not sensible to get your slide processing done in China. Hong Kong and Bangkok are much better places to have it done. Alternatively wait until you get home. Kodachrome film will have to be sent to Japan or Australia. Again, Hong Kong photo shops can do this for you by express air mail – there's a four-day turnaround usually.

Send undeveloped film at your own risk. EMS is a good option, and most professional photographers claim that the dreaded X-ray machines at customs really are film safe.

Prohibited Subjects

Photography from planes and photographs of airports, military installations, harbour facilities and railroad terminals are prohibited; bridges may also be a touchy subject. With the possible exception of military installations, these rules are rarely enforced.

Photography most definitely is prohibited, however, in museums, at archaeological sites and in many temples, mainly to protect the postcard and colour slide industry. It also prevents valuable works of art from being damaged by countless flash photos – but in most cases you're not allowed to take even harmless natural light photos or time exposures. If you're caught taking photos where you shouldn't, generally the film is ripped out of your camera. Start with a new roll if you don't want to lose any previous shots.

HEALTH

Although China presents a few particular health hazards that require your attention, overall it's a healthier place to travel than many other parts of the world. Large cities like Beijing and Shanghai have decent medical facilities – the problem is out in the backwaters like Inner Mongolia, Tibet or Xinjiang.

If you have the time and inclination, the classic medical reference to read is the *Merck Manual*, a weighty volume which covers virtually every illness known to humanity.

Where There Is No Doctor by David Werner (Macmillan, 1994) is useful, though intended for people going to work in an underdeveloped country rather than for the average traveller. Lonely Planet's *Travel with Children* by Maureen Wheeler gives a rundown on health precautions to be taken with kids, or if you're pregnant and travelling.

Medical services are generally very cheap in China, although random foreigner surcharges may be exacted. At least foreigners get better service – Chinese patients usually have to wait for hours in long queues.

In case of accident or illness, it's best just to get a taxi and go to the hospital directly – try to avoid dealing with the authorities

Massage

Massage *(ànmó)* has a long history in China. It's an effective technique for treating a variety of painful ailments, such as chronic back pain and sore muscles. To be most effective, a massage should be administered by someone who has really studied the techniques. An acupuncturist who also practises massage would be ideal.

Traditional Chinese massage is somewhat different from the increasingly popular do-it-yourself techniques practised by people in the West. One traditional Chinese technique employs suction cups made of bamboo placed on the patient's skin. A burning piece of alcohol-soaked cotton is briefly put inside the cup to drive out the air before it is applied. As the cup cools, a partial vacuum is produced, leaving a nasty-looking but harmless red circular mark on the skin. The mark goes away in a few days. Other methods include bloodletting and scraping the skin with coins or porcelain soup spoons.

A related technique is called moxibustion. Various types of herbs, rolled into what looks like a ball of fluffy cotton, are held close to the skin and ignited. A slight variation of this method is to place the herbs on a slice of ginger and then ignite them. The idea is to apply the maximum amount of heat possible without burning the patient. This heat treatment is supposed to be good for such diseases as arthritis.

However, there is no real need to subject yourself to such extensive treatment if you would just like a straight massage to relieve normal aches and pains. Many big tourist hotels in China offer massage facilities, but the rates charged are excessive – around Y100 per hour. You can do much better than that by inquiring locally. Alternatively, look out for the blind masseuses that work on the streets in many Chinese cities. ■

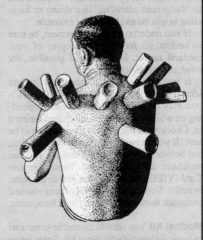

(police and military) if possible. One traveller who broke his leg near Dali made the mistake of calling on the police for help. They took him to the military hospital, where a cast was put on his leg – he was then charged Y10,000 for this service! A civilian hospital would have charged him less than Y100.

The Chinese do not have Rh-negative blood and their blood banks don't store it.

Predeparture Preparations

Health Insurance Although you may have medical insurance in your own country, it is probably not valid in China. But ask your insurance company anyway – you *might* already be covered. A travel insurance policy is a very good idea – the best ones protect you against cancellation penalties on advance-purchase flights, against medical costs through illness or injury, against theft or loss of possessions and against the cost of additional air tickets if you get really sick and have to fly home. Obviously, the more extensive the coverage the higher the premiums, but at a minimum you should at least be covered for medical costs due to injuries. Read the small print carefully since it's easy to be caught out by exclusions – injuries due to 'dangerous activities' like skiing or bicycling might be excluded, for example.

If you undergo medical treatment, be sure to collect all receipts and copies of your medical report, in English if possible, for your insurance company.

If you purchase an International Student Identity Card (ISIC) or Teacher Card (ISTC), you may be automatically covered depending on which country you purchased the card in. Check with the student travel office to be sure. If you're neither a student nor a teacher, but between the ages of 15 and 25, you can purchase an International Youth Identity Card (YIEE), which entitles you to the same benefits. Some student travel offices also sell insurance to others who don't hold these cards.

Medical Kit You should assemble some sort of basic lightweight first-aid kit. Some items which could be included are:

- Antimalarial tablets (south-west China only) and Flagyl (for giardia in Tibet)
- Aspirin or Panadol–for pain or fever.
- Antihistamine (such as Benadryl)–useful as a decongestant for colds and allergies, to ease the itch from insect bites or stings and to help prevent motion sickness. Antihistamines may cause sedation and interact with alcohol, so care should be taken when using them.
- Antibiotics–useful if you're travelling well off the beaten track, but they must be prescribed and you should carry the prescription with you. Some individuals are allergic to commonly prescribed antibiotics such as penicillin or sulpha drugs. It would be sensible to always carry this information when travelling. Ideally, antibiotics should be administered only under medical supervision and should never be taken indiscriminately. Overuse of antibiotics can weaken your body's ability to deal with infections naturally and can reduce the drug's efficacy on a future occasion. Take only the recommended dose as prescribed. It's important that once you start a course of antibiotics, you finish it even if the illness seems to be cured earlier. If you stop taking the antibiotics after one or two days, complete relapse is likely. If you think you are experiencing a reaction to any antibiotic, stop taking it immediately and consult a doctor. Antibiotics can be bought cheaply across the counter in many countries in South-East Asia (Taiwan and Thailand are good places to stock up).
- Kaolin preparation (Pepto-Bismol), Imodium or Lomotil–for stomach upsets.
- Rehydration mixture–for treatment of severe diarrhoea. This is particularly important if you are travelling with children but it is recommended for everyone.
- Antiseptic such as Betadine, which comes as impregnated swabs or ointment, and an antibiotic powder or similar 'dry' spray –for cuts and grazes.
- Calamine lotion–to ease irritation from bites or stings.
- Bandages and Band-aids–for minor injuries.
- Scissors, tweezers and a thermometer (note that mercury thermometers are prohibited by airlines).
- Insect repellent, sunscreen, suntan lotion, chap stick and water purification tablets.
- A couple of syringes - in case you need injections. Ask your doctor for a note explaining why they have been prescribed (it might be useful to get it translated into Chinese too).

Most of these medications are available in China at low cost, but finding them when you urgently need them can often prove problematic.

Acupuncture

Chinese acupuncture (zhēnjiǔ) has received enthusiastic reviews from many satisfied patients who have tried it. Of course, one should be wary of overblown claims. Acupuncture is not likely to cure terminal illness. Nevertheless, it is of genuine therapeutic value in the treatment of chronic back pain, migraine headaches and arthritis.

Acupuncture is a technique employing needles which are inserted into various points of the body. In former times, needles were probably made from bamboo, gold, silver, copper or tin. These days, only stainless steel needles of hairlike thinness are used, causing very little pain when inserted. Dirty acupuncture needles can spread disease rather than cure, so good acupuncturists sterilise their needles or use disposable ones. As many as 2000 points for needle insertion have been identified, but only about 150 are commonly used.

One of the most amazing demonstrations of acupuncture's power is that major surgery can be performed using acupuncture alone as the anaesthetic. The acupuncture needle is inserted into the patient and a small electric current is passed through the needle. The current is supplied by an ordinary torch battery.

The exact mechanism by which acupuncture works is not fully understood by modern medical science. The Chinese have their own theories, but it is by no means certain they really know either. Needles are inserted into various points of the body, each point believed by the acupuncturist to correspond to a particular organ, joint, gland or other part of the body. These points are believed to be connected to the particular area being treated by an 'energy channel', also translated as a 'meridian', but more likely it has something to do with the nerves. By means not fully understood, it seems the needle can block pain transmission along the meridian. However it works, many report satisfactory results.

Acupuncture is practised in hospitals of traditional Chinese medicine, which can be found all over China. Some hospitals in major cities like Guangzhou, Beijing and Shanghai also train Westerners in the technique. In Guangzhou, the Guangzhou Traditional Chinese Medicine Hospital (zhōngyī yīyuàn), on Zhuji Lu near Shamian Island, trains students in acupuncture and herbal medicine. Some hotels also provide acupuncture services at their clinics, but these are likely to be more expensive.

If you're (justifiably) concerned about catching disease from contaminated acupuncture needles, you might consider buying your own before undergoing treatment. Good quality needles are available in major cities in China and in Hong Kong. Needles come in a bewildering variety of gauges – try to determine from your acupuncturist which type to buy. ■

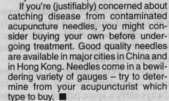

Vaccinations Very few vaccinations are required by law, but there are several that are certainly recommended. If you're arriving within six days after leaving or transiting a yellow-fever-infected area, then a vaccination is required.

The following information should be helpful:

• Smallpox has now been wiped out worldwide, so immunisation is no longer necessary.
• Cholera immunisation is not required by law. Pro-

tection is poor and it lasts only six months. It is contraindicated during pregnancy.

• Yellow fever is not endemic to China but you are required to have a yellow fever vaccination if you have come from an infected area.
• Tetanus and diphtheria boosters are necessary every 10 years and protection is highly recommended.
• Typhoid vaccine is available either as an injection or oral capsules. Protection lasts from one to three years and is useful if you are travelling for long in rural, tropical areas. You may get some side effects such as pain at the injection site, fever, headache and a general unwell feeling. A new single-dose

injectable vaccine, which appears to have few side effects, is now available but is more expensive. Side effects are unusual with the oral form but occasionally an individual will have stomach cramps.

Hepatitis A is the most common travel-acquired illness which can be prevented by vaccination. Protection can be provided in two ways – either with a new vaccine called Havrix or with the antibody gamma globulin. Havrix provides long-term immunity (possibly more than 10 years) after an initial course of two injections and a booster at one year. It may be more expensive than gamma globulin but certainly has many advantages, including length of protection and ease of administration. It is important to know that being a vaccine it will take about three weeks to provide satisfactory protection – hence the need for careful planning prior to travel. Gamma globulin is not a vaccination but a ready-made antibody which has proven very successful in reducing the chances of hepatitis infection. Because it may interfere with the development of immunity, it should not be given until at least 10 days after administration of the last vaccine needed; it should also be given as close as possible to departure because it is at its most effective in the first few weeks after administration and the effectiveness tapers off gradually between three and six months.

You should have your vaccinations recorded in an International Health Certificate. If you are travelling with children, it's especially important to be sure that they've had all necessary vaccinations.

Get your teeth checked and any necessary dental work done before you leave home. Always carry a spare pair of glasses, contact lenses or your prescription in case of loss or breakage.

Basic Rules

Food & Water In many large cities tap water is not too bad (it's chlorinated), but it's still recommended that you don't drink it without boiling first. In rural areas, the water varies from pretty safe to downright dangerous. Especially after a typhoon and the subsequent flooding, there is a problem with sewers overflowing into reservoirs, thus contaminating the tap water used for drinking and bathing. Outbreaks of cholera and typhoid occur most often after floods so you

must be particularly careful at such times – do not even brush your teeth with unboiled water after flooding. Surface water is generally more dangerous than well water, especially if it comes from an area where domestic livestock graze.

Bottled water and soft drinks are widely available in China and should be perfectly safe to drink (how they taste is another matter). There is no problem with contamination of milk products in China, but sometimes yoghurt is stored for prolonged periods without refrigeration – if it smells suspicious, you'd better keep away from it.

Tea and coffee should both be OK since the water should have been boiled. Remember that at high altitude water boils at a lower temperature, so germs are less likely to be killed. You can also boil your own water if you carry an electric immersion coil and a large metal cup (plastic will melt).

Bringing water to a boil is sufficient to kill most bacteria, but 20 minutes of boiling is required to kill amoebic cysts. Fortunately, amoebic cysts are relatively rare and you should not be overly concerned about these, except in Tibet. If you have nothing to boil or purify your water with, you have to consider the risks of drinking possibly contaminated water against the risks of dehydrating – the first is possible, the second is definite.

For emergency use, water purification tablets will help, and this is particularly important in Tibet. Water is more effectively sterilised by iodine than by chlorine tablets, because iodine kills amoebic cysts. However, iodine is not safe for prolonged use, and also tastes horrible.

If you can't find tablets, tincture of iodine (2%) or iodine crystals can be used. Two drops of tincture of iodine per litre or quart of clear water is the recommended dosage; the treated water should be left to stand for 30 minutes before drinking. Iodine crystals can also be used to purify water but this is a more complicated process, as you have to first prepare a saturated iodine solution. Iodine loses its effectiveness if exposed to air or damp so keep it in a tightly sealed container. Flavoured powder will disguise the taste of treated water and is a good idea if you are travelling with children.

Out in the western deserts of Xinjiang or high on the Tibetan Plateau, you really need to drink a great deal of water. In such places it's a good idea to carry a water bottle with you (buy one which doesn't leak!). You are dehydrating if you find you are urinating infrequently or if your urine turns a deep yellow or orange; you may also find yourself getting headaches.

When it comes to food, use your best judgement. To be absolutely safe, everything should be clean and thoroughly cooked – you can get diarrhoea from salads and unpeeled fruit. Chinese food is generally well cooked and raw vegetables are usually pickled. Some of the street markets look pretty grotty, but in general the food is OK.

Shellfish and seafood of any kind pose the greatest risks of all, from spoilage (due to lack of refrigeration) and water pollution. Some of the rivers and bays in China are positively toxic, yet you often see people fishing in them. Better restaurants only buy fish which are raised in commercial ponds, and the fish are kept alive in aquariums until just before cooking – unfortunately, not all restaurants are so scrupulous.

Toilets

Some travellers have given up eating (for a while at least) just to avoid having to use Chinese toilets. Unfortunately, unless your stay in China is extremely brief, you'll have to learn to cope.

Public toilets in China are not the healthiest-looking places – basically they're holes in the ground or ditches over which you squat, and some look like they haven't been cleaned since the Han Dynasty. Many cannot be flushed at all while others are flushed with a conveniently placed bucket of water. Public toilets can often be found in railway stations and the side streets of the cities and towns – many now charge a fee of one or two jiao. Some have very low partitions (without doors) between the individual holes and some have none. Toilet paper is never pro-

vided – always keep a stash with you. Dormitory-style hotel rooms are also not equipped with toilet paper.

While it takes some practice to get proficient at balancing yourself over a squat toilet, at least you don't need to worry about whether the toilet seat is clean. Furthermore, experts who study such things (scatologists?) claim that the squatting position is better for your digestive system. Tourist hotels have Western-style 'sit-down' toilets, a luxury you will come to appreciate.

The issue of what to do with used toilet paper has caused some concern. One traveller wrote:

We are still not sure about the toilet paper...in two hotels they have been angry with us for flushing down the paper in the toilet. In other places it seems quite OK though.

In general, if you see a wastebasket next to the toilet, that is where you should throw the toilet paper. The problem is that in many hotels, the sewage system cannot handle toilet paper. This is especially true in old hotels where the antiquated plumbing system was designed in the pre-toilet paper era. Also, in rural areas there is no sewage treatment plant – the waste empties into an underground septic tank and toilet paper will really create a mess in there. For the sake of international relations, be considerate and throw the paper in the wastebasket.

Remember:

men 男

women 女

Other Precautions A good pair of sunglasses will protect your eyes from the nasty UV rays in the deserts and high-altitude regions of Tibet. Buy them abroad rather than in China. You should also use zinc cream or some other barrier cream for your nose and lips.

If you're sweating profusely, you're going to lose a lot of salt and that can lead to fatigue and muscle cramps for some people. If necessary you can make it up by putting extra salt or soy sauce in your food (a teaspoon a day is plenty), but don't increase your salt intake unless you also increase your water intake.

Everyday Health The normal body temperature is 98.6°F or 37°C; more than 2°C higher is a 'high' fever. A normal adult pulse rate is from 60 to 80 per minute (children from 80 to 100, babies from 100 to 140). You should know how to take a temperature and a pulse rate. As a general rule the pulse increases about 20 beats per minute for each 1°C rise in fever.

Respiration (breathing) rate is also an indicator of illness. Count the number of breaths per minute: between 12 and 20 is normal for adults and older children (up to 30 for younger children, 40 for babies). People with a high fever or serious respiratory illness (like pneumonia) breathe more quickly than normal. More than 40 shallow breaths a minute in an adult usually means pneumonia.

Environmental Hazards

Self-diagnosis and treatment can be risky, so wherever possible seek qualified help. Although we give treatment dosages in this section, they are for emergency use only. Medical advice should be sought before administering any drugs.

Sunburn *(shài shāng)* It's very easy to get sunburnt at high elevations (Tibet), in the deserts (Xinjiang) or the tropics (Hainan Island). Sunburn can be more than just uncomfortable. Among the undesirable effects of frying your hide are premature skin-ageing and possible skin cancer in later years. Sunscreen (UV lotion), sunglasses and a wide-brimmed hat are good means of protection.

Heat Exhaustion *(zhòng shǔ)* Dehydration or salt deficiency can cause heat exhaustion. Take time to acclimatise to high temperatures and make sure you get sufficient

liquids. Salt deficiency is characterised by fatigue, lethargy, headaches, giddiness and muscle cramps, and salt tablets may help. Vomiting or diarrhoea can deplete your liquid and salt levels. Anhydrotic heat exhaustion, caused by an inability to sweat, is quite rare. Unlike the other forms of heat exhaustion, it is likely to strike people who have been in a hot climate for some time rather than newcomers.

Heat Stroke This serious, sometimes fatal, condition can occur if the body's heat-regulating mechanism breaks down and the body temperature rises to dangerous levels. Long, continuous periods of exposure to high temperatures can leave you vulnerable to heat stroke. You should avoid excessive alcohol or strenuous activity when you first arrive in a hot climate.

The symptoms are feeling unwell, not sweating very much or at all and a high body temperature (39°C to 41°C). Where sweating has ceased the skin becomes flushed and red. Severe, throbbing headaches and lack of coordination will also occur, and the sufferer may be confused or aggressive. Eventually the victim will become delirious or convulse. Hospitalisation is essential, but meanwhile get them out of the sun, remove their clothing, cover them with a wet sheet or towel and then fan continually.

Fungal Infections *(pífū bìng)* The most common summertime affliction that visitors to China suffer from is skin disease. This is especially true in the south-east due to the hot, humid climate. The humidity is a bigger problem than the warm weather. The most common varieties of skin problems are 'jock itch' (a fungal infection around the groin), athlete's foot (known to the Chinese as 'Hong Kong feet'), contact dermatitis (caused by a necklace or watchband rubbing the skin) and prickly heat (caused by excessive sweating).

Prevention and treatment of these skin ailments is simply to keep the skin cool, clean, dry and free of abrasions.

For fungal infections, bathe twice daily

and thoroughly dry yourself before getting dressed. Standing in front of the electric fan is a good way to get thoroughly dry. Apply an anti-fungal ointment or powder (ointments are better) to affected area – popular brand names are Desenex, Tinactin or Mycota, all available in Hong Kong.

If you're looking for an excuse to wear kinky underwear, this is it. Your underwear needs to be 'breathable' to reduce sweating, so that means light cotton or silk, or very thin 'see-through' nylon – or none at all.

Wear light, loose-fitting cotton clothing when the weather is really hot and humid – not only better for your skin, but also more comfortable. For athlete's foot, wearing open-toed sandals will often solve the problem without further treatment. Cleaning between the toes with warm soapy water and an old toothbrush also helps. Treat contact dermatitis by removing the offending necklace, bracelet or wristwatch. Avoid anything that chafes the skin, such as tight clothing, especially elastic.

If your skin develops little painful red 'pinpricks', you probably have prickly heat. This is the result of excessive sweating which blocks the sweat ducts, causing inflammation. The treatment is the same – drying and cooling the skin. Bathe often, soak in hot soapy water to get the skin pores open, use a scrub brush to get really clean and dust yourself with talcum powder after drying off. Sleeping in an air-conditioned room will help, but such rooms can be difficult to find if you're on a budget. If all else fails, a trip to the high, cool mountains – or, ironically, to the hot, dry deserts – will do wonders for your itching skin.

Cold Winter in northern China is serious business. Too much cold is probably more dangerous than too much heat, and can lead to the fatal condition known as hypothermia. If you are trekking at high altitudes or simply taking a long bus trip over mountains, particularly at night, be prepared. In regions such as Tibet you should always be prepared for cold even during summer – when the clouds move in, the temperature can drop amazingly fast!

Hypothermia occurs when the body loses heat faster than it can produce it and the core temperature of the body falls. It is surprisingly easy to progress from very cold to dangerously cold due to a combination of wind, wet clothing, fatigue and hunger, even if the air temperature is above freezing. It is best to dress in layers; silk, wool and some high-tech artificial fibres are all good insulating materials. A hat is important, as a lot of heat is lost through the head. A strong, waterproof outer layer is essential, as keeping dry is vital. Carry basic supplies, including food containing simple sugars to generate heat quickly and lots of fluid to drink.

Symptoms of hypothermia are exhaustion, numb skin (particularly toes and fingers), shivering, slurred speech, irrational or violent behaviour, lethargy, stumbling, dizzy spells, muscle cramps and violent bursts of energy. Irrationality may take the form of sufferers claiming they are warm and trying to take off their clothes.

To treat hypothermia, first get victims out of the wind and/or rain, remove their clothing if it's wet and replace it with dry, warm clothing. Give them hot liquids – not alcohol – and some high-energy, easily digestible food. This should be enough for the early stages of hypothermia, but if it has gone further it may be necessary to place sufferers in a warm sleeping bag and get in with them. Do not rub them. Hypothermia dulls sensitivity to pain, and putting someone too near a fire or stove can easily cause burns without anyone realising it. Ditto for putting someone in a too-hot bath – you may wind up parboiling him or her.

Altitude Sickness (*gāo shān fǎnyìng*) Tibet has a few problems all of its own caused by high altitude and thin air. Acute Mountain Sickness (AMS) is the most common problem. Rapid ascent from low altitudes, overexertion, lack of physical fitness, dehydration and fatigue will make it worse. A climber who is elderly, sick or obese is at greater risk. Symptoms include headache, dizziness, lack of appetite, nausea and vomiting. Breathlessness, sleeplessness and a pounding heart are normal at these altitudes and are not part of AMS. If you spend enough time at high elevations, your body will eventually start making more blood cells to carry extra oxygen. If you get altitude sickness, the best cure is to go to a lower altitude. A pain-killer for headache and an anti-emetic for vomiting will also help. The best prevention is to ascend slowly and avoid overexertion in the beginning. Aerobic exercises are good preparation for a trip to high elevations.

AMS is unpleasant, but a far more serious complication is high-altitude pulmonary oedema. This is usually seen only at elevations above 3000 metres about 24 to 72 hours after ascent. Symptoms include coughing up frothy sputum, which usually progresses from white to pink to bloody. A rattling sound in the chest can be heard, often without a stethoscope. The symptoms might be mistaken for pneumonia, but the suddenness of their appearance in a rapidly ascending climber should make you suspect pulmonary oedema. *This is a medical emergency!* Coma and death can follow rapidly – the only effective treatment is to get the victim to a lower elevation as soon as possible. Oxygen helps a little, but only if it's given in the early stages.

Motion Sickness (*yùnchē*) The Chinese are unusually prone to motion sickness – if the person next to you on the bus or ferry starts looking green, move away quickly! Eating lightly before and during a trip will reduce the chances of motion sickness, but the Chinese have the exact opposite idea – the more they throw up, the more they eat.

If you are prone to motion sickness, try to find a place that minimises disturbance – near the wing on aircraft, close to midships on boats, near the centre on buses. Fresh air usually helps, reading and cigarette smoke don't. Commercial anti-motion-sickness preparations, which can cause drowsiness, have to be taken before the trip commences;

when you're feeling sick it's too late. Ginger is a natural preventative and is available in capsule form.

Infectious Diseases

Diarrhoea (*lā dùzi*) Travellers' diarrhoea has been around a long time – even Marco Polo had it. Diarrhoea is often due simply to a change of diet or bacteria or minerals in the local water which your system is not used to. If you do get diarrhoea, the first thing to do is wait – it rarely lasts more than a few days.

Diarrhoea will cause you to dehydrate, which will make you feel much worse. The solution is not simply to drink water, since it will run right through you. You'll get much better results by mixing your water with oral rehydration salt, a combination of salts (both NaCl and KCl) and glucose. Dissolve the powder in *cool* water (never hot!) and drink, but don't use it if the powder is wet. The quantity of water is specified on the packet. Oralit is also useful for treating heat exhaustion caused by excessive sweating. In an emergency you can make up a solution of eight teaspoons of sugar to a litre of boiled water and provide salted cracker biscuits at the same time.

If the diarrhoea persists you can slow down your digestive system with Lomotil or Imodium tablets. The maximum dose for Lomotil is two tablets three times a day. A good Chinese equivalent is berberine hydrochloride (*huáng liǎn sù*). Only use these drugs if absolutely necessary–eg if you *must* travel. For children Imodium is preferable, but under all circumstances fluid replacement is the most important thing to remember. Do not use these drugs if the person has a high fever or is severely dehydrated. Furthermore, the diarrhoea serves one useful purpose – it helps the body expel unwanted bacteria.

Fruit juice, tea and coffee can aggravate diarrhoea – again, water with oral rehydration salts is the best drink. It will help tremendously if you eat a light, fibre-free diet. Yoghurt or boiled eggs with salt are basic staples for diarrhoea patients. Later you may be able to tolerate rice porridge or plain white rice. Keep away from vegetables, fruits and greasy foods for a while. If you suddenly decide to pig out on spicy hot Sichuan food, you'll be back to square one. If the diarrhoea persists for a week or more, it's probably not simple travellers' diarrhoea – it could be dysentery and it might be wise to see a doctor.

In certain situations antibiotics may be indicated:

• Watery diarrhoea with blood and mucous (Imodium or Lomotil should be avoided in this situation).
• Watery diarrhoea with fever and lethargy.
• Persistent diarrhoea for more than five days.

The recommended drugs (adults only) would be either norfloxacin 400 mg twice daily for three days or ciprofloxacin 500 mg twice daily for three days.

The drug of choice in children would be co-trimoxazole (Bactrim, Septrin, Resprim) with dosage dependent on weight. A three-day course is also given.

Ampicillin has been recommended in the past and may still be an alternative.

Giardia (*āmǐbā fùxiè*) This is another type of amoeba which causes severe diarrhoea, nausea and weakness, but doesn't produce blood in the stool or cause fever. Unlike amoebic dysentery, which is most common in the tropics, giardia is found in mountainous and cold regions. Mountaineers often suffer from this problem. Just brushing your teeth using contaminated water is sufficient to make you get it. Many kinds of mammals harbour this parasite, so you can get it easily from drinking 'pure mountain water' unless the area is devoid of animals.

Although the symptoms are similar to amoebic dysentery, giardia will not migrate to the liver and other organs – it stays in the intestine and therefore is much less likely to cause long-term health problems.

It can only be cured with an anti-amoebic drug like metronidazole (Flagyl) – but never drink alcohol while taking this. Without treatment, the symptoms may subside and

you might feel fine for a while, but the illness will return again and again, making your life miserable.

To treat giardia, the proper dosage of Flagyl is different from that for amoebic dysentery. Take one 250-mg tablet three times daily for 10 days. It can sometimes be difficult to rid yourself of giardia, so you might need laboratory tests to be certain you're cured.

Flagyl is not easily obtained in China, though equivalent drugs are available in places like Lhasa where giardia is common. If you're going to be travelling in high mountain areas, it might be prudent to keep your own stock with you.

Bilharzia Bilharzia (schistosomiasis) is found in the central Yangzi River basin. It is carried in water by minute worms. The larvae infect certain varieties of freshwater snails, found in rivers, streams, lakes and particularly behind dams or in irrigation ditches. The worms multiply and are eventually discharged into the water surrounding the snails.

They attach themselves to your intestines or bladder, where they produce large numbers of eggs. The worm enters through the skin, and the first symptom may be a tingling sensation and sometimes a light rash around the area where it entered. Weeks later, when the worm is busy producing eggs, a high fever may develop. A general feeling of being unwell may be the first symptom; once the disease is established, abdominal pain and blood in the urine are other signs.

Avoiding swimming or bathing in freshwater where bilharzia is present is the main method of preventing the disease. Even deep water can be infected. If you do get wet, dry off quickly and dry your clothes as well. Seek medical attention if you have been exposed to the disease and tell the doctor your suspicions, as bilharzia in the early stages can be confused with malaria or typhoid.

If you cannot get medical help immediately, praziquantel (Biltricide) is the recommended treatment. The recommended dose is 40 mg/kg in divided doses over one day. Niridazole is an alternative drug.

Dysentery This is not very common in China – many travellers seem to think they have dysentery when all they have is normal diarrhoea.

Dysentery is caused by contaminated food or water and is characterised by severe diarrhoea, often with blood or mucus in the stool. There are two kinds. Bacillary dysentery is characterised by a high fever and rapid onset; headache, vomiting and stomach pains are also symptoms. It generally does not last longer than a week, but it is highly contagious. Amoebic dysentery is often more gradual in the onset of symptoms, with cramping abdominal pain and vomiting less likely; fever may not be present. It is not a self-limiting disease: it will persist until treated and can recur and cause long-term health problems.

A stool test is necessary to diagnose which kind of dysentery you have, so you should seek medical help urgently. In case of an emergency the drugs norfloxacin or ciprofloxacin can be used as presumptive treatment for bacillary dysentery, and metronidazole (Flagyl) for amoebic dysentery.

For bacillary dysentery, norfloxacin 400 mg twice daily for seven days or ciprofloxacin 500 mg twice daily for seven days are the recommended dosages.

If you're unable to find either of these drugs, then a useful alternative is co-trimoxazole 160/800 mg (Bactrim, Septrin, Resprim) twice daily for seven days. This is a sulpha drug and must not be used by people with a known sulpha allergy.

In the case of children the drug co-trimoxazole is a reasonable first-line treatment. For amoebic dysentery, the recommended adult dosage of metronidazole (Flagyl) is one 750-mg to 800-mg capsule three times daily for five days. Children aged between eight and 12 years should have half the adult dose; the dosage for younger children is one-third the adult dose.

An alternative to Flagyl is Fasigyn, taken as a two-gram daily dose for three days.

Alcohol must be avoided during treatment and for 48 hours afterwards.

Cholera It's not a big problem in China, but cholera tends to travel in epidemics (usually after floods, especially during summer) and outbreaks are widely reported, so you can often avoid problem areas. This is a disease of insanitation, so if you've heard reports of cholera be especially careful about what you eat, drink and brush your teeth with.

Symptoms include a sudden onset of acute diarrhoea with 'rice water' stools, vomiting, muscular cramps and extreme weakness. You need medical help – but treat for dehydration, which can be extreme, and if there is an appreciable delay in getting to hospital then begin taking tetracycline. (See the Medical Kit section for warnings on taking antibiotics.)

The cholera vaccine is not very effective but is still recommended if you are going into an infected area because it will reduce the severity of the disease. The vaccination is good for only four to six months. Cholera vaccinations are cheap and widely available from public health clinics throughout Asia.

Hepatitis *(gān yán)* Hepatitis is a general term for inflammation of the liver. There are many causes of this condition: drugs, alcohol and infections are but a few.

The discovery of new strains has led to a virtual alphabet soup, with hepatitis A, B, C, D, E and a rumoured G. These letters identify specific agents that cause viral hepatitis. Viral hepatitis is an infection of the liver, which can lead to jaundice (yellow skin), fever, lethargy and digestive problems. It can have no symptoms at all, with the infected person not knowing that they have the disease. Travellers shouldn't be too paranoid about this apparent proliferation of hepatitis strains; hep C, D, E and G are fairly rare (so far) and following the same precautions as for A and B should be all that's necessary to avoid them.

Viral hepatitis can be divided into two groups on the basis of how it is spread. The first route of transmission is via contaminated food and water (leading to hepatitis A and E) and the second route is via blood and bodily fluids (resulting in hepatitis B, C and D).

Hepatitis A This is a very common disease in most countries, especially those with poor standards of sanitation. Most people in developing countries are infected as children; they often don't develop symptoms, but do develop life-long immunity. The disease poses a real threat to the traveller, as people are unlikely to have been exposed to hepatitis A in developed countries.

The symptoms are fever, chills, headache, fatigue, feelings of weakness and aches and pains, followed by loss of appetite, nausea, vomiting, abdominal pain, dark urine, light-coloured faeces, jaundiced skin and the whites of the eyes may turn yellow. In some cases you may feel unwell, tired, have no appetite, experience aches and pains and be jaundiced. You should seek medical advice, but in general there is not much you can do apart from resting, drinking lots of fluids, eating lightly and avoiding fatty foods. People who have had hepatitis must forego alcohol for six months after the illness, as hepatitis attacks the liver and it needs that amount of time to recover.

The routes of transmission are via contaminated water, shellfish contaminated by sewerage or foodstuffs sold by food handlers with poor standards of hygiene.

Taking care with what you eat and drink can go a long way towards preventing this disease. But this is a very infectious virus, so if there is risk of exposure, an injection with either Havrix or gamma globulin is recommended.

Hepatitis E This is a very recently discovered virus, of which little is yet known. It appears to be rather common in developing countries, generally causing mild hepatitis, although it can be very serious in pregnant women.

Care with water supplies is the only current prevention, as there are no specific vaccines for this type of hepatitis. At present

it doesn't appear to be too great a risk for travellers.

Hepatitis B This is also a very common disease, with almost 300 million chronic carriers in the world. Hepatitis B, which used to be called serum hepatitis, is spread through contact with infected blood, blood products or bodily fluids, for example through sexual contact, unsterilised needles and blood transfusions. Other risk situations include having a shave or tattoo in a local shop, or having your ears pierced. The symptoms of type B are much the same as type A except that they are more severe and may lead to irreparable liver damage or even liver cancer. Although there is no treatment for hepatitis B, a cheap and effective vaccine is available; the only problem is that for long-lasting cover you need a six-month course. The immunisation schedule requires two injections at least a month apart followed by a third dose five months after the second. Persons who should receive a hepatitis B vaccination include anyone who anticipates contact with blood or other bodily secretions, either as a healthcare worker or through sexual contact with the local population, particularly those who intend to stay in the country for a long period of time.

Hepatitis C This is another recently defined virus. It is a concern because it seems to lead to liver disease more rapidly than hepatitis B.

The virus is spread by contact with blood - usually via contaminated transfusions or shared needles. Avoiding these is the only means of prevention, as there is no available vaccine.

Hepatitis D Often referred to as the 'Delta' virus, this infection occurs only in chronic carriers of hepatitis B. It is transmitted by blood and bodily fluids. Again there is no vaccine for this virus, so avoidance is the best prevention. The risk to travellers is certainly limited.

Typhoid Typhoid fever is another gut infection transmitted in contaminated water and food. Like cholera, epidemics can occur after floods because of sewage backing up into drinking water supplies. Vaccination against typhoid is useful but not totally effective and it is one of the most dangerous infections, so medical help must be sought.

In the early stages of infection, typhoid victims may feel like they have a bad cold or flu on the way, as early symptoms are a headache, a sore throat and a fever which rises a little each day until it is around 40°C or more. Without treatment, the illness will either kill you or begin to subside by the third week.

Chloramphenicol is the recommended antibiotic but there are fewer side effects with Ampicillin. The adult dosage is two 250-mg capsules, four times a day. Children aged between eight and 12 years should have half the adult dose; younger children should have one-third the adult dose.

Patients who are allergic to penicillin should not be given Ampicillin.

Polio Polio is also a disease spread by insanitation and is found more frequently in hot climates. The effects on children can be especially devastating – they can be crippled for

---

Herbal Medicine

Many foreigners visiting China never try Chinese herbal medicine (zhōng yào) because they either know nothing about it or simply don't believe in it. Prominent medical authorities in the West often dismiss herbalists as no better than witch doctors. The ingredients, which may include such marvellous things as snake gall bladder or powdered deer antlers, will further discourage potential non-Chinese customers. Many of the herbs are bitter powders (you may want to load these into empty gelatine capsules if you can't stand the taste). And finally, even true believers are baffled by the wide assortment of herbs available on the shelves of any Chinese pharmacy – it's hard to know where to begin.

Having experimented with Chinese herbs ourselves, we've found several of them to be remarkably effective, but some warnings are in order. Chinese herbalists have all sorts of treatments for stomachaches, headaches, colds, flu and sore throat. They also have herbs to treat long-term problems like asthma. While many of these herbs seem to work, it's much less certain whether Chinese medicine can cure serious illnesses like cancer and heart disease. All sorts of overblown claims have been made for herbal medicines, especially by those who make and sell them. Some gullible Westerners have persuaded themselves that Chinese doctors can cure any disease. A visit to any of China's hospitals will quickly shatter this myth.

Chinese medicine seems to work best for the relief of unpleasant symptoms (pain, sore throat, etc) and for some long-term conditions which resist Western medicines, such as migraine headaches, asthma and chronic backache. But for acute life-threatening conditions, such as a heart attack, it would be foolish to trust your life to herbs.

When reading about the theory behind Chinese medicine, the word 'holistic' appears often. Basically, this means that Chinese medicine seeks to treat the whole body rather than focusing on a particular organ or disease.

Using appendicitis as an example, a Chinese doctor may try to fight the infections using the body's whole defences, whereas a Western doctor would simply cut out the appendix. In this instance the Western technique works better, since removing the appendix surgically is 100% effective, though there is always some risk from the surgical procedure itself. In the case of migraine headaches, on the other hand, Chinese herbs may actually prove more effective than Western medical treatments.

Another point to be wary of when taking herbal medicine is the tendency of some manufacturers to falsely claim that their product contains numerous potent and expensive ingredients.

life. An excellent vaccination is available, and a booster every five years is recommended.

Respiratory Infection The China Syndrome (*liúxíngxìng gǎnmào*), the greatest hazard to your health in China, is a host of respiratory infections which we normally call 'the flu' or just 'the common cold'. You may have heard of the 'Shanghai flu' or various other influenza strains named after Chinese cities. The fact is that China is one vast reservoir of respiratory viruses and much of the population is stricken during the winter, but even during the summer it's easy to get ill.

What distinguishes the Chinese flu from the Western variety is the severity and the fact that the condition persists for months rather than days. Like any bad cold, it starts with a fever, chills, weakness, sore throat and a feeling of malaise normally lasting a few days. After that, a prolonged case of coughing and bronchitis sets in, characterised by coughing up large quantities of thick green phlegm, occasionally with little red streaks (blood). It's the bronchitis that really gets you – it makes sleep almost impossible, and

For example, some herbal formulas may list rhinoceros horn as an ingredient. Rhinoceros horn, widely acclaimed by herbalists as a cure for fever, is practically impossible to buy. Any formula listing rhinoceros horn may, at best, contain water buffalo horn. In any case, the rhino is a rare and endangered species, and you will not wish to hasten its extinction by demanding rhino-horn products.

Another benefit of Chinese medicine is that there are relatively few side effects. Compared with a drug like penicillin which can produce allergic reactions and other serious side effects, herbal medicines are fairly safe. Nevertheless, herbs are still medicines, not candy, and there is no need to take them if you're feeling fine to begin with. In fact, some herbs are mildly toxic and if taken over a long period of time can actually damage the liver and other organs.

Before shopping for herbs, keep in mind that although a broad-spectrum remedy such as snake gall bladder may be good for treating colds, there are many different types of colds. The best way to treat a cold with herbal medicine is to see a Chinese doctor and get a specific prescription. Otherwise, the herbs you take may not be the most appropriate for your condition. However, if you can't get to a doctor, you can just try your luck at the pharmacy.

If you visit a Chinese doctor, you might be surprised by what he or she discovers about your body. For example, the doctor will almost certainly take your pulse and then may tell you that you have a slippery pulse or perhaps a thready pulse. Chinese doctors have identified more than 30 different kinds of pulses. The doctor may then examine your tongue to see if it is slippery, dry, pale or greasy or has a thick coating or maybe no coating at all. The doctor, having discovered that you have wet heat, as evidenced by a slippery pulse and a red greasy tongue, will prescribe the herbs for your condition.

One problem with buying herbs is that there are many fake pharmaceuticals on the market. Counterfeiting is common in China, and the problem extends even to medications. If the herbs you take seem to be totally ineffective, it may be because you've bought sugar pills rather than medicine.

If you spend a good deal of time on buses and boats, you'll get to see how the Chinese deal with motion sickness, nausea and headaches – usually by smearing liniments on their stomach or head. If you want to try these yourself, there are many brands on the market – look for *qīngli ngyóu* and *fēngyóu*, or white flower oil (*b ihuāyóu*), which comes from Hong Kong. A variation on the theme are salves, the most famous being Tiger Balm, which also comes from Hong Kong. And should you strain yourself carrying that heavy backpack around, try applying 'sticky dog skin plaster' (*gǒupí gāoyào*) to your sore muscles. You might be relieved to know that these days it's no longer made from real dog skin. ■

this exhausting state of affairs can continue for as long as you stay in the country. Sometimes it even leads to pneumonia.

Why is it such a serious problem in China? Respiratory infections are aggravated by cold weather, air pollution, chain-smoking and overcrowded conditions, which increase the opportunity for infection. But the main reason is that Chinese people spit a lot, thereby spreading the disease. It's a vicious circle: they're sick because they spit and they spit because they're sick.

During the initial phase of influenza, bed rest, drinking warm liquids and keeping warm are helpful. The Chinese treat bronchitis with a powder made from the gall bladder of snakes – a treatment of questionable value, but there's probably no harm in trying it. If you continue to cough up green phlegm, run a fever and can't seem to get well, it's time to roll out the heavy artillery – you can nuke it with antibiotics. Tetracycline (250 mg) taken orally four times daily for a minimum of five days is usually highly effective, but note the previously mentioned warnings about using antibiotics.

Finally, if you can't get well in China, leave the country and take a nice holiday on a warm beach in Thailand.

No vaccine offers complete protection, but there are vaccines against influenza and pneumococcal pneumonia which might help. The influenza vaccine is good for no more than a year.

Tetanus *(pò shāng fēng)* There seem to be quite a few motor accidents in rural China. Although there is no vaccination that can protect your bus from getting hit by a logging truck, it would be prudent to get a tetanus vaccination before your arrival in China. If you've already been vaccinated once, you still need a booster every five years to maintain immunity.

Rabies *(kuángquǎn bìng)* China still has a serious problem with this, but the Communists deserve much credit for greatly reducing the threat. Since the Communists came to power in 1949, one of their accomplishments has been to systematically wipe out most of the stray dogs which used to roam the streets of China. This was done to control rabies, improve sanitation and preserve food. While dog lovers may not be impressed by these arguments, it's instructive to visit other poor Third World countries where disease-ridden wild dogs roam the streets, often to end their lives by starving to death.

Although the Chinese have reduced the canine population considerably, packs of wild dogs are still common in Tibetan villages and they are indeed dangerous. Other mammals, such as rats, can also transmit the rabies virus to humans. Also, if you have a scratch, cut or other break in the skin you could catch rabies if an infected animal licked that break in the skin.

If you are bitten by an animal that may be rabid, try to get the wound flushed out immediately with soapy water. It would be prudent to seek professional treatment since rabies carries a nearly 100% fatality rate if it reaches the brain. How long you have from the time of being bitten until it's too late varies – anywhere from 10 days to a year depending on where you were bitten. Those bitten around the face and upper part of the body are in the most immediate danger. Don't wait for symptoms to occur – if you think there's a good chance that you've been bitten by a rabid animal, get medical attention promptly, even if it means leaving China.

By all accounts, rabies is a horrible way to go. As the disease works its way through the nervous system towards the brain, the patient experiences terribly painful muscle spasms, especially around the throat. It becomes impossible to drink water – thus, rabies is sometimes called 'hydrophobia'. Death usually occurs from paralysis of the breathing muscles.

A pre-exposure vaccine for rabies exists, though few people bother to get it because the risk of infection is so low. The vaccine will not give you 100% immunity, but will greatly extend the time you have for seeking treatment and the treatment will not need to be nearly so extensive. If you're planning to travel in the Chinese countryside, and especially in Tibet, this might be worth considering.

Tuberculosis (*jiéhé bìng*) The tuberculosis (TB) bacteria is transmitted by inhalation. Coughing spreads infectious droplets into the air. In closed, crowded spaces with poor ventilation (like a train compartment), the air can remain contaminated for some time. In overcrowded China, it's not hard to see why infection rates are among the highest in the world.

In the developed world, TB is usually a relatively mild infection; many people have it at some time in their lives without noticing it and retain a natural immunity afterwards.

The disease is opportunistic – the patient feels fine, but the disease suddenly becomes active when the body is weakened by other factors such as injury, poor nutrition, surgery or old age. It's now spreading rapidly in the developed world, thanks to AIDS and drug abuse, both of which lower natural immunity – people who are in good health are unlikely to catch the disease. It strikes at the lungs and the fatality rate once it is well established in the body is about 10%.

There are good drugs to treat TB, but prevention is the best cure. If you're only going to be in China for a short time there is no need to be overly worried. TB is usually developed after repeated exposures by people who are not well nourished. Budget travellers – those who often spend a long time staying in cramped dormitories and travelling on crowded buses and trains – are at greater risk than tourists who remain relatively isolated in big hotels and tour buses.

The effective vaccine for TB is called BCG and is most often given to schoolchildren because it must be taken before infection occurs. If you want to be vaccinated, you first must be tested to see if you are already immune from a previous infection – if you are, the vaccination will not be necessary. It is thought to be less effective in adults over 35. The only disadvantage of the vaccine is that, once given, the recipient will always test positive with the TB skin test. Even if you never travel, the TB vaccine could be useful – the disease is increasing worldwide.

Eye Infection Trachoma is a common eye infection which is easily spread by contaminated towels (the kind handed out by restaurants and airlines). The best advice about wiping your face is to use disposable tissue paper. If you think you have trachoma, you need to see a doctor – the disease can damage your vision if untreated. Trachoma is normally treated with antibiotic eye ointments for about four to six weeks. Be careful about diagnosing yourself – simple allergies can produce symptoms similar to eye infections, and in this case antibiotics can do more harm than good.

Sexually Transmitted Disease (STD) The Chinese government for decades pretended that prostitution and premarital and extramarital sex simply didn't exist in the PRC, and that sexually transmitted diseases were a foreign problem.

The Cultural Revolution may be over, but the sexual revolution is blooming in China and STDs are spreading rapidly. Gonorrhoea and syphilis are the most common of these diseases; sores, blisters or rashes around the genitals or discharges or pain when urinating are common symptoms. Symptoms may be less marked or not observed at all in women. Syphilis symptoms eventually disappear completely but the disease continues and can cause severe problems in later years, and if untreated can be fatal. The treatment of gonorrhoea and syphilis is with antibiotics.

There are numerous other sexually transmitted diseases, for most of which effective treatment is available. However, there is neither a cure nor a vaccine for herpes and AIDS. Outside of sexual abstinence, using condoms is the most effective preventative. Condoms are available in China – the word is *bǎoxiǎn tào*, which literally translates as 'insurance glove'.

The government announced in early 1993 that foreigners with more than 12 Chinese entry stamps in their passports would have to undergo 'five-minute AIDS tests' right at the border crossing! Exactly how crossing the border 12 times could cause AIDS has not been explained. It seems that Hong Kongers, Taiwanese and others of 'Chinese descent' do not need to undergo the tests – apparently, they are immune to AIDS. There is much suspicion that the real intention was to rake in a little more cash – foreigners must pay for the tests. Whether or not a five-minute AIDS test is accurate has been hotly debated, and at the time of writing it was far from clear whether the rule would actually be enforced or quietly discarded.

The HIV (AIDS) virus can also be spread through infected blood transfusions; most developing countries cannot afford to screen blood for transfusions. It can also be spread by dirty needles – vaccinations, acupuncture, ear piercing and tattooing are potentially as dangerous as intravenous drug use if the equipment is not clean.

Malaria (nüèjì) Malaria is not a big problem in China and you shouldn't worry about it excessively. However, in summer there is a small risk in much of southern China, and a year-round risk in tropical regions like Yunnan and Hainan Island.

If you are travelling in endemic areas it is extremely important to take malarial prophylactics. Symptoms include headache, fever, chills and sweating which may subside and recur. Without treatment malaria can develop more serious, potentially fatal, effects.

Antimalarial drugs do not prevent you from being infected but kill the parasites during a stage in their development.

There are a number of different types of malaria. The two of most concern are falciparum and vivax malaria. Falciparum is responsible for the very serious cerebral malaria; vivax, which is the more common in China, is less dangerous but can lead to chronic ill health if untreated.

The problem in recent years has been the emergence of increasing resistance to commonly used antimalarials such as chloroquine, maloprim and proguanil. Newer

drugs such as mefloquine (Lariam) and doxycycline (Vibramycin, Doryx) are often recommended for chloroquine and multidrug-resistant areas. Expert advice should be sought, as there are many factors to consider when deciding on the type of antimalarial medication, including the area to be visited, the risk of exposure to malaria-carrying mosquitoes, your current medical condition and your age and pregnancy status. It is also important to discuss the side-effect profile of the medication, so you can work out some level of risk versus benefit ratio. It is also very important to be sure of the correct dosage of the medication prescribed to you. Some people have inadvertently taken weekly medication (chloroquine) on a daily basis, with disastrous effects. While discussing dosages for prevention of malaria, it is often advisable to include the dosages required for treatment, especially if your trip is through a high-risk area that would isolate you from medical care.

The locals have some natural immunity to malaria resulting from generations of exposure; foreigners from non-malarial countries have no such resistance. While it is not yet possible to be inoculated against malaria, limited protection is simple: either a daily or weekly tablet (the latter is more common). The tablets kill the parasites in your bloodstream before they have a chance to multiply and cause illness.

The main messages are:

1. Primary prevention must always be in the form of mosquito-avoidance measures. The mosquitoes that transmit malaria bite from dusk to dawn and during this period travellers are advised to:

- wear light-coloured clothing, consisting of long pants and long-sleeved shirts.
- use mosquito repellents containing the compound DEET on exposed areas (overuse of DEET may be harmful, especially to children, but its use is considered preferable to being bitten by disease-transmitting mosquitoes).
- buy mosquito coils (wénxiāng), which are readily available. A more modern innovation are the 'electric mosquito pads' (diàn wénxiāng) on sale at Chinese department stores.
- avoid highly scented perfumes or aftershave.

- use a mosquito net *(wénzhàng)* if one is available. Mosquito repellent is sold in China but you may have trouble finding it, so bring your own.

2. While no antimalarial is 100% effective, taking the most appropriate drug significantly reduces the risk of contracting the disease.

3. No-one should ever die from malaria. It can be diagnosed by a simple blood test. Symptoms range from fever, chills and sweating, headache and abdominal pains to a vague feeling of ill health, so seek examination immediately if there is any suggestion of malaria. Blood tests are needed to determine if you in fact have malaria rather than dengue fever (see next section), and the choice of drugs depends on how well you react to them.

4. Contrary to popular belief, once a traveller contracts malaria he/she does not have it for life. One of the parasites may lie dormant in the liver but this can also be eradicated using a specific medication. Malaria is curable, as long as the traveller seeks medical help when symptoms occur.

Dengue Fever This is a mosquito-borne disease which resembles malaria, but it is not fatal and doesn't recur once the illness has passed. It is fairly common in parts of southern China during summer, and there have even been outbreaks in Taiwan.

A high fever, severe headache and pains in the joints are the usual symptoms – the aches are so bad that the disease is also called breakbone fever. The fever usually lasts two to three days, then subsides, then comes back again and takes several weeks to pass. People who have had this disease say it feels like imminent death.

Despite the malaria-like symptoms, antimalarial drugs have no effect whatsoever on dengue fever. Only the symptoms can be treated, usually with complete bed rest, aspirin, codeine and an intravenous drip. There is no means of prevention other than to avoid getting bitten by mosquitoes, but once you've had dengue fever, you're immune for about a year. The patient should be kept under a mosquito net until after the fever passes – otherwise there is the risk of infecting others.

Cuts & Bites Take good care of all cuts and scratches. In the subtropical south they take longer to heal and can easily get infected.

Treat any cut with care; wash it out with sterilised water, preferably with an antiseptic (Betadine), keep it dry and keep an eye on it. It would be worth bringing an antibiotic cream with you. Cuts on your feet and ankles are particularly troublesome – a new pair of sandals can quickly give you a nasty abrasion which can be difficult to heal. For the same reason, try not to scratch mosquito bites.

Snakes China has a variety of poisonous snakes, the most famous being cobras. *All* sea snakes are poisonous and are readily identified by their flat tails, but opportunities for ocean swimming in China are few and far between. Thanks to American cowboy movies, people often associate snakes with the desert, but they are in fact most common in forested areas, where they have more to eat.

Snakes are not generally aggressive with creatures larger than themselves – they won't chase after you, but they can get nasty if you corner or step on them. To minimise your chances of being bitten while hiking, wear boots, socks and long trousers when walking through undergrowth where snakes may be present. Don't put your hands into holes and crevices.

Snake bites do not cause instantaneous death and antivenins are usually available. Keep the victim calm (sounds easier than it is), wrap the bitten limb tightly, as you would for a sprained ankle, and then attach a splint to immobilise it. Don't wash the wound; any venom remaining on the skin can be used to identify the snake. Then seek medical help, if possible with the dead snake for identification. Don't attempt to catch the snake if there is even a remote possibility of being bitten again. Tourniquets, sucking out the poison and submersion in cold water are now comprehensively discredited.

Bedbugs & Lice Bedbugs live in various places, but particularly in dirty mattresses and bedding. Spots of blood on bedclothes or on the wall around the bed can be read as a suggestion to find another hotel. Bedbugs leave itchy bites in neat rows that swell up, but they generally heal quickly if you don't scratch.

All lice cause itching and discomfort. They make themselves at home in your hair (head lice), your clothing (body lice) or in your pubic hair (crabs). You catch lice through direct contact with infected people or by sharing combs, clothing and the like. Powder or shampoo treatment will kill the lice and infected clothing should then be washed in very hot water.

Women's Health

Gynaecological Problems Poor diet, lowered resistance due to the use of antibiotics for stomach upsets and even contraceptive pills can lead to vaginal infections when travelling in hot climates. Keeping the genital area clean, and wearing skirts or loose-fitting trousers and cotton underwear will help to prevent infections.

Yeast infections, characterised by a rash, itch and discharge, can be treated with a vinegar or even lemon-juice douche or with yoghurt. Nystatin suppositories are the usual medical prescription. Trichomonas is a more serious infection; symptoms are a discharge and a burning sensation when urinating. Male sexual partners must also be treated, and if a vinegar-water douche is not effective medical attention should be sought. Flagyl is the prescribed drug.

The Chinese have various herbal tonics for women only. To help with anaemia and menstrual problems, you could try *sì wù tāng*.

Women travellers often find that their periods become irregular or even cease while they're on the road. Remember that a missed period in these circumstances doesn't necessarily indicate pregnancy. You can go to a clinic or hospital and have a urine test to determine whether or not you are pregnant.

Travel with Children in China

Taking your children to China today is a very different experience from a few years ago. Like everything else in China, change is the order of the day. When the doors swung open, the pioneering Western visitors were a strange sight, so the small minority who brought their children with them were especially weird. These days, in much of China, a Western visitor hardly rates a second glance, and on the beaten tourist trail children too have become boringly familiar. Of course, you don't have to get far off the beaten trail to start to generate the staring crowds, but in general even young children are not unusual.

Many aspects of travel in China have become easier and this holds true for travelling with children as well. Facilities and standards are better and the necessities of travel, such as disposable nappies (diapers) for babies, are more readily available.

On the downside, China is unlikely to rate as a travel favourite for most children. Dry museums and temples are hardly likely to attract most children, and the crowds can at times be overpowering. As usual the answer is to search out the activities which will appeal to children, from clambering over the Great Wall to rowing boats in Beijing parks and riding bicycles around many cities. For older children, travellers' centres like Yangshuo – with everything from watching video movies in the cafes to floating down the river in truck inner tubes – will probably be the highlight of a China visit.

For many visitors to China the national policy of extracting every possible fen from visitors can quickly become annoying and, unfortunately, children simply offer another excuse to charge foreigners inflated prices. Children's prices are rarely available for foreign children, who simply get lumped in with foreign adults and charged at the same inflated level. Even student prices are not available for children unless they have a student card! So, ridiculous though it may seem, it's worth getting your child, even at kindergarten age, an ISIC card to wave at temple, garden and museum entrance counters.

Tony Wheeler

WOMEN TRAVELLERS

In general, foreign women are unlikely to suffer serious sexual harassment in China, but there have been reports of problems in Xinjiang (a Muslim area). Wherever you are, it's worth noticing what local women are wearing and how they are behaving and making a bit of an effort to fit in, as you would in any other foreign country.

We've heard of foreign women being harassed by Chinese men in Beijing's parks or while cycling alone at night, but rape (of foreign women) is not common. This doesn't mean it cannot happen, but most Chinese rapists appear to prefer Chinese victims. The police tend to investigate crimes against foreigners much more closely and more severe penalties (like execution) are imposed if the perpetrator is caught – this provides foreign women with a small but important aura of protection.

Wearing see-through blouses, skimpy shorts or bikinis and going topless at the beach is asking for trouble. While city people in China are hip to the latest fashions (including miniskirts), the countryside is much more conservative. If you want to play safe, wear trousers or a below-the-knee skirt, with a shirt that covers your shoulders. For outdoor wear, sandals are acceptable but thongs (flip-flops) are less so.

DANGERS & ANNOYANCES
Crime & Punishment

Crime is certainly on the rise in China, but for the most part the dangers are exaggerated. Providing you are sensible, keep your wits about you and make it difficult for thieves to get at your belongings you shouldn't have any problems.

Pickpocketing is the most common form of theft and the one you need to carefully guard against. The wholesale theft of luggage is unusual (unless you leave it lying around unattended), but razoring of bags and pockets in crowded places like buses is fairly common. Certain cities are worse than others – Guangzhou, Guiyang and Xi'an are notorious.

The high risk areas in China are railway and bus stations, city and long-distance buses and hard-seat sections of trains. The hard-seat sections of trains in particular can become very anarchic with the onset of darkness – they are sometimes worked by gangs who persuade travellers to hand over their valuables with knives. Some foreign travellers who have tried to resist have been stabbed in incidents such as these.

Be careful in public toilets – quite a few foreigners have laid aside their valuables, squatted down to business, and then straightened up again to discover that someone had absconded with the lot.

Hotels are generally safe. There are attendants on every floor keeping an eye on the rooms and safeguarding the keys. Dormitories obviously require more care. There is no reason to trust your fellow travellers. All Chinese hotels have safes and storage areas for valuables – use them. Don't leave anything you can't do without (passport, travellers' cheques, money, air tickets etc) lying around in dormitories.

A money belt is the safest way to carry valuables, particularly when travelling on buses and trains. During the cooler weather, it's more comfortable to wear a vest (waistcoat) with numerous pockets, but you should wear this under a light jacket or coat since visible pockets invite wandering hands even if sealed with zippers. Keeping all your eggs in one basket is not advised – against possible loss you could leave a small stash of money (say US$50) in your hotel room or buried in your backpack, with a record of the travellers' cheque serial numbers and your passport number. Other things of little or no apparent value to the thief – like film – should be safeguarded, since to lose them would be a real heartbreak to you. Make a copy of your address book before you leave home. And note down ticket numbers – a Swedish couple whose train tickets were stolen in Chengdu were told by the railway booking office that they would have received a refund had they done so.

Small padlocks are useful for backpacks and some dodgy hotel rooms. Bicycle chain locks (preferably not Chinese-made) come in handy not only for hired bikes but for attaching backpacks to railings or luggage racks. The trendy waist-pouches often used by Hong Kong visitors are definitely *not* advisable for valuables. Street tailors are skilled at sewing inside pockets to trousers, jackets and shirts usually for a few yuan, and these can even be sealed with zippers.

Loss Reports If something of yours is stolen, you should report it immediately to the nearest Foreign Affairs Branch of the PSB. They will ask you to fill in a loss report before investigating the case and sometimes even recovering the stolen goods.

If you have travel insurance (recommended), it is essential to obtain a loss report so you can claim compensation. Be warned, however, many travellers have found

Foreign Affairs officials very unwilling to provide one. Be prepared to spend many hours, perhaps a couple of days, to organise it.

Violence

Street fighting in China is extremely common, yet it seldom leads to serious injury – mostly there's just lots of arm-waving, screaming and threats. The reasons are generally simple enough: people are pushing and shoving their way to a front of a queue, the traffic is forever noisily colliding and finally someone just flips out. Don't get involved.

Most Chinese carry knives (at least the men do), but these are seldom used for anything other than slicing bread. Guns are impossible to buy legally (there is a small

---

Kill the Rooster to Frighten the Monkey

'To get rich is glorious,' Deng once famously said. But in the scramble for glory, more and more Chinese are turning to crime. Locals all over the country fret at the increasing incidence of theft and kidnappings. Crime, they mutter, extends from railway station platforms to the corridors of power. No one is immune to temptation in get-rich-quick China. In mid-1995 the vice mayor of Beijing committed suicide while under investigation for fraud. Chen Xitong, Beijing Communist Party chief, was sacked for corruption. Even former 'model workers' are being arrested on charges of extortion and murder.

Cracking down on crime is a priority for the government if it is to stay in power. Official corruption was a major factor in the Tiananmen Square crisis, and most Chinese claim that the problem is worse now than it was then. Widely publicised arrests and drives against corruption are met with public cynicism: the problem is the government itself. Its monopolistic hold on power and brokering of all business deals puts it in a perfect cream-skimming position. Besides, privilege for high officials and their relatives is an age-old tradition in China.

High officials caught with their fingers in the civic pocket sometimes face lengthy jail terms but often get away with a stern rebuke and a temporary demotion. For less well connected criminals it is often the firing squad.

Meanwhile, widescale unemployment and social disaffection is leading to a growing problem in juvenile crime. Murder, rape and theft head the list of juvenile crimes. The official view is that Chinese youngsters are victims of 'spiritual pollution' – influenced by the Western disease of greed and general depravity.

Justice in China is for the most part the domain of the police (though there are signs that China is setting about establishing an impartial legal system), who also decide the penalty. The ultimate penalty is execution, which serves the purpose of 'killing the rooster to frighten the monkey' or, to phrase this in official terms, 'It is good to have some people executed so as to educate others'. The standard manner of execution is a bullet in the back of the head, often at a mass gathering in some sports stadium. This punishment is usually reserved for rapists and murderers. Afterwards a mugshot and maybe even a photo of the extinguished body gets plugged up on a public notice board. Criminals being paraded on the backs of trucks through the streets of Chinese towns are still a common sight. ■

black market in military pistols though). That having been said, there have been cases of armed robbery by gangs on trains – knives are the usual weapons. The police have tried to crack down on this – there have been arrests and executions of offenders. The chance of it happening to you is small and you needn't let this deter you from riding the train, but it's a good idea to be aware that it can happen.

Staring Squads

The programme is *Aliens*, you are the star and cinema-sized audiences will gather to watch. Amazingly, after 15 years of foreign tourism, the Chinese will still stop what they're doing, grab the kids and call out to their friends to see the passing foreigner. It's less likely to occur in major urban centres and tourist sights, but out in rural China it's the same as it ever was.

There is no easy recipe for dealing with crowds of staring strangers. Some travellers take it in their stride, others turn into nervous wrecks and go to Thailand. There is nothing you can do about it: smiling, laughing, waving, scowling or screaming hysterically are all part of the show. It becomes more bearable if you have a travelling companion – solitary travellers can sometimes end up feeling like the elephant man cast adrift in Victorian London.

The best advice, especially if you are on your own, is to keep moving (best of all on a bicycle). Some travellers swear by the Walkman – it helps to insulate you from the caterwauls of locals trying to get your attention as they summon their friends. In close quarters – on trains and buses – try befriending the people closest to you. In almost all cases the staring is pure uninhibited curiosity, and the starers would like nothing more than to strike up a conversation and find out where you are from and how much you make a month if they could break through the language barrier.

Laowai!

Get outside the cosmopolitan centres of Guangzhou, Shanghai and Beijing and you will hear the exclamation *lǎowài!* a couple of dozen times a day. *Lao* means 'old' in Chinese and is a mark of respect; *wai* means 'outside' – together they constitute the politest word the Chinese have for 'foreigner'. Chinese speakers will hear it used in many ways – sometimes with a thick overlay of irony that undermines the respect implied in the word – but generally it is used in startled surprise at suddenly encountering a foreigner in a world that is overwhelmingly Chinese.

There is no point getting annoyed by it: respond with a '*nǐ hǎo*' or a 'Hello' if you want to. Alternatively, just ignore it.

Drinking Water

Can you drink the water? Most Chinese will advise you not to. At the very least it should be boiled first. Boiled water is available free of charge at all Chinese hotels. Mineral water is also widely available at between Y2 and Y3 per bottle.

Noise

In recent years the Chinese government has launched an anti-noise pollution campaign. Look out for billboards emblazoned with a huge crossed-through ear presiding over busy intersections swarming with honking traffic. The government is on a loser with this one. The Chinese are generally much more tolerant of noise than most Westerners. People watch TV at ear-shattering volumes, drivers habitually lean on the horn, telephone conversations are conducted in high-decibel rapid-fire screams and most of China seems to wake uncomplainingly to the sound of jackhammers and earthmoving vehicles. If it's peace and quiet you want, head for the deserts of Tibet or Xinjiang.

Spitting

When China first opened to foreign tourism, many Western travellers were shocked by the spitting, which was conducted noisily by everyone everywhere. Government campaigns to stamp out the practice have been reasonably successful in the major urban centres – there is a lot less public spitting in

Guangzhou, Shanghai and Beijing these days – but out in the country it is still a national sport. Interestingly, English travellers in 19th-century America complained of the same thing.

Apart from the fact that it is very unpleasant to be stuck in, say, a bus with 50 people who feel impelled to spit on the floor every five minutes, the spitting spreads chronic bronchitis, which clogs the lung passages with mucus. This is particularly a problem in the winter months, when almost everyone in China succumbs. If people could agree to stop spitting, the problem would probably diminish very quickly.

Racism

Racism in China is a knotty problem. Most Chinese will swear blind that neither they nor their government is racist. But then very few Chinese you meet will have thought very deeply about the issue, and the Chinese government itself would never allow lively public debate on China's racist policies and attitudes. But, of course, as in most other countries around the world, racism is alive and kicking in China.

The Chinese are a proud people. Being Chinese links the individual to a long historical lineage, for the most part of which, Chinese believe, their country was the centre of the world. Most Chinese believe it is their destiny to once again lead the world. There's nothing new here, except that being Chinese is defined by blood. Chinese public discourse is littered with metaphors of racial purity and fulsome praise for the achievements of the great Chinese people, and this is the stuff that racism thrives on.

Take the dual-pricing system. Whether it is motivated by greed or not, it is fundamentally racist. But for most Chinese, it is simply the rules and they are oblivious to its racist undertones.

Gripes aside, foreigners in China are generally treated well. It is very unusual to encounter direct racism in the form of insults (though it does happen) or be refused service in China. It does help, however, if you are from a predominantly white and prosperous nation. Other Asians and blacks often encounter discrimination in China, and in a famous incident in 1988 Chinese students in Nanjing took to the streets to protest black overseas students dating local Chinese women.

When a Chinese tells you that racism is a 'foreign problem', bear in mind that homosexuality too is a 'foreign problem' – in fact almost everything the Chinese government considers 'unhealthy' is a foreign problem. And if that sounds a little racist, it isn't because there's no racism in China.

Queues

Forget queues. In China a large number of people with a common goal (a bus seat, a train ticket etc) generally form a surging mass. It is one of the more exhausting parts of China travel, and sometimes it is worth paying extra in order to be able to avoid railway and bus stations. Otherwise, take a deep breath and leap in with everyone else. This is China – you have to accept the fact that there's nothing you can do about a billion people!

Beggars

Yes, beggars do exist in China – but there are not as many as there are in countries like India. The beggars tend not to pounce on foreigners – the chief exceptions are the kids, who practically have to be removed with a crowbar once they've seized your trouser leg. Some beggars squat on the pavement beside large posters which detail their sad story. Professional beggars are common – sometimes women clutching babies who regurgitate stories about having lost their train tickets and all their money.

Drugs

China takes a particularly dim view of opium and all of its derivatives. The Chinese suffered severely from an opium epidemic which was started by British traders in 1773 and lasted until the Communists came to power – they haven't forgotten! Several heroin smugglers from Hong Kong were caught in Kunming some years ago – within a week they were scheduled for public execution. The local PSB issued a special invitation for the foreign press to attend.

Marijuana is often seen growing by the roadside in south-western China – it's very poor quality. Hashish is smoked by some of China's minority groups, especially the Uighurs in Xinjiang Province. It's difficult to say what attitude the Chinese police will take towards foreigners caught using marijuana – they often don't care what foreigners do if Chinese aren't involved. Then again, you have to remember the old story about 'kill the rooster to frighten the monkey'. If you plan to use drugs and don't want to become the rooster, discretion is strongly advised!

WORK

There are opportunities to teach English and other foreign languages, or even other technical skills if you're qualified. Teaching in China is not a way to get rich – the pay is roughly US$180 a month, payable in RMB. While this is about four times what the average urban Chinese worker earns, it won't get you far after you've left China. There are usually some fringe benefits like free or low-cost housing and special ID cards that get you discounts on trains and flights. As a worker in China, you will be assigned to a 'work unit', but unlike the locals you'll be excused from political meetings and the God-like controls over your life that the typical Chinese has to endure.

It's become fairly typical for universities to pressure foreigners into working excessive hours. A maximum teaching load should be 20 hours per week, and even this is a lot – you can insist on no more than 15. Chinese professors teach far fewer hours than this – some hardly show up for class at all since they often have outside business interests.

The main reason to work in China is to experience the country at a level not ordinarily available to travellers. Unfortunately, just how close you will be able to get to the Chinese people depends on what the local PSB allows. In Beijing, where the local PSB is almost hysterical about evil foreign 'spir-

itual pollution', your students may be prohibited from having any contact with you beyond the classroom, though you may secretly meet them far away from the campus.

Foreign teachers are typically forced to live in separate apartments or dormitories – Chinese students wishing to visit you at your room may be turned away at the reception desk; otherwise they may be required to register their name, ID number and purpose of visit. Since many people are reluctant to draw attention to themselves like this (and they could be questioned by the PSB later), they may be unwilling to visit you at all.

In other words, teaching in China can be a lonely experience unless you spend all your free time in the company of other expats, but this deprives you of the 'foreign experience' you may be seeking.

Two topics which cannot be discussed in the classroom are politics and religion. Foreigners teaching in Beijing have reported spies being placed in their classrooms. Other teachers have found microphones hidden in their dormitory rooms (one fellow we know took revenge by attaching his Walkman to the microphone wires and blasting the snoops with punk music!).

Rules change – China is opening up slowly, and some provinces are liberalising faster than others. So things might have improved by the time you read this. If you are interested in working in China, contact a Chinese embassy or the universities directly.

Doing Business

At one time, China was the world's most advanced nation. The Chinese invented gunpowder, rockets, the printing press and paper currency. How did such an advanced nation fall so far behind? Probably because the Chinese also invented bureaucracy.

In bureaucratic China, even simple things can be made difficult – renting property, getting a telephone installed, hiring employees, paying taxes etc can generate mind-boggling quantities of red tape. Many foreign business people who have worked in China say that success is usually the result of dogged persistence and finding cooperative officials.

If you have any intention of doing business in China, be it buying, selling or investing, it's worth knowing that most towns and – in large cities – many neighbourhoods have a Commerce Office *(shāngyè jú)*. If you approach one of these offices for assistance, the reaction you get can vary from enthusiastic welcome to bureaucratic inertia. In case of a dispute (the goods you ordered are not what was delivered etc), the Commerce Office could assist you, provided that it is willing.

Anyone thinking of doing serious business in China and setting up a company is advised to do some serious research before going ahead. Do some introductory business reading (see the Books section of this chapter), talk to other foreigners who are already doing business in China and consider talking with a China consultancy of some sort.

ACTIVITIES
Adventure Sports
Western China in particular offers the type of topography to entice mountaineers, whitewater rafters, hang gliding enthusiasts and others who want to pursue their adventurous hobbies in some of the world's highest mountains.

The problem, as always, are those faceless, sombre figures known collectively as 'the authorities'. High-ranking cadres, the PSB, the military, CITS and others in China with the power to extort money know a good business opportunity when they see it. Foreigners have been asked for as much as US$1 million for mountaineering and rafting permits. The amount demanded varies considerably depending on who you're dealing with, and the price is always negotiable.

In many cases, it's doubtful that the law really requires a permit. A Chinese person may climb the same mountain as you without having any authorisation at all and it may be perfectly legal. But many local governments simply make up the law as they go along. In general, when foreigners do something which is deemed unusual – and hang gliding,

bungy jumping, kayaking and the like are unusual in China – a permit will be required and a fee will be charged. The more unusual the activity, the higher the fee demanded.

Hiking
As opposed to mountaineering (which requires equipment such as ropes and ice axes), normal hiking activities can usually be pursued without permits. The Chinese idea of hiking is often different from the Western concept – most of the peaks climbed are hardly wilderness areas. You can expect an admission gate (charging a fee), handrails, concrete steps, Chinese characters painted on the rocks, temples, pavilions, trailside souvenir vendors, restaurants and perhaps a hotel or two. Hiking areas of this sort include some of China's famous mountains like Taishan and Emeishan. Still, it can be good fun and exercise, and it's part of the 'China experience'.

Camel & Horseback Riding
The venues are not numerous, but China does offer some opportunities of this sort. Camel rides for tourists have become popular pastimes in places like Inner Mongolia or the deserts around Dunhuang (Gansu Province). There are chances for beautiful trips by horses in the mountains of Xinjiang, or for that matter in the hills west of Beijing. Costs are negotiable, but in general, the further away from a big city you are, the cheaper it gets.

Exercise & Gymnastics
Swimming pools, gymnasiums and weightlifting rooms are popular ways to keep fit and enjoy yourself. While swimming pools and gymnasiums exist for the Chinese public, they are generally overcrowded and in poor condition. You'll find better facilities at the tourist hotels, but of course it won't be free (unless you're a guest at the hotel). Most hotels in big cities like Beijing permit nonguests to use the workout rooms, pools, saunas or tennis courts on a fee basis. This is not a bad idea if you're staying for a month

or more – monthly fees typically start at around Y450.

Many public swimming pools in China require foreigners to have a recent certificate proving they are AIDS-free before they are allowed to swim.

Winter Sports

Beijing's lakes freeze over for a couple of months during winter and ice skating becomes feasible. Further north in Harbin, January temperatures dip to minus 40°C and ice-boat racing is a favourite pastime for those who can afford it. North-east China is also the venue for skiing, both the downhill and cross-country varieties.

Skiing and ice skating demand specialised shoes, and Westerners with big feet often have difficulty finding the right size. If you want to pursue winter sports, you may need to bring your own equipment, though some local stuff is àvailable.

Golf

Golf courses have invaded the suburbs of Beijing, Shanghai and Guangzhou. As elsewhere, it's a sport of the well-to-do, but that seems to be even more true in China. While green fees are similar to what you'd pay in the West, the cost is astronomical compared with the typical Chinese salary.

University Courses

As China continues to experiment with capitalism, universities have found it increasingly necessary to raise their own funds and not depend so much on state largess. For this reason, most universities welcome fee-paying foreign students. Most of the courses offered are Chinese language study, but other possibilities include Chinese medicine, acupuncture, brush painting and music. If you've got the cash, almost anything is possible.

There is considerable variation in the quality of instruction and the prices charged. Tuition alone typically runs from US$1000 to US$3000 per year, sometimes double that, and it may depend on your nationality. The university is supposed to arrange your accommodation (no, it's not free) – living conditions vary from reasonably comfortable to horrific.

It's worth knowing that you'll probably have to pay some additional fees and service charges you weren't told about when you enrolled. Examples include extra fees for a 'health certificate' or a 'study licence'. Sometimes these fees are imposed by the PSB, which wants its share of the cash, but often the university itself is pocketing the money – the fees vary from reasonable to ridiculous.

If possible, don't pay anything in advance – show up at the school to assess the situation yourself and talk to other foreign students to see if they're satisfied. Once you've handed over the cash, don't expect a refund.

HIGHLIGHTS

With the exception of good beaches, China has something of everything: deserts, grasslands, forests, sacred mountains, imperial remains, crumbling city walls and temples galore. Listed here are some tips for getting started on it all.

Backpacker Getaways

Unlike the South-East Asian trail, which seems to harbour some little getaway with travellers' breakfasts, walks, waterfalls and fabulous beaches at every turn, in China such rest-up retreats are few and far between. In fact, there are only two places that have achieved a legendary status on the travel circuit: Yangshuo (Guangxi Province) and Dali (Yunnan Province).

Yangshuo is a village set amid the famous karst scenery of Guilin. The surrounding countryside alone, which can be explored by bicycle, makes Yangshuo worth a stay of a few days, but there are also river trips, nearby rural markets, caves to explore, cheap accommodation and banana pancakes for breakfast. What more could you ask for? Dali is arguably more exotic, but is essentially a similar deal to Yangshuo. The old walled town, home to the Bai minority, nestles beside the Erhai Lake close to the Cangshan mountains. It is a superb place to rest up for a few days.

There are other parts of Yunnan which have the potential to become legendary backpacker destinations. Lijiang, home to the matriarchal Naxi minority and around six hours by bus from Dali, has already become very popular. Xishuangbanna, on the border of Laos and Myanmar, is also favoured for its minority colours and subtropical weather.

Imperial Splendour

Dynasties have risen and fallen for at least a few millennia in China. Nevertheless, there's not as much imperial debris about as you might expect. Dynasties rarely fell gracefully. Imperial decline was generally marked by rampaging peasant uprisings and pillaging armies led by turncoat generals. More often than not a new dynasty was built on the ashes of the last. Add to this the turmoil of China in the 20th century, the assault on the past led by the Cultural Revolution and finally the rapid modernisation and urbanisation of the nation over the last 15 years and it's a wonder there's anything left to see. Fortunately there is.

China's imperial jewel in the crown is of

Suggested Itineraries

Unless you have a couple of years up your sleeve, oodles of patience and inexhaustible funds, you are only going to be able to see a small part of China on any one trip. It's a good idea to have a loose itinerary to follow. The following suggestions assume you have at least a month in China.

Beijing to Tibet via Xi'an

Beijing – Xi'an – Xining – Golmud – Lhasa

This route has emerged as a very popular one with many travellers, particularly those overlanding from Europe by train and heading for Nepal and India via Tibet. The great thing about this route is that it gives you the best of China's historical sights (Beijing and Xi'an) and at the same time gives you an opportunity to travel out into China's remote and sparsely populated western regions.

Beijing, Xi'an and Lhasa are the main attractions on this route. En route to Xi'an, you can also visit Datong and Taiyuan, though they are not particularly pleasant cities. Xining is worth a day or so, mainly for the nearby lamasery of Ta'ersi. The less time spent in Golmud the better. From Lhasa, it is possible to travel on to Nepal via the Tibetan temple towns of Gyantse, Shigatse and Sakya – some travellers make a detour to the Everest base camp. The journey from Lhasa to Kathmandu is a once-in-a-lifetime trip.

Beijing to Hong Kong via Sichuan, Yunnan and Guangxi

Beijing – Xi'an – Kunming – Guilin (Yangshuo) – Guangzhou – Hong Kong

There are many variations on this route, depending on how much time you have and how much you enjoy travelling on Chinese trains (or, more to the point, trying to get tickets for the trains). A stop-over in Kunming allows travellers to explore Yunnan, which is arguably the most exotic of China's provinces – rich in ethnic colour and some of the best scenery in all China. Also, from Kunming, many travellers opt to travel on to Chengdu (via Dali and Lijiang). From Chengdu there are many options: onwards to Chongqing and from here to Shanghai or Wuhan down the Yangzi River, or onwards to Guizhou and Guilin and on to Hong Kong. You can speed things up on this route with a flight or two.

Hong Kong to Kunming via Guilin

Hong Kong – Guangzhou – Guilin (Yangshuo) – Kunming – Xishuangbanna – Dali – Lijiang

This has long been China's most favoured backpacker trail. The standard routine is a brief stay in Guangzhou (one or two nights), followed by a ferry to Wuzhou, and from there a direct bus to

course Beijing. It has been capital of China for around 500 years (most of the time) and is home to sights such as the Forbidden City, the off-limits palace of Ming and Qing emperors, their eunuch servants, princesses and harems. The Summer Palace in Beijing was established in the late-Qing period but is also a major attraction. Beijing is also the jumping off point for China's most famous imperial legacy – the Great Wall. The wall can actually be viewed from many places, but most visitors approach it from Beijing.

Scattered around China are many other cities that have served as the imperial seat of power at one time or another. Many of them are now heavily industrialised and yield little clues as to what they must have been in the past. One notable exception is Nanjing (the name means 'Southern Capital'; Beijing is the 'Northern Capital'). Nanjing was briefly capital of China in the early years of the Ming Dynasty. Its city walls survive in some places, and nearby at Zijinshan Park is the tomb of the first Ming emperor and other imperial relics.

China's other major imperial drawcard is

Yangshuo (very few travellers bother with Guilin itself). Many travellers end up seduced by Yangshuo and spending much longer than they planned. Onward travel to Kunming can be undertaken by train or by plane. From Kunming, there is a wide range of choices – south to the regional areas of Xishuangbanna and Dehong or north-west to Dali and Lijiang (or both). Other possibilities include flights from Kunming to Chiangmai or Bangkok in Thailand, or a train to Hanoi in Vietnam.

Coastal Routes

If you look at a map of China, an obvious route is one that takes you up (or down) the east of China between Guangzhou and Beijing. It is possible to do this. From Beijing, you might travel to Shandong and from here make a beeline southward via Shanghai and Zhejiang and Fujian provinces to Guangzhou. The only problem with this route is that you are passing through some of the most densely populated regions in the world's most populous nation. There is intense competition for train tickets (where trains are available), and as a result if you don't fly you will inevitably spend days and days bouncing around in crowded buses. To make matters worse, China's coastal cities soon become a blur of smog and chimneys, grey housing estates and factories. It's not a lot of fun.

Yangzi River Routes

Cruises on the Yangzi River have long been touted as one of China's premier attractions. In reality they get mixed reports. Some travellers have even found the Three Gorges (the whole reason for cruising the river) overrated. Whatever the case, the most interesting part of the Yangzi is the section between Chongqing (Sichuan) and Wuhan; the section east of here between Wuhan and Shanghai is of little interest (the Yangzi gets so wide you cannot even see the shores).

Silk Road Route

Beijing/Guangzhou – Shanghai – Kaifeng – Zhengzhou – Xi'an – Liuyuan (Dunhuang) – Ürümqi – Turpan – Kashgar

Kashgar and the Karakoram Highway (to Pakistan) can be approached directly from Beijing, but a fascinating trip is the overland route once used for transporting silk to Europe. It includes little-travelled parts of central China (Kaifeng) and passes through archaeological treasure houses of Xi'an and Dunhuang, before heading into the deserts of Xinjiang. From Ürümqi you will have to travel by bus to Turpan and Kashgar. Onward travel to Pakistan and India is an option. ■

also its most ancient: Xi'an. The Qin Dynasty (221-207 BC) was headquartered here, and later Xi'an was the capital of the Tang Dynasty, when it was known as Chang'an. Today it is the most impressive of China's few remaining walled cities, and the nearby entombed warriors of the Qin Dynasty is one of China's major tourist sights.

Minority Regions

China is around 94% Han Chinese. The remainder of the population belongs to one of China's approximately 60 minorities. Some of these minorities, such as the Hui (Muslim Chinese) and the Man (natives of Manchuria), are ethnically indistinguishable from the Han Chinese and speak only Chinese. Other minorities, such as the Uighurs and the Tibetans, are ethnically distinct and speak languages that have little relation to Chinese.

China's minorities are scattered around the edges of the Chinese empire, and many travellers make a beeline direct to these regions. The provinces richest in minorities are all in the south-west of China, notably in Yunnan and Guizhou. Yunnan alone, which is bordered by Myanmar, Laos and Vietnam, is home to around 20 different minority groups. In large urban areas these minorities are difficult to distinguish from the Chinese, but in the country many still dress in traditional costumes and regularly hold colourful festivals and markets. Notable minority areas in south-west China include Yunnan's Xishuangbanna (mainly Dai), Dali (Bai), Lijiang (Naxi) and Dehong (Burmese, Dai and Jingpo); and in Guizhou, Kaili and further south-east (Dong and Miao).

With a population of close on five million, Tibetans make up one of China's largest minorities. Naturally the place to go is Tibet itself. But there are also large Tibetan communities in parts of China that once belonged to Tibet. In south-western Gansu Province, Xiahe's Labrang Monastery is one of the six major monasteries of the Gelugpa sect of Tibetan Buddhism and is very much a little Tibet. Ta'er Monastery near Xining in

Qinghai Province is another of the six major Gelugpa monasteries

Sacred Mountains

Eulogised through the centuries in countless paintings and poems, the sacred mountains of China were once places of pilgrimage, towering peaks whose vastness inspired the climber with a sense of the frailty of human existence. Nowadays most of them are being turned into major tourist attractions complete with swift-footed armies of souvenir sellers, cable cars and extortionate entry fees. This does not mean that they are not worth the effort; simply that the climber gets few solitary contemplative moments.

Strictly speaking there are nine sacred mountains in total: five Taoist peaks and four Buddhist peaks. Added to this list, however, are peaks that got onto the pilgrimage trail due to a reputation for superlative beauty. These include Huangshan (Anhui Province) and Lushan (Jiangxi Province).

China's Taoist peaks are Huashan (Shanxi Province), Hengshan (Hunan Province), Hengshan (Hebei Province – yes, there are two of them), Taishan (Shandong Province) and Songshan (Henan Province). The Buddhist mountains are Emeishan (Sichuan Province), Wutaishan (Shanxi Province), Putuoshan (Zhejiang Province) and Jiuhuashan (Anhui Province).

China's sacred mountains have been pilgrimage destinations for centuries and all have well-marked trails to the summits. Usually there are stairways carved into rockfaces, and sights en route include poems and inscriptions and numerous temples, many of which have accommodation (unfortunately often off limits to foreigners). The chief attraction is inevitably sunrise at the summit, where camera-toting crowds gather to gaze on the 'sea of clouds'. The most popular with foreign visitors are Huangshan, Taishan and Emeishan.

Cave Art

The Mogao Caves are the most impressive and best-preserved examples of Buddhist cave art anywhere in China. They are set into desert cliffs above a river valley about 25 km south-east of Dunhuang in Gansu Province. Some 492 grottoes are still standing.

The Yungang Buddhist Caves (Shanxi Province) are cut into the southern cliffs of Wuzhoushan, near Datong, next to the pass leading to Inner Mongolia. The caves contain over 50,000 statues and stretch for about one km east to west. On top of the mountain ridge are the remains of a 17th-century Qing Dynasty fortress.

The Grand Buddha at Leshan (Sichuan Province) is the largest Buddha in the world. Seventy-one metres high, it is carved into a cliff face overlooking the confluence of the Dadu and Min rivers. You can go to the top, opposite the head, and then descend a short stairway to the feet for a Lilliputian perspective. Tour boats pass by for a frontal view.

Foreign Concessions

The European powers never managed to colonise China. But by the end of the 19th century the weakness of the Qing government allowed them to grab a large number of 'foreign concessions'. Much of the old architecture is still standing, nowadays often functioning as schools and government offices. In some cities, such buildings are being torn down and replaced with hastily thrown together high-rises. In other cities, such as Guangzhou and Shanghai, some of it is being gentrified.

China's most famous collection of European architecture is lined up facing the sea on the Bund in Shanghai. The city's French Concession, mostly derelict and falling in swathes to modern building projects, also turns up some delightful architectural surprises. Guangzhou, home to China's earliest foreign concession, has an unexpectedly peaceful enclave of European buildings on Shamian Island. Some of the buildings are falling into disrepair, others are being renovated.

Xiamen (Fujian Province) has one of China's most charming collections of colonial architecture on Gulangyu Island. The fact that there are no motorised vehicles on the small island makes this one of the only places in the country where it is possible to take peaceful walks and appreciate the buildings at leisure.

Qingdao (Shandong Province) was ceded to the Germans in 1898, and by 1904 the inevitable brewery was in place along with countless villas and administrative buildings. Qingdao's architectural attractions are scattered (modern construction has taken its toll on the city's charms), but there is still more than enough to keep you busy for a couple of days.

Tianjin became a treaty port for the British in 1858. By the turn of the century they had been joined by the French, Germans, Italians, Belgians and Japanese. The result is a remarkable potpourri of architectural styles divided up into concessions. Along with Shanghai, Tianjin provides some of the best colonial browsing in China.

ACCOMMODATION

One of the main reasons the Chinese threw the door open to tourism in the 1980s is that they badly needed the foreign exchange. Despite all the government's rhetoric about 'Friendship Hotels' and 'Friendship Stores', the purpose of opening up to tourism has always been to rake in money. Hotel prices are steadily rising towards what you'd pay for a similar standard of accommodation in the West – there aren't too many bargains around. On the other hand, quality has improved – rooms are more luxurious, service has improved and hotel staff are friendlier and more used to dealing with foreigners than a few years ago. In the past, it was common for the staff to simply deny that rooms were available even when the place was empty.

Camping

You have to get a long way from civilisation before camping becomes feasible in China. Camping within sight of a town or village in most parts of China would probably result in a swift visit by the PSB. Wilderness camping is more appealing, but most such areas in China require special permits and are difficult to reach. Many travellers have camped successfully in Tibet and remote north-western Sichuan.

The trick is to select a couple of likely places about half an hour before sunset but keep moving (by bicycle, foot or whatever) and then backtrack so you can get away from the road at the chosen spot just after darkness falls. Be sure to get up around sunrise and leave before sightseeing locals take an interest.

Hostels

Youth hostels in the Western sense of the word do not exist in China. The kinds of cheapie dormitories run by the International Youth Hostel Federation (IYHF) – so common in Europe, Australia, Japan and elsewhere – are not permitted in the PRC. In the early days of China travel, many of the government-run hotels had dormitory accommodation. Such hotels are thin on the ground nowadays. Most have been renovated into mid-range or top-end hotels and have only luxury (or pseudo-luxury) doubles.

When dormitories do exist, the staff at the reception desk may be reluctant to tell you. Try a little friendly forcefulness. If this doesn't work, you may have no choice but to look elsewhere – there are many cities in China where none of the hotels that accept foreigners have dormitory accommodation.

One alternative to hotel dormitories is a university foreign student dormitory. These sometimes accept stray foreigners, but in general the rule is that you must have a friend who will vouch for you staying at the university.

Guesthouses

In China guesthouses *(bīnguǎn)* are usually enormous government-run hotels, often with many wings in spacious grounds. Most of them were set up in the 1950s for travelling government officials and overseas dignitaries. Most of these have been renovated over the last five years or so and are being rented out as mid-range accommodation for foreigners, overseas Chinese and affluent locals. They are most definitely not the kind of inexpensive, family-run hotels you find all over Thailand, Indonesia and other parts of Asia.

Hotels

There is no shortage of hotels in China. The problem comes if you are on a budget. In many parts of China, finding a room for less than US$30 a night can be an ordeal. Often inexpensive accommodation is in fact available – if you are Chinese. For foreigners, there are generally rules (enforced by the PSB) concerning which hotels you may or may not stay in, and of course the only ones open to foreigners are the expensive ones.

On the other hand, for travellers on mid-range budgets, China's hotels have improved immensely. Service standards are better, the toilets may actually flush and sometimes there are even minibars and 24-hour hot water. Unless you are in a four or five-star joint venture, however, it is wise not to expect too much, no matter how much you are spending. Many of the finer details of the hotel business still elude Chinese management and staff.

Discounts If you're studying in the PRC, you can get a discount on room prices. Students usually have to show their government-issued 'green card', though sometimes a fake 'white card' will do the trick. Foreign experts working in China usually qualify for the same discounts as students.

If you are really stuck for a place to stay, it sometimes helps to phone or visit the local PSB and explain your problem. Just as the PSB makes the rules, the PSB can break them – a hotel not approved for foreigners can be granted a temporary reprieve by the PSB and all it takes is a phone call from the right official. Unfortunately, getting such an exemption is not the usual practice.

Hotel Etiquette Most hotels have an attendant on every floor. The attendant keeps an eye on the hotel guests. This is partly to prevent theft and partly to stop you from bringing locals back for the night (this is not a joke).

To conserve energy, in many cheaper hotels hot water for bathing is available only in the evening – sometimes only for a few hours a night or once every three days. It's worth asking when or if the hot water will be turned on.

The policy at every hotel in China is to require that you check out by noon to avoid being charged extra. If you check out between noon and 6 pm there is a charge of 50% of the room price – after 6 pm you have to pay for another full night.

Almost every hotel has a left-luggage room (*jìcún chù* or *xínglǐ bǎoguǎn*), and in many hotels there is such a room on every floor. If you are a guest in the hotel, use of the left-luggage room might be free (but not always).

The trend in China over the last few years has been to equip every room – even in the cheap hotels – with TV sets permanently turned to maximum volume. The Hong Kong-style ultra-violent movies are noisy enough, but the introduction of Nintendo-style video games and karaoke microphones (which can be attached to TV sets) has added a new dimension to the cacophony.

Something else to be prepared for is lack of privacy – what happens is that you're sitting starkers in your hotel room, the key suddenly turns in the door and the room attendant casually wanders in. This is becoming less of a problem as hotel workers learn how to handle foreign visitors, but it's still a frequent occurrence. Don't expect anyone to knock before entering. Your best protection is to prop a chair against the door.

It's also worth noting that privacy is another privilege of rank; the high-ranking cadres live in large houses surrounded by high walls and are driven around in cars with drawn curtains. Those of sufficiently high rank stay in huge government guesthouses, exclusive villas surrounded by walls, guards and keep-out signs.

The Chinese method of designating floors is the same as that used in the USA but different from, say, Australia's. What would be the 'ground floor' in Australia is the '1st floor' in China, the 1st is the 2nd, and so on. However, there is some inconsistency – Hong Kong, which uses the British system, has influenced some parts of southern China.

Rental

Most Chinese people live in government-subsidised housing – the price is almost always dirt cheap. For foreigners, the situation is totally different.

If you're going to be working for the Chinese government as a teacher or other type of foreign expert, then you'll almost certainly be provided with cheap or low-cost housing. Conditions probably won't be luxurious, but it should be inexpensive.

The news is not good for those coming to China to do business or work for a foreign company. The cheap apartments available to the Chinese are off limits to foreigners, which leaves you with two choices – living in a hotel or renting a luxury flat in a compound specifically designated for foreigners.

If you live in a hotel, you might be able to negotiate a discount for a long-term stay, but that's not guaranteed. As for luxury flats and villas, monthly rents start at around US$2000 and reach US$5000 or more. Even at these prices, there is a shortage of flats available for foreigners in big cities like Beijing and Shanghai.

Considering the sky-high rents, buying a flat or villa might seem like a good idea for companies with the cash. It's actually possible, but the rules vary from city to city. In Xiamen, for example, only Overseas Chinese are permitted to buy luxury villas – real estate speculators from Taiwan do a roaring trade. Shenzhen has long been in the business of selling flats to Hong Kongers, who in turn rent them out to others. Foreigners can buy flats in Beijing (at astronomical prices), and doing this can actually gain you a residence permit.

As for simply moving in with a Chinese family and paying them rent, forget it – the PSB will swoop down on you (and the hapless Chinese family) faster than ants at a picnic.

FOOD

Chinese cooking is justifiably famous, a fine art perfected through the centuries. Quality, availability of ingredients and cooking styles vary by region, but you'll almost always find something to suit your tastes.

You can also put your mind at ease about food shortages – despite China's long history of famines, the country is not short of food. Famines have resulted from natural disasters (droughts, floods, typhoons) and human disasters (wars, the Cultural Revolution), but in China today the transport system is able to quickly move food to those areas that need it. Your biggest problems with food are likely to be figuring out the menus and being overcharged.

While the Chinese make outstanding lunches, dinners and snacks, many foreigners are disappointed by breakfast. The Chinese do not seem to understand the Western notion of eating light in the morning – a typical breakfast could include fried peanuts, pickled vegetables, pork with hot sauce, fried breadsticks called *yóutiáo*, and rice porridge, all washed down with a glass of beer. Just what you had in mind at 7 am.

Places to Eat

Outside of hotel restaurants, prices are generally low. Beware, however, of overcharging – many places think nothing of charging foreigners double or more.

The other catch is that when Chinese dine out they spend big, and foreigners are expected to do likewise. Travellers in small groups or on their own will often find themselves being pressured to order far more than they can eat. They may also find very expensive dishes landing on their tables. Even the grottiest of Chinese restaurants will often have exotic delicacies costing as much as

Banquets

The banquet is the apex of the Chinese dining experience. When groups of friends get together and eat out they generally follow banquet procedure – extravagant dishes, no rice and lots of toasting.

Dishes are served in sequence, beginning with cold appetisers and continuing through 10 or more courses. Soup is usually served after the main course, usually a thin broth to aid digestion.

The idea is to serve or order far more than everyone can eat. Empty bowls imply a stingy host. Rice rarely appears at a banquet. Don't ask for it – this would imply that the snacks and main courses are insufficient, causing embarrassment to the host.

Never drink alone. Imbibing is conducted via toasts, which will usually commence with general

table toasts and then settle down to frequent toasts to individuals. A toast is conducted by raising your glass in both hands in the direction of the toastee and crying out *ganbei*, literally 'dry glass'. Chinese do not clink glasses. Drain your glass in one hit. It is not unusual for everyone to end up very drunk, though at very formal banquets this is frowned upon.

Don't be late for a formal banquet; it's considered extremely rude. The banquet ends when the food and toasts end – the Chinese don't linger after the meal. You may find yourself being applauded when you enter a large banquet. It is polite to applaud back. ∎

US$100 per serving on their menus. Be sure you know the cost of what you are ordering.

Ten years ago most Chinese restaurants were government-run canteens. All that has changed. Nowadays China is brimming with privately run restaurants – everything from hole-in-the-wall slop shops to upmarket regional cuisines in opulent surroundings. For cheap eats, the best places to look are around train and bus stations. Busy commercial districts will usually harbour some small dumpling and noodle restaurants, and at night many cities have market streets with good food available inexpensively.

Even travellers on a budget shouldn't write off hotel restaurants completely. It is often worth checking the menu (usually in English). The contents often include some very good deals if you pick and choose carefully – the staff will think you are cheapskates, but who cares?

Out on the streets, the problem is the language barrier. A phrasebook is a big help, but the alternative is to point at something one of the other diners is eating – be sure to determine the price before you order. In rural China many restaurants have pick-and-choose kitchens where you wander out back, select your vegetables and meat and have the chef fry it all up. Chinese are often very surprised by the ingredients foreigners choose to throw together, but they will usually oblige all the same.

Main Dishes
See the special colour section on Chinese Cuisine in this chapter.

Chopsticks
If you haven't mastered using chopsticks before going to China, you probably will by the time you leave. In upmarket restaurants, sometimes the staff will bring out the cutlery for foreign guests but generally you will have to click your chopsticks along with the locals. Chopsticks are relatively easy to use and are employed for picking items from communal dishes and for shovelling rice (with the bowl held to the lips) in rapid flicking motions into the mouth – that's a tricky one to master.

In rural China, table manners leave a lot to be desired, but this does not mean you can bring back to the big cities the bad habits you have acquired in the backwoods. Spitting bones on the floor and shouting through mouthfuls of food may be OK in western Sichuan but is frowned upon in a decent restaurant in Shanghai.

Chinese toothpick etiquette is similar to other nearby Asian countries. One hand wields the toothpick and does the picking, the other hand shields the mouth from prying eyes.

Snacks
Western-style cakes and sweetbreads are on sale everywhere – they rarely taste very good. The Chinese are considerably better at making their traditional breads – steamed buns (*mántóu*), clay-oven bread (*shāobǐng*) and fried bread rolls (*yínsī juǎn*) are notable examples. In general, the Cantonese seem to be better at baking than other Chinese – Cantonese specialities such as coconut cakes and custard tarts are excellent.

Desserts
The Chinese do not generally eat dessert, but fruit is considered an appropriate end to a good meal. Western influence has added ice cream to the menu in some upmarket establishments, but in general sweet stuff is consumed as snacks and is seldom available in restaurants.

Fruit
Canned and bottled fruit is readily available everywhere, in department and food stores as well as in dining cars on trains. Good quality fruit – including oranges, mandarins and bananas – is commonly sold in the street markets, though you'll find that the supply and quality drop off severely in winter. Out in the deserts of the north-west, melons are abundant; pineapples and lychees are common along the south-east coast during summer.

Sugarcane is the traditional poor person's candy in China. It is sold at railway and bus stations and is a common on-the-road snack.

The idea is not to eat the purple skin (this is usually shaved off anyway) and not to swallow the pulp – chew on it until it tastes like string, then spit it out.

Self-Catering

In remote places or on long bus trips it helps to have emergency rations such as instant noodles, dried fruit, soup extract, nuts and chocolate. All this stuff is very cheap in China – railway and bus stations are good places to stock up.

The Chinese can obtain rice and other grains with ration coupons (*yōuhuì juàn*), which are not issued to foreigners. These days, few things are actually rationed and the coupons are used mainly for getting a discount.

Food Vocabulary

At the Restaurant The following is a list of Chinese dishes and foodstuffs:

restaurant
  cāntīng
  餐厅
I'm vegetarian.
  Wǒ chī sù.
  我吃素
menu
  cài dān
  菜单
bill (cheque)
  máidān or jiézhàng
  买单/结帐
set meal (no menu)
  tàocān
  套餐
to eat/let's eat
  chī fàn
  吃饭
chopsticks
  kuàizi
  筷子
knife & fork
  dāochā
  刀叉
spoon
  tiáogēng or tāngchǐ
  调羹/汤匙

Rice & Bread

steamed rice
  mǐfàn
  米饭
watery rice porridge
  xīfàn or zhōu
  稀饭
rice noodles
  mǐfěn
  米粉
fried roll
  yínsī juǎn
  银丝卷
steamed buns
  mántóu
  馒头
steamed meat buns
  bāozi
  包子
fried breadstick
  yóutiáo
  油条
boiled dumplings
  jiǎozi
  饺子
prawn cracker
  lóngxiā piàn
  龙虾片

Vegetables

fried rice with vegetables
  shūcài chǎofàn
  蔬菜炒饭
fried noodles with vegetables
  shūcài chǎomiàn
  蔬菜炒面
spicy peanuts
  wǔxiāng huāshēng mǐ
  五香花生米
fried peanuts
  yóuzhà huāshēng mǐ
  油炸花生米
spiced cold vegetables
  liángbàn shíjǐn
  凉拌什锦
Chinese salad
  jiācháng liángcài
  家常凉菜

fried rape in oyster sauce
háoyóu pácài dǎn
蚝油扒菜胆

fried rape with mushrooms
dōnggū pácài dǎn
冬菇扒菜胆

fried bean curd in oyster sauce
háoyóu dòufǔ
蚝油豆腐

spicy hot bean curd
mápó dòufǔ
麻婆豆腐

bean curd casserole
shāguō dòufǔ
沙锅豆腐

bean curd & mushrooms
mógū dòufǔ
磨菇豆腐

garlic & morning glory
dàsuàn kōngxīn cài
大蒜空心菜

fried garlic
sù chǎo dàsuàn
素炒大蒜

fried eggplant
sùshāo qiézi
素烧茄子

fried bean sprouts
sù chǎo dòuyá
素炒豆芽

fried green vegetables
sù chǎo qīngcài
素炒青菜

fried green beans
sù chǎo biǎndòu
素炒扁豆

fried cauliflower & tomato
fānqié càihuā
炒蕃茄菜花

broiled mushroom
sù chǎo xiānme
素炒鲜蘑

black fungus & mushroom
mù'ěr huákǒu mó
木耳滑口磨

fried white radish patty
luóbo gāo
萝卜糕

assorted hors d'oeuvres
shíjǐn pīnpán
什锦拼盘

assorted vegetarian food
sù shíjǐn
素什锦

Eggs

preserved egg
sōnghuā dàn
松花蛋

fried rice with egg
jīdàn chǎofàn
鸡蛋炒饭

fried tomato & eggs
xīhóngshì chǎo jīdàn
西红柿炒鸡蛋

egg & flour omelette
jiān bǐng
煎饼

Beef

fried rice with beef
niúròusī chǎofàn
牛肉丝炒饭

noodles with beef (soupy)
niúròu tāng miàn
牛肉汤面

spiced noodles with beef
niúròu gān miàn
牛肉干面

fried noodles with beef
niúròu chǎomiàn
牛肉炒面

beef with white rice
niúròu fàn
牛肉饭

beef platter
niúròu tiěbǎn
牛肉铁板

beef with oyster sauce
háoyóu niúròu
蚝油牛肉

beef braised in soy sauce
hóngshāo niúròu
红烧牛肉

beef with tomatoes
fānqié niúròu piàn
蕃茄牛肉片

beef with green peppers
qīngjiāo niúròu piàn
青椒牛肉片

beef curry & rice
  gālí niúròu fàn
  咖哩牛肉饭
beef curry & noodles
  gālí niúròu miàn
  咖哩牛肉面

Chicken

fried rice with chicken
  jīsī chǎofàn
  鸡丝炒饭
noodles with chicken (soupy)
  jīsī tāng miàn
  鸡丝汤面
fried noodles with chicken
  jīsī chǎomiàn
  鸡丝炒面
chicken leg with white rice
  jītuǐ fàn
  鸡腿饭
spicy hot chicken & peanuts
  gōngbào jīdīng
  宫爆鸡丁
fruit kernel with chicken
  guǒwèi jīdīng
  果味鸡丁
sweet & sour chicken
  tángcù jīdīng
  糖醋鸡丁
sauteed spicy chicken pieces
  làzi jīdīng
  辣子鸡丁
sauteed chicken with green peppers
  jiàngbào jīdīng
  酱爆鸡丁
chicken slices in tomato sauce
  fānqié jīdīng
  蕃茄鸡丁
mushrooms & chicken
  cǎomó jīdīng
  草蘑鸡丁
chicken pieces in oyster sauce
  háoyóu jīdīng
  蚝油鸡丁
chicken braised in soy sauce
  hóngshāo jīkuài
  红烧鸡块
sauteed chicken with water chestnuts
  nánjiè jīpiàn
  南芥鸡片

sliced chicken with crispy rice
  jīpiàn guōbā
  鸡片锅巴
chicken curry
  gālí jīròu
  咖哩鸡肉
chicken curry & rice
  gālí jīròu fàn
  咖哩鸡肉饭
chicken curry & noodles
  gālí jīròu miàn
  咖哩鸡肉面

Duck

Beijing Duck
  běijīng kǎoyā
  北京烤鸭
duck with white rice
  yāròu fàn
  鸭肉饭
duck with noodles
  yāròu miàn
  鸭肉面
duck with fried noodles
  yāròu chǎomiàn
  鸭肉炒面

Pork

pork chop with white rice
  páigǔ fàn
  排骨饭
fried rice with pork
  ròusī chǎofàn
  肉丝炒饭
fried noodles with pork
  ròusī chǎomiàn
  肉丝炒面
pork & mustard greens
  zhàcài ròusī
  榨菜肉丝
noodles, pork & mustard greens
  zhàcài ròusī miàn
  榨菜肉丝面
pork with crispy rice
  ròupiàn guōbā
  肉片锅巴
sweet & sour pork fillet
  tángcù lǐjī
  糖醋里肌

pork fillet in white sauce
huáliū lǐjī
滑溜里肌

shredded pork fillet
chǎo lǐjī sī
炒里肌丝

spicy hot pork pieces
gōngbào ròudīng
宫爆肉丁

fried black pork pieces
yuánbào lǐjī
芫爆里肌

sauteed diced pork & soy sauce
jiàngbào ròudīng
酱爆肉丁

spicy pork cubelets
làzi ròudīng
辣子肉丁

pork cubelets & cucumber
huángguā ròudīng
黄瓜肉丁

golden pork slices
jīnyín ròusī
金银肉丝

sauteed shredded pork
qīngchǎo ròusī
清炒肉丝

shredded pork & hot sauce
yúxiāng ròusī
鱼香肉丝

shredded pork & green peppers
qīngjiāo ròusī
青椒肉丝

shredded pork & bamboo shoots
dōngsǔn ròusī
冬笋肉丝

shredded pork & green beans
biǎndòu ròusī
扁豆肉丝

pork with oyster sauce
háoyóu ròusī
蚝油肉丝

boiled pork slices
shuǐzhǔ ròupiàn
水煮肉片

pork, eggs & black fungus
mùxū ròu
木须肉

pork & fried onions
yángcōng chǎo ròupiàn
洋葱炒肉片

fried rice (assorted)
shíjǐn chǎofàn
什锦炒饭

fried rice Canton-style
guǎngzhōu chǎofàn
广州炒饭

Seafood

fried rice with shrimp
xiārén chǎofàn
虾仁炒饭

fried noodles with shrimp
xiārén chǎomiàn
虾仁炒面

diced shrimp with peanuts
gōngbào xiārén
宫爆虾仁

sauteed shrimp
qīngchǎo xiārén
清炒虾仁

deep-fried shrimp
zhá xiārén
炸虾仁

fried shrimp with mushroom
xiānmó xiārén
鲜蘑虾仁

squid with crispy rice
yóuyú guōbā
鱿鱼锅巴

sweet & sour squid roll
suānlà yóuyú juàn
酸辣鱿鱼卷

fish braised in soy sauce
hóngshāo yú
红烧鱼

braised sea cucumber
hóngshāo hǎishēn
红烧海参

clams
gé
蛤

crab
pángxiè
螃蟹

lobster
lóngxiā
龙虾

Soup

combination seafood soup
sān xiān tāng
三鲜汤

squid soup
yóuyú tāng
鱿鱼汤

sweet & sour soup
suānlà tāng
酸辣汤

tomato & egg soup
xīhóngshì dàn tāng
西红柿蛋汤

corn & egg thick soup
fènghuáng lìmǐ gēng
凤凰栗米羹

egg & vegetable soup
dànhuā tāng
蛋花汤

mushroom & egg soup
mógu dànhuā tāng
蘑菇蛋花汤

fresh fish soup
shēng yú tāng
生鱼汤

vegetable soup
shūcài tāng
蔬菜汤

cream of tomato soup
nǎiyóu fānqié tāng
奶油蕃茄汤

cream of mushroom soup
nǎiyóu xiānmó tāng
奶油鲜蘑汤

pickled mustard green soup
zhàcài tāng
榨菜汤

bean curd & vegetable soup
dòufǔ cài tāng
豆腐菜汤

wanton soup
húndùn tāng
馄饨汤

clear soup
qīng tāng
清汤

noodle soup
tāng miàn
汤面

Miscellanea & Exotica

kebab
ròu chuàn
肉串

goat/mutton
yáng ròu
羊肉

dog meat
gǒu ròu
狗肉

deer meat (venison)
lùròu
鹿肉

snake
shé ròu
蛇肉

rat meat
lǎoshǔ ròu
老鼠肉

pangolin
chuān shānjiǎ
穿山甲

frog
qīngwā
青蛙

eel
shàn yú
鳝鱼

turtle
hǎiguī
海龟

Mongolian hotpot
huǒguō
火锅

Condiments

garlic
dàsuàn
大蒜

black pepper
hújiāo
胡椒

hot pepper
làjiāo
辣椒

hot sauce
làjiāo jiàng
辣椒酱

ketchup
  fānqié jiàng
  蕃茄酱
salt
  yán
  盐
MSG
  wèijīng
  味精
soy sauce
  jiàng yóu
  酱油
vinegar
  cù
  醋
sesame seed oil
  zhīmá yóu
  芝麻油
butter
  huáng yóu
  黄油
sugar
  táng
  糖
jam
  guǒ jiàng
  果酱
honey
  fēngmì
  蜂蜜

DRINKS
Nonalcoholic Drinks

Tea is the most commonly served brew in the PRC; it didn't originate in China but in South-East Asia. Indian tea is available only in international supermarkets. Coffee addicts will be pleased to find familiar Western brands (Maxwell House, Nescafé) for sale almost everywhere.

Coca-Cola, first introduced into China by American soldiers in 1927, is now produced in China. Chinese attempts at making similar brews include TianFu Cola, which has a recipe based on the root of herbaceous peony. Fanta and Sprite are widely available, both genuine and copycat versions. Sugary Chinese soft drinks are cheap and sold everywhere – some are so sweet they'll turn your teeth inside out. Jianlibao is a Chinese soft

drink made with honey rather than sugar – one of the better brands. Lychee-flavoured carbonated drinks are unique to China and get rave reviews from foreigners. Fresh milk is rare but you can buy imported UHT milk at high prices from Western-style supermarkets in Beijing, Shanghai, Shenzhen and Guangzhou.

A surprising treat is fresh sweet yoghurt, available in many of the more developed parts of China. It's typically sold in what looks like small milk bottles and is consumed by drinking with a straw rather than eating with a spoon. This excellent stuff would make a great breakfast if you could find some decent bread to go with it.

Alcohol

If tea is the most popular drink in the PRC, then beer must be number two. By any standards the top brands are great stuff. The best known is Tsingtao (Qingdao), made with a mineral water which gives it its sparkling quality. It's really a German beer since the town of Qingdao (formerly spelled 'Tsingtao'), where it's made, was once a German concession and the Chinese inherited the brewery. Experts in these matters claim that draft Tsingtao tastes much better than the bottled stuff. Local brews are found in all the major cities of China – notable ones include Zhujiang in Guangzhou and Yanjing in Beijing. San Miguel has a brewery in Guangzhou, so you can enjoy this 'imported' beer at Chinese prices. Real Western imports are sold in Friendship Stores and five-star hotels at five-star prices.

China has probably cultivated vines and produced wine for over 4000 years. Chinese wine-producing techniques differ from those of the West. Quality-conscious wine producers in Western countries work on the idea that the lower the yield the higher the quality of the wine produced. But Chinese workers cultivate every possible sq cm of earth; they encourage their vines to yield heavily and also plant peanuts between the rows of vines as a cover crop for half the year. The peanuts sap much of the nutrient from the soil, and in cooler years the large grape crop fails to ripen sufficiently to produce a wine comparable to Western ones.

Western producers try to prevent oxidation in the wines, but oxidation produces a flavour which the Chinese find desirable and go to great ends to achieve. The Chinese are also keen on wines with different herbs and other materials soaked in them, which they drink for their health and for restorative or aphrodisiac qualities.

The word 'wine' gets rather loosely translated – many Chinese 'wines' are in fact spirits. Rice wine – a favourite with Chinese alcoholics due to its low price – is intended mainly for cooking rather than drinking. Hejie Jiu (lizard wine) is produced in the southern province of Guangxi; each bottle contains one dead lizard suspended perpendicularly in the clear liquid. Wine with dead bees or pickled snakes is also desirable for its alleged tonic properties – in general, the more poisonous the creature, the more potent the tonic effects.

Tibetans have an interesting brew called *chang*, a beer or spirit made from barley. Mongolians serve sour-tasting *koumiss*, made of fermented mare's milk with lots of salt added – most Westerners gag on the stuff. *Maotai*, a favourite of the Chinese, is a spirit made from sorghum (a type of millet) and is used for toasts at banquets – it tastes rather like rubbing alcohol and makes a good substitute for petrol or paint thinner.

Outside the more sophisticated major cities, Chinese women don't drink (except beer) in public – women who hit the booze are regarded as prostitutes. However, Western women can easily violate this social taboo without unpleasant consequences – the Chinese expect weirdness from Westerners anyway. As a rule Chinese men are not big drinkers, but toasts are obligatory at banquets – if you really can't drink, fill your wine glass with tea and say you have a bad stomach. In spite of all the toasting and beer drinking, public drunkenness is strongly frowned upon.

Imported booze – like XO, Johnny Walker, Kahlua, Napoleon Augier Cognac – is highly prized by the Chinese for its prestige value rather than exquisite taste. The snob appeal plus steep import taxes translates into absurdly high prices – don't walk into a hotel bar and order this stuff unless you've brought a wheelbarrow full of cash. If you can't live without Western spirits, be sure to take advantage of your two-litre duty-free allowance on entry to China.

Drinks Vocabulary

fizzy drink (soda)
　qìshuǐ
　汽酒
Coca-Cola
　kěkǒu kělè
　可口可乐
tea
　chá
　茶
coffee
　kāfēi
　咖啡
water
　kāi shuǐ
　开水
mineral water
　kuàng quán shuǐ
　矿泉水
hot water (for tea)
　báikāishuǐ
　白开水
ice cold
　bīngde
　冰的
fruit juice
　guǒzhī
　果汁
beer
　píjiǔ
　啤酒
red grape wine
　hóng pútáo jiǔ
　红葡萄酒
white grape wine
　bái pútáo jiǔ
　白葡萄酒
rice wine
　mǐ jiǔ
　米酒

Chinese Cuisine

China offers a diverse range of culinary styles, and between them almost everything edible ends up in the pot. As the Cantonese proudly declaim: 'If it's got four legs and it's not a table, we'll eat it'. For the most part, however, the pangolins, raw monkey brains and bear paws of legend rarely find their way on to the tables of Chinese restaurants (very few people can afford such 'delicacies'), and the Chinese trick is doing ingenious things with a limited number of basic ingredients.

Chinese cuisine can broadly be divided into four major regional categories which follow a north, south, east, west orientation: Beijing (sometimes called Mandarin) and Shandong, Cantonese and Chaozhou, Eastern (Shanghainese and Jiangzhenese), and Sichuan. There is, however, much disagreement about just what is unique about each regional cuisine.

Sichuan

This is the hottest of the four major categories – it's great stuff if you like spicy food, but keep the drinking water handy. Specialities include frogs' legs and smoked duck – the duck is cooked in peppercorns, marinated in wine for 24 hours, covered in tea leaves and cooked again over a charcoal fire. Other dishes to try are shrimps with salt and garlic, dried chilli beef, bean curd with chilli, fish in spicy bean sauce and aubergines in garlic.

Undoubtedly the most famous Sichuan dish (internationally anyway) is *gōngbǎo jīdīng*, chicken fried with peanuts and chilli pepper. It has become a standard Chinese dish and can be found in restaurants all over China.

Gongbao jiding, chicken with peanuts and chilli pepper, is the most well known Sichuan dish.

Beijing & Shandong

Beijing and Shandong cuisine comes from one of the coldest parts of China. Since this is China's wheat belt, steamed bread and noodles are the staples rather than rice. Basically, northern cuisine combines very simple cooking techniques (steaming and stir-frying) with the sophistication of imperial dishes.

China's most famous northern speciality is Beijing duck, served with pancakes and plum sauce. Another speciality is beggar's chicken, supposedly created by a beggar who stole a chicken earmarked for the emperor and secretly cooked it buried underground (the chicken that is, not the beggar) – the dish is wrapped in lotus leaves and baked all day in hot ashes.

Another speciality is Mongolian hotpot, which throws together meats and vegetables and cooks them in a simmering broth over a burner on the dining table. It's a winter dish. Mongolian barbecue is a variation featuring a slowly roasted goat or lamb carcass along with a hotpot full of spicy vegetables. If you've eaten the Korean dish *bulgogi*, you've got the idea. A warning though – the price of hotpot depends entirely on the ingredients. It can cost Y20 or Y200 depending on what's thrown into the pot, so ask first to avoid unpleasant surprises.

Top: Beijing duck, with pancakes and plum sauce, China's famous northern dish.

Bottom: Mongolian hotpot – meat and vegetables cooked in a simmering broth.

Cantonese & Chaozhou

This is southern Chinese cooking – lots of steaming, boiling and stir-frying. It's the best of the bunch if you're worried about cholesterol and coronaries, as it uses the least amount of oil. It's lightly cooked and not as highly spiced as the other three, with lots of seafood, vegetables, roast pork, chicken, steamed fish and fried rice.

Dim sum is a snack-like variation, served for breakfast and lunch (but never dinner) and consisting of all sorts of little delicacies served from pushcarts wheeled around the restaurant floor. It's justifiably famous and something you should experience at least once, and like many visitors you'll probably get addicted.

The Cantonese are famous for making just about anything palatable: specialities are abalone, dried squid, 1000-year-old eggs (traditionally made by soaking eggs in horse's urine), shark's fin soup, snake soup and dog stew. Other culinary exotica include anteaters, pangolins, cats, rats, owls, monkeys, turtles and frogs. Despite the unusual ingredients, Cantonese food has long been a favourite of Westerners – Chinese restaurants around the world often include a wide selection of Cantonese dishes on the menu.

Top: Dried squid is a popular item in southern cooking. Here it's cooked in curry sauce.

Bottom: Shark's fin soup, a Cantonese speciality.

Eastern

The cuisine of eastern China is probably the least understood of China's regional cuisines – by foreigners at least. It encompasses Shanghai, Zhejiang, Fujian and the so-called lower-Yangzi region of Jiangsu. It is undoubtedly the most diverse of China's regional cuisines and has produced many famous dishes. Wuxi spare ribs is one to look out for: it features the common eastern technique of 'red cooking' in a stock of soy sauce and rice wine to produce a tasty stew. Soups are a celebrated aspect of eastern cuisine, and there are hundreds of varieties. In the coastal regions, seafood is an important ingredient and is generally cooked simply to enhance the natural taste.

It is true that stir-fried dishes in this part of China (famously Shanghai) tend to overdo the oil or lard, but in many restaurants nowadays this is becoming less the case. Cooking standards in major eastern cities have improved immensely over the last 10 years or so, and anyone with some money to throw around can enjoy some of the best cooking in China.

Top: Fresh seafood is an important ingredient in Eastern cuisine.

Bottom: Wuxi spare ribs are cooked in a stock of soy sauce and rice wine.

whisky
wēishìjì jiǔ
威士忌酒

vodka
fútèjiā jiǔ
伏特加酒

Maotai spirit
máotáijiǔ
茅台酒

TOBACCO

The Chinese government is beginning to make good on a long-held promise to do something about public smoking, banning cigarettes in airports and many railway stations. Overall, however, the authorities have a real battle on their hands. In rural China smokers are very cavalier towards non-smokers, and buses and trains are generally thick with wafting cigarette smoke – smokers in buses often simply toss their burning butts into the aisles where they continue to smoulder and occasionally start fires. Hotel rooms are often covered in cigarette burns (it's amazing more hotels don't burn down) – many Chinese guests grind their cigarettes into the carpet.

As with drinking hard liquor, smoking in public has traditionally been a male activity, though more women are starting to smoke. If you cannot tolerate smoking in crowded public places like buses and restaurants, you will either have to leave the country or buy a gas mask – the Chinese will be positively offended if you tell them not to smoke.

For smokers, on the other hand, the good news is that cigarettes are cheap (around US$1 per pack for imported brands such as Marlboro and 555) and you can smoke almost anywhere. Chinese cigarettes are a mixed bag. The cheapest brands can cost less than Y1, while the best brands (such as Red Pagoda Mountain – *hongtashan*) cost double the most expensive imported cigarettes. Curiously, regardless of the price, they all taste very much the same.

ENTERTAINMENT

As an all other fronts, China's entertainment options are improving rapidly. On the nightlife front, bars, discos and karaoke parlours are springing up in all the major cities. More cultural entertainments are being held too.

Cinemas

Upmarket hotels have in-house English-language movies, but elsewhere the situation is fairly dire. Foreign movies are dubbed into Chinese, and Chinese movies – well, they're in Chinese. Hong Kong movies at least usually have inventive English subtitles – 'she my sister you call watermelon fool!' – and can be entertaining when you are in the mood for historical kung fu epics and fast-paced cop dramas.

Discos

Discos have taken China by storm. In rural China, not many Chinese are really sure of the appropriate moves to make to a pounding bass, and it's not unusual to see huge crowds dancing in formation, everyone looking over their shoulders to see what everyone else is doing. But in cities like Guangzhou, Shanghai and Beijing, there are disco complexes (look out for the JJ chain) where the music and the dancers are surprisingly hip to the latest Western trends. See the entertainment entries for Guangzhou, Shanghai and Beijing for some suggestions.

Karaoke

If you don't know what karaoke is by now, China will be a rude awakening. This is *the* entertainment option for moneyed Chinese. Even the plebs are leaping in, yodelling in search of a melody at roadside karaoke stalls. The CCP propaganda department has weighed in with suitably proletarian sing-along hits, Chinese businesspeople from Hainan to Heilongjiang slug back the XO and caterwaul with hostesses on their knees, and no doubt Party leaders get together for wine and songs after a hard day at the office sentencing dissidents and keeping the economic miracle on track. 'Let's get together and sing some songs' is what Chinese say to each other when it's time to unwind.

Much maligned, karaoke can be fun with

◉◉◉◉◉◉◉◉◉◉◉◉◉◉◉◉◉◉◉◉◉◉◉◉◉◉◉◉◉◉◉◉◉◉◉◉

Karaoke

Nowadays karaoke requires little in the way of introduction, even in the benighted West. As most people now know, it is of Japanese origin: a combination of the words *kara*, meaning 'empty', and *oke*, a Japanese contraction of the English word 'orchestra'. The idea is simple enough: the voice track is removed from a particular song, providing the audience with a do-it-yourself pop hit. The results will probably leave you with the impression that 99% of Chinese are completely tone deaf.

From small-time beginnings in Japan, karaoke first took Taiwan and Hong Kong by storm, and then inevitably slipped into China. Today it has become one of the main recreational activities for the Chinese. It's easy to recognise a karaoke parlour: they are usually lit up in neon and have a Chinese sign with the characters for *kālā* (a phonetic rendering of the Japanese) followed by the English letters 'OK'. Sometimes clubs can be identified by the acronym KTV – 'karaoke television'. The latter normally have private booths.

It's actually worth checking out a karaoke parlour or two while you are in China, though they are generally not cheap. There are two menus: one for the drinks and one for the songs. Don't expect much in the way of English songs, though you might get a Carpenters track or two (Rod Stewart's *I Am Sailing* is a popular English number). It usually costs around Y5 to get up on stage and sing a song and the Chinese clamour for the opportunity. It doesn't matter how badly you sing. You'll get a polite round of applause from the audience when you finish, probably a rapturous round of applause if you are a foreigner.

A recent development is the poor-person's karaoke bar, a TV (a video with a bouncing ball following the lyrics) set up by the roadside, where you pay a few jiao to sing into a small PA system. The Chinese government, with characteristic market savvy, has responded to the karaoke boom by setting up a department to produce karaoke numbers that give the public an opportunity to musically express their burning ardour for the Party. Perversely, everyone seems to prefer singing Rod Stewart numbers and the latest Taiwanese and Hong Kong pop hits. ■

◉◉◉◉◉◉◉◉◉◉◉◉◉◉◉◉◉◉◉◉◉◉◉◉◉◉◉◉◉◉◉◉◉◉◉◉

a few drinks under your belt and with the right people. It's not unusual for inebriated Westerners who claim to hate karaoke to have to be pried loose from the microphone once they get going.

Warning One thing to watch out for in karaoke parlours is overpricing and rip-offs. This is not a problem in most places, but in some heavily touristed areas young women work as touts, drawing men into clubs and then fleecing them. It is not sensible to accept invitations to clubs from young women on the streets. In clubs themselves, if you invite a hostess to sit with you it is going to cost money. The same rules apply in China as anywhere else in the world of paid entertainment and sex.

THINGS TO BUY

China is in the grip of a consumer revolution. Gone are the days of ration cards and empty department stores. The new China looks

more and more like Hong Kong by the day. It's still sensible to save your shopping for electronic consumer items for Hong Kong and Singapore, however. For most visitors, shopping in China is restricted to souvenirs.

Shopping Venues

With department stores and shops springing up all over urban China, it is difficult to make specific recommendations. Cities like Guangzhou, Shanghai and Beijing are obviously the best places to shop for Chinese souvenirs, simply because there will be a wide range of products brought together under the single roof of a large store.

Hong Kong Emporia There are some very good shops in Hong Kong dealing in products from China. Quality standards tend to be high and prices, while higher than those in China, are reasonable. See the Hong Kong chapter for details.

Friendship Stores Friendship Stores were set up to cater to foreign needs back in the days when ordinary Chinese basically had no access to imported luxury items. It is a measure of just how far China has come when you think how, just 10 years ago, many Chinese dreamed of simply getting through the doors of a Friendship Store. Nowadays, Friendship Stores are an anachronism and have become one of the many chains of department stores stacked to the rafters with consumer goodies.

For foreign visitors, Friendship Stores are still reasonably good places to scout for souvenirs. In some stores, it is even possible to arrange for postage to your home country.

Department Stores The regular Chinese department stores have a rich stock of cheap, everyday consumer items. They're well worth your time.

Hotel Shops Hotel Shops are still the best places to pick up Western and Japanese film and imported magazines among other things. On the whole, they tend to be expensive places for souvenir shopping but this does depend a lot on the hotel.

Street Markets Blankets spread on the pavement and pushcarts in the alleys – this is where you find the lowest prices. All sales are final, forget warranties and no, they don't accept American Express. Nevertheless, the markets are interesting – be prepared to bargain hard.

Antiques

Many of the Friendship Stores have antique sections and some cities have antique shops, but in the case of genuine antiques you can forget about bargains. Chinese are very savvy when it comes to their own cultural heritage. Only antiques which have been cleared for sale to foreigners may be taken out of the country. When you buy an item over 100 years old it will come with an official red wax seal attached. This seal does *not* necessarily indicate that the item is an antique though. A Canadian who bought

---

More Than Meets the Eye...

Once upon a time in China you got what you paid for. If the sales clerk said it was top-quality jade then it was top-quality jade. Times have changed – now there are all sorts of cheap forgeries and imitations about, from Tibetan jewellery to Qing coins, phoney Marlboro cigarettes, fake Sony Walkmans (complete with fake Maxell cassette tapes), imitation Rolex watches, even fake Garden biscuits (Garden Bakeries is Hong Kong's biggest seller of bread, cakes and biscuits).

China has implemented a major crackdown on counterfeiting, though efforts have been directed mainly towards items that flout international intellectual copyright laws: CDs, pirated software and the like. It's a big country, however, and there are still a lot of illegal consumer goods out there.

At the same time, the government has to contend with more localised problems: the manufacture of fake railway tickets, fake lottery tickets and fake Y100 RMB notes. Cadres frequently pad their expense accounts with fake receipts, one of the many reasons why state-run companies are losing money.

Take care buying anything in China, particularly if you are forking out a large sum for it. Watch out for counterfeit Y100 notes. And if you are after genuine antiques, try to get an official certificate of verification – just make sure the ink is dry. ∎

'real' jade for Y1500 at a Friendship Store in Guilin later discovered in Hong Kong that it was a plastic fake. After six months of copious correspondence and investigation, the Guilin Tourism Bureau refunded the money and closed down the offending store. You'll also get a receipt of sale, which you must show to customs when you leave the country; otherwise the antique will be confiscated. Imitation antiques are sold everywhere. Some museum shops sell replicas, usually at extravagant prices.

Stamps & Coins

China issues quite an array of beautiful stamps – generally sold at post offices in the hotels. Outside many of the post offices you'll find amateur philatelists with books full of stamps for sale; it can be extraordinarily hard bargaining with these guys! Stamps issued during the Cultural Revolution make interesting souvenirs. Old coins are often sold at major tourist sites; many are forgeries.

Paintings & Scrolls

Watercolours, oils, woodblock prints, calligraphy - there is a lot of art for sale in China. Tourist centres like Guilin, Suzhou, Beijing and Shanghai are good places to look out for paintings. Prices are usually very reasonable – even some of the high-quality work available in galleries. Scrolls selling for Y200 are usually rubbish but remain popular purchases all the same.

Oddities

If plaster statues are to your liking, the opportunities to stock up in China are abundant. Fat buddhas appear everywhere, and 60-cm-high Venus de Milos and multi-armed gods with flashing lights are not uncommon.

Lots of shops sell medicinal herbs and spices. Export tea is sold in extravagantly decorated tins – you can often get a better deal buying the same thing in the railway stations.

Getting There & Away

China has 115 ports of entry and exit, offering you a wide choice of travel options. However, the majority of travellers still make their approach and getaway via Hong Kong.

The situation with travelling to or from Hong Kong is so different from the rest of China that it's dealt with separately. See the Hong Kong & Macau chapter of this book for details.

AIR

The air ticket alone can gouge a great slice out of anyone's budget, but you can reduce the cost by finding discounted fares. As a general rule, tickets to Hong Kong are cheaper than tickets directly to China. While Hong Kong is a great place to find cheap air fares, China is not – tickets purchased within China are invariably more expensive (usually much more) than those purchased elsewhere. This reflects the lack of free-market competition in China and the government's general policy of making foreigners pay double for air tickets.

Bargain Hunting

When you're looking for bargain air fares, you have to go to a travel agent rather than directly to the airline, which can only sell fares at the full list price. But watch out – many discount tickets have restrictions (the journey must be completed in 60 days, no flights during holidays, and so on). It's important to ask the agent what restrictions, if any, apply to your ticket.

If you purchase a ticket and later want to make changes to your route or get a refund, you need to see the original travel agent. Airlines only issue refunds to the purchaser of a ticket – if you bought from a travel agent, then that agent is the purchaser, not you. Many travellers do in fact change their route halfway through their trip, so think carefully about buying a ticket which is not easily refunded.

APEX (Advance Purchase Excursion) fares are relatively cheap, but you are locked into a fairly rigid schedule. Such tickets must be purchased two or three weeks ahead of departure, do not permit stopovers and may have minimum and maximum stays as well as fixed departure and return dates. Unless you definitely must return at a certain time, it's best to purchase APEX tickets on a one-way basis only. There are stiff cancellation fees if you try to get a refund on an APEX ticket.

There are plenty of discount tickets which are valid for 12 months, allowing multiple stopovers with open dates. These tickets allow maximum flexibility. Few such tickets are available to China itself, but many are available to Hong Kong. All sorts of special packages are available that allow you a prolonged stopover in Hong Kong on the way to somewhere else. The Hong Kong stopover may cost nothing, or perhaps US$50 extra. Return-trip tickets are usually significantly cheaper than one way.

Open-jaw tickets are a variation on the theme. For example, such a ticket might allow you to fly from your home country to Hong Kong and fly back from Beijing. This saves you the time and expense of backtracking to Hong Kong to catch your return flight.

Round-the-World (RTW) tickets are usually offered by an airline or combination of airlines and let you take your time (six months to a year) moving from point to point on their routes for the price of one ticket. Sometimes this works out to be cheaper than buying all the tickets separately as you go along, but often it's more expensive. The main restriction is that you have to keep moving in the same direction; a drawback is that because you are usually booking individual flights as you go and can't switch carriers, you can get caught out by flight availabilities and have to spend more or less time in a place than you want.

Some airlines offer student discounts on

149

their tickets of up to 25% to student card holders. Besides having an International Student Identity Card (ISIC), an official-looking letter from your school is also required by some airlines. Many airlines also require you to be age 26 or younger to qualify for a discount. These discounts are generally only available on ordinary economy-class fares. You wouldn't get one, for instance, on an APEX or a RTW ticket since these are already discounted.

Frequent-flier deals can earn you a free air ticket or other goodies if you accumulate enough mileage with one airline. First, you must apply to the airline for a frequent-flier account number (some airlines will issue these on the spot or by telephone if you call their head office). Every time you buy an air ticket and/or check in for your flight, you must inform the clerk of your frequent-flier account number, or else you won't get credit. Save your tickets and boarding passes, since it's not uncommon for the airlines to fail to give proper credit. You should receive monthly statements by post informing you how much mileage you've accumulated. Once you've accumulated sufficient mileage to qualify for freebies, you are supposed to receive vouchers by mail. Many airlines have 'blackout periods', or times when you cannot fly for free (Christmas and Chinese New Year are good examples). The worst thing about frequent-flier programs is that these tend to lock you into one airline, and that airline may not always have the cheapest fares or most convenient flight schedule.

Airlines usually carry babies up to two years of age at 10% of the relevant adult fare, a few may carry them free of charge. Reputable international airlines usually provide nappies (diapers), tissues, talcum and all the other paraphernalia needed to keep babies clean, dry and relatively happy. For children between the ages of four and 12 the fare on international flights is usually 50% of the regular fare or 67% of a discounted fare. These days most fares are likely to be discounted.

One thing to avoid are 'back-to-front' tickets. These are best explained by example.

If you are living in Japan (where tickets are very expensive) and you want to fly to Hong Kong (where tickets are much cheaper), you can pay by cheque or credit card and have a friend or travel agent in Hong Kong mail the ticket to you. The problem is that the airlines have computers and will know that the ticket was issued in Hong Kong rather than Japan and they will refuse to honour it. Consumer groups have filed lawsuits over this practice with mixed results, but in most countries the law protects the airlines, not consumers. In short, the ticket is only valid starting from the country where it was issued. The only exception is if you pay the full fare, thus foregoing any possible discounts that Hong Kong travel agents can offer.

Courier flights can be a bargain if you're fortunate enough to find one. The way it works is that an air freight company takes over your entire checked baggage allowance. You are permitted to bring along a carry-on bag, but that's all. In return, you get a steeply discounted ticket. These arrangements usually have to be made a month or more in advance and are only available on certain routes. You aren't likely to find one to China, but you could possibly get one to Hong Kong. Another consideration – such tickets are sold for a fixed date and schedule changes can be difficult or impossible to make. Courier flights are occasionally advertised in the newspapers, or contact airfreight companies listed in the phone book.

Airlines

The attitude of the Chinese government has always been to keep lucrative business for itself. Foreigners are just thrown a few scraps, and even this is done grudgingly. This attitude certainly applies to the airline business – very few foreign carriers are permitted to fly into China, and even this was only reluctantly conceded so that China's own airlines could gain access to foreign markets.

The Civil Aviation Administration of China (zhōngguó mínháng), also known as CAAC, is the official flag carrier of the PRC. (See the Getting Around chapter for more information on CAAC.) On most international routes, CAAC is known as Air China. Despite recent improvements, Air China's standard of service is still considerably lower than most international airlines.

Cathay Pacific (*guótài hángkōng*) is a Hong Kong-based company partly owned by British Airways and (recently) CAAC. Cathay used to be *the* major foreign player in the China market but has seen its market share reduced in recent years. These days, Cathay doesn't fly into China under its own name, but runs a joint venture with CAAC to operate Hong Kong's other airline, Dragonair.

Dragonair (*gǎnglóng hángkōng*) started operations in 1985 with a single aircraft. Owned 100% by the PRC, there was much speculation that it would go bankrupt, and it probably would have if Cathay Pacific hadn't bought into it in 1990. Cathay apparently did this to please the Chinese government and to gain air routes to China. Cathay's influence is certainly visible – these days Dragonair's service is top-notch and prices are lower than CAAC's.

As Dragonair is closely integrated with Cathay Pacific, you can book Dragonair flights from Cathay Pacific offices around the world. Also, you can book combined tickets – a seat from Beijing to Vancouver, for example, flying Dragonair from Beijing to Hong Kong and then switching to a Cathay Pacific flight to Canada. Both flights can be included on a single ticket and luggage checked all the way through. If you're a member of Cathay's frequent-flier program (known as the 'Marco Polo Club'), flights on Dragonair can be credited to your mileage total.

To/From Australia
Australia is not a particularly cheap place to fly out of, but from time to time there are some good deals going. Shop around, as ticket prices vary.

The high season for most flights from Australia to Asia is from 22 November to 31 January; if you fly out during this period expect to pay more for your ticket.

Generally speaking, buying a round-trip air ticket works out cheaper than paying for separate one-way tickets for each stage of your journey, although return tickets are more expensive the longer their validity. Most return tickets to Asia have 28-day, 90-day or 12-month validity.

Cheap flights from Australia to China generally go via one of the South-East Asian capitals, such as Kuala Lumpur, Bangkok or Manila. If a long stopover between connections is necessary, transit accommodation is sometimes included in the price of the ticket, but if it's at your own expense it may work out cheaper buying a slightly dearer ticket.

Quite a few travel offices specialise in discount air tickets. Some travel agents, smaller ones particularly, advertise cheap air fares in the travel sections of weekend newspapers, such as *The Age* and the *Sydney Morning Herald*. Two well-known discounters are STA Travel and the Flight Centre. STA Travel has offices in all major cities and on many university campuses, but you don't have to be a student to use STA Travel's services. The Flight Centre has dozens of offices throughout Australia and New Zealand. Both STA Travel and the Flight Centre regularly publish brochures with their latest deals.

In general, the cheapest way into China is via Hong Kong. The minimum low-season one-way air fare from Australia to Hong Kong is about A$840, or A$1100 return, but flights are often heavily booked months in advance. Hong Kong is a convenient transit point for southern China, but too far south if you just want to get to Beijing or the north of the country.

Air China flies direct from Melbourne and Sydney to Beijing (stopping for a customs control check at Guangzhou Airport) for $A1100/1320 return low/high season.

Malaysia Airlines flies from Melbourne and Sydney for A$1300/1450 low/high season, but you will have to overnight at your own expense in Kuala Lumpur. Cathay Pacific and Qantas offer competitive fares and often have specials.

The departure tax from Australia is A$27 for passengers 12 years and over, and is now included in the price of the ticket so there is no additional charge at the airport.

To/From New Zealand

The Flight Centre has a large central office (☎ 309-6171) at 3A National Bank Tower, 205-225 Queen St, Auckland.

Singapore Airlines and Malaysia Airlines offer low-season return fares to Hong Kong for NZ$1345, and Qantas and Cathay Pacific offer fares from NZ$1400. At the time of writing, Garuda Airlines was offering the cheapest fare to Beijing, NZ$1360 round-trip during low season.

The departure tax from New Zealand is NZ$20. Children under two years of age are exempt.

To/From Europe

Western Europe Fares similar to those from London are available from other western European cities.

Austrian Airlines offers an open-jaw ticket that allows you to fly to Ürümqi (in China's Xinjiang Province), travel overland and fly back from Beijing.

The Netherlands, Belgium and Switzerland are good places for buying discount air fares. In Antwerp, WATS has been recommended. In Zurich, try SOF Travel and Sindbad. In Geneva, try Stohl Travel. In the Netherlands, NBBS is a reputable agency.

CAAC has flights between Beijing and Berlin, Frankfurt, London, Milan, Moscow, Paris, Rome, Stockholm and Zurich. Other international airlines operate flights out of Beijing but there are very few, if any, cut-rate fares from the Chinese end.

Eastern Europe Eastern European countries with functioning airlines that fly to China include Poland (LOT Polish Airlines) and Serbia (JAT Yugoslav Airlines). Both airlines are reputed to be cheap, but travellers have reported problems with lost luggage.

Russia Any air ticket you buy in Russia is likely to be expensive. You're not paying for fine service, you're paying for the lack of competition. Aeroflot is the only Russian

airline, and within Russia it's expensive. Ironically, if you purchase an Aeroflot ticket in some other country (like the UK), it can be very cheap. No matter what you pay for the ticket, be forewarned that Aeroflot has a reputation for frequent cancellations, poor safety and lost luggage.

A direct Moscow to Beijing flight costs US$1200, and foreigners are required to pay in dollars even for domestic flights within Russia – forget any rumours you've heard about cheap rouble-denominated tickets.

CAAC and Aeroflot have flights connecting Irkutsk (Siberia) with Shenyang (in China's Liaoning Province). Both airlines offer flights between Khabarovsk (Siberia) and Harbin (Heilongjiang Province). Both CAAC and Aeroflot offer weekly flights between Moscow and Ürümqi (via Novosibirsk) for US$260 – a tremendous saving!

To/From the UK

Air-ticket discounting is a long-running business in the UK. The various agents advertise their fares and there's nothing under-the-counter about it at all. There are a number of magazines in the UK which have good information about flights and agents. These include: *Trailfinder*, free from the Trailfinders Travel Centre in Earl's Court; and *Time Out*, a London weekly entertainment guide widely available in the UK.

The best deals are available in London. The danger with discounted tickets in the UK is that some of the 'bucket shops' are unsound. Sometimes these backstairs over-the-shop travel agents fold up and disappear after you've handed over the money and before you've got the tickets. Get the tickets when you hand over the cash.

Two reliable London bucket shops are Trailfinders Travel Centre in Earl's Court and STA Travel with several offices.

You can expect a one-way direct London-Hong Kong ticket to cost around £330 and a return ticket around £550 in the low season. Indirect flights are less expensive. The competitive nature of this route ensures that carriers bring out regular specials, with prices from as low as £420 return.

Air China has fares from London to Beijing for around £275 one-way and £450 return.

It's also possible to fly to Melbourne or Sydney via Hong Kong for as low as £385 one-way or £690 return.

To/From the USA

There are some very good open tickets which remain valid for six months or one year (opt for the latter unless you're sure) but don't lock you into any fixed dates of departure. For example, there are cheap tickets between the US west coast and Hong Kong, with stopovers in Japan, Korea or Taiwan, and for very little extra money the departure dates can be changed and you have one year to complete the journey.

However, be careful during the high season (summer and Chinese New Year) because seats will be hard to come by unless reserved months in advance.

Usually, and not surprisingly, the cheapest fares to China are offered by bucket shops owned by ethnic Chinese. San Francisco is the bucket shop capital of America, though some good deals can be found in Los Angeles, New York and other cities. Bucket shops can be found through the Yellow Pages or the major daily newspapers. Those listed in both Roman and Chinese scripts are usually discounters.

A more direct way is to wander around San Francisco's Chinatown, where most of the shops are located, especially in the Clay St and Waverly Place area. Many of these are staffed by recent arrivals from Hong Kong and Taiwan who may speak little English. Inquiries are best made in person, and be sure to compare prices, as cheating is not unknown.

It's not advisable to send money (even cheques) through the post unless the agent is very well established – some travellers have reported being ripped off by fly-by-night mail-order ticket agents.

Council Travel is the largest student travel organisation, and though you don't have to

be a student to use it, it does have specially discounted student tickets. Council Travel has an extensive network in all major US cities and is listed in the telephone book.

One of the cheapest and most reliable travel agents on the US west coast is Overseas Tours (☎ (800) 323-8777 in California, (800) 227-5988 elsewhere), 475 El Camino Real, Room 206, Millbrae, CA 94030. Another good agent is Gateway Travel (☎ (214) 960-2000, (800) 441-1183), 4201 Spring Valley Rd, Suite 104, Dallas, TX 75244. It seems to be reliable for mail-order tickets.

The cheapest fares through these agents are likely to be on Korean Air, the Taiwan-based China Airlines, Philippine Airlines and Thai Airways International. American-based carriers like Delta, Northwest and United also offer competitive fares plus frequent-flier credit, the only drawback being that their open return tickets are usually valid for only six months rather than one year (if you're flying one way or will complete the return journey in six months this hardly matters). At the time of writing, Northwest Airlines was offering the most generous frequent-flier credits.

For direct flights from the USA to China, the general route is from San Francisco (with connections from New York, Los Angeles and Vancouver in Canada) to Tokyo, then Beijing, Shanghai or several other cities in China. It's entirely possible to go through to Beijing and then pick up the return flight in Shanghai. Tickets from the USA directly to Beijing are higher than tickets to Hong Kong, even though the flying distance is actually shorter.

From the US west coast, one-way fares to Hong Kong start at around US$460 and return tickets begin at US$680. To Beijing, return fares start at around US$880. From New York to Hong Kong, fares start at US$560 one-way and US$870 return. Beijing fares start at US$800 one-way and US$1460 return.

In the USA, departure taxes are included in the price of the ticket, so there is no additional charge at the airport.

To/From Canada

Travel CUTS is Canada's national student travel agency and has offices in Vancouver, Victoria, Edmonton, Saskatoon, Toronto, Ottawa, Montreal and Halifax. You don't have to be a student to use their services.

Getting discount tickets in Canada is much the same as in the USA. Go to the travel agents and shop around until you find a good deal. In Vancouver try Kowloon Travel, Westcan Treks and Travel CUTS.

Canadian Airlines is worth trying for cheap deals to Hong Kong, although Korean Air may still be able to undercut it.

In general, air fares from Vancouver to Hong Kong or China will cost about 5% to 10% more than tickets from the US west coast.

In Canada, departure taxes are included in the original price of the ticket and there is no additional charge at the airport.

Besides numerous flights to Hong Kong, CAAC has two flights weekly which originate in Toronto, then fly onward to Vancouver, Shanghai and Beijing (in that order).

To/From Other Asian Countries

Bangladesh Dragonair has flights from Dhaka to Kunming.

Indonesia CAAC has flights originating in Jakarta which continue onwards to Surabaya and then to Guangzhou, Xiamen or Beijing.

Japan CAAC has several flights a week from Beijing to Tokyo, Osaka, Fukuoka and Sendai. Some of these flights are direct and others are via Shanghai. Japan Airlines flies from Beijing and Shanghai to Tokyo, Osaka and Nagasaki. There are flights between Dalian and Fukuoka/Tokyo on All Nippon Airways.

Kazakstan CAAC has flights twice weekly between Ürümqi in Xinjiang Province and Almaty in Kazakstan.

Malaysia CAAC has direct flights from Penang to Guangzhou and Xiamen.

Mongolia During the summer, MIAT (Mongolia's airline) runs three flights weekly from Beijing to Ulaan Baatar for US$160 one way. During the low season (winter), flights are only once weekly.

CAAC has two flights weekly in both directions between Beijing and Ulaan Baatar. There are also two return flights weekly between Ulaan Baatar and Hohhot (the capital of China's Inner Mongolia Province).

Myanmar (Burma) There is a once-weekly flight from Beijing to Rangoon (Yangon) with a stopover in Kunming. You can pick up the flight in Kunming too, but you must have a visa for Myanmar – available in Beijing, not Kunming.

Nepal There are direct flights between Lhasa and Kathmandu twice a week costing US$190. However, you will have to book a three-day Lhasa tour in order to buy the air ticket in Nepal (no problem going the other way). The mandatory tour costs US$125.

Pakistan CAAC has direct flights from Beijing to Karachi three times weekly. There are CAAC flights between Ürümqi in China's Xinjiang Province and Islamabad.

The Philippines CAAC has a twice-weekly flight from Beijing to Manila and a weekly flight from Guangzhou to Manila. The cheapest option is the direct flight from Xiamen to Manila four times a week.

Singapore CAAC has flights from Singapore to Guangzhou, Xiamen and Beijing.

South Korea Asiana Airlines, Korean Air and Air China operate routes from Seoul to Beijing, Dalian, Guangzhou, Qingdao, Shanghai, Shenyang and Tianjin.

Thailand There is a flight from Beijing to Bangkok via Guangzhou (you can pick up the flight in Guangzhou too), but flying to Hong Kong is much cheaper. There is also a very popular flight from Kunming to

Bangkok via Chiang Mai on Thai Airways International–CAAC flies this route too but without the Chiang Mai stop. Some of the Bangkok-Guangzhou flights continue on to Shantou in China's Guangdong Province.

Vietnam China Southern Airlines and Vietnam Airlines fly the China-Vietnam route using fuel-guzzling Soviet-built Tupolev 134 aircraft. The only direct flight between Ho Chi Minh City and China is to Guangzhou. All other flights are via Hanoi. The Guangzhou-Hanoi flight (US$140 one way) takes 1½ hours; Guangzhou-Ho Chi Minh City (US$240 one way) takes 2½ hours. Return airfares cost exactly double.

The Beijing-Hanoi flight on China Southern Airlines stops at Nanning (capital of China's Guangxi Province) en route – you can board or exit the plane there.

LAND

If you're starting from Europe or Asia, it's entirely possible to travel all the way to China and back without ever having to fasten your seatbelt and put out your cigarette. For most travellers, 'overland' to China means from Hong Kong or Macau by rail or bus. However, there are far more interesting routes, including the Vietnam-China border crossing, the Trans-Siberian Railway from Europe, or the exotic Tibet to Nepal, Xinjiang to Pakistan and Xinjiang to Kazakstan routes.

It is not yet possible to travel overland from Myanmar (Burma) to China, but you can enter Myanmar at the Ruili-Muse checkpoint under special circumstances. See the Ruili section in the Yunnan chapter for details.

Trade between China and India occurs at the Indian bordertown of Garbyang, Uttar Pradesh, just north of the Nepalese border; unfortunately, military instability in the Kashmir region has nullified this option for travellers. Another possible border opening getting some press recently was Thailand and Xishuangbanna via a land crossing through either Laos or Myanmar. The logis-

tics of getting this one off the ground look fairly insurmountable, but only time will tell.

The borders with Afghanistan and Bhutan are out of bounds.

The possibility of bringing your own vehicle is a big muddle. Foreigners are not usually allowed to drive cars or motorbikes around China and are therefore not usually allowed to take them in. Bicycles are allowed on some routes but not others – the regulations governing the use of bicycles is in a constant state of confusion. See the following Getting Around chapter for more information on cycling through China.

To/From Hong Kong

Hong Kong's border crossing at Lo Wu is the most popular entrance point for the PRC. For details, see the Hong Kong & Macau chapter.

To/From Macau

On the other side of the border from Macau is the Special Economic Zone (SEZ) of Zhuhai. The Macau-Zhuhai border is open from 7 am to 9 pm, and cyclists can ride across. Most people just take a bus to the border and walk across.

For more details, see the Zhuhai section in the Guangdong chapter.

To/From Pakistan

The Karakoram Highway stretches between Kashgar (in China's Xinjiang Province) and Islamabad. Pakistani visas are compulsory for visitors from most Western countries. Visas are *not* given at the border. If going from China to Pakistan, the closest place to get a Pakistani visa is in Hong Kong or Beijing. Chinese visas can be obtained in your own country, in Hong Kong or in Islamabad.

The following chart provides a rough guide to distances and average journey times:

Route	Distance (km)	Duration
Kashgar-Tashkurgan	280	six hours
Tashkurgan-Pirali	84	90 minutes
Pirali-Khunjerab	35	one hour
(Sino-Pakistan border)		

Route	Distance (km)	Duration
Khunjerab-Sust	86	2¼ hours
Sust-Passu	35	45 minutes
Passu-Gulmit	14	20 minutes
Gulmit-Karimabad	37	one hour
Karimabad (Hunza)-Gilgit	98	two hours
Gilgit-Rawalpindi	631	18 hours

From China to Pakistan From 15 April to late October buses ply this high-altitude route. Landslides are common, so take your hard hat – in 1992 at least one traveller was killed by falling rocks. Also bring some warm clothes – it can be chilly at over 4000 metres.

Buses direct from Kashgar to the Pakistani border post at Sust (in Pakistan) leave from the Chini Bagh Hotel at about 11.30 am all through summer. From June to September buses are laid on, but earlier or later in the season there may not be buses on some days. There's an overnight stop in Tashkurgan (on the Chinese side). The same bus goes on to Sust the next day. The economy bus costs Y260, the high-class one costs Y290. There aren't many food stops, so bring a day's water and snacks.

Everything that goes on top of the bus is inspected by customs at Chini Bagh and stays locked up for the entire journey. So carry on whatever you want for the overnight stop, plus whatever you declared to customs on entering China.

The bus stays overnight at Tashkurgan, where the Chinese customs is located.

From Tashkurgan the road climbs higher for the two-hour stretch to Pirali (elevation 4200 metres), which isn't worth a stop. If you're on a Pakistani bus, you'll have no need to change buses; if you've taken the local bus from Kashgar, you'll need to change to a Pakistani bus from Pirali onwards.

From Pakistan to China From Rawalpindi to Gilgit (a 15-hour trip) there are six buses daily. An ordinary coach costs about 360 rupees, deluxe around 430 rupees. If you can't stand the pace of the bus ride, the flight between Rawalpindi and Gilgit (at least one flight per day, weather permitting) is about 1360 rupees.

From Gilgit to Sust, there's a Northern Areas Transport Company (NATCO) bus which costs 140 rupees; buy your ticket early on the morning of departure as the bus leaves at 8 am. In Sust, the best place to stay is the Mountain View Hotel, which has both dorms and more cushy private rooms.

From Sust to Pirali, there's a NATCO bus for 725 rupees. Get your ticket from the NATCO office first thing in the morning – you'll need to show it to customs. At Pirali everyone changes to a Chinese bus to Kashgar. This bus stops overnight at Tashkurgan. Trucks offer lifts (negotiate the price); ditto for jeeps.

Some cyclists have succeeded in riding across the Pakistani border, some have had to put their bikes on a bus, and some have been refused permission altogether.

For further details, see Lonely Planet's *Karakoram Highway*.

To/From Kazakstan

From Almaty to Ürümqi There is a direct daily bus service between Ürümqi and Almaty, and this is the cheapest way to travel between China and Kazakstan.

On Monday and Saturday there is an international train from Ürümqi to Almaty, which returns the following day. Sleepers cost US$56 for foreigners. In Ürümqi these can be booked through travel agencies.

From Almaty to Yining It's possible to travel overland by bus from Yining (in China's Xinjiang Province) to Panfilov in Kazakstan, and then on to Almaty. The charge at the time of writing was US$30 by bus to Panfilov and then another US$30 on to Almaty, a ridiculous state of affairs when you consider that buses do the trip from Ürümqi for US$48. All things considered, it's probably better to organise things in Ürümqi, where you're less likely to get ripped off.

Local Kazaks, Uighurs, Kyrgyz and others who have relatives on the other side of the border make this trip regularly and inexpensively. If you don't have a relative in Almaty, accommodation is very expensive.

Buses between Yining and Panfilov run daily from 1 May to 1 October via the border town of Korgas *(hùochéng)*, or Khorgos in Russian. This road is actually open all year because of its low elevation, but winter storms could close it for a few days at a time. It's necessary to change buses in Panfilov to reach Almaty.

It may or may not be possible to spend the night in Panfilov, though the chances are that you will be forced to travel between Korgas and Almaty in one day. This is problematic because the border post is only open from 8.30 am to 4 pm. Crossing the other way into China should be no problem provided you have organised a Chinese visa beforehand, but at present this whole region is an unknown, with very few travellers making the trip.

One traveller reported problems with Chinese customs after entering from Korgas: getting into China was no problem, but when he tried to exit in Shenzhen he was told that he had to return to Korgas and exit there. It took him two days of hassle in Shenzhen to get out of China. If you enter China via Korgas, try and make it clear to the customs officials that you will not be exiting the country the same way: say the name of the place you plan to exit followed by ...*chūjìng*.

To/From Kyrgyzstan

Inquire about the possibility of a crossing between Bishkek (the capital of Kyrgyzstan) and Kashgar, via Turugart Pass *(tǔ'ěrgǎtè shānkǒu)*. Government travel agencies have been quoting prohibitively high rates for doing the journey by car, but private entrepreneurs might be able to offer you a better deal.

To/From Nepal

The good news is that the Lhasa-Kathmandu road reopened in 1993 after being closed to foreigners for over three years. The bad news is that there are still a few bureaucratic hurdles to clear, you will have to pay for an unwanted tour in Lhasa and there is a short-age of public transport on the Chinese side. Travel agents in Kathmandu can make all the arrangements.

The first problem is visas. Yes, you can get Chinese visas in Nepal, but you officially have to be booked onto an organised tour and you will definitely not be given more than one month. If possible, get your visa some-place else (Hong Kong etc) and ask for a two-month visa if you plan to do extensive travelling in China.

The next thing is the mandatory Lhasa tour. All foreigners wanting to visit Tibet must book a three-day tour around Lhasa – whether they want it or not – for a cost of roughly US$100. This sounds cheap until you realise that the tour lasts about two hours a day for three days. The tour operator is usually unwilling to go anywhere until there are ten people in the group – if you travel solo, you may have to wait until enough others arrive to make a quorum.

Transport is the next hurdle. Public buses operate on the Nepalese side right up to the border, but there's not much activity on the Tibetan side. People going from Lhasa to Nepal normally get to the border by rented jeep – since the jeeps return home empty, the drivers are more than happy to find travellers waiting at the border looking for rides to Lhasa. Prices average out at Y700 to Y1000 per person to Lhasa, but there is a fair amount of latitude for bargaining. The problem is you might have to wait awhile for an avail-able jeep. There are regular bus services to Shigatse, from where there are daily buses to Lhasa, but buses between Lhasa and the border only run three or four times a month.

Walking from the border to Lhasa is not recommended, but going by bicycle might be feasible. The trouble is the Chinese authorities. Some travellers are allowed to go by bike and some aren't. The Chinese them-selves do not seem to know the rules, and finding out what will be permitted next week or next month requires a knowledge of astrology, crystal ball reading or tarot cards.

For further details about transport on the Chinese side of the border, see the Tibet chapter of this book.

To/From North Korea

There are twice-weekly trains between Beijing and Pyongyang. Visas can be obtained (with difficulty) from the North Korean representative office in Macau. The North Korean consulate in Beijing is also worth a try. Should you succeed in getting a North Korean visa, your time in that country will be both tightly controlled and expensive. For full details, see the Lonely Planet guides *North-East Asia on a Shoestring* and *Korea*.

To/From Vietnam

In the finest bureaucratic tradition, the Vietnamese require a special visa for entering overland from China. These visas cost double and take twice as long to issue as the normal tourist visas needed for entering Vietnam by air. Travellers who have tried to use a standard visa for entering Vietnam overland from China have fared poorly, but sometimes they manage after paying the Vietnamese border guards a considerable bribe.

Exiting from Vietnam to China is much simpler. The Chinese don't require anything more than a standard tourist visa, and Chinese visas do not indicate entry or exit points. However, your Vietnamese visa must have the correct exit point marked on it, a change which can easily be made in Hanoi.

There are two border crossings, as follows:

Friendship Gate The busiest border crossing is at Dong Dang (20 km north of Lang Son in north-east Vietnam), and the nearest Chinese town is Pingxiang, which is not far from Nanning, the capital of Guangxi Province.

On this route, it is necessary to travel to the Vietnamese town of Lang Son by train or bus. From there you can hitch a ride on a motorbike up to Dong Dang. There are regular buses and two trains depart daily from Pingxiang to Nanning; the trip takes three or four hours.

There is also an international train which crosses the border at Friendship Gate, connecting Beijing to Hanoi. This train only runs twice a week and there is no great saving in time.

From Lao Cai to Hekou Inaugurated in 1910, an 851-km metre-gauge railway linked Hanoi with Kunming in China's Yunnan Province, crossing the border at Lao Cai in north-west Vietnam. The railway crossing has been defunct since 1979, but you can cross the border on foot. The border-town on the Chinese side is called Hekou.

Those coming from China will need to have a Vietnamese visa with 'Lao Cai' marked as the entry point. Some travellers without this stamp have paid US$20 for an 'entry permit', but then discovered they were only given a one-week entry stamp (forcing them to immediately seek a visa extension).

Both buses and trains run from Hekou to Kunming. Buses take 14-16 hours on a surprisingly good but mountainous road. Trains to Hanoi from the Kunming's north railway station take around 18 hours. There are two trains daily in each direction on the Lao Cai-Hanoi run.

Trans-Siberian Railway

The Trans-Siberian Railway connects Europe to Asia. It's popularity has declined in recent years due to the general state of chaos in Russia plus rising prices. Nevertheless, it's an option worth considering.

There is some confusion of terms here as there are, in fact, three railways. The 'true' Trans-Siberian line runs from Moscow to the eastern Siberian port of Nakhodka, from where one can catch a boat to Japan. This route does not go through either China or Mongolia. There is also the Trans-Manchurian line which crosses the Russia-China border at Zabaikalsk-Manzhouli, also completely bypassing Mongolia. The Trans-Mongolian line connects Beijing to Moscow, passing through the Mongolian capital city of Ulaan Baatar.

Most readers of this book will not be interested in the first option since it excludes China – your decision is basically between the Trans-Manchurian or the Trans-Mongolian; however, it makes little difference. The

Trans-Mongolian is marginally faster but requires you to purchase an additional visa and endure another border crossing, though you do at least get to see the Mongolian countryside roll past your window.

There are different classes but all are acceptably comfortable. In deluxe class there are two beds per cabin while economy class has four beds.

Which direction you go makes a difference in cost and travelling time. The trains from Beijing take 1½ days to reach Ulaan Baatar. The journey from Moscow to Ulaan Baatar is four days.

There are delays (three to six hours) at both the China-Mongolia and Russia-Mongolia borders. During this time, you can get off the train and wander around the station, which is just as well since the toilets on the train are locked during the whole inspection procedure. You will not have your passport at this time as the authorities take it away for stamping. When it is returned, inspect it closely – sometimes they make errors (like cancelling your return visa for China).

On the Chinese side of the Russian or Mongolian border, about two hours are spent changing the bogies (undercarriage wheels). This is necessary because Russia, Mongolia and all former East Bloc countries use a wider rail gauge than China and the rest of the world. The reason has to do with security – it seems the Russians feared an invasion by train.

Tickets from Europe Travel Service Asia (☎ (07) 371-4963; fax 371-4769), Kirchberg 15, 7948 Dürmentingen, Germany, is recommended for low prices and good service.

In the UK, one of the experts in budget rail travel is Regent Holidays (UK) Ltd (☎ (0117) 921-1711; fax 925-4866), 15 John St, Bristol BS1 2HR. Another agency geared towards budget travellers is Progressive Tours (☎ (0181) 262-1676), 12 Porchester Place, Connaught Square, London W2 2BS.

Several travellers have recommended Scandinavian Student Travel Service (SSTS), 117 Hauchsvej, 1825 Copenhagen V, Denmark. This organisation has branch offices in Europe and the USA, and provides a range of basic tours for student or budget travellers, mostly during summer.

Tickets from China In theory, the cheapest place to buy a ticket is at the office of China International Travel Service (CITS) in the Beijing Tourist Building (☎ 515-8570; fax 515-8603), 28 Jianguomenwai Dajie, hidden behind the New Otani Hotel. A straight Beijing-Moscow economy ticket costs US$280, but there are some tactical hurdles to buying one. First off, CITS offers no advance bookings – you must go to Beijing and make all your arrangements there. If you're lucky, you might get on a train a few days later. If unlucky, you will have to hang around a few weeks waiting for a vacant berth, though that is only likely to happen during the summer crunch period. All tickets bought from CITS are straight through to Moscow (or Ulaan Baatar in Mongolia) – no stopovers are permitted. And contrary to what CITS brochures say, train tickets bought from CITS are nonrefundable.

Your other alternative is to buy from a private travel agent. This will always be more expensive than CITS because the private companies are forced to purchase their tickets from CITS too. However, some travel agents can offer stopover tours.

The best organised of the Trans-Siberian tour agents is Monkey Business, officially known as Moonsky Star (☎ 2723-1376; fax 2723-6653), 4th floor, Block E, Flat 6, Chungking Mansions, 30 Nathan Rd, Tsimshatsui, Kowloon. Monkey Business also maintains an information office in Beijing at Beijing Commercial Business Complex (☎ 329-2244 ext 4406), Room 406, No 1 Building Yu Lin Li. However, it's best to book through its Hong Kong office as far in advance as possible. A booking can be done by telephone or fax and a deposit can be wired to them. One advantage of booking through them is that they keep all their passengers in a group (for mutual protection against theft). Furthermore, they can arrange visas and stopover tours to Mongolia and Irkutsk (Siberia).

Another Hong Kong agent selling Trans-

Mongolian tickets is Time Travel (☎ 2366-6222; fax 2739-5413), 16th floor, Block A, Chungking Mansions, 30 Nathan Rd, Tsimshatsui, Kowloon. Unfortunately, they offer nothing but bare-bones tickets – no visa service, no group tickets (so you might have Russian cabin-mates) and they don't offer stopover tours.

You can organise tickets and visas through Wallem Travel (☎ 2528-6514), 46th floor, Hopewell Centre, 183 Queen's Rd East, Wanchai, Hong Kong. This place does organised tours but is expensive.

Black-Market Tickets Once upon a time, black-market tickets were so common that it seemed like everyone on the train had one. Indeed, you were almost a fool not to buy one. The way it worked was that people with connections would go to Budapest and buy Beijing-Moscow tickets in bulk for around US$50 apiece, then take the tickets to Beijing and sell them for about US$150. A nice little business, while it lasted.

The good old days are gone. If you are approached in either Moscow or Beijing by people plugging black-market tickets on the Trans-Siberian, chances are 90% certain that you will be ripped off. Most likely, you will be sold a rouble-denominated ticket which only Russian nationals can use.

Books A popular book about this journey is the *Trans-Siberian Handbook* by Bryn Thomas, published by Trailblazer Publications and distributed through Roger Lascelles in the UK.

Needs, Problems & Precautions Bring plenty of cash US dollars in small denominations for the journey – only in China can you readily use the local currency. In China, food is plentiful and readily available from both the train's dining car and vendors in railway stations. In both Russia and Mongolia, food quality is poorer, but meals are available on the train. Once you get off the train it's a different story – food can be difficult to buy in both Russia and Mongolia, especially once you get away from the

capital cities. If you don't want to starve, bring plenty of munchies like biscuits, instant noodles, chocolate and fruit. No alcohol is sold on the Russian and Mongolian trains, but a very limited selection of booze can be bought in the Chinese dining car.

Showers are only available in the deluxe carriages. In economy class, there is a washroom. You can manage a bath with a sponge but it's best to bring a large metal cup (available in most Chinese railway stations) and use it as a scoop to pour water over yourself from the washbasin. The metal cup is also ideal for making coffee, tea and instant soup. Hot water is available on the trains.

There is much theft on the train, so never leave your luggage unattended, even if the compartment is locked. Make sure at least one person stays in the compartment while the others go to the dining car. A lot of theft is committed by Russian gangs who have master keys to the compartments, so don't assume that a 'foreign face' is a badge of honesty.

The luggage limit is 35 kg per passenger and there is now some attempt being made to enforce this. Previously, the Trans-Siberian was little more than a freight train because traders were earning a living moving goods back and forth between Beijing and Moscow in the passenger compartments. Of course, the traders haven't given up entirely, and some will try to move their tonnes of 'luggage' into your compartment – don't allow it.

It's important to realise that food in the dining car is priced in local currency. This is true even in Mongolia or Russia. Many foreigners have the mistaken impression that they must pay in US dollars. The railway staff will gladly accept your dollars instead of local currency at some ridiculous exchange rate, which means you'll be paying many times the real price. There are black-market moneychangers at border railway stations, but all the usual dangers of black-market exchanges apply.

Visas can take several days each to issue, even longer if you can't show up at the embassy in person and want to apply through the post. If you just show up in Beijing the day before departure and think you can hop on a train without a visa, you're mistaken.

Russian Visas The burning question that many travellers ask is 'Can I stop off along the way?'. The answer is essentially 'No'. You can get a few days in Moscow on a transit visa, but stopping off elsewhere requires a tourist visa. The same problem applies to Mongolia.

Transit visas are valid for a maximum of 10 days and tourist visas are required if the journey is broken. In practice, you can stay in Moscow for three days on a transit visa and apply for an extension. Trying to extend a tourist visa is much more expensive – the hotel 'service bureau' will do it for you through Intourist, but only with expensive hotel bookings.

With a tourist visa, you can stay in Russia much longer, but you will pay heavily for the privilege. All hotels must be booked through Intourist in advance of arrival. Intourist insists that you stay at good hotels (read 'expensive'). The whole bureaucratic booking procedure takes about three weeks. On a transit visa, you can sleep in the railway station or in one of the rapidly proliferating cheap private hostels.

Before you can get a transit visa, you must have a ticket in hand or a ticket voucher. A transit visa can be issued in three working days for US$40; in two working days for US$60; or the same day for the same price as the two-day service?!

Then there is also the bizarre 'consular fee' for certain nationalities. There is no logic here – Belgians pay a consular fee of US$12 for transit visas and US$33 for tourist visas, but the French pay US$12 for both kinds of visas. The Swiss pay US$18 for a transit visa but get the tourist visa for free. Israelis pay nothing for the transit visa but must pay US$88 for a tourist visa. These fees go up and down like a toilet seat – we can't make any predictions how much you'll actually have to pay.

Someone can apply for the visa on your behalf and use a photocopy of your passport (all relevant pages must be included). If you want to change an already-issued transit visa, this will cost you US$18. Reasons for changing could be if you want go on a different date or change the final destination (Budapest instead of Berlin, for example). Russian embassies are closed during all Russian public holidays: New Year's Day (1 January), Women's Day (8 March), Labour Day (1 & 2 May), Victory Day (9 May), Constitution Day (7 October) and October Revolution (7 & 8 November).

In Beijing, the Russian embassy (☎ 532-2051, 532-1267) is at Beizhongjie 4, just off Dongzhimen and west of the Sanlitun Embassy Compound. Opening hours are Monday to Friday from 9 am to noon. You can avoid the long queues at the Beijing embassy if you apply at the Russian consulate (☎ 6324-2682) in Shanghai, 20 Huangpu Lu, opposite the Pujiang Hotel. However, its opening hours are brief: Tuesday and Thursday from 10 am until 12.30 pm.

The Russian consulate in Budapest is at Nepkoztarsasag utca 104, and is open Monday, Wednesday and Friday from 10 am to 1 pm.

Mongolian Visas The Mongolian embassy in Beijing is open all day, but the visa section keeps short hours only on Monday, Tuesday, Thursday and Friday from 8.30 to 11.30 am. They close for all Mongolian holidays, and they shut down completely for the entire week of National Day (Naadam), which officially falls on 11-13 July. In the UK, the Mongolian embassy (☎ (0171) 937-0150, 937-5235) is at 7 Kensington Court, London W85 DL.

Transit visas cost US$15 if picked up in three days, or US$30 for express service. Tourist visas cost US$25 for three-day service, or US$40 for express service. Indians and Finnish nationalities get them free and Singaporeans can stay two weeks without a visa (figure that one out). One photo is required.

Other Visas Most travellers between Western Europe and Moscow go via Poland, though there are alternative routes via Finland or Hungary. A Polish visa is not needed by most Western nationalities except Canadians. Visas cost US$27. In China, there is a Polish embassy in Beijing and a Polish consulate in Guangzhou. Two photos are needed.

Americans, Canadians and most West Europeans (including UK citizens) don't need a visa for Hungary. Australians, New Zealanders, Greeks and Portuguese do (US$18); two photos are required. Get a tourist rather than transit visa since Hungary is worth visiting.

For Slovakia, you need a visa if you're from Australia, Canada, New Zealand, Israel or South Africa. Visas cost US$21 and two photos are needed.

The Czech Republic requires visas for Australians, Canadians, Israelis, New Zealanders and South Africans.

SEA
To/From Hong Kong
There are numerous ships plying the waters between Hong Kong and China. See the Getting There & Away section of the Hong Kong chapter for details.

To/From Japan
Osaka/Yokohama to Shanghai There is a luxurious boat service between Shanghai and Osaka/Yokohama. The good ship *Suzhou Hao* departs once weekly, one week to Osaka and the next week to Yokohama, and takes two days. Off season it's kind of empty but can be crowded during summer. Fares depend on class – from Osaka 2nd class costs US$270, 1st class is US$540 and a luxury suite costs a whopping US$1600! From Yokohama add about 30% more to these fares. Tickets purchased in Shanghai cost about 30% less than those bought in Japan. Departures from Shanghai are every Tuesday, while departures from Japan are every Friday. For information you can ring up the shipping company's office in Tokyo (☎ (03) 5202-5781; fax 5202-5792), Osaka (☎ (06) 232-0131; fax 232-0211) or Shanghai (☎ (021) 6535-1713). The address of the

shipping office in Shanghai is 777 Dong Changzhi Lu.

Kobe to Tianjin Another ship runs from Kobe to Tanggu (near Tianjin). Departures from Kobe are every Thursday at noon, arriving in Tanggu the next day. Economy/ 1st-class tickets cost US$253/343, or pay US$1355 for your very own stateroom. The food on this boat gets poor reviews so bring a few emergency munchies. Tickets can be bought in Tianjin from the shipping office (☎ 331-2283) at 89 Munan Dao, Hepingqu, or right at the port in Tanggu (☎ 938-3961). In Kobe, the office is at the port (☎ (078) 321-5791; fax 321-5793).

To/From Korea
International ferries connect the South Korean port of Inch'ŏn with three cities in China: Weihai, Qingdao and Tianjin. Weihai and Qingdao are in China's Shandong Province (the closest province to South Korea) and boats are operated by the Weidong Ferry Company. Tianjin is near Beijing and boats are run by the Tianjin Ferry Company.

The phone numbers for Weidong Ferry Company are: Seoul (☎ (02) 711-9111); Inch'ŏn (☎ (032) 886-6171). Phone numbers for Tianjin Ferry Company are: Seoul (☎ (02) 517-8671); Inch'ŏn (☎ (032) 887-3963); Tianjin (☎ (022) 331-6049). In Seoul, tickets for any boats to China can be bought from the Universal Travel Service, otherwise known as UTS (☎ (02) 319-5511; fax 737-2764), Room B-702 in the Dongyang Building (west of the KAL Building). In China, tickets can be bought cheaply at the pier, or from CITS (for a steep premium).

The Inch'ŏn International Ferry Terminal is the next to last stop on the Inch'ŏn-Seoul commuter train (red subway line from the city centre) – the trip takes one hour and from the railway station it's either a long walk or short taxi ride to the terminal. You must arrive at the terminal at least one hour before departure or you won't be allowed to board.

Inch'ŏn to Weihai The trip takes a minimum of 17 hours. Departures from Weihai are

Wednesday and Friday at 5 pm. Departures from Inch'ŏn are on Tuesday and Thursday at 5.30 pm. The cost is US$110 in economy class and up to US$300 in deluxe class. There are also several classes in between.

Inch'ŏn to Qingdao This trip takes a minimum of 24 hours. Departures from Qingdao are on Monday at 11 am. Departures from Inch'ŏn are on Saturday at 5.30 pm. The fare varies from US110 in economy class to US$300 for deluxe service.

Inch'ŏn to Tianjin This popular ferry runs once every five days and the journey takes a minimum of 28 hours. Departures from Tianjin are at 10 am. The boat departs Inch'ŏn at 1 pm. The fare is US$120 to US$230.

The boat doesn't dock at Tianjin proper, but rather at the nearby port of Tanggu. Accommodation in Tianjin is outrageously expensive, but Tanggu has at least one economical place to stay, the International Seamen's Club. Tanggu has trains directly to Beijing.

ORGANISED TOURS

Tour groups are still considered the darlings of the Chinese who have to deal with foreigners. It is much easier for the Chinese if you arrive in a tour group, if all your accommodation is pre-booked, and if everyone sits down at the same time to eat. If there's a government interpreter on hand, someone doesn't have to struggle with a phrasebook or pidgin English. Groups don't make a nuisance of themselves by trying to go to closed places, and they usually channel complaints through the tour leader rather than hassle the desk clerk. Most importantly, tour groups spend more money.

Are tours worth it? Unless you simply cannot make your own way around, then probably not. Apart from the expense, they tend to screen you even more from some of the basic realities of China travel. Most people who come back with glowing reports of the PRC never had to travel proletariat class on the trains or battle their way on

board a local bus in the whole 10 days of their stay. On the other hand, if your time is limited and you just want to see the Forbidden City and the hills of Guilin, then the brief tours from Hong Kong, though expensive, might be worth considering. One advantage of being on a tour is that you may get into places that individuals often can't, such as factories and steam locomotive storage depots.

There are two basic kinds of tours – those for foreigners and those for Overseas Chinese. Officially, the reason for separating foreigners from Overseas Chinese is because the two groups supposedly speak different languages (often not true) and have different interests (sometimes true). Unofficially, the real reason has to do with racism. The Overseas Chinese groups usually receive about a 15% discount, so belonging to the correct gene pool can save you money.

Tours aimed at foreigners are usually organised by CITS, China Travel Service (CTS) or China Youth Travel Service (CYTS), though a few private operators are also getting into the act. An English-speaking guide (or French, German, whatever) is supplied. Tours can be organised for very small groups, but costs are high.

Tours for Overseas Chinese are geared towards large groups and there's a heavy emphasis on shopping, feasting and posing for photos. There's also a tendency towards regimentation – the tour leader (usually female) waves a flag and uses a megaphone to keep the tourist troops in line. The tourists wear some sort of ID badge and a yellow hat (a non-Tibetan version of the Yellow Hat Sect?). Just what language your tour guide will speak is pot luck – some of these groups come from Australia, Canada or the USA and the guides will speak English about half the time. Groups from Hong Kong and Macau are likely to have a Cantonese-speaking guide. Groups from Taiwan might feature a guide who speaks a mixture of Fujianese (similar to Taiwanese) and Mandarin. The prices that Overseas Chinese pay for these tours is not particularly cheap, but you'll eat well and the circus atmosphere is free.

There are innumerable tours you can make from Hong Kong or Macau. The best people to go to if you want to find out what's available are the Hong Kong travel agents, especially China Travel Service (CTS). Essentially the same tours can be booked in Macau.

We could go on endlessly regurgitating all the tours to China. Some people do the one-day tours to the Special Economic Zones (SEZs) – Shenzhen near Hong Kong and Zhuhai near Macau. The tour to Shenzhen costs US$72, which includes admission to Splendid China (which you can easily see for yourself for a fraction of the cost). The Zhuhai tour offers even less to see but costs US$104. The day tours include lunch, transport and all admission fees, but you usually have to pay an additional fee for the visa.

The four-day tour to Guilin and Guangzhou seems to be popular – it costs US$374. CTS flogs an eight-day tour, including Guangzhou, Beijing and Xi'an, for US$907.

In an attempt to spice up the offerings the Chinese have come up with some new formulas. These include honeymoon tours (how many in the group?); acupuncture courses; special-interest tours for botanists, railway enthusiasts, lawyers and potters; trekking tours to Tibet and Qinghai; women's tours; bicycle tours; and Chinese-language courses. Check with your local travel agent – any one of them worth their commission will still tell you that you can't visit China except with an organised tour.

Warning

We have had many negative comments from people who have booked extended tours through CTS and CITS. Although both of these agencies have gradually improved their service, things still sometimes go awry. The most significant complaints have been about ridiculous overcharging for substandard accommodation and tours being cut short to make up for transport delays. Some people have booked a tour only to find that they were the sole person on the tour. No refunds are given if you cancel – you forfeit the full amount. Other travellers report additional charges being tacked on which were not mentioned in the original agreement.

CITS drivers have been known to show up with all their relatives who want to tag along for free, and they sometimes even expect the foreigner to pay for all their meals and accommodation. One traveller reported booking a week-long tour – the female driver showed up with her boyfriend and asked if he could come along. The traveller foolishly agreed. At the first lunch stop, the driver and her boyfriend took off and left the foreigner behind . The couple then apparently spent the rest of the week enjoying a honeymoon at the traveller's prepaid hotel rooms! When the irate traveller finally made her way back to the CITS office to complain, she was given the runaround but no refund – in the end she just left China in a fit of frustration.

Wilderness Tours

Mountaineering, trekking, camping, whitewater rafting, kayaking and cross-country skiing tours to China are organised by various agents in the West, but the prices are too high for low-budget travellers. Trekking is administered and arranged by the Chinese Mountaineering Association (CMA) under the same rules that apply to mountaineering in China. The CMA makes all arrangements for a trek with the assistance of provincial mountaineering associations and local authorities. The all-important point is that CMA can get you permits for peaks that are otherwise off limits to foreigners.

Various travel agents will book you through to these operators. Scan their literature carefully as sometimes the tours can be done just as easily on your own. What you want are places that individuals have trouble getting into.

If you can afford it, a few mountaineering, horse riding, trekking, cycling, sailing and rafting tour operators are:

Australia
Tail Winds Bicycle Touring, 1st floor, Garema Centre, Bunda St, Canberra, ACT 2601 (☎(06) 249-6122)

Taking Off Tours, Suite 3, 618 St Kilda Rd, Melbourne, Vic 3000 (☎ (03) 9521-1475). Good for discount tours and Trans-Siberian Railway tickets from Beijing to Europe.

World Expeditions, 3rd floor, 441 Kent St, Sydney, NSW 2000 (☎ (02) 9264-3366)

UK

Regent Holidays Ltd, 15 John St, Bristol BS1 2HR (☎ (0117) 921-1711; fax 925-4866). A specialist in relatively economical tours.

Voyages Jules Verne, 21 Dorset Square, London NW1 6QG (☎ (0171) 723-4084). Good for more-upmarket tours.

USA

Backroads, 1516 5th St, Berkeley, CA 94710 (☎ (800) 533-2573, (510) 527-1555). Cycling.

Boojum Expeditions, 14543 Kelly Canyon Rd, Bozeman, MT 59715 (☎ (406) 587-0125). Horseback trips.

Earth River Expeditions, 180 Towpath Rd, Accord, NY 12404 (☎ (800) 643-2784, (914) 626-2665). Rafting & trekking.

Mountain Travel, 6420 Fairmount Ave, El Cerrito, CA 94530 (☎ (800) 227-2384, (510) 527-8100). Rafting & trekking.

Nonesuch Whitewater, 4004 Bones Rd, Sebastopol, CA 95472 (☎ (707) 823-6603; fax 823-1954). Rafting & trekking.

Ocean Voyages, 1709 Bridgeway, Sausalito, CA 94965 (☎ (800) 299-4444, (415) 332-4681). Sailing.

REI Adventures, PO Box 1938, Sumner, WA 98390 (☎ (800) 622-2236, (206) 395-8111). Cycling & trekking.

Sierra magazine has an annual outings issue with listings, published by the Sierra Club, 730 Polk St, San Francisco, CA 94109. (☎ (415) 776-2211).

Wilderness Travel, 801 Allston Way, Berkeley, CA 94710 (☎ (800) 368-2794, (510) 548-0420). Trekking.

LEAVING CHINA

In general, there are few hassles on departure. Baggage may be x-rayed even at land and water crossings but the machines are supposedly 'film safe'. Antiques or things which look antique could cause hassles with customs. Lest you need to be reminded, most of China's neighbours (Hong Kong, for example) take a *very* dim view of drugs.

Departure Tax

If leaving China by air, the departure tax is Y105. This has to be paid in local currency, so be sure you have enough yuan to avoid a last-minute scramble at the airport money-changing booth.

Getting Around

AIR

The Civil Aviation Administration of China (CAAC), for many years China's only domestic and international carrier, has officially been broken up and private carriers have been allowed to set up operations in China. This doesn't mean that CAAC is out of business – it now assumes the role of 'umbrella organisation' (whatever that is) for its numerous subsidiaries. Under the CAAC umbrella, you can find numerous airlines, including Air China, China Eastern, China Southern, China Northern, China Southwest, China Northwest, Great Wall, Shanghai, Shenzhen, Sichuan, Xiamen, Xinjiang, Yunnan airlines and several others.

For the most part fleets have been substantially upgraded since the old CAAC days, and extensive work has gone into improving traffic control and safety. However, there are still a few Soviet-built CAAC hand-me-downs in service, mostly on routes in outlying areas like Xinjiang and Tibet. While CAAC claims that these Soviet aircraft are well maintained and completely safe, we couldn't help noticing minor technical difficulties like the air-conditioning system and toilets being out of order. Hopefully, the engines are in better shape.

Reservations

CAAC still publishes a combined international and domestic timetable in both English and Chinese in April and November each year. These can be bought at some CAAC offices in China, but they are much easier to find in Hong Kong (see the Getting There & Away section of the Hong Kong chapter for the location of CAAC offices). Another place to look for timetables is at the CAAC service counters in various airports.

As well as the overall CAAC timetable, former CAAC units and private airlines also publish their own timetables. You can buy these in ticket offices around China.

In theory, you can reserve seats without paying for them. In practice, this doesn't always work. The staff at some booking offices will hold a seat for more than a week – other offices will only hold a seat for a few hours so you can run to the bank and change money. Until you've actually paid for and received your ticket, nothing can be guaranteed. On some routes, competition for seats is keen and people with connections can often jump the queue – if you're only holding a reservation, you might be bounced. If you do decide just to make a reservation rather than purchase a ticket, be sure to get the reservation slip filled out and officially stamped – sometimes they want to hold it but usually you can take it with you and bring it back when you want to pick up the ticket.

If you don't have a reservation and everything is full, you can try flying stand-by. Some seats are always reserved in case a high-ranking cadre turns up at the last moment. If no-one important shows up it should be possible to get on board.

More and more booking offices have been computerised over recent years. These offices allow you to purchase a ticket to or from any other destination on the computer reservation system. If the city you want to fly from is not on the system, however, you'll have to wait until you get there to buy your ticket from the local booking office.

You need to show your passport when reserving or purchasing a ticket, and you definitely need it to board the aircraft. Some airports will even check your Chinese visa, and if it's expired you will be prohibited from boarding.

Incidentally, every flight we took left right on time.

Costs

Foreigners pay 2½ times the Chinese price. Unlike the situation with trains, there is no way around this CAAC regulation, unless you are a foreign resident with all the appropriate paperwork. If you do somehow

🙂🙂🙂🙂🙂🙂🙂🙂🙂🙂🙂🙂🙂🙂🙂🙂🙂🙂🙂🙂🙂🙂🙂🙂🙂🙂🙂🙂🙂

Tales of the Unexpected

Back in the old days CAAC made do with old Soviet hand-me-down aeroplanes and the stewardesses did revolutionary dances in the aisle. Nowadays China's national carrier is upgrading its fleet and its service standards. But it still pays to be prepared for anything when flying CAAC. Being told to carry your luggage on board because it's too big; being thrown a bag of biscuits for your in-flight meal; having to run frantically across the runway to board your flight *(which* plane is it?); and being given life-jacket inflation lessons on flights thousands of km from the nearest body of water large enough to crash a plane in: these are just a sampling of the countless inventive little touches that collectively make CAAC one of the least boring airlines in the world.

Some say that CAAC stands for China Airlines Always Cancels, the standard excuse being 'bad weather'. Evening check-ins generally provide entertaining scenes of hoarse and exhausted crowds who have spent the last eight hours waving their tickets in the air and screaming at the airport staff.

Bear in mind that CAAC is responsible for your meals and hotels whenever a flight is delayed beyond a reasonable amount of time. Just what constitutes 'reasonable' may be subject to interpretation; in general, however, CAAC will take care of you. Delays are so common that almost every airport has a CAAC-run hotel where you can stay for free. Many foreign travellers don't realise this and wind up paying for a hotel when it isn't necessary.

Delays are one thing; crashes are another. It's difficult to obtain reliable statistics, but it's common knowledge that CAAC's safety record is not a good one. The upgrading of the CAAC fleet over recent years (most flights nowadays are done by Boeing 737s) has no doubt improved things somewhat, but frequent China travellers generally make a point of flying as little as possible.

Anyone unfortunate enough to be killed or injured in CAAC domestic crashes isn't likely to receive much in the way of financial compensation. The CAAC timetable states that the maximum amount paid for accidental injury or death will be Y20,000 (less than US$4300) – though you may qualify for a ticket refund too.

Hijackings are another dimension of the CAAC experience. Over the last few years, hijackings to Taiwan have become a frequent occurrence, though with Taiwan sending hijackers back to China for sentencing the situation is improving. Back in the old days, the crew and passengers were encouraged to unite and attack hijackers. Fortunately CAAC officials take a more cautious view of dealing with hijackers nowadays.

The year 1992 was a particularly bad one for CAAC, when it managed to score a fifth of the world's total air passenger fatalities for that year. A Soviet-built tri-jet Yak42 did not quite manage to take to the air in Nanjing – of the 116 passengers, 106 died. But new aircraft have also been falling out of the sky with unusual frequency too. The worst crash was a China Southern Airlines Boeing 737-300, which went down in November 1992 near Guilin, killing all 141 passengers on board. The Chinese refused to allow foreigners to inspect the wreckage and examine the 'black box' flight recorder. It's no secret that China wants to replace imported high-technology equipment with domestically produced stuff – there is much speculation that China is now testing out homemade spare parts in new aircraft. ■

🙂🙂🙂🙂🙂🙂🙂🙂🙂🙂🙂🙂🙂🙂🙂🙂🙂🙂🙂🙂🙂🙂🙂🙂🙂🙂🙂🙂🙂

happen to get the Chinese price and it's discovered, your ticket will be confiscated and no refund given. Children over 12 are charged adult fare. Business-class tickets cost 25% over economy class, and 1st-class tickets cost an extra 60%. Note that it is still impossible to use credit cards to finance your transportation costs; all flights have to be paid for in cash.

There is no such thing as discounting no matter where you buy your tickets. Travel agents charge you full fare, plus extra commission for their services. The service desks in better hotels (three-star and up) can reserve and even purchase air tickets for you with a little advance notice, but they will probably also tack on an additional fee.

There is also an airport tax of approximately Y30 to Y50 on domestic flights.

Cancellation fees depend on how long

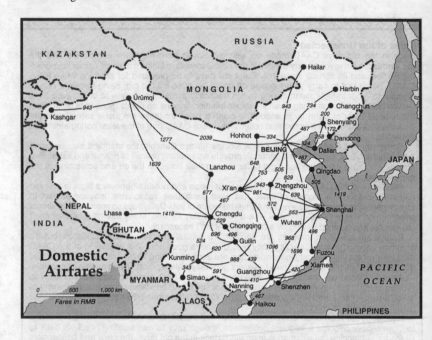

Domestic Airfares

Fares in RMB

before departure you cancel. On domestic flights, if you cancel 24 to 48 hours before departure you lose 10% of the fare; if you cancel between two and 24 hours before the flight you lose 20%; and if you cancel less than two hours before the flight you lose 30%. If you don't show up for a domestic flight, you are entitled to a refund of 50%.

When purchasing a ticket, you may be asked to buy luggage insurance. It's certainly not compulsory though some staff give the impression it is – the amount you can actually claim if your bags are lost is pathetically low.

On domestic and international flights the free-baggage allowance for an adult passenger is 20 kg in economy class and 30 kg in 1st class. You are also allowed five kg of hand luggage, though this is rarely weighed. The charge for excess baggage is 1% of the 1st-class fare for each kg.

On domestic flights, you might get a real meal if you're flying on an Airbus or Boeing, but if the plane is Soviet built there will be no facilities for hot food. In that case, you'll probably be given a little bag or two of sweets and a key ring as a souvenir – it almost justifies the 150% tourist surcharge.

BUS

Long-distance buses are one of the best means of getting around the country. Services are extensive and main roads are usually bumpy but passable. Also, since the buses stop every so often in small towns and villages, you get to see parts of the countryside you wouldn't see if you travelled by train.

Of course, the buses provide stops in places you had never counted on visiting: breakdowns are frequent and can occur anywhere. This is a special treat for the locals, who are temporarily entertained by the rare spectacle of a small herd of big noses while the bus is being repaired (or stripped and sold for scrap metal). It also creates some economic opportunities – enterprising locals are quick to produce baskets of fruit, biscuits and soft drinks to sell to the waiting passengers.

Aside from breakdown, there are sometimes other difficulties which could delay your journey:

One German traveller taking a bus from Wuzhou to Yangshuo was surprised when his bus started competing with the bus ahead for roadside passengers. After getting up perilously close to its rear bumper and blasting furiously on an armoury of horns, his driver managed, in a hair-raising exhibition of reckless abandon and dare-devilry, to sweep around the opposition on a blind bend and be first to get to a group of prospective passengers just around the corner. The other driver, determined not to let his fellow get away with such deviously unsporting behaviour, pulled up and started thumping him through the window.

A decisive knock-out proving elusive in such cramped quarters, the two soon leapt out of their buses to continue the punch-up on the roadside. Things were beginning to look grim for the German's driver, when a wailing siren announced the arrival of the boys in green. Without even a glance at the passengers of the two buses, they handcuffed the two drivers, threw them unceremoniously into the back of their van and drove off. It was five hours before new drivers were dispatched to the scene of the crime.

Safety is another consideration. Accidents are frequent, especially on winding mountain roads. Foreigners have been injured and killed in bus crashes, and there is very little you can do to protect yourself. The government-run buses seem to be somewhat safer than the private ones – government drivers can be imprisoned for causing a bus accident.

If possible, try to avoid sitting at the rear of the bus since it's painful for the shock-absorbers in your back.

Many long-distance buses are equipped with cassette tape players and stereo speakers that allow the drivers to blast out your eardrums with screeching karaoke 'music' – select a seat as far away from these sinister speakers as possible. Alternatively, try buying some classical music or Chinese rock tapes that you like and giving them to the driver in the hope that he'll play them.

Chinese law requires drivers to announce their presence to cyclists, and for this they use a tweeter for preliminaries, a bugle or bullhorn if they get annoyed and an ear-wrenching air horn when they're really stirred up.

While the roads and condition of the buses have improved in recent years, traffic is getting worse, making bus travel a rather slow means of transport. It's safe to reckon times for bus journeys by calculating the distance against a speed of 25 km/h. Things are slowed down further by Chinese driving techniques – drivers are loathe to change gears and appear to prefer coming to an almost absolute standstill on a slope rather than changing from third into second. Petrol-saving ploys include getting up to the highest speed possible and then coasting to a near standstill, before starting the process again. Engines are switched off for stops of any kind, even if it's only a matter of seconds.

Classes

In recent years night buses have become increasingly frequent. These get mixed reviews – they are more dangerous and few but the Chinese can sleep on a crowded jolting bus. On most popular routes, sleeper buses *(wòpù qìchē)* have been introduced – they are usually around double the price of a normal bus service but many travellers swear by them. Some have comfortable reclining seats, while others even have two-tier bunks. On runs of over 12 hours where sleeper buses have not been introduced there should be an overnight stop but this is not always the case. Increasingly, buses are using two drivers and doing torturous two-day excursions in a single stint – the 35-hour run between Golmud and Lhasa is a notorious example.

Privately owned minibuses are increasingly competing with public buses on medium-length routes. Although they're often a bit cramped, you always get a seat (or at least a knee to sit on), though you often have to bargain to get the Chinese price. Drivers will sometimes try to make you pay extra for bulky luggage.

Astronaut-type backpacks are a nightmare to stow on buses as there's little space under the seats, overhead racks hardly big enough to accommodate a loaf of bread and sparse space in the aisles. If you intend doing a lot of bus travel then travel light! In China, unlike other Asian countries, people do not ride on the roof, though luggage is sometimes stowed there.

Reservations

It's a good idea to book a seat in advance. All seats are numbered. You don't actually have a reservation until you've got a fully paid ticket in hand. While some hotels and travel agents book bus tickets, it's often easiest and less error-prone to head for the bus station and do it yourself.

Bus stations are often large affairs with numerous ticket windows and waiting halls. There is a special symbol for a bus station which appears on local maps and is meant to resemble the steering wheel of the bus. The symbol is:

Costs

Bus travel generally works out to be comparable to hard-seat train travel in terms of expense, and at present there is no foreigner double-pricing rule, with the exception of western China (Xinjiang and Tibet are notorious). Gansu Province requires foreigners to purchase 'insurance'.

In terms of how much you'll pay for meals, it's a very mixed bag out there. In about 50% of the cases, drivers take you to the filthiest and most expensive little hovels they can find with the worst food imaginable. It seems that these places are owned by their friends or relatives and the drivers get a commission. It's depressing because buses usually drive right past many perfectly acceptable restaurants, but the drivers refuse to stop. Sometimes you get lucky – there are

at least a few honest drivers out there. Your best defence is to stock up on sufficient munchies before you board the bus.

TRAIN

China's trains are small towns in themselves, with populations typically well over 1000. Though crowded, trains are the best way to get around in reasonable speed and comfort. The network covers every province except Tibet, and that's not for want of trying (experts have advised the Chinese that it is impossible to build a line up to Lhasa – it would involve drilling tunnels through ice). There are an estimated 52,000 km of railway lines in China, most of them built since 1949 when the system had either been blown to bits or was nonexistent in certain regions.

The safety record of the railway system is good – other than getting your luggage pinched or your pocket picked, there isn't much danger on trains. However, the Chinese have a habit of throwing rubbish out the windows even as the train moves through a station. Avoid standing too close to a passing train, lest you get hit by flying beer bottles or chicken bones.

Classes

In socialist China there are no classes; instead you have hard seat, hard sleeper, soft seat and soft sleeper.

Hard Seat Except on the trains which serve some of the branch or more obscure lines, hard seat is not in fact hard but is padded. But it's hard on your sanity and you'll get little sleep on the upright seats. Since hard seat is the only thing the locals can afford it's packed to the gills, the lights stay on all night, passengers spit on the floor and the carriage speakers endlessly drone news, weather, information and music. Hard seat is OK for a day trip; some foreigners can't take more than five hours of it, while others have a threshold of 12 hours or even longer. A few brave, penniless souls have even been known to travel *long-distance* this way – some roll out a mat on the floor under the seats and go to sleep on top of the gob.

As bad as it is, you should try to experience hard seat at least once, and the more crowded the better. This is China as it exists for the masses, a very different world from the glittering tourist hotels.

Hard Sleeper These are comfortable and only a fixed number of people are allowed in the sleeper carriage. The carriage is made up of doorless compartments with half a dozen bunks in three tiers, and sheets, pillows and blankets are provided. It does very nicely as a budget hotel. The best bunk to get is a middle one since the lower one is invaded by all and sundry who use it as a seat during the day, while the top one has little headroom. The top bunks are also where the cigarette smoke floats about and it's usually stinking hot up there in summer even with the fans on fill blast.

The worst possible bunks are the top ones at either end of the carriage or right in the middle; they're right up against the speakers and you'll get a rude shock in the morning at about 6 am. Lights and speakers in hard sleeper go out at around 9.30 to 10 pm. Competition for hard sleepers has become keen in recent years, and you'll be lucky to get one on short notice.

Soft Seat On shorter journeys (such as Shenzhen to Guangzhou) some trains have soft-seat carriages. The seats are comfortable and overcrowding is not permitted. Smoking is prohibited, a significant advantage unless you enjoy asphyxiation. If you want to smoke in the soft-seat section, you can do so only by going out into the corridor between cars. Soft seat costs about the same as hard sleeper and is well worth it. Unfortunately, soft-seat cars are a rarity.

Soft Sleeper Luxury. Softies get the works, with four comfortable bunks in a closed compartment – complete with straps to keep you from falling off in the middle of the night, wood panelling, potted plants, lace curtains, teacup set, clean washrooms, carpets (so no spitting) and often air-con. As for those speakers, not only do you have a volume control, you can turn the bloody things off! Soft sleeper costs twice as much as hard sleeper, and almost the same price as flying (on some routes even *more* than flying!). It's relatively easy to get soft sleeper because few ordinary Chinese can afford it. However, the growing class of *noveaux riches* plus high-ranking cadres (who charge it to their state expense accounts) has upped the demand for soft sleepers, so you might wind up in hard seat no matter how much cash you've got. Travelling in soft sleeper should be experienced once – it gives you a good chance to meet the ruling class.

Train Types
Train composition varies from line to line and also from day to night, and largely depends on the demand for sleepers on that line. A typical high-frequency railway line has about 13 carriages: six hard seat, perhaps one soft seat, three hard sleeper, one soft sleeper, one dining car and one guard/baggage van.

Half or even a whole carriage may be devoted to crew quarters on the longer trips. If the journey time is more than 12 hours then the train qualifies for a dining car. The dining car often separates the hard-seat from the hard-sleeper and soft-sleeper carriages.

The conductor is in a little booth in a hard-seat carriage in the middle of the train – usually carriage No 7, 8 or 9 (all carriages are numbered on the outside). Coal-fired samovars are found in the ends of the hard-class sections, and from these you can draw a supply of hot water. On long trips, however, the water often runs out. The disc-jockey has a little booth at the end of one of the cars with a door marked *Boyinshi*, which apart from the reel-to-reel tape, radio and record player also contains the attendant's bed.

On some of the small branch lines there are various kinds of passenger carriages – some have long bench seats along the walls, others are just cattle cars without seats or windows.

Different types of trains are usually recognisable by the train number:

Nos 1-100 These are special express and usually diesel-hauled. They have all classes and there is a surcharge for the speed and superior facilities. The international trains are included in this group.

Nos 101-399 Trains in this approximate number range make more stops than the special expresses. They have soft and hard sleepers, but fewer of them. The speed surcharge is half that of the special expresses but the difference in overall price is minimal.

Nos 400 & 500 These are slow, and stop at everything they can find. They may have hard wooden seats and no sleepers. They should have soft seats, but these will be equivalent to the hard seats on the fast trains. The trains have antique fittings, lamps and wood panelling, and are usually steam-pulled. There is no speed surcharge as there is no speed.

No 700 These trains take suburban routes.

Apart from the speed breakdown, the numbers don't really tell you much else about the train. As a general rule, the outbound and inbound trains have matching numbers; thus train Nos 79/80 divide into No 79 leaving Shanghai and going to Kunming, and No 80 leaving Kunming and going to Shanghai.

However, there are, for example, at least six different trains listed in the Chinese train timetable under Nos 301/302, and the sequence-number match is not always reliable. Trains also appear to shift numbers from one timetable to the following year's timetable, so train No 175 becomes train No 275. Simple.

Reservations & Tickets

Buying hard-seat tickets at short notice is usually no hassle, though you will not always be successful in getting a reserved seat. Buying a ticket for a sleeper can be problematic – indeed, it can be damn near impossible if you try to do it yourself. If you try to buy a sleeper ticket at the railway station and the clerk just says '*meiyou*,' you'll have to seek the assistance of a travel agent. This can mean CITS, CTS, CYTS and travel agents affiliated with hotels. However, many CITS and CTS offices no longer do rail bookings. If you run into this problem, the best thing is to ask at the reception desk of your hotel

(unless you're staying in a grotty dump). Most hotels have an in-house travel agent who can obtain train tickets. You'll pay foreign-devil rates and a service charge of perhaps Y40 or so, but it's probably worth it to avoid 30 hours in hard-seat hell. You must give your passport to the travel agency when they go to buy your ticket, but an old expired passport will do just fine.

Tickets for sleepers can easily be obtained in major cities, but not in quiet backwaters. There is a three-day advance-purchase limit, presumably to prevent tickets being hoarded by scalpers.

You can buy tickets the night before departure or on the day of departure from the railway station. This often involves long queues, and in large cities the 'queues' can become near riots. Some stations are better than others. Hard-seat tickets bought on the same day will usually be unreserved – you get on board and try and find a seat. If there are no seats, you'll either have to stand or find a place for your bum among the peanut shells, cigarette butts and spittle.

If you're buying a ticket from the railway station, then you should write down clearly on a piece of paper what you want: train number, time, date, class of travel. The appropriate characters and phrases can be copied from a phrasebook. Learn a few key phrases like 'tomorrow' and 'hard sleeper'. English-speaking Chinese people are always willing to translate and there are usually one or two around in the larger places.

If you have a sleeper ticket the carriage attendant will take it from you and give you a metal or plastic chit – when your destination is close he or she will swap it back and give you the original ticket. Keep your ticket until you get through the barriers at the other end, as you'll need to show it there.

Platform Tickets An alternative to all the above is not to bother with a ticket at all and simply walk on to the train. To do this, you need to buy a platform ticket *(zhàntái piào)*. These are available from the station's information booth for a few jiao. You then buy your ticket on the train. This method is usually more hassle than it's worth, but may be necessary if you arrive at the station without enough time to get your ticket.

Black-Market Tickets Black-market train tickets have become something of a cottage industry in China. You simply order a ticket (at the Chinese price plus a commission) from one of the touts standing around the railway station or operating through a cafe or hotel. However, you could be buying a worthless piece of cardboard – ticket counterfeiting has also become a new growth industry in China. It's advisable to have a Chinese-reading person check the ticket before you pay up.

Also note that in some cities (Beijing, for example) the authorities have cracked down hard and will fine foreigners whom they catch using black-market tickets.

Getting Aboard As soon as the train pulls into the station, all hell breaks loose. In the hope of getting a seat, hard-seat passengers charge at the train, often pushing exiting passengers back inside. Some would-be travellers climb through the windows. Railway attendants – often female – try to keep order, sometimes using night sticks or bamboo poles. If you have a reserved seat or sleeper, you can let the crowd fight it out for a while, then peacefully find your carriage and claim your rightful place. If you don't have a reserved seat, you're going to have to join the fray. The sensible option is to head for either the very front or the very rear of the train. Most passengers attack the middle of the train – the part closest to the platform entrance gate.

Upgrading If you get on the train with an unreserved seating ticket, you can seek out the conductor and upgrade *(bǔpiào)* yourself to a hard sleeper, soft seat or soft sleeper if there are any available. You will usually be charged foreigners' prices for this service, and there are risks involved (no sleepers left) but it is sometimes the only way to get a sleeper or even a seat. On some trains it's easy to do but others are notoriously

crowded. A lot of intermediary stations along the railway lines can't issue sleepers, making upgrading the only alternative to hard seat.

If the sleeper carriages are full then you may have to wait until someone gets off. That sleeper may only be available to you until the next major station which is allowed to issue sleepers, but you may be able to get several hours of sleep. The sleeper price will be calculated for the distance that you used it for.

Ticket Validity Tickets are valid for one to seven days, depending on the distance travelled. On a cardboard ticket the number of days is printed at the bottom left-hand corner. If you go 250 km it's valid for two days; 500 km, three days; 1000 km, three days; 2000 km, six days; and about 2500 km, seven days.

Thus if you're travelling along a major line you could (theoretically) buy one ticket and break the journey where you feel like it. This will only work for unreserved hard seats. The advantage of this method is that you can keep away from railway ticket windows for a while; you can get off, find a refreshing hotel and get back on board the next day on the same ticket.

So much for theory – nothing is consistent in China. In some stations, the railway workers won't let you board unless you hold a ticket for the exact date and time of departure. If you buy a ticket for a morning train (unreserved hard seat) and try to take a later train the same day, they may refuse to let you board even though the ticket is still valid!

Given the fact that the rules are subject to the unpredictable whims of various railway workers, you'll probably wind up just buying tickets for the exact time and date you intend to depart.

Timetables
There are paperback train timetables in Chinese but nothing in English. No matter how fluent your Chinese, the timetables are so excruciatingly detailed that it's a drag working your way through them. Even the Chinese complain about this. Thinner ver-

sions listing the major trains can sometimes be bought from hawkers outside the railway stations. Hotel reception desks and CITS offices have copies of the timetable for trains out of their city or town.

Some railway stations require that luggage be x-rayed before entering the waiting area. The reason is that China has to deal with people transporting huge quantities of explosive chemicals, firecrackers and gunpowder for making firecrackers – there have been several disastrous explosions. Occasionally, gory photographs of the results are tacked up in stations.

If the horde of starers in the waiting room is annoying, you can head to the soft-class waiting rooms if you've got a soft-seat or soft-sleeper ticket. Some soft-class waiting rooms require a Y1 ticket which includes free tea.

Just about all railway stations have left-luggage rooms (jìcún chù) where you can safely dump your bags for a few yuan.

Smile – It Helps
As far as foreigners are concerned, many railway staff in China are exceedingly polite and can be very helpful – how they treat their fellow Chinese is another matter. The staff may bend over backwards to assist you, particularly if you smile, behave friendly and look lost. Sometimes they'll invite you to sit with them or even give you their own train seats. Even when all the sleepers are supposedly full, they sometimes manage to find one for foreigners, so it pays to be nice. Unfortunately, many foreigners take out their frustrations on the railway staff – this just makes it tough for all who follow. ■

Costs

Calculation of train prices is a complex affair based on the length of the journey, speed of the train and relative position of the sun and moon. There are a few variables, such as air-con charges or whether a child occupies a berth or not, but nothing worth worrying

about. The express surcharge is the same regardless of what class you use on the train.

The most important thing to remember is the double-pricing system on Chinese trains. Most foreigners are required to pay three times more than People's Republic Chinese for their railway tickets. Other fares apply to Overseas Chinese, Chinese students, foreign students and foreign experts in China. All train fares mentioned in this book are standard tourist price, unless otherwise stated.

Trains are naturally cheaper than planes, but if you get a tourist-price soft sleeper then the gap between train and air travel narrows considerably. Often the difference is so small that, given the savings in time and trouble, it's definitely worth considering flying.

Tourist price is the real crunch – it will clean your wallet out. Maybe a higher price can be justified for the sleepers, since they are hard to get and foreigners are given priority. But to sit in hard-seat hell, it doesn't seem fair – you pay triple to ride in the same agony!

Cheaper Tickets Tourist-price tickets are slips of paper with various details scribbled all over them. Chinese-price tickets are little stubs of cardboard. Getting a Chinese-priced ticket is possible but becoming more difficult. Officially the only foreigners entitled to local Chinese-priced tickets are foreign students studying in the PRC, and certain foreigners authorised to live and work in China.

In the past travellers have been using all sorts of impressive-looking 'student cards' or made-in-Hong-Kong imitations of the 'white card' and 'red card' (which authorises foreigners to pay local price) to pass themselves off as students. Although more railway stations are catching on to these tricks, it's surprising how often they still work. It used to be possible to use a Taiwan student card (Taiwan is officially considered part of China), but this trick no longer works.

Officially, Overseas Chinese, Hong Kongers and Taiwanese are also required to pay tourist prices. In actual practice, anyone who looks Chinese (even Japanese) can usually wind up getting tickets at the local Chinese price. It appears that race is the major consideration.

You can also get a local Chinese person to do it and give them a tip, but exercise caution – they could get into trouble, or they could pocket your money and run away. It's best to have them pay first with their own cash and then reimburse them, though many will not have the cash to do this.

Students are your best bet if you want someone to buy tickets for you – they appreciate any tip you give them and they are usually (but not always) honest.

Most railway workers don't care if you get a Chinese-priced ticket, with the exception of the Guangzhou Railway Station and the Beijing Railway Station, where the rules seem to be enforced. However, if you do get on the train with a Chinese-priced ticket the conductor can still charge you the full fare, or you could be stopped at the railway station exit gate at your destination, have your tickets checked and be charged the full fare. In practice, this seldom happens.

Some railway stations have separate booking offices for foreigners. As a rule they'll charge you tourist price; you can sometimes wangle local price if you speak Chinese or have a fake student ID. On the credit side, you don't have to wait in formidable queues and you can often get a sleeper – so if you do have to pay tourist price, stop bitching and consider your money well spent!

Food The cheapest meals are the 'rice boxes' brought down the carriages on trolleys and sold for about Y4 to Y5.

Trains on longer journeys have dining cars. Meals cost about Y15 for a couple. After about 8 pm when meals are over you can probably wander back into the dining car. The staff may want to get rid of you, but if you just sit down and have a beer it may be OK. One Chinese-speaking traveller recalls getting drunk in the dining car with the train crew, one of whom stood up and loudly cursed the powers that be, saying they were all rotten to the core. He was threatened with ejection from the train at the next stop if he didn't sit down and shut up!

At station stops you can buy food and drinks from the vendors.

We were allowed to spend one night from Zhanjiang to Guilin in the dining car when it wasn't occupied by people eating there. We ended up there after a futile attempt to upgrade to hard sleeper. Eventually we had to pay Y15 each for the sake of staying there, but it was still less horrible than hard seat.

TAXI

Long-distance taxis are usually booked through travel agencies like CITS or from hotels. They generally ask excessive fees – the name of the game is negotiate. If you can communicate in Chinese or find someone to translate, it's not particularly difficult to find a private taxi driver to take you wherever you like for less than half of CITS rates.

In places frequented by tourists it's possible to book private minibuses – with a group this can be worthwhile for getting to certain isolated sites. For example, it's almost essential to book a minibus to see the sights around the desert oasis of Turpan in Xinjiang Province. Drivers can usually be found hanging around bus stations and hotels. Chances are good that you won't have to look for them, as they'll be looking for you.

CAR & MOTORCYCLE

For those who would like to tour China by car or motorbike, the news is bleak – basically it's impossible unless you go with a large group (accompanied by PSB the whole way), apply for permits months in advance and pay through the nose for the privilege. It's not like India, where you can simply buy a motorbike and head off on your own.

That having been said, there are a few hopeful signs. Beijing and Shanghai have recently introduced the concept of drive-away car rental. It's experimental and fraught with bureaucratic hurdles, and the Chinese are making up the rules as they go along. But it seems that armed with nothing more than an international driver's licence, a credit card and wads of cash (for a deposit), you can rent a car in Beijing or Shanghai but nowhere else. The catch – besides the expense – is that you can only drive within the city limits. You can't simply rent a car in Beijing and head off to Xi'an or Lhasa, so don't try it. Tourists are not yet permitted to rent motorbikes or purchase motor vehicles.

Foreign residents (as opposed to tourists) are governed by a different set of regulations. A Chinese driver's licence is required. In order to get one, you must first secure a residence permit. Then you must hand in your native country's driver's licence (not an international driver's licence) – the PSB keeps this licence and issues you a Chinese one. When you leave China, you must turn in your Chinese licence and your native country's licence will be returned to you. To complicate things even more, you need to prove you have a car before the licence can be issued! Foreign residents face the same restrictions about driving outside the city – basically it's forbidden without special permits.

BICYCLE

Probably the first time the Chinese saw a pneumatic-tyred bicycle was when a pair of globe-trotting Americans called Allen and Sachtleben bumbled into Beijing around 1891 after a three-year journey from Istanbul. They wrote a book about it called *Across Asia on a Bicycle*. The novelty was well received by the Qing court, and the boy-emperor Puyi was given to tearing around the Forbidden City on a cycle.

Today there are over 300 million bikes in China, more than can be found in any other country. Some are made for export, but most are for domestic use. It's easy to see why many Chinese would be willing to spend their last yuan for a bike – anything is preferable to being at the mercy of the bus system.

The traditional Chinese bicycle and tricycle are workhorses, used to carry anything up to a 100-kg slaughtered pig or a whole couch...you name it. Until very recently, Chinese bikes all looked the same – heavy gearless monsters made out of waterpipe and always painted black. Although the black beasts are still the most popular design (because they last a long time and are relatively cheap), sleek new multi-geared models in a variety of colours are available. The Chinese are even having success at exporting these, though quality could stand a little improvement.

In Western countries, travel agencies organising bicycle trips advertise in cycling magazines. Bicycle clubs can contact CITS (or its competitors) for information about organising a trip.

Rental

There are now established bicycle hire shops that cater to foreigners in most traveller centres. In touristy places like Yangshuo it's even possible to rent sharp-looking mountain bikes, but elsewhere it's the old black clunkers. The majority operate out of hotels popular with foreigners, but there are also many independent hire shops. Even in towns that don't see much tourist traffic there are often hire shops catering to Chinese who are passing through (however, they are rapidly disappearing as the increasingly affluent Chinese switch to 'modern' transport like taxis). They are usually happy to hire bikes to foreigners as well. Surprisingly, medium-size cities often have better bike-rental facilities than large metropolises.

Day hire, 24-hour hire or hire by the hour are the norm. It's possible to hire for a stretch of several days, so touring is possible if the bike is in good condition. Rates for Westerners are typically Y2 per hour or Y10 to Y20 per day – the price depends more on competition than anything else. Some big hotels charge ridiculous rates, as much as Y10 per hour!

If you hire over a long period you should be able to reduce the rate. Most hire places will ask you to leave some sort of ID. Sometimes they ask for your passport, which is asking a lot. Give them some other ID instead, like a student card or a driver's licence. Old expired passports are really useful for this purpose. Some hire shops may require a deposit, but that should certainly not be more than the actual value of the bike.

If you're planning on staying in one place for more than about five weeks, it's probably cheaper to buy your own bike and either sell it or give it to a friend when you leave.

Before taking a bike, check the brakes (are there any?), get the tyres pumped up hard and make sure that none of the moving parts are about to fall off. Get the saddle raised to maximum leg power. It's also worth tying something on – a handkerchief, for example – to identify your bicycle amid the zillions at the bicycle parks.

A bike licence is obligatory for Chinese but is not necessary for a foreigner. Some cities have bicycle licence plates, and in Beijing bikes owned by foreigners have special licence plates so they can't be sold to a Chinese. Bike-repair shops are everywhere and repairs are cheap (say Y5 a shot) but overcharging of foreigners is common – ask first.

Purchase

Until very recently, there were only four basic types of bike available in China: small wheel, light roadster (14 kg), black hulk (22 kg) and farmers' models (25 to 30 kg). The average price for a one-speed bike is around Y400, about a month's wages for a city worker.

Some travellers have saved themselves the bother of bringing bikes across the border by buying mountain bikes or racers in China. You won't get the range that is available at home or in Hong Kong, but you're likely to save some hassle and quite a bit of money. Mountain bikes are available for around Y700 to Y1400.

In Hong Kong, Flying Ball Bicycle Shop (☎ 2381-5919) at 201 Tung Choi St (near Prince Edward MTR station) in Mongkok is the place to go for both hardware and information about cycling in China.

Freestyle

Prior to 1987, border guards and police officials in remote areas were often puzzled by the sudden appearance of muddy foreign

bikers whizzing through from Guangzhou to Kunming, Shanghai to Xi'an, Kathmandu to Lhasa etc. Unfortunately, now that the novelty has worn off, officials have decided that they need to 'do something' about the influx of foreign bikers. The 'rules' (that is, whims of officials) suggests that at present you can bring bikes from Hong Kong into China by ship (ie, the boat to Guangzhou) but *not* overland into Shenzhen. On the other hand, getting across the border from Macau into China seems to pose no problem. If you do get into the PRC without incident, you have to contend with the possibility of being intercepted by local officials in remote areas and fined.

The legalities of cycling from town to town are open to conjecture. There is absolutely no national law in China which prohibits foreigners from riding bicycles. Basically, the problem is that of 'open' and 'closed' areas. It's illegal for foreigners to visit closed areas without a permit. Fair enough, but foreigners can transit a closed area – that is, you can travel by train or bus through a closed area as long as you don't exit the vehicle in this 'forbidden zone'. The question is: Should riding a bicycle through a closed area be classified as 'transiting' or 'visiting' it?

Chinese law is as clear as mud on this issue. Most of the time, the police won't bother you, but some officials just can't stand seeing foreigners bicycling through China – they expect you to be travelling by taxi and tour bus. After all, foreigners are universally regarded as rich and bicycles are meant for poor peasants. No respectable cadre would be caught dead riding a bicycle – they prefer limousines. Most Chinese can't figure out why foreigners would even want to cycle around China.

If you get caught in a closed area, it is unlikely to be while you are on the road. The long arm of the law keeps firm tabs on transients via hotels. If you're staying overnight in an open place, but you are suspected of having passed through a closed area, the police may pull a raid on your hotel. You can be hauled down to the police station, where you have to submit to a lengthy interrogation, sign a confession and pay a fine. Fines vary from Y50 to Y100. There is some latitude for bargaining in these situations, and you should request a receipt *(shōujù)*. And don't expect the police to give you any tips on which areas are closed and which are open:

It was 10 pm, it was raining, I was in the outskirts and nobody was noticing me, so I quickly hopped into a hotel. I wasn't sleeping yet and they came and took me and my stuff and my bike to the city centre, to a big hotel, of course more expensive, kept my passport and told me to come to the police station next morning.

And there I was and told them about false information and all the mismanagement. I passed through so many road blocks and nobody stopped me, and if I asked a policeman on the street whether the place was open or not, he wouldn't know, so how should I, a tourist who can't speak Chinese, know that this is a closed city?

'No, this is an open city.' Ah?...so what am I doing in the police station? 'You were probably in a closed area.'

I couldn't even lie, I didn't know what was open and what not.

Ze Do Rock

Camping is possible if you can find a spare blade of grass. The trick is to select a couple of likely places about half an hour before sunset, keep pedalling and then backtrack so you can pull off the road at the chosen spot just after darkness falls.

One problem with Western bikes is that they attract a lot of attention. Another problem is the unavailability of spare parts. One Westerner brought a fold-up bicycle with him – but in most places it attracted so much attention that he had to give it to the locals to play with until the novelty wore off. And fold-up bikes just aren't practical for long-distance riding.

It's essential to have a kick-stand for parking. A bell, headlight and reflector are good ideas. Make sure everything is bolted down, otherwise you'll invite theft. A cageless water bottle, even on a Chinese bike, attracts too much attention. Adhesive reflector strips get ripped off.

Hazards

It's difficult to miss the ubiquitous picture displays around Chinese cities exhibiting the gory remains of cyclists who didn't look where they were going and wound up looking like Y5 worth of fried dumplings. These displays also give tips on how to avoid accidents and show 're-education classes' for offenders who have had several accidents. Take care when you're riding and don't give the authorities the opportunity to feature a foreigner in their next display.

Night riding is particularly hazardous. Many drivers in China only use their headlights to flash them on and off as a warning for cyclists up ahead to get out of the way. On country roads look out for those UFO-style walking tractors, which often have no headlights at all.

Your fellow cyclists are another factor in the hazard equation. Most Chinese cyclists have little more than an abstract grasp of basic road courtesy and traffic rules. Be prepared for cyclists to suddenly swerve in front of you, to come hurtling out of a side road or even to head straight towards you against the flow of the traffic. This is not to mention situations where you yourself are the traffic hazard: beware of the cyclist who spots you, glides by staring gape-mouthed, crashes into something in front and causes the traffic following to topple like tenpins.

Dogs, the enemy of cyclists the world over, are less of a problem in China than elsewhere. This is because Fido is more likely to wind up stir-fried than menacing cyclists on street corners. One exception to this rule is Tibet and parts of Qinghai. Be particularly careful if cycling around Lhasa.

In most larger towns and cities bicycles should be parked at designated places on the sidewalk. This will generally be a roped off enclosure, and bicycle-park attendants will give you a token when you park there; the charge is usually five jiao to Y1. If you don't use this service, you may return to find that your bike has been 'towed' away. Confiscated illegally parked bicycles make their way to the police station. There will be a fine in retrieving it, though it shouldn't bankrupt you.

Bicycle theft does indeed exist. The bicycle parks with their attendants help prevent this, but keep your bike off the streets at night, or at least within the hotel gates. If the hotel has no grounds then take the bike up to your room. Most hired bicycles have a lock around the rear wheel which can be pried open with a screwdriver in seconds. You can increase security by buying and using a cable lock, widely available from shops in China.

Off the Road

Most travellers who bring bikes take at least a couple of breaks from the rigours of the road, during which they use some other means of transport. The best option is bus. It is generally no problem stowing bikes on the roofs of buses and there is seldom a charge involved. Air and train transport are more problematic.

Bikes are not cheap to transport on trains; they can cost as much as a hard-seat fare (Chinese price). Boats are cheaper, if you can find one. Trains have quotas for the number of bikes they may transport. As a foreigner you will get preferential treatment in the luggage compartment and the bike will go on the first available train. But your bike won't arrive at the same time as you unless you send it on a couple of days in advance. At the other end it is held in storage for three days free, and then incurs a small charge.

The procedure for putting a bike on a train and getting it at the other end is as follows:

- Railway personnel would like to see a train ticket for yourself (not entirely essential).
- Go to the baggage transport section of the station. Get a white slip and fill it out to get the two or three tags for registration. Then fill out a form (it's only in Chinese, so just fill it out in English) which reads: 'Number/to station x/send goods person/receive goods person/total number of goods/from station y'.
- Take the white slip to another counter, where you pay and are given a blue slip.
- At the other end (after delays of up to three days for transporting a bike) you present the blue slip, and get a white slip in return. This means your bike has arrived. The procedure could take from 20 minutes to an hour depending on who's around. If

you lose that blue slip you'll have real trouble reclaiming your bike.

Chinese cyclists spend ages at the stations mummifying their bicycles in cloth for transport. For the one scratch the bike will get it's hardly worth going through this elaborate procedure.

The best bet for getting your bike on a bus is to get to the station early and put it on the roof. Strictly speaking, there shouldn't be a charge for this, but in practice the driver will generally try to extort a few yuan out of you. Bypass this sort of thing by putting it on the roof and unloading it yourself. The driver won't like it, but you'll normally be allowed to proceed all the same.

Transporting your bike by plane can be expensive, but it's often less complicated than by train. Some cyclists have not been charged by CAAC; others have had to pay 1% of their fare per kg of excess weight.

HITCHING

Hitching is never entirely safe in any country in the world, and we don't recommend it. Travellers who decide to hitch should understand that they are taking a small but potentially serious risk. People who do choose to hitch will be safer if they travel in pairs and let someone know where they are planning to go.

Many people have hitchhiked in China, and some have been amazingly successful. It's not officially sanctioned and the same dangers that apply elsewhere in the world also apply in China. Exercise caution, and if you're in any doubt as to the intentions of your prospective driver, say no. A woman travelling alone would be wise to travel with a male companion.

Hitching in China is rarely free, and passengers are expected to offer at least a tip. Some drivers might even ask for an unreasonable amount of money, so try to establish a figure early on in the ride to avoid problems later. Don't think of hitching as a means to save money – rarely will it be much cheaper than the bus. The main reason to do it is to get to isolated outposts where public transport is poor. There is, of course, some joy in meeting the locals this way, but communicating is certain to be a problem if you don't speak Chinese.

The best way to get a lift is, like anywhere else, to head out to main roads on the outskirts of town. There are usually lots of trucks on the roads, and even army convoys are worth trying. As far as we know, there is no Chinese signal for hitching, so just try waving down the trucks. Unless you speak the local language, you'll need to have where you want to go written down in Chinese characters – otherwise there's no hope of being understood.

BOAT

In the not-too-distant past, travelling around the eastern parts of China by boat was a popular thing to do for both domestic and foreign travellers. This was dictated more by necessity than aesthetics as boats were often the only reliable and cheap form of transport around.

For better or worse, the boats are fast disappearing. Many services have been cancelled, a victim of improved bus and plane transport. In coastal areas, you're most likely to use a boat to reach offshore islands like Putuoshan (near Shanghai) or Hainan Island in the south. The Yantai-Dalian ferry will likely survive because it saves hundreds of km of overland travel. For the same reason, the Shanghai-Ningbo service will probably continue to operate. But elsewhere, the outlook for coastal passenger ships is not too good.

There are also several inland shipping routes worth considering, but these are also vanishing. For details of each trip see the appropriate sections in this book. The best known river trip is the three-day boat ride along the Yangzi River from Chongqing to Wuhan. From Guangzhou to Wuzhou along the West (Xi) River is popular with low-budget travellers as it is the cheapest way to get from Guangzhou to Guilin and Yangshuo, disembarking at Wuzhou and then continuing on by bus to Guilin or Yangshuo. The Li River boat trip from Guilin to

Yangshuo is a popular tourist ride which takes six hours.

You can also travel the Grand Canal from Hangzhou to Suzhou on a tourist boat – the old ferry services have gone the way of the buggy whip. There are no longer passenger boats on the Yellow River.

There are still a number of popular boats between Hong Kong and the rest of China. See the Getting There & Away section of the Hong Kong chapter for details.

LOCAL TRANSPORT

Long-distance transport in China is not really a problem – the dilemma occurs when you finally make it to your destination. As in US and Australian cities where the car is the key to movement, the bicycle is the key in China, and if you don't have one, life is more difficult. Walking is not usually recommended, since Chinese cities tend to be very spread out.

To/From the Airport

Your plane ticket does not include the cost of transport between the CAAC office and the airport; expect to pay around Y25 for airport buses, occasionally more. In many cases, the departure time of the bus will be noted on your ticket.

You can, of course, take a taxi to the airport. Drivers tend to hang out near the airline offices and solicit customers. But watch out as some drivers quote a ridiculously low price and then try to raise it half way to the airport. If you don't pay up, you could be unceremoniously dumped in the middle of nowhere.

Bus

Apart from bikes, buses are the most common means of getting around in the cities. Services are fairly extensive and the buses go to most places you want to go. The problem is that they are almost always packed. If an empty bus pulls in at a stop then the battle for seats ensues, and a passive crowd of Chinese suddenly turns into a stampeding herd. Even more aggravating is the slow traffic. You just have to be patient, never expect anything to move rapidly, and allow lots of time to get to the railway station to catch your train. One consolation is that buses are cheap, rarely more than two jiao.

Good maps of Chinese cities and bus routes are readily available and are often sold by hawkers outside the railway stations. When you get on a bus, point to where you want to go on the map, and the conductor (who is seated near the door) will sell you the right ticket. They usually tell you where to get off.

You may be offered a seat in a crowded bus, although this is becoming less common in the big cities. It's that peculiarly Chinese politeness which occasionally manifests itself, and if you're offered a seat it's best to accept as refusal may offend.

Taxi

Taxis do not cruise the streets (to save petrol) except in large cities, but the situation is improving due to rising affluence. You can always summon a taxi from the tourist hotels, which sometimes have separate booking desks. You can hire them for a single trip or on a daily basis – the latter is worth considering if there's a group of people who can split the cost. Some of the tourist hotels also have minibuses on hand.

While most taxis have meters, they are a pure formality (except in large cities) and usually only get switched on by accident. Sometimes you're better off without the meter – as elsewhere in the world, Chinese taxi drivers don't mind taking you for a 20-km ride to a place just across the street. Taxi prices should be negotiated before you get into the taxi, and bargaining is usual (but keep it friendly as nastiness on your part will result in a higher price!). Don't be surprised if the driver attempts to change the price when you arrive, claiming that you 'misunderstood' what he said – if you want to get nasty, *this* is the time to do it. If your spoken Chinese is less than perfect, write the price down clearly and make sure the driver agrees to avoid 'misunderstandings' later.

It's important to realise that most Chinese cities impose limitations on the number of passengers that a taxi can carry. The limit is usually four, though minibuses can take more, and drivers are usually unwilling to break the rules and risk trouble with the police. We witnessed a vicious argument in Beijing between eight foreigners and a taxi driver – the driver refused to take all eight people in one trip, saying it was illegal and he could get into trouble. He was willing to make two trips, but the foreigners figured that was just his way of trying to charge double and therefore rip them off. The driver was, in fact, telling the truth.

Motorcycle Taxi

The deal is that you get a ride on the back of someone's motorcycle for about half the price of what a regular four-wheeled taxi would charge. If you turn a blind eye to the hazards, this is a quick and cheap way of getting around. It's required that you wear a helmet – the driver will provide one. Obviously, there is no meter so fares must be agreed to in advance.

Motor-tricycle
(*sānlún mótuōchē*)

The motor-tricycle – for want of a better name – is an enclosed three-wheeled vehicle with a driver at the front, a small motorbike engine below and seats for two passengers behind. They congregate outside the railway and bus stations in larger towns and cities. Some of these vehicles have trays at the rear with bench seats along the sides so that four or more people (plus a few chickens) can all be accommodated.

Pedicab
(*sānlúnchē*)

A pedicab is a pedal-powered tricycle with a seat to carry passengers. Chinese pedicabs have the driver in front and passenger seats in the back, the opposite of some countries (Vietnam, for example).

Pedicabs are gradually disappearing in China, victims of the infernal combustion engine. However, pedicabs congregate outside railway and bus stations or hotels in many parts of China. In a few places, pedicabs cruise the streets in large numbers (Lhasa, for example).

Unfortunately, most of the drivers are so aggressive that you have to ask yourself if it's worth bothering with them. Almost without exception a reasonable fare will be quoted, but when you arrive at your destination it'll be multiplied by 10. So if you're quoted a fare of Y5 it becomes Y50, and if you're quoted Y50 it becomes Y500. Another tactic is to quote you a price like Y10 and then demand US$10 – the driver claims that you 'misunderstood'.

The best bet is to write it down (be sure to specify Renminbi, not US$), get the driver to agree three or four times and sign it, and then when he tries to multiply by 10, hand over the exact change and walk away. At this point the smiling friendly driver will suddenly be transformed into an exceedingly menacing beast – you just have to stand your ground. It's worse if there are two of them, so *never* get into a pedicab if the driver wants his 'brother' to come along for the ride (a common strategy). The 'brother' is there to threaten and bully you into paying up when you inevitably baulk at being ripped off.

The situation is less likely to turn ugly when the driver is female, but women pedicab drivers are very rare. And if she happens to have a 'brother' who wants to come along for the ride, find another driver. In many cases, a taxi works out to be cheaper than a pedicab because the chances of being ripped off are much less.

ORGANISED TOURS

Some of the one-day tours are reasonably priced and might be worth the cost for all the trouble they can save you. Some remote spots are difficult to reach and a tour might well be your only option.

Basically, tours come in three varieties: for foreigners, for Overseas Chinese and for local Chinese. See the local branches of CTS, CITS, CYTS and private agencies for details.

If price is the main consideration, going on tour with the local Chinese is by far the cheapest option. Meals might not even be included and the bus could be an old rattletrap, but these tours can be great fun. Don't expect the guides to speak anything but Chinese – possibly just the local dialect. Sometimes the buses will whiz through what Westerners would consider interesting spots and make long stops at dull places for the requisite photo sessions. You might have difficulty getting a ticket if your Chinese isn't good and they think you're too much trouble. The Chinese tours are often booked through hotel service desks or from private travel agencies.

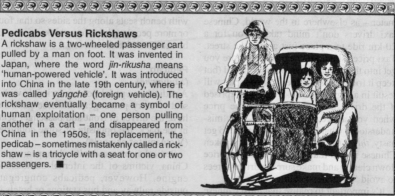

Pedicabs Versus Rickshaws
A rickshaw is a two-wheeled passenger cart pulled by a man on foot. It was invented in Japan, where the word *jin-rikusha* means 'human-powered vehicle'. It was introduced into China in the late 19th century, where it was called *yángchē* (foreign vehicle). The rickshaw eventually became a symbol of human exploitation – one person pulling another in a cart – and disappeared from China in the 1950s. Its replacement, the pedicab – sometimes mistakenly called a rickshaw – is a tricycle with a seat for one or two passengers. ∎

Beijing 北京

As far away as Ürümqi they run on Beijing's clock; around the country they chortle in *putonghua*, the Beijing dialect; in remote Tibet they struggle to interpret the latest half-baked directives from the capital. The Chinese government has announced that if the Dalai Lama were to return he'd be posted to a desk job in – where else? – Beijing. This is where they move the cogs and wheels of the Chinese universe, or try to slow them down if they're moving in the wrong direction.

Tourists often enjoy Beijing – the city offers plenty to see and do, and you can't beat the food or shopping. Those who have slugged it out in hard-seat trains and ramshackle buses through the poverty-stricken interior of China appreciate the creature comforts of Beijing. Other foreigners, having passed their time only in Beijing without seeing the rest of China, come away with the impression that everything is hunky-dory in the PRC and that the Chinese are living high. The Chinese they encounter may, in truth, be doing so.

Whatever impression you come away with, Beijing is not a realistic window on China. It's too much of a cosmetic showcase to qualify. It is, however, a large, relatively clean city, and with a bit of effort you can get out of the make-up department. In between the wide boulevards and militaristic structures are some historical and cultural treasures.

History

Although the area south-west of the city was inhabited by cave dwellers some 500,000 years ago, the earliest records of settlements in Beijing date from around 1000 BC. It developed as a frontier trading town for the Mongols, Koreans and tribes from Shandong and central China. By the Warring States Period it had grown to be the capital of the Yan Kingdom. The town underwent a number of changes as it acquired new war-

Population: 11 million

Highlights:

- The Forbidden City, the centre of power in the Middle Kingdom for over 500 years
- Tiantan, the perfection of Ming architecture and the symbol of Beijing
- The Summer Palace, the lovely gardens of emperors and empresses in a stunning setting beside Kunming Lake
- The Great Wall, ancient China's greatest public works project and now the nation's leading tourist attraction

lords, the Khitan Mongols and the Manchurian Jurchen tribes among them. During the Liao Dynasty Beijing was referred to as Yanjing (capital of Yan), still the name used for Beijing's most popular beer.

Beijing's history really gets under way in 1215 AD, the year that Genghis Khan set fire to the preceding paragraph and slaughtered everything in sight. From the ashes emerged Dadu (Great Capital), alias Khanbaliq, the Khan's town. By 1279 Genghis Khan's grandson Kublai had made himself ruler of most of Asia, and Khanbaliq was his capital. With a lull in the fighting from 1280 to 1300, foreigners managed to drop in along the Silk Road for tea with the Great Khan – Marco Polo even landed a job. The mercenary Zhu

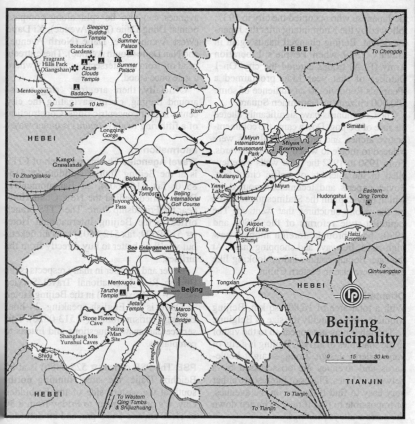

Beijing
Municipality

Yanhang led an uprising in 1368, taking over the city and ushering in the Ming Dynasty. The city was renamed Beiping (Northern Peace) and for the next 35 years the capital was shifted to Nanjing.

In the early 1400s Zhu's son Yong Le shuffled the court back to Beiping and renamed it Beijing (Northern Capital). Many of the structures like the Forbidden City and Tiantan were first built in Yong Le's reign. In fact, he is credited with being the true architect of the modern city.

The first change of government came with the Manchus, who invaded China and estab-

lished the Qing Dynasty. Under them, and particularly during the reigns of the emperors Kangxi and Qianlong, Beijing was expanded and renovated and summer palaces, pagodas and temples were built.

In the last 120 years of the Manchu Dynasty Beijing and subsequently China were subjected to power struggles, invaders and the chaos created by those who held or sought power: the Anglo-French troops who in 1860 marched in and burnt the Old Summer Palace to the ground; the corrupt regime under Empress Dowager Cixi; the Boxers; General Yuan Shikai; the warlords;

the Japanese who occupied the city in 1937; followed by the Kuomintang after the Japanese defeat. Beijing changed hands again in January 1949 when People's Liberation Army (PLA) troops entered the city. On 1 October of that year Mao proclaimed a 'People's Republic' to an audience of some 500,000 citizens in Tiananmen Square.

The Communists have significantly altered the face of Beijing. Down came the commemorative arches, and blocks of buildings were reduced to rubble to widen major boulevards. From 1950 to 1952 the outer walls were levelled in the interests of traffic circulation. Soviet experts and technicians poured in, which may explain the Stalinesque features on the public structures that went up. The capitalist-style reforms of the 1980s and 1990s have brought foreign money, new high-rises, freeways and shopping malls. At this rate, Beijing could wind up looking like everywhere else in eastern China.

Orientation

With a total area of 16,800 sq km, Beijing Municipality is roughly the size of Belgium.

Though it may not appear so to the visitor in the shambles of arrival, Beijing is a city of very orderly design. Long, straight boulevards and avenues are crisscrossed by a network of lanes. Places of interest are either very easy to find if they're on the avenues, or impossible to find if they're buried down the narrow alleys *(hútòng)*.

The central core, once a walled enclosure, still maintains its ancient symmetry based on a north-south axis passing through Qianmen (Front Gate). The major east-west road is Chang'an Jie (Avenue of Eternal Tranquillity).

As for the street names: Chongwenmenwai Dajie means 'the avenue (dajie) outside (wai) Chongwen Gate (Chongwenmen)', whereas Chongwenmennei Dajie means 'the avenue inside Chongwen Gate' (that is, inside the old wall). It's an academic exercise since the gate and the wall in question no longer exist.

A major boulevard can change names six or eight times along its length. Streets and avenues can also be split along compass points: Dong Dajie (East Avenue), Xi Dajie (West Avenue), Bei Dajie (North Avenue) and Nan Dajie (South Avenue). These streets head off from an intersection, usually where a gate once stood.

Officially, there are four 'ring roads' around Beijing, circumnavigating the city centre in four concentric rings. Construction of a fifth ring road *(wǔhuán)* is under way.

Information

Travel Agencies The main branch of CITS is at the Beijing Tourist Building (☎ 515-8570; fax 515-8603), 28 Jianguomenwai Dajie, buried behind the New Otani Hotel near the Friendship Store. The CITS branch office in the Beijing International Hotel (☎ 512-0509; fax 512-0503) sells air tickets, but you'll do better to buy directly from the airlines.

Better and cheaper in many respects is the Beijing Rich International Travel Service (☎ 513-7766 ext 6219) in the Beijing Hotel.

There is an English-speaking 24-hour Beijing Tourism Hotline (☎ 513-0828). This service can answer questions and listens to complaints.

PSB The PSB office (☎ 525-5486) is at 85 Beichizi Dajie, the street running north-south at the eastern side of the Forbidden City. It's open Monday to Friday from 8.30 to 11.30 am and 1 to 5 pm, and on Saturday from 8.30 to 11.30 am; it's closed on Sunday.

Money As for legal money-changing, all hotels – even most budget ones – can change travellers' cheques or US dollars cash.

If you want to cash travellers' cheques and receive US dollars cash in return (necessary if you're going to Russia or Mongolia), this can be done at CITIC, International Building *(guójì dàshà)*, 19 Jianguomenwai Dajie adjacent to the Friendship Store. CITIC will advance cash on major international credit cards. There is a useful branch of the Bank of China on Dong'anmen Dajie – just to the east of the Forbidden City in Wangfujing near the Foreign Languages Bookstore –

which offers many of the same services as CITIC.

American Express The American Express office (☎ 505-2888) is located in Room L115D in the Shopping Arcade at the China World Trade Centre.

Post & Telecommunications The international post & telecommunications building is on Jianguomen Bei Dajie, not far from the Friendship Store. It's open from 8 am to 7 pm. All letters and parcels marked 'Poste Restante, GPO Beijing' will wind up here. The staff even file poste-restante letters in alphabetical order, a rare occurrence in China, but you pay for all this efficiency – there is a Y1 fee charged for each letter received! Overseas parcels must be posted here; a counter sells wrapping paper, string, tape and glue. There's also an international telegraph and telephone service.

There is a small but convenient post office in the CITIC building. Another useful post office is in the basement of the China World Trade Centre.

Most of the tourist hotels sell stamps and some even have 'mini' post offices. You can send overseas packages from these as long as they contain printed matter only.

There are a number of private couriers which offer international express posting of documents and parcels. Some companies to try include: United Parcel Service (☎ 465-1565; fax 465-1897), Room 120A, Lufthansa Centre, 50 Liangmaqiao Lu; DHL (☎ 466-2211; fax 467-7826), 45 Xinyuan Jie, Chaoyang District; and TNT Skypak (☎ 465- 2227; fax 467-7894), 8A Xiangheyuan Zhongli, Chaoyang District.

The Telegraph Building is open 24 hours a day on Xichang'an Jie. Further west on Fuxingmennei Dajie is the International Telephone Office, open daily from 7 am to midnight. However, most of your telecommunication needs can be met at large hotels.

Maps English-language maps of Beijing are handed out for free at the big hotels. They're often part of an advertising supplement for various companies whose locations are, of course, also shown on the map.

It's better to fork out a few yuan for a bilingual map which shows bus routes. These are available from the Friendship Store and hotel gift shops.

If you can deal with Chinese character maps, you'll find a wide variety to choose from.

Embassies Beijing is not a bad place to stock up on visas. There are two major embassy compounds: Jianguomenwai and Sanlitun. For a complete list of embassies in Beijing with addresses and phone numbers, see the Facts for the Visitor chapter at the beginning of this book.

The Jianguomenwai Compound is in the vicinity of the Friendship Store. The Sanlitun Compound is several km to the north-east, near the Great Wall Sheraton Hotel.

Admission Fees

It's important to realise that in many parks, museums and other tourist sites (the Forbidden City being a good example) there are numerous halls and pavilions within the compound, each with its own admission gate charging separate fees.

The locals have the option of buying a cheap general admission ticket for the compound and then buying separate tickets for each pavilion or just one high-priced all-inclusive ticket which grants admission to every pavilion.

For foreigners, the first option is often eliminated – the staff want you to buy the all-inclusive ticket, whether you want it or not. Sometimes it's optional – you can buy the general admission ticket rather than the expensive all-inclusive tourist ticket. This is true for Beihai Park, for example, but at the Summer Palace you don't have the option.

Making your wishes known to the staff at the ticket booth may be difficult if you don't speak Chinese. For what it's worth, the all-inclusive tickets are *tàopiào* in Chinese. The general admission tickets are called 'door tickets' *(mén piào)* or 'common tickets' *(pǔtōng piào)*. ∎

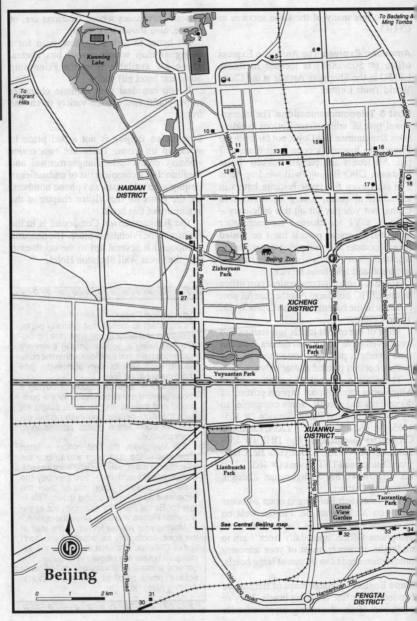

To Badaling &
Ming Tombs

Kunming
Lake

To
Fragrant
Hills

HAIDIAN
DISTRICT

Beisanhuan Zhonglu

Zizhuyuan
Park

Beijing Zoo

XICHENG
DISTRICT

Yuetan
Park

Fuxing Lu

Yuyuantan Park

XUANWU
DISTRICT

Guang'anmennei Dajie

Lianhuachi
Park

Taoranting
Park

See Central Beijing map

Grand
View
Garden

Third Ring Road

Nansanhuan Xilu

FENGTAI
DISTRICT

Beijing

0   1   2 km

Third Ring Road

Fourth Ring Road

Fourth Ring Road

Sihuanbei Lu

8 ■
■ 9

Andingmenwai

Third Ring Road

22 ■
23 ■
24 ■

20 ■
21 ■

25

Ditan
Park

Second Ring Road

**DONGCHENG
DISTRICT**

Jingshan
Park

Workers
Stadium

Forbidden
City

Ritan
Park

**CHAOYANG
DISTRICT**

Chaoyang Lu
29 ■

Chang'an Jie

Tiananmen
Square

Wangfujing Dajie

Dongsi Beidajie

Jianguomen   Dajie

28 ■
Jianguo Lu

**CHONGWEN
DISTRICT**

Qianmen Dajie

Tiantan
Park

Second Ring Road

Longtan
Park

Dongsanhuan Nanlu

38 ■
39 ■
40 ■ 41

36 ■
37

BEIJING 北京

PLACES TO STAY

5 Qinghuayuan Hotel
清华园宾馆

8 Continental Grand Hotel
五洲大酒店

10 Hainan Hotel
海南饭店

11 Yanshan Hotel
燕山大酒店

12 Friendship Hotel
友谊宾馆

14 Big Bell Hotel
大钟寺饭店

15 Jimen Hotel & NASA Disco
蓟门饭店,
NASA 迪斯可

16 Yuanwanglou Hotel
远望楼宾馆

19 Desheng Hotel
德胜饭店

20 Grand Hotel
圆山大酒店

21 Huabei Hotel
华北大酒店

22 Holiday Inn Lido & Watson's
丽都假日饭店,
屈臣氏

23 Yanxiang Hotel
燕翔饭店

24 Grace Hotel
新万寿宾馆

25 Huayuan & Jiali Hotels
华园饭店, 佳丽饭店

26 Shangri-La Hotel
香格里拉饭店

27 Lingnan Hotel
领南饭店

28 China Resources Hotel
华润饭店

29 Furong Hotel
芙蓉宾馆

31 Fengtai Hotel
丰台宾馆

32 Beijing Commercial Business Complex (Hotel)
北京商务会馆

33 Qiaoyuan Hotel
侨园饭店

35 Lihua Hotel
丽华饭店

36 Jinghua Hotel
京华饭店

38 Yongdingmen Hotel
永定门饭店

39 Jingtai Hotel
景泰宾馆

40 Complant Hotel
中成宾馆

41 Park Hotel
百乐酒店

OTHER

1 Summer Palace
颐和园

2 Old Summer Palace
圆明园遗址

3 Beijing University
北京大学

4 Zhongguancun (Bus Stop)
中关村

6 Beijing Language Institute
北京语言学院

7 Chinese Ethnic Culture Park
中华民族园

9 National Olympic Sports Centre
国际奥林匹克体育中心

13 Great Bell Temple
大钟寺

17 Beijing Teachers College
北师大教育管理学院

18 Beijiao (Deshengmen) Long-Distance Bus Station
北郊长途汽车站

30 Fengtai Railway Station
丰台站

34 Yongdingmen (South) Railway Station
永定门火车站
(北京南站)

37 Haihutun Long-Distance Bus Station
海户屯公共汽车站

Libraries The National Library (*běijīng túshūguǎn – xīn guǎn*) holds around five million books and four million periodicals and newspapers, over a third of which are in foreign languages. The library is near the zoo.

Medical Services The International Medical Centre (☎ 465-1561; fax 465-1984) is in the Beijing Lufthansa Centre at 50 Liangmaqiao Lu. Emergency service is available 24 hours a day, but there are normal services during office hours and it's a good

idea to call first for an appointment. Vaccinations and dental services are available here.

Also good is the Sino-German Policlinic (☎ 501-1983) (*zhōngdé zhěnsuǒ*). The clinic is in the basement of Landmark Tower B-1, adjacent to the Sheraton Great Wall Hotel.

Asia Emergency Assistance (☎ 462-9100; fax 462-9111) operates a 24-hour alarm centre. Contact their office for information about their health care plan. The AEA office is in the Tayuan Diplomatic Building, 14 Liangmahe Nanlu, in the Sanlitun Embassy Compound.

Forbidden City & Summer Palace

Forbidden City

(zǐjìn chéng)

The Forbidden City, so called because it was off limits for 500 years, is the largest and best-preserved cluster of ancient buildings in China. It was home to two dynasties of emperors, the Ming and the Qing, who didn't stray from this pleasure dome unless they absolutely had to.

The Beijing authorities insist on calling this place the Palace Museum *(gùgōng)*. Whatever its official name, it's open daily from 8.30 am to 5 pm – last admission tickets are sold at 3.30 pm. Two hundred years ago the admission price would have been instant death, but this has dropped considerably to Y85 for foreigners and Y20 for Chinese. The foreigners' ticket allows admission to all the special exhibition halls, but if you pay Chinese price these cost extra, although it would still work out much cheaper if you could get Chinese price – that appears to be nearly impossible at the Forbidden City unless you have Asian features. Your Y85 includes rental of a cassette tape for a self-guided tour, though you can enter for Y60 without the tape. Tape players are available free but require a refundable Y100 deposit – you can use your own Walkman instead. For the tape to make sense you must enter the Forbidden City from the south gate and exit from the north. The tape is available in a large number of languages.

It's worth mentioning that many foreigners get Tiananmen Gate confused with the Forbidden City entrance because the two are physically attached and there are no signs in English. As a result,

Wumen Gate, the traditional entrance to the Forbidden City, was the setting for important ceremonies during the Qing Dynasty.

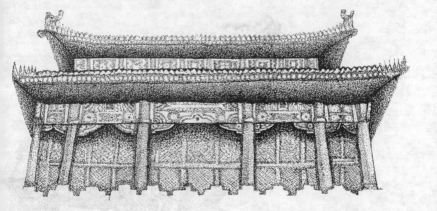

some people wind up purchasing the Tiananmen Gate admission ticket by mistake, not realising that this only gains you admission to the upstairs portion of the gate. To find the Forbidden City ticket booths, keep walking north until you can't walk any further without paying.

The basic layout was built between 1406 and 1420 by Emperor Yong Le, commanding battalions of labourers – some estimate up to a million of them. From this palace the emperors governed China, often rather erratically as they tended to become lost in this self-contained little world and allocated real power to the court eunuchs. One emperor devoted his entire career to carpentry – when an earthquake struck (an ominous sign for an emperor) he was delighted, since it gave him a chance to renovate.

The buildings now seen are mostly post-18th century, as with a lot of restored or rebuilt structures around Beijing. The palace was constantly going up in flames – a lantern festival combined with a sudden gust of Gobi wind would easily do the trick, as would a fireworks display. There were also fires deliberately lit by court eunuchs and officials who could get rich off the repair bills. The moat around the palace, now used for boating, came in handy since the local fire brigade was considered too lowly to quench the royal flames. In 1664, the Manchus stormed in and burned the palace to the ground.

It was not just the buildings that went up in smoke, but rare books, paintings and scrolls. In this century there have been two major lootings of the palace: first by the Japanese forces, and second by the Kuomintang, who, on the eve of the Communist takeover in 1949, removed thousands of crates of relics to Taiwan, where they are now on display in Taipei's National Palace Museum. The gaps have been filled by bringing treasures (old, newly discovered and fake) from other parts of China.

The Bronze Tortoise, symbolising the longevity of the emperor, was used for burning incense.

Summer Palace

(yíhéyuán)

One of the finest sights in Beijing, the Summer Palace includes an immense park that tends to pack out badly during the summer months. The site had long been a royal garden and was considerably enlarged and embellished by Emperor Qianlong in the 18th century. It was later abandoned.

Empress Dowager Cixi began rebuilding in 1888 using money that was supposedly reserved for the construction of a modern navy – but she did restore a marble boat that sits immobile at the edge of the lake. She had this ugly thing fitted out with several large mirrors and used to dine at the lakeside.

In 1900 foreign troops, annoyed by the Boxer Rebellion, had a go at torching the Summer Palace. Restorations took place a few years later and a major renovation occurred after 1949, by which time the palace had once more fallen into disrepair.

The original palace was used as a summer residence. It was divided into four sections: court reception, residences, temples and strolling or sightseeing areas. Three-quarters of the park is occupied by Kunming Lake, and most items of structural interest are towards the east or north gates.

The main building is the Benevolence & Longevity Hall, just off the lake towards the east gate. It houses a hardwood throne and has a courtyard with bronze animals. In it the emperor-in-residence handled state affairs and received envoys.

Along the north shore of the lake is the Long Corridor, over 700 metres long, which is decorated with mythical scenes. If the paint looks new it's because a lot of pictures were whitewashed during the Cultural Revolution.

On artificial Longevity Hill are a number of temples. The Precious Clouds Pavilion on the western slopes is one of the few structures to escape destruction by the Anglo-French forces. It contains some elaborate bronzes. At the top of the hill sits the Buddhist Sea of Wisdom Temple, made of glazed tiles; good views of the lake can be had from this spot.

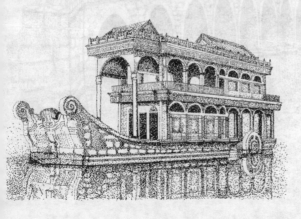

The Boat of Purity & Ease, permanently moored in the lake, was used by Empress Dowager Cixi for dining.

Other sights are largely associated with Empress Cixi, like the place where she kept Emperor Guangxu under house arrest, the place where she celebrated her birthdays and exhibitions of her furniture and memorabilia. A kitsch atmosphere pervades this 'museum'; tourists can have their photos taken, imperial dress-up fashion.

Another noteworthy feature of the Summer Palace is the 17-arch bridge spanning 150 metres to South Lake Island; on the mainland side is a beautiful bronze ox. Also note the Jade Belt Bridge on the mid-west side of the lake and the Harmonious Interest Garden at the north-east end, which is a copy of a Wuxi garden.

You can get around the lake by hiring a small motor or rowing boat. Boating and swimming are popular pastimes for the locals and in winter you can skate on the lakes. As with the Forbidden City moat, it used to be a common practice to cut slabs of ice from the lake in winter and store them for summer use.

The park is about 12 km north-west of the centre of Beijing. The easiest way to get there on public transport is to take the subway to Xizhimen (close to the zoo), then a minibus. Bus No 332 from the zoo is slower but will get you there eventually. Lots of minibuses return to the city centre from the Summer Palace, but get the price and destination settled before departure. You can also get there by bicycle – it takes about 1½ to two hours from the centre of town. Rather than taking the main roads, it's far more pleasant to cycle along the road following the Beijing-Miyun Diversion Canal.

Foreigners are charged an outrageous Y45 for admission. This ticket does *not* get you into everything – there are some additional fees inside. Admission for Chinese costs Y20 – foreigners need to be a Beijing resident with valid ID to get this price.

The 17-arch bridge connects the palace grounds with South Lake Island and the Dragon King's Temple.

Tiananmen Square
(tiān'ānmén guǎngchǎng)

This is the heart of Beijing, a vast desert of pavement and photo-booths. The square is Mao's creation, as is Chang'an Jie leading up to it. During the Cultural Revolution the chairman, wearing a Red Guard armband, reviewed parades of up to a million people here. In 1976 another million people jammed the square to pay their last respects to him. In 1989, army tanks and soldiers cut down pro-democracy demonstrators. Today (if the weather is conducive) the square is a place for people to lounge around in the evening and to fly decorated kites and balloons for the kiddies. Surrounding or studding the square are a strange mishmash of monuments past and present: Tiananmen (Heavenly Peace Gate), the Chinese Revolution History Museum, the Great Hall of the People, Qianmen (Front Gate), the Mao Mausoleum and the Monument to the People's Heroes.

If you get up early you can watch the flag-raising ceremony at sunrise, performed by a troop of PLA soldiers drilled to march at precisely 108 paces per minute, 75 cm per pace. The same ceremony in reverse gets performed at sunset, but you can hardly see the soldiers for the throngs gathered to watch. A digital sign on the square announces the times for the sunrise ceremony for the next two days.

Bicycles cannot be ridden across Tiananmen Square (apparently tanks are OK), but you can walk the bike. Traffic is one way for north-south avenues on either side of the square.

Tiananmen Gate
(tiān'ānmén)

Tiananmen, or Heavenly Peace Gate, is a national symbol. The gate was built in the 15th century and restored in the 17th. From imperial days it functioned as a rostrum for proclaiming to the assembled masses. There are five doors to the gate, and in front of it are seven bridges spanning a stream. Each of these bridges was restricted in its use and only the emperor could use the central door and bridge.

It was from the gate that Mao proclaimed the People's Republic on 1 October 1949. The dominating feature is the gigantic portrait of Mao, the required backdrop for any photo the Chinese take of themselves at the gate. To the left of the portrait is a slogan 'Long Live the People's Republic of China' and to the right 'Long Live the Unity of the Peoples of the World'.

You pass through Tiananmen Gate on your way into the Forbidden City (assuming you enter from the south side). There is no fee for walking through the gate, but to go upstairs and look down on the square costs a whopping Y40 for foreigners, Y10 for Chinese. It's hardly worth it – you can get a similar view of the square from inside Qianmen Gate for a quarter of the price.

Qianmen
(qiánmén)

Silent sentinel to the changing times, Qianmen (Front Gate) sits on the south side of Tiananmen Square. Qianmen guarded the wall division between the ancient Inner City and the outer suburban zone and dates back to the reign of Emperor Yong Le in the 15th century. With the disappearance of the city walls, the gate sits out of context, but it's still an impressive sight.

Qianmen actually consists of two gates. The southern one is called Arrow Tower *(jiàn lóu)* and the rear one is Zhongyang Gate *(zhōngyángmén, also called chéng lóu)*. You can go upstairs into Zhongyang Gate.

Great Hall of the People
(rénmín dàhuì táng)

This is the venue of the rubber-stamp legislature, the National People's Congress. It's open to the public when the Congress is not sitting – to earn some hard currency it's even rented out occasionally to foreigners for conventions! These are the halls of power, many of them named after provinces and regions of China and decorated appropriately. You can see the 5000-seat banquet room where Nixon dined in 1972, and the 10,000-seat

To Summer Palace
& Beijing University

DESHENGMEN

Xisanhuanbei Lu

Zizhuyuan
Park

Baishiqiao Lu

Beijing Zoo

Deshengmen Xi Dajie

Xizhimennei Dajie

XINJIEKOU

Xinjiekou Beidajie

Third Ring Road

Sanlihe Lu

Zhanlan Lu

Xizhimenwai Dajie

Chegongzhuang Dajie

PING'ANLI

Xisi Dajie

XISI

Fuchengmenwai Dajie

Fuchengmennei Dajie

Wenjin Jie

Yuyuantan
Park

Second Ring Road

Yuetan
Park

Xidan Beidajie

Fuxing Lu

Fuxingmenwai Dajie

Fuxingmennei Dajie

Xichang'an Jie

FUXINGMEN

XUANWU
DISTRICT

Qianmen Xi Dajie

Lianhuachi
Park

Guang'anmennei Dajie

Nanheng Jie

Niu Jie

Taoranting
Park

Grand
View
Garden

Central Beijing

0   0.5   1 km

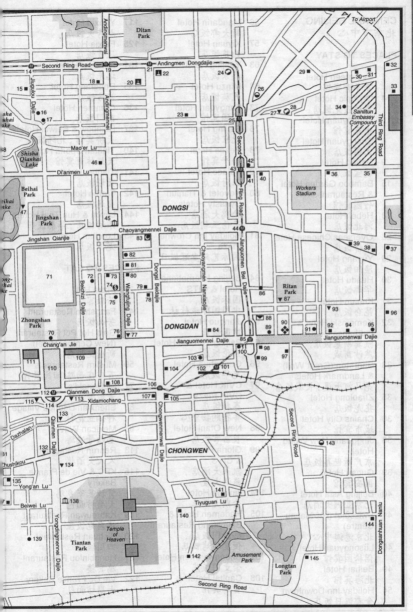

CENTRAL BEIJING
北京市中心

PLACES TO STAY

1 Evergreen Hotel
万年青宾馆
4 Olympic Hotel
奥林匹克饭店
5 Zhongyuan Hotel
中苑宾馆
6 Shangyuan Hotel
上园饭店
9 Debao Hotel
德宝饭店
15 Bamboo Garden Hotel
& Restaurant
竹园宾馆
18 Hebei Hotel
河北饭店
23 Overseas Chinese Hotel
华桥饭店
29 Yuyang Hotel
渔阳饭店
30 Huadu Hotel
华都饭店
31 Kunlun Hotel
昆仑饭店
32 Kempinski Hotel &
Lufthansa Centre
凯宾斯基饭店,
燕沙商城
33 Sheraton (Great Wall)
& Landmark Hotels
亮马河大厦,长城饭店
35 Zhaolong Hotel
兆龙饭店
36 Chains City Hotel
城市宾馆
38 Jingguang New World
Hotel
京广新世界饭店
39 Guoan Hotel
国安宾馆
40 Beijing Asia Hotel
北京亚洲大酒店
41 Swissôtel (HK-Macau
Centre)
北京港澳中心
46 Lüsongyuan Hotel
侣松园宾馆
49 Beihai Hotel
北海宾馆
54 Holiday Inn Downtown
金都假日饭店

56 Mandarin Hotel
新大都饭店
57 Xiyuan Hotel
西苑饭店
63 Yanjing Hotel
燕京饭店
68 Minzu Hotel
民族饭店
73 Fangyuan Hotel
芳园宾馆
76 Beijing Hotel
北京饭店
78 Peace Hotel
和平宾馆
79 Palace Hotel
王府饭店
80 Novotel & Tianlun
Dynasty Hotels
松鹤大酒店,
天伦王朝饭店
81 Holiday Inn Crowne
Plaza
国际艺苑皇冠假日
饭店
84 Beijing International
Hotel & CITS
国际饭店,
中国国际旅行社
92 Jianguo Hotel
建国饭店
94 Beijing Toronto Hotel
京伦饭店
96 Guanghua Hotel
光华饭店
97 CVIK Hotel &
CVIK Plaza
赛特饭店,
赛特购物中心
98 New Otani Hotel
长富宫饭店
99 Gloria Plaza Hotel
& CITS
凯莱大酒店,
旅游大厦
104 Jinlang Hotel
金朗大酒店
105 Hademen Hotel &
Bianyifang Restaurant
哈德门饭店,
便宜坊烤鸭店
107 Chongwenmen Hotel
崇文门饭店
108 Capital Hotel
首都宾馆

117 Yuexiu Hotel
越秀大饭店
125 Feixia Hotel
飞霞饭店
131 Far East Hotel
远东饭店
135 Dongfang Hotel
东方饭店
136 Qianmen Hotel
前门饭店
137 Rainbow & Beiwei Hotels
天桥宾馆,北纬饭店
140 Tiantan Sports Hotel
天坛体育宾馆
141 Tiantan Hotel
天坛饭店
142 Traffic Hotel
交通饭店
144 Leyou & Hua Thai Hotels
乐游饭店,华泰饭店
145 Longtan Hotel
龙潭饭店

PLACES TO EAT

27 Pizza Hut
必胜客
47 Fangshan Restaurant
芳山饭店
58 Gold Hot Pot Restaurant
(New Century Hotel)
新世纪饭店
59 Muslim Restaurants
百万庄西路(回民餐馆)
77 McDonald's
麦当劳
87 Shenxian Douhua Village
神仙豆花村
93 Mexican Wave
墨西哥波涛
113 Renren Restaurant
人人大酒楼
115 KFC & Vie de France
Bakery
肯德基家乡鸡,
大磨坊面包
119 Kaorouwan Restaurant
烤肉宛饭庄
120 Sichuan Restaurant
四川饭店
121 Hongbinlou Restaurant
鸿宾楼
122 Vie De France Bakery
大磨坊面包

132 Pizza Hut
必胜客

133 Qianmen Quanjude
Duck Restaurant
前门全聚德烤鸭店

134 Gongdelin Vegetarian
Restaurant
功德林素菜馆

OTHER

2 Central Nationalities
Institute
中央民族学院

3 National Library
北京图书馆(新馆)

7 Xizhimen (North)
Railway Station
西直门火车站

8 Beijing Exhibition
Centre
北京展览馆

11 Xu Beihong Museum
徐悲鸿纪念馆

13 Song Qingling Museum
宋庆龄故居

16 Bell Tower
钟楼

17 Drum Tower
鼓楼

20 Confucius Temple
孔庙

22 Lama Temple
雍和宫

24 Russian Embassy
苏联大使馆

26 Dongzhimen Long-
Distance Bus Station
东直门长途汽车站

28 Australian Embassy
奥大利亚大使馆

34 Friendship Super-
market
友谊超级商场

37 Chaoyang Theatre
朝阳剧场

42 Poly Plaza
保利大厦

45 China Art Gallery
中国美术馆

48 Prince Gong's
Residence
恭王府

50 Guangji Temple
广济寺

51 Dizhi Auditorium
Cinema
地质电影院

52 White Dagoba Temple
白塔寺

53 Lu Xun Museum
鲁迅博物馆

61 Military Museum
军事博物馆

69 Aviation Building
(CAAC & Airport Bus)
民航营业大厦

70 Tiananmen Gate
天安门

71 Forbidden City
紫禁城

72 PSB
公安局外事科

74 Bank of China
中国银行

75 Foreign Languages
Bookstore
外文书店

82 Capital Theatre
首都剧院

83 Dongsi Mosque
动四清真寺

86 Yabao Lu Clothing
Market
雅宝路

88 International Post &
Telecommunications
国际邮店局

89 International Club
国际俱乐部

90 Friendship Store
& CITIC
友谊商店，国际大厦

91 Xiushui Silk Market
秀水东街

95 China World Trade
Centre & Hotel
国际贸易中心

100 Ancient Observatory
古观象台

102 Beijing Railway Station
北京火车站

103 Beijing Ceroil Plaza
北京中粮广场

109 Chinese Revolution
History Museum
中国革命历史博物馆

110 Tiananmen Square
天安门广场

111 Great Hall of the
People
人民大会堂

114 Qianmen (Front Gate)
前门

126 White Cloud Temple
白云观

127 Beijing West Railway
Station
北京西火车站

128 Tianning Temple
天宁寺

129 Niujie Mosque
牛街礼拜寺

130 Fayuan Temple
法源寺

138 Natural History Museum
自然博物馆

139 Tianqiao Market
天桥市场

143 Majuan Long-Distance
Bus Station
马圈长途汽车站

SUBWAY STATIONS

10 Xizhimen
西直门

12 Jishuitan
积水潭

14 Gulou Dajie
鼓楼大街

19 Andingmen
安定门

21 Yonghegong
雍和宫

25 Dongzhimen
东直门

43 Dongsishitiao
东四十条

44 Chaoyangmen
朝阳门

55 Chegongzhuang
车公庄

60 Gongzhufen
公主坟

62 Junshibowuguan
军事博物馆

64 Muxidi
木樨地

65 Nanlishilu
南礼士路

66 Fuxingmen
复兴门

(Continued)

67	Fuchengmen	阜城门
85	Jianguomen	建国门
101	Beijing Zhan	北京站
106	Chongwenmen	崇文门
112	Qianmen	前门
116	Heping Lu	和平路
118	Xuanwumen	宣武门
123	Xidan	西单
124	Changchun Jie	长春街

auditorium with the familiar red star embedded in a galaxy of lights in the ceiling. There's a sort of museum-like atmosphere in the Great Hall, with objets d'art donated by the provinces, and a snack bar and restaurant.

The hall is on the west side of Tiananmen Square and admission costs a mind-boggling Y40.

Monument to the People's Heroes
(rénmín yīngxióng jìniàn bēi)

On the southern side of Tiananmen Square, this monument was completed in 1958 and stands on the site of the old Outer Palace Gate. The 36-metre obelisk, made of Qingdao granite, bears bas-relief carvings of key revolutionary events (one relief shows the Chinese destroying opium in the 19th century) as well as appropriate calligraphy from Mao Zedong and Zhou Enlai.

Mao Zedong Mausoleum
(máo zhǔxí jìniàn táng)

Chairman Mao died in September 1976 and his mausoleum was constructed shortly thereafter. Known to Beijing expats as the 'Maosoleum', this enormous building is located just behind the Monument to the People's Heroes.

However history will judge Mao, his impact on its course was enormous. Easy as it now is to vilify his deeds and excesses, many Chinese show deep respect when confronted with the physical presence of the man. CITS guides freely quote the old 7:3 ratio on Mao that first surfaced in 1976 – Mao was 70% right and 30% wrong (what, one wonders, are the figures for CITS itself?) and this is now the official Party line.

The mausoleum is open daily from 8.30 to 11.30 am and from 1 to 3.30 pm. Entry is free. Join the enormous queue of Chinese sightseers, but don't expect more than a quick glimpse of the body as you file past the sarcophagus. At certain times of year the body requires maintenance and is not on view.

Whatever Mao might have done to the Chinese economy while he was alive, sales of Mao memorabilia are certainly giving the free market a boost these days. At the souvenir stalls near the mausoleum you can pick up Chairman Mao key rings, thermometers, face towels, handkerchiefs, sun visors, address books and cartons of cigarettes (a comment on his chain-smoking habit?).

Zhongnanhai
(zhōngnánhǎi)

Just west of the Forbidden City is China's new forbidden city, Zhongnanhai. The interior is off limits to tourists, but you can gawk at the entrance. The compound was first built between the 10th and 13th centuries as a sort of playground for the emperors and their retinues. It was expanded during Ming times but most of the present buildings only date from the Qing Dynasty. Empress Dowager Cixi once lived here; after the failure of the 1898 reform movement she imprisoned Emperor Guangxu in the Impregnating Vitality Hall where, ironically, he later died. After the overthrow of the imperial government and the establishment of the republic, it served as the site of the presidential palace.

Since the founding of the People's Republic in 1949, Zhongnanhai has been the site of the residence and offices of the highest-ranking members of the Communist Party.

In 1973, when the new wing of the Beijing Hotel shot up, the PSB suddenly realised that guests with binoculars could observe activity in Zhongnanhai, so a fake building was erected along the western wall of the Forbidden City to short-circuit that possibility.

Old Summer Palace
(yuánmíngyuán)

The original Summer Palace was laid out in the 12th century. By the reign of Emperor Qianlong it had developed into a set of interlocking gardens. Qianlong set the Jesuits to work as architects for European palaces for the gardens – elaborate fountains and baroque statuary.

In the second Opium War (1860), British and French troops destroyed the place and sent the booty abroad. Since the Chinese pavilions and temples were made of wood they did not survive fires, but a marble facade, some broken columns and traces of the fountains remain.

The ruins have long been a favourite picnic spot for foreigners living in the capital and for Chinese twosomes seeking a bit of privacy. More recently, the government has decided to slowly restore the gardens, moats and buildings. It's uncertain yet just how far the restoration will go – will it be allowed to remain as ruins or will it become another tourist circus like the Ming Tombs? At present, it's a very worthwhile place to visit.

The site covers a huge area – some 2½ km from east to west – so be prepared to do some walking. There are three entrance gates to the compound, all on the south side. The western section is the main area, Yuanmingyuan. The south-eastern corner of the site is the Beautiful Spring Garden (Yichunyuan). The eastern section is the Eternal Spring Garden (Changchunyuan) – it's here that you'll find the European Garden with its Great Fountain Ruins, considered the best-preserved relic in the palace and featured prominently on picture postcards.

Admission costs Y5. Minibuses connect the new Summer Palace with the old one, but a taxi will take you for Y10.

Chinese Revolution History Museum
(zhōngguó gémìng lìshǐ bówùguǎn)

If you don't count the Forbidden City and other palaces, this is Beijing's largest museum. It is housed in a sombre building on the east side of Tiananmen Square, and access was long thwarted by special permission requirements. From 1966 to 1978 the museum was closed so that history could be reassessed in the light of recent events.

There are actually two museums here combined into one – the Museum of History and the Museum of the Revolution. Explanations throughout most of the museums are, unfortunately, entirely in Chinese, so you won't get much out of this labyrinth unless you're particularly fluent or pick up an English-speaking student. An English text relating to the museum is available inside.

The Museum of History contains artefacts and cultural relics (many of them copies) from year zero to 1919, subdivided into primitive communal groups, slavery, feudalism and capitalism/imperialism, laced with Marxist commentary. Without a guide you can discern ancient weapons, inventions and musical instruments.

The Museum of the Revolution is split into five sections: the founding of the CCP (1919-21), the first civil war (1924-27), the second civil war (1927-37), resistance against Japan (1937-45) and the third civil war (1945-49).

Military Museum
(jūnshì bówùguǎn)

Perhaps more to the point than the Chinese Revolution History Museum, this traces the genesis of the PLA from 1927 to the present and has some interesting exhibits: pictures of Mao in the early days, Socialist Realist artwork, captured US tanks from the Korean War and other tools of destruction. Explanations are in Chinese only. You must check your bags at the door, presumably to prevent you from liberating a Sherman tank or MiG aircraft.

The museum is on Fuxing Lu on the western side of the city; to get there take the subway to Junshibowuguan. Admission costs Y2.

Natural History Museum
(zìrán bówùguǎn)

This is the largest such museum in China and gets good reviews from travellers. The four main exhibition halls are devoted to flora and fauna, ancient fauna and human evolution. Some of the more memorable exhibits include a human cadaver cut in half (a former dissident?) to show the insides and a complete dinosaur skeleton. There is also plenty of pickled wildlife, though nothing worse than what you see for sale in some of the street markets. Some of the exhibits were donated by the British Museum, the American Museum of Natural History and other foreign sources.

The Natural History Museum is in the Tianqiao area, just west of Tiantan Park and north of the park's west gate entrance. Admission costs Y10. The museum is open daily except Monday, from 8.30 am until 4 pm.

Lu Xun Museum
(lǔ xùn bówùguǎn)

Dedicated to China's No 1 revolutionary thinker, this museum contains manuscripts, diaries, letters and inscriptions by the famous writer. To the west of the museum is a small Chinese walled compound where Lu Xun lived from 1924 to 1926. The museum is off Fuchengmennei Dajie, west of the Xisi intersection on the north-western side of the city.

China Art Gallery
(zhōngguó měishù guǎn)

Back in the post-Liberation days one of the safest hobbies for an artist was to retouch classical-type landscapes with red flags, belching factory chimneys or bright red tractors. You can get some idea of the state of the arts in China at this gallery. At times very good exhibitions of current work including photo displays are held in an adjacent gallery. Check the *China Daily* for listings. The arts and crafts shop inside has an excellent range of woodblock prints and papercuts. The gallery is west of the Dongsi intersection, north-east of the Forbidden City on Chaoyangmennei Dajie.

Xu Beihong Museum
(xú bēihóng jìniàn guǎn)

Here you'll find traditional Chinese paintings, oils, gouaches, sketches and memorabilia of the famous artist, noted for his galloping horse paintings. Painting albums are on sale, as well as reproductions and Chinese stationery. The museum is at 53 Xinjiekou Bei Dajie, Xicheng District, one-half block south of Deshengmen Xi Dajie.

Song Qingling Museum
(sòng qìnglíng gùjū)

Madam Song was the second wife of Dr Sun Yatsen (he divorced the first). Sun went on to become the first president of the Republic of China.

After 1981, Madam Song's large residence was transformed into a museum dedicated to her memory and to that of Dr Sun. The original layout of the residence is unchanged and on display are personal items and pictures of historical interest. The museum is on the north side of Shisha Houhai lake.

Prince Gong's Residence
(gōngwángfǔ)

To find this, you have to get off the main roads into the small alleys running around the Shisha Hai Lakes. Prince Gong's Residence is more or less at the centre of the arc created by the lakes running from north to south. It's reputed to be the model for the mansion in Cao Xueqin's 18th-century classic, *A Dream of Red Mansions* (translated as *The Story of the Stone* by David Hawkes, Penguin, 1980). It's one of the largest private residential compounds in Beijing, with a nine-courtyard layout, high walls and elaborate gardens. Prince Gong was the son of a Qing emperor.

Drum Tower
(gǔlóu)

The tower was built in 1420 and has several drums which were beaten to mark the hours of the day – in effect the Big Ben of Beijing. Time was kept with a water clock. The tower is on Gulou Dong Dajie, one km due north of Jingshan Park.

Behind the Drum Tower, down an alley further north, is the **Bell Tower** (*zhōnglóu*), which was originally built at the same time as the Drum Tower but burnt down. The present structure is 18th-century, and the gigantic bell which used to hang there has been moved to the Drum Tower.

Capital Museum & Library
(*shǒudū túshūguǎn*)

Actually, it's part of the Confucius Temple complex. The museum houses steles, stone inscriptions, bronzes, vases and documents. This place is within walking distance of the Lama Temple. The easiest way to get there is by subway to the Yonghegong station.

Jingshan Park
(*jǐngshān gōngyuán*)

North of the Forbidden City is Jingshan (Coal Hill), which contains an artificial mound made of earth excavated to create the palace moat. If you clamber to the top pavilions of this regal pleasure garden, you get a magnificent panorama of the capital and a great overview of the russet roofing of the Forbidden City. On the east side of the park a locust tree stands in the place where the last of the Mings, Emperor Chongzhen, hanged himself after slaying his family rather than see the palace razed by the Manchus. The hill supposedly protects the palace from the evil spirits – or dust storms – from the north, but didn't quite work for Chongzhen.

Entrance to Jingshan Park is a modest Y0.30, or you can pay over 30 times as much for a souvenir 'tourist passport ticket' – fortunately, this is optional.

Beihai Park
(*běihǎi gōngyuán*)

Approached by four gates, and just northwest of the Forbidden City, Beihai Park is the former playground of the emperors. The park covers an area of 68 hectares, half of which is a lake. The island in the lower middle is

composed of the heaped earth dug to create the lake – some attribute this to the handiwork of Kublai Khan.

The site is associated with the Great Khan's palace, the belly-button of Beijing before the creation of the Forbidden City. All that remains of the Khan's court is a large jar made of green jade, in the Round City near the south entrance.

From the 12th century on, Beihai Park was landscaped with artificial hills, pavilions, halls, temples and covered walkways. Dominating Jade Islet on the lake, the White Dagoba is a 36-metre-high pop-art 'bottle' originally dating from 1651. It was put up for a visit by the Dalai Lama and was rebuilt in 1741.

On the north-east shore of the islet is the handsome double-tiered Painted Gallery – with unusual architecture for a walkway. Near the boat dock is the Fangshan Restaurant, dishing up imperial recipes favoured by Empress Cixi. She liked 120-course dinners with about 30 kinds of desserts. The restaurant is expensive and high class, and reservations are necessary (but check out the decor!).

The main attraction on the north side is the Nine Dragon Screen, five metres high and 27 metres long, made of coloured glazed tiles. The screen was built to scare off evil spirits; it stands at the entrance to a temple which has disappeared. To the south-west of the boat dock on this side is the Five Dragon Pavilion dating from 1651, where the emperors liked to fish, camp and sing songs around the campfire (an ancient form of karaoke).

On the east side of the park are the 'gardens within gardens'. These waterside pavilions, winding corridors and rockeries were summer haunts of the imperial family, notably Emperor Qianlong and Empress Cixi.

Beihai Park is a relaxing place to stroll around, grab a snack, sip a beer, rent a rowing boat (Y10 per hour) or, as the Chinese do, cuddle on a bench in the evening. It's crowded at weekends. Some people dive into the lake when no-one's around – swimming is not permitted. In winter there's skating.

Tiantan Park
(tiāntán gōngyuán)

The perfection of Ming architecture, Tiantan (the Temple of Heaven) has come to symbolise Beijing. Its lines appear on countless pieces of tourist literature and as a brand name for a wide range of products from Tiger Balm to plumbing fixtures. It is set in a 267-hectare park, with four gates at the compass points, and bounded by walls to the north and east. It originally functioned as a vast stage for solemn rites performed by the Son of Heaven, who came here to pray for good harvests, seek divine clearance and atone for the sins of the people.

With this complicated mix in mind, the unique architectural features will delight numerologists, necromancers and the superstitious – not to mention acoustic engineers and carpenters. Shape, colour and sound take on symbolic significance. The temples, seen in aerial perspective, are round and the bases are square, deriving from the ancient Chinese belief that heaven is round, and the earth is square. Thus the north end of the park is semi-circular and the south end is square.

Tiantan was considered highly sacred ground and it was here that the emperor performed the major ceremonial rites of the year. The least hitch in any part of the proceedings was regarded as an ill omen, and it was thought that the nation's future was thus decided.

Round Altar The five-metre-high Round Altar was constructed in 1530 and rebuilt in 1740. It is composed of white marble arrayed in three tiers, and its geometry revolves around the imperial number nine. Odd numbers were considered heavenly, and nine is the largest single-digit odd number. The top tier, thought to symbolise heaven, has nine rings of stones, each ring composed of multiples of nine stones, so that the ninth ring has 81 stones. The middle tier – earth – has the 10th to 18th rings. The bottom tier – humankind – has the 19th to 27th rings, ending with a total of 243 stones in the largest ring, or 27 times nine. The number of stairs and balustrades are also multiples of

nine. If you stand in the centre of the upper terrace and say something, the sound waves are bounced off the marble balustrades, making your voice appear louder (nine times?).

Echo Wall Just north of the altar, surrounding the entrance to the Imperial Vault of Heaven, is the Echo Wall, 65 metres in diameter. This enables a whisper to travel clearly from one end to your friend's ear at the other – that is, if there's not a tour group in the middle.

In the courtyard are the Triple Echo Stones. If you stand on the first one and clap or shout, the sound is echoed once, on the second stone twice, and on the third, three times. Should it return four times, you will almost certainly not get a coveted hard sleeper train ticket that day or any other day that is a multiple of three.

Imperial Vault of Heaven This octagonal vault was built at the same time as the Round Altar, and it is structured along the lines of the older Hall of Prayer for Good Harvests. It used to contain tablets of the emperor's ancestors, which were used in the winter solstice ceremony. Proceeding up from the Imperial Vault is a walkway: to the left is a molehill composed of excess dirt dumped from digging air-raid shelters and to the right is a rash of souvenir shops.

Hall of Prayer for Good Harvests *(qí nián diàn)* The dominant feature of the whole complex is the Hall of Prayer for Good Harvests, a magnificent piece mounted on a three-tiered marble terrace. Amazingly, the wooden pillars ingeniously support the ceiling without nails or cement – for a building 38 metres high and 30 metres in diameter, that's an accomplishment unmatched until Lego was invented.

Built in 1420, the Hall was burnt to cinders in 1889 and heads rolled in apportioning blame. A faithful reproduction based on Ming architectural methods was erected the following year.

The four pillars at the centre represent the

seasons, the 12 in the next ring denote the months of the year, and the 12 outer ones are symbolic of the day, broken into 12 'watches'. Embedded in the ceiling is a carved dragon, a symbol of royalty.

Ditan Park
(dìtán gōngyuán)

Although 'Ditan' sounds just like the Chinese word for 'carpet', in this case it means Temple of the Earth. The park was built around 1530 as a place for the emperors to sacrifice lesser beings to keep on good terms with the earth god. The park experienced many years of neglect but reopened in 1984 as a sort of activities centre for the elderly. The park is just north of the magnificent Lama Temple.

Ritan Park
(rìtán gōngyuán)

Ritan means Temple of the Sun and it's one of Beijing's older parks, having been built in 1530. The park was built as an altar for ritual sacrifice to the sun god. Situated practically right in the middle of Jianguomenwai embassy-land, it's a big hit with diplomats, their families and other local notables.

Yuetan Park
(yuètán gōngyuán)

A small park west of the centre, this one's name means Temple of the Moon. It is another one of Beijing's sacrificial parks, where the emperors reduced the surplus population to appease the moon god. These days the Yuetan is notable for the Emei Restaurant on the north side of the park, which serves hot Sichuan food with no compromise for foreign palates – Sichuan food addicts prefer it to the Sichuan Restaurant itself.

Yuyuantan Park
(yùyuāntán gōngyuán)

Off to the west of Yuetan Park is Yuyuantan (Jade Hole Pool). The park is notable for the palatial Diaoyutai State Guesthouse, the stomping ground of visiting diplomats and high-ranking cadres. Tourists wandering around the main gate will be politely told to

get lost. Just to the south side of the park is the immense TV tower, one of Beijing's most prominent landmarks. The park is just north of the Military Museum.

Taoranting Park
(táoràntíng gōngyuán)

One of several popular venues for crack-of-dawn taiji exercises, Taoranting (Happy Pavilion) Park is in the southern part of Beijing just north of a prominent sewage canal. The park dates back to at least the Qing Dynasty, when it gained fame chiefly because it was one of the very few accessible to the masses (most of the others were the private playgrounds of the emperors).

Zizhuyuan Park
(zǐzhúyuàn gōngyuán)

The park's name means 'Purple Bamboo', a reference to some of what has been planted here. This place doesn't have much history to distinguish it, being mainly former paddy fields, but during the Ming Dynasty there was the Longevity Temple *(wànshòu sì)* at this site. The park is pleasant enough and there is a reasonably large lake which makes a good venue for ice skating in winter. Zizhuyuan is in a prestigious neighbourhood just west of the zoo.

Longtan Park
(lóngtán gōngyuán)

Longtan (Dragon Pool) Park, east of the Temple of Heaven, is of chief interest to travellers staying at the nearby Longtan Hotel – visit at dawn to see outstanding taiji performances.

The west side of Longtan Park has recently been converted into the Beijing Amusement Park, a world of balloons, cotton candy and nauseating rides (don't eat Sichuan food before getting on the Spider). If this appeals to you, at least avoid it on weekends and holidays.

Grand View Garden
(dàguān yuán)

At the south-western corner of town is Grand View Garden, also known as Daguanyuan

Park. Unlike most of Beijing's parks, which date back to imperial days, this one is new – construction started in 1984 and was completed four years later. The park was built as a replica of the family gardens described in the Chinese novel *The Dream of the Red Chamber* (see also Prince Gong's Residence earlier). The book is a Chinese classic written in the late 18th century. While the park is not steeped in history, it could be of interest if you've read the novel. Otherwise, just kick back and enjoy the birds and the trees.

Beijing Zoo
(běijīng dòngwùyuán)
For humans the zoo is OK – an enormous park, pleasant lakes, good birds – but after you've been there you'll probably look as distraught as the animals. No attempt has been made to re-create their natural environments – they live in tiny cages with little shade or water.

Near the zoo are the Beijing Planetarium and the bizarre Soviet-style Beijing Exhibition Hall (irregular industrial displays, theatre, Russian restaurant), which looks like some crazed Communist architect's wedding-cake decoration.

Admission is a modest Y10, but there is an extra fee for the Panda House and other additional charges for special exhibits.

Getting to the zoo is easy enough – take the subway to the Xizhimen station. From there, it's a 15-minute walk to the west or a short ride on any of the trolley-buses.

Lama Temple
(yōnghégōng)
This is by far the most colourful temple in Beijing – beautiful gardens, stunning frescoes and tapestries, incredible carpentry. Get to this one before you're 'templed out' – it won't chew up your day.

The Lama Temple is the most renowned Tibetan Buddhist temple within China, outside Tibet itself (a carefully worded statement!). North-west of the city centre toward Andingmen, it became the official residence of Count Yin Zhen after extensive renovation. Nothing unusual in that – but in 1723

he was promoted to emperor and moved to the Forbidden City. His name was changed to Yong Zheng, and his former residence became Yonghe Palace. In 1744 it was converted into a lamasery and became a residence for large numbers of monks from Mongolia and Tibet.

In 1949 the Lama Temple was declared protected as a major historical relic. Miraculously it survived the Cultural Revolution without scars. In 1979 a large amount of money was spent on repairs and it was restocked with several dozen novices from Inner Mongolia, a token move on the part of the government to back up its claim that the Lama Temple is a 'symbol of religious freedom, national unity and stability in China'. The novices study Tibetan language and the secret practices of the Yellow Sect.

No photography is permitted inside the temple buildings, tempting as it is – the monks are sensitive to the reproduction of

Fresco of Avalokitesvara, in the Tibetan Buddhist Lama Temple.

Buddha images. The temple is open daily, except Monday, from 9 am to 4 pm. You can get there by subway to the Yonghegong station.

Confucius Temple & Imperial College
(kǒng miào/guózijiān)

Just down the hutong opposite the gates of the Lama Temple is the former Confucius Temple and Imperial College. The Confucius Temple is the largest in the land after the one at Qufu. The temple was reopened in 1981 after some mysterious use as a high-official residence and is now used as a museum.

The forest of steles in the temple courtyard look forlorn. The steles record the names of those successful in the civil service examinations (possibly the world's first) of the imperial court.

The Imperial College was the place where the emperor expounded the Confucian classics to an audience of thousands of kneeling students, professors and court officials – an annual rite. Built by the grandson of Kublai Khan in 1306, the former college was the only institution of its kind in China; it's now the Capital Library.

Great Bell Temple
(dàzhōng sì)

The biggest bell in China, this one weighs a hefty 46½ tonnes and is 6¾ metres tall. The bell is inscribed with Buddhist sutras, a total of over 227,000 Chinese characters.

The bell was cast during the reign of Ming Emperor Yong Le in 1406 and the tower was built in 1733. Getting the bell from the foundry to the temple proved problematic – back in those days it wasn't possible to contract the job out to a Hong Kong company. A shallow canal had to be built which froze over in winter – the bell was moved across the ice by sled.

Within the grounds of the monastery are several other buildings (besides the Bell Tower itself). This includes the Guanyin Hall, Sutra-keeping Tower, Main Buddha Hall and Four Devas Hall. This monastery is

one of the most popular in Beijing and was reopened in 1980.

The Great Bell Temple is almost two km due east of the Friendship Hotel on Beisanhuan Xilu north-east of the centre.

White Dagoba Temple
(báitǎ sì)

The dagoba can be spotted from the top of Jingshan and is similar (and close) to the one in Beihai Park. It was used as a factory during the Cultural Revolution but reopened after restoration in 1980. The dagoba dates back to Kublai Khan's days and is now basically just a historical monument. It lies off Fuchengmennei Dajie.

Guangji Temple
(guǎngjì sì)

The Guangji (Universal Rescue) Temple is on the north-western side of the Xisi Dajie intersection, and east of the White Dagoba Temple. It's in good shape and is the headquarters of the Chinese Buddhist Association. It is claimed to contain some of the finest Buddhist statues in China.

Dongsi Mosque
(dōngsì qīngzhēn sì)

This is one of two functioning mosques in Beijing, the other being Niujie Mosque. It's east of Jingshan Park at 13 Dongsi Nan Dajie, just south of the intersection with Chaoyangmennei Dajie.

Niujie Mosque
(niújiē lǐbài sì)

In the south-western sector of Beijing (Xuanwu District), south of Guang'anmennei Dajie, is a Muslim residential area with a handsome mosque facing Mecca. Niujie (Ox St) is an area worth checking out with a feel all its own.

Fayuan Temple
(fǎyuán sì)

In a lane just east of the Niujie Mosque is the Fayuan (Source of Law) Temple. The temple was originally constructed in the 7th century and is still going strong. It's now the China Buddhism College and is open to visitors.

White Cloud Temple
(báiyúnguān)

This is in a district directly south of Yanjing Hotel and west of the moat. It was once the Taoist centre of northern China and is now the most active Taoist temple in Beijing. Check a map for directions. Walk south on Baiyun Lu and cross the moat. Continue south along Baiyun Lu and turn into a curving street on the left; follow it for 250 metres to the temple entrance. Inside are several courtyards, including a pool, a bridge, several halls of worship and Taoist motifs.

Ancient Observatory
(gǔguān xiàngtái)

One interesting perspective on Beijing is the observatory mounted on the battlements of a watchtower, once part of the city walls. Dwarfed by embassy housing blocks, it lies in a wilderness of traffic loops and highways just west of the Friendship Store; it's on the south-west corner of Jianguomennei Dajie and the second ring road.

The observatory dates back to Kublai Khan's days, when it was north of the present site. The Great Khan, as well as later Ming and Qing emperors, relied heavily on astrologers before making any move.

The present Beijing Observatory was built from 1437 to 1446, not only to facilitate astrological predictions but also to aid seafaring navigators. Downstairs are displays of navigational equipment used by Chinese shipping. On the roof is a variety of astronomical instruments designed by the Jesuits.

More recently, government officials were caught off guard when local and foreign rock bands got together and staged a dance party in the ancient tower. The observatory is open Wednesday through Sunday from 9 to 11 am and from 1 to 4 pm.

Chinese Ethnic Culture Park
(zhōnghuá mínzú yuán)

Beijing's answer to Disneyland, this theme park gives you a chance to see China's 56 nationalities in their native habitat. Or rather, to see Han Chinese dressed up in minority costumes. The area is also dressed up with small-scale imitations of famous Chinese scenic spots such as a fake Jiuzhaigou

---

Underground City
(dì xià chéng)

In the late 1960s, with a Soviet invasion apparently hanging over them, the Chinese started to go underground. The shadow-city which resulted was constructed by volunteers and shop assistants living in the Qianmen area – about 2000 people and 10 years of spare-time work with simple tools. It's not one of the most inspiring sights in Beijing, but an estimated 600 people per day pay to catch a glimpse of the 32-km underground system. There are roughly 90 entrances to the complex and entrances are hidden in shops.

Civil defence officials proudly proclaimed that 10,000 shoppers in the Dazhalan area could seek shelter in five minutes in the event of an attack.

Now, pressed for space and trying to maximise the peacetime possibilities of the air-raid shelters (aside from the fact that the shelters are useless in the event of nuclear attack), Beijing has put them to use as warehouses, factories, shops, restaurants, hotels, roller-skating rinks, theatres and clinics.

A few shops are willing to provide access to the tunnels (for a fee). One such place is a shop at 62 Xidamochang Jie, a narrow hutong. To find it, start from Qianmen and walk south a short distance along Qianmen Dajie. The very first hutong on your left (east side of street) is Xidamochang Jie, which parallels Qianmen Dong Dajie. It's about a 10-minute walk. Admission for foreigners costs Y5. A fluorescent wall map reveals the routing of the entire tunnel system. ■

Dragon Waterfall. Perhaps the best thing about the place is the opportunity to sample some ethnic minority speciality foods.

The Chinese Ethnic Culture Park is to the west of the National Olympic Sports Centre.

Places to Stay – bottom end

Hotels Except for a couple of derelict hotels found mostly in outlying parts of town, the grim reality is that Beijing offers little in the way of budget accommodation. In the winter off season you should be able to find something affordable, but during the summer crunch you'll have plenty of competition for the limited space available.

For the sake of definition, any hotel charging under Y400 in the high season would have to be considered 'bottom end' in Beijing. Bargaining for a room is possible in some cases – politely ask for a 'discount'. Many travellers report getting discounts of 30% or more, at least during the off season for a long-term (over one week) stay. Unfortunately, this doesn't always work.

At the present time, the two favourite bottom-end haunts for backpackers are the Jinghua Hotel and Lihua Hotel, about the only two places in town with dormitories. There are plenty of other hotels in the Y300 price range, but try to call ahead first to see if there are any vacant rooms. Of course, there is only a 50% chance that the person answering the phone will speak anything other than Chinese. When the hotel operator answers, ask to speak to the service desk (*zǒng fúwù tái*).

The following list of hotels with rooms priced below Y400 is in alphabetical order. Make allowances for the fact that future renovations (and greed) may drive prices to even more astronomical levels:

Beihai Hotel (běihǎi bīnguǎn), 141 Di'anmen Xi Dajie, 100009. Doubles cost Y210 to Y230 (☎ 601-2229; fax 601-7848).

Beijing Commercial Business Complex (běijīng shāngwù huìguǎn), Building No 1, Yulin Li, Youanmenwai, 100054. Official rates for doubles are Y350 to Y450, but prices as low as Y280 are possible by polite negotiation (☎ 329-2244).

Big Bell Hotel (dàzhōngsì fàndiàn), 18 Beisanhuan Xilu, Haidian District, 100086. Standard doubles are Y280 (☎ 225-3388; fax 225-2605).

Complant Hotel (zhōngchéng bīnguǎn), 1 Dingan Dongli, Puhuangyu, 100075. Standard doubles are Y380 (☎ 762-6688).

Desheng Hotel (déshèng fàndiàn), 4 Beisanhuan Zhonglu. All rooms cost Y252 (☎ 202-4477).

Evergreen Hotel (wànniánqīng bīnguǎn), 25 Xisanhuan Beilu, Haidian District, 100081. Standard doubles cost Y260 (☎ 842-1144).

Fangyuan Hotel (fāngyuán bīnguǎn), 36 Dengshikou Xijie, Dongcheng District, 100006. Double rooms begin at Y198 (☎ 525-6331).

Far East Hotel (yuǎndōng fàndiàn), 90 Tieshuxie Jie, Qianmenwai, Xuanwu District, actually on the west end of Dazhalan (south-west of Qianmen). Double rooms cost Y292 (☎ 301-8811; fax 301-8233).

Feixia Hotel (fēixiá fàndiàn), Building 5, Xibianmen Xili, Xuanwu District, 100053. Rooms cost Y130. One star (☎ 301-2228; fax 302-1764).

Fengtai Hotel (fēngtái bīnguǎn), 67 Zhengyang Dajie, Fengtai District, 100071 (opposite Fengtai Railway Station). Rates are low – Y60 without air-con or Y80 with it (☎ 381-4448).

Furong Hotel (fúróng bīnguǎn), Bailizhuang, Chaoyang Lu, Chaoyang District, 100025. Doubles cost Y180 (☎ 502-2921).

Guanghua Hotel (guānghuá fàndiàn), 38 Dongsanhuan Beilu, Chaoyang District, 100020 (near China World Trade Centre). Rooms cost Y280 to Y332 (☎ 501-8866; fax 501-6516).

Guoan Hotel (guóān bīnguǎn), Guandongdian Beijie, Dongdaqiao, Chaoyang District, 100020. Doubles begin at Y400 (☎ 500-7700).

Hademen Hotel (hādémén fàndiàn), 2A Chongwenmenwai Dajie, 100062. Rates are Y320 to Y450 (☎ 701-2244).

Hainan Hotel (hǎinán fàndiàn), Zhongguancun, Haidian District. Doubles cost Y200 (☎ 256-5550; fax 256-8395).

Hebei Hotel (héběi fàndiàn), 11A Cheniandian Hutong, Andingmennei, 100009. Rooms begin at Y332 (☎ 401-5522).

Hualun Hotel (huálún fàndiàn), 291 Andingmennei, Dongcheng District, 100009. Basic triples cost Y150, but higher-standard doubles are only Y240 (☎ 403-3337).

Huayuan Hotel (huáyuán fàndiàn), 28 Beixiaoyun Lu, Dongsanhuan, 100027. Standard doubles are Y350 (☎ 467-8661).

Jiali Hotel (jiālì fàndiàn), 21B Jiuxianqiao Lu, Chaoyang District, 100016. Standard doubles cost Y300 (☎ 437-3631).

Jimen Hotel (jìmén fàndiàn), Huangtingzi, Xueyuan Lu, Haidian District, 100088. Doubles begin at Y200 (☎ 201-2211).

Jinghua Hotel (jīnghuá fàndiàn), Nansanhuan Xilu (southern part of the third ring road). A favourite with backpackers, dorm beds cost Y26 to Y28. Doubles with private bath are Y140 to Y162. Bus Nos 2 and 17 from Qianmen drop you off nearby (☎ 722-2211).

Jingtai Hotel (jīngtài bīnguǎn), 65 Yongwai Jingtaixi (a small alley running off Anlelin Lu). Rooms without/with attached bath cost Y120/200 but this place is scheduled for renovation – prices may rise to over Y300 (☎ 721-2476, 722-4675).

Leyou Hotel (lèyóu fàndiàn), 13 Dongsanhuan Nanlu, 100021, is east of Longtan Park (south-east Beijing). Doubles go for Y276 to Y380. Take bus No 28 or 52 to the terminus (☎ 771-2266; fax 771-1636).

Lihua Hotel (lìhuá fàndiàn), 71 Yangqiao, Yongdingmenwai. A well-established backpackers' hotel, dorms cost Y25 to Y30 and doubles are Y140 to Y162. Bus No 343 is the easiest to get you there but No 14 will also do (☎ 721-1144).

Lingnan Hotel (lǐngnán fàndiàn), 32 Beiwacun Lu, Haidian District. Doubles begin at Y374 (☎ 841-2288).

Longtan Hotel (lóngtán fàndiàn), 15 Panjiayuan Nanli, Chaoyang District, 100021. Doubles are Y300 while suites are Y510 and Y780. The hotel is opposite Longtan Park in the south of the city (☎ 771-1602; fax 771-4028).

Lüsongyuan Hotel (lǚsōngyuán bīnguǎn), 22 Banchang Hutong, Dongcheng District, 100007. Doubles cost Y298. It can be difficult to find this place – when you approach the hutong from either end, it doesn't seem that there could be a building of such high standard halfway down. The hutong is one way and many taxi drivers are reluctant to drive down it in the wrong direction, but others are willing to do so. The hotel is directly north of the China Art Gallery, second hutong north of Di'anmen, turn left – bus No 104 from Beijing Railway Station comes close (☎ 401-1116, 403-0416).

Overseas Chinese Hotel (huáqiáo fàndiàn), 5 Beixinqiao Santiao, Dongcheng District, 100007. Room rates are Y383 to Y680. Two stars (☎ 401-6688).

Qiaoyuan Hotel (qiáoyuán fàndiàn), Dongbinhe Lu, Youanmenwai. At one time Beijing's largest budget hotel, it is currently under renovation and prices are expected to rise to at least Y300 (☎ 303-8861, 301-2244).

Qinghuayuan Hotel (qīnghuáyuán bīnguǎn), 45 Chengfu Lu, Haidian District, 100083. Doubles cost Y220 (☎ 257-3355).

Shangyuan Hotel (shàngyuán fàndiàn), Xie Jie, Xizhemenwai, Haidian District, 100044. The hotel is near the Xizhimen (north) Railway Station. Doubles are Y278. Two stars (☎ 225-1166).

Tiantan Sports Hotel (tiāntán tǐyù bīnguǎn), 10 Tiyuguan Lu, Chongwen District, 100061. Doubles cost Y300. Take the subway one stop from the main railway station to Chongwenmen, then bus No 39, 41 or 43 (☎ 701-3388; fax 701-5388).

Traffic Hotel (jiāotōng fàndiàn), 35 Dongsi Kuaiyu Nanjie. The 82 comfortable rooms are priced from Y238 to Y268. The hotel is in a narrow alley running south from Tiyuguan Lu – signs in English point the way. Bus No 41 runs on Tiyuguan Lu and drops you off at the alley's entrance. One star (☎ 701-1114, 711-2288).

Wofosi Hotel (wòfósì fàndiàn), Botanical Gardens, 100093; north-west of the centre. Doubles cost Y207 (☎ 259-1561).

Yongdingmen Hotel (yǒngdìngmén fàndiàn), 77 Anlelin Lu. It's currently closed for renovation and prices will probably rise to about Y300. Take bus No 39 from the railway station (☎ 721-3344).

Yuanwanglou Hotel (yuǎnwànglóu bīnguǎn), 13 Beisanhuan Xilu (north third ring road). Standard doubles cost Y300. Two stars (☎ 201-3366).

Ziwei Hotel (zǐwēi bīnguǎn), 40 Shijingshan Lu, Shijingshan District, 100043. Fifteen km west of the Forbidden City. Doubles cost Y400 (☎ 887-8031).

Places to Stay – middle

The following hotels cost under US$100, which by Beijing's pricey standards are considered 'mid-range':

Bamboo Garden Hotel (zhúyuán bīnguǎn), 24 Xiaoshiqiao Hutong, Jiugulou Dajie, 100009. Singles/doubles cost Y579/766 (☎ 403-2229; fax 401-2633).

Beiwei Hotel (běiwěi fàndiàn), 13 Xijing Lu, Xuanwu District (western side of Tiantan Park). Standard rooms are Y420, superior Y630 and suites Y766. Two stars (☎ 301-2266; fax 301-1366).

Chongwenmen Hotel (chóngwénmén fàndiàn), 2 Chongwenmen Xi Dajie, 100062. Standard rooms are Y490, suites Y610 (☎ 512-2211; fax 512-2122).

Debao Hotel (débǎo fàndiàn), Xizhimenwai Dajie (east side of the zoo). Standard doubles cost Y550 (☎ 831-8866; fax 832-4205).

Dongfang Hotel (dōngfāng fàndiàn), 11 Wanming Lu, 100050 (south of Qianmen). Standard doubles are Y450, superior rooms cost Y650. Three stars (☎ 301-4466; fax 304-4801).

Grand Hotel (yuánshān dà jiǔdiàn), 20 Yumin Dongli, Deshengmenwai, Xicheng District. Doubles are Y555 to Y639. Three stars (☎ 201-0033; fax 202-9893).

Holiday Inn Downtown (jīndū jiàrì fàndiàn), 98 Beilishi Lu, Xicheng District, 100037. Rates are Y650 to Y1740. Three stars (☎ 832-2288; fax 832-0696).

Huabei Hotel (huáběi dà jiǔdiàn), Anhuaqiao, 19 Gulouwai Dajie, 100011. Rooms go for Y480 to Y580. Three stars (☎ 202-2266, 202-8888).

Huadu Hotel (huádū fàndiàn), 8 Xinyuan Nanlu, Chaoyang District, 100027. Room rates are Y638 to Y978. Three stars (☎ 500-1166; fax 500-1615).

Hua Thai Apartment Hotel (huátài fàndiàn), Jinsong Dongkou (south-east Beijing). Rooms are actually apartments with kitchen facilities. Twin rooms are Y412; room with four beds costs Y720 (☎ 771-6688; fax 771-5266).

International Hotel (guójì fàndiàn), 9 Jianguomennei Dajie, 100005. Doubles are Y705 to Y830, suites cost Y1000 to Y4980. Four stars (☎ 512-6688; fax 512-9972).

Landmark Hotel (liàngmǎhé dàshà), 8 Dongsanhuan Beilu, 100004. Rates are Y700 to Y1250. Four stars (☎ 501-6688).

Media Centre Hotel (méidìyà zhōngxīn), 11B Fuxing Lu. Room rates are Y650 to Y1300. Three stars (☎ 851-4422).

Minzu Hotel (mínzú fàndiàn), 51 Fuxingmennei Dajie, 100046 (west of CAAC and Xidan). Standard Y700, superior Y1230. Three stars (☎ 601-4466; fax 601-4849).

Olympic Hotel (aòlínpīkè fàndiàn), 52 Baishiqiao Lu, Haidian District, 100081. Doubles cost Y680, suites are Y1360. Three stars (☎ 831-6688; fax 831-8390).

Park Hotel (bǎilè jiǔdiàn), 36 Puhuangyu Lu, 100078. Doubles cost Y550. Three stars but not worth it (☎ 761-2233).

Peace Hotel (hépíng bīnguǎn), 3 Jinyu Hutong, Wangfujing. Standard/deluxe rooms are Y696/1044. Four stars (☎ 512-8833; fax 512-6863).

Qianmen Hotel (qiánmén fàndiàn), 175 Yong'an Lu (south-west of Qianmen). Doubles/suites are Y617/935. Three stars (☎ 301-6688; fax 301-3883).

Rainbow Hotel (tiānqiáo bīnguǎn), 11 Xijing Lu, Xuanwu District, 100050 (south-west of Qianmen). Rooms are priced from Y630 to Y766. Three stars (☎ 301-2266; fax 301-1366).

Tiantan Hotel (tiāntán fàndiàn), 1 Tiyuguan Lu, Chongwen District (east of Tiantan Park). Standard/deluxe rooms cost Y655/697. Three stars (☎ 701-2277; fax 701-6833).

Twenty-First Century Hotel (èrshíyī shìjì fàndiàn), 40 Liangmaqiao. Room prices are from Y560 to Y1250. Three stars (☎ 466-3311).

Yanjing Hotel (yānjīng fàndiàn), 19 Fuxingmenwai Dajie (west Beijing). Standard/deluxe rooms cost Y560/947. Three stars (☎ 853-6688).

Yanxiang Hotel (yānxiáng fàndiàn), 2A Jiangtai Lu, Dongzhimenwai (along the way to the airport in north-east Beijing). Rates are Y480 to Y960. Three stars (☎ 437-6666; fax 437-6231).

Yuexiu Hotel (yuèxiù dà fàndiàn), 24 Dong Dajie, Xuanwumen, 100051. Rates are Y420 and Y550. Three stars (☎ 301-4499; fax 301-4609).

Places to Stay – top end

Keeping up with the top-end hotels in Beijing is like skiing uphill. No sooner does one extravaganza open its doors than the ground-breaking ceremony is held for an even more luxurious pleasure palace. To all the following quoted prices, add 15% surcharge:

Beijing Asia Hotel (běijīng yàzhōu dà jiǔdiàn), 8 Xinzhong Xijie, Gongren Tiyuchang Beilu, 100027. Double rooms cost Y860, suites Y1380. Three stars (☎ 500-7788; fax 500-8091).

Beijing Toronto Hotel (jīnglún fàndiàn), 3 Jianguomenwai Dajie, 100020. Room rates are Y1245 to Y1910. Four stars (☎ 500-2266; fax 500-2022).

Chains City Hotel (chéngshì bīnguǎn), 4 Gongren Tiyuchang Donglu, Chaoyang District, 100027. Standard Y860, superior Y1035. Three stars (☎ 500-7799; fax 500-7668).

China World Hotel (zhōngguó dà fàndiàn), 1 Jianguomenwai Dajie, 100020 (inside China World Trade Centre). Prices are Y2240 to Y3530. Five stars (☎ 505-2266; fax 505-3167).

Continental Grand Hotel (wǔzhōu dà jiǔdiàn), 8 Beichen Donglu, Beisihuan Lu, Andingmenwai, 100101 (in the Asian Games Village). Standard rooms are Y830, superior Y1660 and suites Y2490. Four stars (☎ 491-5588; fax 491-0106).

CVIK Hotel (sàitè fàndiàn), 22 Jianguomenwai Dajie (across from Friendship Store), 341 rooms. Room rates are Y1037 to Y1825. Four stars (☎ 512-3388; fax 512-3542).

Friendship Hotel (yǒuyí bīnguǎn), 3 Baishiqiao Lu, 100873 (at third ring road). Standard rooms cost Y921 to Y1322. Two to four stars (☎ 849-8888; fax 849-8866).

Gloria Plaza Hotel (kǎilái dà jiǔdiàn), 2 Jianguomen Nan Dajie, 100022. Rooms cost from Y1160 up to Y9960. Four stars (☎ 515-8855; fax 515-8533).

Grace Hotel (xīn wànshòu bīnguǎn), 8 Jiangtai Xilu, Chaoyang District, 100016. Twins cost Y1080. Four stars (☎ 436-2288; fax 436-1818).

Great Wall Sheraton (chángchéng fàndiàn), Dongsanhuan Beilu, 100026. Rooms cost Y1870 to Y2280. Five stars (☎ 500-5566; fax 500-3398).

THE EAST

Hilton Hotel (xīěrdùn fàndiàn), 1 Dongfang Lu, Dongsanhuan Beilu, 100027. Room prices are Y1900 to Y2740. Five stars (☎ 466-2288; fax 465-3052).

Holiday Inn Crowne Plaza (guójì yìyuàn huángguān jiàrì fàndiàn), 48 Wangfujing Dajie, Dengshixikou, 100006. Rooms cost Y1245, Y1910 and Y2075. Five stars (☎ 513-3388; fax 513-2513).

Holiday Inn Lido (lìdū jiàrì fàndiàn), Jichang Lu, Jiangtai Lu, 100037 (on the road to the airport). Rooms cost Y1000 to Y1660. Officially only four stars, but perhaps the best hotel in Beijing (☎ 437-6688).

Jianguo Hotel (jiànguó fàndiàn), 5 Jianguomenwai Dajie, 100020. Superior rooms are Y1160 and deluxe twins cost Y2325. Four stars (☎ 500-2233; fax 500-2871).

Jingguang New World Hotel (jīngguǎng xīn shìjiè fàndiàn), Hujialou, Chaoyang District, 100020. Rates are Y1410 to Y3490. Five stars (☎ 501-8888; fax 501-3333).

Kunlun Hotel (kūnlún fàndiàn), 2 Xinyuan Nanlu, Chaoyang District, 100004. Doubles cost Y1245 to Y1495. Five stars (☎ 500-3388; fax 500-3228).

Mandarin Hotel (xīndàdū fàndiàn), 21 Chegongzhuang Lu, 100044 (south of the Beijing Zoo). Standard rooms cost Y830, suites are Y1395. Four stars (☎ 831-9988; fax 831-2136).

Mövenpick Hotel (guódū dà fàndiàn) at Capital Airport. Doubles start at Y954. Four stars (☎ 456-5588; fax 456-5678).

New Otani (chángfù gōng), 26 Jianguomenwai Dajie, 100022. Doubles are Y1660 to Y1825, suites are Y2490 to Y5400. Five stars (☎ 512-5555; fax 512-5346).

Palace Hotel (wángfǔ fàndiàn), 8 Jinyu Hutong, Dongdan Bei Dajie, 100006. Doubles cost Y2158 to Y3154, suites up to Y18,260. Five stars (☎ 512-8899; fax 512-9050).

Poly Plaza (bǎolì dàshà), 14 Dongzhimen Nan Dajie. Rooms cost Y1044 to Y1500. Three stars (☎ 500-1188).

Shangri-La Hotel (xiānggé lǐlā fàndiàn), 29 Zhizhuyuan Lu, Haidian District. Rates are Y1660 to Y3320. Five stars (☎ 841-2211; fax 841-8002).

Swissôtel (běijīng gǎng'aò zhōngxīn) – also called the *Hong Kong-Macau Centre* – Gongren Tiyuchang Beilu & Chaoyangmen Bei Dajie. Doubles are priced from Y1494 to Y1992. Five stars (☎ 501-2288; fax 501-2501).

Tianlun Dynasty Hotel (tiānlún wángcháo fàndiàn), 50 Wangfujing Dajie. Standard/suite rooms are Y1180/1800. Four stars (☎ 513-8888; fax 513-7866).

Places to Eat

The free enterprise system permitted since the early 1980s has generated an explosion of privately owned eateries. That's the good news. The bad news is that prices are rapidly escalating. While there are still plenty of back-alley cafes where you can grab a cheap meal, the days are gone when any backpacker could afford to visit an upmarket restaurant and rub elbows with Beijing's bloated cadres.

Chinese Food Northern cuisine specialities are Beijing duck, Mongolian hotpot, Muslim barbecue and imperial food.

Cheap Eats The hutongs are so packed with small eateries and foodstalls that it would take a book larger than this one to list them all. Good areas to explore include Qianmen region, Wangfujing and around parklands such as Tiantan, Ritan and Beihai Park.

Special mention should go to the Dongan-men Night Market, which gets going from around 6 to 9 pm daily. All sorts of exotic eats from pushcarts are available, including tiny four-legged beasties roasted on a skewer. The night market is at the northern end of Wangfujing near the Bank of China.

Beijing Beijing duck is the capital's most famous invention, now a production line of sorts. Your meal starts at one of the farms around Beijing where the duck is pumped full of grain and soybean paste to fatten it up. The ripe duck is lacquered with molasses, pumped with air, filled with boiling water, dried, and then roasted over a fruitwood fire. The result, force-fed or not, is delicious.

Otherwise known as the 'Old Duck', the *Qianmen Quanjude Roast Duck Restaurant* (☎ 511-2418) *(qiánmén quànjùdé kǎoyā-diàn)* is at 32 Qianmen Dajie, on the east side, near the Qianmen subway station. As the nickname implies, this is one of the oldest restaurants in the capital, dating back to 1864. Price depends on which section of the restaurant you sit in – salubrious surroundings cost more and the cheap section is very crowded. The duck is served in stages. First come boneless meat and crispy skin with a side dish of shallots, plum sauce and crepes, followed by duck soup made of bones and all the other parts except the quack.

The *Bianyifang Duck Restaurant* (☎ 702-0505) *(biànyìfáng kǎoyādiàn)* is another famous house at 2 Chongwenmenwai Dajie near the Hademen Hotel (Chongwenmen subway station). Language is not really a problem; you just have to negotiate half or whole ducks. In the cheap section the locals will show you the correct etiquette, like when to spit on the floor.

Cantonese No self-respecting tourist hotel in Beijing is without a Cantonese restaurant dishing up dim sum to their Hong Kong clientele. Remember that dim sum is for breakfast and lunch only – at night it's mostly seafood.

For something that's not inside a tourist hotel, you might try the *Renren Restaurant* (☎ 511-2978) *(rénrén dà jiǔlóu)* at 18 Qianmen Dong Dajie.

Imperial *(gōngtíng cài* or *mǎnhàn dàcān)* This is food fit for an emperor and will clean your wallet out very fast. In 1982 a group of Beijing chefs set about reviving the imperial pastry recipes, and even went so far as to dig up the last emperor's brother to try their products out on.

Imperial cuisine is served up in the *Fangshan Restaurant* (☎ 401-1889) in Beihai Park. The Summer Palace is home to the *Tingliguan Imperial Restaurant* (☎ 258-2504). There is also an imperial restaurant at Fragrant Hills Park. *Gloria Showcase Restaurant* (☎ 515-8855 ext 333) in the Gloria Plaza Hotel also does imperial cuisine at imperial prices.

Mongolian Hotpot Mongolian hotpot is a winter dish – a brass pot with charcoal inside it is placed at the centre of the table and you cook thick strips of mutton and vegetables yourself, fondue fashion, spicing as you like. Look for the symbol shaped like the hotpot on little foodstalls and restaurants in the hutongs.

Nengren Ju (☎ 601-2560) is appropriately right next to Kublai Khan's creation, the White Dagoba Temple.

In the top-end price category, the New Century Hotel presents the *Gold Hot Pot Restaurant* (☎ 849-1303).

Muslim Muslim barbecue is dirt cheap if you know the right place to look for it. The right place is the west end of Baiwanzhuangxi Lu, a street in a neighbourhood known as Ganjiakou (not far south of the zoo). This is where Beijing's Uighur minority congregates. Restaurants here are very specialised – the way to eat is to collect some Uighur flatbread *(náng)* from the stalls, then sit down in a tea shop or restaurant and order sweat Uighur tea *(sānpào tái* or *bābǎo chá)*, some vegetable dishes, noodles *(miàn)* and kebabs *(ròuchuàn)*. You'll probably have to collect your meal from several proprietors – one restaurant won't have the full range of goodies. It's often best to eat with a small group (two to four persons) so you can get several dishes and sample everything. Alternatively, you can just drift from stall to stall sampling as you go.

Out in tourist hotel-land this type of cuisine costs considerably more. One place you might try is *Hongbinlou* (☎ 601-4832) *(hóngbīnlóu fànzhuāng)* at 82 Xi Chang'an Jie, just east of Xidan intersection.

The *Moslem Restaurant* (☎ 831-3388 ext 5150) in the Xiyuan Hotel can accommodate you and your credit card.

Sichuan The classic place to go is the *Sichuan Restaurant* (☎ 603-3291) *(sìchuān fàndiàn)* at 51 Rongxian Hutong. To get there go south from Xidan intersection (where Xidan meets Chang'an), turn left into a hutong marked by traffic lights and a police box, and continue along the hutong until you find the grey wall entrance. This restaurant is housed in the sumptuous former residence of Yuan Shikai (the general who tried to set himself up as an emperor in 1914).

At the south-west gate of Ritan Park is *Shenxian Douhua Village* (☎ 500-5939) *(shénxiān dòuhuā cūn)* (Jianguomen subway station). Less famous but still excellent is *Dragon Court* (☎ 701-2277 ext 2102) in the Tiantan Hotel. The Great Wall Sheraton Hotel is where you'll find *Yuen Tai Restaurant* (☎ 500-5566 ext 2162). The Beijing Hotel's contribution is *Yiyuan Garden Restaurant* (☎ 513-7766 ext 1383).

Vegetarian The Yangzhou-style *Gongdelin Vegetarian Restaurant* (☎ 511-2542) (*gōngdélín sùcàiguǎn*) at 158 Qianmen Nan Dajie is probably the best in the city. It serves up wonderful vegie food with names to match. How about the 'peacock in pride' or 'the fire is singeing the snow-capped mountains'?

The other notable place is *Vegetarians* (☎ 512-6688) inside the International Hotel (Jianguomen subway station).

Omar Khayyam (☎ 513-9988 ext 20188) is in the Asia Pacific Building at 8 Yabao Lu, next to the International Post & Telecommunications Office in the Jianguomenwai area. Though not exclusively a vegetarian restaurant, it does do vegetarian and halal food.

Western Food All the large tourist hotels serve Western food of varying quality and price. Travellers pining for a croissant or strong coffee will be pleased to know that Beijing is the best place in China to find them.

Fast Food From the day of its grand opening in 1992, *McDonald's (màidāngláo)* has been all the rage with Beijingers. Though prices are low, this is one of Beijing's most prestigious restaurants, the venue for cadre birthday parties and a popular hang-out for the upper crust. McDonald's occupies a prime piece of real estate on the corner of Wangfujing just east of the Beijing Hotel. Business has been so good that a second (but smaller) McDonald's opened in 1993 at the Chang'an Market on Fuxingmenwai Dajie near the Yanjing Hotel. Both branches are open from 7 am until 11 pm.

By comparison, *KFC (kěndéjī jiāxiāng jī)* enjoys a much longer history in Beijing, having spread its wings in 1987. At the time of its opening, it was the largest Kentucky

Fried Chicken in the world. The colonel's smiling face is just across the street from Mao's mausoleum in Tiananmen Square – if this doesn't make the late Chairman turn over in his grave, nothing will. A smaller KFC has hatched one block east of Wangfujing on the south-western corner of Dongsi Xi Dajie and Dongsi Nan Dajie.

Pizza Hut (bìshèngkè) has arrived on the Beijing fast-food scene with two branches. One is on Dongzhimenwai Dajie in the Sanlitun area (next to the Australian embassy). The other hut is less conspicuous – it's at 33 Zhushikou Xi Dajie, the second major road south of Qianmen (first big road south of Dazhalan Dajie).

Uncle Sam's Fastfood (shānmǔ shūshū kuàicān) is on the south side of Jianguomenwai opposite the Friendship Store. At least the pastries and drinks are not bad.

French *Maxim's de Paris* (☎ 505-4853) (*bālí mǎkèxīmǔ cāntīng*) is not just in Paris – a branch can be found within the precincts of the China World Trade Centre (West Wing). Dinner for two – *sacré bleu* – is a cool Y300 or so, excluding that Bordeaux red or the Alsatian Gewürztraminer.

Le Bistrot (☎ 505-2288 ext 6198) is in the same building as Maxim's – perhaps this is Beijing's French Quarter?

German Within the caverns of the enormous Lufthansa Centre (just north of the Great Wall Sheraton) is *Paulaner Brauhaus*, an excellent German restaurant. This place brews its own genuine German beer!

Mexican *Mexican Wave* (☎ 506-3961) is on Dongdaqiao Lu near the intersection with Guanghua Lu. Dongdaqiao Lu is the major north-south road between the Friendship Store and the Jianguo Hotel on Jianguomenwai. Mexican Wave serves set lunches (Western, not Mexican food) from noon until 2.30 pm; dinners (Mexican-style) are from around 6 pm onwards.

Russian The *Moscow Restaurant* (☎ 894-454) (*mòsīkē cāntīng*) is on the west side of the Soviet-designed Exhibition Centre in the zoo district. The vast interior has chandeliers, a high ceiling and fluted columns. You can get a table overlooking the zoo (which has, by the way, no connection with the menu). The food gets mixed reviews, but it's definitely Russian – borsch, cream prawns au gratin, pork à la Kiev, beef stroganoff, black bread, soups and black caviar. It's moderately priced.

Bakeries Chinese bread is about as tasty as a dried-out sponge, but a few entrepreneurs in Beijing have started to introduce edible baked goods to the masses. One fine effort in this direction is *Vie de France (dà mòfáng miànbāo diàn)*, which boasts genuine croissants and prices a fraction of what you'd pay in Paris. This bakery currently has two branches – one is at the Qianmen Zhengyang Market, just south-west of Chairman Mao's mausoleum and adjacent to the enormous KFC. The other branch is on the south-east corner of Xidan and Xichang'an Dajie, across the street from the Aviation Building.

Within the confines of the *Friendship Store*, there is a bakery off to the right as you enter the store. Prices here are also very low but the selection is limited.

Another place to look are some of the big hotels – a few have sent the staff off to Europe for a wintertime crash course in making German black bread and Danish pastries. Unfortunately, hotel prices tend to be high. The deli in the *Holiday Inn Lido* stocks delectable chocolate cake for around Y30 a slice.

Supermarkets Beijing has several notable supermarkets, a good one being *CVIK Plaza* on the south side of Jianguomenwai. It's a department store across the street from the CITIC building and adjacent to SCITE Tower – the supermarket is in the basement.

On the eastern fringe of Jianguomenwai is the China World Trade Centre – go down into the basement to find a fully fledged *Wellcome* supermarket, imported lock, stock and shopping carts from Hong Kong. The Wellcome slogan 'Low everyday prices' doesn't

quite describe the situation in Beijing, but you'll find all the familiar goodies right down to the 'No frills dried lemon peel'.

Just next to the CITIC building is the *Friendship Store* – when you enter the building turn sharply right to find the food section. The supermarket is decidedly mediocre, but new competition may force an improvement soon.

Out in Sanlitun embassy-land there's a small *Friendship Supermarket* serving the diplomatic (and not so diplomatic) crowd – the selection is limited but you can score chocolate chip cookies and other imported delicacies. The store is at 5 Sanlitun Lu. In the same neighbourhood just north of the Great Wall Sheraton Hotel is the enormous *Lufthansa Centre* – yes, it is a ticket office for a German airline, but also a multistorey shopping mall. There is a supermarket of sorts in here, but you may have a hard time finding the food among the Walkmans, computers and colour TVs.

Entertainment

The *China Daily* carries a listing of cultural evenings recommended for foreigners – also worth checking are the free tourist newspapers distributed around hotels.

Acrobatics *(tèjì biǎoyǎn)* Two thousand years old, and one of the few art forms condoned by Mao, acrobatics is the best deal in town.

The best place to catch an acrobatics show is the *Chaoyang Theatre (cháoyáng jùchǎng)* at 36 Dongsanhuan Beilu (at Chaoyang Beilu) in the north-eastern part of Beijing. Shows run from 7.15 to 8.40 pm and cost Y30.

The *International Club* (☎ 532-2188) (guójì jùlèbù) at 21 Jianguomenwai Dajie (west of the Friendship Store) occasionally has performances.

One other place to check is the *Rehearsal Hall of the Beijing Arobatics Troupe* (☎ 303-1769) *(běijīng zájì tuán)* in Dazhalan (the Qianmen area).

Beijing Opera (*píngjù*) It used to be the Marx Brothers, the Gang of Four and the Red Ballet – but it's back to the classics again these days. Beijing opera is one of the many forms of the art and the most famous, but it's only got a short history. The year 1790 is the key date given; in that year a provincial troupe performed before Emperor Qianlong on his 80th birthday. The form was popularised in the West by the actor Mei Lanfang (1894-1961) who played *dan*, or female roles, and is said to have influenced Charlie Chaplin. There is a museum devoted to Mei Lanfang at 9 Huguosi Lu, in western Beijing.

Beijing opera bears little resemblance to its European counterpart. The mixture of singing, dancing, speaking, mime, acrobatics and dancing can go on for five or six hours. The screeching music can be searing to Western ears, but plots are fairly simple and easy to follow.

When you get bored after the first hour or so, and are sick of the high-pitched whining, the local audience is with you all the way –

A character from the lively and dramatic Beijing opera.

spitting, eating apples, breast-feeding an infant in the balcony, or plugging into a transistor radio (important sports match?). It's a lively prole audience viewing entertainment fit for kings.

Special performances are put on for foreigners nightly at 7.30 pm in the *Liyuan Theatre* (☎ 301-6688 ext 8860 or 8986), which is inside the Qianmen Hotel at 175 Yong'an Lu. Ticket prices depend on seat location, starting at Y8. For Y20 you can sit at a table and enjoy snacks and tea while watching the show. For Y40 you get better snacks and a table with better location. Performances here last just 1½ hours with sporadic translations flashed on an electronic signboard. You can get dressed up in an opera costume (with full facial makeup) for a photo-taking session.

The *Laoshe Teahouse* (☎ 303-6830) at 3 Qianmen Xi Dajie has nightly shows though basically it's all in Chinese. The performances vary from comedy acts to musical routines. Prices depend on the type of show and where you sit – the range is typically from Y40 to Y130. Showtime is from 7.30 to 9.30 pm.

Along similar lines is the *Tianqiao Happy Teahouse* (☎ 304-0617) at 113 Tianqiao Market, Xuanwu District. It's open daily except Monday from 7 to 9 pm and has an admission charge of Y80 to Y100.

Discos *NASA Disco* (☎ 201-6622) advertises 'advanced designed style appealing to radicals'. It can accommodate 1500 dancers and is open from 8 pm until 2 am. It's at the corner of Xueyuan Lu and Xitucheng Lu, just north of the third ring road. It's opposite the Jimen Hotel (nearest subway station: Xizhimen). Admission costs Y40, or Y60 on Friday and Saturday.

JJ's Disco (☎ 607-9691) is an enormous Chinese dance venue at 74 Xinjiekou Bei Dajie (Jishuitan subway station). Your admission ticket buys you a chance in JJ's lottery – first prize is a bicycle. The disco operates from 8 pm until 2 am – cover charge is Y50 but rises to Y80 on Friday and Saturday night.

Pubs The legendary *Hard Rock Cafe* (☎ 501-6688) is in the west wing of the Landmark Towers on the third ring road.

The Poacher Inn (☎ 532-3063) is the most British thing in Beijing besides the UK embassy. Admission costs half-price for members – bring a photo on your first visit and become a member straight away. Opening hours are from 2 pm to 3 or 4 am, but it's closed on Sunday – things get hopping about 10 pm. It's on the second floor of the Sanlitun Friendship Store opposite the Belgium embassy.

The *Brauhaus* (☎ 505-2266 ext 6565) in the China World Trade Centre on Jianguomenwai is a small bar with occasional live rock bands. There are just a few tables and drinks are expensive, but there's no cover charge and it is popular with the foreign community. This place shouldn't be mistaken for the Paulaner Brauhaus in the Lufthansa Centre, which is a German restaurant.

Teahouses *San Wei Bookstore* (☎ 601-3204) has a lovely Chinese teahouse on the second floor. Jazz bands sometimes play here and it's open nightly until 10 pm. The bookstore is opposite the Minzu Hotel westwards on Fuxingmen.

Probably of less interest to foreigners is the *Liuhexuan Teahouse* in Longtan Park, by the shores of Longtan Lake.

Theatre Beijing is on the touring circuit for foreign troupes, and these are listed in the *China Daily*. The most likely venue for this type of entertainment is the *Capital Theatre (shǒudū jùcháng)* (☎ 524-9847) at 22 Wangfujing Dajie. The other likely place is the *Experimental Theatre for Modern Drama* (☎ 403-1009) (*zhōngyāng shíyàn jù huà ùyuàn*), 45 Maoer Hutong, Di'anmen Dajie, just east of Qianhai Lake.

Things to Buy
The following is a description of some shopping districts and bargains to be had.

Wangfujing (*wángfǔjǐng*) This prestigious shopping street is just east of the Beijing Hotel – it's a solid block of stores and a favourite haunt of locals and tourists seeking bargains. Westerners now call it 'McDonald's St', after the restaurant which occupies the north-east corner of the main intersection. In pre-1949 days it was known as Morrison St, catering mostly to foreigners. The name Wangfujing derives from a 15th-century well.

Wangfujing's biggest emporium is the Beijing Department Store (*běijīng bǎihuò dàlóu*). Of prime interest to foreign travellers is the Foreign Languages Bookstore (No 235). This is not only *the* place in China to buy English-language books: check out the music tape section upstairs.

Wangfujing is the place to go to buy film, though the Friendship Store also offers very competitive prices. You can even find slide film here, but check the expiration dates. Wangfujing is also a good place to go for photoprocessing or to obtain passport photos in a hurry.

If you're interested in arts & crafts, it's worth looking into the Beijing Arts & Crafts Service Department at 200 Wangfujing.

Xidan (*xīdān*) Officially known as Xidan Bei Dajie, this street west of Zhongnanhai aspires to be a little Wangfujing. There are fewer foreign tourists here and the shops tend to cater mainly to the local market.

Qianmen & Dazhalan (*qiánmén, dàzhàlán*) Dazhalan is a hutong running west from the top end of Qianmen. It's a heady jumble of silk shops, department stores, theatres, herbal medicine, food and clothing specialists and some unusual architecture.

Dazhalan has a remnant medieval flavour to it, a hangover from the days when hutongs sold specialised products – one would sell lace, another lanterns, another jade. This one used to be called Silk Street. The name Dazhalan refers to a wicket-gate that was closed at night to keep prowlers out.

Dazhalan runs about 300 metres deep off the western end of Qianmen. At the far end where the hubbub dies down is a bunch of Chinese hotels, and if you sense something

THE EAST

here...yes, you're right, Dazhalan was the gateway to Beijing's red-light district. The brothels were shut down in 1949 and the women packed off to factories.

Liulichang (*liúlíchǎng*) Not far to the west of Dazhalan is Liulichang, Beijing's antique street. In imperial Beijing, shops and theatres were not permitted near the city centre, but Liulichang was outside the gates. Many of the city's oldest shops can be found along or near this crowded hutong.

Although it's been a shopping area for quite some time, only recently has it been dressed up for foreign tourists. The stores here are all designed to look like an ancient Chinese village. The vast majority of the shops at Liulichang are run by the government but that doesn't mean they are honest. We saw paper fans (not antique) on sale here for Y350 – 100 times the price in a typical Beijing department store. Those goods which are genuine antiques are even more outrageously expensive and cannot be taken out of China without official approval. Nevertheless, Liulichang is worth a look – some of the art books and drawings are a good deal and not easily found elsewhere.

Jianguomenwai (*jiànguómén wài*) The Friendship Store (*yǒuyí shāngdiàn*) at 17 Jianguomenwai (☎ 500-3311) is the largest in the land – this place stocks both touristy souvenirs and everyday useful items. Not long ago, it was *the* place to shop in Beijing – so exclusive that only foreigners and cadres were permitted inside. But these days anyone can go in. The touristy junk is upstairs, but the ground floor is where the really useful items are found – tinned and dried foods, tobacco, wines, spirits, coffee, Chinese medicines and film. The book and magazine section is a gold mine for travellers long-starved of anything to read. To the right are a supermarket and deli.

CVIK Plaza is a huge department store with an enormous selection – the best deal is the supermarket and restaurant in the basement. There are, of course, lots of pricey luxuries on offer: the latest fashion, makeup

and perfumes. Kitchenwares are in basement No 2. CVIK Plaza is on the south side of Jianguomenwai, opposite the CITIC building.

The **Xiushui Silk Market** (*xiùshuǐ dōngjiē*) is on the north side of Jianguomenwai between the Friendship Store and the Jianguo Hotel. Because of the prestigious location amid the luxury hotels, this place is elbow to elbow with foreign tourists at times – go early to avoid crowds and forget it on Sundays. This market is one of the best places to pick up good deals in upmarket clothing – everything from silk underwear and negligees to leather moneybelts. Bargaining is expected here, though it's sometimes difficult because of all the foreign tourists willing to throw money around like water.

Ritan Park is north of the Friendship Store – on the west side of the park and intersecting with it at a 90-degree angle is **Yabao Lu Clothing Market**. This place is enormous – no Beijing department store could hope to match the variety and low prices on offer here. Bargaining is the norm.

Sanlitun (*sānlìtún*) The Sanlitun embassy district is in north-east Beijing, close to the Great Wall Sheraton Hotel. Like Jianguomenwai, the stores here are decidedly upmarket.

Lufthansa Centre falls into a category by itself – it was Beijing's first flashy multistorey shopping mall. The Lufthansa Centre (*yànshā shāngchéng*) is also known as the Kempinski Hotel (*kǎibīnsījī fàndiàn*). You can buy everything here from computer floppy disks to bikinis (but who in China wears the latter?). A supermarket is in the basement.

Miscellaneous If there's anything you think is impossible to buy in Beijing, check out Watson's (*qūchénshì*) in the Holiday Inn Lido out towards the airport. This place sells every vitamin known to humanity, sunscreen (UV) lotion, beauty creams, tampons and the widest selection of condoms in China.

Getting There & Away

Air Beijing has direct air connections to most major cities in the world. Many travellers make use of the direct Beijing-Hong Kong flights on CAAC or Dragonair. For one-way return tickets, CAAC charges US$307/584, while Dragonair is slightly cheaper at US$294/558. Flights tend to be heavily booked, especially on Dragonair. Guangzhou and Shenzhen are both near Hong Kong and have direct flights to Beijing, providing alternative routes. The Beijing-Guangzhou flight is considerably cheaper than Beijing-Shenzhen, and for this reason you can expect all flights to/from Guangzhou to be heavily booked.

For more information about international flights to Beijing, see the introductory Getting There & Away chapter of this book.

In the international arrival hall of Beijing's Capital Airport, there are major delays (over one hour) when it comes to receiving your luggage. This problem may in time be solved when baggage facilities are upgraded, but for the time being you'd be wise to only take a carry-on bag. If this isn't possible, bring a magazine or novel to read while waiting for your luggage.

The CAAC aerial web spreads out in every conceivable direction, with daily flights to major cities and quite a few minor ones. For the most current information, get a CAAC timetable. Domestic flights connect Beijing to the following cities:

Anqing, Beihai, Changchun, Changsha, Changzhou, Chaoyang, Chengdu, Chifeng, Chongqing, Dalian, Datong, Dayong, Dunhuang, Fuzhou, Guangzhou, Guilin, Guiyang, Haikou, Hailar, Hangzhou, Harbin, Hefei, Hohhot, Huangshan, Huangyan, Ji'nan, Jilin, Jinzhou, Kunming, Lanzhou, Lianyungang, Luoyang, Mudanjiang, Nanchang, Nanjing, Nanning, Nantong, Ningbo, Qingdao, Qiqihar, Sanya, Shanghai, Shantou, Shenyang, Shenzhen, Taiyuan, Tianjin, Tongliao, Ürümqi, Wenzhou, Wuhan, Wulanhot, Xi'an, Xiamen, Xiangfan, Xilinhot, Xining, Yanji, Yantai, Yinchuan, Zhanjiang and Zhengzhou

CAAC goes by a variety of aliases (Air China, China Eastern Airlines etc), but you can buy tickets for all of them at the Aviation

Building, 15 Xichang'an Jie (domestic ☎ 601-3336, international ☎ 601-6667). You can purchase the same tickets at the CAAC office in the China World Trade Centre or from the numerous other CAAC service counters such as the one in the Beijing Hotel or the CITS counter in the International Hotel.

Inquiries for all airlines can be made at Beijing's Capital Airport (☎ 456-3604). The individual offices of airlines are:

Aeroflot
   Hotel Beijing-Toronto, 3 Jianguomenwai
   (☎ 500-2412)
Air France
   Room 2716, China World Trade Centre, 1
   Jianguomenwai (☎ 505-1818)
Alitalia
   Rooms 139 & 140, Jianguo Hotel, 5
   Jianguomenwai (☎ 500-2871, 500-2233 ext 139
   or 140)
All Nippon Airways
   Room 1510, China World Trade Centre, 1
   Jianguomenwai (☎ 505-3311)
American Airlines
   c/o Beijing Tradewinds, 114 International Club,
   11 Ritan Lu (☎ 502-5997)
Asiana Airlines
   Room 134, Jianguo Hotel, 5 Jianguomenwai
   (☎ 506-1118)
Austrian Airlines
   Jianguo Hotel, 5 Jianguomenwai (☎ 591-7861 or
   500-2233 ext 8038)
British Airways
   Room 210, 2nd floor, SCITE (CVIK) Tower, 22
   Jianguomenwai (☎ 512-4070)
Canadian Airlines
   Unit S104, Lufthansa Centre, 50 Liangmaqiao
   Lu (☎ 463-7901)
Dragonair
   1st floor, L107, World Trade Tower, 1
   Jianguomenwai (☎ 505-4343)
Ethiopian Airlines
   Room 0506, China World Trade Centre, 1
   Jianguomenwai (☎ 505-0134)
Finnair
   SCITE (CVIK) Tower, 22 Jianguomenwai
   (☎ 512-7180)
Garuda Indonesia
   Unit L116A West Wing, China World Trade
   Centre, 1 Jianguomenwai (☎ 505-2901)
Japan Airlines
   Ground floor, Changfugong Office Building,
   Hotel New Otani, 26A Jianguomenwai
   (☎ 513-0888)

JAT (Yugoslav) Airlines
Room 414, Kunlun Hotel, 2 Xinyuan Nanlu
(☎ 500-3388 ext 414)
Koryo (North Korean Airlines)
Swissôtel Hong Kong-Macau Centre
(☎ 501-1557)
LOT Polish Airlines
Chains City Hotel, 4 Gongren Tiyuchang Donglu
(☎ 500-7215, 500-7799 ext 2002)
Lufthansa
Lufthansa Centre, 50 Liangmaqiao Lu
(☎ 465-4488)
Malaysia Airlines
Lot 115A/B Level One, West Wing Office Block,
China World Trade Centre, 1 Jianguomenwai
(☎ 505-2681)
MIAT – Mongolian Airlines
Room 8-05, CITIC Building, 19 Jianguomenwai
(☎ 507-9297, 500-2255 ext 3850)
Northwest Airlines
Room 104, China World Trade Centre, 1
Jianguomenwai (☎ 505-3505, 505-2288 ext
8104)
Pakistan International Airlines
Room 106A, China World Trade Centre, 1
Jianguomenwai (☎ 505-1681)
Qantas
Suite S120B, East Wing Office Building,
Kempinski Hotel, Lufthansa Centre, 50
Liangmaqiao Lu (☎ 467-4794)
Scandinavian Airlines
18th floor, SCITE (CVIK) Tower, 22
Jianguomenwai (☎ 512-0575)
Singapore Airlines
Room 109, China World Trade Centre, 1
Jianguomenwai (☎ 505-2233)
Swissair
Room 201, SCITE (CVIK) Tower, 22
Jianguomenwai (☎ 512-3555)
Thai Airways International
Room 207, SCITE (CVIK) Tower, 22
Jianguomenwai (☎ 512-3881)
United Airlines
Lufthansa Centre, 50 Liangmaqiao Lu
(☎ 463-1111)

The *Capital Airport Hotel* (☎ 456-4562; fax
456-4563) *(shǒudū jīchǎng bīnguǎn)* is one
km from the airport terminal. Although this
hotel is not especially recommended, you
could find yourself here if your flight is
delayed. Supposedly, the airline should pick
up the tab if the delay is their fault, but don't
count on it. Single/double rooms are
Y280/300.

Bus Many foreigners don't think so, but you

can indeed arrive in or depart from Beijing
by bus. The advantage over the train (besides
cost) is that it's easier to get a seat on a bus.
Sleeper buses are widely available and certainly recommended for those long
overnight journeys. In general arriving by
bus is easier than departing, mainly because
when leaving it's very confusing to try and
figure out which bus station has the bus you
need.

The basic rule is that long-distance bus
stations are on the perimeter of the city in the
direction you want to go. The four major
ones are at Dongzhimen (north-east),
Haihutun (south), Beijiao (north, also called
Deshengmen) and Majuan (east).

In addition, there is a tiny bus station in
the car park in front of Beijing Railway
Station: this is where you catch buses to
Tianjin and the Great Wall at Badaling.
Another tiny bus station is in the car park of
the Workers' Stadium – this is mainly geared
towards buses for destinations within
Beijing Municipality (like Miyun Reservoir).

One of the more useful stations is
Haihutun on the southern side of Beijing. It's
at the intersection of Nansanhuan Zhonglu
(the southern part of the third ring road) and
Nanyuan Lu (which is what Qianmen Lu is
called in the far south of town). Long-distance buses from here head to cities such as
Qingdao and Shanghai.

Beijiao station is on the north side of the
city. It's one km north of the second ring road
on Deshengmenwai Dajie, and is often
referred to as 'Deshengmen station'. Some
long-distance buses depart from here. Otherwise, you might need to take bus No 345
from Deshengmen to the terminus (Changping), from where you can get other
long-distance buses.

Train Foreigners arriving or departing by
train do so at Beijing's main railway station
(běijīng huǒchē zhàn) or the newly opened
west railway station *(běijīng xī zhàn)*, the
largest in China. There are also two other
stations of significance in the city, Yongding

men (south) Railway Station and Xizhimen (north) Railway Station.

There is a Foreigners' Ticketing Office at the Beijing Railway Station. Enter the station and it's to the rear and left side – there's a small sign in English saying 'International Passenger Booking Office'. The ticketing office is inside the foreigners' waiting room. It's open daily from 5.30 to 7.30 am and 8 am to 5.30 pm, and from 7 pm to 12.30 am. At least those are the official times – foreigners have often found the staff unwilling to

Travel Times & Train Fares from Beijing					
Destination	Hard Sleeper (Y)	Hard Seat (Y)	Soft Sleeper (Y)	Soft Seat (Y)	Approx Travel Time (hours)
Baotou	203	125	386	-	15
Beidaihe	105	65	200	99	6
Changchun	256	158	488	-	17
Changsha	331	203	629	-	23
Chengde	-	66	-	99	5
Chengdu	398	245	761	-	34
Chongqing	412	254	782	-	40
Dalian	256	158	488	-	19
Dandong	256	158	488	-	19
Datong	107	65	203	99	7
Fuzhou	503	309	957	-	43
Guangzhou	444	273	845	-	35
Guangzhou (exp)	512	-	973	-	30
Guilin	412	254	782	-	31
Hangzhou	317	183	630	-	24
Harbin	297	183	568	-	20
Hohhot	167	104	317	-	12
Ji'nan	137	84	259	128	9
Kunming	589	362	1120	-	59
Lanzhou	374	231	712	-	35
Liuyuan	551	339	1052	-	59
Luoyang	194	119	369	-	14
Nanjing	264	162	502	-	20
Nanning	492	303	938	-	39
Qingdao	210	129	401	-	17
Qinglongqiao	-	14	-	21	2
Qiqihar	347	213	660	-	23
Shanghai	363	223	689	-	17
Shenyang	203	125	386	192	11
Shijiazhuang	-	51	-	77	4
Suzhou	272	158	543	-	25
Tai'an	149	92	281	-	10
Taiyuan	193	118	365	-	11
Tianjin	-	35	-	54	2
Turpan	656	404	1250	-	72
Ürümqi	670	413	1274	-	75
Xi'an	273	168	521	-	22
Xining	412	254	782	-	44
Yantai	221	128	437	-	18
Yinchuan	290	179	552	-	25
Zhengzhou	171	105	327	162	12

sell tickets in the early morning or after 5 pm. Whether or not you get a ticket here is potluck – sometimes the staff are friendly and helpful, at other times downright hostile. There are lockers inside the waiting room, often full, in which case you'll have to use the left-luggage rooms outside the station (exit station and car park, then to the right). Tickets can be booked several days in advance. Your chances of getting a sleeper (hard or soft) are good if you book ahead.

A big warning – if you arrive in Beijing with a Chinese-priced ticket, you will be given the third degree and almost certainly have to pay a fine. This is in strong contrast to the rest of China, where railway staff don't much care if foreigners use Chinese-priced tickets. A fake student card will not get you out of trouble either – the Beijing railway authorities will also check to make sure you have a student visa if you use a student card.

See the table on the previous page for approximate travel times and train fares out of Beijing for hard seat, hard sleeper and soft sleeper. Variations may arise because of different routings of different trains. For example, the journey to Shanghai can take between 17 and 25 hours depending on the train.

Getting Around

To/From the Airport The airport is 25 km from the Forbidden City, but add another 10 km if you're going to the southern end of town.

For Y12 you can catch the airport shuttle bus from the Aviation Building *(mínháng dàshà)* on Xi Chang'an Jie, Xidan District – this is the location of Air China and China Northwest Airlines, but it's *not* the same place as the CAAC office, which is in the World Trade Centre. The bus departs on the opposite side of the street (south side of Xichang'an Jie), not from the car park of the Aviation Building.

At the airport, you can catch this shuttle bus in front of the terminal building – buy the bus ticket from the counter inside the terminal building, not on the bus itself. The bus terminates at the Aviation Building in Xidan but makes several stops en route – get off at the second stop (Swissôtel-Hong Kong Macau Centre) if you want to take the subway (Dongsishitiao station).

Taxis from the airport to the Forbidden City area cost around Y75 to Y90, plus about Y20 more to the southern side of town.

Bus Sharpen your elbows, chain your wallet to your underwear and muster all the patience you can – you'll need it. Oversized and overstuffed buses are the norm in Beijing – they're sweatboxes in summer but cosy in winter (if you haven't frozen to the bus stop by the time the behemoth arrives). Exiting can be problematic – try the nearest window. Fares are typically two jiao depending on distance, but often it's free because you can't see (let alone reach) the conductor.

There are about 140 bus and trolley routes, which make navigation rather confusing, especially if you can't see out of the window in the first place. A bus map can help.

Buses run from around 5 am to 11 pm. Bus stops are long and far between. It's important to work out how many stops to go before boarding. Avoid these sardine cans at rush hours or on holidays.

Buses are routed through landmarks and key intersections, and if you can pick out the head and tail of the route, you can get a good idea of where the monster will travel. Major terminals are situated near long-distance junctions: the main Beijing railway station, Dongzhimen, Haihutun, Yongdingmen and Qianmen. The zoo (Dongwuyan) has the biggest pile-up, with about 15 bus lines, since it's where inner and outer Beijing get together.

One or two-digit bus numbers are city core, 100-series buses are trolleys and 300-series are suburban lines. If you can work out how to combine bus and subway connections, the subway will speed up part of the trip. Some useful buses are:

No 1 This bus travels east-west across the city along Chang'an, from Jianguo Lu to Fuxing Lu.

No 5 Travels the north-south axis, from Deshengmen/Gulou and down the west side of the Forbidden City to Qianmen; it ends at Youanmen.

No 44 Follows the Circle Line subway in a square on the ring road.

No 15 This one zigzags from the Tianqiao area (west of Tiantan Park) to the zoo and passes several subway stops.

No 7 Runs from the west side of Qianmen gate to the zoo (Dongwuyuan).

No 20 Zigzags from the main Beijing Railway Station to Yongdingmen station via Chang'an and Qianmen Dajie. This bus gets you to the Qiaoyuan Hotel.

No 54 Runs from Beijing's main railway station, terminates at Yongdingmen station and (like bus No 20) is an ideal way to get to the Qiaoyuan Hotel.

No 10 This trolley runs from the main railway station to the zoo via Chongwenmen, Wangfujing, the Art Gallery and Jingshan and Beihai parks.

No 106 Runs from Dongzhimenwai via Chongwenmen Dajie to Yongdingmen station.

No 116 Travels from the south entrance of Tiantan Park up Qianmen Dajie to Tiananmen, east along Chang'an to Dongdan and directly north on Dongdan to the Lama Temple – a good sightseeing bus.

No 332 Covers Dongwuyan (zoo), Minzuxueyuan (Central Nationalities Institute), Weigongcun, Renmindaxue (People's University), Zhongguancun, Haidian, Beijingdaxue (Beijing University) and Yiheyuan (Summer Palace). There are actually two No 332s: regular and express – both make good sightseeing buses. The express bus has fewer stops and is at the head of the queue near the zoo.

Double Decker A special two-tiered bus for tourists and upper-crust locals, the double deckers run in a circle around the city centre. These cost Y2 but you are spared the traumas of normal public buses – passengers are guaranteed a seat! Useful stops along the route include Tiananmen Square, Lufthansa Centre and the National Olympic Sports Centre.

Subway The subway (dì xià tiě) is definitely the best way of travelling around. The Underground Dragon can move at up to 70 km per hour – a jaguar compared with the lumbering buses. Originally constructed as part of Beijing's botched air-raid system, the east-west line (opened in 1969) was for a time restricted to Chinese with special passes. Foreigners were not permitted to ride the subway until 1980. These days anyone can ride, and like most mass transit systems it loses money – several million yuan per year. Unlike most other subways the crime rate is low (there is the odd pickpocket), graffiti is nonexistent, it's very clean, and messy suicides are said to be rare. However, the trains are showing their age – it's a pale shadow to Shanghai's spiffy new subway system.

Beijing Subway Routes

Trains run at a frequency of one every few minutes during peak times. It can get very crowded but it sure beats the buses! The carriages have seats for 60 and standing room for 200. Platform signs are in Chinese and Pinyin. The fare is a flat five jiao regardless of distance. The subway is open from 5 am to 10.30 pm. There are two lines:

Circle Line This 16-km line presently has 18 stations: Beijing Zhan (railway station), Jianguomen, Chaoyangmen, Dongsishitiao, Dongzhimen, Yonghegong, Andingmen, Gulou Dajie, Jishuitan, Xizhimen (the north railway station and zoo), Chegongzhuang, Fuchengmen, Fuxingmen, Changchun Jie, Xuanwumen, Heping Lu, Qianmen and Chongwenmen.

East-West Line This line has 12 stops and runs from Xidan to Pingguoyuan, which is – no, not the capital of North Korea – a western suburb of Beijing whose name translates as Apple Orchard (unfortunately, the apple trees have long since vanished). It takes 40 minutes to traverse the length of the line. The stops are Xidan, Fuxingmen, Nanlishilu, Muxudi, Junshibowuguan (Military Museum), Gongzhufen, Wanshoulu, Wukesong, Yuquanlu, Babaoshan, Bajiaocun, Guchenglu and Pingguoyuan. Fuxingmen is where the Circle Line meets the East-West Line and there is no additional fare to make the transfer. The East-West Line is currently being extended further east and will eventually reach Jianguomenwai and beyond.

Car Resident foreigners are allowed to drive their own cars in the capital and to drive the Beijing-Tianjin highway. Most are not permitted to drive more than 40 km from the capital without special permission. Chauffeur-driven cars and minibuses can be hired from some of the major hotels, but why not just rent a taxi by the day for less money?

It now seems that private car rental in the capital is going to be permitted. You are restricted on just how far you can drive, so find out the rules before you set out. Several companies are ready to dive into this business; one of the first is called First Car Rental Company (☎ 422-3950).

Taxi In 1986 there were fewer than 1000 taxis available in the capital – if you wanted one, it had to be booked hours in advance.

By 1995, the number of taxis exceeded 60,000 and is still increasing rapidly.

In other words, finding a cab is seldom a problem, though surging demand means that during rush hours you may have to battle it out with the other 11 million residents of Beijing. One government brochure claims that 80% of Beijing taxis drivers can speak English. Perhaps they meant 80 drivers – out of the total 60,000, that would be just about the right percentage. If you don't speak Chinese, bring a map or have your destination written down in characters.

The vehicles have a sticker on the window indicating their per-km charge, which varies all the way from Y1 to Y2 with a Y10 minimum. The tiny minivans are the cheapest and therefore most in demand.

There are over 1000 taxi companies in Beijing, some with a fleet of just a few vehicles. For telephone-booking a cab, one of the largest is Beijing Municipal Taxi Company (☎ 831-2288).

Bicycle The scale of Beijing is suddenly much reduced on a bike, which can also give you a great deal of freedom. Hotels often have bike hire, especially budget hotels. Bike hire agencies tend to congregate around hotels and tourist spots – look for signs in English. Prices vary wildly (Y20 per day at the Peace Hotel versus Y80 at the neighbouring Palace Hotel). The renter may demand you leave your passport, but a deposit of about Y100 will usually do.

Make sure the tyres are pumped up, the saddle is adjusted to the correct height (fully extended leg from saddle to pedal) and, most important, that the brakes work. What you get in the way of a bike is potluck. It could be so new that all the screws are loose, or it could be a lethal rustbin. If you have problems later on, adjustments can be made at any bike shop, dirt cheap.

Several shopping areas are closed to cyclists from 6 am to 6 pm; Wangfujing is one. Parking is provided everywhere for peanuts – compulsory peanuts since your velo can otherwise be towed away. Beijing ese peak hours can be rather astounding – a

Top: Baohedian Hall in the Forbidden City, at one time the site of imperial examinations, Beijing

Bottom Left: Monument to the People's Heroes in Tiananmen Square, Beijing

Bottom Right: Bicycle parking zone, Beijing

GLENN BEANLAND

Mutianyu, a good place to view the Great Wall, 90 km from Beijing

roving population of three million plus bicycles, a fact explained by the agony of bus rides. This makes turning at roundabouts a rather skilled cycling procedure. If nervous, dismount at the side of the road, wait for the clusters to unthicken and try again. Beijing in winter presents other problems like slippery roads (black ice), howling headwinds and frostbite.

AROUND BEIJING
Badaling Great Wall
(bādálǐng chángchéng)

The majority of visitors see the Great Wall at Badaling, 70 km north-west of Beijing at an elevation of 1000 metres. This section of the wall was restored in 1957, with the addition of guard rails. Since the 1980s, Badaling has become exceedingly crowded so a cable car was added to enhance the flow of tourist traffic.

The Great Wall Circle Vision Theatre was opened in 1990 – a 360-degree amphitheatre showing 15-minute films about the Great Wall. You'll hear about the wall's history and legends – narration is in English or Chinese and other languages may be added later.

There is an admission fee of Y15. You can spend plenty more for a tacky 'I Climbed the Great Wall' T-shirt, a talking panda doll, a cuckoo clock that plays 'The East Is Red' or a plastic reclining buddha statue with a lightbulb in its mouth. For an additional fee you can get your snapshot taken aboard a camel and pretend to be Marco Polo.

Getting There & Away CITS, CTS, big hotels and everyone else in the tourist business does a tour to Badaling. Prices border on the ridiculous, with some hotels asking over Y300 per person.

There are cheapie Chinese tours (around Y15) departing from a number of venues. Some depart from the south side of Tiananmen Square (near KFC). Others depart from the car park in front of the Beijing Railway Station (west side of station), but don't get confused with the buses heading for Tianjin (which depart from the exact same spot). You can also catch buses from the car park of the Workers' Stadium *(gōngrén tǐyùguǎn)* – this is on Gongren Tiyuchang Beilu next to the Beijing Asia Hotel and the Dongsishitiao subway station. Departures are in the morning only, around 7.30 to 8 am. But first ask about the itinerary – some tour operators don't just go straight to Badaling, but instead really try to give you your money's worth:

Our Chinese tour went to a revolutionary monument, a theme park, movie studio, wax museum, history museum and *finally* the Great Wall. We departed from our hotel at 6.10 am and arrived at the Great Wall at 4.30 pm! All these different sights were not interesting!

Carol M Johnson

Local buses also ply the route to the wall but it's slow going; take bus Nos 5 or 44 to Deshengmen, then No 345 to the terminal (Changping), then a numberless bus to the wall (alternatively, bus No 357 goes part way along the route and you then hitch). Another route is bus No 14 to Beijiao long-distance bus station, which is north of Deshengmen, then a numberless bus to the wall. Going on local buses saves some money but it's a headache even if you speak Chinese.

You can reach the wall by express train from Beijing Railway Station, getting off at Qinglongqiao. There are actually three stations within one km of the wall – Qinglongqiao, New Qinglongqiao and Badaling, but the first is by far the closest to your destination. Qinglongqiao station is notable for the statue of Zhan Tianyou, the engineer in charge of building the Beijing-Baotou line. No trains stop at all three stations and many stop only at Qinglongqiao. You can continue from Qinglongqiao on to Datong, Hohhot and beyond. Coming from the other direction, you can get off the train at Qinglongqiao, look around, and reboard the train to Beijing on the same ticket. You can safely dump your bags in the left-luggage room at Qinglongqiao station while you look around.

There's another approach by slower local trains from Xizhimen (north) Railway Station in Beijing which stop at Badaling or Qinglongqiao and continue to Kangzhuang.

There are several trains on this route with different departure times – check times at the station. It is also possible to catch train No 527 at 9.40 am from Yongdingmen (south) Railway Station and get off at Juyongguan station, but then you'll have to walk several (pleasant) km to the wall. Badaling station is

one km from the wall. The Badaling line is quite a feat of engineering; built in 1909, it tunnels under the wall.

A microbus-style taxi to the wall and back will cost at least Y250 for an eight-hour hire with a maximum of five passengers – you are expected to buy lunch for the driver. Consid-

The Great Wall

Also known to the Chinese as the '10,000 Li Wall' (5000 km), the Great Wall stretches from Shanhaiguan Pass on the east coast to Jiayuguan Pass in the Gobi Desert.

The undertaking was begun 2000 years ago during the Qin Dynasty (221-207 BC), when China was unified under Emperor Qin Shihuang. Separate walls, constructed by independent kingdoms to keep out marauding nomads, were linked up. The effort required hundreds of thousands of workers, many of them political prisoners, and 10 years of hard labour under General Meng Tian. An estimated 180 million cubic metres of rammed earth was used to form the core of the original wall, and legend has it that one of the building materials used was the bodies of deceased workers.

The wall never really did perform its function as a defence line to keep invaders out. As Genghis Khan supposedly said, 'The strength of a wall depends on the courage of those who defend it'. Sentries could be bribed. However, it did work very well as a kind of elevated highway, transporting men and equipment across mountainous terrain. Its beacon tower system, using smoke signals generated by burning wolves' dung, transmitted news of enemy movements quickly back to the capital. To the west was Jiayuguan Pass, an important link on the Silk Road, where there was a customs post of sorts and where unwanted Chinese were ejected through the gates to face the terrifying wild west.

Marco Polo makes no mention of China's greatest tourist attraction. Both sides of the wall were under the same government at the time of his visit. During the Ming Dynasty a determined effort was made to rehash the whole project, this time facing it with bricks and stone slabs – some 60 million cubic metres of them. This Ming project took over 100 years, and the costs in human effort and resources were phenomenal.

The wall was largely forgotten after that. Lengthy sections of it have returned to dust. Other bits were carted off by local peasants to construct their own walls – a hobby that no-one objected to during the Cultural Revolution.

The wall might have disappeared totally had it not been rescued by the tourist industry. Several important sections have recently been rebuilt, dressed up with souvenir shops, restaurants and amusement park rides. Oddly, the depiction of the wall as an object of great beauty is a bizarre one. It's really a symbol of tyranny, like the Berlin Wall used to be. ■

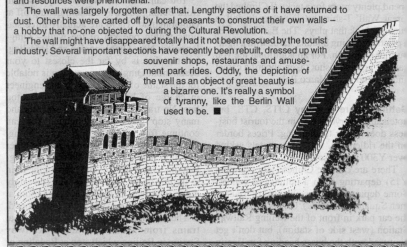

ering that this works out to be less than Y60 per person, it's certainly not unreasonable.

Mutianyu Great Wall
(mùtiányù chángchéng)

To take some of the pressure off crowded Badaling, a second site for Great Wall viewing has been opened at Mutianyu, 90 km north-east of Beijing. This part of the wall is less of a carnival than Badaling, but the recent addition of souvenir shops and a cable car (Y55 for foreigners, Y5 for Chinese) is starting to attract armadas of tour buses. Nevertheless, Mutianyu is the place most preferred by individual travellers and is still much less crowded than Badaling.

Getting There & Away A small number of Chinese tour buses go to Mutianyu – look for them near the KFC near Tiananmen Square, the Beijing Railway Station or the Workers' Stadium. Entrance to the wall at Mutianyu costs Y15. The cable-car ride costs Y30 one way, Y40 for the return trip.

To go by yourself is complicated and doesn't save much money. If you're starting from the Qiaoyuan Hotel area, take bus No 106 (from Yongdingmen) to Dongzhimen (last station). From there walk across the street to the long-distance bus station and take a bus to Huairou, then it's another 20 km by local minibus (these are scarce), taxi or bicycle.

Simatai Great Wall
(sīmǎtái chángchéng)

If you prefer your wall without the benefit of handrails, cable cars and tacky souvenir shops, Simatai is the place to go. Of all the parts of the wall near Beijing which are open to tourism, the 19-km section at Simatai is the least developed (for now). Many consider this part of the wall to be the most beautiful.

This section of the wall dates from the Ming Dynasty and has some unusual features like 'obstacle-walls', which are walls-within-walls used for defending against enemies who'd already scaled the Great Wall. There are 135 watchtowers at Simatai,

the highest being Wangjinglou. Small cannon have been discovered in this area, as well as evidence of rocket-type weapons such as flying knives and flying swords.

Simatai is not for the faint-hearted – this section of the wall is very steep. A few slopes have a 70-degree incline and you need both hands free, so bring a day-pack to hold your camera and other essentials. One narrow section of footpath has a 500-metre drop – it's no place for acrophobics.

In the early 1970s a nearby PLA unit destroyed about three km of the wall to build barracks, setting an example for the locals who used stones from the wall to build houses. In 1979 the same unit was ordered to rebuild the section they tore down.

A small section of the wall at Simatai has already been renovated, but most of it remains in its non-commercialised crumbling condition. Seeing the wall *au naturel* is a sharp contrast to Badaling and Mutianyu, which are so well restored that you may get the impression the wall was built just yesterday to serve CITS tour groups. Perhaps it was.

There is a small restaurant at the car park near the base of the wall, and at the present time prices are still reasonable. It's not a bad idea to come prepared with some snacks and water. There is a Y15 admission charge.

Besides those already mentioned, other parts of the wall open to tourists are the stretches at Jiayuguan in Gansu Province, Shanhaiguan in Hebei Province and Huangyaguan in Tianjin Municipality. Details for visiting these parts of the wall are covered in the relevant chapters of this book.

Getting There & Away Simatai is 110 km north-east of Beijing, and due to the distance and lack of tourist facilities there is little public transport. Buses to Simatai cost Y20 for the round-trip and depart just once daily from the Dongzhimen bus station at 7 am. The journey takes from two to three hours, and the bus departs Simatai at 3 pm (but ask to be sure).

For budget travellers, the best deal around is offered through the Jinghua Hotel – Y70 for the return journey by minibus. Ring up their booking office (☎ 761-2582 after 4 pm) for more details.

If you don't do a tour through the Jinghua Hotel, you can hire a microbus taxi for the day for about Y400. Tour operators also gather at Tiananmen Square and ask ridiculous prices for foreigners.

Ming Tombs
(shísān líng)

The general travellers' consensus on the tombs is that you'd be better off looking at a bank vault, which is, roughly, what the tombs are. The scenery along the way is charming, though, and the approach through a valley is rewarding.

The seven-km 'spirit way' starts with a triumphal arch, then goes through the Great Palace Gate, where officials had to dismount, and passes a giant tortoise (made in 1425) bearing the largest stele in China. This is followed by a guard of 12 sets of stone animals.

Dingling was the first of the tombs to be excavated and opened to the public. In total, 13 of the 16 Ming emperors are buried in this 40-sq-km area, which is why another name for this site is the Thirteen Tombs. Besides Dingling, two other tombs, Changling and Zhaoling, are open to the public.

Aware of the fact that many visitors have found the tombs disappointing, the Beijing municipal government is busy dressing up the area. New facilities include a golf course, the Dingling Museum (with a wax Genghis Khan), the Nine Dragons Amusement Park, the Aerospace Museum, an archery and rifle range, shops, cafes, a 350-room hotel, a swimming pool, an aquarium, a camping ground, a picnic area, a fountain (with 200-metre waterjet), a fishing pier (on the Ming Tombs Reservoir) and a bicycle-racing velodrome. There are also helicopter rides over the tombs and the nearby Great Wall. Plans call for the construction of additional facilities, including a horse-racing track, a cross-country skiing area and Mongolian yurts for use as a summer hotel.

Admission to the Ming Tombs costs Y30 for foreigners.

Getting There & Away The tombs lie 50 km north-west of Beijing and a few km from the small town of Changping. The tour buses usually combine them with a visit to the Great Wall. You can also get there on the local buses. Take bus No 5 or 44 to Deshengmen terminal. West of the flyover is the terminal of bus No 345, which you take to Changping, a one-hour ride (it drops you off near the Aerospace Museum). Then take bus No 314 to the tombs (or get a taxi for the last stretch).

Changping's main railway station is on the main Beijing-Baotou (Inner Mongolia) railway line. There is another station, Changping north station, which is closer to the Ming Tombs, but relatively few trains stop there.

Western Qing Tombs
(qīng xī líng)

These tombs are in Yixian County, 110 km south-west of Beijing. If you didn't see enough of Dingling, Yuling, Yongling and Deling, well, there's always Tailing, Changling, Chongling and Muling – the latter four being part of Xiling.

The tomb area is vast and houses the corpses of the emperors, empresses and other members and hangers-on of the royal family. The tomb of Emperor Guangxu (Chongling) has been excavated – his was the last imperial tomb and was constructed between 1905 and 1915.

Eastern Qing Tombs
(qīng dōng líng)

The Eastern Qing Tombs area is Death Valley – five emperors, 14 empresses and 136 imperial consorts. In the mountains ringing the valley are buried princes, dukes, imperial nurses and so on.

The approach to the tomb area is a common 'spirit way', similar to that of the Ming Tombs but with the addition of marble arch bridges. The materials for the tomb came from all over China, including 20 onne logs pulled over iced roads, and giant stone slabs.

Two of the tombs are open. Emperor Qian-long (1711-99) started preparations when he was 30, and by the time he was 88 he had used up 90 tonnes of silver. His resting place covers half a sq km. Some of the beamless stone chambers are decorated with Tibetan and Sanskrit sutras; the doors bear bas-relief bodhisattvas.

Empress Dowager Cixi also got a head start. Her tomb, Dingdong, was completed some three decades before her death. The phoenix, symbol of the empress, appears above that of the dragon (the emperor's symbol) in the artwork at the front of the tomb – not side by side as on other tombs. Both tombs were plundered in the 1920s.

In Zunhua County (zūnhuà xiàn), 125 km east of Beijing, the Eastern Qing Tombs have a lot more to see in them than the Ming Tombs – although you may be a little jaded after the Forbidden City. Of course, the scenery helps make the visit worthwhile.

The only way to get there is by bus and it's a long ride. Tour buses are considerably more comfortable than the local rattle-traps and take three or four hours to get there; you have about three hours on site. It may be possible to make a one-way trip to Zunhua and then take off somewhere else rather than go back to Beijing. A little way north along the road to Chengde is a piece of the Great Wall.

Halfway to Zunhua the tour bus makes a lunch stop at Jixian, more interesting than Zunhua. Jixian is in Tianjin Municipality – see the Tianjin chapter for details.

Fragrant Hills Park
(xiāngshān gōngyuán)
Within striking distance of the Summer Palace, and often combined with it on a tour, are the Western Hills (xī shān), another former villa-resort of the emperors. The part of the Western Hills closest to Beijing is known as the Fragrant Hills (xiāngshān). This is the last stop for the city buses – if you want to get further into the mountains, you'll have to walk, cycle or take a taxi.

You can scramble up the slopes to the top of Incense-Burner Peak, or take the crowded chairlift (Y15 one way). From the peak you get an all-embracing view of the countryside. The chairlift is a good way to get up the mountain, and from the summit you can hike further into the Western Hills and leave the crowds behind.

The Fragrant Hills area was also razed by foreign troops in 1860 and 1900 but a few bits of original architecture still poke out. A glazed-tile pagoda and the renovated Temple of Brilliance (zhāo miào) – a mock-Tibetan temple built in 1780 – are both in the same area. The surrounding heavily wooded park was a hunting ground for the emperors, and once contained a slew of pavilions and shrines, many of which are now being restored. It's a favourite strolling spot for Beijingers and destined to become another Chinese Disneyland – the hundreds of sou-venir shops are probably a sign of horrors to come. For those who can afford it, it's possi-ble to stay here at the pricey Xiangshan Hotel.

Admission to the park costs a mere Y0.50. There are a couple of ways of getting to the Fragrant Hills by public transport: bus No 333 from the Summer Palace, bus No 360 from the zoo and bus No 318 from Pingguo-yuan (the last stop in the west on the subway).

Azure Clouds Temple
(bìyún sì)
Within walking distance of the North Gate of Fragrant Hills Park is the Azure Clouds Temple, whose landmark is the Diamond Throne Pagoda. Of Indian design, it consists of a raised platform with a central pagoda and stupas around it. The temple was first built in 1366, and was expanded in the 18th century with the addition of the Hall of Arhats, containing 500 statues representing disciples of Buddha. Dr Sun Yatsen's coffin was placed in the temple in 1925 before being moved to Nanjing. In 1954 the govern-ment renovated Sun's memorial hall, which has a picture display of his revolutionary activities.

THE EAST

Sleeping Buddha Temple
(wòfó sì)

About halfway between the Fragrant Hills and the Summer Palace is Sleeping Buddha Temple. During the Cultural Revolution the buddhas in one of the halls were replaced by a statue of Mao (since removed). The drawcard is the huge reclining buddha, five metres long, cast in copper. The history books place it in the year 1331 but it's most likely a copy. Its weight is unknown but could be up to 50 tonnes. Pilgrims used to make offerings of shoes to the barefoot statue.

Xiangshan Botanical Gardens
(xiāngshān zhíwù yuán)

About two km east of Fragrant Hills Park and just to the south of the Sleeping Buddha Temple is the Botanical Gardens. While not spectacular, the gardens are a botanist's delight and a pleasant place for a stroll.

Badachu
(bādàchù)

Directly south of the Fragrant Hills is Badachu, the Eight Great Sites, also known as Eight Great Temples *(bādà sì)*. It has eight monasteries or temples scattered in wooded valleys. The Second Site has the Buddha's Tooth Relic Pagoda, built to house the sacred fang and accidentally discovered when the Allied army demolished the place in 1900.

Since 1994, the ancient culture has been dressed up with a new amusement park ride, a roller-toboggan course. A chairlift carries you up the hill to the top of the toboggan course. The rollerway has a length of 1700 metres and speeds up to 80 km per hour can be achieved.

Admission to Badachu costs Y2. The easiest way to reach the area is to take the east-west subway line to the last stop at Pingguoyuan and catch a taxi (Y10) from there. Alternatively, take bus No 347, which runs there from the zoo (it crosses the No 318 route).

Tanzhe Temple
(tánzhè sì)

About 45 km directly west of Beijing is Tanzhe Temple, the largest of all the Beijing

temples, occupying an area 260 metres by 160 metres. The Buddhist complex has a long history dating back to the 3rd century (Jin Dynasty); structural modifications date from the Liao, Tang, Ming and Qing dynasties. It therefore has a number of features – dragon decorations, mythical animal sculptures and grimacing gods – no longer found in temples in the capital.

Translated literally, Tanzhe means Pool Cudrania – the temple takes its name from its proximity to the Dragon Pool *(lóng tán)* and some rare Cudrania *(zhè)* trees. Locals come to the Dragon Pool to pray for rain during droughts. The Cudrania trees nourish silkworms and provide a yellow dye. The bark of the tree is believed to cure women of sterility, which may explain why there are so few of these trees left at the temple entrance.

The temple complex is open to the public daily from 8.30 am until 6 pm.

Getting There & Away To get there take bus No 336 from Zhanlanguan Lu, which runs off Fuchengmenwai Dajie north-west of Yuetan Park. Take this bus to the terminal at Mentougou and then hitch. A direct route is bus No 307 from Qianmen to the Hetan terminal and then a numberless bus to the temple. Alternatively, take the subway to Pingguoyuan, bus No 336 to Hetan and the numberless bus to the temple.

Jietai Temple
(jiètái sì)

About 10 km south-east of the Tanzhe Temple is a similar but smaller compound, Jietai Temple. The name roughly translates as Temple of Ordination Terrace. The temple was built during the Tang Dynasty, around 622 AD, with major improvements made by later tenants during the Ming Dynasty. The main complex is dotted with ancient pines, all of which have quaint names – Nine Dragon Pine is claimed to be over 1300 years old.

It's roughly 35 km from Jietai Temple to Beijing, and a journey out here is usually combined with a visit to Tanzhe Temple.

Marco Polo Bridge
(lúgōuqiáo)

Publicised by the great traveller himself, the Reed Moat Bridge is made of grey marble, is 260 metres long and has over 250 marble balustrades supporting 485 carved stone lions. First built in 1192, the original arches were washed away in the 17th century. The bridge is a composite of different eras, widened in 1969 – it spans the Yongding River near the little town of Wanping.

Long before CITS, Emperor Qianlong also did his bit to promote the bridge. In 1751 he put his calligraphy to use and wrote 'Morning Moon Over Lugou Bridge', now engraved into stone tablets on the site. On the opposite bank is a monument to Qianlong's inspection of the Yongding River.

Despite the publicity campaign by Polo and Qianlong, the bridge wouldn't have rated more than a footnote in Chinese history were it not for the famed Marco Polo Bridge Incident, which ignited a full-scale war with Japan. On the night of 7 July 1937, Japanese troops illegally occupied a railway junction outside Wanping – Japanese and Chinese soldiers started shooting at each other, and that gave Japan enough of an excuse to attack and occupy Beijing. The Marco Polo Bridge Incident is considered by many as the date of China's entry into WW II.

A relatively recent addition to this ancient site is the Memorial Hall of the War of Resistance Against Japan, built in 1987. Also on the site is the Wanping Castle, the Daiwang Temple and a tourist hotel.

You can get to the bridge by taking bus No 109 to Guang'anmen and then catching bus No 339. It's a 16-km (one-way) bike ride from central Beijing.

Peking Man Site
(zhōukǒudiàn)

Site of those primeval Chinese, Zhoukoudian is 48 km south-west of Beijing. There's an 'Apeman Cave' here on a hill above the village, several lesser caves and some dig sites. There is also a fossil exhibition hall – you'd have to be a fossil yourself to stay here for more than 15 minutes. There are three sections to the exhibition hall – pre-human history, the life and times of Peking Man and a section dealing with recent anthropological research. There are ceramic models, stone tools and the skeletons of prehistoric creatures.

The exhibition hall (☎ 931-0278) is open daily from 9 am to 4 pm, but check before you go. You could get a suburban train from Yongdingmen station and get off at Zhoukoudian. Another possibility is a bus from the Haihutun bus station (south of Tiantan on the corner of Nansanhuan Zhonglu and Nanyuan Lu). If combined with a trip to Tanzhe Temple and Marco Polo Bridge, approaching by taxi is not unreasonable. There is a guesthouse on the site.

Shidu
(shídù)

This is Beijing's answer to Guilin. The pinnacle-shaped rock formations, small rivers and general beauty of the place make it a favourite spot with expatriates like foreign students, diplomats and businesspeople.

Shidu means 'ten ferries' or 'ten crossings'. Shidu is 110 km south-west of central Beijing. At least before the new road and bridges were built, it was necessary to cross the Juma River 10 times while travelling along the gorge between Zhangfang and Shidu village.

Places to Stay The *Longshan Hotel* *(lóngshān fàndiàn)* is opposite the railway station and is the one place which currently accepts foreigners.

Down near Jiudu (the 'ninth ferry') there is a camping ground, conveniently located on a flood-plain.

Getting There & Away This is one of the few scenic areas outside Beijing which can be easily reached by train. Departures are from the south railway station (Yongdingmen) near the Qiaoyuan Hotel – not to be confused with Beijing's main station. If you take the morning train, the trip can be done in one day. The schedule is as follows:

Train No	From	To	Departs	Arrives
595	Yong-dingmen	Shidu	6.07am	8.40am
597	Yong-dingmen	Shidu	5.40pm	8.00pm
596	Shidu	Yong-dingmen	6.41pm	9.03pm
598	Shidu	Yong-dingmen	10.41am	1.05pm

Longqing Gorge
(lóngqìngxiá)

About 90 km north-west of Beijing is Longqing Gorge, which was probably more scenic before the dam and consequent reservoir flooded out the area. Row-boating and hiking are the big attractions during summer. However, from mid-December to the end of January this is the site of Beijing's Ice Lantern Festival *(bīngdōng jié)*. Similar to the more well known and longer-lasting festival at Harbin, the 'lanterns' are huge ice carvings into which coloured electric lights are inserted. The effect (at least during the night) is stunning. Children (including adult children) can amuse themselves on the ice slide.

Tianjin 天津

Like Beijing and Shanghai, Tianjin *(tiānjīn)* belongs to no province – it's a special municipality, which gives it a degree of autonomy, but it's also closely administered by the central government. The city is nicknamed 'Shanghai of the North', a reference to its history as a foreign concession, its heavy industrial output, its large port and its Europeanised architecture. Foreigners who live there now often call it 'TJ' – an abbreviation which mystifies the Chinese.

The city's fortunes are, and always have been, linked to those of Beijing. When the Mongols established Beijing as the capital in the 13th century, Tianjin first rose to prominence as a grain-storage point. Pending remodelling of the Grand Canal by Kublai Khan, the tax grain was shipped along the Yangzi River, out into the open sea, up to Tianjin, and then through to Beijing. With the Grand Canal fully functional as far as Beijing, Tianjin was at the intersection of both inland and port navigation routes. By the 15th century, the town was a walled garrison.

For the sea-dog Western nations, Tianjin was a trading bottleneck too good to be passed up. In 1856 Chinese soldiers boarded the *Arrow*, a boat flying the British flag, ostensibly in search of pirates. This was as much of an excuse as the British and the French needed. Their gunboats attacked the forts outside Tianjin, forcing the Chinese to sign the Treaty of Tianjin (1858), which opened the port up to foreign trade and also legalised the sale of opium. Chinese reluctance to take part in a treaty they had been forced into led the British and French to start a new campaign to open the port to Western trade. In 1860 British troops bombarded Tianjin in an attempt to coerce the Chinese into signing another treaty.

The English and French settled in. Between 1895 and 1900 they were joined by the Japanese, Germans, Austro-Hungarians, Italians and Belgians. Each of the conces-

Population: nine million
Highlights:
- The Antique Market, especially on Sunday, one of the most brilliant markets in China
- Tianjin's 19th-century European buildings, poignant reminders of a not-too-distant past
- Strolling, shopping and eating

sions was a self-contained world with its own prison, school, barracks and hospital.

This palatial life was disrupted only in 1870 when the locals attacked the French-run orphanage and killed, among others, 10 of the nuns – apparently the Chinese thought the children were being kidnapped. Thirty years later, during the Boxer Rebellion, the foreign powers levelled the walls of the old Chinese city.

Meanwhile, the European presence stimulated trade and industry, including salt, textiles and glass manufacture. Heavy silting of the Hai River led to the construction of a new port at Tanggu, 50 km downstream, and Tianjin lost its character as a bustling port.

Since 1949 Tianjin has been a focus for major industrialisation. It produces a wide range of consumer goods – brand names

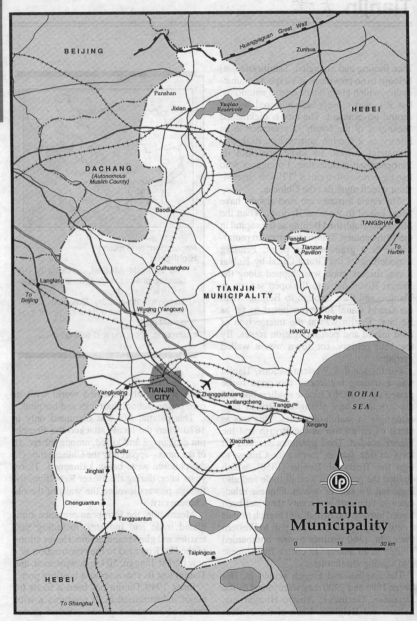

Tianjin
Municipality

0   15   30 km

BOHAI
SEA

from Tianjin are favoured within China for their quality, from Flying Pigeon bicycles to Seagull watches. Plans call for opening China's fourth stock market in Tianjin – the others are in Shanghai, Shenzhen and Chengdu.

The population of Tianjin's city and suburbs is some five million, though the municipality itself takes in a total of over nine million. The hotels are impossibly expensive, but you can travel down here from Beijing in just two hours. A full day in Tianjin is really quite enough.

One of the specialities of the place is the two-day kite-flying festival held in early April or late September.

TIANJIN CITY
Information

CITS (☎ 835-8349; fax 835-2619) is at 22 Youyi Lu (just opposite the Friendship Store) as is their competitor, Tianjin Overseas Tourism Corporation (☎ 835-0821; fax 835-2619). The PSB is at 30 Tangshan Dao, and the Bank of China (☎ 331-1559) is at 80 Jiefang Beilu.

You'll find the international post office, known as the Dongzhan Post Office, next to the main railway station; overseas parcels can be mailed and long-distance phone calls can be made here. For letters, there is another post office conveniently located on Jiefang Beilu, a short walk north of the Astor Hotel. A private courier, DHL (☎ 331-4483; fax 332-3932), is at 195 Machang Dao, Hexi District. TNT Skypak (☎ 332-5462; fax 311-2367) is at 2 Zhejiang Lu, Heping District.

The medical needs of the foreign community are catered for by the International Medical Centre (☎ 331-8888 ext 416), which is in Room 416 of the Hyatt Hotel.

Antique Market
(*gǔwán shìcháng*)
Depending on your tastes, the antique market is the best sight in Tianjin even if you're not into collecting second-hand memorabilia. Just the sheer size and variety of this market makes it fascinating to stroll around.

Among the many items on sale are stamps, silver coins, silverware, porcelain, clocks, photos of Mao, Cultural Revolution exotica (no guns though) and old books.

In China, the one thing you can be certain of is that you can't be certain of anything, especially history, since it is subject to frequent revision according to the politics of the time. Nevertheless, if true, the history behind this market is fascinating. According to the locals, much of what is on display at the antique market was seized during the Cultural Revolution and warehoused – the government is now slowly selling the stuff off to vendors who in turn resell it in Tianjin. These goods supposedly come from all over China. Many of the items carry stickers on the back indicating when, where and from whom the goods were seized.

Just why everything wasn't all immediately destroyed is subject to speculation – possibly it was to be used as evidence at political trials, or maybe some official was a closet antique buff. Or just maybe the Red Guards were aware of the potential resale value. Of course, not all that you see is real – there are fake antiques, fake stickers and so on.

The market is active seven days a week. On weekdays it occupies only a section of central Shenyang Dadao, but on weekends it expands enormously, spilling out into side streets in every direction. It's open from 7.30 am to around 3 pm – get there at 8 am for the widest selection. Sunday morning is best and foreigners residing in Beijing come down here for the day just to shop.

Ancient Culture Street
(*gǔ wénhuà jiē*)
The Ancient Culture Street is an attempt to recreate the appearance of an ancient Chinese city. Besides the traditional buildings, the street is lined with vendors plugging every imaginable type of cultural goody from Chinese scrolls, paintings and chops to the latest heavy-metal sounds on CD. During certain public holidays, street operas are staged here.

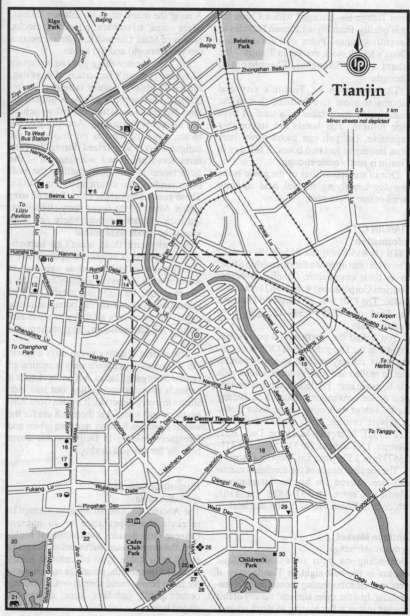

Tianjin

TIANJIN 天津

PLACES TO STAY

15 Furama Hotel
富丽华大酒店
24 Sheraton Hotel
喜来登大酒店
25 Crystal Palace Hotel
水晶宫饭店
27 Tianjin Grand Hotel
天津宾馆
28 Geneva Hotel
津利华大酒店
30 Park Hotel
乐园饭店

PLACES TO EAT

6 Eardrum Fried Sponge-
cake Shop
耳朵眼炸糕店
13 Food Street
食品街

14 Quanjude Restaurant
全聚德烤鸭店
29 18th Street Dough-twists
Shop
桂发祥麻花店

OTHER

1 North Railway Station
北火车站
2 West Railway Station
西火车站
3 Dabeiyuan Monastery
大悲院
4 Zhongshan Park
中山公园
5 Grand Mosque
清真寺
7 North-East Bus Station
东北角发车站
8 Ancient Culture Street
古文化街
9 Confucius Temple
文庙

10 5th Subway Exit
地下铁第五站
11 Nankai Park
南开公园
12 Zhou Enlai Memorial
Hall
周恩来记念馆
16 Tianjin University
天津大学
17 Nankai University
南开大学
18 Renmin Park
人民公园
19 South Bus Station
八里台发车站
20 Shuishang Park
水上公园
21 Zoo
动物园
22 TV Tower
电视塔
23 Natural History Museum
自然博物馆
26 Friendship Store
友谊商店

Within the confines of the street is the small Tianhou Temple (*tiānhòu gōng*). Tianhou (Heaven Queen) is the goddess of the sea, and is known by various names in different parts of China (Matsu in Taiwan and Tin Hau in Hong Kong). It is claimed that Tianjin's Tianhou Temple was built in 1326, but it has seen a bit of renovation since then.

The Ancient Culture Street is a major drawcard for tourists, both foreigners and locals. The street is in the north-western part of town.

Confucius Temple
(*wén miào*)

On the northern side of Dongmennei Dajie, one block west of the Ancient Culture Street, is Tianjin's Confucius Temple. It was built in 1463 during the Ming Dynasty. The temple, and Confucianists in general, took a beating during the Cultural Revolution. In 1993 the buildings were restored and opened to the public.

Grand Mosque
(*qīngzhēn sì*)

Although it has a distinctly Chinese look, this large mosque is an active place of worship for Tianjin's Muslims. The mosque is on Dafeng Lu, not far south of the west railway station.

Dabeiyuan Monastery
(*dàbēiyuàn*)

This is one of the largest and best-preserved temples in the city. Dabeiyuan was built between 1611 and 1644, expanded in 1940, battered during the Cultural Revolution and finally restored in 1980. The temple is on Tianwei Lu in the northern part of the city.

Catholic Church
(*xīkāi jiàotáng*)

This is one of the most bizarre-looking churches you're likely to see. Situated on the southern end of Binjiang Dao, the twin onion domes form a dramatic backdrop to the 'Coca-Cola Bridge' (a pedestrian overpass crossing Nanjing Lu). It's definitely worth a look. Church services are now permitted again on Sundays, which is about the only time you'll have a chance to look inside.

Earthquake Memorial
(kàngzhèn jìniàn bēi)
Just opposite the Friendship Hotel on Nanjing Lu is a curious, pyramid-shaped memorial. Though there's not much to see here, the memorial is a pointed reminder of the horrific events of 28 July 1976, when an earthquake registering eight on the Richter scale struck north-eastern China.

It was the greatest natural disaster of the decade. Tianjin was severely affected and the city was closed to tourists for two years. The epicentre was at Tangshan – that city basically disappeared in a few minutes. Five and six-storey housing blocks have been constructed on the outskirts of Tianjin as part of the rehousing programme.

Hai River Park
(hǎihé gōngyuán)
Stroll along the banks of the Hai River (a popular pastime with the locals) and see photo booths, fishing, early-morning taijiquan, opera-singing practice and old men toting birdcages. The Hai River esplanades have a peculiarly Parisian feel, in part due to the fact that some of the railing and bridge work is French.

Tianjin's sewage has to go somewhere and the river water isn't so pure that you'd want to drink it, but an attempt has been made to clean it up, and trees have been planted along the embankments. Tianjin's industrial pollution horrors are further downstream and are not included in the tour, but some Chinese tourists make their contribution by throwing drink tins and plastic bags into the river.

It's not Venice, but there are tourist boat cruises on the Hai River which commence from a dock not far from the Astor Hotel. The boats cater to Chinese tourists more than foreigners and therefore tend to run mainly during summer weekends and other holiday periods.

At the northern end of town are half a dozen canals that branch off the Hai River. One vantage point is Xigu Park. Take bus No 5, which runs from near the main railway station and passes by the west railway station.

TV Tower
(diànshì tái)
The pride and joy of Tianjin residents, the TV tower dominates the horizon on the southern side of town. Besides its functional purpose of transmitting TV and radio broadcasts to the masses, tourists can go upstairs for a whopping Y80 fee. While the tower looks impressive from the ground, views from the top aren't spectacular in the daytime – after all, Tianjin's flat landscape of old buildings isn't exactly the eighth wonder of the world. However, the view is better at night if the sky is clear.

The TV tower is also topped by a revolving restaurant, but you're liable to get indigestion when you see the bill.

Shuishang Park
(shuǐshàng gōngyuán)
This large park is in the south-western corner of town, not far from the TV tower. The name in Chinese means water park – over half the surface area is a lake. The major activity here is renting rowboats and pedal boats.

It's one of the more relaxed places in busy Tianjin, though not on weekends, when the locals descend on the place like cadres at a banquet. The park features a Japanese-style floating garden and a decent zoo.

Getting to the park from the main railway station requires two buses. Bus No 8 to the last stop gets you close. From there, catch bus No 54, also to the last stop, just outside the park entrance.

Art Museum
(yìshù bówùguǎn)
This museum is easy to get to and pleasant to stroll around. The gallery is housed in an imposing rococo mansion and has a small but choice collection of brush paintings, painting and calligraphy from bygone eras on the ground floor; and folk-art products

such as New Year posters, Zhang family clay figurines and Wei family kites from the Tianjin area on the 2nd floor. The top floor features special displays.

The kites were created by master craftsman Wei Yuan Tai at the beginning of the 20th century, although the kite has been a traditional toy in China for thousands of years. One story has it that Mr Wei's crow kite was so good that a flock of crows joined it aloft. One enthusiastic member of the Kite Society, Ha Kuiming, made a kite with a diameter of eight metres, which required two men to hold it back once it got going.

The Art Museum is at 77 Jiefang Beilu, one stop on bus No 13 from the main railway station.

Other Museums

There are five or so other museums in Tianjin and none are really worth the trouble unless you're an enthusiast. The Natural History Museum (zìrán bówùguǎn) is down the fossil-end of town at 206 Machang Dao.

The History Museum (lìshǐ bówùguǎn), on the south-eastern side of the Hai River, at the edge of a triangular park called the No 2 Workers' Cultural Palace (dì èr gōngrén wénhuà gōng), contains 'historical and revolutionary relics of the Tianjin area'.

Guangdong Guild Hall (guǎngdōng huì guǎn), also known as the Museum of Opera, is considered of historical importance because Sun Yatsen gave an important speech there in 1922.

Zhou Enlai Memorial Hall

(zhōu ēnlái jìniàn guǎn)

Zhou Enlai grew up in Shaoxing in Zhejiang Province, but he attended school in Tianjin, so his classroom is enshrined and there are photos and other memorabilia from his youth (1913-17). The memorial is on the western side of the city in the Nankai District, in the eastern building of Nankai School.

Streetscapes

Far more engrossing than any of the preceding is the fact that Tianjin itself is a museum of European architecture from the turn of the century. One minute you're in little Vienna, turn a corner and you could be in a London street, hop off a bus and you're looking at some vintage French wrought-iron gates or a neo-Gothic cathedral. Unfortunately, recent post-modern architectural horrors are starting to impact on Tianjin's skyline. Poking out of the post-earthquake shanty rubble are an ever-increasing number of high-rise castles made of glass and steel, dressed up with neon at night and punctuated with the wail from a hidden karaoke lounge.

Nevertheless, if you're a connoisseur of architecture, go no further – Tianjin is a textbook of just about every style imaginable. Of course, things have been renamed, and anyone with a sense of humour will be amused with some of the uses to which the bastions of the European well-to-do have been put.

Chinatown

We couldn't resist this misnomer. The old Chinese sector can easily be identified on the bus map as a rectangle with buses running around the perimeter. Roughly, the boundary roads are: Beima (North Horse), Nanma (South Horse), Xima (West Horse) and Dongma (East Horse). Originally there was one main north-south street, crossing an east-west one within that (walled) rectangle.

In this area you can spend time fruitfully exploring the lanes and side streets where traditional architecture remains, and perhaps even find a dilapidated temple or two. Basically, though, this is a people-watching place, where you can get glimpses of daily life through doorways. All along the way are opportunities to shop, window shop and eat to your heart's content.

Places to Stay

First, the good news – Tianjin has many fine hotels of good standard at reasonable prices. The bad news is that the PSB has placed almost all cheap accommodation off limits to foreigners. Examples of the forbidden fruit include the *Chang Cheng Binguan*, *Tianjin Dajiudian*, *Dongfang Fandian* and

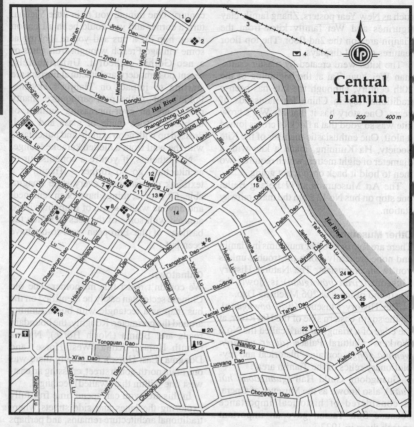

Central
Tianjin

0   200   400 m

the *Baihui Fandian*. However, these places *do* accept Overseas Chinese.

For the big noses, prices border on the ridiculous. So unless you've got an Asian face, heaps of money, or ingratiate yourself into one of the university residences (or a church or bathhouse?), you may end up back at the station.

The only budget place that accepts foreigners is the *Guomin Hotel* (☎ 711-3353) *(guómín fàndiàn)* on the corner of Heping Lu and Chifeng Dao. Acceptable doubles cost Y164.

The *Bohai Hotel* (☎ 712-3391) *(bóhǎi*

fàndiàn) at 277 Heping Lu has suitable rooms for Y328.

Also on the cheaper end by Tianjin standards is the *Furama Hotel* (☎ 431-0961; fax 431-1751) *(fùlìhuá dàjiǔdiàn)* at 104 Qiwei Lu. It's on the east bank of the Hai River not far from the pricey Astor Hotel. Standard/deluxe rooms cost Y280/370, and suites are Y400 to Y500.

The *Tianjin Grand Hotel* (☎ 835-9000; fax 835-9822) *(tiānjīn bīnguǎn)* is on Youyi Lu, Hexi District. And grand it is: 1000 beds in two high-rise blocks built in 1960. Once a well-known cheapie, it's been fully reno-

CENTRAL TIANJIN 天津市中心	8	Goubuli Restaurant 狗不理总店	9	Binjiang Shangsha Department Store 滨江商厦	
PLACES TO STAY	22	Kiessling's Bakery 起士林餐厅	10	Quanyechang Depart- ment Store 劝业场	
12 Bohai Hotel 渤海饭店		**OTHER**	11	Xinhua Bookstore 新华书店	
13 Guomin Hotel 国民大酒店	1	Buses to Beijing 往北京汽车站	14	Zhongxin Park 中心公园	
20 Friendship Hotel 友谊宾馆	2	Wing On Department Store 永安百货	15	Bank of China 中国银行	
23 Tianjin No 1 Hotel 天津第一饭店	3	Main Railway Station 天津火车站	16	PSB 公安局外事科	
24 Astor Hotel 利顺德大饭店	4	Dongzhan Post Office 东站邮局	17	Catholic Church 西开教堂	
25 Hyatt Hotel 凯悦饭店	5	Tianjin Department Store 百货大楼	18	International Market 国际商场	
PLACES TO EAT	6	Antique Market 古玩市场	19	Earthquake Memorial 抗震纪念碑	
7 Chuansu Restaurant 川苏菜馆			21	International Building 国际大厦	

vated and prices have been ramped up. The budget rooms are Y340, but otherwise it's Y620.

The *Tianjin No 1 Hotel* (☎ 331-0707; fax 331-3341) *(tiānjīn dìyī fàndiàn)* is at 158 Jiefang Beilu opposite the Hyatt. The place boasts a bit of old world charm, which perhaps will make you feel better about having to fork out Y439 for a double. Take bus No 13 three stops from the main railway station and walk south.

If you've got money to burn, why not stroll across the street to the *Hyatt Hotel* (☎ 331-8888; fax 331-0021) *(kǎiyuè fàndiàn)* at 219 Jiefang Beilu. Superior/deluxe rooms cost Y1370/1495 and suites begin at Y1825.

Coming back down to earth, there's the *Park Hotel* (☎ 830-9815; fax 830-2042) *(lèyuán fàndiàn)* at 1 Leyuan Lu. It's east of the Friendship Store and, as the name implies, near a park. Doubles cost Y510.

The *Friendship Hotel* (☎ 831-0372; fax 831-0616) *(yǒuyí bīnguǎn)* charges rather unfriendly prices – doubles are Y700. The hotel is at 94 Nanjing Lu.

The *Astor Hotel* (☎ 331-1688; fax 331-6282) *(lìshùndé fàndiàn)* at 33 Tai'erzhuang Lu dates from early this century but has been completely refurbished. Doubles cost from Y1037 to Y1328, suites are Y1411 to Y4714, or rent a cottage for a mere Y7370.

One of the most glamorous places in town is the 346-room *Crystal Palace Hotel* (☎ 835-6888; fax 835-8886) *(shuǐjīnggōng fàndiàn)* at 28 Youyi Lu. Facilities include a swimming pool, tennis court, health club and French restaurant. A standard room is Y1062 and suites are Y1892 to Y5544, to which you must add a 15% surcharge.

Also in the neighbourhood is the *Geneva Hotel* (☎ 835-2222; fax 835-9855) *(jīnlìhuá dàjiǔdiàn)*, 30 Youyi Lu, where doubles cost Y670 to Y1340. The hotel is in the rear – the front side of the building is the World Economy & Trade Exhibition Centre, one of the most perverse architectural nightmares in China.

The *Sheraton Hotel* (☎ 334-3388; fax 335-8740) *(xǐláidēng dàjiǔdiàn)* is on Zijinshan Lu in the south of Tianjin. The hotel dishes up 281 rooms priced between Y1200 and Y1400, plus 49 suites ranging from Y2500 to Y5000. To that add another

15% surcharge, but if it helps the buffet breakfast is thrown in free. Another freebie for guests is a copy of the *China Daily*.

Places to Eat

There are some wonderful digestibles in Tianjin. If you're staying for a while, you can get a small group together, phone ahead and negotiate gourmet delights. 'Tianjin flavour' specialities are mostly in the seasonal seafood line and include crab, prawns, cuttlefish soup and fried carp.

The place to go is *Food Street (shípǐn jiē)*, a covered alley with two levels of restaurants. Old places close and new ones open all the time here, but there are approximately 40 to 50 restaurants on each level. You need to check prices – some of the food stalls are dirt cheap but a few upmarket restaurants are almost absurdly expensive. You can find some real exotica here, like snake (expensive), dog meat (cheap) and eels (mid-range). Mexican food fans take note: this is the only place in China where we found bags of nacho chips for sale! Food Street is a couple of blocks south of Nanma Lu, about one km west of the centre.

Rongji Dajie is an alley just one block north of Food Street and also boasts a fair share of restaurants. The *Quanjude* (☎ 735-0046) is at 53 Rongji Dajie. Upstairs are banquet rooms with moderate to expensive prices. Seafood is expensive (like sea cucumber, a delicacy that chefs love to foist on foreigners). Beijing duck and Shandong food are also served.

The *Tianjin Roast Duck Restaurant* (☎ 730-2660) *(tiānjīn kǎoyā diàn)* is at 146 Liaoning Lu in the city centre. You can get Beijing duck here – either the full works or a cheaper basic duck. This place had Mao Zedong's seal of approval (one doesn't really know if that's positive or positively embarrassing advertising these days), and on the restaurant walls are a couple of black & white photos of a relaxed-looking Mao talking to the chefs and autographing the visitors' book.

The *Chuansu Restaurant* (☎ 730-5142) is at 153 Changchun Dao, between Xinhua Lu and Liaoning Lu, very close to the Tianjin Roast Duck. Spicy hot Sichuan food is the speciality here but other styles are also on the menu.

King of the dumpling shops is *Goubuli* (☎ 730-0810) *(gǒubùlǐ)* at 77 Shandong Lu between Changchun Dao and Binjiang Dao. Very crowded, this place serves some of the finest dumplings in the nation so you might as well dine in style, and it won't cost you an arm or a leg to do so. You can back up the dumplings with tea, soup or beer, and you get upper-crust lacquered chopsticks with which to spear the slippery little devils on your plate. The shop has a century-old history. The staple of the *maison* is a dough bun filled with high-grade pork, spices and gravy, that disintegrates on contact with the palate. Watch for the baozi with the red dot since this indicates a special filling like chicken or shrimp. Frozen versions of this product can be bought from grocery stores all over Tianjin, though backpackers not carrying a microwave oven are unlikely to be customers.

Goubuli has the alarming translation 'dogs won't touch them' or 'dog doesn't care'. The most satisfying explanation of this seems to be that Goubuli was the nickname of the shop's founder, a man with an extraordinarily ugly face – so ugly that even dogs were turned off by him. Former US President George Bush often ate here when he was ambassador to China.

A permanent cake box clipped to a bicycle rack is one of the eccentricities of Tianjin residents and a prerequisite for a visit to friends. Yangcun rice-flour cake is a pastry produced in Wuqing County suburbs since the Ming Dynasty, so they say. It's made from rice and white sugar.

The *Eardrum Fried Spongecake Shop* *(ěrduǒyǎn zhàgāo diàn)* takes its name from its proximity to Eardrum Lane. This shop specialises in cakes made from rice powder, sugar and bean paste, all fried in sesame oil. These special cakes have been named (you guessed it) 'eardrum fried spongecake'.

Another Tianjin speciality that takes its name from a shop's location is the *18th Street*

Dough-Twists (máhuā). The street seems to have been renamed 'Love Your Country Street' *(aìguó dào)*, and the famous shop also seems to have a new label *(guìfā xiáng máhuā diàn)*. However, the dough-twists made from sugar, sesame, nuts and vanilla can be bought all over town – try the shops at the railway station.

Kiessling's Bakery (qǐshìlín cāntīng), built by the Austrians back in foreign concession days (1911), is a Tianjin institution. It's at 33 Zhejiang Lu, south-west of the Astor Hotel. However, you needn't go there, as the cakes are distributed all around the city at various shops and restaurants.

Foreign residents of Tianjin with a bit of cash like to pig out every Sunday at the *Sheraton Hotel*, which does a mean buffet from 11 am until 2 pm. It costs Y120 (no student cards accepted), so don't eat breakfast if you want to get the maximum benefit. On other days there are also lunch and dinner buffets with prices ranging from Y50 to Y80 – sometimes they serve pizza!

The *Hyatt Hotel* also does a memorable breakfast buffet. This one costs Y60 and can fill you up for the rest of the day.

Should you wish to fortify a main meal, an ice cream or a coffee, Tianjin produces a variety of liquid substances. There's Kafeijiu, which approximates to Kahlua, and Sekijiu, which is halfway between vodka and aviation fuel.

Things to Buy

A shopping trip to Tianjin will dispel any doubts about China's commitment to the textile trade. Only Hong Kong can match Tianjin for the amount of clothing on sale, and much of Hong Kong's supply originates in Tianjin.

Adjacent to the main railway station is Wing On Department Store *(yǒng'ān bǎihuò)*, a branch of the Hong Kong company by the same name. It's knee-deep in everything from silk stockings to woollen overcoats.

A massive shopping drag extends from the west railway station south via Beima Lu, where it meets another shopping drag called

Dongma Lu coming from the north railway station. The sprawl of shops snake down the length of Heping Lu as far as Zhongxin Park.

The shopping street to walk on is Binjiang Dao, with alleyways and other commercial streets gathered around it there's something like eight whole blocks of concentrated shopping. Binjiang Dao also has the most active night market. You can find just about anything in the many boutiques, curio stores and emporiums. The area is particularly lively between 5 and 8 pm, when the streets are thronged with excited shoppers and theatre-goers.

On Binjiang Dao itself there are over 100 street stalls selling mostly clothing, plus many more permanent-looking stores. The chief department store on this street is the Binjiang Shangsha, the only large store in the whole city which seems to have trained the staff to give polite service and not bite the tourists.

At the southern end of Binjiang Dao is the four-storey International Market *(guójì shāngcháng)*. It's one of Tianjin's best department stores and features a fine supermarket on the 2nd floor – a clone of Hong Kong's finest. The ground floor has the best bakery in the city. Don't confuse the International Market with the International Building *(guójì dàshà)* at 75 Nanjing Lu.

Also worth looking into is the Friendship Store *(yǒuyí shāngdiàn)* on Youyi Lu in the southern end of town. The ground floor has a notable supermarket – rare items on sale here include imported peanut butter and Diet Coke.

Locals look for everyday Chinese consumer products in the Tianjin Department Store *(bǎihuò dàlóu)* at 172 Heping Lu.

The Quanyechang (Encouraging Industrial Development Emporium) is an old but large department store on the corner of Heping Lu and Binjiang Dao. Besides selling a large variety of consumer goods, the emporium has two theatres and some electronic amusement facilities. The original, smaller Quanyechang has a fascinating balcony interior. If you follow the galleries around they will eventually lead into the main seven-storey block. The older section was founded in 1926.

The Foreign Languages Bookstore (☎ 730-9944) *(wàiwén shūdiàn)* at 130 Chifeng Dao, Heping District, is worth a look to stock up on English-language novels for those long train rides.

Specialities Tianjin is considered famous for its carpets. If you're serious about carpets (that's serious money!) the best bet is to get to a factory outlet. There are eight carpet factories in the Tianjin Municipality. Making the carpets by hand is a long and tedious process – some of the larger ones can take a proficient weaver over a year to complete. Patterns range from traditional to modern. The No 3 Carpet Factory (☎ 238-1712) *(tiānjīn dìtǎn sānchǎng)*, 99 Qiongzhou Dao, is in the Hexi District. Small tapestries are a sideline.

Clay figurines are another local speciality. The terracotta figures originated in the 19th century with the work of Zhang Mingshan; his fifth-generation descendants train new craftspeople. The small figures take themes from human or deity sources and the emphasis is on realistic emotional expressions. Master Zhang was reputedly so skilful that he carried clay up his sleeves on visits to the theatre and came away with clay opera stars in his pockets. In 1900, during the Boxer Rebellion, Western troops came across satirical versions of themselves correct down to the last detail in uniforms. These voodoo dolls were ordered to be removed from the marketplace immediately! Painted figurines are now much watered down from that particular output. The workshop is at 270 Machang Dao, Hexi District (southern end of Tianjin). The Art Gallery on Jiefang Lu has a collection of earlier Zhang family figurines.

Tianjin is also known for its New Year posters. Such posters first appeared in the 17th century in the town of Yangliuqing, 15 km west of Tianjin proper. Woodblock prints are hand-coloured, and are considered to bring good luck and happiness when posted on the front door during the lunar new year

– OK if you like pictures of fat babies done in Day-Glo colour schemes. Rarer are the varieties that have historical, deity or folk-tale representations. There's a salesroom and workshop on Changchun Jie, between Xinhua Lu and Liaoning Lu.

Getting There & Away

Air Dragonair and CAAC both offer direct flights between Hong Kong and Tianjin for HK$2270. CAAC (☎ 730-4045, 730-5888) is at 242 Heping Lu. Dragonair (☎ 330-1234) has a booking office in the Hyatt Hotel. CITS is a booking agent for Dragonair.

The Beijing-Tianjin domestic flight is comical – given the amount of time it takes to get to and from the airports on either end, plus check-in time and security formalities, the two-hour bus journey is faster. Other domestic flights connect Tianjin to:

Changchun, Chengdu, Dalian, Fuzhou, Guangzhou, Haikou, Shanghai, Shantou, Shenyang, Shenzhen, Taiyuan, Ürümqi, Wenzhou, Wuhan, Xi'an and Xiamen

Bus The opening of the Beijing-Tianjin Expressway has greatly reduced travel time between the two cities – the journey takes about 2½ hours. Buses to Beijing depart from in front of Tianjin's main railway station. Costs depend on bus size, but average around Y25. In Beijing, catch the bus to Tianjin from the western side of the car park in front of the Beijing Railway Station. The bus has two great advantages over the train: there are no hassles in buying a ticket and you are guaranteed a seat.

There are three long-distance bus stations, with buses running to places that the average foreign traveller may have little interest in. Bus stations are usually located partway along the direction of travel. The south bus station *(bālǐtái fāchē zhàn)* is on the north-eastern edge of the Shuishang Park, which is south-west of the city centre – this is where you get buses to Tanggu. The west bus station *(xīzhàn fāchē zhàn)* is at 2 Xiqing Dao near Tianjin's west railway station.

Of possible interest to travellers is the north-east bus station (*dōngběijiǎo fāchē zhàn*), which has the most destinations and the largest ticket office. It's very close to the Ancient Culture Street, just west of the Hai River in the northern end of Tianjin. Bus No 24 from the city centre will land you in the general vicinity. From the north-east bus station you can get buses to Jixian, Fengtai (Tianzun Pavilion) and Zunhua (to name just a few places). If you're the sort of person who likes to see everything along the way, a road route worth considering is from Tianjin to Beijing via Jixian. This route is also served by rail.

Train Tianjin is a major north-south train junction with frequent trains to Beijing, extensive links with the north-eastern provinces, and lines southwards to Ji'nan, Nanjing, Shanghai, Fuzhou, Hefei, Yantai, Qingdao and Shijiazhuang.

There are three railway stations in Tianjin: main, north and west. Ascertain the correct station. For most trains you'll want the main railway station. Some trains stop at both the main and west stations, and some only go through the west railway station (particularly those originating in Beijing and heading south). Trains heading for north-eastern China often stop at the north railway station.

If you have to alight at the west railway station, bus No 24 connects the west railway station to the main railway station, passing through the central shopping district.

The main railway station is one of the cleanest and most modern in China. Foreigners can avoid the horrible queues by purchasing tickets on the 2nd floor at the soft-seat ticket office.

Express trains take just under two hours for the trip between Tianjin and Beijing. Local trains take about 2½ hours.

Car Foreigners with their own cars (diplomats, resident businesspeople etc) are permitted to drive along the Beijing-Tianjin highway.

Boat Tianjin's harbour is Tanggu, 50 km (30 minutes by train) from Tianjin proper. This is one of China's major ports, offering a number of possibilities for arriving and departing by boat. See the Tanggu section later in this chapter for details.

Getting Around

To/From the Airport From the city centre, it's about 15 km to Tianjin's Zhangguizhuang Airport. Taxis ask for Y50 or more for the trip. There is a bus from the CAAC ticket office.

Bus A pox on local transport in this city! Tianjin is one of the most confusing places you can take on in China, and things are compounded by the fact that your visit there may turn, by necessity, into a very short one. Your chances of getting on a bus at rush hour are about 2% and you'll get a unique chance to find out what it feels like to be buried alive in a pile of people. If you must use a bus, try and ambush it at the point of origin.

Key local transport junctions are the areas around the three railway stations. The main railway station has the biggest collection: bus Nos 24, 27 and 13, and further out toward the river are Nos 2, 5, 25, 28 and 96. At the west railway station are bus Nos 24, 10 and 31 (Nos 11 and 37 run past the west railway station); at the north railway station are bus Nos 1, 7 and 12.

Another major bus terminal point is around Zhongxin Park, at the edge of the central shopping district. From here you'll get bus Nos 11 and 94, and nearby are bus Nos 9, 20 and 37. To the north of Zhongxin Park are bus Nos 1, 91, 92 and 93.

A useful bus to know is the No 24, which runs between the main and west stations 24 hours a day. Also noteworthy is No 8 – it starts at the main railway station then zigzags across town before finally terminating at Nankai University in the southern part of town.

With the exception of bus No 24, buses run from 5 am to 11 pm.

Subway The subway (*dìxià tiělù*) can be useful – it runs all the way from Nanjing Lu to the west railway station and costs five jiao per ride. Tianjin's subway opened in 1982; the cars shuttle back and forth on a single track. There's nothing to see down in the depths except the subterranean bathroom tiling, but it saves a lot of trauma with the buses.

Taxi Taxis can be found most readily near the railway station and around tourist hotels. Most drivers prefer not to use the meters, so get the fare engraved in stone before heading out.

Tianjin has many motor-tricycles – these cost about Y15 for anywhere in the city. They are particularly useful for manoeuvring through the narrow, traffic-clogged streets in the city centre.

AROUND TIANJIN

Were it not for the abysmal hotel situation, Tianjin would make a fine staging point for trips directly north (to Jixian, Zunhua, Tangshan, Beidaihe and the Great Wall at Huangyaguan), and a launching pad for roaring into the north-east (Manchuria). Preliminary bus tours have been set up for some northern routes, but it's expensive stuff. About the only other place within the Tianjin Municipality that sees many foreign tourists is Tanggu.

Tanggu
(tánggū)

There are three harbours on the Tianjin municipality stretch of coastline: Hangu (north), Tanggu-Xingang (centre) and Dagang (south). Tanggu is about 50 km from Tianjin proper. The Japanese began the construction of an artificial harbour during their occupation (1937-45) and it was completed by the Communists in 1952, with further expansions in 1976 for container cargo. The Tanggu-Xingang port now handles one of the largest volumes of goods of any port in China.

This is one of China's major international seaports, kept open by ice-breakers in winter. The harbour is where 'friends from all over the world' come to drop anchor and get ripped-off by outrageously overpriced hotels.

As for sightseeing, the best advice we can give is to go no further than the ferry pier – the further you go, the worse it gets. Tanggu is a forest of cranes, containers and smokestacks – it's no place to linger.

Nevertheless, you will find foreigners lingering here – not travellers, but businesspeople. Tanggu is booming – many export-oriented industries have set up shop here. The chief focus of all this frenetic activity is the **Economic & Technology Development Zone** (*jīngjì jìshù kāifā qū*). Should you decide to wander around this area in the northern part of Tanggu, you'll see plenty of factories, but also expensive residences and shops catering for the mostly foreign and Overseas Chinese investors and technical experts.

If you insist on seeking out some touristy sights, the city is most proud of its **Bohai Children's World** (*bóhǎi értóng shìjiè*). It's actually a little better than it sounds – almost

---

TANGGU 塘沽

1 Tanggu Main Railway Station
   塘沽火车站
2 Victory Hotel
   胜利宾馆
3 Economic & Technology
   Development Zone
   经济技术开发区
4 South Railway Station
   塘沽南火车站
5 Hot Spring Hotel
   温泉大酒店
6 Beifang Hotel
   北方宾馆
7 Bohai Children's World
   渤海儿童世界
8 Dagu Fort
   大沽炮台
9 International Seamen's Club
   国际海员俱乐部
10 Friendship Store
   友谊商店
11 Passenger Terminal
   天津港客运站

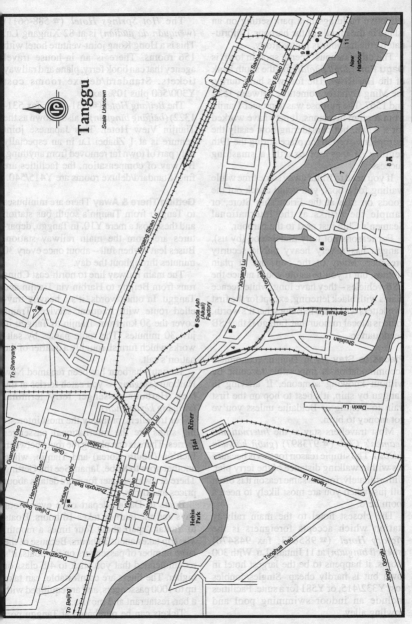

attractive buildings in a park setting on an island in the middle of the harbour. Unfortunately, the harbour is pretty grotty.

The other famous 'scenic spot' in town is **Dagu Fort** (*dàgū pàotái*), on the south bank of the Hai River. The fort was built during the Ming Dynasty, sometime between 1522 and 1567. The purpose was to protect Tianjin from foreign invasions. It may have worked for a while, but considering how easily the Europeans overran the place during the 19th century, it was not exactly a smashing success.

If you need to fritter away some time while waiting for a boat, you could check out the goods on sale at the Friendship Store, or sample the drinks at the International Seamen's Club just next to the harbour.

For reasons not fully understood (by us), Tanggu has a very heavy public security presence. Many of the cops are in plain clothes, but if you're astute you'll notice the PSB vehicles – they have long, white licence plates with black lettering, except for the first two letters which are red. For what it's worth, there is a local rumour that Tanggu is the PSB headquarters.

Places to Stay As in Tianjin, economical accommodation is impossible to come by without knowing someone. If arriving in Tanggu by ship, it's best to hop on the first train to Beijing or Beidaihe unless you've got money to burn.

Most travellers stay at the *International Seamen's Club* (☎ 973897) (*guójì hǎiyuán jùlèbù*). The simple reason for this is because it's within walking distance of the ferry pier. Unfortunately, for this same reason it is often full just when you are most likely to need a room here.

The closest hotel to the main railway station which accepts foreigners is the *Victory Hotel* (☎ 985833; fax 948470) (*shènglì bīnguǎn*) at 11 Jintang Lu. With 300 rooms, it happens to be the largest hotel in town but is hardly cheap. Singles/doubles cost Y332/415, or Y581 for a suite. Facilities include an indoor swimming pool and bowling alley.

The *Hot Springs Hotel* (☎ 588-6611) (*wēnquán dà jiǔdiàn*) is at 82 Xingang Lu. This is a Hong Kong joint-venture hotel with 156 rooms. There is an in-house travel agency that can book ferry, plane and railway tickets. Standard/deluxe rooms cost Y300/560 plus 10% tax.

The *Beifang Hotel* (☎ 531-1301; fax 531-1322) (*běifāng bīnguǎn*) is also known as the Tianjin View Hotel. This Japanese joint venture is at 1 Zhabei Lu in an especially ugly part of town far removed from anything. By way of compensation, the facilities are fine. Standard/deluxe rooms are Y415/540.

Getting There & Away There are minibuses to Tanggu from Tianjin's south bus station and these cost a mere Y10. In Tanggu, departures are from the main railway station. Buses leave when full – about once every 30 minutes throughout the day.

The main railway line to north-east China runs from Beijing to Harbin via Tianjin and Tanggu. In other words, it's a heavily travelled route with frequent service. Trains cover the 50 km from Tianjin to Tanggu in just 30 minutes. The route passes by saltworks which furnish roughly a quarter of the nation's salt.

Tanggu's harbour has been renamed New Harbour (*xīngǎng*) – you catch ferries at the New Harbour passenger ferry terminal (*xīngǎng kèyùn zhàn*).

For travellers, probably the most interesting ships are the international passenger ferries. There is one plying the route between Inch'ǒn (South Korea) and Tianjin, while another goes to Kobe, Japan. See the Getting There & Away chapter for more details about prices and times.

Boats to Dalian depart once every four days and the journey takes 16 hours. Boats to Yantai depart about four times a month. The trip takes about 30 hours. Because of the large number of passengers on the boats, it's recommended that you stick to 4th class or higher. The liners are comfortable, can take up to 1000 passengers, and are equipped with a bar, restaurant and movies.

Tickets can be purchased at Tanggu port

opposite the Tanggu Theatre, but if you're in Tianjin it's safer to buy in advance. In Tianjin, tickets can be bought at 5 Pukou Jie. Difficult to find, Pukou Jie runs west off Tai'erzhuang Lu and is roughly on the same latitude as the enormous smokestack which stands on the opposite side of the river.

Tangshan
(tángshān)

Tangshan was devastated in the earthquake of July 1976 and has since been rebuilt. Over 240,000 people (almost a fifth of Tangshan's population at that time) were killed in the quake and over 160,000 seriously injured; with casualties from Beijing and Tianjin added, the total figures are considerably higher. A new Tangshan has risen from the rubble. As early as 1978 it was claimed that industrial output (steel, cement and engineering) was back to 1976 levels. The present population of the city is around 1½ million. You could stop off in Tangshan for a few hours en route by train from Beijing to Beidaihe. There are direct trains between Tanggu and Tangshan.

Jixian
(jìxiàn)

Jixian is rated as one of the 'northern suburbs' of Tianjin, though it's actually 125 km from Tianjin city. The Jixian area is about 90 km due east of Beijing.

Near the city's west gate is the **Temple of Solitary Joy** *(dúlè sì)*. At 1000 years' vintage, the main multistorey wooden structure, the Avalokitesvara Pavilion, qualifies as the oldest such structure in China. It houses a 16-metre-high statue of a Bodhisattva with 10 heads which rates as one of China's largest terracotta statues. The buddha dates back to the Liao Dynasty and the murals inside are from the Ming Dynasty. The complex has been restored in the interests of mass tourism.

Just east of Jixian is **Yuqiao Reservoir** *(yúqiáo shuǐkù)*, easily the most attractive body of water (not counting the sea) in Tianjin Municipality.

Getting There & Away One way of getting to Jixian is to join a tour from Beijing to the Eastern Qing Tombs and Zunhua – see the Beijing chapter for details. However, this will normally only give you a brief lunch stop in Jixian before pushing on to the tombs. There are also regular long-distance buses from Beijing.

Buses from Tianjin's north-east bus station go to Jixian. There is also a direct Tianjin-Jixian train link.

Panshan
(pánshān)

To the north-west of Jixian is Panshan, a collection of hills ranked among the 15 famous mountains of China. Emperor Qianlong was claimed to have been so taken with the place that he swore he never would have gone south of the Yangzi River had he known Panshan was so beautiful.

The emperor aside, don't expect the Himalayas. Nevertheless, it's still a lovely area, dotted with trees, springs, streams, temples, pavilions and various other ornaments.

The hills are 12 km north-west of Jixian, 150 km north of Tianjin and 40 km west of the Eastern Qing Tombs in Hebei Province. A suburban-type train runs to Jixian from Tianjin; you can also get there by bus from Tianjin's north-east bus station.

Great Wall at Huangyaguan
(huángyáguān chángchéng)

At the very northern tip of Tianjin Municipality (bordering Hebei Province) is Huangyaguan (Yellow Cliff Pass). This is where Tianjin residents head to view the Great Wall. This section of the wall is 41 km long before it crumbles away on each end – the part open to tourists was restored in 1984. In addition to the original structures, a museum was added along with the Hundred Generals Forest of Steles.

Huangyaguan is 170 km north of Tianjin city. Buses go to the wall mostly on weekends, with early morning departures from Tianjin's north-east bus station or sometimes from the main railway station.

Tianzun Pavilion

(tiānzūn gé)

You'd have to be a real temple and pavilion enthusiast to come way out here to see this place. Nevertheless, it's rated as one of Tianjin's big sights. The Tianzun (Heaven Respect) Pavilion is three storeys tall – locals are proud to tell you that the pavilion re-

mained standing when everything else nearby was reduced to rubble by the 1976 Tangshan earthquake.

The pavilion is near Fengtai in Ninghe County, on the eastern border of Tianjin Municipality and Hebei Province. Buses to Fengtai depart from Tianjin's north-east bus station.

Hebei 河北

Wrapping itself around the centrally administered municipalities of Beijing and Tianjin is the province of Hebei (héběi). It is often viewed either as an extension of Beijing, the red-tape maker, or of Tianjin, the industrial giant. This is not far off the mark since, geographically speaking, Beijing and Tianjin take up a fair piece of the pie. In fact, Tianjin used to be Hebei's capital, but when it came under central government administration the next largest city, Shijiazhuang, replaced it.

Topographically, Hebei falls into two distinct parts: the mountain tableland to the north, where the Great Wall runs (and also to the western fringes of the province), and the monotonous southern plain. Agriculture (mainly wheat and cotton growing) is hampered by dust storms, droughts (five years in a row from 1972 to 1977) and flooding. These natural disasters will give you some idea of the weather. It's scorching and humid in summer, and freezing in winter, with dust fallout in spring and heavy rains in July and August.

Coal is Hebei's main resource and most of it is shipped through Qinhuangdao, an ugly port town with iron, steel and machine industries.

As far as tourist sights go, there's the beach resort of Beidaihe, and Chengde with its palaces and temples. Shijiazhuang, the capital city, is a waste of time.

Apart from all these, the best thing to see is the Great Wall, which spans the province before meeting the sea at the exotic market town of Shanhaiguan.

SHIJIAZHUANG
(shíjiāzhuāng)

Shijiazhuang is a railway junction town about 250 km south-west of Beijing and, in spite of being the capital of the province, it's the odd town out in Hebei. Its population is around one million, but at the turn of the century it was just a small village with 500

Population: 53 million
Capital: Shijiazhuang
Highlights:
- Chengde, a small town full of history, including one of the most startling collections of buildings in China
- The trendy beachside resort of Beidaihe for holiday-makers from Beijing
- Shanhaiguan, where the Great Wall meets the sea

inhabitants and a handful of buildings. Railways constructed in this century brought the town relative prosperity and a consequent population explosion.

Shijiazhuang has the biggest officer training school in China; it's about two km west of the city. After the Beijing protests and subsequent killings in 1989, all the new students from Beijing University were taken to this re-education camp for a one-year indoctrination.

Shijiazhuang is an industrial city with little to see, and for most travellers it's a transit point on the way to somewhere else.

Information
Both CITS (☎ 601-4766) and CTS (☎ 601-4570) are in the Hebei Grand Hotel at 23 Yucai Jie.

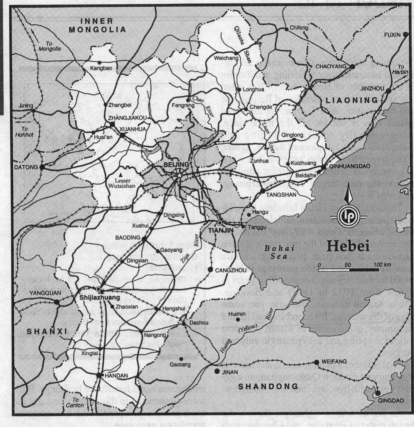

Revolutionary Martyrs' Mausoleum
(lièshì língyuán)

The Martyrs' Mausoleum (☎ 702-3028) is on Zhongshan Lu, west of the railway station. The guerrilla doctor Norman Bethune (1890-1939) is interred here: there is also a photo and drawing display depicting his life and works, and a white memorial. Immediately following the Communist victory in 1949, Bethune (bái qiúēn) became the most famous foreigner in China since Marco Polo. Even today, most Chinese people don't know who Polo is, but they all know Bethune. He goes down in modern

history as the man who served as a surgeon with the Eighth Route Army in the war against Japan, having previously served with the Communists in Spain against Franco and his Nazi allies. Bethune is eulogised in the reading of Mao Zedong Thought: 'We must all learn the spirit of absolute selflessness from Dr Norman Bethune'.

In China, 'Bethune' is also synonymous with 'Canada' – it's about all the Chinese tend to know about the country, and bringing up the name makes for instant friendship if you're Canadian.

More than 700 army cadres and heroes

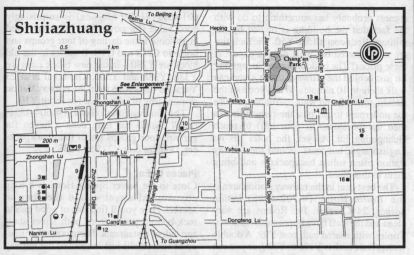

buried in the cemetery died during the Resistance against Japan, the War of Liberation and the Korean War. The area is a large park; in the central alley is a pair of bronze Jin Dynasty lions dating from 1185. There is also a statue of Bethune in the courtyard of the Bethune International Peace Hospital a bit further west of the cemetery.

Hebei Provincial Museum
(héběi shěng bówùguǎn)
This large museum (☎ 604-5642) is opposite

the International Hotel. All explanations are in Chinese.

Places to Stay
Shijiazhuang's hotel prices are strange indeed – many dumps charge more than the upmarket hotels. Always take a look at the room first before putting down the cash; otherwise, you may be disappointed.

Wujing Hotel (☎ 603-2713) *(wǔjǐng bīnguǎn)* is the cheapest place that accepts foreigners – the reason why it can take foreigners probably has something to do with the fact that the building is owned by the military. Beds cost Y15 to Y50. The facilities are a bit tattered but what do you expect at these prices? The building is on Guangming Lu just behind the railway station – you can walk there in 10 minutes. When you exit the station, turn left and walk to Yuhua Lu – use the underpass to get past the railway tracks then up the steps (to your left) to reach Guangming Lu. As yet, the hotel has no English sign, but touts around the railway station often solicit backpackers and bring them to this place.

The best deal in the railway station area is the *Bailin Hotel* (☎ 702-1398) (*bǎilín dàshà*), 24 Chezhan Jie. Rooms are very clean and the staff have impeccable manners. Triples with shared bath cost Y99. A double with private bath is Y176 to Y220, or you can get a suite for Y264 to Y330.

The *Silver Spring Hotel* (☎ 702-6981) (*yínquán fàndiàn*) is also near the railway station. Although the lobby looks fancy, the rooms are a disappointment and not worth the Y270 price tag for a double.

Just next door is the *Hualian Hebei Hotel* (☎ 702-5991) (*huálián héběi fàndiàn*). This place is horribly overpriced – Y280 for a filthy double with broken plumbing. On the positive side, at least the rooms are fairly spacious – consider this a last resort.

The *Lüyou Hotel* (☎ 383-4559) (*lǚyóu bīnguǎn*) is a fair way from the railway station and a bit tattered, but reasonably priced at Y162 for a double. There is no English sign identifying the hotel, but there are plenty of bright lights illuminating the building at night. The hotel is on the south-east corner of Zhonghua Dajie and Cang'an Lu. Bus No 3 from the railway station stops nearby.

Huadu Hotel (☎ 383-1040) (*huádū dàshà*) is the tallest building in town and the pride and joy of Shijiazhuang. Room prices are very cheap for the cushy facilities – doubles are Y249 to Y294, and suites are Y480 to Y585. You'll need a taxi to get here as it's rather far from the railway station.

The *Hebei Grand Hotel* (☎ 601-5961; fax 601-4092) (*héběi bīnguǎn*) is surprisingly good value (for now). The fully renovated guesthouse is the darling of tour groups and home to CITS and CTS. Doubles in the old block are Y280 – in the new block rates are Y338, Y388 and Y560. The hotel is at 23 Yucai Jie – bus No 6 from the railway station stops nearby or take a taxi for about Y10.

The *International Hotel* (☎ 604-4321) (*guójì dàshà*) has long been a haven for geriatric tour groups rather than backpackers. Doubles cost Y275 to Y638.

Places to Eat

Close to the Silver Spring Hotel is a long commercial street called the *Yong'an Market*. Here you'll find lots of good eats at rock-bottom prices from both street stalls and indoor restaurants. There is another line-up of street stalls just in front of the railway station but these seem to operate only in the evening. Upstairs in the railway station itself is a large karaoke and restaurant which supplies much of Shijiazhuang's nightlife.

Getting There & Away

CAAC connects Shijiazhuang to Changsha, Chengdu, Chongqing, Guangzhou, Haikou, Hohhot, Qinhuangdao, Shanghai, Shenyang, Shenzhen, Taiyuan, Wenzhou and Xi'an.

Shijiazhuang is a major rail hub with comprehensive connections: there are lines to Beijing (about four hours), Taiyuan (five hours), Dezhou (five hours) and Guangzhou (30-plus hours).

The long-distance bus station is north-east of the railway station and within walking distance. From there you can get buses to sights outside Shijiazhuang.

Getting Around

To/From the Airport Shijiazhuang's airport is 40 km from town. The CAAC bus costs Y30 and departs from the Airport Centre (booking office) opposite the railway station. The bus is supposed to depart 2½ hours prior to flight time, though from experience we've found it departs 10 minutes earlier than that! A taxi to the airport will cost about Y120 and the ride takes about an hour.

Bus Within the city there are 10 bus lines, but buses tend to be horribly overcrowded.

AROUND SHIJIAZHUANG

There's nothing spectacular in this part of Hebei, but there are a few places that you can visit.

Zhengding

(zhèngdìng)

Ten km north of Shijiazhuang, this town has several magnificent temples and monasteries. The largest and oldest is the Longxing Monastery *(lóngxīng sì)*, noted for its huge, 20-metre-high bronze buddha dating from the Song Dynasty almost 1000 years ago. The multi-armed statue is housed in the Temple of Great Mercy, an impressive structure with red and yellow galleries.

Minibuses to Zhengding cost Y3 and are marked 'Great Buddha Temple' *(dà fó sì)* in Chinese. In Shijiazhuang they congregate in front of the Bailin Hotel opposite the railway station. Bus No 201 from Shijiazhuang Station also goes to the temples. The ride takes a full hour.

Zhaozhou Bridge

(zhàozhōu qiáo)

There's an old folk rhyme about the four wonders of Hebei which goes:

The Lion of Cangzhou
The Pagoda of Dingzhou
The Buddha of Zhengding
The Bridge of Zhaozhou

The bridge is in Zhaoxian County, about 40 km south-east of Shijiazhuang and two km south of Zhaoxian town. It has spanned the Jiao River for 1300 years and is possibly the oldest stone-arch bridge in China (another, believed older, has recently been unveiled in Linying County, Henan Province).

Putting the record books aside, Zhaozhou Bridge is remarkable in that it still stands. It is 50 metres long and 9.6 metres wide, with a span of 37 metres; the balustrades are carved with dragons and mythical creatures. Credit for this daring piece of engineering

goes to a disputed source but, according to legend, the master mason Lu Ban constructed it overnight. Astounded immortals, refusing to believe that this was possible, arrived to test the bridge. One immortal had a wagon, another had a donkey, and they asked Lu Ban if it was possible for them both to cross at the same time. He nodded. Halfway across, the bridge started to shake and Lu Ban rushed into the water to stabilise it. This resulted in donkey-prints, wheel-prints and hand-prints being left on the bridge. Several more old stone bridges are to be found in Zhaoxian County.

Cangyanshan

(cāngyánshān)

About 78 km south-west of Shijiazhuang is a scenic area of woods, valleys and steep cliffs dotted with pagodas and temples. The novelty here is a bizarre, double-roofed hall sitting on a stone-arch bridge spanning a precipitous gorge. It is known as the Hanging Palace, and is reached by a 300-step stairway. The palace dates back to the Sui Dynasty. On the surrounding slopes are other ancient halls.

Xibaipo

(xībǎipō)

In Pingshan County, 80 km north-west of Shijiazhuang, was the base from which Mao Zedong, Zhou Enlai and Zhu De directed the northern campaign against the Kuomintang from 1947 to 1948. The original site of Xibaipo village was submerged by the Gangnan Reservoir and the present village has been rebuilt close by. In 1977 a Revolutionary Memorial Museum was erected. Xibaipo has become a tourist trap, but it's still fun to visit.

CHENGDE

(chéngdé)

Chengde is an 18th-century imperial resort area, also known as Jehol. It's billed as somewhere to escape from the heat (and now the traffic) of summers in the capital and boasts the remnants of the largest regal gardens in China.

Chengde remained an obscure town until 1703 when Emperor Kangxi began building a summer palace here, with a throne room and the full range of court trappings. More than a home away from home, Chengde turned into a sort of government seat, since where the emperor went his seat went too. Kangxi called his summer creation Bishu Shanzhuang (Fleeing-the-Heat Mountain Villa).

By 1790, during the reign of his grandson Qianlong, it had grown to the size of Beijing's Summer Palace and the Forbidden City combined. Qianlong extended an idea started by Kangxi, to build replicas of minority architecture in order to make envoys feel comfortable. In particular he was keen on promoting Tibetan and Mongolian Lamaism, which had proved to be a useful way of debilitating the meddlesome Mongols. The Mongolian branch of Lamaism required one male in every family to become a monk – a convenient method of channelling manpower and ruining the Mongol economy. This helps explain the Tibetan and Mongolian features of the monasteries north of the summer palace, one of them a replica of the Potala Palace in Lhasa.

So much for business – the rest was the emperor's pleasure, which included the usual bouts of hunting, feasting and orgies. Occasionally the outer world would make a rude intrusion into this dream life. In 1793 British emissary Lord Macartney arrived and sought to open trade with China. Qianlong dismissed him with the statement that China possessed all things and had no need of trade.

Chengde has very much slipped back into being the provincial town it once was, its grandeur long decayed, its monks and emperors long gone. The population of over 150,000 is engaged in mining, light industry and tourism. The Qing court has left them a little legacy, but one that needs working on. The palaces and monasteries are tattered – Buddhist statues are disfigured, occasionally beyond recognition, or locked up in dark corners, windows are bricked up, columns are reduced to stumps and the temples are mere facades, impressive from the outsid but shells inside.

All this is being restored, in some case from the base up, in the interests of a projected increase in tourism. It's on the card that Chinese and Western restaurants, high class shops, evenings of traditional musi (with instruments copied from those rescue from tombs around China), horse riding an other things of interest to tourists will b introduced. Meanwhile there's absolutel nothing wrong with ruins – it's just a matte of changing your expectations. Chengde ha nothing remotely approaching Beijing' temples, in case you were expecting some thing along those lines.

The dusty, small-town ambience o Chengde is nice enough and there's som quiet hiking in the rolling countryside Chinese speakers are apparently delighte with the clarity of the local dialect (mayb because they can actually hear it in th absence of traffic).

Information

You'll find CITS (☎ 226827; fax 227484) a 6 Nanyuan Donglu, next to the Yunsha Hotel in a green sheet-metal building tha looks temporary but isn't. Like most resi dents of Chengde, the staff are very friendl and helpful. The PSB (☎ 223091) is o Wulie Lu.

The Bank of China is right next to th Yunshan Hotel and CITS. There is anothe Bank of China on the north side of Zhonghu Lu near the intersection with Nanyingz Dajie.

Imperial Summer Villa
(*bìshǔ shānzhuāng*)

Otherwise known as 'Fleeing-the-Hea Mountain Villa', this park covers 590 hect ares and is bounded by a 10-km wall Emperor Kangxi decreed that there would b 36 'beauty spots' in Jehol; Qianlong deline ated 36 more. That makes a total of 72, bu where are they? At the northern end of th gardens the pavilions were destroyed by

he Forbidden City, home to the 25 emperors of the Ming and Qing dynasties, was off
mits for 500 years.

Chinese opera evolved from the convergence of the comic and balladic traditions in the Northern Song period. Performances now include acrobatics, martial arts, arias and stylised dance.

warlords and Japanese invaders, and even the forests have suffered cutbacks. The park is on the dull side, and hasn't been very well maintained. With a good deal of imagination you can perhaps detect traces of the original scheme of things, with landscaping borrowed from the southern gardens of Suzhou, Hangzhou and Jiaxing, and from the Mongolian grasslands. There is even a feature for resurrecting the moon, should it not be around – a pool shows a crescent moon created by the reflection of a hole in surrounding rocks.

Passing through Lizhengmen, the main gate, you arrive at the **Front Palace**, a modest version of Beijing's palace. It contains the main throne hall, the Hall of Simplicity and Sincerity, built of an aromatic hardwood called *nanmu* and now a museum displaying royal memorabilia, arms, clothing and other accoutrements. The emperor's bedrooms are fully furnished. Around to the side is a door without an exterior handle, through which the lucky bed partner for the night was ushered before being stripped and searched by eunuchs.

The double-storey **Misty Rain Tower**, on the north-west side of the main lake, was an imperial study. Further north is the **Wenjin Chamber**, built in 1773 to house a copy of the *Sikuquanshu*, a major anthology of classics, history, philosophy and literature commissioned by Qianlong. The anthology took 10 years to put together. Four copies were made but three have disappeared; the fourth is in Beijing.

Ninety per cent of the compound is taken up by lakes, hills, mini-forests and plains, with the odd vantage-point pavilion. At the northern part of the park the emperors reviewed displays of archery, equestrian skills and fireworks. Horses were also chosen and tested here before hunting sorties. Yurts were set up on the mock-Mongolian prairies (a throne, of course, installed in the emperor's yurt) and picnics were held for minority princes. So, it's a good idea to pack a lunch, take your tent and head off for the day...the yurts have returned for the benefit of weary tourists.

Eight Outer Temples
(wàibā miào)

To the north and north-east of the imperial garden are former temples and monasteries. So how many are there? The count started off at 11 many years ago, then plummeted to five (Japanese bombers, Cultural Revolution), and now the number varies between five and nine. The outer temples are from three to five km from the garden's front gate; a bus No 6 taken to the north-east corner will land you in the vicinity.

The surviving temples were built between 1750 and 1780. The Chinese-style **Puren Temple** and the vaguely Shanxi-style **Shuxiang Temple** have been totally rebuilt. Get there in the early morning when the air is crisp and cool and the sun is shining on the front of the temples – it's the best time to take photos. Some of the temples are listed here in clockwise order.

Putuozongsheng Temple *(pǔtuózōng shèng zhī miào)* Putuozongsheng (Potaraka Doctrine), the largest of the Chengde temples, is a mini-facsimile of Lhasa's Potala. It was built for the chieftains from Xinjiang, Qinghai, Mongolia and Tibet to celebrate Qianlong's 60th birthday and was also a site for religious assemblies. It's a solid-looking fortress, but unfortunately it is in bad shape – parts are inaccessible or boarded up and gutted by fire. Notice the stone column in the courtyard inscribed in Chinese, Tibetan, Mongolian and Manchurian scripts.

Xumifushou Temple *(xūmǐfúshòu zhī miào)* Xumifushou (the Temple of Sumeru, Happiness and Longevity) was built in honour of the sixth Panchen Lama, who visited in 1781 and stayed here. It incorporates elements of Tibetan and Han architecture and is an imitation of a temple in Shigatse, Tibet. At the highest point is a hall with eight gilded copper dragons commanding the roof ridges, and behind that sits a glazed-tile pagoda.

Puning Temple *(pǔníng sì)* Puning (the Temple of Universal Tranquillity) is also

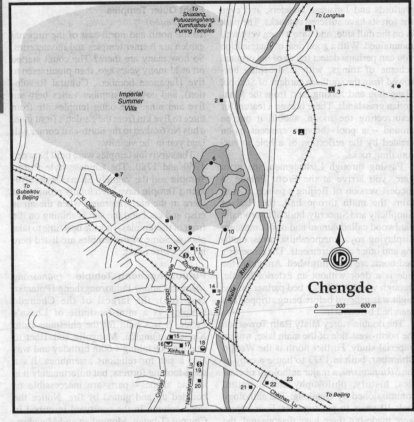

To Shuxiang,
Putuozongsheng,
Xumifushou &
Puning Temples

To Longhua

Imperial
Summer
Villa

To
Gubeikou
& Beijing

Bifenaman Lu

Xi Dajie

Zhonghua Lu

Nanyingzi

Wulie River

Wulie Lu

Wulie River

Chengde

0   300   600 m

Daijie

Xinhua Lu

Cuiqiao Lu

Nancaiyuanzi

Chezhan Lu

To Beijing

modelled on a Tibetan temple. It was built to commemorate Qianlong's victory over Mongol tribes when the subjugated leaders were invited to Chengde. A stele relating the victory is inscribed in Tibetan, Mongol, Chinese and Manchu. The main feature is an Avalokitesvara towering 22 metres; this wooden buddha has 42 arms with an eye on each palm. The temple appears to be used as an active place of worship.

Anyuan Temple (ānyuǎn miào) Only the main hall remains of Anyuan (the Temple of Far Spreading Peace), a copy of a Xinjiang

temple. It contains Buddhist frescoes in a very sad state.

Pule Temple (pùlè sì) Pule (the Temple of Universal Happiness) is definitely the most interesting. You can scramble along the banks of the nearby rivulet to a road that leads off near a pagoda at the garden wall.

The temple was built in 1776 for visits of minority envoys (Kazaks among them). It's in much better shape than the other temples and has been retiled and repainted. At the rear of the temple is the unusual Round Pavilion, reminiscent of Beijing's Temple of Heaven.

CHENGDE 承德

PLACES TO STAY

2 Mongolian Hotel
   蒙古包
8 Qiwanglou Hotel
   绮望楼
11 Mountain Villa Hotel
   山庄宾馆
14 Guesthouse for Diplomatic Missions
   外交人员宾馆
15 Chengde Hotel (Old)
   承德宾馆
17 Xinhua Hotel
   新华饭店
20 Yunshan Hotel
   云山饭店
21 Chengde Hotel (New)
   承德大厦
22 Huilong Hotel
   会龙大厦

PLACES TO EAT

12 Bi Feng Restaurant
   碧峰饭店

OTHER

1 Anyuan Temple
   安远寺
3 Pule Temple
   普乐寺
4 Hammer Rock
   棒槌山
5 Puren Temple
   溥仁寺
6 Misty Rain Tower
   烟雨楼
7 Bifeng Gate
   碧峰门
9 Lizhengmen (Main Gate)
   丽正门
10 Dehui Gate
   德汇门
13 Bank of China
   中国银行
16 Post Office
   邮局
18 Long-Distance Bus Station
   长途汽车站
19 Bank of China
   中国银行
23 Railway Station
   火车站

You can hike to **Hammer Rock** (*bàngchuíshān*) from Pule. It has nothing to do with sharks – the rock is meant to resemble an upside-down hammer. There are commanding views of the area from here. Other scenic rocks to add to your collection include Toad Rock and Monk's Hat Hill. The hiking is pleasant and the scenery is good.

Organised Tours

The only practical way to see all the tourist sights in one day is to take a tour by minibus. Most of these tours start out at 8 am, but a few begin in the afternoon just after lunch, around 1.30 pm. The cheapest sightseeing bus tours cost around Y20 but are Chinese-speaking only. Foreigners are usually welcome to tag along but the tour leaders would be much happier if you could speak Chinese.

The cheapest tours depart from the Lizhengmen Hotel *(lìzhèngmén lǚguǎn)* – this hotel is for Chinese people only but foreigners can join its tours. The tours run daily during the high season (from around May to October) but might only be twice weekly during the winter.

The Mountain Villa Hotel also does tours. These cost around Y30 to Y40 per person. If no tour is available, this hotel can also arrange a car and driver for a personalised tour – this costs Y100 or so and several travellers can split the cost.

Pricey tours are available from CITS in Beijing. A complete tour to Chengde costs Y2000 (two days) for one person, but gets cheaper as the group size increases.

Places to Stay

The *Xinhua Hotel* (☎ 206-5880) *(xīnhuá fàndiàn)*, 4 Xinhua Bei Lu, is a reliable cheapie with rooms for Y120 to Y180.

The old *Chengde Hotel* (☎ 202-5179) *(chéngdé bīnguǎn)* on Nanyingzi Dajie has comfortable doubles for Y100 to Y300. Bus No 7 from the railway station drops you right outside the hotel.

There are two hotels called the Chengde Hotel – the one close to the railway station on Chezhan Lu is the new *Chengde Hotel*

(☎ 227373; fax 208-8808) *(chéngdé dàshà)*. Doubles cost Y220 to Y280.

The *Yunshan Hotel* (☎ 202-6257) *(yúnshān fàndiàn)* at 6 Nanyuan Donglu is a modern tourist hang-out. Doubles cost Y480.

The *Huilong Hotel* (☎ 208-5369) *(huìlóng dàshà)* on Chezhan Lu is a relatively new place. Rooms cost Y160 to Y270.

The *Guesthouse for Diplomatic Missions* (☎ 202-1976) *(wàijiāo rényuán bīnguǎn)*, on Wulie Lu, is in the upmarket league. Doubles cost Y420.

The *Mountain Villa Hotel* (☎ 202-5206) *(shānzhuāng bīnguǎn)* is at 127 Lizhenmen Lu. The Stalinist architecture evokes mixed reactions, but this place certainly has character. Doubles cost Y480. The more expensive rooms are large enough to hold a party in – perhaps that's why they come equipped with mahjong tables. Take bus No 7 from the railway station and from there it's a short walk.

There are two hotels just within the walls of the Imperial Summer Villa. On the west side is the *Qiwanglou Hotel* (☎ 202-2192) *(qǐwànglóu bīnguǎn)* built in Qing Dynasty style. It's a three-star hotel with doubles for Y380 to Y480. Further north and on the east side is the *Mongolian Hotel* (☎ 202-2710) *(ménggǔbāo)*, where doubles cost between Y230 to Y260. It's designed in yurt style with air-con, carpet, telephone and TV – not even Genghis Khan had it this good.

Places to Eat

A fine place to try is the *Bi Feng Restaurant* about 100 metres from the Mountain Villa Hotel. It has fine Chinese food and cheap prices. It's a friendly, family-run business – there's no English menu so just point to something being eaten by others.

There are two main market streets – one just west of the long-distance bus station and the other just north of the post office. The local speciality is food made from haws (the fruit of the hawthorn), such as wine, ice cream and sweets. Chengde Pule beer has an interesting flavour – perhaps it's the mountain water. There are lots of trolleys around town dispensing tasty baked turnip. Fresh

almonds are grown locally – the almond juice sold in plastic containers is also a Chengde product.

The Chinese restaurant on the 2nd floor of the *Yunshan Hotel* has delicious food in generous portions, and is relatively cheap considering the sumptuous surroundings. There is a Western restaurant on the 1st floor of the hotel.

Getting There & Away

Bus Although there are some long-distance buses between Chengde and Beijing, this is generally not the way to do it – most travellers go by train.

Train The regular approach to Chengde is by train from Beijing. The fast train (No 11) departs from Beijing at 7.17 am and arrives in Chengde at 11.51 am. Soft seat is well worthwhile – it's a plush no-smoking car and tea is served to passengers (for a small fee). The same train gets renamed No 12 when it returns to Beijing, leaving Chengde at 2.31 pm. The one-way trip takes less than five hours. There are slower trains which take over seven hours. Tickets for trains leaving Chengde are only sold on the day of departure. Your hotel can buy your ticket, but this usually requires a small fee and you need to trust the staff with your passport (or old expired passport).

Getting Around

There are occasional taxis and pedicabs around town, but most travellers wind up using the minibuses. There are half a dozen bus lines but the only ones you'll probably need to use are the No 7 from the station to the old Chengde Hotel, and the No 6 to the outer temples grouped at the north-eastern end of town. The service is infrequent – you might have to wait 30 minutes or more.

Another good way to get around town and to the outer temples is on a bicycle. There is a rental place opposite the old Chengde Hotel and other rental places pop up periodically – ask at your hotel.

BEIDAIHE, QINHUANGDAO & SHANHAIGUAN

A 35-km stretch of coastline on China's east coast, this region borders the Bohai Sea.

Beidaihe
(běidàihé)

This seaside resort was built by Westerners but is now popular with both Chinese and non-Chinese. The simple fishing village was transformed when English railway engineers stumbled across it in the 1890s. Diplomats, missionaries and businesspeople from the Tianjin concessions and the Beijing legations hastily built villas and cottages in order to indulge in the new bathing fad.

The original golf courses, bars and cabarets have disappeared, though there are signs that these will be revived in the interests of the nouvelle bourgeoisie. Then, as now, Beidaihe is an escape from the hassles of Beijing or Tianjin. Kiesslings, the formerly Austrian restaurant, still sells its time-honoured

---

BEIDAIHE, QINHUANGDAO & SHANHAIGUAN
北戴河，秦皇岛，山海关

1 Beidaihe Railway Station
  北戴河火车站
2 Lianfengshan Park
  联峰山公园
3 Bus Station
  海滨汽车站
4 Pigeon's Nest Park
  鸽子窝公园
5 Seamen's Club
  海员俱乐部
6 Oil Wharf
  油港
7 First Pass Under Heaven
  天下第一关
8 Old Dragon Head
  老龙头

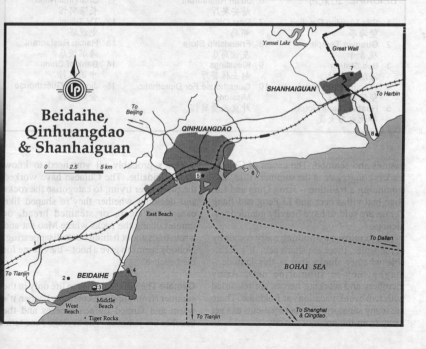

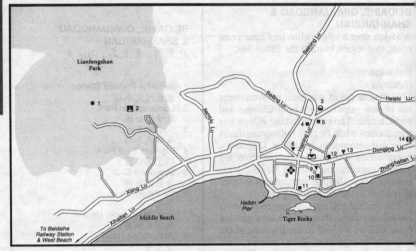

BEIDAIHE 北戴河

1 Sea-Viewing Pavilion
望海亭
2 Guanyin Temple
观音寺
3 Bus Station
海滨汽车站
4 Wanghai Lou Hotel
望海楼宾馆
5 Huabei Dianli Hotel
华北电力大厦

6 Ju'an Restaurant
居安餐厅
7 Post Office
邮局
8 Friendship Store
友谊商店
9 Kiesslings
起士林餐厅
10 Guesthouse For Diplomatic
Missions
外交人员宾馆

11 Changhai Hotel
长海宾馆
12 TV Tower
电视塔
13 Haibin Restaurant
海滨饭店
14 Bank of China
中国银行
15 Jinshan Guesthouse
金山宾馆

pastries and seafood. The cream of China's leaders congregate at the summer villas, also continuing a tradition – Jiang Qing and Lin Biao had villas here and Li Peng and Jiang Zemin are said to have heavily guarded residences.

Just to make sure nothing nasty comes by in the water, there are shark nets. It's debatable whether sharks live at this latitude – maybe they're submarine nets. Army members and working heroes are rewarded with two-week vacations at Beidaihe. There are many sanatoriums where patients can get away from the noise of the city.

That's probably all you need to know about Beidaihe. The Chinese have worked the place over trying to categorise the rocks and deciding whether they're shaped like camels or tigers or steamed bread, or immortalising the rocks where Mao sat and wrote lines about fishing boats disappearing. Nobody seems to give a hoot – they come for the beaches.

Climate The village comes to life only in the summer (from June to September), when it's warm and fanned by sea breezes and the beaches are jammed. The average June tem-

perature is 21°C (70°F). In January, by contrast, temperatures rest at -5°C (23°F).

Other Attractions There are various hikes to vantage points with expansive views of villas or the coast. Some notable viewing places include the Sea-Viewing Pavilion *(wànghǎi tíng)* at **Lianfengshan Park** *(liánfēngshān gōngyuán)*, about 1½ km north of Middle Beach. Right on the shoreline is the **Eagle Pavilion** at Pigeon's Nest Park *(gēziwō gōngyuán)*. People like to watch the sunrise over **Tiger Rocks** *(lǎohǔ shí)*. The tide at the East Beach recedes dramatically and tribes of kelp collectors and shellpickers descend upon the sands. In the high season you can even be photographed in amusing cardboard-cutout racing boats, with the sea as a backdrop.

Places to Stay Many places are open for business only during the brief summer season, and many cheaper hotels do not accept foreigners. One place which operates all year is the *Huabei Dianli Hotel* (☎ 404-2653) *(huáběi diànlì dàshà)*. Rooms rates are from Y150 to Y300.

The *Guesthouse for Diplomatic Missions*

(☎ 404-1287) *(wàijiāo rényuán bīnguǎn)* is the splashy place in town. Recent renovations have pushed the tariff up to Y320 in winter, Y500 in summer.

Also big with moneyed tourists is the *Jinshan Guesthouse* (☎ 404-1678) *(jīnshān bīnguǎn)* on the shorefront on Zhonghaitan Lu. Doubles cost Y380.

The *Wanghai Lou Hotel* (☎ 404-1497) *(wǎnghǎi lóu bīnguǎn)* is a fine place to stay but is only open during summer. Room rates are Y158 and Y580.

A new place right on the beachfront is the *Changhai Hotel (chánghǎi bīnguǎn)*. At the time of our visit, it was closed (too early for the season) but will open during summer.

Places to Eat In season, seafood is served in the restaurants. There's the *Ju'an Restaurant (jū'ān cāntīng)* near the markets, which does a mean beef platter *(niúròu tiěbǎn)*. The *Haibin Restaurant (hǎibīn fàndiàn)* near the TV tower is also good.

Near the Guesthouse for Diplomatic Missions is *Kiesslings (qǐshìlín cāntīng)*, a relative of the Tianjin branch, which only operates from June to August – the bakery is outstanding.

Things to Buy The free markets near the beaches have the most amusing kitsch collection of sculptured and glued shellwork this side of Dalian. Handicrafts such as raffia and basketware are on sale in the stores.

Getting Around Much of Beidaihe is small enough to walk around. Minibuses regularly ply a route between Beidaihe and Qinhuangdao Railway Station which takes you past all the beaches – the cost is Y1 no matter where you get on or get off.

There are a couple of bicycle rental places around town; look for rows of bikes. They charge about Y5 to Y10 per day, and you have to leave a deposit or identification.

Qinhuangdao
(qínhuángdǎo)
Qinhuangdao is an ugly port city that you'd have to squeeze pretty hard to find tourist

attractions in. It has an ice-free harbour, and petroleum is piped in from the Daqing oilfield to the wharves.

Water pollution makes the beach a non-starter – this is *not* the place to get your feet wet. The locals will be the first to suggest that you move along to Beidaihe or Shanhaiguan.

Shanhaiguan
(shānhǎiguān)
Shanhaiguan is where the Great Wall meets the sea. In the 1980s this part of the wall had nearly returned to dust, but it has been rebuilt and is a first-rate tourist drawcard.

Shanhaiguan is a city of considerable charm, though its best to avoid weekends when throngs of camera-clicking Beijingers and local souvenir vendors overrun the place. It was a garrison town with a square fortress, four gates at the compass points and two major avenues running between the gates. The present village is within the substantial remains of the old walled enclosure, making it a picturesque place to wander around. The scenic hills to the north add to the effect. Shanhaiguan has a long and chequered history – nobody is quite sure how

long or what kind of chequers, but plenty of pitched battles and blood it seems.

First Pass Under Heaven *(tiānxià dìyī guān)* Also known as the East Gate *(dōngmén)*, this magnificent structure is topped with a two-storey, double-roofed tower

SHANHAIGUAN 山海关
1 North Street Hotel 北街招待所
2 Jingshan Hotel 京山宾馆
3 First Pass Under Heaven 天下第一关
4 Great Wall Museum 长城博物馆
5 Street Market 南大商业街
6 Bank of China 中国银行
7 Bus Station 汽车站
8 Shangye Hotel 商业宾馆
9 Railway Station 火车站

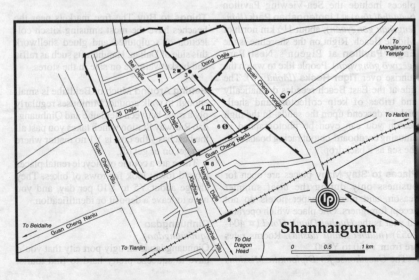

Shanhaiguan

(Ming Dynasty, rebuilt in 1639). The calligraphy at the top (attributed to the scholar Xiao Xian) reads 'First Pass Under Heaven'. The words reflect the Chinese custom of dividing the world into civilised China and the 'barbarians'. The barbarians got the better of civilised China when they stormed this gate in 1644.

A Y5 ticket buys you admission to the top of the wall, and from this vantage point you can see decayed sections trailing off into the mountains. At the watchtower are souvenir shops selling First Pass Under Heaven handkerchiefs, and a parked horse waiting for photos. How about a pair of 'First Pass Under Heaven Wooden Chopsticks' or some 'Brave Lucky Jewellery'?

The nearby Great Wall Museum (*chángchéng bówùguǎn*) displays armour, dress, weaponry and pictures.

Old Dragon Head (*lǎo lóng tóu*) This is where the Great Wall meets the sea. What you see now has been reconstructed – the original wall has long since crumbled away. The name is derived from the legendary carved dragon head that once faced the ocean. It's a four-km hike or taxi ride from the centre of Shanhaiguan. A more viable route is to follow (by road) the wall to the first beacon tower. You can get partway there by bicycle on a dirt road, and you'll pass a small village set in some pleasant countryside.

Yansai Lake (*yànsāi hú*) The lake is also known as Stone River Reservoir (*shíhé shuǐkù*). It's just six km to the north-west of Shanhaiguan. The reservoir is 45 km long and tourists can go boating there. Give them a few years and it could be another Guilin.

Mengjiangnü Temple (*mèngjiāngnü miào*) Six km east of Shanhaiguan (with a regular bus service from the South Gate) is the Mengjiangnü Temple, a Song-Ming reconstruction. It has coloured sculptures of Lady Meng and her maids, and calligraphy on Looking for Husband Rock.

Meng's husband, Wan, was press-ganged into wall building because his views conflicted with those of Emperor Qin Shihuang. When winter came the beautiful Meng Jiang set off to take her husband warm clothing, only to discover that he had died from the backbreaking labour. Meng tearfully wandered the Great Wall, thinking only of finding Wan's bones to give him a decent burial. The wall, a sensitive soul, was so upset that it collapsed, revealing the skeleton entombed within. Overcome with grief, Meng hurled herself into the sea from a conveniently placed boulder.

Organised Tours There are so many Chinese-speaking tours and prices are so competitive that these are worth considering. In the busy summer season, tour operators gather around the railway station in plague proportions and solicit any likely-looking customers, including foreigners. Tours are also available in the off season – if you have no offers, then enquire at your hotel. A couple of hours touring should cost around Y30, subject to some bargaining.

Places to Stay Most popular with foreigners is the *Jingshan Hotel* (☎ 551130) (*jīngshān bīnguǎn*). This beautiful place with doubles for Y100 is highly recommended, at least in the off season. The hotel is right near the First Pass Under Heaven (East Gate).

If the Jingshan is full, take a look at the nearby *North Street Hotel* (*běijiē zhāodàisuǒ*) which charges the same rates. The spacious rooms come with fans and a private bathroom.

The *Shangye Hotel* (*shāngyè bīnguǎn*) is a huge place close to the railway station. Doubles cost Y200.

Getting There & Away
Air Qinhuangdao's little-used airport offers flights to Dalian, Guangzhou and Shanghai.

Train The three stations of Beidaihe, Qinhuangdao and Shanhaiguan are accessible by train from Beijing, Tianjin or Shenyang (Liaoning Province). The trains are frequent but don't always stop at all three stations or always arrive at convenient hours. The usual stop is Shanhaiguan; several trains skip Beidaihe.

One factor to consider is that the hotels at Shanhaiguan are within walking distance of the railway station, whereas at Beidaihe the nearest hotel is at least 10 km from the station. This is no problem if you arrive during daylight or early evening – there are plenty of minibuses meeting incoming trains at Beidaihe Railway Station. However, you can't count on this at night and a taxi could be quite expensive. If you're going to arrive in the dead of night, it's better to do so at Shanhaiguan.

Departing from Shanhaiguan also makes some sense when it comes to ticket sales – the Shanhaiguan Railway Station should be a model for the rest of China. They've tried something new here – having sufficient employees on duty at all times to meet demand. As a result, there are seldom queues and you can get your ticket straight away.

The fastest trains take five hours to Beidaihe from Beijing, and an extra 1½ hours to Shanhaiguan. From Shenyang to Shanhaiguan is a five-hour trip. Tianjin is three to four hours away.

Alternatively, you could get a train that stops at Qinhuangdao and then take a minibus from there to Beidaihe.

Getting Around

Bus Minibuses are fast and cheap, and can be flagged down easily. The fare is Y1 and there are three routes: Beidaihe Railway Station to the Beidaihe bus terminal; Beidaihe bus terminal to Qinhuangdao Railway Station; and Qinhuangdao Railway Station to Shanhaiguan. But watch out for the minibus drivers at Beidaihe Railway Station who like to drop foreigners off at the front door of their hotel for Y15 or so – the regular fare is Y1, so you're paying an extra Y14 to go one more block. To avoid this hassle, pay your fare when everyone else does and don't say anything about getting off at a hotel.

Buses connect Beidaihe, Shanhaiguan and Qinhuangdao. These generally run every 30 minutes from around 6 or 6.30 am to around 6.30 pm (not guaranteed after 6 pm). Some of the important public bus routes are:

No 5 Beidaihe Railway Station to Beidaihe middle beach (30 minutes)

Nos 3 & 4 Beidaihe to Qinhuangdao (45 minutes) then to Shanhaiguan (another 15 minutes)

Shandong 山东

Shandong *(shāndōng)*, the turtle-head bobbing into the Yellow Sea, is a slow starter. The province is relatively poor and beset with economic problems, not the least of which is the unpredictable Yellow River. The river has changed direction some 26 times in its history and flooded many more times. Six times it has swung its mouth from the Bohai Sea (north Shandong) to the Yellow Sea (south Shandong), and wreaked havoc on the residents.

Back in 1899 the Yellow River flooded the entire Shandong Plain, a sad irony in view of the two scorching droughts which had swept the area that same year and the year before. Add to that a long period of economic depression, a sudden influx of demobilised troops in 1895 after China's humiliating defeat in the war with Japan, and droves of refugees from the south moving north to escape famines, floods and drought. Then top it off with an imperial government in Beijing either incapable or unwilling to help the local people, and foreigners whose missionaries and railroads had angered the gods and spirits. All this created a perfect breeding ground for a rebellion, and in the last few years of the 19th century the Boxers arose out of Shandong and their rebellion set all of China ablaze.

Controlling the monstrous river that started it all is still going to take a fair bit of dike building. The other major problem is overpopulation. Shandong, with an area of just 150,000 sq km, is the third most populated province after Henan and Sichuan. And to make matters worse, about two-thirds of Shandong is hilly, with the Shandong massif (at 1545 metres, Taishan is the highest peak) looming up in the south-west, and another mountain chain over the tip of the Shandong Peninsula. The rest is fertile plains.

The Germans got their hands on the port of Qingdao in 1898 and set up a few factories. Shandong Province subsequently took a few quantum leaps towards industrialis-

Population: 80 million
Capital: Ji'nan
Highlights:
* Taishan, one of China's sacred Taoist peaks
* Qufu, the birthplace of Confucius
* Lingering colonial architecture of Qingdao, home of China's most famous brew

ation. The leading industrial town today is still Qingdao; the capital, Ji'nan, takes second place. Zibo, the major coal-mining centre, is also noted for its glassworks and porcelain. The Shengli Oilfield, opened in northern Shandong in 1965, is the second-largest crude oil source in China. As for railway lines, you can count them on the fingers of one hand, but the Shandong Peninsula has some first-class harbours with good passenger links, and there is a dense network of top-notch roads.

Not that many travellers bother with Shandong, which is unfortunate since it has quite a bit to offer. Besides the tourist attractions, an added bonus is that some places (notably Tai'an and Qufu) have very cheap hotels, a godsend for budget travellers in increasingly expensive China. And for those

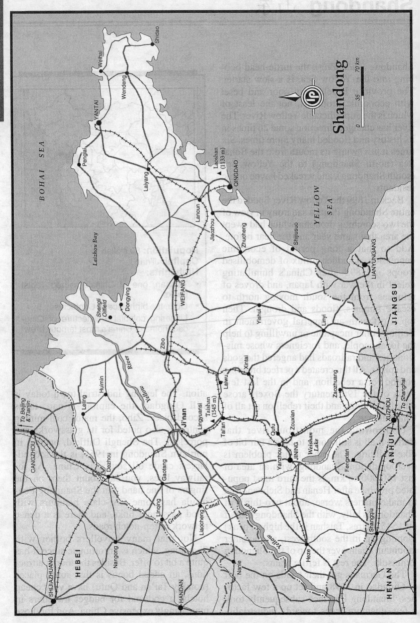

who partake, beer, wine and mineral water from Qingdao, Laoshan and Yantai are the pride of the nation.

JI'NAN
(jì'nán)

Ji'nan (population approximately two million), the capital of Shandong Province, is for most travellers a transit point on the road to other destinations around Shandong. Although the inner-city area (around the new central railway station) is not unpleasant, there is little to see around town and there's a shortage of budget accommodation.

The area has been inhabited for at least 4000 years, and some of the earliest reminders of this are the eggshell-thin pieces of black pottery unearthed in the town of Longshan, 30 km east of Ji'nan.

Modern development in Ji'nan stems from 1899, when construction of the Ji'nan to Qingdao railway line began. The line gave the city a major communications role when completed in 1904. The Germans had a concession near the railway station after Ji'nan was opened up to foreign trade in 1906. Foreign missions were set up here and industrialisation took place under the Germans, the English and the Japanese. Steel, paper, fertiliser, cars and textiles are now produced here. The city is also an important educational centre.

Information

CITS There is an office (☎ 295-5858) in the Qilu Hotel, but Ji'nan CITS caters mainly to tour groups.

Money The Bank of China is in Building 10, Shangye Jie, in the eastern part of town. There are exchange services at the centrally located Pearl and Guidu hotels.

Thousand Buddha Mountain
(qiānfóshān)

The statues were disfigured or just disappeared during the Cultural Revolution, but new ones are gradually being added – Overseas Chinese visitors often donate money to this worthy cause. Thousand Buddha Moun-

tain is on the south side of town. Bus Nos 2 and 31 go there – get off at Qianfoshan Lu.

Shandong Provincial Museum
(shāndōng bówùguǎn)

The museum is adjacent to the Thousand Buddha Mountain. It is divided into history and nature sections – tools, *objets d'art*, pottery, musical instruments.

Golden Ox Park
(jīnniú gōngyuán)

This park on the north side of town is notable for a temple built on a hillside and the city zoo *(jì'nán dòngwùyuán)*. Bus Nos 4, 5, 33 and 35 stop here.

You can make a side trip from here a few km to the north of the No 4 bus terminal to see the dike of the Yellow River, although it's a bit on the dull side.

Daguanyuan Market
(dàguānyuán shìchǎng)

Ji'nan's largest market is a good place to browse around. A couple of blocks to the east is the Ji'nan People's Market *(jì'nán rénmín shāngchǎng)*.

Mystery of the Springs

Ji'nan's 100-plus springs are often quoted as the main attraction, so let's set the record straight on this one. The four main parks-cum-springs are Black Tiger Spring *(hēihǔquán)*, Pearl Spring *(zhūquán)*, Five Dragon Pool *(wǔlóngtán)* and Gushing-from-the-Ground Spring *(bàotúquán)*, all marvellous names but hardly accurate as adjectives. Twenty years ago they might have sprung but now they've virtually dried up. The reasons given vary – droughts, pollution from factories, increased industrial and domestic use and, more quietly, the digging of bomb shelters outside the city.

Daming Lake *(dàmíng hú)* is also affected by this malaise, which the authorities are attempting to 'correct'. Daming Lake has several minor temples, a few teahouses and a restaurant. At Gushing-from-the-Ground Spring there is a small memorial museum

dedicated to the 11th-century patriotic poet
Li Qingzhao.

Places to Stay

Budget travellers are best to avoid Ji'nan
altogether by travelling on to either Tai'an or
Qingdao. Inexpensive hotels in Ji'nan are
uniformly off limits to foreigners.

Around the railway station (the best area
in which to be based), the cheapest option is
the *Ji'nan Hotel* (☎ 793-8981) *(jì'nán fàndiàn)*, 240 Jing 3-Lu. It's a rambling Chinese-
style hotel – just finding the reception
involves numerous stops to ask directions. It

looks like the kind of the place that should
have cheap dormitory beds in one of its old
blocks, but the staff insist that the cheapest
rooms are the standard doubles at Y220,
triples at Y240 and quads at Y280. Students
are eligible for small discounts.

Around five minutes' walk from the Ji'nan
Hotel is the *Pearl Hotel* (☎ 793-2888)
(zhēnzhū dàjiǔdiàn), 164 Jing 3-Lu. The
cheapest doubles cost Y398. Similar in style
and close to the railway station is the *Guidu
Hotel* (☎ 690-0888; fax 690-0999) *(guìdū
dàjiǔdiàn)* at 1 Shengping Lu. The cheapest
rooms are in the auxiliary building next door

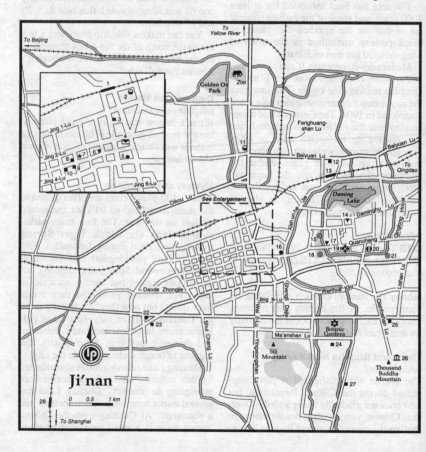

To
Yellow River

To Beijing

Golden Ox
Park

Zoo

Fenghuang-
shan Lu

Beiyuan Lu

To
Qingdao

Jing 1-Lu

Jing 2-Lu

Jing 4-Lu

Jing 6-Lu

Beiyuan Lu

Daming
Lake

See Enlargement

Dikou Lu

Wei 12-Lu

Xisha'an Jie

Daminghu

Qinglong Houjie

Lishan Lu

Quancheng

Wei 2-Lu

Daode Zhongjie

(Sheng) Dajie

Wenhua Xilu

Jing 8-Lu

Shui Chang Lu

Yingxiongshan Lu

Ma'anshan Lu

Botanic
Gardens

Sili
Mountain

Olaofshan Lu

Thousand
Buddha
Mountain

Ji'nan

0   0.5   1 km

To Shanghai

to the hotel, and these come in at US$40 for a standard double. The main building has prices ranging from US$60.

The *Nanjiao Guesthouse* (☎ 295-3931) *(nánjiāo bīnguǎn)* at 2 Ma'anshan Lu is out on the south end of town. Doubles cost from Y220 to Y350; suites are Y360. Getting to the hotel by public transport is an effort – take bus No 34 from the centre and then hike up a hill. The hotel was, so the story goes, flung up for an impending visit by Mao, who then decided to skip Ji'nan.

The *Shungeng Hillview Hotel* (☎ 295-1818) *(shùngēng shānzhuāng)* is in the same neighbourhood, off Shungeng Lu. Doubles cost Y550 to Y650. The best way to get there is by taxi.

Just north of the east railway station is the *Minghu Hotel* (☎ 595-6688) *(mínghú dàjiǔdiàn)* on Beiyuan Lu. This three-star place has rooms for around Y298 to Y498.

The *Qilu Hotel* (☎ 296-6888, 296-7676) *(qílǔ bīnguǎn)* is the prime tourist hotel in town and the home of CITS. Doubles start at Y880. It's on Qianfoshan Lu, right next to Thousand Buddha Mountain Park.

Places to Eat

The area around the station is the best place to seek out cheap eats, though there is nothing particularly special here.

One of the better known eating establishments in town is the *Huiquan Restaurant* *(huìquán fàndiàn)*, 22 Baotuquan Beilu. Be aware that it features sweet and sour carp from the Yellow River which is served while still breathing. Whilst it may be fresh, you may find this more offensive than appetising.

Good Shandong food can be had at *Jufengde Restaurant* *(jùfēngdé fàndiàn)* at the intersection of Wei 4-Lu and Jing 3-Lu. And just outside the south gate of Daming Lake Park is the *Daminghu Restaurant* *(dàmínghú fàndiàn)*, which also serves Shandong food.

JI'NAN 济南		PLACES TO EAT	13	East Railway Station 火车东站
PLACES TO STAY	6	Jufengde Restaurant 聚丰德饭店	15	Five Dragon Pool Spring 五龙潭公园
3 Guidu Hotel 贵都大酒店	14	Daminghu Restaurant 大明湖饭店	16	Ji'nan People's Market 济南人民商场
9 Ji'nan Hotel 济南饭店	17	Huiquan Restaurant 汇泉饭店	18	Gushing-from-the-Ground Spring 趵突泉
10 Pearl Hotel 珍珠大酒店		**OTHER**	19	Department Store 百货大楼
12 Minghu Hotel 明湖大酒店	1	Ji'nan Railway Station 济南火车站	20	Bank of China 中国银行
23 Aviation Hotel 航空大厦	2	Tianqiao Bus Station 天桥汽车站	21	Black Tiger Spring 黑虎泉
24 Nanjiao Guesthouse 南郊宾馆	4	Main Post Office 邮局	22	China Eastern Airlines 东方航空公司
25 Qilu Hotel & CITS 齐鲁宾馆, 中国国际旅行社	5	Daguanyuan Market 大观园市场	26	Shandong Provincial Museum 山东省博物馆
27 Shungeng Hillview Hotel 舜耕山庄	7	PSB 公安局外事科	28	South Railway Station 白马山火车站
	8	CAAC 中国民航		
	11	Long-Distance Bus Station 长途汽车站		

Getting There & Away

Air There are international flights (technically charters) three times a week between Hong Kong and Ji'nan. Domestic flights are available between Ji'nan and all major Chinese cities.

The CAAC ticket office (☎ 692-6624) is at 348 Jing 2 Wei-Lu. China Eastern Airlines (☎ 796-4445, 796-6824) is at 408 Jing 10-Lu. Both offices sell the same tickets.

Bus Ji'nan has at least three bus stations. The main long-distance bus station *(chángtú qìchē zhàn)* in the north of town has buses to Beijing and Qingdao. The Tianqiao bus station *(tiānqiáo qìchē zhàn)* is next door to the main railway station and has minibuses to Tai'an. Minibuses to Tai'an also depart from the huge parking lot in front of the railway station. There is another minibus station in front of the east railway station *(huǒchē dōngzhàn)*, where you catch minibuses to Qufu and rural areas near Ji'nan.

Train Take care when catching trains out of Ji'nan: there are two railway stations. Though most trains use the new main railway station, some trains arrive and depart from the east railway station *(huǒchē dōngzhàn)*.

Ji'nan is a major link in the east China rail system, with over 30 trains passing through daily. From Ji'nan there are direct trains to Beijing (six hours) and Shanghai (13 hours). The trains from Qingdao to Shenyang which pass through Ji'nan sidestep Beijing and go through Tianjin instead.

There are direct trains from Ji'nan to Qingdao and Yantai in Shandong Province, and to Hefei in Anhui Province. There are also direct Qingdao-Ji'nan-Xi'an-Xining trains.

Getting Around

To/From the Airport Flights depart from the Xijiao Airport, 40 km east of the city – a new freeway makes it possible to cover the distance in just 40 minutes. You can catch an airport bus from the CAAC ticket office – try not to miss it because a taxi will cost around Y130.

Bus & Motor-tricycle There are about 25 urban and suburban bus lines in Ji'nan, running from 5 am to 9 pm, and two late-night lines (east-west and north-south) finishing at midnight. There are also plenty of motor-tricycles and taxis. Watch out for the latter, however: they are particularly rapacious.

AROUND JI'NAN

There are a couple of little-visited attractions around Ji'nan.

Four Gate Pagoda

(sìméntǎ)

Thirty-three km south-east of Ji'nan, near the village of Liubu, are some of the oldest Buddhist structures in Shandong. There are two clusters, one a few km north-east of the village and the other to the south. Shentong Monastery, founded in the 4th century AD, holds the Four Gate Pagoda, which is possibly the oldest stone pagoda in China and dates back to the 6th century. Four beautiful light-coloured buddhas face each door.

The Pagoda of the Dragon & the Tiger *(lónghǔtǎ)* was built during the Tang Dynasty. It stands close to the Shentong Monastery and is surrounded by stupas. Higher up is the Thousand Buddha Cliff *(qiānfóyá)*, which has carved grottoes with some 200 small buddhas and half a dozen life-size ones.

Bus No 22 from the city centre heads due south on Yingxiongshan Lu to Four Gate Pagoda. There are some tourist buses on this route, departing from Ji'nan at 8 am and returning at 3 pm.

Divine Rock Temple

(língyánsì)

This temple is set in mountainous terrain in Changqing County, 75 km from Ji'nan. It used to be a large monastery that served many dynasties (the Tang, Song and Yuan, among others) and had 500 monks in its heyday. On view is a forest of 200 stupas commemorating the priests who directed the institution. There's also a nine-storey octagonal pagoda as well as the Thousand Buddha Temple *(qiānfódiàn)*, which contains 40 fine, highly individualised clay arhats – the best Buddhist statues in Shandong.

Buses to Divine Rock Temple depart from Daguanyuan Market in the centre. The one-way trip takes up to three hours. Some buses terminate at Wande station (which is south of Ji'nan and 10 km from Divine Rock Temple) from where you get another bus. If you latch onto a Chinese tour group, tourist buses depart around 7.30 am and return about 4 pm.

TAI'AN
(tài'ān)

Tai'an is the gateway town to the sacred Taishan, possibly the best sight in all of Shandong. It's a sleepy kind of place with a good range of accommodation, making it an ideal base for an assault on Taishan and visit to Qufu, Confucius' birthplace.

On an incidental note, Tai'an is the home town of Jiang Qing, Mao's fourth wife, ex-film actress and notorious spearhead of the 'Gang of Four', on whom all of China's ills are sometimes blamed. She was later air-brushed out of Chinese history and committed suicide in May 1991.

Information

The CITS office (☎ 822-3259) is in a compound just down the road from the Taishan Guesthouse, at 22 Hongmen Lu. It rarely seems to be open, and very few travellers bother with it.

The PSB (☎ 822-4004) is just up the road from the main post office on Qingnian Lu.

Dai Temple
(dài miào)

This temple is south of the Taishan Guest-house. It was traditionally a pilgrimage stop on the road to Taishan, and once served as a resting spot for hiking emperors. The temple covers an area of 96,000 sq metres, and is enclosed by high walls. The main hall is the Temple of Heavenly Blessing (Tiangong), dating back to 1009 AD. It is some 22 metres high and is constructed of wood with double-roof yellow tiling.

The Tiangong was the first built of the 'big three' halls (the others being Taihe Hall at the Forbidden City and Dacheng Hall at Qufu). It was restored in 1956. Inside is a 62-metre-long fresco running from the west to east walls depicting the god of Taishan on his outward and return journeys. In this case the god is Emperor Zhen Zong, who had the temple built. Zhen Zong raised the god of Taishan to the rank of emperor and there is a seven-metre-high stele to celebrate this in the western courtyard. The fresco has been painstakingly retouched by artisans of succeeding dynasties and, though recently restored, is in poor shape – but a majestic concept nonetheless.

The temple complex has been repeatedly restored; in the late 1920s, however, it was stripped of its statues and transmogrified into offices and shops. Later it suffered damage under the Kuomintang. It is gradually coming back together, not as a temple but as an open-air museum with a forest of 200-odd steles. One inscribed stone, originally at the summit of Taishan, is believed to be over 2000 years old (Qin Dynasty). It can be seen at the Eastern Imperial Hall, along with a small collection of imperial sacrificial vessels. Out-of-towners flock to Taishan Temple to copy the masterful range of calligraphy and poetry styles. Also moved from the summit is a beautiful bronze pavilion.

Around the courtyards are ancient cypresses, gingkos and acacias. At the rear of the temple is a bonsai garden and rockery. By the cypress in front of Tiangong Hall, locals and visitors can indulge in a game of luck. A person is blindfolded next to a rock, has to go around the rock three times anti-clockwise, then three times clockwise, and try and grope towards the cypress, which is 20 steps away. They miss every time. Outside the main temple gates, if it's the right season, street hawkers sell watermelons with the display pieces deftly cut into rose shapes.

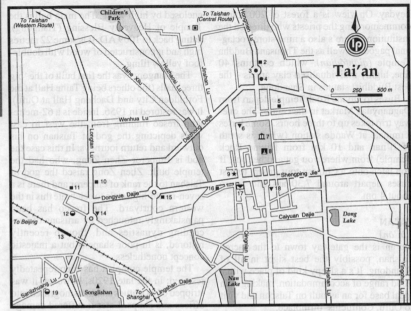

To Taishan (Western Route)

Children's Park

To Taishan (Central Route)

Hongmen Lu

Tai'an

0   250   500 m

Naihe Xilu

Huichüxi Lu

Jinshan Lu

Wenhua Lu

Longtan Lu

Daizhong Dajie

Shengping Jie

Dongyue Dajie

Caiyuan Dajie

Dong Lake

Qingian Lun

Huashan Lu

Yingxiang Lun

To Beijing

Sanlizhuang Lu

To Shanghai

Songlishan

Lingshan Dajie

Nan Lake

TAI'AN 泰安

PLACES TO STAY

2 Taishan Guesthouse
   泰山宾馆
5 Taishan Grand Hotel
   泰山大酒店
10 Longtan Hotel
   龙潭宾馆
11 Liangmao Dasha (Hotel)
   粮贸大厦
15 Waimao Dasha (Hotel)
   外贸大厦
16 Overseas Chinese Hotel
   华侨大厦

PLACES TO EAT

6 California Beef Noodles
   King USA
   美国加州牛肉面
14 Burger Palace
   汉堡包店
18 Duck Restaurant
   迎宾餐厅

OTHER

1 Martyrs' Tomb
   烈士陵园
3 Daizong Archway
   岱宗坊
4 CITS
   中国国祭旅行社

7 Museum
   博物馆
8 Dai Temple
   岱庙
9 PSB
   公安局外事科
12 Minibuses to Ji'nan &
   Bus No 3 (to Taishan)
   往济南汽车，
   三路汽车
13 Railway Station
   火车站
17 Post Office
   邮局
19 Long-Distance Bus
   Station
   长途汽车站

Places to Stay

Tai'an is that rarest of things – a Chinese town with a good range of budget accommodation.

The most popular place in town with budget travellers is the three-star *Taishan Guesthouse* (☎ 822-4678) (*tàishān bīnguǎn*), a five-storey complex with souvenir shops, a bank and a restaurant. Top marks go to the three-bed dorms, which cost Y50 per person. It's a good place to round up a small group for an assault on the mountain. Doubles with private bath are also available for Y280. The hotel is four km from the railway station and just a short walk from the start of the central route trail up Taishan. You can deposit your bags at the hotel's luggage room while you climb the mountain. To get to the hotel, take bus No 3 (Y0.10) or the No 3 minibus (Y0.80) from the railway station to the second-last stop. A taxi is Y10, or you can charter one of the ubiquitous yellow minivans for the same price.

The *Liangmao Dasha* (☎ 822-8212) is one block from the railway station. Like many of the cheapies in Tai'an, it suffers from the usual leaky plumbing and sporadic hot water, but is otherwise OK. It has a bewildering choice of rooms, from triples at Y35 per bed to singles/doubles with bath for Y60/140. There are other, similar budget hotels around the railway station. The *Longtan Hotel* (☎ 822-6511) *(lóngtán bīnguǎn)* is not a bad option, though it is rather more expensive at Y120 for a standard double.

The *Waimao Dasha* (☎ 822-2288) *(wàimào dàshà)* on Dongyue Dajie is one of the better-appointed budget hotels, though the building is showing signs of wear and tear. The rooms are a little overpriced at Y160 for doubles. Basic triples are also available at Y160.

The *Taishan Grand Hotel* (☎ 822-7211) *(tàishān dàjiǔdiàn)*, on Daizhong Dajie, charges Y240 for a double. The best hotel in town is the *Overseas Chinese Hotel* (☎ 822-8112; fax 822-8171) *(huáqiáo dàshà)* on Dongyue Dajie. Standard doubles cost Y680.

Places to Eat

Tai'an is not exactly brimming with great restaurants, but there's some good food around all the same. Hongmen Lu, particularly the section of it between the Dai Temple and the Taishan Guesthouse, is a good area to seek out restaurants. None of them has an English menu, but you can always peek at what other diners are eating.

One of the best treats in town is the *Duck Restaurant (yíngbīn cāntīng)*, as it has been christened by local foreign teachers. There's no English sign, but just look out for the big restaurant south of the Dai Temple. A whole Beijing duck will set you back just Y50 – quite a bargain. The restaurant also does other dishes.

Other restaurants to look out for around town include a *California Beef Noodles King USA (měiguó jiāzhōu niúròumiàn)*, a Taiwanese franchise with branches all over northern China. Just across the road from the railway station is the *Burger Palace* in the Rainbow Plaza *(cǎihóng shāngchǎng)*. This place is the nearest Tai'an gets to a fast-food joint. There's an English menu and the staff try hard to please.

Getting There & Away

Bus Tai'an can be approached by road from either Ji'nan or Qufu and is worth combining with a trip to the latter.

The Tai'an-Qufu buses depart from the long-distance bus stations in both cities (two hours, eight buses daily). There might be a couple of minibuses which run only when full, but the public buses on this route aren't bad. The highway is in excellent condition.

Although there are a few large public buses connecting Tai'an to Ji'nan, these are overcrowded horrors and you're better off travelling by minibus (Y10, 1½ hours). In Ji'nan, departures are from the Tianqiao bus station. In Tai'an, minibuses to Ji'nan depart from right in front of the railway station.

Train There are more than 20 express trains running daily through Tai'an, with links to Beijing, Harbin, Ji'nan, Nanjing, Qingdao, Shanghai, Shenyang, Xi'an and Zhengzhou.

Tai'an Railway Station is about 1¼ hours down the line from Ji'nan, but some special express trains don't stop at Tai'an. The town is a nine-hour ride from Beijing, 11 hours from Zhengzhou and nine from Nanjing. Check the schedule to avoid arriving at some unpleasant hour like 3 am.

Tai'an and Taishan make good stopovers on the way south from Qingdao to Qufu and Shanghai. The trip takes about 9½ hours.

Getting Around

Getting around is easy. The long-distance bus station is near the railway station, so all local transport is directed towards these two terminals.

There are three main bus routes. Bus No 3 runs from the Taishan central route trailhead to the western route trailhead via the railway station, so that just about covers everything. Bus Nos 1 and 2 also end up near the railway station. Minibuses run on the same routes and are more comfortable, but they will leave the station only when full. You can commandeer a minibus and use it as a taxi.

Taxis and pedicabs can be found outside the railway station – the drivers practically kidnap any foreigner they see. Expect the usual problems of overcharging – most destinations around town cost Y10 to Y12.

TAISHAN
(tàishān)

Also known as Daishan, Taishan is the most revered of the five sacred Taoist mountains of China. Once upon a time, imperial sacrifices to heaven and earth were offered from its summit, though only five of China's many, many emperors ever climbed Taishan. Emperor Qianlong of the Qing Dynasty, on the other hand, scaled it 11 times. From its heights Confucius uttered the dictum, 'The world is small'; Mao lumbered up and commented on the sunrise, 'The East is Red'.

Poets, writers and painters have found Taishan a great source of inspiration and extolled its beauties. Today the mountain is what you would expect of a major Chinese tourist attraction – climbers rarely get a moment's peace, as souvenir sellers and bearers grab at their shirt sleeves. Many people do not even bother with the climb, taking the cable car instead.

No matter – the pull of the supernatural (legend, religion and history rolled into one) is enough. The Princess of the Azure Clouds

(Bixia), a Taoist deity whose presence permeates the temples dotted along the route, is a powerful cult figure for the peasant women of Shandong and beyond. Tribes of wiry grandmothers come each year for the ascent. Their target is the cluster of temples at the summit, where they can offer gifts and prayers for their progeny. It's said that if you climb Taishan you'll live to be 100, and some of the grandmothers look pretty close to that already. For the younger set, Taishan is a popular picnic destination. Tourists – foreign and Chinese – gather on the cold summit at daybreak in the hope of catching a perfect

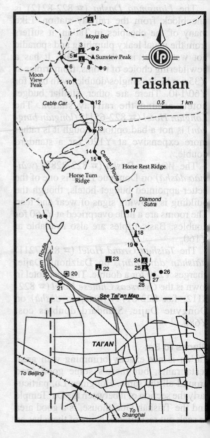

sunrise. In ancient Chinese tradition, it was believed that the sun began its westward journey from Taishan.

Taishan is not a major climb but, with some 6000 steps to negotiate, it can be hard work. Porters with callused shoulders and mishapen backs plod ever upwards with crates of drinks, bedding and the occasional Chinese tourist. It is a job passed from father to son, and the cable car seems to have done nothing to sweep away tradition. One wonders how many backs were broken in the building of the temples and stone stairs on Taishan over the centuries, a massive undertaking accomplished without mechanical aids.

Climate

The peak tourist season is from May to October. But remember that conditions on the mountain vary considerably compared with sea-level Tai'an.

The mountain is frequently enveloped in clouds and haze, which are more prevalent in summer. The best times to visit are in spring and autumn when the humidity is low, though old-timers say that the clearest weather is from early October onwards. In winter the weather is often fine but very cold.

On average, there are 16 fine days in spring, eight in summer, 28 in autumn and 35 in winter. But take care – due to weather changes, you're best advised to carry warm clothing in a small day-pack with you, no matter what the season. You can freeze your butt off on Taishan, though you can hire padded overcoats. The average seasonal temperatures in °C are:

	Winter	Spring	Summer	Autumn
Taishan	-3	20	24	20
Summit	-9	12	17	12

Climbing Taishan

The town of Tai'an lies at the foot of Taishan and is the gateway to the mountain (see the Tai'an section earlier in this chapter).

By Foot The entry fee for Taishan has changed a few times in the last couple of years, and locals maintain that the fee is seasonal. At the time of writing it was Y20 entry, plus a further Y5 environment protection fee.

Upon arrival you have several options, depending on your timing. There are three rest stops to bear in mind: Taishan Guesthouse at the base of the trail; Zhongtianmen Guesthouse halfway up; and the Shenqi Guesthouse on top of Taishan.

You should allow at least two hours for climbing between each of these points – a total of eight hours up and down, at the minimum. Allowing several more hours would make the climb less strenuous and give you more time to look around on top. If you want to see the sunrise, then dump your gear at the railway station or the Taishan Guesthouse in Tai'an and time your ascent so that you'll reach the summit before sundown; stay overnight at one of the summit guesthouses and get up early next morning for the famed sunrise (which, for technical reasons, may not be clearly forthcoming).

Chinese tourists without time or money at their disposal sometimes scale at night (with torches and walking sticks) to arrive at the peak in time for sunrise, descending shortly thereafter. Unless you have uncanny night vision or four hours of battery power, this particular option could lead to you getting lost, frozen, falling off a mountainside, or all three.

There are two main paths up the mountain: the central and the western, converging midway at Zhongtianmen. Most people go up via the central path (which used to be the imperial route and hence has more cultural sites) and down by the western path. Other trails run through orchards and woods.

Taishan is 1545 metres above sea level, with a climbing distance of 7½ km from base to summit on the central route. The elevation change from Zhongtianmen to the summit is approximately 600 metres.

By Minibus & Cable Car Minibuses run from the Tai'an Railway Station to Zhongtianmen, halfway up Taishan, with several

departures each morning. Occasional group tour minibuses run from the Taishan Guesthouse.

Zhongtianmen is less than five minutes' walk from the cable car (*kōng zhōng suǒ dào*), which holds 30 passengers and takes eight minutes to travel from Zhongtianmen to Wangfushan, near Nantianmen. The cable cars operate in both directions. The fare is Y35 one way, or Y70 for a round trip.

Buses come down the mountain hourly between 1 and 5 pm, but don't count on the schedule or the seats.

Central Route

On this route you'll see a bewildering catalogue of bridges, trees, towers, inscribed stones, caves, pavilions and temples (complex and simplex). Half the trip, for Chinese people at least, is seeing the colossal amount of calligraphy scoring the stones en route. Taishan, in fact, functions as an outdoor museum of calligraphic art, with the prize items being the Diamond Sutra (or Stone Valley Sutra) and the Moya Bei at the summit, which commemorates an imperial sacrifice.

The climb proper begins at **No 1 Archway Under Heaven** at the mountain base. Behind that is a stone archway overgrown with wisteria and inscribed 'the place where Confucius began to climb'. **Red Gate Palace**, standing out with its wine-coloured walls, is the first of a series of temples dedicated to the Princess of the Azure Clouds, who was the daughter of the god of Taishan. It was rebuilt in 1626.

Doumu Hall was first constructed in 1542 and has the more poetic name of Dragon Spring Nunnery; there's a teahouse inside.

Continuing through the tunnel of cypresses known as Cypress Cave is **Horse Turn Ridge**, where Emperor Zhen Zong had to dismount and continue by sedan chair because his horse refused to go further – smart horse! Another emperor rode a white mule up and down the mountain and the beast died soon after the descent (it was posthumously given the title of general and its tomb is on the mountain).

Zhongtianmen (Midway Gate to Heaven) is the second celestial gate. Beyond Cloud Bridge and to the right is the place where Emperor Zhen Zong pitched his overnight tents. A little way on is **Five Pine Pavilion** where, one day back in 219 BC, Emperor Qin Shihuang was overtaken by a violent storm and was sheltered by the kind pines. He promoted them to the 5th rank of minister; though the three you see are, of course, not the same ministers!

On the slopes higher up is the **Welcoming Pine**, with a branch extended as if to shake hands. Beyond that is the **Archway to Immortality**. It was believed that those passing through it would become celestial beings. From here to the summit, emperors were carried in sedan chairs – eat your hearts out!

The third celestial gate is **Nantianmen** (South Gate to Heaven). That, and the steep pathway leading up to it, are symbolic of Taishan and of Shandong itself; the picture pops up on covers of books and on maps.

On arrival at Taishan Summit *(dàidǐng)* you will see the **Wavelength Pavilion** (a radio and weather station) and the **Journey to the Stars Gondola** (the cable car). If you continue along Paradise Rd, you'll come to **Sunset Statue** (where a frozen photographer sits slumped over a table with the view beyond dutifully recorded in sunrises and clipped in front of him).

Welcome to Taishan Shopping Centre. Here you'll see fascinating Chinese antics on the precarious rock lookouts – go and check out the **Bridge of the Gods**, which is a couple of giant rocks trapped between two precipices.

The grandmothers' long march ends at the **Azure Clouds Temple** *(bìxiácí)*, where small offerings of one sort or another are made to a bronze statue, once richly decorated. The iron tiling on the buildings is intended to prevent damage by strong wind currents, and on the bronze eaves are *chiwen*, ornaments meant to protect against fire. The temple is absolutely splendid, with its location in the clouds, but its guardians are a trifle touchy about you wandering around, and parts of it are inaccessible. Little is known of the temple's history but we do know that it cost a fortune to restore or make additions, as was done in the Ming and Qing dynasties. The bronze statuette of the Princess of the Azure Clouds is in the main hall.

Perched on the highest point (1545 metres) of the Taishan plateau is **Jade Emperor Temple**, with a bronze statue of a Taoist deity. In the courtyard is a rock inscribed with the elevation of the mountain. In front of the temple is the one piece of calligraphy that you can really appreciate – the **Wordless Monument**. This one will leave you speechless. One story goes that it was set up by Emperor Wu 2100 years ago – he wasn't satisfied with what his scribes came up with, so he left it to the viewers' imaginations.

The main sunrise vantage point is a springboard-shaped thing called **Gongbei Rock**; if you're lucky, visibility could extend to over 200 km, as far as the coast. The sunset slides over the Yellow River side. At the rear of the mountain is **Rear Rocky Recess**, one of the better-known spots for viewing pine trees; there are some ruins tangled in the foliage. It's a good place to ramble and lose the crowds for a while.

Western Route

On this route there's nothing of note in the way of structures, but there's considerable variation in scenery, with orchards, pools and flowering plants. The major scenic attraction is **Black Dragon Pool**, which is just below **Longevity Bridge** (between the bridge and West Brook Pavilion) and is fed by a small waterfall. Swimming in the waters are some rare, red-scaled carp which are occasionally cooked for the rich. Mythical tales revolve around this pool, said to be the site of underground carp palaces and of magic herbs that turn people into beasts. Worth looking into is the **Puzhao Monastery**, founded 1500 years ago along the base of the mountain.

Places to Stay & Eat

The *Zhongtianmen Guesthouse* (☎ 822-6740) *(zhōngtiānmén bīnguǎn)* is a halfway house at Zhongtianmen. Rooms are comfortable but expensive at Y280 for a double. Provided no-one brings a portable stereo or karaoke system, it's a very quiet place.

The *Shenqi Guesthouse* (☎ 822-3866) *(shénqì bīnguǎn)* is a three-star hotel on the summit costing Y350 for a double – expensive, but you're paying for the view. There are also quads with beds for Y60/80 but these are often full. The hotel provides extra blankets and rents out fashionable People's Liberation Army-style overcoats. There's even an alarm bell which tells you when to get up for sunrise. (If you wonder where all those amazing old women go, it seems that there are lodgings – possibly former monasteries – tucked down side trails. They are off limits for foreigners.)

Snacks, drinks and the like are sold on the mountain trail, and the hotel has a pricey restaurant.

QUFU
(qūfù)

As well as being the birthplace of Confucius, Qufu, with its blending of stone, wood and fine imperial architecture, is a worthwhile day trip from Tai'an. Unfortunately, mass tourism has robbed this place of much of its charm, and unless you enjoy being besieged by countless vendors of useless souvenirs, it is not a place to linger.

Following a 2000-year-old tradition, there are two fairs a year in Qufu – in spring and autumn – when the place comes alive with craftspeople, healers, acrobats, pedlars, poor peasants and that new symbol of modernisation, camera-clicking tourists.

The direct descendants of Confucius, the Kong family, resided in Qufu until 1948.

Information

The CITS office (☎ 412-491) is in the Xingtan Hotel, ridiculously located in a remote area south of town far from anything of interest to travellers. Just as well, since this CITS caters almost exclusively to tour groups. There are no train or air tickets on sale here, since neither comes to Qufu (though there is a railway station nearby –

see Getting There & Away further on in this section).

Confucius Temple
(kǒng miào)

The temple started out as a simple memorial hall and mushroomed into a complex one-fifth the size of Qufu. It is laid on a north-south axis, and is over one km long. The main entrance is **Star Gate** *(língxīngmén)* at the south, which leads through a series of portals emblazoned with calligraphy. The third entrance gateway, with four bluish characters, refers to the doctrines of Confucius as heavenly bodies which move in circles without end; it is known as the Arch of the Spirit of the Universe.

QUFU 曲阜	
1	Tomb of Confucius 孔墓
2	Hall for Memorial Ceremony 祭奠堂
3	Ruins of the Ancient Lu State 鲁国址
4	Zhougong Temple 周公庙
5	Yanhui Temple 颜庙
6	Confucius Mansions 孔府
7	Drum Tower 鼓楼
8	Queli Hotel 阙里宾舍
9	Bell Tower 钟楼
10	Tourist Souvenir Market 旅游事业市场
11	Restaurants & Street Market 餐厅，商业街
12	Star Gate 棂星门
13	Yingshi Binguan (Hotel) 影视宾馆
14	Bus Station 汽车站
15	Luyou Binguan (Hotel) 旅游宾馆
16	Confucius Mansions Hotel 孔府饭店

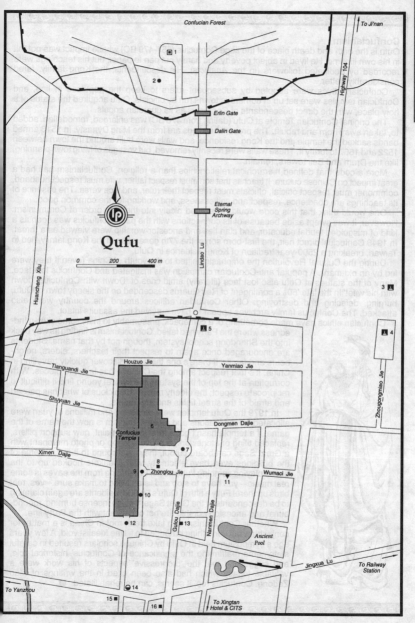

Confucian Forest

To Ji'nan

Highway 104

■ 1

● 2

Erlin Gate

Dalin Gate

Eternal
Spring
Archway

Qufu

0   200   400 m

Lindao Lu

Huancheng Xilu

▲ 3

▲ 4

Zhouyongmiao Jie

○

▲ 5

Tianguandi Jie

Houzuo Jie

Yanmiao Jie

Shuyuan Jie

Dongmen Dajie

Confucius
Temple

6

Ximen Dajie

● 7

8

● 9   Zhonglou Jie

Wumaci Jie

● 10

11

Gulou Dajie

Nanmen Dajie

● 12

13

Ancient
Pool

● 14

Jingxua Lu

To Railway
Station

To Yanzhou

15 ■

16 ■

To Xingtan
Hotel & CITS

THE EAST

Confucianism

Qufu is the birth and death place of the sage Confucius (551-479 BC) whose impact was not felt in his own lifetime. He lived in abject poverty and hardly put pen to paper, but his teachings were recorded by dedicated followers (in the *Analects*). His descendants, the Kong family, fared considerably better.

Confucian ethics were adopted by subsequent rulers to keep the populace in line, and Confucian temples were set up in numerous towns run by officials. Qufu acquired the status of a holy place, with the direct descendants of Confucius as its guardian angels.

The original Confucian Temple at Qufu (dating from 478 BC) was enlarged, remodelled, added to, taken away from and rebuilt. The present buildings are from the Ming Dynasty. In 1513 armed bands sacked the temple and the Kong residence, and walls were built around the town between 1522 and 1567 to fortify it. These walls were recently removed, but vestiges of Ming town planning, like the Drum and Bell towers, remain.

More a code that defined hierarchical relationships than a religion, Confucianism has had a great impact on Chinese culture. It teaches that son must respect father, wife must respect husband, commoner must respect official, officials must respect their ruler, and vice versa. The essence of its teachings are obedience, respect and selflessness, and working for the common good.

One would think that this code would have fitted nicely into the new order of Communism. However, it was swept aside because of its connections with the past. Confucius was seen as a kind of misguided feudal educator, and clan ties and ancestor-worship were viewed as a threat. In 1948 Confucius' direct heir, the first-born son of the 77th generation of the Kong family, fled to Taiwan, breaking a 2500-year tradition of Kong residence in Qufu.

During the Cultural Revolution the emphasis shifted to the youth of China (even if they were led by an old man). A popular anti-Confucian campaign was instigated and Confucius lost face. Many of the statues at Qufu also lost face (literally) amid cries of 'Down with Confucius, down with his wife!' In the late '60s a contingent of Red Guards descended on the sleepy town of Qufu, burning, defacing and destroying. Other Confucian edifices around the country were also attacked. The Confucius family archives appear to have survived the assaults intact.

Confucian ethics have made something of a comeback, presumably to instil some civic-mind-

edness where the Party had failed. Confucianism is finding its way back into the Shandong school system, though not by that name. Students are encouraged once again to respect their teachers, elders, neighbours and family. If there's one thing you discover quickly travelling in China, it's that respect among the Chinese has fallen to pieces. With corruption at the top of the system, the cynical young find it difficult to reciprocate respect; the elderly remain suspicious of what has passed and afraid of the street fights and arguments.

In 1979 the Qufu temples were reopened and millions of yuan were allocated for renovations and repairs. Tourism is now the name of the game; if a temple hasn't got a fresh coat of paint, new support pillars, replaced tiling or stonework, a souvenir shop or photo merchant with a Great Sage cardboard cutout, they'll get round to it soon. Some of the buildings even have electricity, with speakers hooked up to the eaves playing soothing flute music. Emanating from the eaves is some real music – you have to stop and listen twice to make sure – yes, real birds up there! Fully a fifth of Qufu's 50,000 residents are again claiming to be descendants of the Great Sage, though incense burning, mound-burial and ancestor-worship are not consistent with the Party line.

Whether Confucianism can take fresh root in China is a matter for conjecture, but something is needed to fill the idealist void. A few years ago a symposium held in Qufu by Chinese scholars resulted in careful statements reaffirming the significance of Confucius' historical role, and suggesting that the 'progressive' aspects of his work were a valuable legacy which had also been cited in the writings of Mao Zedong. Confucius too, it seems, can be rehabilitated. ■

Throughout the courtyards of the Confucius Temple, the dominant features are the clusters of twisted pines and cypresses, and row upon row of steles. The tortoise tablets record in archaic Chinese such events as temple reconstructions, great ceremonies or tree plantings. There are over 1000 steles in the temple grounds, with inscriptions from Han to Qing times – the largest such collection in China. The creatures bearing the tablets of praise are actually not tortoises but *bixi*, dragon offspring legendary for their strength. The tablets at Qufu are noted for their fine calligraphy; a rubbing once formed part of the dowry for a Kong lady.

Roughly halfway along the north-south axis is the **Great Pavilion of the Constellation of Scholars**, a triple-roofed, Jin Dynasty, wooden structure of ceremonial importance dating from 1190. Further north through Dacheng Gate and to the right is a juniper planted by Confucius – or so the tablet in front of it claims. The small Xingtan Pavilion up from that commemorates the spot where Confucius is said to have taught under the shade of an apricot tree.

The core of the Confucian complex is **Dacheng Hall** which, in its present form, dates back to 1724; it towers 31 metres high on a white marble terrace. The reigning sovereign permitted the importation of glazed yellow tiling for the halls in the Confucius Temple, and special stones were brought in from Xishan. The craftspeople did such a good job on the stone dragon-coiled columns that it is said they had to be covered with silk when the emperor came to Qufu lest he felt that the Forbidden City's Taihe Hall paled in comparison.

The hall was used for unusual rites in honour of Confucius. At the beginning of the seasons and on the great sage's birthday, booming drums, bronze bells and musical stones sounded from the hall as dozens of officials in silk robes engaged in 'dignified dancing' and chanting by torchlight. The rare collection of musical instruments is displayed, but the massive stone statue of the bearded philosopher has disappeared – presumably a casualty of the Red Guards.

At the extreme north end of the Confucius Temple is **Shengjidian**, a memorial hall containing a series of stones engraved with scenes from the life of Confucius and tales about him. They are copies of an older set which date back to 1592.

In the eastern compound of the Confucian Temple, behind the Hall of Poetry and Rites, is **Confucius' Well** (a Song-Ming reconstruction) and the **Lu Wall**, where the ninth descendant of Confucius hid the sacred texts during the anti-Confucian persecutions of Emperor Qin Shihuang. The books were discovered again in the Han Dynasty (206 BC-220 AD) and led to a lengthy scholastic dispute between those who followed a reconstructive version of the last books, and those who supported the teachings in the rediscovered ones.

Confucius Mansions
(kǒng fǔ)

Built and rebuilt many times, the Mansions date from the 16th-century Ming Dynasty, with recent patchwork. The place is a maze of 450 halls, rooms and buildings, and getting around it requires a compass – there are all kinds of side passages to which servants were once restricted.

The Mansions are the most sumptuous aristocratic lodgings in China, indicative of the Kong family's former great power. From the Han to the Qing dynasties, Confucius' descendants were ennobled and granted privileges by the emperors. They lived like kings themselves, with 180-course meals, servants and consorts. Confucius even picked up some posthumous honours.

The town of Qufu, which grew around the Mansions, was an autonomous estate administered by the Kongs, who had powers of taxation and execution. Emperors could drop in to visit – the Ceremonial Gate near the south entrance was opened only for this event. Because of royal protection, copious quantities of furniture, ceramics, artefacts, costumery and personal effects survived and some may be viewed. The Kong family archives, a rich legacy, also seem to have

THE EAST

survived, and extensive renovations of the complex have been made.

The Mansions are built on an 'interrupted' north-south axis. Grouped by the south gate are the former administrative offices (taxes, edicts, rites, registration and examination halls). To the north on the axis is a special gate – Neizhaimen – that seals off the residential quarters (used for weddings, banquets and private functions). East of Neizhaimen is the Tower of Refuge where the Kong clan could gather in case the peasants turned nasty. It has an iron-lined ceiling on the ground floor, and a staircase that is removable to the 1st floor. Grouped to the west of the main axis are former recreational facilities (studies, guest rooms, libraries and small temples). To the east is the odd kitchen, ancestral temple and the family branch apartments. Far north is a spacious garden with rockeries, ponds and bamboo groves. Kong Decheng, the last of the line, lived in the Mansions until the 1940s, when he hightailed it to Taiwan.

Confucian Forest
(kǒng lín)

North of the Confucius Mansions, about 2½ km up Lindao Lu, is the Confucian Forest, the largest artificial park and best-preserved cemetery in China. This timeworn route has a kind of 'spirit-way' lined with ancient cypresses.

It takes about 40 minutes to walk or 15 minutes to go by pedicab, or you can take bus No 1 (infrequent!). On the way, look into the Yanhui Temple *(yán miào)* which is off to the right and has a spectacular dragon head embedded in the ceiling of the main hall, and a pottery collection. The route to the forest passes through the Eternal Spring Archway, its stone lintels decorated with coiled dragons, flying phoenixes and galloping horses dating from 1594 (Ming Dynasty). Visitors, who needed permission to enter, had to dismount at the Forest Gates.

The pine and cypress forest of over 20,000 trees, planted by followers of Confucius, covers 200 hectares and is bounded by a wall 10 km long. Buried here is the Great Sage

himself and all his descendants. Flanking the approach to Confucius' Tomb are a pair of stone panthers, griffins and larger-than-life guardians. The Confucian tumulus is a simple grass mound enclosed by a low wall, and faced with a Ming Dynasty stele. Nearby are buried his immediate sons. Scattered through the forest are dozens of temples and pavilions, and hundreds of sculptures, tablets and tombstones.

Mausoleum of Shao Hao
(shǎo hào líng)

Shao Hao was one of the five legendary emperors supposed to have ruled China 4000 years ago. His pyramidal tomb, four km north-east of Qufu, dates from the Song Dynasty. It is made of large blocks of stone, 25 metres wide at the base and six metres high, and has a small temple on top. Some Chinese historians believe that Qufu was built on the ruins of Shao Hao's ancient capital, but evidence to support this is weak.

Places to Stay

The PSB in Qufu takes a relaxed view of where foreigners put up for the night, though many hotels will not allow you to stay in the really grotty rooms. These hotels have no English signs, however, and are not that easy to find. The best bet is to follow one of the hotel touts.

Close to the bus station, on the corner of Datong Lu, is the *Confucius Mansions Hotel* (☎ 412-985) *(kǒngfǔ fàndiàn)*. Doubles cost Y180, but it is also worth checking to see if the dormitory is still operating. There should be beds available for Y50.

Qufu's main tourist abode is the *Quelí Hotel* (☎ 411-300) *(quèlǐ bīnshè)*, 1 Queli Jie, where doubles start at Y280. The *Xingtan Hotel* (☎ 411-719) *(xìngtán bīnguǎn)* was built with tour groups in mind and as such is badly located (far in the south of town) for individual travellers.

Places to Eat

The food in Qufu is generally of poor quality. The best deals for low prices and reasonable quality seem to be the street markets. The ouristy market just south of Confucius Mansions is one spot, but there is a wider selection on Zhonglou Jie, east of the Queli Hotel.

The name of the Great Sage is invoked in unexpected ways – Sankong (Three Confucius) Beer is the local brew. Can Confucius Fried Chicken be far behind?

Things to Buy

In Qufu Confucius means business. Next to the Confucius Temple, go-get-it vendors peddle everything from Confucius T-shirts to Great Sage cigarette lighters. Elsewhere, it is standard Chinese souvenir fare - the kind of stuff that pops up everywhere, from Yangshuo to Suzhou.

Getting There & Away

Bus Buses and minibuses run between Qufu and the railway station about once every 30 minutes throughout the day. The large public buses cost just Y2 but are packed to the hilt – it's much better to take the minibuses for Y7. The minibuses run later, sometimes as late as 11 pm if there are passengers. Minibuses will also serve as taxis if you pay them enough. There are also minibuses to Yanzhou, but these are somewhat less frequent.

There are direct buses from Qufu to Tai'an (Y12, two hours, eight departures daily) and direct buses from Qufu to Ji'nan (three hours, 13 departures daily).

The bus station in Qufu looks almost like a temple from the outside – you might have trouble recognising it if you don't know the Chinese characters for *qiche zhan*. On the inside it's like a typical Chinese bus station, though there is more tourist junk for sale here than usual. Two nice things we can say about the place: it's usual to give the best seats to foreigners (bus tickets have seat numbers) and the staff force everyone to line up and board in numerical order. We're not sure if this is an expression of Confucianism, but compared with the usual wrestling competitions at Chinese bus stations, it's certainly much appreciated!

Train The situation is a little confused – there's no railway station in Qufu itself. When a railway project for Qufu was first brought up, the Kong family petitioned for a change of routes, claiming that the trains would disturb the Great Sage's tomb. They won – the clan still had pull in those days – and the nearest tracks were routed to Yanzhou, 13 km to the west of Qufu. But the railway builders didn't give up, and finally constructed another station about six km east of Qufu, though still nothing in Qufu itself.

When you want to buy a train ticket to Qufu, just say 'Qufu' and if the ticket clerk says '*méiyǒu*' (no such place), try saying 'Yanzhou'. Qufu (Yanzhou) is on the line from Beijing to Shanghai. There's a fair selection of trains, but some special express trains don't stop here; others arrive at inconvenient times like midnight. Qufu is somewhat less than two hours by train from Tai'an, three from Ji'nan, about seven from Nanjing, and about nine hours from Kaifeng.

CAAC is next in line to disturb the sage's tomb, with an airport planned at Qufu. But for the moment, the trains are the fastest way of getting here.

Getting Around

There are only two bus lines and service is not frequent. Probably most useful for travellers is bus No 1 which travels along Gulou Dajie and Lindao Lu in a north-south direction, connecting the bus station area with the Confucian Forest. Bus No 2 travels east-west along Jingxuan Lu. Pedicabs are a more reliable way of getting around, but expect the usual price hassles.

ZOUXIAN

(*zōuxiàn*)

This is the home town of Mengzi (formerly spelled Mencius; 372-289 BC) who is regarded as the first great Confucian philosopher. He developed many of the ideas of Confucianism as they were later understood. Zouxian is an excellent place to visit – far more relaxed than Qufu. Zouxian is just to the south of Qufu, a short hop on the train from Yanzhou or by bus from Qufu. A visit can easily be done as a day-trip.

ZIBO
(zībó)

Zibo is a major coal-mining centre on the railway line east of Ji'nan. Over two million people live in this city, which is noted for its glassworks and porcelain. Not far from Zibo, at Linzhi, a pit of horses dating back some 2500 years was excavated. They are older than the horses at Xi'an and with one big difference – they are the remains of actual animals. So far, 600 horse skeletons, probably dating from Qi times (479-502 AD), have been discovered. Horses and chariots indicated the strength of the state, so it's not surprising that they were buried in the course of their master's funeral. About 90 horse skeletons are on display in the pit.

QINGDAO
(qīngdǎo)

Qingdao (the name means 'Green Island') is a city on the Bohai Gulf that is being developed as a resort town. For foreign travellers the chief attraction is the city's colonial architecture, the legacy of a German concession. For the most part, however, the city's attractions are overrated. It's not an unpleasant place, but it is also not wildly exciting either. Many of the old German dwellings are in bad shape; others have been torn down to make way for architecturally unexciting hotel and office developments.

History

Qingdao was a simple fishing village until German troops landed in 1897 (the killing of two German missionaries having given them sufficient pretext). In 1898 China ceded the

---

QINGDAO 青岛

PLACES TO STAY

1 Friendship Hotel & Store
   友谊饭店, 商店
2 Peace Hotel
   和平宾馆
4 Jingshan Hotel
   晶山宾馆
10 Qingdao Hotel
   青岛饭店
16 Railway Hotel & Railway Station
   铁道大厦, 火车站
17 Overseas Chinese Hotel
   华侨饭店
18 Zhanqiao Guesthouse
   栈桥宾馆
20 Dongfang Hotel
   东方饭店
23 Xinhao Hill Hotel
   信号山迎宾馆
24 Haiqing Hotel
   海青宾馆
25 Rongshao Hotel
   荣韶宾馆

27 Yellow Sea Hotel & China Eastern Airlines
   黄海饭店,
   东方航空公司
28 Huiquan Dynasty Hotel & CITS
   汇泉王朝大酒店,
   中国国祭旅行社
29 Badaguan Hotel
   八大关宾馆
31 Haitian Hotel
   海天大酒店

PLACES TO EAT

7 Chunhelou Restaurant
   春和楼饭店
8 Muslim Restaurant
   清真餐厅
11 KFC
   肯德鸡

OTHER

3 Passenger Ferry Terminal
   青岛港客运站
5 Brewery
   青岛啤酒厂

6 Xinhua Bookstore
   新华书店
9 Catholic Church
   天主教堂
12 Main Post Office
   邮电局
13 Bank of China
   中国银行
14 PSB
   公安局外事科
15 Local Ferry
   青岛轮渡站
19 Huilan Pavilion
   回澜阁
21 Protestant Church
   基督教堂
22 Longshan Underground Market
   龙山地下商业
26 Qingdao Museum
   青岛博物馆
30 Zhanshan Temple
   湛山寺

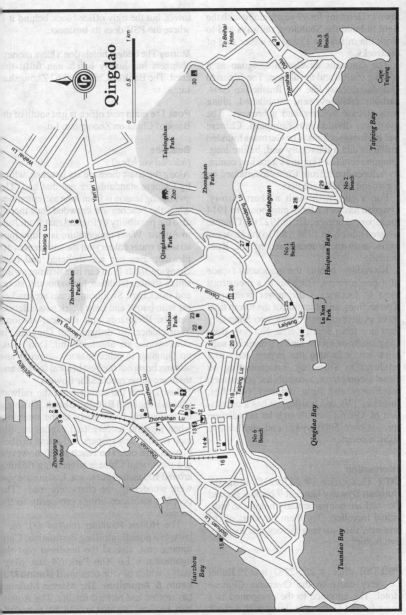

Qingdao

0   0.5   1 km

To Beihai
Hotel

No 3
Beach

Cape
Taiping

Taiping Bay

No 2
Beach

Badaguan

No 1
Beach

Huiquan Bay

Lu Xun
Park

Qingdao Bay

No 6
Beach

Tuandao Bay

Jiaozhou Bay

Zhonggang
Harbour

Zhongshan Lu

Xinhao
Park

Qingdaoshan
Park

Zhongshan
Park

Taipingshan
Park

Zhushuishan
Park

Zoo

Weihai Lu

Yan'an Lu

Liaoning Lu

Liaoning Lu

Liuning Lu

Moyang Lu

Daxue Lu

Wendeng Lu

Zhanshan

Dilin

Jiaozhou Lu

Xuzhou Lu

Shanxi Lu

Taiping Lu

Laiyang
Lu

Sichuan Lu

Shanxi Lu

town to Germany for 99 years, along with the right to build the Shandong railways and to work the mines for 15 km on either side of the tracks.

The Germans developed Qingdao as a coaling station and naval base. The Ji'nan to Qingdao railway line was finished in 1904, harbour facilities were established, along with electric lighting and a brewery. The town was divided into European, Chinese and business sections. The Germans founded missions and a university and, before long, Qingdao rivalled Tianjin as a trading centre, its independence from China maintained by a garrison of 2000 soldiers.

For a city with such a short history, Qingdao has seen a lot of ping pong. In 1914 the Japanese occupied it, in 1922 the Chinese wrested it back. In 1938 it fell to the Japanese again, only to be recaptured by the Kuomintang.

Nowadays, behind the innocuous façade of a beach resort, Qingdao is a monstrous mess of factories – the newer ones sport Korean flags, an indication of the recent tidal wave of investment flowing into Shandong Province from South Korea. Not only does Qingdao brew up the nation's drinking supplies but it is also the largest industrial producer in Shandong, concentrating on diesel locomotives, automobiles, generators, machinery and light industry (watches, cameras, TVs and textiles). It has a population of 1½ million, though its jurisdiction spreads over 5900 sq km and another 3½ million people.

Information

CITS This office (☎ 287-9215) is in the Huiquan Dynasty Hotel at 9 Nanhai Lu, but the staff are not particularly helpful to individual travellers. Try them for tours of the brewery, shell-carving factory and locomotive factory.

PSB This office (☎ 286-2787) is at 29 Hubei Lu, very close to the Overseas Chinese Hotel. The entrance to the compound is a beautiful old German building with a clock tower, but the ugly office block behind it i[s] where the PSB does its business.

Money The budget hotels don't have money changers but luxury hotels can fulfil thi[s] need. The Bank of China is at 62 Zhongsha[n] Lu.

Post The main post office is just south of th[e] Bank of China on Zhongshan Lu.

Beaches
(*hǎishuǐ yùchǎng*)

Along the coast there are six beaches, whic[h] by Chinese standards are not that bad. Th[e] swimming season is from June to Septembe[r] when the beaches are crowded, but there'[s] also the possibility of fog and rain from Jun[e] to August. Water temperature is soupy (an[d] so is the water colour) but the sea breezes ar[e] pleasant. Beaches are sheltered and hav[e] changing sheds (you can hire demure swim[-]suits), shower facilities, photo booths, store[s] and snack bars. Swimming areas are marke[d] off with buoys and have shark nets, lifeboa[t] patrols, lifeguards and medical stations[.] Your chances of drowning at Qingdao, i[n] other words, are absolutely nil. Don't pas[s] up Qingdao in other seasons – spring an[d] autumn bring out the best in local foliage an[d] there are some spectacular flowers.

Just around the corner from the railwa[y] station is the **No 6 Bathing Beach**. This stri[p] is particularly lively early in the morning[,] when joggers, fencers, taiji exponents, ol[d] men reading newspapers and a few Frisbe[e] players turn out. The beach itself, howeve[r,] is a mess, with Chinese advertising floatin[g] around 100 metres out to sea. Just in case yo[u] were wondering, the characters read: 'Th[e] people's insurance brings prosperity to th[e] people'.

The **Huilan Pavilion** (*huílán gé*), on [a] jetty, is a popular strolling destination. Con[-]tinuing east, around the headland past th[e] lighthouse is Lu Xun Park (*lǔ xùn gōng yuán*), which has the combined **Marine Mu[-]seum & Aquarium**. The Marine Museu[m] has stuffed and pickled sea life. The Aquar[-]ium has sea life that would be better of[f] stuffed or pickled. Almost next door is the **Naval Museum** *(hǎijūn bówùguǎn)*, which features naval hardware and lots of add-on entry charges – strictly for naval enthusiasts and the very bored.

The **No 1 Bathing Beach** is, as its name suggests, the premier beach in Qingdao. It has a 580-metre stretch of fine sand, lots of facilities, multi-coloured bathing sheds, restaurants, ridiculous dolphin statues, and high-rise blocks rather like a Chinese version of Australia's Surfers Paradise.

Past the Huiquan Dynasty Hotel and the Ocean Research Institute is the **Badaguan** *(bādàguān)* area, well known for its sanatoriums and exclusive guesthouses. The spas are scattered in lush wooded zones off the coast, and the streets, named after passes (Badaguan literally means Eight Passes Area), are each lined with a different tree or flower. On Jiayuguan Lu it's maples and on Zhengyangguan it's myrtles. The locals simply call them Peach St, Snowpine St or Crab Apple St. The gardens here are extremely well groomed.

As you head out of the Eight Passes Area, Nos 2 and 3 bathing beaches are just east, and the villas lining the headlands are exquisite. **No 2 Beach** is smaller, quieter and more sheltered than No 1 Beach and is preferred when No 1 Beach is overloaded. Facing No 2 Beach are sanatoriums – but at the western headland is a naval installation, so don't take short cuts.

At the eastern end of the No 2 Beach is the former German Governor's Residence. This castle-like villa, made of stone, is a replica of a German palace. It is said to have cost 2,450,000 taels of silver. When Kaiser Wilhelm II got the bill, he immediately recalled the extravagant governor and sacked him.

Xinhao Park

(xìnhàoshān gōngyuán)

Qingdao's city parks are among the best in China, and probably more worthwhile than the crowded and polluted beaches.

Xinhao Park harbours one of Qingdao's most astounding pieces of German architec-

ture, the **Xinhao Hill Hotel** *(xìnhàoshān yíng bīnguǎn)*. At the highest point in the park are the three red golfball-shaped towers known as the mushroom buildings *(mógu lóu)*. Climb up here for an impressive view – it will give you a perspective of just how many old German buildings with red-tiled roofs still exist!

Just across the street from the eastern side of the park on Daxue Lu is what looks like a temple complex, but proves to be the **Qingdao Museum** *(qīngdǎo bówùguǎn)*, with a collection of Yuan, Ming and Qing paintings.

The **Longshan Underground Market** *(lóngshān dìxià shāngyè jiē)* is an amazing shopping arcade built in a tunnel right under the park. The entrance to the arcade is on Longshan Lu at the south-west corner of Xinhao Park near the Protestant church.

Other Parks

North of the Huiquan Dynasty Hotel is **Zhongshan Park** *(zhōngshān gōngyuán)*, which covers 80 hectares, has a teahouse and temple and in springtime is a heavily wooded profusion of flowering shrubs and plants. The city zoo *(dòngwùyuán)* is also within the park's boundaries.

The mountainous area north-east of Zhongshan Park is called **Taipingshan Park** *(tàipíngshān gōngyuán)*, an area of walking paths, pavilions and the magnificent Zhanshan Temple *(zhànshān sì)*. This is the best place in town for hiking.

Just west of Zhongshan Park is **Qingdaoshan Park** *(qīngdǎoshān gōngyuán)*. A notable feature of this hilly park is Jingshan Fort *(jīngshān pàotái)*.

Churches

(jiàotáng)

Off Zhongshan Lu, up a steep hill, is a structure now known simply as the Catholic Church *(tiānzhǔ jiàotáng)* – its double spires can be spotted a long way off. The church is active and services are held on Sunday mornings.

Perhaps not surprisingly, the other main church in town is the Protestant Church *(jīdū jiàotáng*), a single-spired structure with a clock tower. This church is near the southwest entrance of Xinhao Park by the Longshan Underground Market.

Brewery
(qīngdǎo píjiǔchǎng)

No guide to Qingdao would be complete without a mention of the brewery, tucked into the industrial part of town, east of the main harbour. Tsingtao Beer (Tsingtao is the old spelling for Qingdao) has gained a worldwide following.

The brewery was established early this century by the Germans who still supply the parts for 'modernisation' of the system. The flavour of the finest brew in Asia comes from the mineral waters of nearby Laoshan. Unfortunately, unless you are on a tour, it's almost impossible to get into the brewery for a look.

Places to Stay – bottom end

Particularly during the peak summer period it can be very difficult to find cheap accommodation in Qingdao. Try to arrive early in the day and be prepared to run all over town. Most foreigners seem to base themselves close to the ferry terminal.

The *Railway Hotel* (☎ 286-9963) *(tiědào dàshà)*, 2 Tai'an Lu, adjoins the railway station. The 24-storey hotel has 224 rooms, including dormitories from Y48. These are very difficult to get into, however, and you will probably be forced into a standard double, which costs Y240.

The *Friendship Hotel* (☎ 282-8165) *(yǒuyì bīnguǎn)* is next door to the Passenger Ferry Terminal on Xinjiang Lu. It has doubles at Y82 (no bathroom) and six-bed rooms for Y150 (the staff are reluctant to rent out rooms by the bed). Doubles with bathroom and air-con are Y140. To get there from the railway station, first take bus No 6 along Zhongshan Lu to the northern terminal, where it turns around. Then walk back under an overhead bridge near the terminal, turn right, and – if you can find the stop – take the No 21 bus for one stop north. If you can't

find it then just walk the last stretch. Alternatively, a taxi costs Y7.

The *Peace Hotel* (☎ 283-0154) *(hépíng bīnguǎn)* is down an alley and to the left next to the passenger ferry terminal – almost behind the Friendship Hotel. Doubles with no bathroom cost Y110, with bathroom Y270 to Y300. It's a reasonably popular place and has a restaurant.

Finally, not far from No 1 Beach, the *Huiyuan Hotel* (☎ 288-4233) *(huìyuán dàjiǔdiàn)*, 1 Qixia Lu, has a limited number of budget rooms in an annex next to a kindergarten. It's a quiet pension-like place and showers are available in the Huiyuan Hotel at 7 pm. A bed in a simple double costs Y40. Ask for the *hòupèilóu* at the front desk of the Huiyuan. From the station, take a No 6 bus to the *xiǎoyúshān gōngyuán* stop. A taxi costs Y7.

Places to Stay – middle

Most of the accommodation that should be mid-range is dangerously upmarket in price, particularly in peak season. Off season, it's always worth asking for a discount.

Just across the road from Lu Xun Park is the rambling *Rongshao Hotel* (☎ 287-0710) *(róngshào bīnguǎn)*. The rooms are nothing special, but the setting is great. Standard doubles start at Y280 and range up to Y480. Not far away is the *Haiqing Hotel* *(hǎiqīng bīnguǎn)*, a poorly run but well located Chinese-style hotel with doubles at Y210 and Y240.

The *Qingdao Hotel* (☎ 289-1888) *(qīngdǎo fàndiàn)* is at 53 Zhongshan Lu but the entrance is around the corner on Qufu Lu. It barely makes it into the mid-range bracket and certainly doesn't provide value for money – doubles cost Y304 and Y348.

Places to Stay – top end

Qingdao is swarming with top-end accommodation, most of it overpriced and aimed at Chinese on expense accounts and Chinese tourists who think having a holiday involves blowing your life savings on a hotel room.

Badaguan Hotel (bādàguān bīnguǎn), 19 Shan-haiguan Lu (☎ 387-2168; fax 387-1383). From US$80, villas also available.

Beihai Hotel (běihǎi bīnguǎn) (☎ 386-5832). Bad location and overpriced at US$80 for a standard double.

Dongfang Hotel (dōngfāng fàndiàn), 4 Daxue Lu (☎ 286-5888; fax 286-2741). Doubles from Y580.

Haitian Hotel (hǎitiān dàjiǔdiàn), 39 Zhanshan Dalu (☎ 386-6185). Doubles from US$90.

Huanghai Hotel (huánghǎi fàndiàn), 75 Yan'an 1-Lu (☎ 287-0215; fax 287-9795). Doubles from US$80, significant off-peak discounts available.

Huiquan Dynasty Hotel (huìquán wángcháo dàjiǔdiàn), 9 Nanhai Lu (☎ 287-3366; fax 287-1122). Singles US$80, doubles US$115.

Overseas Chinese Hotel (huáqiáo fàndiàn) (☎ 287-9738), 72 Hunan Lu. Good location, doubles from Y550.

Xinhao Hill Hotel (xìnhàoshān yíng bīnguǎn), 26 Longshan Lu in Xinhaoshan Park (☎ 286-6209; fax 286-1985). Renovated German mansion, doubles from US$80.

Zhanqiao Guesthouse (zhànqiáo bīnguǎn), 31 Taiping Lu (☎ 287-0936). Doubles from US$60.

Places to Eat

Qingdao is a tourism city and restaurants are one thing you don't have to look very hard to find. There are good snacks sold on the streets, mainly in the form of kebabs. The local speciality is squid on a stick (diànkǎo yóuyú).

The waterfront area is brimming with restaurants, from No 6 Beach almost all the way to No 1 Beach. The area around No 1 Beach is the best place to come up with cheap eats, however. Try the HL Restaurant for cheap dumplings, though like everywhere else there is no English menu.

Zhongshan Lu is also a good area for restaurants. Just up the road from the prominent KFC (yes, you can get your fingers greasy in Qingdao too) is a Muslim restaurant, the Qīngzhēn Fàndiàn. It's up a sidestreet on the left; there's no English sign but you can't miss the Islamic script. Again, there's no English menu, but try the yángròu paomó, a dish that involves breaking cha-patti-like bread into a bowl and then adding a mutton broth – delicious and cheap.

Look out for the Taiwanese-style noodle shop (táiwān niúròu dàwáng) a few doors down from the Muslim restaurant; its name

literally means the Taiwan Beef Noodle King. The beef noodles are not as authentic as they might be, but they're not bad all the same.

The Chunhelou (☎ 282-7371) (chūnhélóu), 146 Zhongshan Lu, is one of this street's famous eating establishments. It's fairly expensive and only really worth considering if there is a group of you.

Getting There & Away

Air There are so-called international 'charter flights' which follow a regular published schedule – five times weekly between Qingdao and Hong Kong (Y2600). Direct flights between Seoul and Qingdao will be operating by the time you have this book in your hands.

Domestic flights connect Qingdao to Beijing, Changsha, Chengdu, Guangzhou, Haikou, Harbin, Kunming, Ningbo, Shanghai, Shenzhen, Wuhan and Xiamen, among other destinations.

The CAAC office (☎ 288-6047) is at 29 Zhongshan Lu. The booking office of China Eastern Airlines (☎ 287-0215) is adjacent to the Yellow Sea Hotel at 75 Yan'an 1-Lu. The Huiquan Dynasty Hotel also has an air ticketing office.

Bus Buses and minibuses depart from the area next to the massive Hualian Building just across from the railway station. Buses to Yantai (Y25) take 3½ hours for the journey and depart throughout the day. There are also early morning services to Ji'nan (Y50) which take 4½ hours (which is cheaper and faster than by train). Sleeper buses to Shanghai and Beijing are also available.

Train All trains from Qingdao go through the provincial capital of Ji'nan, except for the direct Qingdao to Yantai trains. There are two direct trains daily to Beijing (17 hours). Sleepers can be bought with some persistence at the railway station, and quite frankly you don't have much choice – there is nowhere else to buy tickets. Bear in mind, if you are travelling to Yantai or Ji'nan it is quicker and cheaper to take a bus.

Direct trains to Shenyang (about 26 hours) pass through Ji'nan and Tianjin, sidestepping Beijing. There are direct trains to Xi'an (about 31 hours) which continue to Lanzhou and Xining.

Trains to Dalian and to Shanghai (about 24 hours) will take almost the same time as the boats. There is one train daily to Shanghai. The train is much more expensive than the boat – there's a foreigners' mark-up on the train but not on the boat.

Train No 506 to Yantai departs from Qingdao at 10.10 am, arriving in Yantai at 4.26 pm (over six hours!). It's faster going the other way – train No 508 departs Yantai at 4.46 pm and arrives in Qingdao at the awful time of 8.52 pm. Doing this route by bus is quicker and more convenient.

Boat There are regular boats from Qingdao to Dalian, Shanghai and Inch'ǒn in South Korea. Bookings for all of these can be made at the passenger ferry terminal in the north of town. Inch'ǒn ferries can also be booked at the Huiquan Dynasty Hotel.

The boat to Dalian (on the Liaoning Peninsula), across the Bohai Gulf, is the best way to get there from Qingdao. (It's a long way by train.) The boat takes 19 hours and leaves every three days. Fares start at Y42. There are also boats from Yantai to Dalian – see the Yantai section for details.

Boats from Qingdao to Shanghai leave every four days and take about 26 hours. Fares range from Y53 in 5th class to Y287 in special class. The ship is clean and comfortable, and has friendly and helpful staff.

Getting Around
To/From the Airport Qingdao's airport is 30 km from the city. Taxi drivers ask Y100 (or whatever they think you might possibly pay) for the journey. Buses leave from the China Eastern Airlines ticket office, but *ask* first about the schedule – it's not frequent.

Bus Most transport needs can be catered for by the bus No 6 route, which starts at the north end of Zhongshan Lu, runs along it to within a few blocks of the main railway station and then east to the area above No 3 Beach. The No 6 bus stop closest to the main railway station seems to be the one on Zhongshan Lu, just north of the street leading to the Catholic Church.

Taxi Qingdao taxis are among the cheapest in China; Y7 will get you almost anywhere around town.

AROUND QINGDAO

Forty km north-east of Qingdao is **Laoshan** (*láoshān*), a mountain area covering some 400 sq km. It's an excellent place to go hiking or climbing – the mountain reaches an elevation of 1133 metres. Historical sites and scenic spots dot the area, and the local product is Laoshan mineral water. The Song Dynasty Taiqing Palace (a Taoist monastery) is the central attraction; there are paths leading to the summit of Laoshan from there. With such a large area there's plenty to explore. Due north of the Taiqing Palace is Jiushui, noted for its numerous streams and waterfalls.

An early morning bus runs from Qingdao Railway Station to the Taiqing Palace. Other travel agents around Qingdao have more extended itineraries, including an overnight stop in Laoshan, but it's probably hard to crash these tours unless you speak Chinese.

YANTAI
(yāntái)
Yantai, alias Zhifu (at one time spelled Chefoo), is a busy ice-free port on the northern coast of the Shandong Peninsula. It's a very dull town, and the only real reason to come here would be to take a boat to Pusan in South Korea.

History
Like Qingdao, Yantai started life as a defence outpost and fishing village. It opened for foreign trade in 1862, but had no foreign concessions. Several nations, Japan and the USA among them, had trading establishments here and Yantai was something of a resort area at one time. Since 1949 the port and naval base at Yantai have been expanded

THE EAST

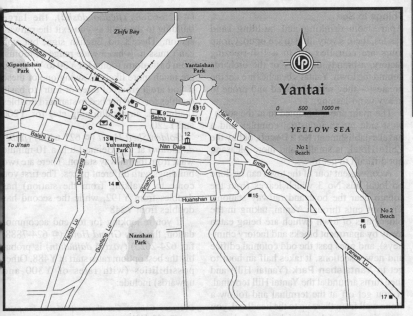

Yantai

Zhifu Bay

Zhifu Lu

Xipaotaishan Park

Yantaishan Park

Baishi Lu

To Ji'nan

Dahuayang Lu

Yuhuangding Park

Nan Dajie

Xinanhe

Huanshan Lu

Nanshan Park

Guolang Lu

Beima Lu

Hai'an Lu

YELLOW SEA

No 1 Beach

Erma Lu

No 2 Beach

Yanwei Lu

0   500   1000 m

---

and, apart from fishing and trading, the town is a major producer of wines, spirits and fruits. Yantai means Smoke-Terrace: wolf-dung fires were lit on the headland to warn fishing fleets of approaching pirates.

Information

There is a CTS office (☎ 624-5625) in the crumbling edifice next to the Overseas Chinese Guesthouse, but it's unlikely the staff will be able help you.

Things to See

Apart from drinking and building sand castles, there's very little to see or do. Group tours are corralled off to a fish-freezing factory, a brandy distillery or the orchards behind the town. Yantai's beaches are not the greatest – they're unsheltered and prone to heavy wind-lashing.

The main one is hemmed in at the south-west side by an industrial complex and a naval establishment. **No 2 Beach**, out by the Zhifu Hotel, is smaller and more pleasant, but difficult to get to.

A convenient tour of the town can be done on local bus No 3 which leaves from the square near the boat and railway stations. The bus cuts through Yantai, taking in the older parts of town (which are being eaten away by apartment blocks and factory chimneys), and goes past the odd colonial edifice and newer sections. It takes half an hour to get to **Yantaishan Park** (Yantai Hill) and then turns around at the Yantai Hill terminal. If you get off at the terminal and follow a stone wall from there up to the headland, you get a nice view of the naval dockyards, heavy shipping and even navy manoeuvres. There's a plush hotel here, and though the sign says 'Welcome You', this doesn't apply to foreigners.

If you carry on round the headland, you hit the esplanade at **No 1 Beach** where there is some distinctively European architecture – former foreign trading or resort housing. You can continue to the bus No 1 route, which will take you back into town.

Tiny **Yuhuangding Park** has a pleasant pagoda (sometimes featured on glossy tourist brochures) and not much else.

The **museum** (bówùguǎn) is not world famous but you can kill 20 minutes there if you have nothing better to do.

Places to Stay

Wandering around looking for accommodation in Yantai is a miserable experience. Most of the official foreigners' accommodation is badly located and overpriced (what a surprise!).

The best deal in town is the *Tiedao Hotel*

(☎ 625-6588) (tiědào dàshà), the large building to the right as you exit the railway station. There's no English sign, but you can't miss it. It has a wide range of rooms, from basic dorm rooms for Y30 to Y40 (you are much more likely to swing one of these if you are a group of three or four) to basic doubles for Y50 per bed to standard doubles (bathroom, air-conditioning etc) for Y200 and Y220.

Golden Shell Hotel (☎ 621-6495) (jīnbèi dàjiǔdiàn) at 172 Beima Lu is a 10-minute walk from the railway station. There are two buildings with different prices. The first you come to (walking from the station) has doubles from Y192, while the second has doubles from Y248

If you're looking for top-end accommodation, the *Asia Grand Hotel* (☎ 624-7888; fax 624-2625) (yàxìyà dàjiǔdiàn) is probably the best option; rates start at Y488. Other possibilities (with rates of Y300 and upwards) include:

Overseas Chinese Guesthouse (huáqiáo bīnguǎn)
　(☎ 622-4431)
Yantai Hotel (yāntái dàjiǔdiàn) (☎ 624-8468)
Yuhuangding Hotel (yùhuángdǐng bīnguǎn)
　(☎ 624-4401)
Zhifu Hotel (zhīfu bīnguǎn) (☎ 624-8421)

Places to Eat

The railway station has a good selection of restaurants. The 'fast-food' restaurant next to the Tiedao Hotel is a reliable option, though like the other restaurants here there is no English menu. The Golden Shell Hotel has a reasonably good restaurant. Otherwise, there is not much to get excited about.

Getting There & Away

Air There are direct flights to a surprisingly large number of destinations, including Beijing, Chengdu, Chongqing, Guangzhou, Haikou, Harbin, Ji'nan, Nanjing, Shanghai, Shantou, Shenzhen, Wuhan, Xiamen and Xi'an. Flight bookings can be made next door to the Tiedao Hotel or at the CAAC office (☎ 622-5908).

Bus There are frequent buses and minibuses between Yantai and Qingdao. The large buses cost Y25, though they often ask for an extra Y5 for 'large luggage', which seems to include a backpack. Minibuses cost Y30. In both Qingdao and Yantai, buses congregate in front of the railway stations and depart when full. The journey takes 3½ hours on an excellent highway. Taxis do the trip for Y60 per person (four per taxi) and take 2½ hours.

Train The Yantai-Qingdao train (only one daily and slower than the bus) terminates in Qingdao – it does not carry on to Ji'nan. By contrast, there are four trains daily in each direction between Yantai and Ji'nan (about eight hours), bypassing Qingdao completely and continuing on to Tianjin, Beijing or Shanghai. There are express trains to Beijing (about 17½ hours) and a direct but slow train to Shanghai.

Boat At the ferry office next to the railway station it is possible to book tickets for boats to Dalian, Tianjin and Pusan (South Korea). Ferries for Dalian leave daily, for Tianjin every two days and for Pusan weekly (every Wednesday). Ticket prices for the Pusan ferry start at US$120. Tickets for the Pusan ferry can also be booked at a booth next to the Peace Hotel in Qingdao.

Getting Around
Yantai's airport is 15 km south of the city. A taxi should cost about Y70 from the railway station area. Airport buses cost Y10. The city bus system is fairly useless and taxis rarely use their meters. Try not to stray too far from the railway station and ferry terminal.

PENGLAI
(pénglái)
About 65 km north-west of Yantai by road is the coastal castle of Penglai, a place of the gods which is often referred to in Chinese mythology. The castle *(pénglái gé)* is perched on a clifftop overlooking the sea and is about 1000 years old. Like much of China's architecture, the castle had been allowed to fall apart, but recently has been fully restored. It's fair to say that this is China's most beautiful castle, and is worth a visit if you've got the time and don't mind the out-and-back ride to get there.

Besides the castle, Penglai is famous for an optical illusion which the locals claim appears every few decades. The last full mirage seen from the castle was in July 1981 when two islands appeared, with roads, trees, buildings, people and vehicles. This phenomenon lasted about 40 minutes.

There are some pebbly beaches in the area, but Penglai isn't considered ideal for bathing.

The most popular place to stay is the *Penglaige Guesthouse* (☎ 643-192) *(pénglǎigé bīnguǎn)* on Zhonglou Beilu. Some small restaurants cater for the domestic tourist market, with seafood being the speciality.

Penglai is a two-hour bus ride from Yantai. Minibuses to Penglai depart from in front of the Yantai Railway Station, though not very frequently.

WEIHAI
(wēihǎi)
About 60 km east of Yantai by road is the obscure port city of Weihai. The British had a concession here around the turn of the century, though little remains today to remind you of its colonial heritage.

Weihai is hardly a place to linger in – it not only lacks scenery, but is horribly expensive. Nevertheless, the port sees plenty of tourist traffic thanks to the opening of a passenger ferry service to Inch'ŏn in South Korea.

Few foreigners spend any length of time in Weihai, but many transit through here in both directions. It's preferable to arrive in Weihai by boat rather than depart this way – otherwise you may get stuck here for the night while waiting for the boat to depart the next day. Since the boat from Korea arrives in Weihai at 9 am, you'll have no problem getting a bus out of town – we suggest you do so as soon as possible. Hotel prices for foreigners are ridiculously expensive at Y500 and upwards. At that price it would be cheaper to fly to Korea.

The introductory Getting There & Away chapter has all the details of the ferry (prices, timetable and so forth).

If you arrive in Weihai without having purchased a ferry ticket in advance, the place to go is CITS (☎ 522-6210), at 44 Dongcheng Lu. Minibuses run from the ferry terminal in Weihai directly to Yantai and Qingdao.

WEIHAI

Jiangsu 江苏

With China's most productive land, Jiangsu *(jiāngsū)* is symbolic of agricultural abundance and has long been known as the land of 'fish and rice' – these two pictographs are even contained in the original Chinese character for the province. The southern part of Jiangsu lies within the Yangzi Basin, a tapestry landscape of greens, yellows and blues contrasting with whitewashed farm houses. Woven into this countryside is a concentration of towns and cities with one of the highest levels of industrial output in China.

As far back as the 16th century, the towns on the Grand Canal set up industrial bases for silk production and grain storage, and are still ahead of the rest of the nation. While heavy industry is based in Nanjing and Wuxi, the other towns concentrate more on light industry, machinery and textiles. They're major producers of electronics and computer components, and haven't been blotted out by the scourges of coal mining or steelworks. Today southern Jiangsu is increasingly being drawn into the rapidly expanding economy of nearby Shanghai.

The stretch from Nanjing down to Hangzhou in Zhejiang Province is heavily touristed, but north of the Yangzi there's not really much to talk about; it's a complete contrast – decayed, backward and lagging behind the rest of the province. In the north the major port is at Lianyungang and there's a big coal works in Xuzhou.

Jiangsu is hot and humid in summer, yet has overcoat temperatures in winter (when visibility can drop to zero). Rain or drizzle can be prevalent in winter, but it's gentle rain, adding a misty soft touch to the land. The natural colourings can be spectacular in spring. Heavy rains fall in spring and summer, but autumn is fairly dry.

NANJING
(nánjīng)

Nanjing (population approximately 4.5 million) is one of China's more attractive

Population: 65 million
Capital: Nanjing
Highlights:
- Nanjing's Zijinshan, with its wealth of historical sights
- Suzhou – redevelopment is rapidly taking its toll, but for the moment Suzhou is still a city of canals and classical gardens
- Lake Taihu, a large, shallow lake with some 90 islands

major cities. It sports a long historical heritage and has twice served briefly as the nation's capital, first in the early years of the Ming Dynasty (1368-1644) and second as the capital of the Republic in the early years of the 20th century. Most of Nanjing's major attractions are reminders of the city's former glory under the Ming.

The construction work that is changing the face of all modern China seems to have affected Nanjing less than many other eastern cities. It remains a place of broad boulevards lined with trees – these give shady relief from the oppressive summer heat, for which Nanjing is justifiably known as one of China's 'three furnaces'.

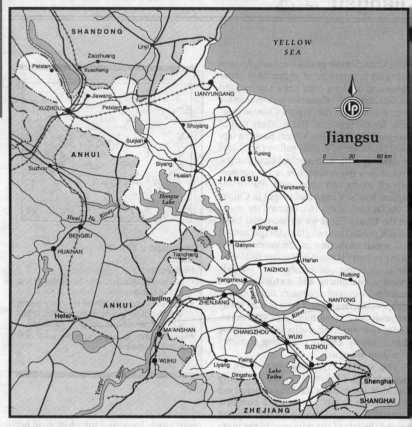

Jiangsu

0   30   60 km

History

The Nanjing area has been inhabited for about 5000 years, and a number of prehistoric sites have been discovered in or around the city. Recorded history, however, begins in the Warring States Period (453-221 BC), when Nanjing emerged as a strategic object of conflict. The arrival of a victorious Qin Dynasty (221-207 BC) put an end to this, allowing Nanjing to prosper as a major administrative centre.

The city's fortunes took a turn for the worse in the 6th century, however, when it was successively rocked by floods, fires,

peasant rebellions and military conquest. With the advent of the Sui Dynasty (589-618) and the establishment of Xi'an as imperial capital, Nanjing was razed, its historical heritage reduced to ruins. Although it enjoyed a period of prosperity under the long-lived Tang Dynasty, it gradually slipped into obscurity.

Until the 14th century, that is: in 1356, a peasant rebellion led by Zhu Yuanzhang against the Mongol Yuan Dynasty (1271-1368) was successful. The peasants captured Nanjing, and 12 years later claimed the Yuan capital, Beijing. Zhu Yuanzhang took the name of Hong Wu and set himself up as the first emperor of the Ming Dynasty, with Nanjing as its capital. A massive palace was built and huge walls were erected around the city.

Nanjing's glory as imperial capital was short-lived. In 1420, the second Ming emperor, Yong Le, moved the capital back to Beijing. From this time, Nanjing's fortunes rose and declined variously as a regional centre, but it was not until the 19th and 20th centuries that the city again entered the centre stage of Chinese history.

In the 19th century, the Opium Wars brought the British to Nanjing, and it was here that the first of the 'unequal treaties' were signed, opening several Chinese ports to foreign trade, forcing China to pay a huge war indemnity, and officially ceding the island of Hong Kong to Britain. Just a few years later, Nanjing became the Taiping capital during the Taiping Rebellion (1851-64), which succeeded in taking over most of southern China. In 1864, the combined forces of the Qing army, British army and various European and US mercenaries had surrounded the city. They laid siege for seven months, before finally capturing it and slaughtering the Taiping defenders.

In the 20th century, Nanjing has variously been the capital of the Republic; the site of the worst war atrocity in Japan's assault on China – the 1937 'Rape of Nanjing' – in which as many as 300,000 people may have died; and the Kuomintang capital from 1945 to 1949, when the Communists 'liberated' the city and made China their own.

Orientation

Nanjing lies entirely on the southern bank of the Yangzi River, bounded in the east by Zijinshan (Purple Mountain). The centre of town is a traffic circle called Xinjiekou, where some of the hotels, including the Jinling Hotel, and most tourist facilities are located. Nanjing Railway Station and the main long-distance bus station are in the far north of the city. The historical sights, including the Sun Yatsen Mausoleum, Linggu Temple and the tomb of the first

Ming emperor Hong Wu, are mainly around Zijinshan, on Nanjing's eastern fringe.

The city has experienced long periods of prosperity – evident in the numerous buildings which successive rulers built – and their tombs, steles, pagodas, temples ·and niches lay scattered throughout the city. If you can get hold of a copy, *In Search of Old Nanking* by Barry Till and Paula Swart (Joint Publishing Company, Hong Kong, 1982) will give you a thorough rundown. Unfortunately, much has been destroyed or allowed to crumble into ruins.

Information

CITS This office (☎ 334-6444) is at 202/1 Zhongshan Beilu. It is basically an air-ticketing office, and its tourist services are directed largely at the tour-group market.

Money The Bank of China is at 3 Zhongshan Donglu, just east of Xinjiekou traffic circle. You can also change money at the Jinling and Central hotels.

Post & Telecommunications The main post office is at 19 Zhongshan Lu, just north of Xinjiekou. The more upmarket tourist hotels also offer postal services. There is a large telephone and telegram office just north of the Drum Tower traffic circle.

Maps Several different versions of the local transport map are available from newspaper kiosks and street hawkers around Nanjing.

Early Remains

Nanjing has been inhabited since prehistoric times. Remains of a prehistoric culture have been found at the site of today's Drum Tower in the centre of the city and in surrounding areas. About 200 sites of small clan communities, mainly represented by pottery and bronze artefacts dating back to the late Shang and Zhou dynasties, have been found on both sides of the Yangzi.

In 212 AD, towards the end of the Eastern Han period, the military commander in charge of the Nanjing region built a citadel

THE EAST

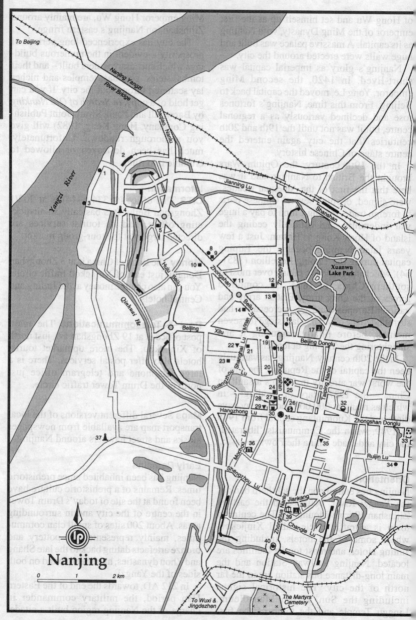

To Beijing

Nanjing Yangzi River Bridge

Yangzi River

Daqiao Nanlu

Jianning Lu

Shanshan Lu

Xuanwu Lake Park

Zhongshan Lu

Hehu Beilu

Qinhuai He

Beijing Xilu

Zhongyang Lu

Baixia Lu

Yunnan Lu

Beijing Donglu

Shanghai Lu

Guangzhou Lu

Zhongshan Lu

Taiping Nanlu

Hangzhong Lu

Zhongshan Donglu

Ruijin Lu

Mochou Lu

Shengzhou Lu

Zhonghua Nanlu

Jiankang Lu

Changle Lu

To Wuxi & Jingdezhen

The Martyrs' Cemetery

Nanjing

0   1   2 km

To Qixia

To Shanghai

Zijinshan

● 41

▣ 43

🏛 44

▣ 42

45

To Yangshan & Tangshanzhen

46

NANJING 南京

PLACES TO STAY

5   Shuangmenlou Hotel
    双门楼宾馆
9   Hongqiao Hotel
    虹桥饭店
10 Nanjing Hotel
    南京饭店
12 Xuanwu Hotel
    玄武饭店
14 Yishi Hotel
    仪事园
21 Nanjing University Foreign Students'
    Dormitory
    南京大学的外国留学生宿舍
23 Nanjing Normal University Nanshan
    Hotel
    南京师范大学的南山宾馆
24 Central Hotel
    中心大酒店
27 Fuchang Hotel
    福昌饭店
30 Jinling Hotel
    金陵饭店

PLACES TO EAT

11 KFC
    肯德鸡
15 Maxiangxing Restaurant
    马祥兴菜馆
20 Sprite Outlet
    梧州酒家
22 Black Cat Cafe
    黑猫餐馆
29 Black Cat Cafe II
    新黑猫餐馆
35 Sichuan Restaurant
    四川酒家

OTHER

1   No 4 Dock
    四号码头
2   Nanjing West Railway Station
    南京西站
3   Zhongshan Dock
    中山码头
4   Monument to the Crossing of the
    Yangzi River
    渡江纪念碑

(Continued)

on Qinglingshan in the west of Nanjing. At that time the mountain was referred to as Shitoushan (Stone Head Mountain) and so the citadel became known as the Stone City. The wall measured over 10 km in circumference. Today, some of the red sandstone foundations can still be seen.

Ming City Wall

Nanjing enjoyed its golden years under the Ming, and there are numerous reminders of the period to be found. One of the most impressive is the Ming city wall measuring over 33 km – the longest city wall ever built in the world. About two-thirds of it still stands. It was built between 1366 and 1386, by over 200,000 labourers. The layout is irregular, an exception to the usual square walls of these times, because much of it is built on the foundations of earlier walls which took advantage of strategic hills. Averaging 12 metres high and seven metres wide at the top, the wall was built of bricks supplied from five Chinese provinces. Each brick had stamped on it the place it came from, the overseer's name and rank, the brickmaker's name and sometimes the date. This was to ensure that the bricks were well made; if they broke they had to be replaced. Some stone bricks were used, but on the whole they were clay.

Ming City Gates

Some of the original 13 Ming city gates remain, including Heping Gate (hépíng mén) in the north and Zhonghua Gate (zhōnghuá mén) in the south. The city gates were heavily fortified and, rather than being the usual weak points of the defences, they were defensive strongholds. The Zhonghua Gate has four rows of gates, making it almost impregnable; it could house a garrison of 3000 soldiers in vaults in the front gate building. Today some of these vaults are used as souvenir shops and cafes, and are wonderfully cool in summer. Zhonghua Gate can be visited, but Heping Gate is now used as a barracks.

Ming Palace Ruins
(mínggùgōng)

Built by Hong Wu, the Ming Palace is said to have been a magnificent structure after which the Imperial Palace in Beijing was modelled. Basically all that remains of it is five marble bridges lying side by side and known as the Five Dragon Bridges, the old ruined gate called Wu Men and the enormous column bases of the palace buildings. There are also some stone blocks and a little stone screen carved with animals and scenery.

The palace suffered two major fires in its first century and was allowed to fall into ruins after the Ming court moved to Beijing. Later the Manchus looted it. During the Taiping Rebellion, bombardments by Qing and Western troops finished it off.

Drum Tower
(gǔlóu)

Built in 1382, the Drum Tower lies roughly in the centre of Nanjing, on a traffic circle on Beijing Xilu. Drums were usually beaten to give directions for the change of the night watches and, in rare instances, to warn the populace of impending danger. The tower originally contained numerous drums and other instruments used on ceremonial occasions. Only one large drum remains today. The ground floor is used for exhibitions of paintings and calligraphy.

Bell Tower
(zhōnglóu)

North-east of the Drum Tower, the Bell Tower houses an enormous bell, cast in 1388 and originally situated in a pavilion on the west side of the Drum Tower. The present tower dates from 1889 and is a small two-storey pavilion with a pointed roof and upturned eaves.

Chaotian Palace
(cháotiān gōng)

Chaotian Palace was originally established in the Ming Dynasty as a school for educating noble children in court etiquette. Most of today's buildings, including the centrepiece

of the palace, a Confucian temple, date from 1866 when the whole complex was rebuilt.

Outside, on the small lane running between the canal and the southern wall of the palace, is a market selling bric-a-brac. On weekends, rows of men sit here at tables playing *xiàngqí* (Chinese chess). At the end of a tiny alley immediately behind the palace is the Jiangsu Province Kunju Theatre *(jiāngsū shěng kūnjùyuàn)*, where excellent – if rather infrequent – performances are held. *(Kunju* is a regional form of classical Chinese opera which developed in the Suzhou-Hangzhou-Nanjing triangle. It is similar to, but slower than, Peking opera and is performed with colourful and elaborate costumes.)

The palace entrance gate is on Mochou Lu on bus route No 4, two stops west from Xinjiekou.

Taiping Museum
(tàipíng tiānguó lìshǐ bówùguǎn)

Hong Xiuquan, the leader of the Taipings, had a palace built in Nanjing, but the building was completely destroyed when Nanjing was taken in 1864. All that remains is a stone boat in an ornamental lake in the Western Garden, inside the old Kuomintang government buildings on Changjiang Lu.

The museum has an interesting collection of documents, books and artefacts relating to the rebellion. Most of the literature is copied, the originals being kept in Beijing. There are maps showing the northward progress of the Taiping army from Guangdong, Hong Xiuquan's seals, Taiping coins, cannon balls, rifles and other weapons, and texts which describe the Taiping laws on agrarian reform, social law and cultural policy. Other texts describe divisions in the Taiping leadership, the attacks by the Manchus and foreigners, and the fall of Nanjing in 1864.

The museum is open daily from 8.30 am to 5.50 pm.

Fuzimiao
(fūzǐ miào)

Fuzimiao is in the south of the city, centred on the site of an ancient Confucian temple. It was a centre of Confucian study for over

1500 years. Fuzimiao has been damaged and rebuilt repeatedly, and what you see here today are newly restored late Qing Dynasty structures or wholly new buildings reconstructed in traditional style. The main Temple of Confucius is behind them on the small square in front of the canal. Five minutes' walk north-west from here are the Imperial Examination Halls, where scholars spent months – or years – in tiny cells studying Confucian classics in preparation for civil service examinations.

Today, Fuzimiao has become Nanjing's main amusement quarter and is a particularly lively and crowded place on weekends and public holidays. There are restaurants, silk stores, souvenir shops, art exhibitions, tacky side-shows in old halls and a bookseller stocking ancient Chinese manuscripts.

You can get to the Fuzimiao area from Nanjing's west railway station by bus No 16, from the docks by trolley-bus No 31 and from Xinjiekou by bus No 2.

Memorial of the Nanjing Massacre
(dàtúshā jìniànguǎn)

The exhibits at the memorial hall document the atrocities committed by Japanese soldiers against the civilian population during the occupation of Nanjing in 1937. They include pictures of actual executions, many taken by Japanese army photographers, and a gruesome viewing hall built over a mass grave of massacre victims. Also on display is furniture used at the signing of Japan's surrender to China – the disproportionately smaller and lower table and chairs given to the Japanese officers carried an unmistakable message.

The exhibits conclude on a more optimistic note, with a final room dedicated to the post-1945 Sino-Japanese reconciliation. The memorial hall is open daily from 8.30 am to 5.00 pm. It's in the city's south-western suburbs on bus route No 7.

Xuanwu Lake Park
(xuánwǔ gōngyuán)

This park is almost entirely covered by the waters of a large urban lake, but you can walk along causeways or take a boat out to its central forested islands, where there are tea-houses, a zoo and a children's fun park. A long path goes around the shores of Xuanwu Lake, beside the old city walls for much of its length. The park's central location makes it a convenient place to escape the hustle – but not necessarily the bustle – of central Nanjing. You can enter Xuanwu Lake Park from the main gate off Zhongyang Lu.

Nanjing Yangzi River Bridge
(nánjīng chángjiāng dàqiáo)

One of the great achievements of the Communists, and one of which they are justifiably proud, is the Yangzi River Bridge at Nanjing, which was opened on 23 December 1968. One of the longest bridges in China, it's a double-decker with a 4500-metre-long road on top and a 6700-metre-long railway line below.

The story goes that the bridge was designed and built entirely by the Chinese after the Russians marched out and took the designs with them in 1960. Given the immensity of the construction it really is an impressive engineering feat, before which there was no direct rail link between Beijing and Shanghai.

Monument to the Crossing of the Yangzi River
(dùjiāng jìniàn bēi)

Standing in the north-west of the city on Zhongshan Beilu, this monument erected in April 1979 commemorates the crossing of the river on 23 April 1949 and the capture of Nanjing from the Kuomintang by the Communist army. The characters on the monument are in the calligraphy of Deng Xiaoping.

Nanjing Museum
(nánjīng bówùguǎn)

Just west of Zhongshan Gate on Zhongshan Donglu, the Nanjing Museum houses an array of artefacts from Neolithic times through to the Communist period. The main building was constructed in 1933 with yellow-glazed tiles, red-lacquered gates and columns, in the style of an ancient temple.

An interesting exhibit is the burial suit made of small rectangles of jade sewn together with silver thread, dating from the Eastern Han Dynasty (25-220 AD) and excavated from a tomb discovered in the city of Xuzhou in northern Jiangsu Province. Other exhibits include bricks with the inscriptions of their makers and overseers from the Ming city wall, drawings of old Nanjing, an early Qing mural of old Suzhou and relics from the Taiping Rebellion. The museum is open from 9 am to 5 pm.

Just east of the museum is a section of the Ming city wall with steps leading up to it from the road. You can walk along the top only as far as Qianhu Lake, where a section of wall has collapsed into the water.

Tomb of Hong Wu
(míng xiàolíng)

This tomb lies east of the city on the southern slope of Zijinshan. Construction began in 1381 and was finished in 1383; the emperor died at the age of 71 in 1398. The first section of the avenue leading up to the mausoleum is lined with stone statues of lions, camels, elephants and horses. There's also a mythical animal called a *xiezhi* which has a mane and a single horn on its head; and a *qilin* which has a scaly body, a cow's tail, deer's hooves and one horn. The second section of the tomb alley turns sharply northward and begins with two large hexagonal columns. Following the columns are pairs of stone military men wearing armour, and these are followed by pairs of stone civil officials. The pathway turns again, crosses some arched stone bridges and goes through a gateway in a wall which surrounds the site of the mausoleum.

As you enter the first courtyard, a paved pathway leads to a pavilion housing several steles. The next gate leads to a large courtyard where you'll find the 'Altar Tower' or 'Soul Tower' – a mammoth rectangular stone structure. To get to the top of the tower, go to the stairway in the middle of the structure. Behind the tower is a wall, 350 metres in diameter, which surrounds a huge earth

mound. Beneath this mound is the tomb vault of Hong Wu, which has not been excavated.

Sun Yatsen Mausoleum
(zhōngshān líng)

For many Chinese, a visit to Sun Yatsen's tomb on the slopes of Zijinshan just east of Nanjing is something of a pilgrimage. Sun is recognised by the Communists and the Kuomintang alike as the father of modern China. He died in Beijing in 1925, leaving behind an unstable Chinese republic. He had wished to be buried in Nanjing, no doubt with greater simplicity than the Ming-style tomb which his successors built for him. But less than a year after his death, construction of this immense mausoleum began.

The tomb itself lies at the top of an enormous stone stairway, 323 metres long and 70 metres wide. At the start of the path stands a stone gateway built of Fujian marble, with a

Lion statue at Sun Yatsen Mausoleum.

roof of blue-glazed tiles. The blue and white of the mausoleum were meant to symbolise the white sun on the blue background of the Kuomintang flag.

The crypt is at the top of the steps at the rear of the memorial chamber. A tablet hanging across the threshold is inscribed with the 'Three Principles of the People', as formulated by Dr Sun: nationalism, democracy and people's livelihood. Inside is a seated statue of Dr Sun. The walls are carved with the complete text of the *Outline of Principles for the Establishment of the Nation* put forward by the Nationalist government. A prostrate marble statue of Sun seals his coffin.

Zijinshan
(zǐjīnshān)

Most of Nanjing's historical sights – the Sun Yatsen Memorial and Tomb of Hong Wu included – are scattered over the southern slopes of Zijinshan, a high forested hill at the city's eastern fringe.

The **Beamless Hall** is one of the most interesting buildings in Nanjing. In 1381, when Hong Wu was building his tomb, he had a temple on the site torn down and rebuilt a few km to the east. Of this temple only the Beamless Hall (so called because it is built entirely of bricks) remains. The structure has an interesting vaulted ceiling and a large stone platform where Buddhist statues used to be seated. In the 1930s the hall was turned into a memorial to those who died in the 1926-28 revolution. One of the inscriptions on the inside wall is the old Kuomintang national anthem.

A road leads either side of the Beamless Hall and up two flights of steps to the **Pine Wind Pavilion**, originally dedicated to the goddess of mercy as part of the Linggu Temple. Today it houses a small shop and teahouse.

The **Linggu Temple** *(línggǔ sì)* and its memorial hall to Xuan Zang is close by; after you pass through the Beamless Hall, turn right and follow the pathway. Xuan Zang was the Buddhist monk who travelled to India and brought back the Buddhist

scriptures. Inside the memorial hall is a 13-storey wooden pagoda model which contains part of his skull, a sacrificial table and a portrait of the monk.

Close by is the **Linggu Pagoda** *(línggǔ tǎ)*, which was built in the 1930s under the direction of a US architect as a memorial to Kuomintang members who died in the 1926-28 revolution. It's a nine-storey octagonal building 60 metres high.

Day Tour

It's possible to combine all of Zijinshan's sights into a single day trip that includes the Tomb of Hong Wu and the Sun Yatsen Mausoleum. You can take bus No 20 from the Drum Tower and get off at the western end of the Avenue of Stone Animals, two stops before the bus reaches the Tomb of Hong Wu. Alternatively, take bus No 9 from just west of Xinjiekou (opposite the Jinling Hotel) and get off at the avenue's eastern end, one stop before the Sun Yatsen Mausoleum. From there you can continue uphill on foot (or in summer by shuttle bus) to the tomb, the mausoleum and the sights around Linggu Pagoda.

Places to Stay – bottom end

The cheapest beds are at the *Nanjing University/Foreign Students' Dormitory (nánjīng dàxué/wàiguó liúxuéshēng sùshè)*, a large white-tiled building on Shanghai Lu, just south of Beijing Xilu. Doubles with communal facilities, including kitchen, cost Y50 or Y55 per bed. Beds in a double with attached bathroom cost Y110. The best way to get there is to take the No 13 bus from the railway station or the long-distance bus station, or you can take a No 3 trolley-bus down Zhongshan Lu and get off just after Beijing Lu.

In the unlikely event that the Nanjing University dormitory is full, the *Nanjing Normal University/Nanshan Hotel (nánjīng shīfàn dàxué nánshān bīnguǎn)* tends to take the overflow, though it is slightly more expensive. To get there from the Nanjing University dorm, walk half a km south along

Shanghai Lu. Turn right into a short market lane, then take the first road left to the main gate of Nanjing Normal University. The hotel is 500 metres inside the campus compound, up to the left from the large grassy quadrangle.

Places to Stay – middle

Most Nanjing accommodation is middle to top end in price; in fact, it's fairly difficult to find a decent room for under Y350. One exception to this rule is the *Shuangmenlou Hotel* (☎ 880-5961) *(shuāngménlóu bīnguǎn)* at 185 Huju Beilu. It's a rambling garden-style hotel, rather inconveniently located in the north-west of town. The cheapest doubles are in an as yet unrenovated old wing and cost Y150. Renovated rooms range in price from Y370 to Y750. The simplest way to get there from the railway station is to take a taxi for around Y10. The unrenovated wing is likely to be renovated soon, which means prices may have increased by the time you arrive here.

Better located is the *Yishi Hotel* (☎ 332-6826) *(yìshì yuán)* on Zhongshan Lu, close to the intersection of Yunnan Lu. It sees very few foreign visitors but offers good value for money with doubles at Y280 and Y310.

The *Hongqiao Hotel* (☎ 330-1466) *(hóngqiáo fàndiàn)* caters largely to tour groups and only just creeps into the middle category. Further renovations were under way at the time of writing that will probably push room rates into the upper end of the market. Doubles cost from Y360 to Y480. Across the road at 259 Zhongshan Beilu you'll find the *Nanjing Hotel* (☎ 330-2302) *(nánjīng fàndiàn)*, the city's oldest tourist establishment. The cheapest doubles cost Y338, and there are other more upmarket rooms available for Y508.

Places to Stay – top end

The *Xuanwu Hotel* (☎ 330-3888; fax 663-9624) *(xuánwǔ fàndiàn)*, a tower block at 193 Zhongyang Lu, opposite the Jiangsu Exhibition Hall, is one of the cheaper top-end options. It may not quite hit the spot as

a luxury hotel, but the smaller corner rooms are good value at US$64. Standard doubles range from US$80 to US$100, while executive suites cost US$120.

The *Central Hotel* (☎ 440-0888; fax 441-4194) *(zhōngxīn dàjiǔdiàn)* at 75 Zhongshan Lu, near the corner of Huaqiao Lu, has rooms from US$100.

The 36-storey *Jinling Hotel* (☎ 445-5888; fax 664-3396) *(jīnlíng fàndiàn)*, at Xinjiekou, is probably the best of Nanjing's top-end hotels. Standard doubles cost US$130 and executive rooms cost US$180. The hotel's numerous amenities include a sauna, fitness centre and swimming pool, and at street level there's a shopping arcade stocking just about any consumer item you're likely to want to buy.

Next door to the Jinling is the old Shengli Hotel, which has been given a complete facelift and is now the *Fuchang Hotel* (☎ 440-0888) *(fúchāng fàndiàn)*. It has a rooftop swimming pool among other amenities and charges US$80 for a standard room, US$140 for a suite.

Places to Eat

Some of Nanjing's livelier eating houses are in the Fuzimiao quarter. The *Yongheyuan Restaurant* (☎ 662-3836) *(yǒnghéyuán chádiǎnshè)* at 122 Gongyuan Jie specialises in sweet and savoury steamed pastries. Nearby, the *Lao Zhengxing Restaurant* *(lǎo zhèngxìng càiguǎn)*, at 119 Gongyuan Jie, just east of the main square by the river, serves typical lower-Yangzi cuisine and was a favourite of Kuomintang officers before the war.

In summer there is an excellent night market at the intersection just south of Xinjiekou, where you can get cheap street food. Here a *shāguō* hotpot or a bowl of noodles washed down with a bottle of the malty local Yali beer will cost you around Y8.

Anyone who has arrived in Nanjing from the backwoods of China can forget all about local delicacies and head over to one of the cluster of restaurants that have sprung up around Nanjing University which cater to adventurous locals and foreign students. The

Black Cat Cafe (hēimāo cānguǎn) was poised to move to bigger and better premises down in Xinjiekou at the time of writing, but the original still lingers on in a small alley opposite the University. (Go down to the new branch for the best pizza south of the Yangzi.) Also next to the campus on Shanghai Lu is *Henry's Home*, celebrated for its breakfasts, but also a reliable lunch or dinner option.

The *Sprite Outlet (wǔzhōu jiǔjiā)* (foreign students also call it the Treehouse) on Guangzhou Lu, 20 metres west of the intersection with Zhongshan Lu, is popular with both foreigners and Nanjing locals. The food is excellent and cheap; the menu is bilingual. Don't be deceived by the deceptively small street-front dining area – there is more seating out the back and in some small rooms.

Worth visiting more for the view than for its food is the vegetarian restaurant at *Jiming Temple*, high on a hill overlooking Xuanwu Lake Park. It's very cheap, but is open only for midday meals. The *Baiyuan Restaurant*, on the northernmost island in Xuanwu Lake, is a bit more upmarket, but it's another good place to relax.

The *Maxiangxing Restaurant* (☎ 663-5807) *(qīngzhēn mǎxiángxìng càiguǎn)*, at No 5 Zhongshan Beilu, serves good cheap Muslim cuisine. The main restaurant is upstairs in a green and cream building on the Drum Tower traffic circle.

A good place to try local specialities is the *Jiangsu Restaurant* (☎ 662-3698) *(jiāngsū jiǔjiā)* at 26 Jiankang Lu near the Taiping Museum. Nanjing pressed, salted duck is slathered with roasted salt, steeped in clear brine, baked dry and then kept under cover for some time; the finished product should have a creamy coloured skin and red, tender flesh.

The *Dasanyuan* (☎ 664-1027) *(dàsānyuǎn jiǔjiā)* at 38 Zhongshan Lu has been recommended for its Cantonese-style cuisine. If you can get a table, the *Sichuan Restaurant* (☎ 664-3651) *(sìchuān fàndiàn)*, at 171 Taiping Lu, is not bad either – but scrutinise the bill before you pay.

Finally, *KFC* has invaded Nanjing in a big way, and despite all the great food available out on the streets, the locals mob these places like they were giving away train tickets to Shanghai. You'll see outlets all over town. *McDonald's* was poised to join the fray at the time of writing.

Entertainment
The best place to ask around about entertainment is the foreign student dormitories or the Black Cat Cafe. The disco in the Zhongshan department store complex was the place to be on Friday nights at the time of writing.

Getting There & Away
Air Nanjing has regular air connections to all major Chinese cities. There are also daily flights to/from Hong Kong.

The main CAAC office (☎ 664-9275) is at 52 Ruijin Lu (near the terminal of bus route No 4), but you can also buy tickets at the CITS office or at the Hongqiao, Jinling or Central hotels, or at the China Eastern Airlines office just north of Xinjiekou. Dragonair (☎ 332-8000) has daily flights to Hong Kong and is in the CITS office.

Bus The long-distance bus station is west of the main railway station, south-east of the wide-bridged intersection with Zhongyang Lu. It's a big chaotic place and even if you can read the posted information (in Chinese) it is all wildly inaccurate. There are direct buses to destinations all over Jiangsu and to major destinations around China. Have the name of the place you want to go written in Chinese to be sure.

Train Nanjing is a major stop on the Beijing-Shanghai railway line, and the station is a disaster area; there are several trains a day in both directions. Heading eastwards from Nanjing, the line to Shanghai connects with Zhenjiang, Changzhou, Wuxi and Suzhou.

An efficient daily express service runs between Nanjing and Shanghai, using two modern double-decker trains:

Train No	From	To	Departs	Arrives
1	Nanjing	Shanghai	8.26 am	12.20 pm
15	Nanjing	Shanghai	9.57 am	2.41 pm
2	Shanghai	Nanjing	1.40 pm	5.42 pm
16	Shanghai	Nanjing	4.30 pm	9.26 pm

The Nos 1 and 2 stop only at Wuxi, while the Nos 15 and 16 also stop at Suzhou. All cars are air-conditioned and a no-smoking rule is vigorously enforced. There is no direct rail link to Hangzhou; you have to go to Shanghai first and then catch a train or bus. Alternatively, there is a direct bus from Nanjing to Hangzhou. Likewise, to get to Guangzhou by rail you must change trains at Shanghai.

Heading west, there is a direct rail link to the port of Wuhu on the Yangzi River. If you want to go further west along the river, then the most sensible thing to do is take the ferry.

Boat There are several departures daily from Nanjing's Yangzi River port downriver (eastward) to Shanghai and upriver (westward) to Wuhan (two days), including a few boats to Chongqing (five days). Most ferries leave from No 4 dock (*sìhào mǎtóu*), one km north of Zhongshan dock, which is at the western end of Zhongshan Beilu.

Getting Around

To/From the Airport Nanjing airport is not far from the centre of town, in the south-east of the city. There is a CAAC bus service, and many of the hotels also have minibuses that run to and from the airport. Taxis charge around Y30 to Xinjiekou, though as a foreigner you may be hard-pressed to get a ride at this price.

Other Taxis cruise the streets of Nanjing and are very cheap – just make sure that the meter is switched on. You can get to Xinjiekou, in the heart of town, by jumping on a No 1 bus or a No 33 trolley-bus from the railway station, or a No 10 or No 34 trolley-bus from the Yangzi docks.

It is no longer easy to rustle up a bicycle for hire in Nanjing, and given the complete chaos on the streets, this is perhaps just as well.

AROUND NANJING
Qixia Temple
(*qíxiá sì*)

Qixia Temple lies 22 km north-east of Nanjing. It was founded by the Buddhist monk Shao Shezhai, during the Southern Qi Dynasty, and is still an active place of worship. Qixia has long been one of China's most important monasteries, and even today is one of the largest Buddhist seminaries in the country. There are two main temple halls: the Maitreya Hall, with a statue of the Maitreya Buddha sitting cross-legged at the entrance, and behind this the Vairocana Hall, housing a five-metre-tall statue of Vairocana.

Behind the temple is a small seven-storey stone pagoda built in 601 AD, and rebuilt during the late Tang period. The upper part has engraved Sutras and carvings of the Buddha; around the base, each of the pagoda's eight sides depicts Sakyamuni. Paths lead through the forest up to small temples and pavilions on Qixiashan itself, from where you can see the Yangzi River.

You reach Qixia from Nanjing by public bus from the Drum Tower bus station or by private minibus from the eastern side of the railway station.

Yangshan Quarry
(*yángshān bēicái*)

The quarry at Yangshan, 25 km east of Nanjing, was the source of most of the stone blocks cut for the Ming palace and statues of the Ming tombs. The attraction here is a massive tablet partially hewn from the rock. Had the tablet been finished it would have been almost 15 metres wide, four metres thick and 45 metres high! The base stone was to be 6½ metres high and 13 metres long. One story goes that Ming Dynasty emperor Hong Wu wished to place the enormous tablet on the top of Zijinshan. The gods had promised their assistance to move it, but when they saw the size of the tablet, even they gave up and Hong Wu had to abandon the project. It seems, however, that Yong Le, the son of Hong Wu, ordered the tablet to be carved; he planned to erect it at his father's tomb. When the tablet was almost finished he realised there was no way it could be moved.

You can get to Yangshan from the bus station on Hanfu Jie (east of Xinjiekou) on bus Nos 9 and 20. Buses to the thermal-springs resort at Tangshanzhen pass Yangshan on the way.

Buddhist Grottoes

The Buddhist grottoes lie about 20 km east of Nanjing. The earliest caves date from the Qi Dynasty (479-502 AD), though there are others from a number of succeeding dynasties right through to the Ming.

GRAND CANAL
(dàyùnhé)

With other, faster, modes of transport available nowadays, tourists are about the only thing being shipped on the Grand Canal. The old Beijing-Hangzhou canal meandered almost 1800 km. Today perhaps half of it remains seasonally navigable. The Party claims that, since Liberation, large-scale dredging has made the navigable length 1100 km. This is an exaggeration. Canal depths are up to three metres and canal widths can narrow to less than nine metres. Put these facts together, think about some of the old stone bridges spanning the route, and you come to the conclusion that it is restricted to fairly small flat-bottomed vessels.

The section of the canal from Beijing to Tianjin has been silted up for centuries. A similar fate has befallen most sections from the Yellow River to Tianjin. The stretch from the Yellow River to Peixian (in northern Jiangsu Province) is also probably silted up.

As a tourist concern, the Grand Canal comes into its own south of the Yangzi, where there is year-round navigation. The Jiangnan section of the canal (Hangzhou, Suzhou, Wuxi, Changzhou, Danyang, Zhenjiang) is a skein of canals, rivers and branching lakes.

Passenger services on the canal have dwindled to a trickle nowadays, unpopular with local travellers now that there are faster ways of getting around. The only option – apart from chartering your own boat – if you want a canal journey is the overnight service that travels between Hangzhou and Suzhou. By all accounts it's a very pleasant trip and improvements have been made on the much maligned sanitation front. (See the Suzhou, Getting There & Away section later in this chapter for more details.)

ZHENJIANG
(zhènjiāng)

Just an hour from Nanjing, Zhenjiang is a drab, industrialised town of over 300,000 people. Its sights are to the north, a fair hike from the railway station. The main attraction is Jinshan Park, where an active Buddhist temple attracts large crowds of worshippers.

Jiaoshan
(jiāoshān)

Also known as Jade Hill because of its dark green foliage (cypresses and bamboo), Jiaoshan is to the east of Zhenjiang on a small island. There's good hiking here with a number of pavilions along the way to the top of the 150-metre-high mount, from where Xijiang Tower gives a view of activity on the Yangzi. At the base of Jiaoshan is an active monastery, with some 200 pieces of tablet engravings, gardens and bonsai displays. Take bus No 4 to the terminal, then a short walk and a boat ride.

Beigushan Park
(běigùshān gōngyuán)

Also on the No 4 bus route, Beigushan Park is home to Ganlu Temple *(gānlù sì)*, which features a Song Dynasty pagoda with expansive views of Zhenjiang – not a view to kill for. The pagoda was once six storeys high but was reduced to four by overzealous Red Guards.

Jinshan Park
(jīnshān gōngyuán)

Jinshan Park packs in the crowds, who congest the flights of stairs that lead up

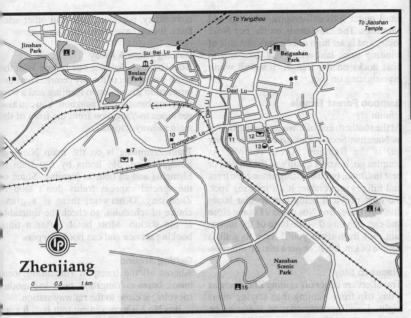

Zhenjiang 镇江

0   0.5   1 km

ZHENJIANG 镇江

1 Jinshan Hotel
  金山饭店
2 Jinshan Temple
  金山寺
3 Museum
  博物馆
4 Ferry Pier to Yangzhou
  轮渡码头
5 Ganlu Temple
  甘露寺

6 Martyrs' Shrine
  烈士墓
7 Zhenjiang Hotel
  镇江宾馆
8 Post Office
  邮局
9 Railway Station
  火车站
10 Zhenjiang Binguan
   (Hotel)
   镇江宾馆

11 Jingkou Hotel
   京口饭店
12 Post Office
   邮电局
13 Long-Distance Bus
   Station
   汽车站
14 Douyao Temple
   都天庙
15 Bamboo Forest
   Temple
   竹林寺

through a Buddhist temple to the seven-storey octagonal Cishou Pagoda. There are four caves at the mount: Buddhist Sea *(fǎhǎi)*, White Dragon *(báilóng)*, Morning Sun *(zhàoyáng)* and Arhat *(luóhàn)*. Fahai and Bailong caves feature in the Chinese fairy tale *The Story of the White Snake*. Take bus No 2 to Jinshan.

Museum
(bówùguǎn)

Between Jinshan Park and the centre of town is the old British consulate, which is now a museum and gallery. It houses pottery, bronzes, gold, silver, Tang Dynasty paintings, and a separate section with photographs and memorabilia of the Japanese war. Its retail outlet sells calligraphy, rubbings and paintings. The museum is on the bus No 2 route, and is set high over a very old area of winding stone-laid alleys that go down to boat docks on the Yangzi. It's well worth investigating on foot.

Bamboo Forest Temple
(zhúlín sì)
At the southern end of town in an area known as Nanshan Scenic Park (nánshān fēngjǐng qū) is the Bamboo Forest Temple. As temples go, it won't qualify as the biggest or best in China, but the setting among the trees and hills is impressive. It's a relaxing spot, the only problem being that regular buses don't go there. Bus Nos 6 and 21 come close and can let you off at the base of the mountain, but from there you'll have to walk a couple of km, hitch, or get a taxi or minibus.

Places to Stay
Travellers are better off visiting Zhenjiang as a day trip from Nanjing than staying overnight. Local accommodation tends to be expensive, and Zhenjiang is a dull place to spend the night.

The Jingkou Hotel (☎ 523-8988) (jīngkǒu fàndiàn) is one of the cheaper places around; it has rooms for Y120 in the old wing, though you will need to exert some pressure to get one of these. Standard renovated doubles start at Y280. The hotel can be a little tricky to find – entry is via a gate on Binhe Lu, which borders a small river.

There is other, more expensive, accommodation available at the Zhenjiang Hotel on the square fronting the railway station. Down the road from the station, the other Zhenjiang Hotel (☎ 523-3888; fax 523-1055) (zhènjiāng bīnguǎn), at 92 Zhongshan Xilu, has standard doubles from US$60.

Finally, the Jinshan Hotel (☎ 562-3888) (jīnshān fàndiàn), 1 Jinshan Xilu, has a quiet location close to Jinshan Park. Doubles range in price from Y210 to Y320.

Things to Buy
There's a very fine Arts & Crafts Store (gōngyìpǐn dàlóu) at 191 Jiefang Lu which stocks

embroidery, porcelain, jade and other artefacts. It may have some antiques.

Getting There & Away
Bus The long-distance bus station is in the south-east corner of the city centre. There are buses from Zhenjiang to Nanjing and a busferry combination to Yangzhou. You can also get buses to Yangzhou from the front of the main railway station.

Train Zhenjiang is on the main Nanjing-Shanghai line, 3½ hours by fast train to Shanghai and an hour to Nanjing. Some of the special express trains don't stop at Zhenjiang. Otherwise, there is a grand choice of schedules, so check the timetable at the station. Most hotels offer a train booking service and can book sleepers.

Getting Around
Almost all the transport (including local buses, buses to Yangzhou, taxis and motortricycles) is close to the railway station.

Bus No 2 is a convenient tour bus. It goes east from the station along Zhongshan Lu to the city centre where the department stores, antique shop and post office are. It then swings west into the older part of town where some speciality and second-hand stores are to be found, goes past the former British consulate and continues on to Jinshan, the terminal.

Bus No 4, which crosses the No 2 route in the city centre on Jiefang Lu, runs to Ganlu Temple and Jiaoshan in the east.

YANGZHOU
(yángzhōu)
Yangzhou, at the junction of the Grand Canal and the Yangzi River, was once an economic and cultural centre of Southern China. It was home to scholars, painters, storytellers, poets and merchants in the Sui and Tang dynasties. Today it is a fairly ordinary Chinese town, with enough sights to keep the traveller busy for a day or so. It is not, however, the major attraction that local tourist literature would have you believe. The main attraction, Shouxi Lake Park, tends to get swamped

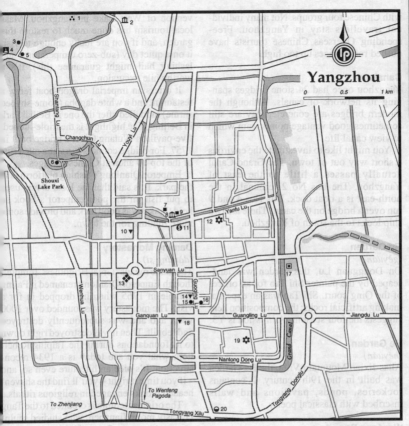

Yangzhou

0   0.5   1 km

To Wenfeng
Pagoda

To Zhenjiang

YANGZHOU 扬州	7	Xiyuan Hotel	14	Caigenxiang Restaurant
		西园饭店		菜根香饭店
1 Tang Dynasty Ruins	8	History Museum	15	Xinhua Bookstore
唐城遗址		扬州市博物馆		新华书店
2 Han Dynasty Tomb	9	Yangzhou Hotel	16	Fuchun Teahouse
Museum		扬州宾馆		富春茶社
汉墓博物馆	10	KFC	17	Tomb of Puhaddin
3 Martyrs' Shrine		肯德鸡		普哈丁墓园
烈士墓	11	Bank of China	18	Gonghechun Dumpling &
4 Daming Monastery		中国银行		Noodle Restaurant
大明寺	12	Ge Garden		共和春铰面店
5 Pingshan Hall		个园	19	He Garden
平山堂	13	No 2 Department Store		何园
6 White Dagoba		第二百货	20	Long-Distance Bus Station
白塔				扬州汽车站

with Chinese tour groups. Not many individual travellers stay in Yangzhou. Free-spending Overseas Chinese tourists have pushed room prices up too high.

Canals

Yangzhou once had 24 stone bridges spanning its network of canals. Although the modern bridges are concrete, they are still sometimes good vantage points from which to view canal life.

You might like to investigate the environs a short way out of town. The Grand Canal actually passes a little to the east of Yangzhou. The bus No 2 terminal in the north-east is a boat dock. Bus Nos 4 and 9 run over a bridge on the canal. There are two ship locks to the south of Yangzhou.

Ge Garden

(gèyuán)

On Dongguan Lu, this garden was landscaped by the painter Shi Tao for an officer of the Qing court. Shi Tao was an expert at making artificial rocks; the composition here suggests the four seasons. Admission is Y3.

He Garden

(héyuán)

Alias Jixiao Mountain Villa, the He Garden was built in the 19th century. It contains rockeries, ponds, pavilions and walls inscribed with classical poetry.

Wenfeng Pagoda

(wénfēng tǎ)

Just south-west of the bus station, this pagoda can be scaled to the seventh level (assemble at 9 am with your grappling-hooks; highly recommended). It offers a bird's-eye view of the flotsam, jetsam and sampans along a canal, as well as an overview of the town. Made of brick and wood, it's been rebuilt several times.

Shouxi Lake Park

(shòu xīhú)

This is the top scenic spot in Yangzhou – in the western suburbs on the bus No 5 route. 'Shouxi' means 'slender west', a slim version of West Lake in Hangzhou. Mass local tourism has done much to restore this garden, and if you are lucky enough to visit it on a quiet day (sub-zero temperatures and lashing hail might guarantee this), it's a worthwhile excursion.

It offers an imperial dragon-boat ferry, a restaurant and a white dagoba (dome-shaped shrine) modelled after the one in Beihai Park in Beijing. The highlight is the triple-arched five-pavilion Wutang Qiao, a bridge built in 1757. For bridge connoisseurs, it's rated one of the top 10 ancient Chinese bridges.

Emperor Qianlong's fishing platform is in the park. It is said that the local divers used to put fish on the poor emperor's hook so he'd think it was good luck and provide some more funding for the town.

Daming Monastery

(dàmíng sì)

The name means 'Great Brightness Temple' though Emperor Qianlong renamed it Fajing Temple in 1765 when he dropped in for a visit. The monastery was founded over 1000 years ago and was subsequently destroyed and rebuilt. Then it was destroyed right down to its foundations during the Taiping Rebellion; what you see today is a 1934 reconstruction. It's nice architecture even so, and – if you time it right – you'll find the shaven-headed monks engaged in religious rituals.

The original temple is credited to the Tang Dynasty monk Jianzhen, who studied sculpture, architecture, fine arts and medicine, as well as Buddhism. In 742 AD two Japanese monks invited him to Japan for missionary work. It turned out to be mission impossible. Jianzhen made five attempts to get there, failing due to storms. On the fifth attempt he ended up in Hainan. On the sixth trip, aged 66, he finally arrived. He stayed in Japan for 10 years and died there in 763. Later, the Japanese made a lacquer statue of Jianzhen, which in 1980 was sent to Yangzhou.

The Chinese have a wooden copy of this statue on display at the Jianzhen Memorial Hall. Modelled after the chief hall of the Toshodai Temple in Nara (Japan), the Jianzhen Memorial Hall was built in 1974 at

Daming Monastery and was financed by Japanese contributions. Special exchanges are made between Nara and Yangzhou; even Deng Xiaoping, returning from a trip to Japan, came to the Yangzhou Monastery to strengthen renewed links between the two countries.

Near the monastery is Pingshan Hall (*píngshān táng*), the residence of the Song Dynasty writer Ouyang Xiu, who served in Yangzhou.

Tomb of Puhaddin
(*pǔhādīng mùyuán*)

This tomb contains documents regarding China's contacts with the Muslims. It's on the east bank of a canal on the bus No 2 route. Puhaddin came to China during the Yuan Dynasty (1271-1368) to spread the Muslim faith, and spent 10 years in Yangzhou, where he died. There is a mosque in Yangzhou.

History Museum
(*yángzhōu shì bówùguǎn*)

The museum lies to the west of Guoqing Lu, near the Xiyuan Hotel. It's in a temple originally dedicated to Shi Kefa, a Ming Dynasty official who refused to succumb to his new Qing masters and was executed. The museum contains items from Yangzhou's past. A small collection of calligraphy and paintings of the 'Eight Eccentrics' is displayed in another small museum just off Yanfu Lu near the Xiyuan Hotel.

Places to Stay

Budget travellers are better off visiting Yangzhou as a day-trip from Nanjing. On a good run it only takes around 1½ hours. There is nothing in the way of budget accommodation in town – hotels are largely geared up to the needs of local and Overseas Chinese tour groups.

The town's two main hotels are next door to each other behind the museum. The garden-style *Xiyuan Hotel* (*xīyuán fàndiàn*) at 1 Fengle Shanglu is said to have been constructed over the site of Qianlong's imperial villa. Room rates are from Y210 to Y420. The *Yangzhou Hotel* (*yángzhōu*

bīnguǎn) has standard doubles from Y380. A new luxury hotel, under construction between Yangzhou and Xiyuan hotels, should be complete by the time you have this book in your hands.

Places to Eat

The most famous culinary export of Yangzhou is Yangzhou fried rice and, as most travellers who have tried it will aver, it tastes just like fried rice – don't expect too much.

Meals are available at Yangzhou's tourist hotels. The *Fuchun Teahouse* (*fúchūn cháshè*), on a lane just off Guoqing Lu, is the place to go to sip tea and eat local snacks. The *Caigenxiang Restaurant* (*càigēnxiāng fàndiàn*) is one of Yangzhou's more famous establishments – it's not the place to be if you are alone or with just one companion. The *Gonghechun Dumpling & Noodle Restaurant* (*gònghéchūn jiǎomiàndàin*), in the south of town on Ganquan Lu, is a better option for inexpensive dining.

Getting There & Away

The nearest airport is in Nanjing. The railway line also gives Yangzhou a miss, which perhaps explains why the city is missing out on China's current tourist and industrial tidal wave. The railway station nearest Yangzhou is in Zhenjiang.

From Yangzhou there are buses to Nanjing (two hours), Wuxi, Suzhou and Shanghai. Most frequent (about every 15 minutes) are minibuses from Zhenjiang (one hour), which make amphibious crossings of the Yangzi. These depart from in front of Zhenjiang Railway Station.

Getting Around

The sights are at the edge of town. If you're in a hurry, you might consider commandeering a motor-tricycle – they can be found outside the bus station. The central area can easily be covered on foot. Bus Nos 1, 2, 3, 5, 6 and 7 terminate near the long-distance bus station. Bus No 1 runs from the bus station up Guoqing Lu and then loops around the perimeter of the inside canal, returning just north of the bus station. Bus No 4 is an east-west bus and goes along Ganquan Lu.

YIXING COUNTY
(yíxīng xiàn)

Yixing County is famed for its tea utensils, in particular its pots. Delicious tea can be made in an aged Yixing teapot simply by adding hot water, or so it is claimed. The potteries of Yixing, in particular of Dingshu, are a popular excursion for Chinese tourists but see very few foreign visitors.

The town of Yixing is *not* an attraction, though most visitors end up passing through the place en route to the nearby karst caves or to Dingshu. There is also a guesthouse in Yixing, if you need to spend the night.

Karst Caves
(shíhuī yándòng)

There are karst caves to the south-west of Yixing township, and if you are in the area, it is worth visiting one or two of them. The drab interiors are lit by the standard selection of coloured neon, but you may wish to supplement this with a torch for navigation. The caves are very wet, so take your raincoat too.

Shanjuan Cave (shànjuǎn dòng) This cave is embedded in Snail Shell Hill (Luoyanshan), 27 km south-west of Yixing. It covers an area of roughly 5000 sq metres, with passages of 800 metres. It's divided into upper, middle and lower reaches, plus a water cave. An exterior waterfall provides special sound effects.

Entry is via the middle cave, a stone hall with a 1000-metre floor space. From here you can mount a staircase to the snail's shell, the upper cave, or wander down to the lower caves and the water cave. In the water cave, you can jump in a rowing boat for a 120-metre ride to the exit called 'Suddenly-See-the-Light'.

Buses run to Shanjuan from Yixing and take approximately one hour.

Zhanggong Cave (zhānggōng dòng) Nineteen km south of Yixing town, Zhanggong Cave is similar in scale to Shanjuan Cave. It

allows you to scale a small hill called Yufengshan from the inside, and come out on the top, with a splendid view of the surrounding countryside with hamlets stretching as far as Lake Taihu.

Buses to Zhanggong from Yixing take half an hour. From Zhanggong you can pick up a passing bus to Linggu – the end of the line. If you're stuck for transport, try to get to Dingshu village, from where bus connections are good.

Linggu Cave (línggǔ dòng) Eight km down a dirt road from Zhanggong Cave, Linggu is the largest and least explored of the three caves. The cave has six large halls arrayed roughly in a semicircle.

Near the Linggu Cave is the Yanxian Tea Plantation (yánxiàn cháchǎng), with bushel lots laid out like fat caterpillars stretching into the horizon, and the odd tea villa in the background. The trip is worth it for the tea fields alone.

There are buses to Linggu from Zhanggong.

Places to Stay

The *Yixing Guesthouse* (yíxīng fàndiàn) caters chiefly to cadres holding meetings. The guesthouse is at the end of Renmin Lu, on the southern edge of Yixing town. If there's not a rash of meetings, or a rare tour bus assault, the guesthouse will be empty. It's a large building, with gardens and some luxury living.

The guesthouse is a half-hour walk from Yixing bus station; turn right from the station, follow the main road south along the lakeside, cross three bridges and turn left then right again to the guesthouse gates.

The long stretch across the bridges is the same road that runs to Dingshu, so if your bus goes to Dingshu ask the driver to let you off closer to the guesthouse. If you don't mind the stroll, and want to see the main drag of Yixing town, another way of getting to the guesthouse is to walk three blocks straight ahead from the bus station, turn right onto Renmin Lu and keep walking until you come to the guesthouse.

Getting There & Away

There are buses from Yixing to Wuxi (2½ hours), Shanghai, Nanjing and Suzhou.

Getting Around

There are no local buses in Yixing. There are buses to the sights out of town and all of them end up in the bus stations of either Yixing town or Dingshu. There are frequent connections between the two stations. Hitchhiking is a possibility.

DINGSHU (JINSHAN)
(dīngshǔ, jīnshān)

Dingshu is the pottery centre of Yixing County, and has enjoyed a reputation as such since the Qin and Han dynasties; some of the scenes you can witness here, especially at the loading dock that leads into Lake Taihu, are timeless. Almost every local family is engaged in the manufacture of ceramics, and behind the main part of town half the houses are made of the stuff.

Dingshu is about 25 km south of Yixing town and has two dozen ceramics factories producing more than 2000 varieties of pottery – quite an output for a population of 100,000. Among the array of products are the ceramic tables and garbage bins that you find around China, huge jars used to store oil and grain, the famed Yixing teapots, and the glazed tiling and ceramic frescoes that are desperately needed as spare parts for tourist attractions – the Forbidden City in Beijing is one of the customers.

Unfortunately, Dingshu's pottery factories and occasional exhibition spaces are scattered around town: you will have to do a lot of walking if you want to see everything. Main attractions include the **Pottery Exhibition Hall** (táocí zhǎnlǎnguǎn), the **Ceramics Research Institute** (táocí yánjiūsuǒ) and a host of factories in the east of town next to Lake Taihu.

Getting There & Away

There are direct buses from Dingshu to Yixing (20 minutes, with departures about every 20 minutes from 6 am to 5 pm), Wuxi (2½ hours), Zhenjiang and Nanjing. Note

Pottery from Dingshu, known China-wide for the quality of its ceramics.

that Dingshu is also known as Jinshan, so try this name if Dingshu draws a blank.

WUXI & LAKE TAIHU
(wúxī, tàihú)

Wuxi and nearby Lake Taihu are possible stopovers between Suzhou and Nanjing. Wuxi itself has little to recommend it – a typical sprawling Chinese urban development with some dirty industry thrown in for good measure – but Lake Taihu is a popular tourist destination, though more for Chinese tourists than Western.

Lake Taihu is a freshwater lake with a total area of 2200 sq km and an average depth of two metres. There are some 90 islands, large and small, within it. The fishing industry is very active, netting over 30 varieties of fish.

Orientation

The city centre proper is ringed by Jiefang Lu. The railway station and main bus station are around 10-minutes' walk north of Jiefang Beilu. A network of canals cuts through the city, including the Grand Canal itself. Accommodation is inconveniently scattered around town and overpriced.

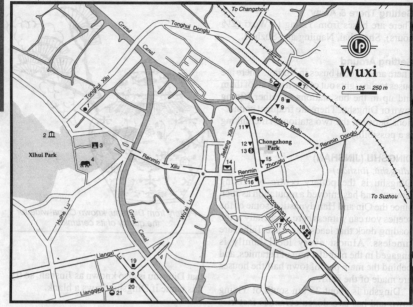

WUXI 无锡

PLACES TO STAY

8 Jinhua Hotel
   锦华大返店
17 Liangxi Hotel
   梁溪饭店
19 Meilidu Hotel
   美丽都大酒店
20 Wuxi Hotel
   无锡饭店

PLACES TO EAT

9 Zhongguo Restaurant
   中国饭店
11 California Fried Chicken
   加州牛肉面

12 Wangyuji Restaurant
   王与记馄饨店
15 KFC
   肯德鸡

OTHER

1 Huishan Clay Figurine
   Factory
   惠山泥人厂
2 Museum
   博物馆
3 Dragon Light Pagoda
   龙光塔
4 Zoo
   动物园
5 North Bus Station
   无锡汽车客运中心站

6 Railway Station
   火车站
7 CITS
   中国国际旅行社
10 Wuxi Antiques Store
   文物商店
13 Bank of China
   中国银行
14 Main Post & Telephone
   Office
   市邮电局
16 Xinhua Bookstore
   新华书店
18 Wuxi Friendship Store
   无锡友谊商店
21 South Bus Station
   无锡汽车站

Information

The CITS office is in a building facing the square in front of the main railway station. Unfortunately, it does not sell railway tickets or have any useful information for the traveller. The best it can do is sell you an air ticket for flights out of Shanghai on China Eastern Airlines.

Xihui Park

(xīhuì gōngyuán)

The vast Xihui Park is west of the city. The highest point in the park, Huishan hill, is 75 metres above sea level, and if you climb the Dragon Light Pagoda *(lóngguāng tǎ)*, the seven-storey octagonal structure at the top, you'll be able to take in a panorama of Wuxi and Taihu. The brick and wood pagoda was built during the Ming Dynasty, burned down during the Qing Dynasty and rebuilt many years later. For sunrises, try the Qingyun Pavilion, just to the east of the pagoda.

The park has a collection of pavilions, snack bars and teahouses, along with a small zoo, a large artificial lake and a cave that burrows for half a km from the east side to the west. The western section of the park rambles off into Huishan, where you'll find the famous Ming Dynasty Jichang Garden *(jìchàng yuán)* ('Ming' refers to the garden layout – the buildings are recent); the Huishan Temple nearby was once a Buddhist monastery.

To get to Xihui Park, you can take bus No 2, 10 or 15.

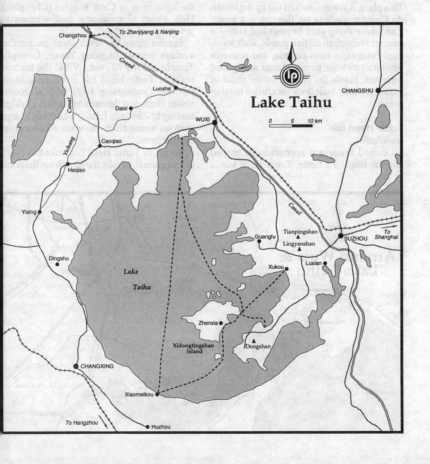

Plum Garden
(méiyuán)

Once a small *peach* garden built during the Qing Dynasty, this has since been renovated, relandscaped and expanded. It is renowned for its thousands of red plum trees which blossom in the spring. Peach and cherry trees grow here too, and rockeries are arrayed at the centre of the garden. The highest point is Plum Pagoda, with views of Taihu. The garden is near the Wuxi bus No 2 terminal.

Li Garden
(lǐyuán)

This place is always packed out by the locals. As Chinese gardens go, this one is a goner. The whole thing goes beyond bad taste – a concrete labyrinth of fish ponds, walkways, mini-bridges, a mini-pagoda, and souvenir vendors hawking garish plaster and gilded figurines. Inside the garden, on the shore of Taihu, is a tour-boat dock for cruises to other points.

Turtle Head Isle
(guītóuzhǔ)

So named because it appears to be shaped like the head of a turtle, Turtle Head Isle is not actually an island but being surrounded on three sides by water makes it appear so. This is the basic scenic strolling area where you can watch the junks on Lake Taihu.

You can walk a circuit of the area. If you continue along the shore, you come to the ferry dock for the Three Hills Isles, passing Taihujiajue Archway and Perpetual Spring Bridge *(chángchūn qiáo)*. A walkway leads to a small lighthouse, near which is an inscribed stone referring to the island's name and several pavilions. The architecture here, like that in the Li Garden, is mostly copied of the classical examples. Inland a bit from the lighthouse is Clear Ripples (Chenglan) Hall, a very nice teahouse from where you get a view of the lake.

Further along the south shore are similar vantage points: Jingsong Tower, Guangfu Temple and the 72 Peaks Villa. The highest point of Turtle Head Isle is the Brightness Pavilion *(guāngmíng tíng)* with all-round vistas. Back past the entrance area is a bridge leading to Zhongdu Island, which has a large workers' sanatorium – no visits without prior appointment.

To get to Turtle Head Isle, take bus No 1 to its terminal, or take the ferry from the dock

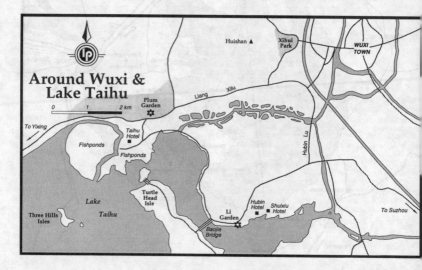

ear Plum Garden. The Chinese like to make
. cycling trip out of it – the road is pleasant,
with no heavy traffic. A possible shortcut is
round the back of Zhongdu Island leading
back towards Taihu Hotel.

Three Hills Isles
(sānshān)

Three Hills Isles is an island park three km
south-west of Turtle Head Isle. If you
aven't seen Wuxi and the lake from every
possible angle by now, try this one. Vantage
points at the top look back toward Turtle
Head Isle and you can work out if it really
does look like a turtle head or not. The Three-
Hill Teahouse *(sānshān cháguǎn)* has outdoor tables and rattan chairs, and views.
Three Hills Isles is a 20-minute ferry ride
from Turtle Head Isle.

Places to Stay – middle

There is no budget accommodation for for-
igners in Wuxi. Touts around the railway
station will take travellers to the *Jinhua
Hotel* (☎ 272-0612) *(jǐnhuá dàfàndiàn)*,
where the cheapest doubles cost Y280. Despite
n abundance of hotels close to the railway
tation, this is the only one that takes foreigners.
The *Liangxi Hotel* (☎ 272-6812) *(liángxī
'ndiàn)*, on Zhongshan Nanlu, is a better
ption. Take bus No 12 from the railway
tation. Doubles cost from Y236.

Places to Stay – top end

In Wuxi itself is the *Meilidu Hotel* (☎ 676-
665) *(měilìdū fàndiàn)*, on the traffic circle
where Liangxi Lu and Liangqing Lu inter-
ect. Rooms start at Y723. Just on the
pposite side of the circle is the four-star
Wuxi Hotel (☎ 676-6789) *(wúxī dàfàndiàn)*,
ith rates from US$100. Neither of these
laces are worth the exorbitant rates they
harge.

All the other tourist hotels are around the
keside and have rates of around US$80
pwards. Some possibilities include:

ubin Hotel (☎ 676-8812) *(húbīn fàndiàn)*
uixiu Hotel (☎ 676-8591) *(shuǐxiù fàndiàn)*
ihu Hotel (☎ 676-7901) *(táihú fàndiàn)*

Places to Eat

Wuxi has no shortage of restaurants, and in
the centre of town you will even find a few
fast-food barns such as *KFC* and *California
Fried Chicken*. For an excellent and economical lunch try the *Zhongguo Restaurant
(zhōngguó fàndiàn)*, just south of the railway
station. One entrance leads into an à la carte
dining area, but look for the rough and ready
section where dumplings are served – ask for
xiǎolóngbāo.

Another place worth popping into is the
*Wangyuji Restaurant (wángyújì húntun
diàn)*. This place is famous for its *húntun*, a
kind of ravioli served in soup – they're very
good and very cheap too.

Things to Buy

Silk products and embroidery are good buys.
There are also some remarkably ugly clay
figurines for sale around the place. A peasant
folk art, they were usually models of opera
stars. Look out for models of obese infants –
symbols of fortune and happiness and just
the thing to fill up your mantelpiece with.

The Wuxi Friendship Store is a good place
to stock up on souvenirs, as is the Wuxi
Antiques Store *(wúxī wénwù shāngdiàn)*, not
far from the railway station. The Huishan
Clay Figurine Factory *(huìshān níǒu gōng-
chǎng)* is near Xihui Park.

Getting There & Away

Air Wuxi has no airport, but you can book
flights out of Shanghai on China Eastern
Airlines from the Wuxi CAAC office.
CAAC's minuscule ticket office is next to the
Wuxi Hotel, but most locals purchase air
tickets from the CITS branch adjacent to the
railway station.

Bus The main long-distance bus station
(wúxī qìchē zhàn) is next to the railway
station. There is another bus station down on
Liangqing Lu *(wúxī qìchē xīzhàn)*, but it has
fewer services and is only worth checking
out if you are based in this part of town.

There are buses to Shanghai, Suzhou,
Dingshu, Yixing and Yangzhou.

Train Wuxi is on the line from Beijing to Shanghai, with frequent express and special-express trains. There are trains to Suzhou (40 minutes), Shanghai (1¾ hours) and Nanjing (2¾ hours). Travellers to Suzhou will be much better off getting a bus.

The railway station ticket office is a real mess. Foreigners are supposed to buy their tickets from Window No 2, but even there you can expect to spend nearly an hour fighting the queue. At the other windows it's even worse. If you have the right ticket, there is a soft-seat waiting room which will help preserve your sanity.

Boat With such a large lake, the area has a wealth of scenery and there are some potentially interesting routes out of town. But canal transport is disappearing in this neck of the woods.

Getting Around

There are about 15 local bus lines. An alternative for faster connections is to grab a motor-tricycle – there are ranks at the main railway station, though these are rapidly being superseded by taxis.

Bus 2 runs from the railway station, along Jiefang Lu, across two bridges to Xihui Park, then way out to Plum Garden, stopping short of the Taihu Hotel. Bus No 2 almost crosses the bus No 1 route at Gongnongbing Square.

Bus No 1 starts on Gongnongbing Lu and runs to Li Garden and the Hubin and Shuixiu hotels. The actual terminal of bus No 1 is further on across a bridge to the scenery on Turtle Head Isle.

A good tour bus is No 10, which does a long loop around the northern part of the city area, taking in four bridges, Xihui Park and the shopping strip of Renmin Lu.

SUZHOU

(*sūzhōu*)

Suzhou (population about 600,000), a famed silk production centre and a celebrated retreat brimming with gardens and canals, is Jiangsu's most famous attraction. Not that this has done anything to hold back the gathering tide of urban renewal. Unfortunately,

much of the city's charm is being swept away by new road, housing and hotel developments. Nevertheless, Suzhou's charming gardens and other historical attractions are worth a couple of days of your time.

History

Dating back some 2500 years, Suzhou is one of the oldest towns in the Yangzi basin. With the completion of the Grand Canal in the Su Dynasty, Suzhou found itself strategically located on a major trading route, and the city's fortunes and size grew rapidly.

Suzhou flourished as a centre of shipping and grain storage, bustling with merchants and artisans. By the 12th century the town had attained its present dimensions, and if you consult the map, you'll see the layout of the old town. The city walls, a rectangle enclosed by moats, were pierced by six gates (north, south, two in the east and two in the west). Crisscrossing the city were six north-south canals and 14 east-west canals. Although the walls have largely disappeared and a fair proportion of the canals have been plugged, central Suzhou retains its 'Renaissance' character.

A legend was spun about Suzhou through tales of beautiful women with mellifluous voices, and through the famous proverb 'In heaven there is paradise, on earth Suzhou and Hangzhou'. The story picks up when Marco Polo arrived in 1276. He added the adjectives 'great' and 'noble', though he reserved his finer epithets for Hangzhou.

By the 14th century Suzhou had established itself as China's leading silk producer. Aristocrats, pleasure-seekers, famous scholars, actors and painters were attracted to the city, constructing villas and garden retreats for themselves.

At the height of Suzhou's development in the 16th century, the gardens, large and small, numbered over 100. If we mark time here, we arrive at the town's tourist formula today – 'Garden City, Venice of the East', a medieval mix of woodblock guilds and embroidery societies, whitewashed housing, cobbled streets, tree-lined avenues and canals.

The wretched workers of the silk sweat-shops, protesting against paltry wages and the injustices of the contract hire system, were staging violent strikes even in the 15th century, and the landlords shifted. In 1860 Taiping troops took the town without a blow. In 1896 Suzhou was opened to foreign trade, with Japanese and international concessions. During WW II, it was occupied by the Japanese and then by the Kuomintang. Somehow Suzhou slipped through the worst ravages of the Cultural Revolution relatively unscathed.

Information

Both CITS (☎ 522-2681) and CTS (☎ 522-5583) are in a separate building in the Suzhou Hotel compound. The PSB office is at 7 Dashitou Xiang. The Bank of China is at 490 Renmin Lu, but all of the major tourist hotels have foreign-exchange counters as well.

North Temple
(běi sìtǎ)

The North Temple has the tallest pagoda south of the Yangzi – at nine storeys it dominates the north end of Renmin Lu. You can climb it for a fine aerial view of the town and the farmland beyond, which grows tea, rice and wheat. The factory chimneys, the new pagodas of Suzhou, loom on the outskirts, and so does the haze and smoke they create.

The temple complex goes back 1700 years and was originally a residence. The pagoda has been burnt, built and rebuilt. Made of wood, it dates from the 17th century. Off to the side of it is Nanmu Hall, which was rebuilt in the Ming Dynasty with some of its features imported from elsewhere. There is a teahouse with a small garden out the back. Entry to the temple costs Y6, Y4 to climb up.

Suzhou Museum
(sūzhōu bówùguǎn)

Situated some blocks east of the pagoda, near the Humble Administrator's Garden, the museum was once the residence of a Taiping leader, Li Xiucheng. It's a good place to visit after you've seen something of Suzhou, as it

helps fill in the missing bits of the jigsaw as you retrace the town's history.

The museum offers some interesting old maps (Grand Canal, Suzhou, heaven & earth), a silk and embroidery exhibition room (with Qing silk samples), Qing Dynasty steles forbidding workers' strikes, and relics unearthed or rescued from various sites around the Suzhou District (funerary objects, porcelain bowls, bronze swords).

Suzhou Silk Museum
(sūzhōu sīchóu bówùguǎn)

Also close to the pagoda, the silk museum doesn't quite live up to its potential. It has some fascinating exhibitions, and the section on old looms and weaving techniques is very interesting, but as a whole it suffers from an air of neglect. Still, it's well worth an hour or so. Inside is a coffee shop and a souvenir shop where you can make purchases.

Temple of Mystery
(xuánmiàoguān)

The heart of what was once Suzhou Bazaar – an area that is being rapidly developed – is the Taoist Temple of Mystery. It was founded in the 3rd century (during the Jin Dynasty and laid out between 275 and 279 AD) with additions during Song times. From the Qing Dynasty onwards, the bazaar fanned out from the temple with small tradespeople and travelling performers using the grounds. The enormous Sanqing Hall, supported by 60 pillars and capped by a double roof with upturned eaves, dates from 1181. It was burnt and seriously damaged in the 19th century. During the Cultural Revolution, the Red Guards squatted here before it was transformed into a library. Today it's been engulfed by souvenir shops; the square in front of it hosts all manner of outdoor industries, including shoe repairing and tailoring.

Gardens
(huāyuán)

Suzhou's gardens are looked upon as works of art – a fusion of nature, architecture, poetry and painting designed to ease the mind, move it, or assist it. Unlike the massive imperial gardens, the classical landscaping of Suzhou reflects the personal taste of officials and scholars south of the Yangzi. Rich officials, once their worldly duties were performed, would find solace here in kingdoms of ponds and rockeries. The gardens were meant to be enjoyed either in solitary contemplation or in the company of a close circle of friends with a glass of wine, a concert, poetry recital or a literary discussion.

The key elements of the gardens are rocks and water. There are surprisingly few flowers and no fountains – just like the Zen gardens of Japan, they give one an illusion of a natural scene with only moss, sand and

rock. These microcosms were laid out by master craftspeople and changed hands many times over the centuries. The gardens suffered a setback during the Taiping Rebellion in the 1860s, and under subsequent foreign domination of Suzhou. Efforts were made to restore them in the 1950s but during the so-called Horticultural Revolution gardeners downed tools, as flowers were frowned upon. In 1979 the Suzhou Garden Society was formed, and an export company was set up to promote Suzhou-designed gardens. A few of the gardens have been renovated and opened to the public.

Each garden is meant to be savoured at a snail's pace. Remember that the flowers are best left unpicked if the garden is to be

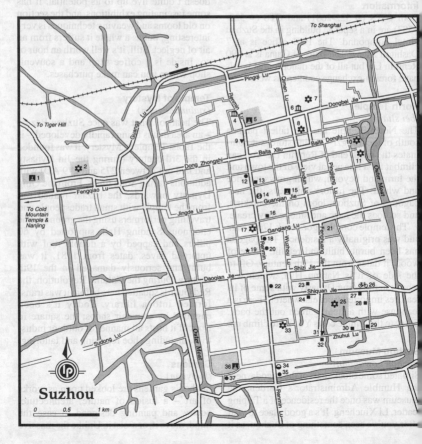

Suzhou

0   0.5   1 km

preserved. The thing to do is take along a Sunday newspaper, a pot of tea, a deck chair, a sketch pad and a bath sponge. Having said that, let us add that it is very hard to wax contemplative when there are thousands of other visitors (mostly Chinese, an amiable enough lot – mostly taking photos of each other or sketching the foliage). Old-timers come here to relax. The size of the crowds depends on the weather, the day of the week and the garden. The gardens are usually open from early morning to dusk (from 7.30 am to 5 pm), and admission is a few yuan.

Humble Administrator's Garden (*zhuó-hèng yuán*) Many consider this Suzhou's second-best garden (after the Garden of the Master of the Nets). The five-hectare garden features streams, ponds, bridges and islands of bamboo; it dates back to the early 1500s. In the same area are the Suzhou Museum and several silk mills. Entry costs Y20.

Lion Grove (*shīzilín*) Just up the street from the Humble Administrator's Garden, this one-hectare grove was constructed in 1350 by the monk Tian Ru and other disciples, as a memorial to their master, Zhi Zheng. The garden has rockeries that evoke leonine forms. The walls of the labyrinth of tunnels bear calligraphy from famous chisels.

Garden of Harmony (*yíyuán*) A small Qing Dynasty garden owned by an official called Gu Wenbin, this one is quite young for a Suzhou garden. It has assimilated many of the features of other gardens and blended them into a style of its own. The garden is divided into eastern and western sections linked by a covered promenade with lattice windows. In the east are buildings and courtyards. The western section has pools with coloured pebbles, rockeries, hillocks and pavilions. The garden is off Renmin Lu, just south of Guanqian Jie.

Blue Wave Pavilion (cānglàngtíng) A bit on the wild side with winding creeks and luxuriant trees, this is one of the oldest gardens in Suzhou. The buildings date from the 11th century, although they have been rebuilt on numerous occasions since. Originally the home of a prince, the property passed into the hands of the scholar Su Zimei, who gave it its name. The one-hectare garden attempts to create optical illusions with the scenery both outside and inside – you look from the pool immediately outside to the distant hills. Admission is only Y2.

Enlightened Way Hall (míngdào táng), the largest building, is said to have been a site for delivery of lectures during the Ming Dynasty. On the other side of Renmin Lu, close by, is the former Confucian Temple.

Garden of the Master of the Nets (wǎngshī yuán) This is the smallest garden in Suzhou – half the size of the Blue Wave Pavilion and a tenth the size of the Humble Administrator's Garden. It's so small, it's hard to find, but well worth the trouble as it's better than all the others combined. Entry is Y4.

Blue Wave Pavilion (Canglangting)

BLUE WAVE PAVILION (CANGLANGTING)
沧浪厅

1 Canglangshengji Arch
   沧浪胜迹坊
2 Lotus Waterside Pavilion
   面水莲亭
3 Steles
   碑纪
4 Waterside House
   面水轩
5 Pavilion of Imperial Stele
   御碑纪
6 Toilet
   公厕
7 Buqi Pavilion
   步碕亭
8 Pavilion for Admiring Fish
   观鱼处
9 Canglangting Garden
   沧浪亭
10 Wenmiaoxiang House
   闻妙香亭
11 Qingxiang Hall
   清香馆
12 Shrine of 500 Sages
   五百名贤祠
13 Enlightened Way Hall
   明道堂
14 Yangzi Pavilion
   仰止亭
15 Cuilinglong Houses
   翠玲珑
16 Kanshan Tower
   看山楼
17 Yaohuajingjie House
   瑶华仙境

This garden was laid out in the 12th century, abandoned, then restored in the 18th century as part of the residence of a retired official. According to one story, he announced that he'd had enough of bureaucracy and would rather be a fisherman. Another explanation of the name is that it was simply near Wangshi Lu.

The eastern part of the garden is the residential area – originally with side rooms for sedan-chair lackeys, guest reception and living quarters. The central part is the main garden. The western part is an inner garden where a courtyard contains the Spring-Rear Cottage *(diànchūn yí)*, the master's study. This section and the study, with its Ming-style furniture and palace lanterns, was duplicated and unveiled at the Metropolitan Museum of Art in New York in 1981.

A miniature model of the whole garden, using Qingtian jade, Yingde rocks, Anhui paper, Suzhou silk and incorporating the halls, kiosks, ponds, blossoms and rare plants of the original design, was produced especially for a display at the Pompidou Centre in Paris in 1982.

The most striking feature of this garden is its use of space. Despite its size, the scale of the buildings is large, but nothing appears cramped. A section of the buildings is used by a cooperative of woodblock artists who find the peaceful atmosphere congenial to work. The entrance is via a narrow alley just west of the Suzhou Hotel.

Garden for Lingering In *(liúyuán)* Extending over an area of three hectares, the Garden for Lingering In is one of the largest Suzhou gardens, noted for its adroit partitioning with building complexes. It dates from the Ming Dynasty and managed to escape destruction during the Taiping Rebellion. A 700-metre covered walkway connects the major scenic spots, and the windows have carefully selected perspectives. The walkway is inlaid with calligraphy from celebrated masters. The garden has a wealth of potted plants. Outside Mandarin Duck (Yuanyang) Hall is a 6½-metre-high Lake Tai piece – it's the final word on rockeries. The garden is about one km west of the old city walls. The bus there will take you over bridges that look down on the busy water traffic.

West Garden Temple
(xīyuán sì)
About 500 metres west of the Garden for Lingering In, this temple was built on the site of a garden laid out at the same time as the Garden for Lingering In and then donated to the Buddhist community. The temple was destroyed in the 19th century and entirely rebuilt; it contains some expressive Buddhist statues.

Cold Mountain Temple
(hánshān sì)
One km west of the Garden for Lingering In, this temple was named after the poet-monk Hanshan, who lived in the 7th century. It was repeatedly burnt down and rebuilt, and holds little of interest except for a stele by poet Zhang Ji immortalising nearby Maple Bridge and the temple bell (since removed to Japan). However, the fine walls and the humpback bridge are worth seeing. The temple was once the site of lively local trading in silk, wood and grain. Not far from its saffron walls lies the Grand Canal. To get to the temple take bus No 4 to the terminal, cross the bridge and walk to the No 6 bus route; or take bus No 5 and then connect with No 6.

Tiger Hill
(hǔqiūshān)
In the far north-west of town, Tiger Hill is likely to be of more interest to Chinese tourists than to those from overseas. The hill itself is artificial, and is the final resting place of He Lu, founding father of Suzhou. He Lu died in the 6th century BC, and myths have coalesced around him – he is said to have been buried with a collection of 3000 swords and be guarded by a white tiger.

Places to Stay – bottom end
The *Lexiang Hotel* (☎ 522-2815) *(lèxiāng fàndiàn)* remains the only budget hotel in Suzhou. Beds in four-bed dorms are Y50,

while doubles with attached bathroom range from Y198 to Y328. Foreigners are automatically shunted into a dorm room. Look for the sign pointing down an alley on Renmin Lu. To get there take bus No 1 from the railway station.

Places to Stay – middle

The south-eastern corner of town is a goldmine of mid-range accommodation. The best value for money is probably the *Friendship Hotel* (☎ 529-1601) *(yǒuyí bīnguǎn)* on Zhuhui Lu. Standard doubles start at Y220.

Just down the street, the *Xiangwang Hotel* (☎ 529-1162) *(xiāngwáng bīnguǎn)* offers a similar deal. Standard doubles are Y220 or Y280. The hotel is on the north-western corner of Xiangwang Lu and Zhuhui Lu.

Walk around the corner and you'll reach the entrance of the *Gusu Hotel* (☎ 519-5127; fax 519-9727) *(gūsū fàndiàn)*, 5 Xiangwang Lu, off Shiquan Jie, a sprawling place with standard doubles from Y260 to Y360.

The *Nanlin Hotel* (☎ 522-4641) *(nánlín fàndiàn)* is at 22 Gunxiufang, off Shiquan Jie. Its very pleasant gardens include a small section with outdoor ceramic tables and chairs. Doubles cost from Y290.

A final possibility is the *Overseas Chinese Hotel* (☎ 720-2883) *(huáqiáo dàjiǔdiàn)* at 518 Renmin Lu, just north of Guanqian Jie. It has standard doubles at Y300.

Places to Stay – top end

The *Bamboo Grove Hotel* (☎ 520-5601; fax 520-8778) *(zhúhuī fàndiàn)*, on Zhuhui Lu, is the pick of Suzhou's top-end accommodation with all the facilities you would expect of a five-star hotel. Room rates start at US$110.

The *Suzhou Hotel* (☎ 520-4646; fax 520-5191) *(sūzhōu fàndiàn)*, 115 Shiquan Jie, does a brisk trade in tour groups, and is a fairly dull place. Rooms start at US$70.

The *Nanyuan Guesthouse* (☎ 522-7661; fax 523-8806) *(nányuán bīnguǎn)*, 249 Shiquan Jie, is inside a walled garden compound. Room prices start at Y522.

Places to Eat

Particularly if you're based in the south-east corner of town, Shiquan Jie and the alleys that run off it is one of the best areas to seek out places to eat. Suzhou is a tourist town, and consequently there is no shortage of expensive places serving up tourist cuisine. On Shiquan Jie, at least there are numerous dumpling and noodle places where you can eat for around Y6 per head. Opposite the Friendship Hotel look out for the *Bamboo Grove Snack Bar (zhúyuán cāntīng)*, which has affordable stir fries. The *Xinjufeng Restaurant (xīnjùfēng càiguǎn)*, near the North Temple, serves bland food. The *My City* ice cream shops are good.

If money is no object, you might try the *Songhelou Restaurant (sōnghè lóu)*, at 141 Guanqian Jie, rated as the most famous restaurant in Suzhou: Emperor Qianlong is said to have eaten there. The large variety of dishes includes squirrel fish, plain steamed prawns, braised eel, pork with pine nuts, butterfly-shaped sea cucumber, watermelon chicken and spicy duck. The waiter will insist that you be parcelled off to the special 'tour bus' cubicle at the back where an English menu awaits. The Songhelou runs from Guanqian Jie to an alley behind, where tour minibuses pull up. Travellers give it mixed reviews.

Most Suzhou hotels also have restaurants. The best can be found in the Bamboo Grove Hotel.

Entertainment

Very popular is the nightly performance of dance and song at the *Garden of the Master of the Nets*. The show lasts from 7.30 to 10.30 pm and tickets can be bought from CITS for Y50. Alternatively, turn up shortly before the performance and buy a ticket on the spot.

Things to Buy

Suzhou-style embroidery, calligraphy, paintings, sandalwood fans, writing brushes and silk underclothes are for sale nearly everywhere, probably even in the gift shop of your hotel. For silk items, try the Silk Mansion on

Renmin Lu, and for other souvenir items, the Suzhou Antiques Store also on Renmin Lu. Check prices against those in the small souvenir shops on Shiquan Jie before making any purchases, however.

The newsagent in the Bamboo Grove Hotel has a good selection of foreign books.

Getting There & Away

Air Suzhou does not have an airport, but China Eastern Airlines (☎ 522-2788) (*dōngfāng hángkōng gōngsī*) has a ticket office at 192 Renmin Lu for booking flights out of Shanghai.

Bus The long-distance bus station is at the southern end of Renmin Lu. Considering that Suzhou is relatively prosperous and supposedly a major tourist attraction, the bus station is surprisingly primitive. There are connections between Suzhou and just about every major place in the region, including Shanghai, Hangzhou, Wuxi, Yangzhou and Yixing.

Train Suzhou is on the railway line from Nanjing to Shanghai. To Shanghai takes about 1¼ hours, to Wuxi 40 minutes and to Nanjing 3¼ hours. For long-distance sleepers, ask your hotel or try CITS.

Boat There are boats along the Grand Canal to Hangzhou. It's basically only foreigners and Overseas Chinese who use them these days – locals prefer to travel by bus or train.

Boats from Suzhou to Hangzhou depart daily at 5 pm and arrive the next morning at 7.30 am. The fare is Y78 for a sleeper in a four-berth room or Y150 in a double. Tickets can be bought through CITS or at the 'civilisation unit' window at the boat booking office. CITS adds a Y20 service charge.

Getting Around

Bus The main thoroughfare is Renmin Lu with the railway station, just off the northern end, and a large boat dock and long-distance bus station at the southern end.

Bus No 1 runs the length of Renmin Lu.

Bus No 2 is a kind of round-the-city bus, while bus No 5 is a good east-west bus. Bus No 4 runs from Changmen directly east along Baita Lu, turns south and runs past the eastern end of Guanqian Jie and then on to the Suzhou Hotel.

Taxi Taxis and motorcycle taxis congregate outside the main railway station, down by the boat dock at the southern end of Renmin Lu, and at Jingmen (Nanxin Bridge) at the western end of Jingde Lu. They also tend to hover around tourist hotels. Drivers generally use their meters. Like elsewhere in China, the pedicab drivers are almost more trouble than they are worth.

Bicycle There is bicycle rental available next door to the Lexiang Hotel for Y10 per day. Rental is also available from a shop just opposite the entrance to the Suzhou Hotel.

AROUND SUZHOU

Some of the local buses go for a considerable distance, such as bus No 11. You could hop on one for a ride to the terminal to see the enchanting countryside.

Grand Canal
(*dàyùn hé*)

The canal proper cuts to the west and south of Suzhou, within a 10-km range of the town. Suburban bus Nos 13, 14, 15 and 16 will get you there. In the north-west, bus No 11 follows the canal for a fair distance. Once you arrive, it's simply a matter of finding yourself a nice bridge, getting out your deck chair and watching the world go by. Unfortunately, parking yourself for too long could make you the main tourist attraction for hordes of Chinese spectators.

Precious Belt Bridge
(*bǎodài qiáo*)

This is one of China's best, with 53 arches, the three central humpbacks being larger to allow boats through. It straddles the Grand Canal, and is a popular spot with fisherfolk. The bridge is not used for traffic – a modern one has been built alongside – and is thought to be a Tang Dynasty construction named after Wang Zhongshu, a local prefect who sold his precious belt to pay for the bridge's construction for the benefit of his people. Precious Belt Bridge is about five km south-east of Suzhou. Bus No 13 will set you on the right track.

Lake Taihu Area

The following places can all be reached by long-distance buses from the station at the southern end of Renmin Lu in Suzhou.

Lingyanshan (*língyán shān*) This is 15 km south-west of Suzhou. There are weirdly shaped rocks, a temple and pagoda (molested by Red Guards), and panoramas of mulberry trees, fertile fields and Lake Taihu in the distance.

The now active Buddhist monastery has a 'Tibetan feel'. It's set aloft a large hill, though in these parts 'large' is relative to totally flat. The monastery dates back to the Ming Dynasty. It was shut down during the Cultural Revolution but was permitted to reopen in 1980.

Lingyanshan is a lovely place to cycle to, though along the way you pass some nightmarish scenes of industrial pollution (these can be intriguing in their own bizarre way).

Tianpingshan (*tiānpíng shān*) This is 18 km south-west of Suzhou and has more of the same – plus some medicinal spring waters.

Guangfu (*guāngfú*) Twenty-five km to the south-west, bordering the lake, Guangfu has an ancient seven-storey pagoda and is dotted with plum trees.

Dongshan (*dōngshān*) Forty km to the south-west of Suzhou, this place is noted for its gardens and the Purple Gold (Zijin) Nunnery, which contains 16 coloured clay arhats and is surrounded by Lake Taihu on three sides.

Xidongtingshan Island (*xīdòngtíng shān*) This town, also called Xishan, is a large island 60 km south-west of Suzhou. Getting

there involves a 10-km ferry ride. Eroded Taihu rocks are 'harvested' here for landscaping. Take a bus from opposite Suzhou Railway Station to Luxian, then catch a ferry across to Zhenxia.

Changshu (*chángshú*) Fifty km north-east of Suzhou, this town is noted for its lace making. To the north-west of the town is Yushan, with historical and scenic spots, including a nine-storey Song pagoda.

Luzhi (*lùzhí*) In this town on the water, 25 km east of Suzhou, the canals provide the main means of commuting – in concrete flat-bottomed boats. The old Baosheng temple has arhats, although that is probably not why you should come here.

XUZHOU

(*xúzhoū*)

Xuzhou does not fall into the category of a canal town, though a tributary of the Grand Canal passes by its north-eastern end. The history of the town has little to do with the canal – Xuzhou is basically a railway junction with little to see beyond a couple of temples. Oh yes, there is something else – the coal mines. If you should accidentally get stuck here on your way to somewhere else, the following sights might keep you amused for a couple of hours:

Dragon in the Clouds Hill

(*yúnlóng shān*)

This hill has half the scenery of Xuzhou: the Xinghua Temple, several pavilions and a stone carving from the Northern Wei Dynasty. If you climb to the top of the hill, to the Xinghua Temple, there's a magnificent panorama of the concrete boxes that compose the Xuzhou valley and the mountains that encircle it. There are even orchards out there somewhere. Set in a grotto off the mountainside is a giant gilded buddha head, the statue of the Sakyamuni Buddha. The park itself has an outdoor shooting gallery, and peanuts and ice-lolly sticks littering the slopes. The hill is a 10-minute walk west of the Nanjiao Hotel, or take bus No 2 or 11.

Monument to Huaihai Campaign Martyrs

(huáihǎi zhànyì lièshì jìniàntǎ)

This revolutionary war memorial and obelisk, which was opened in 1965, is in a huge wooded park at the southern edge of town. The Huaihai battle was a decisive one fought by the People's Liberation Army from November 1948 to January 1949. The obelisk is 38½ metres high and has a gold inscription by Chairman Mao approached by a grand flight of stairs leading up to it. The nearby Memorial Hall contains an extensive collection of weaponry, photos, maps, paintings and memorabilia – over 2000 items altogether – as well as inscriptions by important heads of state, from Zhou Enlai to Deng Xiaoping. The grounds, 100 acres of pines and cypresses, are meant to be 'symbolic of the evergreen spirit of the revolutionary martyrs'. The park is on the bus No 11 route.

LIANYUNGANG

(liányúngǎng)

The town is divided into port and city sections. Yuntai Hill is the 'scenic spot' overlooking the ocean, and there are some salt mines along the shores, as well as a Taoist monastery. The mountain is reputed to be the inspiration for the Flowers and Fruit Mountain in the Ming Dynasty classic *Journey to the West* (but three other places make the same claim). Other sights include the 2000-year-old stone carvings at Kung Wangshan. There's an International Seamen's Club, CITS office and several hotels.

Getting There & Away

CAAC flies between Lianyungang and Beijing, Guangzhou and Shanghai. Buses along the east coast connect Lianyungang with Shanghai. From Xuzhou, a branch line runs east to the major coastal port of Lianyungang (a six-hour ride).

Anhui 安徽

The provincial borders of Anhui (ānhuī) were defined by the Qing government and, except for a few changes to the boundary with Jiangsu, have since remained unchanged. Northern Anhui forms part of the North China plain, settled by the Han Chinese in large numbers during the Han Dynasty. The Yangzi River cuts through the southern quarter of Anhui and the area south of the river was not actually settled until the 7th and 8th centuries.

Anhui's historical and tourist sights are mainly in the south, and hence more accessible from Hangzhou or Shanghai than from the provincial capital, Hefei. Most famous are the spectacular Huangshan (Yellow Mountains), in the far south of the province, and nearby Jiuhuashan. The Yangzi River ports of Guichi and Wuhu are convenient jumping-off points for the Jiuhuashan and Huangshan mountains.

HEFEI

(héféi)

Although the capital of Anhui Province, Hefei is well off the beaten track. The city was a quiet market town before 1949 and has since expanded to become an industrial centre, with a population of over 500,000. It has a few minor attractions, and the system of parks and lakes surrounding the city centre is a pleasant touch; but at best the city can only be recommended as a brief stopover.

Orientation

The railway station and long-distance bus station are in the east of town. Shengli Lu leads down to the Nanfei River (which, along with a series of ponds to the south, forms a circle around the city centre), which you cross to reach the city centre. Changjiang Lu, a thoroughfare which cuts east-west through the city, is the main commercial district. Accommodation for foreigners is concentrated in the city centre and on Meishan Lu

Population: 55 million
Capital: Hefei
Highlights:

- The Huangshan mountains, for many Chinese almost definitive of natural beauty
- Jiuhuashan mountain, a Buddhist sacred mountain and a good antidote to the crowds at Huangshan

in the south-west of town overlooking Yuhua Pond.

Information

There is nothing in the way of useful tourist information around town. The Bank of China is at 155 Changjiang Lu, though money can also be changed at the Anhui Hotel.

Things to See & Do

If you have some time to kill in Hefei, there are some pleasant parks around town. **Xiaoyaojin Park** (xiāoyáojīn gōngyuán), in the north-east corner of town, is the most expansive and has a small, rather depressing zoo. **Baohebin Park** (bāohé gōngyuán), in the south of town, has a series of small tombs and a temple – nothing to get wildly excited about but pleasant enough on a sunny day.

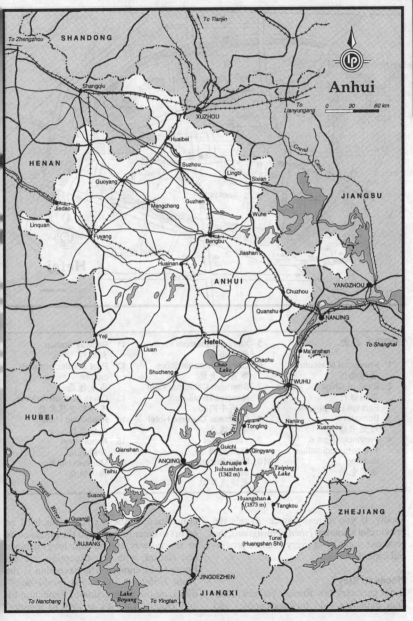

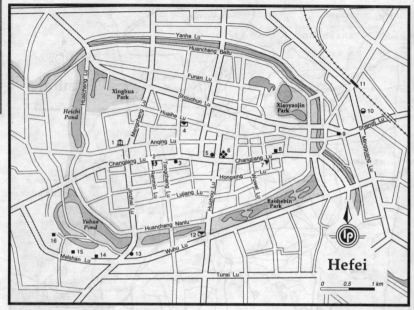

HEFEI 合肥

1 Provincial Museum
省博物馆

2 Bank of China
中国银行

3 Foreign Languages
Bookstore
外文书店

4 Provincial Post &
Telecommunications
Building
省邮电局

5 Xinhua Bookstore
新华书店

6 City Department Store
市百货大楼

7 Southern California Beef
Noodles Restaurant
加州牛肉面

8 Overseas Chinese Hotel
华侨饭店

9 Yinlu Hotel
银路大酒店

10 Long-Distance Bus
Station
长途汽车站

11 Railway Station
火车站

12 Post & Telecommuni-
cations
市电信局

13 China Eastern Airlines
东方航空售票处

14 Friendship Hotel
友谊宾馆

15 Anhui Hotel
安徽饭店

16 Meishan Hotel
梅山饭店

Finally, if you're really stuck, there's the
Provincial Museum (*shěng bówùguàn*), the
good old stand-by of every Chinese provincial capital.

Places to Stay

Hefei gets very few foreign visitors (other
than expenses-paid businesspeople) and

consequently doesn't make much of an
effort to cater to them. All the hotels close
to the railway station and long-distance
bus station, with one exception, are off
limits to foreigners. The exception is the
Yinlu Hotel (☎ 262-8255) (*yínlù dàjiǔdiàn*), on the intersection of Shouchun Lu
and Huaihe Lu (it's around 10 minutes'

walk from the railway station. Clean air-con doubles cost Y168.

Budget travellers will have to head out to the *Meishan Hotel* (☎ 281-3555) *(méishān fàndiàn)*, on Meishan Lu, where beds in basic doubles cost Y40. The Meishan Hotel is a sprawling place and also has expensive villas. To find the cheap rooms, head in through the gate and bear left, looking out for the reception area in a building on your right. The No 10 bus runs from the railway station and stops outside the hotel; alternatively, a taxi (if you can find one with a meter) costs Y8 to Y10.

Most other accommodation has mid-range prices. Closest to the railway station, at 68 Changjiang Lu, is the *Overseas Chinese Hotel* (☎ 265-2221) *(huáqiáo fàndiàn)*, which has a bewildering host of rooms ranging from Y160 for a double in the A block, Y230 in the B block to Y300 in the C block. The *Friendship Hotel* (☎ 282-1707) *(yǒuyì bīnguǎn)* is just down the road from the Meishan Hotel, and has doubles at Y189 and Y221.

The smart set reside at the *Anhui Hotel* (☎ 281-1818; fax 282-2857) *(ānhuī fàndiàn)*, a joint-venture grab at three-star elegance, with the full complement of services, such as English-speaking staff, health centre, coffee shop etc. Rooms range from Y640 to Y860 and upwards for suites and the like.

Places to Eat

Hefei is not exactly the culinary capital of China. The railway station area is particularly dire, being dominated by stalls selling precooked meals in metal trays swarming with flies. The *Southern California Beef Noodles Restaurant (nánjiāzhōu niúróumián)*, more or less opposite the Overseas Chinese Hotel, is a good stand-by, with tasty noodles from Y6. Meishan Lu also has a reasonable selection of restaurants, but don't expect to find anything with an English menu. Finally, the Overseas Chinese Hotel has a decent coffee shop.

Getting There & Away

Air Hefei has a limited selection of flights to major Chinese destinations such as Beijing

(daily), Changchun, Chengdu, Fuzhou, Guangzhou (daily), Haikou, Hangzhou, Huangshan (daily), Shanghai (daily), Shenzhen, Shenyang, Wenzhou Wuhan, Xiamen, Xi'an and even Hong Kong (twice weekly). Bookings can be made at the China Eastern Airlines booking office (☎ 282-2357) at 246 Jinzhai Lu or at the booking office directly opposite the railway station.

Bus The massive bus station just down the road from the railway station has buses to destinations all over China. There are daily departures to nearby destinations such as Hangzhou, Jingdezhen, Wuhan, Nanjing and Huangshan. Sleeper buses head out to cities such as Guangzhou, Shanghai and Qingdao, but bear in mind that long-distance hauls of this sort are only for the truly desperate.

Train Hefei is connected by direct trains to Shanghai (12 hours), Beijing (16 hours), Zhengzhou (13 hours, via Kaifeng), Chengdu (34 hours) and Xiamen (38 hours).

Hard-seat tickets can be purchased by biting and clawing your way to the front of one of the 'queues' in the ticket office of the railway station. For hard-sleeper or soft-sleeper tickets you will have to head over to a white-tiled building about 100 metres to the left after you exit the station. Ticket window No 2 is the place to buy tickets; it is open from 8.30 to 10.30 am and 2.30 to 4.30 pm.

BOZHOU
(bózhōu)

Bozhou lies in Anhui's far north-west, near the border with Henan. It's not a particularly attractive place, but this small regional city has long been one of the most important trading centres for traditional medicine in central China, and attracts merchants and Chinese herbalists from a wide area. The 5th-century BC founder of Taoism, Lao Zi, was supposedly born near Bozhou.

Things to See

Bozhou's main attraction is its very large **Medicinal Market** *(zhōngyào shìchǎng)*, which has some interesting merchandise.

Wandering through the rows of stalls, each specialising in a particular substance, you'll see mounds of pressed herbs and flowers, roots of obscure origin, rocks and other minerals, as well as wasp nests, animal skins, tortoise shells, dried insects and snakes – it's not for the faint-hearted.

The **Underground Pass** (yǐn bīn dìxiàdào) is a 600-metre-long subterranean passageway running parallel to one of the main streets, and once served as a secret route for soldiers. You can walk right through the narrow, damp tunnel, though anyone tall or prone to claustrophobia may find the going a bit confined.

The **Guandi Temple** (huāxìlóu) has an ornate tiled gate built in the Qing Dynasty and a small museum whose collection includes a Han Dynasty burial suit unearthed in 1973 and made from pieces of jade held together with silver thread.

Places to Stay

Most places seem willing to take foreigners. The *Bozhou Hotel* (☎ (05681) 22048) (bózhōu bīnguǎn) on Banjie Lou in the middle of town is Bozhou's main tourist hotel and has a small CITS office. Good doubles cost Y100 a night. The hotel's cheapest beds are Y25 in three-person dorms with communal bathroom.

The *Gujing Hotel* (gǔjǐng dàjiǔdiàn) is another new white-tiled monstrosity on the main corner, one km south of the long-distance bus station. Standard doubles go for Y240. The Medicinal Market is just across the intersection.

Getting There & Away

From the long-distance bus station there are connections to Wuhan, Zhengzhou, Hefei, Shanghai and Nanjing. Bozhou is also on the Zhengzhou-Hefei railway line and all passing trains stop here. Bozhou Railway Station is about 10 km south-east of the city.

HUANGSHAN RANGE

(huángshān)
Huangshan (Yellow Mountains) is the name of the 72-peak range lying in the south of

Anhui Province, 280 km west of Hangzhou. For the Chinese, Huangshan, along with Guilin, is probably the most famous landscape attraction in the country – a local tourist map declares solemnly that it is the 'marvellousest mountain on earth'. Whether you concur with such bold claims or not, in good weather Huangshan is truly beautiful, and the surrounding countryside, with its traditional villages and patchwork paddy fields, is among the best in China.

Huangshan has a 1200-year pedigree as a tourist attraction. The Tang Dynasty emperor Tian Biao gave it its present name in the 8th century. Countless painters and poets have since trudged around the range seeking inspiration and bestowing the peaks with fanciful names, such as Nine Dragons, Taoist

---

HUANGSHAN 黄山

1 Refreshing Terrace Lookout
   清凉台
2 Beihai Hotel
   北海宾馆
3 Xihai Hotel
   西海宾馆
4 Flying Rock
   飞来石
5 Upper Cable-Car Station
   白岭索道站
6 Tianhai Hotel
   天海宾馆
7 Jade Screen Tower Hotel
   玉屏宾馆
8 Mid-Level Temple (hotel)
   半山寺
9 Lower Cable-Car Station
   云谷寺索道站
10 Yungu Hotel
   云谷山庄
11 Mercy Light Temple
   慈光阁
12 Huangshan Hotel
   黄山宾馆
13 Huang Mountain Wenquan Hotel
   黄山温泉大酒店
14 Peach Blossom Hotel
   桃源宾馆
15 Tiandu Hotel
   天都山庄

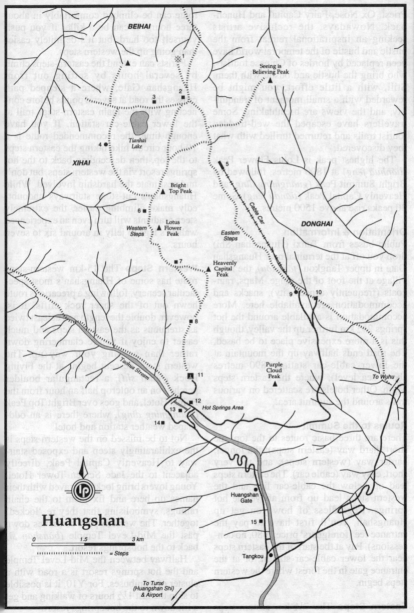

Priest, Ox Nose, Fairy Capital and Hunchback. Nowadays, the reclusive artists seeking an inspirational retreat from the hustle and bustle of the temporal world have been replaced by hordes of Chinese tourists, who bring the hustle and bustle with them. Still, with a little effort, you might be rewarded with a small moment of tranquillity, and the views are breathtaking. Some travellers have escaped the well-trodden tourist trails and returned thrilled with what they discovered.

The highest peak is Lotus Flower Peak *(liánhuā fēng)* at 1800 metres, followed by Bright Summit Peak *(guāngmíng dǐng)* and Heavenly Capital Peak *(tiāndū fēng)*. Some 30 peaks rise above 1500 metres.

Orientation & Information

Public buses from Tunxi (Huangshan Shi) drop you off at the terminal near Huangshan Gate in upper Tangkou *(tāngkǒu)*, the main village at the foot of the range. Maps, raincoats (frequently a necessity), snacks and accommodation are available here. More accommodation is available around the hot springs 2½ km further up the valley, though this is a more expensive place to be based. The road ends halfway up the mountain at the lower cable-car station (890 metres above sea level), where the eastern steps begin. Other hotels are scattered on various trails around the summit area.

Routes to the Summit

There are three basic routes to the top: the short, hard way (eastern steps); the longer, harder way (western steps); and the very short, easy way (cable car). The eastern steps lead up below the cable-car line and the western steps lead up from above the hot springs. Regardless of how you get up Huangshan, you'll first have to pay the entrance fee (foreigners' price: Y80, no concessions). Pay at the start of the eastern steps near the lower cable-car station, or at the entrance gate in the forest where the western steps begin.

Eastern Steps The 7½-km eastern-steps

route can be climbed comfortably in about three hours. It can be a killer if you push yourself too hard, but it's definitely easier than going up the western steps.

Purists can extend the eastern-steps climb by several hours by setting out from Huangshan Gate, where a stepped path crosses the road at several points before connecting with the main eastern-steps trail at the lower cable-car station. If you have enough time, the recommended route is a 10-hour circuit hike taking the eastern steps to the top, then descending back to the hot springs resort via the western steps, but don't underestimate the hardship involved. While Huangshan's cut-stone stairways undoubtedly make climbing easier, the extremely steep gradients will turn even an experienced walker's legs to jelly in around six to seven hours.

Western Steps The 15-km western-steps route has some of Huangshan's most spectacular scenery, following a precarious route hewn out of the sheer rock cliffs. It is, however, double the length and at least twice as strenuous as the eastern steps and much easier to enjoy if you're clambering down rather than gasping your way up. The western steps descent begins at the Flying Rock *(fēilái shí)*, a rectangular boulder perched on an outcrop half an hour from the Beihai Hotel, and goes over Bright Top Peak *(guāngmíng dǐng)*, where there is an odd-shaped weather station and hotel.

Not to be missed on the western steps is the exhilaratingly steep and exposed stairway to Heavenly Capital Peak, directly adjacent to the Jade Screen Tower Hotel. Young lovers bring locks engraved with their names up here and fix them to the chain railings, symbolising that they're 'locked' together. The western path continues down past the Mid-Level Temple *(bànshān sì)* back to the hot springs resort.

Halfway between the Mid-Level Temple and the hot springs resort is a road with a cluster of minibuses. For Y10, it is possible to skip the last 1½ hours of walking and get a lift down to the hot springs resort.

Cable Car The eight-minute cable-car ride is the least painful way up. For Y10, minibuses take you from Huangshan Gate to the lower cable-car station. From here the round-trip cable-car fare is Y70 for foreigners. There are *no* student concessions, *no* one-way tickets, nor are tickets sold at the cable car's upper station. Either get here very early in the day (the service starts at 5.30 am) or later in the day (if you're staying overnight). Queues of over one hour are the norm, and in peak season many people wait as long as two or three hours for a ride – you may as well walk.

Guides & Porters
If you think you're having a hard time, spare a thought for the daily army of lean and agile porters lugging someone else's cargo of 50 kg or more up the mountain – crates of drink bottles, baskets of food, even the odd flabby tourist.

Guides are not really necessary since the mountain paths are very easy to follow. CITS can organise an English-speaking guide for around Y200 per day. Private individuals sometimes offer their services as guides too, but virtually none speak any English besides 'hello'. The truly decadent might make their ascent in a makeshift sedan chair strung between bamboo poles and bounced (literally) along by two porters. The price? Around Y200 to Y300 one-way depending on how hard you bargain.

On the Summit
Paved trails meander around the lookout points of Huangshan's summit area. Imagine a Chinese ink landscape and you will have an idea of what the Chinese tourists are gasping at – gnarled pines, craggy rocks, a rolling sea of clouds, perhaps an ant line of pinprick tourists in the distance toiling up some pointing finger of a peak.

The agreed highlight of Huangshan is the Beihai sunrise: a 'sea' of low cloud blanketing the valley to the north with 'island' peaks hazily reaching for the heavens. Fresh Breeze Terrace (five minutes from the Beihai Hotel) attracts daily sunrise crowds (hotels

supply thick padded jackets for the occasion). It's communal sightseeing at its best and the noise generated by several hundred Chinese tourists is almost as incredible as the sunrise itself. Fortunately, most of them hurry back to eat breakfast shortly afterwards, leaving you to enjoy the mountains in peace.

Places to Stay & Eat
There are five locations with hotels and restaurants in the Huangshan area. Prices and availability of beds can vary a lot according to seasonal demand.

Tangkou *(tāngkǒu)* Tangkou is the best place to be based for an assault on Huangshan. Accommodation up on the mountain and in the hot spring resort is expensive. The three main hotels taking foreigners are on the side road leading down to the village.

The *Free and Unfettered Hotel* (☎ (0559) 556-2571) *(xiāoyáo bīnguǎn)* is probably the best deal in town. The staff are friendly, speak a little English and have beds in functional triples for Y80 or Y90. Standard doubles with attached bathroom cost Y200. There is an English sign pointing down to the hotel (about five minutes' walk) from the main road, which reads 'Xiaoyao Hotel'.

The *Tangkou Hotel* (☎ (0559) 556-2400) *(tāngkǒu bīnguǎn)* is just up the hill from the Free and Unfettered Hotel, 200 metres off the main road. Economy four-bed rooms are Y40 per bed, but not always easy to get. Standard doubles cost Y240.

Further up the hill again and close to the main road is the *Huangshan Yinqiao Hotel* (☎ (0559) 556-2968). It has basic doubles for Y80 and standard doubles for Y100 per bed (or Y200 for the room).

The *Tiandu Hotel* (☎ (0559) 556-2160) *(tiāndū shānzhuāng)*, 700 metres downhill from Huangshan Gate, charges Y60 for a bed in a three-bed room, and Y280 for an air-con double. It's the closest place to the bus terminal.

There is no problem finding food in Tangkou (the restaurant owners will chase you down the street making vivid eating gestures). There is a small restaurant directly opposite the Free and Unfettered Hotel with an English menu. Watch out for overcharging generally in Tangkou – many places specialise in expensive local treats such as mountain frogs and preserved meats.

Hot Springs The hot spring resort, 2½ km further uphill, is a quiet, attractive place to stay but accommodation tends to be a little overpriced. Hot spring baths are available next door to the Huangshan Hotel for Y60 (foreigners' price) in a private bathroom.

The *Huangshan Hotel* (☎ (0559) 556-2202) *(huángshān bīnguǎn)* advertises itself as 'a public service of believable sanitation unit'. Whatever this means, it's the least expensive hotel taking foreigners, with beds in basic doubles for Y50. Doubles with bathroom and air-con cost Y320.

Just across the bridge is the *Huang Mountain Wenquan Hotel* (☎ (0559) 556-2196) *(huángshān wénquán dàjiǔdiàn).* For Y120 all you get is a rather dreary double on the hotel's lowest level, but its rooms for Y280 are much better.

Higher up the hillside is the overpriced *Peach Blossom Hotel* (☎ (0559) 556-2666) *(táoyuán bīnguǎn),* with doubles from US$40 to US$70 and suites for US$120.

The Huang Mountain and the Peach Blossom each have restaurants; as in Tangkou, restaurant touts prowl the streets in pursuit of hungry travellers. Again, watch out for overcharging.

Lower Cable-Car Station There is one hotel here, the *Yungu Hotel* (☎ (0559) 566-2444) *(yúngǔ shānzhuāng),* down the steps from the car park in front of the cable-car station. It has expensive doubles for Y250 and very few foreigners (if any) stay here.

Summit Area Ideally a visit to Huangshan should include a stay on the summit. Unfortunately, the cheaper hotels are officially off limits to foreigners. One place worth trying is the *Shizi Hotel (shīzi fàndiàn),* which has beds in eight-bed dorms for Y40 but is

adamant (most of the time) about not taking foreigners. Some travellers end up camping out.

The *Beihai Hotel* (☎ (0559) 556-2558) *(běihǎi bīnguǎn)* is ridiculously overpriced, but is the cheapest place taking foreigners. Doubles range from Y580 to Y700.

The joint-venture *Xihai Hotel* (☎ (0559) 256-2132/3) *(xīhǎi bīnguǎn),* further west along the trail, is a real 'mountain hotel' designed by Swedish architects. Doubles start at over US$100. All rooms have heating and 24-hour hot water.

The Xihai and the Beihai both have bars and full-service restaurants serving Western and Chinese food but, inconveniently, are open only for a few hours around lunch and dinner time. Cheaper meals are available from stalls and simple restaurants nearby.

Western Steps Highest up is the *Tianhai Hotel (tiānhǎi bīnguǎn)* just down from Bright Top Peak, with basic rooms at Y180.

Further down the mountain at a spectacular 1660-metre-high lookout near Heavenly Capital Peak is the *Jade Screen Tower Hotel* (☎ (0559) 556-2540) *(yùpínglóu bīnguǎn).* The rates and conditions reflect this hotel's relative inaccessibility: a simple double is Y220, and washing arrangements are basic indeed. The next place you'll come to is the small *Mid-Level Temple (bànshān sì)* at 1340 metres. It only has a small dorm, and is best considered as emergency accommodation.

Considering its location, the Jade Screen Tower Hotel has a very cheap dining hall beside the tiny courtyard, and a better restaurant upstairs. The Mid-Level Temple has a teahouse serving simpler meals and refreshments.

Getting There & Away
Air The airport serving Huangshan is at Tunxi (Huangshan Shi). There are flights to Beijing (three a week), Guangzhou (six a week), Hefei (daily), Kunming (via Guilin; twice weekly), Shanghai (daily except Tuesday) and Shenzhen, and there are less frequent flights to Fuzhou, Xiamen and

Xi'an. There are also twice-weekly flights to Hong Kong.

Bus A new paved road means that buses from Tunxi (Huangshan Shi) now only take around 1½ hours to reach Huangshan Gate. In summer other direct buses come from Hefei (eight hours), Shanghai (10 hours), Hangzhou, Suzhou and Jingdezhen. There are also buses from the Yangzi River ports of Wuhu and Guichi.

Train Trains from Hefei and Nanjing via Wuhu pass through Tunxi (Huangshan Shi). For connections from southern destinations, first go to Yingtan (Jiangxi Province) and change trains there.

TUNXI (HUANGSHAN SHI)
(túnxī (huángshān shì))

The old trading town of Tunxi (Huangshan Shi) is roughly 70 km south-east by road from Huangshan. As indicated by its rechristened Chinese name (meaning Huangshan City), Tunxi is significant to travellers only as a jumping-off point for the Huangshan area.

Regular buses run between Tunxi and Tangkou in the Huangshan mountains. There are other scheduled bus services to Shanghai, Hangzhou, Hefei, Nanjing and Jingdezhen, and direct trains to Hefei, Yingtan (via Jingdezhen) and Wuhu. The local airport receives many weekly flights from Beijing, Guangzhou and Shanghai as well as other regional Chinese cities.

JIUHUASHAN
(jiǔhuá shān)

One way to avoid the carnival crowds on Huangshan is to skip it in favour of Jiuhuashan. The scenery here is less spectacular, but it is certainly quieter.

Jiuhuashan is one of China's four sacred Buddhist mountains (together with Pu Tuo in Zhejiang, Emei in Sichuan and Wutai in Shanxi). Third-century Taoist monks built thatched temples at Jiuhuashan, but with the rise of Buddhism these were gradually replaced by stone monasteries. Jiuhuashan owes its importance to a Korean Buddhist disciple Kim Kiao Kak, who arrived in 720 and founded a worshipping place for Ksitigarbha, the guardian of the earth. Annual festivities are held on the anniversary of Kim's death (the 30th day of the 7th lunar month), when pilgrims flock to Jiuhuashan. In its heyday during the Tang Dynasty as many as 5000 monks and nuns worshipped at Jiuhuashan, living in more than 300 monasteries. Today only some 70 temples and monasteries survive in the hills around Jiuhuashan.

Orientation & Information

Jiuhua village lies at 600 metres, about halfway up the mountain (or, as the locals say, at roughly navel height in a giant buddha's potbelly). The bus stops just below the main gate where you must pay an entrance fee to Jiuhuashan (Y30). From here Jiuhua Jie, the narrow main street, leads up past cheap restaurants, souvenir stalls and hotels. The village square is built around a large pond along a side street off to the right. Several 'pictorial' maps in Chinese showing mountain paths can be bought in the village.

Places to Stay

At the bottom of the village is the beautiful, palace-style *Qiyuan Monastery (qǐyuán sì)*. Check here for dormitory accommodation, which may be being phased out. Directly across the square from the monastery is the *Julong Hotel* (☎ (05630) 811-368) *(jùlóng bīnguǎn)*, a standard Chinese tourist operation where standard doubles with bathroom cost Y180. The *Bell Tower Hotel* (☎ (05630) 811-251) *(jiǔhuáshān zhōnglóu fàndiàn)*, at the top of the main street, is a better option. Heated doubles cost Y130 with private bathroom and colour TV. Ask about cheaper dorm accommodation, though it is unlikely to be available.

Getting There & Away

In summer there are direct buses to Jiuhuashan from Huangshan via Qingyang (Y17, six hours, including a ferry across the large Taiping Reservoir), Shanghai and

Nanjing. Outside the tourist season, however, you'll probably have to change in Qingyang, from where there are roughly seven buses daily to Jiuhuashan year-round.

WUHU & GUICHI
(wǔhú, guìchí)

Wuhu is a Yangzi River port and a useful railway junction. Railway lines branch off south to Tunxi, east to Shanghai via Nanjing and, from the northern bank of the river, another line heads north to Hefei. There are also buses to Huangshan and Jiuhuashan from Wuhu. To the west of Wuhu is the Yangzi port of Guichi, which also has buses to Huangshan and Jiuhuashan.

Shanghai 上海

Whore of the East, Paris of China, Queen of the Orient; city of quick riches, ill-gotten gains, fortunes lost in vice and the tumble of a dice; domain of adventurers, swindlers, gamblers, drug runners, idle rich, dandies, tycoons, missionaries, gangsters and backstreet pimps; the city that plots revolution and dances as the revolution shoots its way into town. Shanghai *(shànghǎi)* has always been a dark memory in the long years of forgetting that the Communists brought upon their new China.

Shanghai put away its dancing shoes in 1949. For 40 years, those who returned came to a city whose decaying colonial ambience was the only hint that the city was once symbolic of the West's rape of the East and all that went with it.

Today Shanghai has reawakened. Once again, in sleazy backstreet dives and dance halls the city parties on until daybreak. Massive hotels, department store complexes and office buildings litter the horizon, the first subway line has opened, Mercedes cruise the streets, and child beggars and prostitutes lurk in the shadows.

Shanghai is a city relearning its past and inventing its future. And at this point we make an apology. Almost everything you read here will be changed by the time you have this book in your hands. The juggernaut pace of change in Shanghai is such that even locals despair of keeping up with it. The items included in this chapter were chosen on the basis that they are most likely to last – just remember that there will be much that is new as well.

History

As anyone who wanders along the Bund or through the backstreets of Frenchtown can see, Shanghai (the name means 'by the sea') is a Western invention. At the gateway to the Yangzi, it was an ideal trading port. But when the British opened their first concession there in 1842 after the first Opium War

Population: 13.4 million
Highlights:
- The Bund, the single most evocative symbol of the 'Paris of the East'
- Nanjing Lu: socialism with Chinese characteristics shakes hands with shop-till-you-drop commercialism
- Getting lost on the backstreets of Frenchtown
- Yuyuan Gardens, tacky but fun, with some delicious lunchtime snacks

it was little more than a small town supported by fishing and weaving. The British changed all that. The French followed in 1847; an International Settlement was established in 1863; the Japanese arrived in 1895; and the city was parceled up into settlements, all autonomous and immune from Chinese law. It became in effect China's first fully fledged Special Economic Zone.

In the mid-18th century Shanghai had a population of just 50,000; by 1900 the figure had jumped to a million. By the 1930s, the city claimed some 60,000 foreign residents. The International Settlement sported the tallest buildings in Asia. Shanghai had more motor vehicles than all the rest of China put together. The world's great houses of finance

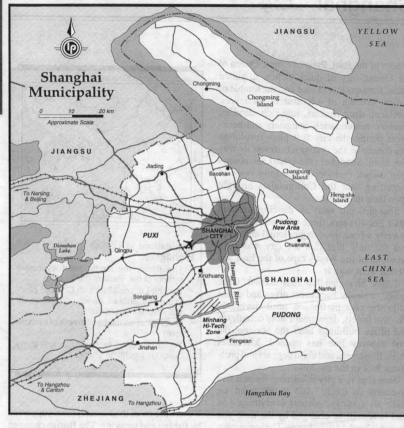

Shanghai
Municipality

0   10   20 km
Approximate Scale

JIANGSU

YELLOW
SEA

Chongming

Chongming
Island

Changxing
Island

Heng-sha
Island

Jiading

Baoshan

JIANGSU

To Nanjing
& Beijing

PUXI

SHANGHAI
CITY

Pudong
New Area

Chuansha

Dianshan
Lake

Qingpu

EAST
CHINA
SEA

Xinzhuang

Huangpu River

SHANGHAI

Nanhui

Songjiang

PUDONG

Minhang
Hi-Tech
Zone

Fengxian

Jinshan

ZHEJIANG   To Hangzhou

Hangzhou Bay

To Hangzhou
& Canton

and commerce descended on the city and erected grand palaces of trade; those who ran them built mansions. The city became a byword for exploitation and vice, in countless opium dens and gambling joints, in myriad brothels. And guarding over it all were the American, French and Italian marines, British Tommies and Japanese bluejackets. Foreign ships and submarines patrolled the Yangzi and Huangpu rivers and the coasts of China. They patrolled the biggest single foreign investment anywhere in the world – the British alone had £400 million sunk into the place. After Chiang

Kaishek's coup against the Communists in 1927, the Kuomintang cooperated closely with the foreign police and with Chinese and foreign factory owners to suppress labour unrest. The Settlement police, run by the British, arrested Chinese labour leaders and handed them over to the Kuomintang for imprisonment or execution, and the Shanghai gangs were repeatedly called in to 'mediate' disputes inside the Settlement.

If it was the Chinese who supported the whole giddy structure of Shanghai, the Chinese who worked as beasts of burden and provided the muscle in Shanghai's port and actories, it was simultaneously the Chinese who provided the weak link. Exploited in work-house conditions, penniless on the streets, sold into slavery, excluded from the high life and the parks created by the foreigners, Shanghai was always a potential hot bed of unrest. And finally, in 1949 – it was inevitable really – the Communists 'liberated' the city.

The Communists eradicated the slums, rehabilitated the city's hundreds of thousands of opium addicts, and eliminated child and slave labour. These were staggering achievements. Unfortunately, they also put Shanghai to sleep. It was not until 1990 that the central government finally allowed Shanghai to go about reinventing itself as a major metropolis.

Climate

The best times to visit Shanghai are spring and autumn. In winter, temperatures can drop well below freezing, with a blanket of drizzle. Summers are hot and humid with temperatures as high as 40°C. So, in short, you'll need silk long johns and down jackets for winter, an ice block for each armpit in summer and an umbrella won't go astray in either season.

Government

Shanghai is politically one of the most important centres in China and one of the political flashpoints. The meeting which founded the Chinese Communist Party (CCP) was held here back in 1921. Shanghai was an important centre of early Communist activity when the Party was still concentrating on organising urban workers. Mao also cast the first stone of the Cultural Revolution in Shanghai, by publishing in the city newspapers a piece of political rhetoric he had been unable to get published in Beijing.

Most extraordinary, during the Cultural Revolution a People's Commune was set up in Shanghai, modelled on the Paris Commune of the 19th century. (The Paris Commune was set up in 1871 and controlled Paris for two months. It planned to introduce socialist reforms such as turning over management of factories to the workers' associations.) The Shanghai Commune lasted just three weeks before Mao ordered the army to put an end to it.

The so-called Gang of Four had their power base in Shanghai. The campaign to criticise Confucius and Mengzi (Mencius) was started here in 1969, before it became nationwide in 1973 and was linked to Lin Biao. And once again, in the emerging power struggle leading up to the imminent death of Deng Xiaoping, commentators are talking of a Shanghai clique – many of Beijing's current top leaders are Shanghai old hands.

Economy

Shanghai's long malaise came to an abrupt end in 1990, with the announcement of massive plans to develop Pudong on the east side of the Huangpu River, though there have been teething problems. Foreign investors complain that costs have risen so sharply that they have been forced to shift production out of Shanghai. But, nevertheless, Shanghai is China's financial centre and an emerging economic powerhouse. By 1998 local planners reckon Pudong will have half as much office space as Singapore. Lujiazui, the area that faces off the Bund on the Pudong side of the Huangpu river, will be a modern highrise counterpoint to the austere old-world structures on the Bund.

Shanghai has a unique opportunity, and the savvy with which locals have grabbed it have many shaking their heads knowingly, saying that Shanghai always had the potential to be a great city. Massive freeway projects crisscross the city, the subway system is proceeding apace, and the indications are that this forward planning will circumvent the infrastructure problems that face other Asian cities such as Bangkok, Jakarta and Taipei.

Population

Shanghai has a population of around 13.4 million people, but that figure is deceptive since it takes into account the whole municipal area of 6100 sq km. Nevertheless, the central core of some 220 sq km has over 7.5

million people, which must rate as one of the highest population densities in China, if not the world.

Orientation

Shanghai municipality covers a huge area, but the city proper is a more modest size. Within the municipality is the island of Chongming, part of the Yangzi River delta worth a footnote because it's the second-largest island in China (or third if you recognise China's claim to Taiwan).

Broadly, central Shanghai is divided into two areas divided by the Huangpu River: Pudong (east of the Huangpu River) and Puxi (west of the Huangpu River). The First Ring Road does a long elliptical loop around the city centre proper, which includes all of commercial west-side Shanghai, the Lujiazui Finance and Trade Zone and the Jinqiao Export Processing Zone of Pudong. A second (Outer) Ring Road will link Hongqiao International Airport (in the west of town) with the new Gaoqiao Free Trade Zone, a port on the Yangzi River in Pudong.

For visitors, the attractions of Shanghai are in Puxi. Here you will find the Bund, the shopping streets, the foreign concessions, hotels, restaurants, sights and nightclubs. Street names are given in Pinyin, which makes navigating easy, and many of the streets are named after cities and provinces. In the central district (around Nanjing Lu) the provincial names run north-south, and the city names run east-west. Some roads are split by compass points, such as Sichuan Nanlu (Sichuan South Rd) and Sichuan Beilu (Sichuan North Rd). Some of the monstrously long roads are split by sectors, such as Zhongshan Dong Erlu and Zhongshan Dong Yilu, which mean Zhongshan East 2nd Rd and Zhongshan East 1st Rd.

There are four main areas of interest in the city: the Bund from Suzhou Creek to the Shanghai Harbour Passenger Terminal (Shiliupu Wharf); Nanjing Donglu (a very colourful neighbourhood); Frenchtown, which includes Huaihai Zhonglu and Ruijin Lu (an even more colourful neighbourhood);

and the Jade Buddha Temple and the side trip along Suzhou Creek.

Information

CITS The main office of CITS (☎ 6321-7200) is on the 3rd floor of the Guangming Building at 2 Jinling Donglu. Train, plane and boat tickets can be booked here, but this is obviously subject to availability. It is often possible to book train tickets for the next day if your destination is Hangzhou, Suzhou or Nanjing. More distant locations, which require sleeper bookings, will take longer to book: sometimes up to a week or more. Boat tickets are easier to book at CITS, but often a lot more expensive than doing it yourself across the road at the boat ticketing office.

Tourist Hotline There is a tourist hotline number (☎ 6439-0630) in Shanghai. This is a new concept in China, so don't expect too much from it. It is essentially geared to dealing with complaints.

PSB The office (☎ 6321-5380) is at 210 Hankou Lu, one block north of Fuzhou Lu, near the corner of Henan Zhonglu.

Money There are money-changing counters at almost every hotel, even cheapies like the Pujiang and the Haijia. Credit cards are more readily accepted in Shanghai than in other parts of China.

Most tourist hotels will accept major credit cards such as Visa, American Express, MasterCard, Diners and JCB, as will bank and friendship stores (and related tourist outlets like the Antique & Curio Store). The enormous Bank of China right next to the Peace Hotel tends to get crowded, but is better organised than Chinese banks else-where around the country. It is also worth a peak inside for its grand interior.

American Express American Express (☎ 6279-8082) has an office at Room 206 Retail Plaza, Shanghai Centre, 1376 Nanjing Xilu.

Post & Telecommunications The larger tourist hotels have post offices from where you can mail letters and small packages.

The express mail service and poste restante is at 276 Bei Suzhou Lu. Letters to London take just two days, or so it advertises.

The international post and telecommunications office is at the corner of Sichuan Beilu and Bei Suzhou Lu. The section for international parcels is in the same building but around the corner at 395 Tiantong Lu.

Express parcel and document service is available from several foreign carriers. You can contact DHL (☎ 6536-2900), UPS (☎ 6248-6060), Federal Express (☎ 6275-0808) or TNT Skypak (☎ 6419-0000).

Long-distance calls can be placed from hotel rooms and do not take long to get through. The international telegraph office, from where you can make long-distance phone calls and send international telexes and telegrams, is on Nanjing Donglu next to the Peace Hotel.

Foreign Consulates There is a growing number of consulates in Shanghai. If you're doing the Trans-Siberian journey and have booked a definite departure date, it's much better to get your Russian visa here than face the horrible queues at the Russian embassy in Beijing.

Australia
. 17 Fuxing Xilu (☎ 6433-4604; fax 6437-6669)
Austria
Suite 514, Shanghai Centre, 1376 Nanjing Xilu (☎ 6279-7196; fax 6279-7198)
Canada
Suite 604, West Tower, Shanghai Centre, 1376 Nanjing Xilu (☎ 6279-8400; 6279-8401)
Denmark
6A, Qihua Tower, 1375 Huaihai Zhonglu (☎ 6431-4301; fax 6471-6343)
France
Room 2008, Ruijin Building, 205 Maoming Nanlu (☎ 6472-3631; fax 6472-5247)
Germany
181 Yongfu Lu (☎ 6433-6951; fax 6471-4448)
Hungary
Room 1810, Union Building, 100 Yan'an Donglu (☎ 6326-1815; fax 6320-2855)
India
2200 Yan'an Xilu (☎ 6275-8885; fax 6472-9589)

Italy
127 Wuyi Lu (☎ 6252-4373; fax 6251-1728)
Japan
1517 Huaihai Zhonglu (☎ 6433-6639; fax 6433-1008)
Korea
2200 Yan'an Xilu (☎ 6219-6417)
New Zealand
15B, Qihua Tower, 1375 Huaihai Zhonglu (☎ 6433-2230; fax 6433-3533)
Poland
618 Jianguo Xilu (tel/fax 6433-9288)
Russia
20 Huangpu Lu (☎ 6324-2682; fax 6306-9982)
Singapore
400 Wulumuqi Zhonglu (☎ 6433-1362; fax 6433-4150)
UK
244 Yongfu Lu (☎ 6433-0508; fax 6433-0498)
USA
1469 Huaihai Zhonglu (☎ 6433-6880; fax 6433-4122)

Bookshops Shanghai is one place where you can replenish your stash – there are numerous foreign-language outlets if you take the tourist hotel bookshops into account. The main Foreign Languages Bookstore is at 390 Fuzhou Lu. The 1st floor has an excellent range of maps and the 2nd floor has probably the widest range of foreign novels in China, with everything from *Space Cops* to Gore Vidal's *Lincoln*. Fuzhou Lu has traditionally been the bookshop street of Shanghai, and there are other bookshops close to the Foreign Languages Bookstore.

A small range of foreign newspapers and magazines is available from the larger tourist hotels (eg Park, Jinjiang, Sheraton Huating) and some shops. Publications include the *Wall Street Journal*, *International Herald Tribune*, *Asiaweek*, *The Economist*, *Time* and *Newsweek*. The latter two make good gifts for Chinese friends.

Get a copy of Pan Ling's *In Search of Old Shanghai* (Joint Publishing Company, Hong Kong, 1982) for a rundown on who was who and what was what back in the bad old days.

Newspapers & Magazines There is quite a number of free magazines available in Shanghai, and there will undoubtedly be more before long. The *Shanghai Star* is a daily English publication that makes for livelier reading than the *China Daily*. Look out also for *Welcome to China – Shanghai*, a free publication with information on hotel restaurants and other items of interest to visitors.

Maps English maps of Shanghai are available at the Foreign Language Bookstore, the Jinjiang Hotel bookshop and occasionally from street hawkers. The best of the bunch is the bilingual *Shanghai Official Tourist Map*, which is produced by the Shanghai Municipal Tourism Administration – unfortunately, it's not easy to track down.

The *Shanghai Traffic Map (shànghǎi shìqū jiāotōng tú)* is only available in Chinese characters but it's the best one for the bus routes. If you don't read Chinese, however, it is a map that requires a lot of perseverance and much cross checking with an English map. It's available from street hawkers, bookshops and hotel gift shops.

An alternative bilingual map is the Hong-Kong-published *Map of Shanghai*, which is sometimes available in China (you can buy it in Hong Kong from most large bookshops). This map has streets and destinations

written in Chinese characters (traditional) as well as English.

Medical Services Shanghai is credited with the best medical facilities and most advanced medical knowledge in China. Western medicines are sold at the Shanghai No 8 Drugstore at 951 Huaihai Zhonglu.

Foreigners are referred to the Shanghai Emergency Centre (☎ 6324-4010) at 68 Haining Lu. Hospital treatment is available at the Huashan Hospital (☎ 6248-9999) at 12 Wulumuqi Zhonglu, which has a Hong Kong joint-venture section; and at the Shanghai First People's Hospital (☎ 6306-9478) at 585 Jiulong Lu in Hongqiao, where there is an Austrian joint-venture section.

What Was What

Until recently, Shanghai was a vast museum, the legacy of late-19th-century colonialism. Nowadays, much of the deadwood is being cleared away for department stores, office blocks and hotels. Even the Bund will get a face-lift as state-appropriated buildings are sold back to their original owners or auctioned off to the highest bidders. It's anyone's guess what Shanghai will look like

Foreign Concessions in Shanghai

in five years time, and difficult not to conjecture that the city will be robbed of much of its charm. But as the Chinese like to say, *Jiùde búqù, xīnde bùlái*' (If the old doesn't go, the new won't come).

For the time being, it is still well worth exploring old Shanghai. The **Chinese city**, for example, is still a maze of narrow lanes, lined with closely packed houses and laundry hanging from windows. The Yuyuan Gardens are in this part of town and well worth a visit. The Chinese City lies on the south-west bank of the Huangpu River, bounded to the north by Jinling Donglu and to the south by Zhonghua Lu.

The **International Settlement** *(shànghǎi zūjiè)*, in its time a brave new world of cooperation by the British, Europeans and Americans (the Japanese were also included but were considered suspect), cuts a broad swathe through the north of the city centre. It extends from the intersection of Yan'an Xilu and Nanjing Xilu north to Suzhou Creek and east to the Huangpu River. Nanjing Lu and the Bund shared pride of place in this settlement. West of Xizang Lu was the Beverly Hills of Shanghai, an elite residential district cluttered with opulent villas.

South of Yan'an Lu and squeezed north of the Chinese city was the **French Concession** *(fǎguó zūjiè)*. Yan'an Lu was known as Avenue Foch in the west, and Avenue Edward VII in the east; the French strip of the Bund (south of Yan'an Lu) was known as the Quai de France. Despite the names, there were never that many French in the concession – 90% of the residents were Chinese, and the most numerous foreigners were White Russians. Nevertheless, Frenchtown remains one of the most interesting parts of Shanghai. The premier district (around the Jinjiang Hotel and on Huaihai Lu) is once again being gentrified, and department stores and boutiques are springing up everywhere. But for Frenchtown at its best, simply strike off on the side streets that head south off Yan'an Lu (see the separate entry for Frenchtown later in this section for more information).

The Bund
(wàitān)

The Bund is an Anglo-Indian term for the embankment of a muddy waterfront. The term is apt. Mud bedevils the city. Between 1920 (when the problem was first noticed) and 1965, Shanghai sank several metres. Water was pumped back into the ground, but the Venetian threat remains. Concrete rafts are used as foundations for high-rises in this spongy mass.

Its muddy predicament aside, the Bund is symbolic of Shanghai. In faraway Kashgar and Lhasa, local Chinese pose for photographs in front of oil-painted Bund façades. Constant throngs of Chinese and foreign tourists pad past the porticos of the Bund's grand edifices with maps in hand. The buildings themselves loom serenely, oblivious to the march of revolutions, a vagabond assortment of neo-classical 1930s downtown New York styles, with a pompous touch of monumental antiquity thrown in for good measure.

To the Europeans, the Bund was Shanghai's Wall Street, a place of feverish trading, of fortunes made and lost. One of the most famous traders was Jardine Matheson & Company. In 1848 Jardine's purchased the first land offered for sale to foreigners in Shanghai and set up shop shortly after, dealing in opium and tea. The company grew into one of the great hongs, and today it owns just about half of Hong Kong.

At the north-western end of the Bund were the British Public Gardens (now called Huangpu Park). Famously, a sign at the entrance announced 'No Dogs or Chinese Allowed'. Or at least that is how posterity remembers it; in actual fact the restrictions on Chinese and dogs were listed in separate clauses of a whole bevy of restrictions on undesirables. The slight, however, remains and will probably never be forgotten.

The Bund today is in the process of yet another transformation. The building identified by a crowning dome is the old Hongkong & Shanghai Bank, completed in 1921 with much pomp and ceremony. The Hongkong & Shanghai Bank has long been

THE EAST

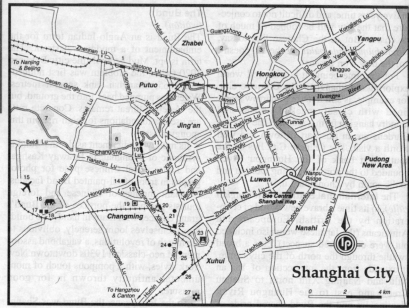

negotiating to get it back, and probably will. For many years it has housed the Shanghai People's Municipal Government. Other Bund fixtures are being sold off, and will no doubt be dusted off and cleaned up.

The statues that once lined the Bund no longer exist; the whereabouts of a pair of bronze lions that once stood outside the Hongkong & Shanghai Bank remain a mystery. It was first thought that they had been melted down for cannons by the Japanese, but later the Chinese claimed they had found them. Perhaps they too will return.

The Tung Feng Hotel, at the bottom of the Bund near Shiliupu Wharf, only hints at its former grandeur and conveys nothing of its former exclusivity. It was once home to the Shanghai Club, the snootiest little gang this side of Trafalgar Square. Membership was confined to upper-crust Brits, men only. The Long Bar, once a Shanghai establishment, has been resurrected in the new Shanghai Centre on Nanjing Xilu. Elsewhere, the foyer of the Tung Feng has been invaded by a KFC – a sign of the times if ever there was one.

Nanjing Lu & the Central District

Nanjing Donglu (Nanjing Road East), from the Peace to the Park hotels, has long been China's golden mile. It may not be Tokyo, and indeed Huaihai Lu now vies with Nanjing Donglu on the prestige front, but for visitors from more remote destinations in China, a wander down Nanjing Donglu is a rude jolt back into the tail end of the 20th century.

Even back in the dull Communist era (let's face it, *that's* long gone), Nanjing Donglu had a distinctly 'shop till you drop' feel about it. Nowadays, the department stores are laying it on thick with opulent window dressings, the racks are near buckling with Japanese electronic goodies, and Esprit, Benetton and McDonald's have shouldered Marx and Mao into the draughty halls of little-visited museums – which was where the capitalist state was meant to end up. Already the unimaginatively named No 10 Department Store (once Wing On's) has

been rechristened the Hua Lian Department Store, and it is probably only a matter of time before the No 1 Department Store (once The Sun) gets a change of moniker in keeping with its shop-front displays.

Nanjing Xilu takes over where Nanjing Donglu ducks south for a breather beside Renmin (People's) Park. The park and the adjacent expanse of Renmin Square were once the Shanghai Racecourse. Nanjing Xilu itself was previously Bubbling Well Rd. Picturesque they may be, but bubbling wells are an inconvenience on busy avenues of commerce, and this one was sealed over.

In general Nanjing Xilu is a lot less interesting to explore than the eastern stretch of road. The area around Renmin Park is being surreptitiously invaded by fast-food outlets and the occasional snob boutique. Beyond the new Chengdu Lu Expressway (a structure of intimidatingly Orwellian proportions), it gives way to office blocks, more shops and hotels, all of which join forces in the impressive Shanghai Centre.

Shanghai Museum
(shànghǎi bówùguǎn)
Formerly housed on Henan Nanlu, the Shanghai Museum has found a new nesting place at 201 Renmin Lu, on Renmin Square. It is an adventurous piece of architecture and by all accounts will house one of the world's best collections of Chinese art.

Frenchtown
(fǎguó zūjiè)
The core of Frenchtown, the former French Concession, is the area around Huaihai Lu and the Jinjiang Hotel. This area is now once again going rapidly upmarket. Isetan have opened a Tokyo-style department store on Huaihai Lu, a huge shopping complex was under construction at the time of writing and the area around the Jinjiang Hotel and the Jinjiang Tower is littered with cafes and boutiques.

Head down the side streets off Yan'an Lu for the tatty, down-at-heel *fin de siècle* architecture, in all its ambient glory. It probably will not last much longer. Already expat

THE EAST

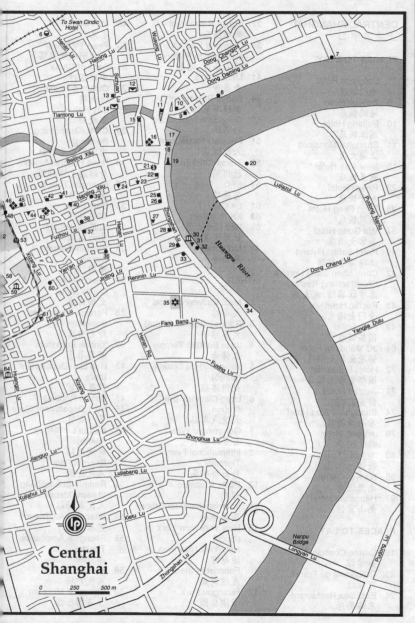

Central Shanghai

0   250   500 m

CENTRAL SHANGHAI
上海市中心

PLACES TO STAY

1 Longmen Hotel
龙门饭店
9 Seagull Hotel
海鸥饭店
10 Pujiang Hotel
浦江饭店
11 Shanghai Mansions
上海大厦
13 New Asia Hotel
新亚饭店
22 Peace Hotel
和平饭店
28 Tung Feng Hotel
东风饭店
37 Wu Gong Hotel
吴宫大酒店
40 Hotel Sofitel Hyland
上海海仑宾馆
42 Chun Shen Jiang Hotel &
Shendacheng Restaurant
春申江宾馆, 沈大成
48 Pacific Hotel
金门大酒店
49 Park Hotel
国祭饭店
64 JC Mandarin Hotel
锦沧文华大酒店
72 Hotel Equatorial
国祭贵都大饭店
73 Jing'an Hotel
静安宾馆
74 Shanghai Hilton Hotel
希而顿酒店
79 Jinjiang Hotel
锦江饭店
80 Jinjiang Tower
新锦江
95 Nanying Hotel
南鹰饭店
97 Hengshan Hotel
衡山宾馆

PLACES TO EAT

18 Coffee Conscious
咖啡馆
23 Croissants de France
可颂坊
24 East Sea Restaurant
东海餐厅
27 Sunya Restaurant
新雅饭店
31 Diamond Restaurant
& Ferries to Pudong
钻石餐厅, 运船
41 McDonald's
麦当劳
44 Sunya Restaurant
新雅粤菜馆
50 Gongdelin Restaurant
功得林
51 People's Restaurant
人民饭店
56 Texas Chicken
德州鸡
57 KFC
肯德鸡
61 LA Cafe
63 KK Roasters
69 Red Rhino
红犀牛餐厅
81 McDonald's
麦当劳

OTHER

2 Main Railway Station
火车站
3 Railway Station (Metro)
火车站
4 Jade Buddha Temple
玉佛寺
5 Hangzhou Lu Station
(Metro)
杭州路站
6 Long-Distance Bus
Station
长途汽车站
7 Gongpinglu Wharf
公平路码头
8 International Ferry
Terminal
外虹桥码头
12 Poste Restante
邮局
14 International Post Office
国祭邮局
15 New York New York
(disco)
New York New York
迪斯可
16 Friendship Store
友谊商店
17 Huangpu Park
黄浦公园
19 Mao Statue
毛象
20 Pearl TV Tower
东方明珠电视塔
21 Bank of China
中国银行
25 Customs House
海关楼
26 City Hall
市政府
29 CITS (Guangming
Building)
中国国祭旅行社
30 Bund History Museum
外滩历史博物馆
32 Huangpu Tour Boats
黄浦上游船
33 Boat Bookings
船售票处
34 Shiliupu Wharf
十六浦码头
35 Yuyuan Gardens &
Bazaar
豫园, 市场
36 Shanghai Antiques &
Curios Store
文物商店
38 Foreign Languages
Bookstore
外文书店
39 Xinhua Bookstore
新华书店
43 Hua Lian Department
Store
花莲百货
45 Baskin Robbins
46 No 1 Department Store
第一百货
47 Xinzha Lu Station
(Metro)
新闸路站
52 Renmin Park
人民公园
53 Renmin Shangchang
Station (Metro)
人民商场站
54 Shanghai Art Theatre
艺术剧院
55 Shanghai Acrobatics
Theatre
杂技场
58 Renmin Square
人民广场
59 Shanghai Museum
上海博物馆

residents are complaining that slabs of old Shanghai are disappearing faster than anyone can keep abreast of.

Site of the 1st National Congress of the Communist Party

(zhōnggòng yīdàhuìzhǐ)

The CCP was founded in July 1921 in a French Concession building at a meeting of delegates from the various Communist and Socialist organisations around China. Given the momentousness of the occasion, the museum is very low profile. There are some photographs and the like with English captions. Opening hours are 8.30 to 11 am and 1 to 4 pm, and it's closed Monday and Thursday mornings. Entry costs Y3.

Sun Yatsen's Residence

(sūn zhōngshān gùjū)

China is simply brimming with Sun Yatsen memorabilia, and here is one of his former residences (he got around), at 7 Xianshan Lu, formerly the Rue Molière. He lived here for six years, supported by Overseas Chinese funds. After Sun's death, his wife, Song Qingling (1893-1981), continued to live here until 1937, constantly watched by Kuomintang plain-clothes police and French police. The two-storey house is set back from the street, furnished as it was back in Sun's days, even though it was looted by the Japanese.

The entry price of Y7 gets you a brief tour of the house. It is open daily from 9 am to 4.30 pm.

Yuyuan Gardens & Bazaar

(yùyuán shāngshà)

At the north-eastern end of the old Chinese city, the Yuyuan Gardens & Bazaar is, while arguably slightly tacky, one of Shanghai's premier sights and well worth a visit. Try not to visit on the weekend, however – the crowds are just too overwhelming for anyone who did not grow up in Shanghai. (See the Places to Eat section for details on the bazaar's justly famous snacks.)

The Pan family, rich Ming Dynasty officials, founded the gardens. The gardens took 18 years (from 1559 to 1577) to nurture into existence and were snuffed out by a bombardment during the Opium War in 1842.

The gardens took another trashing during French reprisals for attacks on their nearby concession by Taiping rebels. Today they have been restored and attract hordes of Chinese tourists. Opening hours are 8.30 am to 4.30 pm daily.

The **Temple of the Town Gods** (*chénghuángmiào*) is a recently restored and overrated attraction in the bazaar area. In fact, the Yuyuan Bazaar itself, a Disneyland version of historical China, is altogether more interesting. Over 100 speciality shops and restaurants jostle shoulders over narrow laneways and small squares in a mock 'olde Cathay' setting. It's a great stop for lunch and some souvenir shopping.

Jade Buddha Temple
(*yùfó sì*)

The Jade Buddha Temple is one of Shanghai's few Buddhist temples. It is active and attracts large numbers of visitors – largely local and overseas Chinese tourists. Built between 1911 and 1918, the centrepiece is a two-metre-high white jade buddha which was installed here after having been lugged by a monk from Myanmar (Burma) to Zhejiang Province in 1882. This seated buddha, encrusted with jewels, is said to weigh 1000 kg. A smaller, reclining buddha from the same shipment reclines on a redwood bed.

No photography is permitted. The temple closes for lunch between noon and 1 pm, and is open daily except on special occasions such as the Lunar New Year in February, when Chinese Buddhists, some 20,000 of them, descend on the place.

Getting There & Away The temple is in the north-west of town, near the intersection of Changshou Lu and Jiangning Lu. One way to get there is to take the subway out to the Shanghai Railway Station and then walk (about one km) or take a taxi. Bus No 19 runs from around the corner of Shanghai Mansions, along Tiantong Lu and on past the temple eventually.

Tomb of Lu Xun (Hongkou Park)
(*hóngkǒu gōngyuǎn*)

Directly north of central Shanghai, up in Hongkou Park, is the Tomb of Lu Xun. While Lu Xun (1881-1936) is almost universally applauded as the foremost of China's 20th-century fiction writers and much admired for his essays too, his tomb is of limited interest. Something of an iconoclast, Lu would no doubt be appalled by the pompous statue that commemorates him. A small museum in the park tells his story (as the Communists see it). It's open daily from 8.30 to 11.30 am and 1.30 to 4 pm.

Bus No 21 travels along Sichuan Lu from the centre of town to Hongkou Park.

Pudong New Area
(*pǔdōng xīnqū*)

Larger than Shanghai itself, the Pudong New Area is on the eastern bank of the Huangpu River. Before 1990, when development plans were first announced, Pudong constituted 350 sq km of boggy farmland supplying vegetables to Shanghai's markets. Now the vegies are grown elsewhere as Pudong has become a Special Economic Zone (SEZ).

Two massive bridges have been constructed to connect Puxi (central Shanghai) with Pudong, as well as numerous tunnels. A huge new coal-burning power plant will be built. The Waigaoqiao harbour area is being upgraded into a major container port. A 24-hour international airport is planned to supplement Shanghai's existing Hongqiao Airport. By 1998, Lujiazui, the waterfront area of Pudong facing the Bund, will have 49 skyscrapers ready to rent out office space. There has been nothing like the development of Pudong in the history of China, or the world probably for that matter.

An economic powerhouse is one thing; an afternoon seeing the sights is another. Obviously there is little to lure you over to Pudong if you are not travelling with a briefcase. The only real attraction at present (and for the foreseeable future) is the Pearl TV Tower, the fantastically prominent and ugly oil-rig lookalike that can be seen from the Bund.

Half-way up is a lookout, which will set you back Y50 – the queues here can be unbelievable.

Other Sights

South-west of central Shanghai, close to the Huangpu River, is the **Longhua Pagoda** (*lónghuá tǎ*). It is said to date from the 10th century and has recently been restored for tourism. It is a hassle to get to. The easiest way is to take the subway to the Caobao Lu subway station then walk or take a taxi.

The Xujiahui area bordering the western end of Frenchtown once had a Jesuit settlement, with an observatory (still in use). **St Ignatius Cathedral**, whose spires were lopped off by Red Guards, has been restored and is open once again for Catholic services. It's at 158 Puxi Lu, in the Xujiahui District.

Further south-west of the Longhua Pagoda are the **Shanghai Botanical Gardens** (*shànghǎi zhíwùyuán*), with an exquisite collection of 9000 miniatures.

The **Shanghai Exhibition Centre** is west of the city centre. Drop in here for a mammoth view of Soviet palace architecture. There are irregular displays of local industrial wares and handicrafts.

Out near the airport is **Shanghai Zoo**, which has a roller-skating rink, children's playground and other recreational facilities. To the west of that is the former **Sassoon Villas**. At Qingpu County, 25 km west of Shanghai, they've made up for the dearth of real antiquities and temples by creating a new scenic area for tourists to visit.

On the way to the town of Jiaxing, by rail or road, is Sunjiang County, 20 km south-west of Shanghai. The place is older than Shanghai itself. On Tianmashan, in Songjiang County, is the **Huzhou Pagoda**, built in 1079 AD. It's the leaning tower of China, with an inclination now exceeding the tower at Pisa by 1½ degrees. The 19-metre-high tower started tilting 200 years ago.

Huangpu River Trip

(*huángpǔ jiāng yóulǎn chuán*)

There are three main perspectives on Shanghai – from the gutters, from the heights (aerial views from the battlements of the tourist fortresses) and from the waters. The Huangpu River offers some remarkable views of the Bund and the riverfront activity.

Huangpu tour boats depart from the dock on the Bund, slightly north of the Peace Hotel. There are several decks on the boat, but foreigners are forced upmarket into special class A or special class B. Departure times are 9 am and 2 pm, with possible extra departures in the summer and on Sunday. The schedule may become erratic in winter due to bad weather. Tickets cost Y45.

Tickets can be purchased from CITS in the Guangming Building or (more cheaply) at the boat dock. The boat takes you on a 3½-hour, 60-km round trip, northward up the Huangpu to the junction with the Yangzi River, to Wusongkou and back again along the same route.

Shanghai is one of the world's largest ports; 2000 ocean-going ships and about 15,000 river steamers load and unload here every year. Coolies used to have the back-breaking task of loading and unloading, but these days the ports are a forest of cranes, derricks, conveyor belts and forklifts. The tour boat passes an enormous variety of craft – freighters, bulk carriers, roll-on roll-off ships, sculling sampans, giant praying-mantis

Statue of Buddha in the Longhua Pagoda.

cranes, the occasional junk and Chinese navy vessels (which aren't supposed to be photographed).

Festivals

There are three events of significance. The Mid-Autumn Festival (15th day of the 8th moon in the lunar calendar) is when they lay on the moon cakes – the festival recalls an uprising against the Mongols in the 14th century when plans for the revolt were passed around in cakes. Moon cakes are usually filled with a mixture of ground lotus, sesame seeds and dates, and sometimes duck egg. The Shanghai Music Festival is in May. The Shanghai Marathon Cup is in March and is one of the top sporting events in the country. The latter two festivals were suspended during the Cultural Revolution. Hotel space may be harder to come by at these times, and at Lunar New Year in February.

Places to Stay – bottom end

Shanghai has the highest real estate values in China, and rapid development is crowding out most of the lower-end accommodation. Nevertheless, a few cheap hotels still hang on by the skin of their teeth. Be warned, in the peak season (summer) most bottom-end places fill up very quickly and it is not unusual to be forced into accommodation that costs upward of Y300 for a double.

The *Pujiang Hotel* (☎ 6324-6388) *(pǔjiāng fàndiàn)* at 15 Huangpu Lu is the only centrally located place that offers dorms and low-cost (by Shanghai standards) rooms. Dorm beds (in airy rooms with attached bathroom) cost Y50, though they are often fully booked by mid-afternoon (around 10 am seems to be the best time to show up). There are also reasonable doubles available for Y300 and Y330. Bus No 64 leaves from in front of the main railway station to the corner of Nanjing Donglu and Jiangsu Zhonglu. Walk left at the Bund and walk over Suzhou Creek to the hotel.

If the Pujiang's full, the *Haijia Hotel* (☎ 6541-1440) *(hǎijiā fàndiàn)*, 1001 Jiangpu Lu, in the north-eastern part of town, usually has vacancies. Beds are Y40 to Y50 per person depending on room size. Very large doubles with air-con and private bathroom are available for Y220, while basic doubles cost Y120. To get there from the Pujiang Hotel area, take bus No 22 east along Daming Donglu (behind the Pujiang). The bus soon turns onto Changyang Lu; when you see/smell the tobacco factory, get off at the next stop, at Jiangpu Lu. The Haijia is a one-minute walk north of Changyang Lu on the left-hand side of Jiangpu Lu.

In the same neighbourhood is the excellent *Changyang Hotel* (☎ 6543-4890) *(chángyáng fàndiàn)* at 1800 Changyang Lu. Doubles range from Y210 to Y260. Bus No 22 from the Bund area runs right past the hotel.

The *Conservatory of Music* (☎ 6437-2577) *(yīnyuè xuéyuàn)*, 20 Fenyang Lu, off Huaihai Zhonglu, is an old stand-by. Unfortunately, renovations have pushed prices up to Y200 for a standard double. The conservatory only has 16 rooms and is often fully booked. Take a subway from the main railway station to Changshu Lu station. To find the rooms walk through the entrance to the conservatory and bear left. The 'dormitory' is an old building on the right with a Chinese sign over the door.

Places to Stay – middle

Mid-range accommodation in Shanghai will cost between Y300 and Y400 for a double.

One of the best deals in central Shanghai is the *Wu Gong Hotel* (☎ 6326-0303; fax 6328-2820) *(wúgōng dàjiǔdiàn)*. Budget rooms cost from Y308, singles from Y352 to Y462, while standard doubles are Y396 to Y462.

The *Chun Shen Jiang Hotel* (☎ 6320-5710) *(chūnshēnjiāng bīnguǎn)*, 626 Nanjing Donglu, has long been known as a good mid-range hotel with a great location. Rooms cost Y390 or Y430.

The *Yangtze Hotel* (☎ 6320-7880; fax 6320-6974) *(yángzi fàndiàn)* is at 740 Hankou Lu, one block east of Renmin Park. It was built back in 1934 and is an old

American-style hotel. Doubles cost from Y390 – quite a bargain for this neighbourhood. From the Shanghai Railway Station it can be reached by subway to the Renmin Shangchang Station.

The *Nanying Hotel* (☎ 6437-8188) *(nányīng fàndiàn)* at 1720 Huaihai Zhonglu is in the south-western part of the city. Very comfortable doubles cost Y320.

Places to Stay – top end

The vast majority of the hotels in Shanghai fall into the top-end (over Y400) category. There is a wide range of choices, ranging from rambling historical ambience to modern amenities. Travellers in Shanghai on business will be better served choosing one of the modern hotels, such as the Portman Shangrila Shanghai, the Shanghai JC Mandarin or the Shanghai Hilton. Travellers on a purely sightseeing visit might want to check out one of the old colonial hotels, such as the Peace Hotel.

Interior renovations at the Park, Shanghai Mansions and Jinjiang have taken their toll, but if there's one place left in Shanghai that will give you a sense of the past, it's the

Peace Hotel (the old Cathay) (☎ 6321-1244; fax 6329-0300) *(hépíng fàndiàn)* at 20 Nanjing Donglu. On the ground floor of the 12-storey edifice are the sumptuous lobby, shops, bookstore, bank, video games parlour, snooker tables, cafe and barber.

The cost of all this history is US$80/110 for standard singles/doubles and climbs all the way to US$380 for a 'national deluxe' suite. The national deluxe suites are laid out in 1930s Art Deco style to represent the concessions of the time – French, British, American and Japanese, not to mention Chinese.

The *Tung Feng Hotel* (☎ 6321-8060) *(dōngfēng fàndiàn)*, 3 Zhongshan Dong 1-Lu, is a grand but lesser-known establishment right on the Bund at Yan'an Donglu. Modernisation has caught up with the place – the KFC on the ground floor does not date from the Kuomintang era. Doubles cost Y500 upwards. There is also another branch (☎ 6323-5304) at Sichuan Zhonglu.

The *Park Hotel* (☎ 6327-5225; fax 6327-6958) *(guójì fàndiàn)*, 170 Nanjing Xilu, overlooks Renmin Park. Erected in 1934, the building is one of Shanghai's best examples

The Cathay

The Peace Hotel is a ghostly reminder of the immense wealth of Victor Sassoon. From a Baghdad Jewish family, he made millions out of the opium trade and then ploughed it back into Shanghai real estate and horses. Sassoon's quote of the day was 'There is only one race greater than the Jews, and that's the Derby'. His office-cum-hotel was completed in 1930 and was known as Sassoon House, incorporating the Cathay Hotel. From the top floors Victor commanded his real estate – he is estimated to have owned 1900 buildings in Shanghai.

Like the Taj in Bombay, the Stanley Raffles in Singapore and the Peninsula in Hong Kong, the Cathay was *the* place to stay in Shanghai. Sassoon himself resided in what is now the VIP section below the green pyramidal tower, complete with Tudor panelling. He also maintained a Tudor-style villa out near Hongqiao Airport just west of the zoo. The likes of Noel Coward (who wrote *Private Lives* in the Cathay) wined and dined in the hotel's Tower Restaurant.

Back in 1949 the Kuomintang strayed into the place, awaiting the arrival of the Communists. A Western writer of the time records an incident in which 50 Kuomintang arrived, carrying their pots and pans, vegetables and firewood, and one soldier was overheard asking where to billet the mules. After the Communists took over the city, the troops were billeted in places like the Picardie (now the Hengshan Guesthouse on the outskirts of the city), where they spent hours experimenting with the elevators, used bidets as face-showers and washed rice in the toilets – which was all very well until someone pulled the chain. In 1953 foreigners tried to give the Cathay to the CCP in return for exit visas. The government refused at first, but finally accepted after the payment of 'back taxes'. ■

of Art Deco architecture from the city's cultural peak. With recent renovations, however, the interior has lost all its old world charm. Singles/doubles start at US$100/110 plus 10% surcharge. The rooms are quite comfortable and the service is efficient.

Shanghai Mansions (☎ 6324-6260; fax 6326-9778) *(shànghǎi dàshà)* is at 20 Suzhou Beilu, near the Pujiang Hotel on the same side of Huangpu River at the junction with Suzhou Creek. It's owned by the Hengshan Group, which also owns the more moderately priced Pujiang and Yangtze hotels. Standard double rooms (no singles) cost US$100 to US$110.

The *Pacific Hotel* (☎ 6327-6226; fax 6326-9620) *(jīnmén dàjiǔdiàn)*, 104 Nanjing Xilu, was previously called the Overseas Chinese Hotel *(huáqiáo fàndiàn)* and most Shanghai residents still call it that. The hotel is easily recognisable by the distinctive clock tower marked with a big red star, and by the fabulously opulent foyer. Doubles cost US$70 to US$95. This is one of Nanjing Lu's more historic hotels.

The traditional-style *Jinjiang Hotel* (☎ 6258-2582; fax 6472-5588) *(jǐnjiāng fàndiàn)* is at 59 Maoming Nanlu. This is not to be confused with its annexe, the adjacent, modern, high-rise *Jinjiang Tower* (☎ 6433-4488; fax 6433-3265) *(xīn jǐnjiāng dàjiǔdiàn)* at 161 Changle Lu. Room rates at the Jinjiang Hotel start at US$100 for a standard double in the south wing, US$155 in the north wing. The Jinjiang Tower has rates from US$190.

The best of Shanghai's modern hotels is probably the *Portman Shangrila Shanghai* (☎ 6279-8888; fax 6279-8999) *(bōtèmàn xiānggélǐlā dàjiǔdiàn)* in the massive Shanghai Centre. Singles/doubles start at US$195/225.

The following Shanghai hotels all have modern facilities and rates from US$60 upwards:

Bailemen Hotel (bǎilèmén dàjiǔdiàn), 1728 Nanjing Xilu (☎ 6256-8686; fax 6256-6869)
Baolong Hotel (bǎolóng bīnguǎn), 70 Yixian Lu (☎ 6542-5425; fax 5663-2710)

Cherry Hill Villa (yīnghuā dùjià cūn), 77 Nonggong Lu (☎ 6275-8350; fax 6275-6457)
City Hotel (chéngshì jiǔdiàn), 5-7 Shanxi Nanlu (☎ 6255-1133; fax 6255-0211)
Cypress Hotel (lóngbǎi fàndiàn), 2419 Hongqiao Lu (☎ 6255-8868; fax 6275-6739)
Dahua Guesthouse (dáhuá bīnguǎn), 914 Yan'an Xilu (☎ 6251-2512; fax 6251-2702)
East Asia Hotel (dōngyà fàndiàn), 680 Nanjing Donglu (☎ 6322-3223)
Equatorial Hotel (guójì guìdū dàfàndiàn), 65 Yan'an Xilu (☎ 6279-1688; fax 6215-4033)
Galaxy Hotel (yínhé bīnguǎn), 888 Zhongshan Xilu (☎ 6275-5888; fax 6275-0201)
Gaoyang Hotel (gāoyáng bīnguǎn), 879 Dong Daming Lu (☎ 6541-3920; fax 6545-8696)
Garden Hotel (huāyuán fàndiàn), 58 Maoming Nanlu (☎ 6433-1111; fax 6433-8866)
Hengshan Hotel (héngshān bīnguǎn), 534 Hengshan Lu (☎ 6437-7050; fax 6433-5732)
Hilton Hotel (jìng'ān xī ěrdùn jiǔdiàn), 250 Huashan Lu (☎ 6248-0000; fax 6255-3848)
Holiday Inn Yinxing (yínxīng jiàrì jiǔdiàn), 388 Panyu Lu (☎ 6252-8888; fax 6252-8545)
Hongqiao State Guesthouse (hóngqiáo yíng bīnguǎn), 1591 Hongqiao Lu (☎ 6437-2170; fax 6433-4948)
Huaxia Hotel (huáxià bīnguǎn), 38 Caobao Lu (☎ 6436-0100; fax 6433-3724)
International Airport Hotel (guójì jīchǎng bīnguǎn), 2550 Hongqiao Lu, Hongqiao Airport (☎ 6255-8866; fax 6255-8393)
JC Mandarin Hotel (jīncāng wénhuà dàjiǔdiàn), 1225 Nanjing Xilu (☎ 6279-1888; fax 6279-1822)
Jianguo Hotel (jiànguó bīnguǎn), 439 Caoxi Beilu (☎ 6439-9299; fax 6439-9714)
Jing'an Hotel (jìng'ān bīnguǎn), 370 Huashan Lu (☎ 6255-1888; fax 6255-2657)
Jinshajiang Hotel (jīnshājiāng dàjiǔdiàn), 801 Jinshajiang Lu (☎ 6257-8888; fax 6257-4149)
Jinshan Hotel (jīnshān bīnguǎn), Jingyi Donglu, Jinshanwei (☎ 5794-1888; fax 5794-0931)
Lantian Hotel (lántiān bīnguǎn), 2400 Siping Lu (☎ 6548-5906; fax 6548-5931)
Longhua Hotel (lónghuá yíng bīnguǎn), 2787 Longhua Lu (☎ 6439-9399; fax 6439-2964)
Magnolia Hotel (báiyùlán bīnguǎn), 1251 Siping Lu (☎ 6545-6888; fax 6545-9499)
Metropole Hotel (xīnchéng fàndiàn), 180 Jiangxi Zhonglu (☎ 6321-3030; fax 6321-7365)
Nanjing Hotel (nánjīng fàndiàn), 200 Shanxi Nanlu (☎ 6322-1455; fax 6320-6520)
New Asia Hotel (xīnyà dàjiǔdiàn), 422 Tiantong Lu (☎ 6324-2210; fax 6326-9529)
New Garden Hotel (xīnyuàn bīnguǎn), 1900 Hongqiao Lu (☎ 6432-9900; fax 6275-8374)
Nikko Longbai Hotel (rìháng lóngbǎi fàndiàn), 2451 Hongqiao Lu (☎ 6255-9111; fax 6255-9333)

Novotel Shanghai Yuanlin (nuòfùtè yuánlín bīnguǎn), 201 Baise Lu (☎ 6470-1688; fax 6470-0008)

Ocean Hotel (yuǎnyáng bīnguǎn), 1171 Dong Daming Lu (☎ 6545-8888; fax 6545-8993)

Olympic Hotel (aòlínpīkè jùlèbù), 1800 Zhongshan Nan 2-Lu (☎ 6439-1391; fax 6439-6295)

Portman Shangri-La (bōtèmàn dàjiǔdiàn), 1376 Nanjing Xilu (☎ 6279-8888; fax 6279-8999)

Qianhe Hotel (qiānhè bīnguǎn), 650 Yishan Lu (☎ 6470-0000; fax 6470-0348)

Rainbow Hotel (hóngqiáo bīnguǎn), 2000 Yan'an Xilu (☎ 6275-3388; fax 6275-7244)

Regal Shanghai Hotel (fùháo wàimào dàjiǔdiàn), 1000 Quyang Lu (☎ 6542-8000; fax 6544-8432)

Ruijin Hotel (ruìjīn bīnguǎn), 118 Ruijin 2-Lu (☎ 6433-1076; fax 6437-4861)

Seagull Hotel (hǎiōu bīnguǎn), 60 Huangpu Lu (☎ 6325-1500; fax 6324-1263)

Seventh Heaven Hotel (qī chóngtiān bīnguǎn), 627 Nanjing Donglu (☎ 6322-0777; fax 6320-7193)

Shanghai Hotel (shànghǎi bīnguǎn), 505 Wulumqi Beilu (☎ 6471-2712; fax 6433-1056)

Silk Road Hotel (sīchóuzhī lù dàjiǔdiàn), 777 Quyang Lu (☎ 6542-9051; fax 6542-6659)

Sofitel Hyland Hotel (hǎilún bīnguǎn), 505 Nanjing Donglu (☎ 6320-5888; fax 6320-4088)

Sunshine Hotel (yángguāng dàjiǔdiàn), 2266 Hongqiao Lu (☎ 6432-9220; fax 6432-9195)

Swan Cindic Hotel (tiāné xìnyí bīnguǎn), 111 Jiangwan Lu, Hongkouqu (☎ 6325-5255; fax 6324-8002)

Tianma Hotel (tiānmǎ dàjiǔdiàn), 471 Wuzhong Lu (☎ 6275-8100; fax 6275-7193)

West Garden Hotel (xīyuán fàndiàn), 2384 Hongqiao Lu, Changning District (☎ 6255-7173)

Westin Taipingyang (wēisītīng tàipíngyáng), 5 Zunyi Nanlu (☎ 6275-8888; fax 6275-5420)

Xianxia Hotel (xiānxiá bīnguǎn), 555 Shuicheng Lu (☎ 6259-9400; fax 6251-7492)

Xijiao Guesthouse (xījiāo bīnguǎn), 1921 Hongqiao Lu (☎ 6433-6643; fax 6433-6641)

Xincheng Hotel (xīnchéng fàndiàn), 180 Jiangxi Zhonglu (☎ 6321-3030; fax 6321-7365)

Xingguo Guesthouse (xīngguó bīnguǎn), 72 Xingguo Lu (☎ 6437-4503; fax 6251-2145)

Yangtze Hotel (yángzi fàndiàn), 740 Hankou Lu (☎ 6322-5115; fax 6320-6974)

Yangtze New World (yángzi jiāng dàjiǔdiàn), 2099 Yan'an Xilu (☎ 6275-0000; fax 6275-0750)

Yunfeng Guesthouse (yúnfēng bīnguǎn), 1665 Hongqiao Lu (☎ 6432-8900; fax 6432-8954)

Places to Eat

The Shanghai restaurant scene has undergone something of a revolution over the last few years. Gone are the government-run, greasy-spoon, grub-for-the-masses joints; Shanghai nowadays is brimming with privately run restaurants, good international hotel food and fast-food outfits. This is both good and bad news (though almost overwhelmingly a plus for anyone who appreciates good food). On the one hand, there is much wider diversity of food available in Shanghai than there was before and foreigners are no longer forced into special cubicles; on the other hand, prices have gone up considerably – travellers on a budget will be limited to snack-tracking and fast-food joints.

For cheap eats, check out the side streets around town, where you will find dumpling shops and small restaurants serving pick-and-choose stir-fried dishes. In the Bund area, Sichuan Zhonglu is a good place to look, as are the sidestreets in the old French Concession.

The Bund & Vicinity Right on the Bund itself, over the Pudong ferry terminal is the *Diamond Restaurant (zuānshílóu dàjiǔdiàn)*. The 2nd floor has a wide range of help-yourself snacks, ranging from dumplings to noodle dishes, all at very affordable prices. On the 5th floor is a more upmarket steak and coffee shop – the outside section provides good views of the Bund.

North of here, at the entrance to Huangpu Park, head over to *Coffee Conscious* (☎ 6329-2636) *(kāngxīsī)*. This place has light snacks and probably the best coffee in Shanghai. It's not cheap, but where else can you get a decent cappuccino or a freshly brewed cup of Sumatra?

Many of the old Nanjing Donglu establishments have been swept away or were in the process of moving at the time of writing. It is no longer a particularly good place to seek out restaurants. One exception is the *Sunya Cantonese Restaurant* (☎ 6320-6277) *(xīnyǎ yuè càiguǎn)*. Expensive banquet-style Cantonese cuisine is available on the upper floors, but inexpensive meals can be had on the ground floor – unfortunately there is no English menu. Close by is the *Singapore Specialties Restaurant (xīnjiāpo fēngwèi cāntīng)*. It has inexpensive curries, fried noodles and the like.

The *Sichuan Restaurant* (☎ 6322-2247) *(sìchuān fàndiàn)* at 457 Nanjing Donglu is a long runner that hopefully will not be squeezed out of business by rising rental costs. It offers lunch from 11 am to 1.45 pm and dinner from 4.45 to 7 pm – get there early.

Not far west of here, on the corner of Zhejiang Zhonglu and Nanjing Donglu, is *Shendacheng (shěndàchéng)*. There's no English sign, but look out for the busy canteen interior. This place specialises in Shanghai snacks – the dumplings are delicious.

Back down on Sichuan Zhonglu is another branch of *Sunya*. It is cheaper than the Nanjing Donglu branch. Also on Sichuan Zhonglu (and at various other locations around town), look out for *Croissants de France*, an excellent little pastry shop with good coffee. It's a great place for breakfast.

Just around the corner from Croissants de France, on Jiangjiu Lu, is the *World of the Snack (xiǎoshí shìjiè)*. This is a narrow lane of snack-food restaurants – everything from dumplings to ice-cream – with pin-up photo menus for easy ordering. The restaurants here are all excellent value.

Another good street for restaurants close to the Bund is Fuzhou Lu. Head in the direction of Renmin Square and look out for the prominent mosque-like structure on the left: the *Daxiyang Moslem Restaurant* (☎ 6322-4787) *(dàxīyáng qīngzhēn)*. Like most big Shanghai restaurants, it has a cheaper downstairs section and high-class dining upstairs.

Nanjing Xilu Nanjing Xilu is very much fast-food-ville. Old standards such as the *People's Restaurant* still linger on, but who bothers nowadays? Appropriately, the People's Restaurant – a notorious bastion of bad service and so-so cooking – now plays second fiddle to a homegrown fast-food outfit downstairs: the *Cowboy Hamburger Restaurant*.

Elsewhere Nanjing Xilu is littered with joints such as *Baskin Robbins*, *KFC* and *TCBY*. Across the road from KFC is a local variant on the theme, *Rong Hua Chicken*.

The sign outside announces, 'Rong Hua Chicken Smells Nice'. Have fun sniffing your chicken.

Up towards the Shanghai Centre, look out for *KK Roasters*, a New Zealand franchise that does roasted chicken and sandwiches and also has excellent coffee.

Yuyuan Bazaar Area If for no other reason than you are hungry, it is worth heading down to the Yuyuan Gardens & Bazaar. There are a couple of fast-food outfits here (*TCBY* and *Mos Burger*), but the real attraction is the excellent snack food. It ranks among the best in China. These snacks are available in the big-name Yuyuan restaurants such as the *Old Shanghai Restaurant* (☎ 6328-9850) *(shànghǎi lǎo fàndiàn)* and the *Green Wave Gallery* (☎ 6326-5947) *(lǜbōláng cāntīng)*, but these places tend to charge extortionate amounts for food that is only marginally better than the stuff served downstairs at streetside vendors. One advantage: they do have English menus.

Wander around the Yuyuan Bazaar and snack track as you go. Certain stalls are famed for a particular snack, and these inevitably have long queues snaking from the counters. The *Hefeng Lou (héfēng lóu)* is a canteen-style operation (no English sign outside unfortunately) with a wide range of savoury snacks on sale. There are photo-menus and some Japanese-style plastic food displays to make ordering easier.

Old French Concession Area This area is rapidly emerging as the best part of town to seek out places to eat. A good starting point is Changle Lu opposite the Jinjiang Tower. There is a string of restaurants here serving good Chinese and foreign food. *The Brasserie* is deservedly popular for its Chinese food and is open late. A few doors down, the *Cafe de Rose* gets the decor right but flounders when it comes to producing decent French cooking.

The *Red Rhino*, on Yan'an Zhonglu, does an interesting mix of Chinese and French cuisine in hole-in-the-wall, ambient surroundings. It's very popular both with locals and expats – you may have to wait for a table. Not far away, at 949 Yan'an Lu, is *Badlands*, an excellent bar-cum-Mexican-eatery, with inexpensive nachos, tacos and burritos.

Huaihai Lu once had a reputation for its confectioneries and bakeries. Many of these have disappeared, as the area steadily dresses up and is invaded by department stores and fast-food joints. The *LA Cafe* (☎ 6358-7097), 4th floor, 188 Huaihai Lu, is a disco by night, but by day operates as an upmarket burger joint, in the Hard Rock Cafe mould. Figure on spending around Y70 per head for your burgers. There are branches of *McDonald's* and the Japanese chain, *Mos Burger*, close by, if Y70 seems over the odds for a burger.

The *Laodachang Bakery & Confectionery* (*lǎodàchāng shípǐndiàn*), at the corner of Huaihai Lu and Chengdu Nanlu, is one of those old bakery establishments that is still in business. The cakes and breads are nothing special, and the place is a little tired these days.

The *Red House* (☎ 6256-5748) (*hóng fángzi xī càiguǎn*) at 37 Shaanxi Nanlu was formerly Chez Louis. It's generally shunned by foreigners nowadays and the food has a bad reputation, but it still lingers on, and who knows, it may get a face-lift and a new chef the way things are going in Shanghai.

Hotel Food For those who don't mind paying international prices, some of the best food in Shanghai is available in the international hotels. The *Blue Heaven Revolving Restaurant* (☎ 6415-4488) in the Jinjiang Tower offers American cuisine, as does *Shanghai Jax* (☎ 6279-8888 ext 8847) in the Portman Shangrila. The Shanghai Centre (same building as the Portman Shangrila) should have a branch of *Tony Roma's*, the ribs specialist, by the time this book is in print.

The Shanghai Centre is also home to the *Thai Restaurant* (☎ 6279-8311). This place has authentic Thai cuisine at international prices.

French cuisine is available at a wide range of international hotels around town. Possi-

bilities include *The Bund* (☎ 6415-4488) in the Jinjiang Tower and the *Teppan Grill* (☎ 6248-0000) in the Shanghai Hilton.

The only place in town serving decent curries and tandoori is the *Bombay Tandoor Restaurant* (☎ 6472-5494) in the New South Building of the Jinjiang Hotel – both the food and décor are excellent.

For Italian food, check out *Luigi's* (☎ 6439-1000) at the Sheraton Huating or *Giovanni's* (☎ 6275-8888) in the Westin Hotel. *Da Vinci's* (☎ 6248-0000) in the Shanghai Hilton also serves high-quality Italian fare.

Shanghai is a popular destination for Japanese tourists and businesspeople, and there are a number of highly rated Japanese restaurants around town – prices, however, are often comparable to those in Tokyo. *Shiki* (☎ 6279-8888 ext 5898) is one possibility; others include *Kampachi* (☎ 6248-1688) in the Hotel Equatorial and the expensive *Sakura* (☎ 6415-1111) in the Garden Hotel.

Most of the major hotels around town have high-quality Cantonese restaurants (popular with Chinese on business trips) and some have restaurants representing the other major regional cuisines of China.

Vegetarian Food Vegetarianism became something of a snobbish fad in Shanghai at one time; it was linked to Taoist and Buddhist groups, then to the underworld, and surfaced on the tables of restaurants as creations shaped like flowers or animals. Khi Vehdu, who ran the Jing'an Temple in the 1930s, was one of the most celebrated exponents. The nearly two-metre-tall abbot had a large following and each of his seven concubines had a house and a car. The Jing'an Temple was eventually divested of its Buddhist statues and turned into a factory.

The *Gongdelin* (☎ 6327-0218) (*gōngdélín shūshíchù*) at 43 Huanghe Lu is probably Shanghai's most famous vegetarian restaurant. It is a branch of the Beijing establishment with the same name. As is usually the case with Chinese vegetarian cuisine, the dishes are designed to resemble and taste like meat – mock chicken, mock duck etc. The restaurant is just around the corner from the Park Hotel on Nanjing Xilu. This place is open until midnight.

The *Juelin Restaurant* (☎ 6326-0115) (*juélín shūshíchù*) at 250 Jinling Donglu is another vegetarian restaurant. It closes early at 7.30 pm. Lunch runs from 11 am to 1.30 pm.

Fast Food Fast food has invaded Shanghai. *KFC* was one of the first to arrive, and now has branches all over the city. *McDonald's* is also well represented, as are other less well known chains such as *Texas Chicken* and *Maxim's*. Others to look out for include *TBCY*, *Baskin Robbins*, *New Zealand Natural Ice Cream*, *Mos Burger* and *Lotteria*. There are local variants on the burgers and fries theme too, such as *Rong Hua Chicken*. A wander around any part of central Shanghai will unearth fast-food dining of one kind or another.

Pub Grub See the Bars & Clubs entry of the following Entertainment section for information on *Malone's American Cafe*, *Shanghai Sally's* and the *Long Bar*. All do excellent pub meals – everything from hamburgers and pizzas to fish and chips. Be prepared to fork out Hong Kong prices for the privilege, however.

Entertainment

Shanghai is emerging as the most spiritually polluted city in China. All the old evils are creeping back with a vengeance. The last couple of years have seen an explosion of nightlife options, with everything from sleazy karaoke parlours to comfy expat bars and discos. None of it comes cheap, however. A night on the town in Shanghai is comparable to a night out in Hong Kong or Taipei.

Bars & Clubs The Shanghai bar and club scene is still in its infancy, and by the time you have this book in your hands there is

likely to be a host of new places that will probably have pushed some of the recommendations here out of business or stolen most of their clientele. At the time of writing, the *Hard Rock Cafe* and *Planet Hollywood* – to name two high-profile newcomers – were poised to open their doors. Others will follow.

Good places to ask around about the latest hot spots in town include *Malone's American Cafe* (☎ 6247-2400), 257 Tongren Lu, a Canadian-run sports bar, *Shanghai Sally's* (☎ 6327-1859), 4 Xiangshan Lu, an English pub, and the *Long Bar* (☎ 6279-8268), in the Shanghai Centre on Nanjing Xilu. Between them, they manage to pack in most of Shanghai's expat community for early evening drinks. They are good places to meet people and find out what's going on.

Other places worth taking a look at include *Jurassic Pub* (☎ 6258-3758), 8 Maoming Nanlu, and *Judy's Place* (☎ 6474-6471), 291 Fumin Nanlu. Jurassic Pub is a dinosaur theme bar with an over-arching Brontosaurus skeleton. Judy's Place is one of Shanghai's pioneering nightlife spots. It has a reputation as one of Shanghai's sleazier entertainment options, but this makes it worth a look in itself if you are new to town.

Popular disco complexes include *New York New York* (☎ 6321-6097), 146 Huqiu Lu, and *LA Café* (☎ 6358-7097), 4th floor, 188 Huaihai Lu. There will undoubtedly be others before long. *JJ Disco* on Yan'an Zhonglu was temporarily closed at the time of writing but will probably reopen. Most discos in Shanghai have a Y50 cover charge.

The *Peace Hotel* bar features an ancient jazz band, more notable for its longevity than its music. There is a Y42 cover charge.

Drinkers on a budget should head up to the Fudan University area. On the corner of Siping Lu and Guoding Lu is *Tribesman Cave*, a funky little bar with inexpensive local beer (Y7 for a Qingdao) and an interesting mix of foreign and Chinese students. It's a good place to meet people. Directly across the road is *Hit*, another popular nightspot. Both places have dancing on the weekends, and entry is free.

Performing Arts Along with Beijing, Shanghai is one of the great cultural centres of China. Nevertheless, having a profound cultural centre in Shanghai takes some determination. With only a few exceptions, much of Shanghai's cultural entertainment is inaccessible to foreigners who do not speak Chinese. Getting hold of schedules for movies and musical performances is also a headache. It will probably still be some time before Shanghai emerges as an international city on this front.

The *Shanghai Art Theatre (shànghǎi yìshù jùyuàn)* is just down the road from the Jinjiang Hotel, and is housed in what used to be the Lyceum Theatre. The theatre was completed in 1931 and was used by the Shanghai Amateur Dramatic Society, a favourite haunt of the Brits. Performances here, however, are unlikely to be accessible to non-Chinese speakers.

The *Conservatory of Music* (☎ 6437-0137) *(yīnyuè xuéxiào)*, at 20 Fenyang Lu off Huaihai Zhonglu, in Frenchtown, is a treat not to be missed by classical music lovers. Performances take place on Sunday evenings at 7 pm. Tickets are usually sold out a few days beforehand, though. Also try the opera at the *People's Opera Theatre* on Jiu Jiang Lu.

There are several professional orchestras in Shanghai, including the Shanghai Philharmonic and the Shanghai National Orchestra. The latter specialises in native instruments.

The Chinese Circus

Circus acts go back 2000 years in the Middle Kingdom; effects are obtained using simple props: sticks, plates, eggs and chairs; and apart from the acrobatics there's magic, vaudeville, drama, clowning, music, conjuring, dance and mime thrown into a complete performance. Happily, it's an art which gained from the Communist takeover and which did not suffer during the Cultural Revolution. Performers used to have the status of gypsies, but now it's 'people's art'.

Most of the provinces have their own performing troupes, sponsored by government agencies, industrial complexes, the army or rural administrations. About 80 troupes are active in China, and they're much in demand. You'll also see more bare legs, star-spangled costumes and rouge in one acrobat show than you'll see anywhere else in China.

Acts vary from troupe to troupe. Some traditional acts haven't changed over the centuries, while others have incorporated roller skates and motorbikes. A couple of time-proven acts that are hard to follow include the 'Balancing in Pairs' with one man balanced upside down on the

head of another and mimicking every movement of the partner below, mirror image, even drinking a glass of water! Hoop jumping is another: four hoops are stacked on top of each other and the person going through the very top hoop may attempt a backflip with a simultaneous body twist.

The 'Peacock Displaying Its Feathers' involves an array of people balanced on one bicycle. According to the Guinness Book of Records, a Shanghai troupe holds the record at 13, though apparently a Wuhan troupe has done 14.

The 'Pagoda of Bowls' is a balancing act where the performer, usually a woman, does everything with her torso except tie it in knots, all the while casually balancing a stack of porcelain bowls on foot, head or both – and perhaps also balancing on a partner. ■

Cinemas In China, foreign movies are generally dubbed into Chinese, Chinese movies very rarely have English subtitles and cinemas are for the most part a dead loss. There are, however, cinemas all over town.

Gyms The largest indoor sports venue in Shanghai is the *Shanghai Gymnasium* at the south-western corner of the city. It has aircon, computer-controlled scoreboards and seats 18,000. All the major hotels also have gyms – the Shanghai Hilton has one of the best.

Acrobatics Chinese acrobatic troupes are among the best in the world, and Shanghai is a good place to see a performance. The *Shanghai Acrobatics Theatre (shànghǎi zájì cháng)* has stunning shows almost every evening. Some people find the animals upsetting, but in general reactions to the shows are enthusiastic. Tickets for the regular shows are around Y10, and the old problem with scalpers no longer seems to exist. Performances start around 7 pm. The theatre is on Nanjing Xilu, a short walk west of the Park Hotel on the same side of the street.

Things to Buy

All Chinese products and popular souvenirs find their way to Shanghai. The city still lags a long way behind other Asian regional centres (such as Hong Kong, Singapore and Bangkok) as a shopping destination, but it seems bent on catching up. The best shopping areas are Nanjing Donglu (of course) and Huaihai Zhonglu, which at the latest count had over 300 shops.

Department Stores Shanghai has some of the best department stores in China. The latest development has been the arrival of flash Tokyo-style operations that bring boutiques and generic brands together under one roof. Check out Isetan at 537 Huaihai Zhonglu for Japanese shopping at its best.

The two most popular department stores are the venerable Hua Lian Department Store (formerly No 10, and before that Wing

On), 635 Nanjing Donglu, and the No 1 Department Store, 830 Nanjing Donglu. They are fascinating places to browse in if you can stand the crowds. Manhattan Plaza, 437 Nanjing Donglu, is a seven-storey smorgasbord of joint-venture shops selling expensive imports – it's probably of more interest to Shanghai residents than to visitors.

The JJ Dickson Centre on Changle Lu is an incredibly expensive shopping centre with nothing but upscale Western shops, including Harvey Nichols, Ralph Lauren, Charles Jourdan, Guy Larouche etc.

For more boutique shopping, Maison Mode at 1312 Huaihai Zhonglu is probably the last say. Brands featured include Yves Saint Laurent and Elizabeth Arden. And by the time you have this book in your hands there will probably be countless more department stores and boutique emporiums scattered around Shanghai.

Supermarkets & Pharmacies If you're craving anything from home or need Western pharmaceutical items, the best place to stock up is the Shanghai Centre. Wellcome is a Hong Kong supermarket chain packed with imported biscuits, chocolates, pasta, cheeses and beverages. Also in the Shanghai Centre is a branch of Watson's, a pharmacy with cosmetics, over-the-counter medicines and health products. Neither of these places are cheap – prices are similar to those you would pay in Hong Kong.

Kids' Stuff There are a number of children's shops around town. At 573 Nanjing Donglu take a look at the Bei Li Children's Clothing Shop. The June 1 Children's Shop can be found at 939 Huaihai Lu (June 1 is Children's Day in China).

Photographic Supplies For photographic supplies, check the shops in the major hotels. Shanghai is one of the few places in China where slide film is readily available. Shanghai's foremost photographic supplies shop is Guan Long at 190 Nanjing Donglu.

THE EAST

Porcelain One of the best places around for porcelain is the Jindezhen Porcelain Artware Co at the corner of Nanjing Xilu and Shanxi Lu.

Souvenirs On the arts and crafts, souvenirs and antiques front, one of the best places to go is the Yuyuan Bazaar. There are a number of shops here with marked prices (asking for a discount or a bit of friendly haggling won't go astray) and a wide range of products. The Shanghai Arts & Crafts Service Centre (☎ 6327-3650), 190-208 Nanjing Xilu, is another place worth checking out, though prices tend be a little high. The Shanghai Arts & Crafts Store, in the Shanghai Exhibition Centre, is largely frequented by tour groups.

Tea & Teapots Tea and the dainty teapots and cups used by the Chinese make excellent gifts, and Shanghai is a good place to buy them. The Yuyuan Bazaar is one of the best places in Shanghai to make purchases. Otherwise, look out for the exclusive Shanghai Huangshan Tea Co at 853 Huaihai Zhonglu. Prices can be surprisingly reasonable. Yixing ware, the most valued of all Chinese teapots, is available at the Huangshan Tea Co.

Getting There & Away

Shanghai has rail and air connections to places all over China, ferries up the Yangzi River and many boats along the coast, and buses to destinations in adjoining provinces.

Air CAAC's useful international flights include those to Brussels, Fukuoka, Hong Kong, Los Angeles, Nagasaki, Nagoya, New York, Osaka, Paris, San Francisco, Tokyo, Toronto and Vancouver. CAAC has announced plans to add direct flights from Shanghai to Seoul, Bangkok and Singapore in the near future. Dragonair also flies between Shanghai and Hong Kong. Northwest and United fly to the USA (with a brief change of aircraft in Tokyo), and Canadian Airlines International can get you to Canada.

Daily (usually several times daily) domestic flights connect Shanghai to every major

city in China. Minor cities are less likely to have daily flights, but if it has an airport the chances are that there will be at least one flight a week, probably more, to Shanghai. The domestic departure tax is Y60.

China Eastern Airlines' main office (☎ domestic 6247-5953, international 6247-2255) is at 200 Yan'an Xilu, and is open 24 hours a day. There are also ticket sales counters at most of the major hotels around town and at the main CITS office in the Guangming Building. Shanghai Airlines (☎ 6255-8558) is at the airport, but travel agents peddle their tickets in the city centre. All domestic flights can also be booked at CITS.

Several other international airlines have Shanghai offices:

Aeroflot
    East Lake Hotel, Donghu Lu (☎ 6471-1665)
Air France
    Hongqiao Airport (☎ 6268-8866)
All Nippon Airways (ANA)
    2F, East Wing, Shanghai Centre (☎ 6279-7000)
Canadian Airlines International
    6th floor, New Jinjiang Tower (☎ 6415-3091)
Dragonair
    Room 202, 2F, Shanghai Centre ☎ 6279-8099)
Japan Airlines
    2F, Ruijin Building, 205 Maoming Lu (☎ 6472-3000)
Korean Air
    Room 104-5, Hotel Equatorial, 105 Yan'an Xilu (☎ 6248-1777)
Lufthansa
    Shanghai Hilton Hotel, 250 Huashan Lu (☎ 6248-1100)
Northwest Airlines
    Suite 207, Level 2, East Podium, Shanghai Centre (☎ 6279-8088)
Singapore Airlines
    Room 208, East Wing, Shanghai Centre, 1376 Nanjing Xilu (☎ 6279-8008)
Thai Airways International
    2F, Shanghai Centre (☎ 6279-7170)
United Airlines
    Suite 204, West Podium, Shanghai Centre (☎ 6279-8009)

Bus The long-distance bus station is on Qiujiang Lu, west of Henan Beilu. There are several buses a day to Hangzhou, Wuxi and Changzhou.

There is another ticket office at Renmin

Square, opposite the junction of Fuzhou Lu and Xizang Zhonglu, which has tickets for buses to Suzhou. The boarding points for the buses are marked on the ticket in Chinese (at the time of writing there were two boarding points for the Suzhou bus: one on Gongxing Lu near Renmin Square, and one on Huangpu Beilu Kou near the main railway station), so check where to board the bus when you buy a ticket.

Because the Shanghai-Nanjing highway corridor is so busy, rail is a better option for getting to towns along this route.

Train Shanghai is at the junction of the Beijing-Shanghai and Beijing-Hangzhou railway lines. Since these branch off in various directions, many parts of the country can be reached by direct train from Shanghai. The problem is getting hold of tickets.

In Shanghai it is virtually impossible to buy anything other than foreigners' price tickets, and it is a nightmare trying to do it yourself at the railway station. The best bet is to first try CITS, which can organise tickets with enough notice. For destinations such as Nanjing, Suzhou and Hangzhou, CITS can generally rustle up tickets for the next day. For journeys further afield, they need more time.

If you need a ticket in a hurry, try the ticketing office in the Longmen Hotel (☎ 6317-0000 ext 5315), next to the railway station, at 777 Hengfeng Lu. The office is open from 7 am to 9 pm, with a break for dinner. (How long? As long as it takes to eat dinner.) Compared with the railway station, it is a very civilised place to buy train tickets, and you rarely have to wait long in line. A final possibility for rail ticket purchases is CYTS at 2 Hengshan Lu. It is open from 9 to 11.30 am and 1 to 4 pm, closed on Sunday.

Most trains depart and arrive at the main railway station (see the Central Shanghai map), but some depart and arrive at the west station (see the Shanghai city map). Be sure to find out which one you should leave from.

Travel times from Shanghai are: Beijing 17½ hours; Fuzhou 22½ hours; Guangzhou 33 hours; Guilin 29 hours; Hangzhou 3½

hours; Kunming 62 hours; Nanjing four hours; Qingdao 24 hours; and Xi'an 27 hours.

There are special double-decker 'tourist trains' operating between Shanghai and Hangzhou, and Shanghai and Nanjing (with stops at Wuxi, Suzhou, Changzhou and Zhenjiang). Even the hard-seat sections of these trains are very comfortable and smoking is forbidden; attendants bring around drinks and food, and it is even possible to request songs from the on-board broadcasting room, providing your tastes run to uplifting oldies like Jingle Bells.

Boat Boats are definitely one of the best ways of leaving Shanghai and they're often also the cheapest. For destinations on the coast or inland on the Yangzi, they may even sometimes be faster than trains, which have to take rather circuitous routes. Smaller, grottier boats handle numerous inland shipping routes.

Boat tickets can be bought from CITS, which charges a commission, or from the ticket office at 1 Jinling Donglu. The situation with tickets is very confusing. CITS charges foreigners 95% over the local price, while the boat ticket office does not always do so (this depends on the shipping company). It is worth comparing prices before buying your ticket.

The Shanghai-Hong Kong route was re-opened in 1980 after a gap of 28 years. Three passenger ships now ply the route: the *Shanghai*, the *Haixin* and the *Jinjiang*. A lot of travellers leave China this way and the 2½-day trip gets rave reviews. There are departures every seven days. There are also once-weekly ferries to Osaka/Yokohama in Japan.

Ships depart from the international passenger terminal to the east of Shanghai Mansions. The address is Wai Hong Qiao Harbour, Taipin Lu No 1. Passengers are requested to be at the harbour three hours before departure. Tickets can be bought from CITS or from the ticket office at 1 Jinling Donglu.

Boats to Putuoshan run every two days,

departing at 3 pm in either direction and taking 12 hours. Tickets cost Y60 to Y132 depending on class. A five-hour rapid ferry service also departs daily at 7 am and costs Y210 or Y300 deluxe. If you take the latter service, you must first take a 7 am bus from inside the Shiliupu Wharf.

The main destinations of ferries up the Yangzi River from Shanghai are Nantong, Nanjing, Wuhu, Guichi, Jiujiang and Wuhan. From Wuhan you can change to another ferry which will take you to Chongqing. If you're only going as far west as Nanjing, take the train, which is much faster than the boat. Daily departures are from Shiliupu Wharf.

If money is more important than time, the most sensible way to head west from Shanghai is along the river. Wuhan, for example, is over 1500 km by rail from Shanghai. For about half the hard-sleeper train fare you can get a berth in 4th class on the boat. For a bit more than a tourist-priced hard-sleeper ticket on a train you'd probably be able to get a bed in a two-person cabin on the boat.

The frequency of coastal shipping varies according to destination. Some of the 5000-tonne liners have staterooms with private bathroom in 1st and special classes, with wood panelling, red velvet curtains, the works. The ship should have a restaurant, bar, snack shops, but this depends on the boat. Second and 3rd class are split into A and B fares, with A having just a bit better accommodation and service than B. Popular destinations include Ningbo and Xiamen.

Unfortunately, many of the coastal shipping services are being superseded by planes, trains and automobiles – many routes have been shut down completely.

Getting Around

Shanghai is not a walker's dream. There are some fascinating areas to stroll around, but new road developments, building sites and shocking traffic conditions conspire to make walking an exhausting, often stressful experience. The buses too are hard work – not particularly easy to figure out, and difficult to squeeze into and out of. The subway

system, on the other hand, is a dream. Unfortunately, so far it only does a north-south sprint through central Shanghai. Travellers with money to spare can at least hop into a taxi.

To/From the Airport Hongqiao Airport is 18 km from the Bund and getting there takes about 30 minutes if you're lucky, or over an hour if you're not. There is a bus from the CAAC office on Yan'an Lu to the airport. Major hotels like the Jinjiang have an airport shuttle. Taxis from the Bund cost approximately Y55, depending on the kind of taxi, the route taken and the traffic conditions.

Bus Buses are often packed to the hilt and at times impossible to board. The closest thing to revolutionary fervour in Shanghai today is the rush-hour bus ambushes. Once on board, keep your valuables tucked away since pickpocketing is easy under such conditions, and foreigners make juicy targets.

Contrary to popular belief, buses are not colour coded – the bus map is. Routes 1 to 30 are for trolley-buses (now supplemented by regular buses). Buses 1 to 199 operate from 5 am to 11 pm. Buses in the 200 and 400 series are peak-hour buses, and 300 series buses provide all-night service. Suburban and long-distance buses don't carry numbers – the destination is in characters. Some useful buses are listed here:

No 18 This bus runs from the front of the main railway station (it originates further north-east at Hongkou or Lu Xun Park) and proceeds south down Xizang Lu, and then south to the banks of the Huangpu..

No 64 This bus gets you to the railway station from the Pujiang Hotel. Catch it near the Pujiang on Beijing Donglu close to the intersection with Sichuan Zhonglu. The ride takes 20 to 30 minutes.

No 65 The No 65 runs from behind the main railway station, passes Shanghai Mansions, crosses Waibaidu bridge, then heads directly south along the Bund (Zhongshan Lu) as far as the Bund can go.

No 49 From the PSB terminal, this bus heads west along Yan'an Lu. Nos 48 and 42 follow similar routes from Huangpu Park, travel south along the Bund, west around the Dongfeng Hotel, then link westbound along Yan'an Lu. No 26 starts in the city centre a few streets west of the Bund, drops to the Yuyuan Bazaar, then goes west along Huaihai Lu.

No 16 This is a good linking bus for all those awkward destinations. It runs from the Jade Buddha Temple to Yuyuan Bazaar, then on to a ferry hop over the Huangpu River.

No 11 This bus travels the ring road around the old Chinese city.

No 71 This bus can get you to the CAAC office, from where you can catch the airport bus. Catch No 71 from Yan'an Donglu close to the Bund.

Subway Shanghai's Metro is being constructed at a feverish pace. The first section opened on 10 April 1995 and runs 16.1 km from the railway station in the north of town through Renmin Square and down to the Jinjiang Amusement Park in the south of town. A second line connecting Hongqiao Airport with the Pudong New Area (running east-west through the centre of town) is slated to open in late 1996. Trains run from

5 am to 9 pm, once every nine minutes at rush hours and every 12 minutes during off-peak hours; tickets cost Y1 to Y2.

Taxi Shanghai taxis are reasonably cheap and easy to flag down, but try to avoid the peak hours of 7 to 9 am and 5 to 7 pm. Fares vary slightly depending on the taxi – flag fall is Y10.80 or Y14.40 depending on the size of the vehicle. It is possible to travel to most destinations within central Shanghai for around Y15 to Y20.

Car Anji Car Rental Company in Shanghai is said to be the first company in China to experiment with renting cars to foreigners at the airport on arrival. If you have never driven in China before, do not even consider driving into town from the airport – Shanghai traffic conditions are anarchic.

Hotel Transport The Sheraton Huating has a free hourly shuttle to the Bund and other central areas. Other major hotels may offer the same service for their guests.

Zhejiang 浙江

Zhejiang is one of the smallest provinces in China. Traditionally one of the most prosperous, Zhejiang *(zhèjiāng)* has always been more important than its size would indicate.

The region falls into two distinct sections. The area north of Hangzhou is part of the lush Yangzi River delta, which is similar to the southern region of Jiangsu Province. The south is mountainous, continuing the rugged terrain of Fujian Province.

Intensely cultivated for a thousand years, northern Zhejiang has lost most of its natural vegetation cover and is a flat, featureless plain with a dense network of waterways, canals and irrigation channels. The Grand Canal also ends here – Zhejiang was part of the great southern granary from which food was shipped to the depleted areas of the north.

The growth of Zhejiang's towns was based on their proximity to the sea and their location in some of China's most productive farmland. Hangzhou, Ningbo and Shaoxing have all been important trading centres and ports since the 7th and 8th centuries AD. Their growth was accelerated when, in the 12th century, the Song Dynasty moved court to Hangzhou in the wake of an invasion from the north.

Silk was one of the popular exports and today Zhejiang is known as the 'land of silk', producing a third of China's raw silk, brocade and satin.

Hangzhou is the province's capital. To the south-east of the city are several places you can visit without backtracking. A road and a railway line run east from Hangzhou to Shaoxing and Ningbo. From Ningbo you could take a bus to Tiantaishan, continue south to Wenzhou and down the coast road into Fujian Province. Jiaxing, on the railway line from Hangzhou to Shanghai, is also open, as is Huzhou in the far north of Zhejiang Province on the shores of Lake Taihu.

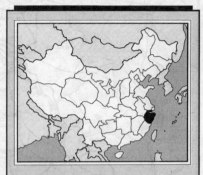

Population: 40 million
Capital: Hangzhou
Highlights:
- Hangzhou's West Lake, one of China's most famous attractions
- Putuoshan island, a rapidly developing but still magical getaway, with temples and walks

HANGZHOU
(hángzhōu)

For the Chinese, Hangzhou, along with Guilin, is the country's most famous tourist attraction. Indeed, if you arrive by train, an announcement is made in Chinese as the train pulls into Hangzhou station proclaiming Hangzhou as the 'tourist capital of China'. This is a warning. Hangzhou is literally swamped with tourists any time of year, but particularly during the peak summer months and on sunny weekends. This has in turn led to rip-off hotel rates and lots of ugly tourist developments around the city's main attraction, West Lake.

West Lake is a large freshwater lake surrounded by hills and gardens, its banks dotted with pavilions and temples. The lake gives rise to what must be one of China's

371

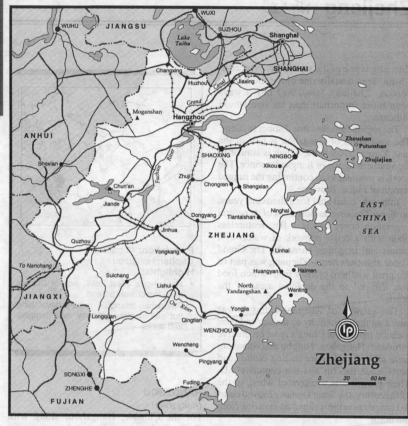

Zhejiang

0   30   60 km

oldest tourist blurbs: 'In heaven there is paradise, on earth Suzhou and Hangzhou'. Be this as it may, the earthly paradise of Hangzhou is a busy place and you will have to work fairly hard to escape the crowds. Even in the reasonably rural areas to the west of the lake, the roads are often crowded with tour buses and cruising taxis.

History

When Marco Polo passed through Hangzhou in the 13th century he described it as one of the finest and most splendid cities in the world. Though Hangzhou had risen to prom-

inence when the southern end of the Grand Canal reached here at the start of the 7th century, it really came into its own after the Song Dynasty was overthrown by the invading Jurchen.

The Jurchen were ancestors of the Manchus, who conquered China five centuries later. The Song capital of Kaifeng, along with the emperor and the leaders of the imperial court, was captured by the Jurchen in 1126. The rest of the Song court fled south, finally settling at Hangzhou and founding the Southern Song Dynasty.

China had gone through an economic revolution in previous years, producing huge and prosperous cities, an advanced economy and a flourishing inter-regional trade. With the Jurchen invasion, the centre of this revolution was pushed south from the Yellow River Valley to the lower Yangzi Valley and to the coast between the Yangzi River and Guangzhou.

While the north remained in the hands of the invaders (who rapidly became Sinicised), in the south Hangzhou became the hub of the Chinese state. The court, the military, the civil officials and merchants all congregated in Hangzhou, whose population rose from half a million to 1¾ million by 1275. The city's large population and its proximity to the ocean promoted the growth of river and sea trade, and of ship-building and other naval industries.

When the Mongols swept into China they established their court at Beijing. Hangzhou, however, retained its status as a prosperous commercial city. It took a beating in the Taiping Rebellion, however: in 1861 the Taipings laid siege to and captured the city; two years later the imperial armies took it back. These campaigns reduced almost the entire city to ashes, annihilated or displaced most of the population, and finally ended Hangzhou's significance as a commercial and trading centre. Few monuments survived the devastation, and most of those that did became victims of the Red Guards a hundred years later. Much of what may be seen in Hangzhou today is of fairly recent construction.

Orientation

Hangzhou is bounded to the south by the Qiantang River and to the west by hills. Between the hills and the urban area is large West Lake, the region's premier scenic attraction. The eastern shore of the lake is the developed touristy district; the western shore is quieter.

Information

CITS This office (☎ 515-2888; fax 515-6667) is at 1 Shihan Lu in a charming old building *(wànghú lóu)* near the Wanghu Hotel. It is not a particularly useful place for independent travellers.

On the Grand Canal in Hangzhou, one of the most popular towns for Chinese tourists in the country.

THE EAST

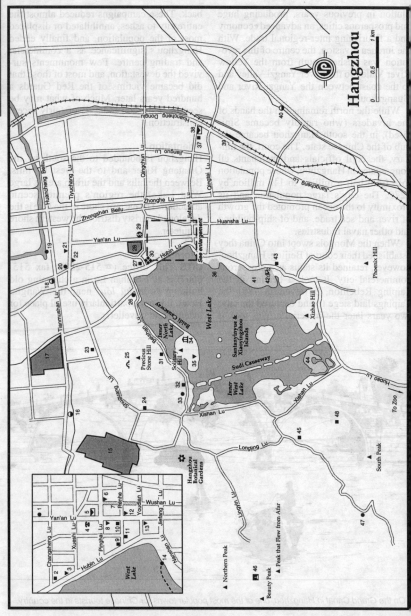

HANGZHOU 杭州

PLACES TO STAY

2 Huaqiao Hotel
   华侨饭店
9 Hubin Hotel
   湖宾饭店
10 Yanling Hotel
   文化中心
11 Huanhu Hotel
   环湖饭店
23 Yellow Dragon Hotel
   黄龙饭店
24 Lingfeng Hotel
   & Overseas
   Student Dorm
   灵峰山庄，
   外国留学生楼
27 Wanghu Hotel
   望湖宾馆
31 Xinxin Hotel
   新新饭店
32 Hangzhou Shangri La
   Hotel
   杭州香格里拉饭店
37 Xinhua Hotel
   新华饭店
43 Qingbo Hotel
   清波饭店
45 Zhejiang Hotel
   浙江宾馆
48 Liu Tong Hotel
   六通宾馆

PLACES TO EAT

3 Paradise Rock
   (restaurant/bar)
   乐园酒吧

6 Dumpling Restaurant
   铰子馆
8 Xi'an Dumpling
   Restaurant
   西安铰子馆
12 KFC
   肯德鸡
13 Roast Duck Restaurant
   烤鸭店
21 KFC
   肯德鸡
22 Boston Fish & Fries
   波士顿快餐
35 Louwailou Restaurant
   楼外楼菜馆

OTHER

1 Overseas Chinese Store
   华侨商店
4 International Telephone
   Office
   长途电话
5 Post Office
   邮局
7 Market Street
   市场
14 Boats to Santanyinyue
   至三潭印月
15 Zhejiang University
   浙江大学
16 West Bus Station
   长途汽车西站
17 Hangzhou University
   杭州大学
18 Long-Distance Bus
   Station
   长途汽车站

19 Hangzhou Passenger
   Wharf
   客运码头
20 CAAC
   民航售票处
25 Yellow Dragon Cave
   黄龙洞
26 CITS
   中国国际旅行社
28 Zhejiang Medical
   College
   浙江医科大学
29 Bank of China
   中国银行
30 Friendship Store
   友谊商店
33 Yue Fei Mausoleum
   岳飞墓
34 Zhejiang Provincial
   Museum
   浙江省博物馆
36 Children's Park
   儿童公园
38 Main Post Office
   邮电局
39 Railway Station
   火车站
40 South Bus Station
   长途汽车南站
41 Liulangwenying Park
   柳浪闻莺公园
42 Bicycle Rentals
   租自行车店
44 Huagang Park
   花港公园
46 Temple of Inspired
   Seclusion
   灵隐寺
47 Dragon Well
   龙井

Money There are money-changing counters at most tourist hotels. The main Bank of China branch is at 140 Yan'an Beilu, near Qingchun Lu.

Temple of Inspired Seclusion

(língyǐn sì)

Lingyin Si, roughly translated as either Temple of Inspired Seclusion or Temple of the Soul's Retreat, is really Hangzhou's main attraction. It was built in 326 AD and, due to war and calamity, has been destroyed and restored no fewer than 16 times.

The Cultural Revolution might have seen it razed for good but for the intervention of Zhou Enlai. Accounts vary as to what exactly happened, but it seems there was a confrontation between those who wanted to save the temple and those who wanted to destroy it. The matter eventually went all the way up to Zhou, who gave the order to save both the temple and the sculptures on the rock face opposite. The monks, however, were sent to work in the fields. In the early

1970s a few of the elderly and invalid monks were allowed to come back and live out their last few years in a small outbuilding on the hillside behind the temple.

The present buildings are restorations of Qing Dynasty structures. At the front of the temple is the Hall of the Four Heavenly Guardians, in the middle of which a statue of Maitreya, the future Buddha, sits on a platform flanked by two dragons. Behind this hall is the Great Hall, where you'll find the magnificent 20-metre-high statue of Siddhartha Gautama. This was sculptured from 24 blocks of camphor wood in 1956 and was based on a Tang Dynasty original. Behind the giant statue is a startling montage of 150 small figures.

Facing the temple is Feilai Feng (*fēilái fēng*), the Peak that Flew from Afar. Some praise must go to the Chinese (or the Indians) for accomplishing the first successful solo flight of a mountain! This name, so the story goes, came from an Indian monk who visited Hangzhou in the 3rd century and said that the hill looked exactly like one in India and asked when it had flown to China. The rocky surface of the hill is chiselled with 330 sculptures and graffiti from the 10th to the 14th centuries. The earliest sculpture dates back to 951 AD and comprises a group of three Buddhist deities at the right-hand entrance to the Qing Lin Cave. Droves of Chinese people clamber over the sculptures and inscriptions to have their photo taken; the most popular backdrop is the laughing Maitreya (the fat buddha at the foot of the ridge). There is a vegetarian restaurant beside the temple.

To get to the temple take bus No 7 to the terminal at the foot of the hills west of Hangzhou. Behind the Lingyin Temple is Northern Peak, which can be climbed via cable car. From the summit there are sweeping views across the lake and city.

Zhejiang Provincial Museum
(*zhèjiāng bówùguǎn*)

This interesting museum is on Solitary Hill Island (*gūshān*), a short walk from the Hangzhou Shangri-La Hotel. Its buildings were part of the holiday palace of Emperor Qianlong in the 18th century. Most of the museum is concerned with natural history there's a large whale skeleton (a female *Rhachianectos glaucus cope*) and a dinosaur skeleton.

Mausoleum of General Yue Fei
(*yuè fēi mù*)

During the 12th century, when China was attacked by Jurchen invaders from the north, General Yue Fei (1103-41) was commander of the Song armies. Despite his successes against the invaders, he was recalled to the Song court where he was executed by a treacherous court official called Qin Gui. Twenty years later, in 1163, Song emperor Xiao Zong rehabilitated him and had his corpse reburied at the present site. Yue was eventually deified.

The mausoleum of this soldier-patriot is in a compound bounded by a red-brick wall on Huanhu Lu, a few minutes' walk west of the Hangzhou Shangri-La Hotel. It was ran sacked during the Cultural Revolution but has since been restored.

Inside is a glazed clay statue of the general and, on the wall, paintings of scenes from his life, including one of his back being tattooed with the words 'Loyal to the Last'.

Precious Stone Hill
(*bǎoshí shān*)

The original Protect Chu Tower (*bǎochù tǎ* was erected on Precious Stone Hill in 938 during the Song Dynasty. It was built to ensure the safe return of Hangzhou's Prince Qian Chu from an audience with the emperor. The present tower is a 1933 reconstruction, 45½ metres high and resembling a stone-age rocket ship. It stands just north of Huanhu Lu (follow the steps) on the northern side of the lake. In the early morning you may find elderly Chinese women practising taijiquan there and old men airing their birds. From the tower there are tracks south along the ridge through bamboo groves; dotted along the tracks are temples and shrines.

Six Harmonies Pagoda
(liùhé tǎ)

To the south-west of the city stands an enormous rail-and-road bridge which spans the Qiantang River. Close by is the 60-metre-high octagonal Six Harmonies Pagoda named after the six codes of Buddhism. As a legacy of the feudal past, the pagoda was slated for demolition during the Cultural Revolution, but since this would have required an army of experts the project was called off. The pagoda was originally built as a lighthouse, although it was also supposed to have some sort of magical power to halt the tidal bore which thundered up the Qiantang River in mid-September every year.

West Lake
(xī hú)

There are 30 lakes in China called Xi Hu, but this one is by far the most famous. Indeed it is the West Lake on which all other west lakes are modelled. In the right weather conditions, West Lake can be a memorable excursion. Unfortunately, West Lake is also a tourist trap. The jostling hordes of holiday makers, souvenir sellers and boat operators can be quite a trial at times.

West Lake was originally a lagoon adjoining the Qiantang River. In the 8th century the governor of Hangzhou had it dredged; later a dike was built which cut it off from the river completely. The result is about three km long and a bit under three km wide. Two causeways, the Baidi and the Sudi, split the lake into sections. The causeways each have a number of arched bridges, large enough for small boats and ferries to pass under. The sights are scattered around the lake, though most of them tend to be uninspiring pavilions or bridges with fanciful names.

The largest island in the lake is Solitary Hill *(gǔshān)* – the location of the Provincial Museum, the Louwailou Restaurant and Zhongshan Park *(zhōngshān gōngyuǎn)*. During the 18th century Zhongshan Park was once part of an imperial palace, but was renamed after 1911 in honour of Sun Yatsen. The Baidi causeway links the island to the mainland.

Most of the other sights are connected with famous people who once lived there – poets, an emperor, perhaps an alchemist who bubbled up longevity pills. One of these sights is the Pavilion for Releasing Crane. It was built in memory of the Song poet Lin Hejing who, it is said, refused to serve the emperor and remained a bachelor his whole life. His only pastimes were planting plum trees and fondling his crane.

Hangzhou's botanical gardens even have a sequoia (a coniferous tree) presented by Richard Nixon on his 1972 visit.

Santanyinyue *(sāntán yìnyuè)* is another island in the lake celebrated for three pools that reflect the moon in mid-August, when the moon is at its largest and roundest.

If you want to contemplate the moon in the privacy of your own boat there are a couple of places around the lake where you can hire paddle boats and go for a slow spin. Boats can also be chartered for a lake cruise from the small docks along the eastern side of the lake. On Sunday and holidays, many Chinese families charter covered boats for picnic outings.

Other Sights
The **Hangzhou Zoo** has Manchurian tigers, though to our untrained eyes they looked no different from other tigers.

About 60 km north of Hangzhou is **Moganshan**. Pleasantly cool at the height of summer, Moganshan was developed as a resort for Europeans living in Shanghai and Hangzhou during the colonial era.

Places to Stay – bottom end
The accommodation situation in Hangzhou is particularly grim, and is likely to get worse rather than better. Be warned also that on weekends and in peak season, it can be difficult to find any accommodation. Try to arrive early in the day if possible.

At the time of writing, the only budget accommodation option was the *Student Dormitory (liúxuéshēng lóu)*, behind the Lingfeng Hotel, close to Zhejiang University. Beds in double rooms cost Y60. Take a No 16 bus to the last stop, and look for the

Lingfeng Hotel around the corner. To find the student accommodation, walk through the foyer of the Lingfeng Hotel and take a door into a courtyard area and walk straight ahead – there are usually a few foreign students about if you have problems locating the place.

CITS was touting the *Guesthouse of Hangzhou University* (☎ 806-6357) (*hángdà zhuānjiā lóu*) as the other budget option in town, but grotty doubles here go for Y270 and Y300. Given the inconvenient location and the state of the rooms, this place is not exactly a bargain.

Places to Stay – middle

Hangzhou accommodation is exclusively middle to top-end. Mid-range options are generally overpriced, but given that there is a shortage of accommodation in Hangzhou hotels can charge whatever they like and get away with it – local tourists pay up without complaint.

Most mid-range hotels are clustered on the eastern edge of the lake close to Hubin Lu. This is a noisy part of town and, despite the high prices, the rooms in all these places tend to be noisy too. One of the quietest (and cheapest) places, the *Renhe Hotel*, is not authorised to take foreigners, though the staff politely claim they would like to.

Two possibilities (neither are particularly worth recommending) are: the *Huanhu Hotel* (☎ 706-7701) (*huánhú fàndiàn*), which has standard doubles at Y300 and Y330; and the *Yanling Hotel* (☎ 706-9769) (*yánlíng bīnguǎn*), which has standard doubles at Y280 and Y330. The latter has no English sign but a large, arched red door leads to a flight of stairs which ascend into the hotel lobby.

South of Hubin Lu, the *Qingbo Hotel* (☎ 707-9988) (*qīngbō fàndiàn*), on Nanshan Lu, is one of the few places in town that comes close to representing value for money, though at Y360 or Y400 for a standard double it is still over the odds. It is easy to miss this place as it is on a turn-off and has no English sign – look for the ground floor ochre finish.

Almost directly opposite is an English sign advertising 'Bicycle Rental'.

The *Xinxin Hotel* (☎ 798-7101) (*xīnxīn fàndiàn*), 58 Beishan Lu, on the northern shore of the lake, is in a quiet location, but is often fully booked. It has doubles from Y180 to Y360 – chances are if any rooms are vacant they will be the Y360 ones.

Places to Stay – top end

There is no shortage of top-end accommodation in Hangzhou, most of it situated around West Lake. The northern and western edges of the lake have the best places to stay. Taxis from the railway station to any of these hotels should cost between Y20 and Y25.

The best of the lakeside hotels is the *Hangzhou Shangri-La Hotel* (☎ 707-7951; fax 707-3545) (*hángzhōu xiānggé lǐlā fàndiàn*), also just called the *Hangzhou Hotel* (*hángzhōu fàndiàn*). It's on the northern side of the lake surrounded by spacious forested grounds. Doubles cost US$145 with a hillside view, or US$190 with a view of the lake.

On the western side of the lake is the *Zhejiang Hotel* (☎ 797-7988; fax 797-1904) (*zhèjiāng bīnguǎn*), a sprawling, mildly disorganised place in a quiet woodland setting. Standard doubles range from Y570 to Y790 and there are singles available from Y360. It's the kind of place to be if you want to spend lots of money and not forget you are in China.

South of the Zhejiang Hotel on the remote west side of the lake is the garden-style *Liu Tong Hotel* (☎ 796-0606; fax 796-0607) (*liùtōng bīnguǎn*), 32 Faxiang Xiang, with rooms costing from Y465. It's a very average attempt at an international hotel.

On the eastern edge of the lake is the *Hangzhou Overseas Chinese Hotel* (☎ 707-4401) (*huáqiáo fàndiàn*), 15 Hubin Lu, a big, tacky place with doubles from Y580. Along similar lines and close by on Wangcheng Xilu is the *Wanghu Hotel* (☎ 707-1024; fax 707-1350) (*wànghú bīnguǎn*), where doubles range from Y740 to Y950; there are some cheaper singles available from Y360.

More centrally located possibilities include the *Dragon Hotel* (☎ 799-8833; fax 799-8090) *(huánglóng fàndiàn)*, where standard doubles are US$130, and the *Xinqiao Hotel* (☎ 707-6688) *(xīnqiáo fàndiàn)*, where standard doubles cost from US$60 to US$80.

Places to Eat

There are lakeside restaurants north of Hubin Lu and Beishan Lu, but bear in mind that these tend to be expensive. For an inexpensive fast-food fix there are a few branches of *KFC* around town, including one next door to the Hangzhou Shangri-La Hotel; it has lakeside views. Another fast-food option is *Boston Fish & Fries* – there's a branch across the road from CAAC.

For cheap eats, Chinese style, check out Yan'an Lu, which runs parallel to Hubin Lu. On Yan'an Lu itself is a fabulous, cheap dumpling shop. An English sign on a gold plate outside announces it as belonging to the *Xi'an Dumpling Enterprises Group*. There's no English menu but ask them for *tāngjiǎo* and you will get a bowl of dumplings in broth to which you add a fiery chilli sauce and soy sauce yourself – it costs just Y3 per bowl. There is another good dumpling shop at the end of the Wushan Lu market street, and it opens fairly late.

See the Hangzhou map for the *Roast Duck Restaurant (kǎoyā diàn)*. You can order à la carte cheaply if you can read the menu. Otherwise ask for the *kǎoyā* (Beijing duck), which costs Y53 per serving (enough for two) – you'd pay three times this elsewhere in Hangzhou. The décor is rough and ready, the staff wander outside to spit on the sidewalk from time to time, but the food is good.

All the major hotels provide high-quality local and Cantonese cuisine, though you will have to go to the Shangri-La for decent Western food.

Paradise Rock, next door to the Overseas Chinese Hotel, has coffee and snacks (good spring rolls) in a very trendy setting (by Hangzhou standards) – a cellular phone is *de rigueur*. It's an interesting place to have a beer (Y15) in the evening and check out the local scene.

Things to Buy

Hangzhou is well known for its tea, in particular *longjing* green tea (grown in the Longjing District, west of West Lake), and for its silk. There is no shortage of places selling Hangzhou silk, tea and tea utensils (as well as lots of other junky items) in shops around the lake. One of the best places to look, however, is the market street on Wushan Lu in the evenings. It's a bit like Patpong Rd without the go-go bars and fake Rolexes – stalls here sell everything from Chairman Mao's *Little Red Book*, to silk shirts, teapots, Tibetan handicrafts, sexy underwear and, at one stall, posters of transsexuals. Interesting browsing, but be prepared to haggle hard if anything catches your eye.

Getting There & Away

Air The CAAC office (☎ 515-4259) is at 160 Tiyuchang Lu. Dragonair (☎ 799-8833 ext 6061) has a representative in the Dragon Hotel on Shuguang Lu. Both CAAC and Dragonair offer daily flights to/from Hong Kong for Y2600. Silk Air (☎ 799-8833 ext 6070) offers direct connections with Singapore and can also be found in the Dragon Hotel.

Hangzhou has regular domestic connections with all major Chinese cities.

Bus The long-distance bus station situation in Hangzhou is a pain. They are scattered around town. If you want to get to Shaoxing or Ningbo by bus, for example, you will need to head over to the east bus station near the railway station. Major destinations such as Shanghai and Hefei can be reached from the main long-distance bus station on Hushu Nanlu just north of the intersection with Huancheng Lu.

Train There are direct trains from Hangzhou to Fuzhou, Nanchang, Shanghai and Guangzhou, and east to the small towns of Shaoxing and Ningbo. For trains to the north you must first go to Shanghai. Hangzhou Railway Station has a separate ticket booking office for foreigners. It's not that easy to find – stand around looking perplexed until someone either offers to sell you a ticket to your destination or takes you to the foreigners' ticket window *(wàibīn shòupiàochù)*. CITS will not book rail tickets.

From Hangzhou to Shanghai takes about three hours, and there are numerous trains daily. Some trains continue through to Suzhou. Trains from Hangzhou to Guangzhou take around 28 hours (depending on the service) and go via Nanchang, the capital of Jiangxi Province, or via the railway junction of Yingtan. From Yingtan a branch line extends to Fuzhou and Xiamen (both in Fujian Province on the south-east coast). There are direct trains from Hangzhou to Fuzhou. There is no direct train from Hangzhou to Xiamen; you must first go to Shanghai. However, you can catch a train to Fuzhou and then catch a bus to Xiamen.

Boat You can take a boat up the Grand Canal from Hangzhou to Suzhou. Boats leave once a day at 5.50 pm from the dock near the corner of Huancheng Lu and Hushu Nanlu, in the northern part of town and arrive early the next morning. Tickets are available from the booking office at the dock. For more details see the Suzhou section in the Jiangsu chapter.

Getting Around
To/From the Airport Hangzhou's airport is 15 km from the city centre; taxi drivers ask around Y50 for the trip.

Bus Bus No 7 is very useful as it connects the railway station to the major hotel area on the eastern side of the lake. Bus No 1 connects the long-distance bus station to the east shore and bus No 28 connects it to the lake's western side. Bus No 27 is useful for getting between the eastern and western sides of the lake.

Taxi Metered taxis are ubiquitous but often not that easy to flag down. Keep a map handy and watch out for circuitous detours. Prices

for taxis depend on the size of the vehicle. Rates are cheap. Figure on around Y10 to Y12 from the railway station to Hubin Lu.

Bicycle Bicycle rental is available from across the street from the Qingbo Hotel. There is a big English sign and the rate is Y2 per hour or Y20 per day. The bikes are fairly clapped out – check the brakes and tyres before you set off. Bear in mind also that the traffic – mainly huge, honking tourist buses and zippy little taxis – is atrocious in Hangzhou, and riding a bike can be really stressful, not to mention dangerous. Take care.

Boat Boat tours of West Lake are popular with the Chinese. You'll hardly have to look for a boat – just stand along the east shore and the boat-ticket vendors will come to you.

SHAOXING
(shàoxīng)
Just 67 km south-east of Hangzhou, Shaoxing is the centre of the waterway system on the northern Zhejiang plain. The waterways are part of the city's charm – Shaoxing is an attractive place, notable for its rivers (subject to flooding), canals, boats and arched bridges. For the Chinese, Shaoxing is famous as a place of 500 bridges (an exaggeration), the birthplace of the 20th-century writer Lu Xun and as the home of Shaoxing wine, a celebrated spirit that tastes remarkably like petrol.

Since early times, Shaoxing has been an administrative centre and an important agricultural market town. From 770 to 211 BC, Shaoxing was capital of the Yue Kingdom.

Information
There is a CITS office (☎ 513-3252; fax 513-5262) at 20 Fushan Xilu. Tourist hotels should be able to change money – if not, the Bank of China is at 225 Renmin Lu.

King Yu's Mausoleum
(yǔ líng)
According to legend, the first Chinese dynasty held power from the 21st to the 16th

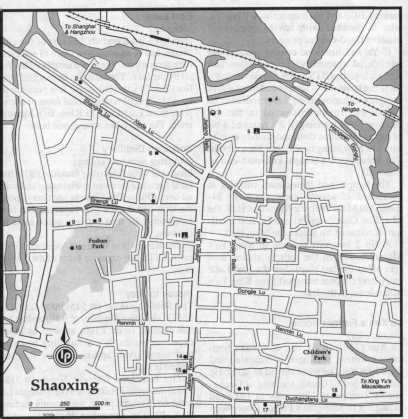

century BC, and its founder was King Yu, who is credited with having engineered massive flood-control projects.

If Yu and his flood-control projects are considered speculative by historians and archaeologists, CITS needs no convincing – Yu is big business. A temple and mausoleum complex to honour the great-grandfather of China was first constructed in the 6th century. Not surprisingly, it's required a bit of renovation since then, and nobody is quite sure just how many times it has been rebuilt. The latest version is eight km south-east of Shaoxing.

The temple and mausoleum complex is composed of several parts: the huge 24-metre-tall Main Hall, the Memorial Hall, the Meridian Gate *(wǔmén)* and Goulou Pavilion. A statue of Yu graces the Main Hall.

A No 2 bus will get you to King Yu's Mausoleum from the railway station area (get off at the last stop). See the East Lake entry later for boat transport from King Yu's Mausoleum to the lake.

Lu Xun's Former Home
(lǔ xùn zǔjū)

Lu Xun (1881-1936), one of China's best-known writers, was born in Shaoxing and lived here until he went abroad to study. He later returned to China, teaching at Guangzhou's Zhongshan University in 1927 and hiding out in Shanghai's French Concession when the Kuomintang decided his books were too dangerous. His tomb is in Shanghai.

You can visit Lu Xun's former residence at 208 Lu Xun Lu. Nearby at 18 Duchangfang Kou is the Lu Xun Memorial Hall *(lǔ xùn jìniàn guǎn)* and adjacent library *(lǔ xùn túshūguǎn)*. Opening hours are daily from 8.30 am to 5.30 pm.

Zhou Enlai's Ancestral Home
(zhōu ēnlái zǔjū)

Zhou Enlai was born in the small town of Huai An in Jiangsu Province, but his ancestral home (a matter of great consequence in the Chinese scheme of things) was here in Shaoxing.

East Lake
(dōng hú)

East Lake is around six km east of the city centre, and is an attractive place of sculpted rock formations. There is a temple *(dōng h sì)* by the lake. The lake can be reached by No 1 bus (it's the last stop). It is possible to travel by 'pedal boat', a local form of transport, from East Lake to King Yu's Mausoleum. The trip takes around one hour.

Shaoxing Distillery
(shàoxīng niàng jiǔ chǎng)

Shaoxing wine *(shàoxīng huādiāo jiǔ)* is the local firewater, brewed in Shaoxing and sold all over China. The Chinese are crazy about the stuff and it even gets exported, but few foreigners take to it – a very quick route to oblivion.

The winery is in the north-western part of town. CITS can organise tours of the distillery.

Places to Stay

The *Shaoxing Hotel* (☎ 515-5888; fax 515-5565) *(shàoxīng fàndiàn)* at 9 Huanshan Lu has doubles from Y180, as well as more expensive suites. It's a rambling place in traditional style, approached by a small arched bridge.

The *Overseas Chinese Hotel* (☎ 513-2323) *(huáqiáo fàndiàn)* at 91-5 Shangda Lu is the main tourist place, with rooms starting at Y240. The *Longshan Hotel (lóngshān fàndiàn)*, close to Fushan Park, also takes foreigners and has rates from Y170.

Getting There & Away

Hangzhou-Ningbo trains and buses all stop in Shaoxing. Most of the foreign tourists you see getting off here are Japanese.

AROUND SHAOXING

Considered one of Shaoxing's 'must see' spots, the **Lanting Pavilion** *(lántíng)* doesn't see many foreign visitors. There are actually several pavilions here, set in pleasant gardens which are worth visiting if you don't mind the trek out there. The gardens were built in 1548.

anting Pavilion is around 10 km south-west f the city, and can be reached by a No 3 bus.

NINGBO
 níngbō)

Like Shaoxing, Ningbo rose to prominence n the 7th and 8th centuries as a trading port rom where ships carrying Zhejiang's xports sailed to Japan, the Ryukyu islands nd along the Chinese coast.

By the 16th century the Portuguese had stablished themselves here, working as ntrepreneurs in the trade between Japan and China, since the Chinese were forbidden to leal with the Japanese.

Although Ningbo was officially opened to Western traders after the first Opium War, its nce-flourishing trade gradually declined as Shanghai boomed. By that time the Ningbo raders had taken their money to Shanghai nd formed the basis of its wealthy Chinese business community.

Ningbo today is a bustling city of over 250,000 people, with fishing, textiles and food processing as its primary industries. Travellers come here mainly in transit on the way to nearby Putuoshan, one of Zhejiang's premier tourist attractions.

Information
There's a CTS office (☎ 732-4145) at 70 Mayuan Lu, adjacent to the Friendship Store, the Asia Gardens and Ningbo hotels.

Places to Stay
The best budget place accepting foreigners s the Yuehu Hotel (☎ 736-3370) (yuèhú fàndiàn) at 59 Yanhu Jie. The hotel is in an nteresting neighbourhood along the shore of Moon Lake. Doubles cost Y110.

The Ningbo Erqing Building (☎ 730-2234) (níngbō èrqīng dàshà), 2 Changchun Lu, is a good two-star hotel with rooms from Y220. Minibuses to the passenger ferry terminal go right by the hotel, but it's within walking distance of the railway station.

The Ningbo Hotel (☎ 732-1688) (níngbō fàndiàn), 65 Mayuan Lu, is two blocks north of the railway station, a massive concrete monster with a wide range of rooms: the cheapest start at Y250. Next door is the upmarket Asia Gardens Hotel (☎ 729-6888; fax 729-2138) (yàzhōu huáyuán bīnguǎn), 72 Mayuan Lu, where rooms start at Y550.

The Huaqiao Hotel (☎ 736-3175) (huáqiáo fàndiàn), 130 Liuting Jie, is within walking distance of the railway station. It represents poor value for money, with rooms from Y350.

Getting There & Away
Air The CAAC ticket office (☎ 733-4202) is at 91 Xingning Lu. There are international flights to Hong Kong four times weekly. Most major Chinese cities have air connections with Ningbo.

Bus There are two bus stations in town. Most long-distance buses depart from the south bus station (qìchē nánzhàn), just one block from the railway station. From here you get buses to Wenzhou (nine hours), Hangzhou (six hours) and Shanghai. Tickets are fairly easy to obtain, though the buses are often crowded.

The north bus station (qìchē běizhàn) is important to travellers mainly because it offers an alternative route (besides direct ferry) to Putuoshan (see the following Putuoshan section for details).

Train Train services between Shanghai and Ningbo are very frequent, but the Ningbo Railway Station ticket office is a nightmare. Ask the staff at your hotel if they can buy the ticket for you – most will do so with at least one day's notice. It's well worth the small service charge. Alternatively, try CTS.

Boat Most useful departures are from the passenger ferry terminal (lúnchuán mǎtóu) near the north bus station. A few boats depart from Zhenhai Wharf (zhènhǎi mǎtóu), which is 20 km (40 to 50 minutes by bus) north-east of Ningbo.

Many travellers are interested in the boat to Putuoshan (see the following Putuoshan section for details). There's a twice-monthly boat to Hong Kong (50 hours).

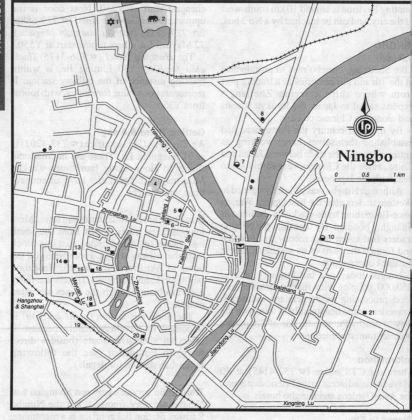

Ningbo

0   0.5   1 km

Getting Around

To/From the Airport Ningbo's Lishe Airport is a 20-minute ride from town. A taxi should cost around Y40.

Other The bus service is extensive; good bus maps are for sale at the railway station. Frequent minibuses (Y1) connect the railway station with the passenger ferry terminal and the north bus station. A taxi across town costs about Y12. Pedicabs are ubiquitous, but the drivers are cut-throat artists.

PUTUOSHAN
(pǔtuóshān)

Putuoshan is the China we all dream about – temples, pagodas, arched bridges, narrow alleys, fishing boats, artisans and monks – the China we see on postcards and in coffee-table books. Distinctly lacking are the noise, pollution, concrete-block housing developments, billboards, political slogans and teeming masses that characterise modern Chinese cities.

The island is small enough for you to reach everywhere on foot, though minibuses

NINGBO 宁波

PLACES TO STAY

12 Yuehu Hotel
    月湖饭店
13 Ningbo Hotel
    宁波饭店
15 Asia Garden Hotels
    亚洲华园
16 Huaqiao Hotel
    华侨饭店
18 Golden Dragon Hotel
    金龙饭店
20 Ningbo Erqing Building
    宁波二轻大厦
21 Yonggang Hotel
    甬港饭店

OTHER

1 Baiguo Garden
   白果园
2 Zoo
   动物园
3 Radio & TV Tower
   电台发射塔
4 Zhongshan Park
   中山公园
5 City Hall
   市政府
6 PSB
   公安局外事科
7 North Bus Station
   汽车北站
8 CAAC
   民航售票处

9 Passenger Ferry
   Terminal
   轮船码头
10 East Bus Station
   汽车东站
11 Main Post Office
   邮电局
14 CTS
   中国旅行社
17 South Bus Station
   汽车南站
19 Railway Station
   火车站

scuttle about the island too. The easternmost part of the island near Fanyin Cave is certainly worthwhile – there are some small but fascinating temples along the route and stunning vistas of the sea. It's also worth investigating the tunnels on the southwestern corner of the island near Guanyin Cave – apparently these once served a military purpose.

Because of its remoteness, Putuoshan sees relatively few foreign visitors, but Chinese tour groups come through here in large enough numbers to threaten the island's serenity. The best way to avoid the crowds is to visit during the off season, which basically means don't come during holidays or in the summer. It's also worth keeping in mind that accommodation on the island is limited, and visiting during peak times could mean an impromptu camping trip.

Places to Stay

It is difficult to provide reliable information on Putuoshan accommodation as prices vary seasonally and according to demand. It is also sometimes very difficult for foreigners to find budget hotel rooms, though some succeed through sheer determination. Unfortunately, most of the island's hotels are off limits to foreigners.

The *Sanshengtang Hotel (sānshèng táng fàndiàn)* is a great place to stay. The outside of the building looks like an old monastery, but rooms are perfectly modern right down to the colour TV sets. Doubles with private bath cost Y150, though significant discounts may be available if you're a student with Chinese ID.

By contrast, the *Xilai Hotel (xīlái xiǎozhuāng)* is an architectural horror – a Chinese version of a modern hotel with full amenities. Rates start at around Y300, though it may be possible to haggle the price down during the off season.

Places to Eat

Forget the expensive hotel food – Putuoshan offers a whole collection of unnamed hole-in-the-wall restaurants where you can have a great meal for only Y15 or so. The biggest concentration of restaurants is along one narrow alley in the centre (see the Putuoshan map), but there are scattered places elsewhere.

Seafood is the speciality, but be careful when you order as some types of fish are very expensive indeed. The usual chicken, pork, duck, rice, tofu (bean curd), stir-fried vegetables etc, are all on offer at rock-bottom prices. Near the Sanshengtang Hotel is a line-up of old women selling fruit for half the price you'd pay in the restaurant alley.

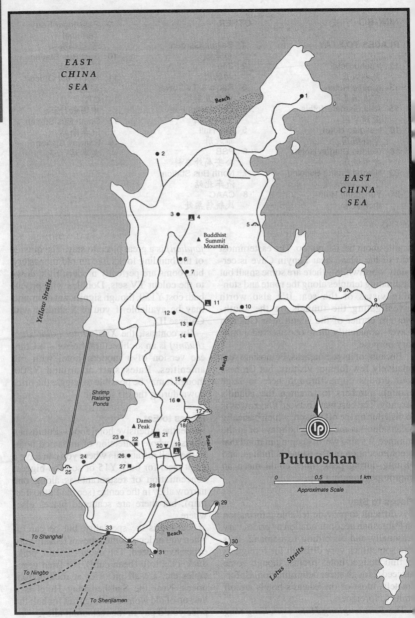

EAST
CHINA
SEA

Beach

EAST
CHINA
SEA

Buddhist
▲ Summit
Mountain

Yellow Straits

Shrimp
Raising
Ponds

Damo
▲ Peak

To Shanghai

To Ningbo

To Shenjiamen

Beach

Beach

Beach

Lotus Straits

Putuoshan

0   0.5   1 km
Approximate Scale

PUTUOSHAN 普陀山

PLACES TO STAY

13 Jinping Villa
锦屏山庄
14 Shuangquan Hotel
双泉饭店
22 Xilai Hotel
西来小庄
27 Sanshengtang Hotel
三圣堂饭店

OTHER

1 Dragon Head
龙头
2 Ridge Mound
岗墩
3 Putuo Goose's Ear
普陀鹅耳枥
4 Wisdom Benefit
Meditation Temple
慧济禅寺
5 Ancient Buddhist Cave
古佛洞

6 Sea Sky Buddhist Nation
海天佛亭
7 Fragrant Cloud Pavilion
香云亭
8 Wisdom & Wealth Cave
善财洞
9 Sanskrit Tidings Cave
梵音洞
10 Viewing Sea Pavilion
望海亭
11 Way Rain Meditation
Temple
法雨禅寺
12 Poplar Branch Convent
杨枝庵
15 Great Multiply Convent
大乘庵
16 Literary Material Hall
文物馆
17 Chaoyang Cave
朝阳洞
18 Fairy's Cave
仙人洞
19 Many Treasures Pagoda
多宝塔
20 Restaurants & Market
餐厅, 市场

21 Universal Benefit
Meditation Temple
普济禅寺
23 Round Open Convent
圆通庵
24 Two Turtles Listen to
the Law Stone
二龟听法石
25 Western Sky Cave
西天洞
26 Administrative Office
管理局
28 Main Interest Pavilion
正趣亭
29 Cannot Agree to Leave
Guanyin Hall
不肯去观音院
30 Guanyin Leap
观音跳
31 South Sky Gate
南天门
32 Seashore Gate
海岸牌坊
33 Passenger Ferry
Terminal
轮船码头

Getting There & Away

As Putuoshan is a small island with no airport, boats are the only option, short of swimming. You can approach from either Ningbo or Shanghai, but Ningbo is closer and offers more frequent service. Many travellers prefer to enter the island from Ningbo and exit to Shanghai, or vice versa. Whatever ship you take, there is a Y10 fee to enter Putuoshan, payable at the pier on arrival.

To/From Shanghai See the Shanghai Getting There & Away section on boats to and from Shanghai, including a new rapid-ferry service that does the trip in five hours.

To/From Ningbo You've got several options. Simplest is the direct ferry, departing from Ningbo's passenger ferry terminal (lún-huán mǎtóu) at 8.30 am. Going in the other direction, departures from Putuoshan are at 7.40 am (there might be an additional afternoon boat during the summer crunch

season). The journey takes just under five hours. Tickets cost Y12 to Y30 – in the crowded economy deck you'll be buried in peanut shells, gob and cigarette butts, so it's better to spend the extra Y18 if you value your sanity.

A less convenient option is to take the boat from Zhenhai Wharf (zhènhǎi mǎtóu), 20 km (40 to 50 minutes by bus) north-east of Ningbo. If you want to use this option, board the bus at Ningbo at 6.40 am at the passenger ferry terminal, and board the ship at Zhenhai Wharf at 7.30 am. There seems to be no great advantage to this route, but it shaves about one hour off the time you spend at sea. You might consider going this way if tickets for the direct boat from Ningbo are sold out.

Another option is to travel by bus from Ningbo to the port of Shenjiamen (shěnjiāmén) on the island of Zhoushan, which is separated from Putuoshan by a narrow strait. The bus from Ningbo gets to Zhoushan Island by vehicular ferry. The total bus journey is roughly four hours and the ferry from Shenjiamen to Putuoshan takes only 30 minutes. The great advantage of this route is that there are several departures throughout the day. Buses to Shenjiamen depart from Ningbo's north bus station (*qìchē běizhàn*). Ferries depart from Shenjiamen at 7.10, 8, 9 and 10 am and 1, 3 and 4 pm. Be careful at Shenjiamen – there are several ferries going to other neighbouring islands, so be sure you get on the one that goes to Putuoshan. The ferries from Putuoshan to Shenjiamen follow a similar schedule, departing at 7, 8, 9 and 10.30 am and 1.15, 2 and 4 pm.

ZHUJIAJIAN
(*zhūjiājiān*)

Just south of Putuoshan is a larger island called Zhujiajian. It has a collection of small temples and fine rural scenery, but it's certainly not the magic sort of place that Putuoshan is. Nevertheless, it might be

worth a visit, particularly if you are travelling during the peak summer season when Putuoshan is packed out. Foreigners of any kind are a rarity in Zhujiajian – expect to be a tourist attraction for the locals.

To reach Zhujiajian, take a bus from Ningbo's north bus station to Shenjiamen (four hours, Y12), then a short ferry ride.

XIKOU
(*xīkôu*)

About 60 km south of Ningbo is the small town of Xikou, the home of Chiang Kaishek.

Zhujiajian

Column Hill
Standing Goat Hill
Fairy Peak
Camphor Isle Bay
Big Hill
Old Hill
Four Column Hill
Back Gate Hill
Big Green Hill
West Peak Island

0   1.5   3 km

EAST CHINA SEA

ZHUJIAJIAN 朱家尖

1 Sisu
  泗苏
2 Ferry Terminal
  轮船码头
3 Cool Hat Pond
  凉帽潭
4 Catch Fish Reef
  钓鱼礁
5 White Cloud Strange Stone
  白云奇石
6 Moon Valley
  月岙
7 Bird Turtle Cave
  鸟龟洞
8 Camphor Tree Isle
  外樟州
9 Full Pond Bird Rock
  满塘鸟石
10 Big Cave Valley
  大洞岙
11 Outer Pond
  外塘
12 Bird Stone Pond
  小鸟石塘
13 Temple Foundation
  寺基
14 Big Isle
  大岙
15 Fishing Lake to Reflect the Moon
  渔湖映月
16 Ten-Mile Golden Sand
  十里金沙
17 King's Crag
  大王岩
18 Little Splash
  小澎安

It has, surprisingly, become a Chinese tourist destination. Not so surprisingly, many visitors from Taiwan also come here.

Despite local rumours that Chiang's body was secretly returned to China for burial at Xikou, his remains in fact reside in Taiwan at Cihu, south of Taipei. Chiang's relatives have persistently maintained that when the Kuomintang 'retakes the mainland', the body will be returned to its proper resting place at Xikou.

TIANTAISHAN
(tiāntái shān)

Tiantaishan is noted for its many Buddhist monasteries, which date back to the 6th century. While the mountain itself may not be considered sacred, it is very important as the home of the Tiantai Buddhist sect, which is heavily influenced by Taoism.

From Tiantai it's a 3½-km hike to the **Gouqingsi Monastery** at the foot of the mountain (you can stay overnight here). From the monastery a road leads 25 km to **Huadingfeng** (over 1100 metres high), where a small village has been built. On alternate days public buses run up to Huadingfeng. From here you can continue by foot for one or two km to the **Baijingtai Temple** on the summit of the mountain.

On the other days the bus goes to different parts of the mountain, passing **Shiliang Waterfall**. From the waterfall it's a good five to six-km walk along small paths to Huadingeng.

Tiantaishan is in the east of Zhejiang. Buses link it with Hangzhou, Shaoxing, Ningbo and Wenzhou.

WENZHOU
(wēnzhōu)

Wenzhou sees very little tourist traffic. It's not an unpleasant place, but it has absolutely nothing to justify the hardship of getting there. There are some reasonably picturesque narrow streets lined with shops and old buildings scattered around town and a couple of minor attractions, but otherwise Wenzhou is very much a pit stop on the long (and seldom travelled) haul along the coast.

Orientation

The city is bounded on the north by the Ou River (oū jiāng) and on the south by the much smaller Wenruitang River. The most interesting areas are along Ou River and major streets like Jiefang Beilu.

Things to See

The major scenic site is **Jiangxin Island** (jiāngxīn dǎo or jiāngxīn gūyǔ) in the middle of the Ou River. The island is a park dotted with pagodas, a lake and footbridges. You can easily reach Jiangxin Island by ferry from the pier (mǎxíng mǎtóu) just west of the passenger ferry terminal.

Jinshan Park (jǐnshān gōngyuán), on the south-west perimeter of the city, is a minor attraction, but might be pleasant on a sunny day.

Places to Stay

Basically, all of Wenzhou's bottom-end accommodation is off limits to foreigners. This leaves a smattering of mid-range and top-end joints. Pick of the pack in terms of value for money and location is the *Huaqiao Hotel* (☎ 822-3911) (huáqiáo fàndiàn) at 77 Xinhe Jie. Singles/doubles start at Y220.

Other possibilities, all with rates of Y350 and upwards, include:

Dongou Hotel (dōngoū dàshà), excellent location on the Ou River (☎ 822-7901)
Ouchang Hotel (oūchāng fàndiàn), 71 Xueshan Lu (☎ 823-4931)
Wenzhou Grand Hotel (wēnzhōu dàjiǔdiàn), 61 Gongyuan Lu (☎ 823-5991)
Xueshan Hotel (xuěshān fàndiàn), also very inconveniently located in Jinshan Park and only reachable by taxi (☎ 822-3981)

Getting There & Away

Air Wenzhou has reasonably good connections with other Chinese cities, but the airport is notoriously bad for heavy fog – pilots often end up flying ridiculously low trying to find the runway.

Bus There are three bus stations in Wenzhou, and even locals are sometimes not sure which station is appropriate for a particular

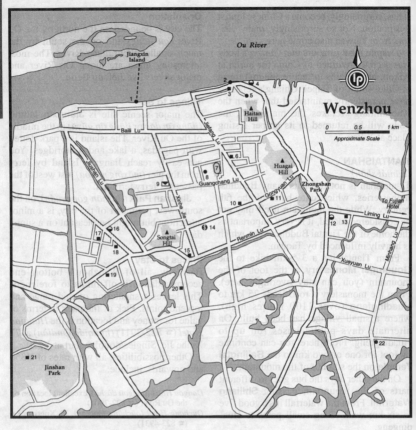

destination. As a general rule, southbound buses arrive at and depart from the south bus station, northbound buses at the west bus station and some (no certainty which) use the east bus station.

Train There are serious plans afoot to extend a railway line from Wenzhou to Jinhua, which is on the main Guangzhou-Shanghai line. So far, the plans remain on the drawing board.

Boat There are passenger ferries between

Wenzhou and Shanghai. For tickets, check at the passenger ferry terminal.

Getting Around
To/From the Airport Wenzhou airport is 27 km south-west of town and the road is in shocking condition. Taxis charge between Y120 and Y160 for the trip. Buses leave from the CAAC office to connect with flights.

Other Taxis are cheap (Y10 to most destinations) and easy to flag down. Pedicabs, on the other hand, are usually more trouble than they are worth.

WENZHOU 温州

PLACES TO STAY

3   Dongou Hotel
    东瓯大厦
6   Mochi Hotel
    墨池饭店
10 Xin'ou Hotel
    新瓯饭店
11 Wenzhou Grand Hotel
    温州大酒店
13 Lucheng Hotel
    鹿城饭店
15 Huaqiao Hotel
    华侨饭店
17 Jiushan Hotel
    九山饭店
18 Xinghua Hotel
    杏花楼饭店
19 Ouchang Hotel
    瓯昌饭店
20 Shuixin Hotel
    水心饭店
21 Jingshan Hotel
    景山宾馆

OTHER

1   Ferries to Jiangxin
    Island
    麻行码头
2   Passenger Ferry
    Terminal
    温州港客运站
4   East Bus Station
    汽车东站
5   Seamen's Club
    国际海员俱乐部
7   Renmin Stadium
    人民广场
8   City Hall
    市政府
9   Post & Telephone
    Office
    邮电局
12 South Bus Station
    汽车南站
14 Bank of China
    中国银行
16 West Bus Station
    汽车西站
22 CAAC
    民航售票处

CHUN'AN COUNTY

(chún'än xiàn)

Chun'an County, in western Zhejiang, is known for its Lake of a Thousand Islands.

Worth investigating would be a route from Hangzhou – you could cross the lake by boat and perhaps take a bus to Huangshan in Anhui Province.

Fujian 福建

The coastal region of Fujian (*fújiàn*), also known in English as Fukkien or Hokkien, has been part of the Chinese empire since the Qin Dynasty (221-207 BC), when it was known as Min. The province has well-established trading ports, which in more recent times have allowed substantial contact with the outside world. Trade transformed the region from a frontier into one of the centres of the Chinese world.

The Fujianese were also the emigrants of China, leaving the Middle Kingdom for South-East Asia in great numbers. Exactly why this happened is unknown. One theory is that the prosperity of the ports caused a population explosion, and as land became scarce the only direction to go was out of China. The other theory is that the money never got beyond the ports, so the interior remained poor but the ports provided a means of escape.

Whatever the reason, ports like Xiamen were stepping stones for droves of Chinese heading for Taiwan, Singapore, the Philippines, Malaysia and Indonesia. In 1718 the Manchus attempted to halt Chinese emigration with an imperial edict recalling all subjects who were in foreign lands. Finding this ineffectual, in 1728 the court issued another proclamation declaring that anyone who did not return to China would be banished and those captured would be executed. Chinese emigration was only made legal by the Convention of Peking, which ended the fourth Opium War in 1860.

Nowadays, many descendants of the original emigrants send money to Fujian, and the Chinese government is trying to build up a sense of patriotism in the Overseas Chinese to get them to invest more money in their 'homeland'.

Just as most Hong Kongers trace their cultural roots to Guangdong Province, most Taiwanese consider Fujian to be their ancestral home. Fujian's local dialect, *minnanhua* (south-of-the-Min-River-language), is essen-

Population: 26 million
Capital: Fuzhou
Highlights:
- Xiamen's Gulangyu Island, with one of China's most charming pockets of colonial architecture
- Nanputuo Temple, just outside Xiamen
- The 'earth buildings' of the Hakka people in remote south-western Fujian
- The walled town of Chongwu, not far from Quanzhou

tially the same as Taiwanese, though both places officially speak Mandarin Chinese. Not surprisingly, the Taiwanese are the biggest investors in Fujian and the most frequent visitors. Some have even built retirement homes in Fujian.

FUZHOU
(*fúzhōu*)

Capital of Fujian province, Fuzhou is a grey industrial sprawl with little of interest to the traveller. That said, it is probably a better place to stay overnight in than Quanzhou. Best of all, however, would be to continue on to Xiamen if time permits.

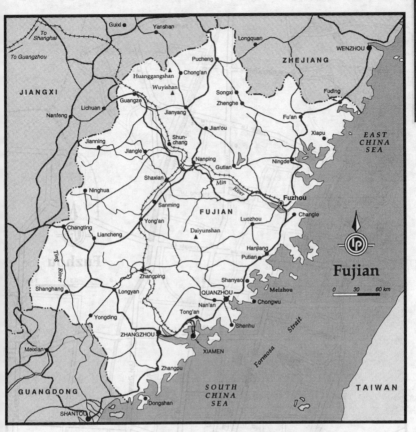

Fujian

0   30   60 km

History

Fuzhou dates back to the 3rd century, when it was known as Yecheng ('smelting city'). Later it emerged as a major commercial port specialising in the export of tea. Its name actually means 'wealthy town' and, in terms of wealth, Fuzhou was second only to Quanzhou. Marco Polo, who passed through Fuzhou towards the end of the 13th century, described Fuzhou as being so 'well provided with every amenity' as to be a 'veritable marvel'. One can only assume that he was referring to the McDonald's at the bottom of Wuyi Lu.

Today, Fuzhou is second only to Xiamen as a centre of Taiwanese investment. The money that the town has recently attracted is reflected in a lot of pricey new hotels and restaurants.

Orientation

Fuzhou city centre sprawls northward from the Min River. Walking from one end of town to the other will take you over an hour. The railway station is situated in the north-east of town, while most of the accommodation is on Wuyi Rd between Hualin Lu and Gutian Lu.

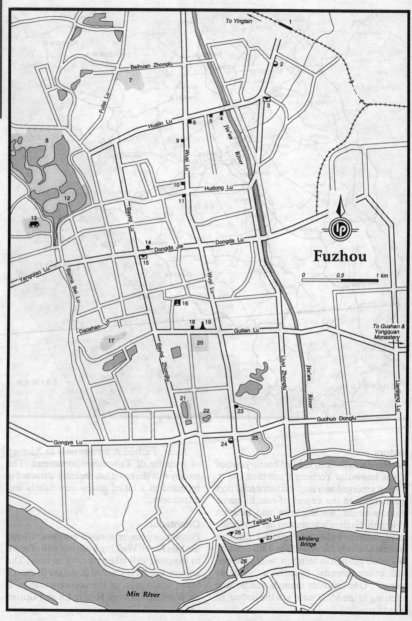

To Yingtan 1

2

3

Beihuan Zhonglu

7

Fufei Lu

Hualin Lu 6 5 4

8

9

Wusi Lu

Jin'an River

10

Hudong Lu

11

Bayiqi Lu

12

13

14 Dongda Jie

Dongda Lu

15

Yangqiao Lu

Baima Bei Lu

16

Daoshan

18 19

17 Gutian Lu

20

Bayiqi Zhonglu

Liuyi Zhonglu

Jin'an River

21

22 23

Guohuo Donglu

Gongye Lu

24 25

To Gushan & Yongquan Monastery

Lianjiang Lu

Fuzhou

0   0.5   1 km

Taijiang Lu

26

27

Minjiang Bridge

28

Min River

FUZHOU 福州	2 North Long-Distance Bus Station 长途汽车北站	19 Mao Statue 毛主席像
PLACES TO STAY	3 Main Post Office 市电政局	20 Wuyi Square 五一广场
4 Hualin Hotel 华林宾馆	7 Pingshan Park 屏山公园	21 Tea Pavilion Park 茶亭公园
5 Taiwan Hotel 台湾饭店	8 Zuohai Park 左海公园	22 Children's Park 儿童公园
6 Material Hotel 物质大厦	12 West Lake Park 西湖公园	23 CAAC 民航售票处
9 Hot Spring Hotel 温泉大饭店	13 Zoo 动物园	24 South Long-Distance Bus Station 福州汽车(南)站
10 Tianfu Hotel 天福大酒店	14 City Library 省图书馆	25 South Park 南公园
11 Minjiang Hotel 闽江饭店	15 Post & Telecommunications Building 邮电大楼	26 McDonald's 麦当劳
18 Yushan Hotel 于山宾馆	16 Haifa Temple 法海寺	27 Jiangbin Park (Ferry for River Tours) 江滨公园 (上游客运码头)
OTHER	17 Bird Park Scenic Area 鸟山风景区	28 Jiefang Bridge 解放桥
1 Fuzhou Railway Station 火车站		

Information

CITS The main CITS office (☎ 755-2052; fax 753-7447) at 73 Dong Dalu is just north of the Overseas Chinese Hotel. There is also a representative office inside the hotel itself. CITS offers tours of Fuzhou and can book air, bus and train tickets.

PSB This office is on Xian Ta Lu, which runs south off Dongda Lu.

Money There is a money-changing counter on the ground floor of the Taiwan Hotel, the Overseas Chinese Hotel and the Hot Spring Hotel.

Things to See

Fuzhou's sights are minor attractions. On a fine day it can be interesting to watch the junks or the squadrons of sampans dredging the riverbed for sand. Across the Min River is **Nantai Island**, where the foreigners established themselves when Fuzhou became an 'unequal' treaty port in the 19th century.

In the centre of town is a windswept square presided over by an enormous **statue**

of Mao Zedong. The statue was erected to commemorate the 9th National Congress of the Communist Party where Maoism was enshrined as the new state religion and Lin Biao was officially declared Mao's successor. Today Mao presides cheerily over rows of massive beer advertisements and is dwarfed by the new buildings that surround him.

In the north-west of Fuzhou is West Lake Park (*xīhú gōngyuǎn*) on Hubin Lu, where you'll find the **Fujian Provincial Museum** (*fújiànshěng bówùguǎn*).

Immediately east of the town, on Drum Hill (*gǔ shān*), is **Yongquan Monastery** (*yǒngquán sì*). The hill takes its name from a large, drum-shaped rock at the summit. The monastery dates back 1000 years and is said to house a collection of 20,000 Buddhist scriptures of which almost 700 are written in blood. There is a spa next to the monastery.

Fuzhou also sports a number of other recently constructed temples built apparently to impress Taiwanese tourists into thinking that China has the same religious freedoms as those enjoyed in Taiwan.

Places to Stay – bottom end

Budget travellers are best off not staying in Fuzhou. There are singles/doubles for Y90/120 at the *Yushan Hotel* (☎ 335-1668) *(yúshān bīnguǎn)*, pleasantly located in a park on Gutian Lu, but these prices are subject to a further 30% foreigners' surcharge. The hotel is also a long way from the railway station and the long-distance bus stations.

Everything else in town is mid-range and up. The one possibility of getting something cheaper is in the railway station area. There are a lot of tatty, local hotels here, none of which officially take foreigners, but some of which will bend the rules for an overnight stay if you pay a little over the odds. If you hang around the railway station, hotel touts will grab you.

Places to Stay – middle

One of the best deals relatively close to the railway station is the *Hualin Hotel* (☎ 784-2920) *(huálín bīnguǎn)* at 36 Hualin Lu. Very comfortable doubles cost Y180; triples are Y225.

Nearby, on the south-east corner of Hualin Lu and Wusi Lu, is the *Material Hotel* (☎ 784-3168) *(wùzhì dàshà)*. It's a cavernous place with singles at Y142 and doubles from Y162 to Y300.

The *Overseas Chinese Hotel* (☎ 755-7603) *(huáqiáo dàshà)* on Wusi Lu is another mid-range option, with standard singles/doubles from Y310.

The *Taiwan Hotel* (☎ 757-0570) *(táiwān fàndiàn)* calls itself the 'Home of Taiwan Compatriots', but all are welcome. Doubles range from Y245 to Y325 and are good value. Facilities include a sauna, bar and disco.

Just north of the Overseas Chinese Hotel on Wusi Lu is the three-star *Minjiang Hotel* (☎ 755-7895) *(mínjiāng fàndiàn)*, where doubles cost Y460. Nearby, the *Tianfu Hotel* *(tiānfú dàjiǔdiàn)* has very good standard doubles from US$42 to US$50 and suites from US$80.

Places to Stay – top end

The *Hot Spring Hotel* (☎ 785-1818) *(wēnquán dàfàndiàn)*, Wusi Lu, is one of the best in town. Standard doubles start at US$110, executive suites at US$145.

Places to Eat

Digging up cheap eats is no problem in Fuzhou. The railway station area is teeming with restaurants serving up steamed dumplings or pick-and-choose stir-fries. The only places with English menus in Fuzhou are the upmarket hotel restaurants. The restaurant on the 4th floor of the Tianfu Hotel is excellent, and affordable if you choose carefully.

It is possible to get a fast-food fix at *California Fried Chicken*, just on the north side of the Overseas Chinese Hotel, or at *McDonald's*, way, way down at the bottom of Wuyi Lu near the Min River.

Getting There & Away

Air The CAAC office (☎ 755-4593) is on Wuyi Lu, and tickets can be bought here or at a few other locations around town. As well as domestic flights to major destinations such as Beijing, Chengdu, Guangzhou, Hangzhou, Kunming, Nanjing, Shanghai and Tianjin, there are also flights to Hong Kong.

Bus There are two long-distance bus stations in town: a north long-distance bus station near the railway station, and one at the southern end opposite the CAAC office. There are buses north and south to all important destinations in Fujian and Zhejiang. The northern route between Fuzhou and Ningbo takes you past some spectacular terraced rice paddies clinging to cloud-shrouded mountainsides, but it's slow-going.

Just south of the Overseas Chinese Hotel are ticket offices for air-con buses. These are long-distance overnighters going to such places as Hangzhou, Shanghai, Guangzhou and Shenzhen. These buses leave from the major hotels.

Train The railway line from Fuzhou heads north and connects the city with the main Shanghai-Guangzhou line at the Yingtan unction. A branch line splits from the Fuzhou-Yingtan line and goes to Xiamen. There are direct trains from Fuzhou to Beijing, Shanghai, Nanchang and Xiamen. The rail route to Xiamen is circuitous, so you'd be better off taking the bus.

Getting Around

Fuzhou is a sprawling city, which makes it difficult to get around by foot. Pedicabs will go anywhere in the central part of the city for Y5 to Y7, but taxis cover similar distances for Y8. The bus network is good and bus maps are available at the railway station or hotels. Bus No 51 travels from the railway station down Wuyi Lu.

XIAMEN

(xiàmén)

Xiamen (population 600,000), or at least the part of it that huddles the harbour, is a Chinese city notable for the fact that it still has some character. There are winding streets, markets, excellent restaurants and restful walks over on the nearby island of Gulangyu. It is well worth spending a day or so exploring the place.

History

Xiamen was founded around the mid-14th century, in the early years of the Ming Dynasty. There had been a town here since Song times, but the Ming built the city walls

Koxinga

When the Ming Dynasty collapsed in 1644, under the weight of the Manchu invasion, the court fled to the south of China. One after the other, a varied succession of Ming princes assumed the title of emperor, in the hope of driving out the barbarians and ascending to the Dragon Throne. One of the more successful attempts (which focused on the port of Xiamen) was by an army led by Zheng Chenggong, known in the West as Koxinga.

Koxinga's origins are a mystery. His father is said to have run away to Japan and married a Japanese woman – Koxinga's mother. His father returned to China as a pirate, raiding the Guangdong and Fujian coasts, and even taking possession of Xiamen. Exactly how and why Koxinga came to be allied with the defunct Ming princes is unknown. One story claims that a prince took a liking to Koxinga when he was young and made him a noble. Another story says that Koxinga was a pirate warrior like his father who, for some reason, teamed up with one of the refugee princes.

Koxinga used Xiamen as a base for his attacks on the Manchus in the north. He is said to have had under his command a fleet of 8000 war junks, 240,000 fighting men and all the pirates who infested the coast of southern China – a combined force of 800,000. He is supposed to have used a stone lion weighing 600 pounds to test the strength of his soldiers; those strong enough to lift and carry it were enlisted in the vanguard of the army. His warriors wore iron masks and armour, and carried long-handled swords to maim the legs of enemy cavalry horses.

Koxinga's army fought its way to the Grand Canal, but was forced to retreat to Xiamen. In 1661 he set sail with his army for Taiwan, then held by the Dutch. He attacked the Dutch settlement at Casteel Zeelandia (not far from Taiwan's west coast city of Tainan) and after a six-month siege the Dutch surrendered. Koxinga hoped to use Taiwan as a stepping stone for invading the mainland and restoring the Ming Dynasty to power but, a year or two later, he died. The Manchus finally conquered the island in the early 1680s.

While Koxinga may have been a pirate and a running dog of the feudal Ming princes, he is regarded as a national hero because he recovered Taiwan from the Dutch, which is roughly analogous to the mainland's ambition to recover the island from the Kuomintang! Those in China who reinterpret (rewrite?) history seem to have forgotten that Koxinga was forced to retreat to Taiwan after his defeats on the mainland and that the 'liberation' of Taiwan was superfluous to his plans. In reality, his story more closely parallels that of the Kuomintang, a regime which fled to Taiwan but awaits the day when it will invade and seize control of the mainland. ■

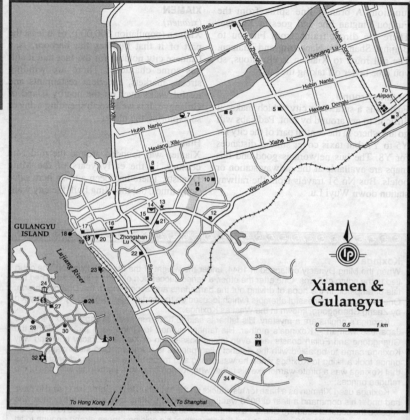

Xiamen & Gulangyu

and established Xiamen as a major seaport and commercial centre. In the 17th century it became a place of refuge for the Ming rulers fleeing the Manchu invaders. From here Ming armies fought their way north again under the command of the pirate-general Koxinga.

Since the early 16th century, the Portuguese, Spanish, Dutch and British had all in turn attempted to establish Xiamen as a base for trade with China. They all met with very limited success. It was not until the Opium War that the tide was turned in favour of the West. In August 1841 a British naval force

of 38 ships carrying artillery and soldiers sailed into Xiamen harbour, forcing the port to open. The Japanese and other Western powers followed soon after, establishing consulates and making the offshore island of Gulangyu a foreign enclave.

Just offshore from Xiamen, the islands of Jinmen and Mazu have been occupied by Taiwan Nationalist troops since the Communist takeover in 1949. When the PLA began bombing them in 1958, the USA's Mutual Security Pact with Taiwan very nearly led to war between China and the USA. Tensions remain high. The government of Taiwan has

XIAMEN & GULANGYU
厦门，鼓浪屿

PLACES TO STAY

3 Xiamen Plaza Hotel
东南亚大酒店
5 Hubin Hotel
湖滨饭店
6 Haixia Hotel
海峡酒店
8 Bailan Hotel
白兰饭店
10 Singapore Hotel
新加坡酒店
12 Xiamen Hotel
夏门宾馆
15 Xiaxi Hotel
夏溪旅社
17 Lujiang & East Ocean
Hotels
鹭江大厦，
东海大厦酒店
21 Xinqiao Hotel
新侨酒店
22 Holiday Inn
假日大酒店
27 Beautiful Island Hotel
of Gulangyu
丽之岛酒店

29 Gulangyu Guesthouse
鼓浪屿宾馆

PLACES TO EAT

9 Chicken Treat
Restaurant
奇肯帝
16 Muslim Restaurant
清真餐厅
20 McDonald's
麦当劳

OTHER

1 CITS
中国国际旅行社
2 Friendship Store
友谊商场
4 Railway Station
厦门火车站
7 Long-Distance Bus
Station
长途汽车站
11 Zhongshan Park
中山公园
13 PSB
公安局外事科

14 Main Post & Telephone
Office
邮电局
18 Ferry Terminal
(to Gulangyu)
轮渡码头 (往鼓浪屿)
19 Bank of China
中国银行
23 Heping Pier (to Hong
Kong)
和平码头 (往香港)
24 Museum
博物馆
25 Bank of China
中国银行
26 Ferry Terminal
(to Xiamen)
轮渡码头 (往厦门)
28 Sunlight Rock
日光岩
30 Musical Hall
音乐厅
31 Statue of Koxinga
郑成功塑像
32 Shuzhuang Garden
菽庄花园
33 Nanputuo Temple
南普陀寺
34 Xiamen University
厦门大学

recently accused the Chinese of a military build-up in the region, and Taiwan has responded with military acquisitions of its own.

Not that you will sense any of this in Xiamen itself. It is a vibrant place, the stores packed with all kinds of consumer goodies. No doubt the city has benefited from significant Taiwanese investment and its designation as a Special Economic Zone in 1980.

Orientation

The town of Xiamen is on the island of the same name, which lies just off the mainland and is connected to it by a long causeway bearing a railway, road and footpath. The first section of the causeway connects the town of Xinglin on the mainland to the town of Jimei at the tip of a peninsula due east of Xinglin. The second section connects Jimei to the north of Xiamen Island.

The interesting part of Xiamen is the western (waterfront) district directly opposite the small island of Gulangyu. This is the old area of town, known for its quaint architecture, parks and winding streets.

The central district includes the railway station. Everything about one km east of the railway station is regarded as the eastern district. Both the central and eastern districts are new development areas and very tacky-looking. Like other recently built Chinese cities, it's a world of concrete high-rises and wide boulevards, thoroughly devoid of trees and lacking imagination.

Information

CITS There are several CITS offices around town, notably next door to the Bank of China on Zhongshan Lu next to the harbour and in the Overseas Chinese Building. They are only really good for booking air tickets, which you can do at countless other places around town.

PSB Opposite the Xinqiao Hotel is a large, red-brick building; the wide footpath on the right-hand side (as you face it) leads to the PSB.

Money The Bank of China is at 10 Zhongshan Lu, near the Lujiang Hotel. There are many black-market moneychangers around town – take care, as rip-offs can occur.

American Express There is an American Express office (☎ 212-0268) in Room 27 on the 2nd floor of the Holiday Inn Hotel.

Gulangyu Island
(gŭlàngyŭ)
Neither Gulangyu nor Xiamen were considered island paradises when Westerners landed in the 1840s. By 1860, however, they had well-established residencies on Gulangyu and, as the years rolled by, churches, hospitals, post and telegraph offices, libraries, hotels and consulates were built. In 1903 the island was officially designated an International Foreign Settlement, and a municipal council with a police force of Sikhs was established to govern it. Today, the only reminders of the settlement are the charming colonial buildings which blanket the island and the sound of classical piano wafting from the villa-style houses. Many of China's most celebrated musicians have come from Gulangyu.

China is hardly a sun-worshipper's paradise, but there are two beaches on Gulangyu: the East Beach and the West Beach. The first is overpopulated and has placid and scungy water, and the second belongs to the army and is off limits. On the beaches are a number of old, disused concrete blockhouses which appear to have ringed the entire island at one time.

At 93 metres, **Sunlight Rock** (rìguāng yán) is the highest point on Gulangyu. It's an easy climb up the steps to the top, where there's an observation platform and a great view across Gulangyu and the harbour. The large colonial building at the foot of Sunlight Rock is the **Koxinga Memorial Hall** (zhèngchénggōng jìniànguǎn). Inside is an exhibition partly dedicated to the Dutch in Taiwan, and the rest to Koxinga's throwing them out. There are no English captions but it is still worth a look and, from the verandas of the upper storeys, there is a fine view across the island. The hall is open daily from around 8 to 11 am and 2 to 5 pm.

The ferry to Gulangyu leaves from the pier just north of Xiamen's Lujiang Hotel. The ferry is free on the downstairs deck, and costs Y0.5 upstairs.

Transport around Gulangyu is by foot; there are no buses, cars or pedicabs. It's a small island and the sights are within easy walking distance of each other.

Nanputuo Temple
(nánpŭtuó sì)
On the southern outskirts of Xiamen town, this Buddhist temple was built during the Tang Dynasty more than a thousand years ago. It was ruined in a battle during the Ming Dynasty but rebuilt during Qing times.

You enter the temple through Tian Wang (Heavenly King) Hall, where the welcoming Maitreya Buddha sits cross-legged, exposing his protruding belly. On either side are a pair of guardians who protect him. Standing behind the Maitreya Buddha is Wei Tuo, another Buddhist deity who safeguards the doctrine. He holds a stick which points to the ground – traditionally, this indicates that the temple is rich and can provide visiting monks with board and lodging (if the stick is held horizontally it means the temple is poor and is a polite way of saying find somewhere else to stay).

Behind Tian Wang Hall is a courtyard and on either side are the Drum and Bell towers. In front of the courtyard is Daxiongbao (Great Heroic Treasure) Hall, a two-storey building containing three buddhas which represent Sakyamuni in his past, present and future lives. The biography of Sakyamuni and the story of Xuan Zang, the monk who made the pilgrimage to India to bring back the Buddhist scriptures, are carved on the lotus-flower base of the buddha figure.

Inlaid in the buildings to the left and right of Daxiongbao Hall are eight stone tablets, inscribed in the handwriting of Emperor Qianlong of the Qing Dynasty. Four tablets are in Chinese and the others in the peculiar Manchu script. All record the Manchu government's suppression of the 'Tian Di Society' uprisings. The tablets were originally erected in front of the temple in 1789, but were inlaid in the walls when the temple was enlarged around 1920.

The Dabei (Great Compassion) Hall contains four Bodhisattvas. Worshippers throw divining sticks at the feet of the statues in order to seek heavenly guidance.

At the rear of the temple complex is a pavilion built in 1936 which stores Buddhist scriptures, calligraphy, woodcarvings, ivory sculptures and other works of art; unfortunately it's closed to visitors. Behind the temple is a rocky outcrop gouged with poetic graffiti; the big red character carved on the large boulder simply means 'Buddha'.

To get to the temple, take bus No 1 from outside the Xinqiao Hotel, or bus No 2 from the intersection of Zhongshan Lu and Siming Lu.

Xiamen University
(xiàmén dàxué)

The university is next to the Nanputuo Temple, and was established with Overseas Chinese funds. The older buildings which face the shoreline are not without charm, though most of the campus is a scattered collection of brick and concrete blocks. The campus entrance is next to the terminal for bus Nos 1 and 2.

The Museum of Anthropology, on the university grounds, is worth a visit if you're down this way. After entering the campus, turn right at the first crossroads and walk until you come to a roundabout. The museum is the old stone building on the left with the cannon at the front. It has a large collection of prehistoric stone implements and pottery from China, Taiwan and Malaya, as well as human fossil remains. There are collections

of porcelain, bronzes, jade and stone implements, coins and inscribed Shang Dynasty bones and tortoise shells. You'll also see some fine calligraphy, exquisite paintings, glazed clay figurines, sculptures, clothing and ornaments from the Shang and Zhou periods through to Ming and Qing times.

Places to Stay

If you are going to stay in Xiamen, stay in the Western district around the harbour. The rest of town is an eyesore and distant from the sights. The harbour area also has the best selection of places to eat.

It is also worth considering staying on Gulangyu Island. There aren't any real budget places to stay on the island, but if you spend around Y130 for a double you'll get value for money.

Places to Stay – bottom end The *Xiaxi Hotel (xiàxī lǚshè)*, inside Xiaxi Market off Zhongshan Lu, combines economy with an excellent location. It has a wide range of rooms, though they will probably try and coerce you to stay in one of the Y100 doubles. Cheaper doubles with bathroom are available for Y68, and there are still-cheaper rooms on the premises but these are frequently 'booked out'. To get there from the railway station take a minibus for Y1. From the bus station it's possible to walk (about 20 minutes). From either the railway station or the bus station a taxi costs Y9-10.

Budget accommodation is also available at the *Hubin Hotel* (☎ 202-5202) *(húbīn fàndiàn)*, where basic rooms start at Y60. It's in a very uninteresting location. The *Bailan Hotel* (☎ 203-1024) *(báilán fàndiàn)* is another badly located hotel, and it just creeps in at the lower end with its singles at Y138 and doubles at Y190.

If you want to splash out and have some peace and quiet for a change, it's worth considering staying on Gulangyu Island. The quaintly named *Beautiful Island Hotel of Gulangyu* (☎ 206-3409) *(lìzhīdǎo jiǔdiàn)* has excellent rooms from Y130 to Y170. The *Gulangyu Guesthouse (gǔlàngyǔ bīnguǎn)* is a beautiful block of decaying colonial

THE EAST

architecture on a hilltop, and has doubles from Y160.

Places to Stay – middle Most Xiamen accommodation is mid-range, shading into top-end. Again, if you're spending money for a decent room, make sure that you stick to the harbour part of town. The *Xiamen Hotel* (☎ 202-2265) *(xiàmén bīnguǎn)* is a rambling old establishment with a certain colonial elegance in a park. Standard doubles cost Y270, while more upmarket rooms are US$55 to US$75.

The *Lujiang Hotel* (☎ 202-2922) *(lùjiāng dàshà)* is opposite the Gulangyu ferry terminal. It is a renovated old colonial building that caters almost entirely to Taiwanese businessmen. Rooms start at US$55.

Xinqiao Hotel (☎ 203-8883) *(xīnqiáo jiǔdiàn)* is an old but classy place at 444 Zhongshan Lu. Rooms start at US$28 for singles and US$48 for doubles.

The *Singapore Hotel* (☎ 202-6668) *(xīnjiāpō jiǔdiàn)* is conveniently located next to Zhongshan Park. Rooms start at US$39.

Places to Stay – top end There is a wide range of top-end accommodation in Xiamen, but much of it is in the eastern part of town and caters to Chinese businesspeople and long-term Western expats. The best place to stay is the *Holiday Inn Crowne Plaza Harbourview Xiamen* (☎ 202-3333; fax 203-6666) *(jiàrì huángguān hǎijǐng dàjiǔdiàn)*. It has some of the best restaurants in town, the best places to have fun at night, and standard doubles are US$130.

Some other top-end hotels with rates of US$80 and upwards include:

Xiamen Mandarin Hotel (xiàmén yuèhuá jiǔdiàn),
    Foreigners' Residential District, Huli (☎ 602-3333; fax 602-1431)
Xiamen Miramar Hotel (xiàmén měilìhuá dàjiǔdiàn),
    Xinglong Lu, Huli (☎ 603-1666; fax 602-1814)
Xiamen Plaza (xiàmén dōngnányǎ dàjiǔdiàn), 908 Xiahe Lu (☎ 505-8888; fax 505-7788)

Places to Eat

Xiamen is teeming with places to eat. The best place to start looking is Zhongshan Lu.

Just north of Xiaxi market street is a canteen operation – the kind you don't see much of in this part of China any more. South of here is the *Qingzhen Restaurant (qīngzhēn cāntīng)*, a large Muslim restaurant with great noodle dishes, dumplings, fried breads and sliced beef. There is no English menu, but out the front you can point to the dumplings, breads and a range of ready-made dishes. Beer and food can be as cheap as Y6 per person. Just around the corner from here in a small alley are a few more Muslim restaurants.

All the alleys off Zhongshan Lu harbour cheap eats, but unfortunately, it seems that most foreigners head straight for the golden gates of *McDonald's*. Down the alley opposite McDonald's is *Yummy Kitchen*, a Japanese fast-food restaurant with katsudon and Japanese-style curry beef; prices start at Y16. *Chicken Treat*, a West Australian fast-food chain, has set up shop on Siming Lu. *Pizza Hut* is hidden away in the park next door to the Gulangyu ferry terminal.

Gulangyu Island is the place to go for seafood. Fresh is best and the meals swim around in buckets and trays outside the restaurants, but they are not cheap. For cheap eats, wander up the hill a little from the Gulangyu Guesthouse, where, on the square formed by an intersection of roads, there are a few places selling beef noodle dishes for Y3 to Y8. Just look for the price lists outside and say *'lāmiàn'*.

If you want to spend big on good food, start at the Holiday Inn. The 24-hour coffee shop has lunch/dinner buffets, *Lao Sichuan* has a dim sum breakfast (around Y40 to Y50 per head) and there is an upmarket Cantonese-style restaurant on the 2nd floor.

Getting There & Away

Air CAAC calls itself Xiamen Airlines in this part of China. There are innumerable ticketing offices around town, some of which are in the hotels. See the Xiamen and Gulangyu map for others.

CAAC offers flights to Hong Kong, Jakarta, Manila, Penang and Singapore. The flight to/from Manila is a popular option at just Y1330. You can also fly between Xiamen and Manila with Philippine Airlines (☎ 202-3333 ext 6742), on the 2nd floor of the Holiday Inn. Silk Air (flights to Singapore) has an office next door to Philippine Airlines. Dragonair (☎ 202-5433) is in the Seaside Building next to the waterfront.

Flights between Taiwan and Xiamen are likely to be permitted before 1997. Discussions were under way at the time of writing. It would be a very short flight to Taipei.

Xiamen has flights to all major domestic destinations around China.

Bus Buses to the towns on the south-east coast depart from the long-distance bus station. Destinations include Fuzhou (Y55), Quanzhou (Y27) and Shantou. You can also get buses straight through to Guangzhou (Y140 to Y170) and Shenzhen (Y120).

There are many privately run air-con buses with ticket offices around the major hotels. Buses to Fuzhou and Quanzhou also run from in front of the park to the right of the Gulangyu ferry office.

Train The 'missing link' in China's railway system is a set of tracks from Guangzhou to Xiamen and up the east coast of Fujian. At present, there is a railway line under construction from Guangzhou to Shantou (close to the Fujian border), but no plans yet for a connection to any cities in Fujian.

The existing railway line from Xiamen heads north and connects with the main Shanghai to Guangzhou line at the Yingtan junction. Another line runs from Yingtan to Fuzhou.

From Xiamen there are direct trains to Yingtan, Shanghai, Fuzhou and possibly Guangzhou. The train to Fuzhou takes a circuitous route, and unless you want to travel by night you're better off taking the bus.

Boat Ships to Hong Kong leave from the Passenger Station of Amoy Port Administration at Heping Pier on Tongwen Lu, about 10 minutes' walk from the Lujiang Hotel. There is a ticket office at the passenger station.

There is one ship, the *Jimei*, between Xiamen and Hong Kong. It departs Xiamen on Monday at 3 pm.

Getting Around
The airport is 15 km east of the waterfront district, or about eight km from the eastern district. Taxis cost around Y50.

Frequent minibuses run between the railway station and Lujiang Hotel for only Y1. The service is extensive but the buses are always extremely crowded. Taxis are available from the railway station and tourist hotels and sometimes cruiseg the streets. Fares for most places in town are Y10.

The interesting western district can be seen on foot. On Gulangyu Island you will have no choice: there are no buses, cars, pedicabs or bicycles – bliss!

AROUND XIAMEN
Jimei School Village *(jíměi xuéxiào cūn)* is a much-touted tourist attraction on the mainland north of Xiamen Island. The school is a conglomeration and expansion of a number of separate schools and colleges set up by Tan Kahkee (1874-1961). Tan was a native of the area who migrated to Singapore when he was young and became a rich industrialist. He set a fine example to other Overseas Chinese by returning some of that wealth to the mother country, and the school now has around 20,000 students. The Chinese-style architecture has a certain appeal which may make a trip worthwhile.

YONGDING
(yǒngdìng)
Yongding is an out-of-the-way place in the south-western part of Fujian. It's in a rural area dominated by small mountains and farmland, and wouldn't be worth a footnote if it weren't for some unusual architecture.

Known as 'earth buildings' *(tǔ lóu)*, these large, circular edifices resemble fortresses and were probably designed for defence. The buildings were constructed by the Hakkas, one of China's ethnic minorities. Coming from Henan Province in northern China, the Hakka people first moved to the Guangdong and Fujian provinces in the south to escape severe persecution in their homelands. The name Hakka means 'guests', and today, Hakka communities are scattered all over South-East Asia.

For some reason, Japanese tourists are drawn like magnets to view the earth buildings – perhaps they know something we don't.

To reach the earth buildings, first take a train or bus to Longyan (*lóngyán*), and from there a bus to Yongding. New hotels are being built in Yongding to accommodate the Japanese tour groups, but prices might be on the high side.

QUANZHOU
(*quánzhōu*)

Quanzhou is sited at what was once a great port city. Marco Polo, back in the 13th century, called it Zaiton and informed his readers that '...it is one of the two ports in the world with the biggest flow of merchandise'.

Not any more. Today Quanzhou is a drab Chinese city, with an ugly snarl of honking traffic and a sprawl of noisy urban development. If you stop at the long-distance bus station, it is highly unlikely that you will be tempted to leave it. Really keen temple

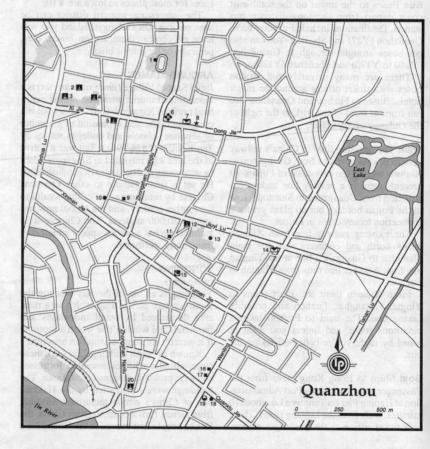

Quanzhou

0   250   500 m

seekers might want to head over to Kaiyuan Temple, Quanzhou's prime attraction. Get a lift on a motorbike or with a pedicab if you do as the traffic will drive you mad if you try to walk.

QUANZHOU 泉州

PLACES TO STAY

9 Quanzhou Hotel
   泉州酒店
11 Overseas Chinese Hotel Quanzhou
   华侨大厦
16 Jianfu Hotel
   建福大厦
17 Quanzhou Overseas Chinese Home
   华侨之家
18 Jinzhou Hotel
   金州酒店

OTHER

1 Gymnasium
   体育场
2 Kaiyuan Temple
   开元寺
3 Renshou Pagoda
   仁寿塔
4 Zhenguo Pagoda
   镇国塔
5 Chengxin Pagoda
   诚心塔
6 Zhonglou Department Store
   钟楼百货
7 Post & Telecommunications Building
   邮电局
8 PSB
   公安局
10 City Hall
   市政府
12 Tongfo Temple
   铜佛寺
13 Workers' Cultural Palace
   工人文化宫
14 Post & Telecommunications Building
   邮电大楼
15 Qingzheng Mosque
   清净寺
19 Long-Distance Bus Station
   泉州汽车站
20 Tianhou Temple
   天后宫

Orientation

The long-distance bus station is in the south-east corner of the city on the intersection of Wenling Lu and Quanxiu Jie. Wenling Lu, to the north, has a rash of hotels. The Kaiyuan Temple is in the north-west of town on the corner of Xinhua Lu and Xi Jie, around two km from the bus station.

Kaiyuan Temple

(*kāiyuǎn sì*)

The Kaiyuan Temple is distinguished by its pair of tall pagodas. It was founded in the 7th century during the Tang Dynasty but reached its peak during Song times when 1000 monks lived here. The present buildings, including the pagodas and the main hall, are more recent. The main hall contains five large, gilded buddhas and on the ceiling above them are peculiar winged apsaras – celestial beings similar to angels. Behind the main hall stands the Guanyin Temple with its saffron-robed buddha.

Within the grounds of the Kaiyuan Temple behind the eastern pagoda is a museum containing the enormous hull of a Song Dynasty seagoing junk which was excavated near Quanzhou.

The temple is on Xi Jie, in the north-west part of town. A ride on a motorbike from the bus station will cost around Y5 or less.

Places to Stay

There should be no need to stay overnight in Quanzhou as it is only a few hours from either Xiamen (a much better place to stay) or Fuzhou by bus. If you get stuck, there is no shortage of hotels, though none of them is particularly cheap. The old stand-by for budget travellers, the Friendship Hotel, was an enormous hole in the ground at the time of writing.

The area around the long-distance bus station is the best place to look. The going rate for hotels is around Y150 for a standard double with bathroom, air-con, TV etc. Some examples include the *Jinzhou Hotel* (☎ 258-6788) (*jīnzhōu dàjiǔdiàn*) on Quanxiu Lu, just around the corner from the bus station; the *Quanzhou Overseas Chinese*

Home (☎ 228-3559) *(quánzhōu huáqiáo zhī jiā)* on Wenling Lu, just north of the bus station; and, a couple of doors up from here, the *Jianfu Hotel* (☎ 228-3511) *(jiànfú dàshà)*.

There are more expensive options with rates of Y280 and upwards in town. The *Overseas Chinese Hotel Quanzhou* (☎ 228-2192) *(quánzhōu huáqiáo dàshà)* is one option; the *Quanzhou Hotel* (☎ 228-9958) *(quánzhōu fàndiàn)* is another.

Getting There & Away

The long-distance bus station has buses to destinations as far away as Shanghai and Guangzhou. Buses to Xiamen (three hours) cost Y13 and buses to Fuzhou cost Y15.

Getting Around

There are city buses, but on a short stopover it's far better to travel by motorbike or pedicab. You'll have no trouble finding them – just step out of the bus station.

AROUND QUANZHOU
Qingyuanshan
(qīngyuánshān)

Qingyuanshan translates as the 'pure water-source mountains'. Regardless of water quality, it's a reasonably scenic mountain area dotted with a few caves, tombs and statues.

The Buddhist caves *(qīngyuán dòng)* on the mountain were destroyed during the Cultural Revolution, though some people still pray in front of the empty spaces where the statues used to be. According to an old woman who lives on the mountain, two Red Guard factions fought each other here during the Cultural Revolution, using mortars. Also found on the mountain is the 'rock that moves' (there's a large painting of it hanging in the dining room of the Overseas Chinese Hotel). It's one of these nicely shaped and balanced rocks which wobbles when you give it a nudge, we're told that to see it move you have to place a stick or a piece of straw lengthways between the rock and the ground and watch it bend as someone pushes on the rock.

The Muslim tomb *(qīngyuánshān shèng-mù)* is thought to be the resting place of two Muslim missionaries who came to China during the Tang Dynasty. There are a number of Muslim burial sites on the north-eastern and south-eastern outskirts of Quanzhou for the thousands of Muslims who once lived at Quanzhou. The earliest dated tombstone belongs to a man who died in 1171. Many tombstone inscriptions are written in Chinese, Arabic and Persian, giving names, dates of birth and quotations from the Koran.

The largest statue on the mountain is a stubby statue of Laotse *(lǎojūn yán)*, the legendary founder of Taoism. Locals claim that Kuomintang soldiers used the statue for target practice but there's no sign of bullet holes.

The highest point in the area reachable by road is now home to a large TV broadcasting tower *(diànshì tái)*.

Getting There & Away Qingyuanshan is certainly too far from Quanzhou to walk, and the hilly terrain makes it impossible to travel by pedicab. The cheapest way for an individual traveller to see the area would be to join a minibus tour with some of the locals or Overseas Chinese. This is best arranged through one of the hotels, though on Sunday and holidays there may be plenty of minibuses looking for passengers around the railway station area. Chartering a taxi or minibus could be worthwhile if you can form a small group.

Chongwu
(chóngwǔ)

Chongwu is a little visited marvel, not far to the north-east of Quanzhou, and is one of China's best preserved walled cities. The granite city walls are around 2.5 km long and average seven metres in height. Scattered around the walls are 1304 battlements; there are four gates into the city.

The city was built in 1387 by the Ming government as a frontline defence against marauding Japanese pirates, and it has survived the last 600 years remarkably well.

There are daily bus services from Quanzhou to nearby Huian from the long-distance bus station. From Huian there are infrequent services to Chongwu.

MEIZHOU
(méizhōu)
About halfway between Quanzhou and Fuzhou is Putian County. Just offshore is the island of Meizhou, known for its scenic beauty and dotted with temples.

Believers in Taoism credit Meizhou as being the birthplace of Mazu, goddess of the sea. Mazu is known by a number of names: Tin Hau in Hong Kong, Thien Hau in Vietnam and so on. As the protector of sailors and fishing folk, Mazu enjoys high prestige and importance in coastal provinces like Fujian.

Mazu's birthday is celebrated according to the lunar calendar, on the 23rd day of the third moon, and at this time the island comes alive. During the summer months, it's also a popular spot for Taiwanese tourists.

You reach Meizhou by first taking a bus to Putian and then a ferry to the island. The temple is simply called the Mazu Temple *(māzǔ miào)*.

WUYISHAN
(wǔyíshān)
Far in the north-west corner of Fujian is Wuyishan, an attractive region of hills, cliffs, rivers and forests. While not really spectacular, it is pretty and has now become the prime scenic spot for Taiwanese tour groups, who descend on the place by the busload. The one advantage this might have is that there are now high-standard (but expensive) hotels in the area. It can get crowded during holiday times; the off season (when it's cold) can be a good time to visit.

From Fuzhou, you can reach Wuyishan by first taking a train to Nanping. From Nanping to Wuyishan takes three hours by bus. An airport is under construction.

zhou to nearby Hutian from the long-distance bus station. From Hutian there are infrequent services to Chongwu.

MEIZHOU
(méizhōu)

About halfway between Quanzhou and Fuzhou is Putian County. Just offshore is the island of Meizhou, known for its scenic beauty and dotted with temples.

Believers in Taoism credit Meizhou as being the birthplace of Mazu, goddess of the sea. Mazu is known by a number of names: Tin Hau in Hong Kong, Thien Hau in Vietnam and so on. As the protector of sailors and fishing folk, Mazu enjoys high prestige and importance in coastal provinces like Fujian.

Mazu's birthday is celebrated according to the lunar calendar, on the 23rd day of the third moon, and at this time the island comes alive. During the summer months it's also a popular spot for Taiwanese tourists.

You reach Meizhou by first taking a bus to Putian and then a ferry to the island. The temple is simply called the Mazu Temple (māzǔ miào).

WUYISHAN
(wǔyíshān)

Far in the north-west corner of Fujian is Wuyishan, an attractive region of hills, cliffs, rivers and forests. While not really spectacular, it is pretty and has now become the prime scenic spot for Taiwanese tour groups, who descend on the place by the busload. The one advantage this might have is that there are now high-standard (but expensive) hotels in the area. It can get crowded during holiday times; the off season (when it's cold) can be a good time to visit.

From Fuzhou, you can reach Wuyishan by first taking a train to Nanping. From Nanping to Wuyishan takes three hours by bus. An airport is under construction.

Liaoning 辽宁

Tourism in Liaoning is the proverbial good news/bad news. The good news is that you won't be tripping over travellers everywhere you go. The bad news is that the province lacks much to see. The industrial city landscapes are supposed to look (starkly) beautiful in winter, with photogenic blacks and whites and some extra-sooty greys. All in all, Liaoning remains a place for those with specialised interests, including history, ornithology, pharmacology and metallurgy.

The situation is not helped by the absurdly high hotel prices. Most of the tourists you bump into are Chinese, Overseas Chinese, South Koreans and a smattering of Japanese pursuing special interests like buying ginseng and eating bear paws (which we don't recommend). The only Western faces you are likely to see are occasional business travellers looking to score a great buy in chemicals or iron ore.

SHENYANG
(shěnyáng)

Shenyang started as a trading centre for nomads as far back as the 11th century, becoming the capital of the Manchu empire in the 17th century. With the Manchu conquest of Beijing in 1644, Shenyang became a secondary capital under the Manchu name of Mukden, and a centre of the ginseng trade.

The city was occupied by the Russians around the turn of the century and was a key battleground during the Sino-Japanese War (1904-05). Shenyang rapidly changed hands, in turn dominated by warlords, the Japanese (1931), the Russians (1945), the Kuomintang (1946) and the Chinese Communist Party (1948).

Now the capital of Liaoning Province, Shenyang is a prosperous city of tall buildings, smokestacks and factories. History buffs will find some well-preserved relics of the Manchu era, but for most travellers Shenyang is no place to linger.

Population: 40 million
Capital: Shenyang
Highlights:
- The North Tomb in Shenyang, an unusual heirloom which dates back to the beginnings of the Manchu era
- The dynamic port city of Dalian, which promises to become the Hong Kong of the north, though it's no place for those on a budget
- Dandong, the gateway to North Korea

Information

You'll find CITS (☎ 680-5858; fax 680-8772) in a building about 100 metres north of the Phoenix Hotel; its official address is 113 Huanghe Nan Dajie. The PSB is just off the traffic circle on Zhongshan Lu near the Mao statue. The Bank of China is at 75 Heping Bei Dajie. The main post office is at 32 Zhongshan Lu, Section 1.

Odd as it might seem, Shenyang has a US consulate (☎ 282-0057; fax 282-0074) at 52 Shisi Wei Lu, Heping District.

Mao Statue (Zhongshan Square)
(zhōngshān guǎngchǎng)

Of all the unusual statues in north-east China (Soviet war heroes, mini-tanks on top of pillars...), this Mao statue takes the cake.

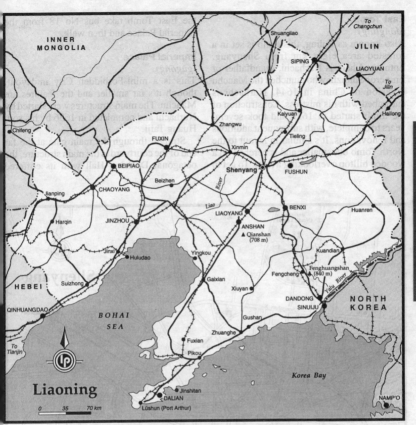

THE NORTH-EAST

Liaoning

0   35   70 km

Like some kind of strange machine, it zooms out of Red Flag Square, a giant epoxy-resin Mao at the helm, flanked by vociferous peasants, soldiers and workers. The last word on the personality cult and the follies of the Cultural Revolution, this is a rare item, erected in 1969. The statue is in Zhongshan Square at the intersection of Zhongshan Lu and Nanjing Jie.

North Tomb
(běilíng)

This is the finest sight in Shenyang. Set in a huge park, the North Tomb is the burial place of Huang Taiji (1592-1643), who founded the Qing Dynasty (although he did not live to see the conquest of China). The tomb took eight years to build, and the impressive animal statues on the approach to it are reminiscent of the Ming tombs. The larger buildings, used as barracks by various warlords, are in a state of disrepair, though some attempt has been made to restore them. The central grassy mound area is known as Zhaoling.

To get to the North Tomb take bus No 220 from the railway station, bus No 213 from the Imperial Palace or bus No 6.

East Tomb
(dōnglíng)

Also known as Fuling, this tomb is set in a forested area eight km from Shenyang. Entombed here is Nurhachi, grandfather of Emperor Shunzhi who launched the Manchu invasion of China in 1644. Nurhachi is entombed with his mistress. Construction of the tomb started in 1626 and took several years to complete, with subsequent additions and renovations. It's similar in layout to the North Tomb but smaller and is perched on a wooded hilltop overlooking a river. To get to the East Tomb take bus No 18 from the Imperial Palace and then walk.

Imperial Palace
(gùgōng)

This is a mini-Forbidden City in layout, though it's far smaller and the features are Manchu. The main structures were started by Nurhachi and completed in 1636 by his son, Huang Taiji.

Straight through the main gate at the far end of the courtyard is the main structure, the octagonal Dazheng Hall with its coffered

Shenyang

0   1   2 km

To East Tomb

0   500 m

ceiling and an elaborate throne. It was here that Emperor Shunzhi was crowned before setting off to cross the Great Wall in 1644. In the courtyard in front of the hall are the Banner Pavilions, formerly administrative offices used by tribal chieftains.

They now house displays of 17th and 18th-century military equipment – armour, swords and bows. The central courtyard west of Dazheng Hall contains a conference hall, some living quarters and some shamanist structures (one of the customs of the Manchus was to pour boiling wine into a sacrificial pig's ear, so that its cries would attract the devotees' ancestors). The courtyard to the western fringe is a residential area added on by Emperor Qianlong in the 18th century, and the Wenshu Gallery to the rear housed a copy of the Qianlong anthology.

The palace functions as a museum, with exhibitions of ivory and jade artefacts, musical instruments, furniture, and Ming and Qing paintings. You must leave bags at the door and photography is prohibited inside. The captions to exhibits are all in Chinese. If you've visited the Forbidden City in Beijing, Shenyang's Imperial Palace may be a disappointment, but Manchu buffs may find it interesting. It's in the oldest section of the city; take bus No 10 from Shenyang's south railway station.

Places to Stay

All the provinces in the north-east have attempted to 'standardise' prices for foreigners. Liaoning pitches in with single rooms starting at Y200 – for that price, you can expect a dump with leaky plumbing.

SHENYANG 沈阳

PLACES TO STAY

3 Friendship Hotel 友谊宾馆
5 Phoenix Hotel 凤凰饭店
6 Liaoning Mansions 辽宁大厦
7 Taishan Hotel 泰山宾馆
9 Jinlong Hotel 金龙宾馆
14 Youzheng Dasha Hotel 邮政大厦宾馆
19 Hua Sha Hotel 华厦饭店
21 Zhongxing Hotel 中兴宾馆
22 Dongbei Hotel 东北饭店
23 Zhongshan Hotel 中山大酒店
24 Liaoning Hotel 辽宁宾馆

OTHER

1 Hang Dynasty Memorial 烈士陵园
2 Zhaoling 昭陵
4 CITS 中国国际旅行社
8 Park Entrance 公园门口
10 Liaoning University 辽宁大学
11 Bainiao Park 百鸟公园
12 North Pagoda 北塔
13 Bitang Park 碧塘公园
15 North Railway Station & Railway Hotel 北火车站，沈铁大厦宾馆
16 East Railway Station 东站
17 City Hall 市政府
18 South Railway Station 南火车站
20 KFC 肯德基家乡鸡

25 Mao Statue 毛主席像
26 PSB 公安局外事科
27 Bank of China 中国银行
28 Imperial Palace 故宫
29 Zoo 动物园
30 Zhongshan Park 中山公园
31 US Consulate 美国领事馆
32 TV Tower & Foreign Languages Bookstore 电视塔，外文书店
33 Qingnian (Youth) Park 青年公园
34 Liaoning Stadium 辽宁体育馆
35 Nanhu (South Lake) Park 南湖公园
36 North East University of Technology 东北工学院
37 Shenyang Sports Centre 沈阳体育中心

There is a good chance that you'll arrive at Shenyang's north railway station, in which case the cheapest and most convenient place to stay is the *Railway Hotel* (☎ 273-2888) *(shēntiě dàshà)*. Rooms with a scenic view of Shenyang's industrial skyline cost Y250.

Just next door to the foregoing is the *Youzheng Dasha Hotel (yóuzhèng dàshà bīnguǎn)*. At Y394 for singles, it's hardly worth it, but at least the location is convenient.

The *Hua Sha Hotel* (☎ 783-3423) *(huáshà fàndiàn)* is a stone's throw from the south railway station at 3 Zhongshan Lu, Section 1. Consider it a bargain at Y200 for a single, but this place is a likely candidate for future renovation and sharp price increases to match. The hotel has a foreign-exchange counter and restaurant.

The *Zhongxing Hotel* (☎ 383-8188; fax 880-4096) *(zhōngxīng bīnguǎn)* is at 86 Taiyuan Beijie, right in the main market area

Northern Warlords

Once known as Manchuria, north-east China has historically been the birthplace of the conquerors. Perhaps it was the harsh climate that caused both the Mongols and Manchus to turn their eyes southwards.

At the turn of this century Manchuria was a sparsely populated region, but it had rich, largely untapped resources. Both the Russians and the Japanese eyed it enviously. After the Chinese were defeated by the Japanese in the Sino-Japanese War of 1894-95, the Liaoning Peninsula was ceded to Japan. Japan's strength alarmed the other foreign powers, Russia among them, and Japan was forced to hand the peninsula back to China. As a reward for this intervention, the Russians were allowed to build a railway across Manchuria to Russia's treaty port of Port Arthur (Lüshun), present-day Dalian. The Russians moved troops in with the railway, and for the next 10 years effectively controlled north-east China.

The Russo-Japanese War of 1904-05 put an end to Russia's domination of Manchuria. Overall control of Manchuria moved into the hands of Zhang Zuolin, a bandit-leader in control of a large and well-organised private army. By the time the Qing Dynasty fell he held the power of life and death in southern Manchuria, and between 1926 and 1928 ran a regional government recognised by foreign powers. Zhang Zuolin was ousted by the Kuomintang's Northern Expedition, which unified southern and northern China, and he was forced to retire.

Zhang's policy in Manchuria had been to limit Japan's economic and political expansion, and eventually to break Japan's influence entirely. But by the 1920s the militarist Japanese government was ready to take a hard line on China.

Zhang Zuolin was assassinated (both the Japanese and the Kuomintang have been blamed for this one); control of Manchuria passed to his son, Zhang Xueliang, with the blessing of the Kuomintang. The Japanese invasion of Manchuria began in September 1931, and the weak Kuomintang government in Nanjing couldn't do anything about it. Chiang Kaishek was too obsessed with his annihilation campaigns against the Communists to challenge the Japanese militarily. Manchuria fell to the Japanese, who renamed it the independent state of Manchukuo – a Japanese puppet state. The exploitation of the region began in earnest: heavy industry was established and extensive railway lines were laid.

The Japanese occupation of Manchuria was a fateful move for the Chinese Communist forces locked up in Shaanxi. The invasion forced Zhang Xueliang and his 'Dongbei' (North-Eastern) army out of Manchuria – these troops were eventually moved into central China to fight the Communists. Up until the mid-1930s Zhang's loyalty to Chiang Kaishek never wavered, but he gradually became convinced that Chiang's promises to cede no more territory to Japan and to recover the Manchurian homeland were empty ones. Zhang made a secret truce with the Communists, and when Chiang Kaishek flew to Xi'an in December 1936 to organise yet another extermination campaign against the Communists, Zhang had Chiang arrested. Chiang was released only after agreeing to call off the extermination campaign and to form an alliance with the Communists to resist the Japanese. Chiang never forgave Zhang and later had him arrested and taken to Taiwan as a prisoner – he wasn't permitted to leave Taiwan until 1992.

a couple of blocks south of the railway station. You can't miss the hotel – it's a brick-red pyramid-shaped skyscraper towering over the market. From the outside it looks frightfully expensive, but it's not (by Shenyang standards). Usual rates are from Y280 to Y580, but the presidential suite will set you back Y1500.

The *Dongbei Hotel* (☎ 386-8120) *(dōngběi fàndiàn)* is at 100 Tianjin Beijie – one block south of Taiyuan Beijie, the main shopping street. It's also known as the Dongning Hotel. It's an old place and doesn't look like it should be expensive, but rooms are not cheap at Y240 for a double.

The giant statue of Mao in Zhongshan Square faces the *Liaoning Hotel* (☎ 782-9166; fax 782-9103) *(liáoníng bīnguǎn)* – it looks almost like he's waving to guests in the hotel lobby. The hotel was constructed in 1927 by the Japanese and boasts 77 suites, a billiard room with slate tables, and art

When WW II ended, the north-east suddenly became the focus of a renewed confrontation between the Communist and Kuomintang troops. At the Potsdam Conference of July 1945 it was decided that all Japanese forces in Manchuria and North Korea would surrender to the Soviet army; those stationed elsewhere would surrender to the Kuomintang.

After the A-bombs obliterated Hiroshima and Nagasaki in August 1945 and forced the Japanese government to surrender, the Soviet armies moved into Manchuria, engaging the Japanese armies in a brief but bloody conflict. The Americans started transporting Kuomintang troops by air and sea to the north, where they could take the surrender of Japanese forces and regain control of north and central China. The US navy moved in to Qingdao and landed 53,000 marines to protect the railways leading to Beijing and Tianjin and the coal mines which supplied those railways.

The Communists, still in a shaky truce with the Kuomintang, also joined the rush for position. Although Chiang Kaishek told them to remain where they were, the Communist troops marched to Manchuria on foot, picking up arms from abandoned Japanese depots as they went. Other Communist forces went north by sea from Shandong. In November 1945 the Kuomintang attacked the Communists even while US-organised peace negotiations were taking place between the two. That attack put an end to the talks.

The Communists occupied the countryside, setting in motion their land-reform policies, which quickly built up their support among the peasants. There was a tremendous growth of mass support for the Communists, and the force of 100,000 regulars who had marched into Manchuria rapidly grew to 300,000, as soldiers of the old Manchurian armies that had been forcibly incorporated into the Japanese armies flocked to join them. Within two years the Red Army had grown to 1½ million combat troops and four million support personnel.

On the other side, though the Kuomintang troops numbered three million and had Soviet and US arms and support, its soldiers had nothing to fight for and either deserted or went over to the Communists who took them in by the thousands. The Kuomintang armies were led by generals whom Chiang had chosen for their personal loyalty to him rather than for their military competence; Chiang ignored the suggestions of the US military advisers whom he himself had asked for.

In 1948 the Communists took the initiative in Manchuria. Strengthened by the recruitment of Kuomintang soldiers and the capture of US equipment, the Communists became both the numerical and material equal of the Kuomintang. Three great battles led by Lin Biao in Manchuria decided the outcome. In the first battle of August 1948, the Kuomintang lost 500,000 people. In the second battle (from November 1948 to January 1949) whole Kuomintang divisions went over to the Communists who took 327,000 prisoners.

The Kuomintang lost seven generals who were killed, captured or deserted; seven divisional commanders crossed sides. The third decisive battle was fought in the area around Beijing and Tianjin; Tianjin fell on 23 January and another 500,000 troops came across to the Communist camp. It was these victories which sealed the fate of the Kuomintang and allowed the Communists to drive southwards. ■

nouveau windows – in short, old but elegant. Doubles cost Y480.

The fanciest place in the city centre is the *Zhongshan Hotel* (☎ 383-3888; fax 383-9189) *(zhōngshān dàjiǔdiàn)*, a gleaming white 27-storey monolith at 65 Zhongshan Lu. It's become a major drawcard for Overseas Chinese – you'll hear more Cantonese and Taiwanese spoken in the lobby than Mandarin. The 257 guest rooms and suites have a starting price tag of Y660.

The *Liaoning Mansions* (☎ 680-9502) *(liáoníng dàshà)* is at 1 Huanghe Dajie, Section 6, going towards the North Tomb. This enormous Soviet-style place features echo-chamber acoustics and looks like Communist Party headquarters (maybe it is). Rooms are Y418.

The *Phoenix Hotel* (☎ 680-5858; fax 680-7207) *(fènghuáng fàndiàn)*, 109 Huanghe Dajie, is just north of the Liaoning Mansions. This is a major staging area for tour groups, with all the modern amenities and the prices to go with it. Singles/doubles are Y535/660 and suites cost Y1200.

Within walking distance of the Phoenix Hotel is the elegant *Jinlong Hotel* (☎ 624-6688) *(jīnlóng bīnguǎn)* at 88 Huanghe Lu. Standard/deluxe rooms are Y298/388, while suites cost all the way up to Y2276. Definitely recommended if you can afford this price range.

Close by the is grotesquely overpriced *Taishan Hotel* *(tàishān bīnguǎn)*, where standard rooms start at Y638. Suites are Y1288 to Y1680.

The *Friendship Hotel* (☎ 680-1122; fax 680-0132) *(yǒuyì bīnguǎn)* is at 1 Huanghe Bei Dajie, Huanggu District, north of the Phoenix Hotel. It's villa-style and geared towards cadres, but you can stay for Y390 and up.

Places to Eat
The areas around the north and south railway stations have numerous noodle and rice places and are the best bet for budget travellers. *KFC* has an outlet on Zhonghua Lu, right in front of the south railway station.

Entertainment
The Shenyang Acrobatic Troupe is one of China's best and is worth chasing up. Ask about tickets at the Zhongxing Hotel. CITS also has details on dates, times and costs for performances.

Things to Buy
The Zhongxing Hotel is part of an enormous complex called the Zhongxing Commercial Centre – it could easily compete with some of Beijing's finest department stores. The building fronts Taiyuan Jie, the major shopping street, where you can stock up on the latest clothing at Giordano and Bossini.

The Foreign Languages Bookstore (☎ 389-1449) is at 195 Qingnian Dajie, near the huge TV tower that dominates Shenyang's skyline. Next door at No 270 is the Xinhua Bookstore, which stocks mostly Chinese-language books.

Getting There & Away
Air The CAAC office (☎ 386-4605) is at 117 Zhonghua Lu, Heping District. CAAC offers international flights between Shenyang and Hong Kong, Seoul and Irkutsk. Aeroflot has a ticket office in the Phoenix Hotel and also offers flights to Irkutsk. A combined Moscow-Irkutsk-Shenyang-Beijing air ticket will save you considerably compared with a direct Moscow-Beijing flight.

Flights from Shenyang to other Chinese cities include those to:

Beijing, Changchun, Changsha, Changzhou, Chaoyang, Chengdu, Chongqing, Dalian, Dandong, Fuzhou, Guangzhou, Guiyang, Haikou, Hangzhou, Harbin, Hefei, Jilin, Ji'nan, Kunming, Lanzhou, Lianyungang, Mudanjiang, Nanjing, Nanning, Ningbo, Qingdao, Qiqihar, Sanya, Shanghai, Shantou, Shenzhen, Taiyuan, Tianjin, Ürümqi, Wenzhou, Wuhan, Xiamen, Xi'an, Yanji, Yantai and Zhengzhou

Bus Given the situation with severely overcrowded trains, consider making your departure by sleeper bus. There are plenty of overnight expresses to Beijing, though you can also exit the bus at Shanhaiguan if you

Top: The symbol of Shanghai, the Bund is one of the most imposing sights in China.
ottom: Dancers go through their paces on the Bund, Shanghai.

Top: The colonial architecture of Shanghai is a reminder of the city's European pas
Bottom: A neon sign announces the Magic Restaurant, one of Shanghai's many eateri

prefer. The best place to find these buses is to simply hang around the entrance of Shenyang's north railway station – women carrying placards saying 'Beijing' in Chinese will approach you and say '*wopu*' ('sleeper'). The buses depart Shenyang at approximately 3 pm and arrive in Beijing about 7 am.

Train By train from Shenyang to Beijing takes nine hours; to Changchun five hours; to Harbin, nine hours; to Dandong, five hours; and to Dalian, six hours.

The situation with railway stations is tricky – there is a north station (*běi zhàn*) and a south station (*nán zhàn*). (The east railway station is a local station, used mainly for freight.) Trains alternate equally between the north and south stations, so you'll have to check the timetable or ask to be certain where you're departing from if you buy the train ticket from a hotel or travel agency. In both stations, tickets for the following day can be booked upstairs. Sleepers out of Shenyang are notoriously difficult to get.

Getting Around

Shenyang cabs are equipped with meters but the drivers prefer not to use them – make sure that they do.

AROUND SHENYANG
Qianshan
(*qiānshān*)
These hills are about 50 km from Shenyang. The name is an abbreviation for Qianlianshan (Thousand Lotuses Mountain).

According to legend, there was once a fairy who wanted to bring spring to the world by embroidering pretty clouds on lotuses. Just as she was making the 999th lotus, the gods found it, accused her of stealing the clouds and had her arrested. The fairy put up a fight and during the struggle all the lotuses dropped to earth, where they immediately turned into green hills. In memory of the fairy, people began to call the mountain 'Thousand Lotuses Mountain' or just Qianshan. Later, when a monk arrived and actually counted the peaks he discovered there were only 999, so he built an artificial one to make a round number.

You can hike around the hills, which have a scattering of Tang, Ming and Qing temples. The mountain, which gets very crowded on Sundays and public holidays, is steep in parts; it takes about three hours to reach the summit. At the southern foot of the mountain (approached along a different bus route) are the **Tanggangzi Hot Springs**. The last Qing emperor, Puyi, used to bathe here with his empresses.

Tanggangzi's hot springs are piped into ordinary baths, and there's a sanatorium for those with chronic diseases. There is some hotel accommodation here.

Getting There & Away Qianshan takes two hours to reach by bus from the Shenyang long-distance bus station. Another approach is from Anshan, which is 25 km from the mountain. The last bus in either direction leaves at 6.30 pm.

The bus drops you off at the entrance to the Qianshan park. Food, drink, Qianshan T-shirts, locally made clickers and knobbly walking sticks are available from hawkers. Maps can be bought from hawkers near the gate or from the ticket office.

DALIAN
(*dàlián*)
Dalian has been known by a variety of names – Dalny, Dairen, Lüshun and Luda. Lüshun is the part further south (formerly Port Arthur, now a naval base), and Lüshun and Dalian comprise Luda. In the late 19th century the Western powers were busy carving up pieces of China for themselves. To the outrage of Tsar Nicholas II, Japan gained the Liaoning Peninsula under an 1895 treaty (after creaming Chinese battleships off Port Arthur in 1894). Nicholas II gained the support of the French and Germans and managed to get the Japanese to withdraw from Dalian; the Russians got the place as a concession in 1898, and set about constructing the port of their dreams and an alternative to the only partially ice-free port of Vladivostok.

To Russia's further dismay, however, the Japanese made a comeback, sinking the

THE NORTH-EAST

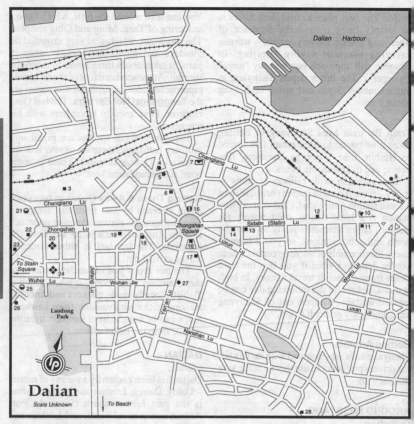

Dalian Harbour

Changjiang Lu

Shanghai Lu

Changjiang Lu

Zhongshan Lu

Sidalin (Stalin) Lu

Zhongshan Square

Luxun Lu

To Stalin Square

Wuhu Lu

Wuhan Jie

Jiefang Lu

Yan'an Lu

Laodong Park

Nanshan Lu

Luxan Lu

Wuwu Lu

Dalian
Scale Unknown
To Beach

Russian East Asia naval squadron in 1902, and decimating the Russian Baltic squadron off Korea in 1905. The same year, Dalian passed back into Japanese hands, and the Japanese completed the port facilities in 1930. In 1945, the Soviet Union reoccupied Dalian and did not withdraw definitively until 10 years later.

Dalian has distinguished itself by being certified as China's 'first rat-free city'. With military precision, local residents planned an intensive eradication campaign and chose April 1986 (when the rats were celebrating peak powers of performance and pregnancy)

as the time of assault. A team of rodent specialists from Liaoning Province was later called in for an official inspection of the city.

More significantly, Dalian was the first of the 14 open coastal cities to offer a package of attractive terms to foreign investors who had expressed great dissatisfaction with previous discriminatory practices.

Dalian is *the* major port for China's north-east provinces, on a par with Tianjin. The city is also an industrial producer in its own right. All this has made Dalian remarkably prosperous – well-stocked shops line the busy thoroughfares. But prosperity has its down-

DALIAN 大连

PLACES TO STAY

3　Holiday Inn
　　九州饭店
6　Dalian Hotel (Fandian)
　　大连饭店
11　Friendship Store &
　　Hotel
　　友谊商店，友谊宾馆
12　Furama Hotel
　　富丽华大酒店
13　Norinco Hotel
　　北方大厦
14　International Hotel
　　国际大酒店
16　Dalian Hotel (Binguan)
　　大连宾馆
17　Grand Hotel
　　大连博览大酒店
18　Gloria Plaza Hotel
　　凯莱大酒店
19　Eastern Hotel
　　东方饭店

22　Nongken Hotel
　　农垦宾馆
23　CAAC & Civil Aviation
　　Hotel
　　民航大厦
28　Nanshan Hotel
　　南山宾馆

PLACES TO EAT

10　International Seamen's
　　Club
　　海员俱乐部

OTHER

1　North Railway Station
　　大连北站
2　Dalian Railway Station
　　大连火车站
4　Xinhua Bookstore
　　新华书店
5　Foreign Languages
　　Bookstore
　　外文书店

7　Post Office
　　邮局
8　East Railway Station
　　大连东站
9　Harbour Passenger
　　Terminal
　　大连港客运站
15　Bank of China
　　中国银行
20　Dalian Shopping Centre
　　大连商场
21　Long-Distance Bus
　　Station
　　长途客运站
24　Zhongxing Shopping
　　Centre
　　中兴大厦
25　Private Buses to
　　Dandong
　　个体服汽车站 (往丹东)
26　CITS
　　中国国际旅行社
27　PSB
　　公安局外事科

side – prices are high and the city resembles one huge construction site. It's easy to get the impression that a new skyscraper is being erected every week, and much of what is being built are upmarket hotels. Unfortunately, the high cost of accommodation makes Dalian a nonstarter for budget travellers.

Information

CITS (☎ 363-5795) is on the 4th floor, 1 Changtong Jie, on the west side of Laodong Park near the Civil Aviation Hotel and CAAC. On the 5th floor of the same building is the Dalian Overseas Tourism Corporation (☎ 368-0857; fax 368-7831), which proved to be both friendlier and more knowledgeable than CITS.

The PSB is on Yan'an Lu, just to the south of Zhongshan Square. The Bank of China is at 9 Zhongshan Square. The post and telephone office is on Changjiang Lu.

TNT Skypak (☎ 280-0524; fax 280-0520) is a private courier service with an office at

35 Changjiang Lu, Zhongshan District. DHL (☎ 272-5883; fax 272-5881) is at 2-11 Gangwan Jie, Zhongshan District.

Stalin Square

(sīdàlín guǎngchǎng)

Stalin seems to be held in high esteem in this part of China. The square commemorates liberation from Japan in 1945 and the memorial was set up in 1954. During the Cultural Revolution, Stalin Square was used for political rallies. It's on the west end of Zhongshan Lu (on the south side) near city hall.

Other Attractions

For the individual traveller, access to the port facilities (probably one of Dalian's top sights) is limited. You'll have to be content with the large **Natural History Museum** *(zìrán bówùguǎn)* with its stuffed sea life. It's east of the north railway station near Shanghai Lu and is open on Tuesday, Thursday, Saturday and Sunday from 8 am to 4 pm. **Laodong Park** *(láodòng gōngyuán)*, in the centre of town, offers good city views. There's also an assortment of handicraft factories, whose products include glasswork and shell mosaics.

Organised Tours

There are a large number of hawkers staked out around the railway station plugging all-day bus tours around the city. Foreigners are welcome, but don't expect the tour guides to speak anything other than Chinese.

Places to Stay – bottom end

Dalian's fortunes have been rising fast, and so have prices – you can easily live more cheaply in Hong Kong! The few hotels which do charge reasonable rates are usually full. You can try your luck at the low end of the hotel battlefield, but if this fails you may find yourself booking a seat on the first train (even aircraft!) to anywhere.

The lower end belongs to the *Friendship Hotel* (☎ 263-4121) *(yǒuyí bīnguǎn)*. This is on the 3rd floor, above the Friendship Store at 137 Sidalin Lu. Doubles cost Y110, a bargain by Dalian standards but the rooms are forever full. You could try arriving at 6 am or so and wait until someone checks out, but you might have to join a queue of other hopefuls.

Places to Stay – middle

The *Eastern Hotel* (☎ 234161; fax 236859) *(dōngfāng fàndiàn)* is at 28 Zhongshan Lu, not far from the railway station. At Y292 to Y430, it's no bargain but still cheaper than most Dalian hotels. For that reason, this place is also usually full.

The *Nongken Hotel* (☎ 363-5599) *(nóngkěn bīnguǎn)* is a one-star hotel charging three-star prices, but at least the staff are friendly. Doubles cost Y268. It's on Zhongshan Lu near the CAAC office.

The seven-storey *Dalian Hotel (Fandian)* (☎ 263-3171; fax 280-4197) *(dàlián fàndiàn)* is at 6 Shanghai Lu. Doubles go for Y368. It's worth noting that there is another Dalian Hotel *(dàlián bīnguǎn)*, with the same name in English but a different Chinese name.

Places to Stay – top end

The *Dalian Hotel (Binguan)* (☎ 263-3111) *(dàlián bīnguǎn)* is at 7 Zhongshan Square. It's an ancient building with a renovated interior. Doubles cost a cool Y748. This hotel was used in a scene in the movie *The Last Emperor*. No doubt when Emperor Puyi was here, the rates were lower.

The *Grand Hotel (bólǎn dàjiǔdiàn)* charges grand prices – singles/doubles are Y765/853, suites are Y1305 to Y2436. The hotel is at 1 Jiefang Jie, just behind the Dalian Hotel (Binguan).

In the same neighbourhood is the luxurious *Gloria Plaza Hotel (kǎilái dà jiǔdiàn)* at 5 Yide Jie. Standard rooms are Y1245 to Y1411, and suites cost Y1494 to Y2490.

The *International Hotel* (☎ 263-4825) *(guójì dàjiǔdiàn)*, 9 Sidalin Lu, has doubles for Y813 plus a 15% service charge.

Next door to the International is the *Norinco Hotel (běifāng dàshà)*. It was under construction at the time of writing so prices were unavailable, but it does not look like it will be cheap.

The *Furama Hotel* (☎ 263-0888; fax 280-4455) *(fùlìhuá dàjiǔdiàn)* at 74 Sidalin Lu is the glitziest hotel in town, with 500 rooms. It's an Overseas Chinese hang-out and even has its own Friendship Store. Costs run from Y1394 to Y2407 a double, or a mere Y12,450 for a suite.

The *Civil Aviation Hotel* (☎ 363-3111) *(mínháng dàshà)*, 143 Zhongshan Lu, is run by CAAC and is next to its ticket office. Singles/doubles cost a whopping Y1062/1147 plus 15% surcharge. If you're booked on one of CAAC's hopelessly delayed flights, you might even get to stay here free.

The *Holiday Inn* (☎ 280-8888; fax 280-9704) *(jiǔzhōu fàndiàn)* costs Y1120 for a 'budget' single. It's unique among Dalian's luxury hotels in that it is conveniently placed right next to the railway station.

The *Nanshan Hotel* (☎ 263-8751) *(nánshān bīnguǎn)*, 56 Fenglin Jie, Zhongshan District, has a dozen villas tucked into very pleasant gardens. It once had the atmosphere of a country club, but has now been renovated and resembles a battleship. Doubles start at Y1200. To get there take the round-the-city unnumbered bus; or take tramcar No 201 and then change to bus No 12 or walk uphill.

Another possibility is the *Bangchuidao Guesthouse* (☎ 263-5131) (*bàngchuídǎo bīnguǎn*) to the east of the town on the coast. It's next to an exclusive beach and there is no way to reach it except by taxi. A lot of tour groups stay here.

Places to Eat

The restaurant on the 3rd floor of the *Eastern Hotel* is not bad and is reasonably priced.

The *International Seamen's Club* (*hǎiyuán jùlèbù*), at the eastern end of Sidalin Lu, has several dining sections on the 2nd floor. It's not cheap, but you can enjoy a peaceful plate of fried dumplings (*guōtiē*).

Xinghai Park, out by the beachfront, has a kind of elevated clubhouse with beach umbrellas. Specialities include giant prawns, fish and beer, and in season there's an open-air view overlooking the windsurfers and sunbathers.

Entertainment

The Copacabana of Dalian is the *International Seamen's Club*, open until 10.30 pm, with dining and banquet rooms, a bar where sailors doze with their stale beers to the chirp of video-game machines and a disco.

Getting There & Away

Air Dalian has both domestic and international air connections. CAAC and Dragonair fly to/from Hong Kong for HK$2410. CAAC and All Nippon Airways go to Osaka, Fukuoka, Sendai and Tokyo. CAAC also flies to Seoul, South Korea. Dragonair (☎ 263-8238 ext 601) has an office on the 6th floor of the International Hotel, 9 Sidalin Lu. All Nippon Airways (☎ 263-9744) also has its office in the International Hotel, but you can book through CITS. CAAC is at 143 Zhongshan Lu next to the Civil Aviation Hotel. Domestic flights are to:

Beijing, Changchun, Changsha, Chengdu, Guangzhou, Haikou, Hangzhou, Harbin, Hefei, Jilin, Ji'nan, Jinzhou, Kunming, Luoyang, Mudanjiang, Nanjing, Ningbo, Qingdao, Qinhuangdao, Qiqihar, Shanghai, Shantou, Shenyang, Shenzhen, Taiyuan, Tianjin, Ürümqi, Wenzhou, Wuhan, Xiamen, Xi'an, Yanji and Zhengzhou

Bus There are buses to Shenyang, Dandong, Lüshun and the odd overnight coach to Beijing. The government-run long-distance bus station is one block south of the railway station. There is a private bus station just next to CITS. Book your ticket peacefully the day before or arrive at the last minute and fight for it.

Several buses leave daily for Dandong between 6 and 8 am, but there is one night bus at 8 pm. The trip takes nine hours.

Train There are nine trains daily to Shenyang and the trip takes six hours. There is also a once-daily express which takes four hours – it departs Dalian at 1.40 pm and tickets are only sold on the day of departure.

Boat The booking office is at the boat terminal, east of the Seamen's Club, and has a left-luggage office (modern facilities, too). Providing you have a ticket, you can sleep in the comfy building beside the booking office. Since the railway lines from Dalian have to go all the way round the peninsula before proceeding south, boats can actually save you time as well as money.

Boats depart Dalian daily for Shanghai at 8.30 am and take 37 hours for the trip. Departures for Yantai are daily at 8 pm and the journey takes eight hours. Boats to Weihai leave Dalian on even-numbered days at 7 pm and take nine hours for the journey. Departures for Longkou are on odd-numbered days at 7 pm and the trip requires 11 hours. Boats to Tanggu (the port of Tianjin) depart once every four days at 3 pm and the ride takes 16 hours. Boats to Qingdao depart once every four days at 7 pm and take 22 hours. The boat to Guangzhou departs Dalian on the 10th and 25th day of every month at 2 pm, requiring 100 hours for the trip.

Even 3rd class is comfortable, but avoid cargo class. Meals are available.

Getting Around

Dalian is notorious for having only two or three traffic lights in the entire city. Crossing a major street is sheer terror. The 'cross-walks' lure you into a false sense of security – drivers will not stop for anything, least of all a pedestrian.

To/From the Airport The airport is 12 km from the city centre.

Bus Bus No 13 runs from the railway station area, behind the Friendship Store, and to the boat terminal. Tramcar No 201 starts from the railway station, heads in the same direction as bus No 13, but turns south before the Friendship Store and proceeds east.

Taxi Drivers have meters but seldom use them. It's usually a flat Y20 for anywhere within the city.

AROUND DALIAN
Parks & Beaches

Even though the traffic is deadly, Dalian is actually a health resort of sorts and beaches with their attached parks are the main attraction. The beach five km to the south-east is for upper-crust tourists and is bordered by the exclusive Bangchuidao Guesthouse. **Laohutan Park** *(lǎohǔtān gōngyuán)* has a rocky beach that's rather poor for swimming (you can get there on bus No 102 from the city centre).

Small **Fujiazhuang Beach** *(fùjiāzhuāng hǎishuǐ yùchǎng)* is the best – it has fine sand and rock outcrops in the deep bay, and is excellent for swimming but has few facilities. Like the other beaches, this one has a sanatorium nearby; the patients sometimes venture out in their pyjamas to assist rubber-booted fishing crews hauling in their catch. The beach is a fair way out of town – take bus No 102 and then change to bus No 5.

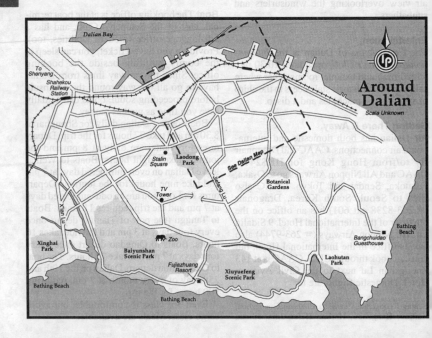

Five km to the south-west is **Xinghai Park** (*xīnghǎi gōngyuán*) – it's a crowded beach and a little on the slimy side, but it's got a good seafood restaurant. Take bus No 2, or else take tramcar No 201 and then change to tramcar No 202.

Jinshitan (Golden Stone Beach) is a new economic development zone north of Dalian, but also has a number of natural scenic wonders which the authorities say will be preserved. For the moment, it's still an attractive beach area with splendid coves and rock formations. Dalian's Municipal Construction Planning Department proposes to 'improve' the scenery with a golf course and possibly an amusement park. The *Jinshitan Hotel (jīnshítān bīnguǎn)* is currently the only accommodation available, but there are plans to add more guesthouses soon.

BINGYU VALLEY
(*bīngyù gōu*)

According to CITS, this is Liaoning's answer to Guilin and Yangshuo. The valley has a number of towering, vertical rock formations with a river meandering between them. It's pretty, but it's not likely to replace Guilin on the travellers' circuit. Still, you might want to have a look.

The valley is 250 km north-east of Dalian. Take a bus from the long-distance bus station to Zhuanghe (*zhuānghé*), a town about halfway between Dalian and Dandong. Then take another bus to Bingyu Scenic Area (*bīngyù fēngjǐn qū*). The Furama Hotel group was building a new hotel at the time of writing, but there's no word yet on prices.

DANDONG
(*dāndōng*)

Dandong lies at the border of Liaoning Province and North Korea. Along with Dalian and Yingkou, this is one of the three key trading and communication ports for the whole north-eastern area. The city has been designated one of Liaoning's major export production centres and the production of things like wristwatches, knitwear, printing and foodstuffs is increasing. This is the home

of Ganoderma wrinkle-killer face cream made from a rare and expensive mushroom. You can buy tussah silk at the silk factory.

Dandong isn't a cultural Mecca, but it's clean, leafy, easy to cover and doesn't suffer from overcrowding. However, there isn't much to see here other than the view of North Korea across the Yalu River. Some travellers come here to continue onwards to Tonghua and the Changbaishan Nature Reserve in Jilin Province.

Information
The CITS office (☎ 27721) is inside the Dandong Guesthouse.

North Korean Border
(*běi cháoxiān*)

Dandong's chief attraction is its location on the North Korean border (for information on visiting North Korea from Dandong, see Sinuiju in the Around Dandong section).

The **Yalu River Park** (*yālù jiāng gōngyuán*) is a favourite picnic site, full of photographers trying to squeeze mum, dad, kids, grandma and grandpa into the standard 'I visited the Sino-Korean border' shot which has to include the bridge as a backdrop. You can even get your portrait taken in the cockpit of a Chinese MiG fighter.

The **Jinjiangshan Park** (*jǐnjiāng shān gōngyuán*) is close to Dandong Guesthouse. From the top of the park there's a panoramic view of the city and North Korea across the river.

Yalu River Boat Cruise
(*yālù jiāng guānguāng chuán*)

If you want to get close to North Korea, an amusing boat ride will take you down the middle of the Yalu River, which is the boundary line. Boats leave at about 9 am (more often on weekends) from a pier at the Yalu River Park. Needless to say, the boat doesn't go anywhere in winter when the river is frozen. Photography is not allowed. The boat passes under the bridge, runs to within 10 metres of the Korean side, and then makes a long loop back down the Chinese side to the pier. There's nothing stunning about what you see: rusty tubs being welded, antiquated tubs being loaded, cheerful schoolkids waving, a steam engine chuffing across the bridge. Sinuiju itself is deliberately hidden behind an embankment topped with trees, to keep foreigners with binoculars and telephoto lenses from stealing North Korea's military secrets.

There are, in fact, two bridges (well, one and a half). The original steel-span bridge was 'accidentally' strafed in 1950 by the Americans, who also accidentally bombed the airstrip at Dandong. The Koreans have dismantled this bridge as far as the mid-river boundary line. All that's left is a row of support columns on the Korean side and half a bridge (still showing shrapnel pockmarks) on the Chinese side. The present bridge runs parallel to the old one.

Places to Stay

The *Yalu River Hotel* (☎ 25901) *(yālü jiāng dàshà)*, 87 Jiuwei Lu, is a shiny, Sino-Japan-

ese joint venture with 300 rooms in the centre of town. Prices are steep, with doubles starting at Y420.

The *Dandong Guesthouse* (☎ 27312, 27313) *(dāndōng bīnguǎn)* is at 2 Shanshang Jie, about two km or half an hour's walk uphill from the railway station. Despite its inconvenient location, the mixture of main buildings and villas set in a park is pleasant. Doubles start at Y400. The rooms all have TV, but if you turn off the telly it's just serenading crickets and the lonesome whistle of steam locomotives shunting outside.

Getting There & Away

Air There are regular flights to Guangzhou, Shanghai and Shenyang. There is a CAAC ticket office east of the Yalu River Hotel.

Bus The bus station is a five-minute walk from the railway station. A bus leaves daily for Tonghua at 6.30 am and takes 10 hours. This bus often fills up, so book your ticket as soon as you arrive in Dandong.

Several buses leave daily between 5.10 and 6.40 am for the nine-hour trip to Dalian.

Dandong
Scale Unknown

Jinjiangshan Park

Yalu River Park

To Sinuiju Railway Station

Yalu River

NORTH KOREA

Shanxia Lu, Sanwei Lu, Wuyi Jie, Liuwei Lu, Saqyi Jie, Zhenba Jie, Xingyi Jie, Xingwu Jie, Xinhua Jie, Zhenwu Lu, Zhenan Lu, Gongye Jie

DANDONG 丹东
1 Dandong Guesthouse & CITS 丹东宾馆, 中国国际旅行社
2 Yalu River Hotel 鸭绿江大厦
3 Long-Distance Bus Station 长途汽车站
4 Post Office 邮局
5 CAAC 中国民航
6 Xinhua Bookstore 新华书店
7 Railway Station 丹东火车站
8 Tour Boat Pier 旅游码头
9 Stadium 体育场

Train There are direct trains to Dandong from Shenyang and Changchun; the trip from Shenyang takes five hours. The combination train from Pyongyang to Moscow and Pyongyang to Beijing passes through Dandong on Saturday at about 3 pm. Buy a platform ticket and watch the international crowds of passengers (mostly Russians, North Koreans and Chinese) buying luxury items.

AROUND DANDONG
Sinuiju
Citizens of the PRC can visit North Korea without a visa, but for Westerners, all questions concerning visas etc have to be sorted out in Beijing or Macau (yes, Macau!), not in Dandong.

Chinese people who have visited Sinuiju universally give it bad reviews 'nothing to see or buy' is what they say. On the other hand, most Westerners find it fascinating. The big posters (in English) in the Sinuiju Railway Station declaring 'Death to the USA' and 'Death to the South Korean Puppet Clique' make for interesting photos. For more information on touring North Korea, see Lonely Planet's *Korea* or *North-East Asia on a shoestring*.

Getting There & Away There are also twice-weekly international trains passing through Dandong and Sinuiju from Beijing to Pyongyang, the capital of North Korea. Dandong CITS arranges quick excursions across the Yalu River to the Korean city of Sinuiju on the other side of the bridge.

Fenghuangshan
About 52 km north-west of Dandong is the town of Fengcheng. The nearby mountain, Fenghuangshan, is 840 metres high and dotted with temples, monasteries and pagodas from the Tang, Ming and Qing dynasties. The Fenghuang Mountain Temple Fair takes place in April and attracts thousands of people. Fenghuangshan is one hour from Dandong by either train or bus. The express train does not stop here, but you do get a view of the mountain.

Wulongbei Hot Springs
(wǔlóngbēi wēnquán)
The springs are about 20 km north of Dandong on the road to Fengcheng. There's a guesthouse here and you could try the springs.

Dagushan
Dagushan, where there are several groups of Taoist temples dating from the Tang Dynasty, lies close to the town of Gushan about 90 km south-west of Dandong.

Jilin 吉林

CHANGCHUN
(chángchūn)

Changchun, with its broad leafy avenues, is a well laid out but rather dull city. The Japanese, who developed it as the capital of 'Manchukuo' between 1933 and 1945, built the uninspiring militaristic structures. In 1945 the Russians arrived in Changchun on a looting spree; when they departed in 1946 the Kuomintang moved in to occupy the cities of the north-east, only to find themselves surrounded by the Communists in the countryside. The Communists had assembled a formidable array of scrounged and captured weaponry, even former Japanese tanks and US jeeps, and Changchun saw more than a few of them in action. The Communists took over the city in 1948.

China's first car-manufacturing plant was set up here in the 1950s with Soviet assistance, starting with 95-horsepower Jiefang (Liberation) trucks, and moving on to make bigger and better things like the now-defunct Red Flag limousines and, most recently, an Audi joint-venture factory. Lesser factories (tractors, locomotives, train coaches, carpet, fur, woodcarving) may be accessible to organised tours.

Travellers have little reason to visit Changchun except to use it as a transit point to somewhere else. The hotel situation is not good – all cheap places are off limits to foreigners.

Information

CTS (☎ 297-1040) has an office inside the Chunyi Guesthouse at 2 Sidalin Dajie, one block from the railway station.

CITS (☎ 564-7052; fax 564-5069) is on the 7th floor of the Yanmao Building, 14 Xinmin Jie, which is adjacent to the Changbaishan Hotel.

The main Bank of China is on the north-west corner of Renmin Square *(rénmín guǎngchǎng)*, which is at the intersection of Xi'an Dalu and Sidalin Dajie. There is a

Population: 25 million
Capital: Changchun
Highlights:

- Tianchi, a lovely crater lake in the stunning Ever-White Mountains, which make up China's largest nature reserve
- Songhuahu Qingshan and Beidahu, two of the leading downhill ski venues in the People's Republic
- Jilin, a city to visit in the bitter cold of winter, when the 'ice-rimmed trees' suddenly transform an industrial landscape to one of unusual beauty

branch Bank of China in the Yanmao Building near the Changbaishan Hotel.

The post office is on Sidalin Dajie, two blocks south of the railway station.

The PSB is on the south-west corner of Renmin Square near the main Bank of China.

Puppet Emperor's Palace & Exhibition Hall
(wěihuánggōng)

No, this place has nothing to do with seeing puppet shows. Henry Puyi was the last person to ascend to the dragon throne. He was two years old at the time and was forced to abdicate just three years later when the 1911 revolution swept the country. He lived

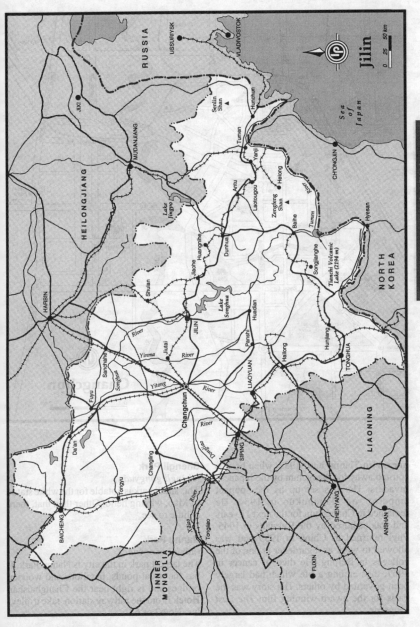

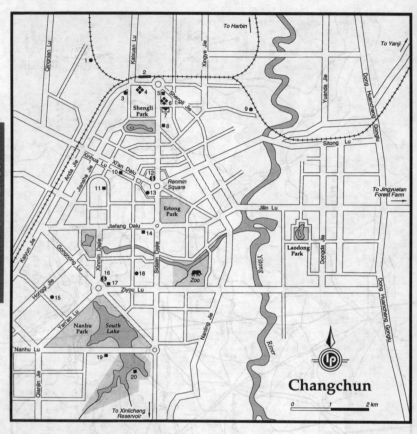

Changchun

in exile in Tianjin until 1932, when he was spirited away to Changchun by the Japanese invaders. He was set up as the 'puppet emperor' of Manchukuo in 1934. He remained in Changchun for the next 11 years and was captured by the Russians in 1945. Puyi returned to China in 1959 and was allowed to work as a gardener at one of the colleges in Beijing. He died of cancer in 1967, thus ending a life which had largely been governed by others. His story was the basis for the award-winning film *The Last Emperor*.

Shengli Park
(shènglì gōngyuán)

This small park is notable for the white statue of Mao, waving hello. Other than that, there is little to see.

Nanhu Park
(nánhú gōngyuán)

The largest park in the city is Nanhu Park. It has the usual ponds, pavilions and wooden bridges and is right near the Changbaishan Hotel. From the railway station, take trolley-bus No 62 or 63.

CHANGCHUN 长春

PLACES TO STAY

2 Railway Station & Railway Hotel
   火车站, 铁联大厦
5 Chunyi Guesthouse & Long-Distance
   Bus Station
   春谊宾馆, 客运中心
8 Paradise Hotel
   乐府大酒店
10 Changchun Hotel
   长春宾馆
11 Dongtian Hotel
   洞天宾馆
14 Jixiang Hotel
   吉香宾馆
17 Changbaishan Hotel
   长白山宾馆
19 Nanhu Guesthouse
   南湖宾馆
20 Overseas Chinese Hotel
   华侨饭店

OTHER

1 Railway Carriage Factory
   客车工厂
3 CAAC
   中国民航
4 Underground Shopping Mall
   春华商城
6 Changchun Shopping Centre
   长春商业城
7 Post Office
   邮局
9 Puppet Emperor's Palace &
   Exhibition Hall
   伪皇宫
12 Bank of China
   中国银行
13 PSB
   公安局外事科
15 Film Studio
   长春电影制片厂
16 Bank of China & CITS
   中国银行, 中国国际旅行社
18 Foreign Language Bookstore
   外文书店

Changchun Film Studio

(chángchūndiànyǐng zhìpiànchǎng)
The studio got its start during the civil war,

making documentaries. You aren't likely to get inside unless you join a CITS tour, but a Chinese tour may be possible.

Places to Stay

The *Railway Hotel* (☎ 298-1318) (tiělián dàshà) is right in the railway station itself. Room rates are Y150 to Y380. Be aware that there are two wings to the building with two separate service desks – if one is 'all full' then try the other.

The *Chunyi Guesthouse* (☎ 297-9966; fax 860171) (chūnyí bīnguǎn), 2 Sidalin Dajie, is one block south of the railway station. They charge Y380 for big, pleasant double rooms with private bath. The staff are friendly.

The *Paradise Hotel* (☎ 891-7071; fax 891-5709) (lèfǔ dà jiǔdiàn), 52 Sidalin Dajie, is just opposite Shengli Park. Although an upmarket place, the cheaper rooms are a bargain at Y166 and Y250. Suites are Y315 to Y8300.

The main tourist place is the *Changbaishan Hotel* (☎ 566-9911) (chángbáishān bīnguǎn). Doubles cost Y620. CITS is in the Bank of China building behind the hotel. Take trolley-bus No 62 or 63.

The *Changchun Hotel* (☎ 892-2661) (chángchūn bīnguǎn), 10 Xinhua Lu, is a short walk west of Renmin Square. Doubles cost Y360.

The *Jixiang Hotel* (☎ 562-0111) (jíxiáng dàjiǔdiàn) is on Jiefang Dalu and gets few foreign visitors. Doubles cost Y380.

The main cadre hang-out is the exclusive *Nanhu Guesthouse* (☎ 568-2501) (nánhú bīnguǎn), where doubles cost from Y400 to Y4000.

Places to Eat

Mouth-watering banquet fare will undoubtedly surface in the classier hotels for a hefty price, but on the streets the level of sanitation will quickly cure your hunger pangs without your having to eat anything at all!

Your best bet for a cheap meal is to descend the steps in front of the railway station into the *Underground Shopping Mall* (chūnhuá shāngchéng), where there are half a dozen Chinese fast-food restaurants. (It's also not a bad place to pick up some cheap clothing.)

The 3rd floor of the *Railway Hotel* has a restaurant which serves cheap, if mundane, set meals. Breakfast should cost you around Y5.

The best restaurant near the railway station area is inside the *Chunyi Guesthouse*. The restaurant in the *Paradise Hotel* can also be recommended.

Things to Buy
The Changchun Shopping Centre (*chángchūn shāngyè chéng*) south of the railway station is the fanciest mall in town. On the ground floor you can find imported chocolates and almost-edible bread.

Getting There & Away
Air The CAAC office is at 2 Liaoning Lu, close to the railway station. There are twice-weekly flights between Changchun and Hong Kong. There are domestic flights between Changchun and the following:

Beijing, Chengdu, Chongqing, Dalian, Fuzhou, Guangzhou, Haikou, Hangzhou, Hefei, Ji'nan, Jilin, Kunming, Nanjing, Shanghai, Shantou, Shenyang, Shenzhen, Tianjin, Ürümqi, Wenzhou, Wuhan, Xiamen, Yanji and Zhengzhou

Bus The long-distance bus station (*kèyùn zhōngxīn*) is south of the railway station and adjacent to the Chunyi Guesthouse. You can catch buses from here to Jilin (2½ hours) – these depart about once every 20 minutes throughout the day.

Train There are frequent trains heading north to Harbin (four hours) and south to Shenyang (five hours). Trains are also frequent to Jilin, and there is an overnight train for Yanji (departs 6.40 pm, arrives 6.30 am), which is the route you take to Changbaishan.

JILIN
(*jílín*)
East of Changchun is the city of Jilin. A Chinese pamphlet puts it in a nutshell:

Under the guidance of Chairman Mao's revolutionary line, it has made rapid progress in industrial and agricultural production...From a desolate consumer city, Kirin (Jilin) has become a rising industrial city with emphasis on chemical and power industries.

The city of Jilin today is home to 1.3 million people. For travellers, the area is mainly of interest for its winter sports and scenery if you can survive the cold.

Information
The CITS office (**☎** 453773) is in the Xiguan Hotel. Its competitor, CYTS (**☎** 456787), is in the Dongguan Hotel.

Most hotels *do not* change money despite the big sign at the reception desks saying 'Foreign Exchange'. The only place that reliably changes money is the Bank of China, adjacent to the Milky Way Hotel.

Ice-Rimmed Trees
(*shù guà*) (*wù sōng*)
Three large chemical plants were built after 1949. The Fengman Hydroelectric Station, built by the Japanese, disassembled by the Russians and put back together by the Chinese, fuels these enterprises, and provides Jilin with an unusual tourist attraction: water passing from artificial Songhua Lake through the power plant becomes a warm, steamy current that merges with the Songhua River and prevents it from freezing. Overnight, vapour rising from the river meets the -20°C weather, causing condensation on the branches of pines and willows on a 20-km stretch of the bank. During the Lunar New Year (late January to mid-February), hordes of Japanese and Overseas Chinese come for the resulting icicle show. To reach this hydroelectric station, take bus No 9 from the roundabout north of the Xiguan Hotel.

Wen Temple
(*wén miào*)
Just east of the Jiangcheng Hotel is the Wen Temple, Jilin's largest. It's also known as the Confucius Temple (*kǒng miào*). From the main railway station take bus No 13.

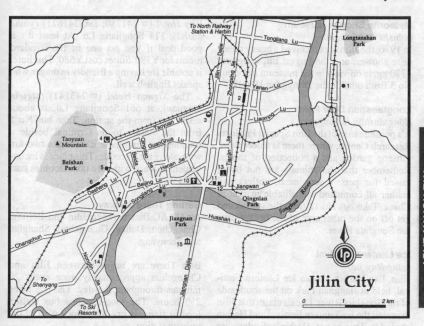

JILIN 吉林

1 Longtanshan Deer Farm
  龙潭山鹿场
2 Main Railway Station
  吉林火车站
3 Long-Distance Bus Station
  岔路乡
4 Mosque
  清真寺
5 Park Entrance
  正门

6 Beishan Railway Station
  北山火车站
7 PSB
  公安局外事科
8 Milky Way Hotel & Bank of China
  银河大厦，中国银行
9 City Hall
  市政府
10 Catholic Church
  天主教堂

11 Dongguan Hotel & CYTS
  东关宾馆，中国青旅行社
12 Jiangcheng Hotel
  江城宾馆
13 Wen Temple
  文庙
14 Xiguan Hotel & CITS
  西关宾馆，国际旅行社
15 Meteorite Shower Museum
  陨石雨博物馆

Beishan Park
(běishān gōngyuán)

If you need a little exercise, go to Beishan Park, a hilly area on the west side of town with temples, pavilions, forests and footpaths. The scenery is mellow enough and is certainly preferable to Jilin's industrial smokestacks. On the west side of the park is **Taoyuan Mountain**, which is worth a short hike.

Bus No 7 from the railway station terminates right in front of the park entrance. If you're on a local train, the Beishan Railway Station is near the park.

Meteorite Shower Museum
(yǔnshí yǔ bówùguǎn)
In 1976, the Jilin area received a heavy meteorite shower, and the largest bit, weighing 1770 kg, is on view in the museum (take bus No 3 from outside the Dongguan Hotel).

Longtanshan Deer Farm
(lóngtánshān lùchǎng)
It's possible to visit the Jilin Special Products Research Centre, where there is a deer farm, ginseng garden and a collection of sables. Remember that the animals are not being raised for pets – deer meat, antlers and leather all command a profitable market in China. Take bus No 12 from the station and get off on the other side of the bridge over the Songhua River.

Ice Lantern Festival
(bīngdēng jié)
Jilin, like Harbin, has an Ice Lantern Festival, held at Jiangnan Park on the south side of the Songhua River. Locals claim that Jilin invented the Ice Lantern Festival and Harbin copied it. True or not, Harbin's displays are now considered superior to those of Jilin, but competition between the two cities should produce better ice sculptures.

Places to Stay
Accommodation is overpriced in Jilin, but it's likely to be most difficult to find a place to stay in January, the peak season for viewing the ice-rimmed trees.

The *Dongguan Hotel* (☎ 454272; fax 445208) *(dōngguān bīnguǎn)*, 2 Jiangwan Lu, is the cheapest but it's hardly a bargain. Threadbare rooms for foreigners cost Y400, but Chinese pay less than a third this price. On the other hand, the restaurant on the 2nd floor offers good food at reasonable prices. The hotel is about three km from the station – take trolley-bus No 10 or a taxi.

Adjacent to the Dongguan Hotel is the upmarket *Jiangcheng Hotel* (☎ 457721; fax 458973) *(jiāngchéng bīnguǎn)*. Living conditions are cosy here, but the Y500 price for a double may cause you to hesitate.

Perhaps the best deal in town is the *Milky Way Hotel* (☎ 241780; fax 241621) *(yínhé dàshà)*, 175 Songjiang Lu. At least it's a good deal if you get one of the standard rooms for Y380. Suites cost Y580. This hotel is notable for having a friendly manager who speaks English well.

The *Xiguan Hotel* (☎ 243141) *(xīguān bīnguǎn)*, at 661 Songjiang Lu, is about seven km from the station. Take bus No 1 from the station to its terminal beside a roundabout; from there it's about a two-km walk along the riverside. This place is inconvenient to reach without a taxi. Doubles start at Y450.

Getting There & Away
Air CAAC flies between Jilin and Beijing, Changchun, Dalian, Guangzhou, Shanghai and Shenyang.

Bus There are buses between Jilin and Changchun approximately once every 20 minutes throughout the day. The trip takes 2½ hours. The long-distance bus station *(chà lù xiāng)* is one long block west of the railway station.

Train There is a direct train service between Jilin and Changchun about once every two hours in each direction. There are also direct trains to Harbin (four hours), Yanji, Shenyang and Dalian.

Getting Around
Although taxis congregate around the railway station and seem to be plentiful on the streets, they are often occupied – allow plenty of time to get where you want to go. Rates are a flat Y20 anywhere within the city.

AROUND JILIN
Songhuahu Qingshan Ski Resort
(sōnghuā hú qīngshān huáxuě cháng)
This resort is at 935 metres elevation, 16 km south-east of Jilin and just east of Fengman. It boasts a 1700-metre cableway, lounge, drying rooms, hotel and restaurant. Any hotel in Jilin can provide further details about snow conditions, lift operation, transport and hire of equipment. During the

summer weekends and holidays, the lake (*sōnghuā hú*) is a popular hang-out for locals.

Beidahu Ski Resort

(*běidàhú huáxuě cháng*)

This new ski area, 20 km from Jilin, is perhaps the best place in China to practice the art of sliding downhill.

Further afield at **Tonghua**, there is a ski field where championships have been held.

TIANCHI

(*tiānchí*)

Tianchi (Lake of Heaven) is in the Changbaishan (Ever-White Mountains) Nature Reserve. The reserve is China's largest, covering 210,000 hectares of dense virgin forest. The forest is divided into a semi-protected area where limited lumbering and hunting are permitted, and a protected area where neither is allowed.

Because of elevation changes, there is wide variation in animal and plant life. From 700 to 1000 metres above sea level there are mixed coniferous and broad-leaf trees (including white birch and Korean pines); from 1000 to 1800 metres, there are cold-resistant coniferous trees such as dragon spruce and fir; from 1800 to 2000 metres is another forest belt; above 2000 metres it's alpine tundra, treeless and windy. For the budding natural scientist there's plenty to investigate. Some 300 medicinal plants grow within the reserve (including winter daphne, Asia bell and wild ginseng); and some very shy animal species make their home in the mountain range (the rarer ones being the protected cranes, deer and Manchurian tiger).

The reserve is a recent creation, first designated in 1960. During the Cultural Revolution all forestry and conservation work was suspended, and technical and scientific personnel were dispersed to menial jobs. Locals had a free-for-all season on the plant and animal life during this period.

Although Changbaishan was only opened to foreigners in 1982, it has been on the Chinese tour map for some time, with something like 40,000 visitors from the north-eastern provinces arriving each year between July and September. It's become particularly popular with South Koreans since 1992, when diplomatic relations with China were established.

Tianchi, at an elevation of 2194 metres, is the prime scenic spot. It's a volcanic crater-lake, five km from north to south, 3½ km from east to west, and 13 km in circumference. It's surrounded by jagged rock outcrops and peaks; three rivers run off the lake, with a rumbling 68-metre waterfall the source of the Songhua and Tumen rivers.

Between 11 am and noon the tour buses roll up to disgorge day-trippers who pose heroically for photos in front of the waterfall, stampede up the mountain, take a lakeside breather and then rush down again between 1 and 2 pm. The beauty of the place is badly marred by picnic detritus, smashed glass and discarded film wrappers.

Apart from midday, when the day-trippers take over, this is a peaceful place to stay for a couple of days and hike around. However, hiking at the lake itself is limited by the sharp peaks and their rock-strewn debris, and by the fact that the lake overlaps the Chinese-North Korean border – there's no tourist build-up yet on the Korean side. Cloud cover starts at 1000 metres and can be prevalent. The highest peak in the Changbaishan range is 2700 metres.

If you're planning to hike off the beaten tourist trail, it's advisable to bring dried food, sunscreen lotion, frog-oil tonic and other medical supplies, plus good hiking gear. High altitude weather is very fickle no matter how warm and sunny it is in the morning – sudden high winds, rain, hail and dramatic drops in temperature are entirely possible by afternoon. In other words, hope for the best but be prepared for the worst.

The hot-spring bathhouse, where water from lake and underground sources is mixed, is close to the hotels. You can take a communal dip or rent a private cubicle. If you cross the nearby river via either the tree trunk or the bridge lower down, there's a forest path which leads to the dark, brooding Lesser Tianchi Lake.

THE NORTH-EAST

Tianchi Legends

Enchanting scenery like that of Tianchi would not be complete in the Chinese world without a legend or mystery of some sort. Of the many myths, the most intriguing is the origin of the Manchu race. Three heavenly nymphs descended to the lake in search of earthly pleasure. They stripped off for a dip in the lake; along came a magic magpie which deposited a red berry on the dress of one of the maidens. When she picked it up to smell it, the berry flew through her lips into her stomach. The nymph became pregnant and gave birth to a handsome boy with an instant gift of the gab. He went on to foster the Manchus and their dynasty.

Dragons, and other things that go bump in the night, were believed to have sprung from the lake. In fact, they're still believed to do so. There have been intermittent sightings of unidentified swimming objects – China's own Loch Ness beasties or aquatic yetis or what have you. Tianchi is the deepest alpine lake in China at a depth estimated at between 200 and 350 metres. Since it is frozen over in winter and temperatures are well below zero, it would take a pretty hardy monster to make it home (even plankton can't). Sightings from the Chinese and North Korean sides point to a black bear, fond of swimming, and oblivious to the paperwork necessary for crossing these tight borders. On a more profound note, Chinese couples throw coins into the lake, pledging that their love will remain as deep as Tianchi, and as long-lived. ■

Places to Stay

The Changbaishan area suffers a severe accommodation shortage during the summer months when South Korean tourists descend on the place in droves. To make things worse, all the cheap places are off limits to foreigners.

Big noses are herded into one of five official tourist hotels, all charging a standard Y220. At present, your options include the *Birch Hotel (yuèhuá lóu)*, the *Nature Reserve Bureau Hotel (bǎohù jú bīnguǎn)*, *Meilinsong Guesthouse (měilínsōng bīnguǎn)*, *Yalin Hotel (yàlín bīnguǎn)* and the *Tianchi Hotel (tiānchí fàndiàn)*. The Tianchi Hotel is the largest, but the Meilinsong Hotel is the only one open during the off season.

If you have a sleeping bag, camping is a possibility, though technically against the rules. Be prepared for possible thunderstorms and try to find a place far from curious spectators and those stern-faced figures collectively known as 'the authorities'.

In Changbaishan, none of the cheap guesthouses would take me in and the staff were most unhelpful. I had my own tent and camped by Lesser Tianchi Lake together with a Danish guy I met on the bus from Baihe. Camping is not permitted but no officials bothered us. There were many curious Chinese tour-

ists of course. The place was quite badly littered and the rusty pedal-boats in the lake disturbed the silence with their squeaking.

Getting There & Away

The *only* season when there's public transport access (when the road from Baihe to Changbaishan isn't iced over) is from late June to September. A winter trip is not impossible, though you might need to rent a snowmobile, or at least a jeep with tyre chains. Chinese hikers come to see the autumn colours – so the peak season with a high local turnover is from mid-July to mid-August.

There are two transit points to Changbaishan: Antu and Baihe. Starting from Changchun, the route via Antu is faster and more common. Before you go, get a weather forecast from someone in Jilin, Changchun or Shenyang (during July and August there will be no problem). Allow about five days for the round trip from, say, Shenyang. Tour buses go up the mountain in July and August, but at other times you may have trouble finding a bus from Baihe. The only other local transport is logging trucks and official jeeps – the latter are expensive to rent, and the drivers of the former are very reluctant to give rides.

Via Antu There are trains to Antu from Changchun – the trip takes 10 hours. The evening train departs from Changchun at 6.40 pm. There are sleepers available on this train, but you might have to book them all the way to Yanji. If you arrive in Antu at night you can sleep in the station waiting room. There is also a small hotel in Antu.

Buses for Baihe depart from 7.20 to 10.30 am. You can also get buses to Baihe from Yanji (further down the railway line) but then you'll have to backtrack. From Antu it takes five hours to travel the 125 km. Unless you arrive early in Baihe, you may find yourself waiting till the next morning for transport to Changbaishan, a further 40 km.

Special tourist buses run from Antu to the Changbaishan Hot Springs area in July and August – some of these have a three-day package trip, but you'll be with a mob of noisy, camera-clicking tourists. There are some trains from Shenyang to Antu.

Via Baihe Baihe is the end of the line as far as trains go – a scrap yard for locos. To get to Baihe from Jilin, Changchun or Shenyang, you must take a train or bus to Tonghua and then change to a train for Baihe. The morning train leaves Shenyang at 6.30 am for Tonghua. From Dandong, there are buses to Tonghua departing at 6.30 am.

The two daily trains between Tonghua and Baihe have two steam locos (one pushing, the other pulling); there are no sleepers, only carriages with soft seats (green velvet) and hard wooden benches (ouch!). The 500-series trains take 10 hours of chugga-lugging to cover the 277 km between Tonghua and Baihe. If you're overnighting, it's worth paying extra for soft seat in lieu of a sleeper. The soft-seat waiting room at Tonghua Railway Station is the lap of luxury. Look for the sign saying 'soft-seat waiting room' beside the packed hard-seat waiting room and ring the red bell.

The early morning train arrives in Baihe at 5.20 am and is met by an excursion bus (*yóulǎn chē*), which takes you about three km into the town with its grubby shacks for breakfast before a change of buses for the two-hour trip to the mountain. Buses usually return from the mountain at 2 pm. There are several cheap places to stay in town, all within a few minutes of the bus station.

Getting Around

The authorities have been constructing roads and bridges in the Tianchi area to improve access for tourism and for forestry and meteorological stations. Buses normally continue past the hotels and the hot-spring bathhouse before dropping passengers off close to the waterfall. From here to the lake is about an hour's hike.

An alternative route for getting from the hotels to Tianchi is to backtrack north for about one km to the crossroads and take the road right (east). It winds on higher and higher, finally turning south, bringing you up onto the ridge of the east side of the valley. The road ends by the meteorological station where you have a splendid view of the lake. From here you head west towards a triangular peak – beyond that small peak it's possible to scramble down to the lake and ford the stream above the waterfall, but take care! Now you are at the end of the main track and can join the crowd back to the hot springs. This walk can be easily completed in one day, but it's always best to get an early start.

AROUND TIANCHI

The Changbaishan region presents you with some possibilities for shaking off the cities and traipsing through the wilderness, and gives you some good reasons for doing so: virgin forest and babbling brooks – and some rough travel and rough trails, as well as rough toilets if you can find one.

The whole zone is the Yanbian (Chaoxian) Korean Autonomous Prefecture. The local people of Korean descent are often indistinguishable in dress from their Chinese counterparts. If you visit this area around mid-August, you can join in the 'Old People Festival'. The Koreans are a fairly lively lot, who enjoy eating spiced cold noodles and dog meat, and singing and dancing and offering hospitality. They can also drink you under the table. Yanbian has the greatest concentration of Korean and Korean-Han groups in China, mostly inhabiting the border areas north and north-east of Baihe, extending up to Yanji.

Transport by rail is safer compared with the winding roads. Apart from public buses, the only other means of getting around is by jeep or logging truck. Off the main track, the trains are puffing black dragons, possibly of Japanese vintage. The fittings are old and the trains have no sleepers.

Food has improved in recent years, and in Korean areas you can sample delicious cold noodles topped with a pile of searing hot spices.

HUNCHUN
(húnchūn)

An isolated backwater if there ever was one, Hunchun, just east of the North Korean border, may yet have its day in the sun. There has been all sorts of talk about a 'free trade zone' encompassing this part of China plus Vladivostok in Siberia and part of North Korea. While the North Korean border remains as sealed as ever, a rail link opened to Siberia in 1993. The train connects the Siberian town of Khasan to Hunchun. Foreigners can indeed make this crossing, but obtaining the necessary tourist visa for Russia is problematic for most Western nationalities.

Heilongjiang 黑龙江

Heilongjiang (Black Dragon River) is China's northernmost province and is known for its subarctic climate. Locals spend January sensibly huddled round their coal-burning stoves drinking vodka – and so would you if it was -30°C outside with howling Siberian gales. Activity slows to a crunch in this snowflake-spitting weather, while the animals pass the season over totally and sensibly hibernating.

This is not to say that you should avoid winter in Heilongjiang, but merely to suggest that it would be a damn good idea! If, however, you can deal with the cold, January and February offers the added attractions of winter sports and a well-known ice festival. You'll be able to get around more freely from May to September. Mohe, in northern Heilongjiang, holds the record for the coldest temperature recorded in China, a mere -52.3°C.

HARBIN
(hā'ěrbīn)

As the provincial capital, Harbin is the educational, cultural and political centre of Heilongjiang. The city now has a population of 2½ million, but at one time it used to be a quiet fishing village on the Songhua River; the name in Manchu means place for drying nets.

In 1896 the Russians negotiated a contract for building a railway line through Harbin to Vladivostok (and Dalian). The Russian imprint on the town remained in one way or another until the end of WW II; by 1904 the 'rail concession' was in place, and with it came other Russian demands on Manchuria. These were stalled by the Russo-Japanese War (1904-05), and with the Russian defeat the Japanese gained control of the railway. In 1917 large numbers of White Russian refugees flocked to Harbin, fleeing the Bolsheviks; in 1932 the Japanese occupied the city; and in 1945 the Soviet Army wrested it back for a year and held it until 1946, when

Population: 36 million
Capital: Harbin
Highlights:
- If you can survive temperatures of -40°C, come in January to witness the amazing Ice Lantern Festival in Harbin
- Yabuli, site of the 1996 Asian Winter Games, is all set to become China's leading ski resort
- Jingbo Lake, an alpine lake that shines like a mirror, from which it takes its name

the Kuomintang troops were finally installed, as agreed by Chiang Kaishek and Stalin.

Harbin has not been totally peaceful since the end of WW II – during the Cultural Revolution, rival factions took to the air to drop bombs on one another.

As the largest former Russian settlement outside the former USSR, Harbin has been acutely aware of Soviet colonial eyes, which explains the large-scale air-raid tunnelling in the city. With the collapse of the USSR in 1991, the tunnels have not been maintained and are likely to be used as warehouses or wine cellars.

Harbin today is largely an industrial city, but thawing relations with Russia have caused a mini-boom in cross-border tourism.

THE NORTH-EAST

You are likely to see Russian faces on the streets of Harbin these days. Their chief motive for visiting the PRC is not tourism, but 'business', otherwise known as smuggling. From Russia they bring an odd selection of goods: deer antlers, live puppies (heavily drugged and stuffed into their luggage), dirty pictures and occasional nasty things like weapons. From China, they buy all manner of consumer goods: clothing, coffee, cosmetics and other items which Russia no longer seems capable of producing. Some of the smugglers supplement their incomes by ripping off other smugglers – the

PSB doesn't seem to care what the Russians do to each other as long as Chinese nationals are not involved.

As for non-Russian tourists, winter is the peak season when mostly Overseas Chinese and Japanese tour groups flock to see the Ice Lantern Festival. Hong Kongers and Taiwanese are particularly drawn to Harbin because of the opportunity to see snow and ice – many come unprepared for the -40°C weather, and are reportedly so blown away by the cold that they never set foot north of the Tropic of Cancer again.

The Daoli District, in the section towards

the banks of the Songhua River, also has the best speciality shops and some market activity, and is worth exploring on foot. Another shopping and market area is to be found north-east of the International Hotel, a short walk away at Dazhi Dajie.

Information

Travel Agencies CITS (☎ 262-2655) is in a separate building in the grounds of the Swan Hotel, at 73 Zhongshan Lu on the No 3 bus route.

The China Harbin Overseas Tourist Corporation (☎ 468-7875; fax 461-4259) is on the 2nd floor of the charming Modern Hotel at 129 Zhongyang Dajie.

Travel agencies can arrange specific tours for diverse tastes, including elderly health build-up, cycling, Chinese law, steam locos, hunting, welding technology and honey production. There are also tours to the Heilong River area (see the Heilong River Borderlands section later in this chapter for details).

Money The Bank of China is on Hongjun Jie near the International Hotel. Although you can exchange foreign currency here, you *cannot* cash travellers' cheques! Fortunately, this can be accomplished just around the corner at a private money-changing agency called *Xinyong Ka* (no English sign).

Daoliqu
(dàolǐqū)

Put wandering around the market areas and the streets high on your list. There's a very different kind of architectural presence in Harbin – Russian spires, cupolas, scalloped turreting and cobblestone streets. The area known as Daoliqu (Daoli District), near Zhongyang Dajie, is especially interesting to investigate.

Harbin has many Orthodox churches *(dōngzhèng jiàotáng)*, but most were ransacked during the Cultural Revolution and have since been boarded up or converted for other uses. A few stray onion-domes punctuate the skyline.

Children's Railway
(értóng gōngyuán)

This railway in the Children's Park was built in 1956. It has two km of track plied by a miniature diesel pulling seven cars with seating for 190; the round trip (Beijing-Moscow) takes 20 minutes. The crew and administrators are kids under the age of 13.

Stalin Park
(sīdàlín gōngyuán)

Down by the river, this is a tacky strip stacked with statues; it's the main perambulating zone, with recreation clubs for the locals. A 42-km embankment was constructed along the edge to curb the unruly Songhua River, hence the surreal-looking Flood Control Monument *(fánghóng jìniàn tǎ)*, which was built in 1958. The sandy banks of the Songhua take on something of a beach atmosphere in summer, with boating, ice-cream stands and photo booths. It's possible to travel on tour boats arranged through CITS but you might like to investigate local docks for a quick sortie down the Songhua.

During winter the river becomes a road of ice (when it's one-metre thick it can support a truck) and the Stalin Park/Sun Island area is the venue for hockey, skating, ice-sailing, sledding and sleighing; equipment can be hired.

Sun Island
(tàiyángdǎo gōngyuán)

Opposite Stalin Park and reached by a ferry hop is Sun Island, a sanatorium-recreational zone still under construction. The island covers 3800 hectares and has a number of artificial features – a lake, hunting range, parks, gardens, forested areas – all being developed to turn this into Harbin's biggest tourist attraction. In summer there's swimming and picnics; in winter it's skating and other sports. There are a number of restaurants and other facilities on Sun Island.

Japanese Germ Warfare Experimental Base – 731 Division
(rìběn xìjūn shíyàn jīdì – 731 yībùduì)

If you haven't visited concentration camps

THE NORTH-EAST

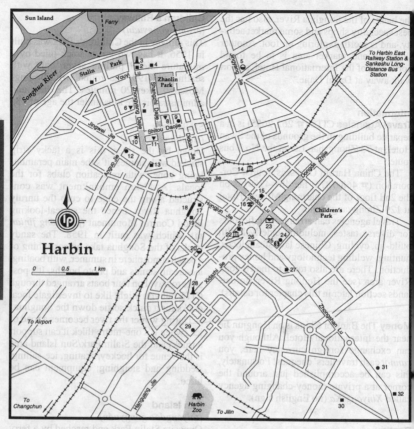

Harbin

such as Belsen or Auschwitz, a similar lesson in the horrors of extermination can be learnt at this base.

In 1939 the Japanese army set up a top-secret, germ-warfare research centre here. Japanese medical experts experimented on Chinese, Soviet, Korean, British and other prisoners. Over 4000 were exterminated in bestial fashion: some were frozen or infected with bubonic plague, others were injected with syphilis and many were roasted alive in furnaces.

When the Soviets took back Harbin in 1945, the Japanese hid all trace of the base.

The secret would probably have remained buried forever, but a tenacious Japanese journalist dragged out the truth in the 1980s. Japan's medical profession was rocked by the news that some of its leading members had a criminal past which had hitherto escaped detection. Another disturbing angle to the story was the claim that the Americans had granted freedom to the perpetrators of these crimes in return for their research data.

To get to the base, take bus No 338 from the main railway station to the terminal, which is close to Pingfang District (about 10 km).

HARBIN 哈尔滨

PLACES TO STAY

1 Friendship Palace Hotel
友谊宫宾馆
2 Songhuajiang Gloria Inn
松花江凯莱酒店
4 Nationality Hotel
民族宾馆
7 Modern Hotel
马迭尔宾馆
13 Holiday Inn
万达假日酒店
15 Power Hotel
怕佛尔饭店
17 Beiyuan Hotel
北苑饭店
19 Tianzhu Hotel
天竹宾馆
21 Overseas Chinese Hotel
华侨饭店
26 International Hotel &
Beifang Hotel
国际饭店，
北方大厦
27 Milky Way Hotel
银河宾馆

30 Flamingo Hotel
双鹤宾馆
32 Swan Hotel & CITS
天鹅饭店，
中国国际旅行社

PLACES TO EAT

6 Huamei Western
Restaurant
华梅西餐厅
8 Beilaishun Restaurant
北来顺饭店
11 Futailou Restaurant
福泰楼饭店

OTHER

3 Flood Control Monument
防洪纪念塔
5 Chengde Square Long-
Distance Bus Station
承德广场长途汽车站
9 Foreign Languages
Bookstore
外文书店
10 PSB
公安局外事科

12 Oriental City
东方娱乐城
14 Martyrs' Museum
东北烈士馆
16 Telephone Office
电信局
18 Main Railway Station
哈尔滨火车站
20 Main Long-Distance
Bus Station (Song-
huajiang Jie)
长途汽车站 (松花江街)
22 Provincial Museum
省博物馆
23 Post Office
邮局
24 Xin Yong Ka
(Moneychanger)
信用卡
25 Bank of China
中国银行
28 Mao Statue
毛主席像
29 Harbin Institute of
Technology
哈尔滨工业大学
31 CAAC
中国民航

THE NORTH-EAST

Steam Locomotives

(zhēngqì jīchē)

For this, you'll need to organise a tour through CITS and be prepared to pay the tariff. Harbin is the centre of northern China's working network of steam locomotives, even though they're being phased out. There is a steam locomotive depot and marshalling yard in Harbin, but ask CITS about tours to areas employing narrow-gauge steam locomotives (Jiamusi, Yichun etc).

Other Attractions

The **Provincial Museum** *(shěng bówùguǎn)* is opposite the International Hotel and has some dull historical and natural history sections; the **Industrial Exhibition Hall** is dead boring; and the **zoo** *(dòngwùyuán)* is lukewarm but does have some Manchurian tigers and red-crowned cranes. The **Martyrs' Museum** *(dōngběi lièshì guǎn)* in the centre

of town has relics from the anti-Japanese campaign.

Ice Lantern Festival

(bīngdēng jié)

If you don't mind the cold, then try not to miss Harbin's main drawcard, the Ice Lantern Festival *(bīngdēng jié)* in Zhaolin Park. Officially, it's held from 5 January to late February, though in reality it may start a week earlier and spill into March.

Fanciful sculptures are made in the shapes of animals, plants, buildings or motifs taken from legends. Some of the larger sculptures have included a crystalline ice bridge and an ice elephant that children could mount from the tail in order to slide down the trunk. At night the sculptures are illuminated from the inside with coloured lights, turning the place into a temporary fantasy-land.

There are ice festivals held in other

Chinese cities, but Harbin's is considered the best.

Music Festival

In warmer times, there's the Harbin Music Festival, a 12-day event that takes place in July (it was suspended during the Cultural Revolution).

Places to Stay

During Harbin's Ice Lantern Festival (January and February) hotel prices are at least 20% higher than what is listed here and rooms of any sort can be difficult to find.

As you exit the main railway station, just off to your right is the 19-storey *Tianzhu Hotel* (☎ 343-2725) *(tiānzhú bīnguǎn)*. This is an excellent place to stay, but there are scary rumours of planned renovation and price hikes. At present, the price range for doubles with attached bath is Y150 to Y350.

The *Beiyuan Hotel* (☎ 340-128, 340-263 *(běiyuàn fàndiàn)* directly faces the railway station. This enormous place dishes up doubles for Y180. Unfortunately, it's often filled to the rooftop with Russians visiting Harbin 'on business'. There have been reports of thefts from rooms – the most likely suspects are some of the guests rather than the Chinese staff. If you stay here, keep your valuables with you or store them in the left luggage rooms at the railway station.

The *Overseas Chinese Hotel* (☎ 364-1341; fax 362-3429) *(huáqiáo fàndiàn)* is at 52 Hongjun Jie, within walking distance of the main railway station. This place often packs out with Hong Kongers and Taiwanese in pursuit of snow and business opportunities. Doubles cost Y310 to Y410.

The *International Hotel* (☎ 364-1441; fax 362-5651) *(guójì fàndiàn)*, 124 Xidazhi Jie is just off Hongjun Jie less than one km from

---

Tigers

China has three subspecies of tiger: the Bengal, the South China and the North-Eastern, or Manchurian. All told there are no more than 400 tigers left in China.

The South China subspecies is the most endangered and numbers only about 50 in the wild and about 30 in zoos both in China and abroad. (Even when India launched its Project Tiger in 1973 there were 1800 Royal Bengal tigers left in its territory – a number that was considered perilously low.) Unlike the Bengal and Manchurian tigers, which are found in several countries, the South China tiger is peculiar to China. Its plight began in the 1950s, with indiscriminate hunting and deforestation. At that time tigers were still fairly numerous in many southern provinces, especially in Hunan, Fujian, Guizhou and Jiangxi. Throughout the '50s and early '60s there were 'anti-pest' campaigns and many areas had their entire tiger populations wiped out. Today the subspecies exists only in the mountainous regions of south-west and south-east Hunan, and in northern Guangdong.

The Manchurian tiger seems doomed since it now numbers only 30 in the wilds of Jilin and Heilongjiang; zoos account for about 100 more and some are still found in Russia and North Korea.

The exact number of Bengal tigers in China is not known; they live in the Xishuangbanna Autonomous Region and southern Yunnan near Myanmar (Burma) and Laos, in a few counties in western Yunnan bordering Myanmar, and in the subtropical mountainous region of south-eastern Tibet and neighbouring Assam. ■

the railway station. Doubles are Y580 but breakfast is thrown in free as a consolation. It's overpriced, but this is glamorous Harbin.

A little further down Zhongshan Lu is the *Milky Way Hotel (yínhé bīnguǎn)*, a three-star place which was closed for renovation at the time of writing.

The *Modern Hotel* (☎ 415-846; fax 414-997) *(mǎdié'ěr bīnguǎn)* is not modern at all – it's an old place with plenty of character. It's been fully renovated and is now a three-star hotel charging a cool Y500 for a double. The hotel is at 129 Zhongyang Dajie in Daoli District, Harbin's most colourful neighbourhood.

The *Friendship Palace Hotel* (☎ 416-146) *(yǒuyí gōng bīnguǎn)* is a classy place at 57 Youyi Lu, next to the Songhua River. Doubles start at Y420.

Close by is the three-star *Songhuajiang Gloria Inn* (☎ 463-8855; fax 463-8533) *(sōnghuájiāng kǎilái jiǔdiàn)* at 257 Zhongyang Dajie. The 304 rooms are said to be the best in Harbin. Prices begin at Y520.

Just next door is the *Nationality Hotel* (☎ 467-4668; fax 467-4058) *(mínzú bīnguǎn)*, 111 Youyi Lu, with 279 rooms. Prices are from Y480.

Also in the three-star category is the *Power Hotel* (☎ 365-3378; fax 362-8609) *(pàfóěr fàndiàn)* at 79 Youzheng Jie, Nangang District. Room rates begin at Y470.

The *Swan Hotel* (☎ 262-0201; fax 262-4895) *(tiāné fàndiàn)*, 73 Zhongshan Lu, is inconveniently far from the centre. Doubles start from Y500. For whatever it's worth, CITS is installed in the same compound and CAAC is nearby. Minibus No 103 running down Zhongshan Lu can take you to the hotel for Y2.

The *Flamingo Hotel* (☎ 263-6698; fax 265-7028) *(shuānghè bīnguǎn)* is also far from anything in the southern part of town at 118 Minsheng Lu. The long commute doesn't bring down the room prices, which start at Y480.

Holiday Inn (wàndá jiàrì jivdiàn) was constructing Harbin's first four-star hotel at the time of writing, and it should be open for business by the time you read this. The hotel is centrally located on Jingwei Jie in the Daoli District.

Places to Eat

A practice almost unique to Harbin is that red lanterns hang above the door outside every restaurant. It's a rating system – the more lanterns, the higher the standard and price.

Harbin has long been famous for expensive culinary exotica, such as grilled bear paws and Siberian tiger testicles. Fortunately for the animals Beijing has suddenly taken an interest in cracking down on the trade in endangered species.

There are a couple of fancy places around Stalin Park. On the edge of Zhaolin Park at 113 Shangzhi Dajie, Daoli District, is the *Beilaishun Restaurant* (☎ 461-9027) *(běiláishùn fàndiàn)*, which serves Muslim beef and mutton dishes upstairs and also hotpot in winter.

The *Futailou Restaurant* (☎ 461-7598) *(fútàilóu fàndiàn)* at 19 Xi Shisandao Jie serves Beijing roast duck and other dishes, but you need to order two days in advance for regional specialities.

If you visit Sun Island, you can get a good meal at the *Sun Island Restaurant (tàiyángdǎo cāntīng)*.

The best (and priciest) lunchroom in town is at the *Huamei Western Restaurant (huáméi xī cāntīng)*, just opposite the Modern Hotel on Zhongyang Dajie.

Entertainment

As elsewhere in China, the emphasis is on drunken karaoke sing-along sessions. One of the better places to pursue this sport is at *Oriental City (dōngfāng yúlè chéng)*, which also boasts a dance hall and sauna. Oriental City is on the corner of Jingwei Jie and Anguo Jie.

Things to Buy

If you're heading into the sub-Siberian wilds, Harbin is the northernmost place in China where you'll be able to stock up on English-language books. The selection is limited, but worth looking into is the Foreign

Languages Bookstore at the corner of Shitou Daojie and Diduan Jie in the Daoli District.

Harbin is famous for furs (mink etc), deer antlers and other products which are sure to infuriate proponents of animal rights. If you get upset by these things, give the department stores a miss. You might, however, want to take a look at the Siberian ginseng, though prices aren't really cheap because the locals recognise the export value.

Getting There & Away

Air CAAC offers three direct flights weekly between Harbin and Hong Kong.

CAAC and Aeroflot both offer international flights to Khabarovsk in Siberia. From Khabarovsk it is supposed to be possible to get connecting flights to Japan and South Korea, but be aware that Aeroflot is notoriously unreliable. Some reports claim that checked luggage on this airline has a tendency to disappear.

Domestic flights from Harbin are:

Beijing, Changsha, Chaoyang, Chengdu, Chongqing, Dalian, Fuzhou, Guangzhou, Haikou, Hangzhou, Heihe, Ji'nan, Jiamusi, Kunming, Nanjing, Ningbo, Qingdao, Shanghai, Shantou, Shenyang, Shenzhen, Ürümqi, Wenzhou, Wuhan, Xiamen, Xi'an, Yanji, Yantai and Zhengzhou.

CAAC (☎ 262-2337) has its office at 87 Zhongshan Lu, close to the Swan Hotel, but there is a small branch office next to the International Hotel. Aeroflot (☎ 264-1441) has an office in the International Hotel, although it seems to be closed when it's supposed to be open.

Bus The main long-distance bus station is on Songhuajiang Jie, not far from the railway station. There is also another long-distance bus station near Sankeshu Railway Station, which takes care of a large proportion of bus departures. Yet another place to get long-distance buses is Chengde Square.

Train There are frequent departures to Beijing, Shanghai and points in between. Harbin to Changchun takes four hours; to

Shenyang, nine hours; and to Beijing, 18 hours. Rail connections to Qiqihar, Mudanjiang and Jiamusi are regular but slow.

For travellers on the Trans-Siberian Railway, Harbin is a possible starting or finishing point.

Getting Around

To/From the Airport Harbin's airport is 46 km from town and the journey takes at least one hour, half of which is spent in the traffic-clogged streets near the city centre.

Buses depart for the airport from the CAAC office and cost Y15; buy tickets on the bus, not inside the office. Buses depart about 2½ hours before scheduled flight departure times.

Taxi drivers congregate around the CAAC office and are as persistent as flies – they practically try to pull you off the bus and into their taxis. Don't believe some of the low fares they may quote you (Y30, for example) – the fare suddenly gets jacked up to reality (Y150) halfway to the airport, and if you don't agree to the change you get dumped out in the middle of nowhere. If you want to go by taxi, it's better to arrange it at the railway station (bargaining is mandatory). However, the sole advantage of booking a taxi at the CAAC office is that you could conceivably share it with some other people heading to the airport.

If you are taking the 7.30 am flight to Beijing, you need to be at the CAAC office at 5 am to catch the bus. Since local buses and taxis don't run at 4.30 am, about the only way you can manage this is to stay at the nearby Swan Hotel, which is within walking distance of the CAAC office. Unfortunately, the Swan Hotel is not cheap.

Bus There are over 20 bus routes in Harbin; buses start running at 5 am and finish at 10 pm (9.30 pm in winter). The most useful one is likely to be No 103; there is both a minibus and a big bus on this route. The minibus costs Y2 and is far superior to the sardine-tin large buses. Bus No 1 or trolley-bus No 3 will take you from the hotel area to Stalin Park.

Boat CITS has a boat tour along the Songhua River which lasts 2½ hours, but it's definitely a summer-only event.

AROUND HARBIN
Ski Resorts
(huáxuě cháng)

Skiers can head for the Qingyun ski field near the city of Shangzhi, some 100 km or so south-east of Harbin. Equipment rentals are available but finding ski boots for big Western feet can be problematic. Make local inquiries to see if the lifts are operating. Shangzhi can be reached by train or bus from Harbin, and the journey takes around six hours. You can stay at the guesthouse or one of the attractive stone cottages.

North of Shangzhi, and approachable by bus, is the Yanzhou County ski field. There's snow for a long time – the main season is from late November to early April.

The Yu Quan hunting grounds, 65 km from Harbin, also have skiing, though there is always the chance you might get blown away by an enthusiastic hunter who mistakes you for a deer.

Yabuli is about 200 km (four hours by train) east of Harbin and will be the site of the 1996 Asian Winter Games. Dagoukui Mountain, the actual ski area, is a 25 km ride by jeep from the main town of Yabuli. Accommodation, meals and ski rental are available at a lodge near the ski area. A package including meals, lodging, ski rental and lift passes costs Y250 to Y400 per day.

Another possibility is cross-country skiing, which probably makes more sense given the lack of mountains in Heilongjiang. The Chinese themselves are not much into this, so you will almost certainly need to bring your own equipment from abroad.

MUDANJIANG
(mǔdānjiāng)

A nondescript city of over one million people, Mudanjiang's only interest to travellers is its function as a staging post for visits to nearby Jingbo Lake (see next section).

Places to Stay

The *Beishan Hotel* (☎ 25734) *(běishān bīnguǎn)* is on Xinhua Lu (opposite the park) about one km north of the railway station. CITS is installed here.

The other place accepting foreigners is the *Mudanjiang Hotel* (☎ 25678) *(mǔdānjiāng bīnguǎn)* on Guanghua Jie, one km east of the railway station.

Getting There & Away

There are flights from Mudanjiang to Beijing, Dalian, Guangzhou, Shanghai, Shenyang and Yantai. The usual approach by rail to Mudanjiang is from Harbin.

JINGBO LAKE
(jìngbó hú)

The name means mirror lake, and it's probably the most impressive sight in Heilongjiang. The lake covers an area of 90 sq km; it's 45 km long from north to south, with a minimum width of 600 metres and a maximum of six km, and is dotted with islets. The nature reserve encompasses a strip of forest, hills, streams, pools and cliffs around the lake and there is a lava cave in the area. The main pastime is fishing (the season is from June to August); tackle and boats can be hired (prices negotiable). Different varieties of carp (silver, black, red-tailed, crucian) are the trophies.

It's best to avoid peak season (July and August). Autumn is nice (when the leaves are changing colour). Get out on the lake in a rowing boat – there are loads of stars at night.

Be sure to visit the Diaoshuilou Waterfall (20 metres high, 40 metres wide). Some foreigners like to come here and amaze the Chinese by diving into the pools. The waterfall is north of Jingbo Villa and within easy hiking distance of it.

The whole area is dotted with forests, hills, pavilions and rock gardens, offering rich opportunities for pleasant walks around the lake. Unfortunately, during the peak summer season you'll have to hike through the jostling mob of photo posers, litter collectors and knick-knack sellers. The Chinese say it's only fun when it's crowded.

THE NORTHEAST

Places to Stay

The centre of operations is *Jingbo Villa* (*jìngbó shānzhuāng*), at the north end of the lake, and the newer *Jingbo Lake Hotel* (☎ 27734) (*jìngbó hú bīnguǎn*). There are other, cheaper hotels around the lake but they aren't allowed to take foreigners.

Getting There & Away

The best approach is by rail from Harbin. Take a train to Dongjing (*dōngjīng*). From there, it's one hour by minibus to the lake.

Some trains only go as far as Mudanjiang. If you get off at Mudanjiang, it's three hours by bus to Jingbo Lake. Buses depart between 6 and 7 am from the square in front of Mudanjiang Railway Station, in summer only (from June to September). There are two or three trains a day between Harbin and Mudanjiang.

From Mudanjiang and Dongjing, there are also slower connections by rail to Tumen (one train daily, about six hours), Suifenhe (one train daily, five hours from Mudanjiang) and Jiamusi (two trains a day, about 10 hours).

SUIFENHE

(*suífēnhé*)

This town achieved commercial importance in 1903 with the opening of the South Manchurian Railway, which was a vital link in the original Trans-Siberian route running from Vladivostok to Moscow via Manchuria.

The railway was later re-routed via Khabarovsk to Vladivostok and Nakhodka. In recent years, cross-border trade has livened up here and there's even some Russian tourism. The grandiose nickname of 'Little Moscow of the East' certainly suits the Russian atmosphere in Suifenhe, but there's little else to do unless you like a lusty international friendship evening, when, according to a local tourist brochure, Russian visitors sing 'Evening in Suburban Moscow'. Although the whole place is Chinese, most of the buildings are Russian leftovers in the elegant, gingerbread style

from the turn of the century – reminders o‹ pre-Revolutionary times.

With the requisite visas, you can indee‹ cross the border to Russia and reach Vladi‹ vostok from here, but obtaining the necessary bits of paper is a monumenta‹ task.

Getting There & Away

There's one train daily (at 6.45 am) from Mudanjiang to Suifenhe; the trip takes abou‹ six hours and the train returns from Suifenh‹ at 1.12 pm.

There is an international passenger train beginning (or ending) at Primorye (Siberia) connecting Pogranichny (Grodekovo) with Suifenhe. Pogranichny is a small town which borders China near Suifenhe, 210 km away from Vladivostok. Pogranichny is connected by bus and taxi with Ussuriysk and Vladi‹ vostok. Suifenhe is connected with Harbin and Mudanjiang by rail. The train from Pogranichny to Suifenhe runs daily, and one‹ way tickets cost US$10. As this is the cheapest way to China, the train is usually packed with Russian traders and their cargoes of deer antlers, drugged puppies and vodka.

DONGNING

(*dōngníng*)

This obscure town near the southernmost corner of Heilongjiang is notable for only one thing – a bus connection that can get you to Vladivostok in Siberia. However, ‹ Russian tourist visa is necessary, though dif‹ ficult to come by.

The bus connects the Russian town of Pokrovka (180 km from Vladivostok) with Dongning. Make local inquiries about the schedule. At the time of writing, the bus wa‹ jam-packed.

WUDALIANCHI

(*wǔdàliánchí*)

Wudalianchi, which means 'five large con‹ nected lakes', is a nature reserve and health spot which has also been turned into ‹ 'volcano museum'. Many Chinese will tell you that Wudalianchi isn't worth the effor‹

The Oroqen

The Oroqen minority lived, until recently, the nomadic life of forest hunters. Recent estimates put their numbers at about 4000, scattered over a vast area. Their traditional tent, called a *xianrenzhu*, is covered with birch bark in the summer and deerskin in the winter. Hunting as well as the raising of reindeer are still their main activities. A major source of income is deer hunting since the deer's embryo, antlers, penis and tail are highly prized in Chinese medicine.

The Oroqen lifestyle is changing rapidly, although they retain their self-sufficiency. Boots, clothes and sleeping bags are made from deerskins; baskets, eating utensils and canoes are made from birch bark; horses or reindeer provide transport. Their food consists mostly of meat, fish and wild plants. Oroqens are particularly fond of raw deer liver washed down with fermented mare's milk. Meat is often preserved by drying and smoking.

Interesting facets of their religion included (and probably still do to a lesser degree) a belief in spirits and consulting shamans. It was once taboo to kill bears. If this happened, perhaps in self-defence, a complicated rite was performed to ask the bear's 'forgiveness' and its bones were spread in the open on a tall frame of willow branches. This 'wind burial' was also the standard funeral for a human. Our word 'shaman' means an 'agitated or frenzied person' in the Manchu-Tungus language. Such persons could enter a trance, become 'possessed' by a spirit and then officiate at religious ceremonies.

It's hard to determine how much of their culture the Oroqens have kept. Official publications trumpet stories of a wondrous change from primitive nomadism to settled consumerism complete with satellite TV. Meng Pinggu, a probably fictional Oroqen, was quoted in the *China Daily*; 'Now we Oroqens can see movies at home'.

The Oroqens – China's Nomadic Hunters by Qiu Pu (Foreign Languages Press, Beijing, 1983) is a surprisingly informative publication, provided you skip the political salad dressing. ■

to get there, but basically that would depend on whether or not you are a hot springs fanatic.

This area has a long history of volcanic activity. The most recent eruptions were during 1719 and 1720, when lava from craters blocked the nearby Bei River and formed this series of five barrier lakes. The malodorous mineral springs are the source of legendary cures and thus the No 1 attraction for hordes of chronically ill, who slurp the waters or slap mud onto themselves. To increase blood pressure, immerse your feet in a basin of the water; to decrease blood pressure, immerse your head. Baldness, cerebral haemorrhages, skin diseases and gastric ulcers are a few of the ailments miraculously cured by drinking the water or

applying mud packs, though some of the cures are only temporary.

As for the volcanoes themselves, don't come expecting Mt Fuji or Krakatoa. Basically, the volcano museum has steam fumaroles, hot springs and a little geothermal activity here and there, but not much else.

To liven up the scenery, there is a sort of Ice Lantern Festival like the one in Harbin, only this one is year-round. The ice sculptures are inside caves which have a steady temperature of -10°C, even during summer. Coloured lights inside the sculptures have a psychedelic effect.

Foreigners are expected to stay at the increasingly expensive *Dragon Spring Hotel* (*lóngquán bīnguǎn*).

To reach Wudalianchi, take a six-hour

train ride northwards from Harbin to Bei'an, where there are regular buses covering the 60 km to the lakes.

HEILONG RIVER BORDERLANDS
(hēilóngjiāng biānjìng)

Much of the north-eastern border between China and Siberia follows the course of the Heilongjiang (Black Dragon River), also known to the Russians as the Amur River. Most places along this river are open to foreigners but ask the PSB anyway just to be sure – international borders and ethnic minority areas are sensitive places. It should be possible to see some Siberian forest and the dwindling settlements of northern tribes, such as the Oroqen, Ewenki, Hezhen and Daur.

In Harbin the CITS office runs boat tours between Huma, Heihe and Tongjiang. Telescopes on the boats will give you a better look at Russian settlements or even at Blagoveshchensk, a large Russian port opposite Heihe.

Assuming you have at least two weeks to spare and are flexible about transport, an independent trip should also be viable during the summer – take some iron rations and insect repellent. Connections between Harbin and this region include the fast option of a flight to Heihe, the much slower option of a train at least as far as Jagdaqi, possibly further, and, of course, buses to the ends of the wilderness.

Mohe
(mòhé)

Natural wonders are the attraction at Mohe, China's northernmost town, sometimes known as the Arctic of China. In mid-June, the sun is visible in the sky for as long as 22 hours. The northern lights (aurora borealis) are another colourful phenomenon seen in the sky at Mohe. China's lowest absolute temperature of -52.3°C was recorded here in 1965; on normal winter days temperatures of -40°C are common.

During May 1987 this area was devastated by China's worst forest fire in living memory. The towns of Mohe and Xilinji were completely gutted, more than 200 people died and over one million hectares of forest were destroyed.

Try for a permit at the PSB in Jagdaqi (jiāgédáqí) in Inner Mongolia. Getting to Mohe requires a train trip north from Jagdaqi to Gulian, followed by a 34-km bus ride.

Heihe
(hēihé)

Heihe's claim to fame is that it borders Russia. Due to the recent thawing in relations between the two countries, there is a steadily increasing amount of cross-border trade and even a fledgling tourist industry. Chinese tour groups are now able to cross the border to Blagoveshchensk. Russian tourists visiting Heihe like to eat Chinese food and stock up on goods which are scarce or nonexistent in Siberia. Chinese tourists don't find much to buy in Russia, but are impressed to see a city where nobody spits and people actually stand in line.

There are still problems for foreigners wishing to visit Blagoveshchensk. A Russian tourist visa is needed, and a re-entry visa for China would also be necessary. All this must be arranged in Beijing, not in Heihe. In theory, one could cross the border at Blagoveshchensk and take a train 109 km to Belogorsk, which is on the Trans-Siberian Railway, then continue on to Europe. This would require a tourist visa.

Flights between Harbin and Heihe run four times weekly. Boats also connect Heihe with Mohe and Tongjiang, but the railway does not reach this far north.

Tongjiang
(tóngjiāng)

Tongjiang lies at the junction of the Songhua and Heilong rivers. They swell to a combined width of 10 km but their respective colours, black for the Heilong and yellow for the Songhua, don't mix until later.

The Hezhen minority, a mere 1300 people, lives almost entirely from fishing in this region. A local delicacy is sliced, raw fish with a spicy vinegar sauce. Apart from carp and salmon, the real whopper here is the huso

CLEM LINDENMAYER

TONY WHEELER

CLEM LINDENMAYER

Top Left: Blind musician in Kaifeng, Henan
Top Right: Bamboo steamers on display on a Xi'an street, Shaanxi
Bottom: Fire buckets at the Great Mosque in Xi'an

NICKO GONCHAROFF

NICKO GONCHAROFF

Top: Shaoshan Railway Station with a portrait of Mao, Hunan
Bottom: Mao's childhood home in Shaoshan

sturgeon (*huáng yú*), which can grow as long as three metres and weigh up to 500 kg!

Tongjiang has boat and bus connections with Jiamusi; boats also connect with Heihe.

Fuyuan
(*fúyuán*)

The earliest sunrise in China starts at 2 am in Fuyuan. Close to Fuyuan is the junction of the Heilong and Wusuli rivers. On the Russian side is the city of Khabarovsk; on the Chinese side there's the tiny outpost of Wusu, which has 20 inhabitants who see visitors only during the salmon season in September.

JIAMUSI
(*jiāmùsī*)

North-east of Harbin is Jiamusi. Once a fishing village, it mushroomed into a city of half a million people. It now smelts aluminium, manufactures farm equipment and refines sugar, and has a paper mill, plastics factory and electrical appliances factory.

One of the few 'sights' is the **Sumuhe Farm**, in the suburbs of Jiamusi. This farm grows ginseng and raises over 700 head of sika and red deer for the antlers. Martens, close kin to the weasel, are also raised. It's not really such a strange combination; in fact the 'three treasures' of the north-east are ginseng, deer antlers and sable pelts. Each of these are also well represented further south in Jilin Province, where production is largely domesticated. Wild ginseng from the Changbaishan area fetches astronomical sums on the Hong Kong market.

A curious item in the north-eastern pharmacopoeia includes frog oil, taken from a substance in the frog's ovary. These and other ingredients will arrive in soups or with stewed chicken if a banquet is ordered at a ritzy hotel.

Places to Stay

The *Huibin Hotel (huìbīn fàndiàn)* on Zhanqian Lu is near the railway station. CITS packs the tourists into the *Jiamusi Hotel* ☎ 223-280) *(jiāmùsī bīnguǎn)* on Guangfu Lu. Still further north of the railway station

is the *Songhuajiang Hotel (sōnghuājiāng fàndiàn)*. The *Jiangtian Hotel (jiāngtiān bīnguǎn)* is where Zhongshan Lu meets the Songhua River.

Getting There & Away

Jiamusi is connected by rail to Harbin (15 hours), Dalian and Mudanjiang. Steamers ply the Songhua River so it may be possible to travel between Harbin and Jiamusi by water.

QIQIHAR
(*qíqíhā'ěr*)

Qiqihar is the gateway to the Zhalong Nature Reserve, a bird-watching area 35 km to the south-east. It's also one of the oldest settlements in the north-east. The town itself is industrialised, with a population of over one million, and produces locomotives, mining equipment, steel, machine tools and motor vehicles. There's not much to see here – a zoo, a stretch of riverside and the ice-carving festival from January to March.

The CITS office (☎ 72016) is in the Hubin Hotel and the staff are very friendly. They can give you a lot of advice about the best places for watching birds.

Places to Stay

The *Hubin Hotel (húbīn fàndiàn)* is one of the cheapest places accepting foreigners. The more modern *Crane City Hotel* (☎ 472-669; fax 475-836) *(hèchéng bīnguǎn)* behind the Hubin at 4 Wenhua Dajie is pricey. You can reach the Hubin Hotel on trolley-bus No 15 – it's seven stops from the railway station.

Getting There & Away

There are flights between Qiqihar and Beijing, Dalian, Guangzhou, Shanghai and Shenyang. Qiqihar is linked directly by rail to Beijing (about 22 hours) via Harbin (about four hours).

ZHALONG NATURE RESERVE
(*zhálóng zìrán bǎohù qū*)

The Zhalong Nature Reserve is at the north-west tip of a giant marsh, and is made up of about 210,000 hectares of reeds, moss and ponds. It lies strategically on a bird-migration path which extends from the Russian Arctic, around the Gobi Desert and down into South-East Asia, and some 180 different species of bird are found there, including storks, swans, geese, ducks, herons, harriers, grebes and egrets. The tens of thousands of winged migrants arrive from April to May, rear their young from June to August, and depart from September to October.

Birds will be birds – they value their privacy. While some of the red-crowned cranes are over 1½ metres tall, the reed cover is taller. The best time to visit is in spring before the reeds have a chance to grow.

The nature reserve, one of China's first, was set up in 1979. In 1981 the Chinese Ministry of Forestry invited Dr George Archibald (director of the ICF, the International Crane Foundation) and Wolf Brehm (director of Vogelpark Walsrode, West Germany) to help set up a crane centre at Zhalong. Of the 15 species of cranes in the world, eight are found in China, and six are found at Zhalong. Four of the species that migrate here are on the endangered list: the red-crowned crane, the white-naped crane, the Siberian crane and the hooded crane. Both the red-crowned and white-naped cranes breed at Zhalong (as do the common and demoiselle cranes), while hooded and Siberian cranes use Zhalong as a stopover.

The centre of attention is the red-crowned crane, a fragile creature whose numbers at Zhalong (estimated to be 100 in 1979) were threatened by drainage of the wetlands for farming. The near-extinct bird is, ironically, the ancient symbol of immortality and has long been a symbol of longevity and good luck in the Chinese, Korean and Japanese cultures. With some help from overseas experts, the ecosystem at Zhalong has been

studied and improved, and the number of these rare birds has risen. Several hand-reared (domesticated) red-crowned and white-naped cranes are kept in a pen at the sanctuary for viewing and study. On the eve of their 'long march' southwards in October large numbers of cranes can be seen wheeling around, as if in farewell. The birds have been banded to unlock the mystery of their winter migration grounds (in either Korea or southern China).

Since the establishment of the ICF George Archibald and Ron Sauey have managed to create a 'crane bank' in Wisconsin, USA, stocking 14 of the 15 known species. They've even convinced the North Koreans to set up bird reserves in the mine-studded demilitarised zone between North and South Korea, and the travel baggage of these two countries includes suitcases full of Siberian crane-eggs picked up in Moscow (on one trip a chick hatched en route was nicknamed 'Aeroflot'). Last on the egg list for the ICF is the black-necked crane, whose home is in remote Tibet and for whom captive breeding may be the final hope.

Places to Stay

The modest *Zhalong Hotel* is relatively cheap and offers tours through the freshwater marshes of the reserve in flat-bottom boats. The area is mainly of interest to the patient binoculared and rubber-booted ornithologist.

Getting There & Away

Zhalong is linked to Qiqihar by a good road, but there's not much traffic along it. There are occasional buses – you'll have to inquire to find them. The other alternative is to get a taxi which is not too expensive (after some bargaining). Hitching may be possible.

CENTRAL CHINA

Shanxi 山西

Shanxi *(shānxī)*, especially the southern half, was one of the earliest centres of Chinese civilisation and formed the territory of the state of Qin. After Qin Shihuang unified the Chinese states, the northern part of Shanxi became the key defensive bulwark between the Chinese and the nomadic tribes to the north. Despite the Great Wall, the nomadic tribes still managed to break through and used Shanxi as a base for their conquest of the Middle Kingdom.

When the Tang Dynasty fell, the political centre of China moved away from the northwest. Shanxi went into a rapid economic decline, though its importance in the northern defence network remained paramount. Strategic importance coupled with isolation and economic backwardness was not an unusual situation for any of China's border regions, then or now.

It was not until the intrusion of the foreign powers into China that any industrialisation got under way. When the Japanese invaded China in the 1930s they carried out development of industry and coal mining around the capital of Taiyuan. True to form, Shanxi was a bastion of resistance to this invasion from the north, this time through the Communist guerrillas who operated in the mountainous regions.

After 1949, the Communists began a serious exploitation of Shanxi's mineral and ore deposits, and the development of places like Datong and Taiyuan as major industrial centres. Some of the biggest coal mines can be found near these cities, and the province accounts for a third of China's known coal deposits.

Shanxi means West of the Mountains and is named after the Taihang range, which forms its eastern border. To the west it is bordered by the Yellow River. The province's population of about 30 million people is relatively light by Chinese standards, unless you consider the fact that almost 70% of the province is mountainous. The Taihang

Population: 30 million
Capital: Taiyuan
Highlights:
- Yungang Buddhist Caves, over 50 of them, crowded with images
- The Hanging Monastery, 75 km southeast of Datong
- The beautiful monastic village of Taihuai near Wutaishan

range, which also includes the Wutaishan mountains, runs from north to south and separates the province from the great North China Plain to the east. The Central Shanxi Basin crosses the central part of the province from north to south in a series of valleys. This is the main farming and economic area. Most of the farmland is used to grow crops, though the north-west is the centre of the province's animal husbandry industry.

Despite its intended future as an industrial bastion, Shanxi's wealth lies in its history. The province is a virtual gold mine of temples, monasteries and cave-temples – a reminder that this was once the political and cultural centre of China. The main attraction for travellers is the Yungang Buddhist Caves at Datong.

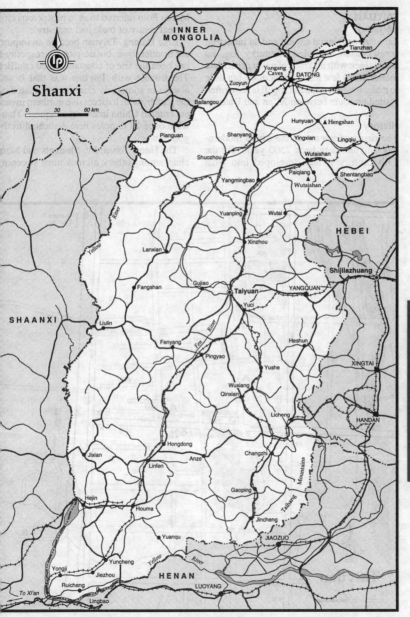

TAIYUAN
(tàiyuán)

Taiyuan, provincial capital and an industrial sprawl often shrouded in murky fog, no doubt thick with all kinds of nasty particulate matter, has a few minor attractions, but little to make it worth a special trip. It is most often visited en route between Xi'an and Datong.

History

The first settlements on the site of modern-day Taiyuan date back 2500 years. By the 13th century it had developed into what Marco Polo referred to as 'a prosperous city a great centre of trade and industry'.

Like Datong, Taiyuan became an import ant frontier town, but despite its prosperity i has been the site of constant armed conflic The trouble with Taiyuan was that it wa always in somebody else's way, situated o the path by which successive northern invad ers entered China intent on conquest. Ther were once 27 temples here dedicated to th god of war.

The Huns, Tobas, Jin, Mongols and Man chus, among others, all took turns sweepin

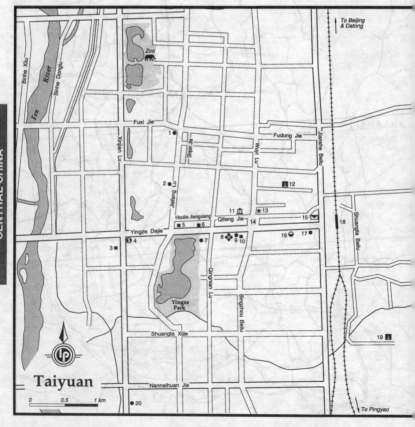

Taiyuan

through Taiyuan. If it wasn't foreign invasion which afflicted the city, then it was the rise and fall of Chinese dynasties during periods of disunity; the town passed from one army to another as different rulers vied for power. Nevertheless, Taiyuan managed to survive.

In the latter part of the 19th century, Taiyuan moved rapidly towards industrialisation, helped by its proximity to some of the world's largest deposits of iron and coal. From 1889 it started to develop as a modern city, with the encouragement of Western powers. In the next 20 years Taiyuan gained a train link to Hebei, electricity and a telephone system, not to mention a university and military academy. Development was pushed along by the warlord Yan Xishan, who ruled Shanxi virtually as his own private empire after the fall of the Manchu Dynasty. The coal mines were also developed by the Japanese invaders during the 1930s and 1940s.

The Communists began the serious industrialisation of Taiyuan, along with other regions of Shanxi, after 1949. Today, the city looks very much like its modern counterparts Zhengzhou and Luoyang, with wide avenues and extensive residential blocks, and the skyline enlivened by numerous factories and smokestacks.

Orientation

Taiyuan lies mainly on the eastern side of the Fen River. The railway station is at the eastern end of Yingze Dajie, Taiyuan's main thoroughfare. The long-distance bus station is roughly half a km west of the railway station on Yingze Dajie, and most tourist sights and facilities are also on or close to this street. The centre of town is May 1st Square.

Information

CITS There is a branch of CITS in the Shanxi Grand Hotel, which mainly handles flight bookings. The main office (☎ 704-2188) is in the south of town on Pingyang Lu in the Guolü Building (*guólǚ dàshà*).

PSB This is on a lane near May 1st Square.

Money The Bank of China has its main branch on Yingze Dajie, east of Xinjian Lu. The tourist hotels also change money.

Post & Telecommunications The main post and telephone office is in a white multi-storey building diagonally opposite the

---

TAIYUAN 太原

1 Foreign Languages Bookstore
外文书店
2 Advanced Rail Booking Office
铁路售票处
3 Shanxi Grand Hotel & CITS
山西大酒店，中国国际路旅行社
4 Bank of China
中国银行
5 Telecommunications Hotel
电信大酒店
6 Yingze Hotel
迎泽宾馆
7 CTS
中国旅行社
8 Friendship Store
友谊商店
9 CAAC
中国民航
10 Bingzhou Hotel
并州饭店
11 Provincial Musuem
山西省博物馆
12 Chongshan Monastery
崇善寺
13 PSB
公安局
14 May 1st Square
五一广场
15 Post & Telephone Office
邮电大楼
16 Long-Distance Bus Station
长途汽车站
17 Tielu Hotel
铁路宾馆
18 Railway Station
火车站
19 Twin Pagoda Temple
双塔寺
20 CITS
中国国际路旅行社

railway station. There is also a modern tele-communications centre on the corner of Yingze Dajie and Jiefang Lu.

Yingze Park
(yíngzé gōngyuán)

The Ming Library *(míngdài cángjīng lóu)*, an ornate building in Yingze Park, is worth seeing. The entrance to the park is on the opposite side of the road, to the west of the Yingze Hotel.

Chongshan Monastery
(chóngshàn sì)

This Buddhist monastery was built towards the end of the 14th century on the site of an even older monastery, said to date back to the 6th or 7th century. The main hall contains three impressive statues; the central figure represents Guanyin, the goddess of mercy, who has 1000 hands and eyes. Beautifully illustrated book covers show scenes from the life of Buddha. Also on display are Buddhist scriptures of the Song, Yuan, Ming and Qing dynasties. The monastery is on a side street running east off Wuyi Lu.

Twin Pagoda Temple
(shuāngtǎ sì)

This temple has two identical Ming Dynasty pagodas, each a 13-storey octagonal structure almost 55 metres high. The pagodas are built entirely of bricks carved with brackets and cornices to imitate Chinese wooden pagodas of ancient times. You can get halfway there by taking the No 19 bus from in front of the railway station and getting off one stop after the railway bridge. From there walk the few steps back to Shuangta Beilu, turn left (south) and follow this road for 20 minutes to the temple.

Provincial Museum
(shānxī shěng bówùguǎn)

This is on Qifeng Jie, north-west of May 1st Square. The museum is in the Chunyang Palace *(chúnyáng gōng)*, which used to be a temple for offering sacrifices to the Taoist priest Lu Dongbin, who lived during the

Tang Dynasty. The temple was built during the Ming and Qing dynasties.

Places to Stay

The *Tielu Hotel* (☎ 404-2847) *(tiělù bīnguǎn)*, a couple of hundred metres down Yingze Dajie from the railway station, is one of the few low-budget places in town that accept foreigners, but it will only allow you to stay in the standard doubles (Y90 per bed) or the suites (Y230).

One of the best deals around is the west block of the *Bingzhou Hotel* (☎ 404-2111) *(bìngzhōu fàndiàn)*, where simple basement doubles cost Y44. How long these rooms will stay available at these rates is anyone's guess. Other rooms range from Y132 to Y162 for doubles and Y252 for a suite. The east block (next door, with a separate reception area) has singles at Y268 and doubles from Y368.

The *Telecommunications Hotel* (☎ 403-3865) *(diànxìn dàjiǔdiàn)*, on a lane behind the huge telecommunications building, is a grotty kind of place but will give you a bed in a shabby double with attached bathroom for Y80. Take the No 1 bus four stops from the railway station.

The *Yingze Hotel* (☎ 404-3211) *(yíngzé bīnguǎn)*, like the Bingzhou, incorporates two massive buildings. The east block was undergoing renovations at the time of writing and will one day emerge phoenix-like from the brick dust and rubble as a four-star hotel. The west block is a typical spruced-up Chinese guesthouse with singles at Y150, doubles at Y280.

The joint-venture *Shanxi Grand Hotel* (☎ 404-3901; fax 404-3525) *(shānxī dàjiǔdiàn)* is a tightly run outfit and the centre of operations for local expats. Singles/doubles cost Y600/680.

Places to Eat

On the Taiyuan street-food menu are local favourites like pigs' trotters *(zhūjiǎo)* stewed in cauldrons and a savoury pancake called *luòbǐng* cooked over coals on a lens-shaped hot-plate. The local variant of Chinese noodles, called *liángpí*, is often served in steaming bowls of spiced soup.

Shipin Jie (Food Street), a pedestrian zone with a Chinese archway and many old-style buildings, has over 30 restaurants serving food in the very cheap to quite upmarket price ranges.

The restaurant on the ground floor of the Telecommunications Hotel is not bad. The *Háohuá Restaurant* on the 7th floor of the Yingze Hotel is pretty good too and has a limited English menu.

Those craving Western cooking should head over to the Shanxi Grand Hotel. The ground-floor coffee shop does surprisingly good hamburgers and salads at affordable prices.

Getting There & Away

Air The local CAAC (☎ 404-2903) is at 38 Yingze Dongdajie. Useful direct flights go to Beijing (daily), Guangzhou (daily), Shanghai and Xi'an. There are also flights to most other major destinations.

Bus Minibuses to Datong (Y25) leave irregularly from outside the railway station; there are scheduled services to Datong and Wutaishan (nine hours) from the long-distance bus station. There are also early-morning sleeper buses *(wòpùchē)* leaving from the square in front of Taiyuan Railway Station to Datong (Y50, 10 hours), Luoyang (Y75), Zhengzhou (Y83), Beijing (Y90, 12 hours) and Tianjin (Y98).

Train The railway station booking office only sells hard-seat tickets, though there is a black market for hard-sleepers to major destinations such as Xi'an, Qingdao, Shanghai, and occasionally Beijing (though these are in great demand). There is a special foreigners' booking office upstairs in a separate building, immediately left as you leave the station ticket office. It is open from 8.30 to 11.30 am and 2.30 to 4.30 pm; same-day hard/soft-class sleeper tickets are usually available. For advance sleeper tickets, go to the advanced rail booking office at 65 Jiefang Lu.

From Taiyuan, Shijiazhuang is the closest train junction on the main Beijing-Guangzhou line, but for southern destinations like Guangzhou, it's best to change trains in Xi'an or Zhengzhou. There are direct trains south to Xi'an via Yuncheng.

Trains go to Datong (eight hours), Beijing (eight hours), Zhengzhou (12 hours), Xi'an (12 hours) and Shijiazhuang (5½ hours).

AROUND TAIYUAN
Jinci Temple
(jìncí sì)
This ancient Buddhist temple is at the source of the Jin River by Xuanwang Hill, 25 km south-west of Taiyuan. It's thought that the original buildings were constructed between 1023 and 1032, but there have been numerous additions and restorations over the centuries, right up to Qing Dynasty times.

As you enter the temple compound the first major structure is the Mirror Terrace, a Ming building used as an open-air theatre. The name is used in the figurative sense to denote the reflection of life in drama.

Zhibo's Canal cuts through the temple complex and lies west of the Mirror Terrace. Spanning this canal is the Huixian (Meet the Immortals) Bridge, which provides access to the Terrace for Iron Statues. At each corner of the terrace stands an iron figure cast in 1097 AD. Immediately behind the statues is Duiyuefang Gate, with two iron statues out the front. Behind the gate is the Offerings Hall built in 1168 to display temple offerings.

A bridge connects the Offerings Hall with the Goddess Mother Hall, the oldest wooden building in the city and one of the most interesting in the temple complex. In front of the hall are large wooden pillars with carvings of fearsome dragons. Inside are 42 Song Dynasty clay figures of maidservants standing around a large seated statue of the sacred lady herself. She is said to be the mother of Prince Shuyu of the ancient Zhou Dynasty, and the temple was built in her memory during the Northern Song period. It's suggested that the original building was constructed by the prince as a place to offer prayers and sacrifices to his mother. Today, people still throw money on the altar in front of the statue. Next to the Goddess Mother Hall is the Zhou Cypress, an unusual tree which has supposedly been growing at an angle of about 30 degrees for the last 900 years.

South of the Goddess Mother Hall is the Nanlao (Forever Young, or Everlasting) Spring over which stands a pavilion. To the west of the spring is the two-storey Shuimu Lou (Water Goddess House), originally built in 1563. On the ground floor is a statue of the goddess cast in bronze. On the upper storey is a shrine with a seated statue of the goddess surrounded by statues of her female servants.

In the north of the temple grounds is the Zhenguan Baohan Pavilion, which houses four stone steles inscribed with the hand writing of the Tang emperor Tai Zong. The Memorial Halls of Prince Shuyu include a shrine containing a seated figure of the prince surrounded by 12 Ming Dynasty female attendants, some holding bamboo flutes, pipes and stringed instruments. In the south of the temple grounds is the Sacred Relics Pagoda, a seven-storey octagonal building constructed at the end of the 7th century.

To get to Jinci Temple you can take a No 8 bus from the long-distance bus station one block east of May 1st Square.

Shuanglin Monastery
(shuānglín sì)

Shuanglin Monastery, 110 km south-west of Taiyuan, is worth the effort of getting to. It contains exquisite painted clay figurines and statues dating from the Song, Yuan, Ming and Qing dynasties. Most of the present buildings date from the Ming and Qing dynasties, while the majority of sculptures are from the Song and Yuan dynasties. There are something like 2000 figurines in total.

A visit to Shuanglin is probably best done as a return day-trip from Taiyuan by train. Take a train to Pingyao, then hire a motor-tricycle out to the temple. Two good train connections are the No 375, departing from Taiyuan at 11.07 am and arriving in Pingyao

at 1 pm, and the No 376, back from Pingyao at 3.59 pm.

WUTAISHAN
(wǔtáishān)

Wutaishan, centred on the beautiful monastic village of Taihuai *(táihuái)*, is one of China's sacred Buddhist mountain areas. Taihuai lies deep in an alpine valley enclosed by the five peaks of Wutaishan, the highest of which is the 3061-metre northern peak, Yedoufeng, known as the roof of northern China. Taihuai itself has 15 or so old temples and monasteries, and many others dot the nearby and more distant mountainsides. Part of the charm of Wutaishan is its relative inaccessibility, which spared the area from the worst of the Cultural Revolution and still keeps development to a minimum.

The Tayuan Temple with its large, white, bottle-shaped pagoda built during the Ming Dynasty is the most prominent in Taihuai. The Xiantong Temple has seven rows of halls, totalling over 400 rooms. The small Guangren Monastery, run by Tibetan monks, contains some fine examples of early Qing wood carvings. The Nanshan Temple, built during the Yuan Dynasty on the nearby slopes of Nanshan, contains frescoes of the fable 'Pilgrimage to the West'.

Other sights include the marble archway of the Longquan Temple and the 26-metre-high buddha and carvings of 500 arhats in the Shuxiang Temple. The Luohou Temple contains a large wooden lotus flower with eight petals, on each of which sits a carved Buddhist figure; the big flower is attached to a rotating disk so that when it turns the petals open up and the figures appear.

Information

Travel to the Wutaishan area requires an Alien Travel Permit, which you can get from the PSB after you arrive. The CITS office at the railway station in Datong can also get you a permit for Y10. Wutaishan CITS is at the Yunfeng Hotel. Chinese-language maps are available locally from shops and hotels.

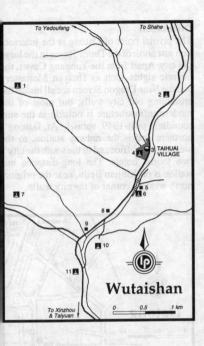

Wutaishan

0   0.5   1 km

To Yedoufeng   To Shahe

3 TAIHUAI VILLAGE

To Xinzhou & Taiyuan

WUTAISHAN 五台山

1 Fenglin Temple
   风林寺
2 Bishan Temple
   碧山寺
3 Bus Station
   汽车站
4 Tayuan Temple
   塔院寺
5 Liangcheng Hotel
   凉城宾馆
6 Puhua Temple
   普化寺
7 Longquan Temple
   龙泉寺
8 Friendship Hotel
   友谊宾馆
9 Yunfeng Hotel & CITS
   云峰宾馆，中国国际旅行社
10 Nanshan Temple
   南山寺
11 Zhenhai Temple
   镇海寺

Places to Stay

There are two foreigners' hotels, both of which are expensive. You might try holding out for a dorm bed – some travellers with student cards have been successful.

The *Friendship Hotel (yǒuyì bīnguǎn)*, about two km below Taihuai, has official rates of Y360 for a double with bathroom. The *Yunfeng Hotel (yúnfēng bīnguǎn)* is three km below the village and has rooms that are only slightly cheaper.

Getting There & Away

There are daily buses to Wutaishan from Taiyuan via Wutai (Y24). The largely unsurfaced and frequently dusty road can make it a rather tortuous nine-hour ride. There is a daily bus to Wutaishan from Datong via Xinzhou (Y28, 9½ hours). A more adventurous way to reach Taihuai from Datong is to get the public bus to Shahe, then a private minibus over the scenic pass road below Yedoufeng.

DATONG

(dàtóng)

Datong's chief attraction is the nearby Yungang Buddhist Caves. Datong itself, on the other hand, is very much an 'unattraction'. It is another Chinese city that has historically enjoyed moments of greatness, and nowadays has very little to show for it. Along with the ravages of time, earthquakes and recent demolition work have robbed Datong of any charm. Today it is one of the country's most depressing cities – ugly, polluted and poor, and all accentuated by its status as one of China's leading producers of coal.

Interestingly, Datong is also caught in a time-warp when it comes to tourism. For anyone who misses the bad old days of China tourism, when three quarters of the country was off limits and the rest was run by CITS, Datong is a little trip down memory lane. CITS really runs the show in this neck of the woods – it's very difficult to do anything without it.

History

In the 5th century AD, the Toba, a Turkic-speaking people, succeeded in unifying all of northern China and forming the Northern Wei Dynasty. They adopted Chinese ways, and under their administration trade, agriculture and Buddhism flourished. Their capital was Datong. It remained as such until 494 AD, when the court moved to Luoyang. Outside the modern-day city is the greatest legacy of the period, the Yungang Buddhist Caves.

Orientation

The pivotal point of Datong is the intersection just north of the Drum Tower in the large old city. Apart from the Yungang Caves, the historic sights such as Huayan Monastery and the Nine Dragon Screen are all inside the crumbling old city walls, but most of the modern infrastructure is outside in the surrounding post-1949 sprawl. At Datong's northern end is the railway station, to the west the post office and in the south the city's two tourist hotels. The long-distance bus station is on Xinjian Beilu, near the original north-western corner of the city walls.

DATONG 大同

1 Railway Station & CITS
火车站，中国国际旅行社
2 Long-distance Bus Station
长途汽车站旧址
3 New Children's Park
新儿童乐园
4 Bank of China
中国银行
5 Yanbei Bus Co (New Bus Station)
雁北公司 (新长途汽车站)
6 PSB
公安局
7 Hongqi Market
红旗商场
8 Post & Telephone Office
邮电大楼
9 Huayan Monastery
华严寺
10 Nine Dragon Screen
九龙壁
11 Shanhua Temple
善化寺
12 Xinkaili Bus Station
(for Yungang Caves)
新开里汽车站
13 Datong Stadium
大同体育场
14 Yaxuyuan Restaurant
雅叙园酒家
15 Yungang Hotel & CITS
云冈宾馆，中国国际旅行社
16 Hongqi Restaurant
红旗大酒店
17 Datong Hotel
大同宾馆
18 Bank of China (Main Branch)
中国银行 (大同支行)

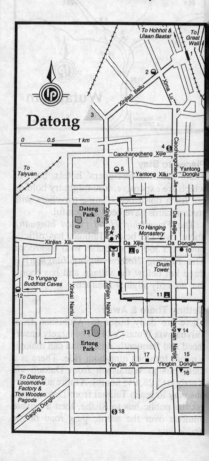

Information

CITS Datong has two CITS offices: a branch at the railway station (☎ 224-460) and another at the Yungang Hotel. Mind you, it is not necessary to go looking for CITS in Datong – the staff at the railway station branch will probably collar you as soon as you leave your train. They broker accommodation and purchase all train tickets for foreigners, and run regular tours of the city and Yungang Caves.

PSB This is on Xinjian Beilu, north of the large department store.

Money The most convenient branch of the Bank of China is on Caochangcheng Xijie. The main office is on Xinjian Nanlu near the end of the No 6 bus route. The Yungang Hotel also offers a money-changing service.

Post & Telecommunications The main post and telephone office is the large central building with the clock tower.

Maps The Xinhua Bookstore, diagonally opposite the main post office, sells maps of Datong with places of interest to tourists shown in English. You can also pick up maps from hawkers around the railway station.

Datong Locomotive Factory
(dàtóng jīchē chǎng)

This factory was the last in China to make steam engines for the main railway lines. In 1989 it finally switched over to the production of diesel and electric engines. However, the factory still maintains a museum housing about seven old steam locomotives.

A factory inspection is reportedly very educational. One US tourist said it reminded him of working in the US shipyards in the 1940s. You may be aghast at the safety conditions. After wandering through the factory you enjoy the ultimate train-buff dream – a ride in the cabin of one of the locomotives.

The factory is on the city's south-western outskirts. You can only see it as part of a CITS tour, and unless there is a big group the tour works out to be fairly expensive – Y260 per person if there are only two of you.

Nine Dragon Screen
(jiǔlóng bì)

This is one of Datong's several 'dragon screens' – tiled walls depicting fire-breathing dragons made from separate glazed-ceramic plates. The Nine Dragon Screen was originally part of the gate of the palace of Ming Dynasty emperor Hong Wu's 13th son, and is eight metres high, over 45 metres long and two metres thick. The Nine Dragon Screen is a short way east of the Da Dongjie/Da Beijie intersection; you can get there on bus No 4 from the railway station.

Huayan Monastery
(huáyán sì)

The Huayan Monastery is on the western side of the old city. The original monastery dates back to 1140 and the reign of Emperor Tian Juan of the Jin Dynasty.

Mahavira Hall is one of the largest Buddhist halls still standing in China. In the centre of the hall are five gilded Ming Dynasty buddhas seated on lotus thrones. The three statues in the middle are carved out of wood; the other two are made of clay. Around them stand Bodhisattvas, soldiers and mandarins. The ceiling is decorated with colourful paintings originally dating from the Ming and Qing dynasties but recently restored and supported by massive wooden beams.

Bojiajiaocang Hall (Hall for the Conservation of Buddhist Scriptures of the Bojia Order) is smaller but more interesting than the main hall. It contains 29 coloured clay figures made during the Liao Dynasty (916-1125 AD) representing the Buddha and Bodhisattvas. The figures give the monastery a touch of magic lacking in other restored temples.

Huayan Monastery is about half a km east of the post office at the end of a small lane running south off Da Xijie. Bus No 4 passes here. Entry to each hall costs Y12.

Shanhua Temple

(shànhuà sì)

The Shanhua Temple is in the south of Datong just within the old city walls. Built during the Tang Dynasty, it was destroyed by fire during a war at the end of the Liao Dynasty. In 1128 more than 80 halls and pavilions were rebuilt, and further restoration was done during the Ming Dynasty. The main hall contains statues of 24 divine generals. There is a small dragon screen within the monastery grounds. Admission is Y10.

Places to Stay

The accommodation situation in Datong is slightly ridiculous. Two hotels are officially allowed to take foreigners and both are expensive and inconveniently located. The CITS office at the railway station acts as a broker for cheaper hotels around town, but the best they can offer is Y160 for a double.

The *Datong Hotel* (☎ (0352) 232-476) *(dàtóng bīnguǎn)*, on Yingbin Xilu, is the only place in town with dorm beds: they cost Y80. Standard doubles cost Y320.

The *Yungang Hotel* (☎ 521-601) *(yúngāng bīnguǎn)* at 21 Yingbin Donglu has doubles from Y350. Ask at CITS about the availability of dorm beds here – at the time of writing everyone was keeping tight-lipped about whether they still exist.

To get to the Datong and Yungang hotels take bus No 15 from the railway station. For the Datong Hotel get off at the 12th stop (just after the bus turns sharply left). For the Yungang Hotel, get off at the stop after that, before crossing the intersection. Taxis cost Y15 to either hotel.

CITS at the railway station can provide accommodation at the *Army Hotel* and the *Railway Hotel*. Both have comfortable doubles for Y160 and are close to the railway station.

Places to Eat

Datong is certainly no gourmet's paradise, but fortunately there are a few good restaurants near the tourist hotels. The *Hongqi Restaurant (hóngqí dàjiǔdiàn)* across the road from the main gate of the Yungang Hotel has expensive and cheaper sections. Another nearby place is the *Yaxuyuan Restaurant (yǎxùyuǎn jiǔjiā)* on Nanguan Nanjie.

Getting There & Away

Air An airport south of the city will probably have commercial flights by the time this book is in print. There is a CAAC booking office (☎ 525-357) on Nanguan Nanjie which can book flights for air routes other than to/from Datong. There is another office in the Yungang hotel.

Bus Foreigners are officially forbidden to travel by bus from Datong. Apparently several buses have been officially designated safe for foreign travellers and you will have to consult with CITS to find out which these are – largely tour buses to sights around Datong.

Train A railway line north-east to Beijing and a northern line to Inner and Outer Mongolia meet in a Y junction at Datong. (Trans-Siberian trains via Ulaan Baatar come through here.) There are daily express trains to Beijing (seven hours), Lanzhou (27 hours), Taiyuan (seven hours) and Xi'an (19 hours). The staff at the CITS office at the railway station can get train tickets for you at very short notice for a service fee of Y30.

AROUND DATONG

Yungang Buddhist Caves

(yúngāng shíkū)

Unless you admire coal dust and grey buildings, the Yungang Buddhist Caves are the only outstanding sight in Datong. The caves are cut into the southern cliffs of Wuzhoushan, 16 km west of Datong, next to the pass leading to Inner Mongolia. The caves contain over 50,000 statues and stretch for about one km east to west. On top of the mountain ridge are the remains of a huge, mud-brick, 17th-century Qing Dynasty fortress. As you approach the caves you'll see the truncated pyramids which were once the watchtowers.

History Most of the caves at Datong were carved during the Northern Wei Dynasty between 460 and 494 AD. Yungang (Cloud Ridge) is the highest part of Wuzhoushan's sandstone range and is on the north bank of the river of the same name. The Wei rulers once came here to pray to the gods for rain.

The Yungang Caves appear to have been modelled on the Dunhuang Caves of Gansu Province, which were dug in the 4th century AD and are some of the oldest in China. Recent studies suggest that the Kongwang grottoes at Lianyungang (a coastal city by the Yellow Sea) were dug 200 years earlier. Buddhism may have been brought to China not only overland along the Silk Road but by sea from Myanmar (Burma), India and Sri Lanka.

It was in India that methods of cutting out cave temples from solid rock first developed. At the Dunhuang Caves the statues are terracotta since the rock was too soft to be carved, but here at Datong are some of the oldest examples of stone sculpture to be seen in China. Various foreign influences can be seen in the Yungang Caves: there are Persian and Byzantine weapons, Greek tridents and the acanthus leaves of the Mediterranean, and images of the Indian Hindu gods Vishnu and Shiva. The Chinese style is reflected in the form of Bodhisattvas, dragons and flying apsaras (celestial beings rather like angels).

Some think the gigantic buddhas at Bamiyan in Afghanistan may have inspired the Yungang statues. The first caves at Yungang had enormous buddhas in the likenesses of five Northern Wei emperors, Daiwu, had been declared a 'living Buddha' in 416 AD because of his patronage of Buddhism.

Work on the Yungang Caves fizzled out when the Northern Wei moved their capital to Luoyang in 494. Datong then declined in importance and the caves appear to have been deliberately abandoned. In the 11th and 12th centuries the Liao Dynasty, founded by northern invaders, saw to some repairs and restoration. Datong itself houses some gems of Liao architecture and sculpture. More repairs to the caves were carried out during the Qing Dynasty. The Datong Caves are probably more impressive than those at Luoyang, and seem to have suffered less vandalism.

From east to west the caves fall into four major groups, though their numbering has nothing to do with the order in which they were constructed.

Caves 1-4 These early caves, with their characteristic square floor plan, are at the far eastern end, separated from the others. Caves 1 and 2 each contain carved pagodas. Cave 3 is the largest in this group, though it contains only a seated buddha flanked by two Bodhisattvas. Between this group of four caves and the others is a monastery dating back to 1652, with pavilions hugging the cliff face.

Caves 5 & 6 Yungang art is seen at its best in these two caves. The walls are wonderfully carved with illustrations of Buddhist tales and ornate processions.

Cave 5 contains a colossal seated buddha almost 17 metres high. The faded paint gives you some idea of the original colour scheme: bronze face, red lips and blue hair. Many of the smaller images in this cave have been beheaded. On the whole, however, the sculptures and paintings in Caves 5 and 6 are better preserved than those in other caves since they're protected from the elements by the wooden towers built over the entrances. Cave 5 also contains a five-storey pagoda perched on the back of an elephant, carved on the upper part of the south wall.

Cave 6 contains a richly carved pagoda covered with scenes from religious stories. The entrance is flanked by fierce guardians. In the centre of the rear chamber stands a two-storey pagoda-pillar about 15 metres high. On the lower part of the pagoda are four niches with carved images, including one of the Maitreya Buddha (the future Buddha). The life story of Gautama Buddha from birth to his attainment of nirvana is carved in the east, south and west walls of the cave and on two sides of the pagoda. A relief on the east wall of the rear chamber of Cave 6 shows

Prince Gautama's encounter with a sick man; the prince rides a horse while his servant protects him with an umbrella (a symbol of royalty) but cannot prevent him from seeing human suffering. Pilgrims walk around the chamber in a clockwise direction.

Cave 8 This cave contains carvings with Hindu influences that have found their way into Buddhist mythology. Shiva, with eight arms and four heads and seated on a bull, is on one side of the entrance. On the other side is the many-armed, multi-faced Indra, perched on an eagle.

Caves 9 & 10 These have front pillars and interesting smaller figures with humorous faces. Some carry musical instruments.

Caves 11-13 These caves, which you can't enter, were apparently carved in 483 AD. Cave 12 contains apsaras with musical instruments and Cave 13 has a 15-metre-high statue of Buddha, its right hand propped up by a figurine.

Caves 16-20 These caves were carved in 460 AD and have oval floors. The roofs are dome-shaped to make room for the huge buddhas – some standing, some sitting, all with saccharine expressions.

The cross-legged giant buddha of Cave 17 represents the Maitreya Buddha. The cave walls are covered with thousands of tiny buddhas; carving them is considered a meritorious act.

The walls of Cave 18 are covered with sculptures of Gautama Buddha's disciples, including one near the Buddha's elbow who has a long nose and Caucasian features.

The seated buddha of Cave 20 is almost 14 metres high. The front wall and the wooden structure which stood in front of it are believed to have crumbled away very early on, and the statue now stands exposed. It is thought to represent the son of Northern Wei emperor Daiwu, who is said to have been a great patron of Buddhism but later, through the influence of a minister, came to favour Taoism. Following a revolt which he

blamed on the Buddhists, Daiwu ordered the destruction of their statues, monasteries and temples, and the persecution of Buddhists. This lasted from 446 to 452 AD. Daiwu was murdered in 452, though he had apparently repented of his cruel persecution. His son is said to have died of a broken heart, having been unable to prevent his father's atrocities, and was posthumously awarded the title of emperor. Daiwu's grandson (and successor) restored Buddhism.

The statue in Cave 20 has distinctly non-Chinese features. The inlaid spot-like *urna*, a hairy wart between the brows which is a distinguishing mark of the Buddha, is missing. A carved moustache is faintly visible.

Next door is Cave 19, which is the largest cave and contains a 16-metre-high seated statue thought to represent Emperor Daiwu. It is possible that he was deliberately carved with his palm facing forwards – the no fear gesture – in an attempt to abate the painful memories of his persecution of Buddhism.

Cave 21 onwards These caves are small and in poor condition. Cave 51 contains a carved pagoda.

Getting There & Away Bus Nos 3 and 10 from the terminal at Xinkaili, on the western edge of Datong, go past Yungang Caves. You can get to Xinkaili on bus No 2 from the railway station or bus No 17 from outside the Datong Hotel. From Xinkaili it's half an hour's ride to the caves.

Many travellers take a CITS tour out to the caves, which costs Y100 per person (minimum of five people) or Y195 with lunch and entrance fees included. The tour also includes the Hanging Monastery.

Admission to the caves is Y20 (or Y5 for students). You are not supposed to take photos – many visitors seem to get away with it anyway but excellent sets of 20 slides of the caves cost only Y25.

The Great Wall
(chángchéng)
The Great Wall is about an hour's drive north of Datong and forms much of the border

separating Shanxi Province and Inner Mongolia. The wall here is completely unrestored, so you'll need to imagine that this long ruin of old bricks and pounded earth was once China's main defence against invasion from the north. You can take a minibus going to Fengzhen from outside the railway station or a public bus from the long-distance bus station; make sure the driver knows where you want to get off. The trip out to the wall is a good opportunity to see some of the sparsely populated countryside of far northern Shanxi.

Hanging Monastery
(xuánkōng sì)
The Hanging Monastery is just outside the town of Hunyuan, 75 km south-east of Datong. Built precariously onto sheer cliffs above Jinlong Canyon, the monastery dates back more than 1400 years. Having been reconstructed several times through the centuries, it now has some 40 halls and pavilions. They were built along the contours of the cliff face using the natural hollows and outcrops, plus wooden beams for support. The buildings are connected by corridors, bridges and boardwalks and contain bronze, iron, clay and stone statues of gods and buddhas. Some long-overdue repairs have been made to the monastery in recent years and some sections have been closed off. Admission to the Hanging Monastery costs Y15.

The CITS tour to the Yungang Caves (see the earlier section) includes the Hanging Monastery. Chinese tours costing Y25 and taking four to five hours leave from around 7 am, from near the long-distance bus station on Yantong Xilu.

Alternatively, you might try taking a direct public bus from Datong to Hunyuan, just 3½ km from the Hanging Monastery, though CITS takes a particularly dim view of this kind of independent travelling. The earliest bus leaves at 9 am and the last bus back to Datong leaves Hunyuan at 3.30 pm. Some travellers stay overnight in Hunyuan and return to Datong the next day. In Hunyuan you can stay at the *Hengshan Guesthouse*

(héngshān bīnguǎn) or the government hostel *(zhèngfǔ zhāodàisuǒ)*.

Wooden Pagoda
(mùtǎ)
This 11th-century pagoda at Yingxian *(yìngxiàn)*, 70 km south of Datong, is one of the oldest wooden buildings in the world. It's said that not a single nail was used in the construction of the nine-storey, 97-metre structure.

Tours of the Hanging Monastery sometimes include the Wooden Pagoda. Getting to Yingxian by public bus is tricky – due to the fact that the local PSB forbids foreigners to travel by local buses, though it might be worth a try.

YUNCHENG
(yùnchéng)
Yuncheng is in the south-western corner of Shanxi Province, near where the Yellow River completes its great sweep through far northern China and begins to flow eastwards. The small city is locally famous for the gutsy little orange tractors that are assembled here and often seen chugging along country roads.

At Jiezhou *(jiězhōu)*, 13 km to the south of Yuncheng, is the large **Guandi Temple**, originally constructed during the Sui Dynasty but destroyed by fire in 1702 and subsequently rebuilt.

Places to Stay
The *Huanghe Hotel (huánghé dàshà)*, near the first street corner on the left as you leave the railway station, has good doubles for Y248 and dorm beds for Y30. The *Yuncheng Hotel* (☎ (0359) 224-779) *(yùnchéng bīnguǎn)*, on Hongqi Lu, has rooms from Y60, and a CITS office.

Getting There & Away
Yuncheng is on the Taiyuan-Xi'an railway line; all trains, including daily express trains, stop here. There are also direct bus connections to Yuncheng from Luoyang (Y22, six hours). The trip includes a ferry ride across the Sanmenxia dam and goes through an

interesting landscape of eroded gorges and small fields levelled out of the loess earth.

Bus No 11 from Yuncheng Railway Station drops you off right at Guandi Temple in Jiezhou.

RUICHENG
(ruìchéng)

At Ruicheng, 93 km south of Yuncheng, is **Yongle Taoist Temple**, which has valuable frescoes dating from the Tang and Song dynasties. The temple was moved to Ruicheng from its original location beside the Yellow River in the early 1960s, when the Sanmenxia dam was built.

Places to Stay

The *Yongle Hotel (yónglè fàndiàn)*, at the town's main intersection, has beds in clean basic doubles for Y35. (Yongle Temple is three km directly south along this road.)

Getting There & Away

From Yuncheng's long-distance bus station there are hourly departures to Ruicheng (Y6, 2½ hours). On the way, the bus passes Jiezhou before climbing the cool sub-alpine slopes of Zhongtiaoshan; it's a nice trip. From Ruicheng you can get an early-morning bus to Xi'an.

Shaanxi 陕西

The northern part of Shaanxi *(shǎnxī)* is one of the oldest settled regions of China, with remains of human habitation dating back to prehistoric times. This was the homeland of the Zhou people, who eventually conquered the Shang and established their rule over much of northern China. It was also the homeland of the Qin, who ruled from their capital of Xianyang near modern-day Xi'an and were the first dynasty to rule over all of eastern China. Shaanxi remained the political heart of China until the 9th century. The great Sui and Tang capital of Chang'an (Xi'an) was built there and the province was a crossroads on the trading routes from eastern China to central Asia.

With the migration of the imperial court to pastures further east, Shaanxi became a less attractive piece of real estate. Rebellions afflicted the territory from 1340 to 1368, again from 1620 to 1644, and finally in the mid-19th century, when the great Muslim rebellion left tens of thousands of the province's Muslims dead. Five million people died in the famine from 1876 to 1878, and another three million in the famines of 1915, 1921 and 1928. It was probably the dismal condition of the Shaanxi peasants that gave the Communists such willing support in the province in the late 1920s and during the ensuing civil war. From their base at Yan'an the Communist leaders directed the war against the Kuomintang and later against the Japanese, before being forced to evacuate in the wake of a Kuomintang attack in 1947.

Some 30 million people live in Shaanxi, mostly in the central and southern regions. The north of the province is a plateau covered with a thick layer of wind-blown loess soil which masks the original landforms. Deeply eroded, the landscape has deep ravines and almost vertical cliff faces. The Great Wall in the far north of the province is something of a cultural barrier, beyond which agriculture and human existence were always precarious ventures.

Population: 30 million
Capital: Xi'an
Highlights:

- The Army of Terracotta Warriors, one of China's premier attractions
- Old Xi'an, with its fascinating Muslim quarter
- Huashan, one of the less-touristed sacred mountains

Like so much of China, this region is rich in natural resources, particularly coal and oil. The Wei River, a branch of the Yellow River, cuts across the middle of the province. This fertile belt became a centre of Chinese civilisation. The south of the province is quite different from the north; it's a comparatively lush, mountainous area with a mild climate.

XI'AN

(xī'ān)

Xi'an (population three million) once vied with Rome and later Constantinople for the title of greatest city in the world. Over a period of 2000 years Xi'an has seen the rise and fall of numerous Chinese dynasties, and the monuments and archaeological sites in

467

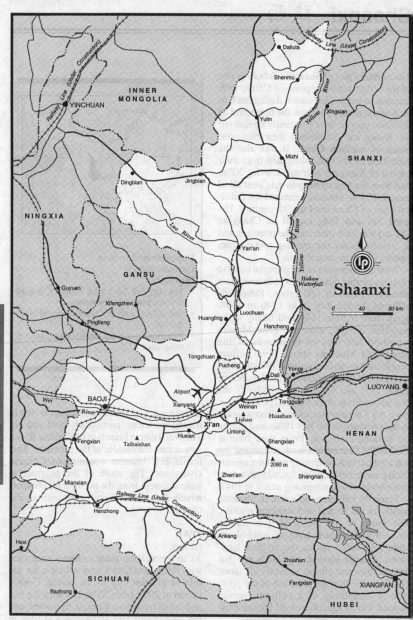

the city and the surrounding plain are a reminder that once upon a time Xi'an stood at the very centre of the Chinese world.

Today Xi'an is one of China's major attractions. The major drawcard is the Army of Terracotta Warriors, but there are countless other sights scattered throughout and around the city. There is also an Islamic element to Xi'an, found in tucked-away mosques and busy market places, that lends the city a touch of the exotic rarely found in Chinese cities further east. These together have made Xi'an an important destination for both independent and tour group travellers.

History

The earliest evidence of human habitation in the Xi'an area dates back 6000 years to Neolithic times, when the then lush plains proved a perfect area for primitive Chinese tribes to establish villages. In time, the legendary Zhou established a capital on the banks of the Fen River near present-day Xi'an.

Xianyang Between the 5th and 3rd centuries BC, China split into five separate states locked in perpetual war, until the state of Qin conquered everyone and everything. Emperor Qin Shihuang became the first emperor of a unified China and established his capital at Xianyang, near modern-day Xi'an. His longing for immortality gave posterity a remarkable legacy – a tomb guarded by an army of thousands of terracotta soldiers.

The Qin Dynasty crumbled shortly after the death of Qin Shihuang. In 207 BC it was overthrown by a revolt led by a commoner, Liu Pang. Pang established the Han Dynasty, which lasted a phenomenal 400 years, during which time the boundaries of the empire were extended deep into central Asia. But the dynasty was never really secure or unified. It collapsed in 220 AD, making way for more than three centuries of disunity and war. Nevertheless, the Han empire set a precedent that lingered on in the dreams of would-be empire builders, a dream that came to fru-

ition in the Sui and the Tang dynasties, which ruled from the city of Chang'an.

Chang'an Chang'an was established in 582 AD on the fertile plain where the capital of the Han Dynasty had once stood. After the collapse of the Han, the north of China was ruled by foreign invaders, and the south by a series of weak and short-lived Chinese dynasties. When the Sui Dynasty united the country, it built the new capital of Chang'an as a deliberate reference back to the glory of the Han period, a symbol of reunification.

The Sui was short-lived and in 618 AD it was replaced by the Tang. Under the Tang, Chang'an became the largest city in Asia, if not the world. It attracted courtiers, merchants, foreign traders, soldiers, artists, entertainers, priests and bureaucrats, and embarked the Tang on a brilliant period of creativity.

The city's design encompassed outer walls which formed a rectangle, 10 km east-west and just over eight km north-south, enclosing a neat grid system of streets and wide avenues. The walls, punctuated by 11 gates, were made of pounded earth faced with sun-dried bricks, and were probably about 5½ metres high and between 5½ nine metres thick at the base. Within these walls the imperial court and government conducted their business inside yet another walled city.

Communications between the capital and the rest of China were developed, mainly by canals which linked Chang'an to the Grand Canal and to other strategic places – another system also developed and improved by the Tang. Roads were built radiating from the capital, with inns for officials, travellers, merchants and pilgrims. This transport infrastructure enabled Chang'an to draw in taxes and enforce its power. Sea ports and caravan routes established the city as a centre of international trade, and a large foreign community established itself there. Numerous foreign religions built temples and mosques, including Muslims, the Zoroastrians of Persia, and the Nestorian Christian sect of Syria. The growth of the government elite and the evolution of a more complex imperial court drew vast numbers of people to serve it. By the 8th century the city had a phenomenal population of two million.

Towards the end of the 8th century the Tang Dynasty and its capital began to decline. From 775 onwards the central government suffered reverses at the hands of provincial warlords and Tibetan and Turkic invaders. The setbacks exposed weaknesses in the empire, and although the Tang still maintained overall supremacy, they gradually lost control of the transport networks

and the tax-collection system on which their power depended. The dynasty fell in 907 AD and China once again broke up into a number of independent states. Chang'an was eventually relegated to the role of a regional centre.

Orientation

Xi'an retains the same rectangular shape that characterised Chang'an, with streets and avenues laid out in a neat grid pattern.

The central block of the modern city is bounded by the city walls. The centre of town is the enormous Bell Tower, and from

here run Xi'an's four major streets: Bei, Nan, Dong and Xi Dajie. The railway station stands at the north-eastern edge of the central city block. Jiefang Lu runs south from the station to intersect with Dong Dajie.

Most of the tourist facilities can be found either along or in the vicinity of Jiefang Lu or Xi and Dong Dajie. However, many of the city's sights like the Shaanxi History Museum, the Big Goose and Little Goose pagodas and Banpo Neolithic Village are outside the central block. Further afield on the plains surrounding Xi'an are sights such as the Entombed Warriors at Xianyang, Famen Temple, the Tomb of Qin Shihuang and the Army of Terracotta Warriors near Lintong.

Information

PSB The PSB is at 138 Xi Dajie, a 10-minute walk west of the Bell Tower. It's open every day except Sunday from 8 am to noon and from 2.30 to 6 pm.

CITS CITS (☎ 526-2066) has its main office on Chang'an Beilu, a few minutes' walk south of the Xi'an Hotel. There are more central CITS branches at the Jiefang Hotel (☎ 742-2219 ext 237) and the Bell Tower Hotel (☎ 727-9200 ext 2842). These mainly organise tours, though other services such as rail ticket bookings are available.

Travel Agencies Many independent travellers use the staff at Mum's Home Cooking

XI'AN 西安		**13**	Bob & Betty's (Fast Food)	**14**	Friendship Store 友谊商店
PLACES TO STAY		**24**	KFC 肯德鸡	**15**	Foreign Languages Bookstore 外文书店
1	Flats of Renmin Hotel 人民大厦公寓	**25**	East Asia Restaurant 东亚饭店	**17**	Post & Telecommunications Building 邮电大楼
5	Jiefang Hotel 解放饭店	**26**	Singapore Fast Food 新加坡快餐	**18**	Drum Tower 鼓楼
9	Grand New World Hotel 古都大酒店	**27**	Laosunjia Restaurant 老孙家饭庄	**19**	Great Mosque 大清真寺
10	People's (Renmin) Hotel 人民大厦	**28**	Xi'an Restaurant 西安饭庄	**20**	City God's Temple 城隍庙
16	May First Hotel 五一饭店	**31**	Three Star & Small World Restaurants 三星，小世界餐厅	**21**	CAAC (China Northwest Airlines) 中国西北航空公司
23	Bell Tower Hotel 钟楼饭店			**22**	PSB 公安局
29	Hotel Royal 西安皇城宾馆	**OTHER**		**32**	Shaanxi Provincial Museum 陕西省博物馆
30	Hyatt Regency Hotel 凯悦宾馆	**3**	Railway Station 火车站		
34	Grand Castle Hotel 长安堡大酒店	**4**	Post Office 邮电局	**33**	Xi'an West Bus Station 西安汽车西站
35	Victory Hotel 胜利饭店	**6**	Long-Distance Bus Station 长途汽车站	**36**	Little Goose Pagoda 小雁塔
37	Xi'an Hotel 西安宾馆	**7**	Bank of China 中国银行	**38**	CITS 中国国际旅行社
PLACES TO EAT		**8**	Advance Rail Booking Office 铁路售票处	**39**	Shaanxi History Museum 陕西历史博物馆
2	Mum's & Dad's Home Cooking	**11**	Temple of the Eight Immortals 八仙安		
12	KFC 肯德鸡				

CENTRAL CHINA

and Dad's Home Cooking as their sole source of travel information – here you get the lowdown on how to get to the sights on a budget and all kinds of other useful information.

Golden Bridge Travel is another useful agency with offices on the 2nd floor of the Bell Tower Hotel (☎ 727-9200 ext 227) and on the 5th floor of the May First Hotel. It also offers tours and can provide discounts on mid-range and top-end hotel bookings in Xi'an if you stop in and visit before checking in anywhere.

Money The main Bank of China (☎ 727-2312) is at 223 Jiefang Lu, just up from Dong 5-Lu. It's open from 9 to 11.45 am and from 2 to 4.30 pm. Two other useful branches where foreigners can change money are on Xi Dajie and Dong Dajie. Many of the hotels also have money-changing services but they often refuse to serve non-guests.

Post & Telecommunications The most convenient post and telephone offices are next to the railway station and on Bei Dajie at the corner of Xixin Jie.

Maps Pick up a copy of the widely available *Xi'an Tourist Map*. A bilingual production, it is exhaustive in its listings – everything from the sights and hotels to the locations of the various KFCs around town.

Bell Tower
(*zhōnglóu*)
The Bell Tower is a huge building in the centre of Xi'an that you enter through an underpass on the north side of the tower. The original tower was built in the late 14th century, but was rebuilt at the present location in 1739 during the Qing Dynasty. A large iron bell in the tower used to mark the time each day, hence the name.

Drum Tower
(*gǔlóu*)
The Drum Tower, a smaller building to the west of the Bell Tower, marks the Muslim quarter of Xi'an. Foreigners pay an entry price of Y5. Beiyuanmen is an interesting old street of traders and craftspeople. It runs north directly from the Drum Tower and has been restored.

City Walls
(*chéngqiáng*)
Xi'an is one of the few cities in China where old city walls are still visible. The walls were built on the foundations of the walls of the Tang Forbidden City during the reign of Hong Wu, first emperor of the Ming Dynasty. They form a rectangle with a circumference of 14 km. On each side of the wall is a gateway, and over each stand three towers. At each of the four corners is a watchtower, and the top of the wall is punctuated with defensive towers. The wall is 12 metres high, with a width at the top of 12 to 14 metres and at the base of 15 to 18 metres.

Air-raid shelters were hollowed out of the walls when the Japanese bombed the city, and during the Cultural Revolution caves were dug to store grain. Most sections have been restored or even rebuilt but others have disappeared completely (though they're still shown on the maps), so unfortunately it's not possible to walk right around Xi'an along the city walls. There are access ramps up to the wall just east of the railway station, and also near Heping Lu and at South Gate (*nánmén*) beside the Provincial Museum. There are also some obscure steps at the eastern end of the south wall; tickets cost Y6.

Big Goose Pagoda
(*dà yàn tǎ*)
This pagoda stands in what was formerly the Temple of Great Maternal Grace in the south of Xi'an. The temple was built about 648 AD by Emperor Gao Zong (the third emperor of the Tang Dynasty) when he was still crown prince, in memory of his deceased mother. The buildings that stand today date from the Qing Dynasty and were built in a Ming style.

The original pagoda was built in 652 AD with only five storeys, but it has been renovated, restored and added to many times. It was built to house the Buddhist scriptures brought back from India by the travelling monk Xuan Zang, who then set about translating them into 1335 Chinese volumes. The impressive, fortress-like wood-and-brick building rises 64 metres. You can climb to the top for a view of the countryside and the city.

The Big Goose Pagoda is at the end of Yanta Lu, at the southern edge of Xi'an. Bus No 41 from the railway station goes straight there. The entrance is on the southern side of the temple grounds. Foreigners pay Y20 at the main gate, plus Y20 to climb the pagoda (student concessions are available).

On the east side of the temple is the newly built Tang Dynasty Arts Museum (tángdài yìshù bówùguǎn) with a collection specifically devoted to the Tang period in Xi'an.

Little Goose Pagoda
(xiǎo yàn tǎ)

The Little Goose Pagoda is in the grounds of the Jianfu Temple. The top of the pagoda was shaken off by an earthquake in the middle of the 16th century but the rest of the structure, 43 metres high, is intact. The Jianfu Temple was originally built in 684 AD as a site to hold prayers to bless the afterlife of the late Emperor Gao Zong. The pagoda, a rather delicate building of 15 progressively smaller tiers, was built from 707 to 709 AD and housed Buddhist scriptures brought back from India by another pilgrim.

You can get to the pagoda on bus No 3, which runs from the railway station through the south gate of the old city and down Nanguan Zhengjie. The pagoda is on Youyi Xilu just west of the intersection with Nanguan Zhengjie. Entry to the grounds is Y10 for foreigners, plus Y10 more to climb to the top of the pagoda for a panorama of Xi'an's apartment blocks and smokestacks.

Great Mosque
(dà qīngzhēnsì)

This is one of the largest mosques in China. The present buildings only date back to the middle of the 18th century, though the mosque might have been established several hundred years earlier. It stands north-west of the Drum Tower and is built in a Chinese architectural style with most of the grounds taken up by gardens. Still an active place of worship, the mosque holds several prayer services each day. The mosque is open from 8 am to noon and from 2 to 6 pm. The courtyard of the mosque can be visited, but only Muslims may enter the prayer hall. Entry is Y15.

The Great Mosque is five minutes' walk from the Drum Tower: go under the arch, then take the second tiny lane leading left to a small side street. From here the mosque is a few steps along to the right past souvenir shops.

Shaanxi Provincial Museum
(shǎnxī shěng bówùguǎn)

Once the Temple of Confucius, the museum houses a fine collection devoted largely to the history of the Silk Road. Among the artefacts is a tiger-shaped tally from the Warring States Period, inscribed with ancient Chinese characters and probably used to convey messages or orders from one military commander to another.

One of the more extraordinary exhibits is the Forest of Steles, the heaviest collection of books in the world. The earliest of these 2300 large engraved stone tablets dates from the Han Dynasty.

Most interesting is the Popular Stele of Daqin Nestorianism, recognisable by the small cross at the top. The Nestorians were an early Christian sect who differed from orthodox Christianity in their belief that Christ's human and divine natures were quite distinct. Nestorian Christianity spread eastwards to China via the Silk Road, and Marco Polo mentions making contact with members of the sect in Fuzhou in the 13th century.

The Popular Stele was engraved in 781 AD to mark the opening of a Nestorian church. The tablet describes in Syrian and Chinese how a Syrian disciple named Raban came to the imperial court of Xi'an in 635. Raban presented Christian scriptures, which were translated and then read by the emperor. The emperor, says the stone, was impressed and ordered that a monastery dedicated to the new religion be established in the city.

Other tablets include the Ming De Shou Ji Stele, which records the peasant uprising led by Li Zhicheng against the Ming, and the 114 Stone Classics of Kaichen from the Tang Dynasty inscribed with 13 ancient classics and historical records.

All of the important exhibits have labels in English. The museum entrance is on a side street which runs off Baishulin Lu, close to the South Gate of the old city wall. It's open from 8.30 am to 6 pm. Admission for foreigners is Y20 and students Y3.

Shaanxi History Museum
(shǎnxī lìshǐ bówùguǎn)

Built in huge classical-Chinese style, the museum was opened in 1992 and is rated by some as the best museum in China. The collection is chronologically arranged and includes material previously housed in the Provincial Museum, though many objects have never been on permanent display before.

The section on the ground floor deals with Chinese prehistory and the early dynastic period, starting with Palaeolithic Langtian Man and the more recent New Stone Age settlements at Lintong and Banpo between 7000 and 5000 years ago. There are many pieces of Neolithic pottery, ancient jade carvings and arrowheads. Particularly impressive are several enormous Shang and Western Zhou Dynasty bronze cooking tripods and other vessels from Yantou, Qin burial objects, bronze arrows and crossbows, ancient ceramic water pipes and four original terracotta warrior statues taken from near the Tomb of Qin Shihuang.

Upstairs, the second section is devoted to Han, Western Wei and Northern Zhou Dynasty relics. There are some interesting goose-shaped bronze lamps and a set of forged-iron transmission gears, which are surprisingly advanced for their time.

The final, third section has mainly artefacts from the Sui, Tang, Ming and Qing dynasties. The major advances in ceramic-making techniques during this period are most evident, with intricately crafted terracotta horses and camels, fine pale-green glazed *misi* pottery and Buddhist-inspired Tang Dynasty statues. There are also items from the Famen Temple, including a gold and silver tea set and some superbly designed Ming and Qing pottery with rose and peony decorations.

To get there from the railway station, take bus No 5 or 14. Foreigners enter and leave the museum via doors to the left of the main entrance. Photography is strictly prohibited and you must deposit (free of charge) any hand luggage in the lockers provided. Admission is Y38, but holders of a valid student card pay only Y10. All exhibits include labels and explanations in English. The museum is open every day from 8.30 am to 5.30 pm.

Old Xi'an

Xi'an's old **Muslim Quarter**, near the Great Mosque, has retained much of its original character. The backstreets to the north and west of the mosque have been home to the city's Hui community for centuries. Walking through the narrow laneways lined with old mud-brick houses, you pass butcher shops, sesame oil factories, smaller mosques hidden behind enormous wooden doors and proud, stringy-bearded men wearing white skull-caps. Good streets to explore are Nanyuan Men, Huajue Xiang and Damaishi Jie, which runs north off Xi Dajie through an interesting Islamic food market.

The **Temple of the Eight Immortals** (bā xiān ān) is Xi'an's largest Taoist establishment and an active place of worship. Scenes from Taoist mythology are painted around the temple courtyard. To get there take a No 10, 11, 28 or 42 bus east along Changle Lu and get off two stops past the city walls, then continue 100 metres on foot and turn right (south) under a green-painted iron gateway into a market lane. Follow this, turning briefly right then left again into another small street leading past the temple. The entrance is on the southern side of the temple grounds. You can also reach the temple by following the street running directly east from Zhongshan Gate.

The **City God's Temple** (*chéng huáng miào*) is built in old-style heavy wooden architecture with a blue tiled roof, and possibly dates from the early Qing period. The building is sadly dilapidated and is currently being used as a warehouse, but this gives it a definite 'unrestored charm'. The temple is 10 minutes' walk west of the Drum Tower at the end of a long covered market running north off Xi Dajie. There's no English sign, so look for the large red Chinese characters above the entrance immediately east of the Xijing Hotel.

Organised Tours

One-day tours allow you to the see all the sights around Xi'an more quickly and conveniently than if you arranged one yourself. Itineraries differ somewhat, but there are two basic tours: a 'Western Tour' and an 'Eastern Tour'. There are also tours of the sights within the city area that leave from the square in front of the railway station. CITS-organised tours are more expensive than those run by other operators, but the cheaper tours usually won't leave until they have enough people and tend to give you less time at each place.

Eastern Tour The Eastern Tour (*dōngxiàn yóulǎn*) is the most popular as it includes the Army of Terracotta Warriors as well as the Tomb of Qin Shihuang, Banpo Neolithic Village and Huaqing Pool.

Both Golden Bridge Travel and CITS do Eastern Tours for Y95 with transport only, or Y280 including lunch and all entry tickets. The coach leaves Xi'an around 9 am and returns by 5 pm. An English-speaking guide is provided and you usually get two hours at the warriors and Qin Shihuang's tomb, although many tourists complain that the CITS tour spends too long at the boring Huaqing Pool. Essentially the same tour can be done for far less by taking one of the Chinese minibus tours; you can buy tickets for Y40 at a kiosk in front of the railway station.

Western Tour The longer Western Tour (*xīxiàn yóulǎn*) includes the Xianyang City Museum, some of the Imperial Tombs, the Qian Tomb and sometimes also Famen Temple. It's less popular than the Eastern Tour and consequently you will have to get a group of people to make your own tour with either Golden Bridge Travel or CITS – the cost for one person alone is Y860.

Places to Stay – bottom end

Two hotels vie for the coveted title of backpacker crash pad – the Flats of Renmin Hotel in the north-west of town and the Victory Hotel in the south. The former is the most popular, and is the best place to be based if you want to meet other travellers and have easy access to banana pancakes. Travellers coming in from Beijing and Chengdu by train will be greeted by touts from the nearby restaurants who will take you to the hotel and then cordially invite you to breakfast, lunch and dinner (in their restaurant). Both hotels come in for occasional criticism on the sanitation front – if you are fastidious about such things, stay at the May First Hotel.

The *Flats of Renmin Hotel* (☎ 722-2352) (*rénmín dàshà gōngyù*) is at No 9 Fenghe Lu. Beds in mini-dorm quads (with free breakfast) go for Y35, while air-con doubles with bathroom cost Y100. There's 24-hour hot water for showering and a relatively cheap laundry service. If no-one meets you at the station, take bus No 9 and get off after six stops. A taxi from the station should cost between Y10 and Y12.

The *Victory Hotel* (☎ 721-3184) (*shènglì fàndiàn*), just south of Heping Gate, is an old stand-by and still gets a regular trickle of foreign custom. Beds in simple triples/quads start at Y34, while air-con doubles with bathroom cost Y140. Bus Nos 5 and 41 (among others) go past the hotel from the railway station.

Places to Stay – middle

The *May First Hotel* (☎ 723-1844) (*wǔyī fàndiàn*) is at 351 Dong Dajie, a short distance from the Bell Tower. It has an excellent location, is clean and friendly, and has singles at Y121, doubles at Y150 and deluxe doubles at Y190. All rooms have attached bathrooms and air-con. An inexpensive laundry service is available.

The *Jiefang Hotel* (☎ 721-2369) (*jiěfàng fàndiàn*), diagonally across the wide square to your left as you leave the railway station, has a convenient location that for some travellers is the deciding factor. The Jiefang has doubles at Y260, triples at Y260 and quads at Y320.

The enormous *People's (Renmin) Hotel* (☎ 721-5111) (*rénmín dàshà*) is at 319 Dongxin Jie. Built in the classic early-1950s Stalinist architectural style (with Chinese characteristics), it has been renovated into a fairly upmarket accommodation option. The cheapest doubles cost Y350 and range up to Y470 or Y660 for a suite.

Places to Stay – top end

Not surprisingly, there has been a boom in top-end accommodation in Xi'an in recent years, with the result that many of the hotels seem a little deserted – scope for significant discounts, especially in the low season months (November to March). Most top-end hotels in Xi'an levy a 15% service charge and tax.

Top-end hotels (and there are dozens of them) include:

Bell Tower Hotel (*zhōnglóu fàndiàn*); managed by Holiday Inn group; rates from US$70/75 for singles/twins (☎ 727-9200; fax 721-8767)

Empress Hotel (*huánghòu dàjiŭdiàn*); rates from US$50 (☎ 323-2999; fax 323-6988)

Grand Castle Hotel (*cháng'ān chéngbǎo dàjiŭdiàn*); rates from US$100 (☎ 723-1800; fax 723-1500)

Grand New World Hotel (*gǔdū xīnshìjiè dàjiŭdiàn*); rates from US $110 (substantial discounts available) (☎ 721-6868; fax 721-9754)

Hotel Royal (*xī'ān huángchéng bīnguǎn*); rates from US$90 (☎ 723-5311; fax 723-9754)

Hyatt Regency Hotel (*kǎiyuè fàndiàn*); rates from US$150 (☎ 723-1234; fax 721-6799)

Shangrila Hotel (*xiānggélǐlā fàndiàn*) (☎ 323-2981; fax 323-5477)

Sheraton Hotel (*xǐláidēng dàjiŭdiàn*); rates from US$90 (☎ 426-1888; fax 426-2188)

Singapore Hotel (*shénzhōu míngzhū jiŭdiàn*); rates from US$80 (☎ 323-3888; fax 323-5962)

Places to Eat

The travellers' restaurant scene is almost exclusively centred on two restaurants across from the Flats of Renmin Hotel: *Dad's Home Cooking* and *Mum's Home Cooking*. These are two separate establishments and competition between them is fierce. Try them both and decide for yourself which you prefer. Both offer good food at reasonable prices and provide useful services for travellers. Dad's is perhaps a little more relaxed about sharing custom with its new next-door neighbour.

The *Small World Restaurant* and the *Three Star Restaurant* just north of the Victory Hotel also provide travellers' essentials (pancakes, cheap beer and free information), but have fallen on hard times now that most travellers are based up in the north of town at the Flats of Renmin Hotel.

It's easy to forget that there's a lot of good street food available in Xi'an. In winter the entire population seems to get by on endless bowls of noodles, but at other times of the year there are all kinds of delicious snacks to be had. Much of the local street food is of Islamic origin, and some common dishes are: *fěnrèròu*, made by frying chopped mutton in a wok with fine-ground wheat; dark brown sorghum or buckwheat noodles called *héletiáo*; and *mǐgāo*, deep-fried rice cakes with a sweet rose-water filling. Best of all, however, is *yángròu pàomó*, a soup dish that involves breaking (or grating) a flat loaf of bread into a bowl and adding a delicious mutton stock.

For Muslim-Chinese 'haute cuisine' try the 3rd-floor section of the *Laosunjia Restaurant* (*lǎosūnjia fànzhuāng*) on the corner of Duanlumen and Dong Dajie. Downstairs, in the inexpensive plebs dining area, they have the yangrou paomo (among other things) mentioned above. The restaurant is opposite the Friendship Store and is readily identified by its green dome roof with an Islamic moon-crescent on top. They serve a delicious local hotpot called *shuànguōzi*, made by dipping uncooked meat and vegetable slices into a boiling chafing dish.

The cheap downstairs restaurant in the

May First Hotel *(wǔyī fàndiàn)* is good for staple northern China food like pork dumplings and hearty bowls of noodles. It's popular with locals and always busy. The upstairs restaurant is not worth bothering with.

The *East Asia Restaurant* (☎ 721-8410) *(dōngyà fàndiàn)* was founded in 1916 in Shanghai, but moved to Xi'an in 1956. The restaurant's better sections on the 2nd and 3rd floors have arguably the city's best Chinese cuisine. The East Asia is south-east of the Bell Tower at 46 Luoma Shi, a lane running off Dong Dajie.

The *Xi'an Restaurant* (☎ 721-6262) *(xī'ān fànzhuāng)* is at 298 Dong Dajie. In the cheap section downstairs, the house specialty is a salty fried dumpling called *guōtiē*. Upstairs is geared mainly to banquets, but there is also a section for general guests with a shorter menu in English. The food ranges from mediocre to outstanding.

The Bell Tower Hotel has a breakfast buffet for Y55, and its *Xi'an Garden Cantonese Restaurant* serves reasonably good food.

CITS can organise a Tang Dynasty evening with banquet-style Xi'an cuisine and traditional dancing. At US$40 per head it is somewhat overpriced, but those who have tried it say it is fun.

Fast Food If you must, *KFC* has invaded Xi'an in a big way – there are branches all over town. Another, more palatable, option is *Singapore Fast Food*, a hawker-style variation on the fast-food theme – air-con and laminex – but the food is good. Also worth checking out is *Bob & Betty's* at 285 Dong Dajie. It has excellent burgers, pizzas and coffee at affordable prices.

Things to Buy

Huajue Xiang *(huàjuè xiàng)* is a narrow alley running beside the Great Mosque with many small souvenir and 'antique' shops – it's great for browsing. This is one of the best places in China to pick up souvenirs like name chops or a pair of chiming steel balls. Bargaining is the order of the day.

The Friendship Store is east of the Bell Tower, on Nanxin Jie just north of the intersection with Dong Dajie. It has everything from perfume and kitsch watches to life-size terracotta soldiers. Prices are, shall we say, slightly inflated.

Around town you'll also find worthy conversation pieces like carved-stone ink trays used in Chinese calligraphy and a wide range of jade products from earrings to cigarette holders. There are plenty of silks too, but you're probably better off buying these closer to their source (Suzhou, Shanghai etc) than in Xi'an. Street hawkers sell delicate miniature wire furniture and ingenious little folded bamboo-leaf insects such as crickets and cicadas, which make cheap and attractive souvenirs.

Getting There & Away

Air Xi'an is one of the best-connected cities in China – it's possible to fly to almost any major Chinese destination. Here, CAAC is called China Northwest Airlines *(zhōngguó xīběi hángkōng gōngsī)*. Its booking office is inconveniently located on the south-eastern corner of Xiguan Zhengjie and Laodong Lu, 1½ km from West Gate. It's open from 8.30 to 11.30 am and 3 to 8 pm. It's more convenient to book tickets with CITS or in any of the air booking offices in the major hotels around town – the Bell Tower Hotel has an efficient office on the ground floor.

There's also another CAAC-affiliated company calling itself 'Shaanxi United Airlines', whose small booking office is conveniently located beside the People's (Renmin) Hotel gate.

On the international front, there are flights to Hong Kong for Y2240 with Dragonair and Y2180 with China Northwest, and daily flights to Nagoya in Japan. Dragonair (☎ 426-9288) has an office in the lobby of the Sheraton Hotel. Singapore Airlines should have a direct connection with Singapore by the time you have this book in your hands.

Bus The most central long-distance bus station is opposite Xi'an Railway Station.

Some useful connections are to Huashan, Ankang, Yan'an and Ruicheng (south-western Shanxi). Evening buses with sleeping berths go to Zhengzhou, Yichang, Yinchuan and Luoyang from here, though travelling by train will be much more comfortable.

There is also a large bus station on Huancheng Nanlu, west of the South Gate.

Train There are direct trains from Xi'an to Beijing, Chengdu, Guangzhou, Hefei, Qingdao, Shanghai, Taiyuan, Ürümqi and Wuhan. For Chongqing and Kunming change at Chengdu.

The foreigners' ticket office is on the 2nd floor of the railway station above the ticket office for Chinese. Same-day tickets can sometimes be bought immediately at window Nos 1 and 2, but for other tickets you must first book at the windows near the stairs. Travellers with student cards can buy tickets downstairs at Chinese prices.

CITS can organise tickets with a minimum of fuss providing you give them two or three days' notice, and it's also worth asking around at the foreigners' restaurants for information on buying tickets.

Direct trains to Beijing take around 17 hours, to Guangzhou around 22 hours and to Chengdu around 19 hours. For travellers to Luoyang and Zhengzhou, there is an air-con tourist train that leaves at 10.50 am and arrives in Zhengzhou at 7.23 pm the same day.

Getting Around

To/From the Airport Xi'an's Xiguan Airport is around 40 km north-west of Xi'an. CAAC's shuttle buses run only between the airport and its ticket office (Y15, 50 minutes each way), from where you can pick up a taxi or local bus to your hotel. Taxis demand at least Y130 in either direction and will try to gouge you for even more if you arrive at an inconvenient hour of the day.

Bus Xi'an's packed public buses are a pickpocket's paradise, so watch your wallet when you ride them. More comfortable minibuses run on the same routes and charge around Y2 for most central destinations. Local buses go to all the major sights in and around the city, such as Banpo Neolithic Village and the Army of Terracotta Warriors.

Taxi Taxis are abundant and reasonably cheap if you can convince the driver to use the meter – flag fall is between Y4.80 and Y5.60, though there is usually a Y2 surcharge on top of this. At the railway station and airport, prices are negotiable.

Bicycle Bicycle hire is available at the Flats of Renmin Hotel (and at the nearby foreigners' restaurants) and at the Victory Hotel. Prices average Y1 per hour or Y10 per day. Mum's Home Cooking was talking about investing in some decent bikes – check to see if they have got around to it. Bike rental is also available at the Bell Tower Hotel for Y2 per hour.

AROUND XI'AN

Most of the really interesting sights are outside the city. The two biggest drawcards are the Banpo Neolithic Village and the Army of Terracotta Warriors near the Tomb of Qin Shihuang.

Banpo Neolithic Village

(bànpō bówùguǎn)

Formally rated as Xi'an's No 2 attraction surpassed only by the Army of Terracotta Warriors, the Banpo Neolithic Village gets very mixed reports from travellers. The general consensus is that it's tacky and boring, but the occasional traveller comes away singing its praises. The best advice is to limit your visit to the Neolithic village itself (Y15) and avoid the adjacent Matriarchal Clan Village (Y40), where matriarchs in Neolithic garb, high heels and reinforced stockings seem to be shooting for a Guinness Book of Records 'tacky recreation of the Stone Age' award.

Banpo is the earliest example of 'Yangshao culture' (named after the village where the first of these was discovered) so far unearthed. It appears to have been occupied

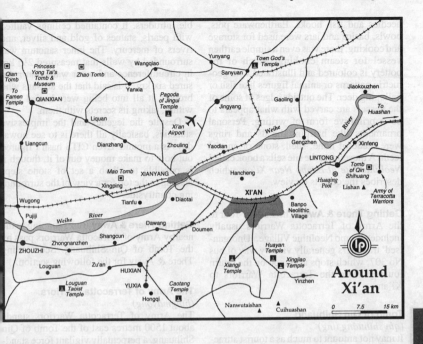

Around Xi'an

from 4500 BC until around 3750 BC. The village was discovered in 1953 and is on the eastern bank of the Chan River in a suburb of Xi'an. A large hall has been built over what was part of the residential area of the village, and there are adjacent buildings housing pottery and other artefacts. Pottery found south of the Qinlingshan mountains has suggested that even earlier agricultural villages may have existed there, but this is speculation.

The Banpo ruins are divided into three areas: a residential area, a pottery-manufacturing area and a cemetery. These include the remains of 45 houses or other buildings, over 200 storage cellars, six pottery kilns and 250 graves.

The earlier houses are half underground, in contrast to the later houses, which stand at ground level and have a wooden framework. Some huts are round, others square, with doors facing south in both cases. There is a hearth or fire-pit in each house. The main

building materials were wood for the framework and mud mixed with straw for the walls.

The residential part of the village was surrounded by an artificial moat, 300 metres long, about two metres deep and two metres wide. It protected the village from attacks by wild animals and from the effects of heavy rainfall in what was originally a hot and humid environment. Another trench, about two metres deep, runs through the middle of the village. To the east of the residential area is the pottery kiln centre. To the north of the village lies the cemetery, where the adult dead were buried along with funerary objects like earthen pots. The children were buried in earthen pots close to the houses.

The villagers survived by hunting, fishing and gathering, but had begun to farm the surrounding land and keep domestic animals. Their stone tools included axes, knives, shovels, millstones, arrowheads and fishing-net sinkers. Bone objects included needles and fish hooks. Earthenware pots, bowls, basins and jars were used for storage and cooking; there was even a simple earthen vessel for steam cooking. Much of the pottery is coloured and illustrated with geometric patterns or animal figures like fish or galloping deer. The outside edges of some of the vessels are carved with what appears to be a primitive form of writing. Personal ornaments like hairpins, beads and rings were made of bone, shell, stone or animal teeth. A museum at the site sells a book called *Neolithic Site at Banpo Near Xi'an*, which describes the objects on view.

Getting There & Away The Eastern Tour to the Army of Terracotta Warriors usually includes Banpo Neolithic Village. 'Unorganised' travellers generally visit by way of bus No 307, which stops at Banpo on the return journey from the Terracotta Warriors to Xi'an.

Tomb of Qin Shihuang
(qín shǐhuáng líng)

It may not amount to much as a tourist attraction, but in its time the Tomb of Qin Shihuang must have been one of the grandest mausoleums the world has ever seen.

In the year 246 BC, at the age of 13, Ying Zheng ascended the throne of the state of Qin and assumed the title 'Shi Huang', or First Emperor. One by one he defeated his enemies, until in 221 BC the last of them fell. Qin Shihuang united the country, standardised the currency and the written script. On the down side, he acquired a reputation for purges, mass book-burning parties, enforced labour in massive construction projects, and in general behaviour that has made him a byword for tyranny among the Chinese. His rule lasted until his death in 210 BC. His son only held out for four years, before being overthrown by the revolt which established the Han Dynasty.

His tomb, as one might expect, was a grand affair. Historical accounts describe it as containing palaces filled with precious stones and ingenious defenses against possible intruders. It contained ceilings vaulted with pearls, statues of gold and silver, and rivers of mercury. The inner sanctum was surrounded by walls that measured 2½ km in circumference and outer walls that measured six km. It is said that the artisans who brought it all into being were buried alive within, taking its secrets with them.

Despite the legends and the impressive statistics, basically all there is to see nowadays is a mound. Even CITS hasn't figured out how to make money out of it, though it is possible to climb a set of stone steps leading to the top for a view of the surrounding countryside.

Getting There & Away Buses running to the nearby Army of Terracotta Warriors pass by the Tomb of Qin Shihuang. See Getting There & Away for the following section.

The Army of Terracotta Warriors
(bīngmǎyǒng)

The Army of Terracotta Warriors stands about 1500 metres east of the Tomb of Qin Shihuang, a perpetually vigilant force standing guard over the ancient imperial necropolis.

In 1974 peasants digging a well uncovered what turned out to be perhaps the major archaeological discovery of the 20th century: an underground vault of earth and timber that eventually yielded thousands of life-size terracotta soldiers and their horses in battle formation. In 1976, two other, smaller vaults were discovered close to the first one.

The first underground vault measures about 210 metres east to west and 60 metres from north to south. The pit varies in depth from five to seven metres. Walls were built running east to west at intervals of three metres, forming corridors. In these corridors, on floors laid with grey brick, are arranged the terracotta figures. Pillars and beams once supported a roof.

The 6000 terracotta figures of warriors and horses face east in a rectangular battle array. The vanguard appears to be three rows of 210 crossbow and longbow bearers who stand at the easternmost end of the army. Close behind is the main force of armoured soldiers holding spears, dagger-axes and other long-shaft weapons, accompanied by 35 horse-drawn chariots. Every figure differs in facial features and expressions. The horsemen are shown wearing tight-sleeved outer robes, short coats of chain mail and windproof caps. The archers have bodies and limbs positioned in strict accordance with an ancient book on the art of war.

Many of the figures originally held real weapons of the day, and over 10,000 pieces have been sorted to date. Bronze swords were worn by the figures representing the generals and other senior officers. Surface treatment made the swords resistant to rust and corrosion so that after being buried for more than 2000 years they were still sharp.

Arrowheads were made of a lethal metal alloy containing a high percentage of lead.

The second vault, excavated in 1976, contained about 1000 figures. The third vault contained only 68 warriors and one war chariot, and appeared to be the command post for the soldiers in the other vaults. Archaeologists believe the warriors discovered so far may be part of an even larger terracotta army still buried around Qin Shihuang's tomb. Excavation of the entire complex and the tomb itself could take decades.

Almost as impressive is a pair of bronze chariots and horses unearthed in 1980 just 20 metres west of the Tomb of Qin Shihuang and now housed in a small museum *(qín yǒng bówùguǎn)* within the enclosure of the warriors site.

Visitors are not permitted to take photos at the site (ostensibly to protect the figures from light damage caused by camera flashes, but one suspects also to boost postcard and slide sales) and people who infringe this rule can expect to have their film confiscated. If you decide to take a few sly shots and get caught, try to remember that the attendants are just doing their job.

The management realises that the same foreign tourists who marvel at the warriors will also pay good money to see them, and as a result ticket prices have been raised progressively in recent years. Admission to Vault 1 costs Y60; an additional Y20 is required for Vaults 2 and 3 (these can be missed unless you didn't see enough terracotta warriors in Vault 1); the museum costs Y15; and there is a final Y40 for a 'Circle Vision' documentary on the warriors and their excavation. Student discounts are available.

Getting There & Away You can see the site as part of a tour from Xi'an (see Organised Tours in the Xi'an section earlier in this chapter). Alternatively, it is possible to do it yourself by public bus. From the railway station take a No 306 bus, which travels via Huaqing Pool, for Y3.5. The No 307 bus does the return journey to Xi'an via Banpo Neolithic Village.

The world-famous terracotta warriors army, near Xi'an.

Huaqing Pool
(huáqīng chí)

The Huaqing Pool is 30 km east of Xi'an below Lishan. Water from hot springs is funnelled into public bathhouses that have 60 pools accommodating 400 people. During the Tang Dynasty these natural hot baths were a favoured retreat of emperors, who often came here to relax with their concubines.

The Huaqing Pool leaves most visitors cold. If you don't fancy strolling around the gardens with swarms of excited Chinese tourists, try the museum up the road or take a walk on one of the paths leading up through the forest behind the complex. There is a Taoist temple on Lishan dedicated to the 'Old Mother' Nu Wa, who created the human race and patched up cracks in the sky after a catastrophe. On the mountain's summit are beacon towers built for defence during the Han Dynasty. A cable car will whiz you up there for Y30, Y25 to come down. Admission to Huaqing Pool is Y33 for foreigners.

The 'Guifei Surfing Pool' at Huaqing pipes hot spring water into personal bathtubs, where you can have a soak at an exorbitant price – very few non-Chinese bother.

Getting There & Away The No 306 bus, which runs from the Xi'an Railway Station to the Army of Terracotta Warriors, stops at Huaqing Pool. The Eastern Tour organised from Xi'an visits the Huaqing Pool (see Organised Tours in the Xi'an section), but some tours stop for an excessively long two hours. Buses back to Xi'an can be caught from the parking lot opposite the entrance.

Xianyang
(xiányáng)

This little town is half an hour's bus ride from Xi'an. The chief attraction is Xianyang City Museum *(xiányáng shì bówùguǎn)*, which houses a remarkable collection of 3000 miniature terracotta soldiers and horses, discovered in 1965. Each figure is about half a metre high. They were excavated from a Han Dynasty tomb. Admission

to the Entombed Warriors is Y30, with an extra ticket needed for entry to the special exhibition hall.

Getting There & Away To get to Xianyang Museum from Xi'an, take bus No 3 from the railway station to the terminal and then get bus No 59. Get off at the terminal in Xianyang. Up ahead on the left-hand side of the road you'll see a clock tower. Turn right at this intersection and then left at Xining Jie. The museum is housed in a former Ming Dynasty Confucian temple on Zhongshan Jie, which is a continuation of Xining Jie. The entrance is flanked by two stone lions. It's about a 20-minute walk from the bus terminal.

Imperial Tombs

Apart from the tomb of Qin Shihuang, a large number of other imperial tombs dot the Guanzhong plain surrounding Xi'an. The easiest way to get there is by tour from Xi'an (see the Xi'an Organised Tours section for details).

In these tombs are buried the emperors of numerous dynasties, as well as empresses, concubines, government officials and high-ranking military leaders. Construction of an emperor's tomb often began within a few years of his ascension to the throne and didn't finish until he died.

Zhao Tomb *(zhāo líng)* The Zhao Tomb set the custom of building imperial tombs on mountain slopes, breaking the tradition of building tombs on the plains with an artificial hill over them. This burial ground on Jiuzongshan, 70 km north-west of Xi'an, belongs to the second Tang emperor, Tai Zong, who died in 649 AD.

Of the 18 imperial mausoleums on the Guanzhong plain, this is probably the most representative. With the mountain at the centre, the tomb fans out to the south-east and south-west. Within its confines are 167 lesser tombs of the emperor's relatives and high-ranking military and government officials.

The Xi'an Incident

Nowadays, Lishan is hardly worth the effort of going there, as Chiang Kaishek would probably attest. His visit turned out to be most inauspicious. On 12 December 1936 he was arrested in Lishan by his own generals, supposedly clad only in his pyjamas and dressing gown, on the slopes of the snow-covered mountain up which he had fled. A pavilion marks the spot and there's a simple inscription, 'Chiang was caught here'.

In the early 1930s Kuomintang General Yang Huzheng was the undisputed monarch of those parts of Shaanxi not under Communist control. In 1935 he was forced to share power when General Zhang Xueliang arrived with his own troops from Manchuria in the wake of the Japanese occupation. Zhang assumed the office of 'Vice-Commander of the National Bandit Suppression Commission'.

In October and November 1935 the Kuomintang suffered severe defeats at the hands of the Communists and thousands of soldiers went over to the Red Army. Captured officers were given a period of 'anti-Japanese tutelage' and were then released. Returning to Xi'an, they brought Zhang reports of the Red Army's desire to stop the civil war and unite against the Japanese. Chiang Kaishek, however, stubbornly refused to turn his forces against the Japanese and continued his war against the Communists. On 7 December 1936 he flew to Xi'an to oversee another 'extermination' campaign against the Red Army.

Zhang Xueliang flew to Yan'an, met Zhou Enlai and became convinced of the sincerity of the Red Army's anti-Japanese policies. A secret truce was established. On the night of 11 December Zhang met the divisional commanders of his Manchurian army and the army of General Yang. A decision was made to arrest Chiang Kaishek. The following night the commander of Zhang's bodyguard led the attack on Chiang Kaishek's residence at the foot of Lishan and took him prisoner along with most of his general staff. In the city the 1500 'Blueshirts' (the police force controlled by Chiang's nephew and credited with numerous abductions, killings and imprisonments of Chiang's opponents) were disarmed and arrested.

A few days later, Zhang sent his plane to collect three representatives of the Red Army and bring them to Xi'an: Zhou Enlai, Ye Jianying and Bo Gu. Chiang Kaishek feared he was going to be put on trial and executed, but instead the Communists and the Manchurian leaders told him their opinions of his policies and described the changes they thought were necessary to save the country. Whatever Chiang did or did not promise to do, the practical result of the Xi'an Incident was the end of the civil war.

Zhang released Chiang Kaishek on Christmas Day and flew back with him to Nanjing to await punishment. It was a face-saving gesture to Chiang. Zhang was sentenced by a tribunal to 10 years' imprisonment and 'deprivation of civil rights for five years'. He was pardoned the next day. The extermination campaign against the Red Army was called off and the Kuomintang announced that their first task now was to recover the territory lost to the Japanese.

Nevertheless, Chiang began organising what he hoped would be a quiet decimation of the Communist forces. By June 1937 Chiang had moved the sympathetic Manchurian army out of Shaanxi and replaced it with loyal Kuomintang troops. He planned to disperse the Communists by moving the Red Army piecemeal to other parts of the country, supposedly in preparation for the war against the Japanese. The Communists were only extricated from their precarious position by Japan's sudden and all-out invasion of China in July 1937. Chiang was forced to leave the Red Army intact and in control of the north-west.

Chiang never forgave Zhang Xueliang and never freed him. Thirty years later he was still held prisoner on Taiwan. General Yang was arrested in Chongqing and towards the end of WW II was secretly executed. Another reminder of this period is the office which the Communist Party set up in Xi'an to liaise with the Kuomintang. The office was disbanded in 1946, and after 1949 it was made into a memorial hall to the Eighth Route Army. It's on Beixin Lu, in the north of the city's central block. ∎

Burying other people in the same park as the emperor was a custom dating back to the Han Dynasty. Tai Zong won support and loyalty from his ministers and officials by

bestowing on them the great favour of being buried in attendance on the Son of Heaven.

Buried in the sacrificial altar of the tomb were six statues known as the 'Six Steeds of

Zhaoling', representing the horses which the emperor used during his wars of conquest. Some of the statues have been relocated to museums in Xi'an.

Qian Tomb (*qián líng*) One of the most impressive tombs is the Qian Tomb, 85 km north-west of Xi'an on Liangshan. This is the joint resting place of Tang emperor Gao Zong and his wife Empress Wu Zetian. Gao Zong ascended the throne in 650 AD after the death of his father, Emperor Tai Zong. Empress Wu was actually a concubine of Tai Zong, who also caught the fancy of his son, who made her his empress. Gao died in 683 AD, and the following year Empress Wu dethroned her husband's successor, Emperor Zhong Zong. She reigned as an all-powerful monarch until her death around 705 AD. Nowadays it's fashionable to draw comparisons between Empress Wu and the late Jiang Qing, Mao's disgraced last wife.

The tomb consists of three peaks; the two on the south side are artificial, but the higher northern peak is natural and is the main part of the tomb. Walls used to surround the tomb but these are gone. South-west of the tomb are 17 smaller tombs of officials.

The grounds of the imperial tomb boast a number of large stone sculptures of animals and officers of the imperial guard. There are 61 (now headless) statues of the leaders of minority peoples of China and of the representatives of friendly nations who attended the emperor's funeral.

The two steles on the ground each stand over six metres high. The 'Wordless Stele' is a blank tablet; one story goes that it symbolises Empress Wu's absolute power, which she considered inexpressible in words.

Prince Zhang Huai's Tomb (*zhāng huái mù*) Of the smaller tombs surrounding the Qian Tomb only five have been excavated. Zhang was the second son of Emperor Gao Zong and Empress Wu. For some reason the prince was exiled to Sichuan in 683 and died the following year, aged 31 (a pillow across the face perhaps?). Empress Wu posthumously rehabilitated him. His remains were

brought to Xi'an after Emperor Zhong Zong regained power. Tomb paintings show horsemen playing polo, but these and other paintings are in a terrible state.

Princess Yong Tai's Tomb (*yǒng tài gōng zhǔ mù*) Nearby is the Tomb of Princess Yong Tai with tomb paintings showing palace servants. The line engravings on the stone outer coffin are extraordinarily graceful. Yong Tai was a granddaughter of the Tang emperor Gao Zong, and the seventh daughter of Emperor Zhong Zong. She was put to death by Empress Wu in 701 AD, but was rehabilitated posthumously by Emperor Zhong Zong after he regained power.

Mao Tomb (*mào líng*) The Mao Tomb, 40 km from Xi'an, is the resting place of Emperor Wu, the most powerful ruler of the Han Dynasty, who died in 87 BC. The cone-shaped mound of rammed earth is almost 47 metres high, and is the largest of the Han imperial tombs. A wall used to enclose the mausoleum but now only the ruins of the gates on the east, west and north sides remain. It is recorded that the emperor was entombed with a jade cicada in his mouth and was clad in jade clothes sewn with gold thread, and that buried with him were live animals and an abundance of jewels.

Famen Temple
(*fǎmén sì*)
Famen Temple is 115 km north-west of Xi'an and was built during the Eastern Han Dynasty in about 200 AD.

In 1981, after torrential rains had weakened the temple's ancient brick structure, the entire western side of the 12-storey pagoda collapsed. The subsequent restoration work produced a sensational discovery. Below the pagoda in a sealed crypt (built during the Tang Dynasty to contain four sacred finger bones of the buddha, known as *sarira*) were over 1000 sacrificial objects and royal offerings, including stone-tablet Buddhist scriptures, gold and silver items and some 27,000 coins. These relics had been completely forgotten for over 1000 years. A museum housing part of the collection has been built on the site. After the excavations had finished the temple was reconstructed in its original form.

The best way to visit Famen Temple is to take a Western Tour from Xi'an (see the Xi'an Organised Tours section). Some tours don't include the temple so check before you book. Foreigners' entry prices are Y10 to the temple, Y15 to the crypt and Y15 to the museum; the pagoda itself is not open to the public.

HUASHAN
(huáshān)

The 2200-metre-high granite peaks of Huashan, 120 km east of Xi'an, tower above the plains to the north, forming one of China's sacred mountain areas. A tortuous 15-km stepped path leads to the top; in one famous section called Green Dragon Ridge the way has been cut along a narrow rock ridge with sheer cliffs on either side. At the top a circuit trail links Huashan's four main summit peaks. From Huashan village at the base of the mountain it usually takes between six and nine hours to reach the top, so it's best to stay overnight at one of the mountain hotels. Several narrow and almost vertical 'bottle-neck' sections are dangerous when the route is crowded, particularly under wet or icy conditions. The gate ticket price for foreigners is Y35, plus another Y5 'registration fee'.

Places to Stay & Eat

It's best to be based in Huashan village as rates on the mountain have become expensive in recent years. There is a good CITS-run hotel on the left, 20 metres before you come to the entrance gate; doubles with bath cost Y50 per person and singles are Y80. The *Xiyue Hotel (xīyuè fàndiàn)*, a short way down the street, has cheaper rates if it is not full. The *Huashan Guesthouse (huáshān bīnguǎn)* on Jianshe Lu near the bus station has doubles for Y180; the back rooms have mountain views. There are many cheap tourist restaurants along the street leading up to the entrance gate.

Unfortunately, many of the hotels along the climb have gone upmarket and those that haven't are often off limits to foreigners. The official foreigners' abode is the *East Peak Guesthouse (dōngfēng fàndiàn)*, which has rates of Y400 and upwards.

Getting There & Away

If you're coming from Xi'an, the best access to Huashan is by bus from the long-distance bus station (2½ hours). Although Huashan village is on the Xi'an-Luoyang railway line, most trains don't stop at the local station, so you will probably have to get off at Mengyuan, 15-odd km east of Huashan. From Mengyuan there are regular minibuses to Huashan.

HUANGLING
(huánglíng)

Halfway between Xi'an and Yan'an is the town of Huangling. The tomb on nearby Qiaoshan is supposedly that of the Yellow Emperor Huang Di. Huang is said to be the father of the Chinese people, one of the 'Five Sovereigns' who reigned about 5000 years ago and by wars of conquest unified the Chinese clans. He is credited with numerous inventions and discoveries: silkworm cultivation, weaving, writing, the cart, the boat, the compass, building bricks and musical instruments. You can stay overnight in this town if you're taking the bus up from Xi'an to Yan'an.

YAN'AN
(yán'ān)

Yan'an, 270 km from Xi'an in northern Shaanxi Province, is just a small city of 40,000 people, but together with Mao's birthplace at Shaoshan it has special significance as a major Communist pilgrimage spot. Between the years 1936 and 1947 this was the headquarters of the Chinese Communists. The Long March from Jiangxi ended in 1936 when the Communists reached the northern Shaanxi town of Wuqi. The following year they moved their base to Yan'an.

Very few travellers indeed make it up into

this part of Shaanxi. Accommodation is fairly expensive and onward transport (unless you are heading up to Inner Mongolia) is a hassle.

Orientation

Yan'an is spread out along a Y-shaped valley formed where the east and west branches of the Yan River meet. The town centre is clustered around this junction, while the old Communist army headquarters is at Yangjialing on the north-western outskirts of Yan'an. The railway station is at the far southern end of town about seven km from the centre.

Things to See

At the **Former Revolutionary Headquarters** (*gémìng jiùzhǐ*) you can see the assembly hall where the first Central Committee meetings were held and the nearby simple dugouts built into the loess earth where Mao, Zhu De, Zhou Enlai and other senior Communist leaders lived, worked and wrote. The nearby **Yan'an Revolutionary Museum** (*yán'ān gémìng jìniànguǎn*) has an extensive collection of revolutionary paraphernalia – old uniforms, weaponry and many photographs and illustrations. There's even a horse (stuffed) that was allegedly ridden by Mao himself. Unfortunately, there are no English labels. The **Precious Pagoda** (*bǎotǎ*), built during the Song Dynasty, stands on a prominent hillside south-east of the river junction. The **Ten Thousand Buddha Cave** (*wànfó dòng*) dug into the sandstone cliff beside the river has relatively intact Buddhist statues and wall inscriptions. The CITS (☎ 216-285) at the Yan'an Hotel organises tours.

Places to Stay

The *Liangmao Hotel* (☎ (0911) 212-777) (*liángmào dàshà*) at 120 Qilipu Dajie near the railway station is a new and friendly place with doubles at Y180. Its dining hall is good value. The *Yan'an Hotel* (☎ 213-123) (*yán'ān bīnguǎn*) is a typical 1950s-style Chinese hotel catering largely to visiting People's Liberation Army officers. Foreign-

ers are expected to stay in doubles with attached bathroom for Y240, though there may be a little latitude for bargaining – at least the hotel restaurant is cheap.

Getting There & Away

Regular flights to Yan'an ceased after the railway line opened in 1992, and only the odd charter now flies here. From the long distance bus station in Xi'an there are some 12 buses daily to Yan'an (Y29). It's a rough ride. A railway line links Yan'an with Xi'an via an interesting route along the Luo River which it crosses on numerous bridges. Trains leave at 8.44 am and arrive at 5.16 pm.

YULIN

(*yúlín*)

Yulin lies on the fringe of Inner Mongolia's Mu Us Desert in far northern Shaanxi. During the Ming Dynasty, Yulin was a fortified garrison town and patrol post serving the Great Wall.

Until now Yulin's remoteness and relative poverty have kept the old town largely untouched by the 'white-tile' trend in Chinese architecture, which is rapidly destroying what remains of the country's older buildings. Along the narrow brick lanes near the unrestored bell tower are traditional family houses with tiny courtyards hidden behind low enclosure walls and old stone gates. The city's old Ming walls are mainly still standing, though in places their original outer brick layer has been removed (probably for housing).

A large three-tier **fortress** and beacon tower (*zhènběitái*) lie 7½ km north of town.

Places to Stay & Eat

In Yulin, two hotels (out of a total of three) accept foreigners. The *Yulin Hotel (Fandian)* (*yúlín fàndiàn*), two km north of the bus station on Xinjian Lu quotes Y100 for double. The *Yulin Hotel (Binguan)* (☎ (0912) 223-974) (*yúlín bīnguǎn*), on Xinjian Lu, two km just outside the city walls, is the appointed abode for the occasional foreigner who turns up, and charges

YULIN 榆林

1 Yulin Hotel (Binguan)
榆林宾馆
2 Bank of China
中国银行
3 Yulin Hotel (Fandian)
榆林饭店
4 Bell Tower
钟楼
5 PSB
公安局
6 Ten-Thousand Buddha Cave
万佛楼
7 Long-Distance Bus Station
长途汽车站
8 Pagoda
塔

Y180 for a double. Both have good, cheap dining halls.

Getting There & Away

Air Air links with Xi'an were discontinued at the time of writing, but it may be worth inquiring as to whether they have been re-established.

Bus There is one direct daily bus each way between Xi'an and Yulin, but it's more convenient and less tiring to stop in Yan'an. There are three normal buses each day between Yan'an and Yulin (Y30) and one sleeping-berth bus (Y51). There is one daily bus at 5.30 am to Yinchuan (Y46, 14 hours) following a route close to the Great Wall. There are also half-hourly buses to the railhead at Daliuta, from where you can catch a train to Baotou in Inner Mongolia.

Train Scheduled services should arrive in Yulin around 1999, when a planned railway line north of Yan'an is due to be completed.

CENTRAL CHINA

Henan 河南

Henan *(hénán)*, or at least the northern tip of it, which is intersected by the Yellow River, is allegedly where it all began. The beginnings of the Chinese civilisation can be traced back here, about 3500 years ago, when primitive settlements began to coalesce into a true urban sprawl (without the honking traffic, of course).

Today, Henan is one of China's smallest provinces, and also one of the most densely populated, with over 80 million jostling for living space and train tickets. Only Sichuan Province has more human mouths to feed. For the traveller, Henan's charms are limited. The province is at its best in the city of Kaifeng, a delightful old-world surprise, and at the Longmen Caves near Luoyang.

History

It was long thought that the Shang Dynasty (1700-1100 BC) was founded by tribes who migrated from western Asia. Excavations of Shang Dynasty settlements in Henan, however, have shown these towns to be built on the sites of even more ancient settlements. The Shang probably emerged from a continuous line of development that reaches back into prehistoric times.

The first Shang capital, perhaps dating back 3800 years, is believed to have been at Yanshi, west of modern-day Zhengzhou. Around the middle of the 16th century BC the capital was moved to Zhengzhou, where the walls of the ancient city are still visible. Later the capital moved to Yin, near the modern town of Anyang, in the north of Henan.

The only clues as to what Shang society was like are found in the remnants of their cities, in divining bones inscribed with a primitive form of Chinese writing, and in ancient Chinese literary texts. Apart from the walls at Zhengzhou, all that has survived of their cities are the pounded-earth foundations of the buildings, stone-lined trenches where wooden poles once supported thatched

Population: 80 million
Capital: Zhengzhou
Highlights:
- Kaifeng, a delightful blast from the past
- Shaolin Monastery, for those with an interest in kungfu
- Buddhist Longmen Cave complex near Luoyang

roofs, and pits used for storage or as underground houses.

Henan once again occupied centre stage during the Song Dynasty (960-1279), but political power deserted it when the government fled south from its capital at Kaifeng in the wake of an invasion from the north in the 12th century. Nevertheless, with such a large population on the fertile (though periodically flood-ravaged) plains of the unruly Yellow River, Henan remained an important agricultural area.

Henan's urban centres dwindled in importance and population with the demise of the Song. It was not until the Communist takeover in 1949 that they once again expanded. Zhengzhou was transformed into a sizable industrial city, as was Luoyang. Kaifeng and Anyang have been slower to respond to the call of the hammer and anvil

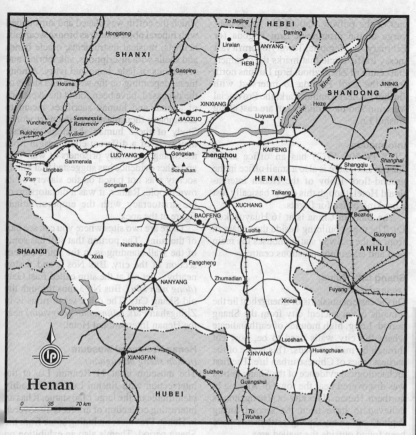

Henan

0   35   70 km

ZHENGZHOU
(zhèngzhōu)
Provincial capital of Henan since 1949, Zhengzhou is a sprawling paradigm of ill-conceived town planning – in short, a typical Chinese provincial capital. It sports broad, neatly intersecting boulevards, a People's Park, a towering anachronistic Mao statue, a provincial museum and an oversized railway station.

While Zhengzhou lags far behind Guangzhou, Shanghai and Beijing, it is nevertheless valiantly holding up its end in the latest Chinese revolution: there's a high technol-ogy science park on the outskirts of town and a reasonably large number of expats are in town working on a massive World Bank-funded dam project close to Luoyang. For the traveller, however, Zhengzhou is at best an overnight stop en route to more worth-while attractions.

Orientation
All places of interest to travellers lie within the section of the city east of the railway line.

The liveliest part of town is around the railway and long-distance bus stations, with street stalls, restaurants and markets. North-east of the railway station, five roads converge at the prominent Erqi Pagoda (or February 7th Memorial Tower) to form a vast messy traffic circle that marks the commercial centre of Zhengzhou. Erqi Lu runs north from the Erqi Pagoda to intersect with Jinshui Lu near Renmin Park; the Provincial Museum and the Holiday Inn are east along Jinshui Lu.

Information

CITS (☎ 595-2072) has an office at 15 Jinshui Lu. There is also a small office in the ground-floor lobby of the Henan International Hotel, though this one is basically just a booking office for flights.

The Bank of China is at 16 Huayuankou Lu. The tower building beside the square in front of the railway station houses the main post and telecommunications centre.

Shang City Ruins

(shāngdài yízhǐ)

On the eastern outskirts of Zhengzhou lie the remains of an ancient city from the Shang period. Long, high mounds of earth indicate where the city walls used to be, now cut through by modern roads. This is one of the earliest relics of Chinese urban life. The first archaeological evidence of the Shang period was discovered near the town of Anyang in northern Henan. The city at Zhengzhou is believed to have been the second Shang capital, and many Shang settlements have been found outside the walled area.

Excavations here and at other Shang sites suggest that a 'typical' Shang city consisted of a central walled area containing large buildings (presumably government buildings or the residences of important people, used for ceremonial occasions) surrounded by a ring of villages. Each village specialised in such products as pottery, metalwork, wine or textiles. The village dwellings were mostly semi-underground pit houses, while the buildings in the centre were rectangular and above ground.

Excavations have also uncovered Shang tombs. These are rectangular pits with ramps or steps leading down to a burial chamber in which the coffin was placed and surrounded with funeral objects such as bronze weapons, helmets, musical instruments, oracle bones and shells with inscriptions, silk fabrics, and ornaments of jade, bone and ivory. Among these, depending on the wealth and status of the deceased, have been found the skeletons of animal and human sacrifices meant to accompany their masters to the next world. Study of these human skeletons suggests they were of a different ethnic origin from the Shang – possibly prisoners of war. This and other evidence has suggested that Shang society was not based on the slavery of its own people. Rather, it was a dictatorship of the aristocracy with the emperor/father-figure at the apex.

There are two sites where you can see part of the ruins. The portion that still has some of the wall standing is in the south-eastern section of the city. Bus Nos 2 and 8 stop nearby – get off at the stop called East Gate *(dōng mén kǒu)*. Bus No 3 runs through the old Shang City. The other set of ruins is in Zijingshan Park *(zǐjīngshān gōngyuán)* near the Henan International Hotel.

Henan Provincial Museum

(hénán shěng bówùguǎn)

The museum is at 11 Renmin Lu, at the intersection with Jinshui Lu, and is readily identifiable by the large Mao statue. It has an interesting collection of artefacts discovered in Henan Province, including some from the Shang period. There's also an exhibition on the February 7th revolt but, unfortunately, there are no English captions. The Erqi Pagoda, in the centre of Zhengzhou, commemorates the 1923 strike organised by workers building the railway from Wuhan to Beijing. The strike was bloodily suppressed.

Yellow River

(huánghé)

The Yellow River is just 24 km north of Zhengzhou and the road passes near the village of Huayuankou, where in April 1938 Kuomintang general Chiang Kaishek ordered his troops to blow up the river dikes to halt the Japanese advance. This desperately ruthless tactic was successful for only a few weeks and at the cost of drowning some one million Chinese people and making another 11 million homeless and starving. The dike was repaired with Ameri-

can help in 1947 and today the point where it was breached has an irrigation sluice gate and Mao's instruction, 'Control the Yellow River', etched into the embankment.

The river has always been regarded as

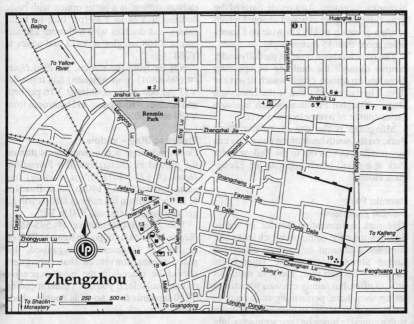

'China's sorrow' because of its propensity to flood. It carries masses of silt from the loess plains and deposits them on the riverbed, causing the water to overflow the banks. Consequently, the peasants along the riverbank have had to build the dikes higher and higher each century. As a result, parts of the river flow along an elevated channel which is often as much as 1½ km wide and sometimes more than 15 metres high.

The river has been brought partially under control through the building of upstream dams and irrigation canals which divert the flow. The largest of these is the Longyang Dam in Qinghai Province, which is also a major source of hydroelectric power.

Mangshan is the site of **Yellow River Park**, on the south bank of the river. You can buy minibus tickets out to the Yellow River Park at a small booth opposite the Zhengzhou Hotel.

Renmin Park
(rénmín gōngyuán)
This park is interesting not for its scenic beauty but for the entrance, which looks like someone's attempt to recreate either the Lunan Stone Forest or the Tiger Balm Gardens – enough said. The park itself has little to offer, but family circuses sometimes set up shop here, performing such feats as wrapping their bodies in wire or lying down with a concrete block on their stomach while Dad takes to it with a sledgehammer. You can play that venerated Chinese sport of ping pong on the concrete tables in the park if you've got some bats and a ball. The entrance to the park is on Erqi Lu.

Places to Stay – bottom end
Budget travellers are better off heading to Kaifeng, which is only 1½ hours away by bus. There's cheap accommodation in Zhengzhou, but it's all clustered in the grotty railway station area.

Opposite the railway station is *Zhongyuan Mansions (zhōngyuán dàshà)*, a cavernous white tower with untold numbers of rooms in two adjoining hotels, both of which are more than a bit run-down but handy if you're just passing through. Prices depend on what is available and how many of you there are – it might be anything from Y18 to Y58 per bed. This is a sleazy, noisy part of town.

The *Zhengzhou Hotel* (☎ 696-9941) (zhèngzhōu fàndiàn), to the left as you leave the railway station, is a better option with basic doubles at Y24 to Y38 (per bed, no bathroom), and doubles with bathroom and air-con at Y108, singles at Y113 and suites at Y284.

Not far from the station, the *Erqi Hotel* (☎ 696-8801) (èrqī bīnguǎn) has triples at Y33 per bed, basic doubles at Y76 per bed, and doubles with air-con and bathroom from Y124 to Y210.

Places to Stay – middle
Good mid-range accommodation is thin on the ground in Zhengzhou. The *Friendship Hotel* (☎ 622-8807) (yǒuyì fàndiàn) has clean doubles from Y140 to Y308. Bus Nos 6, 24 and 32 from the railway station will all get you there. Taxis cost Y10 to Y15.

The *Henan Guesthouse* (☎ 595-5522) (hénán bīnguǎn) is opposite Renmin Park on Jinshui Lu. Hopelessly disorganised, this place seems convinced that foreigners should be placed in the most expensive rooms available. If you don't mind spending Y250 upwards for a no-frills double, check it out.

Places to Stay – top end
The *Asia Hotel* (☎ 698-8888) (yàxìyà dàjiǔdiàn), a joint venture facing the Erqi Pagoda, has rates from Y498 for a double and Y458 for a single (foreigners pay Y100 more for their rooms). It's close to the station, but has little else to recommend it.

Over in the city's eastern suburbs, on Jinshui Lu, is the *International Hotel Henan* (☎ 595-6600; fax 595-0161) (hénán guójì fàndiàn). Rooms start at Y442 for a double and Y680 for a suite. Sharing the same compound is the *Regent Palace* (☎ 595-0122) (lìjīng dàshà), where doubles cost Y350.

The latest arrival on the Zhengzhou accommodation scene is the new *Holiday Inn Crowne Plaza Zhengzhou* (☎ 595-0055;

fax 599-0770) *(hénán zhōngzhōu huáng-guān jiàrì bīnguǎn)*. This place started life as the Russian foreign experts' hotel back in the '50s, was resuscitated as the Zhongzhou Hotel in the '60s, and now – after three years of renovations – is being managed by the Holiday Inn group. Rates start from US$95.

Places to Eat
Food stalls around town sell bowls of opaque noodles called *liáng fěn*. Popular in Henan, as in many parts of north-western China, it's dismal fare. Try it in soup with a tossing of vinegar or hot chilli.

The station area is the best for cheap eats. The Zhongyuan Mansions block has a couple of 'grub for the masses' joints and armies of hole-in-the-wall slop-shops. Next door to the Erqi Hotel, look out for *Fast Food World*, which has a notable McDonald's rip-off, right down to the golden arches.

The classier restaurants are clustered in the fashionable end of town, on Jinshui Lu between Chengdong Lu and Huayuankou Lu. Restaurants here come and go in popularity and open and close regularly. The most popular at the time of writing was the *Flower Restaurant (huāyuán fàndiàn)*.

The Holiday Inn has a *Patisserie* and a Western restaurant in the foyer serving reasonably inexpensive hamburgers, steaks and the like.

Getting There & Away
Air The CAAC office (☎ 696-4789) is at 51 Yima Lu, but there are ticket outlets scattered all over town, notably in the Holiday Inn, International Hotel, Henan Hotel and even in the Zhongyuan Mansions. From Zhengzhou there are scheduled flights to over 20 cities in China, including Beijing (daily), Guangzhou (daily), Guilin, Kunming, Qingdao, Shanghai (daily), Wuhan and even Ürümqi. The airport is on the eastern outskirts of the city.

Bus From the Zhengzhou long-distance bus station (diagonally opposite the railway station) there are air-con buses to Luoyang (Y17, three hours) approximately every half hour, six scheduled departures to Kaifeng (two hours) and several to Anyang (4½ hours) every day.

There are also overnight sleeping-berth coaches *(wòpùchē)* to Beijing, Wuhan, Xi'an and destinations in Shandong Province, though these long hauls are better done by train if possible. Minibuses leave irregularly from the square in front of the railway station for Shaolin (Y12). There are also regular services to Kaifeng from the east bus station.

Train Zhengzhou is one of the most important junctions in the Chinese rail network, and numerous express and rapid trains run via the city; you could well find yourself here 'in transit' for a few hours. The ticket office at Zhengzhou Railway Station is often crowded out, but foreigners can buy tickets more easily at counter Nos 1 and 2 or at the advance booking office at 193 Erqi Lu. Convenient connections are to Beijing (12 hours), Guangzhou (23 hours), Luoyang (four hours), Shanghai (14 hours), Wuhan (nine hours) and Xi'an (10 hours), as well as Taiyuan and Datong.

Travellers to Xi'an are best off taking the two-tiered 'tourist train'. It leaves Zhengzhou daily at 10.20 am and arrives in Xi'an just before 7 pm.

Getting Around
Since most of the sights and tourist facilities are well away from the city centre, you can forget walking. Unfortunately, no bicycle rental is available. Bus No 2 gets you from the railway station to the Henan International Hotel, while the No 3 runs through the old Shang City. Taxis (both red sedan and yellow minivan) are readily available. The red taxis have meters but drivers rarely use them (reckon on between Y10 and Y15); minivans generally cost between Y7 and Y10.

AROUND ZHENGZHOU
Shaolin Monastery
(shàolín sì)
David Carradine never trained here, but China's most famous martial arts tradition

was indeed developed by Buddhist monks at Shaolin Monastery, 80 km west of Zhengzhou.

Each year, thousands of Chinese enrol at Shaolin's martial art schools. Large classes of enthusiastic young trainees, many no older than nine or 10, can often be seen in the monastery grounds ramming a javelin through their imaginary opponent's body or kicking into a sparring dummy with enough force to wind an elephant.

According to legend, Shaolin was founded in the 5th century AD by an Indian monk, Bodhidharma, who preached Chan (Zen) Buddhism. The story goes that for relief between long periods of meditation, Bodhidharma's disciples imitated the natural motions of birds and animals, developing these exercises over the centuries into a form of unarmed combat. The monks have supposedly intervened continually throughout China's many wars and uprisings – always on the side of righteousness, naturally – and, perhaps as a result, their monastery has suffered repeated sackings. The most recent round of destructive visits was in 1928 when a local warlord had a go, then again in the early '70s by bands of Red Guards.

In spite of the fires and vandalism many of the monastery buildings are still standing, though most have had any original charm restored out of them. One of the most impressive and photogenic sights is the **Forest of Dagobas** (*shǐǎolín tǎlín*) situated outside the walls past the temple, each dagoba built in remembrance of a monk.

Nowadays Shaolin is something of a tourist trap catering to the hordes of Chinese tourists who are bussed in every day. The way from the main bus parking area to the monastery is thick with food stalls, ice-cream sellers, street photographers and small souvenir shops selling imitation scimitars along with other junk. There's a martial arts museum and a giant buddha for the kids to play on.

The monastery sits on Songshan, a mountain sacred to Taoists. On the same mountain is the Taoist **Zhongyue Temple**, supposedly founded during the Qin Dynasty, and site of the oldest surviving pagoda in China.

The main gate-ticket is Y15; it costs another Y10 to get into Shaolin temple itself.

Places to Stay It's possible to spend the night at Shaolin at the *Wushu Hotel (wǔshù*

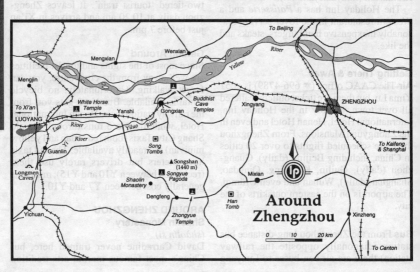

Around Zhengzhou

0   10   20 km

bīnguǎn), a place with special foreigners' rates of around Y150. You may bump into the occasional foreigner studying at Shaolin.

Getting There & Away Shaolin is well off the main road between Zhengzhou and Luoyang. One way of getting there is to take one of the frequent but unscheduled private minibuses from in front of the railway station in either city. Minibuses from Zhengzhou cost Y12, and (depending on what route they take) sometimes stop at either Zhongyue Temple, the tombs near Dahuting or the Songyue Pagoda.

Public buses to Shaolin leave roughly half-hourly from the long-distance bus stations in both Zhengzhou (Y8) and Luoyang (Y5), and are generally cheaper and quicker than minibuses.

Gongxian County
(gǒngxiàn)

Gongxian County, between Zhengzhou and Luoyang, is home to a series of Buddhist caves and to tombs built by the Northern Song emperors. Construction of the caves began in 517 AD. Additions continued through the Eastern and Western Wei, Tang and Song dynasties, and today there are 256 shrines containing over 7700 Buddhist figures.

The Song Tombs are scattered over an area of 30 sq km, and in them repose seven of the nine Northern Song emperors (the other two were carted off by the Jin armies who overthrew the Northern Song in the 12th century). Some 800 years on, all that remain of the tombs are ruins, burial mounds and the statues which line the sacred avenues leading

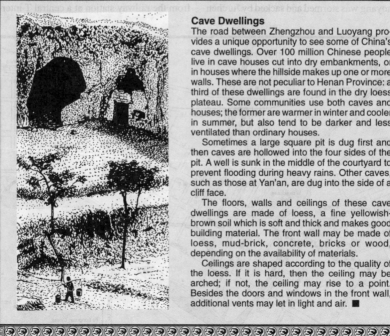

Cave Dwellings

The road between Zhengzhou and Luoyang provides a unique opportunity to see some of China's cave dwellings. Over 100 million Chinese people live in cave houses cut into dry embankments, or in houses where the hillside makes up one or more walls. These are not peculiar to Henan Province: a third of these dwellings are found in the dry loess plateau. Some communities use both caves and houses; the former are warmer in winter and cooler in summer, but also tend to be darker and less ventilated than ordinary houses.

Sometimes a large square pit is dug first and then caves are hollowed into the four sides of the pit. A well is sunk in the middle of the courtyard to prevent flooding during heavy rains. Other caves, such as those at Yan'an, are dug into the side of a cliff face.

The floors, walls and ceilings of these cave dwellings are made of loess, a fine yellowish-brown soil which is soft and thick and makes good building material. The front wall may be made of loess, mud-brick, concrete, bricks or wood, depending on the availability of materials.

Ceilings are shaped according to the quality of the loess. If it is hard, then the ceiling may be arched; if not, the ceiling may rise to a point. Besides the doors and windows in the front wall, additional vents may let in light and air. ■

up to the ruins. About 700 stone statues are still standing, and together they comprise the main attraction of the tombs. Experts see a progression of styles from the simplicity of late-Tang forms to the life-like depiction of public figures and animals.

Buses running between Zhengzhou and Luoyang pass by the turn-off for the tombs, though the tombs themselves are some distance from the highway. From Gongxian it is also possible to charter a taxi or motor-tricycle out to the tombs and/or the Buddhist cave temples on the Zhengzhou to Luoyang road and rail route, but be prepared for some intense bargaining.

LUOYANG
(luòyáng)

Founded in 1200 BC, Luoyang was the capital of 10 dynasties until the Northern Song Dynasty moved its capital to Kaifeng in the 10th century AD. In the 12th century Luoyang was stormed and sacked by Jurchen

invaders from the north and never quite recovered from the disaster. For centuries it languished with only memories of greatness. By the 1920s it had just 20,000 inhabitants. It took the Communists to bring life back to Luoyang, constructing a new industrial city that now houses over a million people.

In other words, today it's hard to imagine that Luoyang was once the centre of the Chinese world and home to over 1300 Buddhist temples. There are reminders of Luoyang's historical greatness scattered about town, but the main point of interest is the Longmen Caves, 16 km out of town.

Orientation

Luoyang is spread across the northern bank of the Luo River. Luoyang Railway Station, a large new white-tiled building with a loud chiming clock, is in the north of the city. Luoyang's chief thoroughfare is Zhongzhou Lu, which meets Jinguyuan Lu leading down from the railway station at a central T-inter-

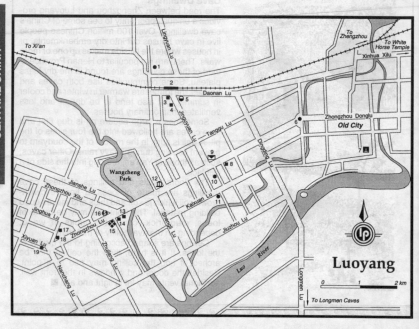

section. The old city is east of the old west gate at Xiguan and sections of the original walls can still be seen. Throughout the maze of narrow streets and winding laneways stand many older houses. It is an interesting area to explore on foot.

Information

The CITS office (☎ 491-3701) is at 6 Xiyuan Lu, not far from the New Friendship Hotel. There is also a branch on the 2nd floor of the

---

LUOYANG 洛阳

1 CAAC
   中国民航售票处
2 Railway Station
   火车站
3 Luoyang Hotel
   洛阳旅社
4 Tianxiang Hotel
   天香旅社
5 Long-Distance Bus Station
   长途汽车站
6 Xiguan (West Gate)
   西关
7 Wenfeng Pagoda
   文峰塔
8 Xuangong Hotel
   旋宫大厦
9 Post Office
   邮电局
10 Xinhua Bookstore
   新华书店
11 PSB
   公安局
12 Luoyang Museum
   洛阳博物馆
13 Peony Hotel
   牡丹大酒店
14 Huacheng Hotel
   花城饭店
15 Friendship Store
   友谊商店
16 Bank of China
   中国银行
17 New Friendship Hotel
   新友谊宾馆
18 Friendship Hotel
   友谊宾馆
19 CITS
   中国国际旅行社

Peony Hotel. The PSB is on the corner of Kaixuan Lu and Tiyuchang Lu.

The Bank of China is on the corner of Yanan Lu and Zhongzhou Xilu (opposite the Friendship Store). The main post and telephone office is at the T-intersection of Zhongzhou Lu and Jinguyuan Lu.

White Horse Temple
(báimǎ sì)

Founded in the 1st century AD, the White Horse Temple was the first Buddhist Temple constructed on Chinese soil. Today, Ming and Qing structures stand at the site of the original temple.

Five hundred years before the journey of Xuan Zhuang, the Tang Dynasty monk whose travels are fancifully immortalised in the classic *Journey to the West*, two envoys of the Han Dynasty court went in search of Buddhist scriptures. In Afghanistan they met two Indian monks and together they returned to Luoyang. The story goes that they carried Buddhist scriptures and statues on the backs of two white horses. In due course the temple was founded to house the scriptures and statues, and it was named after the horses. The temple is 13 km east of Luoyang. The sensible way to get there is to take a minibus from in front of the station for Y5. Alternatively, take bus No 5 or 9 to Xiguan traffic circle at the edge of the old city walls, then walk east to the stop for bus No 56, which will take you to the temple.

Wangcheng Park
(wángchéng gōngyuán)

At the rear of the park are a tiny zoo and two Han Dynasty tombs. Paintings and bas-reliefs can still be seen on the stone doors but the coffins have long gone. There's also an underground 'theme park' with moving dinosaur models and an assortment of polystyrene ghouls. The Peony Festival centred in Wangcheng Park is held from April 15 to 25, when thousands of Chinese tourists descend on Luoyang to view the peony flowers. If nature fails to provide sufficiently resplendent blooms, fake peonies are attached to the bushes.

Luoyang Museum
(luòyáng bówùguǎn)
The museum is next to the park and houses a collection of early bronzes, Tang figurines and implements from the Stone Age. There are some eye-catching pieces but no English captions. Bus No 2 from the railway station area goes to the museum.

Longmen Caves
(lóngmén shíkū)
In 494 AD the Northern Wei Dynasty moved its capital from Datong to Luoyang. At Datong the dynasty had built the impressive Yungang Caves. Now in Luoyang, the dynasty commenced work on the Longmen Caves. Over the next 200 years, more than 100,000 images and statues of Buddha and his disciples were carved into the cliff walls on the banks of the Yi River, 16 km south of the city. It was an ideal site. The hard texture of the rock, like that at Datong, made it eminently suitable for carving. The caves of Luoyang, Dunhuang and Datong represent the peak of Buddhist cave art.

Apart from natural erosion, at Luoyang there has been much damage done to the sculptures during the 19th and 20th centuries by Western souvenir hunters who beheaded just about every figure they could lay their saws on. These heads now grace the museums and private paperweight collections of Europe and North America. Among these were two murals which were entirely removed and can now be seen at the Metropolitan Museum of Art in New York and the Atkinson Museum in Kansas City. Oddly enough, the caves appear to have been spared the ravages of the Cultural Revolution. Even during the most anarchic year of 1967 the caves were reported to be open, no-one was watching over them and anybody could go in and have a look.

The art of Buddhist cave sculpture largely came to an end around the middle of the 9th century as the Tang Dynasty declined. Persecution of foreign religions in China began, with Buddhism as the prime target. Although Buddhist art and sculpture continued in China, it never reached the heights it had enjoyed previously.

Binyang Caves *(bīnyáng dòng)* The main caves of the Longmen group are on the west bank of the Yi River. They stretch out along the cliff face on a north-south axis. The three Binyang Caves are at the northern end, closest to the entrance. All were begun under the Northern Wei and, though two were finished during the Sui and Tang dynasties, the statues all display the benevolent expressions which characterised the Northern Wei style.

Ten Thousand Buddha Cave *(wànfó dòng)* Several minutes' walk south of the Binyang Caves is the Tang Dynasty Ten Thousand Buddha Cave, built in 680. In addition to the legions of tiny bas-relief buddhas which give the cave its name, there is a fine big buddha and images of celestial dancers. Other images include musicians playing the flute, *pípá* (a plucked stringed instrument), cymbals and *zheng* (a 13 to 14-stringed harp).

Lotus Flower Cave *(liánhuā dòng)* This cave was carved in 527 AD during the Northern Wei Dynasty and has a large standing buddha, now faceless. On the ceiling are wispy apsaras drifting around a central lotus flower. A common symbol in Buddhist art, the lotus flower represents purity and serenity.

Ancestor Worshipping Temple *(fèngxiān sì)* This is the largest structure at Longmen and contains the best works of art. It was built between 672 and 675 AD, during the Tang Dynasty. The roof is gone and the figures lie exposed to the elements. The Tang figures tend to be more three-dimensional than the Northern Wei figures, standing out in high relief and rather freer from their stone backdrop. Their expressions and poses also appear to be more natural but, unlike the other-worldly figures of the Northern Wei, the Tang figures are meant to be awesome.

The seated central buddha is 17 metres

high and is believed to be Vairocana, the supreme, omnipresent divinity. The face is thought to be modelled on that of the all-powerful Empress Wu Zetian of the Tang Dynasty.

As you face the buddha, to the left are statues of the disciple Ananda and a bodhisattva wearing a crown, a tassel and a string of pearls. To the right are statues (or remains) of another disciple, a bodhisattva, a heavenly guardian trampling on a spirit and a guardian of the buddha.

Medical Prescription Cave South of the Ancestor Worshiping Temple is the tiny Medical Prescription Cave, whose entrance is filled with 6th-century stone steles inscribed with remedies for common ailments.

Guyang Cave Adjacent to the Medical Prescription Cave is the much larger Guyang Cave, cut between 495 and 575 AD. It's a narrow, high-roofed cave featuring a buddha statue and a profusion of sculpture, particularly of flying apsaras. This was probably the first cave of the Longmen group to be built.

Shiku Cave This cave is a Northern Wei construction. It's the last major cave and has carvings depicting religious processions.

Getting to the Caves The caves are 13 km south of town and can be reached from the Luoyang Railway Station area by bus No 81 or from the Friendship Guesthouse by bus No 60, which leaves from the far side of the small park opposite the hotel. Bus No 53 from the Xiguan traffic circle also goes past the caves. Minibuses head out to the caves from the railway and bus station area.

Half-day minibus tours including the Longmen Caves, White Horse Temple and possibly other sights around Luoyang depart sporadically from in front of the railway station. The price is negotiable, but Chinese tourists seem to pay about Y25. Some hotels run their own tours out to the caves as well.

Places to Stay
Directly opposite the railway station is the *Luoyang Hotel (luòyáng lǚshè)*, where doubles without bathroom cost Y44 and singles cost Y40. It's a depressing, noisy place. The *Tianxiang Hotel* (☎ 394-0600) *(tiānxiāng lǚshè)* is a far better choice, even though all its posted prices are subject to a 100% foreigners' surcharge. Beds in a basic quad are Y22 or from Y26 to Y30 in a triple. Air-con singles with attached bathroom are Y70 and beds in similar doubles are also Y70. Suites are available for Y300.

Less conveniently located is the *Huacheng Hotel (huāchéng fàndiàn)* at 49 Zhongzhou Xilu, where beds in triple rooms start at Y20 and doubles from Y45. Bus Nos 2, 4 and 11 run past it – get off at the stop after the Peony Hotel.

The *Xuangong Hotel* (☎ 393-7189) *(xuángōng dàshà)*, a very drab mid-range hotel, is in a good central location on Zhongzhou Lu near its junction with Jinguyuan Lu. This tower-block hotel has doubles with bathroom from Y190.

Over in the west of town, on Xiyuan Lu, are two Friendship Hotels. Catering largely to tour groups, both have prices of Y480 upwards for standard doubles. The *Friendship Hotel* (☎ 491-2780) *(yǒuyì bīnguǎn)* also has singles at Y295. The *New Friendship Hotel* (☎ 491-3770) *(xīn yǒuyì bīnguǎn)* has economy doubles at Y380. Bus No 4 from the main railway station passes close to the hotels (get off at the seventh stop). For a taxi, expect to pay around Y60 from Luoyang Airport or Y15 to Y20 from the main railway station.

The *Peony Hotel* (☎ 491-3699) *(mǔdān dàjiǔdiàn)* is a high-rise joint venture at 15 Zhongzhou Xilu. It's popular with foreign tour groups and expats, and although it falls short of delivering international standards room rates start at Y510.

Places to Eat
Luoyang is situated far enough west to give the local street food a slight Islamic touch. Cheap common snacks include *jiānpào*, small fried pastries filled with chopped herbs

and Chinese garlic, and *dòushāgāo*, a sweet 'cake' made from ground yellow peas and jujubes (Chinese dates), sold by street vendors for about Y0.50 a slice. At night the street stalls around the railway station sell cheap and very good *shāguō*, a kind of meat and vegetable casserole cooked with bean noodles in a small earthenware pot.

You'll find better 'sit-down' restaurants along Zhongzhou Lu. The Tianxiang Hotel has a good and inexpensive restaurant with an English menu. The Peony Hotel has an excellent coffee shop (Y6 for a bottomless coffee) with passable meals – try the nasi goreng.

Getting There & Away

Air It's possible to book air tickets at various places around town, though Luoyang is not so well connected by air with the rest of China (consider flying to or from Zhengzhou). The Peony Hotel has a small ground-floor office, as does the Tianxiang Hotel and the Friendship hotels. There are flights to Xi'an (four a week), Guangzhou, Beijing, Xiamen and Fuzhou. There are also charter flights to Hong Kong.

Bus The long-distance bus station is diagonally opposite the main railway station. There are daily buses to Zhengzhou (Y17, air-con; three hours) and Shaolin (Y8). You can also get direct buses to Anyang and Ruicheng (in south-western Shanxi Province) from here.

Coach buses fitted with sleeping berths leave in the evening from outside the railway station for Xi'an (10 hours), Taiyuan (11 hours), Wuhan (15 hours) and Yantai in Shandong Province (23 hours).

Train From Luoyang there are direct trains to Beijing (13 hours), to Shanghai (18 hours) and to Xi'an (eight hours). Note that there is also now a two-tiered tourist train running between Zhengzhou and Xi'an daily – it stops in Luoyang en route to Xi'an at 12.27 pm and arrives in Xi'an around 7 pm the same day.

There are some direct trains north to

Taiyuan and south to Xiangfan and Yichang. Yichang is a port on the Yangzi River, where you can pick up the Chongqing to Wuhan ferry.

Getting Around

Bicycle hire seems to have disappeared in Luoyang (like many Chinese cities unfortunately) but you might try asking at the Tianxiang Hotel. Red-cab and yellow-minivan taxis are abundant and rarely cost more than Y10. The bus system is also less crowded than in many Chinese cities.

ANYANG
(ānyáng)

Anyang, north of the Yellow River near the Henan-Hebei border, is now believed to be the site of Yin, the last capital of the ancient Shang Dynasty and one of the first centres of an urban-based Chinese civilisation.

Peasants working near Anyang in the late 19th century unearthed pieces of polished bone inscribed with an ancient form of Chinese writing, which turned out to be divining bones with questions addressed to the spirits and ancestors. Other inscriptions were found on the undershells of tortoises as well as on bronze objects, suggesting that the late Shang capital once stood here in the 14th century BC.

The discoveries attracted the attention of both Chinese and Western archaeologists, though it was not until the late 1920s that work began on excavating the site. These excavations uncovered ancient tombs, the ruins of a royal palace, workshops and houses – proof that the legendary Shang Dynasty had indeed existed.

Museum of the Yin Ruins
(yīnxū bówùyuàn)

A museum has recently been established at the Yin site, but its collection is disappointingly limited; it includes reassembled pottery and oracle bone fragments as well as jade and bronze artefacts. An excavation site is being prepared for public viewing. Bus No 1 from near the corner of Jiefang Lu and Zhangde Lu goes past the museum turn-off.

Places to Stay & Eat

The *Fenghuang Hotel (fēnghuáng bīnguǎn)* on Jiefang Lu near its intersection with Xihuancheng Lu charges Y45 for a double. There's a good restaurant on the ground floor. If you're turned away, the only official foreigners' abode is the *Anyang Guesthouse* (☎ 422-219) *(ānyáng bīnguǎn)* at 1 Youyi Lu. Rooms range from Y60 to Y250.

Getting There & Away

From Anyang long-distance bus station there are connections to Zhengzhou (4½ hours), Linxian (leaving half-hourly), Taiyuan (a rough 10-hour ride across the Taihangshan) and Luoyang. Anyang is on the main Beijing-Zhengzhou railway line. Other rail links go to Taiyuan (13 hours) and Linxian (one daily at 8.30 am).

AROUND ANYANG

To the west of Anyang, in the foothills of the Taihangshan close to Henan's border with Shanxi Province, lies **Linxian County** *(línxiàn)*.

Linxian is a rural area which rates with Dazhai and Shaoshan as one of the 'holy' places of Maoism, since this is the location of the famous Red Flag Canal. To irrigate the district, a river was re-routed through a tunnel beneath a mountain and then along a new bed built on the side of steep cliffs. The Communists insist that this colossal job, carried out during the Cultural Revolution, was done entirely by the toiling masses without the help of engineers and machines.

The statistics are impressive: 1500 km of canal was dug, hills were levelled, 134 tunnels were pierced, 150 aqueducts were constructed and enough earth was displaced to build a road one metre high, six metres wide and 4000 km long. All this was supposedly done by hand and was a tribute to Mao's vision of a self-reliant China.

On the other hand, it might equally be regarded as an achievement worthy of Qin Shihuang, who pressed millions into building the Great Wall. The endless back-breaking toil of peasants and workers could certainly have been put to more productive use and the profits might have paid for a pump with which to pipe the water straight over the hill.

KAIFENG

(kāifēng)

Once the prosperous imperial capital of China during the Northern Song Dynasty (960-1126), Kaifeng is a charming city with a population of around 600,000. It doesn't see a great deal of tourist traffic and it deserves more than it gets. Kaifeng has been somewhat left behind in China's modernisation drive. While the locals tut with embarrassment about the lack of fast-food outfits and five-star hotels, for the foreign visitor there is much in Kaifeng that has disappeared from other parts of China.

It would be a good idea to get there soon, however. Even Kaifeng is slowly being nudged into the modern world, and whole blocks are being demolished to make way for the dreams of China's civic planners. Eroded, pounded-earth city walls surround Kaifeng on all sides, but these are frequently interrupted by roads or new buildings.

A small Christian community also lives in Kaifeng alongside a much larger local Muslim minority; you may come across their churches and mosques in Kaifeng's back-streets.

Orientation

The long-distance bus station and the railway station are both outside and about one km to the south of the old city walls; the rest of Kaifeng is mostly within the walled area. The city's pivotal point is the intersection of Sihou Jie and Madao Jie; the street market here is particularly lively at night. The surrounding restaurants, shops and houses are of mainly traditional Chinese wooden architecture. Not far away are the Kaifeng Guesthouse and the Xiangguo Temple.

Information

The PSB is on Dazhifang Jie, 50 metres west of Zhongshan Lu. CITS (☎ 595-5131) has an

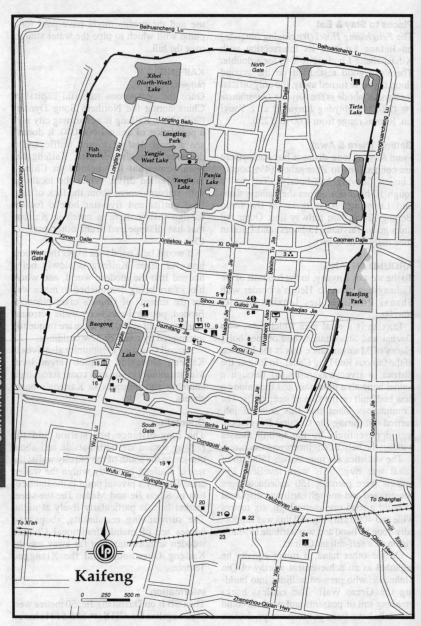

CENTRAL CHINA

Kaifeng

0   250   500 m

To Xi'an

To Shanghai

To Shanghai

Kaifeng-Qixian Hwy

Zhengzhou-Qixian Hwy

Pota Xijie

Huili River

Telubeiyan Jie

Beihuancheng Lu

Beihuancheng Lu

North Gate

Tieta Lake

Xibei (North-West) Lake

Longting Beilu

Longting Park

Fish Ponds

Longting Xilu

Yangjia West Lake

Yangjia Lake

Panjia Lake

Beidamen Dajie

Beiman Dajie

Donghuancheng Lu

Xinhuancheng Lu

Ximen Dajie

West Gate

Xinjiekou Jie

Xi Dajie

Caomen Dajie

Beixing Tu Jie

Shudian Jie

Bianjing Park

Baogong Lake

Dazhifang Jie

Yingbin Lu

Zhongshan Lu

Sihou Jie

Gulou Jie

Madao Jie

Wusheng Jiao Jie

Mujiaqiao Jie

Ziyou Lu

Wolong Jie

South Gate

Binhe Lu

Dongguai Jie

Wuyi Lu

Wufu Xijie

Siyinglang Jie

Ximenguan Jie

Gongyuan Jie

KAIFENG 开封	12	Californian Beef Noodles 加州牛肉面	10	Xiangguosi Market 相国寺市场
PLACES TO STAY	19	Tianjin Restaurant 天津饭馆	11	Post Office 邮电局
6 Dajintai Hotel 大金台旅馆		**OTHER**	13	PSB 公安局
8 Kaifeng Guesthouse 开封宾馆	1	Iron Pagoda 铁塔	14	Yanqing Taoist Temple 延庆观
18 Dongjing Hotel 东京大饭店	2	Longting (Dragon Pavilion) 龙亭	15	Museum 博物馆
20 Bianliang Hotel 汴梁旅社	3	Ruins of Kaifeng Synagogue 开封犹太教堂遗址	16	West Bus Station 汽车西站
22 Bian Hotel 汴大旅社	4	Bank of China 中国银行	17	CITS 中国国际旅行社
PLACES TO EAT	7	Post Office 邮电局	21	Long-Distance Bus Station 长途汽车站
5 Jiaozi Guan Restaurant 饺子馆	9	Xiangguo Temple 相国寺	23	Railway Station 火车站
			24	Fan Pagoda 繁塔

office at 14 Yingbin Lu, next to the Dongjing Hotel. The Bank of China is on Gulou Jie about half a km north of the Kaifeng Guesthouse.

There are post and telephone offices near the corner of Zhongshan Lu and Ziyou Lu, and on the corner of Mujiaqiao Jie and Wusheng Jiao Jie.

Xiangguo Temple
(xiàngguó sì)
This temple is next door to a large Chinese-style market. Originally founded in 555 AD but frequently rebuilt over the next 1000 years, Xiangguo Temple was completely destroyed in 1644 when the Yellow River floodgates were opened in a disastrous attempt to halt a Manchu invasion. The current buildings date from 1766 and have had a thorough going-over since then. There's an enormous old cast-iron bell on the right as you go in; entry costs Y5.

Iron Pagoda
(tiě tǎ)
Built in the 11th century, the Iron Pagoda is actually made of normal bricks but covered in specially coloured tiles that look like iron.

You can climb to the top of this impressive structure. The tiles on the lower levels have damaged buddha images, possibly the result of Red Guard sledgehammers. Take bus No 3 from near the long-distance bus station to the route terminal; it's a 15-minute walk from there.

Other Sights
The large local **museum** *(kāifēng bówùguǎn)* on Yingbin Lu just south of Baogong Lake might once have been worth a look, but it is now virtually empty (apart from a work-manlike display on Kaifeng's revolutionary history) – 'no money', the staff complain.

Longting Park *(lóngtíng gōngyuán)* is covered mostly by lakes; on its drier northern rim near the **Longting** (Dragon Pavilion) there is a small children's fun park with sideshows and bumper-car rides; old men often sit here playing Chinese chess in the shade.

The very small **Yanqing Taoist Temple** *(yánqìng guān)* has interesting architecture and a strange, 13-metre-high pagoda. The oldest existing building in Kaifeng is **Fan Pagoda** *(fán tǎ)*, south-east of the railway station.

Places to Stay

Kaifeng is one of those rare things in modern China – a place where budget travellers get a wider range of accommodation than those with lots of money to throw around. There seem to be absolutely no constraints on where foreigners choose to stay.

The *Bianliang Hotel* (☎ 393-1522) *(biànliáng lǚshè)* is on Zhongshan Lu, about 100 metres up from the railway station, and has doubles with crude bathrooms for Y44 and dorm beds from Y5.5 to Y8.5. There's hot water for a few hours in the evening.

The *Bian Hotel (biàn dàlǚshè)* is the big four-storey building you see to the left as you leave the bus station. Despite its grand appearance this place is rather basic inside – none of the rooms come with private bathroom – but with singles from Y16.50 and doubles for Y18.50 one can hardly complain.

Another good-value place is the *Dajintai Hotel (dàjīntái lǚguǎn)* on Gulou Jie (nearly opposite the Bank of China). It has a central yet quiet location in a small courtyard just behind the street front, and offers double

rooms with bathroom (including 24-hour hot water) for Y44. Basic no-frills doubles are available for Y13 per bed.

In the mid-price range is the *Bianjing Hotel (biànjīng fàndiàn)*, on the corner of Dong Dajie and Beixing Jie, at the north-eastern edge of town in the Muslim quarter. It's an older prefab concrete building with little character of its own, but there's plenty of activity on the surrounding streets. There's also a popular restaurant in the back of the hotel compound. There are dorm beds from Y17, while doubles with attached bathroom start at Y105. To get there take bus No 3 from the long-distance bus station and get off at the sixth stop.

The *Kaifeng Guesthouse* (☎ 595-5589) *(kāifēng bīnguǎn)* on Ziyou Lu, plonk in the centre of town, is a Russian-built structure with an unusual amount of charm. There is a bewildering array of rooms in the various buildings around a central square. Standard doubles range from Y96 to Y150 in the pleb wings. Tour groups put up in Building 2, where rooms start at Y280.

Kaifeng's Israelites

Father Nicola Trigault translated and published the diaries of the Jesuit priest Matteo Ricci in 1615, and based on these diaries he gives an account of a meeting between Ricci and a Jew from Kaifeng. The Jew was on his way to Beijing to take part in the imperial examinations, and Trigault writes:

'When he (Ricci) brought the visitor back to the house and began to question him as to his identity, it gradually dawned upon him that he was talking with a believer in the ancient Jewish law. The man admitted that he was an Israelite, but he knew no such word as 'Jew'.'

Ricci found out from the visitor that there were 10 or 12 families of Israelites in Kaifeng. A 'magnificent' synagogue had been built there and the five books of Moses had been preserved in the synagogue in scroll form for over 500 or 600 years. The visitor was familiar with the stories of the Old Testament, and some of the followers, he said, were expert in the Hebrew language. He also told Ricci that in a province which Trigault refers to as 'Cequian' at the capital of 'Hamcheu' there was a far greater number of Israelite families than at Kaifeng, and that there were others scattered about. Ricci sent one of his Chinese converts to Kaifeng, where he confirmed the visitor's story.

Today several hundred descendants of the original Jews live in Kaifeng and, though they still consider themselves Jewish, the religious beliefs and the customs associated with Judaism have almost completely died out. The original synagogue was destroyed in a Yellow River flood in 1642. It was rebuilt but destroyed by floods again in the 1850s. This time there was no money to rebuild it. Christian missionaries 'rescued' the temple's scrolls and prayer books in the late 19th century, and these are now in libraries in Israel, Canada and the USA. ■

South of Baogong Park on Yingbin Lu is the *Dongjing Hotel* (☎ 398-9388; fax 595-6661) *(dōngjīng dàfàndiàn)*. It's one of those Chinese attempts to bring international comforts to the weary traveller and to throw in some local colour at the same time. The result is akin to a caring prison complex with souvenir shops. The staff speak some English and do their best. Prices for doubles in the hotel's four separate wings vary from Y120 to Y280, and Y390 for a suite. Bus No 9 from the railway station goes past here.

Places to Eat

Despite its small size, Kaifeng offers a fair variety of street food, which is particularly good at the night market near the corner of Sihou Jie and Madao Jie. Worth sampling there is *ròuhé*, a local snack of fried vegetables and pork (or mutton in its Islamic version) stuffed into a 'pocket' of flat bread.

The eating places around the railway station offer the same generic slop that railway stations all over China serve up. The simple *Tianjin Restaurant (tiānjīn fànzhuāng)* five minutes' walk up Zhongshan Lu offers a good alternative.

As its name suggests, the busy government-run *Jiaozi Guan Restaurant (jiǎozi guǎn)* specialises in jiaozi, Chinese dumplings with a meat or vegetable filling. The dumplings here are nothing short of amazing and cost virtually nothing. Upstairs there's a much wider selection of dishes. It's on the corner of Shudian Lu and Sihou Jie in a three-storey traditional Chinese building with a quaint old wooden balcony.

For fast food with a Chinese touch, try *California Beef Noodles (jiāzhōu niúròumiàn)*, opposite the Xiangguosi Market. The noodles (Taiwan-style) are not bad.

Getting There & Away

Bus Private minibuses to Zhengzhou collect passengers from in front of the railway station. The best option, however, is to head over to the west bus station, opposite the Dongjing Hotel. The journey to Zhengzhou takes just under two hours and costs around Y7.

Buses to Luoyang are less frequent, and it may work out quicker changing at Zhengzhou. From the bus station in front of the railway station, there are three regular daily buses to Anyang (Y25) via Zhengzhou and a daily bus to Bozhou.

Train Kaifeng lies on the railway line between Xi'an and Shanghai and trains are frequent. Expresses to Zhengzhou take about 1½ hours and about 13 hours to both Shanghai and Xi'an. You can also get direct trains south to Bozhou and Hefei in Anhui Province from here.

Getting Around

Buses are less crowded than in many other parts of China and cover all sights of likely interest to tourists. Pedicabs and minivans are also widely available and fairly cheap.

CENTRAL CHINA

Hubei 湖北

Site of the great industrial city and river port of Wuhan, slashed through by the Yangzi River and its many tributaries, and supporting a population of almost 50 million, Hubei *(húběi)* is still one of China's most important provinces. But for most travellers, it's mainly a transit point, or the end point of the Yangzi cruise down from Chongqing.

The province actually comprises two quite different areas. The eastern two-thirds is a low-lying plain drained by the Yangzi and its main northern tributary, the Han River. The western third is an area of rugged highlands with small cultivated valleys and basins dividing Hubei from Sichuan. The plain was settled by the Han Chinese in 1000 BC. Around the 7th century it was intensively settled and by the 11th it was producing a rice surplus. In the late 19th century it was the first area in the Chinese interior to undergo considerable industrialisation.

WUHAN
(wŭhàn)

Not many people go out of their way to get to Wuhan, but a lot of people pass through the place, since this is the terminal of the Yangzi ferries from Chongqing. Livelier, less grimy and more modern than Chongqing, Wuhan is now enjoying a boom in foreign and local investment that may help it catch up to the comparatively sparkling, cosmopolitan citadels of Nanjing and Shanghai.

With a population of nearly four million, Wuhan is one of China's largest metropolises. It's actually a conglomeration of what were once three independent cities: Wuchang, Hankou and Hanyang.

Wuchang was established during the Han Dynasty, became a regional capital under the Yuan and is now the seat of the provincial government. It used to be a walled city but the walls have long since gone. Hankou, on the other hand, was barely more than a village until the Treaty of Nanjing opened it to foreign trade. There were five foreign

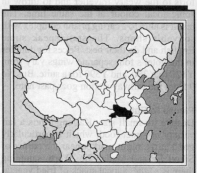

Population: 50 million
Capital: Wuhan
Highlights:

- A major port on the Yangzi River, Wuhan is probably the most cosmopolitan and lively of China's interior cities
- Yichang, access point for the massive Three Gorges Dam project and cruises upriver to Chongqing via the soon-to-be-submerged Three Gorges
- Shennongjia district, a relatively untravelled mountainous region boasting some of Hubei's wildest scenery

concession areas in Hankou, all grouped around present-day Zhongshan Lu. Arriving in 1861, the British were the first on the scene, followed by the Germans in 1895, the Russians in 1896, the French in 1896 and the Japanese in 1898. With the building of the Beijing-Wuhan railway in the 1920s, Hankou really began to expand and became the first major industrial centre in the interior of China. Many of the European-style buildings from the concession era have remained, particularly along Yanjiang Dadao in the north-east part of town. Government offices now occupy what were once the foreign banks, department stores and private residences.

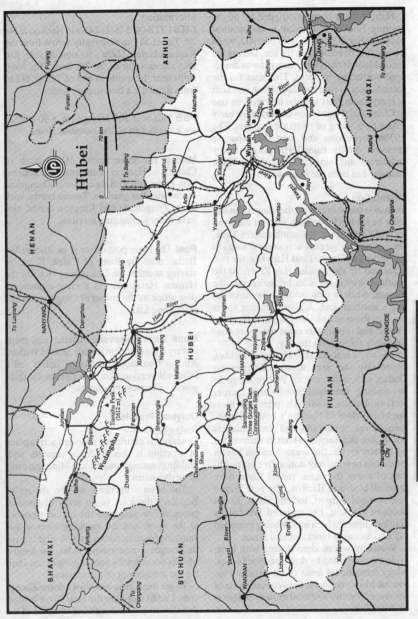

Hanyang has been outstripped by neighbouring Hankou and today is the smallest municipality. It dates back to 600 AD, when a town first developed on the site. During the second half of the 19th century it was developed for heavy industry. The plant for the manufacture of iron and steel which was built at Hanyang in 1891 was the first modern one in China and it was followed during the early 1900s by a string of riverside factories. The 1930s depression and then the Japanese invasion totally ruined Hanyang's heavy industries and since the revolution light industry has been the main activity.

Orientation

Wuhan is the only city on the Yangzi that can truly be said to lie on both sides of the river. From Wuchang on the south-eastern bank, the metropolis spreads across the Yangzi to the sectors of Hankou and Hanyang, the two separated by the smaller Han River. To the south of Wuhan an older bridge crosses the Yangzi, while a new bridge now links the city's northern end. A shorter bridge spans the Han River to link Hanyang with Hankou. Ferries and speedboats cross the rivers continuously throughout the day.

The city's real centre is Hankou *(hànkǒu)*, especially the area around Zhongshan Dadao, although 'central' Wuhan seems to be shifting gradually northwards, across Jiefang Dadao, Hankou's principal thoroughfare. Most of Hankou's hotels, department stores, restaurants and street markets are within this sector, which is surrounded by quieter residential areas. Hankou has an enormous new railway station five km north-east of town; the main Yangzi River ferry terminal is also in Hankou. The new Tianhe International Airport, located about 30 km north of Hankou, has replaced Wuchang's Nanhu Airport, which is now being parcelled off into lucrative blocks of real estate.

Wuchang is a modern district with long, wide avenues lined by drab concrete blocks. Many recreational areas and the Hubei Provincial Museum are on the Wuchang side of the river. The city's second railway station is in Wuchang.

Information

CITS CITS (☎ 578-2124) is in Hankou at No 26, Taibei Yi Lu, diagonally across from the Ramada Hotel. There's no sign outside: just take the elevator to the 7th floor. Bus No 9 stops near the southern end of Taibei Yi Lu: from there it's a five-minute walk.

PSB This is at 206 Shengli Lu, a 10-minute walk north-east of the Jianghan Hotel.

Money The main branch of the Bank of China is in Hankou in an ornate old concession-era building on the corner of Zhongshan Dadao and Jianghan Lu. Tourist hotels, such as the Qingchuan and Jianghan hotels, also have money-changing services.

Post The main post office is on Zhongshan Dadao near the Bank of China. If you're staying at either the Changjiang Hotel or the Hankou Hotel there is a more convenient post office on the corner of Qingnian Lu and Hangkong Lu.

Maps There are several different city maps of varying usefulness on sale around Wuhan. Xinhua Bookstores and some hotels sell a bilingual version that indicates, in English, places of interest to tourists.

Guiyuan Temple
(guīyuǎn sì)

Doubling as a curiosity shop and active place of worship is this Buddhist temple, with buildings dating from the late Ming and early Qing dynasties.

The main attractions are the statues of Buddha's disciples in an array of comical poses. A few years ago the statues were out in the open, and the smoking incense and sunshine filtering through the skylights gave the temple a rare magic. Alas, no longer. Monks occasionally bang a gong or tap a bell for the amusement of the masses.

To get there, take bus No 45 down Zhongshan Dadao and over the Han River bridge; there's a stop within walking distance of the temple. The temple is on Cuiweiheng Lu at the junction with Cuiwei Lu; a trinket market lines Cuiwei Lu.

Yangzi River Bridge
(wǔhàn chángjiāng dàqiáo)
Wuchang and Hanyang are linked by this great bridge – it's over 1100 metres long and 80 metres high. The completion of the bridge in 1957 marked one of Communist China's first great engineering achievements, because until then all road and rail traffic had had to be laboriously ferried across the river. A second trans-Yangzi road bridge in northern Wuhan was completed in mid-1995.

Hubei Provincial Museum
(húběishěng bówùguǎn)
The museum is a must if you're interested in archaeology. Its large collection of artefacts came from the Zhenghouyi Tomb, which was unearthed in 1978 on the outskirts of Suizhou City. The tomb dates from around 433 BC, in the Warring States Period. The male internee was buried with about 7000 of his favourite artefacts, including bronze ritual vessels, weapons, horse and chariot equipment, bamboo instruments and utensils, and gold and jade objects.

The museum is beside Donghu (East Lake) in Wuchang. Take bus No 14 from the Wuchang ferry (the dock closest to the bridge) to the terminal, then walk back along the road about 10 minutes, where there's a sign for Mao Zedong's villa. The museum is down that road.

In summer you can do a scenic day-trip that includes the museum, taking a ferry over from Hankou to the Zhonghua Lu pier in Wuchang, then boarding bus No 36 to Moshan Hill. Take another ferry across the lake to East Lake Park, walk to the museum, then get bus No 14 to Yellow Crane Tower, and finally get a ferry back to Hankou.

Mao Zedong's Villa
(máozédōng biéshù)
If you've just come up from Hunan, you may have had your fill of Mao by now. But if not, you may find a stroll through this bucolic hideaway of the Chairman worth your time and the Y20 entrance fee. The tour takes in his living quarters, offices, private swimming pool and a meeting room where key decisions were made during the Cultural Revolution. Mao stayed here more than 20 times between 1960 and 1974, including nearly a year and a half between 1966 and 1969. Jiang Qing joined him, but only three times: apparently she didn't like the place. If you're lucky, you may get a guided tour from one of the frosty, politically correct female guides.

The buildings are in pretty poor shape and have obviously been neglected for decades. But the tree-filled grounds and the gardens are quite nice and have become a haven for a variety of birds. To get there, keep going past the provincial museum for about 10 minutes: there are plenty of signs to show you the way.

Wuhan University
(wǔhàn dàxué)
Wuhan University is beside Luojia Hill in Wuchang. It was founded in 1913, and many of the charming campus buildings originate from that early period. The university was the site of the 1967 'Wuhan Incident' – a protracted battle during the Cultural Revolution with machine gun nests on top of the library and supply tunnels dug through the hill. For a bit of Cultural Revolution nostalgia take bus No 12 to the terminal.

Places to Stay – bottom end
Nearly all the really low-end places in Wuhan have slammed their doors to foreigners, leaving few options. The cheapest choice is probably in Wuchang at the Dadongmen Hotel (☎ 887-7402) (dàdōngmén fàndiàn) at the intersection of Wuluo Lu and Zhongshan Lu, convenient to Wuchang Railway Station. It's a large place with plenty of good basic rooms ranging in price from Y25 per bed in a double to Y15 in quads, or Y30 for a single. The Dadongmen's major drawbacks are the traffic noise –

CENTRAL CHINA

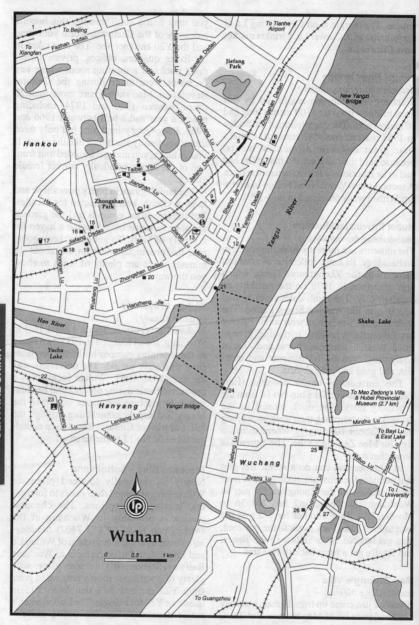

Hankou

To Beijing

To Xiangfan

Fazhan Dadao

Qingnian Lu

Hankou Lu

Hankou Lu

Xinhua Lu

Chongren Lu

Zhongshan Park

Taibei Lu

Xima Lu

Qiuchang Lu

Huangpuiche Lu

Jianshe Dadao

Sanyangjiao Lu

Zhongshan Dadao

Jiefang Park

To Tianhe Airport

New Yangzi Bridge

Taibei Lu

Yilu

Jianghan Lu

Jianghan Dadao

Jiefang Dadao

Shengli Jie

Lanjiang Dadao

Yangzi River

Jiefang Dadao

Shundao Jie

Zhongshan Dadao

Hanzheng Jie

Wushang Lu

Qianlu Lu

Minsheng Lu

Han River

Yuchu Lake

Hanyang

Cuiweilu Lu

Cuiwei Lu

Lanjiang Lu

Yaolu Di

Yangzi Bridge

Shahu Lake

To Mao Zedong's Villa & Hubei Provincial Museum (2.7 km)

Minzhu Lu

To Bayi Lu & East Lake

Wuchang

Jiefang Lu

Ziyang Lu

Wuluo Lu

Zhongnan Lu

To University

To Guangzhou

Wuhan

0   0.5   1 km

WUHAN 武汉

PLACES TO STAY

2 Ramada Hotel Wuhan
华美达酒店
3 Xinhua Hotel
新华酒店
6 Victory Hotel
胜利饭店
8 Jianghan Hotel
江汉饭店
11 Xieli Hotel
协力宾馆
15 Hankou Hotel
汉口饭店
16 Yangtze Hotel
长江大酒店
18 Wuhan Asia Hotel
武汉亚州大酒店
20 Yin Feng Hotel
银丰宾馆
25 Dadongmen Hotel
大东门饭店

26 Marine Hotel
航海宾馆

OTHER

1 New Hankou Railway Station
汉口新火车站
4 CITS
中国国际旅行社
5 Old Hankou Railway Station
汉口旧火车站
7 PSB
公安局外事科
9 Laotongcheng Restaurant
老通城酒楼
10 Bank of China
中国银行
12 Yangzi Ferry Terminal
武汉港客运站
13 Main Post Office
邮局

14 Long-Distance Bus Station
长途汽车站
17 Chi Chi's Disco
琪琪
19 CAAC
中国民航售票处
21 Hankou-Wuchang Ferries
汉口武昌渡船
22 Hanyang Railway Station
汉阳火车站
23 Guiyuan Temple
归元寺
24 Zhonghua Lu Pier
中华路码头
27 Wuchang Railway Station
武昌火车站

though rooms not fronting the street are quieter – and its location in Wuchang, as most of the city action is in Hankou.

In Hankou, the *Victory Hotel* (☎ 281-2780) *(shènglì fàndiàn)*, an old British-built guesthouse on the corner of Shengli Jie and Siwei Lu, has moved decidedly upmarket since it had a thorough renovation some years ago. Standard doubles now cost Y440, but at the back they've still got a few cheap rooms around a leafy courtyard for Y100. The place is a bit out of the way, but there are plenty of buses along Shengli Jie.

Places to Stay – middle

Pretty much in central Hankou, the uninspiring *Xinhua Hotel* (☎ 585-4567) *(xīnhuá jiǔdiàn)* on Jianghan Beilu has doubles starting at Y148, though they may try and tack on a 30% service charge for foreigners. Just north of and across from the massive Hankou ferry terminal, the *Xieli Hotel (xiélì bīngguǎn)* has decent doubles for Y180, good to keep in mind for those late-night Yangzi river cruise arrivals in Wuhan.

Costing a bit more but definitely worth it is the *Yin Feng Hotel* (☎ 589-2700) *(yínfēng bīngguǎn)*, centrally located at 400 Zhongshan Dadao. Doubles/triples are Y208/260 and feature clean wooden floors, sparkling bathrooms and great water pressure for excellent showers. Over in Wuchang diagonally across from the railway station on Zhongshan Lu, the *Marine Hotel (hánghǎi bīngguǎn)* has doubles/triples for Y158/198.

Places to Stay – top end

The *Jianghan Hotel* (☎ 281-1600) *(jiānghàn fàndiàn)* at 245 Shengli Jie, just around the corner from the old (now disused) Hankou Railway Station, is the place to stay if you can afford it. Built by the French in 1914 as the Demin Hotel, it's one of the best examples of colonial architecture in this part of China. Room rates range from US$83 for a double to US$230 for a suite, plus a 10% surcharge. The hotel has its own post office, shops and an excellent restaurant.

The *Yangtze Hotel* (☎ 586-2828) *(chángjiāng dàjiǔdiàn)* on the north-west corner of

CENTRAL CHINA

Jiefang Dadao and Qingnian Lu has doubles from US$85 a night. Immediately opposite is the *Hankou Hotel* (☎ 585-7834) *(hànkǒu fàndiàn)*, which is similar but somewhat cheaper. Both are quite good hotels, but this intersection now resembles a freeway junction due to an adjacent noisy traffic overpass.

Although its location is a bit inconvenient, the US-style *Ramada Hotel Wuhan* (☎ 283-7968) *(huáměidá jiǔdiàn)* at 9 Taibei Yi Lu offers four-star service for US$75 for a double, though prices seem negotiable. It's also Wuhan's best spot for Western food (see the following Places to Eat section). The fanciest spot in town is now undoubtedly the *Wuhan Asia Hotel* (☎ 586-8777) *(wǔhàn-yàzhōu dàjiǔdiàn)* at 616 Jiefang Dadao, where a double room will set you back over Y800. A lot of Wuhan's foreign business community calls this hotel home, but this may change after the five-star Wuhan Holiday Inn opens for business.

Places to Eat

Wuhan has some pretty good eating houses in all price ranges. Popular local snacks include fresh catfish from the nearby Dong Hu (East Lake) and charcoal-grilled whole pigeons served with a sprinkling of chilli. Locals swear the best spot to go for seafood is a series of floating restaurants on Ba Yi Lu, which runs towards East Lake. Good streets for night food are Minsheng Lu and Jianghan Lu, both running off Zhongshan Dadao. If you have a craving for Western food, there's no better spot than the Ramada Hotel's coffee shop.

The *Laotongcheng Restaurant (lǎotōng-chéng jiǔlóu)* at 1 Dazhi Lu on the corner with Zhongshan Dadao serves a tasty snack called *dòupí*. While it may look like a stuffed omelette, it's actually made with a bean curd base – its name translates as 'bean skin' – and is served rolled around a filling of rice and diced meat. The Laotongcheng was apparently a favourite of Mao's, though presumably he didn't have to push and shove with the proletariat to get his doupi. Doupi is no great delicacy, but at Y2.50 a serving you can't go wrong.

Entertainment

Wuhan nightlife is beginning to take off with discos and nightclubs opening all over Hankou. One of the top spots with locals is *Chi Chi's* , a former movie theatre that now rocks to deafening disco and Chinese pop tunes. Despite the Y20 cover charge, young Chinese flock to this place, especially on weekend nights, lured by foreign disc jockeys, the chance to display their karaoke prowess on stage (at Y50 per song!) and a nightly 'Star Wars' light show that has to be seen to be believed. Chi Chi's is located on Jiefang Dadao, about a 10-minute walk from the Wuhan Asia Hotel.

Getting There & Away

The best way of getting to eastern destinations such as Nanjing and Shanghai is by air or river ferry rather than the circuitous rail route.

Air CAAC (☎ 385-7949) has its main ticket office in Hankou at 151 Liji Beilu. It offers air connections to virtually all major cities in China, including daily flights to Beijing, Guangzhou, Kunming, Shanghai and Shenzhen, and several each week to Nanjing, Fuzhou, Xi'an, Chengdu and Hong Kong (Y1600). Several regional airlines have ticket offices north of the CAAC office on Liji Beilu and Hangkong Lu. Buses to Tianhe International Airport leave 4 to 5 times throughout the day from the China Southern Wuhan Ticket Office at Hangkong Lu, just north of the Yangtze Hotel. The fare is Y10. A taxi to the airport should cost between Y100 and Y120.

Bus The main long-distance bus station is in Hankou on Jiefang Dadao between Xinhua Lu and Jianghan Lu. There are daily departures to Nanchang, Changsha, Xiamen, Xiangfan (north-western Hubei), Hefei and Bozhou (northern Anhui). There are also numerous buses throughout the day to Yichang, with a partially completed four-lane highway cutting travel time down to around seven hours. This should get even shorter when the full length of the roadway is finished, possibly by late 1996.

Train Wuhan is on the main Beijing-Guangzhou line; express trains to Kunming, Xi'an and Lanzhou run via the city. All trains that go through Wuhan to other destinations stop at both Hankou and Wuchang railway stations; it's usually more convenient to get off at Hankou even though the new station is a fair way out. At Hankou station, hard and soft sleepers must be booked in the small ticket office between the waiting hall and the main ticket office. There is also a railway ticket office in central Hankou at the northern end of where Zhongshan Dadao briefly divides (opposite the No 7 bus stop). They only have some sleeper tickets and might not serve foreigners, but it's worth a try. There are usually a few locals hanging about who will help – for a slight fee. Note that many southbound trains originating at Wuhan actually depart from Wuchang station rather than Hankou. Tickets for these must be bought at Wuchang. Window 14 is for foreigners.

Some sample hard-sleeper-ticket prices for foreigners are: Beijing, Y273; Guangzhou, Y247; and Kunming, Y392.

Boat You can take ferries from Wuhan along the Yangzi River either west to Chongqing or east to Shanghai (see the Yangzi River section below for details).

Getting Around

Bus routes crisscross the city but getting where you want to go may mean changing at least once. A useful bus is the No 38, which passes the Jianghan Hotel to and from the new Hankou Railway Station. Bus No 9 runs from the train station down Xinhua Lu to the Yangzi ferry terminal. Motor-trikes and pedicabs wait outside the two main railway stations and the Yangzi boat terminal, as well as the smaller ferry docks. The Hankou-Wuchang ferries are usually a more convenient, and always much faster, way of crossing the river than taking a bus over the Yangzi bridge. The large boats take 15 to 20

minutes to make the crossing, while smaller speedboats, which carry around 15 people, do it in five minutes for Y5.

YANGZI RIVER: WUHAN TO CHONGQING & SHANGHAI

Wuhan more or less marks the halfway point in the long navigable stretch of the Yangzi River from Chongqing down to Shanghai. From Wuhan numerous ferries go up and down the river, some running its entire length.

Boat tickets can be bought at the main Yangzi ferry terminal in Hankou or the service desks at tourist hotels. CITS can also help book tickets, but mostly for luxury tourist cruises which are priced in US dollars and can cost 10 times more than the standard ferries. Although some private ferries now have 1st-class cabins, most companies still follow socialist doctrine, only offering 2nd, 3rd and 4th class. Second class is a two-person cabin, 3rd class is a 10-person dormitory and 4th class is a 20-person dormitory. Food and beer are sold on board; you can also get off at any of the many stops along the way for provisions.

Following are Chinese ticket prices and travel times from Wuhan to selected destinations. Prices for foreigners are usually (but not always) 50% higher than the Chinese price.

	2nd Class (Y)	3rd Class (Y)	4th Class (Y)	Journey Time
Chongqing	457	191	138	4 days
Jiujiang	85	36	27	1 night
Nanjing	204	86	62	36 hours
Shanghai	301	127	91	48 hours
Wuhu	179	76	55	30 hours
Yichang	177	74	54	32 hours
Yueyang	78	33	24	1 night

Heading downriver on leaving Wuhan, the steamer passes through Huangshi in eastern Hubei Province. This town lies on the southern bank of the river and is being developed as a centre for heavy industry. Nearby is an ancient mining tunnel dating back to the Spring and Autumn Period; it contained

The Three Gorges (Sanxia) Dam

When completed in about 2008, the Three Gorges (Sanxia) Dam will be the world's largest water storage reservoir. First put forward more than a decade ago, the dam proposal was finally given the go-ahead by the Chinese government only in 1992. This colossal project involves the construction of a two-km-wide, 185-metre-high dam wall across the Yangzi River at Sandouping, 38 km upstream from the existing Gezhou Dam. The aims of the project are to supply electricity, to improve the river's navigability and to protect against flooding.

The Three Gorges Dam is a cornerstone in government efforts to channel economic growth from the dynamic coastal provinces towards the more backward Chinese hinterland. The dam's hydroelectric production – reckoned to equal almost one-fifth of China's current generating capacity – is intended to power the continuing industrialisation of the upper Yangzi Basin.

Navigation upriver from Yichang has always been hindered by rather unfavourable conditions for shipping. Although passing the dam itself will be an inconvenience for ships – the Three Gorges Dam will have five passage locks compared with just one lock on the Gezhou Dam – the navigability of the upper Yangzi will be drastically improved by the widening of shipping lanes and the creation of a more constant water level within the new lake. Inundation will eliminate strong river currents, and obstacles dangerous to navigation such as sand bars and submerged rocks will disappear completely.

At least as important will be the dam's role in flood control. The Yangzi is prone to repeated flooding, often causing great loss of life. Several catastrophic floods have occurred this century, in 1931, 1935, 1954 and more recently in 1991, when over 2000 people are believed to have perished.

However, the massive scale of the Three Gorges Dam project has caused disquiet among environmentalists and economists, arousing some of the most outspoken criticism of government policy in China since 1989.

The social and environmental implications of the dam, which will create a vast 550-km-long lake stretching deep into Sichuan Province, are profound indeed. When the backwaters build up behind the dam wall, the great inland port of Chongqing will become the world's first metropolis situated on the banks of a major artificial lake. An estimated two million people living in the inundated areas will need to be relocated. Some destruction of the natural and scenic splendour of the Three Gorges will be unavoidable, though how the dam will affect Yangzi River tourism – still in its infancy – is uncertain.

Construction of the dam will be enormously expensive, with a final cost probably somewhere in the vicinity of US$20 billion. Economists at home and abroad have warned that it may be imprudent for China to concentrate such investment into one single project.

Fears about the dam project have heightened with the recent release of information about two dams that collapsed in Henan Province in 1975. After 20 years as a state secret, it is now apparent that as many as 230,000 people died in the catastrophe.

Planners insist that the Three Gorges Dam will be constructed according to safety regulations that would make a similar disaster impossible – still, the collapse of the walls holding back the world's largest water storage reservoir in one of the world's most densely populated pieces of real estate is a thought that must give even the most gung-ho supporters of the Three Gorges project nightmares. ∎

numerous mining tools, including bronze axes. Near the border with Jiangxi on the north bank is the town of Wuxue, noted for the production of bamboo goods.

The first major town you come to in Jiangxi is Jiujiang, the jumping-off point for nearby Lushan. The mouth of Lake Boyang is situated on the Yangzi River and at this point on the southern bank of the river is Stone Bell Mountain, noted for its numerous Tang Dynasty stone carvings. This was also the place where Taiping troops were garrisoned for five years defending Jinling, their capital.

The first major town you approach in Anhui Province is Anqing, on the north bank in the foothills of the Dabie Mountains. Next comes the town of Guichi, from which you can get a bus to the spectacular Huangshan (Yellow Mountains). The town of Tongling lies in a mountainous area in central Anhui on the southern bank, west of Tongguanshan. Tongling has been a copper-mining centre for 2000 years and is a source of copper for the minting of coins. Still in Anhui Province, and at the confluence of the Yangzi and Qingyi rivers, is Wuhu, also a jumping-off point for Huangshan. Just before Anhui Province ends is the city of Manshan, the site of a large iron and steel complex.

In Jiangsu Province the first large city you pass is Nanjing, followed by Zhenjiang, then the port of Nantong at the confluence of the Tongyang and Tonglu canals. The ferry then proceeds along the Yangzi and turns down the Huangpu River to Shanghai. The Yangzi empties into the East China Sea.

WUDANGSHAN
(wŭdāng shān)

The Wudangshan mountains stretch for 400 km across north-western Hubei Province. The highest summit is the 1600-metre-high Tianzhu Peak, situated south-east of Shiyan, whose name translates as Pillar Propping Up the Sky or Heavenly Pillar Peak.

The Wudangshan are a sacred range to the Taoists, and a number of Taoist temples were built here during the construction sprees of the Ming emperors Cheng Zu and Zhen Wu. Noted temples include the Golden Hall on Heavenly Pillar Peak, which was built entirely of gilded copper in 1416; the hall contains a bronze statue of Ming emperor Zhen Wu, who became a Taoist deity. The Purple Cloud Temple stands on Zhanqifeng Peak, and the Nanyan Temple perches on the South Cliff. From Changsha and Yichang there are both trains and buses to Xiangfan; trains and buses from there to Shiyan pass through Wudangshan Village.

SHENNONGJIA
shénnóngjià)

The Shennongjia district in remote north-western Hubei has the wildest scenery in the province. With heavily forested mountains reaching over 3000 metres, the area is famous for the sightings of wild, ape-like creatures, a Chinese equivalent of the Himalayan Yeti or the North American Bigfoot. The stories are interesting, but the creatures seem to be able to distinguish between peasants and scientists – molesting the former and evading the latter. The best way into the Shennongjia area is by bus from Yichang to Songbai, a ride of 250 km. If there are four or more of you, you might consider hiring a van in Yichang. There are one or two travel outfits near the Yichang Railway Station that specialise in tours of Shennongjia.

YICHANG
(yíchāng)

Situated just below the famous Three Gorges, Yichang is the gateway to the Upper Yangzi and was a walled town as long ago as the Sui Dynasty. The city was opened to foreign trade in 1877 by a treaty between Britain and China and a concession area set up along the river front south-east of the old city.

Today Yichang is best known for the nearby Gezhou Dam, and the city's economy has taken off due to the massive Three Gorges hydroelectric project now being built at Sandouping, 40 km upstream. A steady flow of Yangzi River tourists passing through town is also swelling local coffers. Unless you have a special fondness for dams, there's really not much worth seeing in Yichang, but it's a useful jumping-off point for more interesting places.

Places to Stay

Across from the Dagongqiao bus and ferry terminal, the *Da Gong Hotel (dàgōng fàndiàn)* may well be the only cheap place in town that takes foreigners. Even then, you'd do well to be polite and keep a smile on your face, or they may decide you're not worth the trouble. Beds in doubles without bath are Y36, and start at Y56 for low-end rooms with attached bathrooms. The hotel is up a small driveway set back from Yanjiang Dadao and

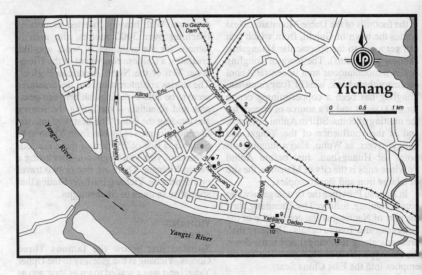

YICHANG 宜昌

1　Three Gorges Hotel
　　三峡宾馆
2　Railway Station
　　火车站
3　Post Office
　　邮局
4　Sunshine Hotel
　　阳光大酒店
5　Long-Distance Bus Station
　　长途汽车站
6　Children's Park
　　儿童公园
7　CITS
　　中国国际旅行社
8　Taohualing Hotel
　　桃花岭饭店
9　Da Gong Hotel
　　大公饭店
10　Dagongqiao Bus/Ferry Terminal
　　大公桥客运站
11　CAAC Office
　　中国民航售票处
12　Yichang Ferry Terminal
　　宜昌港

has no English sign, but there's a big red lighted sign in Chinese at night that's easy to spot.

Just down the steps from the railway station and to the left, the *Sunshine Hotel* *(yángguāng dàjiǔdiàn)* has clean, though slightly tattered, doubles for Y234 and up. There are a number of other hotels around here, but none of them seem to welcome foreign friends.

If these two don't work out, you may be stuck with the *Taohualing Hotel* (☎ 442-244) *(táohuālíng bīnguǎn)* in the middle of town on Kangzhuang Lu. Run-down doubles in the old wing start at Y342 and nicer rooms at over Y400. The *Three Gorges Hotel* (☎ 224-911) *(sānxiá bīnguǎn)* is fairly far north at 38 Yanjiang Dadao and has similar prices, though the rooms look better. Take bus No 11 from the station or No 2 from the dock.

Getting There & Away

Yichang has a small airport with two flights a week to Wuhan.

The long-distance bus station is to the left of the railway station along Dongshan

Dadao. There are day buses and night sleepers to Wuhan and one 6 am bus daily to Songbai in the Shennongjia area. Buses to Wuhan also leave from the Dagongqiao bus and ferry terminal on Yanjiang Dadao.

The town is linked by a 40-km section of track to the rail junction at Yaqueling (*yāquèlǐng*). There are direct trains daily between Yichang and Beijing, Zhengzhou, Xi'an, Wuhan and Huaihua. Trains to Huaihua stop en route at Zhangjiajie City (formerly Dayong). If you can't get on these, you will probably have to change trains at Yaqueling. The long-distance bus station also has buses to Yaqueling. Make sure to somehow let the driver know you're headed to the railhead, as it is located far outside the town of Yaqueling. You'll probably then be

dropped off next to the railway tracks and pointed in the direction of the station. Walk along the tracks for 10 minutes and you'll get there.

All passing river ferries call in at Yichang ferry terminal. Travellers often find the two-day boat trip through the Yangzi gorges between Chongqing (Sichuan Province) and Yichang quite long enough, and some disembark or board here rather than spend an extra day on the river between Yichang and Wuhan. If you're going upriver, the Chinese-price fares to Chongqing are: Y234 (2nd class), Y109 (3rd class) and Y84 (4th class). There is also an express ferry that gets you to Chongqing in 38 hours for similar prices. Bus Nos 3 and 4 run from the railway station to near the ferry terminal.

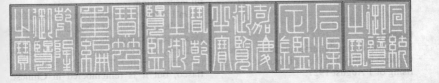

Jiangxi 江西

Jiangxi (*jiāngxī*) was incorporated into the Chinese empire at an early date, but it remained sparsely populated until the 8th century. Before this, the main expansion of the Han Chinese had been from the north into Hunan and then into Guangdong. When the building of the Grand Canal from the 7th century onwards opened up the southeastern regions, Jiangxi became an important transit point on the trade and shipment route overland from Guangdong.

Before long the human traffic was diverted into Jiangxi, and between the 8th and 13th centuries the region was rapidly settled by Chinese peasants. The development of silver mining and tea growing allowed the formation of a wealthy Jiangxi merchant class. By the 19th century, however, its role as a major transport route from Guangzhou was much reduced by the opening of coastal ports to foreign shipping, which forced the Chinese junk trade into a steady decline.

Jiangxi also bears the distinction of having been one of the most famous Communist guerrilla bases. It was only after several years of war that the Kuomintang were able to drive the Communists out onto their 'Long March' to Shaanxi.

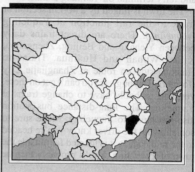

Population: 35 million
Capital: Nanchang
Highlights:
- Jingdezhen, China's most famous area for the production of pottery and ceramics
- Lushan, a hill resort where mountain vistas have inspired artists and Communist leaders alike

NANCHANG
(nánchāng)

The fairly nondescript capital of a province that sees little in the way of foreign visitors, Nanchang has been called 'the poor person's Beijing'. There is little to see, and the city can be a very miserable place on a cold, rainy day. Still, there are far worse Chinese cities, and the side streets that run off the broad boulevards can make for interesting exploring.

History

Nanchang is largely remembered in modern Chinese history for the Communist-led uprising of 1 August 1927.

After Chiang Kaishek staged his massacre of Communists and other opponents in March 1927, what was left of the Communist Party fled underground and a state of confusion reigned. At this time the Party was dominated by a policy of urban revolution, and the belief was that victory could only be won by organising insurrections in the cities. Units of the Kuomintang Army led by Communist officers happened to be concentrated around Nanchang at the time, and there appeared to be an opportunity for a successful insurrection.

On 1 August, a combined army of 30,000 under the leadership of Zhou Enlai and Zhu De seized the city and held it for several days until they were driven out by troops loyal to the Nanjing regime. The revolt was largely a fiasco, but it is remembered in Chinese

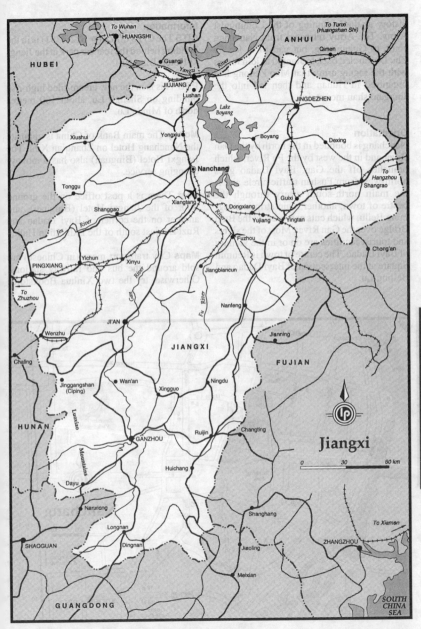

history as the beginning of the Communist Army. The Army retreated from Nanchang south to Guangdong, but part of it, led by Zhu De, circled back to Jiangxi to join forces with the ragtag army that Mao Zedong had organised in Hunan and then led into the Jinggangshan mountains.

Orientation

Nanchang is bounded in the north by the Gan River and in the west by the Fu River, which branches off the Gan. Bayi Dadao goes north-west from Fushan traffic circle and is the main north-south artery through the centre of town; another main strip is Yangming Beilu, which cuts east-west to the Bayi Bridge over the Gan River. Most of the sights and tourist facilities are on or in the vicinity of Bayi Dadao. The centre of town is Renmin Square at the intersection of Bayi Dadao and Beijing Lu.

Information

CITS The CITS office (☎ 622-4391) is in the building behind the rear car park at the Jiangxi Hotel (Binguan).

PSB This is in the new cream-tiled high-rise building on Shengli Lu, about 100 metres north of Minde Lu.

Money The main Bank of China is opposite the Nanchang Hotel on Zhanqian Xilu. The Jiangxi Hotel (Binguan) also has a money-changing service.

Post There is a post office on the ground floor of the Jiangxi Hotel (Binguan), and another on the corner of Bayi Dadao and Ruzi Lu, just south of the Exhibition Hall.

Maps City transport maps (in Chinese) are sold around the bus and railway stations. Otherwise, try the two Xinhua Bookstores

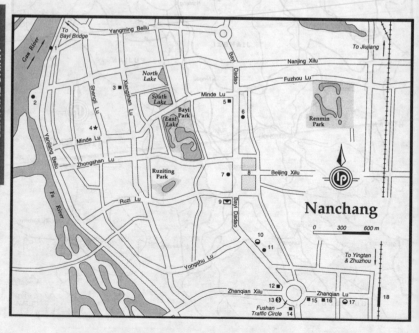

on Bayi Dadao: one at Renmin Square and the other between the bus station and Fushan traffic circle.

Things to See

On Bayi Dadao in the heart of Nanchang is **Renmin Square**. Here you'll find the **Monument to the Martyrs**, a sculpture of red-tiled flags and a stone column topped with a rifle and fixed bayonet. Opposite the square is the **Exhibition Hall**, an immense

---

NANCHANG 南昌

1	Nanchang Port 南昌港客运站
2	Tengwang Pavilion 腾王阁
3	Xiangshan Hotel 象山宾馆
4	PSB 公安局外事科
5	Jiangxi Hotel (Binguan) 江西宾馆
6	Memorial Hall to the Martyrs of the Revolution 烈士纪念馆
7	Exhibition Hall 展览馆
8	Renmin Square 人民广场
9	Post Office 邮电局
10	Long-Distance Bus Station 长途汽车站
11	CAAC Booking Office 中国民航
12	Nanchang Hotel 南昌宾馆
13	Bank of China 中国银行
14	Poyanghu Hotel 鄱阳湖大酒店
15	Lucky Hotel 吉利大酒店
16	Jingjiu Hotel 京九宾馆
17	Minibuses to Jiujiang 往九江小型车
18	Railway Station 火车站

---

building adorned with a giant red star – a nostalgic tribute to Stalinist architecture.

Pride of the city is the massive **Tengwang Pavilion**, erected in 1989, allegedly on the same site as 28 previous reconstructions. Originally built in the Tang period, the modern nine-storey granite pavilion is situated on the banks of the Fu River and houses exhibit rooms, teahouses and the inevitable souvenir shops. On the top floor is a traditional Chinese music and dance theatre. Entry costs Y10 for Chinese and students, Y20 for foreigners.

Most of the other sights are reminders of the Communist Revolution and include the **Memorial Hall to the Martyrs of the Revolution** on Bayi Dadao, north of Renmin Square; the **Residence of Zhou Enlai & Zhu De** on Minde Lu; and the **Former Headquarters of the Nanchang Uprising**, now a museum, near the corner of Shengli and Zhongshan Lu.

Places to Stay

The cheapest deal around is at the *Nanchang Hotel* (☎ 621-9698) *(nánchāng bīnguǎn)*, where three-bed/four-bed dorms are available for Y15 per bed. There will need to be a group of you to swing one of these. Standard doubles cost from Y100 to Y180, and the cheaper ones are good value.

The old backpacker stand-by, the *Xiangshan Hotel* (☎ 677-2246) *(xiàngshān fàndiàn)*, on Xiangshan Beilu, has gone up in price but is still not a bad deal, though it is a long way from the bus and railway stations. It has an enormous range of rooms from Y108 to Y286. Take bus No 5 for nine stops from the railway station; the bus stop is almost outside the hotel.

The *Poyanghu Hotel* (☎ 622-9688) *(póyánghú dàjiǔdiàn)*, on the south-west side of Fushan traffic circle, is a massive and fairly recent construction that is rapidly falling apart. It has basic doubles at Y120, and other more luxurious rooms from Y160 to Y310. It's convenient for the bus and railway stations.

There are a couple of new mid-range hotels just down from the railway station: the

CENTRAL CHINA

Jingjiu Hotel (☎ 627-6708) (*jīngjiǔ bīnguǎn*) has standard doubles at Y248; and the *Lucky Hotel* (☎ 621-9683) (*jílì dàjiǔdiàn*) has very similar rooms for Y218. There is very little between them.

Two local establishments go by the English name Jiangxi Hotel, although their names in Chinese use different words (and characters) for hotel. The *Jiangxi Hotel* (☎ 622-1131) (*jiāngxī bīnguǎn*), at 78 Bayi Dadao, is where most foreign tourists seem to stay. The building is an interesting relic of early 1960s socialist architecture. Renovations had effectively closed the place down at the time of writing but you can expect rooms to start at US$80 for a standard double when it reopens. The other *Jiangxi Hotel* (☎ 621-2123) (*jiāngxī fàndiàn*) is a dreary, overpriced place just down the road.

Places to Eat

As usual the railway station area is a good hunting ground for cheap eats. It's pointless making any suggestions – all over Nanchang there are restaurants selling dumplings, fried breads and the like. So few foreign travellers pass through here there are no reasonably priced restaurants with English menus.

Getting There & Away

Air The most convenient CAAC office (☎ 622-3656) is on Bayi Dadao, next to the long-distance bus station. There is also an office next to the Jiangxi Hotel (Binguan). Scheduled flights go to Beijing, Guangzhou, Hong Kong, Kunming, Ningbo, Shanghai, Wenzhou and Xi'an. The airport is at Xiangtang, 40 km south of the city centre.

Bus Nanchang's long-distance bus station is on Bayi Dadao between Renmin Square and Fushan traffic circle. From here there are air-con buses to Changsha (Y60, seven daily), Jiujiang (Y19, six daily) and the porcelain-producing centre of Jingdezhen (Y30, eight daily). There are also direct buses to the mountain resorts of Jinggangshan in Jiangxi's south-western mountains (Y45, five per day) and Lushan hill station to the north (Y27).

Minibuses to Jiujiang (Y15) run through the day as soon as there are enough passengers to make the trip worthwhile (the trip usually takes an hour). The departure point is between the Jingjiu Hotel and a small rash of barbershops which have young women waving from the doorways.

Train Counter No 9 at Nanchang Railway Station is for foreigners. Nanchang lies just off the main Guangzhou-Shanghai railway line but most trains make the short detour north via the city. There are also direct trains to Fuzhou once daily. Express trains run daily to the Yangzi River port of Jiujiang (2½ hours), though the new highway between Nanchang and Jiujiang makes it quicker and cheaper to do the trip by bus.

Boat The small Nanchang ferry terminal is just south of the Bayi Bridge. An alternative way of getting to Jingdezhen is to catch a 6.30 am boat across Lake Boyang to the town of Boyang, then take a bus to Jingdezhen. In summer, tourist cruise boats also leave from here.

Getting Around

From Nanchang Railway Station, the most useful public transport routes are trolley-bus Nos 2 and 201, which go up Bayi Dadao past the long-distance bus station, and bus No 5, which runs north along Xiangshan Beilu. The city has few pedicabs and motor-tricycles, but there are plenty of taxis at the stations and better hotels.

JINGDEZHEN

(*jǐngdézhèn*)

Jingdezhen is an ancient town once famous for the manufacture of much-coveted porcelain. The city has maintained its position as a major producer of Chinese ceramics, but quality seems to have been compromised by mass production. The skyline of Jingdezhen is dominated by chimney stacks belching out coal smoke from countless firing kilns. While the centre of town is pleasant enough, the outskirts are depressing.

In the 12th century the Song Dynasty fled

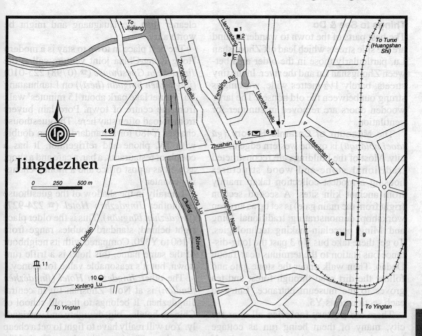

JINGDEZHEN 景德镇

PLACES TO STAY

1 Jingdezhen Hotel
(Binguan)
景德镇宾馆
2 Jingdezhen Guesthouse
景德镇宾馆合资
6 Jingdezhen Hotel
(Fandian)
景德镇饭店

8 Huaguang Hotel
华光饭店

OTHER

3 CITS
中国国际旅行社
4 Bank of China
中国银行
5 Post Office
邮电局

7 Xinhua Bookstore
新华书店
9 Railway Station
火车站
10 Long-Distance Bus
Station
长途汽车站
11 Museum of Ceramic
History
陶瓷历史博览区

south in the wake of an invasion from the north. The Song court moved to Hangzhou and the imperial potters moved to Jingdezhen, near Gaolin village and the rich supply of kaolin clay. Today some 10% of Jingdezhen's 300,000 people are employed in the ceramics industry. For a rundown on the history of pottery in China see the Facts about the Country chapter.

Orientation

Most of Jingdezhen lies on the eastern bank of the Chang River, and the main arteries are Zhongshan Lu and Zhushan Lu. Various restaurants and hotels may be found in the city centre.

Good bus maps are available from newspaper stands, the Xinhua Bookstore and around the railway station.

Things to See & Do

The best parts of the town to wander around are the side streets which lead off Zhongshan Lu, particularly those in the older area between Zhongshan Lu and the river. In the tiny streets, barely 1½ metres wide, washing is strung out between the old houses. The large wooden doors are removed in summer for ventilation.

The **Museum of Ceramic History** *(gŭ táocí bólǎnqū)* is on the western edge of the city. Most of the buildings are reconstructed traditional stone-and-wood structures housing a modest collection taken mainly from ancient kiln sites. A second section (right from the main gate) is set up as an open workshop demonstrating traditional Qing and Ming porcelain-making technologies. To get there take bus No 3 past the long-distance bus station to the terminus near Taodu Dadao. Then walk under the stone gate and follow the dirt road through forest and tea groves to the museum entrance. Entry to each section costs Y5.

There are **pottery factories** all over the city, many of them being run as cottage industries within enclosed courtyards. If you're interested in a tour of the city's porcelain factories, contact CITS at No 8 Lianhuatang Lu. Tours may include the Art Porcelain Factory *(yìshù táochǎng)*, the Porcelain Sculpture Factory *(měidiāo táochǎng)* or the modern Weimin Porcelain Factory *(wèimín táochǎng)*, where you can see the whole process of porcelain production.

Places to Stay

The rock-bottom cheapest deals in town are clustered in the miserable railway station area. Directly opposite the railway station is the distinctly downmarket *Huaguang Hotel (huáguāng fàndiàn)*. Beds in grotty doubles with shower are Y28; a dorm bed costs a low Y7, but as usual you will have to fight to get one.

The inappropriately named *Wen Yuan Grand Hotel (wényuàn dàfàndiàn)* is next door to the railway station and was not taking foreigners at the time of writing. It seems cleaner than the Huaguang and might be worth a try.

The best place in town to stay is a modern Hong Kong-China joint venture called the *Jingdezhen Guesthouse* (☎ (0798) 225-010) *(jǐngdézhèn bīnguǎn (hézī))* on Lianhuatang Lu, a quiet lake park about 15 minutes' walk from the centre of town. Porcelain buyers from abroad often stay here. The guesthouse charges Y480 for a standard air-con double with TV, phone and refrigerator. It has a couple of restaurants, a bar, a cafe and a shop, as well as a post office and a money-changing counter.

Literally in the shadow of the guesthouse is another *Jingdezhen Hotel* (☎ 224-927) *(jǐngdézhèn bīnguǎn)*. This is the older place right behind; standard doubles range from Y160 to Y320. Compared with its neighbour of the same name, this hotel is a trifle run-down, but it's reasonable value for money.

The other *Jingdezhen Hotel (jǐngdézhèn fàndiàn)* is at No 1 Zhushan Lu in central Jingdezhen. It belongs to the old school of Chinese hotels – big, draughty and unfriendly. You will really have to fight to get a cheap room here. The best price they offer is Y96 for a damp, run-down double with a barely functioning bathroom. Prices range upwards to Y240, but they are really not worth the expense. Bus No 2 goes past the hotel.

Places to Eat

There is no shortage of cheap eats in Jingdezhen. One place that deserves a special mention, however, is the *New Century Restaurant (xīn shìjì cāntīng)* on Lianshe Beilu, about five minutes' walk up the hill from the Jingdezhen Hotel (Fandian). The food is excellent and reasonably priced, and there is an English menu. Mr Zheng is the owner and resident English speaker – he is starved of opportunities to use his English.

Things to Buy

Porcelain products are sold everywhere around the city, piled up on pavements, lined up on street stalls and tucked away in antique shops, particularly those on Lianshe Nanlu, up from the Jingdezhen Hotel (Fandian). The

Porcelain Friendship Store *(yǒuyì shāngdiàn)* is at 13 Zhushan Lu.

Getting There & Away

Jingdezhen is a bit of a bottle-neck as far as transportation is concerned. There is no airport, train tickets are difficult to buy and bus services are limited.

Bus Minibus services for Jiujiang and Nanchang leave from the bottom of Maanshan Lu, a couple of minutes' walk from the Jingdezhen Hotel (Fandian).

The long-distance bus station also has services to Yingtan (four hours), Jiujiang (4½ hours) and Nanchang (6½ hours), as well as to more distant destinations such as Shanghai, Hangzhou and Guangzhou. Most buses leave by 8 am and after that the bus station effectively closes down. There are no buses to Mt Huangshan.

Train Jingdezhen Railway Station is rather like a vast, deserted crypt of the dead, and there is little in the way of tickets available either. Everything but hard-seat tickets (no seat allocation) is reserved for those with connections with the ticket sellers. This is one town where it is worth calling in to CITS, who can organise hard-sleeper and soft-sleeper tickets – it's worth it for a long trip.

If you're heading north there are trains to Shanghai and Nanjing via Tunxi (Huangshan Shi, 3½ hours) and Wuhu.

There is one daily express train to Nanchang (six hours), but for better connections first go to the railway junction at Yingtan (3½ hours).

Getting Around

Real taxis are almost nonexistent in Jingdezhen, but there are plenty of pedicabs and motor-tricycles. The centre of town is small enough to walk around in anyway.

Bus No 2 runs from the long-distance bus station, through the centre of town past the Jingdezhen Hotel (Fandian) and out to the railway station.

JIUJIANG
(jiǔjiāng)

Jiujiang is a stopover on the road to Lushan; if you are travelling from Nanchang, you can safely miss the place altogether by taking a direct bus. Travellers arriving in Jiujiang by ferry from Chongqing or Shanghai may need to stay overnight. Jiujiang is most definitely not a place to linger, though many locals labour happily under the illusion that the two lakes in the centre of town make their city something of a scenic wonder.

Situated close to Lake Boyang, which drains into the Yangzi, Jiujiang has been a port since ancient times. It was once a leading market town for tea and rice in southern China. After it was opened to foreign trade in 1862, the city developed into a port serving nearby Hubei and Anhui provinces. Today, Jiujiang is a medium-sized city, second in importance to Nanchang on a provincial level.

Orientation & Information

Jiujiang stretches out along the southern bank of the Yangzi River. Two interconnected lakes divide the older north-eastern part of the city from a newer industrial sprawl off to the south. The long-distance bus station is on the city's eastern side and the railway station over to the west, while the main river port is more conveniently situated close to the heart of town.

There is a CITS office (☎ 822-3390) at the Nanhu Guesthouse.

Things to See

The small **Nengren Temple** *(néngrénsì)* on Yuliang Nanlu is worth a short visit. In the temple grounds is a disused Yuan Dynasty pagoda *(dàshèngtǎ)*.

The **museum** is housed in quaint old buildings on **Yanshuiting** *(yānshuǐtíng)*, a tiny island in Gantang Lake. It's near the centre of town and is connected to the shore by a short bridge. The museum has small exhibits of clothing, ceramics and imperial knights' armour and weaponry, but there are no captions in English.

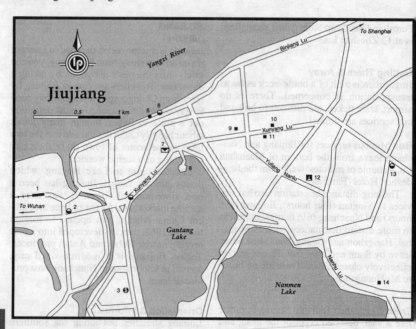

Jiujiang

To Shanghai

Yangzi River

Binjiang Lu

0   0.5   1 km

Xunyang Lu

Yuliang Nanlu

Nannu Lu

To Wuhan

Xunyang Lu

Gantang Lake

Nanmen Lake

JIUJIANG 九江	OTHER	6 Minibuses to Lushan
		往庐山小型车
PLACES TO STAY	1 Railway Station	7 Post Office
	火车站	邮局
9 Dongfeng Hotel	2 Minibuses to Lushan	8 Yanshuiting Island
东风饭店	开往庐山汽车	烟水亭
10 Jinlong Hotel	3 Bank of China	12 Nengren Temple
金龙饭店	中国银行	能仁寺
11 Bailu (White Deer) Hotel	4 Minibuses to Nanchang	13 Long-Distance Bus
白鹿宾馆	往南昌小型车	Station
14 Nanhu Guesthouse,	5 Yangzi River Ferry	长途汽车站
CITS & Minibus Station	Terminal	
南湖宾馆, 中国国际	轮船客运码头	
旅行社, 小型汽车站		

Places to Stay

The *Dongfeng Hotel* (☎ 822-5512) *(dōng-fēng fàndiàn)*, on Xunyang Lu, was still a budget option at the time of writing, though half the hotel was being jack-hammered into mid-range comfort. If you are lucky, you may be able to get a bed in a four-bed dorm

for Y15 or a bed in a double for Y26. Singles cost Y50, while doubles range from Y50 to Y98. It's in a very noisy area; rooms facing the back are a bit quieter. Bus Nos 1 and 4 run past the hotel from both the long-distance bus station and the railway station.

Most other hotels around town are mid-range in price and are in the same area as the Dongfeng Hotel. The *Jinlong Hotel* (☎ 822-4057) *(jīnlóng fàndiàn)* is good value at Y96 for standard doubles and Y128 for a 'suite'. The *Bailu (White Deer) Hotel* (☎ 822-2088) *(báilù bīnguǎn)* is a Chinese version of a luxury hotel with doubles from Y160 to Y180 and suites from Y360 to Y640, all with a 40% foreigners' surcharge. This place is basically falling apart and not worth the prices they charge. The Bailu also has tours to Lushan – see the following Lushan section for details.

The *Nanhu Guesthouse* (☎ 822-5041) *(nánhú bīnguǎn)*, at 28 Nanhu Lu, is the old bastion of draughty comforts for cadres and foreign guests. Renovations are proceeding apace and it might be worth checking out if you have extra cash to throw around.

Getting There & Away
Bus Minibuses for Lushan leave from the car park next to the ferry terminal whenever they have enough passengers. Scheduled public buses to Lushan leave from the long-distance bus station (gate 3) between 7.30 am and 1.30 pm. The fare for all Lushan buses is about Y8. Most of the hotels in town offer one-day tours of Lushan for Y25. Tour minibuses depart early in the morning from the minibus stand near the railway station.

There are at least five departures to Jingdezhen each day from the long-distance bus station. The 4½-hour trip includes a short ferry ride across the mouth of Lake Boyang. Daily buses go to Nanjing and Nanchang, among other places. Minibuses to Nanchang can also be picked up at the northwest point of Gantang Lake for Y15 – the trip takes two hours.

Train There are several Jiujiang-Nanchang express trains each day; the train takes 2½ hours, which is slightly slower than the minibus services. A railway line is being built across the Yangzi through southern Anhui. When finished (1997 is the projected completion date) it will directly link the provincial capital of Hefei with Jiujiang and Nanchang.

Boat There is a massive ferry terminal in Jiujiang, and most long-distance boats plying the Yangzi call in here. Ferry tickets upriver to Chongqing cost Y524 (2nd class), Y219 (3rd class) and Y157 (4th class); downriver fares to Shanghai are Y234 (2nd class), Y98 (3rd class) and Y71 (4th class). (First class still doesn't exist in nominally socialist China.)

Getting Around
Bus Nos 1, 4 and 14 run from the long-distance bus station to the railway station via the centre of town. You can get pedicabs and motor-tricycles from around the bus and railway stations, and the dock.

LUSHAN
(lúshān)
Lushan was established as a mountain resort town by European and American settlers late last century as an escape from lowland China's sweaty summers. They left a fascinating hotchpotch of colonial buildings, from quaint stone cottages reminiscent of southern Germany to small French-style churches and more grandiose hotels built in classical Victorian style.

Despite this, Lushan is not a particularly attractive proposition as a travel destination. For much of the year it is bitterly cold and shrouded in heavy fog, and then for the summer season, which sees it at its best, it is inundated with Chinese tourists.

For the Chinese, however, Lushan is rich with significance. Its mountain vistas have been the subject of poems and paintings, and on the historical front it has been the site of some epoch-making events. China's post-1949 revolutionaries found Lushan's cool uplands a good place for Party conferences. It was here in 1959 that the Central Committee of the Communist Party held its fateful meeting which eventually ended in the dismissal of Peng Dehuai, sent Mao almost into a political wilderness and provided the seeds of the rise and fall of Liu Shaoqi and Deng Xiaoping.

In 1970, after Mao had regained power, another meeting was held in Lushan, this time of the Politburo. Exactly what happened is shrouded in as much mist as the mountains, but it seems that Lin Biao clashed with Mao, opposed his policies of *rapprochement* with the USA and probably proposed the continuation of the xenophobic policies of the Cultural Revolution. Whatever happened, by the following year Lin was dead.

Orientation & Information

The point of arrival in Lushan is the charming resort village of Guling *(gǔlǐng)*, perched 1167 metres high at the northern end of the range. Two km before Guling is the entrance gate, where you must pay an entry fee (Y60, which should cover entry fees for all sights). Guling village is where the shops, post office, bank and the long-distance bus station are located. Nestled into the surrounding hills are scores of tourist hotels, sanatoriums and factory work units' holiday hostels. The

CITS office, uphill from the Lushan Hotel, is quite well organised and helpful. Detailed maps of Lushan showing roads and walking tracks are available from shops and hawkers in Guling.

Things to See

Lushan has enough sites of historical and scenic interest to keep you here for a couple of days.

Built by Chiang Kaishek in the 1930s as a summer getaway, **Meilu Villa** *(měilú biéshù)*

LUSHAN 庐山

PLACES TO STAY

4 Guling Hotel
  牯岭饭店
6 Meilu Villa Hotel
  美庐别墅村
8 Lushan Hotel
  庐山宾馆
9 Yunzhong Guesthouse
  云中宾馆
11 Lushan Mansion
  庐山大厦
14 Lulin Hotel
  芦林饭店

OTHER

1 Jiexin Park
  街心公园
2 Long-Distance Bus Station
  长途汽车站
3 Bank & Post Office
  银行，邮局
5 CITS
  中国国际旅行社
7 Meilu Villa
  美庐别墅
10 People's Hall
  人民剧院
12 Three Ancient Trees
  三宝树
13 Museum
  博物馆
15 Botanical Garden
  植物园

was named after the general's wife, Song Meilu. It's not a particularly grand house, but well worth a visit. Although the original gardens were probably much more spacious and better maintained than today, the villa has evidently been kept much as it was.

The **People's Hall** (*rénmín jùyuàn*), built in 1936 and the venue for the Chinese Communist Party's historic 1959 and 1970 get-togethers, has been turned into a museum. On display are photos of Mao, Zhou and other members of the Party elite taking it easy between meetings. The main auditorium is decked out with the predictable red flags and Mao-era decor.

At Lushan's north-western rim, the land falls away abruptly to give some spectacular views across the densely settled plains of Jiangxi. A long walking track south around these precipitous slopes passes the **Xianren Dong Cave** (*xiānrén dòng*) and continues to the **Dragon Head Cliff** (*lóngshǒuyá*), a natural rock platform tilted above a vertical drop of hundreds of metres.

A place of interest to Chinese visitors is the **Three Ancient Trees** (*sānbǎoshù*) not far by foot from Lulin Lake; 500 years ago Buddhist monks planted a ginkgo and two cedar trees near their temple, now an abandoned ruin. Tourists used to climb onto the branches to have their photos taken, but a fence now protects the trees from this indignity.

The **Lushan Museum** (*bówùguǎn*) beside Lulin Lake commemorates the historic 1970 meeting with a photo collection and Mao's huge bed. Scrolls and inscribed steles displaying the poetry and calligraphy of Li Bai and other Chinese poet-scholars who frequented Lushan can also be seen, as well as exhibits on local geology and natural history. Unfortunately, none of the labels are in English.

The **Botanical Garden** (*zhíwùyuán*) is mainly devoted to sub-alpine tropical plants that thrive in the cooler highland climate. In the open gardens there are flowering rhododendrons, camellias and conifers, and hothouses with a cactus collection and species of palm and hibiscus.

Organised Tours

From Jiujiang, return day-trips cost Y25 and give you about five hours in Lushan; one hotel in Jiujiang that has regular tours is the Bailu (White Deer) Hotel. Tours normally include several of the pavilions, a nature hike and the museum. These tours are much more bearable if there is more than one of you.

Places to Stay

Hotel prices in Lushan vary considerably according to season. Off season (from October to May), when Lushan is usually cold, drizzly and miserable, very few people stay overnight and there are some good deals to be had. In season is a different matter. In the height of summer, budget travellers can forget about Lushan – it would probably be cheaper to stay in Jiujiang and do a day-trip.

The best place to try for reasonably priced accommodation is the *Guling Hotel* (*gǔlíng fàndiàn*). It's right in Guling village around the corner from the bank, shops, restaurants and bus terminal. Most other places open to foreigners are more upmarket, though it is worth checking around Guling village if you are looking for a bargain.

Other options include:

Lushan Hotel (*lúshān bīnguǎn*); large old colonial-era hotel now managed as a joint venture
Meilu Villa Hotel (*měilú biéshù cūn*); cottages scattered throughout lovely old pine forest
Yunzhong Guesthouse (*yúnzhōng bīnguǎn*); summer holiday camp setting

Places to Eat

There are plenty of places to eat in Lushan. Remember that Lushan is a prime tourist attraction for Chinese, who spend big on meals; if you are on a budget, check prices first. Don't expect any English menus.

Getting There & Away

In summer there are daily buses to Nanchang (Y27) and Jiujiang (Y8), but from November to late March direct buses to Nanchang from here are sporadic. During the tourist season numbers can be very high, so try to arrive early in the day to get a room.

Getting Around
If you like country walking, exploration on foot is the ideal way to go. Paths and small roads crisscross Lushan, so getting around is easy. It's also the best way to avoid the hoards of Chinese tourists who bus up by the truckful from the sticky lowlands in summer.

YINGTAN
(yīngtán)
Nanchang is north of the main Shanghai-Guangzhou railway line and though most trains make the short detour, you may have to catch some at the railway junction town of Yingtan. If you do stop here, walk down the main street leading from the railway station. The street ends in a T-intersection in front of a park. Turn right for the old part of town by the river. You might try getting a boat to the other side and exploring.

Places to Stay & Eat
There are three cheap Chinese hotels, including an *Overseas Chinese Hotel (huáqiáo fàndiàn)*, on the main street near the railway station. Dormitory beds go for Y15, and rooms for Y70 and upwards. There are lots of food stalls on the street beside the railway station.

Getting There & Away
The long-distance bus station is on the main street next to the Overseas Chinese Hotel. There are buses to Jingdezhen and trains to Fuzhou, Guangzhou, Kunming, Shanghai and Xiamen. There is also a branch line to Jingdezhen via Guixi.

JINGGANGSHAN (CIPING)
(jǐnggǎng shin)
The remote Jinggangshan region, in the Luoxiao mountains along the Hunan-Jiangxi border, played a crucial role in the early Communist movement. After suffering a string of defeats in an urban-based revolution in the cities, Mao led a core of 900 men into the refuge of these misty hills in 1927. They were soon joined by other companies

of the battered Communist Army led by Zhu De, and from here began the Long March.

Orientation & Information
The main township, Ciping (also called Jinggangshan), up in the mountains at 820 metres, is an attractive place built around a small lake. The local CITS (☎ 222-504) is in the grounds of the Jinggangshan Hotel (Binguan). The Xinhua Bookstore near the museum sells a Chinese tourist map of Ciping which also shows hiking trails in the hills.

Things to See
The **Jinggangshan Revolutionary Museum** *(jǐnggǎngshān gémìng bówùguǎn)* is devoted to the Kuomintang and Communists' struggle for control of the Hunan-Jiangxi area in the late 1920s. The collection includes Nationalist and Communist Army war paraphernalia and has exhibits showing military strategies and troop movements. The explanations are all in Chinese, but the collection is graphic enough for you to get the gist of things. Entry costs Y2.

The **Former Revolutionary Quarters** *(gémìng jiùzhǐ qún)* in Ciping served as the Communist centre of command between 1927 and 1928. Mao lived temporarily in one of the four crude mud-brick buildings.

Jinggangshan is a major scenic area with large expanses of natural highland forest; the area boasts an interesting species of square-stemmed bamboo and some 26 kinds of alpine azaleas that bloom from late April. There are some great walks into the hills around Ciping, such as to **Five Fingers Peak** *(wǔzhǐfēng)*, a mountain featured on the back of the Y100 banknote, and to the **Five Dragon Pools** *(wǔlóngtán)*.

Places to Stay & Eat
The *Jinggangshan Hotel (jǐnggǎngshān fàndiàn)*, a short walk down from the bus station, has beds in four-person dorms for Y15 and doubles with shower for Y65.

The other *Jinggangshan Hotel (jǐnggǎngshān bīnguǎn)* is where the Party top brass choose to stay – Mao, Lin Biao, Deng and Li

Peng have all put up here. Renovations have made this hotel expensive – Y200 and upwards for a double. The hotel is 15 minutes' walk from the bus station; go downhill, turn right at the first road, then right again. There's no sign on the main gate.

There are good cheap restaurants on the main street down from the bus station. For something a bit more romantic, try the place on the island in the middle of the lake.

Getting There & Away
From Nanchang there are five direct buses to Ciping/Jinggangshan each day (eight hours). It's a pleasant ride through lush countryside with high bamboo fences, old stone bridges, water wheels and flocks of ducks waddling about the rice paddies. A daily bus from Ciping goes to Hengyang in Hunan Province via the beautiful Huangyang Pass, but the road is prone to icing over in cold weather.

Hunan 湖南

Most people pass through Hunan on their way to somewhere else, but the province has its attractions. The Zhangjiajie nature reserve in the western part of the province offers some of the most bizarre mountain scenery in China, rivalling the karst peaks of Guangxi. Shaoshan, birthplace of Mao Zedong, makes for an interesting visit and is a beautiful, relaxing village as well. Up north, Yueyang is a major stop for Yangzi River cruises, and the city has a unique port feel to it.

Hunan *(húnán)* lies on some of the richest land in China. Its main period of growth occurred between the 8th and the 11th centuries when the population increased fivefold, spurred on by a prosperous agricultural industry and migrations from the north. Under the Ming and the Qing dynasties it was one of the empire's granaries, and vast quantities of Hunan's rice surplus were shipped to the depleted northern regions.

By the 19th century Hunan was beginning to suffer from the pressure of population. Land shortage and landlordism led to widespread unrest among the Chinese farmers and the hill-dwelling minority peoples. The increasingly desperate economic situation led to the massive Taiping Rebellion of the mid-19th century and the Communist movement of the 1920s.

The Communists found strong support among the poor peasants of Hunan, and also a refuge on the mountainous Hunan-Jiangxi border in 1927. Some of the most prominent Communist leaders were born in Hunan: Mao Zedong, Liu Shaoqi (both of whose villages can be visited), Peng Dehuai, Hu Yaobang and others. Hua Guofeng, a native of Shanxi, became an important provincial leader in Hunan.

Most of the inhabitants are Han Chinese. Hill-dwelling minorities can be found in the border regions of the province. They include the Miao, Tujia, Dong (a people related to the Thais and Lao) and Yao. In the far north of

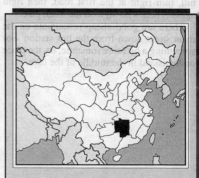

Population: 60 million
Capital: Changsha
Highlights:

- Shaoshan, birthplace of Mao Zedong, offers a fascinating look at 'Mao Mania' and a relaxing rural respite from the rigours of the road
- Zhangjiajie/Wulingyuan Scenic Area, home to bizarre and beautiful rock formations
- Yueyang, a major Yangzi River city with a unique port feel and interesting back alleys
- Changsha – several Maoist pilgrimage spots offer yet more chances to retrace the Chairman's footsteps and get a feel for the formative years of Communist China

the province there is, oddly enough, a pocket of Uighurs.

CHANGSHA
(chángshā)

The site of Changsha has been inhabited for 3000 years. By the Warring States Period (453-221 BC) a large town had grown up here. The town owes its prosperity to its location on the fertile Hunan plains of central

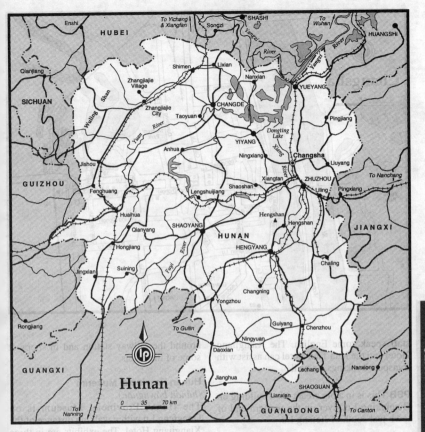

Hunan

China and on the Xiang River, where it rapidly grew as a major trading centre of agricultural produce.

In 1904 the city was opened to foreign trade as a result of the 1903 Treaty of Shanghai between Japan and China. The 'most-favoured nation' principle allowed foreigners to set themselves up in Changsha, and large numbers of Europeans and Americans came to build factories, churches and schools. The medical centre was originally a college established by Yale University.

Today greater Changsha has a population of 5.5 million people.

Orientation

Most of Changsha lies on the eastern bank of the Xiang River. The railway station is at the far east of the city. From the station Wuyi Lu leads to the river, neatly separating the city's northern and southern sections. From Wuyi Lu you cross the Xiang River bridge to the western bank, passing over Long Island in the middle of the river. Most of the sights are on the eastern side of the river.

Information

CITS The local CITS office (☎ 443-9757) is located to the left of the Lotus Hotel. The

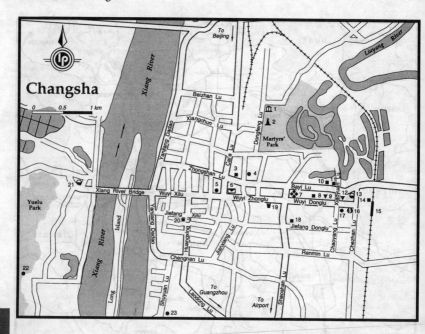

Changsha

staff speak some English. The Xiangjiang Hotel and the Hua Tian Hotel can assist with transport bookings, as well.

PSB This is in a big cream-tiled building on Huangxing Lu, over on the western end of town just south of Jiefang Lu.

Money The Bank of China is next to the CAAC office on Wuyi Donglu. You can also change money at the Xiangjiang Hotel and the Lotus Hotel.

Post & Telecommunications The main post and telecommunications office is on the north-east corner of Wuyi Zhonglu and Cai'e Lu in the centre of town. There are other post offices at the railway station and the Xiangjiang Hotel.

Maps Several colourful variations of the local city transport map are on sale at kiosks

around the railway station and in shops at some of the hotels.

Hunan Provincial Museum
(*húnán bówùguǎn*)
The Hunan Provincial Museum is on Dongfeng Lu within walking distance of the Xiangjiang Hotel. The exhibits are in three main buildings. The first section covers revolutionary history while the two other buildings are devoted to the 2100-year-old Western Han tombs at Mawangdui, some five km east of the city centre, which were fully excavated by 1974.

Not to be missed are the mummified remains of a Han Dynasty woman. Her preserved body, which was found wrapped in more than 20 layers of silk and linen, is housed in the basement and is viewed from the floor above through Perspex. The organs have been removed and are laid out on display. Another building houses the enormous solid outer timber casks.

CHANGSHA 长沙

PLACES TO STAY

Large quantities of silk garments and fabrics were found in the tomb, as well as stockings, shoes, gloves and other pieces of clothing. One of the most interesting objects, now on display in the museum, is a painting on silk depicting the underworld, earth and heaven.

The museum is open daily from 8 am to noon and from 2.30 to 5.20 pm. Entry to all three sections is Y10 for students and Chinese and, unfortunately, Y30 for foreigners. Minibus No 3 runs from the railway station and then heads north on Dongfeng Lu past the museum.

Maoist Pilgrimage Spots

Scattered about the city are a number of Maoist pilgrimage spots. The **Hunan No 1 Teachers' Training School** (*dìyī shīfàn xuéxiào*) is where Mao attended classes between 1913 and 1918, and where he returned as a teacher in 1920-21. The school was destroyed during the civil war but has since been restored. Follow the arrows for a self-guided tour of Mao's dorm room, study areas, halls where he held some of his first political meetings and even an open-air bathing well. The school is still in use, so you also get a chance to see China's educational system in action. To get there take the No 1 bus from outside the Xiangjiang Hotel.

The **Former Office of the Hunan (Xiang District) Communist Party Committee** (*zhōnggòng xiāngqū wéiyuánhuì jiùzhǐ*) is now a museum that includes Mao's living quarters and an exhibition of photos and historical items from the 1920s. Nearby is a long wall in which are carved large-scale versions of Mao's poems that reproduce his characteristic expansive brushstrokes.

Other Sights

If rabid excesses of Communist propaganda suit your sense of humour, try to fit in a visit to the **Lei Feng Memorial Museum** (☎ 875-244) (*léifēng jìniànguǎn*), about one hour's bus ride west of Changsha. Lei Feng was a young soldier who in 1963, one year after dying in a traffic accident at age 22, was lionised by the Communist Party as a model

CENTRAL CHINA

worker, warrior, Party member and all-round PRC citizen. The masses were urged by top Party officials to 'learn from Comrade Lei', whose feats included washing his fellow soldiers' laundry in his spare time, helping old ladies cross the street and making sure everyone in his home town and army platoon was up-to-date on the latest Party doctrine. Lei was dredged up again by the Beijing leadership in 1990, in a bid to counter the widespread disillusionment with the Party that followed the Tiananmen Square massacre.

Although the museum exhibits have no English captions, such photos as Lei gently smiling over a washtub of dirty socks or the cartoon-like renderings of him and his parents facing down evil landlords and Japanese invaders speak for themselves. In all, the museum has somehow managed to assemble five rooms of photos, diary entries and objects to catalogue Lei's life, which is quite a feat when one considers that no-one had really heard of this guy until a year after he died. The head of the museum has admitted that some of the photos were 'later restaged', although it's not clear if this was before or after Lei's death.

To get there, take the No 12 bus from the railway station to the terminus at Rongwanzhen, where you can switch to the No 15 minibus, which makes its final stop just two minutes' walk south of the museum.

Back in Changsha, the **Loving Dusk Pavilion** (*àiwǎntíng*) is in Yuelu Park on the western bank of the Xiang River, from where you can get a good view of the town. **Long Island** (*júzizhōu*), or Long Sandbank, from which Changsha takes its name, lies in the middle of the Xiang River. The only remaining part of the old city walls is **Tianxin Pavilion** (*tiānxīngé*) in the south of the city.

Places to Stay

Unhappily for backpackers, the hotels in Changsha that take foreigners are mostly upmarket places. There's plenty of good, cheap accommodation for locals, of course, but they're quite determined in excluding non-Chinese from their registers. This includes the Binhua Hotel, which used to turn a blind eye but now has a PSB guard hanging around the front door. It still may be worth trying, but don't be disappointed if you are vigorously waved away.

The cheapest option, if they'll let you have the room, is a triple for Y135 at the *Nanhai Hotel* (☎ 229-7888) (*nánhǎi bīnguǎn*) on Bayi Lu. But they may try to push you into doubles which start at Y225. If so, the *Lotus Hotel* (☎ 440-1888) (*fúróng bīnguǎn*) has bottom-range singles and doubles for Y145/160, though you must ask for them, as these rooms are not listed on the rate card. For your money, you get plenty of hot water, good service and a central location.

Adjacent to the north side of the railway station, the *Chezhan Hotel* (*chēzhàn dàshà*) has decent doubles/triples for Y168/160, and an added bonus: if you stay there, they'll book your train tickets, which they get direct from the railway station, for Chinese prices. The hotel even has a doorway onto the platform, just before the exit gate. If you're taking a train, this one's hard to beat.

The *Xiangjiang Hotel* (☎ 444-6888) (*xiāngjiāng bīnguǎn*) is at 2 Zhongshan Lu. It's a three-star hotel, but they have a few doubles in a newly redone wing for US$28. Standard doubles start at US$48. To get there, take bus No 1 from the railway station, which has a stop just past the hotel driveway.

The best luxury deal in town is the four-star *Hua Tian Hotel* (☎ 444-2888) (*huátiān dàjiǔdiàn*) at 16 Jiefang Donglu, just off Shaoshan Lu. Business travellers praise the Hua Tian for its service and clean rooms. Rates range from US$58 for a standard double to US$388 for a deluxe suite.

Places to Eat

Hunanese food, like that of neighbouring Sichuan Province, makes use of plenty of chillies and hot spices. The *Kaiyunlou Restaurant* (*kāiyúnlóu jiǔjiā*) is on Wuyi Donglu near the corner of Chaoyang Lu. Although government-run, it's cheap and surprisingly good, but it doesn't have an English menu. There are also several good Hunan-style fast-food places on Chezhan Lu just south of the railway station. For late night snacks, there's a decent noodle stand that sets up around 9 pm out in front of the *Kiddies Restaurant* on Wuyi Lu. The bigger hotels, such as the Lotus and Xiangjiang, also have good restaurants.

The adventurous might like to sample betel nut *(bīnglang)*, sold at small street stalls all around town. When chewed, the woody flesh, which has an overpowering, spicy-sweet taste, produces a mild, semi-narcotic effect. Once should be enough to satisfy your curiosity.

Entertainment

Changsha also now boasts its first Western-style bar, the *Ocean-shore Music Bar* *(hǎi'ànxiàn yīnyuè jiǔláng)* on Wuyi Zhong-lu, which comes complete with draught beer, black-painted walls and bands playing several times a week. The owners are dedicated to helping promote Chinese and western rock and roll, and will be happy to throw on the latest discs for you if there isn't any live music going that night.

Getting There & Away

Air The main CAAC office (☎ 229-9821) is at 5 Wuyi Donglu, one block west of the railway station. The Lotus Hotel also has a CAAC booking office. Together, CAAC and their associated local airline, China Southern Airlines, have daily flights to Beijing, Chengdu, Guangzhou and Shanghai. Other useful flights include Kunming, Nanjing, Shenzhen and Xi'an. There are also four to five flights a week to Hong Kong (Y1640). CAAC buses leave for the airport about two hours before scheduled flights. The fare is Y12.50.

Bus The long-distance bus station is conveniently located near the railway station. There are frequent departures for Yueyang and Hengyang and several to Nanchang and Shaoshan. There are also daily sleeping-berth coaches to Guangzhou (18 hours), Hefei (30 hours), Zhangjiajie (10 hours), Zhuhai (21 hours), Nanjing (30 hours) and

Zhengzhou (26 hours). The bus station closes at 8 pm.

Train There are two Guangzhou-Changsha-Beijing express trains daily in each direction, as well as a daily train to Shanghai. Other important routes via Changsha are Beijing-Guilin-Kunming and Guangzhou-Xi'an-Lanzhou. Not all trains to Shanghai, Kunming and Guilin stop in Changsha, so it may be necessary to go to Zhuzhou first and change there. If you're heading to Hong Kong, there's an overnight Changsha-Shenzhen air-conditioned express train that gets into Shenzhen around 9.30 am. A hard sleeper berth costs around Y160, Chinese price, which you may be able to get at the Chezhan Hotel. There is also a train daily to Shaoshan (Y10), leaving at 7 am. Counter No 6 at the Changsha Railway Station is for foreigners.

SHAOSHAN

(shāoshān)

The village of Shaoshan, about 130 km south-west of Changsha, has a significance to Chinese Communism which far overshadows its minute size, for this is where Mao Zedong was born. In the '60s, during the Cultural Revolution's headier days, some three million pilgrims came here each year, and a railway line and a paved road were built from Changsha to transport them. After Mao's death, the numbers declined. But in recent years, as memories of the Cultural Revolution's excesses gradually fade, the village has seen a tourist revival. In 1993 Shaoshan held celebrations to mark the centenary of Mao's birth.

Shaoshan is hardly typical of Chinese villages, considering the number of tourists who have passed through since it was established as a national shrine. Despite the obvious impact of tourism, however, the surrounding countryside has retained its original rural charm. Traditional adobe houses dot this landscape of mountains and lush rice paddies. Apart from its historical significance, Shaoshan is a great place to get away from those grim, grey cities.

Orientation

There are two parts to Shaoshan: the new town clustered around the railway and bus stations and the original Shaoshan village about five km away. From the railway station you can catch minibuses to the main sites. Public buses and motor-tricycles also meet the train from Changsha. The long-distance bus station is on Yingbin Lu, just north of the railway station.

Mao's Childhood House

(*máozédōng tóngzhì gùjū*)

This is the first building you come to as you reach Shaoshan, and it is the village's principal shrine. It's a fairly large structure with mud walls and a thatched roof. It's no different from millions of other mud-brick dwellings in China, except for the painstaking restoration. Exhibits include a few kitchen utensils and original furnishings and

Mao Zedong

Mao was Hunan's main export. Mao was born in the Hunanese village of Shaoshan, not far from Changsha, in 1893. His father was a poor peasant who had been forced to join the army because of heavy debts. After several years of service he returned to Shaoshan, and by careful saving through small trading and other enterprises managed to buy back his land.

As 'middle' peasants Mao's family owned enough land to produce a surplus of rice with which they were able to buy more land. This raised them to the status of 'rich' peasants.

Mao began studying in the local primary school when he was eight years old and remained at school until the age of 13, meanwhile working on the farm and keeping accounts for his father's business. His father continued to accumulate wealth (or what was considered a fortune in the little village) by buying mortgages on other people's land.

Several incidents influenced Mao around this time. A famine in Hunan and a subsequent uprising of starving people in Changsha ended in the execution of the leaders by the Manchu governor. This left a lasting impression on Mao, who '...felt that there with the rebels were ordinary people like my own family and I deeply resented the injustice in the treatment given to them'. He was also influenced by a band of rebels who had taken to the hills around Shaoshan to defy the landlords and the government, and by a radical teacher at the local primary school who opposed Buddhism and wanted people to convert their temples into schools.

At the age of 16, Mao left Shaoshan to enter middle school in Changsha, his first stop on the path to power. At this time he was not yet an anti-monarchist. He felt, however, even at an early age, that the country was in desperate need of reform. He was fascinated by stories of the ancient rulers of China, and learned something of foreign history and geography.

In Changsha, Mao was first exposed to the ideas of revolutionaries and reformers active in China, heard of Sun Yatsen's revolutionary secret society and read about the abortive Canton uprising of 1911. Later that year an army uprising in Wuhan quickly spread and the Qing Dynasty collapsed. Yuan Shikai made his grab for power and the country appeared to be slipping into civil war. Mao joined the regular army but resigned six months later, thinking the revolution was over when Sun handed the presidency to Yuan and the war between the north and south of China did not take place.

Mao became an avid reader of newspapers and from these was introduced to socialism. He decided to become a teacher and enrolled in the Hunan Provincial First Normal (Teachers' Training) School, where he was a student for five years. During his time at the Teachers' Training School, he inserted an advertisement in a Changsha newspaper 'inviting young men interested in patriotic work to make contact with me...' Among them was Liu Shaoqi, who later became president of the PRC, Xiao Chen, who became a founding member of the Communist Party, and Li Lisan.

'At this time,' says Mao, 'my mind was a curious mixture of ideas of liberalism, democratic reformism and utopian socialism...and I was definitely anti-militarist and anti-imperialist'. Mao graduated from the Teachers' Training School in 1918, and went to Beijing, where he worked as an assistant librarian at Beijing University. In Beijing he met future co-founders of the Chinese

bedding, as well as photos of Mao's parents. In front of the house is a pond, and on the other side is a pavilion where Chinese tourists pose for photos with the house in the background.

Museum of Comrade Mao
(máozédōng tóngzhì jìniànguǎn)

Devoted to the life of Mao, the museum opened in 1967 during the Cultural Revolution. Unfortunately there are no English captions, but the exhibits are graphic enough. There were originally two wings, exact duplicates, so that more visitors could be accommodated at the same time. Today only one set of exhibits exists. Admission is Y2.

Other Sights

If you came looking for Mao souvenirs, there are **tourist markets**, both uphill from Mao's

Communist Party: the student leader Zhang Guodao, Professor Chen Duxiu and university librarian Li Dazhao. Chen and Li are regarded as the founders of Chinese Communism. It was Li who gave Mao a job and first introduced him to the serious study of Marxism.

Mao found in Marxist theory a programme for reform and revolution in China. On returning to Changsha, he became increasingly active in Communist politics.

He became editor of the *Xiang River Review*, a radical Hunan students' newspaper, and also took up a post as a teacher. In 1920 he was organising workers for the first time and from that year onwards considered himself a Marxist. In 1921, Mao went to Shanghai to attend the founding meeting of the Chinese Communist Party. Later he helped organise the first provincial branch of the Party in Hunan, and by the middle of 1922 the Party had organised trade unions among the workers and students.

Orthodox Marxist philosophy saw revolution spreading from the cities as it had in the Soviet Union. The peasants, ignored through the ages by poets, scholars and political soothsayers, had likewise been ignored by the Communists. But Mao took a different stand and saw the peasants as the lifeblood of the revolution. The Party had done very little work among them but in 1925 Mao began to organise peasant trade unions.

This aroused the wrath of the landlords and Mao had to flee to Guangzhou (Canton), where the Kuomintang and Communists held power in alliance with each other. Mao proposed a radical redistribution of the land to help the peasants, and supported (and probably initiated) the demands of the Hunan Peasants Union to confiscate large landholdings. Probably at this stage he foresaw the need to organise and arm them for a struggle against the landlords.

In April 1927, Chiang Kaishek launched his massacre of the Communists. The Party sent Mao to Changsha to organise what became known as the 'Autumn Harvest Uprising'. By September the first units of a peasant-worker army had been formed, with troops drawn from the peasantry, Hengyang miners and rebel Kuomintang soldiers. Mao's army moved south through Hunan and climbed up into the Jinggangshan mountains to embark on a guerrilla war against the Kuomintang. This action eventually culminated in the 1949 Communist takeover. ■

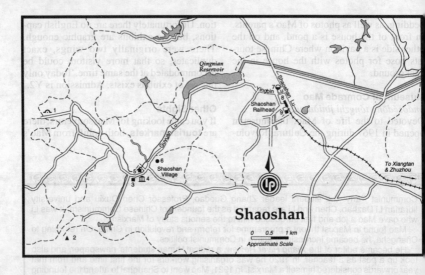

Shaoshan

0   0.5   1 km

Approximate Scale

childhood house and diagonally across from the Shaoshan Guesthouse, which should satiate any craving for Maoist kitsch. Fancy a Chinese fan that unfolds to reveal a jolly profile of the Chairman? Or how about a set of Mao chopsticks decorated with His picture? Of course there are also more conventional Maobilia such as Mao badges, Mao rings and Mao bracelets, as well as those Mao portrait good-luck charms that Chinese drivers attach to their windscreens and car mirrors.

Dripping Water Cave *(dīshuǐdòng)* is three km up from Shaoshan village. Retreating to his native Shaoshan in June 1966, Mao lived in this cave for 11 days, probably thinking up new slogans for the Cultural Revolution he had just begun. Nearby are the Mao clan's family tombs. You can get a bus up here from the parking lot opposite the Shaoshan Guesthouse.

Shaoshan Peak *(shāofēng)* is the prominent, conical-shaped mountain visible from the village. There is a lookout pavilion on the summit, and the 'forest of steles' on the lower slopes has stone tablets engraved with Mao's poems. The area is less frequented than other sites in Shaoshan and has some nice walks along quiet paths through pine forests and stands of bamboo. From Shaoshan village take a minibus south to the end of the road at Feilaichuan *(fēiláichuán)*.

Places to Stay

The recently renovated *Shaoshan Guesthouse (shāoshān bīnguǎn)* (☎ 568-5127) in Shaoshan village is in a convenient location. The guesthouse has doubles/triples for Y100/105 and dorm beds for Y15. Keep an eye out for possible overcharging here. Up the road is the cheaper *Hongri Hotel (hóngrì fàndiàn)*, a smaller, family-run hotel. They have clean, no-frills accommodation for Y10 per bed in small dorms, and doubles for Y20. It also has a cheap restaurant downstairs. There is also a row of little restaurants to the right of the Shaoshan Guesthouse. Meals are a bit pricey in Shaoshan, as the steady flow of tourists means food must be shipped in.

Back in the new town, just south of the railway station, the *Yinfeng Hotel (yínfēng bīnguǎn)* has beds in a triple for Y40 and doubles for Y100.

SHAOSHAN 韶山

1 Dripping Water Cave
   滴水洞
2 Shaoshan Peak
   韶山峰
3 Hongri Hotel
   红日饭店
4 Museum of Comrade Mao
   毛泽东同志纪念馆
5 Shaoshan Guesthouse
   韶山宾馆
6 Mao's Childhood House
   毛泽东同志故居
7 Long-Distance Bus Station
   长途汽车站
8 Railway Station
   火车站
9 Yinfeng Hotel
   银峰宾馆

Getting There & Away

Bus Changsha has three morning buses to Shaoshan leaving between 8 and 9 am, and one in the afternoon. From the Shaoshan bus station there are two morning buses and one afternoon bus back to Changsha daily, this last bus leaving at 2.10 pm. The trip costs Y9 and takes three to four hours. There are also daily buses to Xiangtan, from where you can catch a train to Changsha or Huaihua. You may also be able to catch a minibus to Changsha from Shaoshan village, though these seem to be fairly infrequent.

Train There is one train daily from Changsha. The train leaves at 7 am and departs from Shaoshan station at 4 pm, so you can easily do Shaoshan as a day-trip. The one-way fare is Y5 and the journey takes three or more hours. There are hard seats only. Coming back, the second to last car offers 'tea seating' *(cházuò)*: for only Y5 extra, you get a steady supply of tea and a bit of extra elbow room.

YUEYANG

(yuèyáng)

Yueyang is a port of call for river ferries plying the Yangzi between Chongqing and Wuhan. The Wuhan-Guangzhou railway passes through this small provincial city, so if you're heading to Guangzhou you can get off the boat here instead of going all the way to Wuhan.

Orientation & Information

Yueyang is situated just south of the Yangzi River on the north-eastern shore of Dongting Lake, where the lake flows into the river. Yueyang has two quite separate sections. Yueyang proper is really the southern part, where the railway and bus stations, as well as most of the hotels and sites, are located. Some 17 km away to the north at Chenglingji *(chénglíngjī)* is the city's main port. Most Yangzi ferries dock here, but there are also two smaller local docks in the main (southern) part of Yueyang, where long-distance ferries also call in.

Things to See

Yueyang has a 'port city' atmosphere, and its back streets make interesting exploring. The city's chief landmark is the **Yueyang Pavilion** *(yuèyáng lóu)*, a temple complex and park originally constructed during the Tang Dynasty and subsequently rebuilt. Housed within the pavilion is a gold replica of the complex. The park is something of a Mecca for Japanese tourists, apparently because of a famous poem written in its praise which Japanese kids learn at school. Also on the shoreline, but more to the south, is the **Cishi Pagoda** *(císhì tǎ)* is a brick tower dating back to 1242. To get there, take the No 22 bus down Baling Lu to the lake, get off and walk south on Dongting Nanlu. Keep to the left hand side of the street so the buildings don't block your line of sight, and after about 10 minutes you'll see the pagoda, which lies up a lane to the right in a residential courtyard. Be prepared to see the lower portions adorned with drying laundry.

Yueyang borders the enormous **Dongting Lake** *(dòngtíng hú)*. At 3900 sq km, it is the second-largest body of fresh water in China. There are several islands in the lake; the most famous is **Junshan Island** *(jūnshān dǎo)*, where the Chinese grow 'silver needle tea'.

CENTRAL CHINA

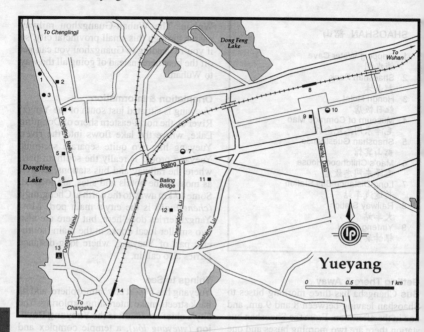

Yueyang

When the tea is added to hot water, it's supposed to remain on the surface, sticking up like tiny needles and emitting a fragrant odour.

You can board boats for the 45-minute ride to Junshan Island at either Nanyuepo dock (*nányuèpō mǎtou*), centrally located at the end of Baling Lu (bus No 22 more or less gets you there), or at the Yueyang Pavilion ferry dock (*yuèyáng lóu lúnchuán kèyùnzhàn*), just north of the Pavilion on Dongting Beilu. The latter has more frequent sailings. For both docks, the earliest boats leave around 7.30 am and the last boat back from the island departs at 4.30 pm. The return fare is only Y10, and it's worth a visit not only for the tea plantations but for the other farming activity on the island. There are also fast boats which get there in 10 minutes for Y20 return.

Places to Stay

Probably the best deal in town is the *Xuelian Hotel* (☎ 225-677) (*xuělián bīnguǎn*) on Dongting Beilu just north of Yueyang Pavilion. Beds in quads cost Y18, in doubles Y28, and doubles with bathroom attached start at Y56. The hotel and surrounding buildings are of quaint traditional Chinese architecture and are set in one of the more scenic parts of town. From the railway station, take the No 22 bus to the Yueyang Pavilion and walk north a few minutes to get there.

Nearer the city centre, the *Xiangwan Hotel* (*xiāngwǎn bīnguǎn*) has beds in doubles for Y28. It's just off Baling Daqiao on Desheng Lu, and the No 17 bus passes it on the way from the new railway station. South of the new railway station on Nanhu Dalu is the *Dahua Hotel* (*dàhuá dàjiǔdiàn*), with doubles/triples for Y88/99. As the station is pretty far out to the east, this place is really only convenient if you need to catch an early train.

On a side street just off Dongting Beilu, the *Yueyang Tower Hotel* (☎ 235-188) (*yuèyáng lóu bīnguǎn*) is a friendly place offering

YUEYANG 岳阳

1 Yueyang Pavilion Ferry Dock
  岳阳轮船客运站
2 Xuelian Hotel
  雪莲宾馆
3 Yueyang Pavilion
  岳阳楼
4 Yueyang Tower Hotel
  岳阳楼宾馆
5 Yueyang Hotel & CITS
  岳阳宾馆，中国国际旅行社
6 Nanyuepo Dock
  南岳坡码头
7 West Bus Station
  汽车西站
8 New Railway Station
  新火车站
9 Dahua Hotel
  大华大酒店
10 Long-Distance Bus Station
  长途汽车站
11 Xiangwan Hotel
  湘宛宾馆
12 Yunmeng Hotel
  云梦宾馆
13 Cishi Pagoda
  慈氏塔
14 Old Railway Station (Not in use)
  旧火车站

doubles with private bath for Y120. The No 22 bus to the Yueyang Pavilion will get you there. The *Yunmeng Hotel* (☎ 221-115) *(yúnméng bīnguǎn)* down at 25 Chengdong Lu has similar rooms to the Yueyang Tower, but for Y180 and up, and smiles at the reception desk are harder to find, as well.

The classiest and probably most central place in town is the *Yueyang Hotel* (☎ 223-011) *(yuèyáng bīnguǎn)* on Dongting Beilu. The local CITS has an office here, and there's a Friendship Store next door. Singles/doubles cost Y200/288. From the railway station, take bus No 22 and get off just after turning right onto Dongting Beilu.

Places to Eat

Yueyang's better restaurants often display their menu outside in cages! Their speciali-ties include hedgehog, snakes, pheasant, frogs, egrets and assorted rodents, but don't let it put you off – not all local cuisine is so exotic.

There are some good fish and seafood restaurants, particularly on Dongting Beilu, which also has a swath of cheap spots for dumplings, noodles and breakfast. There are also food stalls and small restaurants near the Nanyuepo dock and just south of the new railway station.

Getting There & Away

Yueyang is on the main Guangzhou-Beijing railway line. There are trains to Wuhan (four hours), Changsha (two hours) and Guang-zhou (14 hours). A direct train to Guilin (No 213) leaves daily at 3.45 pm. There are also daily buses to Changsha and Wuhan from the newly opened long-distance bus station. The west bus station also has buses to Changsha in addition to more-local destina-tions, but the bulk of longer-length routes seems to have shifted to the long-distance bus station.

Most of the large Yangzi ferries dock at Yueyang's northern port at Chenglingji. All tickets must be bought at the ticket office here. Private minibuses to Yueyang Railway Station regularly meet arriving boats. Bus Nos 1 and 22, which leave from an intersec-tion about 200 metres inland from the ferry terminal, also take you to the trains.

There are usually four boats daily to Chongqing from Chenglingji. Boats to Wuhan leave twice daily, in the morning. The Yueyang Pavilion ferry dock usually has one to two sailings daily in either direction. Though boats are less frequent, sailing from the Pavilion ferry dock is more convenient if you're in town, not to mention aesthetically more pleasing: Chenglingji is a pit.

Upriver to Chongqing usually takes four full days. Chinese ticket prices from Yue-yang are: 2nd class Y485, 3rd class Y183, and 4th class Y131. In a departure from egalitarian tradition, a 1st-class cabin is also offered for Y970, though this isn't available on all boats. Downriver to Wuhan normally takes just under 10 hours. Chinese ticket

CENTRAL CHINA

prices from Yueyang are: 2nd class Y78, 3rd class Y33, and 4th class Y124. Sailing to Chongqing, you'll find prices out of Chenglingji are a bit lower. You may be able to buy a Chinese-price ticket. However, more-bureaucratically-minded ticket sellers may tack on a surcharge anywhere from 50% to 100% – the amount does not seem to be fixed.

ZHUZHOU
(zhūzhōu)

Formerly a small market town, Zhuzhou underwent rapid industrialisation following the completion of the Guangzhou-Wuhan railway line in 1937. As a major railway junction and a port city on the Xiang River, Zhuzhou has since developed into an important coal and freight reloading point, as well as a manufacturing centre for railway equipment, locomotives and rolling stock. The only reason foreigners usually come here is to change trains. Although there's really nothing much in Zhuzhou to see, it's a pleasant enough place for a short stopover.

Places to Stay & Eat

The joint-venture *Qingyun Hotel (qìngyún dàshà)* opposite the railway station has triples for Y198. After that it's Y348 and up for a double. More affordable is the *Zhuzhou Guesthouse*(☎ 821-888) *(zhūzhōu bīnguǎn)* on Xinhua Xilu. They've got doubles for Y170. You might be able to persuade them to give you a bed in a triple for around Y60, but don't count on it. To get there from the railway station head right past the Qingyun Hotel. At the next main intersection turn left and continue past the traffic roundabout. The hotel is just before the bridge off a little side street to the right.

Across from the long-distance bus station, the shabbily upmarket *Hongdu Hotel* (☎ 822-3760) *(hóngdūgúojì dàjiǔdiàn)* has singles/doubles starting at Y168/198. To get there, walk past the Qingyun to the intersection at Xinhua Xilu, turn right, cross the bridge and go straight for another 10 minutes. It's on the right.

The Qingyun Hotel has good, if somewhat pricey, dim sum on the 2nd floor, as well as

a rather expensive rooftop restaurant. Near the railway station are cheaper food stalls and small restaurants.

Getting There & Away

Zhuzhou is at the junction of the Beijing-Guangzhou and the Shanghai-Kunming railway lines. From Changsha it's just one hour by express train.

You can catch buses to Xiangtan (from where you can then get a bus to Shaoshan) at the long-distance bus station on Xinhua Xilu. It's a 15-minute walk to the railway station: turn right and cross the railway bridge, then turn left again at the next intersection.

HENGYANG
(héngyáng)

With a population of over 800,000, Hengyang is Hunan's second largest city. It's on the railway junction where the Guilin-Changsha and Beijing-Guangzhou lines intersect, and people travelling from Guangzhou to Guilin often find themselves here briefly between train connections. Hengyang has important lead and zinc-mining industries, but was badly damaged during WW II. Despite post-1949 reconstruction, Hengyang still lags noticeably behind its neighbour down the Xiang River, Zhuzhou.

If you find yourself here for a full day, you might want to go to Nan Yue Mountain, about an hour's bus ride away. Locals claim it's worth the trip.

Places to Stay & Eat

Hengyang, like Zhuzhou, is quite strict about where foreigners can stay. Close to the railway station is the *Huiyan Hotel (huíyàn bīnguǎn)*, at 26 Guangdong Lu, which charges Y118 for a nice double room. There are rooms for Y98, but these seem harder to get. From the railway station it's a 10-minute walk straight along the main road.

Across the river, where the city centre lies, your other option is the *Yan Cheng Hotel* (☎ 226-921) *(yànchéng bīnguǎn)* at 91 Jiefang Lu, where doubles start at Y160. Bus

No 1 runs past the hotel, but a taxi might be best for the first time, as the main sign is only in Chinese.

Upon emerging from the train station, you may be besieged by touts promising to get you into cheaper local hotels. Think twice about this, as you may well end up walking with them only to get turned back when the hotel staff see you're not Chinese.

The Huiyan has a restaurant next door that serves great steamed dumplings and some other fairly cheap dishes. Check prices first, though, as they have a few seafood delights priced at Y200 and up. Some of the small eating places around the railway station are a bit on the sleazy side, so choose carefully.

Getting There & Away

Hengyang is a major railway junction with direct trains to Wuhan, Guangzhou and Guilin among other places. Trains to Changsha take three hours, and tourist-price hard seats cost Y24.

HUAIHUA
(huáihuà)

Huaihua is a small, drab town built around a railway junction in western Hunan. It's not the sort of place you'd choose to come to, but if you're on the way to or from Zhangjiajie, Yaqueling or Liuzhou there are train connections from here. Beijing-Kunming, Chengdu-Guangzhou and Shanghai-Chongqing express trains run via Huaihua. There are also slower trains from Guiyang, Guangzhou, Zhengzhou and Liuzhou, terminating in Huaihua. There is a daily train to Zhangjiajie which leaves at 8.50 am. You can also catch a train to Sanjiang, in northern Guangxi Province, from Huaihua.

The *Tianfu Hotel (tiānfù fàndiàn)* is the second hotel on your right upon exiting the railway station: look for the multicoloured sign that includes the words 'Tianfu Restaurant'. With doubles/triples at Y136/150, it's among the cheapest and most conveniently located of the few hotels that take foreigners. To your left across the square as you exit the train station, the *Huairong Hotel*

(huáiróng bīnguǎn) has doubles for Y120, but this price is probably only for Chinese guests.

WULINGYUAN SCENIC AREA/ ZHANGJIAJIE
(wǔlíngyuán fēngjǐngqū)

Parts of the Wuling mountains *(wǔlíngshān)* in north-western Hunan were set aside in 1982 as nature reserves collectively known as the Wulingyuan Scenic Area, encompassing the localities of Zhangjiajie, Tianzishan and Suoxiyu. Of these, Zhangjiajie is the best known, and many Chinese refer to this area by that name.

The first area of its kind in China, Wulingyuan is home to three of the province's minority peoples, the Tujia, Miao and Bai, many of whom continue to speak their languages and maintain their traditional culture.

The mountains have gradually eroded to form a peculiarly spectacular landscape of craggy peaks and huge rock columns rising out of the luxuriant subtropical forest. There are waterfalls, limestone caves (including Asia's largest cave chamber), fresh clearwater streams, and rivers suitable for organised rafting trips. There are many possible short and extended hikes, but even if you don't intend doing any walking it's a nice place to spend some time.

Several towns serve as access points to Wulingyuan, but the most popular way in is via **Zhangjiajie City** (formerly known as **Dayong**) and Zhangjiajie Village. The city is near the railway line, while Zhangjiajie Village is situated nearly 600 metres above sea level in the Wuling foothills, surrounded by sheer cliffs and vertical rock outcrops.

A fee of Y45 (for both locals and foreigners alike) must be paid at the main entrance gate to the Zhangjiajie forest reserve just past the village. Chinese maps showing walking trails, some with key tourist sites marked in English, are on sale in both Zhangjiajie City and Village. The scenery is spectacular, but don't expect to view it alone: Wulingyuan has been targeted as a major national tourist area and is usually swarming with both Chinese and overseas tour groups. The local

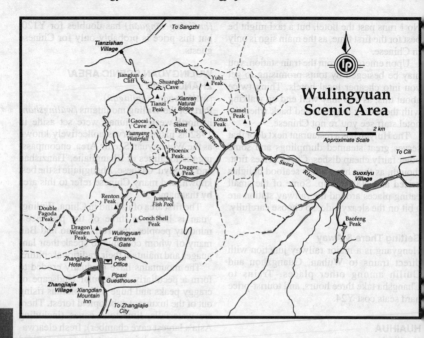

Wulingyuan Scenic Area

0   1   2 km
Approximate Scale

government recently opened an airport to further the tourist trade, and more hotels and karaoke nightspots will doubtless soon join the already considerable number both inside and outside the park.

Places to Stay & Eat

You'll probably find it more convenient and interesting to stay in Zhangjiajie Village, but in Zhangjiajie City a number of hotels also take foreigners.

Diagonally opposite the bus station is the *Dule Hotel (dūlè bīnguǎn)*, where a spartan double room is Y108 a night and beds in a triple are Y18. The *Wuling Guesthouse (wǔlíng bīnguǎn)* on Jiefang Lu (past the Puguang Temple) charges Y240 for very nice double rooms with bathroom, TV and lots of hot water. Further down Jiefang Lu, the *Dragon International Hotel (xiánglóng guójì jiǔdiàn)* is a tacky establishment masquerading as a four-star hotel. Doubles start

at Y420, plus a 20% service charge, and go up steadily from there.

In Zhangjiajie Village most places seem willing to take foreigners. Just uphill from where the buses stop is the *Zhangjiajie Hotel (zhāngjiàjiè bīnguǎn)*, which has basic but clean doubles for Y132, including a 10% service charge. You may also be able to bargain them down to Y80 if you're very persistent. The hotel also has a new three-star addition next door which offers more upmarket air-con doubles for Y280.

Better value though is the *Xiangdian Mountain Inn (xiāngdiàn shānzhuāng)*, uphill from the bridge, 50 metres off the main road. This hotel has modern, clean doubles/triples for Y120/150, no service charge and nice touches such as towels and balconies. It's also quieter, as the Zhangjiajie Hotel sits amid several karaoke clubs.

The *Pipaxi Guesthouse (pípāxī bīnguǎn)* also offers a quiet setting and has somewhat fancy doubles for Y240 and Y340 and suites for Y600. The Pipaxi is situated just outside Zhangjiajie Village, so you can save yourself a 10-minute walk back uphill by getting dropped off here. There are simple eating houses scattered around the village, and the better hotels also have their own restaurants.

For those hiking overnight in Wulingyuan, there are places to stay inside the park along the popular trail routes. As the park tickets are only good for one entry, local visitors often do a two to three-day circuit hike, going in at Zhangjiajie Village and hiking or busing it to villages within park boundaries such as Tianzishan and Suoxiyu, both of which have a bewildering choice of hotels and hostels.

If you're just interested in day hiking, a stay in Zhangjiajie will do just fine. One way to skirt the crowds and the entrance fee is to walk up the road past the Xiangdian Mountain Inn and several other hotels, and follow the stream up into the foothills. It takes a bit of bushwhacking, but there are nice views to be had, and some peace and quiet in which to enjoy them.

Getting There and Away

With the opening of the new airport in late 1994, there are now direct flights linking Zhangjiajie City with Beijing, Changsha, Chongqing, Guangzhou, Shanghai and Shenzhen. More destinations, including Guilin and Wuhan, are expected to be added by early 1996.

There are direct trains from Zhangjiajie City to Changsha (15 hours), Zhengzhou (23 hours) and Guangzhou (27 hours). The Changsha train leaves around 4.30 pm and gets you in the next morning at 7.30 am. If you're coming from the Yangzi port of Yichang, there is a direct afternoon train (originating from Zhengzhou) that stops at Zhangjiajie around 11.30 pm before continuing on to the railway junction at Huaihua. If you're heading south to Sanjiang or Liuzhou in Guangxi Province, you must change trains at Huaihua. CITS in Zhangjiajie City (☎ 227-295), located on the 4th floor of 34 Jiefang Lu, can help you book hard and soft sleepers, as well as air tickets.

Buses leave the Zhangjiajie City bus station for Changsha throughout the day. The 10-hour trip costs Y36.60, Y67 for air-con buses. Sleeper buses are also available, leaving at around 5 pm and arriving in Changsha at 5 am, for Y70.

Minibuses to Zhangjiajie Village pick up incoming passengers at the railway station. The trip takes over an hour and costs Y10. The minibuses first stop at the bus station in Zhangjiajie City, which lies across the river, 14 km from the railway station. They then continue on to the Zhangjiajie Village. At the Zhangjiajie City bus station, you can also get buses to Tianzishan and Suoxiyu villages.

CENTRAL CHINA

THE SOUTH

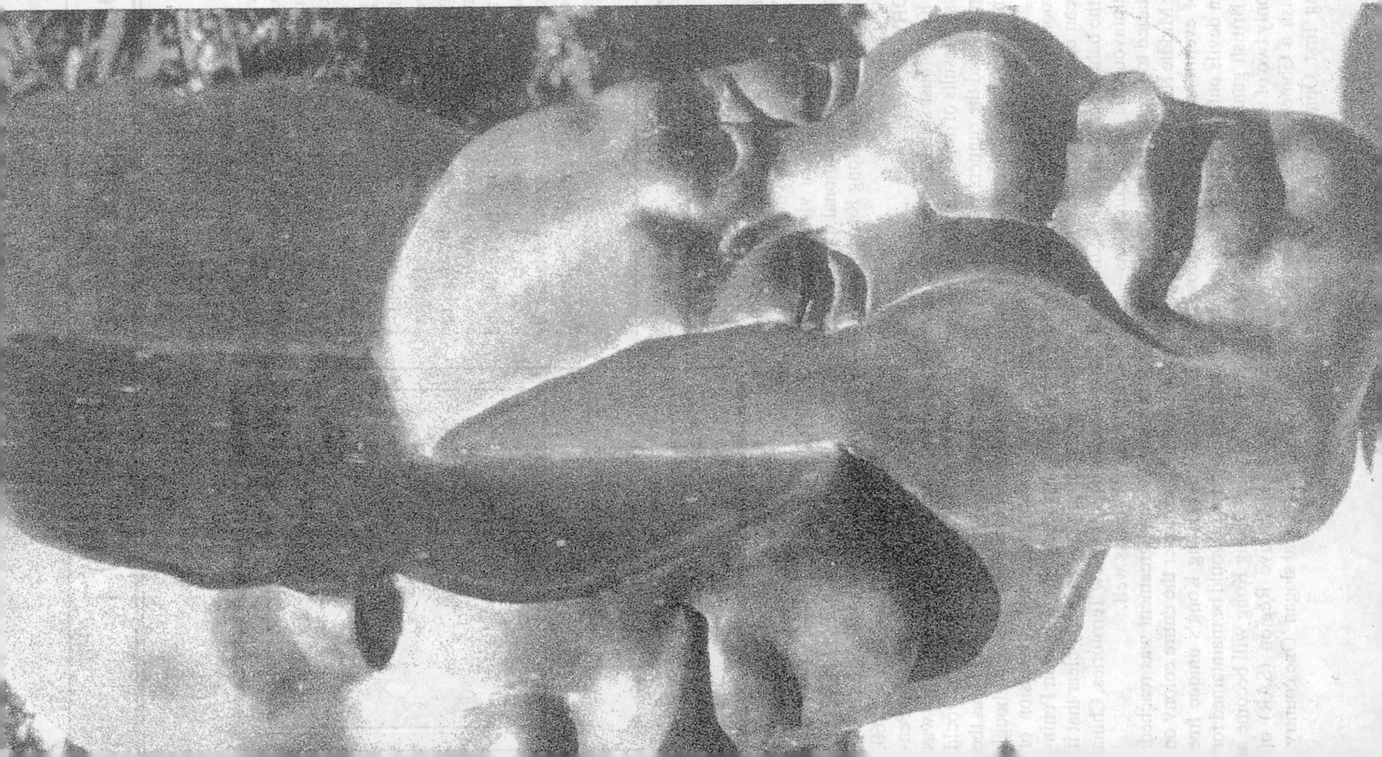

Hong Kong & Macau 香港, 澳门

Hong Kong is a curious anomaly. It's an energetic paragon of the virtues of capitalism and yet it will soon become part of what is officially the largest Communist country in the world. Currently a British colony, Hong Kong will be handed back to China in 1997. Sixty km west of Hong Kong, on the other side of the Pearl River's mouth, is the oldest European settlement in the East – the tiny Portuguese territory of Macau. Its 16 sq km consists of a peninsula joined to the Chinese mainland, and the islands of Taipa and Coloane, which are joined together by a causeway and linked to central Macau by two bridges. Macau is slated to be handed back to China in 1999.

Population: 6 million
Highlights:
- A sampan ride in Aberdeen Harbour
- A trip on the Peak Tram to Victoria Peak
- Dim sum in a good restaurant
- Shopping in the many shopping centres

Hong Kong

Hong Kong's political and economic system is significantly different from that of the PRC. Thus, much of what you've read elsewhere in this book (about visas, currency, accommodation, international phone calls etc) does not apply to Hong Kong.

HISTORY

Hong Kong must stand as one of the more successful results of dope running. The dope was opium and the runners were backed by the British government. European trade with China goes back over 400 years. As the trade mushroomed during the 18th century and European demand for Chinese tea and silk grew, the balance of trade became more and more unfavourable to the Europeans – until they started to run opium into the country.

The Middle Kingdom grew alarmed at this turn of events and attempted to throw the foreign devils out. The war of words ended when British gunboats were sent in. There were only two of them, but they managed to demolish a Chinese fleet of 29 ships. The ensuing first Opium War went much the same way and, at its close in 1842, the island of Hong Kong was ceded to the British.

Following the second Opium War in 1860, Britain took possession of the Kowloon Peninsula. Finally, in 1898, a 99-year lease was granted for the New Territories. What would happen after the lease ended in 1997 was the subject of considerable speculation. Although the British supposedly had possession of Hong Kong Island and the Kowloon Peninsula for all eternity, it was pretty clear that if they handed back the New Territories, China would want the rest as well.

In late 1984, an agreement was reached: China would take over the entire colony on 1 July 1997 but Hong Kong's unique free enterprise economy would be maintained for at least 50 years. Hong Kong will become a Special Administrative Region (SAR) of China with the official slogan 'One country, two systems'.

China has repeatedly reassured Hong Kong's population that 'nothing will change', but few believe this. A belated attempt by Britain to increase the number of democratically elected members of Hong Kong's Legislative Council (LEGCO) caused China to threaten to dismiss the council and appoint leaders approved by Beijing. Indeed, the last few years have seen repeated denunciations of Britain by the Chinese leadership bordering on the hysterical. These public tantrums have done much to undermine confidence among Hong Kong residents. Well aware of China's previous record of broken promises and harsh political repression, Hong Kongers are emigrating in droves.

Still, Hong Kong continues to prosper, even though nervousness about 1997 has caused much capital to flee to safe havens overseas. Trade with both the West and the rest of China is booming. Service industries such as banking, insurance, telecommunications and tourism now employ 75% of Hong Kong residents. All the polluting sweatshop factories have moved just across the border to Shenzhen and other cities in China. Part of the reason for Hong Kong's prosperity is that it is a capitalist's dream; it has lax controls and a maximum tax rate of 15%.

ORIENTATION

Hong Kong's 1070 sq km are divided into four main areas – Kowloon, Hong Kong Island, the New Territories and the outlying islands.

Hong Kong Island is the economic heart of the colony but comprises only 7% of Hong Kong's land area. Kowloon is the densely populated peninsula to the north – the southern tip of the Kowloon peninsula is Tsimshatsui, where herds of tourists congregate. The New Territories, which officially include the outlying islands, occupy 91% of Hong Kong's land area. Much of it is rural and charming, but tourists seldom visit this scenic part of Hong Kong.

Western visitors should have few problems getting around Hong Kong – English is widely spoken and most street signs are bilingual. If you've been brushing up on your Mandarin, be aware that less than half the population can speak it – most speak Cantonese as their native tongue.

VISAS

Most visitors to Hong Kong do not need a visa. British passport holders are permitted to stay visa-free for 12 months, citizens of all Western European nations can stay for three months and citizens of the USA and most other countries get one month. Visas are still required for Eastern Europeans and citizens of Communist countries (including China).

But beware – these visa regulations will almost certainly be changed after 1 July 1997. Western nationalities will probably not require a visa for a short visit, but it seems most unlikely that UK citizens will continue to get a 12-month visa-free stay. China is silent on the issue, but our best guess is that foreigners will not be allowed to stay over one month unless they have a work permit.

For visa extensions, you should inquire at the Immigration Department (☎ 2824-6111), 2nd floor, Wanchai Tower Two, 7 Gloucester Rd, Wanchai. In general, they do not like to grant extensions unless there are special circumstances – cancelled flights, illness, registration in a legitimate course of study, legal employment, marriage to a local etc.

Hong Kong is currently the best place to pick up a visa for China, and this will probably continue for a while after 1997.

FOREIGN CONSULATES

Hong Kong is a good place to pick up a visa for someplace else or replace a stolen or expired passport. The following consulates could come in handy:

Australia
    23rd & 24th floor, Harbour Centre, 25 Harbour Rd, Wanchai (☎ 2827-8881)
Austria
    Emperor House, Central (☎ 2522-8086)
Belgium
    33 Garden Rd, Central (☎ 2524-3111)

CHINA

To Guangzhou

SHENZHEN

Lak Ma Chau

San Tin

Hau Hoi Wan (Deep Bay)

Ponds

Ponds

Lau Fau Shan

Yuen Long

Kam Tin

Ching Chung Koon Temple

NEW TERRITORIES

Castle Peak (583 m)

Tuen Mun

Tai Lam Chung Reservoir

Tsuen Wan

Lung Kwu Chau Island

Sham Tseng

Tsing Yi Island

Brother Islands

Chek Lap Kok Island *(New Airport)*

Discovery Bay

Pak Mong

Peng Chau Island

Tung Chung

Po Lin Monastery

Mui Wo

Tai O

Ngong Ping

Lantau Island

Silvermine Bay

Hei Ling Chau Island

West Lama Channel

Yung Shue Wan

Shek Pik Reservoir

Cheung Sha Wan

Hung Shir Ye Beach

Lama Island

Lantau Channel

Soko Islands

Shek Kwu Chau Island

Cheung Chau Island

OUTLYING ISLANDS

THE SOUTH

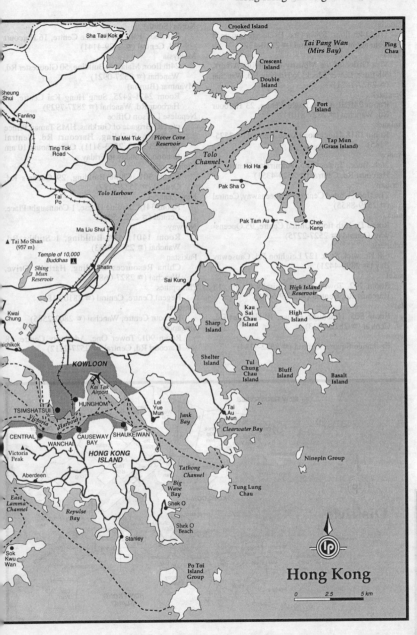

Hong Kong

0   2.5   5 km

Canada
11th-14th floor, Tower One, Exchange Square, 8 Connaught Place, Central (☎ 2810-4321)

China
Visa Office of the Ministry of Foreign Affairs, 5th floor, Lower Block, 26 Harbour Rd, Wanchai (☎ 2827-1881)

Denmark
Room 2402B, Great Eagle Centre, 23 Harbour Rd, Wanchai (☎ 2827-8101)

Finland
Room 1818, Hutchison House, Central (☎ 2525-5385)

France
26th floor, Tower Two, Admiralty Centre, 18 Harcourt Rd, Central (☎ 2529-4351)

Germany
21st floor, United Centre, 95 Queensway, Central (☎ 2529-8855)

India
Room D, 16th floor, United Centre, 95 Queensway, Central (☎ 2527-2275)

Indonesia
6-8 Keswick St & 127 Leighton Rd, Causeway Bay (☎ 2890-4421)

Israel
Room 702, Tower Two, Admiralty Centre, 18 Harcourt Rd, Central (☎ 2529-6091)

Italy
Room 805, Hutchison House, 10 Harcourt Rd, Central (☎ 2522-0033)

Japan
Exchange Square, Central (☎ 2522-1184)

Korea (South)
5th floor, Far East Finance Centre, 16 Harcourt Rd, Central (☎ 2529-4141)

Malaysia
24th floor, Malaysia Building, 50 Gloucester Rd, Wanchai (☎ 2527-0921)

Myanmar (Burma)
Room 2421-2425, Sung Hung Kai Centre, 30 Harbour Rd, Wanchai (☎ 2827-7929)

Nepalese Liaison Office
c/o HQ Brigade of Gurkhas, HMS Tamar, Prince of Wales Building, Harcourt Rd, Central (☎ 2863-3253, 2863-3111). Office hours 10 am to noon, Monday to Friday

Netherlands
Room 301, China Building, 29 Queen's Rd, Central (☎ 2522-5127)

New Zealand
Room 3414, Jardine House, 1 Connaught Place, Central (☎ 2525-5044)

Norway
Room 1401, AIA Building, 1 Stubbs Rd, Wanchai (☎ 2574-9253)

Pakistan
China Resources Building, Harbour Drive, Wanchai (☎ 2827-0681)

Philippines
Regent Centre, Central (☎ 2810-0183)

Portugal
Harbour Centre, Wanchai (☎ 2802-2585)

Singapore
Room 901, Tower One, Admiralty Centre, 18 Harcourt Rd, Central (☎ 2527-2212)

Districts

South Africa
27th floor, Sunning Plaza, 10 Hysan Ave, Causeway Bay (☎ 2577-3279)

Spain
8th floor, Printing House, 18 Ice House St, Central (☎ 2525-3041)

Sri Lanka
22nd floor, 43 Queen's Rd East, Wanchai (☎ 2866-2321)

Sweden
Room 804, Hong Kong Club Building, Chater Rd, Central (☎ 2521-1212)

Switzerland
Room 3703, Gloucester Tower, The Landmark, 11 Pedder St, Central (☎ 2522-7147)

Taiwan
Chung Hwa Travel Service, 4th floor, Lippo Tower, 89 Queensway, Central (☎ 2525-8315)

Thailand
8th floor, Fairmont House, 8 Cotton Tree Drive, Central (☎ 2521-6481)

UK
c/o Overseas Visa Section, Hong Kong Immigration Department, 2nd floor, Wanchai Tower Two, 7 Gloucester Rd, Wanchai (☎ 2824-6111)

USA
26 Garden Rd, Central (☎ 2523-9011)

MONEY
Exchange Rates
The unit of currency in Hong Kong is the HK$, divided into 100 cents. Bills are issued in denominations of $10, $20, $50, $100, $500 and $1000. Coins are issued in denominations of $5, $2, $1, 50 cents, 20 cents and 10 cents. Exchange rates are as follows:

Australia	A$1	=	HK$5.74
Belgium	BFr1	=	HK$0.26
Canada	C$1	=	HK$5.69
China	Y1	=	HK$0.94
France	FF1	=	HK$1.57
Germany	DM1	=	HK$5.36
Japan	¥100	=	HK$7.36
Netherlands	G1	=	HK$4.79
New Zealand	NZ$1	=	HK$5.13
Sweden	Kr1	=	HK$1.18
Switzerland	SFr1	=	HK$6.66
UK	UK£1	=	HK$11.98
USA	US$1	=	HK$7.74

Hong Kong has no exchange controls – locals and foreigners can send large quantities of money in or out as they please with no restrictions, and even play the local stock-market while they're at it. Hong Kong is, in fact, the financial centre of Asia simply because it is so unregulated. Whether or not China will interfere with this financial freedom after 1997 is the big question that keeps bankers awake at night.

Hong Kong is also a dream come true for money changing. All major and many minor foreign currencies can be exchanged. Foreigners can open bank accounts in various currencies (or in gold!), and international telegraphic transfers are fast and efficient. International credit cards are readily accepted.

Banks give the best exchange rates, but they vary from bank to bank. Excellent rates can be found at Wing Lung Bank, 4 Carnarvon Rd, Tsimshatsui, next to the New Astor Hotel. Another good bank for changing money is the Hang Seng Bank, which has numerous branches all over the city (the small branches in the MTR stations do not change money). However, the Hang Seng charges HK$50 per transaction, so the rates are good only if you change over US$200.

The Hongkong Bank gives relatively poor rates for a bank and tacks on a HK$30 service charge for each transaction.

Licensed moneychangers in the tourist districts operate 24 hours a day but give relatively poor exchange rates, which are clearly posted. However, you can often get a better rate by bargaining (but be sure to ask politely)! The moneychangers in Chungking Mansions in Tsimshatsui are known to give the best exchange rates.

Try not to change more money than necessary at the airport as the exchange rate there is poor.

Bank hours are from 9 am to 4 pm Monday to Friday, and from 9 am to noon or 1 pm on Saturday.

Costs
Hong Kong is an expensive place, but there are ways to limit the damage. If you stay in dormitories, eat budget meals and resist the urge to shop, you can survive (just barely) on

under HK$200 per day. However, most travellers will spend more.

In general, tipping is not expected in Hong Kong. A 10% service charge is usually added to restaurant bills in upmarket establishments, and this is a mandatory 'tip'. In taxis you should round the fare up to the nearest HK$0.50 or dollar.

If you shop for cameras, electronics and other big ticket items in the Tsimshatsui tourist zone, bargaining is essential because the shops will try to charge double. However, bargaining is *not* the norm in Hong Kong. It's only normal in places where tourists congregate. Out in the suburban shopping malls or the street markets of Mongkok and Shamshuipo, everything has a price tag and there is little scope for bargaining.

HONG KONG TOURIST ASSOCIATION

The enterprising HKTA is definitely worth a visit. They're efficient and helpful and have reams of printed information, free or fairly cheap.

You can call the HKTA hotline (☎ 2801-7177) from 8 am to 6 pm from Monday to Friday, or from 9 am to 5 pm on weekends and holidays. For shopping advice and inquiries on HKTA members, there's a different phone (☎ 2801-7278) staffed from 9 am to 5 pm Monday to Friday, and 9 am to 12.45 pm on Saturday (closed Sunday and holidays). You'll find HKTA offices at:

Star Ferry Terminal, Tsimshatsui. Open 8 am to 6 pm Monday to Friday, and from 9 am to 5 pm weekends and holidays.
Shop 8, Basement, Jardine House, 1 Connaught Place, Central. Open 9 am to 6 pm weekdays, and 9 am to 1 pm on Saturday. Closed on Sunday and holidays.
Buffer Hall, Kai Tak Airport, Kowloon. Open 8 am to 10.30 pm daily. Information is provided for arriving passengers only.
Head Office, 35th floor, Jardine House, 1 Connaught Place, Central (☎ 2801-7111). This is a business office – not for normal tourist inquiries.

HKTA Offices Overseas Overseas branches of the HKTA can be found in the following countries:

Australia
    Level 5, 55 Harrington St, The Rocks, Sydney (☎ (02) 9251-2855)
Canada
    347 Bay St, Suite 909, Toronto, Ontario M5H 2R7 (☎ (416) 366-2389)
France
    Escalier C, 8ème étage, 53 rue Francois 1er, 75008, Paris (☎ (01) 47 20 39 54)
Germany
    Humboldt Strasse 94, D-60318 Frankfurt am Main (☎ (069) 959 12 90)
Italy
    c/o Sergat Italia Srl, Casella Postale 620, 00100 Roma Centro (☎ (06) 6880-1336)
Japan
    4th floor, Toho Twin Tower Building, 1-5-2 Yurakucho, Chiyoda-ku, Tokyo 100 (☎ (03) 3503-0731)
    8th floor, Osaka Saitama Building, 3-5-13 Awaji-machi, Chuo-ku, Osaka 541 (☎ (06) 229-9240)
Korea
    c/o Glocom Korea, Suite 1006, Paiknam Building, 188-3 Ulchiro 1-ga, Chung-gu, Seoul (☎ (02) 778-4403)
New Zealand
    PO Box 2120, Auckland (☎ (09) 575-2707)
South Africa
    c/o Development Promotions Pty Ltd, PO Box 9874, Johannesburg 2000 (☎ (011) 339-4865)
Singapore
    13th floor, 13-08 Ocean Building, 10 Collyer Quay, Singapore 0104 (☎ 532-3668)
Sweden
    c/o Airline Marketing Service, PO Box 12179, S-102 25, Stockholm (☎ (0) 8653-5711)
Taiwan
    9th floor, 18 Chang'an E Rd, Section 1, Taipei (☎ (02) 581-2967)
    Hong Kong Information Service (☎ (02) 581-6061)
Spain
    c/o Sergat Espana SL, Pau Casals 4, 08021 Barcelona (☎ (93) 414-1794)
UK
    5th floor, 125 Pall Mall, London, SW1Y 5EA (☎ (0171) 930-4775)
USA
    5th floor, 590 Fifth Ave, New York, NY 10036-4706 (☎ (212) 869-5008)
    10940 Wilshire Blvd, Suite 1220, Los Angeles, CA 90024-3915 (☎ (310) 208-4582)

POST & TELECOMMUNICATIONS
Sending Mail

All post offices are open Monday to Saturday from 8 am to 6 pm, and are closed on Sunday and public holidays. The GPO is where you go to collect poste restante letters – it's in Central just to the west of the Star Ferry Terminal. In Tsimshatsui, there are two convenient post offices just east of Nathan Rd: one at 10 Middle Rd and another in the basement of the Albion Plaza, 2-6 Granville Rd.

Telephone

If you want to call overseas, it's cheapest to use an international direct dialling (IDD) telephone. You can place an IDD call from most phone boxes but you'll need stacks of coins. A better alternative is to buy a Phonecard, which comes in denominations of HK$50, HK$100 and HK$250. Every 7-Eleven store in Hong Kong has an IDD phone and sells the requisite Phonecards. You can also find card phones at a Hong Kong Telecom office. There's a Hong Kong Telecom at 10 Middle Rd in Tsimshatsui and another in the basement of Century Place at D'Aguilar and Wellington in Central (Lan Kwai Fong area).

To make an IDD call from Hong Kong, first dial 001, then the country code, area code and number. When calling Hong Kong from abroad, the country code is 852.

For calls to countries that do not have IDD service, you can call from a Hong Kong Telecom office – first pay a deposit and they will hook you up (minimum three minutes) and give you your change after the call is completed.

If you don't have the cash on hand, an easy way to make collect calls or bill to a credit card is to use a service called Home Country Direct. This service connects you immediately to an operator in your home country, so there is no language barrier. You can call Home Country Direct by dialling one of the following numbers:

Country	Home Country Direct
Australia	800-0061
Canada	800-1100
France	800-0033
Germany	800-0049
Hawaii	800-1188
Indonesia	800-0062
Italy	800-0039

Japan	(IDC) 800-0181
	(KDD) 800-0081
Macau	800-0853
Malaysia	800-0060
Netherlands	800-0031
New Zealand	800-0064
Norway	800-0047
Portugal	800-0351
Singapore	800-0065
South Korea	800-0082
Spain	800-0034
Sweden	800-0046
Taiwan	800-0886
Thailand	800-0066
UK	800-0090
USA	(AT&T) 800-1111
	(MCI) 800-1121
	(Sprint) 800-1877

Some useful phone numbers and prefixes include the following:

Ambulance, fire, police, emergency	999
Operator-assisted calls	010
Credit card calls	011
International dialling assistance	013
Police business & taxi complaints	2527-7177
Directory assistance	1081
Time	18501
Weather	187-8066

Fax, Telex & Telegraph

All your telecommunications needs can be taken care of at Hong Kong Telecom. Many hotels and even hostels have fax machines and will allow you to both send and receive for a reasonable service charge.

BOOKSHOPS

Hong Kong is an excellent place to stock up on books. This is at least partially due to the lack of censorship – no doubt that will change in 1997. At present, some of Hong Kong's notable bookshops include:

Bookazine Company, Basement, Jardine House, 1 Connaught Place, Central (opposite HKTA office) (☎ 2523-1747)

Cosmos Books LTD, 30 Johnston Rd, Wanchai (☎ 2528-3605)

Government Publications Centre, Government Offices Building, Queensway, Central (near the Admiralty MTR station)

South China Morning Post Bookshop, Star Ferry Terminal, Central

Swindon Books, 13 Lock Rd, Tsimshatsui

Times Books, Basement, Golden Crown Court, corner Carnarvon and Nathan Rds, Tsimshatsui

LIBRARIES

The main library is at City Hall, High Block, Central, just one street to the east of the Star Ferry Terminal. However, many people prefer the American Library (☎ 2529-9661), 1st floor, United Centre, 95 Queensway, Central.

CULTURAL CENTRES

The HKTA can give you the latest schedule of events. You can reserve tickets by calling the URBTIX hotline (☎ 2734-9009) and pick them up from any URBTIX outlet within three days. Except for the Fringe Club and Hong Kong Stadium, all of the following cultural centres are also URBTIX outlets:

Academy for the Performing Arts, 1 Gloucester Rd, Wanchai (☎ 2584-1514)
Arts Centre, 2 Harbour Rd, Wanchai (☎ 2877-1000)
City Hall Theatre, Edinburgh Place, Central (next to the Star Ferry Terminal) (☎ 2921-2840)
Hong Kong Coliseum, 9 Cheong Wan Rd, Hunghom, Kowloon (☎ 2355-7234)
Hong Kong Cultural Centre, 10 Salisbury Rd, Tsimshatsui (☎ 2734-2010)
Hong Kong Stadium, 55 Eastern Hospital Rd, So Kon Po (300 metres due east of the horse race track at Happy Valley) (☎ 2895-7895)
Queen Elizabeth Stadium, 18 Oi Kwan Rd, Wanchai (☎ 2591-1347)
Sai Wan Ho Civic Centre, 111 Shau Kei Wan Rd (adjacent to Sai Wan Ho MTR station), Hong Kong Island (☎ 2568-5998)
Shatin Town Hall, 1 Yuen Ho Rd, Shatin, New Territories (☎ 2694-2536)
Sheung Wan Civic Centre, 5th floor, Sheung Wan Urban Council Complex, 345 Queen's Rd, Sheung Wan, Hong Kong Island (☎ 2853-2678)
Tsuen Wan Town Hall, 72 Tai Ho Rd, Tsuen Wan, New Territories (☎ 2414-0144)
Tuen Mun Town Hall, 3 Tuen Hi Rd, Tuen Mun, New Territories (☎ 2452-7328)

TRAVEL AGENCIES

There are lots of travel agencies, but some agencies we've personally tried and found to offer competitive prices include:

Phoenix Services, Room B, 6th floor, Milton Mansion, 96 Nathan Rd, Tsimshatsui (☎ 2722-7378; fax 2369-8884)

Shoestring Travel, Flat A, 4th floor, Alpha House, 27-33 Nathan Rd, Tsimshatsui (☎ 2723-2306; fax 2721-2085)
Traveller Services, Room 1012, Silvercord Tower One, 30 Canton Rd, Tsimshatsui (☎ 2375-2222; fax 2375-2233)

MEDIA

In descending order of quality, Hong Kong's three local English-language daily newspapers are the *Eastern Express*, *South China Morning Post* and *Hong Kong Standard*. Also printed in Hong Kong are the *Asian Wall St Journal*, *International Herald Tribune* and *USA Today International*. Imported news magazines are readily available.

There are two English-language and two Cantonese TV stations in Hong Kong. Star TV offers satellite TV broadcasting.

EMERGENCY

The general emergency phone number for ambulance, fire and police is 999. You can dial this without a coin.

There are some excellent private hospitals in Hong Kong, but their prices reflect the fact that they must operate at a profit. Some of the better private hospitals include:

Adventist, 40 Stubbs Rd, Wanchai (☎ 2574-6211)
Baptist, 222 Waterloo Rd, Kowloon Tong (☎ 2337-4141)
Canossa, 1 Old Peak Rd, Mid-Levels, Hong Kong Island (☎ 2522-2181)
Grantham, 125 Wong Chuk Hang Rd, Deep Water Bay, Hong Kong Island (☎ 2554-6471)
Hong Kong Central, 1B Lower Albert Rd, Central (☎ 2522-3141)
Matilda & War Memorial, 41 Mt Kellett Rd, The Peak, Hong Kong Island (☎ 2849-6301)
St Paul's, 2 Eastern Hospital Rd, Causeway Bay (☎ 2890-6008)

Public hospitals are cheaper, although foreigners pay more than Hong Kong residents. Public hospitals include:

Queen Elizabeth Hospital, Wylie Rd, Yaumatei, Kowloon (☎ 2710-2111)
Princess Margaret Hospital, Lai Chi Kok, Kowloon (☎ 2310-3111)
Queen Mary Hospital, Pokfulam Rd, Hong Kong Island (☎ 2819-2111)

Prince of Wales Hospital, 30-32 Ngan Shing St, Shatin, New Territories (☎ 2636-2211)

ACTIVITIES

If you'd like a morning jog with spectacular views, nothing beats the path around Victoria Peak on Harlech and Lugard Rds. Part of this is a 'fitness trail' with various exercise machines (parallel bars and the like).

If you like easy runs followed by beer and good company, consider joining Hash House Harriers (☎ 376-2299; fax 813-6517), 3rd floor, 74 Chung Hom Kok Rd, Stanley, Hong Kong Island.

Anyone who is serious about sports should contact the South China Athletic Association (☎ 2577-6932), 88 Caroline Hill Rd, Causeway Bay. The SCAA has numerous indoor facilities for bowling, tennis, squash, ping-pong, gymnastics, fencing, yoga, judo, karate, billiards and dancing. Outdoor activities include golf, and there is also a women's activities section. Membership is very cheap and there is a discounted short-term membership available for visitors.

Another excellent place you can contact is the Hong Kong Amateur Athletic Association (☎ 2574-6845), Room 913, Queen Elizabeth Stadium, 18 Oi Kwan Rd, Wanchai. All sorts of sports clubs have activities here or hold members meetings.

KOWLOON

Kowloon, the peninsula pointing out towards Hong Kong Island, is packed with shops, hotels, bars, restaurants, nightclubs and tourists. Nathan Rd, the main drag of Kowloon, has plenty of all. Start your exploration from Kowloon's southern tip, the tourist ghetto known as Tsimshatsui. Adjacent to the Star Ferry Terminal is the **Hong Kong Cultural Centre**. Just next door is the **Museum of Art**. Both are closed on Thursday, otherwise operating hours are weekdays (including Saturday) from 10 am to 6 pm, and Sunday and holidays from 1 pm to 6 pm.

Adjacent to the preceding is the **Space Museum**, which has several exhibition halls and a Space Theatre (planetarium). Opening times for the exhibition halls are weekdays (except Tuesday) from 1 pm to 9 pm, and from 10 am to 9 pm on weekends and holidays. The Space Theatre has about seven shows each day (except Tuesday), some in English and some in Cantonese, but headphone translations are available for all shows. Check times with the museum.

The lower end of Nathan Rd is known as the **Golden Mile**, which refers to both the price of real estate here and also its ability to suck money out of tourist pockets. If you continue north up Nathan Rd you come into the tightly packed Chinese business districts of Yaumatei and Mongkok.

Hidden behind Yue Hwa's Park Lane Store on Nathan Rd is **Kowloon Park**, which every year seems to become less of a park and more like an amusement park. The swimming pool is perhaps the park's finest attribute – it's even equipped with waterfalls.

The **Museum of History** is in Kowloon Park near the Haiphong Rd entrance. It covers all of Hong Kong's existence from prehistoric times (about 6000 years ago give or take a few) to the present and contains a large collection of old photographs. The museum is open Monday to Thursday and Saturday from 10 am to 6 pm, and Sunday and public holidays from 1 to 6 pm. It is closed on Friday. Admission costs HK$10.

The **Kowloon Mosque** stands on Nathan Rd at the corner of Kowloon Park. It was opened in 1984 on the site of an earlier mosque constructed in 1896. Unless you are Muslim, you must obtain permission to go inside. You can inquire by ringing up (☎ 2724-0095).

The **Science Museum** is in Tsimshatsui East at the corner of Chatham and Granville Rds. This multilevel complex houses over 500 exhibits. Operating hours are 1 to 9 pm Tuesday to Friday, and 10 am to 9 pm on weekends and holidays. The museum is closed on Monday.

The most exotic sight in the Mongkok district is the **Bird Market**. It's on Hong Lok St, an obscure alley on the south side of Argyle St, two blocks west of Nathan Rd.

THE SOUTH

To Mongkok
& Shamshuipo

Dundas St
Hamilton St
Pitt St
Waterloo Rd
Waterloo Rd

Princess Margaret Rd

Kowloon

0   100   200 m

Yaumatei
MTR
Station

Shek Lung St
Man Ming La
Tung Kun St

Reclaimed
Land

Public Square St

King's
Park

Kansu St
Market St
Pak Hoi St
Saigon St
Wai Ching St
Ferry St
Canton Rd
Battery St
Reclamation Rd
Shanghai St
Temple St
Ningpo St
Nanking St

Wylie Rd

Jordan Rd

Gascoigne Rd

Hong Chong Rd

Bowring St
Parkes St
Pilkem St

Jordan
MTR
Station

Jordan
Path

Austin Rd

Austin Rd

Reclaimed
Land

Hillwood Rd

Hunghom
Railway
Station

Kowloon Park

Nathan Rd

Kimberley Rd

Granville Rd

Cameron Rd

Carnarvon Rd

Prat Ave

Chatham Rd

Tsimshatsui
East

Coliseum

Haiphong Rd

Kowloon Park Drive

Canton Rd

Ashley Rd

Hankow Rd

Lock Rd

Mody Rd

Cross-Harbour
Tunnel

Peking Rd

Middle Rd

Mody Rd

Tsimshatsui
MTR
Station

Ocean Terminal

Salisbury Rd

Star Ferry Pier

Victoria
Harbour

KOWLOON

PLACES TO STAY

1 STB Hostel
2 YMCA International House
3 Booth Lodge
4 Caritas Bianchi Lodge
7 Fortuna Hotel
8 Nathan Hotel
12 New Lucky Mansions
13 Shamrock Hotel
14 Bangkok Royal Hotel
16 Tourists Home
19 Holiday Inn Crowne Plaza
21 Lee Garden Guesthouse
22 Star Guesthouse
26 Hyatt Regency
27 Golden Crown Guesthouse
28 Mirador Arcade
29 Lyton House Inn & Frank's
   Mody House
30 Chungking Mansions
31 Kowloon Hotel
32 Sheraton
33 The Peninsula
34 YMCA
35 Omni, The Hongkong Hotel
40 Regent Hotel
42 New World Hotel

PLACES TO EAT

10 Night Market
24 Orchard Court
25 Java Rijsttafel

OTHER

5 Tin Hau Temple
6 Jade Market
9 Queen Elizabeth Hospital
11 Yue Hwa Chinese Products
15 China Hong Kong City
   (Ferries to China)
17 Science Museum
18 Cross-Harbour Bus Stop
20 Empire Centre
23 Kowloon Mosque
36 HK Tourist Association
37 Star Ferry Bus Terminal
38 Hong Kong Cultural Centre
39 Space Museum
41 New World Centre

China has indicated that the market will be closed or moved after 1997.

The **Wong Tai Sin Temple** is a very large and active Taoist temple built in 1973. It's right near the Wong Tai Sin MTR station. The temple is open daily from 7 am to 5 pm. Admission is free but a donation of HK$1 (or more) is expected.

The **Laichikok Amusement Park** is standard dodgem cars, shooting galleries and balloons for the kiddies, but the ice skating rink may be of interest for the sports-minded. There is a theatre within the park's grounds that has Chinese opera performances. Operating hours for the park are Monday to Friday from noon to 9.30 pm, and from 10 am to 9.30 pm on weekends and holidays. From the Kowloon Star Ferry Terminal take bus No 6A, which terminates near the park. Otherwise, it's a 15-minute walk from the Mei Foo MTR station. Admission is HK$15.

Adjacent to the Laichikok Amusement Park is the **Sung Dynasty Village**, which is promoted as an authentic re-creation of a Chinese village from 10 centuries ago. The village is open from 10 am to 8.30 pm daily. Admission costs HK$120. It drops to HK$80 on weekends and public holidays between 12.30 pm and 5 pm.

HONG KONG ISLAND

The north and south sides of the island have very different characters. The north side is an urban jungle, while much of the south is still surprisingly rural (but developing fast). The central part of the island is incredibly mountainous and protected from further development by a country park.

North Side

Central is the bustling business centre of Hong Kong. A free shuttle bus from the Star Ferry Terminal brings you to the lower station of the famous Peak Tram on Garden Rd. The tram terminates at the top of **Victoria Peak**, and the ride costs HK$14 one way or HK$21 return. It's worth repeating the peak trip at night – the illuminated view is spectacular if the weather cooperates. Don't just admire the view from the top – wander

THE SOUTH

Pier 1
(To Lamma Island)

Macau Ferry
Pier

Shun Tak
Centre

Victoria
Hotel ■

Reclaimed Land

Connaught Road West

Pier Rd

Western
Market

Sheung Wan
MTR Station

Man Wa Lane

Wing Lok Street

China
Travel
Service

Bonham Strand

Queen's Road West

Cleverly Street

Jervois Street

Wing On St

Lok Ku Road

Upper Lascar Row

Cat
Street
Galleries

Cat Street

Connaught Road Central

Des Voeux Rd Central

Bus
Terminal

Central
Market

Queen Victoria St

Ladder Street

Man Mo
Temple ■

Hollywood Road

Wellington Street

Li Yuen St
West

Li Yuen St
East

Chiu Lung St

Aberdeen Street

Peel Street

Graham Street

Queen's Road Central

Stanley Street

Theatre
Lane

Pedder St

Caine Road

Lyndhurst Terrace

Pottinger Street

Seymour Road

Staunton Street

Club
Sri Lanka ▼

Photo Scientific
& Color Six ■

D'Aguilar Street

HK
Telecom

Robinson Road

Shelley Street

Wanderlust
Books

Ashoka
Restaurant

Wyndham Street

Lan Kwai
Fong

Mosque Street

La Bodega
Bar

Fringe Club

Gloucester Street

Duddell Street

Conduit Road

Government
House

Robinson Road

Aberlady Road

Upper Albert Road

Zoological &
Botanical Gardens

— · — · — MTR Subway Route

————— Tram Route

++++++ Hillside Escalator Link

- - - - - Ferry Route

Central
Hong Kong

0   100   200 m

To New Territories (Hoverferries)

To Cheung Chau, Peng Chau & Lantau Islands

To Tsimshatsui

To Hunghom & Discovery Bay

Pier 6

Pier 7

Jordan Road Ferry

Star Ferry Pier

Victoria Harbour

Queen's Pier

Hoverferry to Tsimshatsui East

Exchange Square

GPO

South China Morning Post Bookshop

Jardine House

HKTA

Edinburgh Place

City Hall

HMS Tamar Naval Centre

Prince of Wales Building

Swire House

Mandarin Oriental Hotel

Central MTR Station

Ice House Street

Cenotaph

Furama Kempinski Hotel

Naval Dockyard

The Landmark

Chater Road

Statue Square

Legco Building

Jackson Road

Chater Garden

Murray Road

Lambeth Walk

Harcourt Road

Far East Finance Centre

Hong Kong & Shanghai Bank Building

Queen's Road

Battery Path

Thai Consulate

Lippo Centre

Admiralty MTR Station

To Wanchai & Causeway Bay

St John's Cathedral

Bank of China

Garden Road

Cotton Tree Drive

Queensway

Flagstaff House & Teaware Museum

Lower Albert Road

US Consulate

Peak Tram Terminal

Pacific Place

Island Shangri-La Hotel

Hong Kong Park

up Mt Austin Rd to **Victoria Peak Garden** or take the more leisurely stroll around Lugard and Harlech Rds – together they make a complete circuit of the peak. You can walk right down to Aberdeen on the south side of the island or you can try Old Peak Rd for a few kilometres' return to Central. The more energetic may want to walk the **Hong Kong Trail**, which runs along the top of the mountainous spine of Hong Kong Island from the Peak to Big Wave Bay.

There are many pleasant walks and views in the **Zoological & Botanical Gardens** on Robinson Rd overlooking Central. Entry is free to the **Fung Ping Shan Museum** in Hong Kong University (closed Sunday).

Hong Kong Park is just behind the city's second-tallest skyscraper, the Bank of China. It's an unusual park, not at all natural but beautiful in its own weird way. Within the park is the **Flagstaff House Museum**, the oldest Western-style building still standing in Hong Kong. Inside, you'll find a Chinese teaware collection. Admission is free.

Between the skyscrapers of Central you'll find **Li Yuen St East** and **Li Yuen St West**, which run parallel to each other between Des Voeux and Queen's Rds. Both streets are narrow alleys, closed to motorised traffic and crammed with shops and stalls selling everything imaginable.

The **Hillside Escalator Link** is a mode of transport that has become a tourist attraction. The 800-metre moving walkway (known as a 'travelator') runs from the Vehicular Ferry Pier alongside the Central Market and up Shelley St to the Mid-Levels.

West of Central in the Sheung Wan district is appropriately named **Ladder St**, which climbs steeply. At the junction of Ladder St and Hollywood Rd is **Man Mo Temple**, the oldest temple in Hong Kong. A bit further north near the Macau Ferry Terminal is the indoor **Western Market**, a four-storey red brick building built in 1906 and now fully renovated.

At the Western Market you can hop on Hong Kong's delightfully ancient double-decker trams, which will take you eastwards to Wanchai, Causeway Bay and Happy Valley.

Just east of Central is **Wanchai**, known for its raucous nightlife but relatively dull in the daytime. One thing worth seeing is the **Arts Centre** on Harbour Rd. The **Pao Sui Loong Galleries** are on the 4th and 5th floors of the centre and international and local exhibitions are held year-round with the emphasis on contemporary art.

Wanchai's **Police Museum**, 27 Coombe Rd, emphasises the history of the Royal Hong Kong Police Force. Opening hours are Wednesday to Sunday 9 am to 5 pm, and Tuesday from 2 to 5 pm. It's closed on Monday and admission is free.

The **Hong Kong Convention & Exhibition Centre** is an enormous building on the

WANCHAI-CAUSEWAY BAY

PLACES TO STAY

1	Grand Hyatt
3	New World Harbour View Hotel
9	Luk Kwok Hotel
11	Harbour Hotel
12	Excelsior Hotel
15	Noble Hostel
19	Leishun Court
20	Phoenix Apartments
21	Emerald House
23	Charterhouse Hotel

OTHER

2	Hong Kong Convention & Exhibition Centre
4	Australian Consulate
5	China Resources Centre (visa for China)
6	Central Plaza
7	Immigration Department
8	Arts Centre
10	Neptune Disco
13	World Trade Centre
14	Daimaru Household Square
16	Sogo Department Store
17	Mitsukoshi Department Store
18	Matsuzakaya Department Store
22	Times Square
24	Queen Elizabeth Stadium
25	South China Athletic Association

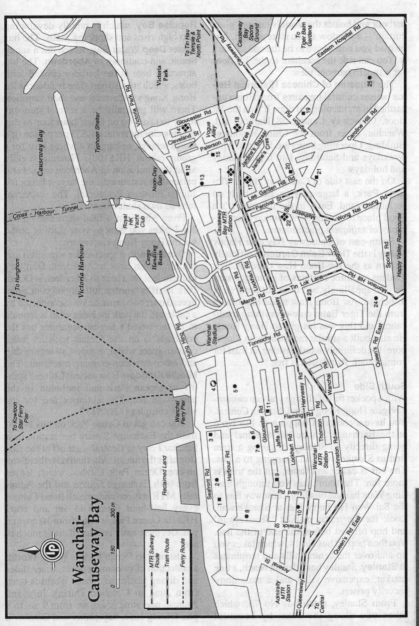

Wanchai-
Causeway Bay

0   150   300 m

MTR Subway
Route
Tram Route
Ferry Route

harbour and boasts the world's largest 'glass curtain' – a window seven storeys high. Just be glad you don't have to be the one to wash it. You can ride the escalator to the 7th floor for a superb harbour view.

The **Museum of Chinese Historical Relics** houses cultural treasures from China unearthed in archaeological digs. It's on the 1st floor, Causeway Centre, 28 Harbour Rd, Wanchai. Enter from the China Resources Building. Operating hours are 10 am to 6 pm weekdays and Saturday, 1 to 6 pm Sunday and holidays.

On the east side of Causeway Bay is **Victoria Park**, a large playing field built on reclaimed land. Early in the morning it's a good place to see the slow-motion choreography of *taijiquan* practitioners.

South-east of Causeway Bay near Happy Valley is the **Tiger Balm Gardens**, officially known as the Aw Boon Haw Gardens. The gardens are three hectares of grotesque statuary in appallingly bad taste but are a sight to behold. Aw Boon Haw made his fortune from the Tiger Balm cure-everything medication and this was his gift to Hong Kong. He also built a similar monstrosity in Singapore. It's definitely worth visiting, at least for comic relief. Admission is free.

South Side

With a pocket full of change you can circumnavigate Hong Kong Island. Start in Central. You have a choice of hopping on bus No 6 at the Exchange Square bus terminal and going directly to Stanley, or taking a tram first to Shaukeiwan and changing to a bus. The bus is easier and faster, but the tram is more fun. The tram takes you through hustling Wanchai and bustling Causeway Bay to the Sai Wan Ho Ferry Pier at Shaukeiwan. Look for the trams marked 'Shaukeiwan' and hop off just before the end of the line. You then hop on bus No 14, which takes you up and over the central hills and terminates at **Stanley**. Stanley has a decent beach, a fine market, expensive villas and a maximum-security prison.

From Stanley, catch bus No 73, which takes you along the coast by beautiful

Repulse Bay, which is rapidly developing into high-rises and shopping malls. The bus passes **Deep Water Bay**, which has a sandy beach, and continues to **Aberdeen**. The big attraction here is the harbour choked with boats, which are also part-time residences for Hong Kong's fishermen and their families. There will generally be a several sampans ready to take you on a half-hour tour of this floating city for about HK$35 per person (it's worth seeing), or bargain a whole boat for a group (about HK$100). Floating regally amid the confusion in Aberdeen are several palace-like restaurants, the largest being the Jumbo Floating Restaurant. The restaurant runs its own shuttle boat.

From Aberdeen, a final short ride on bus No 7 takes you back to your starting point, via the Hong Kong University.

Ocean Park, a spectacular aquarium and funfair, is also close to Aberdeen. Don't try to include it on a tour to Aberdeen – Ocean Park itself is worth a full day of your time. Spread over two separate sites, connected by a cable car, the park includes what is reputed to be the world's largest aquarium but the emphasis is on the funfair with its roller coaster, space wheel, octopus, swinging ship and other astronaut-training machines. The **Middle Kingdom** is an ancient Chinese spin-off of Ocean Park and included in the admission fee. The entrance fee for the whole complex is HK$130.

You can get to Ocean Park on bus No 70 from the Exchange Square bus station near the Star Ferry in Central – get off at the first stop after the tunnel. Alternatively, there's an air-con Ocean Park Citybus which leaves from both Exchange Square and the Admiralty MTR station (underneath Bond Centre) every half-hour from 8.45 am and costs HK$10. Ocean Park is open from 10 am to 6 pm. Get there early because there is much to see.

Just next to Ocean Park is **Water World**, a collection of swimming pools, water slides and diving platforms. Water World is open from June to October. During July and August, operating hours are from 9 am to 9 pm. During June, September and October it is open from 10 am to 6 pm. Admission for adults/children is HK$60/30 during the day, but in the evening falls to HK$40/20. Take bus No 70 and get off at the first stop after the tunnel. If you take the Ocean Park Citybus, be sure to get off at the first stop.

Shek O, on the south-east coast, has one of the best beaches on Hong Kong Island. To get there, take the MTR or tram to Shaukeiwan, and from Shaukeiwan take bus No 9 to the last stop.

NEW TERRITORIES

You can explore most of the New Territories by bus and train in one very busy day, assuming that you don't take time out for hiking or swimming (both worthwhile and recommended activities).

You start out by taking the MTR to the last stop at **Tsuen Wan**. The main attraction here is the **Yuen Yuen Institute**, a Taoist temple complex, and the adjacent Buddhist **Western Monastery**. You reach the institute by taking minibus No 81 from Shiu Wo St, which is two blocks south of the MTR station. Alternatively, take a taxi, which is not expensive.

Chuk Lam Sim Yuen is another large monastery in the hills north of Tsuen Wan. The instructions for getting there are almost the same as for the Yuen Yuen Institute. Find Shiu Wo St and take maxicab No 85.

At Tsuen Wan you have an option. You can continue west to Tuen Mun, or north to **Tai Mo Shan** (elevation 957 metres), Hong Kong's highest peak. To reach Tai Mo Shan, take bus No 51 from the Tsuen Wan MTR station – the bus stop is on the overpass that goes over the roof of the station, or you can also pick it up at the Tsuen Wan Ferry Pier. The bus heads up Route Twisk (Twisk is derived from Tsuen Wan Into Shek Kong). Get off at the top of the pass, from where it's uphill on foot. You walk on a road but it's unlikely you'll encounter traffic. The path is part of the **MacLehose Trail**, which is 100 km long. The trail runs from Tuen Mun in the west to the Sai Kung Peninsula in the east and walking the entire length would take several days.

If you choose not to visit Tai Mo Shan, from Tsuen Wan take bus No 60M or 68M to the bustling town of **Tuen Mun**. Here you can visit Hong Kong's largest shopping mall, the Tuen Mun Town Centre. From here, hop on the Light Rail Transit (LRT) system to reach **Ching Chung Koon**, a temple complex on the north side of Tuen Mun.

You then get back on the LRT and head to Yuen Long. From here, take bus No 54, 64K or 74K to the nearby walled villages at **Kam Tin**. These villages with their single stout entrances are said to date from the 16th century. There are several walled villages at Kam Tin but most accessible is **Kat Hing Wai**. Drop about HK$5 into the donation box by the entrance and wander the narrow little lanes. The old Hakka women in traditional gear require payment before they can be photographed.

The town of Sheung Shui is about eight km east on bus No 77K. Here you can hop on the KCR and go one stop south to **Fanling**. The main attraction in this town is the **Fung Ying Sin Kwun Temple**, a Taoist temple for the dead.

At Fanling, get on the Kowloon-Canton Railway (KCR) and head to Tai Po Market station. From here, you can walk 10 to 15 minutes to the **Hong Kong Railway Museum**. You can get back on the KCR and go south to the Chinese University, where there's the Art Gallery at the **Institute of Chinese Studies**. Admission is free.

The KCR will bring you to Shatin, a lively, bustling city where you can visit the huge **Shatin Town Centre**, one of Hong Kong's biggest shopping malls. Also, this is where you begin the climb up to the **Temple of 10,000 Buddhas** (which actually has over 12,000).

All this should fill your day, but there are other places to visit in the New Territories. The **Sai Kung Peninsula** is one of the least spoilt areas in the New Territories – great for hiking and you can get from village to village on boats in the Tolo Harbour. Also, the best beaches in the New Territories are in the eastern New Territories around the Sai Kung Peninsula, including **Clearwater Bay**.

THE SOUTH

OUTLYING ISLANDS

There are 235 islands dotting the waters around Hong Kong, but only four have bedroom communities and are thus readily accessible by ferry.

While very tranquil during the week, the islands are packed on weekends and holidays. Cars are prohibited on all of the islands except Lantau, and even there vehicle ownership is very restricted.

Cheung Chau

This dumbbell-shaped island has a large community of Western residents who enjoy the slow pace of island life and relatively low rents. Were it not for the Chinese signs and people, you might think you were in some Greek island village.

The town sprawls across the narrow neck connecting the two ends of the island. The bay on the west side of the island (where the ferry lands) is an exotic collection of fishing boats much like Aberdeen in Hong Kong Island. The east side of the island is where you'll find Tung Wan Beach, Cheung Chau's longest. There are a few tiny but remote beaches that you can reach by foot, and at the southern tip of the island is the hideaway cave of notorious pirate Cheung Po Tsai.

The big *gwailo* (Western) nightlife spot is the *Garden Cafe/Pub* (☎ 2981-4610) at 84 Tung Wan Rd, in the centre of the island.

Lamma

This is the second largest of the outlying islands and the one closest to the city. Lamma has good beaches and a very relaxed pace on weekdays, but on weekends it's mobbed like anywhere else. There are two main communities here, Yung Shue Wan in the north and Sok Kwu Wan in the south. Both have ferry service to Central.

Both Yung Shue Wan and Sok Kwu Wan are lined with seafood restaurants, so you won't starve. The *Waterfront Bar* in Yung Shue Wan is a lively place for nightlife and good food, or you can try its quieter competition, the *Island Bar*.

Lantau

This is the largest of the islands and the most sparsely populated – it's almost twice the size of Hong Kong Island but the population is only 30,000. You could easily spend a couple of days exploring the mountainous walking trails and enjoying uncrowded beaches.

Mui Wo (Silvermine Bay) is the major arrival point for ferries. As you exit the ferry, to your right is the road leading to the beach. It passes several eateries and hotels along the way.

From Mui Wo, most visitors board bus No 2 to **Ngong Ping**, a plateau region 500 metres above sea level in the western part of the island. It's here that you'll find the impressive **Po Lin Monastery**. It's a relatively recent construction and almost as much a tourist attraction as a religious centre. Just outside the monastery is the world's largest outdoor Buddha statue. It's possible to have a vegetarian lunch at the monastery dining hall and you can spend the night here. The main reason to stay overnight is to launch a sunrise expedition to climb Lantau Peak (elevation 934 metres).

Another place to visit is Tai O, a village at the western end of the island, reachable by bus No 1.

The two-km-long **Cheung Sha Wan** on Lantau Island is Hong Kong's longest beach. You'll have it to yourself on weekdays, but forget it on weekends.

On Lantau's north shore is the 19th-century **Tung Chung Fort**, which still has its old cannon pointing out to sea. The bad news here is that just off the coast construction is proceeding on Hong Kong's new airport, which is due to receive its first flight on 1 July 1997, the day China takes over. Lantau will soon be connected to Kowloon with a bridge and the island's character will surely change for the worse.

You may also want to visit **Discovery Bay** in the north-eastern part of the island. This is a very upscale housing development complete with high-rises, shopping mall, yacht club and golf course. Jet-powered ferries run from Discovery Bay to Central every 20 minutes, but there are no places to stay and tourism is actively discouraged. The main reason for visiting isn't to see Discovery Bay but to walk for one hour southwards along the coastline to find the **Trappist Haven Monastery**. Walking about another 1½ hours from there over a dangerously slippery trail brings you out to Mui Wo, from where you can get ferries back to Central.

Peng Chau

This is the smallest of the outlying islands that are readily accessible. It's also the most traditionally Chinese, with narrow alleys, an outdoor meat and vegetable market and a very tiny gwailo community. The **Tin Hau Temple** was originally built in 1792. A climb to the top of **Finger Hill** (elevation 95 metres) will reward you with a view of the entire island and nearby Lantau.

South of the main ferry pier and right along the shoreline are the two best Western restaurants and pubs, the *Sea Breeze Club* and adjacent *Forest Pub*. There are no places to stay in Peng Chau unless you can rent a holiday flat.

ORGANISED TOURS

There are dozens of these, including boat tours. All can be booked through the HKTA, travel agents, large tourist hotels or directly from the tour company.

PLACES TO STAY

For budget travellers, the situation is grim – accommodation in Hong Kong is expensive. Solo backpackers may want to seek out dormitories, some of which are very basic. There are a couple of YHA dormitories, which charge only HK$25 per bed, but all are very inconveniently located. The same is true for camping sites – they exist, but you'll spend an hour or two commuting to the city.

Guesthouses are the salvation for most budget travellers. Some guesthouses (not many) have dormitories where beds go for HK$70 to HK$100, with discounts for long-term (one week or more) rentals. Private rooms the size of closets are available for as little as HK$150 but you can easily spend

twice that. It definitely pays for two people to share a room, as this costs little or no extra. A 'mid-range' Hong Kong hotel would be anything priced between HK$400 and HK$1000, but even rooms at these prices are becoming rare.

The majority of cheap accommodation is on the Kowloon side. With a few exceptions, the places on Hong Kong Island are mid-range to top-end hotels. Rentals are about 20% cheaper if you pay by the week, but stay one night first to make sure that the room is acceptable – noisy neighbours and rats will not be obvious at first glance.

At mid-range and top-end hotels, you can get sizable discounts (up to 30%) by booking through some travel agencies. One such place is Traveller Services (☎ 2375-2222), but a few other agents do it as well.

At the airport, there is a hotel reservation desk, but they deal only with the more expensive hotels. However, they always have good deals, particularly if you arrive late at night. You'll always get a better price if you book at this desk rather than straight through the hotels. Even budget travellers can use their free courtesy phone to call around and see who has vacancies.

Kowloon – Guesthouses

Chungking Mansions There is probably no other place in the world like Chungking Mansions, the bottom-end accommodation ghetto of Hong Kong. It's a huge high-rise dump at 30 Nathan Rd in the heart of Tsimshatsui with approximately 80 guesthouses. It's divided into five blocks labelled A to E, each with its own derelict lift. If you stand around the lobby with your backpack, chances are that the touts from the guesthouses will find you before you find them.

With few exceptions, there is little difference in prices for private rooms, but dormitories are of course significantly cheaper. The price range for a private room is roughly HK$150 to HK$250, while dorm beds go for about HK$60 to HK$80. The following is a complete list of Chungking's guesthouses, and those places offering dormitory accommodation are indicated:

A Block, 17th floor: *United Guesthouse*, Flat A6

A Block, 16th floor: *Travellers' Hostel*, dorm beds HK$70, doubles with/without attached bath HK$150/170 (☎ 2368-7710)

A Block, 15th floor: *Happy Guesthouse*; *Ocean Guesthouse*; *Park Guesthouse* (☎ 2368-1689); *Spring Guesthouse*

A Block, 14th floor: *New Grand Guesthouse*, Flat A2; *New Hawaii Guesthouse*, Flat A6 (☎ 2366-6127); *Tokyo Guesthouse*, Flat A5

A Block, 13th floor: *Ashoka Guesthouse*, Flat A4 (☎ 2724-4646); *Capital Guesthouse*, Flat A6; *Rhine Guesthouse*, Flat A1

A Block, 12th floor: *Double Star Guesthouse*, Flat A6; *Peking Guesthouse*, Flat A2 (☎ 2723-8320); *Super Guesthouse*, Flat A5, dorm beds start at HK$70

A Block, 11th floor: *New International Guesthouse* (☎ 2369-2613)

A Block, 8th floor: *New Asia Guesthouse*, Flat A6; *New Mandarin Guesthouse*, Flat A9 (☎ 2366-1070); *Tom's Guesthouse*, Flat A5; *Sun Ying Guesthouse*, Flat A1

A Block, 7th floor: *Double Seven Guesthouse*; *First Guesthouse*; *Pay Less Guesthouse*; *Welcome Guesthouse* (☎ 2721-7793)

A Block, 6th floor: *London Guesthouse*, Flat A1 (☎ 2724-5000); *New World Hostel*, Flat A4, dorm beds HK$70, doubles HK$180 (☎ 2723-6352)

A Block, 4th & 5th floors: *Chungking House*, the most upmarket place in Chungking Mansions with singles at HK$270 to HK$300, doubles HK$370 to HK$400 (☎ 2366-5362; fax 2721-3570)

B Block, 17th floor: *Mr Li Guesthouse*

B Block, 16th floor: *New Carlton Guesthouse*; *Tom's Guesthouse*

B Block, 15th floor: *Carlton Guesthouse* (☎ 2721-0720); *China Guesthouse*; *New Shangri-la Guesthouse*; *OK Guesthouse*; *Shangri-la Guesthouse*

B Block, 14th floor: *Dashing Guesthouse*

B Block, 13th floor: *New Washington Guesthouse* (☎ 2366-5798)

B Block, 12th floor: *Columbia Guesthouse*; *Hong Kong Guesthouse*

B Block, 11th floor: *Hong Kong Guesthouse*; *Kowloon Guesthouse*

B Block, 10th floor: *Kowloon Guesthouse*

B Block, 9th floor: *Grand Guesthouse* (☎ 2368-6520)

B Block, 7th floor: *Brother's Guesthouse*; *Jinn's Ti Guesthouse*; *New York Guesthouse* (☎ 2339-5986)

B Block, 6th floor: *Travellers Friendship Hostel*, dorm beds first night cost HK$80, the second HK$70 and anything thereafter is HK$60 (☎ 2311-0797, 2311-2523)

B Block, 5th floor: *Chungking Lodge*

B Block, 4th floor: *Harbour Guesthouse*

B Block, 3rd floor: *Dragon Inn*; *New Delhi Guesthouse*

C Block, 16th floor: *Garden Guesthouse*; *Tom's Guesthouse* (☎ 2367-9258)

C Block, 15th floor: *Carlton Guesthouse*

C Block, 13th floor: *New Grand Guesthouse* (☎ 2311-1702); *Osaka Guesthouse*

C Block, 11th floor: *Marria Guesthouse*

C Block, 10th floor: *Kowloon Guesthouse*

C Block, 9th floor: *New Harbour Guesthouse*

C Block, 7th floor: *Jinn's Ti Guesthouse*; *New Chungking Guesthouse*

C Block, 6th floor: *New Brother's Guesthouse* (☎ 2724-0135)

C Block, 4th floor: *Maharaja Guesthouse*; *Ranjeet Guesthouse*

D Block, 16th floor: *New Shanghai Guesthouse*

D Block, 13th floor: *New Guangzhou Guesthouse*

D Block, 8th floor: *Fortuna Guesthouse* (☎ 2366-4524)

D Block, 6th floor: *Regent Inn Guesthouse*

D Block, 5th floor: *Royal Inn*; *Royal Plaza Inn* (☎ 2367-1424)

D Block, 4th floor: *Head Sun Guesthouse*; *Lai Wei Guesthouse*; *Mt Everest Guesthouse*

D Block, 3rd floor: *Princess Guesthouse*

E Block, 14th floor: *Far East Guesthouse* (☎ 2368-1724)

E Block, 13th floor: *Mandarin Guesthouse*

E Block, 12th floor: *International Guesthouse*

E Block, 8th floor: *Yan Yan Guesthouse*

E Block, 6th floor: *Regent Inn Guesthouse* (☎ 2722-0833)

Mirador Arcade You can avoid the stigma of staying in Chungking Mansions by checking out Mirador Arcade at 58 Nathan Rd. There are numerous places here. The complete lineup from top floor to bottom is as follows:

14th floor: *Man Hing Lung*, Flat F2. All rooms come equipped with private bath, air conditioning and TV, and this is our personal favourite in Mirador. Doubles cost HK$300 to HK$360. If you arrive by yourself and want a roommate, the management can put you in with another traveller thus cutting the bill in half (☎ 2722-0678; fax 2311-6669); *Wide Sky Hotel* (☎ 2312-1880)

13th floor: *Kowloon Hotel*, Flat E1 (☎ 2311-2523; fax 2368-5241); *London Guesthouse*, Flat F2, dorm beds HK$55, doubles HK$250 (☎ 2368-4681; fax 2739-0187); *Cosmic Guesthouse*

12th floor: *Ajit Guesthouse*, Flat F3, very friendly and clean with rooms for HK$150 to HK$200 (☎ 2369-1201)

9th floor: *City Guesthouse*, dorm beds HK$70, doubles HK$220 (☎ 2724-2612)

7th floor: *Mini Hotel*, Flat F2, dorm beds HK$70, doubles HK$240 (☎ 2367-2551)

6th floor: *Man Lee Tak Guesthouse*

6th floor: *Oriental Pearl Hostel*, Flat A3, doubles HK$300 (☎ 2723-3439; fax 2723-1344)

5th floor: *Mei Lam Guesthouse*, Flat D1, singles HK$220, doubles HK$280 to HK$360 (☎ 2721-5278)

3rd floor: *Lily Garden Guesthouse*, Flat A9, doubles HK$220 (shared bath), doubles (private bath) HK$280 (☎ 2367-2708; fax 2312-7681); *Blue Lagoon Guesthouse*, Flat F-2, dorm beds HK$60 to HK$80, doubles (shared bath) HK$240 to HK$250, doubles (private bath) HK$260 to HK$280 (☎ 2721-0346); *Garden Hostel*, dorm beds HK$70 to HK$80, doubles HK$200 – it's easier to find this place if you enter from Mody Rd (a sign marks the entrance) (☎ 2721-8567)

New Lucky Mansions Located at 300 Nathan Rd (entrance on Jordan Rd), Yaumatei, this is a better neighbourhood than most of the other guesthouses. The rundown from top floor to bottom is as follows:

14th floor: *Great Wall Hotel*, also known as *Sky Guesthouse*, very posh doubles for HK$450 (☎ 2388-7645)

11th floor: *Ocean Guesthouse*, singles/doubles HK$300/350 (☎ 2385-0125)

10th floor: *Nathan House*, doubles HK$300 (☎ 2780-1302)

9th floor: *Overseas Guesthouse*, singles/doubles with shared bath HK$220/230, clean and friendly; *Tung Wo Guesthouse*, singles HK$170, cheap but not so nice

5th floor: *Hoi Pun Uk House*, doubles HK$300, good but currently no English sign, owner speaks Mandarin (☎ 2780-7317)

3rd floor: *Hitton Inn*, double with private bath HK$260 (☎ 2770-4880); *Hakkas Guesthouse*, singles/doubles HK$250/260, nice rooms and owner speaks English well (☎ 2770-1470); *Galai Guesthouse*, no English sign, doubles HK$300

Other Guesthouses *Golden Crown Guesthouse* (☎ 2369-1782), Golden Crown Mansion, 5th floor, 66-70 Nathan Rd, Tsimshatsui, has dormitory beds for HK$80, singles from HK$200 and doubles from HK$280. But before you stay, take a look at neighbouring *Wahtat Travel & Trading Co* (☎ 2366-9495; fax 2311-7195), which is also on the 5th

floor of Golden Crown Mansion – there are superclean singles/doubles here for HK$250/300.

The *STB Hostel* (☎ 2710-9199; fax 2385-0153), 2nd floor, Great Eastern Mansion, 255-261 Reclamation St, Mongkok, is run by the Student Travel Bureau. Dorm beds are HK$100. There are pricier doubles costing HK$400 to HK$450, and triples for HK$450 to HK$560.

Star Guesthouse (☎ 2723-8951; fax 2311-2275), 6th floor, 21 Cameron Rd, is immaculately clean. *Lee Garden Guesthouse* (☎ 2367-2284) is on the 8th floor, D Block, 36 Cameron Rd, close to Chatham Rd. Both guesthouses are run by the same owner, the charismatic Charlie Chan. Rooms with shared bath are HK$260 to HK$300, and with private bath they jump to HK$320 to HK$400.

The Lyton Building, 32-40 Mody Rd, has two decent guesthouses but neither is cheap. *Lyton House Inn* (☎ 2367-3791) is on the 6th floor of Block 2 and costs HK$400 for a double. *Frank's Mody House* (☎ 2724-4113) is on the 7th floor of Block 4 and has doubles for HK$350 to HK$550.

Tourists Home (☎ 2311-2622) is on the 6th floor, G Block, Champagne Court, 16 Kimberley Rd. Doubles are from HK$300 to HK$350. All rooms have an attached private bath.

Kowloon – Hotels
The small number of mid-range hotels includes the following:

Bangkok Royal, 2-12 Pilkem St, Yaumatei (Jordan MTR station), 70 rooms, singles HK$420 to HK$600, doubles & twins HK$500 to HK$680 (☎ 2735-9181; fax 2730-2209)

Booth Lodge, 11 Wing Sing Lane, Yaumatei, 54 rooms, doubles HK$500 to HK$800 – run by the Salvation Army (☎ 2771-9266; fax 2385-1140)

Caritas Bianchi Lodge, 4 Cliff Rd, Yaumatei, singles HK$590, doubles HK$690 (☎ 2388-1111; fax 2770-6669)

Caritas Lodge, 134 Boundary St, Mongkok (near Prince Edward MTR station), singles/doubles HK$450/520 (☎ 2339-3777; fax 2338-2864)

Eaton, 380 Nathan Rd, Yaumatei (Jordan MTR station), 392 rooms, doubles & twins HK$770 to HK$1650, suites HK$1750 (☎ 2782-1818; fax 2782-5563)

Fortuna, 355 Nathan Rd, Yaumatei (Jordan MTR station), 187 rooms, singles HK$780 to HK$1300, doubles & twins HK$1170 to HK$1400 (☎ 2385-1011)

Imperial, 30-34 Nathan Rd, Tsimshatsui, 215 rooms, singles HK$700 to HK$1150, doubles & twins HK$800 to HK$1250, suites HK$1900 to HK$2400 (☎ 2366-2201; fax 2311-2360)

International, 33 Cameron Rd, Tsimshatsui, 89 rooms, singles HK$430 to HK$750, twins HK$560 to HK$950, suites HK$1250 to HK$1450 (☎ 2366-3381; fax 2369-5381)

King's Hotel, 473 Nathan Rd, Yaumatei, 72 rooms, singles HK$410 to HK$430, doubles & twins HK$520 to HK$550 (☎ 2780-1281; fax 2782-1833)

Nathan, 378 Nathan Rd, Yaumatei, 186 rooms, doubles & twins HK$880 to HK$950, suites HK$1150 to HK$1300 (☎ 2388-5141; fax 2770-4262)

Shamrock, 223 Nathan Rd, Yaumatei, 148 rooms, singles HK$520 to HK$850, doubles & twins HK$600 to HK$950, suites HK$800 to HK$1050 (☎ 2735-2271; fax 2736-7354)

YMCA International House, 23 Waterloo Rd, Yaumatei, 333 rooms, singles HK$270 to HK$300, twins HK$720 to HK$930, suites HK$1020 to HK$1300 (☎ 2771-9111; fax 2771-5238)

YMCA, 41 Salisbury Rd, Tsimshatsui, singles HK$730, doubles & twins HK$860 to HK$1060, suites HK$1450 to HK$1690 (☎ 2369-2211; fax 2739-9315)

YWCA, badly located near Pui Ching and Waterloo Rds in Mongkok – official address is 5 Man Fuk Rd, up a hill behind a Caltex petrol station. There are 169 rooms for women only, singles HK$300 to HK$500, doubles & twins HK$600 to HK$650 (☎ 2713-9211; fax 2761-1269)

The vast majority of Kowloon hotels are in the top-end category, as follows:

Ambassador, 26 Nathan Rd, Tsimshatsui, 313 rooms, doubles & twins HK$1100 to HK$2000, suites HK$3000 to HK$4300 (☎ 2366-6321; fax 2369-0663)

BP International, 8 Austin Rd, Tsimshatsui, 535 rooms, doubles & twins HK$980 to HK$1700, suites HK$2200 to HK$2800 (☎ 2376-1111; fax 2376-1333)

Concourse, 22 Lai Chi Kok Rd, Mongkok (Prince Edward MTR station), 359 rooms, doubles & twins HK$980 to HK$1580, suites HK$2180 (☎ 2397-6683; fax 2381-3768)

Grand Tower, 627-641 Nathan Rd, Mongkok, 549 rooms, doubles & twins HK$1050 to HK$1750, suites HK$2900 to HK$4150 (☎ 2789-0011; fax 2789-0945)

Guangdong, 18 Prat Ave, Tsimshatsui, 245 rooms, doubles & twins HK$1100 to HK$1400, suites HK$1700 to HK$2800 (☎ 2739-3311; fax 2721-1137)

Holiday Inn Crowne Plaza, 70 Mody Rd, Tsimshatsui East, 594 rooms, singles HK$1700 to HK$3150, twins HK$1800 to HK$3250, suites HK$3300 to HK$10,000 (☎ 2721-5161; fax 2369-5672)

Holiday Inn Golden Mile, 46-52 Nathan Rd, Tsimshatsui, 600 rooms, singles HK$1550, doubles & twins HK$1900 to HK$2150, suites HK$4800 to HK$8000 (☎ 2369-3111; fax 2369-8016)

Hyatt Regency, 67 Nathan Rd, Tsimshatsui, 723 rooms, doubles & twins HK$1900 to HK$2500, suites HK$5000 to HK$15,000 (☎ 2311-1234; fax 2739-8701)

Kimberley, 28 Kimberley Rd, Tsimshatsui, 532 rooms, doubles & twins HK$1150 to HK$1650, suites HK$1900 to HK$3800 (☎ 2723-3888; fax 2723-1318)

Kowloon Shangri-La, 64 Mody Rd, Tsimshatsui East, 717 rooms, doubles & twins HK$2150 to HK$3550, suites HK$3000 to HK$16,000 (☎ 2721-2111; fax 2723-8686)

Kowloon, 19-21 Nathan Rd, Tsimshatsui, 735 rooms, singles HK$1080 to HK$2000, twins HK$1200 to HK$2100, suites HK$2750 to HK$3080 (☎ 2369-8698; fax 2739-9811)

Majestic, 348 Nathan Rd, Yaumatei, 387 rooms, doubles & twins HK$1100 to HK$1480, suites HK$2500 (☎ 2781-1333; fax 2781-1773)

Metropole, 75 Waterloo Rd, Yaumatei, 487 rooms, doubles & twins HK$1080 to HK$1580, suites HK$2700 to HK$5200 (☎ 2761-1711; fax 2761-0769)

Miramar, 130 Nathan Rd, Tsimshatsui, 500 rooms, doubles & twins HK$1300 to HK$1800, suites HK$3800 to HK$13,500 (☎ 2368-1111; fax 2369-1788)

New Astor, 11 Carnarvon Rd, Tsimshatsui, 148 rooms, doubles & twins HK$980 to HK$1400, suites HK$3000 (☎ 2366-7261; fax 2722-7122)

New World, 22 Salisbury Rd, Tsimshatsui, 543 rooms, singles HK$1650 to HK$2400, doubles & twins HK$1850 to HK$2400, suites HK$2600 to HK$5800 (☎ 2369-4111; fax 2369-9387)

Newton, 58-66 Boundary St, Mongkok, 175 rooms, doubles & twins HK$990 to HK$1390, suites HK$2800 (☎ 2787-2338; fax 2789-0688)

Nikko Hongkong, 72 Mody Rd, Tsimshatsui East, 461 rooms, doubles & twins HK$1800 to HK$2800, suites HK$4500 to HK$12,500 (☎ 2739-1111; fax 2311-3122)

Omni Marco Polo, Harbour City, Canton Rd, Tsimshatsui, 440 rooms, doubles & twins HK$1600 to HK$1800, suites HK$2700 to HK$6500 (☎ 2736-0888; fax 2736-0022)

Omni Prince, Harbour City, Canton Rd, Tsimshatsui, 396 rooms, doubles & twins HK$1600 to HK$2150, suites HK$2700 to HK$3100 (☎ 2736-1888; fax 2736-0066)

Omni, The Hongkong Hotel, Harbour City, 3 Canton Rd, Tsimshatsui, 665 rooms, doubles & twins HK$1900 to HK$3500, suites HK$3100 to HK$11,000 (☎ 2736-0088; fax 2736-0011)

Park, 61-65 Chatham Rd South, Tsimshatsui, 430 rooms, singles HK$1200 to HK$1400, doubles & twins HK$1300 to HK$1500, suites HK$2000 to HK$4000 (☎ 2366-1371; fax 2739-7259)

Pearl Seaview, 262-276 Shanghai St, Yaumatei, 253 rooms, singles HK$780 to HK$930, doubles & twins HK$850 to HK$1050, suites HK$1600 to HK$2400 (☎ 2782-0882; fax 2388-1803)

Peninsula, Salisbury Rd, Tsimshatsui, 300 rooms, twins HK$2450 to HK$3200, suites HK$4500 to HK$25,000 (☎ 2366-6251; fax 2722-4170)

Prudential, 222 Nathan Rd, Yaumatei (Jordan MTR station), 434 rooms, singles HK$1000 to HK$1550, twins HK$1080 to HK$1630, suites HK$1950 to HK$3380 (☎ 2311-8222; fax 2311-4760)

Ramada, 73-75 Chatham Rd South, Tsimshatsui, 205 rooms, doubles & twins HK$980 to HK$1680, suites HK$2280 to HK$3480 (☎ 2311-1100; fax 2311-6000)

Regal Airport, Sa Po Rd, Kowloon (next to airport), 389 rooms, doubles & twins HK$1300 to HK$2050, suites HK$2800 to HK$7500 (☎ 2718-0333; fax 2718-4111)

Regal Kowloon, 71 Mody Rd, Tsimshatsui East, 592 rooms, singles HK$1000 to HK$2280, doubles & twins HK$1480 to HK$2280, suites HK$3500 to HK$9000 (☎ 2722-1818; fax 2369-6950)

Regent, Salisbury Rd, Tsimshatsui, 602 rooms, doubles & twins HK$2000 to HK$3100, suites HK$3600 to HK$20,000 (☎ 2721-1211; fax 2739-4546)

Renaissance, 8 Peking Rd, Tsimshatsui, 500 rooms, doubles & twins HK$1950 to HK$2800, suites HK$3200 to HK$13,000 (☎ 2375-1133; fax 2375-6611)

Royal Garden, 69 Mody Rd, Tsimshatsui East, 422 rooms, doubles & twins HK$1800 to HK$2550, suites HK$3300 to HK$7600 (☎ 2721-5215; fax 2369-9976)

Royal Pacific, China Hong Kong City, 33 Canton Rd, Tsimshatsui, 675 rooms, doubles & twins HK$980 to HK$2280, suites HK$1880 to HK$8000 (☎ 2736-1188; fax 2736-1212)

Sheraton, 20 Nathan Rd, Tsimshatsui, 790 rooms, doubles & twins HK$2100 to HK$3200, suites HK$3000 to HK$7500 (☎ 2369-1111; fax 2739-8707)

Stanford Hillview, 13-17 Observatory Rd, Tsimshatsui, 163 rooms, doubles & twins HK$990 to HK$1500, suites HK$2200 (☎ 2722-7822; fax 2723-3718)

Stanford, 118 Soy St, Mongkok, 194 rooms, doubles & twins HK$980 to HK$1380 (☎ 2781-1881; fax 2388-3733)

Windsor, 39-43A Kimberley Rd, Tsimshatsui, 166 rooms, doubles & twins HK$1050 to HK$1400, suites HK$2400 (☎ 2739-5665; fax 2311-5101)

HK Island – Hostel

Ma Wui Hall (☎ 2817-5715), on top of Mt Davis on Hong Kong Island, offers stunning views and is the most accessible of the YHA hostels. The drawback is that it's 'centrally located' in the relative sense only. From the Star Ferry Pier in Central it's still a good hour's journey but travellers say it's 'almost worth it'. Before embarking on the trek, ring up first to be sure a bed is available. To get there, take bus Nos 5B or 47 to the 5B terminus at Felix Villas on Victoria Rd. Walk back 100 metres and look for the YHA sign. You've then got a 20 to 30-minute climb up the hill! Don't confuse Mt Davis Path with Mt Davis Rd! There are 112 beds here and the nightly cost is HK$50. You need a YHA card (which can be purchased at the hostel) and it's open from 7 am to 11 pm.

HK Island – Guesthouses

Noble Hostel (☎ 2576-6148) is surely one of the best guesthouses in Hong Kong, but it is often full. Due to popular demand, the owner has expanded to five locations. There are two offices where you can check in – one at Flat C1, 7th floor, 37 Paterson St, Paterson Building, Causeway Bay. The other is nearby at Flat A3, 17th floor, 27 Paterson St. Singles with shared bath are HK$250; doubles with shared bath are HK$300; doubles with private bath are HK$350 to HK$380. If the guesthouse is full, the manager will try to help you find another place to stay.

The *Phoenix Apartments*, 70 Lee Garden Hill Rd, Causeway Bay (look for the New Phoenix Shopping Centre on the ground floor), has a number of elegant and reasonably priced guesthouses. The catch here is that most are short-time hotels, where rooms

THE SOUTH

are rented by the hour. One hotel proudly advertises 'Avoidance of Publicity & Reasonable Rates'. Nevertheless, rooms are available for overnighters, and as long as the sheets have been changed recently it's not a bad place to stay.

Nearby is *Emerald House* (☎ 2577-2368), 1st floor, 44 Leighton Rd, where clean doubles with private bath and round beds (no kidding) are HK$350. Enter the building from Leighton Lane just around the corner.

Leishun Court at 116 Leighton Rd, Causeway Bay, is another relatively cheap option. The building houses a number of low-priced guesthouses, mostly on the lower floors. *Fuji House* (☎ 2577-9406), 1st floor, is excellent at HK$250 for a room with private bath. On the same floor is the *Villa Lisboa Hotel* (☎ 2576-5421). On the 3rd floor is *Sam Yu Apartment*.

HK Island – Hotels

In terms of mid-range hotels, there's even less available on Hong Kong Island than in Kowloon. Figure on HK$450 at the minimum. Again, check with travel agents for discounts. Some places to check out include:

Emerald, 152 Connaught Rd West, Sheung Wan, 316 rooms, singles HK$500, doubles & twins HK$600 to HK$800, suites HK$850 to HK$1200 (☎ 2546-8111; fax 2559-0255)

Harbour, 116-122 Gloucester Rd, Wanchai, 200 rooms, singles HK$500 to HK$800, doubles & twins HK$680 to HK$950, suites HK$1400 (☎ 2507-2702)

YMCA – Harbour View International, 4 Harbour Rd, Wanchai, 320 rooms, doubles & twins HK$620 to HK$850, suites HK$950 to HK$1050 (☎ 2802-1111)

YWCA – Garden View International, 1 MacDonnell Rd, Central, 130 rooms, doubles & twins HK$693 to HK$814, suites HK$1180 (☎ 2877-3737)

Top-end hotels on Hong Kong Island include the following:

Century Hong Kong, 238 Jaffe Rd, Wanchai, 511 rooms, twins HK$1600 to HK$2100, suites HK$3100 to HK$8500 (☎ 2598-8888; fax 2598-8866)

Charterhouse, 209-219 Wanchai Rd, Wanchai, 237 rooms, doubles & twins HK$1450 to HK$2000, suites HK$1800 to HK$2700 (☎ 2833-5566; fax 2833-5888)

City Garden, 231 Electric Rd, North Point (Fortress Hill MTR station), 615 rooms, singles HK$1200 to HK$1700, doubles & twins HK$1330 to HK$1830, suites HK$2900 (☎ 2887-2888; fax 2887-1111)

Conrad, Pacific Place, 88 Queensway, Central (Admiralty MTR station), 513 rooms, doubles & twins HK$2250 to HK$3500, suites HK$4400 to HK$20,000 (☎ 2521-3838; fax 2521-3888)

Evergreen Plaza, 33 Hennessy Rd, Wanchai, 331 rooms, doubles & twins HK$1000 to HK$1500, suites HK$1900 to HK$4600 (☎ 2866-9111; fax 2861-3121)

Excelsior, 281 Gloucester Rd, Causeway Bay, 897 rooms, doubles & twins HK$1400 to HK$2100, suites HK$2800 to HK$6500 (☎ 2894-8888; fax 2895-6459)

Furama Kempinski, 1 Connaught Rd, Central, 516 rooms, doubles & twins HK$1700 to HK$2650, suites HK$2750 to HK$8000 (☎ 2525-5111; fax 2845-9339)

Grand Hyatt, 1 Harbour Rd, Wanchai, 572 rooms, doubles & twins HK$2650 to HK$3850, suites HK$5100 to HK$25,000 (☎ 2588-1234; fax 2802-0677)

Grand Plaza, 2 Kornhill Rd, Quarry Bay (Tai Koo MTR station), 248 rooms, doubles & twins HK$1100 to HK$1650, suites HK$1900 to HK$3200 (☎ 2886-0011; fax 2886-1738)

Harbour View International House, 4 Harbour Rd, Wanchai, 320 rooms, doubles & twins HK$850 to HK$2350 (☎ 2802-0111; fax 2802-9063)

Island Shangri-La, Pacific Place, 88 Queensway, Central (Admiralty MTR station), 565 rooms, doubles & twins HK$2500 to HK$3350, suites HK$5300 to HK$25,000 (☎ 2877-3838, 2521-8742)

JW Marriot, Pacific Place, 88 Queensway, Central (Admiralty MTR station), 604 rooms, doubles & twins HK$2350 to HK$3300, suites HK$5000 to HK$15,000 (☎ 2810-8366; fax 2845-0737)

Luk Kwok, 72 Gloucester Rd, Wanchai, 198 rooms, singles HK$1300 to HK$1500, twins HK$1400 to HK$1600, suites HK$2700 (☎ 2866-2166; fax 2866-2622)

Mandarin Oriental, 5 Connaught Rd, Central, 538 rooms, doubles & twins HK$2250, suites HK$5000 to HK$22,000 (☎ 2522-0111; fax 2810-6190)

New Cathay, 17 Tung Lo Wan Rd, Causeway Bay, 223 rooms, singles HK$630 to HK$1050, doubles & twins HK$850 to HK$1100, suites HK$1600 to HK$1800 (☎ 2577-8211; fax 2576-9365)

New Harbour, 41-49 Hennessy Rd, Wanchai, 173 rooms, doubles & twins HK$880 to HK$1300, suites HK$1500 to HK$1700 (☎ 2861-1166; fax 2865-6111)

New World Harbour View, 1 Harbour Rd, Wanchai, 862 rooms, singles HK$1880 to HK$3080, twins HK$2130 to HK$3330, suites HK$4180 to HK$14,000 (☎ 2802-8888; fax 2802-8833)

Newton, 218 Electric Rd, North Point (Fortress Hill MTR station), 362 rooms, singles HK$1000 to HK$1800, doubles & twins HK$1100 to HK$2000, suites HK$3300 (☎ 2807-2333; fax 2807-1221)

Park Lane, 310 Gloucester Rd, Causeway Bay, 815 rooms, doubles & twins HK$1800 to HK$3000, suites HK$4000 to HK$12,000 (☎ 2890-3355; fax 2576-7853)

Regal Hongkong, 88 Yee Wo St, Causeway Bay, 425 rooms, doubles & twins HK$1900 to HK$2650, suites HK$3800 to HK$15,000 (☎ 2890-6633; fax 2881-0777)

Richmond, 1A Wang Tak St, Happy Valley, 111 rooms, doubles & twins HK$1800 to HK$2200, suites HK$3900 to HK$5000 (☎ 2574-9922)

Ritz-Carlton, 3 Connaught Rd, Central, 216 rooms, doubles & twins HK$2250 to HK$3350, suites HK$4500 to HK$15,000 (☎ 2877-6666; fax 2877-6778)

South China, 67-75 Java Rd, North Point, 204 rooms, doubles & twins HK$780 to HK$1450 (☎ 2503-1168; fax 2512-8698)

South Pacific, 23 Morrison Hill Rd, Wanchai, 293 rooms, singles HK$1200 to HK$1800, doubles & twins HK$1350 to HK$1800, suites HK$3300 to HK$4800 (☎ 2572-3838; fax 2893-7773)

Victoria, Shun Tak Centre, 200 Connaught Rd West, Sheung Wan, 535 rooms, doubles & twins HK$1900 to HK$2650, suites HK$3200 to HK$10,000 (☎ 2540-7228; fax 2858-3398)

Wesley, 22 Hennessy Rd, Wanchai, 251 rooms, doubles & twins HK$1100 to HK$1800 (☎ 2866-6688; fax 2866-6633)

Wharney, 57-33 Lockhart Rd, Wanchai, 335 rooms, doubles & twins HK$1450 to HK$1750, suites HK$2800 to HK$3000 (☎ 2861-1000; fax 2865-6023)

New Territories

The Hong Kong Youth Hostel Association (HKYHA) operates several hostels in the New Territories. All are in fairly remote locations and it isn't practical to stay in these places and commute to the city. The only reason for staying would be to enjoy the countryside and do a bit of exploring and hiking. You'll need a YHA card – these can be bought at the hostels (bring a photo). You

are also strongly advised to ring up first to make sure that a bed is available.

The following four places are all YHA-operated:

Bradbury Lodge (☎ 2662-5123), Ting Kok Rd, Tai Mei Tuk, Tai Po, is the most easily reached hostel in the New Territories. There are 80 beds costing HK$35, but no camp sites. Take the KCR to Tai Po Market station, then bus No 75K to Tai Mei Tuk (last stop). Walk south (the sea will be to your right) for four minutes to reach the hostel.

Sze Lok Yuen (☎ 2488-8188) is on Tai Mo Shan Rd. There are 92 beds costing HK$25 each, and 200 campsites. Take the No 51 bus (Tsuen Wan Ferry Pier-Kam Tin) at Tsuen Wan MTR station and alight at Tai Mo Shan Rd. Follow Tai Mo Shan Rd for about 45 minutes, and after passing the car park turn on to a small concrete path on the right-hand side, which leads directly to the hostel. This is a good place from which to climb Tai Mo Shan, Hong Kong's highest peak. Because of the high elevation, it can get amazingly cold at night, so be prepared.

Pak Sha O Hostel (☎ 2328-2327), Hoi Ha Rd, Sai Kung East Peninsula, has 112 beds priced at HK$25. There are campsites for 150 tents. Take bus No 92 from the Choi Hung Estate bus terminal and get off at the Sai Kung terminal. From Sai Kung, take bus No 94 (last one is at 7 pm) towards Wong Shek Pier, but get off at Ko Tong village. From there, walk 100 metres along Pak Tam Rd to find Hoi Ha Rd on the left. The walk along Hoi Ha Rd to the hostel is signposted and takes about 40 minutes.

Also on the Sai Kung Peninsula is *Bradbury Hall* (☎ 2328-2458), in Chek Keng. There are 100 beds costing HK$25, plus 100 campsites. From Choi Hung Estate bus terminal, take bus No 92 to the Sai Kung terminal. From Sai Kung, take bus No 94 (last one is at 7 pm) to Yellow Stone Pier, but get off at Pak Tam Au. There's a footpath at the side of the road leading to Chek Keng village (a 45-minute walk). The hostel is right on the harbour just facing the Chek Keng Ferry Pier. An alternative route is to take the ferry from Ma Liu Shui (adjacent to

THE SOUTH

the Chinese University railway station) to Chek Keng Ferry Pier.

Cheung Chau Island
There is a solid line-up of booths offering flats for rent opposite the ferry pier. Small flats for two persons begin at HK$300 but easily double on weekends and holidays.

Cheung Chau has one upmarket place to stay, the *Warwick Hotel* (☎ 2981-0081) with 70 rooms. Doubles cost HK$780 on a weekday and HK$1180 on weekends.

Lamma Island
There are several places to stay in Yung Shue Wan. Right by the Yung Shue Wan Ferry Pier is the *Man Lai Wah Hotel* (☎ 2982-0220), where doubles cost HK$350 on weekdays, rising to HK$700 on weekends. *Lamma Vacation House* (☎ 2982-0427) is at 29 Main St and offers coffin-sized rooms for HK$150 or cushier flats for HK$300 – prices double on weekends.

On nearby Hung Shing Ye beach is *Concerto Inn* (☎ 2982-1668; fax 2836-3311), an upmarket place with rooms for HK$680 to HK$880.

Lantau Island
As you exit the ferry in Silvermine Bay, turn right and head towards the beach. Here you'll find several hotels with a sea view. The line-up of places to stay includes *Sea House* (☎ 2984-7757), which has rather dumpy-looking rooms starting from HK$300 on weekdays, HK$500 on weekends. One of the best places around is the *Mui Wo Inn* (☎ 2984-1916) with doubles from HK$300 to HK$400 on weekdays, and HK$550 to HK$700 on weekends. Top of the line is the *Silvermine Beach Hotel* (☎ 2984-8295), which has doubles ranging from HK$820 to HK$1200.

There are two places to stay in Ngong Ping. The *Po Lin Monastery* offers dormitory beds for HK$200 (price includes vegetarian meals), but it's not a friendly place. A better deal is the nearby *S G Davis Youth Hostel* (☎ 2985-5610; 48 beds), which costs HK$25, but a YHA card is required.

The youth hostel also has a campsite for 20 tents.

PLACES TO EAT
Hong Kong offers incredible variety when it comes to food. You should at least once try dim sum, a uniquely Cantonese dish served only for breakfast or lunch but never dinner. Dim sum delicacies are normally steamed in a small bamboo basket. Typically, each basket contains four identical pieces, so four people would be an ideal number for a dim sum meal. You pay by the number of baskets you order. The baskets are stacked up on pushcarts and rolled around the dining room. You choose whatever you like from the carts, so no menu is needed.

In Cantonese restaurants tea is often served free of charge, or at most you'll pay HK$1 for a big pot which can be refilled indefinitely. On the other hand, coffee is seldom available except in Western restaurants or coffee shops and is never free.

Kowloon
There are a lot of restaurants concentrated in the tourist area of Tsimshatsui.

Breakfast If your hotel doesn't serve breakfast, you may find it difficult to eat before 9 am, when most of the restaurants open. The window of the *Wing Wah Restaurant* (☎ 2721-2947) is always filled with great-looking cakes and pastries. It's at 21A Lock Rd near Swindon's Bookstore and the Hyatt Regency. Either take it away or sit down with some coffee. Prices are very reasonable. Inexpensive Chinese food is also served and – a rare treat for a Hong Kong budget Chinese cafe – there is an English menu.

A very similar cafe with cakes, coffee and other delicacies is the nearby *Kam Fat Restaurant* at 11 Ashley Rd. Prices here are slightly higher than Wing Wah but the atmosphere is also better.

Deep in the bowels of *every* MTR station you can find *Maxim's Cake Shops*. The cakes and pastries look irresistible, but don't sink your teeth into the creamy delights until you're back on the street as it is prohibited

Top: Souvenirs can be found on Cat Street in Hong Kong Central.
Bottom Left: Jardine House in Central, when the colony was still flying the Union Jack
Bottom Right: The Bank of China, the second-tallest skyscraper in Hong Kong

An old woman makes her way through the Largo do Senado, the square in the centre of Macau.

to eat or drink anything in the MTR stations or on the trains – HK$1000 fine if you do.

There is a chain of bakeries around Hong Kong with the name *St Honore Cake Shop*, but there's no English sign on their stores although you'll soon recognise their ideogram. You can find one at 12 Cameron Rd and 8 Canton Rd in Tsimshatsui.

If you're up early before the aforementioned places open, 7-Eleven operates 24 hours and does good coffee, packaged breads and microwave cuisine.

American *Planet Hollywood* (☎ 2377-7888), 3 Canton Rd, claims to be 'the galaxy's ultimate dining experience'. Never mind the food – this place wins awards for its knockout decor. The T-shirts make a good souvenir.

Dan Ryan's Chicago Grill (☎ 2735-6111), Shop 200, Ocean Terminal, Harbour City, Canton Rd, Tsimshatsui, is a trendy spot with prices to match.

Chinese – Dim Sum This is normally served from around 11 am to 3 pm, but a few places have it available for breakfast. The following places are chosen for reasonable prices:

Canton Court, Guangdong Hotel, 18 Prat Ave, Tsimshatsui, dim sum served from 7 am to 4 pm (☎ 2739-3311)

Eastern Palace, 3rd floor, Omni The Hongkong Hotel, Shopping Arcade, Harbour City, Canton Rd, Tsimshatsui, dim sum served from 11.30 am to 3 pm (☎ 2730-6011)

Harbour View Seafood, 3rd floor, Tsimshatsui Centre, 66 Mody Rd, Tsimshatsui East, dim sum served from 11 am to 5 pm, restaurant closes at midnight (☎ 2722-5888)

New Home, 19-20 Hanoi Rd, Tsimshatsui, dim sum served from 7 am to 4.30 pm (☎ 2366-5876)

North China Peking Seafood, 2nd floor, Polly Commercial Building, 21-23 Prat Ave, Tsimshatsui, dim sum served from 11 am to 3 pm (☎ 2311-6689)

Orchard Court, 1st & 2nd floors, Ma's Mansion, 37 Hankow Rd, Tsimshatsui, dim sum served from 11 am to 5 pm (☎ 2317-5111)

Tai Woo, 14-16 Hillwood Rd, Yaumatei, dim sum served from 11 am to 4.30 pm (☎ 2369-9773)

Chinese – Street Stalls The cheapest place to enjoy authentic Chinese cuisine is the *Temple St Night Market* in Yaumatei. It starts at about 8 pm and begins to fade at 11 pm. There are also plenty of mainstream indoor restaurants with variable prices.

Fast Food *Oliver's* is on the ground floor of Hong Kong Pacific Centre, 28 Hankow Rd, and in the basement at 100 Nathan Rd. It's a great place for breakfast – inexpensive

Dim sum seller. With a few friends, dim sum is the best way to eat lunch in Hong Kong.

bacon, eggs and toast. The sandwiches are equally excellent, though it gets crowded at lunch time.

McDonald's occupies key strategic locations in Tsimshatsui. Late-night restaurants are amazingly scarce in Hong Kong, so it's useful to know that two McDonald's in Tsimshatsui operate 24 hours a day: at 21A Granville Rd, and 12 Peking Rd. There is also a McDonald's at 2 Cameron Rd, and another in Star House just opposite the Star Ferry Pier. McDonald's is one of the cheapest places to eat in Hong Kong.

Domino's Pizza (☎ 2765-0683), Yue Sun Mansion, Hunghom, does not have a restaurant where you can sit down to eat. Rather, pizzas are delivered to your door within 30 minutes of phoning in your order.

Other fast food outlets in Kowloon include:

Café de Coral, mezzanine floor, Albion Plaza, 2-6 Granville Rd, Tsimshatsui; 16 Carnarvon Rd, Tsimshatsui
Fairwood Fast Food, 6 Ashley Rd, Tsimshatsui; Basement Two, Silvercord Shopping Centre, Haiphong & Canton Rds
Hardee's, arcade of Regent Hotel, south of Salisbury Rd at the very southern tip of Tsimshatsui
Jack in the Box, Shop G60-83, Tsimshatsui Centre, 66 Mody Rd, Tsimshatsui East
Ka Ka Lok Fast Food Shop, 55A Carnarvon Rd, Tsimshatsui; 16A Ashley Rd, but enter from Ichang St, Tsimshatsui
KFC, 2 Cameron Rd, Tsimshatsui; 241 Nathan Rd, Yaumatei
Pizza Hut, Lower Basement, Silvercord Shopping Centre, Haiphong & Canton Rds, Tsimshatsui; Shop 008, Ocean Terminal, Harbour City, Canton Rd, Tsimshatsui
Spaghetti House, 57 Peking Rd; 38 Haiphong Rd, Tsimshatsui
Wendy's, Basement, Albion Plaza, 2-6 Granville Rd, just off Nathan Rd, Tsimshatsui

Indian The greatest concentration of cheap Indian restaurants is in Chungking Mansions on Nathan Rd. Despite the grotty appearance of the entrance to the Mansions, many of the restaurants are surprisingly plush inside. A meal of curried chicken and rice, or curry with chapattis and dhal, will cost around HK$30 per person.

Start your search for Indian food on the ground floor of the arcade. The bottom of the market belongs to *Kashmir Fast Food* and *Lahore Fast Food*. These open early, so you can have curry, chapattis and heartburn for breakfast. Neither of these two offers any kind of cheery atmosphere, so it's no place to linger.

Up on the mezzanine floor is *Nepal Fast Food* – connoisseurs of budget Indian fast food say this is one of the best.

Upstairs in Chungking Mansions are many other places with better food and a more pleasant atmosphere. Prices are still low, with set meals from HK$35 or so. The following are worth a try:

Delhi Club, 3rd floor, the best in C Block (☎ 2368-1682)
Karachi Mess, halal food, looks like you've stepped right into Pakistan (☎ 2368-1678)
Kashmir Club, 3rd floor, A Block, highly rated and even offers free home delivery (☎ 2311-6308)
Royal Club Mess, 5th floor, D Block, Indian and vegetarian food (☎ 2369-7680)
Taj Mahal Club Mess, 3rd floor, B Block, excellent (☎ 2722-5454)

Nearby is the excellent Koh-I-Noor (☎ 2368-3065) at 3-4 Peninsula Mansion, 16C Mody Rd.

Indonesian The *Java Rijsttafel* (☎ 2367-1230), Han Hing Mansion, 38 Hankow Rd, Tsimshatsui, is a good place to enjoy a 'rijsttafel', literally meaning a rice table. This place packs out with Dutch expats.

There is also the *Indonesian Restaurant* (☎ 2367-3287) at 66 Granville Rd, Tsimshatsui.

Italian A great Italian restaurant is *Valentino* (☎ 2721-6449) at 16 Hanoi Rd. Also highly rated is *La Taverna* (☎ 2376-1945), Astoria Building, 36-38 Ashley Rd, Tsimshatsui.

The Pizzeria (☎ 2369-8698 ext 3322) is an Italian eatery on the 2nd floor of the Kowloon Hotel at 19-21 Nathan Rd, Tsimshatsui.

Korean There are several excellent and easily accessible Korean restaurants. A good one is *Seoul House* (☎ 2314-3174), 35 Hill-wood Rd, Yaumatei.

Another place is *Manna*, a chain restaurant with outlets in Tsimshatsui at 83B Nathan Rd (☎ 2721-2159); Lyton Building, 32B Mody Rd (☎ 2367-4278); and 6A Humphrey's Ave (☎ 2368-2485).

Two other centrally located Korean restaurants are *Arirang* (☎ 2956-3288), Shop 210, 2nd floor, The Gateway, Canton Rd, Tsimshatsui, and *Korea House* (☎ 2367-5674), Empire Centre, 68 Mody Rd, Tsimshatsui East.

Kosher The *Beverly Hills Deli* (☎ 2369-8695), Level 2, Shop 55, New World Centre, Salisbury Rd, is where you'll find gefilte fish and lox. It's good, but *not* cheap.

Malaysian The *Singapore Restaurant* (☎ 2376-1282), 23 Ashley Rd, Tsimshatsui, does Malaysian-style cooking. It's coffee-shop style, but forget the decor because the food is excellent and cheap (by Hong Kong standards). It's open from 11 am until midnight.

Mexican *Someplace Else* (☎ 2369-1111 ext 5), Sheraton Hotel, 20 Nathan Rd, is part bar and part Mexican restaurant. The Tex-Mex luncheons are worth trying, but in the evening it becomes very busy. Operating hours are from 11 am until 1 am.

Thai Thai food is devastatingly hot but excellent. A reasonably priced and good Thai restaurant is *Royal Pattaya* (☎ 2366-9919), 9 Minden Ave, Tsimshatsui. Also good is *Sawadee* (☎ 2376-3299), 6 Ichang St, Tsimshatsui.

Vegetarian *Bodhi* (☎ 2739-2222), Ground floor, 56 Cameron Rd, Tsimshatsui, is one of Hong Kong's biggest vegetarian restaurants with branches at 36 Jordan Rd, Yaumatei, and 1st floor, 32-34 Lock Rd (also can enter at 81 Nathan Rd), Tsimshatsui. Dim sum is dished out from 11 am to 5 pm.

Also excellent is *Pak Bo Vegetarian Kitchen* (☎ 2366-2732), 106 Austin Rd, Tsimshatsui.

Another to try is *Fat Siu Lam* (☎ 2388-1308), 2-3 Cheong Lok St, Yaumatei

Self-Catering If you're looking for the best in cheese, bread and other imported delicacies, check out the delicatessen at *Oliver's* on the ground floor of Ocean Centre on Canton Rd. Another branch is on the ground floor of the Tung Ying Building, Granville Rd (at Nathan Rd).

Numerous supermarkets are scattered about. A few in Tsimshatsui and Yaumatei to look for include:

Park'n Shop, south-west corner of Peking Rd & Kowloon Park Drive; 2nd basement, Silvercord Shopping Centre, 30 Canton Rd

Wellcome, inside the Dairy Farm Creamery (ice-cream parlour), 74-78 Nathan Rd; north-west corner of Granville and Carnarvon Rds

Yue Hwa Chinese Products, Basement, 301 Nathan Rd, Yaumatei (north-west corner of Nathan and Jordan Rds), both Western products and Chinese exotica (tea bricks and flattened chickens)

Hong Kong Central

The place to go for reasonably priced eats and late-night revelry is the neighbourhood known as Lan Kwai Fong. However, it's such a conglomeration of pubs and all-night parties that it's covered in the Entertainment section.

Breakfast To save time and money, there are food windows adjacent to the Star Ferry that open shortly after 6 am. It's standard commuter breakfasts consisting of bread, rolls and coffee with no place to sit except on the ferry itself. As you face the ferry entrance, off to the right is a *Maxim's* fast food outlet, also with no seats.

If you'd prefer something better, *Jim's Eurodiner* (☎ 2868-6886), Paks Building, 5-11 Stanley St, does outstanding morning meals between 8 and 10.30 am for around HK$20 to HK$30. From noon until 10 pm it's standard Western fare.

Of course, all the big hotels serve breakfast, often a sumptuous buffet.

Chinese – Dim Sum All of the following places are in the middle to lower price range:

Luk Yu Tea House (☎ 2523-5464), 26 Stanley St, Central, dim sum served from 7 am to 6 pm
Tai Woo (☎ 2524-5618), 15-19 Wellington St, Central, dim sum served from 10 am to 5 pm
Zen Chinese Cuisine (☎ 2845-4555), Lower ground 1, The Mall, Pacific Place, Phase I, 88 Queensway, Central, dim sum served from 11.30 am to 3 pm

Fast Food Domino's Pizza (☎ 2521-1300), 9 Glenealy, Central, has no restaurant facilities but delivers to any address within a two-km radius.

Famous fast food chains have the following outlets in Central:

Café de Coral, 10 Stanley St; 18 Jubilee St; 88 Queen's Rd
Fairwood, Ananda Tower, 57-59 Connaught Rd
Hardee's, Grand Building, 15 Des Voeux Rd; Regent Centre
KFC, 6 D'Aguilar St; Pacific Place, 88 Queensway, Central
Maxim's, Swire House, 9 Connaught Rd
McDonald's, 38-44 D'Aguilar St; Basement, Yu To Sang Building, 37 Queen's Rd; Sanwa Building, 30-32 Connaught Rd; Shop 124, Level 1, The Mall, Pacific Place, 88 Queensway, Central
Pizza Hut, B38, Basement 1, Edinburgh Tower, The Landmark, 11 Queen's Rd
Spaghetti House, Lower ground floor, 10 Stanley St

French Wine, cheese, the best French bread and bouillabaisse can be found at Papillon (☎ 2526-5965), 8-13 Wo On Lane. This narrow lane intersects with D'Aguilar St (around No 17) and runs parallel to Wellington St.

Indian The ever-popular Ashoka (☎ 2524-9623) is at 57 Wyndham St. Just next door in the basement at 57 Wyndham St is the excellent Village Indian Restaurant (☎ 2525-7410).

Greenlands (☎ 2522-6098), 64 Wellington St, is another superb Indian restaurant offering all-you-can-eat buffets.

Club Sri Lanka (☎ 2526-6559) in the basement of 17 Hollywood Rd (almost at the Wyndham St end) has great Sri Lankan curries. Their fixed-price all-you-can-eat deal is a bargain compared with most Hong Kong eateries.

Kosher The Shalom Grill (☎ 2851-6300), 2nd floor, Fortune House, 61 Connaught Rd, serves up kosher and Moroccan cuisine. If you're in the mood for a Jerusalem felafel or a Casablanca couscous, this is the place.

Malaysian If you like Malaysian food, you should love Malaya (☎ 2525-1675), 15B Wellington St, Central. It has Western food too, but it's considerably more expensive.

Self-Catering A health-food store with great bread and sandwiches is Eden's Natural Synergy (☎ 2408-2616), Mappin House, Central.

For imported delicacies, check out Oliver's Super Sandwiches with three locations: Shop 104, Exchange Square II, 8 Connaught Place; Shop 201-205, Prince's Building, 10 Chater Rd (at Ice House St); Shop 8, Lower ground floor, The Mall, Pacific Place, 88 Queensway, Central.

The largest stock of imported foods is found at the Seibu Department Store, Lower ground 1, Pacific Place, 88 Queensway, Central (Admiralty MTR station). Besides the imported cheeses, breads and chocolates, tucked into one corner is the Pacific Wine Cellar. This is the place to get wine, and there are frequent sales on wine by the case. It's open from 11 am until 8 pm.

Of special interest to chocolate addicts is See's Candies with two stores in Central: B66 Gloucester Tower, The Landmark, 11 Pedder St; and Shop 245, Pacific Place, Phase II, 88 Queensway, Central (Admiralty MTR station).

ENTERTAINMENT
Kowloon
Rick's Cafe (☎ 2367-2939), Basement, 4 Hart Ave, is popular with the backpacker set.

Jouster II (☎ 2723-0022), Shops A&B, Hart Ave Court, 19-23 Hart Ave, Tsimshatsui, is a fun multi-storey place with wild decor. Normal hours are noon to 3 am, except on Sunday, when it's open from 6 pm to 2 am. Happy hour is anytime before 9 pm.

Ned Kelly's Last Stand (☎ 2376-0562), 11A Ashley Rd, open 11 am to 2 am, became famous as a real Australian pub complete with meat pies. Now it is known mainly for its Dixieland jazz and Aussie folk music bands.

Amoeba Bar (☎ 2376-0389), 22 Ashley Rd, Tsimshatsui, is a local new-wave place with live music from around 9 pm, and it doesn't close until about 6 am.

The *Kangaroo Pub* (☎ 2312-0083), 1st & 2nd floors, 35 Haiphong Rd, Tsimshatsui, is an Aussie pub in the true tradition. This place does a good Sunday brunch.

Mad Dog's Pub (☎ 2301-2222), Basement, 32 Nathan Rd, is a popular Aussie-style pub. From Monday to Thursday it's open from 7 am until 2 am, but from Friday to Sunday it's 24-hour service.

HK Island – Lan Kwai Fong

Running off D'Aguilar St in Central is a narrow, L-shaped alley closed to cars. This is Lan Kwai Fong, and along with neighbouring streets and alleys it is Hong Kong's No 1 eating, drinking, dancing and partying venue. Prices range from economical to outrageous.

Club 64 (☎ 2523-2801), 12-14 Wing Wah Lane, is an old favourite, though it's not as good as in the past because the authorities no longer permit customers to sit outdoors.

As you face the entrance to Club 64, off to your left are some stairs (outside the building, not inside). Follow the stairs up to a terrace to find *Le Jardin Club* (☎ 2526-2717), 10 Wing Wah Lane. This is an excellent place to drink, relax and socialise.

Facing Club 64 again, look to your right to find *Bon Appetit* (☎ 2525-3553), a Vietnamese restaurant serving up reasonably priced meals.

Top Dog (☎ 2868-9195/6), 1 Lan Kwai Fong, produces every kind of hot dog imaginable. Opening hours are late and the management's policy is to stay open 'until nobody is left in the street'.

As the name implies, late-night hours are kept at *Midnight Express* (☎ 2525-5010, 2523-4041), 3 Lan Kwai Fong. This place has a combination menu of Greek, Indian and Italian food (check out the kebabs), with deliveries available from Monday to Saturday. Opening hours are 11.30 am to 3 am the next day, except on Sunday, when it opens at 6 pm.

While *glasnost* is already yesterday's buzzword, you can still find it at *Yelt's Inn* (☎ 2524-7796), 42 D'Aguilar St. This place boasts Russian vodka, a bubbly party atmosphere and extremely loud music.

If it's fine Lebanese food, beer and rock music you crave, what better place to find it than in *Beirut* (☎ 2804-6611)? It's at 27 D'Aguilar St.

If you prefer Europe to the Middle East, visit *Berlin* (☎ 2530-3093), 19 Lan Kwai Fong. This place features loud disco music with members of the audience invited to sing along – think of it as disco karaoke.

Post 97 (☎ 2810-9333), 9 Lan Kwai Fong, is a very comfortable eating and drinking spot. During the daytime it's more of a coffee shop, and you can sit for hours to take advantage of the excellent rack of Western magazines and newspapers. It can pack out at night, and the lights are dimmed to discourage reading at that time.

Next door in the same building and under the same management is *1997* (☎ 2810-9333), known for really fine Mediterranean food. Prices are mid-range.

Graffiti (☎ 2521-2202), 17 Lan Kwai Fong, is a very posh and trendy restaurant and bar, but high drink prices don't seem to have hurt business.

It's raging revelry at *Acropolis* (☎ 2877-3668), on the ground floor of Corner II Tower, 21 D'Aguilar St. Shoulder to shoulder crowds, loud music and reasonably cheap drinks contribute to the party atmosphere.

The California Entertainment Building is at the corner of Lan Kwai Fong and D'Aguilar St. There are numerous places to eat here at varying price levels, but it tends to be upmarket. Note that the building has two blocks with two separate entrances, so if you don't find a place mentioned in this book be sure to check out the other block.

Top-flight food at high prices can be found at Koh-I-Noor (☎ 2877-9706), an Indian restaurant. Il Mercato (☎ 2868-3068) steals the show for Italian food. Both are in the California Entertainment Building. Prices are mid-range.

The California (☎ 2521-1345), also in the California Entertainment Building, is perhaps the most expensive bar mentioned in this book. Open from noon to 1 am, it's a restaurant by day, but there's disco dancing and a cover charge Wednesday to Sunday nights from 5 pm onwards.

The American Pie (☎ 2521-3381) is the locale for desserts in Hong Kong – not only pies, but all sorts of killer desserts like cakes, tarts, puddings and everything else containing sinful amounts of sugar, not to mention superb coffee and tea. If you're on a diet, don't even go near the place. It's an upmarket place charging upmarket prices. You'll find it on the 4th floor of the California Entertainment Building.

The Jazz Club (☎ 2845-8477), 2nd floor, California Entertainment Building, has a great atmosphere. Bands playing blues and reggae are a feature here, as well as friendly management and customers. Beer is reasonable at HK$40 a pint, but a cover charge is tacked on for special performances, sometimes up to HK$250 (half-price for members).

DD II (☎ 2524-8809) is short for 'disco disco'. This trendy place is in the California Entertainment Building. It's open from 9.30 pm until 3.30 am.

The Cactus Club (☎ 2525-6732), 13 Lan Kwai Fong, does passable Mexican food. It seems like more of a pub than a restaurant, with top-grade beer and tequila imported from Mexico. Their Mescal, brewed from the peyote cactus, is pretty strong stuff – tastes like it still has the needles in it.

Supatra's (☎ 2522-5073) at 46 D'Aguilar St is Lan Kwai Fong's top venue for Thai food.

Al's Diner (☎ 2869-1869), 27-37 D'Aguilar St, is a Hong Kong institution. The place

looks like it was lifted lock, stock, burgers and French fries from a New York diner of the 1950s. The food is fine but none of it comes cheaply.

Schnurrbart (☎ 2523-4700) at 29 D'Aguilar St is a Bavarian-style pub. There are a couple of other German pubs on either side.

Oscar's (☎ 2804-6561), 2 Lan Kwai Fong, is a very posh cafe and bar combination. Specialities include pizza, pasta and sandwiches on pita bread. Food is available from noon until 11 pm and the place stays open until 2 am. Bring lots of money.

HK Island – Central

Just outside of Lan Kwai Fong is Fringe Club (☎ 2521-7251), 2 Lower Albert Rd. It's an excellent pub known for cheap beer and an avant-garde atmosphere. Live music is provided nightly by various local folk and rock musicians.

The Mad Dogs Pub (☎ 2525-2383), 33 Wyndham St, Central, is just off the trendy Lan Kwai Fong. It's a big two-floor Australian-style pub serving pub grub and drinks.

The legendary Hard Rock Cafe (☎ 2377-8168), 11 Chater Rd, Central, has its happy hour from 3 to 7 pm.

LA Cafe (☎ 2526-6863), Ground floor, Shop 2, Lippo Centre, 89 Queensway (near the Admiralty MTR station), has a large loyal following of late-night rowdies. The mostly Mexican luncheons are not to be discounted either – great guacamole, burritos and other Tex-Mex delights, but it isn't cheap.

La Bodega (☎ 2877-5472), 31 Wyndham St, is an unusual place. It's a comfortable bar with a Mediterranean flavour. Although moderately expensive, drinks are half-price on Friday until somebody goes to the toilet! A Spanish-style band (with Filipino musicians) provides the entertainment.

The Bull & Bear (☎ 2525-7436), Ground floor, Hutchison House, 10 Harcourt Rd, Central, is a British-style pub and gets pretty lively in the evening. It is open from 8 am to 10.30 am, and again from 11 am to midnight.

Portico (☎ 2523-8893), Lower ground floor, Citibank Plaza, 3 Garden Rd, has fine live music every Saturday night from around 10 pm.

HK Island – Wanchai

Most of the action is concentrated at the intersection of Luard and Jaffe Rds.

Joe Bananas (☎ 2529-1811), 23 Luard Rd, has become a trendy disco nightspot and has no admission charge, but you may have to queue to get in. Happy hour is from 11 am until 9 pm (except Sunday) and the place stays open until around 5 am.

Neptune Disco (☎ 2528-3808), Basement, 54-62 Lockhard Rd, is pure disco and heavy metal from 4 pm until 5 am. To say this place is popular is an understatement. To survive the night, spend the previous week doing aerobic exercises and bring your dancing shoes and earplugs.

To accommodate the spillover crowd, there is now *Neptune Disco II* (☎ 2865-2238), 98-108 Jaffe Rd. This place has live bands and a weekend cover charge of HK$80.

New Makati (☎ 2866-3928) at 100 Lockhart Rd is a Filipino fun-rage party place which has also become an instant hit with Westerners.

West World (☎ 2824-0523), also known as *The Manhattan*, is known for its fine late-night dancing music. Admission is free except on Friday and Saturday, when it costs HK$140 (one drink included). It's on the 4th floor of the New World Harbour View Hotel – ask at the front desk where to find the lift.

The Big Apple Pub & Disco (☎ 2529-3461), 20 Luard Rd, is a thumping disco. There is a weekend cover charge of HK$60 for men, HK$40 for women. From Monday to Friday it operates from noon until 5 am, and on weekends and holidays it's open from 2 pm until 6 am.

JJ's (☎ 2588-1234 ext 7323), Grand Hyatt Hotel, 1 Harbour Rd, Wanchai, is known for its rhythm & blues bands. There is a cover charge after 9 pm.

Old Hat (☎ 2861-2300), 1st floor, 20 Luard Rd, keeps some of the latest hours around – it's open 24 hours on Friday and Saturday nights, so you can stay up all

evening and have breakfast there. Also in the same building is *La Bamba* (☎ 2866-8706), which has live bands and good food.

Crossroads (☎ 2527-2347), 42 Lockhart Rd, Wanchai, is a loud disco that attracts a young crowd. Dancing is from 9 pm to 4 am. There is a cover charge, but one drink is included.

At 54 Jaffe Rd just west of Fenwick Rd is *The Wanch* (☎ 2861-1621). It stands in sharp contrast to the more usual Wanchai scene of hard rock and disco. This is a very pleasant little folk-music pub with beer and wine at low prices, but it can get crowded.

THINGS TO BUY

It's very easy in Hong Kong to decide suddenly that you need all sorts of consumer goods you don't really need at all. Try not to let the flashy stores tempt you into an uncontrollable buying binge.

Hong Kong resembles one gigantic shopping mall, but a quick look at price tags should convince you that the city is not quite the bargain it's cracked up to be. Imported goods like Japanese-made cameras and electronic gadgets can be bought for roughly the same price in many Western countries. However, what makes Hong Kong shine is the variety – if you can't find it in Hong Kong, then you don't need it.

The HKTA advises tourists to shop where they see the HKTA red logo on display. This means that the shop is an 'ordinary member' of the HKTA. From our experience, many of the 'ordinary members' charge high prices for rude service, while many nonmembers are quite all right.

The worst neighbourhood for shopping happens to be the place where most tourists shop. Tsimshatsui, the tourist ghetto of Kowloon, is the most likely place to be cheated. Notice that none of the cameras or other big ticket items have price tags. This is *not* common practice elsewhere in Hong Kong. If you go out to the Chinese neighbourhoods where the locals shop, you'll find price tags on everything.

Clothing is the best buy in Hong Kong. All the cheap stuff comes from China and most is decent quality, but check zippers and stitching carefully – there is some real junk around. You'll find the cheapest buys at the street markets at Tong Choi St in Mongkok and Apliu St in Shamshuipo. Another good place for cut-rate clothes is the mezzanine floor of Chungking Mansions (not the ground floor). Better quality stuff is found in Tsimshatsui on the eastern end of Granville Rd. Two Chinese chain stores with Italian names, Giordano's and Bossini, offer quality clothing at reasonable prices.

Yue Hwa Chinese Products at 301 Nathan Rd, Yaumatei (corner of Nathan and Jordan Rds) is a good place to pick up everyday consumer goods. It's also one of the best places to get eyeglasses made.

The Golden Shopping Centre, Basement, 146-152 Fuk Wah St, Shamshuipo, has the cheapest collection of desktop computers – be sure to check out the adjacent annex building. Another good place to explore is Mongkok Computer Centre at Nelson and Fa Yuen Sts in Mongkok. For laptop computers, the best shopping centre in Kowloon is Star Computer City in Ocean Terminal, Tsimshatsui. On Hong Kong Island, the main computer centre is Windsor House, Great George St, Causeway Bay. A smaller but excellent collection of computer shops is at Jos Mart on Hennessy Rd, Wanchai.

If it's a camera you need, don't even waste your time on Nathan Rd in Tsimshatsui. Photo Scientific (☎ 2522-1903), 6 Stanley St, Central, is the favourite of Hong Kong's resident professional photographers. But if you're in a hurry and want to buy in Tsimshatsui, the best seems to be Kimberley Camera Company (☎ 2721-2308), Champagne Court, 16 Kimberley Rd.

Apliu St in Shamshuipo has the best collection of electronics shops selling personal stereos, CD players and the like.

HMV (☎ 2302-0122) at 12 Peking Rd in Tsimshatsui has the largest collection of CDs in Hong Kong, and prices are very reasonable. There is another branch on the 10th floor of Windsor House, Great George St, Causeway Bay. KPS is also a good chain store for discounted CDs and tapes with branches around the city – most convenient is the shop in the basement of the Silvercord Shopping Centre on Canton Rd, Tsimshatsui. Tower Records (☎ 2506-0811), 7th floor, Shop 701, Times Square, Matheson St, Causeway Bay, also has a good CD collection.

Flying Ball Bicycle Shop (☎ 2381-5919), 201 Tung Choi St (near Prince Edward MTR station), Mongkok, is the best bike shop in Asia.

Hong Kong is a good place to pick up a decent backpack, sleeping bag, tent and other gear for hiking, camping and travelling. Mongkok is by far the best neighbourhood to look for this stuff though there are a couple of odd places in nearby Yaumatei. Some places worth checking out include:

Grade VI Alpine Equipment, 115 Woosung St, Yaumatei (☎ 2782-0202)
Mountaineer Supermarket, 395 Portland St, Mongkok (☎ 2397-0585)
Rose Sports Goods, 39 Fa Yuen St, Mongkok (☎ 2781-1809)
Tang Fai Kee Military, 248 Reclamation St, Mongkok (☎ 2385-5169)
Three Military Equipment Company, 83 Sai Yee St, Mongkok (☎ 2395-5234)

Finally, if you want to see a good shopping mall where the locals go, visit Cityplaza in Quarry Bay. Take the MTR to the Tai Koo station.

GETTING THERE & AWAY
Air
Hong Kong is a good place to buy discounted air tickets, but watch out – there are swindlers in the travel business. The most common trick is a request for a nonrefundable deposit on an air ticket. So you pay a deposit for the booking, but when you go to pick up the tickets they say that the flight is no longer available but that there is another flight at a higher price, sometimes 50% more!

It is best not to pay a deposit but, rather, to pay for the ticket in full and get a receipt clearly showing that there is no balance due and that the full amount is refundable if no ticket is issued. Tickets are normally issued the next day after booking, but for the really cheapie tickets (actually group tickets) you must pick these up yourself at the airport from the 'tour leader' (whom you will never see again once you've got the ticket). One note of caution: when you get the ticket from the tour leader, check it carefully. Occasionally there are errors, such as being issued a ticket with the return portion valid for only 60 days when you paid for a ticket valid for one year.

Some budget fares available in Hong Kong follow, but realise that these are discounted fares and may have various restrictions upon their use:

Destination	One Way (HK$)	Return (HK$)
Auckland	4300	5800
Beijing	2270	4308
Darwin	2800	5050
Frankfurt	3300	5700
Jakarta	1700	3200
London	3300	5700
Manila	950	1520
New York	3800	6800
San Francisco	2800	4400
Seoul	1500	2500
Singapore	1500	2200
Sydney	3800	5400
Taipei	1030	1420
Tokyo	1950	2880

CAAC runs numerous direct flights between Hong Kong and every major city in China. Many of these flights are technically called 'charter flights'. It's important to know if your flight is designated a 'charter' because it means that the tickets have fixed-date departures and are nonrefundable.

The following are the one-way fares between China and Hong Kong on CAAC, and flights marked with an asterisk are 'charters':

Destination	Fare (HK$)	Destination	Fare (HK$)
Beijing	2370	Chengdu*	2160
Beihai*	1070	Chongqing*	2000
Changchun*	2350	Dalian	2510
Changsha*	1390	Fuzhou	1550
Guangzhou	600	Nanjing*	1620
Guilin*	1670	Nanning*	1670
Guiyang*	1230	Ningbo	1620
Haikou*	1200	Qingdao*	2320
Hangzhou	1550	Shanghai	1710
Harbin*	2620	Shantou	1110
Hefei*	1520	Shenyang	2800
Huangshan*	1520	Taiyuan*	2000
Ji'nan*	2180	Tianjin	2370
Kunming	1630	Wuhan*	1450
Lanzhou*	2400	Xi'an	2040
Luoyang*	1770	Xiamen	1290
Meixian*	1040	Zhanjiang*	1100
Nanchang*	1120	Zhengzhou*	1880

You can purchase a ticket from a travel agent or CAAC itself. Travel agents seldom give discounts on CAAC tickets because CAAC charges the agents almost full fare. There are two CAAC offices in Hong Kong (see the airline list later in this section).

It is possible to buy all of your CAAC tickets from CTS in Hong Kong (both international and domestic), and even from some non-Chinese airlines that have reciprocal arrangements with CAAC. While this should work OK for international flights, this is generally *not* a good idea for Chinese domestic flights.

First of all, it saves you no money whatsoever. Secondly, the tickets issued outside China need to be exchanged for a proper stamped ticket at the appropriate CAAC office in China and a few of these offices get their wires crossed and refuse to honour 'foreign' tickets. Furthermore, CAAC flights are often cancelled but you'll have to return the ticket to the original seller in order to get a refund.

Dragonair typically charges HK$100 less than CAAC on one-way tickets, and double that amount for round-trip tickets. Dragonair has flights from Hong Kong to 14 cities in China: Beijing, Changsha, Chengdu, Dalian, Guilin, Haikou, Hangzhou, Kunming, Nanjing, Ningbo, Shanghai, Tianjin, Xi'an and Xiamen.

In Hong Kong, any travel agent with a computer can book you onto a Dragonair flight but you can contact the ticketing offices of Dragonair directly (see the airline list below). Within China, Dragonair tickets

THE SOUTH

can be bought from CITS or a number of Dragonair representatives listed in this book.

Airport departure tax is HK$50, but you're excused from paying if you can convince them that you're under age 12. If departing by ship, departure tax is HK$26, but it's included in the purchase price of the ticket.

There are often horribly long queues at immigration, and more than a few travellers have missed their flights because of this. On departure, allow yourself an hour to clear immigration. The problem seems to be most acute during lunch hour, when there are insufficient staff to handle the stampede.

You need to reconfirm your onward or return fight if you break your trip in Hong Kong. This can be accomplished at one of the following airline offices:

Aeroflot, New Henry House (Res ☎ 2537-2611, Info 2769-6031)

Air France, Room 2104, Alexandra House, 7 Des Voeux Rd, Central (Res ☎ 2524-8145, Info 2769-6662)

Air India, 10th floor, Gloucester Tower, 11 Pedder St, Central (Res ☎ 2522-1176, Info 2769-8571)

Air Lanka, Room 602, Peregrine Tower, Lippo Centre, 89 Queensway, Central (Res ☎ 2521-0708, Info 2769-8571)

Air Mauritius, c/o Mercury Travel Ltd, St George's Building, Ice House St & Connaught Rd, Central (☎ 2523-1114)

Air New Zealand, Suite 902, 3 Exchange Square, 8 Connaught Place, Central (Res ☎ 2524-9041, Info 2769-6046)

Air Niugini, Room 705, Century Square, 1-13 D'Aguilar St, Central (Res ☎ 2524-2151, Info 2769-6038)

Alitalia, Room 2101, Hutchison House, 10 Harcourt Rd, Central (Res ☎ 2523-7047, Info 2769-7417)

All Nippon Airways, Room 2512, Pacific Place, 88 Queensway, Central (Res ☎ 2810-7100, Info 2769-8606)

Ansett Australia Airlines, Alexandra House, 7 Des Voeux Rd, Central (Res ☎ 2527-7883, Info 2769-6046)

Austrian Airlines, Room 1503, Queen's Place, 74 Queen's Rd, Central (☎ 2521-5175)
Room 713, Carnarvon Plaza, 20 Carnarvon Rd, Tsimshatsui (☎ 2723-0011)

Asiana Airlines, Gloucester Tower, The Landmark, 11 Pedder St, Central (Res ☎ 2523-8585, Info 2769-7113)

British Airways, 30th floor, Alexandra House, 7 Des Voeux Rd, Central (Res ☎ 2868-0303, Info 2868-0768)
Room 112, Royal Garden Hotel, 69 Mody Rd, Tsimshatsui East (☎ 2368-9255)

CAAC, Ground floor, 17 Queen's Rd, Central (☎ 2840-1199)
Ground floor, Mirador Mansion, 54-64B Nathan Rd, Tsimshatsui (☎ 2739-0022)

Canadian Airlines International, Ground floor, Swire House, 9-25 Chater Rd, Central (Res ☎ 2868-3123, Info 2769-7113)

Cathay Pacific, Ground floor, Swire House, 9-25 Chater Rd, Central
Sheraton Hotel, 20 Nathan Rd, Tsimshatsui (Res ☎ 2747-1888, Info 2747-1234)

China Airlines (Taiwan), Ground floor, St George's Building, Ice House St & Connaught Rd, Central
G5-6 Tsimshatsui Centre, Tsimshatsui East (Res ☎ 2868-2299, Info 2843-9800)

Continental Micronesia, Room M1, New Henry House, 10 Ice House St, Central (Res ☎ 2525-7759, Info 2769-7017)

Delta Airlines, Pacific Place, 88 Queensway, Central (☎ 2526-5875)

Dragonair, Room 1843, Swire House, 9 Connaught Rd, Central
12th floor, Tower 6, China Hong Kong City, 33 Canton Rd, Tsimshatsui (☎ Res 2590-1188, Info 2769-7727)

Emirates Airlines, Gloucester Tower, The Landmark, 11 Pedder St, Central (Res ☎ 2526-7171, Info 2769-8571)

Garuda Indonesia, 2nd floor, Sing Pao Centre, 8 Queen's Rd, Central (Res ☎ 2840-0000, Info 2769-6681)

Gulf Air, Room 2508, Caroline Centre, 28 Yun Ping Rd, Causeway Bay (☎ Res 2882-2892, Info 2769-8337)

Japan Airlines, 20th floor, Gloucester Tower, 11 Pedder St, Central
Harbour View Holiday Inn, Mody Rd, Tsimshatsui East (Res ☎ 2523-0081, Info 2769-6524)

Japan Asia, 20th floor, Gloucester Tower, 11 Pedder St, Central (Res ☎ 2521-8102)

KLM Airlines, Room 701-5 Jardine House, 1 Connaught Place, Central (☎ Res 2822-8111, Info 2822-8118)

Korean Air, Ground floor, St George's Building, Ice House St & Connaught Rd, Central
11th floor, South Seas Centre, Tower II, 75 Mody Rd, Tsimshatsui East
G12-15 Tsimshatsui Centre, Salisbury Rd, Tsimshatsui East (☎ 2368-6221)

Lauda Air, Pacific House, On Lan St, Central (Res ☎ 2525-5222, Info 2769-7017)

Lufthansa Airlines, 6th floor, Landmark East, 12 Ice House St, Central (Res ☎ 2868-2313, Info 2769-6560)

Malaysia Airlines, Room 1306, Prince's Building, 9-25 Chater Rd, Central (Res ☎ 2521-8181, Info 2769-7967)

Northwest Airlines, 29th floor, Alexandra House, 7 Des Voeux Rd, Central (☎ 2810-4288)

Philippine Airlines, Room 603, West Tower, Bond Centre, Central (Res ☎ 2524-9216)

Room 6, Ground floor, East Ocean Centre, 98 Granville Rd, Tsimshatsui East (Res ☎ 2369-4521, Info 2769-6263)

Qantas, Room 1422, Swire House, 9-25 Chater Rd, Central (Res ☎ 2524-2101, Info 2525-6206)

Royal Brunei Airlines, Room 1406, Central Building, 3 Pedder St, Central (☎ 2869-8608)

Royal Nepal Airlines, Room 704, Lippo Sun Plaza, 28 Canton Rd, Tsimshatsui (☎ 2375-9151)

Scandinavian Airlines, Room 1410, Harcourt House, Gloucester Rd, Wanchai (Res ☎ 2375-9151, Info 2375-3152)

Singapore Airlines, United Centre, Queensway, Central (☎ Res 2520-2233, Info 2769-6387)

South African Airways, 30th floor, Alexandra House, Central (Res ☎ 2877-3277, Info 2868-0768)

Swissair, 8th floor, Tower II, Admiralty Centre, 18 Harcourt Rd, Central (Res ☎ 2529-3670, Info 2769-8864)

Thai Airways International, United Centre, Pacific Place, 88 Queensway, Central

Shop 124, 1st floor, World Wide Plaza, Des Voeux Rd and Pedder St, Central

Shop 105-6, Omni, The Hongkong Hotel, 3 Canton Rd, Tsimshatsui (☎ Res 2529-5601, Info 2769-7421)

United Airlines, 29th floor, The Landmark, Gloucester Tower, Des Voeux Rd & Pedder St, Central

Ground floor, Empire Centre, Mody Rd, Tsimshatsui East (Res ☎ 2810-4888, Info 2769-7279)

Varig Brazilian, Central Plaza, Gloucester Rd, Wanchai (Res ☎ 2511-1234, Info 2769-6048)

Vietnam Airlines, c/o Cathay Pacific Airlines, Ground floor, Swire House, 9-25 Chater Rd, Central

Sheraton Hotel, 20 Nathan Rd, Tsimshatsui (Res ☎ 2810-6680, Info 2747-1234)

Virgin Atlantic, Lippo Tower, 89 Queensway, Central (☎ 2532-6060)

Land

Shenzhen is the city just across the border from Hong Kong. The border checkpoint is open daily from 6 am to midnight. You have a choice of crossing the border by bus or train – bicycles, it seems, are forbidden to enter China by this route.

Bus A new superhighway connects Hong Kong to Guangzhou (Canton) – the bus journey takes 3½ hours and costs HK$170. Departures in Kowloon are from the bus station on the ground floor of China Hong Kong City (the same building where you get ferries to Guangzhou). There are also departures from the Admiralty station on Hong Kong Island and City One in Shatin (New Territories). Departures from China Hong Kong City are at 8, 8.30, 9 and 9.30 am. From Guangzhou, you catch these buses at the Garden Hotel; departures are at 2.30, 3.30, 4 and 4.30 pm. Schedules can change, but in Hong Kong you can ring up City Bus (☎ 2736-3888) for the latest information. The same company also operates buses to places in Shenzhen, including Shenzhen Airport, Safari Park, Windows of the World, Shenzhen Bay and Central Shenzhen.

Train The KCR train takes 30 minutes to run from Hunghom station in Kowloon to the border checkpoint at Lo Wu. You walk across the border to the city of Shenzhen, and from there you can take a local train to Guangzhou and beyond. Coming from the other direction, be aware that there are no money-changing facilities on the Hong Kong side of the border. Take care of it before passing through Chinese customs on the Shenzhen side or else you might not have enough cash for the train to Kowloon.

Alternatively, there are express trains straight through between Hunghom station in Kowloon and Guangzhou for HK$190 – these depart four times daily. There is also a Kowloon-Zhaoqing train. You pass through immigration and customs at the point of departure – therefore, you must arrive at the railway station at least 30 minutes before departure or you will not be allowed to board. The staff are very strict about enforcing this!

Sea

Hong Kong has one of the most spectacular harbours in the world, so departing or arriving this way can be fun. Luxury cruise liners frequently visit Hong Kong, though this option is basically for elderly millionaires. For those of more humble means, there are economical boats between Hong Kong and several other cities in China. There are special discounts for children on all these boats – inquire if interested.

Hong Kong – Guangzhou The Hong Kong-Guangzhou boat is one of the most popular ways to enter or exit China. The journey takes about nine hours, and the boats leave at 9 pm from China Hong Kong City in Kowloon, and from the Zhoutouzui Wharf in Guangzhou. There is no service on the 31st day of the month. Prices are: deluxe class HK$724, special class HK$294, 1st class HK$259, 2nd class HK$214 to HK$224 and 3rd class HK$184.

There is also a jet-powered catamaran which completes the journey in just 3½ hours. Departures from Hong Kong are daily at 8.15 am, and departures from Guangzhou are at 1 pm. The fare is HK$190 on weekdays and HK$215 on weekends.

Hong Kong – Haikou There are six trips monthly and the journey takes 24 hours. In Hong Kong, check-in is from noon to 12.45 pm. In Haikou, check-in is from 8 to 9 am. Fares are: special A class HK$538, special B class HK$488, 1st class HK$428, 2nd class HK$388, 3rd class HK$288.

Hong Kong – Sanya The new luxury cruiser *Star Pisces* has over 600 rooms and makes frequent runs between Hong Kong and Sanya on Hainan Island. The journey takes only half a day.

Hong Kong – Shanghai There is one trip every five days and the journey takes 62 hours. Some of the boats stop in at Ningbo en route. In Hong Kong check-in time is at noon, but in Shanghai departure time is not fixed, so ask.

In Shanghai, tickets can be bought from CITS or the China Ocean Shipping Agency (☎ 329-0088) on the 3rd floor at 13 Zhongshan Dongyi Lu. Rates are: special A class HK$1650, special B class HK$1520, 1st A class HK$1400, 1st B class HK$1270,

2nd A class HK$1200, 2nd B class HK$1100, 3rd A class HK$1010, 3rd B class HK$920.

Hong Kong – Shenzhen Airport The jet-powered catamaran departs six times daily in each direction. Although the journey *officially* takes one hour, it usually takes two hours, so you must depart Hong Kong at least three hours before your scheduled flight time. VIP cabins cost HK$1650 per person, seats on the super deck are HK$275 and the main deck is HK$175.

Hong Kong – Taiping (Opium War Museum) The jet-powered catamaran takes two hours (minimum) to complete the journey. Departures from Hong Kong are daily at 9.15 am and 2.20 pm. Departures from Taiping are at 11.50 am and 4.50 pm. Fares from Hong Kong are HK$226 and HK$186. Fares from Taiping are HK$158.

Hong Kong – Wuzhou Wuzhou is the gateway to Guilin. The boat journey takes 12 hours, and departures from Hong Kong are at 8 am on even-numbered dates. Departures from Wuzhou are at 7.30 am on odd-numbered dates. The fare is HK$360.

Hong Kong – Xiamen The journey takes 22 hours. Hong Kong check-in time is Tuesday and Friday from 12.30 to 1 pm, and departures are at 2 pm. In Xiamen, departures are on Monday and Thursday at 3 pm. Tickets cost: 1st class HK$550, 2nd class HK$500, 3rd class HK$450.

Hong Kong – Zhaoqing The journey takes 12 hours. Departures from Hong Kong are on odd-numbered dates at 7.30 pm, with no service available on the 31st day of the month. Departures from Zhaoqing are on even-numbered dates at 7 pm. Fares are: special A class HK$671, special B class HK$378, 1st class HK$338, 2nd class HK$303, 3rd class HK$248.

There is also a jet-powered catamaran which completes the journey in five hours. Departures from Hong Kong are at 7.45 am on even-numbered dates. From Zhaoqing departures are at 2 pm on odd-numbered dates, with no service available on the 31st day of the month. Fares are from HK$188 to HK$353.

GETTING AROUND
To/From the Airport
The Airbus (airport bus) services are very convenient and are significantly cheaper than taxis. A taxi to Tsimshatsui costs about HK$40 plus HK$5 per bag. There are five bus services – A1 to Tsimshatsui (HK$12); A2 to Wanchai, Central and the Macau Ferry Terminal (HK$17); A3 to Causeway Bay (HK$17); A5 to Tai Koo Shing (HK$17); and A7 to Kowloon Tong MTR station (HK$6.50). The buses operate every 15 to 20 minutes, from 7.40 am to midnight, and depart from right outside the arrivals area. There's plenty of luggage space on board and the buses go past most major hotels.

The A1 service to Tsimshatsui in Kowloon goes down Nathan Rd right in front of Chungking Mansions, then turns around at the Star Ferry Terminal and heads back, making numerous stops en route. There is an Airbus brochure at the departure area with a map showing the bus route.

Bus
Before setting out to travel anywhere by bus, ensure you have a good pocketful of small change – the exact fare normally must be deposited in a cash box and nobody has change. There are plenty of buses with fares starting from HK$1 and going up to HK$30.60 for the fancy 'City Buses' which take you to the New Territories.

Most services stop around 11 pm or midnight, but bus Nos 121 and 122 are 'Cross Harbour Recreation Routes' which operate through the Cross-Harbour Tunnel every 15 minutes from 12.45 to 5 am. Bus No 121 runs from the Macau Ferry Terminal on Hong Kong Island, then through the tunnel to Chatham Rd in Tsimshatsui East before continuing on to Choi Hung on the east side of the airport.

Bus No 122 runs from North Point on Hong Kong Island, through the Cross-Harbour Tunnel, to Chatham Rd in Tsimshatsui East, the northern part of Nathan Rd and on to Laichikok in the north-west part of Kowloon.

Minibus & Maxicab
Small red and yellow minibuses supplement the regular bus services. They cost HK$2 to HK$7 and you pay as you exit. They generally don't run such regular routes but you can get on or off almost anywhere.

Maxicabs are just like minibuses except they are green and yellow and they do run regular routes. Two popular ones are from the car park in front of the Star Ferry in Central to Ocean Park or from HMS Tamar (east of the Star Ferry) to the Peak. Fares are between HK$1 and HK$8 and you pay as you enter.

Mass Transit Railway
The MTR operates from Central across the harbour and up along Kowloon Peninsula. It is very fast and convenient but fairly pricey. The ticket machines do not give change (get it from the ticket windows) and single-journey tickets are valid only for the day they are purchased. Once you go past the turnstile, you must complete the journey within 90 minutes or the ticket becomes invalid. The MTR operates from 6 am to 1 am.

If you use the MTR frequently, it's very useful to buy a Common Stored Value Ticket for HK$70, HK$100 or HK$200. These tickets remain valid for nine months. The Tourist Souvenir Ticket is a rip-off at HK$25 because it gives you only HK$20 worth of fares!

Smoking, eating or drinking are not allowed in the MTR stations or on the trains (makes you wonder about all those Maxim's Cake Shops in the stations). The fine for eating or drinking is HK$1000, while smoking will set you back HK$2000. Busking, selling and soliciting are forbidden. There are no toilets in the MTR stations.

Kowloon-Canton Railway
The KCR runs from Hunghom station in Kowloon to Lo Wu, where you can walk

Sheung Shui
Luk Keng
69K
76K
Fanling
70
77K
Tai Mei Tuk
75K
Lau Fau Shan
655
54
64K
Kam Tin
Wong Shek Pier
94
Yuen Long
Tai Po
Nai Chung
Pak Tam Chung
94
LRT
51
NEW TERRITORIES
99
94
68M
Sai Kung
92
Tuen Mun
70
Tsuen Wan
92
60X
68X
6A
KOWLOON
91
12
Choi Hung
Kai Tak Airport
Clearwater Bay
A1
A2
A3
5B
4
7
Central
Admiralty
Causeway Bay
3
Shaukeiwan
Mt Davis
HK University
2
15
11
Tiger Balm Gardens
Victoria Peak
70
HONG KONG ISLAND
72
262
61
Wah Fu
Aberdeen
73
6
14
9
Ocean Park
Repulse Bay
Shek O
6
73
Stanley

Public Bus Route Numbers

0   2.5   5 km

across the border into Shenzhen. Apart from being a launch pad into China, the KCR is also an excellent alternative to buses for getting into the New Territories.

The Common Stored Value Tickets which are used on the MTR are valid on the KCR too, but not for Lo Wu station, which requires a separate ticket.

Tram

There is just one major tram line, running from east-west along the northern side of Hong Kong Island. As well as being ridiculously picturesque and fun to travel on, the tram is quite a bargain at HK$1.20 for any distance. You pay as you get off.

In addition to the major tram line there is a spur route off to Happy Valley. Some trams don't run the full length of the line, but basically you can just get on any tram that comes by. They pass frequently and there always seem to be half a dozen trams actually in sight.

Light Rail Transit

The LRT operates only on routes in the western part of the New Territories, in and around Tuen Mun. Fares are HK$3.20 to HK$4.70.

Taxi

On Hong Kong Island and Kowloon, the flagfall is HK$13 plus HK$1.10 for every 0.2 km. In the New Territories, flagfall is HK$11, thereafter HK$1 for every 0.2 km. There is a luggage fee of HK$5 per bag but not all drivers insist on this.

If you go through either the Cross-Harbour Tunnel or Eastern Harbour Tunnel, you'll be charged an extra HK$20. The toll is only HK$10, but the driver is allowed to assume that he won't get a fare back so you have to pay.

Note: Taxis cannot pick up or put down passengers where there's a painted yellow line in the road.

Bicycle

Bicycling in Kowloon or Central would be suicidal, but in quiet areas of the islands or the New Territories a bike can be quite a nice way of getting around. The bike rental places tend to run out early on weekends.

Some places where you can rent bikes and ride in safety include: Shek O on Hong Kong Island; Shatin and Tai Mei Tuk (near Tai Po) in the New Territories; Mui Wo (Silvermine Bay) on Lantau Island; and on the island of Cheung Chau.

Boat

With such a scenic harbour, commuting by ferry is one of the great pleasures of Hong Kong. You have a wide choice of boats, though the one most familiar to tourists is the Star Ferry.

Star Ferry There are three routes on the Star Ferry, but by far the most popular one shuttles between Tsimshatsui and Central. The boats cost a mere HK$1.40 (lower deck) or HK$1.70 (upper deck), except for the Hunghom ferry, which is HK$1.70 and HK$2, respectively. The schedule for all three ferries is as follows:

Tsimshatsui – Central, every five to 10 minutes from
    6.30 am until 11.30 pm
Tsimshatsui – Wanchai, every 10 to 20 minutes from
    7.30 am to 10.50 pm
Hunghom – Central, every 12 to 20 minutes (every 20
    minutes on Sunday & holidays) from 7 am to 7.20
    pm

Hoverferries The schedule for hoverferries is as follows:

Tsimshatsui East – Central (Queen's Pier), every 20
    minutes from 8 am to 8 pm
Tsuen Wan – Central, every 20 minutes from 7.20 am
    to 5.20 pm
Tuen Mun – Central, every 10 to 20 minutes from 6.45
    am to 7.40 pm

Kaidos A *kaido* is a small to medium-sized ferry which can make short runs on the open sea. Few kaido routes operate on regular schedules, preferring to adjust supply according to demand. There is sort of a schedule on popular runs like the trip between Aberdeen and Lamma Island. Kaidos run most frequently on weekends and holidays when everyone tries to get away from it all.

A *sampan* is a motorised launch which can accommodate only a few people. A sampan is too small to be considered seaworthy but can safely zip you around typhoon shelters like Aberdeen Harbour.

Bigger than a sampan, but smaller than a kaido, is a *walla walla*. These operate as water taxis on Victoria Harbour. Most of the customers are sailors living on ships anchored in the harbour.

Outlying Island Ferries The HKTA can supply you with schedules for these ferries. Fares are higher on weekends and holidays and the boats can get crowded. From Central, most ferries go from the Outlying Islands Piers just west of the Star Ferry Piers on Hong Kong island.

Macau

The lure of Macau's casino gaming tables has been so actively promoted that its other attractions are almost forgotten, but it is a fascinating blend – steeped in history and Old World elegance, but prosperous and changing fast. It has a very different look and feel from Hong Kong, and is well worth the one-hour boat trip to get there. Better yet, spend at least one night – this is a place to enjoy and relax.

HISTORY

Portuguese galleons visited Macau in the early 1500s, and in 1557, as a reward for clearing out a few pirates, China ceded the tiny enclave to the Portuguese.

For centuries, it was the principal meeting point for trade with China. In the 19th century, European and American traders could operate in Guangzhou (just up the Pearl River) only during the trading season. They would then retreat to Macau during the off season.

When the Opium Wars erupted between the Chinese and the British, the Portuguese

Population: 400,000
Highlights:
- Ruins of St Paul's, the symbol of Macau
- Monte Fort, with its great views over Macau
- Colonial architecture
- Gambling in one of the casinos

stood diplomatically to one side and Macau soon found itself the poor relation of the more dynamic Hong Kong.

Macau's current prosperity is given a big boost from the Chinese gambling urge which every weekend sees hordes of Hong Kongers shuttling off to the casinos. Although the government doesn't publicly admit it, prostitution is also a significant source of revenue.

About 95% of Macau's people are Chinese, 3% are Portuguese and 2% are foreigners employed in what is loosely called the 'entertainment industry'. Whether or not the Portuguese and foreigners will be permitted to remain after 1999 is a largely unanswered question.

LANGUAGE

Portuguese may be the official language but Cantonese is the real one. Mandarin Chinese is spoken by about half the population. Bus and taxi drivers almost never speak English. On the other hand, virtually all Portuguese in Macau can speak English well.

There is no real need to learn Portuguese,

but it can be helpful (and fun) to know a few words for reading maps and street signs. The following words should come in handy:

alley	*beco*
avenue	*avenida*
bay	*baía*
beach	*praia*
big	*grande*
bridge	*ponte*
building	*edificio*
bus stop	*paragem*
cathedral	*sé*
church	*igreja*
courtyard	*pátio*
district	*bairro*
fortress	*fortaleza*
friendship	*amizade*
garden	*jardim*
guesthouse	*hospedaria/vila*
guide	*guia*
hill	*alto or monte*
hotel	*pousada*
island	*ilha*
lane	*travessa*
lighthouse	*farol*
lookout point	*miradouro*
market	*mercado*
moneychanger	*casa de cambio*
museum	*museu*
of	*da, do*
pawnshop	*casa de penhores*
pier	*ponte-cais*
police station	*esquadra da polícia*
post office	*correios*
restaurant (small)	*casa de pasto*
path	*caminho*
road	*estrada*
rock, crag	*penha*
school	*escola*
small hill	*colina*
square	*praça*
square (small)	*largo*
steep street	*calçada*
street	*rua*

VISAS

For most visitors, all that's needed to enter Macau is a passport. Everyone gets at least a 20-day stay on arrival, or 90 days for Hong Kongers. Visas are not required for people from the following countries: Australia, Austria, Belgium, Brazil, Canada, Denmark, Finland, France, Germany, Greece, Hong Kong, India, Ireland, Italy, Japan, Luxembourg, Malaysia, Mexico, Netherlands, New Zealand, Norway, Philippines, Singapore, South Africa, South Korea, Spain, Sweden, Switzerland, Thailand, UK and USA.

All other nationalities must have a visa, which can be obtained on arrival in Macau. Visas cost M$205 for individuals, M$410 per family, M$102.50 for children under 12 and M$102.50 per person in a bona fide tour group (usually 10 persons minimum). People holding passports from countries which do not have diplomatic relations with Portugal must obtain visas from an overseas Portuguese consulate before entering Macau.

An exception is made for Taiwanese, who can get visas on arrival for free despite their lack of diplomatic relations. The Portuguese consulate (☎ 2802-2585) in Hong Kong is at Harbour Centre, Harbour Rd, Wanchai.

Visa Extensions

After your 20 days are up, you can obtain a one-month extension if you can come up with a good reason (emergency poker game?). A second extension is not possible, though it's easy enough to go across the border to China and then come back again. The Immigration Office (☎ 577-338) is on the 9th floor, Macau Chamber of Commerce Building, Rua de Xangai 175, which is one block to the north-east of the Hotel Beverly Plaza.

MONEY

Macau issues its own currency, the pataca, written as M$. The pataca is divided into 100 avos and is worth about 3% less than the HK$. HK$ are accepted everywhere on a 1:1 basis with patacas, which means, of course, that you'll save a little by using patacas.

Although Hong Kong coins are acceptable in Macau, you'll need pataca coins to make calls at public telephones. Get rid of

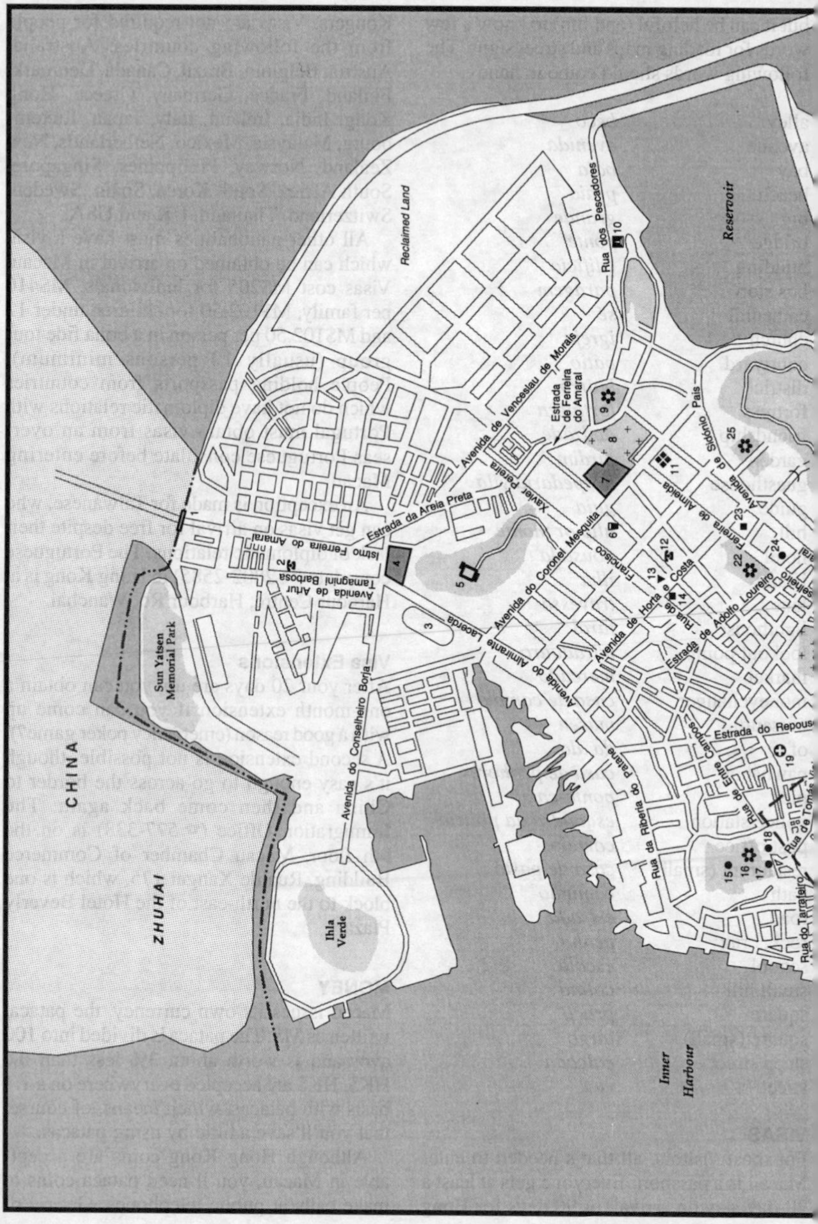

THE SOUTH

CHINA

ZHUHAI

Sun Yatsen
Memorial Park

Ilha
Verde

Inner
Harbour

Reclaimed Land

Reservoir

Rua dos Pescadores

Estrada de Ferreira
do Amaral

Estrada da Areia Preta

Istmo Ferreira do Amaral

Avenida de Venceslau de Morais

Xavier Pereira

Avenida de Artur Tamagnini Barbosa

Avenida do Conselheiro Borja

Rua da Ribeira do Patane

Avenida do Almirante

Avenida do Coronel Mesquita

Avenida de Horta e Costa

Francisco

Avenida de Adôlo Loureiro

Sidônio Pais

Avenida de Almeida

Ferreira do Amaral

Estrada do Repouso

Estrada do Repouso

Rua dos

Rua do Tarrafeiro

MACAU PENINSULA

PLACES TO STAY

PLACES TO EAT

OTHER

Airport
& Coloane

Outer Harbour

Jetfoil
Pier

Avenida da Amizade

Macau
Peninsula

0   0.5   1 km

Reclaimed Land

Rua de Xangai

Avenida da Amizade

Avenida do Infante D'Henrique

Avenida da Amizade

Estrada de São Francisco

Rua Nova à Guia

Estrada D. Ricardo Rodrigues

Rua de São Francisco

Baía da
Praia Grande

See Central Macau Map

Nam Van Lakes

Avenida do Bom Parto

Rua da Praia do Bom Parto

To Taipa, Airport
& Coloane

Praia Grande

Rua de S. Domingos

Rua de Almeida Ribeiro

Rua das Estalagens

Rua das Lorchas

Rua de S. Paulo

Rua do Almirante Sérgio

Avenida da República

Rua do Campo

Rua de S. Tiago da Barra

Rua da Barra

Rua da Praia

THE SOUTH

MACAU PENINSULA

PLACES TO STAY

14	Fu Hua Hotel
20	Holiday Hotel
23	Mondial Hotel
26	Estoril Hotel
29	Royal Hotel
30	Guia Hotel
32	Nam Yue Hotel
38	Mandarin Oriental Hotel
39	Kingsway Hotel
40	Grandeur Hotel
45	Pousada Ritz Hotel
46	Bela Vista Hotel
52	Pousada de Sao Tiago

PLACES TO EAT

13	McDonald's III
27	Restaurante Violeta
34	McDonald's II & Yaohan Department Store
43	A Lorcha Restaurant
47	Henri's Galley & Cafe Marisol
48	Ali Curry House
51	Pele Restaurant

OTHER

1	Barrier Gate
2	CTM Telephone Company
3	Canidrome
4	Lin Fung Miu (Lotus Temple)
5	Mong-Ha Fortress
6	Talker Pub & Pyretu's Bar
7	Kun Iam Temple
8	Our Lady of Piety Cemetery
9	Montanha Russa Garden
10	Macau-Seac Tin Hau Temple
11	Pak Vai Plaza
12	CTM Telephone Company
15	Casa Garden Fundacao Oriente
16	Camões Grotto & Gardens
17	Future Bright Amusement Centre
18	Old Protestant Cemetery
19	Kiang Wu Hospital
21	St Michael's Cemetery
22	Lou Lim Ioc Gardens
24	Sun Yatsen Memorial House
25	Flora Garden
28	Vasco da Gama Garden
31	Guia Lighthouse
33	Jai Alai Casino
35	HK-Macau Ferry Pier
36	Heliport
37	Macau Forum
41	Maritime Museum
42	A-Ma Temple
44	Penha Church
49	Governor's Residence
50	Barra Hill

your patacas before departing Macau – they are hard to dispose of in Hong Kong, though you can change them at the Hang Seng Bank.

There is a convenient moneychanger at the Jetfoil Pier (where most tourists arrive) and at the Chinese border. Banks are normally open on weekdays from 9 am to 4 pm, and on Saturday from 9 am until noon. If you need to change money when the banks are closed, the major casinos (especially the Lisboa) can accommodate you 24 hours a day.

Costs

As long as you don't go crazy at the blackjack tables or slot machines, Macau is cheaper than Hong Kong. Indeed, it's cheaper than almost anywhere else on the east coast of China. However, it's important to avoid weekends when hotel prices double and even the ferries charge more. As in China, tipping is not the usual custom though hotel porters and waiters may have different

ideas. Upmarket hotels hit you with a 10% service charge and 5% 'tourism tax'.

Most stores have fixed prices, but if you buy clothing, trinkets and other tourist junk from the street markets, there is some scope for bargaining. On the other hand, if you buy from the ubiquitous pawnshops, bargain ruthlessly. Pawnbrokers are more than happy to charge whatever they can get away with – charging five times the going price for second-hand cameras and other goods is not unusual!

MACAU GOVERNMENT TOURIST OFFICE

The MGTO (☎ 315-566) is well organised and extremely helpful. It's at Largo do Senado, Edificio Ritz No 9, near the Leal Senado building in the square in the centre of Macau.

Macau also maintains overseas tourist representative offices, including the Macau

Tourist Information Bureau (MTIB), as follows:

Australia

MTIB, 449 Darling St, Balmain, Sydney, NSW 2041 (☎ (02) 9555-7548, (1800) 252-448; fax 9555-7559)

Belgium

Tourism Delegation, Avenue Louise, 375 Bte 9, 1050 Brussels (☎ (02) 647-1265; fax 640-1552)

Canada

MTIB, Suite 157, 10551 Shellbridge Way, Richmond, BC, V6X 2W9 (☎ (604) 231-9040; fax 231-9031)

13 Mountain Ave, Toronto, Ontario M4J IH3 (☎ (416) 466-6552)

France

MTIB Consultant, Atlantic Associates, SARL, 52 Champs Élysées, 75008, Paris (☎ (01) 4256-4551; fax 4651-4889)

Germany

Macau Tourism Representative, Shafergasse 17, D-60313, Frankfurt-am-Main (☎ (069) 234-094; fax 231-433)

Hong Kong

MTIB, Room 3704, Shun Tak Centre, 200 Connaught Rd (Macau Ferry Pier) – closed for lunch from 1 to 2 pm (☎ 2540-8180)

Italy

MTIB Consultant, Bruce Renton Associates, Maffeo Pantaleoni 25, Rome 00191 (☎ (06) 3630-9117)

Japan

MTIB, 4th floor, Toho Twin Tower Building, 5-2 Yurakucho 1-chome, Chiyoda-ku, Tokyo 100 (☎ (03) 3501-5022; fax 3502-1248)

Malaysia

MTIB, 10.03 Amoda, 22 Jalan Imbi, 55100, Kuala Lumpur (☎ 245-1418; fax 248-6851)

New Zealand

MTIB, PO Box 42-165, Orakei, Auckland 5 (☎ (09) 575-2700; fax 575-2620)

Philippines

MTIB, 664 EDSA Extension, Pasay City, Metro Manila (☎ (02) 521-7178; fax 831-4344)

Portugal

Macau Tourist Representative, Avenida 5 de Outubro 115, 5th floor, 1000 Lisbon (☎ (01) 793-6542; fax 796-0956)

Singapore

MTIB, 11-01A PIL Building, 140 Cecil St, Singapore 0106 (☎ 225-0022; fax 223-8585)

South Korea

MGTO Representative, Glocom Korea Ltd, 1006 Paiknam Building, 188-3 Ulchiro 1-ga, Chunggu, Seoul 100-191 (☎ (02) 778-4401; fax 778-4404)

Spain

ICEP, Gran Via 27, 1st floor, 28013 Madrid (☎ (01) 522-9354; fax 522-2382)

Taiwan

MGTO Representative, Compass Public Relations Ltd, 11th floor, 65 Chienkuo North Rd, Section 2, Taipei (☎ (02) 516-3008; fax 515-1971)

Thailand

MTIB, 150/5 Sukhumvit 20, Bangkok 10110, or GPO Box 1534, Bangkok 10501 (☎ 258-1975)

UK

MTIB, 6 Sherlock Mews, Paddington St, London W1M 3RH (☎ (0171) 224-3390; fax 224-0601)

USA

MTIB, 3133 Lake Hollywood Drive, Los Angeles, CA, or PO Box 1860, Los Angeles, CA 90078 (☎ (213) 851-3402, (800) 331-7150; fax 851-3684)

Suite 2R, 77 Seventh Ave, New York, NY 10011 (☎ (212) 206-6828; fax 924-0882)

PO Box 350, Kenilworth, IL 60043-0350 (☎ (708) 251-6421; fax 256-5601)

999 Wilder Ave, Suite 1103, Honolulu, HI 96822 (☎ (808) 538-7613)

POST & TELECOMMUNICATIONS

Postal Rates

Domestic letters cost M$1 for up to 20 grams. For international mail Macau divides the world into zones. Zone 1 is east Asia, including Korea and Taiwan; Zone 2 is everywhere else. There are special rates for the rest of China and Portugal. Printed matter receives a discount of about 30% off the regular rates. Registration costs an extra M$12.

Sending Mail

The GPO on Leal Senado is open from 9 am to 8 pm, Monday to Saturday. Large hotels like the Lisboa also sell stamps and postcards and can post letters for you. Scattered around Macau are several red-coloured 'mini-post offices', which are basically machines that sell stamps. The current postal rates are posted clearly on the machines.

Telephone

Companhia de Telecomunicações (CTM) runs the Macau telephone system, and for the most part the service is good. However, public pay phones can be hard to find, being mostly concentrated around the Leal

Senado. Most large hotels have one in the lobby, but this is often insufficient and you may have to stand in line to use it.

Local calls are free from a private or hotel telephone. At a public pay phone, local calls cost M$1 for five minutes. All pay phones permit international direct dialling (IDD). The procedure for dialling Hong Kong is totally different to all other countries. You first dial 01 and then the number you want to call – you must *not* dial the country code.

The international access code for every country *except* Hong Kong is 00. To call into Macau from abroad, the country code is 853.

Telephone cards from CTM are sold in denominations of M$50, M$100 and M$200. A lot of phones which accept these cards are found around Leal Senado, the Jetfoil Pier and at a few large hotels. You can also make a call from the telephone office at Largo do Senado, next to the GPO. The office is open from 8 am until midnight Monday to Saturday; and from 9 am until midnight on Sunday.

Some other useful phone numbers in Macau include:

Directory assistance (Macau)	181
Directory assistance (Hong Kong)	101
Time	140

Fax, Telex & Telegraph

Unless you're staying at a hotel that has its own fax, the easiest way to send and receive a fax is at the GPO (not the telephone office) at Leal Senado. The number for receiving a fax at this office is (853) 550-117, but check because the number can change. The person sending the fax must put your name and hotel telephone number on top of the message so the postal workers can find you. The cost for receiving a fax is M$7.50 regardless of the number of pages.

Telex messages are sent from the telephone office next to the GPO. The telephone office also handles cables (telegrams).

BOOKSHOPS

Macau's best bookshop for English-language publications is Livraria Sao Paulo

(☎ 355-010), Travessa do Bispo 11 R/C. For Portuguese-language publications, check out the nearby Livraria Portuguesa (☎ 566-442), Rua de Sao Domingos 18-20.

TRAVEL AGENCIES

Most likely, you'll only visit a travel agent if you want to book a day tour around Macau. However, China Travel Service and a few other agencies do visas for China in 24 hours. The current line-up of agents includes:

Able Tours
  Travessa do Padre Narciso 5-9 (☎ 566-939; fax 566-938; HK 2545-9993)
Asia
  Rua da Praia Grande 23-B (☎ 565-060; HK 2548-8806)
China Travel Service
  Xinhua Building, Rua de Nagasaki (☎ 705-506; fax 706-611; HK 2540-6333)
Estoril Tours
  Mezzanine floor, New Wing, Lisboa Hotel, Avenida da Amizade (☎ 710-361; fax 567-193; HK 2581-0022)
Feliz
  14th floor, Rua de Xangai 175 (☎ 781-697; fax 781-699; HK 2541-1611)
Guangdong Macau Tours
  Rua da Praia Grande 37-E (☎ 588-807; fax 323-771; HK 2832-9118)
Hi-No-De Caravela
  Rua de Sacadura Cabral 6A-4C (☎ 338-338; fax 566-622; HK 2368-6781)
International Tourism
  Travessa do Padre Narciso 9, Loja B (☎ 975-183; fax 974-072; HK 2541-2011)
Lotus
  Edificio Fong Meng, Rua de Sao Lourenço (☎ 972-977)
Macau Mondial
  Avenida do Conselheiro Ferreira de Almeida 74-A (☎ 566-866; fax 574-531)
Macau Star Tours
  Room 511, Tai Fung Bank Building, Avenida de Almeida Ribeiro 34 (☎ 558-855; HK 2366-2262)
Macau Mondial
  Avenida do Conselheiro Ferreira de Almeida 74-A (☎ 566-866; fax 574-531)
Macau Star
  Room 511, Avenida de Almeida Ribeiro (☎ 558-855; fax 586-702; HK 2922-3013)
Mirada
  9 Rua do General Castelo Branco (☎ 261-582)

Peninsula
Rua das Lorchas 14, Inner Harbour (☎ 316-699;
fax 362-944)
Presidente
Avenida da Amizade 355 (☎ 781-334; fax 781-335)
Sintra Tours
Room 135, Lisboa Hotel, Avenida da Amizade
(☎ 710-361; fax 710-353; HK 2540-8028)
STDM
Room 134, Lisboa Hotel, Avenida da Amizade
(☎ 710-461; fax 710-353; HK 2540-8028)
TKW
4th floor, Rua Formosa 27-31, Apt 408 (☎ 591-122; fax 576-200; HK 2723-7771)
Vacations International
Mandarin Oriental Hotel shopping arcade,
Avenida da Amizade (☎ 336-789, 567-888 ext
3004; fax 314-112)

FILM & PHOTOGRAPHY
You can find most types of film, cameras and accessories in Macau, and photoprocessing is of a high standard. The best store in town for all photographic services, including visa photos, is Foto Princesa (☎ 555-959), Avenida Infante D'Henrique 55-59, one block east of Rua da Praia Grande.

HEALTH
Medical treatment is available at the Government Hospital (☎ 514-499, 313-731), north of San Francisco Garden.

EMERGENCY
The emergency phone number is ☎ 999, and if you want the police, dial ☎ 573-333.

CULTURAL EVENTS
Macau has its own collection of holidays, festivals and cultural events, including some imported from Portugal.

The International Music Festival is held during the third week of October. The Macau Marathon is held in the first week of December.

The biggest event of the year is no doubt the Macau Grand Prix. As in Monte Carlo, the streets of the town make up the race track. The race is a two-day event held on the third weekend in November – accommodation can be scarce as a three-humped camel at this time.

Other holidays and festivals are as follows:

New Year's Day
The first day of the year is a public holiday.
Chinese Lunar New Year
As elsewhere in China, this is a three-day public holiday in late January or early February.
Lantern Festival
Not a public holiday, but a lot of fun, this festival occurs two weeks after the Chinese New Year.
Procession of Our Lord of Passion
Not a public holiday, but interesting to watch. The procession begins in the evening from St Augustine's Church and goes to the Macau Cathedral. The statue is kept in the cathedral overnight and the procession returns to St Augustine's the following day.
Feast of the Earth God Tou Tei
A minor holiday for the Chinese community in March or April.
Tomb Sweep Day
A major public holiday in April.
Easter
A four-day public holiday starting on Good Friday and lasting until Monday.
Anniversary of the 1974 Portuguese Revolution
This public holiday on 25 April commemorates the overthrow of the Michael Caetano regime in Portugal in 1974 by a left-wing military coup.
Procession of Our Lady of Fatima
Celebrated on 13 May, this commemorates a miracle that took place at Fatima, Portugal in 1917. It is not a public holiday. The procession begins from Santa Domingo Church and ends at Penha Church.
A-Ma Festival
This is the same as the Tin Hau Festival in Hong Kong and occurs in May. It's not a public holiday.
Festival of Tam Kong
A relatively minor holiday usually celebrated in May.
Camões and Portuguese Communities Day
Held on 10 June, this public holiday commemorates 16th-century poet Luis de Camões.
Dragon Boat Festival
As in Hong Kong, this is a major public holiday held in early June.
Procession of St John the Baptist
The procession for the patron saint of Macau is held on 10 June.
Feast of St Anthony of Lisbon
This June event celebrates the birthday of the patron saint of Lisbon. A military captain, St Anthony receives his wages on this day from a delegation of city officials, and a small parade is held from St Anthony's Church. This is not a public holiday.

Battle of 13 July
Celebrated only on the islands of Taipa and Coloane, this holiday commemorates the final defeat of pirates in 1910.

Ghost Month
This festival, in August or September, is an excellent time to visit temples in Macau.

Mid-Autumn Festival
A major public holiday in September.

Portuguese Republic Day
A public holiday on 5 October.

Cheung Yeung Festival
A public holiday in October, also celebrated in Hong Kong.

All Saints' Day
Held on 1 November. Both All Saints' Day and the following day (All Souls' Day) are public holidays.

Portuguese Independence Day
Celebrated on 1 December, a public holiday.

Winter Solstice
Not a public holiday, but an interesting time to visit Macau. Many Macau Chinese consider the winter solstice more important than the Chinese New Year. There is plenty of feasting and temples are crammed with worshippers.

Christmas
Both the 24th and 25th of December are public holidays.

ACTIVITIES

Future Bright Amusement Centre (☎ 989-2318) has Macau's only ice skating rink and is also a venue for bowling. It is on Praca Luis de Camões, on the south side of the Camões Grotto & Gardens.

Up around the Guía Lighthouse is the best track for jogging. It's also the venue for early-morning taiji exercises.

Bicycles are available for hire on Taipa and Coloane, but not on the Macau Peninsula. The Westin Resort on Coloane also boasts a golf course. Hotels offering tennis facilities include the Hyatt Regency, Mandarin Oriental, New Century and Westin Resort, but there is also a public tennis court at Hac Sa Beach on Coloane.

The Hash House Harriers do various weekend jogs around Macau, with a drinking party thrown in at the end. Stop in at expat pubs such as Pyretu's and Talker to find out where the Hash is meeting.

Spectator sports are best seen at the Macau Forum (near the Jetfoil Pier) and the Taipa Stadium (next to the Jockey Club on Taipa).

MACAU PENINSULA

There's far more of historical interest to be seen in Macau than Hong Kong. And unlike the rest of China, churches are a major part of the scenery. Although Buddhism and Taoism are the dominant religions, Portuguese influence has definitely had an impact and Catholicism is very strong in Macau. Many Chinese have been converted and you are likely to see Chinese nuns.

Ruins of St Paul's

This is the symbol of Macau – the façade and majestic stairway are all that remain of this old church. It was designed by an Italian Jesuit and built in 1602 by Japanese refugees who had fled anti-Christian persecution in Nagasaki. In 1853 the church was burned down during a catastrophic typhoon.

The spectacular facade of St Paul's, Macau

Monte Fort

The fort overlooks the ruins of St Paul's and almost all of Macau from its high and central position. It was built by the Jesuits. In 1622, a cannonball fired from the fort conveniently landed in a Dutch gunpowder carrier during an attempted Dutch invasion, demolishing most of their fleet.

Kun Iam Temple

This is the city's most historic temple. The 400-year-old temple is dedicated to Kun Iam, the queen of heaven and goddess of mercy. You'll find it on Avenida do Coronel Mesquita. In the study are 18 wise men in a glass case – the one with the big nose is said to be Marco Polo.

Old Protestant Cemetery

Lord Churchill (one of Winston's ancestors) and the English artist George Chinnery are buried here, but far more interesting are the varied graves of missionaries and their families, traders and seamen with the often detailed accounts of their lives and deaths. One US ship seems to have had half its crew 'fall from aloft' while in port.

Camões Grotto & Gardens

This serves as a memorial to Luis de Camões, the 16th-century Portuguese poet who has become something of a local hero, though his claim is not all that strong. He is said to have written his epic *Os Lusiadas* by the rocks here, but there is no firm evidence that he was ever in Macau. A bust of Camões is in the gardens, which provide a pleasant, cool and shady place. The gardens are popular with the local Chinese and you may find old men sitting here playing checkers.

Barrier Gate

This used to be of interest because you could stand 100 metres from it and claim that you'd seen into China. Now you can stand on the other side and claim you've seen Macau.

Leal Senado

Known in English as the Loyal Senate, this graceful building looks out over the main town square and is the main administrative body for municipal affairs. At one time it was offered (and turned down) a total monopoly on all Chinese trade! The building also houses the National Library.

Guía Fortress

This is the highest point on the Macau Peninsula, and is topped with a lighthouse and 17th-century chapel. The lighthouse is the oldest on the China coast, first lit up in 1865.

St Dominic's Church

Arguably the most beautiful church in Macau, this 17th-century building has an impressive tiered altar. There is a small museum at the back, full of church regalia, images and paintings.

Lou Lim Ioc Gardens

These peaceful gardens with an ornate mansion (now the Pui Ching School) are a mixture of Chinese and European influences, with huge shady trees, lotus ponds, pavilions, bamboo groves, grottoes and odd-shaped doorways.

A-Ma Temple

Macau means the City of God and takes its name from A-Ma-Gau, the Bay of A-Ma. A-Ma Temple (Ma Kok Miu), which dates from the Ming Dynasty, stands at the base of Penha Hill near the southern end of the peninsula. According to legend, A-Ma, goddess of seafarers, was supposed to have been a beautiful young woman whose presence on a Guangzhou-bound ship saved it from disaster. All the other ships of the fleet, whose rich owners had refused to give her passage, were destroyed in a storm. The boat people of Macau come here on a pilgrimage each year in April or May.

Macau Maritime Museum

There are a number of boats on exhibit here, including a *lorcha*, a type of sailing cargo-vessel used on the Pearl River. The museum offers short cruises for M$15. The Maritime Museum is on the waterfront opposite the A-Ma Temple.

THE SOUTH

Rua D Belchior Carneiro

Calçada de S Paulo

L da Companhia

Rua Colonos

C Botelho

Rua Santo Antonio

Rua de S Paulo

Rua dos Faitioes

R Nossa Senhora do Amparo

Rua de Cinco Outubro

Rua do Teatro

T Armazem Velho

Rua Palha

Rua das Estalagens

Rua de S Domin

Largo da S

Rua Nova do Comercio

Rua Visconde Paco de Arcos

Rua do Pagode

Rua Camilo Pessanha

Rua Mercadores

T do Soriano

Largo do Senado

Travessa Pagode

Rua da Madeira

Avenida de Almeida Ribeiro

Rua da Caldeira

Travessa Caldeira

Rua da Felicidade

T Aterro Novo

Rua Cules

Calçada do Tronco Velho

Macau-Guangzhou Ferry Wharf

Travessa Auto Novo

Rua de Felicidade

T da Felicidade

Rua Allandega

Rua das Lorchas

Rua do Bocage

Rua Gamboa

Inner Harbour

Praca Ponte e Horta

Patio Francisco Antonio

Travessa Chan Loc

Rua do Barao

Rua do Seminario

Rua Prata

Rua de S Lourenço

Travess

Traves

1
2
3
24
23
25
26
27
28
29
30
31
32
33
34
35
36
37
38
39
40
41
42
62
63
64
65
66
67
68
69
70
71
72
73
74
75
76

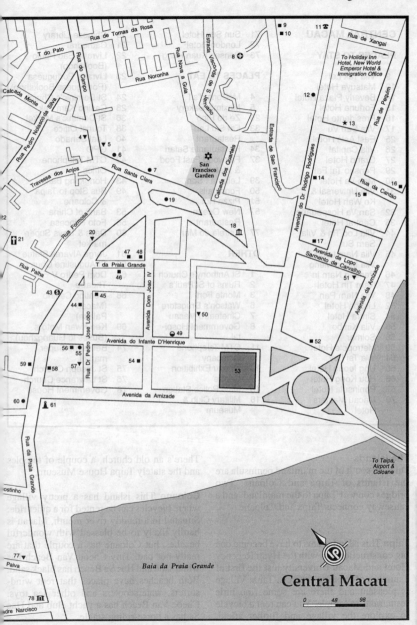

Central Macau

0   48   98

Baia da Praia Grande

To Taipa,
Airport &
Coloane

CENTRAL MACAU

PLACES TO STAY

9	Vila Tak Lei
10	Matsuya Hotel
14	Beverly Plaza Hotel
15	Fortuna Hotel
16	Presidente Hotel
17	Vila San Vu
25	East Asia Hotel
26	Vila Capital
27	Grand Hotel
29	Pensao Tai Fat
30	Man Va Hotel
31	Vila Universal & Ko Wah Hotel
32	San Va Hospedaria
35	Central Hotel
44	Vila Loc Tin & Vila Sam Sui
45	Vila Nam Loon & Vila Meng Meng
46	Pensao Nam In
47	Nam Tin Hotel
48	Vila Nam Pan
52	Lisboa Hotel
54	Sintra Hotel
56	Vila Kimbo
58	Solmar
59	Metropole Hotel
64	Vila Tai Loy
65	Ung Ieong Hotel
66	Hou Kong Hotel
67	Peninsula Hotel
70	Macau Masters Hotel
71	Sun Sun Hotel
72	London Hotel
73	Pensao Kuan Heng

PLACES TO EAT

4	McDonald's I
5	Maxim's Bakery
20	Ze do Pipo
33	Fat Siu Lau Restaurant
34	Restaurante Safari
37	Fairwood Fast Food & Watson's
39	Leitaria I Son
50	Foodstalls
51	Pizza Hut
57	New Ocean Restaurant
77	Estrela do Mar

OTHER

1	St Anthony's Church
2	Ruins of St Paul's
3	Monte Fort
6	Watson's Drugstore
7	Cineteatro Macau
8	Government Hospital
11	CTM Telephone Company
12	Macau Exhibition Centre
13	Main Police Station
18	Military Club & Museum
19	Chinese Library
21	Cathedral
22	Livraria Sao Paulo (Bookshop)
23	Livraria Portuguesa (Portuguese Bookshop)
24	St Dominic's Church
28	Casino Kam Pek
36	St Dominic's Market
38	Tourist Office
40	Leal Senado
41	GPO
42	CTM Telephone Office
43	Hongkong Bank
49	Bus Stop to Taipa & Coloane
53	Bank of China
55	Foto Princesa
60	Days & Days Supermarket
61	Jorge Alvares Statue
62	St Augustine Church
63	Dom Pedro V Theatre
68	Floating Casino (Macau Palace)
69	Kee Kwan Motors (Buses to Guangzhou)
74	Belissimo Super market
75	St Joseph Church
76	St Lawrence Church
78	Government House

The Islands

Directly south of the mainland peninsula are the islands of Taipa and Coloane. Two bridges connect Taipa to the mainland, and a causeway connects Taipa and Coloane.

Taipa This island seems to have become one big construction site with the Hyatt Regency Hotel and Macau University just the first of a number of massive projects. Taipa Village is pleasant and there are some fine little restaurants to sample. You can rent a bicycle to explore the village and further afield.

There's an old church, a couple of temples and the stately Taipa House Museum.

Coloane This island has a pretty village where bicycles can be rented for a quiet ride. Situated in a muddy river mouth, Macau is hardly likely to be blessed with wonderful beaches, but Coloane has a couple that are really not bad. Tiny Cheoc Van Beach has white sand and Hac Sa Beach has black sand. Both beaches have places that rent windsurfers, waterscooters and other sea toys. Cheoc Van Beach has a yacht club and Hac Sa has a horse-riding stable.

THE SOUTH

Coloane Park is most notable for its aviary, and as the starting point on the Coloane Trail which is over eight km in length. The path leads to the top of Alto Coloane, the highest point in Macau.

ORGANISED TOURS

A typical city tour (booked in Macau) of the peninsula takes three to four hours and costs about M$100 per person, often including lunch. Bus tours out to the islands run from about M$50 per person. You can also book a one-day bus tour across the border into Zhuhai in China, which usually includes a trip to the former home of Dr Sun Yatsen in Zhongshan County. Given the lack of interesting sights in Zhuhai, it hardly seems worth the bother.

PLACES TO STAY

During weekends, hotel prices can double and rooms of any kind can be scarce. Some bargaining is possible during the mid-week, especially in the winter off season.

With the mid to upper-range places, you can get discounts of 20% or more by booking through a Hong Kong travel agent. The best place to do this is at the numerous travel agencies in Shun Tak Centre (the Macau Ferry Pier) at Sheung Wan, Hong Kong Island.

Places to Stay – bottom end

All places listed are on the Central Macau map.

One block back from the Floating Casino is an alley called Rua do Bocage. At No 17 you'll find *Ung Ieong Hotel* (☎ 573-814), though a sign on the door says Restaurante Ung Ieong. Auditorium-sized singles/ doubles go for M$41/68 and some rooms have attached bath. Before you pay, go upstairs and take a look – it's quite run-down.

Also down at the bottom end is *San Va Hospedaria* on Rua de Felicidade. A double with shared bath costs M$70.

Two blocks to the south of the Floating Casino, on Rua das Lorchas, is a large square (now buried beneath an indoor market) called Praca Ponte e Horta. Around the

square are several places to stay. On the east end of the square is *Pensao Kuan Heng* (☎ 573-629, 937-624), 2nd floor, Block C, Rua Ponte e Horta. Singles/doubles are M$150/250 and it's very clean and well managed.

The *Vila Tai Loy* (☎ 937-811) is at the corner of Travessa das Virtudes and Travessa Auto Novo. At M$200, it's barely in the budget class, but the rooms are attractive and the manager is friendly.

Also in this vicinity is *Pensao Tai Fat*, Rua da Caldeira 41-45, where rooms cost M$200.

Moving to the east side of the peninsula, the area between the Lisboa Hotel and Rua da Praia Grande has some budget accommodation. Intersecting with Rua da Praia Grande is a small street called Rua Dr Pedro Jose Lobo, where there's a dense cluster of guesthouses, including *Vila Meng Meng* (☎ 710-064), on the 3rd floor at No 24. If you don't mind a shared bathroom, you can get an air-conditioned room for M$130. Next door is the *Vila Nam Loon*, where rooms start at M$150.

Also on Rua Dr Pedro Jose Lobo, the *Vila Sam Sui* (☎ 572-256) seems very nice and just barely qualifies as budget with rooms for M$200.

Just above Foto Princesa (a camera shop) at Avenida do Infante D'Henrique 55-59 is *Vila Kimbo* (☎ 710-010), where singles go for M$130 and up.

Running off Avenida D Joao IV is an alley called Travessa da Praia Grande. At No 3 you'll find *Pensao Nam In* (☎ 710-024), where singles with shared bath are M$110, or M$230 for a pleasant double with private bath.

Behind the Lisboa Hotel on Avenida de Lopo Sarmento de Carvalho is a row of pawnshops and a couple of guesthouses. The *Vila San Vu* is friendly and has good rooms for M$200.

Places to Stay – middle

For the sake of definition, a mid-range hotel in Macau is anything priced between M$200 and M$500. Unless otherwise noted, all places are on the Central Macau map.

THE SOUTH

An excellent place to stay is the *East Asia Hotel* (☎ 922-433; fax 922-430), Rua da Madeira 1-A. This is one of the city's classic colonial buildings – the outside maintains its traditional façade, but it's been fully remodelled on the inside. Spotlessly clean singles/twins are M$320/360 with private bath and fierce air-conditioning. The dim sum restaurant on the 2nd floor does outstanding breakfasts.

Almost next door to the East Asia Hotel is the *Vila Capital* (☎ 920-154) at Rua Constantino Brito 3. Singles/twins are M$250/300.

On Rua Dr Pedro Jose Lobo, near Vila Sam Sui, *Vila Loc Tin* has moved upmarket – rooms are M$250.

In Travessa da Praia Grande, *Nam Tin Hotel* (☎ 711-212) looks cheap but isn't – singles are M$330! *Vila Nam Pan* (☎ 572-289) on the corner has also gotten too pricey, with singles for M$250, but try polite bargaining.

The *Central Hotel* (☎ 373-838) is centrally located at Avenida de Almeida Ribeiro 26-28, a short hop west of the GPO. The hotel looks better on the outside than it does on the inside – go upstairs and look at the rooms before you decide to stay. Singles/doubles with private bath cost from M$250/300.

The *London Hotel* (☎ 937-761) on a large square called Praca Ponte e Horta (two blocks south of the Floating Casino) has singles for M$230. Rooms are comfortable and clean.

A few doors to the south of the Floating Casino you'll find an alley called Travessa das Virtudes. On your left as you enter the alley is the *Hou Kong Hotel* (☎ 937-555), which has doubles/twins for M$260/350. The official address is Rua das Lorchas 1.

Just a block to the north of the Floating Casino, at Avenida de Almeida Ribeiro 146, is the *Grand Hotel* (☎ 921-111; fax 922-397), where singles/twins cost M$380/480.

One block to the east of the Floating Casino is a street called Travessa Caldeira, where you'll find the *Man Va Hotel* (☎ 388-655), Rua da Caldeira 32. Doubles cost M$280 but this place is perpetually full.

In the same neighbourhood is the very clean and very friendly *Vila Universal* (☎ 573-247) at Rua de Felicidade 73. The manager speaks English well and doubles/twins cost M$200/252.

Next door at Rua de Felicidade 71, close to Travessa Auto Novo, is *Ko Wah Hotel* (☎ 375-599), which has doubles from M$202 to M$212. Reception is on the 4th floor – check out the ancient lift.

Just on the north side of the Floating Casino on Rua das Lorchas is the *Peninsula Hotel* (☎ 318-899; fax 344-933). Singles/twins are M$350/400. This hotel is large, clean and popular.

Stretching the definition of 'mid-range' is the *Macau Masters Hotel* (☎ 937-572; fax 937-565; 75 rooms), Rua das Lorchas 162 (next to the Floating Casino). Doubles are M$440, twins M$550 to M$1000.

One more place to look around is the area north of the Lisboa Hotel on a street called Estrada de Sao Francisco. You have to climb a steep hill to get up this street, but the advantage is that the hotels have a little sea breeze and it's quiet. Up here you'll find the fancy *Matsuya Hotel* (☎ 575-466; fax 568-080; 41 rooms), where doubles/twins cost M$330/390 and suites are M$650.

Next to the Hotel Matsuya at Estrada de Sao Francisco 2-A is *Vila Tak Lei* (☎ 577-484), where doubles go for M$300. However, with some bargaining you can shave off about M$50.

On the top-end of the middle is *Guia Hotel* (☎ 513-888; fax 559-822; 89 rooms) at Estrada do Eng Trigo 1-5 (see the Macau Peninsula map). Twins are priced from M$470 to M$600, triples are M$650 and suites cost M$750 to M$930.

The *Metropole Hotel* (☎ 388-166; fax 330-890; 112 rooms) has a prime location at Rua da Praia Grande 63. Doubles are M$460 and twins are M$600.

The *Mondial Hotel* (☎ 566-866; fax 514-083; 141 rooms) is on a side street called Rua de Antonio Basto, east of the Lou Lim Ioc Gardens (see the Macau Peninsula map). It's rather far from the centre but still not cheap. In the old wing, doubles go for M$360 to

M$480, and there are suites for M$850. In the new wing, twins are M$580 to M$630 and suites cost M$1050 to M$2300.

Places to Stay – top end

Most of these hotels have a telephone number in Hong Kong which you can call to make a booking. However, you can often get a better deal booking top-end places from the travel agencies inside Shun Tak Centre (the Macau Ferry Pier) in Hong Kong. During the summer travel season, many upmarket hotels are solidly booked, even during weekdays. Just where all these rich high-rollers come from is a mystery. The map location for most hotels is shown as CM (Central Macau) or MP (Macau Peninsula); the others are on Taipa or Coloane Island. The list of top-end places includes:

Bela Vista, Rua Comendador Kou Ho Neng; eight rooms; twins M$1800, suites M$4850 (☎ 965-333; fax 965-588; HK 2881-1688) (MP)

Beverly Plaza, Avenida do Dr Rodrigo Rodrigues; 300 rooms; twins M$740 to M$900, suites M$1600 to M$1800 (☎ 782-288; fax 780-684; HK 2739-9928) (CM)

Fortuna, Rua da Cantao; 368 rooms; twins M$780 to M$980, suites M$1800 (☎ 786-333; fax 786-363; 2517-3728) (CM)

Fu Hua, Rua de Francisco Xavier Pereira 98; 140 rooms; twins M$680, triples M$730 (☎ 553-838; fax 527-575; HK 2559-0708) (MP)

Grandeur, Rua de Pequim; 350 rooms; twins M$800 to M$1000, suites M$1300 to M$7000 (☎ 781-233; fax 785-896; HK 2857-2846) (MP)

Holiday Inn, Rua de Pequim; 451 rooms; twins M$700 to M$1200, suites M$2400 to M$9600 (☎ 783-333; fax 782-321; HK 2736-6855) (CM) – don't confuse this place with the similarly named Holiday Hotel

Hyatt Regency, Estrada Almirante Marques Esparteiro 2, Taipa Island; 326 rooms; standard rooms M$990 to M$1380, suites M$2800 to M$10,000 (☎ 831-234; fax 830-195; HK 2559-0168)

Kingsway, Rua de Luis Gonzaga Gomes; 410 rooms; twins M$680 to M$880, suites M$1080 to M$3380 (☎ 702-888; fax 702-828) (MP)

Lisboa, Avenida da Amizade; 1050 rooms, twins M$600 to M$1100, suites M$1650 to M$7000 (☎ 377-666; fax 567-193; HK 2559-1028) (CM)

Mandarin Oriental, Avenida da Amizade; 435 rooms; twins M$1080 to M$1680, suites M$3500 to M$17,500 (☎ 567-888; fax 594-589; HK 2881-1688) (MP)

Nam Yue, International Centre, Avenida do Dr Rodrigo Rodrigues; 388 rooms; twins M$680 to M$880, suites M$1680 to M$3380 (☎ 726-288; fax 726-626; HK 2559-0708) (MP)

New Century, Avenida Padre Tomas Pereira 889, Taipa Island; 600 rooms, 28 apartments; twins M$1100 to M$1650, suites M$3000 to M$20,000, apartments M$20,500 to M$29,000 (☎ 831-111; fax 832-222; HK 2581-9863)

New World Emperor, Rua de Xangai; 405 rooms; twins M$870 to M$990, suites M$1480 to M$4680 (☎ 781-888; fax 782-287; HK 2724-4622) (CM)

Pousada de Coloane, Cheoc Van Beach, Coloane Island; 22 rooms; twins M$600 to M$680 (☎ 882-143; fax 882-251; HK 2540-8180)

Pousada de Sao Tiago, Avenida da Republica; 23 rooms; twins M$1080 to M$1380, suites M$1600 to M$3000 (☎ 378-111; fax 552-170; HK 2739-1216) (MP)

Pousada Ritz, Rua da Boa Vista 2; 31 rooms; twins M$1180 to M$1280, suites M$1680 to M$8880 (☎ 339-955; fax 317-826; HK 2739-6993) (MP)

Presidente, Avenida da Amizade; 340 rooms; twins M$620 to M$850, suites M$2800 to M$3800 (☎ 553-888; fax 552-735; HK 2857-1533) (CM)

Royal, Estrada da Vitoria 2-4; 380 rooms; twins M$750 to M$880, suites M$1850 to M$2980 (☎ 552-222; fax 563-008; HK 2543-6426) (MP)

Sintra, Avenida Dom Joao IV; 240 rooms; twins M$560 to M$820, suites M$1180 (☎ 710-111; fax 510-527; HK 2546-6944) (CM)

Sun Sun, Praca Ponte e Horta 14-16; 178 rooms; twins M$600 to M$820, suites M$980 to M$1650 (☎ 939-393; fax 938-822)

Westin Resort, Estrada de Hac Sa, Coloane Island; 208 rooms; twins M$1300 to M$1650, suites M$4000 to M$16,000 (☎ 871-111; fax 871-122; HK 2803-2015)

PLACES TO EAT

Given its cosmopolitan past, it's not surprising that the food is an exotic mixture of Portuguese and Chinese cooking. There is also a little influence from other European countries and Africa. The English-speaking waitresses are invariably from the Philippines.

The most famous local speciality is African chicken baked with peppers and chillies. Other specialties include *bacalhau*, which is cod, served baked, grilled, stewed or boiled. Sole, a tongue-shaped flatfish, is another Macanese delicacy. There's also ox tail and ox breast, rabbit prepared in various ways, and soups like *caldo verde* and *sopa a*

THE SOUTH

alentejana made with vegetables, meat and olive oil. The Brazilian contribution is *feijoadas*, a stew made of beans, pork, potatoes, cabbage and spicy sausages. The contribution from the former Portuguese enclave of Goa on the west coast of India is spicy prawns.

The Portuguese influence is visible in the many fine imported Portuguese red and white wines, port and brandy. Mateus Rosé is the most famous but even cheaper are bottles of red or white wine.

A long, lazy Portuguese meal with a carafe of red to wash it down with is one of the most pleasant parts of a Macau visit. The menus are often in Portuguese, so a few useful words are *cozido* (stew), *cabrito* (kid), *cordeiro* (lamb), *carreiro* (mutton), *galinha* (chicken), *caraguejos* (crabs), *carne de vaca* (beef) and *peixe* (fish).

Another Macau pleasure is to sit back in one of the many little *pastelarias* (cake shops) with a glass of *chá de limão* (lemon tea) and a plate of cakes – very genteel! These places are good for a cheap breakfast.

People eat early in Macau – you can find the chairs being put away and that the chef has gone home around 9 pm.

Henri's Galley (☎ 556-251) is on the waterfront at Avenida da República 4, on the south end of the Macau Peninsula. The adjacent *Ali Curry House* is also worth a visit.

For good, cheap Portuguese and Macanese food, the *Estrela do Mar* (☎ 322-074) at Travessa do Paiva 11, off the Rua da Praia Grande, is the place to go, as is the *Solmar* (☎ 574-391), at 11 Rua da Praia Grande. Both places are famous for African chicken and seafood.

Fat Siu Lau (☎ 573-580) serves Portuguese and Chinese food. It's at Rua de Felicidade 64, once the old red-light Street of Happiness. The speciality is roast pigeon.

An excellent place is *Restaurante Safari* (☎ 322-239) at Patio do Cotovelo 14, a tiny square off Avenida de Almeida Ribeiro across from the Central Hotel. It has good coffee-shop dishes as well as spicy chicken, steak and fried noodles.

Ze do Pipo (☎ 374-047), 95A Rua da Praia Grande (near Rua do Campo), is a two-storey splashy Portuguese restaurant with all the trimmings. Once you get past the mirrors and the marble, it's not a bad place to eat, but check the menu prices first.

Chinese-style yoghurt and milkshakes are dished up at *Leitaria I Son* (☎ 573-638), next to the Macau Government Tourist Office.

Lots of people hop over to Taipa Village for the excellent restaurants found there, though it's no longer cheap. One place to try is *Pinocchio's* (☎ 827-128). Other popular Taipa Village restaurants include the very Portuguese *Restaurante Panda* (☎ 827-338), *Galo Restaurant* (☎ 827-318) and *O'Manuel* (☎ 827-571).

At Hac Sa Beach on Coloane Island, *Fernando's* (☎ 882-264) deserves honourable mention for some of the best food and nightlife in Macau. Fernando recommends the clams.

ENTERTAINMENT
Gambling
Even if gambling holds no interest for you, it's fun to wander the casinos at night. The largest and most fun arena for losing money is the *Lisboa Hotel*. Cheating at gambling is a serious criminal offence, so don't even think about it.

There's also horse racing on Taipa Island at the *Jockey Club*. Dog races are held at the *Canidrome* (yes, they really call it that) at 8 pm on Tuesday, Thursday, Saturday and Sunday.

Pubs
There are two adjacent pubs that can claim to be the centre of Macau's nightlife. Both are near the Kun Iam Temple on the same street, Rua de Pedro Coutinho. At No 104 is *Talker Pub* (☎ 550-153, 528-975). Just next door at No 106 is *Pyretu's Bar* (☎ 581-063). Most of Macau's pubs open around 8 pm but don't get moving until after 9 pm and may not close until well after midnight.

A hot spot which is open on Friday and Saturday night only is the *Jazz Club*, Rua Alabardas 9, near St Lawrence Church. Live

School children at the entrance to the Sacred Heart Church, Guangzhou, Guangdong

GLENN BEANLAND

GLENN BEANLAND

GLENN BEANLAND

Top Left: Sculpture of the Five Rams in Yuexiu Park, Guangzhou, Guangdong
Top Right: The Sacred Heart Church, an imitation Gothic cathedral, is made entirely of granite, Guangzhou.
Bottom: The five-storey Zhenhai Tower in Yuexiu Park offers views over Guangzhou.

music is normally performed here between 11 pm and 2 am.

There is a sedate pub of sorts inside the *Military Club*, which is known for its rustic atmosphere. Other notable pubs include:

Africa Pub, Rua de Xangai 153 (next to the Immigration Office) (☎ 786-369)
Bar Da Guia, Mandarin Oriental Hotel (☎ 567-888)
Casa Pub, Estrada de Cacilhas 25, R/C 4, Edificio Hoifu Garden (☎ 524-220)
Kurrumba Bar, Rua do Tap Siac 21 (☎ 569-752)
Oskar Pub, Holiday Inn Hotel (☎ 783-333)
Panguiao Bar, Calçada do Gaio 14 (☎ 304-620)
Paprika Bar, Rua de Ferreira do Amaral 34-A (☎ 381-799)
RJ Bistro, Rua da Formosa 29-E R/C (☎ 339-380)

THINGS TO BUY

Pawnshops are ubiquitous in Macau, and it is possible to get good deals on cameras, watches and jewellery, but you must be prepared to bargain without mercy. In Macau, at least, the nasty reputation of pawnbrokers is well deserved!

The Macau Government Tourist Office has a number of good souvenir items for sale at low prices. Some of the items to consider are Macau T-shirts, books, sets of postcards and other tourist paraphernalia.

St Dominic's Market, in the alley behind the Central Hotel, is a good place to pick up cheap clothing.

If you've got the habit, Macau is cheap for Portuguese wine, imported cigarettes, cigars and pipe tobacco. However, Hong Kong's customs agents only allow you to bring in one litre of wine and 50 cigarettes duty-free.

GETTING THERE & AWAY
Air

Macau's controversial new airport opened in early 1996. There are serious doubts that the airport will ever generate enough passengers to pay for itself. Despite official denials, a newly built airport 20 km away in Zhuhai will siphon off much of Macau's business.

Very few airlines have shown much interest. Fledgling Air Macau (51% owned by CAAC) is offering flights connecting Macau to both Beijing and Shanghai. There are also proposed flights to two cities in Taiwan, Taipei and Kaohsiung, offered by EVA Air and Trans-Asia Airways. No-one is yet certain when (or if) the flight schedule can be expanded to include other cities.

For Hong Kongers in a hurry to lose their money, East Asia Airlines runs a helicopter

The bizarre and kitsch architecture of Macau's most popular gambling palace, the Lisboa Hotel.

service. Flying time from Hong Kong is 20 minutes at a cost of HK$1206 on weekdays, HK$1310 on weekends – quite an expense just to save the extra 30 minutes required by boat. There are up to 17 flights daily between 9.30 am and 10.30 pm. In Hong Kong, departures are from Shun Tak Centre (☎ 2859-3359), 200 Connaught Rd, Sheung Wan; in Macau, departures are from the Jetfoil Pier (☎ 725-939).

Land

Macau is an easy gateway into China. You simply take a bus to the border and walk across. Bus No 3 runs between the Jetfoil Pier and the Barrier Gate at the Macau-China border. You can also catch a bus directly from Macau to Guangzhou, though this won't save any time because you've got a long stopover at the border while your fellow passengers go through the immigration queues. Tickets for the Guangzhou bus are sold at Kee Kwan Motors next to the Floating Casino.

Sea

The vast majority of visitors to Macau make their arrival and departure by boat.

Guangzhou-Macau There are two ships which run on alternate days, the *Dongshanhu* and the *Xiangshanhu*.

In Macau, departures are from the pier near the Floating Casino (*not* the Jetfoil Pier). The boat leaves Macau at 8.30 pm and arrives in Guangzhou the next morning at 7.30 am. Fares are M$96 in 2nd class, M$120 in 1st class and special class costs M$176. There is an extra M$8 charge on holidays.

In Guangzhou, departures are from Zhoutouzui Wharf. Fares are exactly the same as in Macau. From Guangzhou, the boat departs at 8.30 pm.

Hong Kong-Macau Macau is separated from Hong Kong by 65 km of water. There are departures about once every 15 minutes during daylight hours, and every 30 minutes

at night. The boats operate from 7 am to 9.30 pm.

You have three types of boats to choose from. There are jetfoils, turbocats (jet-powered catamarans) and high-speed ferries. Jetfoils take 55 minutes. The turbocats come in two varieties: so-called jumbo-cats, which take 65 minutes, and tri-cats, which take 55 minutes. Slowest are the high-speed ferries (95 minutes), but they are also the cheapest. Smoking is prohibited on the jetfoils and turbocats.

Most of the boats depart from the huge Macau Ferry Pier next to Shun Tak Centre at 200 Connaught Rd, Sheung Wan, Hong Kong Island – this is easily reached by MTR to the Sheung Wan station. However, there are a few boats from the China Hong Kong City Ferry Pier in Kowloon.

Luggage space on the jetfoils is limited to what you can carry. You'll be OK just carrying a backpack or one suitcase, but oversized baggage will need to be checked in as on an aircraft.

On weekends and holidays, you'd be wise to book your return ticket in advance because the boats are sometimes full. Even Monday morning can be difficult for getting seats back to Hong Kong, but there is normally no problem on weekdays. If you can't get a seat on the jetfoil or turbocat, you might have a chance with the high-speed ferries, which have a lot more room.

Jetfoil tickets can be purchased up to 28 days in advance in Hong Kong at the pier and at MTR Travel Services Centres, or booked by phone (☎ 2859-6569) if you have a credit card. Turbocat tickets can be purchased 28 days in advance at the pier (no phone bookings), at China Travel Service in Hong Kong or at the Lisboa Hotel in Macau.

There are three different classes on the high-speed ferries and turbocats (economy, first and VIP). The VIP cabin seats up to six persons, and the cost per ticket is the same whether one or six persons occupy the cabin. The jetfoils have two classes (economy and first). The Hong Kong government charges HK$26 departure tax, which is included in the price of your ticket. Macau charges

M$22 departure tax, also included in the ticket price. The following prices are what you pay in Hong Kong:

Vessel	Weekday (HK$)	Weekend (HK$)	Night (HK$)
High-Speed Ferry	30/55/71	35/55/71	no night fare
Jetfoil	123/136	134/146	152/166
Turbocat	123/223/ 1336	134/234/ 1396	146/246/ 1476

GETTING AROUND

Macau is fairly compact and it's relatively easy to walk almost everywhere, but you'll definitely need motorised transport to visit the islands of Taipa and Coloane.

To/From the Airport

At the time of writing this was not yet sorted out, but no doubt some sort of easy bus and taxi service will be made available.

Bus

There are minibuses and large buses, and both offer air-con and frequent service. They operate from 7 am until midnight. Buses on the Macau Peninsula cost M$2.

Arguably the most useful bus to travellers is the No 3, which takes in the China border crossing, the Jetfoil Pier and the central area near the GPO. There are numerous other routes. Unfortunately, these change so frequently that Macau's map makers have given up – most maps of the city do not show bus routes. Nevertheless, a detailed map (preferably bilingual) will be of some help in navigation.

Buses to Taipa cost M$2.50, to Coloane Village it's M$3.20 and to Hac Sa Beach (on Coloane) it's M$4. At the time of writing, Bus Nos 11, 26, 26A, 28A, 33 and 38 all go to Taipa and/or Coloane.

Taxi

Macau taxis all have meters, and drivers are required to use them. Flagfall is M$8 for the first 1.5 km, thereafter it's M$1 every 250 metres. There is a M$5 surcharge to go to

Taipa, and M$10 to go to Coloane, but there is no surcharge on return trips. Taxis can be dispatched by radio if you ring up (☎ 519-519). Not many taxi drivers speak English, so it would be helpful to have a map with both Chinese and English or Portuguese.

Car

The mere thought of renting a car for sightseeing on the Macau Peninsula is ridiculous – horrendous traffic and the lack of parking space makes driving more of a burden than a pleasure. However, between a group, car rental might make sense for exploring on Taipa and Coloane.

As in Hong Kong, driving is on the left-hand side of the road. Another local driving rule is that motor vehicles must always stop for pedestrians at a crosswalk if there is no traffic light. It's illegal to beep the horn.

Happy Mokes (☎ 439-393, 831-212) is across from the Jetfoil Pier in Macau. Bookings can be made at its Hong Kong office (☎ 2540-8180). A Moke costs M$280 on weekdays and M$310 on weekends and holidays.

You can also rent mokes from Avis Rent A Car (☎ 336-789, 567-888 ext 3004) at the Mandarin Oriental Hotel. It's probably not necessary on weekdays, but you can book in advance at the Avis Hong Kong office (☎ 2541-2011).

Bicycle

You can hire bicycles out on the islands of Taipa and Coloane. On the peninsula, there are no places to hire bikes and, anyway, it wouldn't be pleasant riding with the insane traffic.

Pedicabs

The pedicabs are essentially for touristy sightseeing and photo opportunities. The vehicles have to be bargained for and it's hardly worth the effort – if there are two of you make sure the fare covers both. Typical fees are M$20 for a short photo opportunity, or about M$100 per hour.

Guangdong 广东

Guangdong's close proximity to Hong Kong has made it a major gateway into China. It has also made it China's most affluent province. Back in 1979, Guangdong was China's 10th largest province in economic terms. A high level of economic integration between Guangdong's Pearl River Delta and Hong Kong, however, has led to record economic growth – some economists refer to the area as Greater Hong Kong.

The Cantonese, as the people of Guangdong are called, are regarded somewhat suspiciously by Chinese in the north of China, and are sometimes even referred to as 'southern barbarians'. Trade with the 'foreign barbarians' first started in Guangdong, and it was the Cantonese who spearheaded Chinese emigration to the USA, Canada, Australia and South Africa in the mid-19th century, spurred on by the gold rushes in those countries and by the wars and growing poverty in their own country. In Chinatowns around the world, it is mostly Cantonese food which is eaten and the Cantonese dialect which is most spoken.

The economic successes of Hong Kong and ethnic Chinese around the world have been important factors in Guangdong's dizzying growth. Hong Kong and other Overseas Chinese businesspeople have invested heavily in the province. At the same time, the Hong Kong entertainment industry (films and music in particular) has helped to create a strong regional culture. When China-watchers worry (or rub their hands in glee) about the possible decentralisation of power in China and the rise of regionalism, it is Guangdong that is chief among their examples.

After all, Guangdong was a latecomer to the Chinese empire. It was not integrated until 214 BC, during the Qin Dynasty. Since then the province has been the site of 15 rival national governments, giving the province a reputation for unruliness and revolt.

Today Guangdong is an economic power-

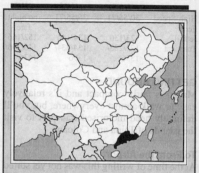

Population: 59 million
Capital: Guangzhou (Canton)
Highlights:
- Decaying colonial ambience on Guangzhou's Shamian Island
- Fear and loathing, the bizarre and the disgusting (plus vegetables) at Guangzhou's Qingping Market
- Ancestor Temple at Foshan
- Limestone crags at Zhaoqing, the poor cousin of Guilin

house rather than a sightseeing destination. Most foreigners visiting the province are there on business or in transit to other, less developed parts of China. The Special Economic Zones (SEZs) of Shenzhen and Zhuhai – though fabulous success stories – offer little to see, and Guangzhou is for the most part an urban sprawl that resounds to the sound of jackhammers and car horns.

GUANGZHOU

Known also as Canton, Guangzhou (*guǎngzhōu*) is the capital of Guangdong Province and one of the most prosperous cities in China. There may not be much in the way of sights, but wandering the streets of Guang-

Guangdong

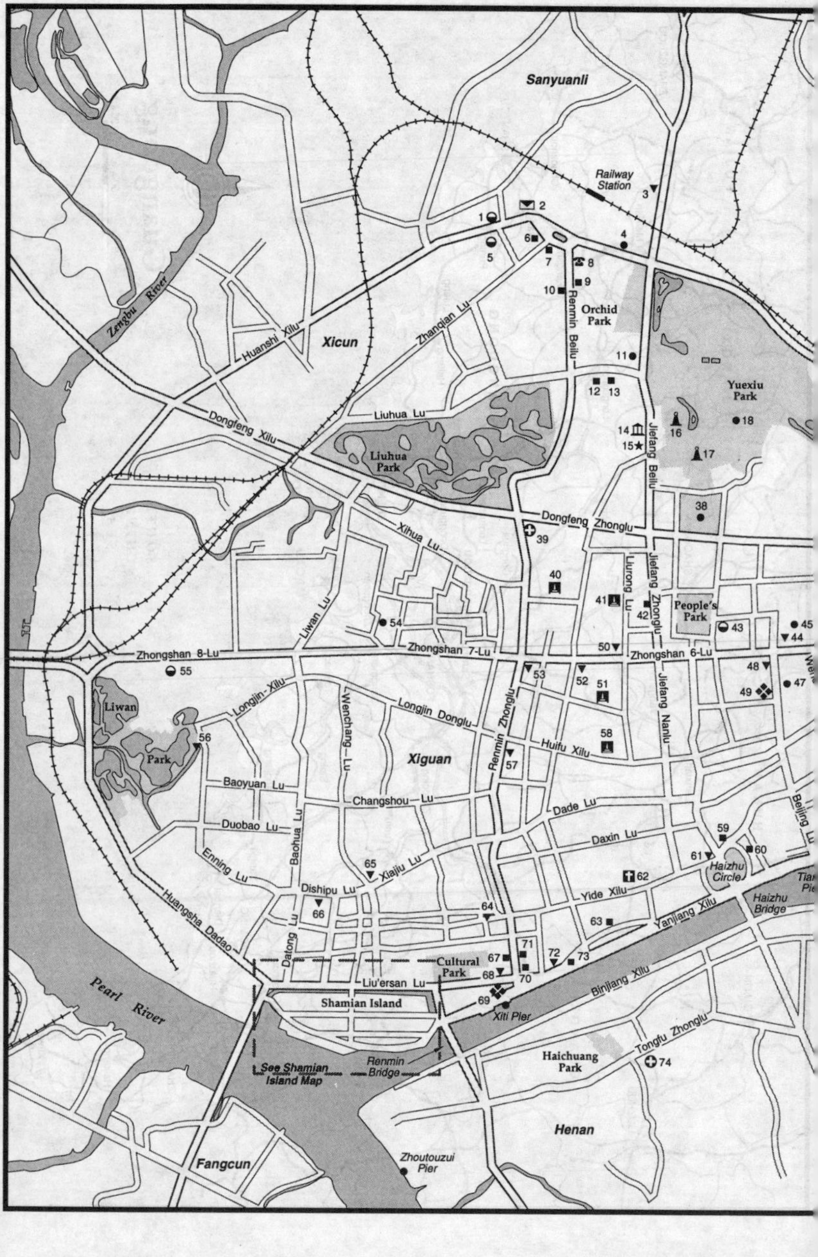

Sanyuanli

Railway
Station   ▼3

1 ☎   ✉ 2
6 ☎   ▼4
5 ●   7
☎ 8
☐ 9
10 ●   Renmin Beilu   Orchid Park

Xicun   Zhangjian Lu

11 ●
Liuhua Lu   12 ▪ 13 ▪
Yuexiu
Park

Dongfeng Xilu   14 🏛   Jiefang Beilu   ● 18
Liuhua Park   15 ★   16 ●
Huaineh Xilu   17 🏯

Zengbu River   38 ●
Dongfeng Zhonglu
Xihua Lu   39 ▼
40 🏛
41 🏛   42 🏛   People's
Park
● 54   Liwan Lu   Liurong Lu   Jiefang Zhonglu   43 ◡   ● 45
Zhongshan 8-Lu   Zhongshan 7-Lu   50 ▼   ▼ 44
◡ 55   53 ▼   Zhongshan 6-Lu   48 ▼
52 ▼ 51   49 ●   ● 47
Longjin Xilu   Longjin Donglu   🏛   58 🏛
56   57 ▼   Huifu Xilu
Liwan   Baoyuan Lu   Renmin Zhonglu
Park   Changshou Lu   Dade Lu
Duobao Lu   Daxin Lu   59 ●
Enning Lu   65   Xiajiu Lu   61 ●   ● 60
Huangsha Dadao   Baohua Lu   Dishipu Lu   62 ⛪   Haizhu
Circle
66   63 ▪   Yide Xilu   Yanjiang Xilu   Haizhu Bridge
64 ▼   Binjiang Xilu
71 ▼   72 ▪ 73
Datong Lu   Cultural   67 ▪
Park   68 ▪ 70
Liu'ersan Lu   69 ●
Xiti Pier   Tongfu Zhonglu
Shamian Island   Haichuang
Park   74 ⊕
See Shamian
Island Map   Renmin
Bridge
Henan

Pearl River
Fangcun   Zhoutouzui
Pier

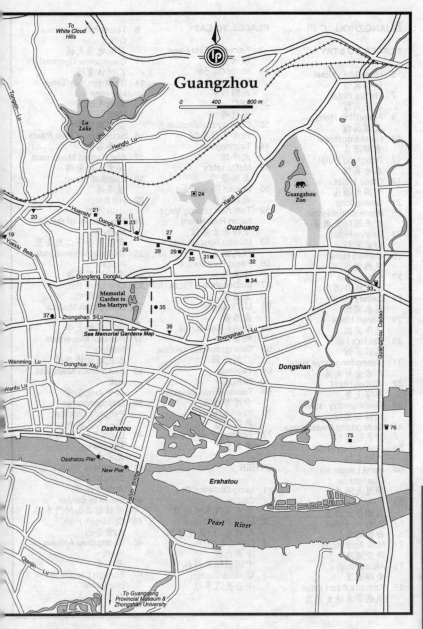

Guangzhou

To
White Cloud
Hills

Tonsin-Lu

Lu
Lake

Luhu Lu

Hengtu Lu

Huanshi
Donglu

Yuexiu Beilu

Xianli Lu

24

Guangzhou
Zoo

Ouzhuang

21

22
23

25

26

27

28 29

30 31

32

34

19

20

Dongfeng Donglu

Memorial
Garden to
the Martyrs

35

33

37

Zhongshan 3-Lu

36

See Memorial Gardens Map

Zhongshan 1-Lu

Dongshan

Guangzhou Diadao

Wenming Lu

Donghua·Xilu

Wanfu Lu

Dashatou

Dashatou Pier

New Pier

Haiyin Bridge

Ershatou

75

76

Pearl   River

Qianlin Lu

To Guangdong
Provincial Museum &
Zhongshan University

THE SOUTH

GUANGZHOU 广州

PLACES TO STAY

6 Hong Mian Hotel
红棉宾馆
7 Liuhua Hotel
流花宾馆
9 Friendship Hotel
友谊宾馆
10 Hotel Equatorial
贵都酒店
12 Dongfang Hotel
东方宾馆
13 China Hotel
中国大酒店
21 Guangdong
International Hotel
广东国际大酒店
23 Baiyun Hotel
白云宾馆
26 Garden Hotel
花园酒店
27 Holiday Inn
文化假日酒店
28 Cathay Hotel
国泰宾馆
29 Ocean Hotel
远洋宾馆
30 Hakka's Hotel
嘉应宾馆
31 Guangdong Jinye Hotel
广东金页大厦
32 Yuehai Hotel
粤海大厦
34 Pine Forestry Hotel
松林业宾馆
42 Guangdong Guesthouse
广东迎宾馆
59 Guangzhou Hotel
广州宾馆
60 Hotel Landmark
Guangzhou
华厦大酒店
63 Furama Hotel
富丽华大酒店
67 Baigong Hotel
白宫酒店
71 New Asia Hotel
新亚酒店
73 Aiqun Hotel
爱群大厦
75 Ramada Pearl Hotel
凯施华美达大酒店

PLACES TO EAT

3 Fairwood Fast Food
快活快餐
19 North Garden
Restaurant
北园酒家
20 KFC
肯德鸡
36 Cowboy Steakhouse
西部牛仔餐馆
44 Taipingguan
太平馆
48 McDonald's
麦当劳
50 Xiyuan Restaurant
西园饭店
52 Tsai Ken Hsiang Vege-
tarian Restaurant
菜根香素菜馆
53 Muslim Restaurant
回民饭店
56 Panxi Restaurant
泮溪酒家
57 McDonald's & Pizza Hut
麦当劳
61 McDonald's
麦当劳
64 Snake Restaurant
蛇餐馆
65 Guangzhou Restaurant
广州酒家
66 Taotaoju
陶陶居
68 Taiwan Fried Chicken
台湾香鸡城
70 Xinhua Hotel
新华酒店
72 Timmy's Fast Food
添美食

OTHER

1 Long-Distance Bus
Station
广东省汽车客运站
2 Main Post Office
邮政总局 (流花邮局)
4 CAAC & CITS
中国民航，
中国国际旅行社
5 Minibus Station
小公共汽车站
8 Telecommunications
Office
国际电话大楼
11 Guangzhou Gymnasium
广州体育场
14 Southern Yue Tomb
Museum
南越王汉墓
15 PSB
公安局外事科
16 Sculpture of Five Rams
五羊石像
17 Sun Yatsen Monument
孙中山纪念碑
18 Zhenhai Tower
镇海楼
22 Hill Bar
小山酒吧
24 Mausoleum of the 72
Martyrs
黄花岗七十二烈士墓
25 Nanfang International
Plaza
南方国祭商厦
33 One Love Bar
红风车酒吧
35 Zhongshan Medical
College
中山医科大学
37 Peasant Movement
Institute
农民运动讲习所
38 Sun Yatsen Memorial
Hall
孙中山纪念堂
39 Guangzhou No 1
People's Hospital
第一人民医院
40 Bright Filial Piety
Temple
光孝寺
41 Temple of the Six
Banyan Trees
六榕寺花塔
43 Buses to Baiyun
开往白云山的汽车站
45 Children's Park
儿童公园
46 Guangzhou Antique
Store
粤龙堂
47 Foreign Languages
Bookstore
外文书店

zhou is an interesting lesson in what China is transforming itself into – a place of Dickensian extremes of poverty and wealth.

In the space of less than a decade, Guangzhou has gone from a quiet backwater full of decaying colonial buildings and regiments of blue-suited cyclists into a bustling Asian metropolis that looks more and more like Bangkok or Taipei as every day passes. Don't expect to like what you see. The city's few saving graces subsist in a couple of expansive parks and pockets of historical ambience that linger on in a few temples and on Shamian Island, a foreign concession that is being gracefully gentrified.

Like so many other coastal Chinese cities, Guangzhou is also becoming an expensive travel destination. For travellers on a budget there are a handful of hotels that continue to keep their prices down and their doors open to foreigners, but this is unlikely to last for very much longer. Guangzhou is in a hurry to get rich and hasn't much time for laggards.

History

The first town to be established on the site of present-day Guangzhou dates back to the Qin Dynasty (221-207 BC). The first foreigners to come here were the Indians and Romans, who appeared as early as the 2nd century AD. By the Tang Dynasty (500 years later) Arab traders were visiting and a sizable trade with the Middle East and South-East Asia had grown.

Initial contact with modern European nations was made in the early 16th century when the Portuguese were allowed to set up base downriver in Macau in 1557. Then the Jesuits came and in 1582 were allowed to establish themselves at Zhaoqing, a town north-west of Guangzhou, and later in Beijing itself. The first trade overtures from the British were rebuffed in 1625, but the imperial government finally opened Guangzhou to foreign trade in 1685.

In 1757, by imperial edict, China's foreign trade was restricted to Guangzhou and the Co Hong, a Guangzhou merchants' guild, gained exclusive rights to it. Westerners were restricted to Shamian Island, where they had their factories. Their lives there were rulebound and the Co Hong saw to it that trade flourished in China's favour. In 1773 the British decided to shift the balance of trade by unloading 1000 chests of Bengal opium at Guangzhou. The import proved popular and soon became a drain on China's silver reserves.

In 1839 opium was still the key to British trade in China. The emperor appointed Lin Zexu commissioner of Guangzhou with orders to stamp out the opium trade once and for all. Despite initial successes (the British surrendered 20,000 chests of opium), the Chinese war on drugs led to a British military reaction known as the Opium War. The British military action was ended by the Convention of Chuen Pi, which ceded Hong Kong Island to the British. A later treaty ceded the island and a piece of Kowloon 'in perpetuity'.

In the 19th century, Guangzhou became a cradle of revolt. The leader of the anti-dynastic Taiping Rebellion, Hong Xiuquan (1814-64), was born at Huaxian, north-west of Guangzhou, and the early activities of the Taipings centred on this area. Guangzhou was also a stronghold of the republican forces after the fall of the Qing Dynasty in 1911. Sun Yatsen, the first president of the Republic of China, was born at Cuiheng

THE SOUTH

village south-west of Guangzhou. In the early 1920s, Sun headed the Kuomintang (Nationalist Party) in Guangzhou, from where the republicans mounted their campaigns against the northern warlords. Guangzhou was also a centre of activities for the fledgling Communist Party.

Contemporary Guangzhou, however, swings to the tinkle of cash registers rather than the drum roll of protest and revolt. The city has hitched a ride with the Hong Kong-Shenzhen-Zhuhai economic juggernaut and is doing very well out of it. In recent times the Cantonese have been happy to leave the turbulence of politics to their northern compatriots.

Orientation

Central Guangzhou is bounded by a circle road (Huanshi Lu – literally 'circle-city road') to the north and the Pearl River to the south. This is not the full extent of the city, of course, but most hotels, commercial areas and places of interest lie within these boundaries. Accommodation tends to cluster around the railway station (in the north), on Huanshi Donglu (in the north-east) and in and around the old foreign concession of Shamian Island (in the south). If you want to come away with a reasonably decent impression of Guangzhou, Shamian Island is the best to be based in.

According to Chinese convention, Guangzhou's major streets are usually split into numbered sectors (Zhongshan 5-Lu etc). Alternatively they are labelled by compass points: *bei* (north), *dong* (east), *nan* (south) and *xi* (west) – as in Huanshi Donglu, which will sometimes be written in English as Huanshi East Road.

Information

Travel Agencies There is an enormous CITS office (☎ 666-6271) at 179 Huanshi Lu, next to the main railway station. This office is being made increasingly redundant by all the hotel booking services and private operations in town. Think of it as the equivalent of a money-losing state-run industry. The whole operation is poorly run, and

doesn't deserve to survive all that much longer. It does, however, occasionally manage to rustle up tickets for trains, buses and boats and is open from 8.30 am to 6.30 pm.

Most of the major hotels have ticketing agencies. The office in the Garden Hotel is one of the more efficient, providing air, boat and train tickets with a minimum of fuss.

Tourist Hotline A relatively new development in the Chinese tourism industry, Guangzhou, like Shanghai, now has a tourist hotline (☎ 667-7422). It has been set up mainly to deal with complaints relating to overcharging and theft.

PSB The PSB (☎ 333-1060) is at 863 Jiefang Beilu, opposite the road which leads up to the Zhenhai Tower.

Money Every large tourist hotel cashes travellers' cheques and changes Hong Kong and US dollars; some will provide cash advances on credit cards. Guangzhou's once notorious black marketeers are almost nonexistent nowadays.

American Express Guangzhou's American Express office (☎ 331-1771; fax 331-3535) is in the ground-floor lobby of the Guangdong International Hotel.

Post & Telecommunications All the major tourist hotels have post offices where you can send letters and packets containing printed matter.

If you're posting parcels overseas, go to the post office at 43 Yanjiang Xilu, near the riverfront and Shamian Island. Get the parcel contents checked and fill out a customs form.

Adjacent to the railway station is the main post office, known locally as the Liuhua post office (*liúhuā yóu jú*).

DHL (☎ 335-5034) has an office in Guangzhou, as does UPS (☎ 775-5778). Federal Express (☎ 386-2026) can be found in the Garden Hotel, Room 1356-7, Garden Tower.

The telecommunications office is across from the railway station on the east side of

Renmin Beilu. Most hotels have direct-dial international services – calls to Hong Kong are very cheap. All the main tourist hotels have 'business centres' offering domestic and international telephone, fax and telex facilities.

Guangzhou's area code is 020.

Consulates There are several consulates which can issue visas and replace stolen passports.

Australia
    Room 1503-4, Main Building, Gitic Plaza, 339 Huanshi Donglu (☎ 331-2738; fax 331-2198)
France
    Unit 1160, China Hotel, Liuhua Lu (☎ 667-7522; fax 666-5390)
Japan
    Garden Hotel Tower, 368 Huanshi Donglu (☎ 333-8999)
Poland
    Near the White Swan Hotel on Shamian Island (☎ 886-1854)
Thailand
    Room 316, White Swan Hotel, Shamian Island (☎ 888-6968 ext 3310)
USA
    1 Shamian Nanjie, Shamian Island (☎ 888-8911; fax 886-2341)
Vietnam
    13 Taojin Beilu (behind the Guangzhou Friendship Store) (☎ 358-1000 ext 101)

Medical Services The Guangzhou Red Cross Hospital has an emergency number (☎ 444-6411) with English speakers. Use it for emergencies only.

For general treatment of non-emergencies, try the medical clinic for foreigners at the Guangzhou No 1 People's Hospital (☎ 333-3090) (*dìyī rénmín yīyuàn*), 602 Renmin Beilu.

If you're staying on Shamian Island or the riverfront, a nearby hospital is the Sun Yatsen Memorial Hospital (☎ 888-2012) (*sūn yìxiān jìniàn yīyuàn*), 107 Yanjiang Xilu, next to the Aiqun Hotel. Not much English is spoken here but the medical facilities are pretty good and the prices low.

Just next to Shamian Island and the Qingping Market is the Guangzhou Hospital of Traditional Chinese Medicine (☎ 888-6504) (*zhōngyī yīyuàn*) at 16 Zhuji Lu. If you want to try acupuncture and herbs, this is the place to go. Many foreigners come here to study Chinese medicine rather than to be treated.

Warning While it is fairly safe to walk the streets of Guangzhou, remember that the city is inundated with poor peasants in search of riches. Some of them turn to crime. Pickpocketing is a problem, as is bag snatching. Be sensible and keep alert, even in places where you would not normally think of being so – hotel lobbies and so on. The railway station area is commonly regarded as the most dangerous part of town.

Peasant Movement Institute
(*nóngmín yùndòng jiǎngxí suǒ*)
In the early days of the Communist Party members from all over China trained at the Peasant Movement Institute, which was built in 1924. It was set up by Peng Pai, a high-ranking Communist leader who believed that if a Communist revolution was to succeed in China then the peasants must be its main force. Mao Zedong – of the same opinion – took over as director of the institute in 1925 or 1926. Zhou Enlai also lectured here.

The buildings were restored in 1953 and are now used as a revolutionary museum. There's not a great deal to see: a replica of Mao's room, the soldiers' barracks and rifles, and old photographs. The institute is at 42 Zhongshan 4-Lu.

Memorial Garden to the Martyrs
(*lièshì língyuán*)
The Guangzhou Communist uprising of 11 December 1927 was one of several across China that were responses to Chiang Kaishek's massacre of Communists in Shanghai and Nanjing in April of the same year. It was unsuccessful, and some 5700 people are estimated to have been killed during or after the uprising. The memorial garden is laid out on Red Flower Hill (Honghuagang), which was one of the execution grounds. It is a minor attraction.

THE SOUTH

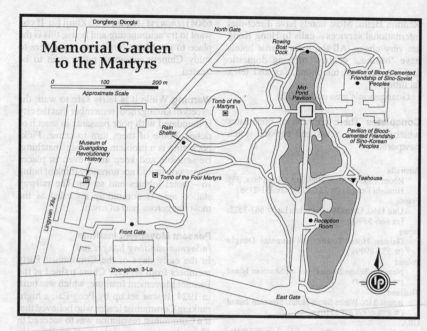

Memorial Garden to the Martyrs

Dongfeng Donglu

North Gate

Rowing Boat Dock

Pavilion of Blood-Cemented Friendship of Sino-Soviet Peoples

Mid-Pond Pavilion

Tomb of the Martyrs

Pavilion of Blood-Cemented Friendship of Sino-Korean Peoples

Rain Shelter

Museum of Guangdong Revolutionary History

Tomb of the Four Martyrs

Teahouse

Reception Room

Front Gate

Zhongshan 3-Lu

East Gate

0   100   200 m
Approximate Scale

Mausoleum of the 72 Martyrs & Memorial of Yellow Flowers

(*huánghuā gāng qīshí'èr lièshì mù*)

This memorial commemorates the victims of the unsuccessful Guangzhou Uprising of 27 April 1911, just five months before the Qing Dynasty collapsed and a Republic of China was declared.

Built in 1918, it was the most famous revolutionary monument of pre-Communist China. A motley collection of architectural symbols of freedom and democracy, the memorial is essentially an exercise in architectural bad taste. An Egyptian obelisk jostles shoulders with a replica of the Liberty Bell, a miniature Trianon of Versailles and a Statue of Liberty.

Sun Yatsen Memorial Hall

(*sūn zhōngshān jìniàn táng*)

This large hall on Dongfeng Lu was built in honour of Sun Yatsen, with donations from Overseas Chinese and from Guangzhou citizens. It dates from 1931.

Temple of the Six Banyan Trees

(*liù róng sì huā tǎ*)

The six banyan trees of the temple's name (celebrated in a poem by Su Dongpo, a renowned poet who visited the temple in the 11th or 12th century), are no longer standing, but the temple remains a popular attraction for its octagonal Flower Pagoda. At 55 metres, the pagoda is the tallest in the city – although from the outside it only appears to have nine storeys, inside it has 17. The pagoda was constructed in 1097.

Originally the temple, which may date back as long ago as the 6th century AD, was associated with Hui Neng, the sixth patriarch of the Zen Buddhist sect. Today it serves as the headquarters of the Guangzhou Buddhist Association. It is an active temple – be sensitive about taking photographs of monks and worshippers.

THE SOUTH

Bright Filial Piety Temple
(guāngxiào sì)

This temple is one of the oldest in Guangzhou. The earliest Buddhist temple on this site possibly dates as far back as the 4th century AD. The place has particular significance for Buddhists because Hui Neng was a novice monk here in the 7th century. The temple buildings are of much more recent construction, the original buildings having been destroyed by fire in the mid-17th century.

Five Genies Temple
(wǔ xiān guān)

This Taoist temple is held to be the site of the appearance of the five rams and celestial beings in the myth of Guangzhou's foundation – see the section on Yuexiu Park for the story.

The stone tablets flanking the forecourt commemorate the various restorations that the temple has undergone. The present buildings are comparatively recent, as the earlier Ming Dynasty buildings were destroyed by fire in 1864.

The large hollow in the rock in the temple courtyard is said to be the impression of a celestial being's foot; the Chinese refer to it by the name of Rice-Ear Rock of Unique Beauty. The great bell, which weighs five tonnes, was cast during the Ming Dynasty – it's three metres high, two metres in diameter and about 10 cm thick, probably the largest in Guangdong Province. It's known as the 'calamity bell', since the sound of the bell, which has no clapper, is a portent of calamity for the city.

At the rear of the main tower stand life-size statues with archaic Greek smiles; these appear to represent four of the five genies. In the temple forecourt are four statues of rams, and embedded in the temple walls are inscribed steles.

The temple is just south of Huaisheng Mosque at the end of an alleyway whose entrance is on Huifu Xilu. It is open daily from 8.30 to 11.30 am and from 2.30 to 5.30 pm.

Sacred Heart Church
(shí shì jiàotáng)

This impressive church is built entirely of granite and dates back to 1888. Designed by the French architect Guillemin, the church is an imitation of a European Gothic cathedral. Four bronze bells suspended in the building to the east of the church were cast in France; the original coloured glass was also made in France, but almost all of it is gone. It's on the north side of Yide Xilu, west of Haizhu Circle.

The Zion Christian Church, at 392 Renmin Zhonglu, is another church which may be of interest. The building is a hybrid, with a traditional European Gothic outline and Chinese eaves. It's an active place of worship.

Huaisheng Mosque
(huáishèng sì guāngtǎ)

The original mosque on this site is said to have been established in 627 AD by the first Muslim missionary to China, possibly an uncle of Mohammed. The present buildings are of recent construction. The name of the mosque means 'Remember the Sage', in memory of the prophet. Inside the grounds of the mosque is a minaret, which because of its flat, even appearance is known as the Guangta, or Smooth Tower. It stands on Guangta Lu, which runs eastwards off Renmin Zhonglu.

Mohammedan Tomb & Orchid Park
(mùhǎnmòdé mù)

At the top of Jiefang Beilu, the Mohammedan Tomb is thought to be the tomb of the Muslim missionary who built the original Huaisheng Mosque. The tomb is in a secluded bamboo grove behind the Orchid Park; continue past the entrance to the garden, walk through the narrow gateway ahead and take the narrow stone path on the right. Behind the tomb compound are Muslim graves and a monumental stone arch. The tomb came to be known as the 'Tomb of the Echo' or the 'Resounding Tomb' because of the noises that reverberate in the inner chamber.

The park itself is devoted to orchids (over 100 varieties) as the name suggests. It is well worth a visit in summer but is a dead loss in winter.

Qingping Market
(qīngpíng shìchǎng)

Qingping Market came into existence in 1979. Although such private (capitalist) markets are a feature of all Chinese cities today, it was one of Deng Xiaoping's more radical economic experiments at that time.

The market is like a take-away zoo. Near the entrance you'll find the usual selection of medicinal herbs and spices, dried starfish, snakes, lizards, deer antlers, dried scorpions, leopard and tiger skins, bear paws, semi-toxic mushrooms, tree bark and unidentifiable herbs and plants. Further up you'll find the live ones waiting to be butchered. Sad-eyed monkeys rattle at the bars of their wooden cages, tortoises crawl over each other in shallow tin trays, owls sit perched on boxes full of pigeons, and fish paddle around in tubs aerated with jets of water. There are also bundles of frogs, giant salamanders, pangolins (anteaters), dogs and raccoons, alive or contorted by recent violent

death – which may just swear you off meat. This market will definitely upset the more sensitive traveller!

The market is on the north side of Liu'ersan Lu and spills out into Tiyun Lu, which cuts east-west across Qingping Lu.

Shamian Island
(shāmiàn)

Shamian means 'sand surface', which is all this island was until foreign traders were permitted to set up their warehouses (factories) here in the middle of the 18th century. Land reclamation has increased its area to its present size: 900 metres from east to west, and 300 metres from north to south. The island became a British and French concession after they defeated the Chinese in the Opium Wars, and is covered with decaying colonial buildings which housed trading offices and residences.

The French Catholic church has been restored and stands on the main boulevard. The old British church at the western end of the island has been turned into a workshop, but is betrayed by bricked-up Gothic-style windows. Today most of the buildings are used as offices or apartment blocks, and the

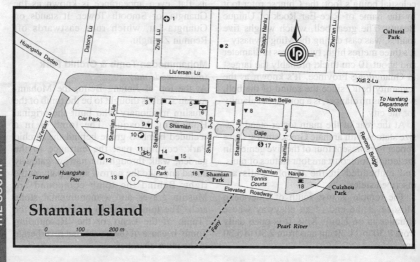

Shamian Island

0   100   200 m

Pearl River

area retains a quiet residential atmosphere detached from the bustle across the canals.

Slowly but surely the island is being gentrified. Sidewalk cafes, bars and the

---

SHAMIAN ISLAND 沙面

PLACES TO STAY

4 Guangdong Victory Hotel
  胜利宾馆
7 Guangdong Victory Hotel
  (new annexe)
  胜利宾馆 (新楼)
13 White Swan Hotel
  白天鹅宾馆
14 Guangzhou Youth Hostel
  广州青年招待所
15 Shamian Hotel
  沙面宾馆

PLACES TO EAT

3 Bakery
  面包店
5 Hot Gossip Bar & Coffee Shop
  嘉宾廊西餐厅
8 New York Silver Palace Restaurant
  银宫大酒楼
9 Li Qin Restaurant
  利群饮食店
16 Lucy's Bar & Restaurant
  露西西餐
18 Chicago Coffee Shop
  芝加哥咖啡馆

OTHER

1 Hospital of Traditional Chinese
  Medicine
  中医医院
2 Qingping Market
  清平市场
6 Post Office
  邮局
10 Polish Consulate
  波兰领事馆
11 Happy Bike Rental Station
  租自行车店
12 US Consulate
  美国领事馆
17 Bank of China
  中国银行

---

occasional boutique are starting to spring up, while police patrol to keep beggars off the island.

Cultural Park
(wénhuà gōngyuán)
The Cultural Park – just north-east of Shamian Island – was opened in 1956. Inside are merry-go-rounds, a roller-skating rink, an aquarium with exhibits from Guangdong Province, nightly dance classes, acrobatic shows, films and live performances of Cantonese opera (sometimes in full costume).

Haichuang Park
(hǎichuáng gōngyuán)
Haichuang Park across the river would be a nondescript park but for the remains of what was once Guangzhou's largest monastery, the **Ocean Banner Monastery**. It was founded by a Buddhist monk in 1662, and in its heyday the monastery grounds covered 2½ hectares. After 1911 the monastery was used as a school and soldiers' barracks. It was opened to the public as a park in the 1930s. Though the three colossal images of the Buddha have gone, the main hall remains and is now used at night as a dance hall (live band). During the day the grounds are full of old men chatting, playing cards and chequers, and airing their pet birds.

The large stone which decorates the fish pond at the entrance on Tongfu Zhonglu is considered by the Chinese to be a tiger struggling to turn around. The stone came from Lake Tai in Jiangsu Province, brought here by a wealthy Cantonese merchant in the last century. It was sold to a private collector after WW II and disappeared from public view, finally returning to the park in 1951.

Yuexiu Park
(yuèxiù gōngyuán)
This is the biggest park in Guangzhou, covering 93 hectares, and includes the Zhenhai Tower, the Sun Yatsen Monument, the Sculpture of the Five Rams and a soon-to-be-completed water theme park.

The **Sculpture of the Five Rams**, erected in 1959, is the symbol of Guangzhou. It is

THE SOUTH

said that long ago five celestial beings wearing robes of five colours came to Guangzhou riding through the air on rams. Each carried a stem of rice, which they presented to the people as an auspicious sign from heaven that the area would be free from famine forever. Guangzhou means Broad Region, but from this myth it takes its other name, City of Rams, or just Goat City.

The **Zhenhai Tower**, also known as the Five Storey Pagoda, is the only part of the old city wall that remains. From the upper storeys it commands a view of the city to the south and the White Cloud Hills to the north. The present tower was built during the Ming Dynasty. Because of its strategic location it was occupied by the British and French troops at the time of the Opium wars. The 12 cannons in front of the tower date from this time. The tower now houses the City Museum, with exhibits which describe the history of Guangzhou from Neolithic times until the early part of this century.

The **Sun Yatsen Monument** is south of the Zhenhai Tower. This tall obelisk was constructed in 1929, four years after Sun's death. It is built of granite and marble blocks and, while there's nothing to see inside, a staircase leads to the top, where there's a good view of the city. On the south side of the obelisk the text of Dr Sun's last testament is engraved in stone tablets.

Yuexiu's historical attractions will soon be overshadowed by the arrival of an 'American-style' water theme park. The park will contain – wait for it – water slides, a wave pool, an Olympic-size swimming pool, a 24-lane bowling alley, a children's playground and shopping arcades. The whole thing will cost over US$15 million, and completion is targeted for mid-1996.

Southern Yue Tomb Museum
(nán yuè wáng mù)
The Southern Yue Tomb Museum is also known as the Museum of the Western Han Dynasty of the Southern Yue King's Tomb. It stands on the site of the tomb of Emperor Wen, the second ruler of the Southern Yue Kingdom dating back to 100 BC. The South-

ern Yue Kingdom is what the area around Guangzhou was called during the Han Dynasty (206-220 AD). It's an excellent museum with English explanations. More than 500 rare artefacts are on display.

Chen Clan Academy
(chén shì shū yuàn; chén jiā cí)
This family shrine is housed in a large compound built between 1890 and 1894. The compound encloses 19 traditional-style buildings along with numerous courtyards, stone carvings and sculptures.

Liuhua Park
(liúhuā gōngyuán)
This enormous park on Renmin Beilu contains the largest artificial lake in the city. It was built in 1958, a product of the ill-fated Great Leap Forward. The entrance to the park is on Renmin Beilu.

Guangzhou Zoo
(guǎngzhōu dòngwùyuán)
The Guangzhou Zoo was built in 1958 and is one of the better zoos you'll see in China, which is perhaps not saying much. It's on Xianlie Lu, north-east of the Mausoleum of the 72 Martyrs.

Guangdong Provincial Museum
(guǎngdōng shěng bówùguǎn)
This museum is on Yan'an 2-Lu on the south side of the Pearl River, and houses exhibitions of archaeological finds from Guangdong Province.

Zhongshan University
(zhōngshān dàxué)
Also on Yan'an 2-Lu, the university houses the Lu Xun Museum *(lǔ xùn bówùguǎn)*. Lu Xun (1881-1936) was one of China's greatest modern writers; he was not a Communist, though most of his books were banned by the Kuomintang. He taught at the university in 1927.

Guangzhou Fair
(zhōngguó chūkǒu shāngpǐn jiāoyì huì)
Apart from the Chinese New Year, this is the

biggest event in Guangzhou. Otherwise known as the Chinese Export Commodities Fair, it is mostly of interest to businesspeople who want to conduct foreign trade with China. The fair is held twice yearly, usually in April and October, in spring and autumn, each time for 20 days. You need an invitation to attend.

The Guangzhou Fair is important to travellers for one reason – accommodation becomes a real problem at that time and many hotels double the room prices.

Pearl River Cruises
(zhūjiāng yóulǎnchuán)
The northern bank of the Pearl River is one of the most interesting areas of Guangzhou, filled with people, markets and dilapidated buildings. A tourist boat ride down the Pearl River runs daily from 3.30 to 5 pm and costs Y10. Boats leave from the pier just east of Renmin Bridge. They take you down the river as far as Ershatou and then turn around and head back to Renmin Bridge.

From April to October there are night cruises for tourists. Departures are from Pier 2 (just south of the Nanfang Department Store). Bookings can be made at many hotels around town, including the Shamian Hotel on Shamian Island.

The White Swan Hotel on Shamian Island also offers an evening cruise from 6 to 9 pm, including dinner on the boat.

Places to Stay – bottom end
On Shamian Island, near the massive White Swan Hotel, is the *Guangzhou Youth Hostel* (☎ 888-4298) *(guǎngzhōu qīngnián zhāodàisuǒ)* at 2 Shamian 4-Jie. By default, this place wins the title of 'backpackers' headquarters' in Guangzhou since there is little else in this price range that is open to foreigners. Since renovations have been carried out, everything but the dorm beds is often booked out by Chinese visitors. Dorm beds range from Y65 to Y75, fairly grotty singles/doubles are available for Y75, while quality doubles range from Y150 to Y185.

One other possibility for budget travellers is to scout around the railway station area,

which is the haunt of touts who carry photo books or simple placards advertising inexpensive rooms. Some of these places are Chinese only, some don't seem to care who they take. The *Meishan Hotel (méishan dàshà)*, just around the corner from the station on Jiefang Beilu, was taking foreigners at the time of writing and had basic doubles for Y90. Shamian Island, however, is an altogether more pleasant area to be based and you are much more likely to meet other travellers there.

Places to Stay – middle
Pearl River Area The *Shamian Hotel* (☎ 888-8124; fax 886-1068) *(shāmiàn bīnguǎn)*, at 50 Shamian Nanjie, is only a few steps to the east of the Guangzhou Youth Hostel on Shamian Island. Doubles with twin beds start at Y190. This place is popular and at times can be booked up by tour groups.

Also on Shamian Island are two branches of the *Guangdong Victory Hotel* (☎ 886-2622; fax 886-2413) *(shènglì bīnguǎn)*. Both of them are fairly upmarket, though the branch at 54 Shamian Lu is the cheaper of the two, with rooms from HK$300 upwards. The branch at 53 Shamian St (despite the consecutive number they are on the same side of the road and around five minutes' walk from each other) has standard rooms at HK$432, triples at HK$489 and deluxe rooms at HK$616.

The *Aiqun Hotel* (☎ 886-6668; fax 888-3519) *(àiqún dàjiǔdiàn)* is at 113 Yanjiang Xilu (on the corner of Changdi Lu). Opened in 1937 but fully refurbished, this grand old place overlooks the Pearl River. Given the high standards, prices are reasonable (for Guangzhou anyway) at Y240/320 for singles/doubles, or Y400 for a deluxe twin with riverfront view.

The *Bai Gong Hotel* (☎ 888-2313; fax 888-9161) *(bái gōng jiǔdiàn)* is a pleasant and friendly place to stay, though the staff speak little English and it's in a very noisy part of town, near the river at 17 Renmin Nanlu. Singles are Y188 or Y288, doubles Y238 or Y288, and triples cost Y388. From the railway station, take bus No 31 and get off at the river.

Across the street from the Bai Gong is the *New Asia Hotel* (☎ 888-4722) *(xīnyà jiǔdiàn)*, at 10 Renmin Nanlu, where singles range from Y198 to Y238, doubles from Y238 to Y268, and triples are Y380. It's a huge, elegant-looking place that's popular with Hong Kongers but attracts few foreigners. There is no English sign on the hotel and the staff's English-speaking ability consists of 'Hello', but it's not a bad place to stay.

Just to the south of the New Asia is the *Xinhua Hotel* (☎ 888-2688) *(xīnhuá dàjiǔdiàn)* at 4 Renmin Nanlu. This is another large, Chinese-speaking place geared towards the Hong Kong crowd. Singles/doubles are reasonably priced at Y198/238.

Further to the east of here and close to the Hotel Landmark is the *Guangzhou Hotel* (☎ 333-8168; fax 333-0791) *(guǎngzhōu bīnguǎn)*, Haizhu Square. Standard doubles range from Y380 to Y420, and suites are available for Y560.

Railway Station Area Certainly one of the best deals in this neighbourhood is the *Friendship Hotel* (☎ 667-9898; fax 667-8653) *(yǒuyí bīnguǎn)* at 698 Renmin Beilu. On 'side B' of the hotel, doubles are Y168, while those on 'side A' cost Y300. The adjoining Apollo Fast Food Restaurant is a cheap place to eat.

The *Liuhua Hotel* (☎ 666-8800; fax 666-7828) *(liúhuā bīnguǎn)* is the large building directly opposite the railway station at 194 Huanshi Xilu. It's a busy place that caters overwhelmingly to local Chinese – don't expect much English to be spoken. Standard doubles range in price from Y380 to Y538. The cheaper rooms are on the ground floor and can be noisy – look the room over first before deciding whether you want to stay here.

Across the road from the Liuhua is the *Hong Mian Hotel* (☎ 666-3989; fax 666-4879) *(hóngmiǎn dàjiùdiàn)*, a very similar setup. Standard twins/triples cost Y295/340.

North-East Area One of the best deals in

this part of town is the *Pine Forestry Hotel* (☎ 776-1888; fax 778-5594) at 748 Dongfeng Donglu. Standard doubles cost Y238. Almost next door, the *Silk Hotel* offers similar rates.

At 422 Huanshi Donglu, *Guangdong Jinye Hotel* (☎ 777-2888; fax 778-7759) *(guǎngdōng jīnyè dàshà)* has standard doubles at Y268 and Y298, or Y468 for a suite. It's a nondescript kind of place with nothing in particular to recommend it.

The *Hakkas Hotel* (☎ 777-1688; fax 777-0788) *(jiāyìng bīnguǎn)*, 418 Huanshi Donglu, is reasonably good value at the lower end of the business market. Singles/doubles start at US$38/41 and range up to US$70 for a suite.

Places to Stay – top end

Pearl River Area Some top-end hotels in the Pearl River Area are:

Furama Hotel (fùlìhuá dàjiǔdiàn), 316 Changdi Lu; standard doubles US$80, suites US$150 (☎ 886-3288; fax 886-3388)

Hotel Landmark Guangzhou (huáshà dàjiǔdiàn); standard doubles start at US$120, suites from US$180 (☎ 335-5988; fax 333-6197)

White Swan Hotel (báitiāné bīnguǎn), 1 Shamian Nanjie; standard/deluxe doubles US$120/140, executive suites US$190 to US$250 (☎ 888-6968; fax 886-1188)

Railway Station Area Around the railway station, are the following top-end hotels:

China Hotel (zhōngguó dàjiǔdiàn); superior/deluxe doubles cost US$130/148 (☎ 666-6888; fax 667-7014)

Dongfang Hotel (dōngfāng bīnguǎn), 120 Liuhua Lu; singles cost US$100, doubles US$120 to US$130 (☎ 666-2946; fax 666-2775)

Guangdong Guesthouse (guǎngdōng yíng bīnguǎn), 603 Jiefang Beilu; standard/deluxe doubles cost US$60/70, while suites start at US$128 (☎ 333-2950; fax 333-2911)

Hotel Equatorial (guìdū jiǔdiàn), 931 Renmin Beilu; standard doubles start at US$75 (☎ 667-2888; fax 667-2583)

North-East Area The north-east part of the city has the highest concentration of top-end hotels and is probably the best area to be based in. The relatively new *Guangdong*

International Hotel is probably the pick of the pack for business travellers, offering personal fax machines in each of the deluxe rooms and conference facilities.

Baiyun Hotel (báiyún bīnguǎn), 367 Huanshi Donglu; wide range of rooms, from singles at US$35 to 'honeymoon doubles' at US$38 to standard/superior doubles at US$55/68 and deluxe rooms/superior suites at US$73/143 (☎ 333-3998; fax 333-6498)

Cathay Hotel (guótài bīnguǎn), 376 Huanshi Donglu; standard/superior doubles cost HK$400/700 (☎ 386-2888; fax 384-2606)

Garden Hotel (huāyuán jiǔdiàn), 368 Huanshi Donglu; doubles cost US$120 to US$125, suites start at US$250 (☎ 333-8989; fax 335-0467)

Guangdong International Hotel (guǎngdōng guójì dàjiǔdiàn); singles/doubles from US$115, executive rooms from US$140 (☎ 331-1888; fax 331-3490)

Holiday Inn (wénhuà jiàrì jiǔdiàn), 28 Guangming Lu; rooms start at US$120 (☎ 776-6999; fax 775-3126)

Ocean Hotel (yuǎnyáng bīnguǎn), 412 Huanshi Donglu; standard rooms start at US$70 (☎ 776-5988; fax 776-5475)

Yuehai Hotel (yuèhǎi dàshà), 472 Huanshi Donglu; doubles start at US$50 (☎ 777-9688; fax 778-8364).

Places to Eat

The Chinese have a saying that to enjoy the best in life, one has to be 'born in Suzhou, live in Hangzhou, eat in Guangzhou and die in Liuzhou'. Suzhou is renowned for beautiful women, Hangzhou for scenery and Liuzhou for its coffins. While most travellers would sensibly pass on a Liuzhou coffin, Guangzhou is certainly one of the best places in China to stuff your face.

There are restaurants scattered all over Guangzhou. Many of the famous old restaurants have been renovated and, like the new multi-storey Cantonese dining complexes, tend to be fairly expensive. Travellers on a budget will be better off tracking down inexpensive eats on the back alleys than in the big restaurants.

Chinese Food Many of the cheap eateries on Shamian Island have gone decidedly upmarket in recent years. Most budget trav-

ellers head for *Li Qin Restaurant (lì qún yǐn shídiàn)*. It's distinguished by a large tree growing right inside the restaurant and out through the roof. Prices are inexpensive and the food is excellent. It's only a tiny place, but the restaurant next door takes the overflow. For affordable dim sum on Shamian, head over to the *New York Silver Palace (yíngōng dàjiǔlóu)*

There are a couple of good places close to the riverfront. Foremost is the *Datong* (☎ 888-8988) *(dàtóng jiǔjiā)* at 63 Yanjiang Xilu, just around the corner from Renmin Lu. The restaurant occupies all of an eight-storey building overlooking the river. Specialities of the house are crisp fried chicken and roast suckling pig. The crisp-roasted pig skin is a favourite here. This is a great place for morning dim sum.

Close to the Datong Restaurant is the *Yan Yan Restaurant* (☎ 888-5967) *(rénrén càiguǎn)*, 28-32 Xihao 2-Lu, a side street which runs east from Renmin Lu. Look for the pedestrian overpass which goes over Renmin Lu up from the intersection with Yanjiang Lu. The steps of the overpass lead down into a side street and the restaurant is opposite them.

One of the city's best-known restaurants is the *Guangzhou* (☎ 888-8388) *(guǎngzhōu jiǔjiā)*, 2 Wenchang Nanlu near the intersection with Dishipu Lu. The four storeys of dining halls and private rooms are built around a central garden courtyard, where potted shrubs, flowers and landscape paintings are intended to create the effect of 'eating in a landscape'. Specialities of the house include shark fin soup with shredded chicken, chopped crabmeat balls and braised dove. This is an expensive restaurant and reservations are sometimes necessary.

For excellent Muslim-Chinese cuisine, check out the *Five Rams Muslim Restaurant (wǔyáng huímín fàndiàn)*, a huge place right on the corner of Renmin Lu and Zhongshan Lu. Head upstairs (as usual) for classier dining.

North of Zhongshan Lu is Dongfeng Lu, which runs east-west across the city. At 202 Xiaobei Lu, which crosses Dongfeng, is the

North Garden Restaurant (☎ 333-0087) *(běiyuán jiǔjiā)*. This is another of Guangzhou's 'famous houses', a measure of its success being the number of cars and tourist buses parked outside. Operations have been expanded from the beautiful courtyard restaurant and overflow into a hideous structure next door with tacky golden columns.

In the west of Guangzhou, the *Panxi* (☎ 881-5718) *(bànxī jiǔjiā)*, 151 Longjin Xilu, is one of the largest restaurants in the city. It's noted for its dumplings, stewed turtle, roast pork, chicken in tea leaves and a crabmeat-sharkfin consommé. Its famed dim sum is served from about 5 to 9.30 am, at noon and again at night.

In the same general direction is the *Taotaoju* (☎ 881-5769) *(táotáojū)*, 20 Dishipu Lu. Originally built as a private academy in the 17th century, it was turned into a restaurant in the late 19th century. Tao Tao was the name of the proprietor's wife. Dim sum is the speciality here; you choose sweet and savoury snacks from the selection on trolleys that are wheeled around the restaurant. Tea is the preferred beverage and is said to be made with Guangzhou's best water – brought in from the Nine Dragon Well in the White Cloud Hills.

Just north of Zhongshan Lu and west of People's park, at 344 Beijing Lu, is *Taipingguan* (☎ 333-2938) *(tàipíngguǎn cāntīng)*, a long-running establishment with an affordable ground-level fast-food section (limited English menu available) and classier offerings upstairs.

The *South Garden Restaurant* (☎ 444-9211) *(nányuán jiǔjiā)* is at 142 Qianjin Lu and the menu features chicken in honey and oyster sauce or pigeon in plum sauce. Qianjin Lu is on the south side of the Pearl River; to get to it you have to cross Haizhu Bridge and go down Jiangnan Dadao. Qianjin Lu branches off to the east.

Just to the west of Renmin Lu at 43 Jianglan Lu is the *Snake Restaurant* (☎ 888-3811) *(shé cānguǎn)*, with the snakes on display in the window. The restaurant was originally known as the 'Snake King Moon' and has an 80-year history. To get to the restaurant you have to walk down Heping Lu, which runs west from Renmin Lu. After a few minutes turn right into Jianglan Lu and follow it around to the restaurant on the left-hand side. Creative snake recipes include fricasseed assorted snake and cat meats, snake breast meat stuffed with shelled shrimp, stir-fried colourful shredded snakes, and braised snake slices with chicken liver.

Vegetarian Food The *Tsai Ken Hsiang Vegetarian Restaurant* (☎ 334-4363) *(càigēnxiāng sùshíguǎn)*, 167 Zhongshan 6-Lu, is one of the few places in Guangzhou where you don't have to worry about accidentally ordering dogs, cats or monkey brains.

Fast Food Guangzhou is swarming with fast-food restaurants nowadays. Remember that eating at these places is going to work out more expensive than eating in snackeries on the streets: in China eating at a fast-food restaurant is a modern, chic thing to do, and high prices keep away the riff-raff.

Some of the familiar names have established themselves – *KFC*, *McDonald's* and even *Pizza Hut* – but there is also a host of other less familiar variations on the burger and French fries theme. Some of the Hong Kong franchise chains, such as *Fairwood Fast Food* and *Café de Coral* do fast-food Cantonese. These make a decent lunch, and with a drink should set you back around Y20. If the crowds get to you at the Renmin Lu branch of McDonald's, try the *Chicago Steak Beer House* just over the road on the 2nd floor – the steaks aren't brilliant but the curry dishes will have you dreaming of Malaysia; wash it down with a Newcastle Brown Ale.

Other chains to look out for include *Timmy's* (pretty awful), *Da Lu*, *Taiwan Fried Chicken* (one of the best), *Dragon Ball* and *Albie & Gibie* (with two merry parrots as its logo).

Pub Grub There are a few places around town where you can get imported beers and eat Western-style meals. Pick of the pack is the *Hill Bar* next to the Baiyun Hotel on

Huanshi Donglu. The food is excellent and remarkably inexpensive. Try the fish and chips at Y20 – a bargain. The steaks here are also highly rated.

Very similar are *Lucy's*, *Hot Gossip* and the *Chicago Café* down on Shamian Island. There are English menus and English-speaking staff, and while these places are not such good value as the Hill Bar, it's worth calling into one of them if you've been in China for a while and need a break from noodles and rice.

The *Cowboy Steakhouse (xību niúzǎi píjiǔ niúpái chéng)* is a funky place with live music (pretty awful), steaks and beer, and staff dressed in cowboy attire. It's at 90 Zhongshan 2-Lu. There's no English sign but look out for it on the 2nd floor above a collection of sports and clothing stores.

Hotel Food Guangzhou's international hotels are among the best in China to eat elegant Chinese cuisine or to escape Chinese cuisine altogether. Naturally, which ever way you incline, you will be paying international prices for the privilege.

For Italian cuisine head over to *The Pizzeria* in the Garden Hotel. Pasta dishes are also available here and it is popular with the expat community. Barbecue with a Gallic touch can be had at *Le Grill* in the Guangdong International Hotel. *Cafe La* at the same hotel has a French smorgasbord in the evenings. Singapore and Malay cooking can be had at the *Gourmet Court* in the Furama Hotel.

All the major hotels have a selection of Chinese dining with English menus available.

Entertainment

There's been an explosion of entertainment options in Guangzhou over recent years. For straight drinking check out any of the bars in the international hotels (boring and expensive usually) or any of the pubs listed in the Pub Grub entry above. For late night carousing one of the most popular places around is *One Love (hóngfēngchē)*. It has a Y10 cover charge, an inky black dance area with a hip

DJ, and a large beer garden and live music area upstairs. It's good value for money and a fantastic opportunity to see an 'underground' bar in China. You can find it on the north-west corner of Dongfeng Donglu and Guangzhou Dadao. Friday and Saturday nights see the place at its liveliest.

JJ Disco (☎ 380-9911), 18 Jiao Chang Lu, has to be seen to be believed. Space-pod lights lead you into a warehouse-size dance complex with laser light shows. On a Friday or Saturday night this place is packed with sweaty bodies, and this despite the Y80 cover to get in. Techno beat is featured with happy-happy Filipino DJs. It's well worth a look.

Another dance club that was popular at the time of writing is *Hit* (☎ 331-3889) at 1 Tongxin Lu (just off Huanshi Donglu). Hidden away in an extremely tacky castle structure, it's essentially a small-scale JJ clone, but at least the cover charge is cheaper at Y50.

Red Ants is way out east on Guangzhou Dadao, not far from the Ramada Hotel. One of Guangzhou's pioneering alternative bars, it seems to have declined in popularity, but may still be worth checking out. Ask about *Awol* and *Grasshopper*, other popular bars in the area.

Finally, for anyone who wants a total Chinese experience (karaoke, tacky floor shows, dancing and lucky draws all rolled into one), the *Taojin Bar*, behind the Baiyun Hotel near the corner of Hengfu Lu, can make for a surprising night out. It's located in a disused underground car park (follow the fairy lights down a long ramp) – anything and everything goes on here. There's no cover charge, but drinks are a little pricey.

Things to Buy

The intersection of Beijing Lu and Zhongshan Lu was traditionally the principal shopping area in the city, but the whole of central Guangzhou is gradually being transformed into a huge shopping mall. The section of Renmin Nanlu down by the river is crammed with fashionable boutiques, the Haizhu traffic circle has a ritzy shopping complex, and the north-east part of town on Huanshi Donglu, where all the best hotels are, is also emerging as a top-notch shopping district.

The days when you needed to seek out a Friendship Store to stock up on goodies from the West are long gone: you can buy imported beer and Snickers bars at corner shops today. The Friendship Stores still exist, however, and now house modern supermarkets, as well as antiques sections and the like.

For souvenir shopping, try the Friendship Stores, but also take a look at the Guangzhou Antique Shops at 146 and 162 Wende Beilu. They have a reasonable range of items from collectibles to affordable souvenirs. Shamian Island also has a number of hole-in-the-wall souvenir shops. Remember to bargain. If you are heading on to Yangshuo, save your shopping for there – prices will be cheaper.

The Foreign Languages Bookstore at 326 Beijing Lu is a waste of time unless you want to pick up a copy of *Vanity Fair* or *Mill on the Floss*: the store is almost entirely given over to dictionaries and English language teaching materials. For reading material head off to the newsagents in the Guangdong International Hotel, the Garden Hotel or the White Swan. Some popular novels are available as well as current issues of *Time*, *Newsweek*, *The Economist*, *Far Eastern Economic Review* and even some French and German publications.

Getting There & Away

Air The CAAC office is at 181 Huanshi Lu, to your left as you come out of the railway station. It has separate telephone numbers for domestic (☎ 666-2969) and international (☎ 666-1803). You can also book air tickets at various locations around town, including the White Swan Hotel and the Garden Hotel. The office is open from 8 am to 8 pm daily.

International Flights There are at least four daily flights (usually more) from Hong Kong on CAAC. The flight takes 35 minutes.

There are direct flights between Guang-

zhou and a number of other foreign cities, including Bangkok, Hanoi, Jakarta, Kuala Lumpur, Manila, Melbourne, Penang, Singapore, Surabaya and Sydney.

Singapore Airlines (☎ 335-8999) has an office on the mezzanine floor of the Garden Hotel, 368 Huanshi Donglu. Malaysia Airlines (☎ 335-8828) is also in the Garden Hotel, Shop M04-05. Vietnam Airlines (☎ 382-7187) also has an office in Guangzhou.

Domestic Flights Virtually every destination in China that has an airport is connected with Guangzhou. For domestic flights, the airport departure tax is Y30.

Bus Buses ply both international and domestic routes. A small sample of what's on offer includes the following:

To/From Hong Kong If you want to get to Hong Kong with a minimum of fuss, head over to one of the major hotels and book one of the services that use the Guangzhou-Shenzhen superhighway. On a good run you can be in Kowloon in just 3½ hours. Customs procedures are normally routine and painless. The cost varies from HK$170 to HK$190. The Garden Hotel has a booking office on the ground floor.

To/From Macau Kee Kwan Motors, across the street from the Floating Casino in Macau, sells bus tickets direct to Guangzhou. It is necessary to change buses at the border. The trip takes about five hours in all. It is often quicker to arrange the trip yourself: take a taxi or bus to the Macau-Zhuhai border, then change to a minibus to Guangzhou.

To/From Shenzhen Privately owned aircon minibuses line up opposite the Shenzhen Railway Station near the Hong Kong border. The fare price is posted on a sign where the minibuses line up, and at the time of writing was Y50. Payment can be made in either HK dollars or RMB. The trip takes around three hours.

From Guangzhou to Shenzhen, minibuses operate from the bus station across the street from the Guangzhou Railway Station. The east side of the bus station (closest to the Liuhua Hotel) is where the big government-run buses are. These are cheaper but slower and less comfortable. Minibuses depart from the west side of the bus station.

To/From Zhuhai Air-con buses between Guangzhou and Zhuhai cost Y42. See the Shenzhen entry above for their departure point in Guangzhou. See the Zhuhai section later in this chapter for information on buses there.

Train Both international and domestic trains service Guangzhou. Getting sleepers on the domestic routes can be difficult. It's also worth knowing that the staff in Guangzhou's railway station are strict about foreigners using Chinese-priced tickets – if you don't have what appears to be a valid red (white) card, you won't be allowed to board.

Whatever you do, be careful near the railway station. The whole area is a den of thieves – everything from pickpockets to bag slitters and purse snatchers. There are people selling black-market (Chinese price) tickets outside the station, but the tickets are printed in Chinese so be sure you know what you're buying.

To/From Hong Kong The express train between Hong Kong and Guangzhou is comfortable and convenient. The train covers the 182-km route in 2½ hours. However, it is much cheaper to take a local train to Shenzhen and then another local train to Guangzhou.

Timetables change, but the following was current at the time of writing:

Train No	From	To	Departs	Arrives
96	Kowloon	Guangzhou	7.50 am	10.30 am
98	Kowloon	Guangzhou	8.35 am	11.15 am
92	Kowloon	Guangzhou	12.25 pm	3.05 pm
94	Kowloon	Guangzhou	2.10 pm	4.50 pm
91	Guangzhou	Kowloon	8.15 am	10.55 am
93	Guangzhou	Kowloon	10.00 am	12.40 pm
95	Guangzhou	Kowloon	4.13 pm	6.53 pm
97	Guangzhou	Kowloon	6.00 pm	8.40 pm

To/From Shenzhen The local train from Shenzhen to Guangzhou is cheap and reasonably fast. Since the opening of the superhighway, tickets have become much easier to come by. The trip takes between 2½ and three hours.

If you buy a ticket in Guangzhou, check which station it leaves from. Most Shenzhen services stop and terminate at Guangzhou's east railway station. It's a long way from the centre of town. If you arrive here, just follow the crowd to take a bus or minibus to the main railway station. Express trains all leave and arrive at Guangzhou's main railway station.

In Guangzhou, you can buy train tickets from CITS several days in advance. Otherwise, you can join the queues at the railway station.

To/From Beijing Trains head north from Guangzhou to Beijing, Shanghai and every province in the country except Hainan Island and Tibet. CITS is not always able (or willing perhaps) to organise advance sleeper tickets, though they are worth a try. If you don't mind paying over the odds in service fees and the like, it is worth trying the travel agents in the international hotels or the independent operators on Shamian Island for tickets.

In Hong Kong it is possible to book domestic railway tickets at CTS for more than double the price. The fastest express trains to Beijing take 33 hours (if on time), but most trains require 36 hours or more.

Boat Guangzhou is the major port on China's southern coast. It offers high-speed catamaran services or slower overnight ferries to a number of destinations.

To/From Hong Kong Two types of ships ply the route between Hong Kong and Guangzhou: jetcats (jet-powered catamaran) and slow, overnight ferries. See the Hong Kong chapter for information on departures from Hong Kong.

The jetcat (named *Liwanhu*) takes 3½ hours to travel between Hong Kong and Guangzhou. In Guangzhou, departures are from Zhoutouzui Wharf daily at 1 pm. Tickets can be bought at the wharf and some major hotels if you give them enough advance notice. The ticket costs HK$178 on weekdays or HK$200 on weekends.

The Pearl River Shipping Company runs two overnight ferries between Hong Kong and Guangzhou – the *Tianhu* and the *Xinghu*. This is an excellent way to get to Guangzhou from Hong Kong and saves you the cost of one night's accommodation. The ships are clean and fully air-conditioned with comfortable beds, and there is a good Chinese restaurant. The boats alternate on the runs between Hong Kong and Guangzhou, and leave at 9 pm and arrive at 6 am from both cities.

Tickets in Guangzhou can be bought at the Zhoutouzui Wharf and cost from HK$151 to HK$466. If you can't get a cabin or a bunk, then buy a seat ticket and go to the purser's office as soon as you are on board. The purser distributes leftover bunks and cabins, but get in quick if you want one.

Bus No 31 (not trolley-bus No 31) will drop you off near Houde Lu in Guangzhou, which leads to Zhoutouzui Wharf. To get from the wharf to the railway station, walk up to the main road, cross to the other side and take bus No 31 all the way to the station.

To/From Macau There is a direct overnight ferry between Macau and Guangzhou. Two ships – the *Dongshanhu* and the *Xiangshanhu* – run on alternate days.

In Guangzhou, departures are from Zhoutouzui Wharf daily at 8.30 pm. The fare is HK$91 in 3rd class, HK$106 in 2nd class, HK$136 in 1st and HK$186 in special class.

To/From Wuzhou/Yangshuo Ferry connections between Guangzhou and Wuzhou have improved in recent years. It is possible to buy a combined bus/boat ticket, but there are plenty of buses available in Wuzhou for Yangshuo and Guilin, many of them timed with the arrival of boats from Guangzhou.

The quickest way to get to Wuzhou is the rapid ferry service, which takes between 4½ and five hours. The cost is Y158 and

departures are at 7.30 and 8 am, and 12.30 and 2.15 pm. Take a morning service and you should be in Yangshuo in time for a late dinner and a beer. Tickets are sold at the Dashatou Wharf and departures are from the Rapid Ferry Terminal, which is 100 metres east of Dashatou.

The old 24-hour service is still running but most of the ferries have been upgraded, so you can do the trip in a bit more comfort than was the case in the past: Y77 will get you a two-bed cabin; Y50 a four-bed cabin; penny pinchers can sleep with the masses for Y35. Boats depart from Dashatou Wharf at 12.30, 2.30 and 9 pm.

To/From Liuzhou There is a daily boat service from Dashatou Wharf at 8 am. The cost is Y87 or Y101 – it's a long trip to a dull destination.

To/From Zhaoqing Wuzhou-bound ferries (see above) stop at Zhaoqing. The slow ferries take 10 hours to get there, while the new rapid services take just two hours. The Zhaoqing rapid service costs Y68.

To/From Other Destinations In theory there should be a boat service from Guangzhou to Shanghai via Xiamen every five days and another service from Guangzhou to Dalian via Qingdao twice monthly. Staff at Zhoutouzui Wharf insisted that both services have been indefinitely suspended. Ask for the latest information.

Zhoutouzui Wharf also has daily services to Haikou and once-weekly services to Sanya and Wenzhou.

Getting Around

Guangzhou proper extends for 60 sq km, with most of the interesting sights scattered throughout, so seeing the place on foot is impractical. Besides, the pollution and traffic in Guangzhou makes getting around on foot a miserable experience.

To/From the Airport Guangzhou's Baiyun airport is 12 km out of town near the Baiyun Hills. Inexpensive airport buses run from the

CAAC office near the railway station to the airport. It's impossible to find these at the airport itself, or if you do, to board one. The jostling crowds at the airport are almost as bad as those at the railway station.

Just outside the entrance to the airport is a taxi ramp. Taxis leaving from here are metered. Don't go with the taxi touts unless you want to be ripped off. When you get into a taxi, tell the driver '*dǎ biǎo*' (turn on the meter). The cost should be between Y30 and Y40 depending on the size of the taxi and where you are headed in town.

Bus Guangzhou has an extensive network of motor and electric trolley-buses which will get you just about anywhere you want to go. The problem is that they are almost always packed. Once an empty bus pulls in at a stop, a battle for seats ensues and a passive crowd suddenly turns into a stampeding herd. Bumper-to-bumper traffic also serves to slow public transport down during peak hours and can make getting around Guangzhou a frustrating experience.

Good Chinese maps of the city with bus routes are sold by hawkers outside the railway station and at some of the tourist hotel bookshops. Get one! There are too many bus routes to list them all here, but a few of the important routes are:

No 31 Runs along Gongye Dadao Bei, east of Zhoutouzui Wharf, crosses Renmin Bridge and goes straight up Renmin Lu to the main railway station at the north of the city.

No 30 Runs from the main railway station eastwards along Huanshi Lu before turning down Nonglin Xia Lu to terminate in the far east of the city. This is a convenient bus to take if you want to go from the railway station to the Baiyun and Garden hotels.

No 5 Starting from the main railway station, this bus takes a similar route to No 31, but instead of crossing Renmin Bridge it carries on along Liu'ersan Lu, which runs by the northern side of the canal separating the city from Shamian Island. Get off here and walk across the small bridge to the island.

Minibus Minibuses seating 15 to 20 people ply the streets on set routes. If you can find out where they're going, they're a good way to avoid the crowded buses. The front window usually displays a sign with the destination written in Chinese characters.

Taxi Taxis are abundant on the streets of Guangzhou but demand is great, particularly during the peak hours: from 8 to 9 am and during lunch and dinner hours.

Taxis are equipped with meters and drivers use them unless you've negotiated a set fee in advance – this shouldn't be necessary, even at the airport. The cost varies depending on what type of vehicle it is. The per-km cost (after flag fall) is displayed on a little sticker on the right rear window. Depending on the vehicle, a trip from the railway station to Shamian Island should cost between Y15 and Y20.

Taxis can be hired for a single trip or chartered on an hourly or daily basis. The latter is worth considering if you've got the money or if you're in a group which can split the cost. If you hire for a set period of time, negotiate the fee in advance.

Bicycle Shamian Island has at least two places to rent bicycles – finding bikes for rent elsewhere in the city is pretty much a lost cause. The Happy Bike Rental Station is opposite the White Swan Hotel and across the road from the Guangzhou Youth Hostel. Costs are Y2 per hour, Y20 per day, with a Y400 deposit. Take a look at the traffic on the streets of Guangzhou before you go ahead and hire a bike.

AROUND GUANGZHOU
White Cloud Hills
(*báiyún shān*)

The White Cloud Hills, in the north-eastern suburbs of Guangzhou, are an offshoot of Dayu Ling, the chief mountain range of Guangdong Province. The hills were once dotted with temples and monasteries, though no buildings of any historical significance remain. The hills are popular with the local people, who come here to admire the views

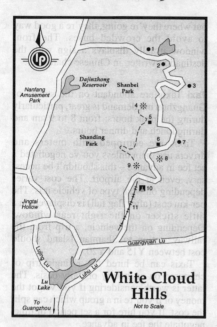

Nanfang
Amusement
Park

Dajinzhong
Reservoir

Shanbei
Park

Shanding
Park

Jingtai
Hollow

Guangyuan Lu

Luhu Lu

Luhu Lu

Lu
Lake

To
Guangzhou

White Cloud Hills

Not to Scale

WHITE CLOUD HILLS 白云山

1 Liaoyang Clinic
  疗养院
2 Mingzhu Building
  明珠楼
3 White Cloud Billowing Pines
  白云松涛
4 Star Touching Peak
  摩星岭
5 Shanzhuang Inn
  山庄旅舍
6 Twin River Villa
  双溪别墅
7 Dripping Water Crag
  滴水岩
8 Southern Sky First Peak
  天南第一峰
9 Cheng Precipice
  白云晚望
10 Nengren Temple
  能仁寺
11 Cable Car
  白云索道

and slurp cups of tea. The Cloudy Rock Teahouse by a small waterfall on the hillside is recommended if you want to do the same.

At the southern foot of the hills is Lu Lake (*lù hú*), also called Golden Liquid Lake, which was built for water storage in 1958 and is now used as a park.

The highest peak in the White Cloud Hills is Star Touching Hill (*mōxīng líng*). At 382 metres it's considerably smaller than Hong Kong's famed Victoria Peak (554 metres), but anything higher than a kiddy's sandcastle is a mountain in the Pearl River Delta area. On a clear day, you can see a panorama of the city – the Xiqiao Hills to one side, the North River and the Fayuan Hills on the other side, and the sweep of the Pearl River. Unfortunately, clear days are becoming a rarity in Guangzhou.

The Chinese rate the evening view from Cheng Precipice as one of the eight sights of Guangzhou. The precipice takes its name from a Qin Dynasty tale:

It is said that the first Qin Emperor, Qin Shi Huang, heard of a herb which would confer immortality on whoever ate it. Cheng On Kee, a minister of the emperor, was dispatched to find it. Five years of wandering brought Cheng to the White Cloud Hills where the herb grew in profusion. On eating the herb, he found that the rest of it disappeared. In dismay and fearful of returning empty-handed, Cheng threw himself off the precipice, but having been assured immortality from eating the herb, he was caught by a stork and taken to heaven.

The precipice, named in his memory, was formerly the site of the oldest monastery in the area. However, these days the precipice is usually just called the White Cloud Evening View (*báiyún wǎnwàng*).

Getting There & Away The White Cloud Hills are about 15 km from Guangzhou and make a good half-day excursion. Express buses leave from Guangwei Lu, a little street running off Zhongshan 5-Lu to the west of the Children's Park, about every 15 minutes. The trip takes between 30 and 60 minutes, depending on traffic. There is also a cable car from the bottom of the hill near Lu Lake.

Nanhu Amusement Park
(nánhú lèyuán)

Nanhu is a minor attraction with roller coasters, water slides, dodgem cars, a skating rink and go-carts. The park also has a tree-shaded lake and a good restaurant. It is best to avoid Nanhu on the weekends for obvious reasons.

Air-con minibuses depart from near the main entrance of the railway station and go directly to the amusement park.

Lotus Mountain
(liánhuā shān)

Lotus Mountain is an old quarry site 46 km to the south-east of Guangzhou. It is a possible day-trip from Guangzhou, though you should expect it to be crowded with local and Hong Kong tourists. It is of more interest to Guangzhou long-termers than to travellers with a busy itinerary.

The stonecutting at Lotus Mountain ceased several hundred years ago and the cliffs have eroded to a state where it looks almost natural. Pagodas, pavilions and stone steps have been added, creating some pleasant walks with good views of the Pearl River.

Getting There & Away Both bus and boat connections are available, but the boat is more interesting. The once-daily boat leaves Guangzhou at 8 am and takes about 2½ hours to reach Lotus Mountain. It returns to Guangzhou at 4 pm, giving you about five hours on the mountain.

The boat leaves from the Tianzi Pier *(tiānzǐ mǎtóu)* on Yanjiang Lu, one block east of Haizhu Square and the Haizhu Bridge. It's not a bad idea to buy a ticket one day in advance. Buses depart from the railway station area in Guangzhou. In theory the bus should be faster than the boat, but with Guangzhou's traffic jams it works out about the same.

The major hotels in Guangzhou also run tours to Lotus Mountain, as does CTS in Hong Kong. Naturally it is cheaper to do it yourself.

Jinsha Park
(jīnshātān dùjià cūn)

Jinsha Park is gradually being developed into a standard Chinese tourist trap – picnic ground and beach with changing rooms, restaurants and soft drink stands – but the attraction is the cruise there and back. It's unlikely you will be tempted to swim at the 'beach' (on the Pearl River); only do so if you've had a hepatitis vaccination.

The boat leaves from the No 1 ferry pier, opposite the Nanfang Department Store on Yanjiang 1-Lu, at 9.30 am. It drops passengers off at Jinshan Park about noon and returns at 3 pm. Alternatively, you can stay on the boat, which turns around at Jinxi, a small town of no significance but not without some charm from the distance of the boat.

Conghua Hot Springs
(cōnghuà wēnquán)

Conghua Hot Springs is unlikely to be of much interest to foreign visitors. Nowadays the hot spring water is piped into the bathrooms of fairly expensive tourist hotels, and the area has generally been developed into an ugly resort.

There is no shortage of hotels in the area, and visitors are greeted by touts representing the smaller, cheaper establishments (reckon on Y100 to Y150 for a double). Prices of Y300 and upwards prevail at the better hotels.

Getting There & Away Buses to Conghua depart throughout the day from the long-distance bus station on Huanshi Xilu near Guangzhou Railway Station. Some buses go directly to the hot springs, but most of the buses terminate in the town of Conghua, an ugly place 16 km from the hot springs. In that case, you have to catch another bus (20 minutes) to the hot springs *(wēnquán)*.

Foshan
(fóshān)

Foshan, just 28 km south-west of Guangzhou, is a medium-size city complete with factories and snarled honking traffic. There would be no reason to go there at all if it were not for its Ancestor Temple, which has emerged as a popular destination for local and Overseas Chinese tourists.

Like all tourist attractions worth their salt in China, there is a legend connected with Foshan (Buddha Hill). In this case, the story involves three buddha statues which mysteriously disappeared only to be rediscovered hundreds of years later in the Tang Dynasty (618-907 AD). Foshan also has a reputation as a handicrafts centre. The locally produced papercuts are common tourist souvenirs.

Information CITS (☎ 335-3338; fax 335-2347) is in the Foshan Hotel at 75 Fenjiang

Nanlu. CTS (☎ 222-3828) is in the Overseas Chinese Hotel at 14 Zumiao Lu.

Lianhua Market *(liánhuā shìchǎng)* This market is considerably smaller than the Qingping Market in Guangzhou, but it's similar. It sells dried fish, turtles, frogs, lizards, dogs and snakes.

Ancestor Temple *(zǔ miào)* Foshan's number one tourist attraction, the Ancestor Temple, attracts large tour groups from Hong Kong and elsewhere. It is one of those temples that has been through so many rebuildings that its name and function have drifted apart from each other. The original 11th-century temple may have been a place of ancestor worship, but from the mid-14th century it has enshrined a 2500-kg bronze statue of Beidi, the Taoist god of the water and all its denizens, especially fish, turtles and snakes.

Because South China was prone to floods, people often tried to appease Beidi by honouring him with temples and carvings of

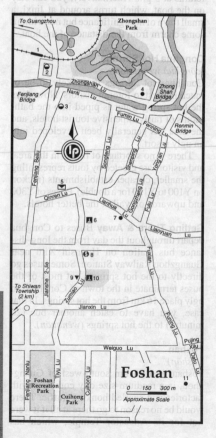

FOSHAN 佛山

1 Railway Station
火车站
2 Buses to Guangzhou
开往广州的汽车站
3 Long-Distance Bus Station
长途汽车站
4 Renmin Athletic Field
人民体育场
5 Post Office
邮电局
6 Renshou Pagoda
仁寿寺
7 Market
莲花市场
8 Bank of China & New Stadium
中国银行，新广场
9 Rose Restaurant
玫瑰酒家
10 Ancestors' Temple
祖庙
11 City Hall
市政府

turtles and snakes. In the courtyard is a pool containing a large statue of a turtle with a serpent crawling over it, into which the Chinese throw small notes and the odd drink can.

The temple also has an interesting collection of ornate weapons used on ceremonial occasions during the imperial days. The Foshan Museum is in the temple grounds, as is the Foshan Antique Store and an arts & crafts store. The temple is open daily from 8.30 am to 4.30 pm.

Getting There & Away Foshan is easily visited as a day-trip from Guangzhou. There are frequent minibuses from the west bus station (*guǎngfó qìchē zhàn*) on Zhongshan Balu. Alternatively, there are less frequent services from the long-distance bus terminal next to the Liuhua Hotel, near the railway station. Minibuses take a little over an hour (depending on the traffic).

Train services between Guangzhou and Foshan, faster than the buses (30 minutes), are an alternative to the maddening traffic. However, the time consumed organising a ticket at Guangzhou's chaotic railway station and waiting for the train is likely to exceed that wasted sitting on the bus in a traffic jam. There are six departures daily.

For the busy business traveller, there are now direct express trains to/from Hong Kong. These cost Y190 and take three hours. Currently, there are two trains daily, departing from Kowloon's Hunghom Railway Station at 4.28 and 6.10 pm. Going the other way, departures from Foshan are at 11.50 am and 1.32 pm.

Getting Around You won't have to look too hard for the two-wheeled taxis – they will be looking for you. Motorcycle drivers wearing red safety helmets greet minibuses arriving from Guangzhou and practically kidnap disembarking passengers. The drivers assume that every foreigner wants to head for the Ancestor Temple. If that's not where you want to go, make that clear straight away.

There aren't too many pedicabs, but you will see them about town. Foshan's pedicabs are really designed for hauling freight – there are no seats, just a cargo area behind the driver. Fares are negotiable.

Shiwan
(*shìwān*)
Two km south-west of Foshan, Shiwan township is known mostly for its porcelain factories. Although there is nothing of outstanding scenic interest here, you might want to take a look if you have an interest in pottery. Bus Nos 9 and 10 go to Shiwan. You can catch bus No 9 in front of the Ancestor Temple, or No 10 on Fenjiang Xilu. From the Ancestor Temple, you could walk to Shiwan in 30 minutes.

The only hotel accepting foreigners is the Taocheng Hotel (*táochéng bīnguǎn*) at the corner of Heping Lu and Yuejin Lu.

Xiqiao Hills
(*xīqiáo shān*)
Another scenic spot, these hills are 68 km south-west of Guangzhou. Seventy-two peaks (basically hills) make up the area. There are 36 caves, 32 springs, 28 waterfalls and 21 crags. The summit is very rocky but, rising to a piddling 345 metres, it's certainly not a difficult climb.

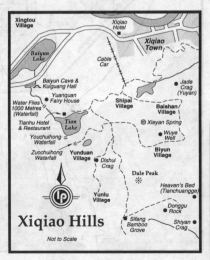

Xiqiao Hills

At the foot of the hills is the small market town of Xiqiao and around the upper levels of the hills are scattered several centuries-old villages. One of the big sights (at least for the Chinese) is a waterfall called Water Flies 1000 Metres *(fēi liútiān chǐ)*. Most of the area is made accessible by stone paths. It's popular with Chinese tourists, but foreigners of any kind are rare.

Getting There & Away Buses to the hills depart from the Foshan bus station on Daxin Lu, which runs west off Jiefang Nanlu.

SHENZHEN
(shēnzhèn)

'The mountains are high and the emperor is far away', says an ancient Chinese proverb. Just a stone's throw from the mountainous skyscrapers of downtown Hong Kong yet more than 2300 km from Beijing, Shenzhen gives new meaning to proverbial wisdom.

The name 'Shenzhen' refers to three places: Shenzhen City (opposite the border crossing at Lo Wu); Shenzhen Special Economic Zone (SEZ); and Shenzhen County, which extends several km north of the SEZ. None of them are particularly interesting to visit, and the majority of foreigners who come here are businesspeople. Shenzhen City is perhaps worth a couple of hours of your time if you are en route between Hong Kong and Guangzhou, but most travellers sensibly give the place a miss.

The northern part of the SEZ is walled off from the rest of China by an electrified fence to prevent smuggling and to keep back the hordes of people trying to emigrate illegally into Shenzhen and Hong Kong. There is a checkpoint when you leave the SEZ. You don't need your passport to leave but you will need it to get back in, so don't leave it in your hotel if you decide to make a day-trip outside Shenzhen.

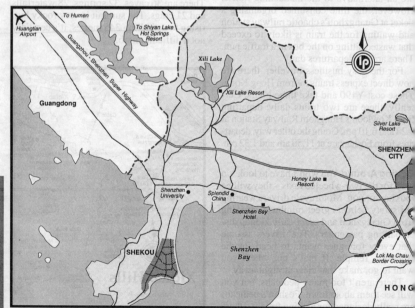

History

Hong Kong's border town, Shenzhen, is officially labelled a Special Economic Zone, or SEZ. Shenzhen came into existence in 1980 along with three other SEZs: Zhuhai (near Macau), Shantou in the eastern part of Guangdong Province and Xiamen in Fujian Province.

The Shenzhen SEZ was initially deemed a failure, largely on ideological grounds. Today, with most of China a failure – on ideological grounds at least – Shenzhen is probably the foremost east-coast success story, and is rapidly emerging as one of China's largest cities. China's average economic growth rate in the last decade was 10% – one of the world's highest – while Guangdong Province has managed 18%. However, Shenzhen tops them all with a phenomenal 45%, a dizzying rate of growth possibly unmatched anywhere else in the world.

Information

CITS There are two branches of CITS. The one most convenient for arriving travellers is the office in the railway station. The main CITS office (☎ 557-7970) is at 2 Chuanbu Jie, just west of Heping Lu. It has no English sign and is of little use to individual travellers.

PSB The Foreign Affairs Branch of the PSB (☎ 557-2114) is on the west end of Jiefang Lu, on the north side of the street.

Post & Telecommunications The main post office is at the north end of Jianshe Lu and is often packed out. Telecommunications facilities are in a separate building on Shennan Donglu, but many hotels now offer international direct dial (IDD) service right from your room. Rates to Hong Kong are very cheap.

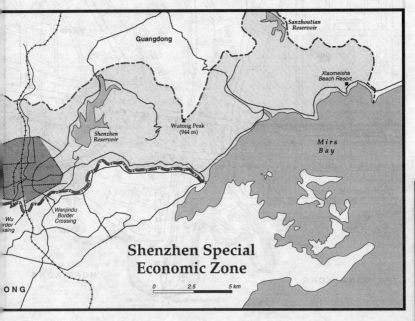

Shenzhen Special Economic Zone

For direct dialling to Shenzhen, the area code is 0755.

Money Shenzhen effectively operates with a dual currency system – Chinese yuan and Hong Kong dollars. The Hong Kong dollar is the preferred currency, though RMB is accepted at most hotels, restaurants and shops.

Hotels change money but this magic can also be performed at the border crossing with Hong Kong. The Bank of China is at 23 Jianshe Lu.

Places to Stay – middle

There is no real budget accommodation in Shenzhen. Most of the cheaper hotels have rates that start at Y200 for a standard double. Staff in the cheaper hotels are often not used to dealing with foreigners either. There is a 10% service charge for almost all Shenzhen hotels.

The cheapest place in town that accepts foreigners is the *Yat Wah Hotel (rìhuá bīnguǎn)*. It has a good location on the north-west corner of Shennan Lu and Heping Lu, just to the west of the railway tracks. The

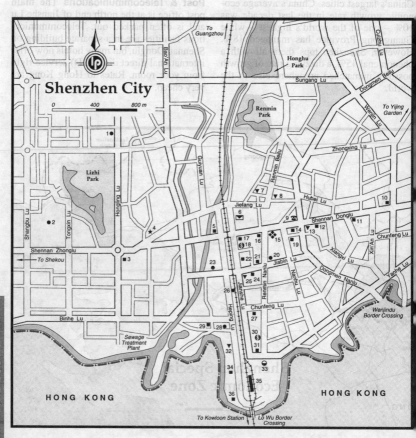

outside looks a bit tattered, but the interior is all right. Room prices are Y145 for doubles and Y168 for triples. There is a 20% discount from Monday to Friday.

Other mid-range hotels around town include:

Heping Hotel (hépíng jiǔdiàn), 63 Chuanbu Jie; doubles/triples start at HK$175/225 (☎ 225-2111, 222-8149)

Nanyang Hotel (nányáng jiǔdiàn); doubles from HK$332 (☎ 222-4968)

Overseas Chinese Hotel (huáqiáo dàshà); doubles HK$238 (☎ 557-3811)

Petrel Hotel (hǎiyàn dàjiǔdiàn); doubles from HK$230 (☎ 223-2828; fax 222-1398)

Shen Tieh Building (shēntiě dàshà); doubles/singles from HK$220 (☎ 558-4248)

Shenzhen Hotel (shēnzhèn jiǔdiàn), 156 Shennan Donglu; doubles from HK$250 (☎ 223-8000; fax 222-2284)

Wah Chung International Hotel (huázhōng guójì jiǔdiàn), 140 Shennan Donglu; singles/doubles from HK$248 and HK$348; triples from HK$448 (☎ 223-8060)

Places to Stay – top end

Century Plaza Hotel (xīndū jiǔdiàn); standard/deluxe doubles cost HK$900/1000 (☎ 222-0888; fax 223-4060)

Far East Grand Hotel (yuǎndōng dàjiǔdiàn), 104 Shennan Donglu; singles/doubles from HK$380/460 (☎ 220-5369; fax 220-0239)

Forum Hotel (fùlín dàjiǔdiàn), 67 Heping Lu; doubles from HK$980 (☎ 558-6333; fax 556-1700)

Guangdong Hotel (yuèhǎi jiǔdiàn); standard doubles from HK$530; suites from HK$880 (☎ 589-5108; fax 576-9381)

Hotel Oriental Regent (jīngdū jiǔdiàn); doubles from Y690, suites from Y1150 (☎ 224-7000; fax 224-7290)

Landmark Hotel (shēnzhèn fùyuàn jiǔdiàn) (☎ 217-2288; fax 229-0473)

SHENZHEN CITY 深圳市

PLACES TO STAY

3 New World Hotel
  昌都大厦
5 Yatwah Hotel
  日华宾馆
10 Nam Fong International Hotel
  南方国际大酒店
11 Tung Nam International Hotel
  东南国际大酒店
12 Far East Grand Hotel
  远东大酒店
14 Airlines Hotel & Guangdong Hotel
  航空，广东酒店
16 Wah Chung Hotel
  华中国际酒店
17 Shenzhen Hotel
  深圳酒店
19 Landmark Hotel
  富苑酒店
21 Petrel Hotel
  海燕大酒店
22 Nanyang Hotel
  南洋酒店
24 Friendship Hotel
  友谊宾馆

26 Shen Tieh Building
  深铁大厦
27 Century Plaza Hotel
  新都酒店
29 Heping Hotel
  和平酒店
31 Shangri-La Hotel
  香格里拉大酒店
34 Forum Hotel
  富临大酒店
36 Overseas Chinese Hotel
  华侨大厦

PLACES TO EAT

7 McDonald's
  麦当劳
8 Royal Pizza
  皇室
13 Wendy's
  温蒂
25 Pan Hsi Restaurant
  泮溪酒家
32 Fairwood Fast Food
  大快活

OTHER

1 Xinhua Bookstore
  新华书店

2 Shenzhen City Hall
  深圳市政府
4 PSB
  公安局外事科
6 Post Office
  邮局
9 Telecommunications Building
  电信大楼
15 Oriental Sunshine Shopping Complex
  东方天虹商场
18 Bank of China (large)
  中国银行
20 International Trade Centre
  国贸大厦
23 People's Gymnasium
  人民体育馆
28 CITS Main Office
  中国国际旅行社
30 Bank of China (small)
  中国银行
33 Minibuses
  小型车
35 Railway Station & Dragon Inn
  火车站

THE SOUTH

Shangri-La Hotel (xiānggé lǐlā dàjiǔdiàn); doubles from Y1155 (☎ 223-0888; fax 223-9878)

Places to Stay – resorts

These Chinese-oriented paradise escapes are unlikely to be of much interest to the average foreign visitor (Why not fly to Thailand or Malaysia instead?). They offer discos, saunas, swimming pools, golf courses, horseback riding, roller coasters, supermarkets, palaces, castles, Chinese pavilions, statues and monorails. The huge (and surprisingly cheap) dim sum restaurants become nightclubs in the evening, with Las Vegas-style floor shows.

Those interested might contact *Honey Lake Resort* (☎ 774-5061; fax 774-5045) *(xiāngmì hú dùjià cūn)*; *Shenzhen Bay Hotel* (☎ 660-0111; fax 660-0139) *(shēnzhèn wān dàjiǔdiàn)*; *Shiyan Lake Hot Springs Resort* (☎ 996-0143) *(shíyán hú wēnquán dùjià cūn)*; *Silver Lake Resort Camp* (☎ 222-2827; fax 224-2622) *(yín hú lǚyóu zhōngxīn)*; *Xiaomeisha Beach Resort* (☎ 555-0000) *(xiǎoméishā dàjiǔdiàn)*; or *Xili Lake Resort* (☎ 666-0022; fax 666-0521) *(xīlì hú)*.

Places to Eat

Shenzhen has a thriving upmarket dining scene, but there are also cheap eats available around town. The railway station has a number of affordable restaurants on its 3rd floor. At the back of the railway station on Heping Lu, there are a number of cheap restaurants selling dumplings and the like. Up around the Jiefang Lu area are street vendors selling tasty chicken legs and fruit.

Jiefang Lu itself is fast-food city. The enormous *McDonald's* has to be seen to be believed – the 'queues' here are worse than those at the railway station. Most of the fast-food places have separate counters for those paying in Hong Kong dollars, and these counters are far and away the easiest to make your order. The RMB counters are a chaotic free for all. *Royal Pizza* on Jiefang Lu is one of the quieter fast-food places on Jiefang Lu, and the pizzas are not bad.

Dim sum breakfast and lunch is available in all but the scruffiest hotels. Usually the dim sum restaurants are on the 2nd or 3rd floor rather than by the lobby. Prices are slightly lower than in Hong Kong. You'll have to pay in Hong Kong dollars in the better hotels but you may get away with RMB elsewhere.

One of Shenzhen's best restaurants is the *Pan Hsi Restaurant* (☎ 223-8081) *(bànxī jiǔjiā)* at 33 Jianshe Lu.

Getting There & Away

Air Shenzhen's new Huangtian Airport is rapidly becoming one of China's busiest. There are flights to most major destinations around China, but it is often significantly cheaper to fly from Guangzhou.

Air tickets can be purchased at the Airlines Hotel *(hángkōng dàjiǔdiàn)*, at 130 Shennan Donglu in central Shenzhen, and at many other locations around town, including a small office on the 2nd floor of the railway station.

Bus From Hong Kong, there are buses to Shenzhen run by Citybus, by Motor Transport Company of Guangdong & Hong Kong Ltd at the Canton Rd bus terminal, and by CTS. For most travellers, buses are not a good option unless you are on a tour.

There are long-distance buses to Shantou, Chaozhou and other coastal cities, departing from the Overseas Chinese Travel Service *(huáqiáo lǚyóu bù)*, next to the Overseas Chinese Hotel on Heping Lu. Deluxe air-con buses to Shantou cost Y130 and take nine hours.

There are frequent minibuses between Guangzhou and Shenzhen. In Guangzhou, buses depart from next to the Liuhua Hotel, across the street from the railway station. In Shenzhen, departures are from just east of the railway station next to the Hong Kong border crossing. The fare is Y40 and the ride takes three hours.

Train The Kowloon-Guangzhou (Canton) Railway (KCR) offers the fastest and most convenient transport to Shenzhen from Hong Kong. See the Hong Kong chapter for details.

There are frequent local trains between Guangzhou and Shenzhen and the journey takes about three hours. Tourist prices are Y20 (hard seat) and Y46 (soft seat). The trains are often packed and there are long queues to buy tickets.

Boat Hoverferries run between Hong Kong and Shekou, a port on the west side of Shenzhen. There are three daily departures from the ferry terminal at China Hong Kong City on Canton Rd in Tsimshatsui, Kowloon, at 8 and 10.15 am, and 3.30 pm. There are four additional departures from the Macau Ferry Terminal on Hong Kong Island at 8.20 and 9.30 am, and at 2 and 4.30 pm.

There is one jetcat (jet-powered catamaran) daily from Macau to Shekou. It departs from Macau at 8.30 am and arrives at 10 am. The cost is M$79.

There are three daily jetcats running between Shekou and Zhuhai SEZ (north of Macau).

Getting Around

To/From the Airport There are shuttle buses between the airport and the Airlines Hotel (see Getting There & Away above). Minibuses and taxis are also available, but remember that in Shenzhen's traffic, getting to the airport can take a long time.

There is a rapid boat service (jetcat) between the airport and Hong Kong which takes 60 minutes, at least twice as fast as the bus. The sole ticketing agent in Hong Kong is the branch office of CTS (☎ 736-1863) in Kowloon's China Hong Kong City Ferry Terminal on Canton Rd. In Shenzhen, you can purchase tickets right at the airport. The price is steep and based on season. There are eight sailings daily.

Bus Shenzhen has some of the best public transport in China. The city bus services are dirt cheap and not nearly as crowded as elsewhere in China.

The minibuses are faster. These are privately run and cheap, but if you can't read the destination in Chinese characters, you will need help.

Taxi Taxis are abundant but not so cheap, because their drivers have been spoilt by free-spending tourists. There are meters, but drivers often demand a negotiated fee instead. Payment can be made either in RMB or Hong Kong dollars.

AROUND SHENZHEN CITY

At the western end of the SEZ, near Shenzhen Bay, are a couple of tacky attractions that may be of interest to the occasional visitor: Splendid China (*jǐnxiù zhōnghuá*) and China Folk Culture Villages (*zhōngguó mínsú wénhuà cūn*). Splendid China miniaturises the sights of China, and China Folk Culture Villages has people dressed up as China's ethnic minorities in recreations of their villages. Curiosity piqued? The two of them are adjacent to each other not far from Shekou ferry terminal.

From the railway station there are frequent minibuses or, if you're entering Shenzhen by hoverferry, you could take a taxi from Shekou.

HUMEN

(*hǔmén*)

The small city of Humen on the Pearl River is of interest only to history buffs curious about the Opium wars that led directly to Hong Kong's creation as a British colony. At the end of the first Opium War, after the Treaty of Nanking, there was a British Supplementary Treaty of the Bogue, signed on 8 October 1843. The Bogue Forts (*shājiǎo pàotái*) at Humen is now the site of an impressive museum. There are many exhibits, including large artillery pieces and other relics, and the actual ponds in which Commissioner Lin Zexu had the opium destroyed.

The only problem with this place is getting there. No buses go directly to Humen, but buses and minibuses travelling from Shenzhen to Guangzhou go right by. You could ask to be let off at the Humen access road, and then get a taxi, hitch or walk the five km into town.

ZHUHAI
(zhūhǎi)

From any hilltop in Macau, you can gaze to the north and see a mass of modern buildings just across the border in China. This is the Zhuhai SEZ. Like the Shenzhen SEZ, Zhuhai was built from the soles up on what was farmland less than a decade ago. The areas near the beach have several high-class resort playgrounds catering to Chinese residents of Hong Kong and Macau as well as the occasional foreigner.

Zhuhai is changing, and the speed of development is almost frightening. Travellers from the 1980s (even *late* 1980s) remember Zhuhai as a small agricultural town with a few rural industries and a quiet beach. Nowadays, high-rise hotels, factories and workers' flats have crowded out the few remaining farms, and half the beach has been paved over to make way for a new waterfront freeway.

Zhuhai is so close to the border that a visit can be arranged as a day-trip from Macau, and you can see many of the sights just

travelling by foot. Or you can use Zhuhai as an entry or exit point for the rest of China.

Orientation

Zhuhai is divided into three main districts. The area nearest the Macau border is called Gongbei, the main tourist zone. To the north-east is Jida, the eastern part of which has Zhuhai's harbour *(jiǔzhōu gǎng)*. The northernmost section of the city is called Xiangzhou, an area of worker flats and factories.

Information

There is a CTS office (☎ 888-6748) next door to the Huaqiao Hotel. It specialises in tours for Overseas Chinese. The PSB (☎ 222-2459) is in the Xiangzhou District on the south-west corner of Anping Lu and Kangning Lu.

The most useful post office is on Qiaoguang Lu, in Gongbei. You can make IDD calls from your own room in most hotels. The area code for Zhuhai is 0756.

ZHUHAI 珠海

PLACES TO STAY

6	Jiari Hotel 假日酒店
9	Zhuhai Hotel 珠海宾馆
14	Huaqiao Hotel 华侨宾馆
15	Yindo Hotel 银都酒店
17	Zhuhai Quzhao Hotel 拱北大厦
18	Good World Hotel 好世界酒店
19	Guangdong Hotel 粤海酒店
21	Overseas Chinese Hotel 华桥大酒店
22	Bu Bu Gao Hotel 步步高大酒店
23	Lianhua Hotel 莲花大厦

25	Gongbei Palace Hotel 拱北宾馆
26	Jiuzhou Hotel 九州酒店
27	Traffic Hotel 交通大厦
29	Friendship Hotel 友谊酒店

OTHER

1	Bus Station 香州汽车站
2	Post Office 邮局
3	Xiangzhou Harbour 香州码头
4	Martyrs Museum 烈士陵园
5	PSB 公安局
7	Shijingshan Tourist Office 石景山旅游中心

8	Jiuzhou Cheng (Shopping Mall) 九州城
10	Zhuhai Amusement Park 珠海游乐场
11	Helicopter Pad 直升机场
12	Jiuzhou Harbour 九州港
13	Resort Reception 度假村总服务台
16	Bank of China 中国银行
20	Gongbei Market 拱北市场
24	Post Office 邮局
28	Bus Station 长途汽车站
30	Border/Customs 海关

THE SOUTH

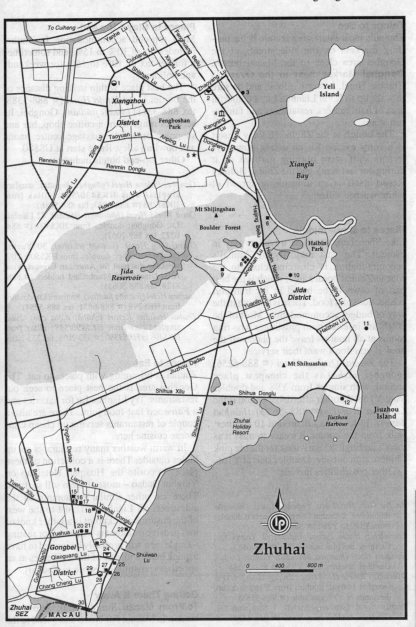

Mt Shijingshan

Boulder Forest

Jida
Reservoir

Xiangzhou
District

Fengboshan
Park

Xianglu
Bay

Yeli
Island

Haibin
Park

Jida
District

Mt Shihuashan

Zhuhai
Holiday
Resort

Jiuzhou
Harbour

Jiuzhou
Island

Gongbei
District

Zhuhai
SEZ

MACAU

Zhuhai

0   400   800 m

Things to See

Zhuhai's most interesting feature is the bustling markets on the side streets of the Gongbei area close to the Macau border. **Gongbei Market**, next to the Overseas Chinese Hotel, is worth a look, and be sure to walk up to it via Lianhua Lu, a colourful area of hairdressers, restaurants and family-run stores.

The **beach** at the Zhuhai Holiday Resort is a sorry excuse for an outing nowadays (resort staff were burning garbage on it during our last visit), and the Zhuhai Holiday Resort itself is an uninspiring sprawl of white-washed villas.

Places to stay – middle

Like Shenzhen, very few travellers stay in Zhuhai. The vast majority of Zhuhai's accommodation is clustered close to the Macau/Zhuhai border area, which is the best part of town to be based in for transport connections and food. There is nothing in the way of budget accommodation. Most of the hotels are infested with prostitutes who ring rooms at all hours – leave the phone off the hook if you don't want their services.

The *Zhuhai Quzhao Hotel* (☎ 888-6256) *(gǒngbèi dàshà)* is the cheapest place around, with singles from Y98 and doubles from Y168. Another affordable option is the *Lianhua Hotel* (☎ 888-5673) *(liánhuā dàshà)*, 13 Lianhua Lu, around 10 minutes' walk from the border. It's easy to miss it as there's no English sign – look for the big pink Chinese sign outside. Doubles start at Y166.

Other possibilities include:

Bu Bu Gao Hotel (or *Popoko Hotel*) *(bùbùgāo dàjiǔdiàn)*, 2 Yuehai Donglu, Gongbei; doubles from Y180 to Y260 (☎ 888-6628).
Friendship Hotel (yǒuyì jiǔdiàn), 2 Youyi Lu, Gongbei; doubles from Y180 (☎ 888-6683)
Huaqiao Hotel (huáqiáo bīnguǎn), Yingbin Dadao, Gongbei; doubles from Y234 (☎ 888-5123)
Overseas Chinese Hotel (huáqiáo dàjiǔdiàn), next to Gongbei Market; doubles from Y280 to Y480; discounts of 30% available (☎ 888-5183)
Traffic Hotel (jiāotōng dàshà), 1 Shuiwan Lu, Gongbei; doubles from Y180 (☎ 888-4474)

Places to Stay – top end

Most top-end accommodation in Zhuhai includes tax of 10% to 15%, and sometimes a further tax of 10% to 15% for weekends and holidays.

The best place within striking distance of the border is the *Yindo Hotel* (☎ 888-3388; fax 888-3311) *(yíndū jiǔdiàn)*, Gongbei. Its services range from a coffee shop, bar and shopping arcade to massage centre, sauna and bowling alley. Rates start at US$80.

Other top-end hotels include:

Gongbei Palace Hotel (gǒngbèi bīnguǎn); standard singles/twins HK$430/500; villas from HK$1288 (☎ 888-6833; fax 888-5686)
Good World Hotel (hǎo shìjiè jiǔdiàn), 82 Lianhua Lu, Gongbei; doubles from HK$300 (☎ 888-0222; fax 889-2061)
Guangdong Hotel (yuèhǎi jiǔdiàn), 30 Yuehai Donglu, Gongbei; doubles from HK$500; 20% weekday discount for American Express, Visa, JCB, Diners and MasterCard holders (☎ 888-8128; fax 888-5063)
Jiuzhou Hotel (jiǔzhōu jiǔdiàn), Shuiwan Lu; doubles from HK$298 (☎ 888-6851; fax 888-5254)
Zhuhai Holiday Resort (zhūhǎi dùjià cūn), Jida; singles/twins from HK$498/538; villas from HK$498 to HK$3380 (☎ 333-2038; fax 333-2036)

Places to Eat

Zhuhai is brimming with places to eat. The Gongbei area is the best place to seek out restaurants. Try Lianhua Lu for bakeries and a *Fairwood* fast-food joint. There are also a couple of restaurants serving up cheap Cantonese cuisine here.

In warm weather many restaurants set up tables outside. There is a collection of these places opposite the Huaqiao Hotel up on Yingbin Dadao – most of them sell seafood. There are other similar restaurants on the sidestreets off Lianhua Lu. Just to the west of the customs checkpoint is another knot of inexpensive restaurants with outdoor seating – single men will probably be invited to have a quick bonk with one of the waitresses as an appetiser (prostitution is rife in Zhuhai).

Getting There & Away

To/From Macau Simply walk across the border. In Macau, bus Nos 3 and 5 lead to the

Barrier Gate, from where you make the crossing on foot. Taxis from the Hong Kong ferry area cost around HK$22. The Macau-Zhuhai border is open from 7 am to 9 pm.

To/From Guangzhou Buses to Zhuhai depart from the bus station across the street from the railway station, just west of the Liuhua Hotel. The large government buses are cheaper, but less frequent, slower and more crowded. Minibuses from this bus station are air-conditioned, cost Y30 and leave according to a posted schedule. Unscheduled minibuses cost Y25 and cruise in front of the station in a circular direction (south on Renmin Beilu then back on Zhanqian Lu) looking for passengers. All buses and minibuses accept payment in RMB.

Going the other way, buses from Zhuhai to Guangzhou depart from the main bus terminal on Youyi Lu, directly opposite the customs building (the border checkpoint). There are frequent buses through the day from 6.30 am to 5 pm, and air-con services cost Y42.

To/From Hong Kong Jetcats (jet-powered catamarans) between Zhuhai and Hong Kong do the trip in about 70 minutes. From the ferry terminal at China Hong Kong City on Canton Rd in Tsimshatsui boats depart at 7.45, 9.30 and 11 am, and 2.30 and 5 pm. Boats from the Macau Ferry Terminal in Central depart at 8.40 am, midday and 4 pm. It is, however, only marginally slower (and less expensive) to take a ferry to Macau and then a taxi to Zhuhai.

Going the other way, departures are from Jiuzhou Harbour in Zhuhai at 8 and 9.30 am, and 1, 3 and 5 pm to Tsimshatsui and at 10.30 am, 2 and 5.30 pm to Central. The cost is Y140.

To/From Shenzhen A high-speed ferry operates between the port of Shekou in Shenzhen and Jiuzhou Harbour (*jiǔzhōu gǎng*) in Zhuhai (Jida). There are departures approximately hourly between 7 am and 5 pm in each direction. The cost is Y84.

Getting Around
Bus Zhuhai has a decent public transport system. The routes are clearly shown on the Zhuhai city map and you shouldn't have any trouble figuring it out. Minibuses ply the same routes and cost Y2 for any place in the city. Minibuses will stop in the public bus stops and most other places, but cannot stop right in major intersections.

Taxi You are most likely to use taxis to shuttle between your hotel and the boats at Jiuzhou Harbour. Don't bother with the taxis lined up outside the customs area or those at the harbour – walk for five minutes and flag one down. Taxi drivers cruising the streets use their meters. From the customs area to Jiuzhou Harbour costs around Y17.

AROUND ZHUHAI
In the village of Cuiheng, north of the city limits of Zhuhai, is **Dr Sun Yatsen's Residence** (*sūn zhōngshān gùjū*). Republican, enemy of the Qing Dynasty and China's most famous revolutionary, Dr Sun Yatsen was born in a house on this site on 12 November 1866. That house was torn down after a new home was built in 1892. This second house is still standing and open to the public.

There are frequent minibuses to Cuiheng departing from Gongbei near the border checkpoint.

ZHONGSHAN CITY
(*zhōngshān shì*)
The administrative centre of the county by the same name, Zhongshan City is also known as Shiqi. An industrial city, there is little to see or do here, though you may pass through the place if you are doing the circuit from Cuiheng to Zhongshan Hot Springs.

If you get stranded here for an hour or so, the one and only scenic spot in town is **Zhongshan Park**, which is pleasantly forested and dominated by a large hill (*yāndūn shān*) topped with a pagoda. It's visible from most parts of the city so it's easy to find.

AROUND ZHONGSHAN

The Zhongshan Hot Springs (*zhōngshān wēnquán*) resort has indoor hot springs and a golf course. If you're a real enthusiast of either activity, you might want to spend a night here. Otherwise, you'll probably just want to look around briefly and then head back to Gongbei. Accommodation is available at the *Zhongshan Hot Springs Hotel* (☎ 668-3888; fax 668-3333) from Y300 for doubles plus 10% service charge.

A minibus drops you by the entrance to the resort, then it's a ½-km walk to the hotel. For a couple of yuan you can hire someone to

carry you on the back of a bicycle. You won't have to look for them as they'll be looking for you. To get back to Gongbei, flag down any minibus you see passing the resort entrance.

ZHAOQING

(*zhàoqìng*)

Zhaoqing, home to some craggy limestone rock formations similar to those around Guilin, is rated highly among the attractions of Guangdong. Be this as it may, Yangshuo it ain't. Zhaoqing is a big city, replete with innumerable hotels, karaoke parlours and

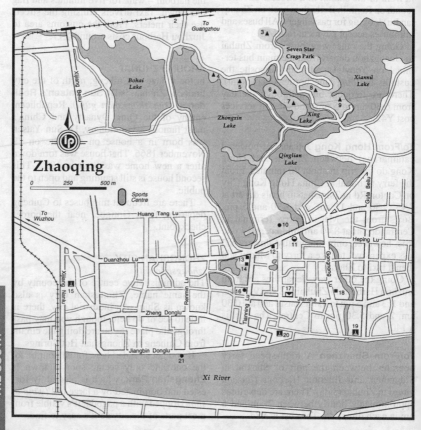

blinking neon advertising. Don't expect a peaceful retreat from the push and shove of Guangzhou.

Nevertheless, Sinophiles will note that Zhaoqing is a tourist attraction of some long-standing. For almost 1000 years people have been coming to Zhaoqing to scribble graffiti on its cliffs or inside its caves (generally sensitively expressed poetic tributes to the very rock formations they were defacing). Nowadays, tour groups from Hong Kong often overnight here, but individual travellers rarely visit.

Orientation

Zhaoqing, 110 km west of Guangzhou on the Xi River, is bounded to the south by the river and to the north by the immense Seven Star Crags Park. Zhaoqing is a sprawling city, but the main attractions can be easily seen on foot.

Things to See

Zhaoqing's premier attraction, the **Seven Star Crags** (*qī xīng yán*), is a group of limestone towers – a peculiar geological formation abundant in the paddy fields of Guilin and Yangshuo. Legend has it that the crags were actually seven stars that fell from the sky to form a pattern resembling the Big Dipper. The artificial lakes were built in 1955, and the park is adorned with concrete pathways, arched bridges and little pavilions.

On Tajiao Lu in the south-east, the nine-storey **Chongxi Pagoda** (*chóngxī tǎ*) was in a sad state after the Cultural Revolution, but was restored in the 1980s. On the opposite bank of the river are two similar pagodas.

The Seven Star Crags **Yuejiang Temple** (*yuèjiāng lóu*) is a restored temple about 30 minutes' walk from the Chongxi Pagoda, just back from the waterfront at the eastern end of Zheng Donglu.

By a lake in the western part of town off Zheng Xilu is the small **Plum Monastery** (*méi ān*).

Finally, 20 km east of Zhaoqing and one of the best scenic spots in Guangdong, at least equal to the Seven Star Crags, is **Dinghushan** (*dǐnghú shān*). Apart from its streams, brooks, pools, hills and trees, the mountain is noted for the Qingyuan Temple, built towards the end of the Ming Dynasty. Dinghushan can be visited as a day-trip from Zhaoqing.

THE SOUTH

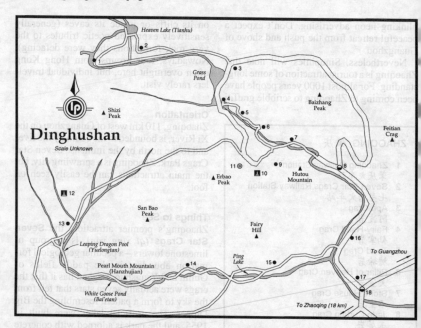

Heaven Lake (Tianhu)

Grass Pond

Baizhang Peak

Feitian Crag

Shizi Peak

Dinghushan
Scale Unknown

Erbao Peak

Hutou Mountain

San Bao Peak

Fairy Hill

Leaping Dragon Pool (Yuelongtan)

Pearl Mouth Mountain (Hanzhujian)

White Goose Pond (Bai'etan)

Ping Lake

To Guangzhou

To Zhaoqing (18 km)

Places to Stay
Very few foreign travellers overnight in Zhaoqing, and although hotels are thick on the ground it is difficult to come up with a bargain. Zhaoqing is too integral a part of the Hong Kong tour-group circuit.

The least expensive hotel around is the *Flower Tower Hotel* (☎ 223-2412) (*huātǎ jiǔdiàn*), 5 Gongnong Beilu. Doubles range from Y96 to Y196.

The *Duanzhou Hotel* (☎ 223-2281) (*duānzhōu dàjiǔdiàn*), 77 Tianning Beilu, is a reasonable mid-range option with standard doubles at Y168 and Y220. The *Jinye Hotel* (☎ 222-1338; fax 222-1368) (*jīnyè dàshà*) is similarly priced, with doubles from Y195 to Y280.

Huaqiao Hotel (☎ 223-2952) (*huáqiáo dàshà*), 90 Tianning Beilu, has an excellent location but is expensive at Y330 upwards for standard doubles.

The *Star Lake Hotel* (☎ 222-1188; fax 223-6688) (*xīnghú dàshà*), 37 Duanzhou 4-

Lu, is the best of Zhaoqing's hotels and has a full range of near international-class services from HK$430.

Places to Eat
Just take a stroll along Duanzhou Lu for affordable eats. Look out for the restaurants selling *zōngzi* – rice, pork and other oddments steamed in a lotus leaf; these triangular snacks can be seen hanging outside the restaurants.

There are some good dim sum restaurants on Tianning Lu. Look out for the one directly opposite the Duanzhou Hotel. Ordering is simple as the food comes around on a trolley – all you have to do is point.

Getting There & Away
Bus There are buses to Zhaoqing from Guangzhou's west bus station and from the long-distance bus station near the railway station. The fare is Y28. There are half a dozen buses a day and the trip takes about

DINGHUSHAN 鼎湖山

1 Cliff-Face Plank Path
   (Lantianzhandao)
   连天栈道
2 No 1 Hydroelectric Station
   水电一站
3 No 2 Hydroelectric Station
   水电二站
4 Twin Rainbow Bridge
   (Shuanghongfeiqian)
   双虹飞堑
5 Tingpu Pavilion
   听瀑亭
6 Sun Yatsen Swimming Area
   孙中山游泳处
7 Half Mountain Pavilion
   半山亭
8 Bus Station
   鼎湖山汽车站
9 Tea Flower Pavilion (Huachage)
   花茶阁
10 Qingyun Temple
   庆云寺
11 Gulong Spring
   古龙泉
12 White Cloud Temple
   白云寺
13 Leaping Dragon Nunnery (Yuelong'an)
   跃龙庵
14 Lion's Roar Rock (Shihoushi)
   狮吼石
15 Crane Viewing Pavilion
   望鹤亭
16 Archway
   牌楼
17 Kengkou Store
   坑口商店
18 Kengkou Bus Station
   坑口汽车站

three hours, traffic permitting. Try to avoid returning to Guangzhou on a weekend afternoon.

Privately run minibuses operate between Zhaoqing and Guangzhou. In Zhaoqing the minibus ticket office is inside the main gate of the Seven Star Crags Park.

Train Be careful – there are two railway stations in Zhaoqing. All trains stop at the main railway station (*zhàoqìng huǒchē zhàn*)

but only train Nos 351 and 356 stop at the Seven Star Crags Railway Station (*qīxīngyán huǒchē zhàn*). If you get into a taxi and say you want to go to the railway station, drivers will automatically assume you mean the main railway station.

Trains from Guangzhou take two to three hours. All trains also stop at Foshan. Train Nos 69 and 70 connect Zhaoqing and Shenzhen – you do not need to get off at Guangzhou if you wish to go straight through.

Boat This is the best way to get to Zhaoqing nowadays. There are direct high-speed ferries from Guangzhou to Zhaoqing from the Dashatou ferry terminal or from close to the ticket office just off Shamian Island. Ferries take two hours, cost Y68 and leave at 8 am and 2.15 pm. Slow boats from Guangzhou leave from Dashatou and take 10 hours.

In the tourist season (summer and holidays), there are direct boats to/from Hong Kong.

Getting Around

The local bus station is on Duanzhou Lu, a few minutes' walk east of the intersection with Tianning Lu. Bus No 1 runs to the ferry dock on the Xi River. Bus Nos 4 and 5 go to the Plum Monastery.

The main railway station is well out of town near the north-west corner of the lake. A taxi into town costs Y12 or you can grab a minibus for Y2.

Aside from walking, the best way to get around Zhaoqing is by bicycle. There is a hire place diagonally opposite the main entrance to the Seven Star Crags, and another south of the Duanzhou Hotel in Tianning Lu. They ask exorbitant fees if you have a foreign face, but will accept Y10 per day.

ZHANJIANG

(*zhànjiāng*)

Zhanjiang is a major port on the southern coast of China, and the largest Chinese port west of Guangzhou. It was leased to France in 1898 and remained under French control until WW II. Today the French are back, but this time Zhanjiang is a base for their oil-exploration projects in the South China Sea.

Very few foreigners come to Zhanjiang, and when they do they are usually en route to Hainan. This is eminently sensible: Zhanjiang is a drab, urban conglomeration with expensive room rates and nothing to recommend it.

Orientation

Zhanjiang is divided into two parts. The northern Chikan District (chìkǎn qū) and the southern (xiáshān qū). There is no need to bother with the northern part of town at all, however, as the harbour, bus station and most of the hotels are conveniently close together in the southern part of town.

Places to Stay

The southern part of town is the most convenient for travellers and has the widest selection of hotels.

For budget travellers the *Friendship Hotel* (☎ 228-6622) (yǒuyì bīnguǎn) is the best option. Singles/doubles/triples are Y85/150/160. It's a fairly grotty, noisy place but will do for an overnight stay.

Most of the other hotels that take foreigners are mid-range in price. The *Canton Bay*

Hotel (☎ 228-1966) (guǎngzhōuwān huáqiáo bīnguǎn), 16 Renmin Lu, is well located, and has clean, air-con rooms ranging from Y160 to Y240 and upwards. The *Jade Garden Hotel* (☎ 222-7627) (cuìyuán fàndiàn), 124 Minzhi Lu, is a friendly place with doubles at Y180, Y200 and Y220.

The *Haiwan Hotel* (☎ 222-2266) (hǎiwān bīnguǎn) on Renmin Lu is also the location of the International Seamen's Club and boasts a karaoke bar. Singles cost Y168, while doubles range from Y198 to Y280. The *Haifu Grand Hotel* (☎ 228-0288) (hǎifù dàjiǔdiàn) is one of those places that strives to be upmarket and doesn't quite hit the mark. Standard doubles cost Y290, while rooms with a view of the sea cost Y300. There is a 10% service charge.

ZHANJIANG 湛江

1 South Railway Station
   湛江火车站
2 Hualian Hotel
   花莲大厦
3 Friendship Hotel
   友谊宾馆
4 Haibin Amusement Park
   海滨游乐中心
5 Children's Park
   儿童公园
6 Cuiyuan Hotel
   翠园饭店
7 Qingshaonian Park
   青少年公园
8 Canton Bay Hotel & Southwest Airlines
   广东湾酒店, 西南航空
9 Haifu Grand Hotel
   海富大酒店
10 Bank of China
   中国银行
11 Haiwan Hotel & Seamen's Club
   海湾宾馆, 海员俱乐部
12 Long-Distance Bus Station
   霞山汽车客运站
13 Zhangang Hotel
   湛港宾馆
14 Zhanjiang Harbour Passenger
   Terminal
   湛江港客运站

Zhanjiang

To Airport

0   0.5   1 km
Approximate Scale

Xiachi
Wenming Donglu
Minzhi Lu
Renmin Nan Dadao
Dongan Lu

Xiashan District

Jiefang Donglu
Guangdong
Jianshe Lu
Youyi Lu

THE SOUTH

Getting There & Away

Air The CAAC office (☎ 222-4415) is at 23 Renmin Nan Dadao. It is also possible to make bookings from the China Southwest Airlines booking office almost next door to the Canton Bay Hotel.

There are flights out of Zhanjiang to Guangzhou, Shenzhen, Beijing, Shanghai, Kunming, Wuhan, Chengdu, Chongqing, Guiyang, Sanya and Shantou.

Bus The long-distance bus station only sells tickets to Guangzhou on clapped-out Chinese buses (Y60), but tickets for deluxe services (reclining seats and videos) can be bought at the Southwest Airlines office next door to the Canton Bay Hotel for Y120. The trip takes 10 to 11 hours and most buses travel by night. There are also bus services to Shenzhen. Getting from Zhanjiang to Zhaoqing by bus is a lost cause.

Train Trains to Guilin, Nanning and Guangzhou leave from the south railway station. From Zhanjiang to Guilin takes about 13 hours. From Zhanjiang to Nanning takes about 9½ hours.

Boat There are combination bus-boat tickets to Haikou on Hainan Island on sale at the bus station. However, it is more convenient – and not much more expensive – to take a direct boat to Haikou; tickets are on sale at the harbour. Fast boats leave at 9.30 am and 2.30 pm. For more details see the Getting There & Away section for Haikou in the Hainan Island chapter.

Getting Around

There are two railway stations and two long-distance bus stations, one each in the northern and southern parts of town. The southern railway station is the main one.

Bus No 1 runs between the two parts. This bus may be designated by a double-headed arrow (surrounded by calligraphy) rather than by a numeral.

There are many motorcycles, some with sidecars, cruising the streets; Y5 is enough for all locations within a couple of km from where you embark.

SHANTOU
(shàntóu)

Shantou, one of China's four original SEZs – along with Shenzhen, Zhuhai and Xiamen – is a little-visited port with a unique culture. The local dialect is known as *chaoshan* in Mandarin – a combination of Chaozhou and Shantou – or *taejiu* by the people themselves and is the language of many of the Chinese who emigrated to Thailand. These Thai-Chinese have started to return, and it's not unusual to see Thai written in the hotels and on business signs.

Unfortunately, however, for foreign visitors there is little to see and do. Shantou is basically a transit point on the little-travelled haul between Guangdong and Fujian. If you find yourself in town, the harbour area is the most interesting but nothing to get excited about.

History

Shantou was previously known to the outside world as Swatow. As early as the 18th century the East India Company had a station on an island outside the harbour, when the town was little more than a fishing village on a mudflat. The port was officially opened up to foreign trade in 1860 with the Treaty of Tianjin, which ended another Opium War. The British were the first to establish themselves here, though their projected settlement had to relocate to a nearby island due to local hostility. Before 1870 foreigners were living and trading in Shantou town itself. Many of the old colonial buildings still survive, though in a state of extreme dilapidation.

Orientation

Most of Shantou lies on a peninsula, bounded in the south by the ocean and separated from the mainland in the west and the north by a river and canals. The bulk of the tourist amenities are in the western part of the peninsula.

THE SOUTH

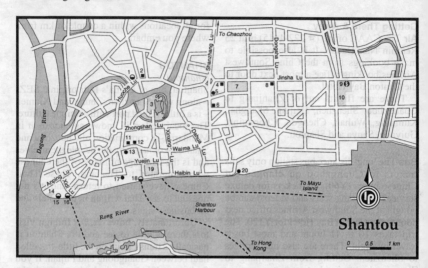

SHANTOU 汕头市

PLACES TO STAY

2 Hualian Hotel
   滑联酒店
4 Swatow Peninsula Hotel
   鮀岛宾馆
6 Huaqiao Hotel, CTS &
   Bank of China
   华侨大厦，中国旅行社，
   中国银行
8 International Hotel
   国际大酒店
11 Xinhua Hotel
   新华酒店
12 Taiwan Hotel
   台湾宾馆

OTHER

1 Long-Distance Bus
   Station
   汽车客货运站
3 Zhongshan Park
   中杉公园
5 CAAC
   民航售票处
7 Jinsha Park
   金砂公园
9 Bank of China (Main
   Branch)
   中国银行
10 Longhu Amusement
   Park
   龙湖乐园
13 Xinhua Bookstore
   新华书店

14 Xidi Park
   西堤公园
15 Local Ferry
   西堤客运公司客运站
16 Buses to Guangzhou
   往广州汽车站
17 International Seamen's
   Club
   国际海员俱乐部
18 Shantou Wharf Pass-
   enger Terminal
   汕头港客运站
19 Renmin Square
   人民广场
20 Stone Fort
   石炮台

Information

You'll find the PSB on Yuejin Lu at its eastern end, near the corner of Nannai Lu. The CTS office (☎ 823-3966) is in the Huaqiao Hotel. It sells bus tickets to Guangzhou, Shenzhen and Xiamen, boat tickets to Hong Kong and air tickets to wherever CAAC flies.

The Bank of China has a branch in the Huaqiao Hotel. There's a post office at 415 Zhongshan Lu, near the intersection with Shanzhang Lu.

Places to Stay

The *Swatow Peninsula Hotel* (☎ 823-1261) *(túodǎo bīnguǎn)* on Jinsha Lu is the best bargain in town. Very comfortable rooms with private bath and *no* TV (what a blessing!) are Y96. There are also plusher doubles from Y160 to Y206. If you push hard enough (with a smile of course) you may get a room without a bath for Y60 – remember that the cheaper rooms get taken quickly by locals.

Not far away, the *Huaqiao Hotel* (☎ 831-9888) *(huáqiáo dàshà)* on Shanzhang Lu has a complicated pricing system, and even though rooms start at Y120, if you look really pitiful and broke they'll relent and give you a bed in a triple for less than this: it's luck of the draw.

Other places around town are generally mid-range. The *Xinhua Hotel* (☎ 827-3710) *(xīnhuá jiǔdiàn)*, at 121 Waima Lu, has basic doubles with Y152 and better rooms from Y178 to Y196. Next door, the *Taiwan Hotel* (☎ 827-6400) *(táiwān bīnguǎn)* has singles/doubles at Y182/221, and rooms 'with a view' for Y234. Opposite the bus station is the *Hualian Hotel* (☎ 822-8389) *(huálián jiǔdiàn)*, where doubles are Y152 to Y196.

There are a number of top-end hotels in town. Pick of the bunch is the *International Hotel* (☎ 825-1212; fax 825-2250) *(guójì dàjiǔdiàn)* on Jinsha Zhonglu. It has standard doubles from Y900, deluxe doubles from Y1200 and suites from Y2100.

Places to Eat

Street markets set up at night and this is where you'll find the cuisine Shantou is famous for. Rice noodles (called *kwetiaw* locally) are also a speciality. All along Minzu Lu are a number of stalls specialising in delicious wonton *(húndùn)*.

If you're staying at the Swatow Peninsula Hotel, check out the *Western Restaurant* in the back. There's excellent food at low prices, although as usual, no English menu.

Getting There & Away

Air The CAAC office (☎ 825-1915) is at 46 Shanzhang Lu, a few minutes' walk south of the intersection with Jinsha Lu. It's usually more convenient to buy from CTS next door in the Huaqiao Hotel.

Shantou has international flights to Bangkok, Singapore and Hong Kong (twice daily).

Domestic flights are available to Beijing, Guangzhou, Chengdu, Chongqing, Fuzhou, Guilin, Haikou, Nanjing, Kunming, Shanghai, Shenyang, Wenzhou, Wuhan and Xi'an.

Bus As is the case in many parts of China nowadays, services from the long-distance bus station are supplemented by a wide variety of private services. The services running from the bus station are generally more basic and include Xiamen (Y40), Fuzhou (Y170 - sleeper), Guangzhou (Y50-100) and Nanning (Y145) among many, many others. Most hotels also offer bus services. Around the corner from the long-distance bus station, on Huoche Lu, just before the bridge, is a collection of private bus companies with sleeper buses to destinations all over Guangzhou and Fujian.

Finally, although buses to Xiamen usually leave in the morning and evening, you can head off there almost any time of day by catching a bus from opposite the Hualian Hotel. Prices are subject to a little negotiation but hover between Y40 and Y50. You will have to change buses a few times, but your fare will be carried over.

Train A railway line from Shantou to Guangzhou is slowly being built, and is years away from completion.

Boat There are boats plying the route between Hong Kong and Shantou. In Hong Kong, departures are from China Hong Kong City Ferry Terminal in Tsimshatsui, Kowloon. In Shantou, departures are from Shantou Wharf Passenger Terminal (☎ 827-1513) *(shàntóu gǎng kèyùn zhàn)*, one block west of the Gymnastic Hotel. The ship runs approximately four times weekly in each direction and the cruise takes 14 hours.

Getting Around

Pedicabs and motor-tricycles hover outside the long-distance bus station and tourist hotels and charge about Y3 for most trips in the town centre. Taxis cost about Y15 to Y20. The local public buses are the usual horror, but there are minibuses for Y2 going anywhere in the city. Generally you won't have to bother with any of this – it doesn't take long to explore the city on foot.

AROUND SHANTOU

Not far out of the city is **Mayu Island** (*māyǔ dǎo*), which makes a good day-trip. A boat leaves from the waterfront at 9 am every day and returns at 2.30 pm. The hour-long ride takes you through the fishing area with close-ups of the fisherfolk and their equipment. On an ordinary weekday the boat is filled with people toting bags of food and sacrificial offerings. Follow the crowd from the landing to the Temple of the Mother of the Heavenly Emperor (*tiānhòu miào*), built in 1985 with funds supplied by Overseas Chinese. The site has apparently always been holy to this deity, and this is where the fisherfolk burn incense before they leave in the morning.

Evidently the island has been developed to keep pace with the worshippers' enthusiasm; there are hotels and restaurants, as well as marked trails for getting around the island. There are no cars, and the beaches and views are refreshing after spending several months in large Chinese cities. According to the villagers, the island was settled mainly during the Japanese occupation, although there were a few people living here before then.

CHAOZHOU
(*cháozhōu*)

Chaozhou is an ancient commercial and trading city dating back 1700 years. It is

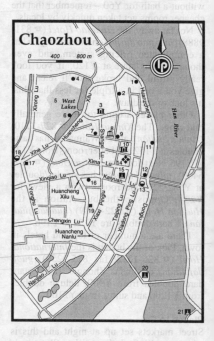

CHAOZHOU 潮州

1 Jinshan Ancient Pine
  金山古松
2 Loyalty Arch
  忠节坊
3 Prince Xu's Palace
  许驸马府
4 Athletic Field
  体育场
5 Xihu Park
  西湖公园
6 Hanbi Building
  涵碧楼
7 Huangshang Ancient Library
  黄尚书府

8 Museum
  博物馆
9 City Hall
  市正府
10 Children's Palace
  青年宫
11 Passenger Ferry Terminal
  朝州港客运站
12 Guangjimen City Wall
  广济门城楼
13 East Bus Station
  东汽车站
14 Friendship Store
  友谊商店
15 Kaiyuan Temple
  开元寺

16 Kouchi Nunnery
  叩齿庵
17 Chezhan Hotel & Restaurant
  车站饭店
18 West Bus Station
  西汽车站
19 Overseas Chinese Hotel
  华侨饭店
20 Phoenix Temple
  凤凰寺
21 Phoenix Pagoda
  凤凰塔

situated on the Han River and surrounded by the Golden and Calabash hills. It can be explored in a couple of hours and is best visited as a day-trip from Shantou.

The chief sight is the **Kaiyuan Temple** (*kāiyuán sì*), which was built during the Tang Dynasty to house a collection of Buddhist scriptures sent here by Emperor Qian Long. The temple was reduced almost to rubble during the Cultural Revolution, but has since been restored with help from Overseas Chinese donors.

On the cliffs at the foot of the Calabash Hills by the shores of the West Lake are the **Moya carvings** depicting local landscapes and the customs of the people, as well as poems and calligraphy; they date back 1000 years. South-east of Chaozhou is the seven-storey **Phoenix Pagoda** (*fènghuáng tǎ*) built in 1585.

Still further south-east of Chaozhou is the more difficult to reach **Sanyuan Pagoda** (*sānyuán tǎ*).

Getting There & Away

Minibuses run out to Chaozhou from in front of the Hualian Hotel in Shantou. The trip takes around one hour and costs Y7.

Hainan Island 海南岛

Hainan Island (*hǎinán dǎo*) is a large tropical island off the southern coast of China. It was administered by the government of Guangdong Province until 1988, when it became Hainan Province.

Like Xishuangbanna in Yunnan Province, Hainan is popular as a winter refuge, but it certainly isn't the 'Asian Hawaii' dished up in some tourist brochures. Full-throttle development of tourist facilities has taken place over the last few years, with the result that there is basically nowhere to stay besides upmarket, resort-style hotels. Even the island's attractions have been customised to the needs of limousine-bus tourists, of whom there are hordes. In sum, Hainan is an interesting place to see the Chinese tourism revolution in full swing, but if it's beaches you want try Malaysia or Thailand, and if it's China's ethnic minorities you are interested in head for Yunnan or Guizhou.

Population: five million
Capital: Haikou
Highlights:
• Li and Miao minority villages around Tongzha (for the intrepid, Chinese-speaking traveller only)

CLIMATE

Hainan is the southernmost tip of China (Sanya, in the south, is roughly on the same latitude as Vientiane in Laos), and can be relied on to be warm even when the rest of China is freezing. At the height of China's frigid winter, average temperatures of 21°C prevail. From as early as March through to November, the weather becomes hot and humid.

Typhoons can play havoc with a tight itinerary. They usually descend on the island between May and October; during the past 50 years there has been at least one every year. Although they bring the island vital rain, typhoons also have an awesome capacity for destruction. Bear in mind that typhoons can cripple all transport and communication with the mainland for several days at a time.

ECONOMY

Historically, Hainan has always been a backwater of the Chinese empire, a miserable place of exile and one of the poorest regions in the country. When Li Deyu, a prime minister of the Tang Dynasty, was exiled to Hainan he dubbed it 'the gate of hell'.

Times are changing – the entire island of Hainan has been established as a Special Economic Zone (SEZ) and has emerged as an enclave of free-market bedlam. One of the most famous fiascos occurred when the provincial government imported 90,000 duty-free Japanese cars in 1989 and resold them on the mainland at 150% profit. Real estate values jumped 20-fold between 1989 and 1993, and recent estimates of growth for the province hover around 22%. A desolate patch of land on the west of the island is being developed as the Yangpu Economic Development Area, a deep-water harbour that planners envisage as becoming a modern city of 250,000 residents.

At the cutting edge of Hainan's market

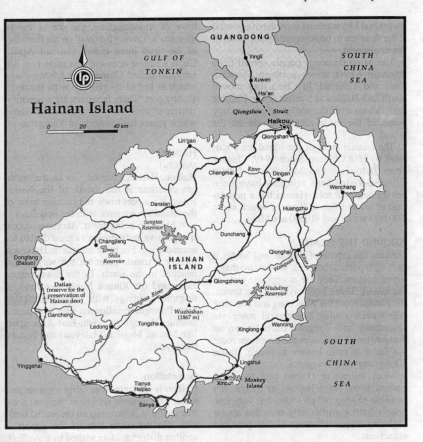

Hainan Island

GULF OF
TONKIN

GUANGDONG

Yingli

Xuwen

Hai'an

Qiongzhou ← Strait → *Qiongzhou*

SOUTH
CHINA
SEA

0   20   40 km

Haikou
Qiongshan

Lin'gao

Chengmai

River

Dingan

Wenchang

Danxian

Nandu

Songtao Reservoir

Dunchang

Huangzhu

Changjiang

Shilu Reservoir

HAINAN
ISLAND

Qionghai

Dongfang
(Basuo)

Datian
(reserve for the
preservation of
Hainan deer)

Qiongzhong

Niululing Reservoir

Wanquan River

Xinhua

Changhua River

Wuzhishan
(1867 m)

Xinglong

Wanning

Gancheng

Ledong

Tongzha

Xinglong

SOUTH
CHINA
SEA

Yinggehai

Lingshui

Tianya
Haijiao

Xincun

Monkey Island

Sanya

reforms is tourism. For the time being Chinese tourists account for around 80% of the market. Local authorities would like to turn this around and attract big-spending foreigners. Resort-style hotels are springing up all over the island.

POPULATION & PEOPLE

The original inhabitants of the island, the Li and Miao minority peoples, live in the dense tropical forests covering the Limulingshan mountains that stretch down the centre of the island. The Li probably settled on Hainan

3000 years ago after migrating from Guangdong and Guangxi provinces. Although there has been a long history of rebellion by the Li against the Chinese, they aided the Communist guerrillas on the island during the war with the Japanese. Perhaps for this reason the island's centre was made an 'autonomous' region after the Communists came to power.

Until recently the Li women had a custom of tattooing their bodies at the age of 12 or 13. Today, almost all Li people except the elderly women wear standard Han dress. However, when a member of the Li dies, traditional Li costume is considered essential if the dead are to be accepted by ancestors in the afterworld.

The Miao (Hmong) people spread from southern China across northern Vietnam, Laos and Thailand. In China they moved south into Hainan as a result of the Chinese emigrations from the north, and now occupy some of the most rugged terrain on the island.

The coastal areas of the island are populated by Han Chinese. Since 1949, Chinese from Indonesia and Malaysia and later Chinese-Vietnamese refugees have been settled here. All told, Hainan has a population of around five million, of which about 700,000 are Li and 40,000 are Miao.

AROUND THE ISLAND

Haikou, the capital of Hainan, and Sanya, a port with popular beaches, are the two major urban centres. They are at opposite ends of the island. Three highways link the towns: the eastern route via Wenchang and Wanning (the fastest route); the central route via Dunchang and Tongzha (also known as Tongshi); and the less popular western route via Danxian (also known as Nada), Basuo (Dongfang) and Yinggehai.

Most visitors to Hainan take the rapid eastern route from Haikou to Sanya. It's possible to stop off en route, but very few people bother, particularly now that a new highway bypasses most of the possible attractions.

The central route across the island is only worth taking if you have plenty of time on your hands. The ethnic minority areas of central Hainan are not readily accessible and transport links are slow. The best mountain scenery is between Sanya and Qiongzhong. There is little of interest beyond Qiongzhong.

Not many travellers bother with the western route. It offers very little in the way of amenities. Attractions include the Institute of Tropical Plants (rèdài zhìwù yánjiūsuǒ) near Danxian (dànxiàn) and the Nature Reserve for the Protection of the Hainan Deer at Datian. To the east of Datian is the town of Xiaodongfang, the site of the Li minority's 'Loving Festival' on the third day of the third lunar month (around April). China's largest open-cut iron mine is at Shi Lu (also called Changjiang) (chāngjiāng), which is linked by railway with Basuo, a shabby port. There is reportedly a beautiful stretch of road between Basuo and Sanya which passes the saltworks at Yinggehai.

HAIKOU
(hǎikǒu)

Haikou, Hainan's capital, lies on the northern coastline at the mouth of the Nandu River. It's a port town and handles most of the island's commerce with the mainland.

It has little going for it. Accommodation is expensive and there isn't a great deal to see around town. For most travellers, Haikou is merely a transit point on the way to the beaches in the south. In the town centre, along and off Xinhua Nanlu, are rows of original buildings with the unmistakable Sino-Portuguese influence seen in Chinese colonies throughout South-East Asia: spots like Macau, Melaka (Malaysia) and Penang (Malaysia).

Orientation

Haikou is split into three fairly separate sections. The western section is the port area. The centre of Haikou has all the tourist facilities. On the south side of the airport is another district seldom visited by travellers.

Information

Tourist Offices Haikou is pretty much a dead loss when it comes to travellers' information. The main CTS office (☎ 677-3288) is in a dilapidated building hidden behind the Overseas Chinese Hotel I.

Money The Bank of China is in the International Financial Centre at 33 Datong Lu. There is a newer branch next door in the International Commercial Centre. There are moneychangers outside nearly every tourist hotel.

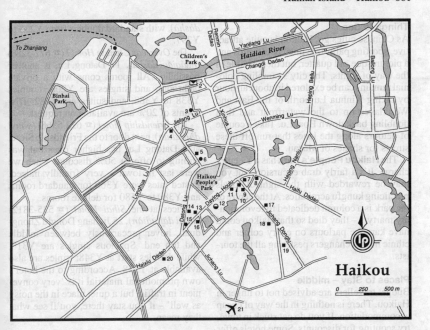

HAIKOU 海口

PLACES TO STAY

4 Friendship Hotel
   & Store
   友谊大酒店,商店
5 Overseas Chinese
   Hotel I
   华侨大厦
7 Haikou Hotel
   海口宾馆
8 East Lake Hotel
   东湖大酒店
9 Nanhai Hotel
   南海酒店
10 Ocean Hotel
   海洋宾馆

11 Seaview Hotel
   望海国际大酒店
13 CAAC Hotel & Ticket
   Office
   民航酒店售票处
14 International Financial
   Centre
   国际金融大厦
16 Taoyuan Hotel
   桃园酒店
17 Wuzhishan Hotel
   五指山大厦
18 Shu Hai Hotel
   蜀海酒店
19 Sihai Hotel
   四海大酒店
20 Ambassador Hotel
   国宾大酒店

OTHER

1 Haikou New Harbour
   海口新港
2 Main Post & Telephone
   Office
   市邮电局
3 Xinhua Bookstore
   新华书店
6 CTS
   中国旅行社
12 Long-Distance Bus
   Station
   长途汽车站
15 International Commer-
   cial Centre
   国际金融大厦
21 Haikou Airport
   海口机场

Post The post and telecommunications building is south of the long-distance bus station on Daying Jie. There is another post and telecommunications centre on Jiafang Xilu, near the Xinhua Bookstore. Most upmarket hotels also offer postal services.

Things to See

As Chinese cities go, Haikou is quite attractive, sporting palm-tree lined boulevards and a picturesque old quarter, but there is little in the way of sights. The city's rambling colonial remains can be explored in about an hour by taking Xinhua Lu north of the East and West lakes up to the waterfront and then doubling back down Boai Lu. Take a couple of detours along the lanes that run off these streets for shades of Macau.

The **Haikou People's Park** has a Y1 entry charge. It's a fairly drab excursion, but you may be rewarded with the sight of locals practicing kungfu acrobatics. At the centre of the park is a column dedicated to revolutionary martyrs – they died so that Haikou could have karaoke parlours on every corner and ethnic moneychangers pestering all the tourists.

Places to Stay – middle

Budget travellers are advised not to linger in Haikou. There is nothing in the way of cheap accommodation. If you do get stuck in town, try scouting for discounts. Some hotels offer discounted rates from 20% to 50%.

Haikou's cheapest hotels can be found on Jichang Donglu. The *Wuzhishan Hotel* (☎ 535-5101) *(wǔzhǐshān bīnguǎn)* has serviceable rooms with all mod cons (air con, TV, bathroom etc) for Y150 for singles and Y200 for doubles. Close by, on the other side of the road, the *Ocean Hotel (hǎiyáng bīnguǎn)* has singles from Y190 to Y248 and doubles from Y228 to Y280. It's the only place we stumbled across in town that charged by the hour – now, why would they do that?

Quite a bit further south on Jichang Donglu – and in an area dominated by hairdressing salons with lurid pink lighting – is the *Shu Hai Hotel* (☎ 535-1904) *(shǔhǎi jiǔdiàn)*, where standard doubles are Y180.

Another option is the *Taoyuan Hotel* (☎ 677-2998) *(táoyuán jiǔdiàn)* on Daying Houlu opposite the CAAC office. Singles start at Y180, while doubles range from Y280 to Y680. Over the road is the *CAAC Hotel* (☎ 677-2608) *(hǎikǒu hángkōng*

dàshà), with standard doubles from Y233 to Y297.

The *Overseas Chinese Hotel I* (☎ 677-3288) *(huáqiáo dàshà)*, 17 Datong. Lu, is another possibility. All rooms come with a private bathroom, and singles are Y208, doubles Y338 to Y388, and suites are Y582. Discounts of 20% are available on request.

The *Friendship Hotel* (☎ 622-5566) *(yǒuyì dàjiǔdiàn)*, next door to the Friendship Store, at 2 Datong Lu, has higher rates but was willing to offer a 50% discount when we were last in town – very friendly indeed. Posted rates were Y360 for standard rooms and Y380 to Y580 for deluxe rooms.

Prices at the *Sihai Hotel* (☎ 535-3812) *(sìhǎi dàjiùdiàn)*, 25 Jichang Donglu Zhongduan, hover precariously between middle and top end. Spacious singles are Y318, while doubles start at Y348; triples are also available at Y348. According to the hotel's own promotional material it is 'very convenient in traffic, but a quiet place in the noisy as well' – if you stay there, you'll see what they mean.

Places to Stay – top end

The *East Lake Hotel* (☎ 535-3333; fax 535-8827) *(dōnghú dàjiǔdiàn)*, 8 Haifu Dadao, is a typical lower end upmarket Haikou hotel. Standard doubles cost Y368; luxury doubles start at Y700.

The *Wanghai International Hotel* (☎ 677-3381; fax 677-3101) *(wànghǎi guójì dàjiǔdiàn)* is popular with the Chinese business set, and has singles from Y385, doubles from Y498 and suites from Y994.

Close by, the *Haikou Hotel* (☎ 677-2266; fax 677-2232) *(hǎikǒu bīnguǎn)* seems to be the busiest hotel in town; or at least the large and very sleazy lobby coffee shop is. Rooms range from Y408 to Y1280.

Haikou's premier lodging is the *Haikou International Commercial Centre* (☎ 679-6999; fax 677-4751) *(hǎikǒu gúojì shāngyè dàshà)*, a new structure that offers health-club facilities, banking, shopping and restaurants. Essentially, the rooms are serviced apartments intended for long-term leasing, but they are also available at daily rates. A standard suite is US$175 per day.

The *International Financial Centre* (☎ 677-3088) *(guójì jīnróng dàshà)*, 33 Datong Lu, is a very similar setup to the similarly named Commercial Centre next door. Amenities include everything from a swimming pool to a bowling alley. Doubles start at Y538 and climb all the way up to Y1478 for the executive suite.

Places to Eat

Depending on where you are in town, there are not as many street-side economical restaurants as in other Chinese cities. The trend seems to be towards upmarket hot-pot restaurants and their ilk. All the hotels have restaurants and, if you are not watching your budget too closely, can be relied on to serve up good food. The problem with these places for non-Chinese speakers is that virtually none of them has an English menu – a sure sign that very few foreigners are passing through.

If you want to save money, there are fruit sellers on the street vending bananas, mangos, sugar cane and so on. Jichang Donglu is the best place to seek out reasonably priced restaurants, and in the evening a lot of pick-and-choose places set up shop on the pavements. Next to the long-distance bus station in a dilapidated building is the *Chezhan Kuaican (chēzhàn kuàicān)*, which serves excellent meals from around Y12. There's no English menu, of course, but take a look at what other diners are eating.

The *Kuaihuolin Delicious Food Town (kuàihuólín)* is next door to the Ocean Hotel on Jichang Donglu. It serves up set meals in fast-food surroundings, with prices from around Y12. The English menu is much more limited than the Chinese menu, but still provides a couple of pages of choices.

Upmarket eats with an English menu? The International Commercial Centre is the best bet. The restaurants are on the 2nd floor and all of them are good. The best coffee in town can be had in the ground-floor coffee shop of the Wanghai International Hotel, though at Y18 per pot it is getting close to international prices.

Entertainment

Haikou has a certain reputation...This is the balmy tropics of China and businessmen come here to do deals and loosen their ties. Anyone who thinks they are coming to Bangkok or Manila, however, is wrong. The nightlife scene is *very* Chinese, and essentially limited to karaoke parlours (look out for the signs saying KTV). Holidaying Chinese men cruise for escorts in the lobby coffee shop of the Haikou Hotel. It's a rather depressing place to sit and nurse a beer or a coffee. The nightclub at the *Wanghai International Hotel* has an expensive variety show, as does the nightclub at the *Sihai Hotel*.

Getting There & Away

Air There are daily flights between Haikou and Hong Kong (HK$1200) on CAAC and Dragonair. Dragonair (☎ 677-4373) has a representative in Room 2 on the 5th floor of the International Financial Centre. The CAAC flights are technically charters and therefore do not appear in the CAAC timetable.

The CAAC office (☎ 677-2608), in a large building which also houses the CAAC Hotel, is on Daying Houlu. Just a few doors down is the China Southwest Airlines office. Between them they have regular flights between Haikou and the following cities: Beijing, Changsha, Chengdu, Dalian, Fuzhou, Guangzhou, Guiyang, Harbin, Jinnan, Kunming, Lanzhou, Nanning, Ningbo, Qingdao, Shanghai, Shenyang, Shenzhen, Tianjin, Wuhan, Xiamen, Xi'an and Zhengzhou.

Bus The long-distance bus station has departures to all major destinations on the island as well as offering combination ferry/bus journeys to many destinations on the mainland. Also worth looking out for are the private operators running buses to Sanya. Superluxury buses depart from near the Ocean Hotel on Jichang Donglu, take just three hours and cost Y90.

Luxury buses (ask for *háohuá*) from the bus station charge around Y70 for the run to Sanya and take four to five hours for the journey. There are cheaper services available for around Y40, but take a couple of hours longer and are terrifically crowded and uncomfortable.

The ticket windows on the left-hand side of the bus station sell combination ferry/bus tickets to Guangzhou, Shenzhen and Zhuhai. Ticket prices vary according to the comfort you travel in. For Guangzhou, it is possible to choose between ordinary (Y66), standard luxury (Y109), super luxury (Y139) and luxury sleeper (Y178) services. Luxury services to Shenzhen cost Y165 and to Zhuhai Y140.

Boat There are two harbours in Haikou, but most departures are from Haikou New Harbour (*hǎikǒu xīngǎng*) at the terminus of bus No 7. From the centre of town to the harbour by taxi costs around Y15.

Boats leave Haikou about once an hour for the 1½-hour trip to Hai'an on the Leizhou Peninsula, where there are bus connections with Zhanjiang. Combined bus/boat tickets are available at the harbour and vary in price depending on which window you make the purchase – there are lots of them. It's best to simply buy a boat ticket for Y20 and deal with finding a bus later – it's difficult and time-consuming to find your bus in Hai'an. All up the trip to Zhanjiang takes between six and seven hours.

The long-distance bus station sells tickets for two daily boat services directly from Haikou to Zhanjiang at 8 and 8.30 am. The journey takes around six hours and the cheapest ticket is Y33. Alternatively, take one of the fast boat services, which leave at 9.30 am and 2.30 pm for both Zhanjiang and Beihai in Guangxi Province (separate boats). Tickets are on sale at the harbour and cost Y88. The trip takes between 3½ and four hours.

Boats between Haikou and Guangzhou run every two days. Departures are at 9 am from Guangzhou's Zhoutouzui Wharf and the trip takes 25 hours. Starting from 4th

class and moving upmarket, prices are Y112, Y134 and Y154. It's worth paying a little extra to avoid the large dorm below deck, a particularly gruesome place to spend a rough night at sea. Third class will get you into an eight-bed dorm on deck. Watch out for petty thievery and take your own food – the food on board is poor. In Haikou, tickets can be purchased at the long-distance bus station (ticket window 16).

Boat services from Haikou to Hong Kong run every three or four days and cost between Y330 and Y600. For information on getting from Hong Kong to Haikou, see the Getting There & Away chapter.

Getting Around
To/From the Airport Haikou Airport is two km south of the city centre and taxi fares range between Y15 and Y30, depending on your bargaining skills. The fare should be Y15 but taxi drivers hang around at the airport precisely so they can charge people more. Bus No 7 runs between the airport and Haikou New Harbour.

Bus The central area of Haikou is small and easy to walk around, but there is also a workable bus system. The fare is two jiao for any destination in the city.

Taxi Taxis are reasonably abundant in Haikou, but bear in mind that meters are virtually unheard of and you will need to bargain your fare. Figure on an average fare of Y15 for any place in the city.

WENCHANG
(*wénchāng*)
The coconut plantations at Dongjiao (*dōngjiāo yēlín*) and Mt Jianhua (*jiànhuáshān yēlín*) are a short ride out of town at Qinglan Harbour (*qīnglán gǎng*). Minibuses by the riverside in Wenchang will take you to Qinglan, where you can take a ferry to the stands of coconut palms and mile after mile of beach. Another way to get to the same plantation is to take the direct bus to Dongjiao from Haikou's long-distance bus station.

Unfortunately, the beaches in this area are being developed as resorts and accommodation prices are very high.

Buses leave for Wenchang from Haikou's long-distance bus station; or you can catch a Sanya-bound bus from outside the Overseas Chinese Hotel or East Lake Hotel. The 73 km could be done as a day trip.

XINGLONG
(xīnglóng)

Since 1952, over 20,000 Chinese-Vietnamese and Overseas Chinese refugees (mostly from Indonesia or Malaysia) have settled at the **Xinglong Overseas Chinese Farm** *(xìnglóng huáqiáo cūn)*. Tropical agriculture, rubber and coffee are important cash crops here. Many of the residents speak English and may be able to organise transport to Miao villages. Local guides (including the motorbike drivers) are usually not worth the money they ask.

Xinglong is only worth considering as an overnight stopover if you are happy to spend a lot of money on accommodation. The spring baths here – piped into the hotels – are very popular with local tourists, which has driven prices beyond what most travellers would consider reasonable. If you are still interested, the hotels are concentrated in an area three km from the town.

From the bus stop to the hotels costs Y2 on the back of a motorbike, or Y4 in a motorbike with sidecar.

XINCUN
(xīncūn)

Xincun is populated almost solely by Danjia (Tanha) minority people, who are employed in fishing and pearl cultivation. In recent years, typhoons have repeatedly blown away the pearl and oyster cultivation farms, but the harbour area, fish market and nearby Monkey Island are worth an afternoon ramble.

Buses travelling the eastern route will drop you off at a fork in the road about three km from Xincun. It should then be easy to get a lift on a passing minibus and hitch or walk into Xincun. Frequent minibuses run directly from Lingshui and Sanya to Xincun.

MONKEY ISLAND
(hóuzi dǎo)

About a thousand Guangxi monkeys *(Macaca mulatta)* live on this narrow peninsula near Xincun. The area is under state protection and a special wildlife research centre has been set up to investigate all the monkey business.

A shack on the beach at Xincun functions as a booking office selling return ferry tickets. It also sells a booklet put together in Chinese by the research centre. It includes exhaustive monkey data and an appendix which lists the monkeys' favourite plants like a menu.

The ferry put-puts from Xincun to Monkey Island in 10 minutes. From the island pier, motorbikes with sidecars will take you to the monkey enclosure *(hóuzi yuán)*. You can also get there on foot: walk along the beach road to the left for about one km, then follow the road leading uphill to the right for another 1½ km.

At the entrance a stall sells tickets, and peanuts for the monkeys. Apart from feeding times at 9 am and 4 pm, it's a case of the monkeys seeing you and not vice versa. You can often hear them crashing around and chattering in the shrubs on the hillside; occasionally a wild, woolly head pops out of the top branches to see what's happening or to scream at you.

SANYA
(sānyà)

Sanya is a busy port and tourist resort on the southern tip of Hainan Island. The town lies on a peninsula parallel to the coast and is connected to the mainland on one side by two bridges.

The harbour area is protected to the south-east by the hilly Luhuitou Peninsula. On the western outskirts of Sanya there's a community of around 5000 Hui, the only Muslim inhabitants of Hainan.

Most travellers will find Sanya disappointing. There is construction work taking place everywhere, throwing up yet more hotels, and the sights are for the most part boring.

Things to See

Sanya's attractions are overrated. Even the beaches are poor by South-East Asian standards. For Chinese tourists, the popular beaches are at Dadonghai, Luhuitou Peninsula and Tianya Haijiao.

The beach at **Dadonghai** (dàdōnghǎi) is the best of the lot, but is consequently crowded and well on the way to being overdeveloped. There is even a ticket office

selling tickets for the beach (Y5), though nobody seems to bother with this. Dadonghai is around three km east of Sanya and is easily reached by bus (Y1).

The beaches on the **Luhuitou Peninsula** (lùhuítóu) are poor, but they make for pleasant enough walks. Luhuitou means 'deer turns its head', and the name refers to a legend of a Li hunter who pursued a deer to the peninsula where, realising it was trapped, it turned its head back and promptly changed into a beautiful maiden. The two then 'got married and settled down' as the promotional material says. The deer, the maiden and the

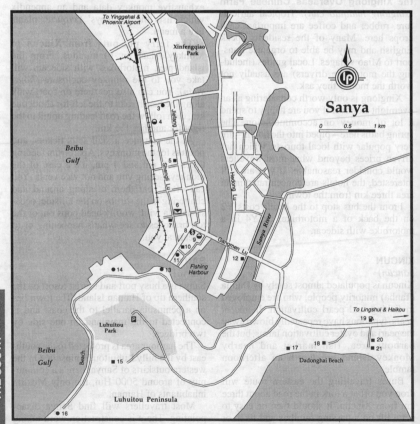

THE SOUTH

hunter are immortalised in stone, drawing huge crowds daily; entry is Y15.

On the tip of Luhuitou Peninsula is the

SANYA 三亚
PLACES TO STAY
5   Sanya Hotel   三亚宾馆
7   Haisheng Hotel   海生纠店
10 Guiya Hotel   贵亚大酒店
12 Sanya International Hotel   三亚国际大酒店
15 Luhuitou Hotel   鹿回头宾馆
17 Jinling Holiday Resort   金陵渡假村
18 Seaside Holiday Inn Resort   滨海渡假村
20 Dadonghai Hotel   大东海大酒店
21 South China Hotel   南中国大酒店
OTHER
1   Cuiyuan Restaurant   翠园酒家
2   Railway Station   火车站
3   Sanya Market   三亚商场
4   Sanya Bus Station   三亚汽车站
6   Post & Telephone Office   邮店局
8   Bank of China   中国银行
9   Buses to Haikou   往海口汽车站
11 Boat Ticket Office   三亚港客运站
13 Granny Ferry   小渡船
14 Customs Building   海关楼
16 Marine Research Station   海学研究所
19 Petrol Station   加油站

Hainan Experimental Marine Research Station, which specialises in pearl cultivation. The use of pearls in China can be traced back 4000 years; cultured pearls were created over 900 years ago during the Song Dynasty.

The beach at **Tianya Haijiao** (*tiānyà hǎijiǎo*) (literally 'edge of the sky, rim of the sea'), about 24 km west of Sanya, is not bad, but you would probably be arrested if you tried swimming there. Chinese tourists flock to the beach dressed in their Sunday best to have their pictures taken in front of rocks with carved characters. Entry to the beach is Y16 – it's not worth it. Catch any bus travelling west from Sanya bus station. The trip takes about 45 minutes.

To the east of Sanya is Dragon Tooth Bay (*yálóng wān*), another sightseeing spot crowded with Chinese tour buses.

South of Sanya are **Xidao Dongdao** (*xīdǎo dōngdǎo*) (Eastern & Western Hawksbill islands), two coral islands clearly visible from Luhuitou Peninsula. Boats from the harbour head out to the islands for Y80. Island inhabitants use coral for housing and tacky souvenirs. A site close to these islands has been opened to foreigners for scuba-diving and snorkelling.

Places to Stay

Be warned, there is nowhere to stay for travellers on a budget. Most of the hotels in and around Sanya cater mainly to package tourists, and the cheaper places don't take foreigners.

If you want to keep costs to a minimum and want a good location, the best bet is the *Seaside Holiday Inn Resort* (☎ 213-898) (*bīnhǎi dùjiàcūn*) in Dadonghai. Standard doubles are Y250, and deluxe doubles are Y320. There are many other hotels in the Dadonghai area (in fact there is really nothing but hotels in Dadonghai). All sport room rates of around Y350 upwards for a double and there is little to distinguish one from another. The *South China Hotel* (☎ 213-888) (*nánzhōngguó dàjiǔdiàn*) is rated as the best of the lot and has singles at

THE SOUTH

Y588, standard doubles for Y718 and deluxe doubles for Y888.

Finding a hotel in Sanya itself will bring costs down slightly, but it's not a very pleasant place to stay. The *Sanya Hotel* (☎ 274-703) *(sānyà bīnguǎn)* is in the centre of town on Jiefang Lu, and has singles from Y130, doubles from Y180 and triples at Y240.

Also in Sanya and popular with Overseas Chinese tourists is the *Haisheng Hotel* (☎ 247-804) *(hǎishèng dàjiǔdiàn)*, an average mid-range hotel with rates of Y266 for standard doubles and Y310 for triples.

Sanya's luxury option is the *Sanya International Hotel* (☎ 273068) *(sānyà guójì dàjiǔdiàn)*. It's poorly located close to town next to the Sanya River. Standard doubles start at Y420.

Places to Eat

Sanya and its environs are swarming with restaurants. Most of them are seafood restaurants like the *Jumbo Seafood Restaurant*, a huge floating affair. Remember that Sanya is a resort town, and most Chinese arrive in big groups and spend freely and rowdily on the best in the house. You will often find yourself being pressured to order far more than you can possibly eat. All the major hotels have both Chinese and Western restaurants, though you are unlikely to dig up any credibly authentic Western food.

Budget travellers are best off seeking out street stalls. Gangmen Lu has dozens of stalls that set up tables and chairs outside, and are pleasant enough places to sit and have a meal on balmy evenings. Most of them are of the pick-and-choose variety, and have lots of fresh seafood. Jiangang Lu, down near the harbour, is another place to seek out restaurants. None of them have English menus, and it would be impossible to make specific recommendations. Take a stroll and see what's on offer.

Things to Buy

Southern Hainan is famous for its cultured pearls, but watch out for fakes. Tourists have been known to pay 100 times the going price for authentic-looking plastic.

Getting There & Away

Air Phoenix Airport – as it has been recently named – is open for domestic flights, and international flights are also anticipated at some later date.

Also anticipated are daily flights to Guangzhou and Shenzhen. Reception at the major hotels may be able to book plane tickets; otherwise try the CAAC office, which is inconveniently located at the western end of town. It is very likely that a new CAAC office will be opened in a better location when the renovated airport is completed.

Bus From Sanya bus station there are frequent buses and minibuses to most parts of Hainan. Deluxe buses for Haikou (Y80) also depart from the Sanya, Luhuitou and Dadonghai hotels. The express buses to Haikou take around 3½ hours to cover the 320-km route.

Train The railway line is mostly used for hauling freight, but there is sporadic passenger service between Sanya and Dongfang on the west coast. Travel by this method is very slow.

Boat Boat services are being cut back at Sanya now that the new highway offers rapid road connections with Haikou. Soon, almost all boat services will operate from Haikou.

Getting Around

The airport is a 20-minute drive from the town by taxi. Reckon on paying around Y40.

Motorbikes with sidecars cruise the streets all day. The real fare is usually half the asking fare. The same applies for rickshaws, a slow and bumpy mode of transport.

Given that Sanya's attractions (such as they are) are so widely spread out it is worth getting together with a few people and hiring a vehicle and driver. The minibuses down by the long-distance bus station charge Y150 for a full-day, six-destinations excursion. It's not a bad deal.

THE SOUTH

TONGZHA

(tōngzhá)

Tongzha, also known as Tongshi, is the capital of the Li and Miao Autonomous Prefecture, which in itself makes it sound like it's worth a visit. It might be, if you have time to hike out of town and seek out the villages. It is, however, a drab stopover on the central route between Haikou and Sanya. Minorities in Tongzha are suitably dressed in tidy ethnic attire, working in the hotels and putting on dance routines for visiting tourists. Intrepid travellers might want to try taking local buses from Tongzha to Mao'an, Maodao or Maogan, and seek out real Li and Miao villages.

Near Tongzha, at 1867 metres, Mt Five Fingers *(wǔzhǐshān)* is Hainan's highest mountain. Tourist minibuses run up to the mountain from Tongzha.

QIONGZHONG

(qióngzhōng)

The route between Tongzha and Qiongzhong passes through thick forest. Qiongzhong is a small hilltown with a lively market; the nearby waterfall at Baihuashan drops over 300 metres.

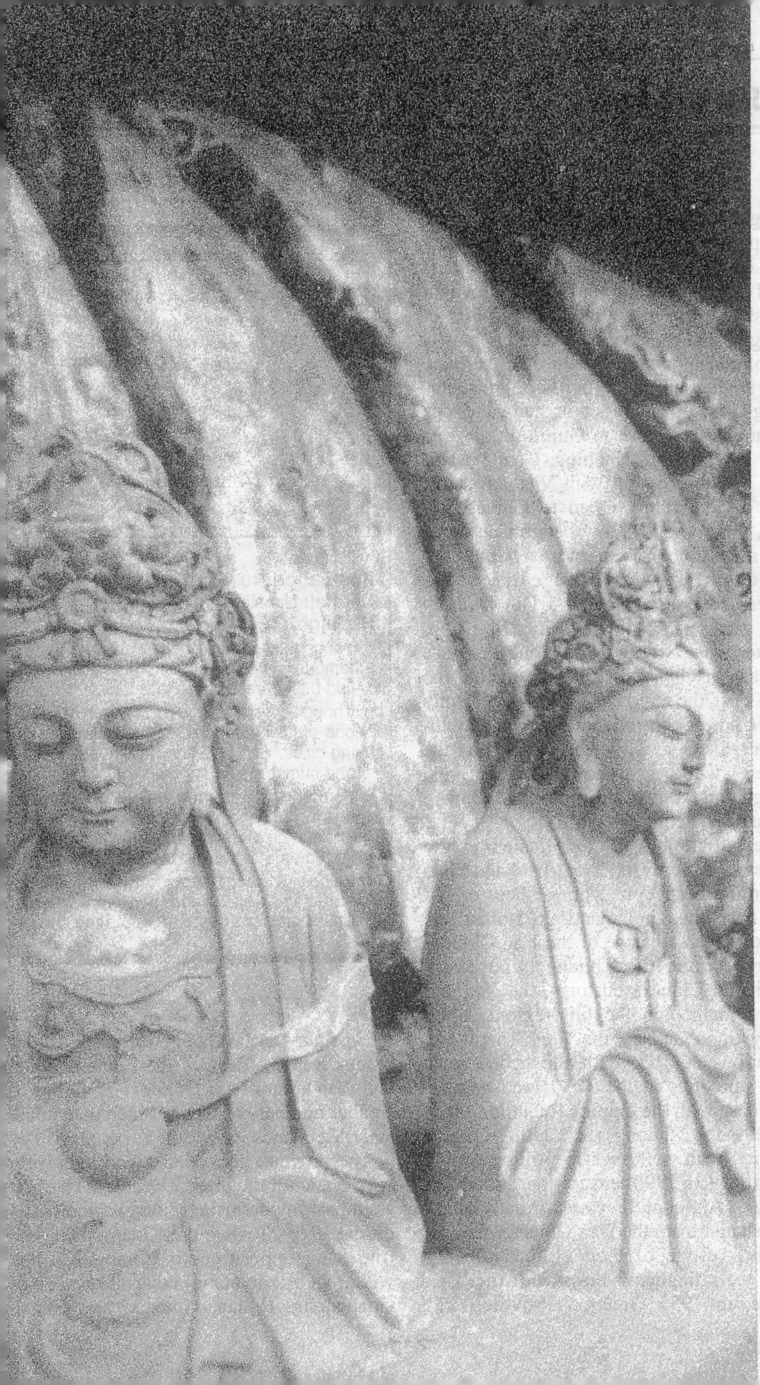

THE SOUTH-WEST

Guangxi 广西

Guangxi's most famous attraction is Guilin, perhaps the most eulogised of all Chinese sightseeing areas. While most travellers spend some time in the nearby town of Yangshuo, few make it to other parts of Guangxi, and the province remains mostly unexplored. For the adventurous, there are minority regions in the northern areas bordering Guizhou and less touristed karst rock formations like those in Guilin on the Zuo River not far from Nanning. Guangxi also has a border crossing with Vietnam at the town of Pingxiang. Open to Chinese for years, this route has now been made much more accessible to Western travellers.

Guangxi (guǎngxī) first came under Chinese sovereignty when a Qin Dynasty army was sent southwards in 214 BC to conquer what is now Guangdong Province and eastern Guangxi. Like the rest of the south-west, the region had never been firmly under Chinese control; the eastern and southern parts of Guangxi were occupied by the Chinese, while a system of indirect rule through chieftains of the aboriginal Zhuang people prevailed in the west.

The situation was complicated in the northern regions by the Yao (Mien) and Miao (Hmong) tribespeople, who had been driven there from their homelands in Hunan and Jiangxi by the advance of the Han Chinese settlers. Unlike the Zhuang, who easily assimilated Chinese customs, the Yao and Miao remained in the hill regions, often cruelly oppressed by the Han. There was continuous conflict with the tribes, with major uprisings in the 1830s and another coinciding with the Taiping Rebellion.

Today the Zhuang are China's largest minority, with well over 15 million people (according to a 1990 census) concentrated in Guangxi. Although they are virtually indistinguishable from the Han Chinese, the last outward vestige of their original identity being their linguistic links with the Thai people, in 1955 Guangxi Province was

Population: 40 million
Capital: Nanning
Highlights:

- Yangshuo – a backpackers' Mecca, justly famous for its gorgeous karst scenery and laid-back rural atmosphere
- Though overrated and pricey, Guilin is still one of China's more aesthetically pleasing cities, with tree-lined avenues, parks and numerous karst peaks
- Longsheng/Sanjiang – two mountain towns that serve as jumping-off points for exploration of minority villages, spectacular terraced fields and beautiful scenery
- Beihai, a sleepy seaside town boasting attractive white sand beaches where China's tourists come for fun in the sun

reconstituted as the Guangxi Zhuang Autonomous Region. Besides the Zhuang, Miao and Yao minorities, Guangxi is home to smaller numbers of Dong, Maonan, Mulao, Jing (Vietnamese Gin) and Yi peoples.

The province remained a comparatively poor one until the present century. The first attempts at modernising Guangxi were made during 1926-27 when the 'Guangxi Clique' (the main opposition to Chiang Kaishek within the Kuomintang) controlled much of Guangdong, Hunan, Guangxi and Hubei.

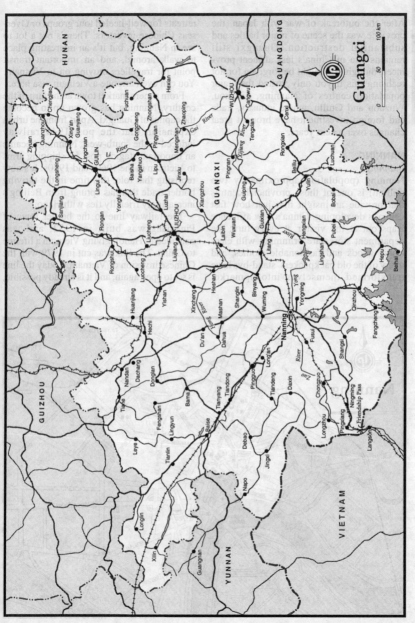

After the outbreak of war with Japan, the province was the scene of major battles and substantial destruction. Guangxi still remains one of China's less affluent provinces, though you might be forgiven for not realising this if you only visited the major population centres of Nanning, Liuzhou, Wuzhou and Guilin, where industry, trade and foreign investment have brought great changes over recent years.

NANNING
(nánníng)

Nanning (population approximately two million) is one of those provincial centres that provide an insight into just how fast China is developing. China's new affluence leaps out at the visitor at every turn: the department stores are brimming with electronic goods and fashionable clothes, and many of the old backpackers' stand-bys have transformed themselves into upmarket retreats for well-heeled tour groups or Overseas Chinese investors. There's not a lot to see in Nanning, but it's an interesting place to walk around, and an important transit point for travellers moving on to Vietnam. You can even arrange a Vietnam visa here.

From a mere market town at the turn of the century, Nanning has grown up to become the capital of Guangxi. Apart from the urban expansion that the post-1949 railway induced in the south-west, Nanning became an important staging post for shipping arms to Vietnam in the 1960s and 1970s. It's now reprising that role, this time in the thriving border trade that has sprung from Beijing's increasingly friendly ties with Hanoi.

The railway line to the border town of Pingxiang was built in 1952, and was extended to Hanoi, giving Vietnam a lifeline to China. The link was cut in 1979 with the Chinese invasion of Vietnam. Today the line is set to open again, and it is already possible,

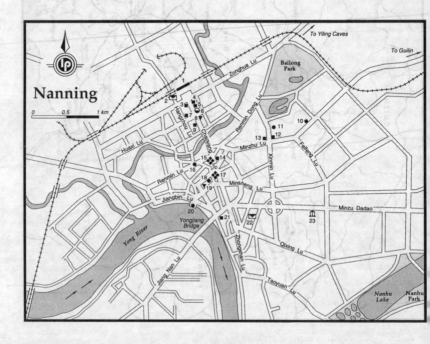

with the appropriate paperwork, to travel to Pingxiang by train, cross the Vietnam border and continue by train or bus to Hanoi from Langsön just over the border.

The population of Nanning is more than 63% Zhuang, though for the most part it is impossible to distinguish them from their Han counterparts. The only colourful minorities you're likely to encounter in town are the occasional Miao and Dong selling silver bracelets and earrings on the overhead pedestrian passes near the railway station.

Information

CITS The office (☎ 281-6197) is at 40 Xinmin Lu, across from the Yongzhou Hotel. The new Family and Individual Traveller (FIT) department there is good news for travellers. The English-speaking staff are friendly, helpful and, perhaps best of all, can help you get your hands on the formerly elusive Vietnam visa.

Vietnam Visas If you need a visa, the staff at the FIT department at CITS in Nanning can set you up with one for around Y400, about the same as what it costs in Hong

Kong. But while in Hong Kong more money means a quicker visa, in Nanning you will have to wait five working days. FIT also offers five-day individual or group tours to Hanoi and Haiphong, and a nine-day tour that also takes in Saigon.

Maps Nanning city maps are available at shops and stalls near the railway and long-distance bus stations.

Guangxi Provincial Museum

(guǎngxī bówùguǎn)

Down on Minzu Dadao, the museum offers a peaceful browse through 50,000 years of Guangxi history up to the Opium wars. There's a wealth of minority costumes and artefacts, as well as several full-size examples of Dong and Miao architecture in the tree-filled back yard. The museum also makes for a quiet, relaxing break from the hectic city streets. To get there, take a No 6 bus, which runs along Chaoyang Lu from the railway station, into Minzu Dadao and past the museum. Opening hours are from 8.30 to 11.30 am and 2.30 to 5 pm daily. Admission is Y2.

NANNING 南宁

PLACES TO STAY

3 Yingbin Hotel
  迎宾饭店
4 Milky Way Hotel
  银河大厦
5 Airways Hotel/CAAC
  中国民航酒店 ,
  中国民航
7 Tian Hu Hotel
  天湖饭店
9 Phoenix Hotel
  凤凰宾馆
12 Majestic Hotel
  明圆饭店
13 Yongzhou Hotel
  邕州饭店
21 Yongjiang Hotel
  邕江饭店

PLACES TO EAT

8 American Fried Chicken
  华越美餐馆
19 Muslim Restaurant
  清真饭馆

OTHER

1 Railway Station
  火车站
2 Post Office
  邮局
6 Long-Distance Bus
  Station
  南宁汽车站
10 Exhibition Hall
  展览馆
11 CITS
  中国国际旅行社

14 Chaoyang Square
  朝阳广场¡
15 Electronics Store
  (Friendship Store)
  南宁友谊商店
16 Nightmarket Area
  夜市
17 Nanning Department
  Store
  南宁百货大楼
18 Xinhua Bookstore
  新华书店
20 Ferry Dock
  南宁客运码头
22 Main Post Office
  电信大楼
23 Guangxi Provincial
  Museum
  广西省博物馆

Bailong Park
(báilóng gōngyuán)

Also known as Renmin Park, the park has now reverted to its old name, Bailong, which means White Dragon. It's a pleasant enough place for a stroll, with a lake, a couple of pagodas, a restaurant and boat hire. Close to the main entrance is a flight of stairs leading up to a viewing platform complete with funny mirrors and an old cannon. Entrance to the park is Y0.5, and it's open until 10.30 pm daily.

Dragon Boat Races

As in other parts of the south-west (and Guangdong and Macau), Nanning has dragon boat races on the fifth day of the fifth lunar month (sometime in June), when large numbers of sightseers cheer on the decorated rowing vessels along the Yong River. The rowers pull to a steady cadence of drum beats maintained by a crewmate at one end of the boat.

Places to Stay – bottom end

Nanning is getting expensive, and most hotels are pricing themselves out of the backpacker market, but there are still a few cheap picks around the railway station.

Opposite the railway station is the *Yingbin Hotel (yíngbīn fàndiàn)*, probably the cheapest place open to foreigners, with basic doubles starting at Y26 and dorm beds for Y10. There's no English sign for this place, but it takes foreign guests all the same.

A little further up Chaoyang Lu, next to the CAAC booking office, is the *Airways Hotel (mínháng fàndiàn)*, which has dorm beds for Y32 and singles/doubles starting at Y70/90, the latter having attached bathrooms. If the Airways is full, you can try the *Phoenix Hotel (fènghuáng bīnguǎn)* across the road. It asks a pricey Y50 for a bed in a triple with shared bathroom; dank singles and doubles with bathrooms and satellite TV start at Y80/100.

Places to Stay – middle & top end

For Y150 and up, there are more options available. In the railway station area the *Milky Way Hotel (yínhé dàxià)* and the *Tian Hu Hotel (tiānhú fàndiàn)* both have dingy but fairly comfortable doubles with air-con, satellite TV and bathrooms for Y140 or Y150.

Less conveniently located, the *Yongjiang Hotel* (☎ 280-8123) *(yōngjiāng fàndiàn)* has air-con doubles for Y180. The *Yongzhou Hotel* (☎ 280-2338) *(yōngzhōu fàndiàn)* has doubles starting at Y120, and some cosy, quiet rooms at Y220 and up.

Forget about the *Majestic Hotel* (☎ 283-0808) *(míngyuán fàndiàn)* unless you're set to bleed cash. Formerly called the Ming Yuan, this hotel has been reborn as a four-star monster where the cheapest rooms start at HK$750.

Places to Eat

If you are in the railway station area on Chaoyang Lu, you can't miss the *American Fried Chicken* restaurant. It's run by some young Vietnamese-Americans of Chinese extraction (figure that one out), and serves up some good dishes. Their Vietnamese noodle soup is worth a try. For some excellent food and cheap beer try the *Muslim Restaurant (qīngzhēn fàndiàn)*. It has a limited English menu, and the friendly staff will probably also let you into the kitchen to point out what you want.

There's also a lively row of restaurants offering both northern and southern dishes on Hangzhou Lu. Not much in the way of English menus here, but that doesn't stop the owners from trying to lure you off the street.

Nanning, like Guilin and Liuzhou, is famous for its dog hotpot *(gǒuròu huǒguō)*, and while most travellers are inclined to give doggy dishes a miss the canine cuisine district is just over the Chaoyang Stream and south of Chaoyang Lu. In the evenings this area teems with roadside stalls specialising in dog hotpot.

Getting There & Away

Air Domestic airlines fly daily to Guangzhou and Beijing, five days a week to Shanghai, four days a week to Kunming and Shenzhen, and once a week to Guilin. There are also three flights each week to Hong Kong (Y1350). Other flights available include Chengdu, Shenyang, and Hanoi. Flights to Wuzhou may start by early 1996.

The CAAC office (☎ 252-1459) is at 82 Chaoyang Lu. But unless you like chaos and crowds, you may do better to try the Nanning Air Service (☎ 280-2911), next to CITS at 40 Xinmin Lu.

Bus Daily buses to Wuzhou, from Nanning's long-distance bus station, cost Y43 and take up to nine hours. Overnight sleeper buses take you there a bit more quickly for Y69.40. Sleepers to Guangzhou are Y120 and take 20 hours (although it's a long trip, having a place to actually lie down brightens the picture a bit, and it's the cheapest way to get to Guangzhou from Nanning).

There are also regular buses to Liuzhou (Y25, five hours) and Beihai (Y22, five hours). Buses to Pingxiang also take around five hours and cost Y22, while Fangcheng buses cost Y15. An interesting though rigorous option is the sleeper berth bus service to Kunming via Guangnan. Tickets are around Y200. Regular buses to Guangnan just over the Guangxi-Yunnan border are Y56. The roads are bad and the whole journey can take up to 36 hours.

Train Trains bound for Beijing allow for connections with Changsha, Guilin, Liuzhou, Wuhan (Hankou) and Zhengzhou. Other major destinations with direct rail links with Nanning are Beijing, Shanghai and Xi'an. There are also direct connections with Zhanjiang (eight hours) in Guangdong Province. Zhanjiang is a coastal town with ferry connections to Hainan Island. Train service to Beihai, where you can also catch a ferry to Hainan, should start sometime in 1996.

Direct trains from Nanning to Guilin take around seven hours and cost Y40 for a hard-seat ticket. There are various trains leaving for Liuzhou throughout the day. Hard-seat tickets for the four-hour trip cost Y23. Getting these Chinese prices may be tough: everyone at the railway station will likely

point you toward ticket window No 6, where you will have to cough up double – at least the line is usually shorter.

There is a service to Chongqing via Guiyang every other day. It's around 12 hours to Guiyang and another eight hours on to Chongqing. Hard-sleeper tickets to Guiyang are around Y192, to Chongqing Y265. You can also get trains to Kunming, but staff will only sell you a berth up to Guiyang. After that it's hard seat: you have to try and upgrade to a sleeper in Guiyang. A new railway line between Nanning and Kunming is nearing completion, though service is not expected to start for several years. This will not only cut travel time to Kunming but also alleviate some of the pressure of the overworked Guilin-Guiyang-Kunming line.

There are two trains daily for Pingxiang. The faster one, at Y38, leaves at 7.30 am and arrives at 12.30 pm. The slower train, which leaves at 10.40 am, takes seven hours, so it pays to get up early.

Boat There used to be ferries connecting Nanning to Wuzhou as well as Guangzhou. But when we last checked, the service had been suspended indefinitely due to a lack of passengers, and the ticket window had disappeared. Should service resume, the trip takes 36 hours to Wuzhou and 48 hours to Guangzhou.

Getting Around
Bicycle hire places have all closed up shop, driven out of business by the abundance of taxis and motorcycle taxis (a ride on the back or sidecar of a motorcycle or motor-tricycle). Taxi rides usually start at Y10, the motorcycle taxis around Y5.

AROUND NANNING
Yiling Caves & Wuming
(*yílíng yán*)
Twenty-five km to the north-west of Nanning are the Yiling Caves, with their stalagmites and galactic lights; 15 minutes is enough for the caves, but the surrounding countryside is worth exploring.

Wuming is 45 km from Nanning, on the same road that leads to the Yiling Caves. A few km further up is Lingshui Springs, which is a big swimming pool.

To get to either Wuming or the Yiling Caves, take a minibus from the square on the left-hand side of Chaoyang Lu just over the Chaoyang Stream.

Guiping & Jintiancun
(guìpíng/jīntiáncūn)
If you want to break up the journey between Nanning and Wuzhou, Guangxi residents recommend a stop in Guiping, said to have beautiful mountain scenery as well as places to stay overnight.

Just 25 km north-west of Guiping is Jintiancun, the birthplace of Hong Xiuquan. Hong was a schoolteacher who declared himself a brother of Jesus Christ and eventually led an army of over a million followers against the Qing Dynasty in what came to be known as the Taiping Rebellion, one of the bloodiest civil wars in human history.

Zuo River Scenic Area
(zuǒjiāng fēngjǐngqū)
The Zuo River area, around 190 km southeast of Nanning, provides the opportunity to see karst rock formations like those in Guilin, with the added attraction that this area is home to around 80 groups of Zhuang minority rock paintings. The largest of these is in the area of Mt Huashan *(huāshān bìhuà)*, which has a fresco 45 metres high and 170 metres across grouping around 1300 figures of hunters, farmers and animals.

This area is still relatively unexplored by Western travellers, and it may be worth considering one of the two-day tours offered by Nanning's FIT department (located at CITS) for around Y400 per person. Alternatively, take a bus from the Nanning square on Chaoyang Lu to Ningming City Wharf *(níngmíng xiànchéng mǎtóu)*, and from there haggle to join up with one of the boat tours for the approximately one-hour ride to Huashan.

The *Huashan Ethnic Culture Village* (☎ (0781) 728-195) *(huāshān mínzúshānzhài*

dùjiàcūn), in neighbouring Panlong, offers rooms in Dong-style wooden cabins, but at tourist prices of around Y200. You may be able to find something cheaper in the area.

Pingxiang
(píngxiáng)
Pingxiang is the staging post for onward transport to Vietnam. It's basically a border trading town, and after you've taken a wander through the bustling markets there's not a lot to see. There are places to stay, but they're no bargains. The *Xiangxiang Hotel* *(xiángxīng bīnguǎn)* on Beida Lu has doubles for Y120. Nearby on Nanda Lu, the *Nan Yuan Hotel (nányuán bīnguǎn)* charges foreigners Y160 for a double.

Nevertheless, there's no real need to stay in Pingxiang. An early-morning bus or train from Nanning will get you into Pingxiang around midday, and at this point you should be able to hitch a lift to the Friendship Pass *(yǒuyì guān)* on the Vietnamese border.

There are minibuses and private transport running from around the long-distance bus station – you shouldn't have to pay more than Y5 for a ride. From the Friendship Pass it's a 10-minute walk to Vietnam. Onward transport to Hanoi by train or bus is via the Vietnamese town of Langsön.

Beihai
(běihǎi)
Beihai is a coastal town that sees few Western travellers. This may change with the recently opened ferry service to Hainan Island and the advent of a direct rail link from Nanning, due to start service in 1996. Beihai itself is worth a couple of days, providing you don't expect too much of the beaches, touted as the best in China. The town is easy-going, people seem pretty friendly and the main tourist draw, Silver Beach, is a good place to get a tan and see how the Chinese pursue their fun in the sun.

Silver Beach *(yíntān)* Southern Thailand it is not, but Silver Beach, which lies about 10 km south-east of Beihai city, does have sparkling white sands and fairly clean water.

Designated a national tourist site, the beach and the road leading to it are also home to some of the oddest resort villas you're likely to see in China: ersatz Swiss chalets, German castles and French villas vie with the obligatory concrete hulk hotels for space along the shoreline. To get there from Beihai, catch a minibus at Renmin Jüchang, off Heping Lu, one block west of the Beihai Yinbinguan. The ride takes about 20 minutes, and costs Y2.

Places to Stay Across from the Beihai bus station on Beibuwan Zhonglu, the *Shuhai Lo (shŭhăi lóu)* offers doubles for Y90 and dorm beds for Y30. Look for the English sign in front that says 'guest room department'. A few doors down to the right is the *Jinwan Hotel (jīnwān bīnguăn)*, which has doubles for Y160 and dorm beds in triples starting at Y25.

For a more upscale stay, try the *Beihai Yingbinguan (běihăi yíngbīnguăn)* at 32 Beibuwan Zhonglu. Singles/doubles start at Y180/240, but this place is clean, quiet and well run. And well it should be: this is where the cadres stay when they come down for a dose of Beihai's sea breezes.

Getting There & Away Daily buses connect Beihai to Nanning, Liuzhou and Guilin. (See the Getting There & Away sections on these cities for more information.) There are also sleeper buses to Guangzhou for Y112. Boats for the 12-hour journey to Haikou on Hainan Island leave daily at 6 pm from the Beihai ferry terminal *(běiháng kèyùnzhàn)*. Cabins for four persons are around Y125 per head, while dorm-style beds are around Y100. Beihai is served by daily flights to and from Guangzhou, Shenzhen and Haikou, and twice weekly to and from Guilin, Changsha, Guiyang and Hong Kong.

GUILIN
(guìlín)
Guilin has always been famous in China for its scenery and has been eulogised in innumerable literary works, paintings and inscriptions since its founding as the most beautiful spot in the world – the world of course meaning China. Rapid economic growth and a booming tourist trade have pared some of Guilin's charm, but it is still one of China's greener, more scenic cities.

If you can handle the hectic traffic, most of Guilin's limestone karst peaks and parks are a short bicycle ride away. There is also a wealth of restaurants to choose from, and a fair number have English menus to boot. Unfortunately, locals don't shy from cashing in on Guilin's popularity. Most tourist sights levy exploitative entry fees for foreigners, and many travellers tell of being grossly overcharged at restaurants throughout town.

The city was founded during the Qin Dynasty and developed as a transport centre with the building of the Ling Canal, which linked the important Pearl and Yangzi river systems. Under the Ming it was a provincial capital, a status it retained until 1914 when Nanning became the capital. During the 1930s and throughout WW II Guilin was a Communist stronghold, and its population expanded from about 100,000 to over a million as people sought refuge here. Today it's home to around 600,000.

If you're itching to get to the heart of karst country, you may do best to skirt the crowds, high prices and heat of the city and go straight to Yangshuo, approximately one-hour south of Guilin by bus. But for those in the mood for a bit of city life, a day or two of cycling around Guilin can be enjoyable.

Orientation
Most of Guilin lies on the western bank of the Li River. The main artery is Zhongshan Lu, which runs roughly parallel to the river on its western side. At the southern end of this street – that is, Zhongshan Nanlu – is Guilin Railway Station, where most trains pull in. Zhongshan Lu itself is a rapidly developing stretch of tourist-class hotels, opulent department stores and expensive restaurants – a good place for a browse, but be sure to check prices before you order a bite to eat.

Closer to the centre of town is Banyan Lake, to the west of Zhongshan Lu, and Fir

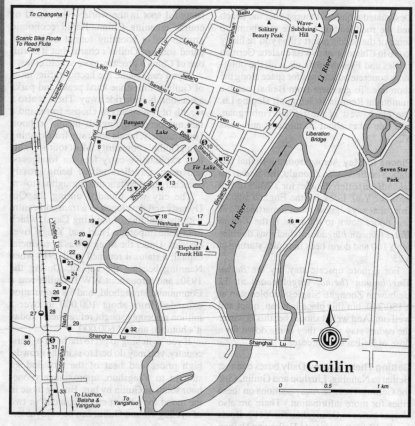

Guilin

Lake on the eastern side. Further up around the Zhongshan Lu/Jiefang Lu intersection, you'll find the CITS office, the PSB and places to hire bicycles, as well as one of Guilin's original upmarket hotels and landmarks, the Li Jiang Hotel.

Jiefang Lu runs east-west across Zhongshan Lu. Heading east, it runs over Liberation (Jiefang) Bridge to the large Seven Star Park, one of the town's chief attractions. Most of the limestone pinnacles form a circle around the town, though a few pop up within the city limits. For the best views of the surrounding karst formations you either have

to climb up the hills, or get to the top of the Li Jiang or Hong Kong hotels, which give you 360-degree vistas.

Information

CITS This office (☎ 222-648) is at 14 Ronghu Beilu, facing Banyan Lake. The staff are friendly, reasonably helpful and are now better equipped to serve both independent travellers and tours.

PSB This office is on Sanduo Lu, a side street which runs west off Zhongshan Lu, in

GUILIN 桂林

PLACES TO STAY

1 Guilin Royal Garden Hotel
帝苑酒店
2 Universal Hotel
3 Sheraton Hotel
文华大酒店
7 Ronghu Hotel
榕湖饭店
8 Holiday Inn Guilin
桂林宾馆
9 Hubin Hotel
湖滨饭店
12 Li Jiang Hotel
漓江饭店
14 Tailian Hotel
台联酒店
16 Guishan Hotel
桂山大酒店
17 Yu Gui Hotel
玉桂宾馆
19 Osmanthus Hotel
丹桂大酒店
20 Taihe Hotel
泰和饭店

23 Xingui Hotel
新桂饭店
24 Jingui Hotel
京桂宾馆
25 Hidden Hill Hotel
隐山饭店
29 South Stream Hotel
南溪饭店
30 Hong Kong Hotel
香江饭店
33 Overseas Chinese Hotel
华侨大厦

PLACES TO EAT

15 Nighttime Food Stalls
夜间摊子
18 Yiyuan Restaurant
怡园饭店

OTHER

4 PSB
公安局
5 CITS
中国国际旅行社

6 Ancient South Gate
古南门
10 Bank of China
中国银行
11 Xinhua Bookstore
新华书店
13 Guilin Department Store
桂林百货大楼
21 Long-Distance Bus Station
长途汽车站
22 Bank of China
中国银行
26 Post Office/International Phones
邮电局
27 Guilin South Bus Station
城南站
28 Guilin Railway Station
火车站
31 Bank of China
中国银行
32 CAAC
中国民航

the area between Banyan Lake and Jiefang Lu.

Money The main branch of the Bank of China is on Shanlu Beilu and this is where you will have to go if you want a cash advance on your credit card. For changing money and travellers' cheques, you can use the branches at the corner of Shanghai Nanlu and Zhongshan Nanlu – next to the railway station – and at Zhongshan Lu near Yinding Lu. Tourist hotels, including the Hidden Hill, also have foreign-exchange services which you can usually use even if you're not staying at the hotel.

Post & Telecommunications The post and telecommunications building is on Zhongshan Lu. There is a second post office on the north corner of the large square in front of the railway station; it has convenient direct-dial international telephone service that is considerably cheaper than dialling from the business centres of the tourist hotels. Some of the large hotels, such as the Li River Hotel, have post offices.

Dangers & Annoyances In Guilin it's always hunting season, and your wallet is the quarry. Whether it's a fourfold price hike in the cost of a meal, a wildly circuitous taxi ride or extortionate entry fees, almost every traveller can count on having to deal with overcharging. Stay alert to potential rip-offs and calmly negotiate prices first. Be wary of students wanting to practice English with you. While most are no doubt sincere, some travellers have lost money to smooth-talking 'English students' selling art or offering to act as guides or arrange railway tickets. Signs of possible scam artists include a willingness to discuss ways of spending your money and a reluctance to talk near police or in hotel lobbies. Also, watch out for pickpockets, especially around the railway station.

Solitary Beauty Peak
(dúxiù fēng)
The 152-metre pinnacle is at the centre of the town. The climb to the top is steep but there are good views of the town, the Li River and surrounding hills. The nephew of a Ming emperor built a palace at the foot of the peak in the 14th century, but only the gate remains. The site of the palace is now occupied by a teachers' college.

Bus No 1 goes up Zhongshan Lu past the western side of the peak. Alternatively, take bus No 2, which goes past the eastern side along the river. Both buses leave from Guilin Railway Station.

Wave-Subduing Hill
(fúbō shān)
Close to Solitary Beauty and standing beside the western bank of the Li River, this peak offers a fine view of the town. Its name is variously described as being derived from the fact that the peak descends into the river, blocking the waves, and from a temple that was established here for a Tang Dynasty general who was called Fubo Jiangjun, the wave-subduing general.

On the southern slope of the hill is Returned Pearl Cave (huánzhū dòng). The story goes that the cave was illuminated by a single pearl and inhabited by a dragon; one day a fisherman stole the pearl but he was overcome by shame and returned it.

Near this cave is Thousand Buddhas Cave (qiānfó dòng), a typical Chinese exaggeration – there seem to be a couple of dozen statues at most, dating from the Tang and Song dynasties. Bus No 2 runs past the hill.

Seven Star Park
(qīxīng gōngyuán)
One of China's nicer city parks, Seven Star Park is on the eastern side of the Li River. Cross Liberation Bridge (jiěfàng qiáo) and continue to the end of Jiefang Donglu to get there.

The park takes its name from its seven peaks, which are supposed to resemble the star pattern of the Ursa Major (Big Dipper) constellation. There are several caves in the peaks, where visitors have inscribed graffiti for centuries, including a recent one which says, 'The Chinese Communist Party is the core of the leadership of all the Chinese People'. It takes a lot of imagination to see the 'Monkey Picking Peaches' and 'Two Dragons Playing Ball' in the stalagmites and stalactites. Back outside, there are lots of trails in and around the hills, and sprawling lawns to sit or picnic on. You may want to avoid the pitiful zoo, which is enough to bring tears to any animal lover.

To get to the park take bus No 9, 10 or 11 from the railway station. From the park, bus No 13 runs back across the Li River, past Wave-Subduing Hill and down to Reed Flute Cave.

Reed Flute Cave
(lúdí yán)
Some of the most extraordinary scenery Guilin has to offer is underground at the Reed Flute Cave, which with its multi-coloured lighting and fantastic stalactites and stalagmites resembles a set from Journey to the Centre of the Earth. At one time the entrance to the cave was distinguished by clumps of reeds used by the locals to make musical instruments, hence the name.

One grotto, the Crystal Palace of the Dragon King, can comfortably hold about 1000 people, though many more crammed in here during the war when the cave was used as an air-raid shelter. The dominant feature of the cave is a great slab of white rock hanging from a ledge like a cataract, while opposite stands a huge stalactite said to resemble an old scholar. The story goes that a visiting scholar wished to write a poem worthy of the cave's beauty. After a long time he had composed only two sentences and, lamenting his inability to find the right words, turned to stone.

The other story is that the slab is the

Dragon King's needle, used as a weapon by his opponent the Monkey King. The Monkey King used the needle to destroy the dragon's army of snails and jellyfish, leaving their petrified remains scattered around the floor of the cave. You can no doubt invent your own stories.

Though the cave is worth visiting, some travellers may be put off by the laughably high entrance fee of Y44, in contrast to Y16 for locals. Also, the horde of hawkers that swarm around the exit of the cave may leave you with a deep-seated hatred for the phrase 'hello, postcard'.

The cave is on the north-western outskirts of town. Take bus No 3 from the railway station to the last stop. Bus No 13 will take you to the cave from Seven Star Park. Otherwise, it's a pleasant bicycle ride. Follow the route of bus No 3 along Lujun Lu, which runs into Taohua Jiang Lu. The latter parallels a small river and winds through fields and karst peaks, and lets you avoid the traffic of Zhongshan Lu.

Other Hills

Time to knock off a few more peaks. North of Solitary Beauty is **Folded Brocade Hill** *(diécǎi shān)*. Climb the stone pathway which takes you through the cooling relief of Wind Cave, with walls decked with inscriptions and Buddhist sculptures. Some of the damage to faces on the sculptures is a legacy of the Cultural Revolution. There are great views from the top of the hill. Bus No 1 runs past the hill.

There's a good view of **Old Man Hill** *(lǎorén shān)*, a curiously shaped hill to the north-east, from Wave-Subduing Hill. The best way to get there is by bicycle as buses don't go past it. At the southern end of town, one of Guilin's best known sights is **Elephant Trunk Hill** *(xiàngbí shān)*, which actually does resemble an elephant dipping its trunk into the Li River.

At the southern end of Guilin, **South Park** *(nán gōngyuán)* is a pretty place. You can contemplate the mythological immortal who is said to have lived in one of the caves here; look for his statue.

There are two lakes near the city centre, **Banyan Lake** *(róng hú)* on the western side and **Fir Lake** *(shān hú)* on the eastern side. Banyan Lake is named after an 800-year-old banyan tree on its shore. The tree stands by the restored South City Gate *(nán mén)* originally built during the Tang Dynasty. This is one of the nicer neighbourhoods in town.

Places to Stay – bottom end

For those on a backpacker's budget, Guilin is lacking – the lower end of the market is served primarily by Yangshuo. A few formerly Chinese-only places have recently opened to foreigners, at least giving you some options for under Y100.

Across from the railway station, the *South Stream Hotel (nánxī fàndiàn)* has singles for Y60, doubles for Y90 and beds in three-person dorm rooms for Y20. Dingy and damp they can be, but you're not going to find much cheaper in Guilin any more. Five minutes' north of the railway station, on Yinding Lu, the *Xingui Hotel (xīnguì fàndiàn)* has singles/doubles starting at Y56, though it tacks on a Y10 per room 'service charge' for foreign guests.

Nearby on Zhongshan Lu, the *Jinggui Hotel (jīngguì bīnguǎn)* offers doubles from Y80, and dorm beds for Y25. Also in the same area, The *Hidden Hill Hotel (yǐnshān fàndiàn)* has air-con doubles starting at Y100.

To the north on Ronghu Lu, the *Hubin Hotel (☎ 282-2837) (húbīn fàndiàn)* has decidedly downscale singles/doubles for Y80/100.

The old backpackers' stand-by, the *Overseas Chinese Hotel (☎ 383-3573) (huáqiáo dàshà)*, has decided it's now a classier establishment. You may still be able to wheedle an Y80 double with shared bathroom, but staff will probably push you toward the Y180 doubles.

There are numerous Chinese hotels north and south of the railway station on Zhongshan Lu that officially don't take foreigners, but may soon do so, or might even make an exception for you. They will probably double their price, but given the low base, it still could be worth a try.

Places to Stay – middle

Most of the low-end places mentioned above also have nicer rooms for Y100 to Y200, but there are also a couple of mid-range spots for those setting their sights a bit higher.

Close to the long-distance bus station is the *Taihe Hotel* (☎ 333-5504) *(tàihé fàndiàn)*. Doubles with air-con and TV cost Y120 and triples are also available from Y150. At the higher end of the middle range, the *Yu Gui Hotel* (☎ 282-5499) *(yù guì bīnguǎn)* has clean singles/doubles with all the features for Y150/230. Some of the rooms also have nice views of the Li River and Elephant Trunk Hill.

Places to Stay – top end

No shortage of choice here, at least in terms of price, but only some of the expensive spots are worth it. Just north of the long-distance bus station on Zhongshan Lu, the *Osmanthus Hotel* (☎ 383-4300) *(dānguì dàjiǔdiàn)* is one of the better top-end deals, with nicely furnished doubles from US$55.

The *Li Jiang Hotel* (☎ 282-2881) *(lǐjiāng fàndiàn)* at 1 Shanhu Beilu was once the main tourist hotel in Guilin. It's right in the middle of town and the roof provides a panoramic view of the encircling hills. Standard doubles are US$65, deluxe rooms closer to US$100; there are no singles available. It has the full works: post office, barber, bank, restaurants, tour groups and bellboys in monkey suits.

In the same price and value range, the *Ronghu Hotel* (☎ 282-3811) *(rónghú fàndiàn)* at 17 Ronghu Lu has singles/doubles for US$65/70. This spot seems to be favoured by Overseas Chinese tour groups. Looking out over Banyan Lake, it's in a nice part of town, though a bit inconvenient unless you have a bicycle.

At 14 Ronghu Lu, the US four-star *Holiday Inn Guilin* (☎ 282-3950) *(guìlín bīnguǎn)* has doubles posted at US$110, but when occupancy is low it offers a 20% discount.

The *Universal Hotel* (☎ 228-228) at 1 Jiefang Lu is a fairly new luxury hotel with rooms for US$80 to US$100.

Though its 19th-floor revolving restaurant has a great view of the city and surrounding peaks, the Hong Kong-managed *Hong Kong Hotel* (☎ 383-3889) *(xiāngjiāng fàndiàn)* is looking a bit run-down to be charging US$80 for a double.

Across the river, the formally ritzy *Guishan Hotel* *(guìshān dàjiǔdiàn)* is showing a bit of wear and tear, but boasts a bowling alley. Doubles start at US$90, but discounts are possible if occupancy is low.

The five-star *Sheraton Guilin Hotel* (☎ 282-5588) *(wénhuá dàjiǔdiàn)* at 9 Binjiang Nanlu asks a minimum of US$105 for a double, though some guests have opined that a star should be pared from its ranking.

Places to Eat

Guilin is traditionally noted for its snake soup, wild cat or bamboo rat, washed down with snake-bile wine. You could be devouring some of these animals into extinction, and we don't recommend that you do! The pangolin (a sort of Chinese armadillo) is a protected species but still crops up on restaurant menus. Other protected species include the muntjac (Asian deer), horned pheasant, mini-turtle, short-tailed monkey and gemfaced civet. Generally the most exotic stuff you should come across is eels, catfish, pigeons and dog.

For a quick bite of more down-to-earth fare, there are a couple of places between the railway station and the long-distance bus station on Zhongshan Lu with reasonable prices and English menus. Don't worry too much about finding these places; the staff will let you know where they are.

At night, on Zhongshan Lu north of Nanhuan Lu, the street comes alive with pavement stalls serving up all sorts of wok-fried goodies. Just point at what you want, and they'll do the rest. At all the above places, make sure you set prices first: too many travellers have had a fine meal ruined by confronting a bill for over Y100 when Y25 would do.

There is an outstanding, inexpensive Sichuan restaurant on Nanhuan Lu called the *Yiyuan Restaurant (yíyuán fàndiàn)*. Although there is no English sign, you'll easily spot the place by its tasteful all-wood exterior. The owner is a local Chinese woman who speaks excellent English and will be happy to explain and help you choose dishes. She especially imports all her spices from Sichuan Province, and you can taste the difference.

For an OK cup of coffee and an excellent view of Guilin, try the revolving restaurant on the 19th floor of the Hong Kong Hotel. For pizza, try the pizzeria at the Universal Hotel; pizzas cost about Y30.

For dim sum, the Tailian Hotel is considered by locals and Overseas Chinese as the best place in town, as long as you get there around 8 am: too much later and all the best dishes will have been snatched up.

Getting There & Away

Guilin is connected to many places by air, bus, train and boat. Give serious thought to flying in or out of this place, as train connections are not good.

Air CAAC has an office (☎ 384-4007) at the corner of Shanghai Lu and Minzhu Lu. Go in through the doorway on the corner and head up to the 2nd floor.

Guilin is well connected to the rest of China by air and destinations include: Beihai, Beijing, Chengdu, Chongqing, Fuzhou, Haikou, Hangzhou, Hong Kong, Guangzhou, Guiyang, Kunming, Lanzhou, Qingdao, Shanghai, Shenzhen Shenzou, Ürümqi, Wulumqi, Xiamen and Xi'an.

Probably the most popular travellers' option is the Guilin-Kunming flight, which saves considerable travelling time and saves mucking about trying to get tickets on a train that is frequently booked out.

Internationally, Guilin is linked only to Hong Kong. Curiously, it's much cheaper to fly Guilin-Guangzhou plus Guangzhou-Hong Kong than direct Guilin-Hong Kong, despite the extra departure tax. (Of course, you would be risking an additional landing and takeoff in China.) More direct overseas flights are likely to open up when a new international airport 30 km west of the city is completed, though the opening date is said to be 'not for a while, maybe in 1999'.

CAAC runs buses from the Shanghai Lu office to the airport for Y5, leaving one to two hours before scheduled flight times. A taxi to the airport costs about Y40.

Bus For short local runs (ie, Yangshuo, Xing'an), minibuses depart regularly from the railway station. Buses to Yangshuo should set you back Y5, and the trip takes just over an hour.

The long-distance bus station is north of the railway station on Zhongshan Lu. Buses to Longsheng leave approximately every half-hour from 6.50 am to 5.50 pm; two buses a day leave for Sanjiang at 8.40 am and 2.20 pm. There is one bus daily for Xing'an at 11.40 am.

Frequent buses leave for Liuzhou from 6.20 am until 1.40 pm, and from Liuzhou you can connect with buses to Nanning. There is also a sleeper bus to Nanning leaving daily at 4 pm.

For Wuzhou and Guangzhou, ordinary, deluxe and sleeper buses are available. The sleepers may be your best bet, especially for the 16-hour marathon to Guangzhou. Deluxe buses to Guangzhou leave in the early morning and afternoon, and cost around Y87; sleepers leave at 4 pm and 5.30 pm, and cost Y130. Buses for Wuzhou leave pretty much hourly between 6.40 am and 8 pm, and cost Y56.50 for a deluxe and Y87.20 for a sleeper. You can also catch buses daily to Zhuhai and every other day to Shenzhen, though there are no sleepers for these rides, which last nearly 20 hours..

Behind the railway station is the Guilin South bus station, where buses and minibuses leave on a regular basis for Longsheng and other relatively local destinations.

Train There are useful train connections to Guilin, but some of these (like the Kunming-Guiyang-Guilin-Shanghai route) tend to involve long hauls on unbelievably crowded carriages. Guilin Railway Station has a separate ticket office for foreigners; this means you'll have to pay tourist price but at least you avoid the impossible queues and will normally be able to pick up a ticket. You may

THE SOUTH-WEST

also be able to swing a hard-sleeper ticket from the cafes and travel outfits in Yangshuo.

Direct trains out of Guilin include those to Beijing (31 hours); Changsha (11 hours); Guangdong (13 hours); Guangzhou (15 hours); Guiyang (18 hours); Kunming (about 29 hours); Liuzhou (four hours); Nanning (seven hours); Shanghai (35 hours); Xi'an (36 hours); and Zhanjiang. For Chongqing change trains at Guiyang.

There are two trains a day to Kunming: one starts from Shanghai and the other from Guangzhou. In either case, the trains are generally very crowded. The 'Well-Mannered Youth Window' ticket counter at Guilin Railway Station seems to have no problems in supplying hard-sleeper tickets providing you are happy to pay tourist prices. These are usually for the train from Guangzhou, which stops in Guilin around 1 am. Tourist-price tickets from Guilin to Kunming are around Y300 for hard sleeper and a shocking Y586 for soft sleeper.

Getting Around
Bus & Taxi Most of the city buses leave from the terminal at Guilin Railway Station and will get you to many major sights, but a bicycle is definitely better, especially in the searing summer heat.

Taxis are available from the major tourist hotels for about Y20 per trip, depending on the distance. Pedicabs charge Y5 to Y10 per trip.

Bicycle Bicycles are definitely the best way to get around Guilin. There are plenty of bicycle-hire shops – just look along Zhongshan Lu for the signs. There are some near the long-distance bus station and near the railway station, one next to the Overseas Chinese Hotel and another on the grounds of the Li Jiang Hotel. Most charge between Y10 and Y15 per day, and require Y200 or your passport as security.

AROUND GUILIN
The Ling Canal (*líng qú*) is in Xing'an County, about 70 km north of Guilin. It was built during the 2nd century BC in the reign

of the first Qin emperor, Qin Shihuang, to transport supplies to his army. The canal links the Xiang River (which flows into the Yangzi River) and the Tan River (which flows into the Pearl River), thus connecting two of China's major waterways.

You can see the Ling Canal at **Xing'an**, a market town of about 30,000 people, two hours by bus from Guilin. A daily bus departs from the long-distance bus station at 11.40 am. Minibuses to Xing'an also leave from in front of the railway station. The town is also connected to Guilin by train. Two branches of the canal flow through the town, one at the northern end and one at the southern end. The total length of the Ling Canal is 34 km.

LI RIVER
(*lí jiāng*)
The Li River is the connecting waterway between Guilin and Yangshuo and is one of the main tourist attractions of the area. A thousand years ago a poet wrote of the scenery around Yangshuo: 'The river forms a green gauze belt, the mountains are like blue jade hairpins'. The 83-km stretch between the towns is hardly that but you do see some extraordinary peaks, sprays of bamboo lining the riverbanks, fishers in small boats and picturesque villages.

As is the Chinese habit, every feature along the route has been named. **Paint Brush Hill** juts straight up from the ground with a pointed tip like a Chinese writing brush. **Cock-Fighting Hills** stand face to face like two cocks about to engage in battle. **Mural Hill** just past the small town of Yangti is a sheer cliff rising abruptly out of the water; there are supposed to be the images of nine horses in the weathered patterns on the cliff face.

A popular tourist trip is the boat ride from Guilin down the Li River to Yangshuo. Although popular with tour groups (fleets of boats do the run daily in the high season), low-budget travellers have been put off by the exorbitant ticket prices, which presently come in at Y400, including lunch and the bus trip back to Guilin from Yangshuo. This must rank as one of Guilin's worst cases of price gouging, as the most luxurious local trip costs only Y127.

Tour boats depart from Guilin from a jetty across the road from the Yu Gui Hotel each morning at around 8 am, although when the water is low you have to take a shuttle bus to another pier downriver. For trips booked through hotels, buses usually pick you up at around 7.30 to 8 am, and take you to the boat. The trip lasts all day, and some people find

that the time drags towards the end. It's probably not worth it if you're going to be spending any length of time in Yangshuo, where you can organise local boat trips.

YANGSHUO
(yángshuò)
Just 1½ hours from Guilin by bus, Yangshuo has, along with Dali in Yunnan, become one of those legendary backpacker destinations

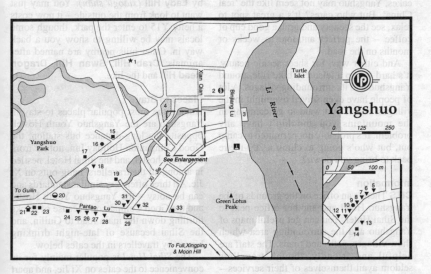

that most travellers have heard about long before they even set foot in China. Set amid limestone pinnacles, it's a small town that is admittedly getting bigger on the back of its popularity. Although not as quaint as it once was, Yangshuo is still a great laid-back base from which to explore other small villages in the nearby countryside.

With its Western-style cafes, Hollywood movies, Bob Marley tunes and banana pancakes, Yangshuo may not seem like the 'real China'. But who cares? It's a great spot to relax, see the scenery and grab a good cup of coffee – the perfect antidote to weeks or months on the road.

And either way, for sheer scenic beauty, it's hard to top a leisurely bike ride around Yangshuo and its surrounding villages. A lot of people have even stayed overnight in the villages, and if you want to go camping in the mountains you shouldn't have any problem. It's probably not permitted to camp out, but who's going to climb a 200-metre peak to bring you down?

Information

CITS There's an office on the grounds of the Yangshuo Hotel and another office next to the Sihai Hotel. You can get useful maps of Yangshuo and the surrounding area which show villages, paths and roads. The staff are helpful and friendly, though travellers seldom avail themselves of their services – enterprising locals working from the cafes are generally more in touch with the needs of independent travellers.

Money The Bank of China on Binjiang Lu will change cash and travellers' cheques, as well as receive wire transfers.

Post & Telecommunications The post office, on the main road across from Xi Jie, has English-speaking staff and long-distance phone services that are much cheaper than those offered by the cafes and hotels.

Things to See

The main peak in Yangshuo is **Green Lotus Peak** *(bìlián fēng)*, which stands next to the Li River in the south-eastern corner of the town. It's also called Bronze Mirror Peak *(tóngjìng fēng)* because it has a flat northern face which is supposed to look like an ancient bronze mirror.

Yangshuo Park *(yángshuò gōngyuán)* is in the western part of the town, and here you'll find **Man Hill** *(xīláng shān)*, which is supposed to resemble a young man bowing and scraping to a shy young girl represented by **Lady Hill** *(xiǎogū shān)*. You may just want to look from the outside – it now costs a hefty Y15 to enter the park, though some locals may be willing to show you a back way in. Other hills nearby are named after animals: **Crab Hill**, **Swan Hill**, **Dragon Head Hill** and the like.

Places to Stay

Among the most popular places to stay in Yangshuo are the Yangshuo Youth Hostel, opposite the long-distance bus station, the Good Companion Holiday Inn, not far from the youth hostel, and the Sihai Hotel, nestled in among all the travellers' hang-outs on Xi Jie. All three offer very similar standards and can be noisy – the Yangshuo Youth Hostel and the Good Companion because of trucks hurtling down the main road to Guilin, and the Sihai because of late-night drinking binges by travellers in the cafes below.

The *Sihai Hotel* is popular mainly for its convenience to the cafes on Xi Jie, and apart from the noise in the evenings and the dampness of the rooms in the winter months it's a good spot. The Sihai has 'luxury' doubles for Y40 per person, as well as singles/doubles with shared bathroom starting at Y15/20.

The *Yangshuo Youth Hostel*, which has recently been renovated, has beds for Y15 in a five-bed dorm and for Y25 in a three-bed dorm, both with attached bath. Dorm beds in rooms without attached bath are Y10. Beds in singles and doubles range from Y30 to Y60.

Just up the street, the *Good Companion Holiday Inn* still offers dorm beds for Y5 and beds in doubles/triples for Y9/7. Cheap prices, but the service can be pretty frosty.

On the main road toward the east end of

town lies one of Yangshuo's better bets: the *Zhuyang Hotel*. It's friendly, very clean, and provides little touches, like towels and tea, that the other places lack. Singles/doubles with attached bathroom are Y30/60, while a bed in a triple costs Y10.

The *Xilang Hotel* is set back from the street and is very quiet at night. It's a bit run-down, but it's a friendly place with reasonable rates. Singles are Y14 and doubles/triples with attached bathroom are Y16/18 per bed. Dorm beds are available for Y10.

Having been targeted by a Sino-Malaysian joint venture, the *Yangshuo Hotel* was to be reborn in late 1995 as the *Yangshuo Resort Hotel*, replete with swimming pool, bar, three-star rating and doubles starting at US$50! You knew it was only a matter of time...

There are also several formerly Chinese-only hotels along the main road which have opened up to foreign guests, including the *Golden Dragon Hostel* (☎ 882-2674) and the *South Comfortable Hostel*. They're not bad, but tend to charge a bit more and offer a bit less than their more seasoned competitors. Another new hotel is the *Green Leaf Hotel* (☎ 882-2860), with singles/doubles for Y50/Y100.

Places to Eat

Xi Jie teems with tiny cafes offering interesting Chinese/Western crossovers as well as perennial travellers' favourites, such as banana pancakes, muesli and pizza. For anyone who has been wandering around China for a while it's a good chance to have a break from oily stir-fried vegetables and grab a cup of coffee.

One popular cafe is *Lisa's*. Local fame has made Lisa a tad cheeky, but she and her staff are all smiles, the food is generally excellent and the place is often packed when other spots are not, though that doesn't mean the others aren't worth trying.

Across from Lisa's, the *Mei You Cafe* promises 'mei you bad service, mei you warm beer', and it delivers. Just up the street, *Minnie Mao's* has won travellers' praise for tasty dishes and some of the most attentive

service in town. Just south of the Sihai Hotel off a small side street, *Susannah's* also draws a steady stream of customers. It's claim to fame is that it was the first Western restaurant in town and Jimmy Carter ate there in 1987!

Other popular places include the cluster of cafes up on the corner of Xi Jie and the main road: *Green Lotus*, *Paris Café* and *MC Blues Bar*. They all have outdoor seating and are good places to sit and watch the world go by. MC Blues has the added attraction of over 150 tapes, and staff are usually happy to let you choose what you like.

The places on the main road are where some of Yangshuo's original cafes started. They don't enjoy the popularity of some of the places on Xi Jie, but cafes like *Gan Bei*, *The Hard Seat* and the *Hard Rock* are all friendly spots for a meal or a cup of coffee. The *Wild Swans* cafe also has a full-fledged bookstore, with both new and second-hand paperbacks.

There are a slew of other cafes as well, making for fierce competition – by the time you read this it's a safe bet some of names will have changed, but at least you won't lack for choice.

If you get tired of the 'international' spots, you'll find a number of *yóutiáo* (fried bread sticks) and noodle vendors on Xie Jie closer to the main road and around the long-distance bus station.

Things to Buy

Yangshuo is a good place to do some souvenir shopping. Good buys include silk jackets (at much cheaper prices than in Hong Kong), hand-painted T-shirts, scroll paintings and batiks (from Guizhou). Name chops cost Y10 to Y60 on average. Everything on sale should be bargained for. The paintings available in Yangshuo, for example, are generally poor quality (even if you think they look good) and a starting price of Y150 can easily go below Y100.

If you are in the market for a chop, bear in mind that it is not the size of the stone that is important in determining a price but the quality of the stone itself. Often the smaller pieces are more expensive than the hefty chunks of rock available.

Student Cards Several places around Yangshuo, most notably the Merry Planet Language Club, offer brief courses in Chinese language, taiji or medicine that will allow you to walk away with a student ID card. Travellers who paid the Y30 fee have gleefully told of subsequently nabbing Chinese-price tickets at railway and bus stations, hotels and parks. Railway station staff in Guilin and other major cities already seem wise to this scam, and how long it will work elsewhere is open to question, but you can probably still save money at parks and other tourist sights.

Getting There & Away

Air The closest airport is in Guilin, and the CAAC office is near the Xilang Hotel. Cafes can also drum up tickets for you. Check the Guilin Getting There & Away section earlier in this chapter for details on the flights available.

Bus There are frequent buses and minibuses running to Guilin through the day. The best option is the minibus service which operates from the square in front of the long-distance bus station. Buses leave as soon as they fill up, which could be anywhere from five to 15 minutes, and the trip takes a little over an hour. They charge Y5 per person, and Y1 per piece of luggage.

If you're heading to Guangzhou you can take a bus/boat combination from Yangshuo for around Y100; buses to Wuzhou leave in the morning and evening. The morning bus allows you to connect with the evening boat leaving Wuzhou; the evening bus is less convenient as it leaves you to sit out in the wee small hours of the morning waiting for the first boat of the day. From Yangshuo you can only book 3rd-class tickets. If you want your own 2nd-class cabin you should book in Wuzhou when you arrive – the 5 pm boat usually has beds in cabins for Y77.50. Tickets for the five-hour high-speed ferry

ride to Guangzhou also must be booked in Wuzhou.

You can arrange the Wuzhou-Hong Kong high-speed ferry in Yangshuo. Combined bus/boat tickets are available from CITS and most cafes/travel outfits for around Y500. Most people catch the morning bus and overnight in Wuzhou, though accommodation is not included in the price of the ticket.

There are several buses a day to/from Yangshuo's long-distance bus station to Liuzhou for around Y16. Overnight sleeper buses direct to Guangzhou leave throughout the afternoon and cost around Y90. Though still a bumpy ride, the sleepers have reportedly taken some of the nightmare out of this journey.

Train The nearest railway station is in Guilin. Almost any cafe or travel outfit around Yangshuo will organise train tickets, and some offer hard sleepers for high-demand routes like Guilin to Kunming at around Y240. When eyeing these prices, bear in mind that locals usually have to go through 'the back door' in Guilin to get the tickets. This also means that sometimes a 'guaranteed' hard-sleeper ticket can turn into a less-than-enticing hard seat, which has led some travellers to make the day-trip up to the foreign ticket counter at the Guilin Railway Station just to be sure.

CITS can also get you a hard sleeper to Kunming, but you have to take a bus to Liuzhou and board the train there. The bus/train package costs Y360. To get any of these tickets you'll probably have to book at least two to three days in advance.

Getting Around

Yangshuo itself is small enough to walk around without burning up too many calories, but if you want to get further afield then hire a bicycle. Just look for rows of bikes and signs near the intersection of Xi Jie and the main road. The charge is about Y5 per day.

AROUND YANGSHUO

The highway from Guilin turns southward at Yangshuo and after a couple of km crosses the Jingbao River. South of this river and just to the west of the highway is **Moon Hill** *(yuèliang shān)*, a limestone pinnacle with a moon-shaped hole. To get to Moon Hill by bicycle, take the main road out of town towards the river and turn right on the road about 200 metres before the bridge. Cycle for about 50 minutes – Moon Hill is on your right and the views from the top are incredible!

A series of caves have been opened up not far from Moon Hill: the **Black Buddha Caves** *(hēifó dòng)*, **New Water Caves** *(xīnshuǐ dòng)* and **Dragon Cave** *(jùlóng tán)*. If you head out to Moon Hill, you will undoubtedly be intercepted and invited to visit the caves. Tours cost around Y25 per head, though prices can drop if there are more of you. You go through the caves and then climb down a steep chimney via a rope and ladder to an underground pool fed by a river. You can walk along the river through the mountain for a few hours and come out on the other side. The Dragon Cave demands an outlandish Y46. Not cheap for a damp and muddy trek.

In Yangshuo there are also several women offering guided tours of Moon Hill, the caves and other famous spots, as well as their home villages. Some will even bring you home and cook you lunch! These mini-tours have garnered rave reviews from some travellers and may be worth a try, though you usually need to get at least three people together to make it worth your guide's while.

River Excursions

There are many villages close to Yangshuo which are worth checking out. A popular riverboat trip is to the picturesque village of **Fuli** *(fúlǐ)*, a short distance down the Li River, where you'll see stone houses and cobbled lanes. There are a couple of boats a day to Fuli from Yangshuo for around Y20 (foreigners' price), although most people tend to cycle there – it's a pleasant ride and takes around an hour.

An alternative mode of transport to Fuli is by inner tube. Inner-tube hire is available at Minnie Mao's for about Y5 per day. It takes

around three or four hours to get to Fuli this way. Several places also offer rafting trips and kayak hire, both popular options in the warm summer months.

On market days in Fuli, be very careful of pickpockets; young males work in groups of three or four, brushing up against travellers in the press of the crowd and relieving their pockets of valuables.

A host of cafes and local travel agents also organise boat trips to **Yangti** *(yángtí)* and **Xingping** *(xīngpíng)*.

About three hours upstream from Yangshuo, the mountain scenery around Xingping is even more breathtaking, and there are many caves in the area. People residing in some of the caves manufacture gunpowder for a living.

Many travellers take their bicycles out to Xingping by boat and cycle back – it's a picturesque ride of about three hours, and the whole package costs Y20 to Y30 depending on how many of you there are. Any number of cafes can organise boat tickets for you.

It's possible to spend the night in Xingping. One small hotel sits on a point that juts out into the river; basic rooms are Y10 to Y20 per person. A couple of doll's house restaurants with bilingual menus keep everyone fed (take care that they don't overcharge).

Markets

Villages in the vicinity of Yangshuo are best visited on market days, and these operate on a three-day, monthly cycle. Yangshuo is on the same cycle as Xingping. Thus, markets take place every three days starting on the first of the month for Baisha (1, 4, 7 etc), every three days starting on the second of the month for Fuli (2, 5, 8 etc), and every three days starting on the third of the month for Yangshuo and Xingping (3, 6, 9 etc). There are no markets on the 10th, 20th, 30th and 31st of the month.

LONGSHENG & SANJIANG
(lóngshèng/sānjiāng)

Around four and seven hours respectively by bus to the north-west of Guilin, Longsheng and Sanjiang are close to the border of

THE SOUTH-WEST

Guizhou Province and are a good introduction to the rich minority cultures of this province. The Longsheng area is home to a colourful mixture of Dong, Zhuang, Yao and Miao minorities, while Sanjiang is mainly Dong.

Longsheng and Sanjiang are best visited with an overnight stay in each. Trying to do either as a day-trip from Guilin would leave you with no time to get out of town and see the sights.

Longsheng

Longsheng's main attraction is definitely not the town itself, a cluster of concrete hulks that clash with the mountain backdrop. Not far out of town, however, are the Dragon's Backbone Rice Terraces *(lóngjǐ fītián)* and a nearby hot spring *(wēnquán)*. The hot spring is a tacky tourist highlight and can be safely missed, though local buses running out to the hot spring pass through rolling hills sculptured with precipitous rice terraces and studded with Yao minority villages. The area is reminiscent of Banaue in northern Luzon, Philippines. It's possible to desert the bus around six or seven km from the hot spring and take off into the hills for some exploring. When you return from the day's outing, Longsheng at least offers cheap accommodation and even cheaper food at its lively night market.

Things to See Though the region around Longsheng is covered with terraced rice fields, the **Dragon's Backbone Rice Terraces** sees these feats of farm engineering reach all the way up a string of 800-metre

LONGSHENG 龙胜

PLACES TO STAY

- 4 Longsheng All-Autonomous Government Hotel
     龙胜各族自治县政府招待所
- 5 Business Hotel
     商业宾馆
- 6 Longsheng Tourist Corp Hostel
     龙胜县旅游公司客房部
- 8 Moon Hotel
     月亮宾馆
- 9 Xiantao Hotel
     仙桃大酒店
- 10 Hualong Hotel
     华隆大酒店
- 11 Riverside Hotel
     凯凯旅社

OTHER

- 1 Minibus Station
     小公共汽车站
- 2 Jinhui Restaurant
     金徽饭店
- 3 PSB
     公安局
- 7 Longsheng Tourist Corp
     龙胜县旅游公司
- 12 Bus Station
     汽车站

peaks. A half-hour climb to the top delivers an amazing vista, if the Yao women who invariably tag along to peddle their trinkets give you a moment's peace to enjoy it.

Buses to the terraces leave from opposite the Jinhui Restaurant. Though the trip is only about 20 km, some of the buses stop midway at the town of Heping to try and pull in more passengers, which can make the ride last up to 1½ hours! Locals pay Y3, but you'll probably have a tough time getting your fare below Y5. Expect a Y8 per-person entry fee at the terraces.

There are some other tourist sights around Longsheng, including **forest reserves**, **Dong and Yao villages** and unusual **stone formations**. Staff at the Longsheng Tourist Corp, located next to the Longsheng Tourist Corp Hostel, can give you a somewhat fanciful map and perhaps tell you how to get to these spots, though they'll probably want you to rent your own van, which could get pricey.

Places to Stay Longsheng is betting its future on tourism, and now sports a host of hotels that welcome foreign guests. Leading the low end in both price and aesthetics is the *Longsheng Tourist Corp Hostel (lóngshèng xiàn lǚyǒu zǒnggōngsī zhāodàisuǒ)*. Beds in doubles/triples start at Y10/8 for foreigners. To get there, walk downhill from the bus station and turn right at Xinglong Xilu to cross the bridge into town. Keep going until the second intersection, where the road ends, and turn left. Look for an English sign that says 'Room Service Department'.

Downhill from the bus station, just before the bridge is the *Riverside Hotel (kǎikǎi lǚshè)*. It's run by an English teacher who seems happy to help travellers with information on getting to the local sights. She's even made up a map of the surrounding area for her guests. Rooms are very basic, and cost Y10 per bed.

More upmarket accommodation can be had at the *Business Hotel (shāngyè bīnguǎn)*, just down the street from the Longsheng Tourist Corp Hostel. Singles/doubles with

bathrooms are Y35/40. *The Moon Hotel (yuèliàng bīnguǎn)*, which is one block nearer the bridge on Xinglong Beilu, has air-con doubles/triples for Y50/60.

Up the hill from the Longsheng Tourist Corp Hostel, on Shengyuan Lu, the ponderously named *Longsheng All-Autonomous Government Hotel (lóngshèng gèzú zìzhìxiàn zhèngfǔ zhāodà isuǒ)* offers a quiet refuge from the pervasive karaoke that rocks Longsheng's main streets until around midnight. Sanctuary costs Y80 for a double and Y30 for a bed in a triple, bathrooms attached.

Places to Eat Longsheng is not a culinary wonderland. Past the Moon Hotel, the *Jinhui Restaurant) (jīnhuī fàndiàn)* serves up some decent dishes and has an English menu, albeit one pinched from the Hong Kong Hotel in Guilin. Negotiate the prices down, and forget about ordering the sea cucumber or crab. Just past the bridge on Xinglong Xilu, street stalls appear around 8 pm, offering point-and-choose meals by lantern light. There are also some noodle shops on Xinglong Beilu.

Getting There & Away From Guilin, you can catch buses and minibuses to Longsheng from the long-distance bus station, the south bus station (behind the railway station) and in front of the railway station. The long-distance bus station has buses departing approximately on the half-hour between 6.50 am and 5.50 pm. Buses from the railway station and the south bus station are less frequent but do the trip a bit faster. From Longsheng to Guilin, buses leave the bus station every 15 to 20 minutes from 6 am to 5.40 pm. The fare is Y9.60. There is also a daily Longsheng-to-Liuzhou bus which leaves at 6.50 am and costs Y24.50.

Buses and minibuses leave from the Longsheng bus station for Sanjiang approximately every hour from 6.30 am to 5 pm. You can also catch these at the corner of Guilong Lu and Xinglong Lu, down the road from the bus station. The fare is Y6.60 and the bumpy but scenic journey takes three hours.

Sanjiang

If arriving in Sanjiang leaves you wondering why you made the trip, don't worry. Like Longsheng, the idea is to get out and about. About 20 km to the west of town, Chengyang Wind & Rain Bridge *(chéngyáng qiáo)* and the surrounding Dong villages are as peaceful and attractive as Sanjiang is not.

Chengyang Wind and Rain Bridge Over 80 years old, this elegant covered bridge is considered by the Dong to be the finest of the 108 such structures in Sanjiang county, and took the local villagers 12 years to build. It looks out over a lush valley dotted with Dong villages and water wheels.

If you want to really enjoy and explore the area, you can stay at the Chengyang Bridge National Hostel, which is just to the left of the bridge on the far side of the river. See the following Places to Stay section for details.

From the Sanjiang bus station, you can catch hourly buses to Lin Xi *(lín xī)*, which go right past the bridge, or if there are several of you, hire a van to take you out there for around Y60 for the round trip. Bus service stops around 5 pm, so if you need to get back to Sanjiang later than that you'll have to hitchhike. The first bus of the day to Sanjiang passes by the bridge around 7.30 to 8 am.

Places to Stay With the advent of the Chengyang Bridge National Hostel, there's no need to stay in Sanjiang unless you're catching a very early bus out of town. If so, your quietest option is the *Guesthouse of the People's Government of the Sanjiang Dong Autonomous County (sānjiāng dòngzú zìzhìxiàn rénmín zhèngfǔ zhāodaisuo)*. Doubles are Y21, or Y48 with bathroom attached. To get there, follow the road that runs between the Department Store Hotel and the bus station uphill, and bear left. Walk about 10 minutes and it's on your right, across from a Dong drum tower.

Right in town on the opposite corner of the long-distance bus station, the *Hostel of the Department Store (sānjiāng bǎihuò zhāodàisuǒ)* has noisy three and four-bed dorms

for Y5/7, and doubles with attached bathroom for Y18.

Further down the street, the *Chengyang Bridge Hotel (chéngyáng qiáo bīnguǎn)* (not to be confused with the National Hostel at the bridge itself) has slightly more upmarket singles/doubles starting at about Y100.

Opened in mid-1994, the *Chengyang Bridge National Hostel* (☎ (0772) 861-2444) *(chéngyáng qiáo zhāodàisuǒ)* is an all-wood Dong-style building with beds for Y15 and nice doubles with shared bath for Y50, and friendly staff who speak some English. Even if you don't spend the night, a cup of tea or a simple meal on the hostel's riverside balcony is a great way to enjoy the scenery. The only fly in the ointment is the karaoke-crazed staff, but a few polite words may persuade them to croon softly.

Getting There & Away The Sanjiang bus station has several buses to Guilin between 7 and 8.30 am and five buses to Liuzhou between 6.40 and 11 am. Buses to Longsheng leave every 40 to 50 minutes between 6.40 am and 4.40 pm.

Sanjiang to Kaili If you have time on your hands, it's worth considering entering Guizhou Province through the backdoor, via local bus. From Sanjiang take the 10 am bus to Long'e (Y8.5), which is just across the Guizhou border. Though the journey is only approximately three hours, you'll almost certainly have to overnight in Long'e, as the onward bus to Liping leaves at 6 am. The hotel on the square where the buses stop has beds in triples for Y5.

The four-hour journey to Liping costs Y10, and passes through some beautiful mountains, as well as the town of Zhaoxing, which itself may be worth a visit. From Liping there is one bus to Kaili daily at 6 am, and sometimes buses run in the afternoon as well.

One as yet untested option might be to take a bus to Fulu, from where you can get on a boat to Congjiang. Congjiang has connections to Rongjiang and Kaili. Another possibility is to take a train to Tongdao in Hunan Province and from there travel onwards by bus to Liping (there are minibuses running to the railway station west of Sanjiang half-hourly throughout the day).

LIUZHOU
(liǔzhōu)

Liuzhou, with a population of over 730,000, is the largest city on the Liu River and an important south-west China railway junction. The place dates back to the Tang Dynasty, at which time it was a dumping ground for disgraced court officials. The town was largely left to its mountain wilds until 1949, when it was transformed into a major industrial city.

Liuzhou is Guilin's poor cousin, with similar but less impressive karst scenery on the outskirts of town. It sees few foreigners, and those that do visit may meet with sullen stares from the locals, though some will venture the ubiquitous 'Hello!'. Hotels that take foreign guests are also few and far between.

Things to See

There are a few sights around town worth taking a look at if you have time on your hands. Along Feie Lu near the long-distance bus station is **Yufeng Hill** *(yúfēng shān)*, or Fish Peak Mountain, in Yufeng Park. It's very small as mountains go (33 metres), and derives its name from the fact that it looks like a 'standing fish'. Climb to the top for a smoggy vista of Guangxi's foremost industrial city.

Next door to Fish Peak Mountain is **Mt Ma'an** *(mǎān shān)*, or Horse Saddle Mountain, which provides similar views.

Liuhou Park *(liǔhòu gōngyuán)* is a more pleasant park in the north of the city. It has a lake and a small temple erected to the memory of Liu Zongyuan (772-819), a famous scholar and poet. Bus No 2, 5 or 6 will get you to the park, or you can walk there from the long-distance bus station in around 20 minutes.

Places to Stay & Eat

A few minutes' walk from the main railway station down Feie Lu is the large *Nanjiang Hotel (nánjiāng fàndiàn)*, which will take foreigners. Singles/doubles with hard beds, your own TV and mouldy bathroom cost Y40/64. There are dorm beds, but not for foreign friends.

Close to the long-distance bus station is the *Educational Building Hotel (jiàoyù dàshà)*, where a bed in a triple with shared bathroom is Y63 and doubles with attached bathroom cost a steep Y163. Right next door to the long-distance bus station you may notice the *Transport Hotel*, but despite its English sign it does not take foreigners.

The *Liuzhou Hotel (liǔzhōu fàndiàn)* rounds out this limited selection. Its cheapest doubles start at Y100, and after that it's a quick jump up to Y380 for TV and air-con. To get there take bus No 2 to the Liuhou Park, turn right into Youyi Lu and look out for the hotel on the left.

For food, your best bet may be the lively night market across from the Educational Building Hotel. Starting around 8 pm there are numerous stalls serving up tasty dumplings and noodles fried with your choice of fresh ingredients – just point to what you want. The railway station area also has dumpling and noodle places. The Liuzhou Hotel has a few restaurants, but the prices will probably put you off. Just a cup of coffee, albeit brewed, costs Y18.

Up on Liuzhou Square is what may be Liuzhou's first foray into Western-style bars, the *Old Place (lǎo dìfāng)*. It serves up a few decent Western dishes and has draught beer! As the few foreigners who work in Liuzhou tell it, the Old Place is becoming the new hang-out for the local arty-yuppie crowd, which could make for an interesting evening.

Getting There & Away

Air The CAAC booking office on Feie Lu offers flights four days a week to Guangzhou, and twice weekly to Beijing and Shanghai. At the time of writing, flights to Guiyang were expected to start soon, and other destinations may be offered in 1996, though CAAC staff seemed far from certain.

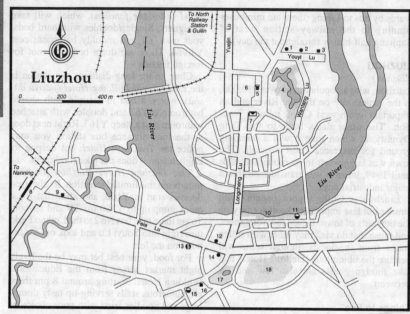

LIUZHOU 柳州

PLACES TO STAY

3 Liuzhou Hotel
   柳州饭店
9 Nanjiang Hotel
   南疆饭店
16 Educational Building
   Hotel
   教育大厦

OTHER

1 Xinhua Bookstore
   新华书店

2 CITS
   中国国际旅行社
4 Liuzhou Park
   柳州公园
5 Old Place Bar
   老地方酒吧
6 Liuzhou Square
   柳州广场
7 Post Office
   邮电局
8 Main Railway Station
   火车站
10 Riverside Park
   江滨公园
11 Ferry Dock
   航运码头

12 CAAC
   民航售票处
13 Bank of China
   中国银行
14 Xinhua Bookstore
   新华书店
15 Long-Distance Bus
   Station
   汽车总站
17 Yufeng Park
   鱼峰公园
18 Ma'an Hill
   马鞍山

Bus There is a daily 2.15 pm bus direct to Yangshuo from the long-distance bus station. The journey takes around five hours and costs Y16.40. Frequent buses to Guilin

(Y21.50) also pass through Yangshuo, but this may change when current construction of a direct Liuzhou-Guilin road is completed. Other destinations include Beihai (Y36),

Fangcheng (Y37.40), Guangzhou (Y76 or Y106 for a sleeper bus), Guiping (Y23.40), Longsheng (Y25), Nanning (Y23), Pingxiang (Y42.70), Sanjiang (Y18.90), Shenzhen (Y88.50), Wuzhou (Y34.80) and Zhuhai (Y91.50).

Train Liuzhou is a railway junction which connects Nanning to Guilin. Trains from Guilin to Kunming pass through Liuzhou. If you're coming up from Nanning you'll have to change trains in Liuzhou to get to Kunming. All trains heading out of Nanning pass through Liuzhou, and you could hook up with any one of these to get to a number of major destinations. Possibilities include Beijing, Changsha, Guangzhou, Guiyang, Shanghai and Xi'an.

The hard-seat fare from Liuzhou to Guilin is around Y25, and the trip takes approximately four hours. Hard-seat tickets for the five-hour trip to Nanning are Y23.

Boat There are nightly boats for Guangzhou leaving at 8 and 9 pm. The 12-hour journey takes you through Guiping and Wuzhou, and costs Y100 for a 3rd-class dorm-style bed; no cabins are available. Tickets seem to be in good supply, and can be bought at the ferry dock.

Getting Around
Liuzhou is a bit large for walking around, particularly at the height of summer when the place is like a blast furnace! Unfortunately, there are no bicycle-hire places either. Pedicabs, motor-tricycles, motorcycle taxis and taxis can be found at the bus station and outside the main railway station. Bus No 2 will take you to the Liuzhou Hotel, and bus No 11 links the long-distance bus station to the main railway station. Bus maps can be bought from sidewalk hawkers at both railway stations.

WUZHOU
(wúzhōu)
For most travellers, Wuzhou is a pit stop on the road between Yangshuo and Guangzhou or Hong Kong. Although it's not one of

Guangxi's major attractions, Wuzhou has some pleasant parks and interesting street life which can make for an enjoyable overnight stop.

Situated at major and minor river junctions, Wuzhou was an important trading town in the 18th century. In 1897 the British dived in there, setting up steamer services to Guangzhou, Hong Kong and later Nanning. A British consulate was established which gives some idea of the town's importance as a trading centre at the time, and the town was also used by British and US missionaries as a launching pad for the conversion of the 'heathen' Chinese.

The period after 1949 saw some industrial development with the establishment of a paper mill, food-processing factories, and machinery and plastics manufacturing, among other industries. During the Cultural Revolution, parts of Guangxi appear to have become battlegrounds for Red Guard factions claiming loyalty to Mao. In something approaching a civil war, half of Wuzhou was reportedly destroyed.

Today, Wuzhou has some fine street markets, tailors, tobacco, herbs, roast duck and river life to explore. Wuzhou also has one of Guangxi's more unusual sights in the Snake Repository.

Information
The post office is on Nanhuan Lu, just before the bridge. Good maps of the city, with bus routes, are usually available at shops near the long-distance bus station. Failing that, try the Xinhua Bookstore on Danan Lu, across from the New World Hotel. CITS has an office at the Beishan Hotel, but you shouldn't have to deal with it at all if you're just passing through – all onward tickets can easily be purchased at the boat dock or long-distance bus station.

Snake Repository
(shécáng)
Wuzhou has what it claims is the world's largest snake repository, a major drawcard for Overseas Chinese tourists and a sight that pulls in the occasional Western traveller.

More than one million snakes are transported annually to Wuzhou (from places like Nanning, Liuzhou and Yulin) for export to the kitchens of Hong Kong, Macau and other snake-devouring parts of the world. To get there, walk along Shizhi Lu from next to the Wuzhou Hotel; it's about two km away. Snake and cat fights are staged for visiting groups of Overseas Chinese tourists – something you may wish to avoid if you have any feelings or respect for animals. The repository is open daily from 8 am to 6 pm. Admission is Y4.

Sun Yatsen Park
(zhōngshān gōngyuán)
Just north of the river up Zhongshan Lu, which then turns into Wenhua Lu, Sun Yatsen Park is worth a look as the site of China's earliest memorial hall for the founder of the Republic of China. The hall was constructed in 1928 and commemorates an important speech given by Sun Yatsen in Wuzhou.

Western Bamboo Temple
(xīzhú yuán)
Just north of town bordering Sun Yatsen Park is the Western Bamboo Temple, where around 40 Buddhist nuns live. The vegetarian restaurant, open for breakfast and lunch, is highly rated by travellers who have taken the time to wander up here. You can walk to the temple by taking Wenhua Lu into Sun Yatsen Park. From the park gate walk about 10 minutes until you reach an old brick building with an English sign saying 'temple' on the left-hand side. Then just follow the signs.

Places to Stay
The steady flow of Hong Kong Chinese into Wuzhou has pushed hotel prices up, and in several places room rates are quoted in HK dollars.

If you want or need to overnight in Wuzhou, the best bottom-end choice is the *Yuanjiang Hotel (yuānjiāng jiǔdiàn)* on

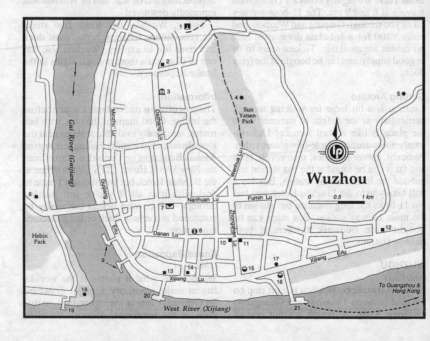

Xijiang Lu, a five-minute walk down from the bus station and ferry dock area. Singles/ doubles with attached bathroom range from Y50 to Y90, while singles/doubles with common washing facilities are from Y40 to Y60. Close by, the *Xinxi Hotel (xīnxī lǚdiàn)* offers slightly lower rates, but is a bit dank and gloomy.

The somewhat more upscale *Hebin Hotel (hébīn fàndiàn)*, lies west across the Gui River near the bridge. Doubles cost around Y105 a night, but it's a bit of a concrete hulk. The best reason to stay here is to catch the early morning high-speed ferry to Hong Kong (see Getting There & Away in this section).

Originally the top spot in town, the *Beishan Hotel (běishān fàndiàn)*, at 12 Beishan Lu up Dazhong Lu to the north of the city centre, is better off given a miss. It's overly expensive for what it offers, and is a fair trudge out of town.

Wuzhou's newest hotel, the *New World Hotel (xīnjiè dàjiǔdiàn)* doesn't seem worth the HK$328 it charges for a standard room. Across the street, the *Triumphal Arch Hotel (kǎixuánmén dàjiǔdiàn)* already looks as if it's glory days have passed, but singles and doubles start at a more reasonable Y98/138.

The *Wuzhou Hotel (☎ 222-193) (wúzhōu dàjiǔdiàn)* is also showing signs of wear and tear, and isn't much of a bargain either. Standard doubles start at Y210. But the place is worth noting for its coffee shop in the lobby (see the following Places to Eat section).

Places to Eat

There's no shortage of small restaurants, especially in the vicinity of the boat docks and bus station. The illuminated mirages by the riverbank are floating restaurants à la Aberdeen (Hong Kong), with extravagant names such as *Water City Paradise*.

If that doesn't appeal to you, there are other small restaurants along the eastern bank of the Gui River on Guijiang Erlu. For a slightly upmarket snack and a cup of coffee after a long bus or boat journey head over to the ground-floor coffee shop at the *Wuzhou Hotel*. A good cup of coffee costs only Y6, and the food is not bad either.

WUZHOU 梧州

PLACES TO STAY

2 Beishan Hotel
   北山饭店
6 Hebin Hotel
   河滨饭店
10 New World Hotel
   新世界大酒店
11 Triumphal Arch Hotel
   凯旋门大酒店
12 Wuzhou Hotel
   梧州大酒店
13 Yuanjiang Hotel
   鸳江酒店
14 Xinxi Hotel
   新西旅店

OTHER

1 Western Bamboo Temple
   西竹圆
3 Museum
   博物馆
4 Sun Yatsen Memorial Hall
   中山纪念堂
5 Snake Repository
   蛇仓
7 Post Office
   邮电局
8 Bank of China
   中国银行
9 Waterside Restaurants
   河边餐厅
15 Long-Distance Bus Station
   客运站
16 Long-Distance Bus Station
   客运站
17 Ferry Tickets (for Guangzhou)
   梧港客运站
18 Yuanjiang Pavilion
   鸳江亭
19 Ferry Dock (for Hong Kong)
   往香港船
20 Ferry Dock (for Guangzhou)
   客运站码头
21 Ferry Dock (for Guangzhou)
   客轮码头

Getting There & Away

Air Wuzhou is expected to have its own airport in early 1996. But aside from a flight to Nanning, CAAC staff were wary of predicting what routes would open up.

Bus Buses from Wuzhou to Yangshuo leave from the two long-distance bus stations to the left of the ferry dock area, and cost Y43.40. Buses leave at 7.20 and 7.50 am, and at 6.40 and 8 pm, making it generally possible to catch a bus after coming in on any of the boats from Guangzhou. High-speed ferries from Hong Kong connect with the evening buses. There are also bus connections to Beihai (Y69), Guangzhou (Y56), Guilin (Y51), Liuzhou (Y58), Nanning (Y62) and Shenzhen (Y84).

The bus trip from Wuzhou to Yangshuo takes a bumpy seven hours, with another two hours to Guilin. The scenically impressive Wuzhou-to-Nanning run takes eight to nine hours.

Boat There is a high-speed ferry service between Wuzhou and Hong Kong on odd

days of the month (1, 3, 5, 7 etc), leaving at 7 am and arriving in Hong Kong at around 3 pm on the same day. (From Hong Kong, boats leave at 8 am on even dates.) Tickets are around HK$400. From Yangshuo, CITS and several local hotels can arrange tickets for the trip; for more details see the Yangshuo Getting There & Away section earlier in this chapter and the Getting There & Away chapter at the start of this book.

Boats to Guangzhou leave at 3, 5, 7 and 8 pm, and the cheapest tickets are for the crowded (but bearable) dorm-style accommodation at Y44.50. Two-bed/four-bed cabins are Y56.50/77.50, but are only available on one or two boats per evening. Boats leave from both the docks just past the long-distance bus stations, or from a pier diagonally across the street from the Yuanjiang Hotel.

There are now also high-speed ferries that make the trip to Guangzhou in four to five hours. Boats leave at 7.40 am and 1.30 pm. Tickets are Y159.50. High-speed boats also serve Shenzhen (242.50) and Zhuhai (199.50).

Guizhou 贵州

Until recent times Guizhou (*guìzhōu*) was one of the most backward and sparsely populated areas in China, and it is still among the poorest. It is also one of the most rewarding provinces to visit. Mountains and plateaus make up some 87% of Guizhou's topography, which has an average altitude of 1000 metres above sea level. The star attraction close to Guiyang is the Huangguoshu Falls, China's biggest. The neighbourhood also presents many opportunities for hiking and stumbling around some of China's least-visited villages.

About 65% of Guizhou's population is Han and the rest a mixture of minorities such as Miao, Bouyei, Dong, Yi, Shui, Hui, Zhuang, Bai, Tujiao and Gelao. Between them these minorities celebrate nearly 1000 festivals each year which preserve fascinating customs and elaborate skills in architecture, dress and handicrafts.

Surprisingly for a province so rich in minority culture, Guizhou is neglected by most travellers. According to the Guizhou Tourism Administration, the province's total number of foreign visitors to date is just over 100,000. One of the reasons is probably the difficulty of travel in the province; another is that very little English is spoken.

However, the south-east of Guizhou in particular deserves more attention from adventurous travellers, especially since now almost all counties and towns are open to foreigners. Around 72% of the population in this region is Miao, Dong and a mixture of other minorities. Those who strike off from Guilin to Guiyang by local buses, for example, will find themselves travelling through countless tiny villages with drum towers and wind and rain bridges. With the exception of the buses and trucks that ply the roads, life in this part of China seems to go on as it has for centuries past.

Although Chinese rulers set up an administration in the area as far back as the Han Dynasty, they merely attempted to maintain

Population: 36 million
Capital: Guiyang
Highlights:
- Huangguoshu Falls, China's highest at 74 metres, sit among scenic countryside and interesting minority villages
- The south-east region, home to several minority groups, offering great chances for village-hopping and festival-watching

some measure of control over the non-Chinese tribes who lived here and Chinese settlement was confined to the north and east of the province. The eastern areas were not settled until the 16th century, when the native minorities were forced out of the most fertile areas. Another wave of Chinese immigration in the late 19th century brought many settlers in from overpopulated Hunan and Sichuan. But Guizhou remained impoverished and backward, with poor communications and transport.

When the Japanese invasion forced the Kuomintang to retreat to the south-west, the development of Guizhou began; roads to the neighbouring provinces were constructed, a rail link was built to Guangxi and some industries were set up in Guiyang and Zunyi.

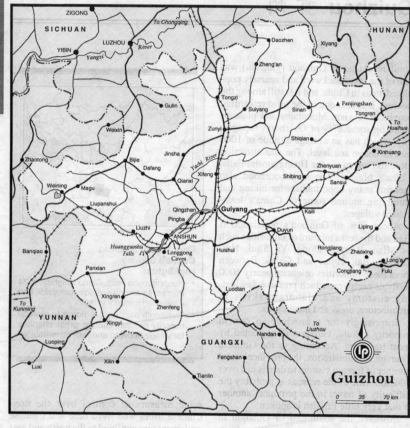

Guizhou

0   35   70 km

Most of the activity ceased with the end of WW II, and it was not until the construction of the railways in the south-west under Communist rule that some industrialisation was revived.

Chinese statistics continue to paint a grim picture of backwardness and poverty. Eight million of the province's population live below the national poverty line. Between 60% and 70% of the population are illiterate and nearly 30% of the villages are not accessible by road.

Unfairly, blame has been laid at the door of the minorities, who have been castigated

by state-run media for 'poor educational quality'. More self-righteous arguments have been levelled at cave dwellers because 'the temptations of modern life have failed to lure these Miao out of their dark, unhealthy cave'. These self-sufficient minorities living without TV, radio, electricity etc are certainly poor, but they show few signs of embracing consumer life and throwing away their cultural identity as a reward for assimilation with the Han.

The province's most famous export is Maotai liquor, named for the village of its origin in Renhuai County. This fiery white spirit is sold in distinctive white bottles with a diagonal red label. Guizhou is also, like Yunnan, a major tobacco-producing area.

FESTIVALS

Festivities among the minorities in Guizhou offer plenty of scope for exploration. Festivals take place throughout the lunar calendar at specific sites and are technicolour spectaculars which can feature bullfighting, horse racing, pipe playing, comic opera, singing contests and gigantic courting parties.

There are several festivals in Guiyang during the first lunar month (usually February or March), fourth lunar month (around May) and sixth lunar month (around July). Some of these take place in Huaxi.

A good starting point for festival forays is Kaili, on the railway line east of Guiyang. A profusion of festivals is held in nearby minority areas such as Leishan, Xijiang, Danxi, Qingman and Panghai. The town of Zhijiang, about 50 km from Kaili, is also a festival centre.

Further east on the railway line is Zhenyuan, which is renowned for its festivals between April and July. This town was once an important staging point on the ancient post road from central China to Southeast Asia.

GUIYANG
(guìyáng)
Guiyang, the capital of Guizhou Province, has a mild climate all year round; its name means Precious Sun and may be a reference to the fact that the sun rarely seems to shine through the clouds and drizzle. Despite this, Guiyang remains a much underrated Chinese city. Most travellers give the place a miss, but it's worth lingering for a day or so. There's good food available, lively market and shopping areas and a few interesting sights around town.

A few old neighbourhoods and temples remain amid the mushrooming high-rise towers, and with some effort the place can be appreciated for the funky conglomeration of city and village that it is. Guiyang is also a jumping-off point for the Huangguoshu Falls or via Kaili to the minority areas of the southeast.

Orientation
Guiyang is a sprawling kind of place that at first glance seems to lack a centre of any kind. It doesn't take long to get on top of things, however.

Zunyi Lu heads up from the railway station and links up with Zhonghua Lu, the road that cuts through the centre of town and is home to Guiyang's main shopping area. Yan'an Lu intersects Zhonghua Lu, and it is along this road that you will find the Bank of China, CITS, the expensive Guiyang Plaza Hotel and, on the other end, the long-distance bus station. There are more hotels further up Zhonghua Lu near the intersection with Beijing Lu.

Information
CITS This office is at 20 Yan'an Zhonglu (☎ 582-5873) and is one of China's more helpful and friendly branches of CITS. The staff have maps and info on minority areas, though they still can't help you book train tickets. It's located on the ground floor of a crumbling white plaster and brick building.

PSB The office (☎ 682-1231) is located in a white-tiled building complex on Zhongshan Xilu, quite close to the intersection with Zhonghua Lu. This is the place to report thefts or seek visa extensions. As nearly all of Guizhou is now open to foreigners, there shouldn't be any need to get permits for travel within the province.

Money The Bank of China has several branches around town that will change money: on Yan'an Donglu, near the Guiyang Plaza Hotel; across from the CAAC ticket office; and the main branch up on Ruijin Beilu. The latter can also help with credit card withdrawals and wire transfers. The CAAC office also has a foreign-exchange counter. The Guiyang Plaza Hotel has an efficient exchange service, though the hotel, at the end of Yan'an Donglu, is quite a trudge from the railway station.

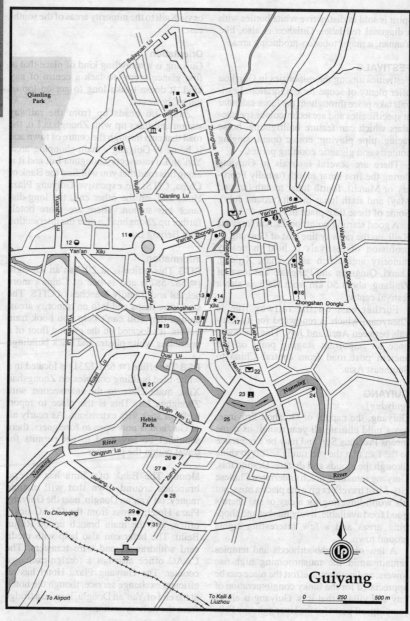

Guiyang

GUIYANG 贵阳

PLACES TO STAY

1 Guizhou Park Hotel
贵州公园饭店
2 Bajiaoyuan Hotel
八角岩饭店
3 Yunyan Hotel
云岩宾馆
6 Guiyang Plaza Hotel
金筑大酒店
18 Jingdu Hotel
京都饭店
19 Jinqiao Hotel
金桥饭店
21 Hebin Hotel
河滨宾馆
30 Sports Hotel
体育宾馆

PLACES TO EAT

20 Jiangnan Dumplings
江南饺子馆
31 Guizhou Beijing Duck
Restaurant
贵州北京烤鸭店

OTHER

4 Museum
博物馆
5 Bank of China
中国银行
7 Post & Telecommuni-
cations Office
电信局
8 Bank of China
中国银行
9 Foreign Languages
Bookstore
外文书店
10 CITS
中国国际旅行社
11 Xinhua Bookstore
新华书店
12 Long-Distance Bus
Station
贵阳汽车站
13 Advance Rail Ticket
Office
火车预售处
14 PSB
公安局
15 Hua Jia Pavilion
华家阁

16 Wen Chang Pavilion
文昌阁
17 Department Store
百货大楼
22 Post & Telecommuni-
cations Building
邮电大楼
23 Qianming Temple
黔明寺
24 Jiaxiu Pavilion
甲秀楼
25 People's Square/Mao
Statue
人民广场
26 CAAC
中国民航
27 Guizhou Exhibition
Centre
省展览馆
28 Chaoyang Cinema
朝阳影剧院
29 Guizhou Gymnasium
省体育馆
32 Railway Station
贵阳站

Post & Telecommunications The post and telecommunications building is up on the intersection of Zunyi Lu and Zhonghua Nanlu. You can make international phone calls from the international and long-distance hall, located to the left of the main doors. If the lines are really long, try the post and telecom office at the intersection of Zhonghua Lu and Yan'an Lu.

Bookshop There's a branch of the Foreign Languages Bookstore on Yan'an Donglu. It's not particularly well stocked, but if you're desperate for reading material there should be something worth picking up. Several employees of the store hold an English-speaking and lecture session there every Sunday morning and warmly welcome any foreign visitors; they may even offer to pay you to address the crowd!

Dangers & Annoyances Guiyang has a reputation among Chinese as one of China's most dangerous cities for theft. It's probably a good idea to be particularly careful at night. The railway station is a favoured haunt of pickpockets, and travellers have reported problems in the station. Take care.

Things to See

The distinctive architectural characteristics of Guiyang's handful of Mussolini-modern buildings are the columns like the ones at the Provincial Exhibition Hall. The main street, Zunyi Lu, leading north from the railway station harbours one of the largest glistening white statues of Mao Zedong in China. For details on the scenic bus tour around the city, see the Getting Around section.

Qianling Park (*qiánlíng gōngyuán*) is worth a visit for its forested walks and for the late Ming Dynasty **Hongfu Monastery** *(hóngfú sì)*, perched near the top of 1300-metre-high Qianling Mountain. The monastery has a vegetarian restaurant in the rear courtyard that's open from 11 am to around 4 pm, making the park a good place to head out to for lunch. From the Jinqiao Hotel or the railway station area take a No 2 bus. The park is open from 8 am to 10.30 pm, and admission is Y1.

Guiyang's two other park attractions, **Huaxi Park** *(huāxī gōngyuán)* and **Nanjiao Park** *(nánjiāo gōngyuán)*, are nothing to get particularly excited about, and if you are short of time give them a miss. Both of them have caves and strolling areas. Not far from the CAAC office is the **Hebin Park** *(hébīn gōngyuán)*, which has benches under shade trees along the river and a Ferris wheel which offers good views of Guiyang for Y6.

Guiyang is a pleasant enough place to stroll around (if it's not raining), and apart from the markets and shopping district there are a few pavilions and pagodas scattered around town. These include the **Wen Chang Pavilion**, **Jiaxiu Pavilion**, **Hua Jia Pavilion** and the **Qianming Temple**. Check the map for their locations. They're all within easy walking distance of the centre of town.

Places to Stay – bottom end

Unfortunately, budget accommodation is in short supply in Guiyang. Contrary to popular opinion the hard/soft sleeper waiting room upstairs in the railway station is not a place to crash out, and if you try it you'll be asked to leave.

Your cheapest option is a bed in a quad at the *Jinqiao Hotel* (☎ 582-9951) *(jīnqiáo fàndiàn)*, somewhat inconveniently located on Ruijin Zhonglu, a good 30 minutes' walk from the railway station. Beds cost Y35, and although it's a long trek to the showers, the rooms themselves are actually pretty nice. It's a steep jump in price if you want your own bathroom, however. Doubles start at Y168 and don't seem a particularly good deal at that price. Bus Nos 1 and 2 run from the railway station past the hotel.

Another low-budget possibility is a

double for Y76 at the *Jingdu Hotel (jīngdū fàndiàn)*, located on Gongyuan Lu, diagonally across from the PSB compound. The rooms come with washroom attached, so it's not a bad deal if there are two of you, though this hotel has quite obviously seen better days.

Near the entrance to Hebin Park, the *Hebin Hotel* (☎ 584-1855) *(hébīn bīnguǎn)* has a few basic doubles for Y80, but they tend to fill up quickly. There are also three doubles located in the building's glass turret, complete with 180-degree picture windows, for Y120. After these, it's a straight jump up to Y248 for a standard air-con double.

Places to Stay – middle

Most of Guiyang's accommodation is midrange in standard, even if some of the prices quoted for rooms are definitely top-end. Pick of the bunch in terms of value for money is the *Sports Hotel* (☎ 582-1779) *(tǐyù bīnguǎn)* on the grounds of the Guizhou Gymnasium. It's next door to the big restaurant on the railway-station side of the complex. Enormous and very clean doubles with TV and bathroom start at Y135. If you want a night of comfort, they're well worth the money. The hotel is just a short walk from the railway station.

Up near the corner of Zhonghua Beilu and Beijing Lu are three hotels catering to the well-heeled. The cheapest of the bunch is the *Bajiaoyan Hotel* (☎ 682-2651) *(bājiǎoyán fàndiàn)*. It has clean doubles with bathroom for Y100 and Y130, and suites from Y220. Though somewhat of a concrete hulk, it's a quiet place and not a bad deal for the price. This is less true for the two other hotels close by. The *Yunyan Hotel* (☎ 682-3325) *(yúnyán bīnguǎn)*, a cadre-style place, has singles/doubles starting at Y172 and triples at Y240. Staying here does give you access to a swimming pool in front of the hotel, though actually swimming there will cost you extra. The *Guizhou Park Hotel* (☎ 682-2888) *(guìzhōu fàndiàn)* is the lap of luxury, with standard doubles ranging from Y320 to Y508. Ask about the presidential suite for

Y4800 – maybe they have special rates for backpackers.

The *Guiyang Plaza Hotel* (☎ 682-5888) *(jīnzhù dàjiǔdiàn)* is basically a half-hearted attempt to produce a homegrown Holiday Inn. There's a foreign exchange counter, a coffee shop, restaurants and shops. Singles/doubles/triples cost Y450/480/750. But if you're spending this kind of money, go to the Guizhou Park, where they seem to have a better idea of what a luxury hotel should be.

Places to Eat

Guiyang, like Kunming, is a great city for snack tracking. Just follow Zunyi Lu up to Zhonghua Nanlu and peer into the side alleys for noodle, dumpling and kebab stalls. There's also a decent, if small, night market on Ruijin Lu between the Jinqiao and Hebin Hotels.

Next door to the Sports Hotel on the grounds of the Guizhou Gymnasium is a good Chinese restaurant with fairly reasonable prices. Try their chicken and peanuts dish *(gōngbǎo jīdīng)*. There's no English menu, but it's a popular place so there should be a representative selection of what's available on other diners' tables.

North of the post and telecommunications building on Zhonghua Nanlu is a dumpling shop that is worth a special recommendation. The Jiangnan Dumplings Restaurant *(jiāngnán jiǎozǐguǎn)* has great steamed dumplings *(zhēngjiǎo)* and the speciality of the house is chicken soup *(qìguōjī)*; interesting sweets are also available. Prices are very reasonable. If you're going for dinner, make it an early one, as they close up shop by 8 pm.

For a special night out, try the *Guizhou Beijing Duck Restaurant (guìzhōu běijīng kǎoyādiàn)*, across the road from the Sports Hotel near the railway station. The duck here is really excellent, and although you'll be looking at around Y58 for a whole duck it's money well spent.

Getting There & Away

Air The CAAC office (☎ 582-3000) is at 170 Zunyi Lu. Flights from Guiyang include:

Beijing, Changsha, Chengdu, Guangzhou, Guilin, Haikou, Kunming, Shanghai, Shenzhen, Wuhan, Xiamen and Xi'an. China Southwest has two flights a week to Hong Kong for HK$1450, or US$194.

Bus The long-distance bus station is quite a long way from the railway station, and if you're looking at getting out of Guiyang quickly you're better off using the bus services that operate from the railway station. There are frequent buses to Xingyi (from where there are onward buses to Kunming) between 8 am and 6 pm for Y35. There is also a nightly sleeper bus at 6 pm which costs Y56. It takes about 12 hours to get from Guiyang to Xingyi. Buses to Anshun leave every half-hour from 7 am to 10 pm. The journey takes 2 hours and costs Y8. For the five-hour trip to Kaili, there are buses approximately hourly from 6.30 am to 5.30 pm. The fare is Y25. Buses to Zunyi leave every 30 minutes from 7 am to 9 pm. The ride takes 5 hours and costs Y15. The travel times to both Kaili and Zunyi should improve gradually as extensive roadworks are completed.

The long-distance bus station has similar schedules and prices for buses to Anshun and Xingyi and, in addition, has sleepers for Xingyi at noon and 4 and 6 pm. Buses to Zunyi leave hourly between 6 am and noon. At the time of writing, the bus service to Kaili had been cancelled. Take bus No 1 or 2 from the railway station to get here.

It's also possible to take tour buses to Huangguoshu Falls and the Longgong Caves from the railway station, the long-distance bus station and most of the hotels. They generally depart at 6 or 7 am and cost Y45. If you don't want to stay overnight at the falls, this is definitely the most hassle-free way of getting out there.

Train Direct trains run to Kunming, Shanghai, Guilin, Liuzhou (Guangxi), Nanning (Guangxi), Zhanjiang (Guangdong) and Chongqing. Some sample hard sleeper fares for foreigners from Guiyang are: Kunming, Y169; Chengdu, Y237; and Guilin, Y172.

Foreigners are required to purchase tickets at a special booth in the soft-sleeper waiting room, located upstairs on the left-hand side of the railway station. Though you'll have to pay foreign prices, there are no crowds or lines here, making it one of the more pleasant places in China to buy a train ticket, especially if the ticket seller is in a good mood.

The advance rail ticket office for locals only (if you're planning to have someone buy a ticket for you) is on the second floor of a large yellow-tiled building on Gongyuan Lu.

Getting Around

If you want to do a city-loop tour, then across the square from the railway station are two round-the-city buses, Nos 1 and 2. They follow the same route but No 2 goes clockwise while No 1 goes anticlockwise. These buses will get you to most places – the round trip from the railway station costs Y0.80 and takes about 45 minutes. You can get a good window seat since you get on at the terminal; the same cannot be said if you choose to alight at random for a foot-sortie. The main shopping street is on the bus No 1 route heading north, but this area is more fun to explore on foot. Note that minibuses with route numbers on the windscreen do not follow the same route as larger buses bearing the same numbers.

ANSHUN
(ānshùn)

Spending a day or two in Anshun isn't the worst of fates. The karst valley setting is pleasant and some of the narrow streets are lined with interesting old wooden houses. It is also the best place from which to visit Huangguoshu Falls and Longgong Caves.

Once an opium-trading centre, Anshun remains the commercial hub of western Guizhou but is now known for its batiks. The town's main attraction is the **Wen Temple** (wénmiào), north-west of the railway station. The temple, which dates back to the Ming Dynasty, underwent restoration work in 1668.

Anshun lacks a CITS branch, but its domestic cousin, China Travel Service (☎ 224-379), has an office at the Minzu Hotel. It organises trips to Huangguoshu and the surrounding area and has information on minor attractions in the region. From town, the bus station and the railway station are three and four km away, respectively. The No 1 minibus will take you into town for Y0.50 to Y1 depending on where you alight.

Places to Stay

There are basically only three options for foreigners staying in Anshun. Near the bus station, the Xixiushan Hotel (xīxiùshān bīnguǎn) has doubles with common washrooms for Y60 and doubles with attached bath for Y120. These prices are double what Chinese pay, and you may be able to bargain them down somewhat.

The Minzu Hotel (mínzú fàndiàn) on Tashan Donglu, on the eastern side of town near the highway to Guiyang, has doubles in the old wing for Y50, though you can probably bargain the price down to Y40 without too much trouble. Doubles/triples in the new building cost Y170/220. There's a Muslim restaurant on the 2nd floor.

The main tourist joint, inconveniently located on the northern outskirts of Anshun, is the Hongshan Hotel (☎ 333-088) (hóngshān bīnguǎn) at 43 Hongshan Donglu. It's a bit lacking in the electricity and plumbing departments, but it's solid. The hotel gardens overlook the Hongshan Reservoir. This place has used some recent partial renovations as an excuse to hike prices for its cheapest rooms up to Y200.

Behind the bus station on Guihuang Lu, which is the highway linking Guiyang and Huangguoshu, is the Jiaotong Hotel (jiāotōng fàndiàn). This place wasn't taking foreigners at the time of writing but seems like a possible candidate, so it might not hurt to check.

Getting There & Away

Bus The simplest option is probably the minibuses that run to Anshun from the Guiyang Railway Station. They leave every 30 minutes and cost Y8. Alternatively, you can head out to the long-distance bus station, where buses run approximately every 30 minutes between 7 am and 6.30 pm. The trip takes about two hours along the Guihuang Expressway, Guizhou's first and only real highway, built specifically to whisk tourists up to Huangguoshu Falls.

From Anshun, Huangguoshu Falls and Longgong Caves are 46 and 32 km away, respectively. There are minibuses running from the long-distance bus station to Huang-guoshu for Y5, though prices are fairly flexible and may require a little bargaining. Buses to Longgong are occasional at best, so

you may have to join up with one of the local tours running from the bus station or the hotels.

If you don't feel like heading back to Guiyang to book a railway sleeper, you might want to consider travelling onwards from Anshun to Kunming by bus. From Anshun there is a 6.45 am direct bus that arrives in Kunming around midnight, roads permitting. There is also a sleeper bus that leaves at 1 pm, getting into Kunming around 6 am the next day. The day bus costs Y44.50, the sleeper Y75.

More interesting might be travelling from Anshun or Huangguoshu to Xingyi in the south-west of Guizhou. Xingyi is worth a visit in itself (see the listing at the end of this chapter), and there are direct buses from there to Kunming (12 hours). There is a daily bus from Anshun to Xingyi which leaves around 6 to 7 am: the time varies from day to day. The ride takes around eight hours and costs Y21.50. There are probably other ways

Anshun

0   250   500 m

of doing this trip. Once you make it to Yunnan, onward transport to Kunming should be no problem.

Train Most of the trains running between Guiyang and Anshun at present arrive in Anshun in the evening. One exception is the No 571, which links Guiyang and Dawan. It departs at 8.50 am and stops in Anshun at 11.20 am. If you are headed to Guiyang and miss the last bus, you can catch the No 92 train, which stops in Anshun around 8 pm and pulls into Guiyang just after 10 pm.

If you're thinking of travelling onwards from Anshun to Kunming by train, bear in mind that it's almost impossible to get hold of hard-sleeper tickets in Anshun itself. If comfort is important to you, you'll be better off heading back to Guiyang and organising your ticket there.

AROUND ANSHUN
Huangguoshu Falls
(huángguǒshù dàpùbù)

Located 46 km south-west of Anshun, China's premier cataract reaches a width of 81 metres, with a drop of 74 metres into the Rhinoceros Pool, and is the foundation of Guizhou's fledgling tourist industry. If, like some travellers, you feel the falls are overrated, don't worry. Huangguoshu also provides an excellent chance to go rambling through the superb rural minority areas on foot.

Once you're there, you'll have no transport problems as everything you need is within walking range or, if you wish to go further, hiking range. Take a raincoat if you're off to the waterfalls and a warm jacket or sweater if you're descending into caves, which can be chilly.

The thunder of Huangguoshu Falls can be heard for some distance, and the mist from the falls carries up to Huangguoshu village during the rainy season, which lasts from May to October. The falls are at their most spectacular about four days after heavy rains. The dry season lasts from November to April, so during March and April the flow of water can become a less impressive trickle.

The main falls are the central piece of a huge waterfall, cave and karst area, covering some 450 sq km. It was explored by the Chinese only in the 1980s as a preliminary to harnessing the hydroelectric potential. They discovered about 18 falls, four subterranean rivers and 100 caves, many of which are now being gradually opened up to visitors.

At the edge of the falls is **Water Curtain Cave** *(shuǐlián dòng)*, a niche in the cliffs which is approached by a slippery (and dangerous) sortie wading across rocks in the Rhinoceros Pool – from the cave you'll get an interior view of the gushing waters through six 'windows'. Admission to the main waterfall area is Y30.

One km above the main falls is **Steep Slope Falls** *(dǒupō pùbù)*, which is easy to reach. Steep Slope Falls is 105 metres wide and 23 metres high and gets its name from the crisscross patterning of sloping waters. Eight km below Huangguoshu Falls are the **Star Bridge Falls** *(tiānxīng qiáo)*, for which there are occasional minibuses leaving from Huangguoshu village.

Huangguoshu (Yellow Fruit Tree) is in the Zhenning Bouyei and Miao Autonomous County. The Miao are not in evidence around the falls, but for the Bouyei, who favour river valleys, this is prime water country. The Bouyei are the 'aboriginals' of Guizhou. The people are of Thai origin and related to the Zhuangs in Guangxi. They number two million, mostly spread over the south-western sector of Guizhou Province. Bouyei dress is dark and sombre, with colourful trimmings; 'best' clothes come out on festival or market days. The Bouyei marry early, usually at 16, but sometimes as young as 12. Married women are distinguished by headgear symbols.

The Bouyei are very poor, showing signs of malnutrition and wearing clothes that are grubby and tattered. The contrast with the postcard minority image of starched and ironed costumes, or the ring-of-confidence sparkling teeth, is obvious. The Bouyei tribespeople can also be shy and suspicious of foreigners.

Batik (cloth wax-dyeing) is one of the skills of the Bouyei. The masonry at Huangguoshu is also intriguing – houses are composed of stone blocks but no plaster is used; the roofs are finished in stone slates.

There is a Bouyei festival in Huangguoshu lasting 10 days during the first lunar month (usually February or early March). Attendance is put at around 10,000 people.

Longgong Caves

About 32 km from Anshun is a spectacular series of underground caverns called **Longgong** *(lónggōng)*, or Dragon Palace, which form a network through some 20 mountains. Charter boats tour one of the largest waterfilled caves, often called the Dragon Cave. The caverns lie in Anshun County, at the Bouyei settlement of Longtan *(lóngtǎn zhài)* (Dragon Pool). Other scenic caves in the vicinity include **Daji Dong**, **Chuan Dong** and **Linlang Dong**. Admission is Y30.

Places to Stay & Eat

At the bus park near the Huangguoshu Falls are some food stalls. Below them, down the cliff, is a teahouse and souvenir shop. The viewing area for the falls is a short downhill walk from the bus park. Further away from the bus park is *Huangguoshu Guesthouse (huángguǒshù bīnguǎn)*, which has actually become two hotels. The 'new' Huangguoshu Guesthouse is up a driveway to the right and, being the more expensive of the two, sports an English sign at the entrance to show foreigners which way to turn. Rooms here start at Y190 for a standard double. The old guesthouse, which actually doesn't look too different from the new one, has doubles for Y140, though they may try and tack on a 30% 'service charge' for foreign friends. The old guesthouse also has 5 to 7 bed dorms for Y86, but these are almost always booked up.

All is not lost however. Just before the bridge on the way into town from Anshun is the *Tianxing Hotel (tiānxīng fàndiàn)* a quiet, friendly place with beds for Y10. Rooms with attached bath are Y20 per bed, making prices comparable to the Chinese-only hotels located in the village. Note that some tour buses come into town from the opposite direction, passing the Huangguoshu Guesthouse on the way in. In this case, to find the Tianxing Hotel, walk through town, cross the bridge and look for a large concrete gate on the left side of the road: there is no sign, but the hotel lies within. Some travellers have managed to get beds for Y10 in the Chinese hotels, while others have been turned away. If you try, go for a hotel on the waterfall side: apparently one has a little pathway that gives you free access to the waterfall viewing area!

Along the town main road there are several restaurants that have verandas at the back where you can eat, sip a cold beer and enjoy a great view of the falls.

Getting There & Away

You can get to Huangguoshu Falls and Longgong Caves from either Guiyang or Anshun. There are a few direct buses to the falls from the Guiyang long-distance bus station and the railway station around 7 am, though these take about 3 to 4 hours to get there. Otherwise, catch a bus or a train to Anshun and hitch up with a minibus there. Minibuses run every 30 minutes from the Guiyang Railway Station to Anshun, a distance of 106 km from Guiyang.

Alternatively, local tour buses leave from the Guiyang Railway Station at 7 am. They take in both the falls and Longgong Caves for Y42 to Y55, depending on the type of bus. This does not include entry fees. Tours also run from nearly all the hotels listed in the Guiyang Places to Stay section. These buses will get you to Huangguoshu in around 2 to 3 hours, as opposed to the five hours required if you take public transportation.

From the Anshun long-distance bus station there are several direct buses to Huangguoshu between 6 and 8 am, and one each at 10 am and noon. The fare is Y4.50. The 7 am and noon buses to Zhenfeng and Qinglong all pass through Huangguoshu. There are also frequent minibuses running from the bus station from 8 am to 5 pm for Y5. Both buses and minibuses take the local road to Huangguoshu rather than the expressway, so the 46-km ride takes around 1½ hours but does pass through some interesting small towns.

Minibuses run from Huangguoshu to Anshun and on to Guiyang from 7 am to 7 pm. Buses leave as soon as they are full. Try to get one that takes the Guihuang Expressway rather than a local bus. These aren't that hard to find, as there are usually a fair number of visitors headed directly back to Anshun or Guiyang.

KAILI
(kǎilǐ)

Around 195 km almost directly east of Guiyang, Kaili is a fairly uninspiring kind of place but it's the gateway to the minority areas of south-eastern Guizhou. The bus journey between here and Liping in the far south-east of Guizhou takes you through some of the most fascinating minority regions in this part of China. It should be possible to stop over in some of these towns

without arousing the ire of local PSB agents as nearly all of Guizhou Province is now open to foreigners.

Particularly recommended are Leishan, Yongle and Rongjiang. Liping is a good base for exploring nearby Dong villages. Buses also run from Kaili to the Miao area of Shibing, from where there are cruises on the Wuyang River, something that the local tourist authorities are promoting heavily. This whole area sees few Western travellers.

About 32 km from Anshun is a spectacular series of underground caver.

Things to See

There's really not a great deal in this category. There's a pagoda in the **Dage Park** *(dàgé gōngyuán)*, which is not surprising as the park's name means 'big pagoda park'. The only other thing to check out is the drum tower down in **Jinquanhu Park** *(jīnquánhú gōngyuán)*, at the very southern end of town, where you can also find the moderately interesting **Minorities Museum** *(zhōu mínzú bówùguǎn)*.

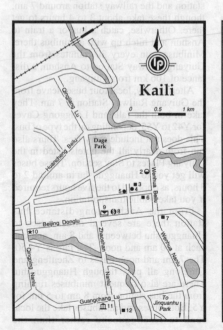

KAILI 凯里

1 Railway Station
　火车站
2 Long-Distance Bus Station
　长途汽车站
3 Yingpanpo National Hotel
　营盘坡宾馆
4 CITS
　中国国际旅行社
5 Minorities Souvenir Shop
　民族商店
6 Shiyou Guesthouse
　石油招待所
7 Zhenhua Guesthouse
　振华招待所
8 Bank of China
　中国银行
9 Post Office
　邮电局
10 PSB
　公安局
11 Minorities Museum
　贵州民族博物馆
12 Kaili Hotel
　凯里宾馆

Festivals

Kaili and the areas around it are host to a large number of minority festivals – over 130 annually, according to CITS. One of the biggest is the Lusheng Festival, held from 11 to 18 of the first lunar month. The *lusheng* is a reed instrument used by the Miao people. Activities include playing the lusheng (of course), dancing, drumming, bull fighting and horse racing. Participants are said to number 30,000. The festival is held in Danxi.

A similar festival is held midway through the seventh lunar month in Qingman. Participants number 20,000. The Miao new year is celebrated on the first four days of the 10th lunar month in Kaili, Guading, Danxi and other Miao areas by some 50,000 people. CITS in Kaili should be able to provide you with a list of local festivals and their dates. After that, you're probably better off on your own.

Places to Stay

If you're looking to save a few yuan, head for the *Zhenhua Guesthouse (zhènhuá zhāodàisuǒ)*, south of the long-distance bus station at the corner of Wenhua Nanlu and Beijing Donglu. Beds in doubles/triple/quad dorm rooms cost Y7/5/4. If you want your own washroom, there are doubles available for Y30. The Zhenhua is nothing special, but then again you can't expect too much for these prices.

Also south of the long-distance bus station is the *Shiyou Guesthouse (shíyóu bīnguǎn)* with doubles for Y40, and beds in triples/quads for Y14/12. The triples have their own bathrooms. Not far from there is the *Yingpanpo National Hotel (yìngpànpō mínzú bīnguǎn)*, which has two-bed dorms for Y20 in the old wing and more upmarket doubles in the new wing for Y226, though you might be able to bargain them down. To find this place, look for a big gate at the three-way intersection, enter and follow the road up and to the right. CITS has an office in the hotel compound. The staff speak passable English and can fill you in on minority activities and destinations, and they have decent maps in English of the area. Be careful if they try and get you onto one of their 'minority tours' however, unless you're interested in a visit to a Dong village, complete with dance performance for a mere Y600 per head.

The only other option is the forlorn-looking *Kaili Hotel (kǎilǐ bīnguǎn)* down in the south of town, where doubles start at a 'discount price' of Y180. No bargains there.

Getting There & Away

There are numerous trains departing Guiyang that pass through Kaili, including three between 8 and 11 am. Try and avoid the No 586, which leaves around 8.50 am and takes five hours, as opposed to just over three hours for most other trains. A hard seat ticket is Y8 to Y12, depending on which train you take. From Kaili to Guiyang, there are five trains between 10 am and 6 pm.

Buses to Kaili leave frequently from in front of the Guiyang Railway Station between 6.30 am and 5.30 pm. The journey takes around five hours and costs Y25. The Minzu Hotel runs a comfortable minibus from the hotel to the Guiyang railway station at 7 am for Y30. The same bus heads back to Kaili at around 1 to 2 pm.

The Kaili long-distance bus station has frequent buses to Guiyang between 6 am and 1 pm. There is one bus a day, leaving around 7 am, to Shibing and Zhenyuan. Liping and Congjiang are served by one to two buses daily, leaving Kaili between 6 and 7 am. There are two to three buses each morning for Leishan, and hourly buses to Rongjiang between 6.30 am and 1.30 pm.

AROUND KAILI

The minority areas of south-eastern Guizhou are relatively unexplored by Western travellers, and the following are some places that are worth checking out. Very little English is spoken in this part of the world and you're not likely to bump into many other travellers, but if that's your kind of thing strike off somewhere on a local bus.

Shibing & Zhenyuan
(shībǐng/zhènyuán)

Shibing is basically an overgrown Miao village that offers opportunity for walks in the surrounding countryside and visits to even smaller Miao villages. The major attraction in the area are cruises on the **Wuyang River** (wǔyáng hé), which pass through Guilin lookalike countryside (karst rock formations) before ending up in Zhenyuan. From here you could take a bus back to Shibing or Kaili, or a bus on to Tianzhu, which in turn offers the interesting prospect of an undoubtedly rough bus journey down to Jinping and on to Liping. From Liping it is possible to travel (slowly) all the way to Guilin, passing through Dong minority villages en route.

Places to Stay & Eat There's basic accommodation in Shibing at the *Shibing Guesthouse* (shībīng zhāodàisuǒ) and in Zhenyuan at the *Zhenyuan Guesthouse* (zhènyuán zhāodàisuǒ). Both are small towns and you'll have no problems finding the hotels.

Chong'an
(chóngān)

Lying about two hours north of Kaili by bus, this hamlet's claim to fame is its Friday market, and travellers who have seen it say it's one not to miss. There are also some nice walks to be had along the river and into Miao villages nearby. There's one hotel in town taking foreigners, with dorm beds for Y5 to Y8. Buses to Shibing pass through Chong'an.

KAILI TO LIPING

Liping, in the far south-east of Guizhou, is a fairly uninteresting town, but the road between it and Kaili is crammed with sights and some beautiful countryside. Ideally, it would be best to get off the bus and spend at least a couple of hours in some of the minority villages like Leishan, Tashi, Chejiang, Rongjiang, Maogong and Gaojin. You may not be able to catch an onward bus until the following day, but the scenery should keep you from wanting to hurry anyway. Accommodation in these small spots is usually limited to a hotel either attached or next to the bus station. If you wander around looking lost, someone will either put you on the next bus or take you to the local hotel. Most of these towns have Dong wind and rain bridges and drum towers, many of which you'll see from the bus.

If you decide to head straight to Liping, the bus ride takes around 9 hours and costs Y20. Liping has basic accommodation in the *Liping Guesthouse* (lìpíng zhāodàisuǒ) – reckon on Y5 to Y10 for a bed. It's located at the traffic circle at the centre of town, near where the long-distance buses stop.

LIPING TO GUILIN

This is really only an option for travellers with time to kill. Buses in this part of the world are very infrequent and travel at a snail's pace over roads that only barely qualify as such. Buses run from Liping to Diping (dìpíng), also known as Long'e (lóngé), at 7 am. To Diping, it takes around four hours, passing through the town of Zhaoxing (zhàoxīng), an incredible Dong minority village with a total of five drum towers. There's a hotel in Zhaoxing, and a stop in the village would require you stay in it as there is only one bus a day travelling between here and Diping. Diping, another Dong village, also requires an overnight stop, as the bus on to Sanjiang in Guangxi Province doesn't leave until the next morning. The hotel at the square where the buses stop has dorm beds for Y5. From Sanjiang there are buses on to Longsheng or direct to Guilin. See the Sanjiang section of the Guangxi chapter for more information.

ZUNYI
(zūnyì)

Around 163 km north of Guiyang, Zunyi is worth a mention and even possibly a visit for those who have a particular interest in Chinese Communist Party history. For everyone else it's a fairly drab, industrialised Chinese town with few attractions.

Hemmed into the Jiangxi Soviet by Kuomintang forces, on 16 October 1934 the Communists set out on a Herculean one-

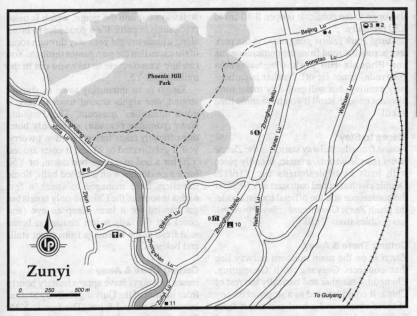

ZUNYI 遵义

1   Railway Station
    火车站
2   Zuntie Hotel
    遵铁大厦
3   Long-Distance Bus Station
    长途汽车站
4   CAAC
    中国民航
5   Bank of China
    中国银行
6   Zunyi Guesthouse
    遵义宾馆
7   Zunyi Conference Site
    遵义会议会址
8   Catholic Church
    天主教堂
9   Workers' Cultural Palace
    工人文化宫
10 Baiyun Temple
    百云寺
11 Xiangshan Hotel
    湘山宾馆

year, 9600-km tramp from one end of China to the other. By mid-December, having reached Guizhou, they marched on Zunyi, a prosperous mercantile town. Taking the town by surprise, the Communists were able to stock up on supplies and take a breather. On 15-18 January 1935, the top-level Communist leadership took stock of their situation in the now-famous Zunyi Conference. The resolutions taken largely reflected the views of Mao Zedong, who was elected a full member of the ruling Standing Committee of the Politburo and chief assistant to Zhou Enlai in military planning. It was a crucial factor in Mao's rise to power.

Things to See

The main sight is the **Zunyi Conference Site** *(zūnyì huìyì huìzhǐ)*. It's around five km to the south of the railway station and is home to a collection of CCP memorabilia. The meeting rooms and living quarters are also open to the public. It is open 8.30 am to 4.30 pm daily.

Zunyi Park (zūnyì gōngyuán) is the park area across the road from the conference site and **Phoenix Hill Park** (fènghuángshān gōngyuán) is not far off. Neither is particularly exciting, but will probably make for a pleasant enough stroll if you have some time to kill.

Places to Stay

Across from the railway station is the *Zuntie Hotel* (zūntiě dàshà), a basic, friendly place with beds in triples/quads for Y16/12. Doubles with attached bath start at Y50. Near the conference site the official tourist abode, the plush *Zunyi Guesthouse* (zūnyì bīnguǎn), has doubles from Y120.

Getting There & Away

Zunyi is on the main northern railway line that connects Guiyang with Chongqing, Chengdu, Shanghai and basically the rest of China. It could be used as a stopover on any of these routes, and a hard-seat ticket from Guiyang is Y8.

Alternatively, buses leave Guiyang's long-distance bus station hourly between 6 am and noon. You can also catch buses to Zunyi from in front of the Guiyang Railway Station: there's one about every half hour between 7 am and 9 pm. Zunyi's long-distance bus station is next door to the Zuntie Hotel, and there are minibuses leaving for Guiyang throughout the day starting at 7 am, though they start to thin out around 6 pm. The ride takes 5 hours and costs Y15.

XINGYI
(xīngyì)

Xingyi is mainly a stopover in the far south-west of Guizhou for those travelling between Guiyang and Kunming by bus. The main attraction in the area is the 15-km-long **Maling Gorge** (mǎlíng héxiǎgǔ), which some travellers say is more interesting than Huangguoshu Falls. There are steps and

walkways cut into the gorge, which is quite precipitous in parts. It's a good idea to bring along a torch to light your way through some of the caves that the path passes through. You can hire a motorcycle to take you out to the trailhead for Y5.

Xingyi is an interesting town to wander around, and sights around town include a good minorities' museum. The *Panjiang Hotel* (pánjiāng bīnguǎn) is the only hotel that officially takes foreigners (don't worry, you'll get directed to it) and it costs around Y20 for a bed in a three-bed dorm, or Y50 for a nice double with attached bath. Some travellers have managed to sneak a few nights in some of the Chinese-only hotels but got hassled for it later. Keep an eye (and nose) out for tasty warm cinnamon bread sold fresh in the mornings from street stalls and bakeries.

Getting There & Away

Buses to Xingyi leave approximately hourly from in front of the Guiyang Railway Station between 6 am and 6 pm. The fare is Y35. There is also one sleeper bus nightly at 6 pm for Y56. From the long-distance bus station regular buses leave frequently from 6 am to 6 pm for Y30. You can also catch sleepers from here at noon and 4 and 6 pm for Y52. The journey to Xingyi takes 12 hours.

If you're going from Anshun, you can catch the daily bus at 6.30 or 7 am: the actual departure time varies depending on the date. The seven-hour trip takes in some beautiful scenery, so it's probably best to do it in the daytime. The fare is Y21.50.

From Xingyi, buses leave the bus station at 6 am for the 12-hour ride to Kunming. There is also a 6 pm bus, but it's not a sleeper, which could make for a long, dark, bumpy ride. In addition, a number of independent bus companies around town run services to Kunming throughout the day. Tickets are Y25 to Y30. From Kunming's long-distance bus station there are morning buses to Xingyi.

Yunnan 云南

Yunnan *(yúnnán)* is without doubt one of the most alluring travel destinations in China. It's the most geographically varied of all of China's provinces, with terrain as widely divergent as tropical rainforest and icy Tibetan highlands. It is also the sixth-largest province in China and the home of a third of all China's ethnic minorities and half of all China's plant and animal species. If you could only go to one province, this one might well be it.

Yunnan is also well known for its mild climate year-round – its name is a reference to this reputation, meaning South of the Clouds. The provincial capital, Kunming, is similarly referred to as the 'Spring City'.

Despite the best government efforts, there are numerous pockets of the province that have successfully resisted Chinese influence and exhibit strong local identities. Even Kunming has a flavour all its own that seems more than half a world away from Beijing, though this gap is in danger of being bridged by rapid economic growth.

When Qin Shihuang and the Han emperors first held tentative sway over the south-west, Yunnan was occupied by a large number of non-Chinese aboriginal peoples who lacked any strong political organisation. But by the 7th century AD the Bai people had established a powerful kingdom, the Nanzhao, south of Dali. Initially allying its power with the Chinese against the Tibetans, this kingdom extended its power until, in the middle of the 8th century, it was able to challenge and defeat the Tang armies. It took control of a large slice of the south-west and established itself as a fully independent entity, dominating the trade routes from China to India and Burma. The Nanzhao kingdom fell in the 10th century and was replaced by the kingdom of Dali, an independent state which lasted until it was overrun by the Mongols in the mid-13th century. After 15 centuries of resistance to northern rule, this part of the south-west was finally

Population: 35 million
Capital: Kunming
Highlights:

- Though modernising, Kunming still has intriguing back streets, great food and some worthwhile sights
- The narrow stone streets of 'old town' Lijiang give a fascinating glimpse into Naxi minority culture and history
- Tiger Leaping Gorge, a two to three-day trek amid dramatic cliffs and waterfalls
- Dali, one of China's best places to kick back and relax, surrounded by ancient wooden buildings and flagstone streets
- Old wooden architecture and customs still survive in the quaint town of Tengchong, which also has adjacent hot springs and (dormant) volcanoes
- Ruili, a sometimes-wild bordertown that offers lots of chances for exploring nearby temples, villages and forests
- Xishuangbanna, a taste of tropical South-East Asia in China and home of the colourful Dai people

integrated into the empire as the province of Yunnan.

Even so it remained an isolated frontier region, with scattered Chinese garrisons and settlements in the valleys and basins, a mixed

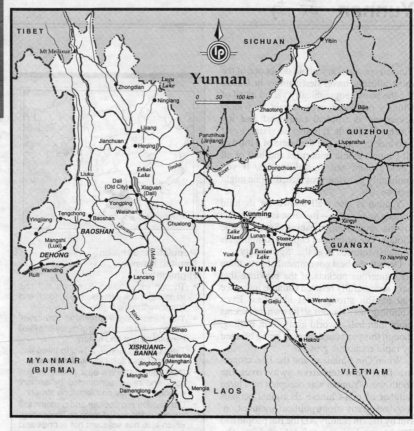

Yunnan

aboriginal population occupying the high-lands, and various Dai (Thai) and other minorities along the Lancang (Mekong) River. Like the rest of the south-west, it was always one of the first regions to break with the northern government. During China's countless political purges, fallen officials often found themselves exiled here, which added to the province's rebellious character.

Today, however, Yunnan Province looks to be firmly back in the Chinese fold. It is a province of 35 million people, including a veritable constellation of minorities (25 registered): the Zhuang, Hui, Yi, Miao, Tibet-

ans, Mongols, Yao, Bai, Hani, Dai, Lisu, Lahu, Wa, Naxi, Jingpo, Bulang, Pumi, Nu, Achang, Benglong, Jinuo and Dulong.

KUNMING
(kūnmíng)

While Kunming and its surrounding districts boast a fair number of interesting sights, they pale in comparison with some of Yunnan's jewels, such as Lijiang or Xishuangbanna. But the city is still a fine place to wander around on foot, once you get off the wide boulevards. It is unfortunate that much of Kunming's charm is under threat: in recent years, like much of China, the city has been treated to a major face-lift. For the locals this spells 'progress', but for Western visitors in search of the old Kunming it means the quaint back alleyways lined with fascinating wooden buildings are rapidly disappearing. There is enough still standing to make it worth getting lost in the backstreets, but the next decade will likely see the last remnants of old Kunming succumb to the wrecking ball.

For now the city remains an interesting place to linger for a few days. There is some great food available, and the streets are vibrant with shoppers, peddlers, roadside masseurs, karaoke stalls and the occasional street performer.

Kunming's total population is around 3½ million, though only a million or so inhabit the urban area. At most, minorities account for 6% of Kunming's population, although the farming areas in the outlying counties are home to some Yi, Hui and Miao groups. There are also a fair number of Vietnamese refugees-turned-immigrants from the Chinese-Vietnamese wars and border clashes that started in 1977.

At an elevation of 1890 metres, Kunming has a milder climate than most other Chinese cities, and can be visited at any time of year. Light clothes will usually be adequate, but it's wise to bring some woollies during the winter months, when temperatures can suddenly drop, particularly in the evenings – there have even been a couple of light snowfalls in recent years. There's a fairly even spread of temperatures from April to September. Winters are short, sunny and dry. In summer (from June to August) Kunming offers cool respite, although rain is more prevalent.

History

The region of Kunming has been inhabited for 2000 years. Tomb excavations around Lake Dian to the south of the city have unearthed thousands of artefacts from that period – weapons, drums, paintings, and silver, jade and turquoise jewellery – that suggest a well-developed culture and provide clues to a very sketchy early history of the city. Until the 8th century the town was a remote Chinese outpost, but the kingdom of Nanzhao, centred to the north-west of Kunming at Dali, captured it and made it a secondary capital. In 1274 the Mongols came through, sweeping all and sundry before them. Marco Polo, who put his big feet in everywhere, gives us a fascinating picture of Kunming's commerce in the late 13th century:

At the end of these five days journeys you arrive at the capital city, which is named Yachi, and is very great and noble. In it are found merchants and artisans, with a mixed population, consisting of idolaters, Nestorian Christians and Saracens or Mohametans... The land is fertile in rice and wheat...For money they employ the white porcelain shell, found in the sea, and which they also wear as ornaments about their necks. Eighty of the shells are equal in value to...two Venetian groats. In this country also there are salt springs...the duty levied on this salt produces large revenues to the Emperor. The natives do not consider it an injury done to them when others have connection with their wives, provided the act is voluntary on the woman's part. Here there is a lake almost a hundred miles in circuit, in which great quantities of fish are caught. The people are accustomed to eat the raw flesh of fowls, sheep, oxen and buffalo...the poorer sorts only dip it in a sauce of garlic...they eat it as well as we do the cooked.

In the 14th century the Ming set up shop in Yunnanfu, as Kunming was then known, building a walled town on the present site. From the 17th century onwards, the history of this city becomes rather grisly. The last Ming resistance to the invading Manchu took place in Yunnan in the 1650s and was crushed by General Wu Sangui. Wu in turn rebelled against the king and held out until his death in 1678. His successor was overthrown by the Manchu emperor Kangxi and killed himself in Kunming in 1681. In the 19th century, the city suffered several bloodbaths, as the rebel Muslim leader Du Wenxiu, the Sultan of Dali, attacked and besieged the city several times between 1858 and 1868. A large number of buildings were destroyed and it was not until 1873 that the rebellion was finally and bloodily crushed.

The intrusion of the West into Kunming

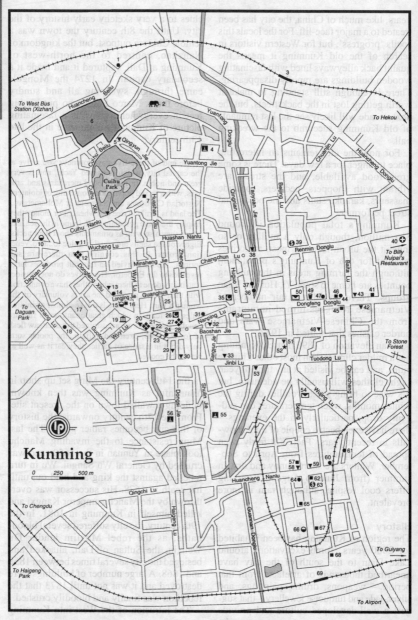

Kunming

0   250   500 m

To West Bus
Station (Xizhan)

To Hekou

To Billy
Nuipal's
Restaurant

To Daguan
Park

To Stone
Forest

To Chengdu

To Haigeng
Park

To Guiyang

To Airport

KUNMING 昆明

PLACES TO STAY

7 Green Lake Hotel
翠湖宾馆
9 Golden Flower Hotel
金花宾馆
16 Yunnan Hotel
云南饭店
28 Chun Cheng Hotel
春城饭店
41 Camellia Hotel
茶花宾馆
45 Holiday Inn Kunming
樱花酒楼
46 Kunming Hotel
昆明饭店
57 Kunhu Hotel
昆湖饭店
62 Golden Dragon Hotel
金龙饭店
65 King World Hotel
锦华大酒店
67 Three Leaves Hotel
三叶饭店
68 Railroad Travel Service
铁路旅行社

PLACES TO EAT

5 Tong Da Li Restaurant
通达利餐馆
8 Laozhiqing Restaurant
老知青食馆
11 Wucheng Vegetarian
Restaurant
武成素食店
13 Shanghai Noodle
Restaurant
上海面店
20 Ice Cream Shop
冰淇淋店
22 Qiaoxiangyuan Rest-
aurant
桥香园饭店
23 Muslim Restaurants
清真饭店
29 Yunnan Across-the-
Bridge Noodles
Restaurant
云南过桥米线
30 California Noodle
King USA
美国加州牛肉面大王

32 Beijing Restaurant
北京饭店
33 Nanlaisheng Coffee
Shop
南来盛咖啡馆
34 Minsheng Restaurant
民生饭店
38 Yingjianglou Muslim
Restaurant
映江楼饭店
42 Cooking School
学厨饭店
43 Yunnan Typical Local
Food Restaurant
根兴饭店
48 Bai Ta Dai Flavour
Restaurant
白塔傣味餐厅
51 Mengzi Across-the-
Bridge Noodles
Restaurant
蒙自过桥米线
53 Guangshengyuan
Restaurant
冠生园饭店
58 Yuelai Cafe
悦来餐厅
59 Wei's Place
哈哈餐厅

OTHER

1 Yunnan Minorities
Institute
云南少数民族学院
2 Kunming Zoo
昆明动物园
3 North Railway Station
火车北站
4 Yuantong Temple
圆通寺
6 Yunnan University
云南大学
10 Xiaoximen Bus Station
小西门汽车客运站
12 Dongfeng Department
Store
东风百货商店
14 Arts Theatre
艺术剧院
15 Buses to Western Hills
& Bamboo Temple
往西山，筇竹寺的车
17 Guofang Sports Ground
国防体育场

18 Advance Ticket Booking
Office
火车票预售处
19 Yunnan Provincial
Museum
云南省博物馆
21 Wuhua Mansions
Department Store
五华大厦
24 Kunming United Airlines
昆明联合航空公司
25 Flower & Bird Market
花鸟市场
26 Nancheng Mosque
南城清真古寺
27 Kunming Department
Store
昆明百货商店
31 Xinhua Bookstore
新华书店
35 Mosque
清真寺
36 Yunnan Antique Store
云南文物店
37 Foreign Languages
Bookstore
外文书店
39 Bank of China
中国银行
40 Yan'an Hospital
延安医院
44 CAAC
中国民航售票处
47 China Southern &
Shanghai Airlines
上海航空公司
49 Golden Triangle Bar
金角酒吧
50 Post & Telecommuni-
cations Office
邮电局
52 PSB
公安局
54 International Post Office
国际邮局
55 East Pagoda
东寺塔
56 West Pagoda
西寺塔
60 CITS
中国国际旅行社
61 Thai Airways
泰国航空公司

(Continued)

63 Bank of China
    中国银行
64 China Southwest Airlines
    西南航空公司
66 Long-Distance Bus Station
    长途汽车总站
69 Main Railway Station
    火车站

began in the middle of the 19th century when Britain took control of Burma, and France took control of Indochina, providing access to the city from the south. By 1900 Kunming, Hekou, Simao and Mengzi were opened to foreign trade. The French were keen on exploiting the region's copper, tin and timber resources, and in 1910 their Indochina railway, started in 1898 at Hanoi, reached the city.

Kunming's expansion began with WW II, when factories were established here and refugees fleeing the Japanese poured in from eastern China. In a bid to keep China from falling to Japan, Anglo-American forces sent supplies to Nationalist troops entrenched in Sichuan and Yunnan. Supplies came overland on a dirt road carved out of the mountains in 1937-38 by 160,000 Chinese with virtually no equipment. This was the famous Burma Road, a 1000-km haul from Lashio to Kunming (today, the western extension of Kunming's Renmin Lu, leading in the direction of Heilinpu, is the tail end of the Road).

In early 1942 the Japanese captured Lashio, cutting the supply line. Kunming continued to handle most of the incoming aid during 1942-45 when US planes flew the dangerous mission of crossing the 'Hump', the towering 5000-metre mountain ranges between India and Yunnan. A black market sprang up and a fair proportion of the medicines, canned food, petrol and other goods intended for the military and relief agencies were siphoned off into other hands.

The face of Kunming has been radically altered since then, with streets widened and office buildings and housing projects flung up. With the coming of the railways, industry has expanded rapidly, and a surprising range of goods and machinery available in China now bears the 'made in Yunnan' stamp. The city's produce includes steel, foodstuffs, trucks, machine tools, electrical equipment, textiles, chemicals, building materials and plastics.

Orientation

The jurisdiction of Kunming covers 6200 sq km, including four city districts and four rural counties (which supply the city with fruit and vegetables). The centre of the city is the traffic circle at the intersection of Zhengyi Lu and Dongfeng Lu. This is where you'll find the local trendies, cinemas, karaoke bars and department stores overflowing with the latest fashions and electronic goods. Surprisingly, it is still possible to find a few rows of old wooden houses in nearby neighbourhoods. To the south-west of the intersection down to Jinbi Lu there are some interesting old alleys and some great places to eat. Jinbi Lu itself is a fascinating tree-lined street crowded with shops and restaurants, though it is rumoured the trees will soon fall to a road-widening project.

To the north of the intersection are Cuihu Park, a pleasant place for a wander, Yuantong Temple and the Kunming Zoo, the inhabitants of which, like those of most Chinese animal incarceration sites, would probably be better off put out of their misery. East of the intersection is Kunming's major north-south road, Beijing Lu. At the southern end is the main railway station, the long-distance bus station and the Kunhu Hotel, one of the few cheap places to stay in Kunming. At about the halfway point Beijing Lu is intersected by Dongfeng Donglu, which is where the luxurious Kunming Hotel and Holiday Inn Kunming can be found.

Information

CITS The travel service (☎ 314-8308) is just east of Beijing Lu in a large white-tiled building at 220 Huancheng Nanlu. Like CITS offices elsewhere in China, this one emphasises group tours and is not able to offer a lot of assistance to individual travellers. A few years back some travellers successfully made reservations by telex to Beijing for tickets on the Trans-Siberian, but CITS staff seemed shocked that such a transgression had taken place.

PSB The Foreign Affairs Branch is at 93 Beijing Lu and is open from 8 to 11.30 am and from 2.30 to 4.30 pm, seven days a week. It's a tiny office with a small plaque in English on the wall outside. The officers on duty usually speak excellent English, and are quite friendly. They also have current lists of all the open counties and cities in Yunnan (happily, the list keeps getting longer).

Money The Kunming, Green Lake, Camellia, King World, Holiday Inn and Golden Dragon hotels each have foreign-exchange counters. Changing money in the hotels is generally more convenient than trudging up to the Bank of China on Renmin Donglu, though the bank recently opened a branch near the Golden Dragon Hotel. There are still one or two hopeful moneychangers in front of the Kunming Hotel, but be very careful of rip-offs, which occur frequently by sleight of hand. Beware of moneychangers handing you back a US$100 bill and telling you it's a fake – it has often been discreetly swapped for a US$1 bill.

Post & Telecommunications There is an international post office on the east side of Beijing Lu. It's halfway between Tuodong Lu and Huancheng Nanlu and has a very efficient poste restante and parcel service – this is where poste restante mail ends up. Every poste restante letter or parcel that comes in is listed in a ledger that's kept on the counter. To claim a letter, you must show your passport or ID. At least one of the clerks speaks English. You can also make telephone calls here. There is another post office to the north of this one, on Beijing Lu near the intersection with Dongfeng Donglu.

With Kunming's hotels in the grip of a renovation frenzy, it's probably not a good idea to use a hotel as a poste restante address

unless you are absolutely sure that it is still standing and will be open.

Consulates Thailand, Laos and Myanmar now all have visa-issuing consulates in Kunming. When we last checked, PSB officials said exit permits were not needed to go into Laos or Myanmar. But given the flexibility of rules in China, it would be wise to check for yourself. Visa details for each country follow.

Laos The Lao consulate (☎ 317-6623) is on the 2nd floor of Building Three at the Camellia Hotel. Unless you have a sponsor in Laos (doesn't everyone?) you'll probably only be able to get a seven-day transit visa. This is just enough time to cross the border at Mengla, make your way down to Vientiane and on to Thailand. (It actually may take a few days more, but travellers who have overextended their stay have met with little real trouble.) The visa costs US$28 and takes three to five days to process. You must bring four (yes, four) photos, and already have a visa from a third country stamped in your passport. Even though Thailand grants most nationalities a grace period of 30 days before requiring a visa, you may have to get one stamped in your passport anyway, just to satisfy the Lao officials. Office hours are Monday to Friday, 8.30 to 11.30 am and 2.30 to 4.30 pm.

Myanmar The office (☎ 312-6309) is just above the Lao consulate, on the 3rd floor of Building Three. Myanmar seems to be really gearing up for tourists: the consulate can grant you a four-week visa in 24 hours, and possibly on the same day, for Y165. There are two catches: first you are required to change US$300 into Myanmar kyat at the government's scandalously low rate; and the visas are not good for land crossings: you are supposed to fly in via Yangon (Rangoon) only. If there are several of you, you might try your luck at the Ruili border crossing. See the Ruili section for more information. The consulate is open Monday to Friday from 8.30 am to noon and 1 to 4.30 pm.

Thailand The Thai consulate (☎ 396-8916), on the 2nd floor of the north wing at the Golden Dragon Hotel, can arrange two-month visas for Y110 in three working days. Travellers from most countries won't need one unless they plan to spend more than 30 days in Thailand (which actually is not all that hard to do).

Maps There are at least three varieties of map, some with a smattering of English names, available from hotels and the Foreign Languages Bookstore. The *Kunming Tourist Map* has street and hotel names in English and shows bus lines, while the *Yunnan Communications and Tourist Map* has the names of nearly every town in the province written out in English.

Medical Services The Yan'an Hospital (*yán'ān yīyuàn*) on Renmin Lu has a foreigners' clinic (☎ 317-7499 ext 311) on the 1st floor of Building Six, at the back of the compound.

Tang Dynasty Pagodas

To the south of Jinbi Lu are two Tang pagodas, of which the West Pagoda (*xīsì tǎ*) is more worth visiting. The East Pagoda (*dōngsì tǎ*) was, according to Chinese sources, destroyed by an earthquake; Western sources say it was destroyed by the Muslim revolt. It was rebuilt in the 19th century, but there's little to see. The more interesting West Pagoda is on Dongsi Jie, a bustling market street – you'll probably have to walk your bicycle through the crowds. The West Pagoda has a compound that is a popular spot for old people to get together, drink tea and play cards and mahjong. It's not a bad stop to catch your breath and sip a cup of tea. Look out for a red gateway hidden among the trees and karaoke signs: the pagoda is about 20 metres in along a narrow corridor. The temple is open from 9 am to 9 pm.

Yunnan Provincial Museum

(*yúnnánshěng bówùguǎn*)
The museum, on Wuyi Lu, houses an exhibition centred on Yunnan's minorities, as well as a collection of artefacts from tomb excavations at Jinning on the southern rim of Lake Dian. All things considered, the museum is probably not worth the foreigners' entry fee of Y10. The exhibits are for the most part fairly tacky shop mannequins dressed in minority colours, and fuzzy photographs of minority festivals. The museum is open Monday to Thursday.

Yuantong Temple

(*yuántōng sì*)
The Yuantong Temple, to the north-east of the Green Lake Hotel, is the largest Buddhist complex in Kunming, and is a target for pilgrims. It is over 1000 years old, and has seen many renovations. Leading up to the main hall from the entrance is an extensive display of flowers and potted landscapes. The central courtyard holds a large square pond intersected by walkways and bridges, and has an octagonal pavilion at the centre. To the rear of the temple a new hall has been added, enshrining a statue of Sakyamuni, a gift from the king of Thailand. There's a vegetarian restaurant on the grounds that serves lunch and dinner. The temple is open from 8 am to 5 pm, though the restaurant doors don't close until 9 pm. Admission is Y5 for overseas visitors, Y1 for locals. Watch out for pickpockets outside the temple and for the elderly women inside who do their best to stop foreigners taking pictures of the Buddhist statuary.

Kunming Zoo

(*dòngwùyuán*)
Close to Yuantong Temple is the zoo, and as Chinese zoos go it's not too shabby. The grounds are pleasantly leafy and high up, and provide a bird's-eye vista of the city. Most travellers find the animals' living conditions depressing – animal lovers are better off giving the place a miss.

Cuihu Park

(*cuìhú gōngyuán*)
A short distance south-west of the zoo, the Cuihu Park is worth a stroll if you can avoid paying the foreigners' entry fee of Y8.

Sunday sees the park at its liveliest, when it is host to an English Corner and hordes of families at play.

Mosques

(qīngzhēnsì)

Today, while Kunming's Buddhist shrines, desecrated during the Cultural Revolution, are humming with renovations for the tourist trade, the local Muslim population seems to have been left out of the action. There are a few mosques around the city centre, none of which see much activity. This may change, however. The oldest of the lot, the 400-year-old Nancheng Ancient Mosque *(nánchéng gǔsì)* is slated to be torn down so that a new, larger version may be put in its place. Whether or not this actually comes to pass is hard to say, but it may be worth stopping by to see what's developed. The mosque is hidden down an alleyway immediately north of the Kunming Department Store, at 51 Zhengyi Lu.

There's another mosque nearby, wedged between Huguo Lu and Chongyun Jie, though it looks to be more of an historical landmark rather than a place of active worship.

Organised Tours

Several tour outfits cover the area faster than public minibuses would, but you must be prepared to pay for them. They generally feature a lot of sights that most Western travellers find rather boring, like the Black Dragon Pool and various caves (a national obsession). More central sights like Yuantong Temple are just a short bicycle ride away – it hardly makes sense to join a tour to see them. Some tour operators refuse to take foreigners on their tours, claiming the language barrier causes too much trouble.

There are various tours to the Stone Forest running from in front of the railway station, and from near the Three Leaves, Golden Dragon and Kunhu Hotels on Beijing Lu – avoid them. You'll spend the whole morning rummaging around in caves where you'll be charged exorbitant foreigners' entry fees, followed by a marathon midday lunch. If you're lucky you may even get an hour or so

Kunming's Muslims

Unlike Muslims in other parts of China, who generally formed settlements at the termini of trade routes used by Arab traders, Yunnan's sizable Muslim population dates back to the 13th-century Mongol invasion of China. Ethnically indistinguishable from the Han Chinese, the *hui*, as Muslims are known, have had an unfortunate history of repression and persecution, a recent low point being the years of the Cultural Revolution. The Cultural Revolution failed to spark off a revolt of any kind, though unsuccessful protests were registered in Beijing. The turbulent years of the mid-19th century, which witnessed the massive Taiping and Nian rebellions, were another matter. Heavy land taxes and disputes between Muslims and Han Chinese over local gold and silver mines triggered a Muslim uprising in 1855.

The Muslims made Dali the centre of their operations and laid siege to Kunming, overrunning the city briefly in 1863. Du Wenxiu, the Muslim leader, proclaimed his newly established kingdom Nanping Guo, or the Kingdom of the Pacified South. But the Muslim successes were short-lived. In 1873 Dali was taken by Qing forces and Du Wenxiu was captured and executed, having failed in a suicide attempt. ∎

in the Stone Forest before being whisked back to Kunming. That said, the occasional traveller has come back satisfied with the experience – an interesting initiation into Chinese tourism rituals.

There's also an outfit up at No 73 Renmin Xilu in town called Yunnan Exploration (☎ 531-2203) that can organise jeep tours, hiking, backcountry skiing, bicycle trips and other more exotic outdoor activities, most of which take place far away from Kunming. What's on offer looks interesting, though probably beyond the budgets of many travellers.

Places to Stay – bottom end

Kunming's hotel situation is bleak for budget travellers. Only three hotels have dormitories – all other accommodation open to foreigners is mid-range, at least in terms of price.

Long frequented by budget travellers, the *Camellia Hotel* (☎ 316-8000) *(cháhuā bīnguǎn)* on Dongfeng Donglu closed down its dormitory accommodation for several years in a bid to move more upmarket. But a ceaseless barrage of backpackers apparently changed someone's mind: three seven-bed dorm rooms were opened up in mid-1995. At Y30 per bed, it's pretty much the cheapest spot in town, and as such it can be difficult to get in sometimes. Also in high demand are the hotel's Y140 doubles, which have TV and attached bathrooms. Sad to say, these are almost among the cheapest such rooms in Kunming. There are also standard doubles for Y220, which some travellers have resorted to in hopes they'll get a dorm bed or a Y140 double the next day.

The Camellia has bicycle hire, a foreign-exchange counter and poste restante. Staff are generally friendly: if they seem curt with you, remember that they deal everyday with a constant stream of foreigners pulling their hair out, demanding rooms, and camping out in the lobby. To get there from the railway station, take a No 2 or 23 bus to Dongfeng Lu, then change to the No 5 bus heading east and get off at the second stop.

Near the railway station on Beijing Lu, the *Kunhu Hotel* (☎ 313-3737) *(kūnhú fàndiàn)* also has dorm beds for Y30, and draws a fair amount of travellers as a result. They certainly don't go there for the service, which can be so terrible it may even make you laugh (or want to strangle someone). Unfortunately the dorm rooms look out onto Beijing Lu, so they're quite noisy. The hotel also has dingy doubles with attached bath for Y152. On the plus side, the common bathrooms are fairly clean, dorm beds are easier to get than at the Camellia, and next door are several cafes where you can relax, sip coffee and trade tales with fellow travellers.

The hotel is two stops from the railway station on bus No 2, 23 or 47.

The only other budget option is the *Golden Flower Hotel* (☎ 532-6900) *(jīnhuā bīnguǎn)* way out on Xichang Lu. A bed in a seven-person room is Y40, which is akin to robbery, but may have to do if you're shut out of the Camellia and Kunhu. At least you may get a laugh from the silly 'minority' headdresses worn by staff behind the check-in counter. Standard doubles are Y200. The hotel is in a courtyard set back from Xichang Lu, but there is a gateway with an English sign out front. Getting here by bus is a hassle. Take the No 3 bus to the intersection of Jinbi Lu and Xichang Lu, and change to the No 22 bus which runs up Xichang Lu and past the hotel.

Places to Stay – middle

Your best bet here is probably the *Chun Cheng Hotel* (☎ 316-1773) *(chūnchéng fàndiàn)* on Dongfeng Xilu. Also known as the Spring City Hotel, it has spacious clean doubles with attached bathroom for Y166 – pretty good value for money. There are also doubles with common washroom for Y82, which are not such a good deal.

Right next to the main railway station, the *Railroad Travel Service (tiělù lǚxíngshè)* has doubles with bath for Y138. The hotel is fairly new, so it's not a bad place to stay as long as you don't mind wading through the railway station crowds on your way in and out of the building. The *Three Leaves Hotel (sānyè fàndiàn)* is a short walk from the railway station and directly opposite the long-distance bus station on Beijing Lu. Decent standard doubles with air-con and satellite TV are Y198.

Places to Stay – top end

Several former proletarian stand-bys have received luxury face-lifts and so, as usual, there is plenty to choose from in this category. (If Kunming's tourist authorities had their way, probably every hotel in town would be a four-star or higher.)

The *Kunming Hotel* (☎ 316-2063) *(kūnmíng fàndiàn)* at 145 Dongfeng Donglu has a north and a south wing; both are fairly expensive, though the south wing is the cheaper of the two. Only doubles are available in the north wing, and prices start at Y670. The south wing has singles/doubles for Y350. The hotel has some useful facilities: airline ticket bookings, poste restante, post office, photocopying, a snooker room, bike hire, several high-end restaurants and a couple of shops. To get there from the main station, take bus No 23 to the intersection of Dongfeng Lu and Beijing Lu, and then take a bus east or walk. From the west bus station (xīzhàn) take bus No 5.

Diagonally opposite the Kunming Hotel is Kunming's superluxury monster: the *Holiday Inn Kunming* (☎ 316-5888) (*yīnghuā jiàrì jiǔdiàn*). It is still the best of Kunming's hotels, sporting some excellent restaurants, a Western-style pub, a super-chic disco and one of the better breakfasts in town. You can expect the usual Holiday Inn standards and room rates (US$95 to US$112 for a double).

The *Green Lake Hotel* (☎ 515-7326) (*cuìhú bīnguǎn*) on 6 Cuihu Nanlu is in an older section of Kunming. It used to be quiet and quaint, but has lost some of its character with the construction of a 20-floor, four-star addition in the back. Doubles in the old building are actually pretty reasonable at US$33, especially when compared with US$100 for a room in the new section. The hotel has a bar, a coffee shop and both Western and Chinese restaurants. The food in these places has a good reputation.

Down on Beijing Lu, the *Golden Dragon Hotel* (☎ 313-2793) (*jīnlóng fàndiàn*) is a Hong Kong-China joint venture. Only doubles are available and these start at US$80, while suites start at US$140 and reach the giddy heights of US$600 (plus 10% service charge). A 15% discount is sometimes available on request. Both CAAC and Dragonair have offices here and there is a business centre on the premises as well. The Golden Dragon, once Kunming's premier upmarket hotel, is gradually losing custom to the other new hotels around Kunming and some complain that standards are slipping.

Down the road from the Golden Dragon is another luxury hotel: the *King World Hotel* (☎ 313-8888) (*jǐnhuá dàjiǔdiàn*). Doubles range from US$80 for a standard to US$198 for a superior suite, plus 15% service charge.

The hotel features an expensive revolving restaurant (the highest above sea level in China, the hotel proudly points out) on the top floor.

The *Yunnan Hotel* (☎ 361-3888) (*yúnnán fàndiàn*) on Dongfeng Xilu, near the Yunnan Provincial Museum and the Zhengyi Department Store, was Kunming's first tourist hotel. It recently made a break with its humble beginnings and now its cheapest rooms are Y480. But if you're going to spend this much, the old wings at the Cuihu or Kunming Hotel will probably give you more for your money.

Places to Eat

Local Cuisine There are several eating places near the Kunming and Camellia hotels on Dongfeng Donglu that feature bilingual menus. The *Cooking School* (*xuéchú fàndiàn*) on Dongfeng Lu specialises in local fish and vegetable dishes, but it must save its novice chefs for the foreigners: the place gets the thumbs down from most travellers who have eaten there. On the other hand, the *Yunnan Typical Local Food Restaurant* (*gēnxīng fàndiàn*) has a good range of dishes, including across-the-bridge noodles, and gets good reviews from both locals and foreigners.

Several small restaurants in the vicinity of Yunnan University's main gate are highly recommended, especially the popular *Tong Da Li Restaurant* (*tóngdàlì cāntīng*). Coming out of the Yunnan University gate, go left on the main road and then take the first left onto a small back street; Tong Da Li is the second restaurant on the right. There's a slew of little restaurants on this street, most of which have outdoor seating and are overflowing with happy diners. They're worth a try as well. This area is about 15 minutes' walk north of the Green Lake Hotel.

Two of the better known places for steampot chicken are the *Chun Cheng Hotel* and the *Dongfeng Hotel* (*dōngfēng fàndiàn*), around the corner of Wuyi Lu and Wucheng Lu, in the direction of the Green Lake Hotel. Several small, private restaurants on Beijing Lu opposite the long-distance bus station sell cheaper versions of steampot chicken. Steampot chicken is served in dark-brown Jianshui County casserole pots, and is imbued with medicinal properties depending on the spicing – caterpillar fungus (chóngǎo), pseudo-ginseng.

The best Hui, or Chinese Muslim, food in Kunming is reportedly served at the Yingjianglou Muslim Restaurant (yìngjiānglóu fàndiàn) at 360 Changchun Lu. It's still running strong after many years and can be found in an interesting, bustling part of town. An English menu is available and one of the staff speaks English. Try the cold sliced beef – it comes with a delicious sauce.

A good restaurant to try Kunming's famous noodle dish is the Minsheng Restaurant (mínshēng fàndiàn). Prices are either Y5 or Y10, but you'll almost certainly be pressured into taking the Y10 option – relax, it's worth it. Close to the Yunnan Provincial Museum and set back from the main road a little is the Qiaoxiangyuan Restaurant (qiáoxiāng yuán). The noodles here are also very good and are similarly priced to those of the Minsheng Restaurant.

The Yunnan Across-the-Bridge Noodles Restaurant (guòqiáo mǐxiàngguǎn) on Nantong Jie serves huge bowls at rock-bottom prices. The decor is, shall we say, basic – the predominant noise is a chorus of hissing and slurping; tattered beggars circulate among

---

Kunming Food

Kunming has some great food, especially in the snack line. Regional specialities are herb-infused chicken cooked in an earthenware steampot (qìguōjī), Yunnan ham (xuānwèi huǒtuǐ), across-the-bridge noodles (guòqiáo mǐxiàn), goat cheese (rǔbǐng) and various Muslim beef and mutton dishes. Some travellers wax enthusiastic about toasted goat's cheese, another local speciality. It probably depends on how long you've been away from home – the cheese is actually quite bland and sticks to your teeth.

Gourmets with money to burn may perhaps be interested in a whole banquet based on Jizhong fungus (mushrooms) or 30 courses of cold mutton, not to mention fried grasshoppers or elephant trunk braised in soy sauce.

The chief breakfast in Kunming, as throughout most of Yunnan, is noodles (choice of rice or wheat), usually served in a meat broth with a chilli sauce.

Yunnan's best-known dish is across-the-bridge noodles. You are provided with a bowl of very hot soup (stewed with chicken, duck and spare ribs) on which a thin layer of oil is floating, along with a side dish of raw pork slivers (in classier places this might be chicken or fish) and vegetables, and a bowl of rice noodles. Diners place all of the ingredients quickly into the soup bowl, where they are cooked by the steamy broth.

Across-the-bridge noodles is the stuff of which fairy tales are made, as the following story proves:

Once upon a time there was a scholar at the South Lake in Mengzi (Southern Yunnan) who was attracted by the peace and quiet of an island there. He settled into a cottage on the island, in preparation for official examinations. His wife, meanwhile, had to cross a long wooden bridge over the lake to bring the bookworm his meals. The fodder was always cold in winter by the time she got to the study bower. Oversleeping one day, she made a curious discovery. She'd stewed a fat chicken and was puzzled to find the broth still hot, though it gave off no steam – the oil layer on the surface had preserved the temperature of the broth. Subsequent experiments showed that she could cook the rest of the ingredients for her husband's meal in the hot broth after she crossed the bridge.

It is possible to try across-the-bridge noodles in innumerable restaurants in Kunming. Prices generally vary from Y5 to Y15 depending on the side dishes provided. It's usually worth spending a bit more, because with only one or two condiments it lacks zest. ■

the stainless-steel-topped tables, pursued by management. Never mind the beggars or the decor – the food is absolutely delicious!

A more recent phenomenon in Kunming is the discovery of ethnic cuisines. At present there are at least two Dai minority restaurants in Kunming. The food is spicy and uses sticky rice as its staple. Popular with over-seas students studying in Kunming is the *Laozhiqing Restaurant (lǎozhīqīng shíguǎn)* next to the main entrance to Cuihu Park. It's an open-fronted place complete with minia-ture chairs.

The *Bai Ta Dai Flavour Restaurant (bái-tádaiwèi cāntīng)*, nestled down an alley near the Kunming Hotel, has tasty food, an English menu and cold draught beer. Prices are a bit high, but it's a good place to try Dai cuisine – an opportunity you won't get again unless you head down to Xishuangbanna.

Finally, a few doors down from the Kunhu Hotel on Beijing Lu are several pleasant cafes catering to travellers and hip locals. The No 1 spot is the *Yuelai Cafe*, where the outside tables are almost always full, even though it's house policy to never hassle passing travellers by trying to drag them in off the street. Prices are very reasonable. Almost next door, the *Happy Cafe*, which used to be known as the Pizza Hut, also serves all the traveller's favourites. The pizzas aren't bad, though their appearance has thrown a few Western customers, who thought they were being served pancakes.

Around the corner on Huancheng Nanlu, *Wei's Place (hāhā cāntīng)* is a bit more like a hip Western bar in atmosphere, but it also has good food, and diners at the outdoor tables are spared the traffic roar of Beijing Lu.

Other Chinese Cuisine There is a string of eateries on Xiangyun Jie between Jinbi Lu and Nanping Lu. At the Nanping end at No 77 is the *Beijing Restaurant (běijīng fàn-diàn)* with northern-style seafood, chicken and duck. Further down are lots of street vendors and small private restaurants.

Pick of the pleb restaurants is the *Shang-hai Noodle Restaurant (shànghǎi miànguǎn)* at 73 Dongfeng Xilu, in a yellow-fronted building. To the left side you'll get cheap noodles; to the right are steampot chicken, cold cuts and dumplings.

Aside from the various temples in and around town, there's an interesting vegie alternative in the *Wucheng Vegetarian Res-taurant (wǔchéng sùshi chān)*, in a small red wooden building at 162 Wucheng Lu. Steaming vegetable noodle dishes are tasty and cheap at Y2 a bowl. There's no English sign, but you should be able to pick out the place from the crowds milling outside. It's just a short walk up Wucheng Lu from the Dongfeng Department Store, on the left side of the street.

Snacks Kunming used to be a good place for bakeries, but many of these seem to be disappearing. Exploration of Kunming's backstreets might turn up a few lingerers, however.

In the vicinity of the long-distance bus station and in many of the side streets running off Beijing Lu are roadside noodle shops. Generally you get a bowl of rice noodles for around Y2 and a bewildering array of sauces with which to flavour the broth – most of them are hot and spicy.

Another place to go snack hunting is Huguo Lu, north of Nantaiqiao, for simmer-ing noodle bars and a teahouse. The intersection of Changchun and Huguo yields lots of small eateries. Also try Shuncheng Jie, an east-west street running south of Dong-feng Xilu near the Chun Cheng Hotel. Here you'll find literally dozens of Muslim restau-rants, dumpling shops and noodle stands.

Western Food If your stomach is crying out for Western food that tastes like the real thing, there is one option outside the Holiday Inn's tasty but expensive restaurants. Tucked away in the north-eastern Xinying Xiaoqu district is *Billy Niupai's* (☎ 331-1748) *(bǐlì niúpá)*, where you can get steaks, burgers, pasta and even tacos that should successfully satisfy a homesick appetite. Figure on around Y50 for a full Western meal. The restaurant imports some of its food via the

Holiday Inn – you can even get chips made with imported potatoes if you wish. The decor is strictly American Cowboy, but pleasant for all that. It's probably best to take a taxi, if for no other reason than you'll probably need the cab driver to help you find the place. The ride should cost around Y15 to Y20 from the Kunhu Hotel.

For a *real* heart-starting cup of coffee, seek out the wooden stools of the *Nanlaisheng Coffee Shop (nánláishèng kāfēiguǎn)* at 299 Jinbi Lu. Cakes and breads are also available, as well as hearty French-style loaves. Coffee tickets and bread are sold at the front of the shop; take your coffee ticket into the kitchen at the back to pick up the black, freshly brewed coffee (milk costs extra, sugar is free). This is a good place to meet local foreign residents.

The big hotels all sport coffee shops. For a no-holds-barred breakfast buffet, head down to the *Holiday Inn Kunming*, where you can eat as much as you can stuff in for Y70. If you're a caffeine addict you'll love their coffee deal – Y20 for as many refills as you can stomach, and the coffee is excellent. The ground-floor coffee shop in the *Golden Dragon Hotel* is not quite in the same league, but the coffee is good. The *Yuelai* and *Happy* cafes also serve Yunnan coffee and breakfast sets.

Entertainment

If you're not an ardent fan of karaoke bars, the nightlife options for Kunming are fairly dismal but then again where aren't they in China?

Wei's Place on Huancheng Nanlu attracts a fairly good crowd of both foreigners and locals in the evenings, and has a good Western music selection. Not far from the Kunming Hotel, the *Golden Triangle Bar* sounds promising, but is an expensive place for a drink by Chinese standards: Qingdao is Y12 a bottle. Up the street, the *Bluebird Cafe* has similar prices. Both spots fill up at night, mostly with local patrons. Over at the Holiday Inn, *Charlie's* bar is frequented by Kunming's expat community, but prices are even higher, averaging around Y25 per beer.

You might be able to chase up minority dancing displays (more often held for the benefit of group tours), travelling troupes or Yunnan Opera. CITS sometimes has information on these events. The Arts Theatre on Dongfeng Xilu is a likely venue.

Things to Buy

You have to do a fair bit of digging to come up with inspiring purchases in Kunming. Yunnan specialities are jade (related to Burmese), marble (from the Dali area), batik, minority embroidery (also musical instruments and dress accessories) and spotted brass utensils.

Other crafts to consider are some of the basic utilitarian items that are part of everyday Yunnanese life: the large bamboo waterpipes for smoking angel-haired Yunnan tobacco, local herbal medicines (Yunnan White Medicine *(yúnnán báiyào)* is a blend of over 100 herbs and is highly prized by Chinese throughout the world) and the *qìguō* or ceramic steampot.

Yunnanese tea is also an excellent buy and comes in several varieties, from bowl-shaped bricks of smoked green tea called *tuōchá*, which have been around since at least Marco Polo's time, to leafy black tea that rivals some of India's best.

One of the main shopping drags is Zhengyi Lu, which has the Zhengyi Department Store, the Overseas Chinese Department Store and the Kunming Department Store, but these mainly sell consumer goods. Other shopping areas are Jinbi Lu by the Zhengyi Lu intersection (lots of small speciality shops), and Dongfeng Donglu, between Zhengyi Lu and Huguo Lu.

The Flower & Bird Market *(huāniǎo shìcháng)* is definitely worth a visit. It's tucked away on Tongdao Jie, one of numerous little streets and alleys lying between Zhengyi Lu and Wuyi Lu, just north of the Kunming Department Store. Pet supplies, fishing gear and flowers dominate the cramped rows of tiny stalls, but there is a bizarre assortment of other items such as old coins, wooden elephants, tacky wall murals and so-called 'antiques' on sale. Just walking around here is rewarding: if you actually find something you want to buy, consider it an added bonus.

The Yunnan Antique Store (*yúnnán wénwù shāngdiàn*), on Qingnian Lu, has some pottery, porcelain and handicrafts, but it's pretty dull. Better to look among the privately run shops on Beijing Lu and Dongfeng Donglu. Outside the Kunming Hotel you will probably be ambushed by minority women flogging their handiwork – bargain if you want a sane price. Both the Green Lake and Kunming hotels sell batik which you can also find in Dali. Delve into the smaller shops around Jinbi Lu if you're into embroidery. For Yunnan herbal medicines, check the large pharmacy on Zhengyi Lu (on the east side, several blocks up from the Kunming Department Store). The southern end of Beijing Lu also has a few herbal medicine shops.

Kunming is a fairly good place to stock up on film, and one of the few places in Yunnan where slide film is available. Fuji and other film can be bought at the larger tourist hotels.

Getting There & Away

Air CAAC (☎ 313-7465) is at 146 Dongfeng Donglu, next door to the Kunming Hotel. There is also an office in the Golden Dragon Hotel which can take bookings and issue tickets but not for the next day. China Southern Airlines (☎ 317-4682) has its main office on the other side of the Kunming Hotel, as well as numerous branches around the city. For internal flights, other alternatives include Shanghai Airlines (☎ 313-8502), close to CAAC on Dongfeng Donglu, Kunming United Airlines (☎ 316-4590) on Dongfeng Xilu, and China Southwest Airlines, at 36 Beijing Lu.

Kunming is well connected by air to the rest of China, and most flights (even within Yunnan) are on Boeing 737 and 757 jets. Flights include Beijing, Chengdu, Chongqing, Guangzhou, Guilin, Haikou, Lanzhou, Nanjing, Nanning, Qingdao, Shanghai, Shenzhen, Xiamen, Xi'an and Wuhan.

Within the province, Yunnan Airlines (☎ 316-4415) flies to Baoshan, Jinghong (Banna), Lijiang, Mangshi (Dehong), Xiaguan and Zhaotong. Service on this surprisingly comprehensive network is quite good, and the planes are generally well maintained. Most destinations are served at least three times a week, and Jinghong and Mangshi have daily flights. At the time of writing flights to Lijiang had just begun and those to Xiaguan had not yet started. Lijiang will probably see three flights a week, while service to Xiaguan could well be daily. Tickets for Yunnan Air flights can be booked at any domestic airline ticket office.

Due to the wider availability of flights, it's now often possible to book flights to Xishuangbanna, the Dehong region and most other popular destinations at short notice. However, during peak seasons it pays to book at least a week in advance. During April (Water-Splashing Festival) and summer, the flights to Xishuangbanna (Jinghong) can be booked rock solid for two to three weeks, and the CAAC office jammed with maniacs pushing, shoving and trying to pull rank. At times like this it is best to make your plans for Xishuangbanna as flexible as possible: consider the bus option, or book your flight several weeks ahead and spend the intervening time in Dali or elsewhere. For more details on this flight, see the Jinghong Getting There & Away section.

As well as internal flights, CAAC and several foreign carriers have international flights to Hong Kong (Y1710, daily), Bangkok (Y1540, daily), Yangon (Rangoon) (Y2800, once a week), Vientiane (Y1420, once a week) and Singapore (Y3480, twice a week). At the time of writing service to Chiang Mai in Thailand had been suspended but was likely to resume, so it's worth looking into.

Thai Airways International (☎ 313-3315) has an office at 32 Chuncheng Lu. It's advisable to reconfirm your flight, as travellers have been bumped off flights before. Dragonair (☎ 313-3104) has an office in the Golden Dragon Hotel and has twice-weekly (Thursday and Sunday) flights to Hong Kong.

Bus The bus situation in Kunming can be a little confusing at first. There seem to be buses leaving from all over the place. However, the long-distance bus station on Beijing Lu is the main centre of operations, and this is the best place to organise bus tickets to almost anywhere in Yunnan or further afield. Exceptions to this are more local destinations like Lake Dian.

The most popular bus routes from Kunming are Dali, Lijiang, Jinghong (in the Xishuangbanna Prefecture in the south) and the Dehong Prefecture (in the west). The long distances involved make sleeper buses a popular option. These have reclining seats or even double-tiered bunks in some cases. If you're looking at an overnight trip, they are definitely worth the extra cost. Very few travellers go straight from Kunming to Lijiang; it makes better sense to take a sleeper bus to Dali first and then move on to Lijiang.

Day buses direct to Dali leave between 7 and 9 am and cost around Y50. The trip takes around 11 hours. Most travellers opt for the sleepers, which generally leave from 6.30 to 8 pm and cost from Y75 to Y85. If you can't get on a bus to Dali (not likely), you can take a bus to Xiaguan, which is 30 minutes by public bus from Dali. There are numerous night buses to Xiaguan from 6.30 pm, and prices range from Y54 for a regular night bus to Y75 for a sleeper. For the 15-hour Lijiang trip, buses leave at 1 and 4 pm and prices range from Y81 to Y111 (sleeper).

The marathon trip to Jinghong in Xishuangbanna takes 24 to 28 hours, depending on the length of the numerous meal breaks and various unscheduled but inevitable stops. The trip used to include an overnight stop, but now nearly all buses drive straight through. Sleepers to Jinghong cost Y180 and leave at 2 pm. The travel agency next door to the Three Leaves Hotel has comfortable sleeper buses that can get you to Jinghong in 24 hours (or so they claim). Buses leave at 11 am and 4 pm and cost Y180. There are also day/night buses that cost Y90 and leave at around 7 to 8 am. These are marginally more comfortable than standard buses, with slightly more leg room and a 'better class' of

passenger (less spitting and chain-smoking). Others might want to try the cheaper day/night bus leaving at 7.30 am: 24 to 30 hours in a lightly cushioned seat (which may recline a bit if you're lucky) for Y80.

Both options for getting to the Dehong region involve long hauls, so it's worth considering doing at least one leg of the trip by air (to Mangshi). Sleeper buses leave for Baoshan from the long-distance bus station at 2.30, 4.30 and 6.30 pm and cost Y115. There is also a night bus for Y88. The journey takes around 18 bumpy hours. Buses direct to Ruili take even longer (30 hours): sleepers (Y171) leave at 9.40 am, between 2 and 3 pm and between 7 and 9 pm.

If you're headed to Vietnam, there are night buses to the border town of Hekou, leaving at 10 pm. The trip takes 14 hours and costs Y51. Before buying a ticket, check at the railway station: hard-sleeper train tickets to Hekou are relatively easy to get and would assure you of an infinitely more pleasant journey. Travellers looking to go overland to Laos have to go to Jinghong first, from where there are buses to Mengla, near the border crossing.

It is possible to travel by bus to several destinations in neighbouring provinces from the long-distance bus station. Sleeper buses to Guiyang (in Guizhou Province) leave at 1 pm, take around 20 hours and cost Y95. It is possible to break the trip by travelling first to Xingyi, an interesting town just over the border, and staying overnight there. Buses cost Y45, leave at 7 and 8.30 am and take about nine hours to get there. There's also a night bus leaving at 7.30 pm, but this puts you into Xingyi in the middle of the night.

Another interesting option is the bus service to Nanning in Guangxi Province. Limits seem to have been relaxed on foreigners travelling this route, so getting tickets should be no problem. There is one sleeper bus a day for Nanning (Y212), leaving at 1 pm. Roads are rough, so be prepared for at least 36 hours of bumps and halts. On the off chance you can't buy a ticket for Nanning, get a bus to Guangnan (Y51), a border town with onward connections to Nanning.

Finally, the long-distance station also has buses to the Stone Forest, and this is probably the best way to visit it. For more information see the Stone Forest section later in this chapter.

Train Rail options out of Kunming include Beijing, Chengdu, Chongqing, Guangzhou and Shanghai. You can also take a train down the narrow-gauge railway to the border crossing with Vietnam at Hekou. A new rail link with Nanning is currently under construction, though direct service is not expected to start for several years yet. This should dramatically cut travelling time between Yunnan and Guangxi and Guangdong provinces.

During peak season Kunming can become a real trap for railway travellers. Make a point of booking your tickets at least four days in advance. The No 12 window at the main railway station is the place to buy sleeper tickets. There is an advance booking office at 142 Xichang Lu (open from 8 to 11.30 am and 1.30 to 5 pm), but it only sells hard-seat tickets. The main station sells tickets from 6.30 pm for trains departing the next day, but these are a real rarity. Unless you can get your hands on a black-market ticket (there doesn't seem to be much of a market for them in Kunming), getting hold of a ticket at local prices is almost impossible.

The Kunming-Shanghai train (No 80) travels via Guiyang, Guilin, Zhuzhou, Nanchang and Hangzhou. The whole trip (3069 km) takes just over 60 hours. A foreigners' price hard sleeper for Guilin costs Y300, while onwards to Shanghai costs around Y560. For Beijing (No 62), via Guiyang, Changsha and Zhengzhou (3182 km), a hard sleeper will set you back Y570. For Chongqing (No 92), trains pass through Guiyang, taking around 24 hours; a hard sleeper costs Y250. Alternatively you might travel to Panzhihua (Jinjiang), from where the No 86/83 train leaves daily for Chongqing via Chengdu at 5.40 pm, though this is a much more round-about way of doing things. Guangzhou trains take 49 hours and cost

Y390 for a hard sleeper. A hard-sleeper train from Kunming to Guiyang (13-plus hours) costs Y160 (take the Beijing, Chongqing, Guangzhou or Shanghai trains, or the No 324, which leaves at 7.49 pm). Trains to Emei take 21 hours and cost Y220 for a hard sleeper; on the same route, trains to Chengdu (Nos 66 and 68) take around 24 hours and cost Y240.

The No 313 train to Hekou leaves from the north railway station (*huǒchē běi zhàn*) at 9.30 pm. The journey takes 17 hours and a hard-sleeper ticket should cost you around Y150. From Hekou, trains to Kunming leave at 2.45 pm.

Getting Around
Most of the major sights are within a 15-km radius of Kunming. Local transport to these places is awkward, crowded and time-consuming; it tends to be an out-and-back job, with few crossovers for combined touring. If you wish to take in everything, you'd be looking at something like five return trips, which would consume three days or more. You can simplify this by pushing Black Dragon Pool, Anning Hot Springs and the Golden Temple to the background, and concentrating on the trips of high interest – the Bamboo Temple and Western Hills, both of which have decent transport connections with special express buses in the mornings. Lake Dian presents some engrossing circular-tour possibilities on its own. Better yet, buy a map, hire a good bicycle and tour the area by bike (though there are some steep hills lurking out there...).

Bus The best option for getting out to the Bamboo Temple and the Western Hills is to head over to the Yunnan Hotel – buses and minibuses leave from in front of the hotel in the morning. Departure times depend on how fast the bus fills up: afternoon buses can sit around for hours.

Public buses run out to most of the other major sights. Options include No 10 to the Golden Temple and the No 9 to Black Dragon Pool, both from the north railway station; the No 44 from Kunming Railway

Station to Haigeng Park; and the No 4 from the Zoo to Daguan Park.

Bicycle Bikes are a fast way to get around town. Both the Kunming and Camellia hotels offer have a large selection (and both require large deposits of between Y200 and Y400!) The Kunhu also has a few bikes for rent, though they've seen better days.

AROUND KUNMING
Golden Temple
(jīndiàn)

This Taoist temple is perched amid a pine forest on Phoenix Song Mountain, 11 km north-east of Kunming. The original was carted off to Dali; the present one dates from the Ming Dynasty and was enlarged by General Wu Sangui, who was dispatched by the Manchus in 1659 to quell the uprisings in the region. Wu Sangui turned against the Manchus and set himself up as a rebel warlord, with the Golden Temple as his summer residence.

The pillars, ornate door frames, walls, fittings and roof tiles of the six-metre-high temple are all made of copper; the entire structure, laid on a white Dali marble foundation, is estimated to weigh more than 300 tonnes. In the courtyard are ancient camellia trees. At the back is a 14-tonne bronze bell, cast in 1423. The gardens around the temple offer secluded areas for picnicking. In the compound are teahouses and a noodle stand.

To get there, take bus No 10 from the Kunming's north railway station. Many travellers ride hired bikes to the temple – it's fairly level-going all the way to the base of the hill. Once you get there, you'll have to climb an easy hill path to the temple compound.

Black Dragon Pool
(hēilóng tán)

Eleven km north of Kunming is this uninspiring garden, with old cypresses, dull Taoist pavilions and no bubble in the springs. But the view of the surrounding mountains from the garden is inspiring. Within walking distance is the **Kunming Botanical Insti-**

tute, where the collection of flora might be of interest to specialists. Take the No 9 bus here from the north railway station.

Bamboo Temple
(qióngzhú sì)

Twelve km north-west of Kunming, this temple dates back to the Tang Dynasty. Burned down and rebuilt in the 15th century, it was restored from 1883 to 1890 when the abbot employed the master Sichuan sculptor Li Guangxiu and his apprentices to fashion 500 *luohan* (arhats or noble ones). These life-size clay figures are stunning – either

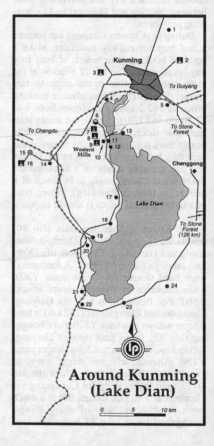

Around Kunming (Lake Dian)

very realistic or very surrealistic – a sculptural tour de force.

Down one huge wall come the incredible surfing buddhas, some 70-odd, riding the waves on a variety of mounts – blue dogs, giant crabs, shrimp, turtles, unicorns. One gentleman has metre-long eyebrows; another has an arm that shoots clear across the hall to the ceiling.

In the main section are housed row upon row of standing figures. The statues have been done with the precision of a split-second photograph – a monk about to chomp into a large peach (the face contorted almost into a scream), a figure caught turning around to emphasise a discussion point, another about to clap two cymbals together, yet another cursing a pet monster. The old, the sick, the emaciated – nothing is spared; the expressions of joy, anger, grief or boredom are extremely vivid.

So lifelike are the sculptures that they were considered in bad taste by Li Guangxiu's contemporaries (some of whom no doubt appeared in caricature), and upon the project's completion he disappeared into thin air. As for the bamboo of the temple's name, there was actually none on the grounds until very recently, when bamboo was transplanted from Chengdu. The main halls were restored in 1958 and again, extensively, in 1981.

By far the easiest way to get there is to take a bus from in front of the Yunnan Hotel. Buses run from 8 am to around 3 pm, leaving as soon as they are full. The ride takes 30 minutes and costs Y5.

Anning Hot Springs
(ānníng wēnquán)

Forty-four km south-west of Kunming, most travellers sensibly give this place a wide berth. The local tourist authorities proclaim (in their Chinese-language promotional material) the hot spring as 'No 1 under the heavens', but the hot spring and the surrounding area, which includes some Miao minority villages, are not particularly interesting. There are various hotels and guesthouses here that pipe the hot spring water into the rooms, but reports have it that couples are not accepted in some of them – this rule may have changed. Nearby, and possibly worth a look, is the **Caoxi Monastery**. It's over the river and a couple of km or so to the south in a bamboo grove on Cong Hill.

Buses to the springs run approximately hourly from the Xiaoximen bus station between 8 am and 6 pm. Returning, the last bus is at 5 pm.

Lake Dian
(diān chí)

The shoreline of Lake Dian, to the south of Kunming, is dotted with settlements, farms and fishing enterprises; the western side is hilly, while the eastern side is flat country. The southern end of the lake, particularly the south-east, is industrial, but other than that there are lots of possibilities for extended touring. The lake is an elongated one, about 150 km in circumference, about 40 km from north to south, and covering 300 sq km. Plying the waters are *fanchuan*, pirate-sized junks with bamboo-battened canvas sails. It's mainly an area for scenic touring and hiking, and there are some fabulous aerial views from the ridges up at Dragon Gate in the Western Hills.

Daguan Park
(dàguān gōngyuán)

Daguan, or Grand View, Park is at the northernmost tip of Lake Dian, three km south-west of the city centre. It dates back to 1682, when a Buddhist temple was constructed there. Shortly after, in 1690, work began on the park and the Daguan Tower. It covers 60 hectares and includes a nursery with potted plants, children's playground, rowing boats and pavilions. The **Daguan Tower** *(dàguān lóu)* provides good views of Lake Dian. Its façades are inscribed with a 180-character poem by Qing poet Sun Ranweng rapturously extolling the beauty of the lake. Bus No 4 runs to Daguan Park from Yuantong Temple via the city centre area.

At the north-eastern end of the park is a dock where you can get boats to Dragon Gate

Village and Haigeng Park. Boats leave when full and the 40-minute ride should cost Y5. From Dragon Gate Village you can hike up the trail to Dragon Gate and the Western Hills, and then catch a minibus back into town near the summit at the Tomb of Nie Er. From Haigeng, take the No 44 bus to Kunming's main railway station.

Western Hills
(xī shān)

The Western Hills spread out across a long wedge of parkland on the western side of Lake Dian; they're also known as the 'Sleeping Beauty Hills', a reference to their undulating contours, which are thought to resemble a reclining woman with tresses of hair flowing into the sea. The path up to the summit passes a series of famous temples – it's a steep approach from the north side. The hike from Gaoyao bus station at the foot of the Western Hills to Dragon Gate takes 2½ hours. If you're pushed for time, there's a connecting bus from Gaoyao to the top section, or you could take a minibus direct from in front of the Yunnan Hotel to Dragon Gate. Alternatively, it is also possible to cycle to the Western Hills in about an hour – to vary the trip, consider doing the return route across the dykes of upper Lake Dian.

At the foot of the climb, about 15 km from Kunming, is **Huating Temple** *(huátíng sì)*, a country temple of the Nanzhao kingdom believed to have been constructed in the 11th century, rebuilt in the 14th century, and extended in the Ming and Qing dynasties. The temple has some fine statues and excellent gardens. There is a Y10 entry fee.

The road from the Huating Temple winds from here up to the Ming Dynasty **Taihua Temple** *(tàihuá sì)*, again housing a fine collection of flowering trees in the courtyards, including magnolias and camellias. Entry here costs Y8.

Between the Taihua Temple and Sanqing Taoist Temple near the summit is the **Tomb of Nie Er** (1912-36) *(nièěr zhīmù)*, a talented Yunnan musician. Nie composed the national anthem of the PRC before drowning in Japan en route for further training in the

Soviet Union. From here you can catch a chairlift to the top (Y20), if you want to skip the fairly steep ascent to the summit. If you decide to visit the restaurant at the top, watch that you are not overcharged.

The **Sanqing Temple** (*sānqīng gé*) near the top of the mountain was a country villa for a prince of the Yuan Dynasty, and was later turned into a temple dedicated to the three main Taoist deities.

Further up is **Dragon Gate** (*lóngmén*), a group of grottoes, sculptures, corridors and pavilions hacked from the cliff between 1781 and 1835 by a Taoist monk and co-workers, who must have been hanging up there by their fingertips. At least that's what the locals do when they visit, seeking out the most precarious perches for views of Lake Dian. The tunnelling along the outer cliff edge is so narrow that only one or two people can squeeze by at a time, so avoid public holidays and weekends! Entry to the Dragon Gate area (which includes Sanqing Temple) costs Y20.

From Kunming to the Western Hills the most convenient mode of transport is by minibus. These leave from outside the Yunnan Hotel between 8 am and 1 pm, leaving as they fill up. The 30-minute ride costs Y4.

Alternatively, you can use the local bus service to get there: take bus No 5 from the Kunming Hotel to the terminus at Liangjiahe, and then change to bus No 6, which will take you to the Gaoyao bus station at the foot of the hills. Buses to the Kunming Steel Plant (*kūngāng*) also run past Gaoyao, and leave from in front of the Arts Cinema (near the Yunnan Hotel), or from Xiaoximen.

From the Western Hills to Kunming you can either take the bus or scramble down from the Dragon Gate area directly to the lakeside along a zigzag dirt path and steps that lead to Dragon Gate Village, also known as Shan Yi Village (*shānyìcūn*). When you reach the road, turn right and walk about 100 metres to a narrow spit of land which leads across the lake. Continuing across the land spit, you arrive at a narrow stretch of water and a small bridge. The opposite bank is one

giant construction zone and will eventually be the base for a cable car being built to link Haigeng with Dragon Gate. Proceed by foot through this area along the lakeside road that runs back to Haigeng Park, where you can catch the No 44 bus to the Kunming Railway Station.

The tour can easily be done in reverse; start with the No 44 bus to Haigeng Park, walk to Dragon Gate Village, climb straight up to Dragon Gate, then make your way down through the temples to the Gaoyao bus station, where you can get bus No 6 back to the Xiaoximen station. Alternatively, bus No 33 runs along the coast through Dragon Gate Village, or you can take a boat from Daguan Park.

Haigeng Park & Yunnan Nationalities Village
(*hǎigěng gōngyuán/yúnnán mínzúcūn*)

On the north-eastern side of the lake, the local tourist authorities have thrown together a string of model minority villages here with the aim of finally representing all 26 of Yunnan's minorities. It's a rather expensive cultural experience for the visitor, with a Y20 general entry fee and Y10 per village. There are also various song-and-dance performances throughout the day, some of which also cost extra. As for the villages, while they show you what the minorities' architecture and costumes look like, it's impossible to get any feel for how these people really live. Add in the hordes of gawking tourists, and the place feels a bit more like a zoo. If you're at all averse to tourist-board fabrications of ethnic cultures, give the place a miss and spend an extra day in Xishuangbanna or Dehong, where you can see the real thing.

However, with the advent of the Nationalities Village, what little remains of Haigeng Park – a narrow strip of greenery along the lakefront – has become a good place to escape the crowds and enjoy the scenery. The roller coaster is covered with weeds, and most of the lakefront restaurants are shuttered, giving the place a ghost town feel. There are great views of the lake and the Western Hills, and plenty of spots to kick back, read a book or have a picnic. And when you're ready, you can tackle the hike up to Dragon Gate.

Bus No 44 runs to Haigeng Lu from one street north of the Kunming Railway Station.

Zheng He Park
(zhènghé gōngyuán)

At the south-east corner of the lake, this park commemorates the Ming Dynasty navigator Zheng He (known as Admiral Cheng Ho throughout most of the world). A mausoleum here holds tablets describing his life and works. Zheng He, a Muslim, made seven voyages to over 30 Asian and African countries in the 15th century in command of a huge imperial fleet (for details, see the section on the town of Quanzhou in Fujian Province).

From the Xiaoximen station take the bus to Kunyang: the park is on a hill overlooking the town. Or for a change of pace, take a train from the north railway station to Haikou, and then a local bus to Kunyang. You can complete a full circuit by catching a bus onto Jincheng and Chenggong. There's also accommodation in Kunyang for around Y20 per bed if you feel like moving at a more relaxed pace.

Jinning County
(jìnníng xiàn)

This is the site of archaeological discoveries from early Kunming, and you'll find it at the southern end of the lake. Bronze vessels, a gold seal and other artefacts were unearthed at **Stone Hill**, and some items are displayed at the Provincial Museum in Kunming. The bus to Kunyang runs via Jincheng to Jinning.

Chenggong County
(chénggòng xiàn)

This is an orchard region on the eastern side of the lake. Climate has a lot to do with Kunming's reputation as the florist of China. Flowers bloom all year round, with the 'flower tide' in January, February and March which is the best time to visit. Camellias, azaleas, magnolias and orchids are not usually associated with China by Westerners although many of the Western varieties derive from south-west China varieties. They were introduced to the West by adventuring botanists who carted off samples in the 19th and 20th centuries. Azaleas are native to China – of the 800 varieties in the world, 650 are found in Yunnan. During the Spring Festival (February/March) a profusion of blooming species can be found at temple sites around Kunming – notably the Taihua, Huating and Golden temples, as well as Black Dragon Pool and Yuantong Hill.

Take the No 5 bus east to the terminus at Juhuacun, and change there for the No 12 bus to Chenggong.

STONE FOREST
(shílín)

The Stone Forest, around 120 km south-east of Kunming, is a massive collection of grey limestone pillars, split by rain water and eroded to their present fanciful forms, the tallest standing 30 metres high. Marine fossils found in the area suggest that it was once under the sea. Legend has it that the immortals smashed a mountain into a labyrinth for lovers seeking some privacy and picnicking Chinese couples take heed of this myth (it can get busy in there!).

The maze of grey pinnacles and peaks, with the odd pool, is treated as an oversized rockery, with a walkway here, a pavilion there, some railings along paths and, if you look more closely, some mind-bending weeds. The larger formations have titles like Baby Elephant, Everlasting Fungus, Baby Buffalo, Moon-Gazing Rhino, Sword Pond. The maze is cooler and quieter by moonlight, and would enthral a surrealist painter.

There are actually several stone forests in the region – the section open to foreign tourists covers 80 hectares. Twelve km to the north-east is a larger (300-hectare) rock series called Fungi Forest, with karst caves and a large waterfall.

The Stone Forest is basically a Chinese tourist attraction and some Westerners find it grossly overrated on the scale of geographical wonders. The important thing, if you venture there, is to get away from the main tourist area – within a couple of km of the centre are some idyllic, secluded walks.

The villages in the Lunan County vicinity are inhabited by the Sani branch of the Yi tribespeople. Considering that so many other 'ethnic' areas of Yunnan are now open, you could be disappointed if you make the trip just to see the Sani branch of the Yi tribespeople who live in this area. Their craftwork (embroidery, purses, footwear) is sold at stalls by the entrance to the forest, and Sani women act as tour guides for groups. Off to the side is Five-Tree Village, which is an easy walk and has the flavour of a Mexican pueblo, but the tribespeople have been somewhat influenced by commercialism. For those keen on genuine village and farming life, well, the Stone Forest is a big place – you can easily get lost. Just take your butterfly net and a lunch box along and keep walking – you'll get somewhere eventually.

There is a Y33 entry fee for foreigners into the main Stone Forest.

Activities

The Shilin and Yunlin hotels put on Sani song-and-dance evenings when there are enough tourists around. Surprisingly, these events turn into good-natured exchanges between Homo Ektachromo and Sani Dollari, and neither comes off the worse for wear. The short performances display ethnic costumes and musical instruments. The hotels usually charge a fee of around Y25 for the performances, which start around 7.30 to 8 pm. The Torch Festival (wrestling, bullfighting, singing and dancing) takes place on 24 June at a natural outdoor amphitheatre by Hidden Lake.

Places to Stay

The *Shilin Hotel* (*shílín bīnguǎn*), near the main entrance to the Stone Forest, is a villa-type place with a souvenir shop and dining hall. A double room costs Y250 (Y200 in the off season, whenever that is), and triples are Y300. Before you despair, wait: there's a 'Common Room Department' (*pǔtōng kèfáng*) at the rear section of the hotel compound, with dormitory accommodation for Y30 per bed. It's on the other side of the hill, across from a restaurant and a couple of souvenir shops.

Rates are a bit cheaper at the *Yunlin Hotel* (*yúnlín fàndiàn*), which is a little less than a km down the road that forks to the right after you cross the bridge. In addition to Y150 doubles and Y200 triples, the Yunlin has one concrete cell with four soft beds for Y20 per person.

Near the bus terminal are several smaller hotels with basic rooms for Y20 to Y30 per person: these have similar bathing facilities to the dorm rooms at the Shilin and Yunlin but are not as clean. They may or may not accept foreign guests.

Places to Eat

Several restaurants next to the bus terminal specialise in duck roasted in extremely hot clay ovens with pine needles. A whole duck costs Y40 to Y50 and takes about 20 minutes to cook – have the restaurant staff put a beer in their freezer and it'll be just right when the duck comes out. The ducks are massaged with a local sesame oil mixture before roasting.

Near the main Stone Forest entrance is a cluster of food vendors that purvey a variety of pastries and noodles from dawn to dusk. The *Shilin Hotel* and *Yunlin Hotel* offer fixed-price meals that aren't bad. Western breakfasts are available at either hotel.

Getting There & Away

There is a variety of options for getting to the Stone Forest. Your fastest options might be a minibus from the Camellia Hotel: one group of travellers made it there nonstop in two hair-raising hours. In most cases the trip takes around three hours one way – much longer going there if you sign on with a tour bus. If you're feeling adventurous, you can a try a bus/train/hitchhiking combination.

It's best to take an overnight stop in the forest for further exploration, though if you're just looking at the forest itself then a day-trip will do.

Bus The best way to get to the Stone Forest is to head down to the long-distance bus station in Kunming and buy a one-way ticket for Y18.50. There are four buses leaving between 7.30 and 8.30 am.

The Kunming Hotel and Three Leaves Hotel sell tickets for tour buses to Shilin for Y20, but if you take this option you'll be stuck with a tour that takes in at least three caves en route (complete with special foreigner entry fees); once you've pigged out on the obligatory lunch, you'll be lucky to have had two hours wandering around the forest. It's much better to buy the tickets at the long-distance bus station and leave yourself the option of staying overnight or returning the same day, as you please.

At the time of writing the Camellia Hotel was running a minibus that went straight to the Stone Forest, skipping the caves and other nonsense. Check to see if this service is still operating: if so, it's your fastest way there.

Getting back from the Stone Forest to Kunming is fairly simple. There are usually minibuses waiting along the road outside the entrance, and once they're full, they tend to go straight back to Kunming. There are also local buses leaving at 7 am and between 2.30 and 3.30 pm, but these can be cancelled if they don't look like filling up. You could also try hitching back to Kunming from the Stone Forest.

Bus & Train The old French narrow-gauge line that runs all the way from Kunming to Hanoi (Chinese trains now terminate at Hekou near the Vietnamese border) is an interesting alternative way of getting to Shilin. Trains bound for Kaiyuan stop at the town of Yiliang, which is only 45 minutes by bus from Shilin. Stations along the way sport steep roofs and painted shutters in the French style. Train Nos 311 and 313 travel by night, arriving at 11.30 pm and 1 am respectively. A more sensible option is the No 501, which leaves at 8.30 am from the Kunming's north railway station, pulling into Yiliang at 11 am. Buses from Yiliang are infrequent (be prepared for a wait of a couple of hours), and

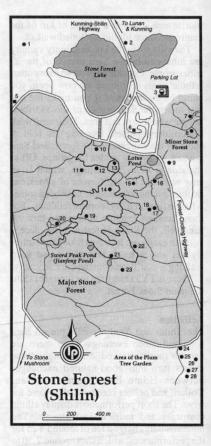

Stone Forest (Shilin)

0   200   400 m

often only go as far as Lunan, from where you will have to hitch to Shilin.

There are plans to open the line all the way to Hanoi before 1997, and with the consequent increased traffic this may become a more viable route.

LUNAN
(lùnán)
Lunan is a small market town about 10 km from the Stone Forest. It's not worth making a special effort to visit, but if you do go, try and catch a market day (Wednesday or Saturday), when Lunan becomes a colossal jam

STONE FOREST (SHILIN)
石林

1 Five-Tree Village
五木村
2 Truck Stop
卡车站
3 Bus Departures
汽车站
4 Local Handicraft Stalls
工艺摊
5 Yunlin Hotel
云林宾馆
6 Shilin Hotel & CITS
石林宾馆,
中国国际旅行社
7 Inscription of Mao
Zedong's poem `Ode to
the Plum Blossom'
泳梅石
8 Rock Arrowhead Point
to the Sky
石簇擎天

9 Figure of Monk Tanseng
唐僧石
10 Lion Pond
狮子池
11 Sweet Water Well
甜水井
12 Stone Buffalo
小水牛
13 Stone Screen
石屏风
14 Open Stage
舞场
15 Resting Peak for Wild
Geese
落雁峰
16 Stone Prison
石监狱
17 Phoenix Combing Its
Wings
凤凰梳翅
18 Stone Mushroom
灵芝石
19 Steps to the Sky
笋天阶

20 Lotus Peak
莲花峰
21 Two Birds Feeding
Each Other
双鸟渡食
22 Stone Bell
石钟
23 Rhinoceros Looking
at the Moon
犀牛望月
24 Wife Waiting for Her
Husband
望夫石
25 Goddess of Mercy
观音石
26 Camel Riding on an
Elephant
骆驼骑象
27 Swan Gazing Afar
天鹅远嘱
28 Old Man Taking
a Stroll
漫步从容

of donkeys, horse carts and bicycles. The streets are packed with produce, poultry and wares, and Sani women are dressed in their finest.

To get to Lunan from the Stone Forest, head back towards Kunming and turn left at the first major crossroads, then go straight on at the second crossroads but veering to the right. You'll have to hitch a truck or hire a three-wheeler (Y5 to Y10 or some foreign cigarettes for a 20-minute ride). Plenty of trucks head that way on market day, some from the parking lot near the forest.

XIAGUAN
(xiàguān)

Xiaguan lies at the southern tip of Erhai Lake, about 400 km west of Kunming. It was once an important staging post on the Burma Road and is still a key centre for transport in north-west Yunnan. Xiaguan is the capital of Dali Prefecture and is also referred to as Dali City (dàlǐ shì). This confuses some travellers, who think they are already in Dali, book into a hotel and head off in pursuit of a

banana pancake only to discover they haven't arrived yet. Nobody stays in Xiaguan unless they have an early bus the next morning. Upon arriving, turn left out of the long-distance bus station, and at the first intersection make a left. Just up from the corner, diagonally opposite the Dali Hotel, is the station for the No 4 local bus, which runs to the real Dali. Ignore the big sign telling you to wait at the street corner, and walk up to where the buses are. If you want to be sure, ask for dàlǐ gùchéng (Dali Old City). The trip takes 30 minutes and costs Y1.20.

Things to See

Xiaguan has developed into an industrial city specialising in tea processing, cigarette making and the production of textiles and chemicals. There is little to keep you here other than transport connections.

There are good views of the lake and mountains from **Erhai Park** (érhǎi gōngyuán). You can reach the park on foot or by motor-tricycle for around Y3. Local travel agents around the bus station also sell tickets for day-trips up and down Erhai Lake, taking in all the major sights. Prices for the all-day tours range from Y60 to Y80.

Places to Stay

Some travellers end up staying a night in Xiaguan in order to catch an early-morning bus from the long-distance bus station. If this is the case, there are three hotels close to the bus station, all much the same.

Right next to the bus station is the *Keyun Hotel (kèyùn fàndiàn)*. It has four-bed dorms for Y19 a bed, triples for Y24 a bed and doubles for Y38. Singles cost Y50. More upmarket singles/doubles with attached bathroom are also available at Y130. Turn left after you exit the bus station and on the far corner of the first left is the *Dali Hotel (dàlǐ fàndiàn)*, which is the cheapest of the three. Four-bed dorms cost Y10 a bed, while singles/doubles are Y25/36. Diagonally opposite (back towards the long-distance bus station) is the *Xiaguan Hotel (xiàguān bīn-guǎn)*, the most upmarket of the three. Basic triples are available for Y30 per bed and doubles with bathroom are Y190.

Those seeking luxury need go no further than across the street and to the right of the bus station to the *Jinpeng Hotel (jīnpéng dàjiǔdiàn)*. The hotel had not yet opened at the time of writing, but was expected to offer air-con doubles with TV, direct-dial long-distance telephone and satellite TV, for a price of around Y400 to Y500. Perhaps not coincidentally, the hotel's opening date matched that of Xiaguan's new airport.

Getting There & Away

At the time of writing Xiaguan's new airport was scheduled to open in late 1995. CAAC staff seemed pretty much in the dark regarding scheduling, but at the start there will probably only be three to four flights per week. The one-way fare from Kunming will be around Y400. A railway link with Kunming is also under construction. Xiaguan should fare well, but it remains to be seen how the small town of Dali will cope with the ensuing deluge of visitors.

Unless you're making for one of the typical traveller's destinations (ie Kunming or Lijiang), you'll probably have to head into the Xiaguan long-distance bus station to organise your onward transport. There's really no point in coming here to organise a bus ticket for Kunming as there are services available from Dali itself, but for the record buses leave from 7 to 7.30 am and 7 to 8.30 pm. Prices range from Y40 for a creaking, bone-jarring ordinary bus to Y75 for a sleeper with two-tiered bunks.

Other bus options include Baoshan for Y20 (six hours; buses leave at 7.30 and 10.30 am, noon and 6 pm) and Mangshi (Luxi) for Y45 (12 hours; buses leave at 7 and 8 am; the latter is a sleeper for Y75). The Mangshi buses continue on to Ruili, for a total travel time of around 15 hours. Consider breaking the journey up by staying overnight in Baoshan.

Buses for Lijiang leave at 7, 8 and 10.30 am (these stop in Dali to pick up passengers, and tickets can also be booked in Dali). There is also one bus a day to Zhongdian, leaving at 6.30 am. The ride takes 10 hours and costs Y32. But if you're headed in this direction, it would make far more sense to head to Lijiang first and rest up there for a couple of days.

For the interesting possibility of buses from Xiaguan to Xishuangbanna, you can try getting a 6.30 am bus to Jingdong, where there are onward buses that should put you into Jinghong the following night. Roads are very bad along this route, and travel times have been known to stretch to three or four days. Staff at the long-distance bus station seemed reluctant to sell tickets to foreigners for this trip, but the situation looks likely to ease up. PSB staff in Dali didn't seem to even know whether this route was open, redirecting our queries to the bus station. If you still can't wangle a ticket here, you may want to try the Baoshan-Jinghong route, which overnights in Lincang, a city included on the PSB's latest list of open municipalities and counties.

For Mt Jizu, buses run to Binchuan at 8 am, take around two hours and cost Y10.

AROUND XIAGUAN

All of Dali Prefecture is open nowadays, so you shouldn't have any problems with nasty PSB officials if you wander off the beaten track. The chief attraction for travellers is Mt Jizu, an ancient Buddhist pilgrimage site.

Mt Jizu

(jīzú shān)

Mt Jizu (or to translate its Chinese name, Chicken-Foot Mountain) is one of China's sacred mountains and a major attraction for Buddhist pilgrims, both Chinese and Tibetan. At the time of the Qing Dynasty there were approximately 100 temples on the mountain and somewhere in the vicinity of 5000 resident monks. The Cultural Revolution's anarchic assault on the traditional past did away with much that was of interest on the mountain, though renovation work on the temples has been going on since 1979. Today, it's estimated that more than 150,000 tourists and pilgrims clamber up the mountain every year to watch the sunrise. Jinding, or the Golden Summit, is at a cool 3240 metres so you will need some warm clothing.

Sights along the way include the **Zhusheng Temple** *(zhùshèng sì)*, about an hour's walk up from the bus stop at Shazhi. This is the most important temple on the mountain. **Zhongshan Temple** *(zhōngshān sì)*, about halfway up the mountain, is a fairly recent construction and holds little of interest. Just before the last ascent is the **Huashou Gate** *(huáshǒu mén)*. At the summit is the **Lengyan Pagoda**, a 13-tier Tang Dynasty pagoda that was restored in 1927, and some basic accommodation at the **Jinding Temple** next to the pagoda – a sleeping bag might be a good idea at this altitude.

To reach Mt Jizu from Xiaguan you should first take a bus to Binchuan, which is 70 km east of Xiaguan. Buses leave at 8 am from the long-distance bus station. From Binchuan take another bus or minibus to the foot of mountain. If you turn up in Binchuan, the locals will probably guess your destination. If you should need to overnight in Binchuan, there are a few hotels around with dorm beds for as low as Y5.

Accommodation is available at the base of the mountain, about halfway up and on the summit. Prices average Y10 to Y15 per bed. Food gets fairly expensive once you reach the summit so you may want to bring some of your own. A popular option for making the ascent is to hire a pony. The ponies were originally used to carry supplies up until a local hit on the idea of hiring them out to the big noses with the bulging wallets. Travellers who have done the trip claim it's a lot of fun. A cable car to the summit was also scheduled to open by early 1996.

Some travellers have hiked from Wase on the eastern shore of Erhai Lake to Mt Jizu. It is certainly a possibility, but it isn't recommended, and should only be undertaken by experienced hikers. Locals in Dali claim that it is easy to get lost in the mountainous terrain and in bad weather the hike could turn into a bad experience. Take care, and talk to locals in Dali about your plans before you go.

Weishan

(wēishān)

Weishan is famous for the Taoist temples on nearby Mt Weibao *(wēibǎo shān)*. There are reportedly some fine Taoist murals here. It's 61 km due south of Xiaguan, so it could be done as a day-trip.

Yongping

(yǒngpíng)

Yongping is 103 km south-west of Xiaguan on the old Burma Road. The Jinguang Monastery *(jīnguāng sì)* is the attraction here.

DALI

(dàlǐ)

Dali is a perfect place to tune out for a while and forget about trains, planes and bonejarring buses. The stunning mountain backdrop, Erhai Lake, the old city, cappuccinos, pizzas and the herbal alternative (you can pick it yourself) to cheap Chinese beer make it, alongside Yangshuo, one of the few places in China where you can well and truly take a vacation from travelling.

Dali lies on the western edge of Erhai Lake

THE SOUTH-WEST

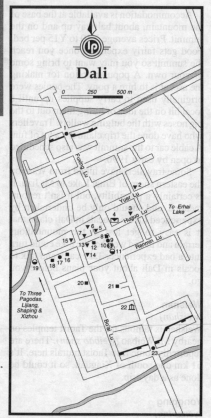

Dali

0   250   500 m

Fuxing Lu

Yuer Lu

Huguo Lu

To Erhai
Lake

Renmin Lu

Bo'ai Lu

To Three
Pagodas,
Lijiang,
Shaping &
Xizhou

DALI 大理

PLACES TO STAY

8 Jinhua Hotel
 金花大酒店
12 No 2 Guesthouse
 第二 招待所
16 No 3 Guesthouse (Sunny Garden)
 第三招待所 (桑尼园)
18 No 4 Guesthouse (Yu'an Garden)
 第四招待所 (榆安园)
20 Old Dali Inn
 大理四季客栈
21 Dali Hotel
 大理宾馆

PLACES TO EAT

2 Apricot Flower Restaurant
 李花餐厅
3 Yunnan Cafe
 云南 咖啡馆
5 Tibetan Cafe
 西藏餐厅
6 Jim's Peace Cafe
 吉母和平饭店
7 Old Wooden House
 如意饭店
13 Marley's Cafe
14 Cafe de Jack
 樱花阁
15 Happy Cafe

OTHER

1 North Gate
 北门
4 Post Office
 邮电局
9 Dali Prefecture Transport Co
 Ticket Office
 长途客车售票处
10 Bank of China
 中国银行
11 Buses to Xiaguan
 往下关的公共汽车
17 PSB
 公安局
19 Local Buses to Shaping
 往沙平的公共汽车
22 Dali Museum
 大理博物馆
23 South Gate
 南门

---

at an altitude of 1900 metres, with the imposing Cangshan Mountain range (average 4000 metres) behind it. For much of the five centuries in which Yunnan governed its own affairs, Dali was the centre of operations, and the old city still retains a historical atmosphere that is hard to come by in other parts of China. Certainly the area has become a Mecca for travellers, but it's easy enough to escape the crowds on the narrow backstreets lined with old stone houses.

The main inhabitants of the region are the Bai, who number about 1½ million, according to a 1990 census. The Bai people have long-established roots in the Erhai Lake region, being thought to have settled the area some 3000 years ago. In the early 8th century they grouped together and succeeded in defeating the Tang imperial army, establishing the Nanzhao kingdom. The kingdom held power, exerting considerable influence throughout south-west China and even, to a lesser degree, south-east Asia (the kingdom controlled upper Burma for much of the 9th century), through to the mid-13th century when it fell before the undefeatable Mongol hordes of Kublai Khan. It was this event that brought Yunnan back into the imperial Chinese ambit.

Orientation

Dali is a midget-sized city which has preserved some cobbled streets and traditional stone architecture within its old walls. Unless you are in a mad hurry (in which case use a bike), you can get your bearings just by taking a walk for an hour or so. It takes about half an hour to walk from the South Gate across town to the North Gate. Many of the sights around Dali couldn't be considered stunning on their own, but they do provide a destination towards which you can happily dawdle even if you don't arrive. Huguo Lu is the main strip for cafes – locals call it 'foreigner's street' (*yángrén jiē*) – and this is where to turn for your café latté, burritos, ice-cold beer and other treats.

Maps of Dali and the Erhai Lake area are available at street stalls near the corner of Huguo Lu and Fuxing Lu.

Information

PSB The office is between the No 3 and No 4 guesthouses on Huguo Lu. Previous goodwill has been overtaxed by some travellers, so this is no longer the place to get a second or third visa extension.

Money The Bank of China is in the centre of town, near the corner of Huguo Lu and Fuxing Lu. The bank generally will only change money Monday to Friday – this is

probably one of the few reasons you would want to keep track of what day it is in Dali.

Post & Telecommunications The post office is at the corner of Fuxing Lu and Huguo Lu. This is the best place to make international calls, as it has direct dial and doesn't levy a service charge.

Dali Museum
(*dàlǐ bówùguǎn*)

This small collection of archaeological pieces relating to Bai history is nothing to get particularly excited about, but is certainly worth a browse in between coffees or fruit shakes on Huguo Lu. There's an interesting permanent art exhibition at the back of the museum, featuring various artists who have leapt onto the Yunnan school of art bandwagon. The museum is open from 8.30 am to 5 pm and admission is Y1.

Three Pagodas
(*sān tǎsì*)

Standing on the hillside behind Dali, the pagodas look pretty, particularly when seen reflected in the nearby lake. They are, in fact, among the oldest standing structures in south-western China. The tallest of the three, Qianxun Pagoda, has 16 tiers that reach a height of 70 metres. It was originally erected in the mid-9th century by Xi'an engineers. It is flanked by two smaller pagodas that are 10-tiered and each measure 42 metres high.

The temple behind the pagodas, **Chongsheng Temple**, is laid out in the traditional Yunnanese style, with three layers of buildings lined up with a sacred peak in the background. The temple has been recently restored and converted into a museum that chronicles the history, construction and renovation of the pagodas. Also on exhibit are marble slabs that have been cut and framed so that the patterns of the marble appear to depict landscapes.

Many travellers find the pagodas more impressive from a distance. Up close there's not all that much to see except for a seemingly endless row of souvenir and trinket stands.

Festivals

If you don't mind crowds, probably the best time to be in Dali is during the Third Moon Fair *(sānyùe jíe)*, which begins on the 15th day of the third lunar month (usually April) and ends on the 21st day. The origins of the fair lie in its commemoration of a fabled visit by Guanyin, the Buddhist goddess of mercy, to the Nanzhao kingdom. Today it's more like an extra festive market, with people from all over Yunnan arriving to buy, sell and make merry.

The Three Temples Festival *(ràosānlíng)* is held between the 23rd and 25th days of the fourth lunar month (usually May). The name of the festival refers to making a tour of three temples and this is basically what the participants do. The first day involves a walk from Dali's South Gate to the Xizhou Shengyuan Temple at the foot of Mt Wutai. Here the walkers stay up until dawn, dancing and singing, before moving on to Jingui Temple at the shore of the Erhai Lake. The final day involves walking back to Dali by way of Majiuyi Temple.

The Torch Festival *(huǒbǎ jíe)* is held on the 24th day of the sixth lunar month (usually July). Flaming torches are paraded at night through homes and fields. Other events include fireworks displays and dragon-boat racing.

Places to Stay

The addition of several new, low-budget hotels has greatly improved the accommodation situation in Dali. Even so, places tend to fill up quickly, and those visiting during the peak summer months may find themselves trekking around town in search of a bed on their first day.

The most popular pick with travellers is the *No 4 Guesthouse*, also known as the *Yu'an Garden (yú'ān yuán)*. Perched at the top of Huguo Lu, this idyllic little spot has it all – bamboo pavilions, 24-hour hot water, a lovely Thai-style cafe, washing machines, a score of laundry lines, friendly staff, and dorm beds for Y15. Doubles are also available for Y25 per bed, but these tend to suffer from poor ventilation. The only problem

with the No 4 is that it always seem to be full, and it may take a day or two on the waiting list before you secure a spot.

Don't despair, there are other options, none of them terrible. Just down from the No 4 Guesthouse, the friendly *No 3 Guesthouse*, or *Sunny Garden (sāngní yuán)* as it's also called, is obviously modelled along the lines of its successful neighbour. Unfortunately, the hotel is crammed into an area about half the size of the No 4, which gives some travellers a touch of claustrophobia. When we visited, the management was also fairly chaotic, though this should improve with time (and practice). Beds in six or seven-bed dorms are Y12, singles/doubles Y30/40.

Closest to all the action on Huguo Lu, the *No 2 Guesthouse (dìer zhāodàisuǒ)* has long been Dali's old stand-by. Though a bit lacking in charm, it's actually not a bad place to stay, especially if you get a room on the 2nd or 3rd floor of the old wing. First-floor rooms tend to be damp and dark. Beds in doubles/triples with common washroom are Y16. Singles are Y32. There are also doubles with attached bath in the old wing for Y90, but these are mostly on the 1st floor, and not really worth the money. Hot water is available from 8 pm until around midnight, and sometimes, if you're lucky, there may even be some left over in the morning. The No 2 also has standard doubles, with 24-hour hot water, in the new building for Y180.

The *Dali Hotel (dàlǐ bīnguǎn)* is a bit further away, on Fuxing Lu, but the exercise of walking the 10 minutes or so to Huguo Lu may give you the illusion of having earned your banana pancake. It has beds in triples for Y35 – not great value, but an acceptable option if all the other places are booked up. Basic doubles with attached bath go for Y105, while standard doubles with all the mod cons are Y230.

Sticking out like a sore thumb at the corner of Huguo Lu and Fuxing Lu, the newly opened *Jinhua Hotel (jínhuā dàjiǔdiàn)* probably won't see much in the way of backpacker traffic. Standard doubles with air-con, satellite TV and all the rest, start at Y245. Sporting red-capped doormen and a marble staircase, the Jinhua definitely seems out of sync with the rest of Dali. But if you're in the mood for luxury, or are toting the kids around, this might be a good choice.

Welcome relief to Dali's cheap bed shortage may come from *The Old Dali Inn (dàlǐ sìjìkèzhàn)*, a delightful little place hidden away up Bo'ai Lu. When we last visited, the hotel was waiting for approval to take foreign guests, and the management was quite anxious to do so (all the signs already had English translations). Beds in four-bed dorms are Y10, and comfortable doubles with bath are Y120, and all rooms are housed in classic Dali-style stone buildings grouped around a flower-laden courtyard. It's definitely worth stopping by to check if the hotel has successfully parted the sea of red tape to enter the foreign travellers' market.

Dali is also getting its own five-star hotel, an enormous luxury monster that is thankfully parked several km south of town. A China-Taiwan joint venture, it stands out clearly against the mountain backdrop when viewed from the lake, and should be open by the time you read this. Though poorly located for those who want to be in the heart of Dali's street life, the hotel will probably do well from the hordes of tour groups that will start flying in to Xiaguan's new airport for blitzkrieg tours of the Erhai Lake region.

Places to Eat

The top section of Huguo Lu, clustered around the entrance to the No 2 Guesthouse, is where most of the travellers' hang-outs are. Most of them are good value for money, and have good food and pleasant staff, all of which are a welcome relief if you've been on the road for a while. If you're a misanthropic type and want to avoid the other travellers, you can eat with the locals in any number of Chinese restaurants around town.

It's difficult to make recommendations – as in Yangshuo, restaurants wax and wane in popularity for all kinds of reasons. One place that seems certain to keep drawing a steady crowd is the *Yunnan Cafe*, about five minutes' walk down Huguo Lu. Formerly called the Coca Cola Restaurant (until the long arm of Coca-Cola Inc sniffed out the use of its name and dispatched warnings to Dali), it still serves the best pizzas, Mexican food, desserts and coffee in town. Travellers routinely plant themselves on the rooftop sun deck until the night-time chill or closing time drives them away. The cafe also has a book exchange and rental service (the sale prices are high to discourage people from buying the books and exhausting the library – a point that seems too complex for some travellers to grasp). Xiangxia, who runs the place, is a fluent English speaker and a mine of useful information on Dali. And if you're looking to soothe travel-weary muscles, Dr Mu Qingyun gives incredible massages from his office on the 2nd floor.

Other favourites when we were in town last were the *Tibetan Cafe*, which serves a fine iced coffee; *Cafe de Jack*, known for its amazing chocolate cake with ice cream; and *Marley's Cafe*, which draws the afternoon crowd (the seats outside get the sun). The *Old Wooden House*, across from Marley's, has good outside seating and its bolognaise is definitely worth trying – a roving Italian gave them the recipe. For an interesting afternoon of conversation, you can try *Mr China's Son*, a cafe opened by an old gentleman who has penned an English-language account of his trials and tribulations during the Cultural Revolution.

Basically, it's a good idea to move around a bit and share your patronage. Most of the cafes have decent food and they all try hard to please. If you're a fan of Japanese food, try the *Happy Cafe* next door to the Tibetan Cafe – it serves the Japanese travellers' market and is a good place to meet wandering souls from Tokyo, Osaka and so on. True party-goers should head to *Jim's Peace Cafe* for rock and roll and late-night sessions. Jim is part-Tibetan, a very cool guy, and mixes up some potent concoctions – look out for his No 1 Special.

Things to Buy

Dali is famous for its marble, and while a slab of the stuff in your backpack might slow you down a bit, local entrepreneurs produce everything from ashtrays to model pagodas in small enough chunks to make it feasible to stow one or two away in your pack.

Huguo Lu has become a mini Khao San Rd in its profusion of clothes shops. It won't take you long to decide whether the clothes are for you or not – you could outfit yourself for a time-machine jaunt back to Woodstock here but bear in mind that the shopkeepers can also make clothes to your specifications, so you're not necessarily just stuck with the ready-made hippie stuff. Prices are very reasonable.

Most of the 'silver' jewellery sold in Dali is really brass. Occasionally it actually is silver, though this will be reflected in the starting price. The only advice worth giving, if you're in the market for this kind of thing, is to bargain hard.

Batik wall hangings have become popular in Dali. Several places near the No 2 Guesthouse on Huguo Lu have a good collection, but don't believe the proprietors when they tell you they make the stuff themselves and start justifying the extortionate prices they charge by telling how many hours they worked on a piece. Most of the batik, as in Yangshuo, comes from Guizhou where it can be bought for a song. Check with cafe owners and other locals about prices before you set out shopping.

Getting There & Away

The opening of Xiaguan's new airport will bring Dali to within 45 minutes' flying time from Kunming. Flights are initially expected to only run three to four times per week, but will probably pick up as tourists become aware of the new air route. The one-way fare should be around Y400.

Many travellers will probably still opt for the overnight sleeper bus service from Kunming. Sleepers direct to Dali leave from Kunming's long-distance bus station at 6.30 and 8 pm, take around 11 hours and cost Y75 to Y85, depending on the bus and whether you take an upper or lower berth. Though the road gets a bit bumpy, this is altogether not a bad ride, and you usually will meet fellow

travellers to share any mild misery you may feel. The long-distance bus station also has sleepers to Xiaguan leaving half-hourly from 6.30 to 9 pm.

If you want to catch the scenery, there are several day buses direct to Dali leaving between 7.30 and 9 am for Y45 and Y56, the latter being for 'luxury coaches' – don't take this too literally.

Back to Kunming, there are at least two sleeper buses nightly between 6 and 8 pm leaving from in front of the No 2 Guesthouse. Tickets are sold at the Dali Prefecture Transport Co booking office near the corner of Huguo Lu and Fuxing Lu, and from several travel agencies along Huguo Lu. Day buses to Kunming leave at 6.20 and 8 am, and cost Y45.

Buses to Lijiang leave at 7.20 and 11 am. Tickets for the five-hour trip cost Y20 (Y25 for minibuses) and can be bought from the Dali Prefecture Transport Co. You can also catch any one of numerous buses to Lijiang that originate in Xiaguan. Some of the independent travel agencies also sell tickets to Lijiang.

To catch buses to other points, such as Baoshan, Ruili or Jinghong, you have to go to Xiaguan. Tickets for most of these routes can be bought in Dali. If you buy your ticket at the Dali Prefecture Transport Co they will let you ride the 6.20 am Kunming bus down to Xiaguan to make your connection, though if you're catching a very early bus you'll probably have to stay in Xiaguan the night before anyway.

The No 4 local bus to Xiaguan runs every 10 minutes, and there's a stop right in front of the Bank of China. The trip takes around 30 minutes and costs Y1.20.

Getting Around

Bikes are the best way to get around. Prices average Y4 per day for standard Chinese models, Y8 for mountain bikes. The No 2 Guesthouse and Jim's Peace Cafe have the largest selection of bikes for hire – an important consideration if you're doing some long-distance cycling and you need to find a good bike.

Numerous travel agencies near the No 2 Guesthouse have tours to sights around Dali. Some of the cafes also offer trips, mostly in the form of boat outings across Erhai Lake to Wase, which has an open-air market every five days. Private entrepreneurs run cruises around the lake daily if there is enough demand. During festivals, many of the cafes arrange transport, which can spare you the fight to board jam-packed local buses out to festival sites at nearby villages.

AROUND DALI
Goddess of Mercy Temple
(*guānyīn táng*)

The temple is built over a large boulder said to have been placed there by the goddess of mercy to block an invading enemy's advance. It is five km south of Dali.

Erhai Lake
(*érhǎi hú*)

The lake is a 40-minute walk from town or a 10-minute downhill zip on a bike. You can watch the large junks or the smaller boats with their queue of captive cormorants waiting on the edge of the boat for their turn to do the fishing. A ring placed around their necks stops them from guzzling the catch.

From Caicun, the lakeside village east of Dali, there's a ferry at 4.30 pm to Wase on the other side of the lake. You can stay overnight and catch a ferry back at 6 am. Plenty of locals take their bikes over.

Since ferries crisscross the lake at various points, there could be some scope for extended touring. Close to Wase is Putuo Island (*pǔtuó dǎo*) with the Lesser Putuo Temple (*xiǎopǔtuó sì*). Other ferries run between Longkan and Haidong, and between Xiaguan and Jinsuo Island. Ferries appear to leave early in the morning (for market) and return around 4 pm; timetables are flexible.

Zhonghe Temple
(*zhōnghé sì*)

Zhonghe is a long, steep hike up the mountainside behind Dali. When you finally get there, you might be received with a cup of tea and a smile. Then again, you might not. Branching out from either side of the temple is a trail that winds along the face of the mountains, taking you in and out of steep lush valleys and past streams and waterfalls.

Gantong Temple
(*gǎntōng sì*)

This temple is not far south of the town of Guanyintang, which is about six km from Dali in the direction of Xiaguan. From Guanyintang follow the path uphill for three km. Ask friendly locals for directions.

Qingbi Stream
(*qīngbì xī*)

This scenic picnic spot near the village of Qiliqiao is three km from Dali in the direction of Xiaguan. After hiking four km up a path running close to the river, you'll reach three ponds.

Xizhou
(*xǐzhōu*)

Among the 101 things to do while you're in Dali, a trip to Xizhou would have to rate fairly high. It's an old town around 25 km north of Dali, with even better preserved Bai architecture than Dali. A local bus would be the easiest option for getting there, but a bicycle trip with an overnight stop in Xizhou (there's accommodation in town) is also a good idea.

Butterfly Spring
(*húdié quán*)

Butterfly Spring is a pleasant spot about 30 km north of Dali. The inevitable legend associated with the spring is that two lovers committed suicide here to escape a cruel king. After jumping into the bottomless pond, they turned into two of the butterflies which gather here en masse during May.

If you're energetic you could cycle to the spring. Since it is only four km from Shaping, you could also combine it with a visit to the Shaping Market.

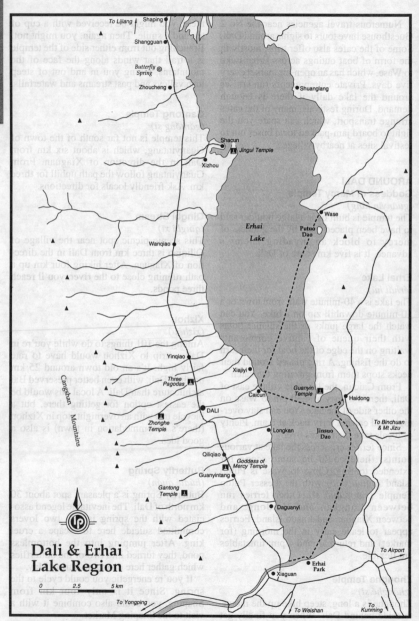

To Lijiang

Shaping

Shangguan

Butterfly Spring

Zhoucheng

Shuanglang

Wase

Putuo Dao

Erhai Lake

Shacun

Jingui Temple

Xizhou

Wanqiao

Yinqiao

Xiajiyi

Three Pagodas

Caicun

Guanyin Temple

Haidong

To Binchuan & Mt Jizu

DALI

Zhonghe Temple

Longkan

Jinsuo Dao

Qiliqiao

Guanyintang

Goddess of Mercy Temple

Gantong Temple

Daguanyi

To Airport

Cangshan Mountains

Dali & Erhai Lake Region

Erhai Park

Xiaguan

To Yongping

To Weishan

To Kunming

0   2.5   5 km

Shaping Market
(shāpíng gǎnjí)

Every Monday the town of Shaping, about 30 km north of Dali, is host to a colourful market. It's a good place to take some snaps. The market starts to rattle and hum at 10 am and ends around 2.30 pm. You can buy everything from tobacco, melon seeds and noodles to meat, pots and wardrobes. In the ethnic clothing line, you can look at shirts, headdresses, embroidered shoes and money belts. Expect to be quoted ridiculously high prices on anything you set your eyes on, get into a bargaining frame of mind, and you should have a good time.

Getting to Shaping Market from Dali is fairly easy. Some of the hotels and cafes in town run minibuses out there on market day. Usually they leave at 9 pm, though it's a good idea to ask around and book the day before. Alternatively you can walk up Huguo Lu to the main road and catch a local bus from up here, although bear in mind that market day is not going to be the ideal time to take a spin on the local buses.

DALI TO LIJIANG

Most travellers take a direct route between Dali and Lijiang. However, a couple of places visited by Chinese tourists might make interesting detours for foreigners. Transport could be a case of potluck with buses or hitching.

Jianchuan
(jiànchuān)

This town is 92 km north of Dali on the Dali-Lijiang road. Approaching from the direction of Dali, you'll come to the small village of Diannan about eight km before Jianchuan. At Diannan, a small road branches south-west from the main road and passes through the village of Shaxi (23 km from the junction). Close to this village are the Shibaoshan Grottoes *(shíbǎoshān shíkù)*. There are three temple groups: Stone Bell *(shízhōng)*, Lion Pass *(shīzi guān)* and Shadeng Village *(shādēng cūn)*.

Heqing
(hèqìng)

About 46 km south of Lijiang, Heqing is on the road which joins the main Dali-Lijiang road just above Erhai Lake at Dengchuan. In the centre of town is the Yunhe Pavilion, a wooden structure built during the Ming Dynasty.

LIJIANG
(lìjiāng)

North of Dali, bordering Tibet, the town of Lijiang is set in a beautiful valley and is another great spot to while away a few days or weeks. Your initial response when you pull into the bus station and start the long trudge up to the square might be 'Get me out of here!' First impressions of Lijiang are likely to be of an underwhelming, dusty Chinese town, especially if you've just come from Dali. It's not until you get into the old town – a delightful maze of cobbled streets, rickety old wooden buildings, gushing canals and the hurly-burly of market life – that you realise Lijiang is more than a boring Chinese urban sprawl in the middle of nowhere.

Lijiang Earthquake

The Lijiang area was heavily damaged by a severe earthquake in February 1996, after our visit. Many buildings, particularly those in the old part of the city, were destroyed. Some of the hotels, restaurants and sites mentioned in this section may no longer be open. Check with the CITS office or the PSB in Kunming for more information. ∎

There are a number of interesting sights around Lijiang, some of which can be reached by bicycle. You can also use a bike to get out of town to the mountains, where you can hike around. You may need time to acclimatise to the height (2400 metres).

Yunnan was a hunting ground for famous foreign plant-hunters such as Kingdon Ward and Joseph Rock. Rock, an Austro-American, lived almost continuously in Lijiang between 1922 and 1949. Hef is still remembered by some locals. A man of quick and violent temper, he commissioned local carpenters to build special chairs and a desk to accommodate his stocky frame. He burdened his large caravans with a gold dinner service and a collapsible bathtub from Abercrombie & Fitch. He also wrote a definitive guide to Hawaiian flora before devoting the rest of his life to researching Naxi culture and collecting the flora of the region.

The Ancient Nakhi Kingdom of Southwest China (Harvard University Press, 1947) is Joseph Rock's definitive work; the two volumes are heavy-duty reading. For a lighter treatment of the man and his work, take a look at *In China's Border Provinces: The Turbulent Career of Joseph Rock, Botanist-Explorer* (Hastings House, 1974) by J B Sutton.

Another venerable work on Lijiang worth reading if you can find it is *The Forgotten Kingdom* (John Murray Co, 1955) by Peter Goulart. Goulart was a White Russian who studied Naxi culture and lived in Lijiang from 1940 to 1949.

Orientation

Lijiang is separated into old and new towns that are as different as day and night. The approximate line of division is Lion Hill, the bump in the middle of town that's topped by a radio mast. Everything west of the hill is the new town, and everything east of the hill is the old town. The easiest way into the old town is to head up to the cinema, turn west into a small square that also serves as the town's night market, and head south. The old town is a delightful maze of twists and turns – although it's small, it's easy to get lost in there which, of course, is part of the fun. Enjoy!

Information

Some travel information can be gleaned from the cafes near Mao Square and in the old town. At the time of writing, CITS (☎ 25999) was planning to open a Family-Independent Traveller (FIT) Department in Lijiang, across the street from the entrance

to the Guluwan Hotel. These offices represent a bid by China's travel monolith to cater to individual or small-group travellers. The Lijiang staff are generally quite helpful, and should be able to give you ideas for local outings and book plane and even train tickets (though it sounds too good to be true). Stop by the office to see if this latter dream has become a reality.

The PSB is opposite the Lijiang Hotel, though some travellers have also been sent up to another office next to the north bus station. There seems to be no problem extending visas in Lijiang.

LIJIANG 丽江

PLACES TO STAY

6 Guluwan Hotel
古路湾宾馆
7 No 2 Guesthouse &
North Bus Station
第二招待所，北站
10 Red Sun Hotel
红太阳宾馆
12 Lijiang Hotel
丽江宾馆
14 Jiamei Hotel
佳美宾馆
19 Lijiang Grand Hotel
格兰饭店
32 Yunshan Hotel
云杉饭店

PLACES TO EAT

5 Ma Ma Fu's Cafe
马马虎餐厅
8 Ali Baba's Cafe
阿里巴巴餐厅

23 No 40 Restaurant
40 号饭店
27 Old Market Inn
纳西餐厅
28 Tower Cafe

OTHER

1 Black Dragon Pool Park
黑龙潭公园
2 Shop & Dongba
Museum
东巴博物馆
3 Dongba Research
Institute
东巴研究所
4 Yunling Theatre
云岭剧场
9 Mao Square
毛主席广场
11 CAAC
民航售票处
13 Bank of China
中国银行
15 Hospital
二门诊所

16 PSB
公安局
17 Bank of China
中国银行
18 Xinhua Bookstore
新华书店
20 Cinema
电影院
21 Post Office
邮电局
22 Night Market Area
夜市
24 Naxi Music Perform-
ances
纳西音乐
25 Radio Mast
狮子山
26 Old Market Square
四方街
29 Bicycle Hire
出租单车
30 Sports Ground
体育场
31 Long-Distance Bus
Station
长途汽车站

The Bank of China is on Xin Dajie almost opposite the intersection of the road that leads off to the Lijiang Hotel and the PSB. There is also a small branch just next to the entrance of the Lijiang Hotel. It is possible to change travellers' cheques at both branches.

Old Town

Crisscrossed by canals and a maze of narrow streets, the old town is not to be missed. Arrive by mid-morning to see the market square full of Naxi women in traditional dress. Parrots and plants adorn the front porches, old women sell griddle cakes in front of tea shops, men walk past with hunting falcons proudly keeping balance on their gloved fists, more old women energetically slam down the trumps on a card table in the middle of the street. You can buy embroidery and lengths of striped cloth in shops around the market.

Above the old town is a beautiful park

which can be reached on the path leading past the radio antenna. Sit on the slope in the early morning and watch the mist clearing as the old town comes to life.

Black Dragon Pool Park
(hēilóngtǎn gōngyuán)

The park is on the northern edge of town. Apart from strolling around the pool, you can visit the Dongba Research Institute, which is part of a renovated complex on the hillside. There is a small museum here with Dongba scrolls and artefacts – admission is Y2. At the far side of the pond are renovated buildings used for an art exhibition, a pavilion with its own bridge across the water and the Ming Dynasty Wufeng Temple. Entry to the park costs Y6.

Museum of Naxi Culture

Mr Xuan Ke, a Naxi scholar who spent 20 years in labour camps following the suppression of the Hundred Flowers movement, has

The Naxi

Lijiang is the base of the Naxi (also spelt Nakhi and Nahi) minority, who number about 278,000 in Yunnan and Sichuan. The Naxi are descended from Tibetan nomads and lived until recently in matriarchal families, though local rulers were always male. Women still seem to run the show, certainly in the old part of Lijiang.

The Naxi matriarchs maintained their hold over the men with flexible arrangements for love affairs. The *azhu* (friend) system allowed a couple to become lovers without setting up joint residence. Both partners would continue to live in their respective homes; the boyfriend would spend the nights at his girlfriend's house but return to live and work at his mother's house during the day. Any children born to the couple belonged to the woman, who was responsible for bringing them up. The father provided support, but once the relationship was over, so was the support. Children lived with their mothers; no special effort was made to recognise paternity. Women inherited all property, and disputes were adjudicated by female elders. The matriarchal system appears to have survived around Yongning, north of Lijiang.

There are strong matriarchal influences in the Naxi language. Nouns enlarge their meaning when the word for 'female' is added; conversely, the addition of the word for 'male' will decrease the meaning. For example, 'stone' plus 'female' conveys the idea of a boulder; 'stone' plus 'male' conveys the idea of a pebble.

Naxi women wear blue blouses and trousers covered by blue or black aprons. The T-shaped, traditional cape not only stops the basket always worn on the back from chafing, but also symbolises the heavens. Day and night are represented by the light and dark halves of the cape; seven embroidered circles symbolise the stars. Two larger circles, one on each shoulder, used to depict the eyes of a frog, which until the 15th century was an important god to the Naxi. With the decline of animist beliefs, the frog eyes fell out of fashion, but the Naxi still call the cape by its original name: 'frog-eye sheepskin'.

The Naxi created a written language over 1000 years ago using an extraordinary system of pictographs. The most famous Naxi text is the Dongba classic *The Creation*, and ancient copies of it and other texts can still be found in Lijiang, as well as in the archives of some US universities. Dongba were Naxi shamans who were caretakers of the written language and mediators between the Naxi and the spirit world. The Dongba religion eventually absorbed itself into an amalgam of Lamaist Buddhism, Islam and Taoism. The Tibetan origins of the Naxi are confirmed by references in Naxi literature to Lake Manasarovar and Mt Kailas, both in Western Tibet. ■

turned his Lijiang family home into a small repository for Naxi and Lijiang cultural items. Besides clothing and musical instruments (including an original Persian lute that has been used in Naxi music for centuries), his home displays Dr Joseph Rock's large, handmade furniture and has a small library of out-of-print books on Lijiang. Dr Rock was a close family friend.

Xuan Ke speaks English and is always willing to discuss his original ideas about world culture (for example, that music and dance originated as rites of exorcism). He has taken an active role in working to preserve traditional Chinese music, which he maintains is in danger of being wiped out by the corrosive influence of popular music and its evil offspring, karaoke. His home is in the old town, at No 11 Jishan Alley, diagonally opposite the No 40 Restaurant.

Festivals

The 13th day of the third moon (late March or early April) is the traditional day to hold a Fertility Festival (why not?). July brings Hub Jie (*huǒbǎ jíe*), the Torch Festival, also celebrated by the Bai in the Dali region. The origin of this festival can be traced back to the intrigues of the Nanzhao kingdom, when the wife of a man burned to death by the king eluded the romantic entreaties of said monarch by leaping into a fire.

Places to Stay

The first place you're likely to come across when you arrive in town is the *Yunshan Hotel (yúnshān fàndiàn)*, also known as the *No 3 Guesthouse*, next to the new bus station. Formerly one of Lijiang's better bargains, the Yunshan has fallen victim to rising prices and slipping standards. Given its inconvenient location in a boring part of town, there's not much reason to stay here: even if you're catching an early bus you can usually board at the north bus station, which is near Lijiang's other accommodation. The Yunshan has beds in three-bed dorms with TV for Y20, and in two-bed dorms for Y35. Doubles with attached bathroom are Y150.

The very basic *No 2 Guesthouse (dièr zhāodàisuŏ)* next to the north bus station is the budget option, with hard beds in five-bed dorms for Y10. Beds in quads/triples/doubles are Y14/16/18. If you want your own bathroom, you have to walk back a bit further to the *Guluwan Hotel (gǔlùwā bīnguǎn)*, the No 2 Guesthouse's answer to Lijiang's airport-inspired hotel boom. Basic doubles with attached bathroom are Y80, which is actually not a bad deal if there are two of you. Standard doubles with all mod cons are Y180. The Guluwan has a small travel agency on the grounds, as well as an air-ticket booking office (check to see how much their commission is – it might be better to try CITS across the street). The Guluwan Hotel is at the end of the driveway; the No 2 Guesthouse is the red brick building on your right just past the bus ticket window.

Adjacent to Mao Square, diagonally opposite the entrance to the Guluwan Hotel, the *Red Sun Hotel* is the next-cheapest choice for budget travellers. Beds in six to eight-bed dorms cost Y18, while those in quads are Y20, and in doubles Y24. The hotel also has triples/doubles with attached washroom for Y60/75 per bed. The Red Sun manages to snare a fair number of travellers due to its prominent location, but has received mixed reports. Some find the place perfectly fine while others, having endured several nights of ear-shattering karaoke, warn to avoid it like the plague.

The *Lijiang Hotel (lìjiāng bīnguǎn)*, also known as the *No 1 Hotel (dìyī zhāodàisuŏ)*, is probably Lijiang's leader in terms of friendly service. It's also more expensive, with the cheapest choice being a bed in a five-bed dorm for Y24. Beds in clean quads/triples/doubles are Y30/35/40. In the more luxurious block at the back, nicely furnished doubles/triples with attached bath cost Y180/240. As long as there are no small-scale construction projects on the grounds, the Lijiang Hotel should be the quietest of the town's low-end places to stay.

Just east of the Lijiang Hotel, the *Jiamei Hotel (jiāměi bīnguǎn)* offers doubles and triples with attached bath, telephone and 24-hour hot water for Y120. The rooms are nothing special, but are fair value all the same.

Hovering ominously at the northern edge of the old town, the brand-new *Lijiang Grand Hotel (gélán dàjiǔdiàn)* is a hulking luxury monster with facilities and prices (US$80 for a double) that seem completely at odds with the rest of Lijiang. The hotel is a Chinese-Thai joint venture managed in part by several Europeans.

Places to Eat

Like Dali, Lijiang has a legion of small, family-operated restaurants catering to the fantasies of China backpackers. Kitchens are tiny and waits can be long (if one of the ubiquitous Dutch tour groups is in town, forget it), but the food is usually interesting. There are always several 'Naxi' items on the menu, including the famous 'Naxi omelette' and 'Naxi sandwich' (goat's cheese, tomato and fried egg between two pieces of local *baba* flatbread). Try locally produced *yinjiu*, a lychee-based wine with a 500-year history – it tastes like a decent semi-sweet sherry.

Mao Square Most people stumble across the restaurants lining Mao Square first. *Peter's*, a former favourite with travellers, has taken a nosedive following the departure of founder Crystal and her American husband Tom. Food is acceptable, but the place is gloomy and all traces of personality seem to have been surgically removed. At the northern edge of the square, *Ma Ma Fu's* and *Ali Baba's* are both better bets, with good food and friendly people. They are also good spots to find out about details on Tiger Leaping Gorge and Lugu Lake.

Old Town There are some great places to eat in the old part of town. *The Old Market Inn* comes up tops for its friendly service and wonderful atmosphere. Seats downstairs look out onto the market square, allowing you to take in the market sights and sounds over a cold beer or hot Yunnan coffee. At the western edge of the square, across the stream and hidden up an alley, is *The Tower Cafe*, which has a wide range of tasty dishes in a courtyard setting: a bit like eating at someone's home. Try their outstanding potato croquettes.

Walking along Xinyi Jie into the old quarter you will come across *Din-Din's*, then *Mimi's Cafe* and the *No 40 Restaurant*. Mimi's seems to have passed its heyday, but the other spots do a fairly steady trade despite the competition from the market square cafes. The 2nd floor of the No 40 Restaurant gives good views of old town rooftops, good for contemplating over a coffee following a lengthy discourse with Mr Xuan Ke, who lives nearby.

Other Elsewhere around Lijiang and off the travellers' circuit look out for places serving baba, the Lijiang local speciality – thick flatbreads of wheat, served plain or stuffed with meats, vegetable or sweets. Morning is the best time to check out the baba selection. In the old town, you can buy baba from street vendors. East of the cinema across the bridge is a night market where you can get a steaming bowl of tasty noodles for Y2, roasted potatoes dipped in chilli powder for Y0.30, and other assorted snacks. There are several smaller restaurants just before the entrance to the Black Dragon Lake Park. Xin Dajie has several pastry shops.

Entertainment
One of the few things you can do in the evening in Lijiang is attend performances of the Naxi orchestra. Performances are held nightly in a beautiful old building inside the old town, usually from 8 to 10 pm. What's distinctive about the group is not only that all 20 to 24 members are Naxi, but that they play a type of Taoist temple music that has been lost elsewhere in China. The pieces they perform are supposedly faithful renditions of music from the Han, Song and Tang dynasties, played on original instruments (in most of China such instruments didn't survive the Communist revolution: several of this group hid theirs by burying them underground).

This is a rare chance to hear Chinese music as it must have sounded in classical China. Xuan Ke usually speaks for the group at performances, explaining each musical piece and describing the instruments. There are taped recordings of the music available: a set of two costs Y30. If you're interested, make sure you buy the tape at the show – tapes on sale at shops around town, and even in Kunming, are pirated copies, from which the orchestra receives no revenue.

You can usually turn up on your own and watch a performance, but you might want to arrive 15 minutes early to ensure a good seat. Tickets are Y10. Staff at Din-Din's will show you the way to the theatre at no extra cost, though they would probably appreciate it if you had dinner with them first. To get to the performance venue, from the No 40 Restaurant, turn left and then right, crossing a small courtyard to enter a narrow alley. At the end of the alley, you will see a large white wall with the words 'Naxi Music' written on it; the main door is just to the left.

Eyeing the popularity of the Naxi orchestra, CITS and other travel agencies have hopped on the bandwagon, organising various 'minority music concerts'. Usually incorporating some sort of staged dancing and costumes, these shows are designed to show minority culture to tourists through an official lens, and are better off skipped. Better to support the original Naxi Orchestra, whose members managed to retain both their skills and their instruments throughout the officially sanctioned insanity of the Cultural Revolution.

Getting There & Away

Air With the opening of a new airport 25 km to the east of town, Yunnan Airlines can now fly you from Kunming to Lijiang in 45 minutes. At the time of writing, there were only three flights a week, but this number is likely to increase. In Lijiang, tickets can be booked at the CAAC ticket office, the Guluwan Hotel (which levies a service charge) and CITS. Yunnan Airlines has a bus service to and from the airport for Y5.

Bus The bus situation in Lijiang is complicated by the existence of two bus stations. If you're staying up around the Lijiang Hotel or the No 2 Guesthouse, check to see what's on offer at the north bus station before making the long trek down to the main long-distance bus station. The ticket window is just inside the entrance to the Guluwan Hotel.

Most buses originate from the north station and then stop at the main bus station before heading out. This means departure times from the north stop are generally 15 minutes ahead of those from the main station. But be warned: sometimes the north bus station sells tickets for buses running from the main bus station. There should be a connecting bus if this is the case, but it would be a good idea to check – ask at one of the cafes on Mao Square if you're really confused.

Buses for Dali leave at 6.20 and 6.30 am from the main bus station – the north station has a connecting bus service leaving about 15 minutes before departure time. The ride takes over five hours and costs Y20. The long-distance bus station also has buses to Xiaguan at 7.50 and 10 am which pass through Dali. Minibuses originate from the north bus station at 12.45, 1.45, 2.45 and 3.15 pm, though these times are somewhat flexible. The ride is a bit quicker at four to five hours, and costs Y25. Several local bus companies also run buses to Dali: check on Xin Dajie just north of the Bank of China to see what's on offer. Most buses to Dali continue onto Xiaguan.

The other most popular destinations are Kunming and Jinjiang (for rail connections with Chengdu). Buses for Kunming leave at 7 am (Y50) and 1.30 pm (Y81): the latter is a night bus with reclining seats that gets you into Kunming at around 4.30 am. Sleeper buses to Kunming leave at 3.30 and 5.15 pm (3.15 and 5 pm from the north bus station) and cost Y111. Jinjiang buses leave at 6.30 am (6.20 from the north bus station) which, failing a major breakdown, will allow you to connect with the 5.40 pm, 9.25 pm or 12.12 am trains to Chengdu. During the rainy season (July to September), the Lijiang-Jinjiang road is often washed out and Chengdu-bound travellers have no alternative but to return to Kunming to catch a train or plane onward. At the time of writing it was still impossible for foreigners to book tickets of any kind for the train here. This may change with the opening of the FIT Department of CITS: staff said they should be able to help with train ticket bookings, but you'll have to check to see if they weren't being overambitious.

Buses to Zhongdian leave from the north bus station at 6.30 am and 12.45 pm, stopping at the main station before continuing on the six-hour ride. Tickets cost Y20. Other buses from Lijiang's north station include: Qiaotou at 6.30 am and 1.45 pm (Y11); Shigu at 2.45 pm (Y6.70) and Ninglang at 6.50 am (Y21).

Getting Around

The modern part of town is a tedious place to walk around. The old town, however, is best seen on foot. Bike hire is readily available around town at Mao Square and south of the post office on Xin Dajie.

Lijiang (nicknamed 'Land of Horses') is famous for its easily trained horses, which are usually white or chestnut with distinctive white stripes on the back. It might be possible to arrange an excursion on horseback.

AROUND LIJIANG
Monasteries

Lijiang's monasteries are Tibetan in origin and belong to the Red Hat sect. Most of them were extensively damaged during the Cul-

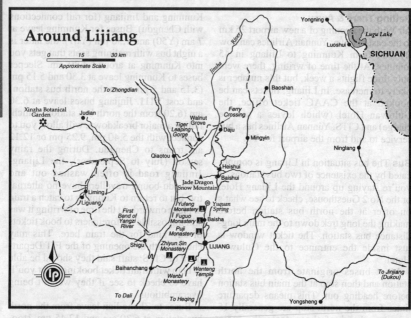

Around Lijiang

0   15   30 km
Approximate Scale

tural Revolution and there's not much monastic activity to be seen nowadays. Nevertheless, it's worth hopping on a bicycle and heading out of town for a look.

Puji Monastery (*pǔjí sì*) Around five km north-west of town (on a trail that passes the two ponds to the north of town) are a few monks at the Puji Monastery who are usually happy to show the occasional stray traveller around.

Yufeng Monastery (*yùfēng sì*) This small lamasery is on a hillside about five km past the town of Baisha. The last three km of the track require a steep climb. If you decide to leave your bike at the foot of the hill, don't leave it too close to the village below – the local kids have been known to let the air out of the tyres!

The monastery sits at the foot of Mt Yulongxue and was established in 1756. The monastery's main attraction nowadays is the

Camellia Tree of 10,000 Blossoms (*wànduǒ shānchá*). Ten thousand might be something of an exaggeration, but locals claim that the tree produces at least 4000 between February and April. A monk on the grounds risked his life to keep the tree secretly watered during the years of the Cultural Revolution.

Fuguo Monastery (*fùguó sì*) Also not far from the town of Baisha, this was once the largest of Lijiang's monasteries. Much of it was destroyed during the Cultural Revolution. In the monastery compound look out for the Hufa Hall; the interior walls have some interesting frescoes.

Wenbi Monastery (*wénbǐ sì*) The Wenbi Monastery involves a fairly steep uphill ride to the south-west of Lijiang. The monastery itself is not that interesting, but there are some good views and pleasant walks in the near vicinity.

Frescoes

Lijiang is famed for its temple frescoes. Most travellers are probably not going to want to spend a week or so traipsing around seeking them out, but it may be worth checking out one or two of them.

For the most part the frescoes were carried out during the 15th and 16th centuries by Tibetan, Naxi, Bai and Han artists. Many of them were subsequently restored during the later Qing Dynasty. They depict variously Taoist, and Chinese and Tibetan Buddhist themes and can be found on the interior walls of temples in the area. The best example is said by experts to be the fresco in Baisha's Dabaoji Hall. Again, the Red Guards came through here slashing and gouging during the Cultural Revolution, but there's still a lot left to see.

In Baisha ask around for the **Dabaoji Hall** (dàbǎojī gōng), the **Liuli Temple** (liúlí diàn) or the **Dading Pavilion** (dàdìng gé). Check the little shop for reasonably priced Naxi scrolls and paintings.

In the nearby village of Longquan (lóng-quán) frescoes can also be found on the interior walls of the **Dajue Temple** (dàjué gōng). See the earlier Fuguo Monastery section for other frescoes.

Baisha

(báishā)

Baisha is a small village on the plain north of Lijiang in the vicinity of several old temples (see the preceding Frescoes section). Before Kublai Khan made it part of his Yuan Empire (1271-1368), it was the capital of the Naxi kingdom. It's hardly changed since then and though at first sight it seems nothing more than a desultory collection of dirt roads and stone houses, it offers a close-up glimpse of Naxi culture for those willing to spend some time nosing around.

The star attraction of Baisha will probably hail you in the street. Dr Ho (or He) looks like the stereotype of a Taoist physician and there's a sign outside his door: 'The Clinic of Chinese Herbs in Jade Dragon Mountains of Lijiang'.

Jade Dragon Snow Mountain

(yùlóngxuě shān)

Soaring 5500 metres above Lijiang is Mt Satseto, also known as Yulongxue Shan (Jade Dragon Snow Mountain). Thirty-five km north of Lijiang, the peak was climbed for the first time in 1963 by a research team from Beijing. A chairlift has recently opened which brings you about halfway up a nearby

The Dr Ho Phenomenon

Dr Ho gets extremely mixed reports from travellers, but it's worth bearing in mind before you head out to Baisha that the majority of them are negative: words like 'charlatan' seem to roll easily off the tongue after a visit. It's not entirely the venerable doctor's fault. Bruce Chatwin, a travel writer who was among the first to stumble across and mythologise Dr Ho as the 'Taoist physician in the Jade-Dragon Mountains of Lijiang', is at least partly responsible. Chatwin did such a romantic job on Dr Ho that he was to subsequently appear in every travel book (including this one) with an entry on Lijiang; journalists and photographers turned up from every corner of the world; and Dr Ho, previously an unknown doctor in an unknown town, had achieved worldwide renown.

If you visit, the doctor's son Baisha will drag you off the street for your obligatory house call on Dr Ho. Unfortunately the attention has gone to the doctor's head somewhat – try not to hold it against him. You will be shown as many press clippings proving his international fame as your attention span allows, and you will probably be given some of the doctor's special tea. The true market value (not to mention medicinal value) of this tea has never been ascertained, but locals estimate Y0.20 to Y0.50. Dr Ho has the canny trick of handing out his tea and asking guests to pay as much as they think it's worth. It has made him the wealthiest soul in Baisha – although this is not saying a great deal. Look out for the John Cleese quote: 'Interesting bloke; crap tea'. ■

slope, from where you can rent horses which will take you to a large meadow. There, if the weather is clear, you will be greeted by a stunning view of Yulongxue Shan, and probably groups of Naxi women dancing and singing. The latter is clearly aimed at garnering tourist yuan, but it's still pleasant. This trek, aimed mainly at Chinese tourists, is an expensive one. Getting out to the mountain will either require hitching, hiring your own van for around Y100, or catching a ride on one of the infrequent private buses to Daju. Getting this same bus back could be tricky. Once there, the chairlift ride will cost Y50, the horse rental another Y20.

Alternatively, you can reach the snow line on one of the adjoining peaks if you continue along the base of the hillside near Baisha but ignore the track to Yufeng Monastery. On the other side of the next obvious valley, a well-worn path leads uphill to a lake. It might be a good idea to ask locals about conditions in this area before setting out.

Shigu & The First Bend of the Yangzi
(shígǔ/chángjiāng dìyīwān)
The small town of Shigu sits on the first bend of China's greatest river. Shigu means stone drum in Chinese, and the stone drum itself is a marble plaque shaped like a drum that commemorates a 16th-century Naxi victory over a Tibetan army. The other plaque on the river's edge celebrates the People's Army crossing of the river here in 1936 in the Great March to the north.

Buses to Shigu leave at 2.45 pm from Lijiang's north bus station, and take three hours. This would probably require an overnight stay. At the time of writing, the morning bus service had been suspended, but it's probably worth checking to see if it has resumed. Alternatively, try buses bound for Judian or get a bus as far as Baihanchang and hitch from this point.

Tiger Leaping Gorge
(hǔtiào xiá)
After making its first turn at Shigu the mighty Yangzi River (at this point known as the Jinsha River) surges between the Haba Mountains and the Jade Dragon Snow Mountain, through what is one of the deepest gorges in the world. The entire gorge measures 16 km, and from the waters of the Yangzi to the mountaintops is a giddy 3900 metres.

The hike through the gorge is very popular, though you'll probably only encounter several other travellers on the trail. All up, plan on spending three or four days away from Lijiang doing the hike. One American hiked through the gorge in one day, but if you didn't bring your superhero suit you'll have to stay overnight at Walnut Grove. It's worth spending an extra day in Daju, a good town with the *Tiger Leaping Gorge Hotel* – a great place to stay.

Gorge Trek The first thing to do is to check with the Old Market Inn or Ma Ma Fu's in Lijiang for the latest gossip on the mini-trek, particularly the transport side of things, which is where problems arise. It's difficult to recommend which end of the gorge to start at (Qiaotou or Daju), but we will say this: while finishing at Qiaotou has the advantage of easier transport links back to Lijiang, you should consider the fact that, even if you have to wait a day or two for a bus to Lijiang from Daju, there are much worse places to hang around for a couple of days.

Ideally you can do the walk in two days, though some travellers, enchanted with Walnut Grove, have lengthened it to over a week. From Qiaotou walk north from the China Hotel, which is where the bus from Lijiang drops you off (and where you'll stay overnight if you came in on the 1.45 pm bus). Cross the bridge, turn right and you are on the Tiger Leaping Gorge trail. A six to eight-hour walk will bring you to the small town of Walnut Grove. This section of the hike can be hair-raising during the rainy months of July and August, when landslides and swollen waterfalls can place themselves in your path. Ask locals in Lijiang about conditions.

Walnut Grove is the approximate halfway point, and there are two hotels nestled among the walnuts. The *Spring Guesthouse*, which incorporates *Sean's Cafe*, is the spot for more lively evenings and socialising. *Chateau de Woody*, the other option, is considered the quiet alternative. Both places have beds for Y5, and both have won praise from travellers. Food and beer are also available here. Supplies of bottled water can be chancy; it's probably best to bring your own.

The next day's walk is slightly shorter at four to six hours. The first two or three hours should bring you to a plateau that is more or less opposite Daju. The trail divides here and you should be careful to take the steep path leading up to a village. From here there is a path that descends down to the ferry.

From the ferry drop-off point to Daju is a fairly straightforward walk to the south. The *Tiger Leaping Gorge Hotel*, Daju's premier vacationer's residence, costs Y5 a bed and is on the left-hand side as you walk southward out of town; it's about 600 metres from the department store. It has good food and is a good place to hang out for at least a day. Nearby, the *Snowflake Hotel* also has beds in fairly clean rooms for Y5.

If you're doing the walk the other way round and heading for Qiaotou, walk north through town, aiming for the white pagoda at the foot of the mountains.

Warning Many travellers have become sick on the Tiger Leaping Gorge trek. It's probably a good idea to bring your own bottled water and watch where you eat in Qiaotou.

Getting There & Away Buses run to Qiaotou daily from the main long-distance bus station in Lijiang at 6.50 am and 2 pm for Y11 (a shuttle bus runs from the north bus station 20 minutes prior to departure to connect with it). The 6.50 am bus continues on to Zhongdian. There is no public bus service to Daju. Ali Baba's and sometimes Ma Ma Fu's have minibuses running there around 8 am, returning to Lijiang in the afternoon. Check with the cafes to make sure. Some of the travel outfits around the Lijiang Hotel and Guluwan Hotel may also be running mini-buses to Daju or Qiaotou.

Lugu Lake
(lúgū hú)
This remote lake overlaps the Yunnan-Sichuan border and is a centre for several Tibetan, Yi and Mosu (a Naxi subgroup) villages. The Mosu still practise matriarchy, and many of the Naxi customs now lost in Lijiang are still in evidence here. The lake itself is fairly high at 2685 metres and is usually snowbound over the winter months. The best times to visit the lake are April-May and September-October, when the weather is dry and mild.

Things to See In addition to just admiring the gorgeous scenery, you can visit several islands on the lake via large dugout canoes, which the Mosu call 'pig troughs' *(zhūcáo)*. The canoes, which are rowed by Mosu who also serve as guides, generally take you out to **Liwubi Island** *(lǐwùbǐ dǎo)*, the lake's largest. Out to the island and back is Y10 per person, Y15 if you want to be rowed around the island as well. The canoes can hold around seven people, but the price should be the same regardless of how many of you there are. Canoes leave from near the Mosu Yuan Hotel.

Twelve km west of the lake is **Yongning Monastery** *(yǒngníng sì)*, a lamasery with at least 20 lamas in residence. There is also a hot spring *(wēnquán)* up around here.

Places to Stay & Eat Visitors to Lugu Lake arrive at the lakeside village of Luoshui *(luòshuǐcūn)*, where you can stay in Mosu homes for around Y10 per bed. Most of the homes are equipped to take guests, so you won't be short of options. There are no showers. Food is cooked up for you by the Mosu: little fish, potatoes and eggs are the order of the day.

There are also three guesthouses in Luoshui, all very similar – only triples and quads are available, for Y15 and Y10 per bed respectively. There is no running water: you can wash up from a cistern in the courtyard. Of the three the *Mosu Yuan (mósuōyuàn)* seems to be the centre of action: occasional Mosu song-and-dance performances are held here, and morning buses to Ninglang leave from out in front of the hotel.

Finally, there are also several guesthouses in Yongning, which makes a good base from which to hike out to the nearby hot spring. Beds average around Y20.

Getting There & Away From Lijiang it's a nine-hour bus trip to Ninglang, the Lugu County seat. Sometimes minibuses meet buses coming in from Lijiang to take travellers onward to Lugu Lake, but there's still a good chance you'll have to overnight here. And anyway, it's not a bad idea to break up the journey.

There are several places to stay in Ninglang. Probably most convenient is the recently opened *Lugu Hotel (lùgú fànzhuāng)*, which has beds in doubles/triples for Y8/10, as well as standard doubles for Y150. It's right in the centre of town, about three minutes' walk from the bus station, and near lots of shops and restaurants. Travellers used to frequent the *Government Guesthouse (zhèngfǔ zhāodàisuǒ)*, which has dorms beds for Y8 to Y15 and standard doubles for Y140. The problem here is that the hotel is about one km from the bus station up a fairly steep hill: transport links are not convenient and there's not much in the way of places to eat nearby. Also, tour groups tend to book this place solid, so getting a room can sometimes be a hassle.

From Ninglang it's another four or five hours by bus to Lugu Lake. There are two bus stations on the main street quite close to one another. Check in both for the next bus to Lugu. There is also an English speaker in the Government Guesthouse who is usually happy to provide information. Coming back from Lugu Lake, buses to Ninglang leave in the morning from in front of the Mosu Yuan Hotel.

Some travellers have tried hiking from Yongning on to Muli in Sichuan Province, from where there is bus transport to Xichang on the Kunming-Chengdu line. But be warned: it's a dangerous route with no accommodation. You'll need to bring a tent, a warm sleeping bag and all your own pro-

visions. There's also no reason to expect the Tibetan tribespeople (all armed) you come across en route to be friendly either. One Canadian traveller we met had a frightening experience with locals while hiking this route and headed back to Yongning. Most travellers head back to Lijiang the same way they came.

ZHONGDIAN
(zhōngdiàn)

Zhongdian, 198 km north-west of Lijiang, is basically the last stop in Yunnan for more hardy travellers looking at a rough five or six-day journey to Chengdu via the Tibetan townships and rugged mountain terrain of western Sichuan. It is also a jumping-off point for those looking to slip into Tibet by the back door. There are rumours that the Yunnan route into Tibet will open up in coming years, but it is unlikely. The route is quite dangerous and the PSB is still keeping a vigilant eye out for errant backpackers nearing the provincial border.

Whether Zhongdian merits a trip in itself is a difficult question. If you don't have time to make it into Tibet, Zhongdian, a principally Tibetan town with a heavy Han overlay and a sprinkling of Bai, Hui (Muslim) and Naxi, is worth a look. It's perhaps worth visiting in combination with the Tiger Leaping Gorge trek. Start at Daju and then take a bus from Qiaotou at the end of the trek to Zhongdian. The bus journey from Qiaotou takes only three or four hours.

In mid-June Zhongdian plays host to a horse-racing festival that sees several days of dancing, singing, eating and of course, horse racing. The horses are actually more akin to ponies, and the races don't exactly proceed at thoroughbred speed. But travellers who have witnessed the event have raved about it. Accommodation can be a bit tight around this time, so you may want to arrive a day or two early. If you are in Lijiang, you can probably ask CITS to help you book a room.

Zhongdian is at 3200 metres and very close to the Tibetan border. About an hour's walk north of town is the Songzanlin Monastery *(sōngzànlín sì)*, a 300-year-old Tibetan monastery complex with several hundred monks.

Places to Stay & Eat

Almost all travellers head to the *Tibet Hotel* (*yŏngshēng fàndiàn*), a clean and friendly spot. Dorm beds here cost Y8 to Y15, and there are doubles for Y38 that come with satellite television. Getting there is easy: just follow the signs from the bus station.

Next to the bus station is the *Transport Hostel* (*jiāotōng zhāodàisuǒ*) where you can get a bed in an eight-bed dorm for Y5. Beds are Y8 in a six-bed dorm, and Y12 in triples. The hotel also has doubles with attached bath in the new wing for Y80. If these are full, you can walk a bit further to the *Kangben Hotel* (*kāngběn jiǔló*), a Tibetan-style place which has dorm beds for Y8 and doubles with common washing facilities for Y30. To get there, turn left after you exit the bus station and walk down to the four-way intersection. The hotel is on the far-left corner.

It gets cold in Zhongdian, particularly between November and March, so if you're here around this time you may want to ask for extra quilts or an electric blanket.

Up in the north of town are some Sichuan-style restaurants and a little place cranking out pretty good dumplings. Near the bus station, the *Lhasa Cafe* has obviously set itself up to be *the* travellers' hang-out. Reports on the food have been mixed, but it's a good place to go for info: there's a little book there where wandering backpackers have jotted down their nuggets of travel wisdom. Travellers have reported the existence of a *Chocolate Cafe*, also near the bus station. Whether this is the same as the Lhasa Cafe (which was boarded up when we were last in the area but apparently later reopened) you'll have to find out for yourself. Whichever it is, the apple pie and mashed potatoes come highly recommended.

There are also a few Tibetan and Naxi restaurants south of the bus station. Be wary of hotpot meals – numerous travellers have been ripped off by locals charging ridiculous sums. Check the price of everything when you order.

Getting There & Away

Buses for Zhongdian leave daily from Lijiang's north bus station at 6.30 am and 12.45 pm, cost Y20 and take anywhere from four to six hours. Another alternative is to travel from Xiaguan, from where buses leave daily at 6.30 am, cost Y32 and take around 10 hours. Buses to Zhongdian pass through Qiaotou, at the southern end of the Tiger Leaping Gorge trek.

Onward travel from Zhongdian offers some interesting possibilities. The one that is no longer illegal is the arduous bus-hopping trek to Chengdu, in Sichuan. If you're up for this you're looking at a minimum of five to six days' travel at some very high altitudes – you'll need warm clothes. The first stage of the trip is Zhongdian to Xiangcheng (*xiāngchéng*) in Sichuan, a journey of around 12 hours. You could break this up with a stop in Derong (*déróng*) just over the Sichuan border and only about seven hours from Zhongdian. From Xiangcheng, head to Litang (*lĭtáng*) (10 hours), though if roads are bad you may be forced to stay overnight in Daocheng (*dàochéng*). From Litang it's 12 hours to Kangding (*kāngdìng*) and another 12 hours on to Chengdu. Accommodation on the way is rough and your fellow passengers are likely to be chain-smoking phlegm removalists whose idea of fun is leaving the windows open and letting the sub-zero mountain breezes ruffle their hair. Have fun! For details on this trek, see the Litang to Zhongdian section in the Sichuan chapter.

The other destination from Zhongdian is Tibet and, who knows, by the time you have this book in your hands the miraculous may have occurred and this route may be open – don't count on it, though. For more information see the Road Routes section of the Tibet chapter.

AROUND ZHONGDIAN

There are probably numerous as yet unexplored possibilities for trips out of Zhongdian. At present the two most popular options are **Baishui Tai** (*báishuǐ tái*) and **Mt Meilixue** (*méilǐxuě shān*). The former is a limestone deposit plateau 108 km to the south-east of Zhongdian with some breathtaking scenery and Tibetan villages en route. Mt Meilixue straddles the Yunnan-Tibet border and, at 6740 metres, rates as Yunnan's highest peak. Getting to the mountain can be a problem in the winter months. If you are planning to head to Mt Meilixue, try and combine it with a visit to Deqin (*déqīn*), the last major town before the mountain. There is an important Tibetan monastery here. At the time of writing this area was still closed to foreigners, but with much of Yunnan now open, this may change.

Getting There & Away

Transport to sights around Zhongdian is still pretty touch and go. If it is possible to rustle up a group of travellers with similar interests, there are jeeps and minibuses for hire for Y250 to Y350 per day. There are also Chinese day tours of area sights which you should be able to join.

JINJIANG

(*jīnjiāng*)

Jinjiang is the tiny railhead for the large town of Panzhihua, just over the border in Sichuan Province.

Accommodation in this jolly little hamlet is provided courtesy of various fleapits, the most convenient being the *Railway Hotel* (*tiělù lǚxíngshè*). It's directly opposite the railway station; dorm beds cost between Y12 and Y30. Make an effort to get on a train before you book in anywhere – a stay in Jinjiang is not recommended.

For travellers Jinjiang is an important junction for the Lijiang-Chengdu route. To reach Jinjiang from Chengdu, one of the better trains is the No 85/84 which leaves Chengdu at 6.15 pm and reaches Jinjiang at 9.40 am the next day. This will give you time to get to Lijiang without having to stay overnight in Jinjiang. A hard sleeper for this trip costs Y144, a soft sleeper Y280. At Jinjiang station the minibus drivers are likely to assault you in droves for the trip to Lijiang.

Travelling in the other direction, from Lijiang to Chengdu, you can forget about

getting train tickets of any kind before you get to Jinjiang. The bus station in Lijiang won't sell them to you and there doesn't seem to be a black market for them either. To make matters worse this is a busy line and even the hard-seat tickets get booked out from time to time. This situation may improve if the FIT Department of the Lijiang CITS comes through on its pledge to help foreigners book train tickets, but you'll have to check for yourself.

Leaving Lijiang on the morning bus may allow you to connect with the No 86/83 to Chengdu departing at 5.40 pm. If you miss that, you can try for the No 68, which leaves at 8 pm, or the No 322, departing Jinjiang at 9.25 pm. After that your last chance is the No 66, which leaves at midnight. If you want anything other than a hard seat, look for the entrance to the toilet to the right of the inquiries booth, turn left into the door just in front of the toilet (remember, this is China), and to the back of the courtyard on the right-hand side is an office selling hard and soft-sleeper tickets.

XISHUANGBANNA REGION

(*xīshuāngbǎnnà*)

The region of Xishuangbanna is in the deep south of Yunnan Province, next to the Myanmar and Lao borders. The name Xishuangbanna is a Chinese approximation of the original Thai name, Sip Sawng Panna (12 rice-growing districts). The place has a laid-back south-east Asian feel to it and it's easy to watch the weeks slip by as you make your way around small villages, tropical forests and the occasional stupa.

In recent years Xishuangbanna has become China's own mini-Thailand, and Chinese tourists have been heading down in droves for the sunshine, Dai minority dancing, water-splashing festivals (held daily nowadays), as well as the ubiquitous tour group lures, such as the 'forest of one tree', the 'king of tea trees' and other trees that suggest something less prosaic than a mere tree. But it's easy to get away from the crowds by jumping on a public bus to some small town, and making it your base for exploring the surrounding countryside and villages.

Xishuangbanna Dai Autonomous Prefecture, as it is known officially, is subdivided into the three counties of Jinghong, Menghai and Mengla. Mengla County is still closed to foreign tourists at present and permits seem to be a bit hit or miss, though they can be applied for at the PSB office in Jinghong. You can easily buy a ticket to Mengla in Jinghong, and may make it there and back without running afoul of the PSB, but be ready for fines and a swift ejection all the same. However, if you're headed to the border crossing with Laos, south of Mengla, and have a Lao visa stamped in your passport, then you should have no trouble.

Xishuangbanna has wet and dry seasons. The wet season is between June and August, when it rains ferociously almost every day. From September to February there is less rainfall but thick fog descends during the late

evening and doesn't lift until 10 am or even later at the height of winter. Between May and August there are frequent and spectacular thunderstorms.

Between November and March temperatures average about 19°C. The hottest months of the year are from April to September, when you can expect an average of 25°C.

Like Hainan Island, Xishuangbanna is home to many unique species of plant and animal life. Unfortunately, recent scientific studies have demonstrated the devastating effect of previous government policies on land use; the tropical rainforest areas of Hainan and Xishuangbanna are now as acutely endangered as similar rainforest areas elsewhere on the planet. The jungle areas that remain still contain dwindling numbers of wild elephants, tigers, leopards and also golden-haired monkeys. The Tropical Plant Research Institute in Jinghong has gardens with a limited selection of plants that

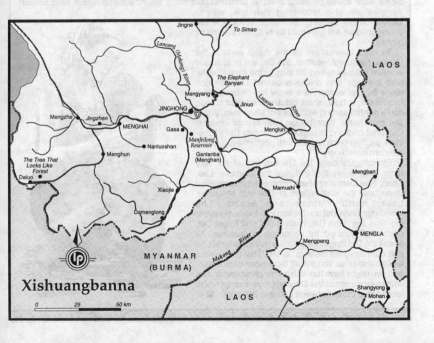

Xishuangbanna

0   25   50 km

gives an idea of the spectacular flora that once covered the land.

About one-third of the 800,000-strong population of this region are Dai; another third or so are Han Chinese and the rest are a hotchpotch of minorities which includes the Miao, Zhuang, Yao and lesser known hill tribes such as the Aini, Jinuo, Bulang, Lahu and Wa.

Festivals

Festivals celebrated by the Dai attract hordes of foreigners and Chinese alike. The Water-Splashing Festival held around mid-April (usually 13 to 15 April) washes away the dirt, sorrow and demons of the old year and brings in the happiness of the new. The first day of the festival is devoted to a giant market. The second day features dragon-boat

The Dai

The Dai people are concentrated in this pocket of Yunnan and exercise a clear upper hand in the economy of Xishuangbanna. During the Cultural Revolution many Dai people simply voted with their feet and slipped across the border to join their fellow Dai who are sprinkled throughout Thailand, Laos, Myanmar and Vietnam. Not only the Dai but also most of the other minorities in these areas display a nonchalant disregard for borders and authority in general.

The Dai are Buddhists who were driven southwards by the Mongol invasion of the 13th century. The Dai state of Xishuangbanna was annexed by the Mongols and then by the Chinese, and a Chinese governor was installed in the regional capital of Jinglan (present-day Jinghong). Countless Buddhist temples were built in the early days of the Dai state and now lie in the jungles in ruins. During the Cultural Revolution Xishuangbanna's temples were desecrated and destroyed. Some were saved by being used as granaries, but many are now being rebuilt from scratch.

Temples are also recovering their role, with or without official blessing, as village schools where young children are accepted for religious training as monks.

To keep themselves off the damp earth in the tropical rainforest weather, the Dai live in spacious wooden houses raised on stilts in the classic style, with the pigs and chickens below. The common dress for Dai women is a straw hat or towel-wrap headdress; a tight, short blouse in a bright colour; and a printed sarong with a belt of silver links. Some Dai men tattoo their bodies with animal designs. Betel-nut chewing is popular and many Dai youngsters get their teeth capped with gold; otherwise they are considered ugly.

Ethnolinguistically, the Dai are part of the very large Thai family that includes the Siamese, Lao, Shan, Thai Dam and Ahom peoples found scattered throughout the river valleys of Thailand, Myanmar, Laos, north Vietnam and Assam. The Xishuangbanna Dai are broken into four subgroups, the Shui Dai, Han Dai, Huayai Dai and Kemu Dai, each distinguished by variations in costume. All speak the Dai language, which is quite similar to Lao and northern Thai dialects. In fact Thai is as useful as Chinese once you get off the beaten track a little, and you might have fun with a Thai phrasebook. The written language of the Dais employs a script which looks like a cross between Lao and Burmese. ■

racing (races in Jinghong are held on the Mekong River below the bridge), swimming races and rocket launching. The third day features the water-splashing freakout – be prepared to get drenched all day by the locals, and remember, the wetter you get, the more luck you will receive. In the evenings there is dancing, launching of hot-air paper balloons and game playing.

During the Tanpa Festival in February, young boys are sent to the local temple for initiation as novice monks. At approximately the same time (between February and March), Tan Jing Festival participants honour Buddhist texts housed in local temples.

The Tan Ta Festival is held during the last 10-day period of October or November, with temple ceremonies, rocket launches from special towers and hot-air balloons. The rockets, which often contain lucky amulets, blast off with a curious droning sound like mini-space shuttles before exploding high above; those who find the amulets are assured of good luck.

The farming season (from July to October) is the time for the Closed-Door Festival, when marriages or festivals are banned. Traditionally, this is also the time of year that men aged 20 or older ordain as monks for a period of time. The season ends with the Open-Door Festival, when everyone lets their hair down again to celebrate the harvest.

During festivals, booking airline tickets to Jinghong can be extremely difficult. You can try getting a flight into Simao, 162 km to the north, or take the bus. Hotels in Jinghong town are booked solid, but you could stay in a nearby Dai village and commute. Festivities take place all over Xishuangbanna, so you might be lucky further away from Jinghong.

SIMAO
(sīmáo)

Simao, an uninteresting little town, used to be Xishuangbanna's air link with the outside world. Nowadays Jinghong has its own airport and very few travellers stop here. True, the occasional traveller flies from Kunming to Simao and does the final leg to Jinghong by bus, but it's doubtful whether it's worth the effort unless you absolutely can't get a flight to Jinghong. The scenery between Simao and Jinghong is not exactly a Sumatran jungle, and if you're travelling further afield from Jinghong you'll get to see plenty of Xishuangbanna scenery anyway.

Getting There & Away
Air The CAAC office (☎ 223-234) is just off the main street at the northern corner of Hongqi Square. There are three flights weekly between Kunming and Simao and the one-way fare is Y360.

Bus Not too many travellers head for Simao by bus, though most pass through briefly on the way from Kunming to Jinghong or vice versa. There are buses from Simao to Baoshan and Xiaguan, but most of these originate in Jinghong anyway.

JINGHONG
(jǐnghóng)

Jinghong, the capital of Xishuangbanna Prefecture, lies beside the Lancang River (Mekong River). It's a sleepy town with streets lined with palms, which help mask the Chinese-built concrete boxes until they merge with the stilt-houses in the surrounding villages. It doesn't have much to keep you longer than a couple of days. It's more a base for operations than a place to hang out, though it's not without a certain laid-back charm that somehow endures despite the steady flood of tourist traffic.

Information
CITS The travel service (☎ 31165) is just next to the entrance to the Xishuangbanna Guesthouse. The staff are friendly, and can help answer questions about sights and accommodation in the region. CITS also offers several one-day tours for around Y80 to Y90 per person that generally take in one to two towns and sights en route. These may suit travellers who are on a rushed itinerary

and don't want to waste time mucking about with public transport, or who are in the mood to rub shoulders with their Chinese counterparts.

PSB This is opposite Peacock Park in the centre of town. Staff there politely refused to issue permits to Mengla when we last visited, though you may have better luck – the situation seems fluid, to say the least. They did confirm, however, that those with visas for travel in Laos can happily wend their way to Mengla, no permit needed.

Money The Bank of China is on Jinghong Nanlu, next door to the Banna Mansion Hotel.

Post & Telecommunications The post office is in the centre of town at the intersection of Jinghong west and south roads (Xilu and Beilu). Phone lines in Xishuangbanna have improved dramatically, and staff are only slightly flustered if you announce plans to place an international call. You can also direct dial from most of the hotels, but as usual their rates are noticeably higher.

Chunhuan Park
(chūnhuān gōngyuán)
Chunhuan Park, in the south of Jinghong down past the Dai restaurants, is a fairly poor excuse for an outing. The park contains a couple of replica stupas, Dai dancing girls

JINGHONG 景洪

PLACES TO STAY

2   Communications Hotel
    交通饭店
8   Banna Mansion Hotel & Bank of China
    版纳大厦，中国银行
10 Jingyong Hotel
    景咏宾馆
11 Xishuangbanna Guesthouse & CITS
    版纳宾馆，中国国际旅行社
15 Wanli Dai Restaurant & Hotel
    婉丽傣味楼
16 Dai Building Hotel
    傣家花苑小楼
17 Dai Guesthouse
    傣家旅店
18 Dai Hotel
    傣乡旅店

OTHER

1   Bridge Over the Mekong
    大桥
3   Long-Distance Bus Station
    长途汽车站
4   No 2 Bus Station
    第二客运站
5   Tropical Plant Research Institute
    热代所
6   Medicinal Botanical Gardens
    药用植物园
7   Post Office
    邮电大楼
9   PSB
    公安局
12 Workers' Cultural Palace
    工人文化宫
13 CAAC
    民航售票处
14 Mei Mei Cafe
    美美咖啡厅
19 Manting Temple
    曼听佛寺

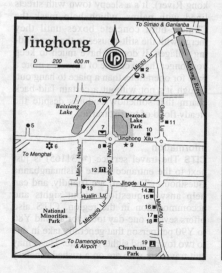

Top Left: The karst scenery of Yangshuo, Guangxi
Top Right: Making bamboo steamers in Ruili, Yunnan
Bottom: The limestone pillars of the Stone Forest near Kunming, Yunnan

Buddhist Temple near Ruili, Yunnan

(you'll probably get to see a water-splashing festival now held daily by popular demand if you hang around) and a pitiful elephant in chains. Just before you get to the park entrance is the **Manting Temple** *(mántīng fósì)*. It's claimed to date back 1100 years. Across from the park is the 'Peacock Minority Customs Tourist Village' where you can watch Chinese tour groups gather for daily water-splashing festivals, courtesy of your local travel agent.

Tropical Plant Research Institute
(rèdài zuòwù yánjiùsuǒ)
A short bicycle ride out of town, the institute is one of Jinghong's better attractions. A modest entry fee of Y5 gets you into the institute's inner sanctum, only recently opened to the public, where you can view over 1000 different types of plant life. Unless you're a botanist, telling them all apart could be tricky – of the few signs around, more than half are in Chinese only, and the rest carry only the scientific names in English. Still, it's easy to get a feel for the impressive variety of plants that make up Yunnan's tropical forests, and the grounds makes for a pleasant stroll. The Y5 admission also gets you into the **Zhou Enlai Memorial**, a bizarre 2001-like sculpture commemorating a 1961 visit by China's best-loved premier. After you come out, check out the shop where the entry tickets are sold: it sells a number of agricultural products grown on the premises, including tea, Chinese medicine and outstanding ground coffee. If you ask nicely, the shop staff may brew you a cup unless they're very busy (hard to imagine).

A little way back towards town and on the opposite side of the road is the **Medicinal Botanical Gardens in Xishuangbanna**. Staff at the gate might try to deter you from entering by telling you it's boring. It's not a trick to keep you out...they're telling the truth.

Peacock Lake Park
(kǒngquèhú gōngyuán)
This artificial lake in the centre of town isn't much but the small park next to it is pleasant.

There's also a zoo, but as usual the total lack of effort to reproduce even traces of the animals' original habitat tend to leave you feeling as depressed as the animals themselves look to be. The English Language Corner takes place here every Sunday evening, so this is your chance to exchange views or practise your English with the locals.

National Minorities Park
(mínzú fēngqíng yuán)
If you come in to Jinghong by plane, you'll pass this place on the way into town. It's not that far south of the CAAC booking office. On the map of Jinghong provided by the Banna Hotel bicycle hire service it's mysteriously referred to as the 'Minority Flirtation Expression'. Intrigued? If so, head down on Friday or Saturday when, from 7 to 11 pm, there are minority dances and so on.

Bridge Over the Mekong
(mǐgòng qiáo)
The bridge is no technical wonder, and the views of the river from it are not even that good, but it's there and it is a bridge over the Mekong after all. If rumour is correct, there was an attempt some years ago by a member of a disaffected minority to blow up the bridge. Jinghong is such a splendidly torpid town, it's hard to imagine the excitement. The no-photography rule has been dropped.

Places to Stay
Jinghong definitely does not suffer a lack of hotel space, though most places have little to set them apart from their rivals. But there are a few which stand out from the crowd.

The *Xishuangbanna Guesthouse (xīshuang-bǎnnà bīnguǎn)*, in the centre of town, used to be one of those exceedingly rare Chinese hotels that travellers reminisced about after they had left. It's not quite that idyllic any more – if you want to gaze out over the Mekong you'll have to pay at least Y150 – but you can still lounge in the shade of the surrounding palms, and there are some reasonably priced rooms. Doubles with balcony, bathroom and TV in building Nos 6, 7 and 9 are not a bad deal at Y50: similar triples are Y60. Doubles and triples in the Bamboo House are more basic, and cost the same. After that it's Y150 to Y240 for standard doubles in the Riverview Buildings which, whether from earthquakes, shifting silt or shoddy construction, already seem to be falling apart. Repeated cracks in the wall have been repeatedly plastered up, and the metal plates of the walkways keep getting wider as they shift further away from the walls. If you get a dorm room on the ground floor, you may want to leave any valuables with the front desk: some travellers have had possessions stolen here.

If you're in the market for real basic accommodation with a Dai flavour head down to Manting Lu. It's a long walk from the bus station (around 25 minutes), in the south of town. There are numerous places to choose from, most of which charge Y10 per bed. The first and oldest is the *Wanli Dai Restaurant (wǎnlì dǎiwèilóu cāntīng)*. This used to be the 'in spot' with backpackers, but it seems to have fallen on hard times, perhaps because of the indifferent service of the staff.

A bit further south, on the same side of the street, the newly opened *Dai Building Hotel (dǎijiāhuā yuàn xiǎolóu)* looks to be an up-and-coming backpacker hang-out – one of the first signs you see upon entering the courtyard is for 'Cold Beer'. All accommodation is in separate bamboo bungalows on stilts. Doubles and triples are around Y25 a bed. Another five minutes' walk down the street, right next to each other, are the *Dai Guesthouse (dǎijiā lǚdiàn)* and the *Dai Hotel (dǎixiāng lǚdiàn)*, both with dorm beds for Y10. None of the Dai hotels have hot water: if this is one of your basic needs you'll have to head for one of the Chinese hotels.

Right next to the long-distance bus station, the *Communications Hotel (jiāotōng fàndiàn)*, has some good mid-range rooms and cheap dorms. Beds in a four-bed room range from Y10 to Y15, while doubles with bathroom, fan and TV cost Y80. More upmarket standard doubles are Y120.

A more centrally located place with dormitory accommodation is the *Jingyong Hotel (jǐngyǒng bīnguǎn)*, on Jinghong Donglu.

Beds are Y10 in a quad, and Y15 in a triple. Clean doubles with fan and attached bath are available for Y60. If it's air-conditioning you're after, it will cost you Y160 for a double.

Finally, right in the heart of town, the *Banna Mansion Hotel (bǎnnà dàshà)* is Jinghong's luxury option, with air-con doubles for Y260, and triples for Y280. Smiling doormen and the lobby bathroom attendants are complimentary.

Places to Eat

As with accommodation, Manting Lu is the place for Dai-style food. The road is lined with restaurants, most of which are pretty similar. One drawback (or bonus, depending on how you view it) is that the majority of these restaurants dish up Dai dance performances along with their culinary specialities. This explains why the words 'singing and dancing hall' are tacked onto a lot of restaurant names. These places are filled nearly every night with Chinese tourists whooping it up, hollering, playing drinking games and generally being festive. Once is worth a try, but you might not want to sit through the show every evening.

One place that serves Dai food but spares diners the dancers is the *Wanli Dai Restaurant (wǎnlì dàiwèilóu cāntīng)*, which also has cheap accommodation. Try the roast fish, eel or beef cooked with lemon grass or served with peanut-and-tomato sauce. Vegetarians can order roast bamboo shoot prepared in the same fashion. Other mouthwatering specialities include fried river moss (sounds rather unappetising but is excellent with beer) and spicy bamboo-shoot soup. Don't forget to try the black glutinous rice. The upstairs balcony is a pleasant place to sit with a beer in the winter and read about the sub-zero temperatures in Beijing.

Elsewhere around town is pretty much standard Chinese fare. Walk up from Manting Lu and turn left in the direction of the CAAC booking office and you will find a host of tiny Chinese restaurants; most of them are pretty good for lunch. Next to the bus station there are also some good restaurants – look out for the place specialising in dumplings.

Street markets sell coconuts, bananas, papayas, pomelos (a type of grapefruit) and pineapples. The pineapples, served peeled on a stick, are probably the best in China. The covered market near the Banna Hotel is at its busiest in the morning.

If the heat has you gasping, duck into the air-conditioned lobby bar at the *Banna Mansion Hotel* for a decent cup of Yunnan coffee. It's not exactly a great bargain at Y8 per cup, but then you won't be dripping sweat into your coffee cup either.

Finally, for good food, strong coffee, really cold beer and (you guessed it) banana pancakes, stop by the *Mei Mei Cafe* on Manting Lu, a pleasant little hole in the wall just down from the intersection with Jingde Lu. You'll be greeted with a smile, and usually find fellow travellers with whom to swap tall tales. This is just as well, as the cafe's minimal kitchen facilities can sometimes cause a bit of a backlog on food orders, especially around dinner time.

Getting There & Away

Air More flights and bigger planes (737s) mean that it's a lot easier to fly to Jinghong from Kunming than it used to be. It's often even possible to book the day before. If one airline or travel agent in Kunming says the flights are all full, check with another place: travel agencies tend to snap up large blocks of seats ahead of time, and often fail to fill them all. In April (Water-Splashing Festival), however, allow for several days' advance booking, as this is a very popular time for Chinese to visit. There are normally several flights daily to Jinghong (Banna). The flight takes 50 minutes and the one-way fare is Y520. Flights back are also daily and can be booked at the CAAC booking office in Jinghong. The airport is five km south of the city; CAAC buses leave from next to the booking office about an hour before scheduled departures.

Bus There are daily buses from Kunming to Jinghong. Somewhat better roads and the advent of sleeper buses mean that the trip can now be done in one haul of 24 hours or more – the only overnight stops along the way are now unintentional.

Sleepers to Jinghong leave from the Kunming long-distance bus station at 2 pm and 8 pm, take 27 hours, and cost Y180. So-called luxury buses, with reclining seats, cost Y118 to Y125. A more downmarket, and more painful, alternative is the day/night bus: Y80 buys you a somewhat-cushioned seat for the 24 to 30-hour ride. The travel agency next door to the Three Leaves Hotel in Kunming has more comfortable sleeper buses that make it to Jinghong in 24 hours; tickets are also Y180.

Buses back to Kunming are available from various travel services around town, and the long-distance bus station. The latter has sleepers at 2 and 7 pm, and luxury buses at 7, 8.30 and 11 am. The No 2 bus station, just south-west of the long-distance station, also has sleepers, leaving at 11.40 am and 5 pm.

If you're torn between the bus and the plane, don't let other travellers give you any crap about missing the scenery on the flight. There are some good views from the bus window, but nothing that won't stop you nodding off to sleep and certainly nothing much that will make you sit up and decide that the 24 hours of inhaling second-hand smoke and bouncing up and down in lieu of sleep were worth it.

The Jinghong long-distance bus station also has buses running to Xiaguan, Baoshan and Ruili. With more than 80 counties and cities now open in Yunnan, the PSB has decided to stop discouraging travellers from making this arduous journey (though they may still think you're crazy to do so, since you must have enough money to fly). The trip to Xiaguan takes two days, with an overnight stop, usually in Zhenyuan. The fare is Y80. Baoshan is also a two-day journey (Y89), with the town of Lincang playing midway host to frazzled passengers. The marathon to Ruili takes three full days, with stops in Lincang and Baoshan, and costs Y126. Serious thought should be given to breaking this trip up in Baoshan, if for no other reason than to preserve at least traces of pink in your lungs. Roads are quite poor on these routes, and the buses, all of the standard hard-seat variety, little better. If you choose this option, don't do it to save time – many travellers have found their two-day trip stretch to three and even four days as they encounter landslides, floods and (surprise, surprise) bus breakdowns.

The Jinghong long-distance bus station has buses running to towns around Xishuangbanna, but it is mainly useful for more distant destinations. The best place to get out of Jinghong and explore other parts of Xishuangbanna is the No 2 bus station, which has frequent buses, minibuses and minivans from 7 am to around 5 pm. Timetables are flexible to say the least. Most of the buses that run locally from the long-distance bus station call in at the No 2 bus station to pick up extra passengers, so you'll get something one way or another.

Getting Around
Jinghong is small enough that you can walk to most destinations, but a bike makes life much easier. The Xishuangbanna Guesthouse hires out bikes for Y8 a day, Y18 for mountain bikes. The Jingyong Hotel rents standard Chinese versions for Y6 a day. The bikes from the Xishuangbanna Guesthouse are better, however.

AROUND JINGHONG
The possibilities for day-trips and longer excursions out of Jinghong are endless. Some travellers have hiked and hitched from Menghai to Damenglong, some have cycled up to Menghai and Mengzhe on mountain bikes (it's almost impossible on bikes without gears), and one French photographer hitched up with a local medicine man and spent seven days doing house calls in the jungle.

Obviously, it's the longer trips that allow you to escape the hordes of tourists and get a feel for what Xishuangbanna is about. But even with limited time there are some interesting possibilities. Probably the best is an overnight (or several nights) stay in Gan-

lanba (also known as Menghan). It's only around 27 km from Jinghong, and not that hard to cycle to, even on a local bike. The trip takes two to three hours.

Most other destinations in Xishuangbanna are only two or three hours away by bus, but generally they are not much in themselves – you need to get out and about. The best advice is to get yourself a good bike or some sturdy hiking boots, pick up a map, put down this book, and get out of town.

Nearby Villages
Before heading further afield, there are numerous villages in the vicinity of Jinghong that can be reached by bicycle. Most of them are the kinds of places you happen upon by chance, and it's difficult to make recommendations. On the other side of the Mekong are some small villages, and a popular jaunt involves heading off down Manting Lu – if you go far enough you'll hit a ferry crossing point on the Mekong. There are also villages in this area, and many travellers have been invited into Dai homes for tea and snacks.

Mengyang
(měngyáng)
Mengyang is 34 km north-east of Jinghong on the road to Simao. It's a centre for the Hani, Lahu and Floral-Belt Dai. Chinese tourists stop here to see a banyan tree shaped like an elephant.

From Mengyang it's another 19 km to Jinuo, which is home base for the Jinuo minority. Travellers have reported that the Jinuo are unfriendly, so you'll probably have to stay in Mengyang. Some minorities dislike tourists, and if this is the case with the Jinuo they should be left alone.

The Jinuo, sometimes known as the Youle, were officially 'discovered' as a minority in 1979. The women wear a white cowl, a cotton tunic with bright horizontal stripes and a tubular black skirt. Ear-lobe decoration is an elaborate custom – the larger the hole and the more flowers it can contain the better. The teeth are sometimes painted black with the sap of the lacquer tree, which serves the dual dental purpose of beautifying the mouth and preventing tooth decay and halitosis. Previously, the Jinuo lived in long houses with as many as 27 families occupying rooms on either side of the central corridor. Each family had its own hearth, but the oldest man owned the largest hearth, which was the first at the door. Long houses are rarely used now and it looks like the Jinuo are quickly losing their distinctive way of life.

Ganlanba (Menghan)
(gānlánbà)

Ganlanba, or Menghan as it's sometimes referred to, lies on the Mekong south-east of Jinghong. In the past the main attraction of Ganlanba was the boat journey down the Mekong from Jinghong. Improved roads sank the popular boat trip (locals prefer to spend an hour on a bus to three hours on the boat), and the only way to travel down the river now is to charter a boat at special tourist prices that most tourists can't afford.

Nevertheless, Ganlanba remains a wonderful retreat from hectic Jinghong. The town itself is fairly forgettable, but if you come on a bike (it is also possible to hire one in Ganlanba) there is plenty of scope for exploration in the neighbourhood. Check the visitors' book in the Dai Bamboo House for some ideas.

Places to Stay The family-run *Dai Bamboo House* is a house on stilts with a dorm for Y10 per bed and small doubles for Y24; all beds are on the floor in the traditional Dai style. The friendly family serves Dai food on tiny lacquered tables: just give them notice several hours before dinner. It's a favourite with almost everyone who stays here, and many people end up staying longer than they had intended. Search out the visitors' books, which have several helpful maps of the area drawn by previous guests. The Bamboo House is on the right-hand side (heading away from Jinghong) of the main road that runs through town.

Getting There & Away Minivans leave from in front of the Jinghong No 2 bus station as they fill up. The ride costs Y6 and takes around 45 minutes. It's possible to cycle the distance in a brisk two hours or a leisurely three hours, and it's a pleasant enough ride.

Getting Around The only way to do this is by bicycle or hiking. If you didn't bring your own bike, you can rent one at the Dai Bamboo House. If they're all out, take the lane next to the Bamboo House and follow it down towards the river. After passing through a small market area you'll reach another main road. On the right-hand corner is a bicycle repair stand where you can hire bicycles for Y5 a day.

Around Ganlanba

The stately Wat Ban Suan Men, south-west of town, is said to be 730 years old and is one of the best surviving examples of Dai temple architecture in Yunnan. Follow the road closest to the Mekong southwards out of town and then take a path that follows the river. Check at the Dai Bamboo House for information before you leave.

There are numerous temples and villages in the area that are worth exploring. There's an old decaying temple on the road into town from Jinghong, and to the south of this, overlooking the Mekong, is a white stupa. Most travellers who have spent any time here recommend striking off aimlessly on day-trips and seeing what turns up.

Menglun
(měnglún)

Menglun is the next major port of call east of Ganlanba. The major attraction for Chinese visitors is the **Tropical Plant Gardens** *(rèdài zhíwùyuán)*. It's a pleasant enough place, though concrete pathways and guides toting bullhorns quickly dash any hopes of communing with nature. But the gardens are nicely laid out, and the tour groups give it a somewhat festive atmosphere.

After going about two-thirds of the way into town, you'll come to a road leading downhill on the right side. Follow this until you reach a footbridge across the Mekong. The ticket booth is just in front of the bridge and the entry fee is Y20 (foreigners' price).

Places to Stay For dirt-cheap (though not dirt-free) accommodation you can try the *Friendship Hotel (yǒuyí lǔshè)* on the right side of the road leading to the Tropical Plant Gardens. Beds there are Y5. There is also budget accommodation within the gardens. After crossing the bridge, follow the main path for about 15 minutes until you arrive at a group of buildings and a fork in the road. Take the right fork and you will find a Dai-style hostel with dorms beds for Y12 to Y15. For a more upmarket stay, take the left fork, go over the hill and to the left of the pond, where there is a damp but clean Chinese hotel that has doubles with attached bath for Y88.

Getting There & Away From Jinghong there are buses to Menglun (Y10) approximately hourly between 7 am and 3 pm. The buses pass through Ganlanba. Minivans occasionally leave from the main street of Ganlanba to Menglun, and also charge Y10. Some travellers have also cycled here from Ganlanba. Cycling onwards to Mengla could be more difficult because of the PSB. A permit for Mengla might make a difference, but it's hard to say.

Mengla

Mengla may not be a very inspiring town, but it is likely to see an increasing number of travellers passing through en route to Laos via the border crossing at Mohan. As the bus journey from Jinghong, or even Menglun, will take the better part of the day, you will probably have to overnight here. Downhill from the bus station, the *Binya Hotel (bīnyà bīnguǎn)* has hard dorm beds for Y10. Nearby the *Nanjiang Hotel (nánjiāng bīnguǎn)* offers a more upmarket alternative, with doubles with attached bath for Y60.

CITS has an office with at least one or two English-speaking staff at the *Mengla Hotel (měnglà bīnguǎn)*, which is about two km uphill from the bus station. The Mengla has dorm beds for around Y20, and doubles with bath and TV for Y60. The location is inconvenient, but a pedicab should get you there for Y3 to Y4.

Laos Border Crossing Though only recently opened to foreigners, this crossing has already seen a fair amount of traffic. From Mengla, there are buses to Mohan (Y8). Once your passport is stamped and you've waved goodbye to the border guards, you can jump on a tractor or truck to take you into Laos for around Y2. If you can't find a bus to Mohan, get on one to Shangyong, from where it should be relatively easy to arrange another ride.

Getting There & Away There are four or five direct buses a day between Jinghong and Mengla, leaving between 6.30 am and 3 pm. The 200-km ride takes anywhere from five to seven hours and the fare is Y20.

Damenglong
(dà měnglóng)
Damenglong is about 70 km south of Jinghong and a few km from the Myanmar border. It's another sleepy village that serves well enough as a base for hikes around the surrounding hills. It's also one of those places where, after three hours of bouncing up and down in a terminally ill bus, you arrive, thinking 'Is this *it*?' The village is not much (it rouses itself somewhat for the Sunday market), but the surrounding countryside, peppered with decaying stupas and little villages, is worth a couple of days' exploration. You can hire bikes at the Damenglong Hotel for Y5 a day.

The town's laid-back feel may change in the next few years, however. The border crossing point with Myanmar (poetically named 2-4-0) has been designated as the entry point for a planned highway linking Thailand, Myanmar and China. The road is supposedly due to open in 1998. If and when it does, things should definitely pick up in Damenglong. Just before we last visited, a group of Hong Kong investors was apparently sniffing around for a spot to build a tourist hotel.

Manfeilong Pagoda *(mánfēilóng tǎ)* This pagoda, built in 1204, is Damenglong's premier attraction. According to legend, the temple was built on the spot of a hallowed footprint left by Sakyamuni, who once visited Xishuangbanna – if you're interested in ancient footprints you can look for it in a niche below one of the nine stupas. Unfortunately, in recent years a 'beautification' job has been done on the temple with a couple of cans of silver paint – it probably sounded like a good idea at the time, but now that the paint has started to flake off it creates a very tacky effect.

If you're in Xishuangbanna in late October or early November, check for the precise dates of the Tan Ta Festival. Manfeilong Pagoda is host to hundreds of locals at this time in celebrations that include dancing, rockets, paper balloons and so on.

Manfeilong is easy to get to: just walk back along the main road towards Jinghong for two km until you reach a small village with a temple on your left. From here there's a path up the hill; it's about 20 minutes' walk.

Black Pagoda *(hēitǎ)* Just down from the stone mythical beasts that have mysteriously set up camp in the centre of town is a Dai monastery with a path beside it leading up to the Black Pagoda. The pagoda itself is not black at all – it's covered in flaking silver paint. Take a stroll up, but bear in mind that the real reason for the climb is less the pagoda itself than the superb views of Damenglong and the surrounding countryside. An English-speaking Malaysian monk is said to spend most of his time around here, though we didn't run into him.

Places to Stay & Eat The officially sanctioned foreigners' residence is the low-key *Damenglong Guesthouse (dàměnglóng zhāodàisuǒ)*. To get there, walk uphill from the black beasts at the traffic circle to the end of the road, where sits the local government building. The hotel is in the grounds to the left, just past some ornamental frogs. Basic dorm beds are Y10.

At the time of writing, construction work was being finished on a new bus station, just on the left as you enter town from Jinghong. It will incorporate a hotel, which may give travellers an alternative to the Damenglong Guesthouse.

The food situation in Damenglong is OK. Down from the bus station, near the steps leading up to the Black Pagoda are a couple of decent restaurants. The Chinese signs proclaim them to be Dai restaurants, but it's the old story of going out the back, pointing to your vegies and getting them five minutes later in a little pool of oil.

There are also two somewhat trendy (for Damenglong) veranda restaurants, one on each side of the road. The one on the left has an English sign saying 'Dai Hotel & Restaurant', but it's actually only the latter. The food is tasty, and it's a fun place to watch the town creep its way through the day (unless the staff are putting the karaoke machine through its paces).

There is also a cold drinks cafe at the traffic circle, where you can get a Coke with ice for Y5. The ice cubes tend to be a little brown, but the staff insist the water has been well boiled, and we suffered no ill effects.

Getting There & Away There are buses to Damenglong (Y10, 2½ hours) every half hour between 7 am and 5 pm from the No 2 bus station in Jinghong. Buses for the return trip are on a similar schedule, though the last bus tends to leave a bit earlier, around 3 to 4 pm.

Around Damenglong
The village of Xiaojie, about 15 km before Damenglong, is surrounded by Bulang, Lahu and Hani villages. Lahu women shave their heads; apparently the younger Lahu women aren't happy about this any more and use caps to hide their shaven heads. The Bulang are possibly descended from the Lolo in northern Yunnan. The women wear black turbans with silver decorations; many of the designs are of shells, fish and marine life.

There's plenty of room for exploration in this area, although you're not allowed over the border.

Menghai
(ménghǎi)
This uninspiring place serves as a centre for trips into the surrounding area. The Sunday

market attracts members of the hill tribes and the best way to find it is to follow the early-morning crowds. There are a couple of drab hotels. One near the old bus station at the centre of town has beds for Y5. About one km further down the street, near the smaller but more active bus station, the *Liangyuan Hotel (liángyuán bīnguǎn)* has beds in triples for Y20 and doubles/triples for Y60.

Buses and minibuses run from the No 2 bus station in Jinghong to Menghai approximately every half hour between 7 am and 5 pm. The fare is Y7 and the trip takes about 90 minutes. Minibuses to Jinghong, Menghun and Jingzhen leave from a smaller bus station, at the western end of Menghai.

Menghun
(měnghùn)

This tiny village is about 26 km south-west of Menghai. The Sunday market here begins buzzing around 7 am and lingers on through to noon. The swirl of hill tribes and women sporting fancy leggings, headdresses, earrings and bracelets alone makes the trip worthwhile. Although the market seems to be the main attraction, a temple and footpaths that wind through the lush hills behind the White Tower Hotel are also worth an extra day or two.

Places to Stay & Eat Right at the centre of town where the buses let you off, the *Yun Chuan Restaurant/Hotel (yúnchuān fàndiàn)* is nothing to get excited about, but the rooms are acceptable. Further down on the right side of the street, the *Phoenix Hotel (fènghuáng fàndiàn)* is cheaper (Y4 a bed), but very noisy and better off given a miss. The more secluded *White Tower Hotel* is roomier, quieter and looks out over a lily pond. Beds in doubles here cost Y10, but you can probably talk the price down. From the main intersection, take the road uphill, walk through the archway, then bear left along a small path heading downhill. Apparently one foreigner had a camera stolen from here, so be careful with your belongings.

There are several good Dai restaurants along the main street, some of which have English menus.

Getting There & Away Buses from Jinghong to Daluo pass through Menghun, and leave the Jinghong No 2 bus station every half hour between 7 and 5 pm. The fare to Menghun is Y11. Going back you just have to wait on the side of the road until a bus passes by. Normally you shouldn't have to wait too long.

Unless you have a very good bike with gears, cycling to Menghai and Menghun is not a real option. The road up to Menghai is so steep that you'll end up pushing the bike most of the way.

Intrepid travellers have hitched and hiked all the way from here to Damenglong. This should be no problem, providing you don't inadvertently stray over the Myanmar border at some point. A mountain bike would be the best way to do it. Hitching and walking should take a leisurely seven days.

Jingzhen
(jǐngzhen)

In the village of Jingzhen, about 14 km north-west of Menghai, is the **Octagonal Pavilion** *(bājiǎo tíng)*, first built in 1701. The original structure was severely damaged during the Cultural Revolution, so the present renovated building isn't exactly thrilling. Take a close look at the new paintings on the wall of the temple. There are some interesting scenes which appear to depict People's Liberation Army (PLA) soldiers causing death and destruction during the Cultural Revolution; adjoining scenes depict buddha vanquishing PLA soldiers, one of whom is waving goodbye as he drowns in a pond.

Jingzhen is a pleasant rural spot for walks along the river or the fish ponds behind the village. Frequent minibuses from the minibus centre in Menghai go via Jingzhen.

Nanluoshan
(nánlúoshān)

Nanluoshan lies south of the road between Jinghong and Menghai (17 km from Menghai). It's best done as a day-trip from Menghai, providing you start early and return to the main road before dusk. The bus will drop you off close to a bridge; cross the bridge and follow the dirt track about six km uphill until you join a newly constructed main road.

About one km before the junction, you'll round a bend in the road and see a fence with a stile and stone benches beyond. This is the turn-off for the steps down to the overrated **King of Tea Trees** *(cháwáng)* – the name says it all! According to the Hani, their ancestors have been growing tea for 55 generations and this tree was the first one planted. The tree is definitely not worth descending hundreds of steps to see; it is half dead and covered with moss, graffiti and signs forbidding graffiti. A crumbling concrete pavilion daubed with red paint completes the picture.

The highway has been bulldozed out of the mountain for the comfort of tourists who can now visit the hill tribes further up the mountain. Repeated exposure to tour buses is certain to cause changes among the Hani and Lahu villagers there. If you leave the main road, there's some pleasant hiking in the area, but don't expect villagers to automatically give you a bed for the night. A Hani villager did invite us into his stilt house for an excellent meal and some firewater that left us wobbling downhill.

The Hani (also known in adjacent countries as the Akha) are of Tibetan origin, but according to folklore they are descended from frogs' eyes. They stick to the hills, cultivating rice, corn and the occasional poppy. Trading takes place at weekly markets where the Dai obviously dominate the Hani, who seem only too keen to scamper back to their mountain retreats. Hani women wear headdresses of beads, feathers, coins and silver rings. At one remote market the women were very nervous and it was only when their backs were turned that I could inspect their headdresses, which were made with French (Vietnamese), Burmese and Indian coins from the turn of the century.

BAOSHAN REGION
(bǎoshān dìqū)

Travellers who pass through the Baoshan area tend to do so quickly, generally staying overnight in Baoshan city on the way to Ruili

and Wanding, but the area is worth a bit more time than that. There are some worthwhile historical sights, the old quarters of Tengchong and Baoshan make for some good browsing, distinctive minority groups are in abundance (as in other parts of southern Yunnan), and the Tengchong area is rich in volcanic activity, with hot springs and volcanic peaks.

As early as the 4th and 5th centuries BC (two centuries before the northern routes through central Asia were established), the Baoshan area was an important stage on the southern Silk Road – the Sichuan-India route. The area did not really come under Chinese control until the time of the Han Dynasty when, in 69 AD, it was named the Yongchang Administrative District.

Baoshan
(bǎoshān)

Baoshan is a small city that's easily explored on foot. There are pockets of traditional wooden architecture still standing in the city area and some good walks on the outskirts of town. It has innumerable speciality products that range from excellent coffee to leather boots and pepper and silk. Tea aficionados might like to try the Reclining Buddha Baoshan Tea, a brand of national repute.

Information Baoshan is not exactly geared up for a large-scale invasion of foreign visitors, and little in the way of information is available. Shops in the long-distance bus station sell maps of Baoshan Prefecture which include Baoshan city and Tengchong as well as regional sights, with some explanations in English. Otherwise you're pretty much on your own. The Bank of China is next to the Yindou Hotel, and the post office is not far away.

Things to See Baoshan is an interesting city to wander aimlessly in. The streets are lively and, in many areas, lined with old traditional homes. The major sight within easy walking distance of the centre of town is **Taibao Park** *(tàibǎo gōngyuán)*. It's flanked to the south

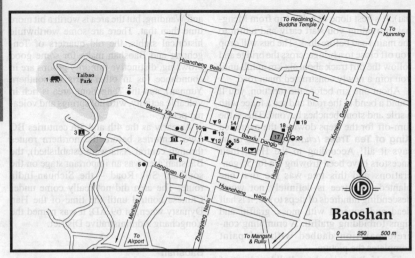

by the **Wenbi Pagoda** (*wénbǐ tǎ*) and to the east by the **Yuhuang Pavilion** (*yùhuáng gé*). All three are worth a look. The Yuhuang Pavilion dates back to the Ming Dynasty and has a small museum next door to it. The small viewing pagodas in the park provide good views of Baoshan, the Wenbi Pagoda and Yiluo Pond. There are paths in the park strik-

ing off to the north, west and south. The northern path doubles back to the south and eventually takes you past a very mediocre zoo (keep walking). Continuing to the south you will reach **Yiluo Pond** (*yìluó chí*), also known as the Dragon Spring Pond (*lóngquán chí*). The best thing about the latter are the views of the 13-tiered Wenbi Pagoda.

The Last Word

In the Baoshan post office the staff were using the postage scales to weigh three deep-fried chickens. It was a unique undertaking (perhaps the stuff of which *Guinness Book of Records* attempts are made), and the customers, who seemed to vaguely approve of the proceedings, waited patiently in line, lighting up cigarettes and grinding their phlegm contentedly into the concrete underfoot. Finally, one of the girls dragged herself away from the chickens, sauntered over my way and glanced at my letter. She sighed wearily, as if to say 'not *another* one', and shook her head: 'The address is not central enough – you'll have to write it again.' I refused. She insisted. I refused again. She took a new envelope and placed it in front of me. I ignored it and pushed my original letter towards her. She eyed it suspiciously and turned it over: 'Your name should be after your address, not before it.' I crossed out my name at the head of the address and re-wrote it at the bottom. 'Happy?' I asked her. She scowled, thrust my letter onto the scales and handed it back to me dripping with deep-fried chicken oil. As always, it's the people behind the counter who get the last laugh in China. ■

Places to Stay There are plenty of inexpensive places to stay in Baoshan. Right next to the long-distance bus station is the *Keyun Hotel (kèyùn zhùsùbù)*, which has beds in a clean three-bed dorm for Y16 and in a four-bed dorm for Y12. Doubles with common bathroom are Y56. Really good value is the *Lanyuan Hotel (lányuàn dàjiǔjiā)*, which is two or three minutes north of the bus station on the other side of the road. Look for the blue sign with 'Lanyuan Restaurant' on it – don't worry, it really is a hotel. The Lanyuan has beds in doubles/triples for Y5/8. But the best deal may be the doubles with attached bathroom for Y28 and Y44. Rooms are clean, airy and, depending on who your neighbours are for the night, quiet.

Along Baoxiu Xilu are a few sprawling Chinese-style hotels. They all take foreign-

ers and most seem fairly friendly even though they're probably uninspiring places to stay. The first is the *Yongchang Hotel (yǒngchāng bīnguǎn)*, which has dorm beds for Y10. A host of other rooms are available: singles from Y40 to Y120 and doubles from Y30 to Y100. Triples with bath are Y90. Don't expect anything more than a bed in the cheaper rooms. Not far up the road is the *Lanhua Hotel (lánhuā bīnguǎn)*, which has beds in three-bed dorms for Y8. Doubles/triples with attached bathroom come in at Y60 and deluxe singles at Y80. The *Baoshan Guesthouse (bǎoshān bīnguǎn)* is where the pedicab drivers will probably take you if you stumble off the bus looking dazed and confused. It has beds in triples for Y30 and, over in the north wing, slightly upmarket doubles for Y100 (bathroom attached).

Baoshan's premier accommodation is brought to you by the Bank of China. The *Yindou Hotel (yíndū dàjiǔdiàn)* is a money-making venture set up by the bank. It offers doubles with international telephone, 24-hour hot water, air-con and satellite TV for Y140. It's probably not a bad deal if you're looking for comfort. But if you're en route to Tengchong, hold out a bit longer: you can get a comparable room there for half the price.

Places to Eat Baoxiu Lu and the road to the south running parallel to it are good places to seek out cheap restaurants. Look for the place selling dumplings and noodles down the road from the Yindou Hotel towards the bus station. Next door to the Baoshan Guesthouse is an across-the-bridge noodle restaurant that is worth checking out, though it closes quite early. Most of the hotel restaurants are probably better left alone.

As in Kunming there are plenty of road-side snacks available. There's a tiny coffee shop across from the Yongchang Hotel. While its coffee is very sweet and very instant, it's only Y3 per cup, and the place offers you a chance to rest your feet for a few moments. Cold drinks are also served. *A Splendid Tea House* in the long-distance bus compound is notable as a place to avoid. It has terrible coffee, and the owner has a penchant for serenading her guests on a clapped-out karaoke machine at 100 decibels. It is also the entrance for one of the worst discos in China.

Getting There & Away You can fly in and out of Baoshan, though very few Western travellers do; mysteriously, there are no references to this air link in CAAC timetables. Ask in Kunming for details or at the Baoshan CAAC office, which is rather inconveniently located at the intersection of Longquan Lu and Minhang Lu. Look for a large yellow-tiled building. The only English you'll see is on the vertical sign, which says 'Civil Aviation Hotel' at the very bottom. The ticket office is on the 1st floor, facing Longquan Lu. There are three flights weekly to Kunming, and tickets cost Y400. The airport is around nine km south of town.

The Baoshan long-distance bus station is a huge new construction, and there are buses running from here to a host of destinations around Yunnan. There are numerous late-afternoon buses making the 18-hour haul to Kunming, several of them sleepers. Fares are Y66 for your standard bone-rattler, Y84 for luxury buses and Y122 for sleepers. Buses for Xiaguan (Dali) leave at 6.50, 9 and 11 am and 3.30 pm and cost Y20; the journey takes around six hours. Buses to Tengchong also leave daily at 6.50, 9 and 11 am. The 167-kilometre ride usually takes a stunning eight hours at least, including six solid hours of jolting mountain ascents and descents that should reduce the average traveller's kidneys to mush. The experience will cost you Y20. Buses on to Yingjiang, past Tengchong leave at 6.30 and 6.50 am: the former is a sleeper, which costs Y35. There are several buses to Ruili between 6.50 and 10.30 am. The ride takes seven to eight hours, some of it over a newly finished roadway, and costs Y35. Buses to Ruili pass through Mangshi and Wanding.

Across the street at the city bus station you can catch a bus to Jinghong in Xishuangbanna daily at 6.30 am. This odyssey takes two full days: the bus overnights at Lincang,

and arrives in Jinghong sometime the following night, depending on road conditions, which are dubious at the best of times. Lincang is on the PSB's list of approved destinations for foreigners, so you should have no trouble along this route. The fare is Y89.

Getting Around Baoshan can comfortably be explored on foot, which is probably why there is no evidence of bicycle-hire stands around town. This is a pity because a bicycle would be the ideal way to get to some of the sights around Baoshan. With any luck, an enterprising local may fill this gap as increasing numbers of foreigners pass through the area.

Around Baoshan

Just 17 km north of town, the **Reclining Buddha Temple** *(wòfó sì)* is one of the most important historical sights in the vicinity of Baoshan. The temple dates back to the Tang Dynasty, having a history of some 1200 years. The reclining buddha itself, in a cave to the rear of the temple area, was severely damaged during the Cultural Revolution and has only recently been restored.

The only problem is getting to the temple. There are no local buses or minibuses. A motorcycle with sidecar, can take two people there and back for Y40. Taxis ask around Y70 to Y80. It would be a fairly comfortable bicycle trip if you could get hold of a bike.

Tengchong

(téngchōng)

Not many travellers get to this town on the other side of the Gaoligong Mountain range, but it's an interesting place. There are some 20 volcanoes in the vicinity and lively geothermal activity – lots of hot springs. It's also prime earthquake territory, having experienced 71 earthquakes measuring over five on the Richter scale since 1500 AD.

The town itself has preserved, on a larger scale, the kind of traditional wooden architecture that has survived only in pockets in Kunming and Baoshan. It's not exactly Dali,

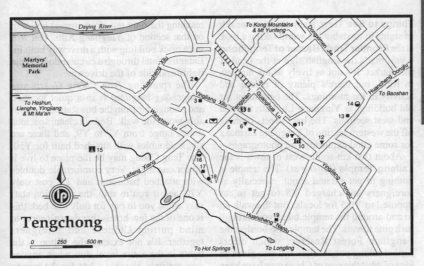

Tengchong

TENGCHONG 腾冲

PLACES TO STAY

3 Hongyan (Swan Goose)
   Hotel
   鸿雁族社
7 Tengyun Hotel
   腾云宾馆
13 Gonglu Hotel
   公路招待所
17 Teng Chong Guest-
   house
   腾冲宾馆
19 Taian Hotel
   泰安宾馆

PLACES TO EAT

5 Youyi Restaurant
   友谊饭店
6 Burmese Cafe
   缅甸咖啡厅
9 Qiao Wei Restaurant
   桥味餐厅
12 Chunhua Huishiguan
   春华会族食馆

OTHER

1 Frontier Trade Bazaar
   of Tengchong
   腾冲边境货物商场
2 PSB
   公安局

4 Post Office
   邮电局
8 Bank of China
   中国银行
10 Workers' Cultural Palace
   工人文化宫
11 Bicycle Rental
   自行车出租
14 Long-Distance Bus
   Station
   长途汽车站
15 Laifeng Temple
   来凤寺
16 Minibuses to Yingjiang
   往盈江的中巴车
18 Hot Springs Bus Ticket
   Office
   热海车售票处

but there's a definite charm to some of the narrow backstreets. The town is at an altitude of 1650 metres and can get quite crisp in the evenings during the winter months.

Information Tengchong has a small travel office at the front gate of the Teng Chong Guesthouse. The staff don't speak much English, but can provide you with maps of the county, and maybe some assistance. Maps are also sold at the store in the hotel courtyard. The post office is on Fengshan Lu. The Bank of China towers over the town's main intersection. The bank won't change travellers' cheques, so unless you have cash, change money before you get to Tengchong.

Things to See There's not exactly a wealth of sights in town but it's worth taking a look at the **Frontier Trade Bazaar of Tengchong** – yes, that's the English sign at the head of the market. It's not as lively as the markets in Ruili, but there's plenty of colour and activity in the mornings. The best street for old buildings is Yingjiang Lu, both the east and west sections. The backstreets running off the western section of Yingjiang Lu make for some good exploring and photographs.

About two km south-west of town is the **Laifeng Temple** (*láifēng sì*). The temple is nothing to get excited about, especially as foreigners are charged Y5 to get in, as opposed to Y0.5 for locals. But the walk up to and around the temple takes you through lush pine forests. The temple also borders the Fengshan Forest Reserve, which offers further hiking possibilities and also gives an idea of what this part of China may have been like before the trees gave way to farms.

Places to Stay Tengchong's accommodation options are fairly spread out. South of the bus station, the *Gonglu Hotel* (*gōnglù zhāodàisuǒ*) has beds for Y7 to Y15. It's a noisy place, and the rooms are nothing special, but it's the closest place to the bus station. The hotel has no English sign – look for the ubiquitous bus steering wheel logo at the top of the entry gate.

Close to the centre of town, the *Tengyun Hotel* (*téngyún bīnguǎn*) is a slightly dilapidated place with dorm beds for Y5 to Y8 in pleasant old wooden buildings, and doubles/triples in the (somewhat) newer wing for Y26/30. None of the rooms have bathrooms, which is too bad, as the common ones are particularly pungent. Again, there are no English signs for this hotel, but you can pick out the entrance by looking for the little Burmese cafe on the right-hand side. Up on Yingjiang Xilu is the wonderful *Hongyan Hotel* (Swan Goose Hotel) (*hóngyàn lǚshè*). Rooms are clustered around a little courtyard, and beds are Y5 in doubles and triples, singles are Y6, and 'suites' Y10. The place often seems to be booked up. To find it, start looking to your left about 20 metres before

reaching the only tall (four-storey) building on that section of Yingjiang Xilu. You will see a brick building with a driveway built in. Enter the hotel through a circular door on the right-hand side of the driveway.

The sprawling *Teng Chong Guesthouse* (*téngchōng bīnguǎn*) is in a quiet location and, though far from the bus station, is probably worth the walk. Beds in clean, spacious dorms range from Y7 to Y9, and there are singles/doubles with attached bath for Y50. The Teng Chong may be the place to live it up for one night. Very comfortable doubles with attached bathroom and TV cost only Y70, and if you're solo, the reception staff may allow you to pay for only one bed: this is one of the few hotels that doesn't seem to mind putting Chinese and foreigners together. It's not exactly the Hilton – the lights in the entire hotel dim when anyone uses the only elevator – but for the money it's great value.

Lastly, the *Taian Hotel* (*tàiān bīnguǎn*), a Sino-Burmese joint venture, has what appear to be fairly decent doubles and triples with attached washroom for Y80/90. Consistent with the rest of Tengchong hotels, there is no English sign. But it's hard to miss this place – a white-tiled five-storey lump of curves and right angles hovering over the intersection of Huancheng Donglu and Huancheng Nanlu.

Places to Eat There are scores of tiny, inviting eateries housed in Tengchong's wooden buildings. Look out for the *Youyi Restaurant* (*yǒuyì fàndiàn*) on Fengshan Lu just before Yingjiang Donglu. There's no English sign, but it's an open-fronted place and fairly easy to find. Ask for their delicious Shandong-style steamed dumplings (*zhengjiǎo*) – they are unlike dumplings anywhere else in China. Also try their spicy pickled vegetables (*shuǐyāncài*). You can also head out to the back of the restaurant and invent your own meal.

Up on Guanghua Lu you can get tasty Burmese-style dishes at the *Qiao Wei Restaurant* (*qiáowèi cānguǎn*). There's no menu: just head into the kitchen. It also prepares

Chinese food, so if you want Burmese cooking, ask for *miǎndiàn wèi*.

Towards the long-distance bus station, near the corner of Huancheng Donglu and Guanghua Lu, is the *Chunhua Huishiguan (chūnhuá huíshíguǎn)*, a Muslim place that seems to be worth checking out. It has a green and white sign and light-green doors. For sweet coffee, excellent samosas, Mekong whisky, and the likely chance of chatting with some of Tengchong's itinerant Burmese jewellery peddlers, stop by the *Burmese Cafe* at the entrance to the Tengyun Hotel. There is an English sign out front, and usually at least one English speaker within.

Getting There & Away Tengchong's long-distance bus station must be the only bus station in the whole of the south-west that has a board with English information about bus times and prices. Ignore it – it's completely out of date, though it's a nice thought.

There are several buses from the long-distance bus station to Baoshan between 7.30 and 11 am. The price is Y20. The journey should take around eight hours, though it often takes longer, and will leave your bones vibrating well into the night. Buses to Ruili run via Yingjiang and Zhangfeng, cost Y12 and take eight to nine hours. Alternatively, if you have time on your hands, travel to Yingjiang (stopping to have a browse in Lianghe on the way), stay overnight there and travel on to Ruili by bus the next day. Buses to Yingjiang leave at 7.30 and 10.30 am and 12.30 pm. There are also buses to Mangshi at 7.30 am (five hours, Y13) and to Kunming. The latter is a sleeper, leaving at 10 am and arriving in Kunming around 24 hours later. The fare is Y160.

You should also be able to get a minibus to Yingjiang at the intersection of Fengshan Lu and Huancheng Nanlu, near the Teng Chong Guesthouse. Buses run from 8 am to around 4 pm, leaving as they fill up. You can also hire vans here to take you to the Kong Mountain volcanoes, Mt Yunfeng and other sights in the area. (See the following Around Tengchong section).

Getting Around Tengchong is small enough to walk around, but a bicycle would be useful for getting to some of the closer sights outside town – the surrounding scenery alone justifies a ride. If you're interested, there is a bicycle shop on Guanghua Lu, diagonally opposite the Qiao Wei Restaurant, that rents bikes for Y1 per hour, with a deposit of Y200. There's no sign out front, but just look for a mass of bicycles parked in front of a yellow wooden building.

Around Tengchong

There's a lot to see around Tengchong but, as in Baoshan, the area has only recently opened and getting out to the sights is a bit tricky. Catching buses part of the way and hiking up to the sights is one possibility, while some of the closer sights can be reached by bicycle. Your other option is a hired van, which may be affordable if there are several of you. The *Five Continent Travel Service (wǔzhōu lǚxíngshè)* at the entrance to the Teng Chong Guesthouse can arrange such transport, or you can head down to the minibus stand at the intersection of Huancheng Nanlu and Fengshan Lu, where van drivers often sit around puffing cigarettes and waiting for some business to walk their way.

Heshun Village *(héshùn xiāng)* If you come into Tengchong from Ruili and Yingjiang, just four km before pulling into town you pass through the village of Heshun. It's worth hiking or cycling back to take a closer look at the village. The Chinese make much fuss of the fact that it has been set aside as a kind of retirement village for Overseas Chinese, but for the average Western visitor it's likely to be of more interest as a quiet, traditional Chinese village with cobbled streets. There are some great old buildings in the village, providing lots of photo opportunities. You may also get a chance to meet some older English-speaking Chinese.

Mt Yunfeng *(yúnfēng shān)* Mt Yunfeng is a Taoist mountain dotted with temples and monastic retreats, 47 km to the north of Tengchong. The temples were built in the early 17th century, and the best example is said to be the Yunfeng Temple at the summit. Getting there is not so easy. The only budget option is to take a bus to Ruidian *(ruìdiàn)* – after passing through the town of Gudong *(gúdōng)*, you will come to a turn-off for the mountain. After getting off here you will have to either walk or hitch the remaining nine to 10 km to reach the base of the mountain. Buses to Ruidian leave the Tengchong bus station at 7.30 am and 1 and 5 pm. Hiring a vehicle to take you there and back will cost around Y300.

Volcanoes *(huǒshānqún)* Tengchong County is renowned for its volcanoes, and although they have been behaving themselves for many centuries the seismic and geothermal activity in the area probably indicates that they won't always continue to do so. The closest one to town is Mt Ma'an *(mǎān shān)*, around five km to the north-west. It's just south of the main road that runs to Yingjiang.

Around 22 km to the north of town, near the village of Mazhan *(mǎzhàn)* is a cluster of volcanoes: the Kong Mountains *(kōngshān huǒshānqún)*. Buses to Gudong run past Mazhan. From Mazhan you can either walk or take a motor-tricycle (Y5) to the volcano area. Alternatively, hire a van to take you there and back for around Y150.

Hot Springs The 'Sea of Heat' *(rèhǎi)* as the Chinese poetically refer to it, is a cluster of hot springs, geysers and streams around 12 km south-west of Tengchong. In addition to the usual indoor baths, there is an outdoor hot spring as well as a warm-water pool, sitting just above a river. Two hotels at the entrance to the springs have simple doubles for Y30 to Y50, and restaurants serving up local specialities, so it's easy to make this a relaxing overnight trip. However, in summer a fairly active mosquito community can wreak havoc with sleep – you may wish to opt for just a day's sojourn if the weather is hot.

Charter vans run to the hot springs daily at 9 am from in front of a small travel agency just south of the Teng Chong Guesthouse. They return to Tengchong around 2 pm. The one-way fare is Y6. The travel agency has maps of the springs as well as of Tengchong itself. If you have trouble finding the travel agency, walk around to the Huancheng Nanlu side, and look inside the shop until you see a sign board promoting the 'Tengchong Hot Sea'.

DEHONG REGION
(déhóng zhōu)

Dehong Prefecture, like Xishuangbanna, borders Myanmar and is heavily populated by distinctive minority groups, but for some reason it doesn't seem to have captured travellers' imaginations to the extent that Xishuangbanna has. It's in the far west of Yunnan and is definitely more off the beaten track than Xishuangbanna – you're unlikely to see the busloads of Chinese tourists who have overrun Xishuangbanna in recent years, and even less likely to bump into more than a couple of other backpackers. Most Chinese in Dehong are there for the Myanmar trade that comes through the towns of Ruili and Wanding. Burmese jade is a commodity that many Chinese have grown rich on in recent years, but there are countless other items being spirited over the border that separates China and Myanmar, some of them illicit.

Many minority groups are represented in Dehong, but among the most obvious are the Burmese, the Dai and the Jingpo (known in nearby Myanmar as the Kachin, a minority long-engaged in armed struggle against the Myanmar government). Throughout Dehong it is possible to see signs sporting numerous languages: Chinese, Burmese, Dai and English. This is a border region that is getting rich on trade – in the markets you can see old Indian men selling jewellery, tinned fruits from Thailand, Burmese papier-mâché furniture, young bloods with huge wads of foreign currency, and Chinese plain-clothes police trying not to look too obvious.

The Rebel

He slid into the chair opposite me and glanced around nervously. 'The walls have ears,' I almost expected him to say. But no, it was something altogether more mundane: what did I do? I was writing a book about China. 'China? Why not Myanmar?' he asked, looking slightly surprised. I explained that it had been a foolish mistake on my part but, now that I had already started, it was a bit late to change. But my newly acquired friend from Burma wasn't convinced: 'I take you to Kachin rebel camp in Myanmar,' he said. 'We dye your hair black. You wear Chinese clothes. We travel at night. Maybe the border guards they shoot at you – no problem. We take you rebel camp. You write Kachin rebels good people.' After expressing reservations about dyeing my hair, I exchanged business cards with him, and we agreed to keep in touch. ∎

Yingjiang

(*yíngjiāng*)

Yingjiang is a possible stopover if you're heading to Ruili from Tengchong. It's not really worth a special effort (it might be described as a *very* pale shadow of Ruili), but the locals are friendly and, even though there's not a lot to do, it's a good place to break up the bus ride.

Things to See There's nothing much really. Take a minibus out to **Jiucheng** (*jiùchéng*, literally, old town) to see an old Chinese town. It's only a 20-minute ride, and it's fairly picturesque. Back on the road to Ruili, a couple of km out of town, is an old stupa: **Laomian Pagoda** (*lǎomiǎn tǎ*). The name means old Burmese stupa/pagoda, which is a fairly accurate description. Locals claim it's a nice place to visit in the evenings 'with someone you care about' – see if you can find the local PSB and invite one of the boys in green along.

Places to Stay & Eat Opposite the long-distance bus station is the drab *State Guesthouse* (*guóyíng lǚshè*). Locals claim it is a den of iniquity, but unfortunately we didn't come across anything particularly iniquitous. It's Y4 for a bed in a three or five-bed dorm, Y16 for a double and Y10 for a single. None of the rooms have showers. You also need to take a bit of a hike if you want to use the toilet.

Better still, give the State Den of Iniquity a miss and walk into town (turn right after you exit the bus station) for the *Yingxiang Hotel* (*yíngxiáng lǚshé*). It's on the right-hand side of the road, just after the road makes a bit of a turn to the right. This clean and friendly place has singles/doubles for Y12/18 and singles with bathroom and TV for Y30. The hot water is solar heated and doesn't really get warm until mid-afternoon. And don't expect a nice hot shower if it's been raining that day.

Yingjiang's answer to the Hilton is the *Great Wall Hotel* (*chángchéng bīnguǎn*), where the cheapest rooms cost Y60 (no carpet!) and the most expensive are Y120. All rooms have their own TVs and bathrooms. To get there, keep walking from the Yingxiang Hotel and turn right at the first major intersection; the Great Wall is on the corner of the next intersection. Across the street, the *Bright Pearl Hotel* (*míngzhū dàjiǔdiàn*) has similar standards and rates.

Yingjiang is not a gastronomical experience that merits a postcard to mum and dad, but the cheap noodle stores over near the bus station will keep you alive for another day.

Getting There & Away There is one bus daily at 9.30 am to Yingjiang from Ruili. From Tengfeng, buses leave at 7.30 and 10.30 am and 12.30 pm. Unless you're taking the early bus from Tengchong, you will probably have to stay overnight in Yingjiang as most outbound buses stop around noon. Up to around 4 pm you may be able to catch a minibus across from the bus station to Zhangfeng, where you can connect with buses to Ruili. The whole journey should cost Y25 and take around five hours. Direct buses from Yingjiang to Ruili leave at 7, 8.30 and 11 am and cost Y16. Going the other way, there are several buses to Tengchong between 7 am and noon. The trip takes around three hours and costs Y12. There is one bus daily to Baoshan leaving at 7 am. You can even get a sleeper bus from here to Kunming, departing daily at 7 am. The 29-hour odyssey costs Y170.

Ruili
(ruìli)

Ruili is without a doubt one of the more interesting towns in south-western China. It's just a few km from Myanmar and has a real border-town feel about it. There's a great mix of Han Chinese, minorities and Burmese traders, and travellers tend to linger longer than they intended just for the atmosphere. At first sight it doesn't seem like much, and the place is getting dustier with all the new construction, but it's worth giving it a couple of days. Compared with the rest of China, Ruili seems unrestricted, as though people get away with a lot more here. That this atmosphere is generated by proximity to Myanmar and it's repressive military junta makes Ruili all the more interesting. There are some interesting minority villages nearby; the stupas are in much better condition than those in Xishuangbanna, and it's

worth travelling onwards to Wanding and Mangshi, either as day-trips or as overnight stops.

Information The shop next to the reception area of the Ruili Guesthouse has maps and a few brochures on Ruili, but there's very little else in the way of information available. The travel agency on the grounds of the Ruili Guesthouse also has maps and brochures, but it can't do much unless you're part of a large group. The PSB is just up the road from the guesthouse. Heading down the road you'll find the telecommunications building, from where you can make direct-dial international calls. The Bank of China is not far from the long-distance bus station. In case you're headed to Myanmar, the bank will let you cash travellers' cheques for US dollars, which should come in handy across the border.

Myanmar Border Crossing At the time of writing, Ruili was not really set up for regular forays by foreigners across the border, though things looked likely to change soon. If you have a multiple-entry visa for China, the Chinese border guards

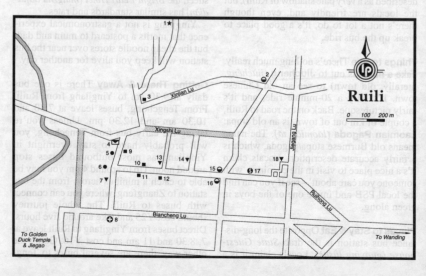

Ruili

0   100   200 m

To Golden
Duck Temple
& Jiegao

To Wanding

will probably let you walk across to the Myanmar border checkpoint, where US$10 will buy you a one-day visa to tour the town of Muse, but no further. By the time you have this book in your hand, some local travel

agencies may be able to take foreigners across the border via guided tours, which could help you get around the multiple-entry visa requirement. You'll have to ask around.

If you already have a Myanmar tourist visa, you can get across, but on one condition: there have to be at least two of you. Myanmar government regulations stipulate that only 'package tours' can enter the country at the Ruili-Muse checkpoint. Apparently, even two scruffy-looking backpackers constitute a package, but if you're solo, it's no go. This bureaucratic hurdle may eventually be torn down, so it wouldn't hurt to ask around.

Things to See There is really not a lot to see in Ruili itself though it's a great town to wander around, and is small enough that you can cover most of it in an hour or so. The market street in the west of town is the most colourful by day, especially in the morning, while by night the market street just around the corner from the Ruili Guesthouse is the liveliest place to hang out. Most of Ruili's sights are outside town, and you'll need a bicycle to get out and see them.

Places to Stay While everywhere else in Dehong and Baoshan has rock-bottom prices for accommodation, Ruili is the exception to the rule. However, a slew of new hotels has made for stiff competition, and some prices have actually come down in recent years, albeit slightly.

Probably the best deal in town is the *Mingrui Hotel (míngruì bīnguǎn)*, where a bed in a triple with bathroom will cost you only Y20. Beds in doubles are Y30, and if the hotel is not very full, you'll probably get a room to yourself. Rooms are airy and clean, and you can use the hotel's scenic rooftop washing machine – hang your socks while gazing at the Burmese hills. The Mingrui is also the only spot in town for bicycle rental.

Across the street, the *Limin Hotel (lìmín bīnguǎn)* has beds in triples with common washroom for Y20. Similar doubles are Y50, while standard doubles with attached bath are Y100. One other place that takes foreign-

---

RUILI 瑞丽

PLACES TO STAY

3 Ruili Guesthouse
   瑞丽宾馆
9 Yongchang Hotel
   永昌大酒家
10 Mingrui Hotel
   明瑞宾馆
11 Limin Hotel
   利民宾馆
12 Nanyang Hotel
   南洋宾馆

PLACES TO EAT

7 Burmese Restaurants
   缅甸餐厅
13 Jue Jue Cold Drinks Shop
   觉觉冷饮店
14 Noodle Shops
   面条店
18 Burmese Restaurants
   缅甸餐厅

OTHER

1 PSB
   公安局
2 Buses to Zhangfeng
   往章凤的汽车
4 Post Office
   邮电大楼
5 Xinhua Bookstore
   新华书店
6 Cinema
   电影院
8 Hospital
   医院
15 Minibus Stand
   小型车站
16 Long-Distance Bus Station
   长途汽车站
17 Bank of China
   中国银行

ers and has dormitory accommodation is the *Ruili Guesthouse (ruìlì bīnguǎn)*. Being a bit further away from the main strip, it offers refuge from the blaring discos and evil roadside karaoke stands. Beds in quads and doubles are Y20 each. Bathrooms and showers are on the 1st floor. There are also doubles for Y160 – not good value for money.

The *Yongchang Hotel (yǒngchāng dàjiǔdiàn)* attracts fewer travellers (possibly because of it's location), but is also a comfortable, clean place to stay. Standard doubles here are Y130, and triples Y150. There is also one four-bed room for Y160. Back on the main strip, the *Nanyang Hotel (nányáng bīnguǎn)* has doubles for Y90, though you'd probably be better off with a Y60 double at the Mingrui.

If all of the above are full (not likely) or not to your taste, there are many other hotels to choose from, including several down on Biancheng Lu. Standard doubles at these places all share a sense of shabby luxury, and usually cost between Y100 and Y130.

Places to Eat Reports concerning the existence of decent curries in Ruili are greatly exaggerated, but there is some good food available all the same. Take a stroll up the market street around the corner from the Ruili Hotel in the evening and check out all the hotpot stands – as always with hotpot, confirm prices beforehand. For good Burmese food, there are several restaurants in a small alley off Jiegang Lu. The one at the top of the north-western corner is particularly good, and sees a lot of Burmese patrons. This is also the spot to go for Thai Mekong whisky, served Thai style with soda water and ice. More Burmese places, with outdoor seating in the evenings, can be found just south of the cinema on Renmin Jie.

The noodle stalls on the street off Nanlao Jie just west of the bus station are also very good. For nice iced coffee and fruit juice drinks, or something stronger, try the *Jue Jue Cold Drinks Shop (juéjué léngyǐndiàn)*. There's no English sign, but the shop is at the corner of the side street just east of the

Mingrui Hotel, and shouldn't be too hard to find.

Take the opportunity to try a freshly squeezed lime juice from one of the numerous stands dotting the town. At Y5 a glass it's a bit more than your average drink, but the taste is superb, and the Chinese and Burmese who run the stands will get a kick out of watching you down your glass in several seconds.

Entertainment Ruili may be only a small town, but by Chinese standards it packs a lot of punch on the entertainment level. For the Chinese, Ruili has a reputation as one of *the* happening places in Yunnan, and young people with money head down here just for a few nights out. But where discos used to be the venue of choice, now massage parlours have taken over. Prostitution is rampant in Ruili, and it's difficult to find a sleaze-free bar or dance hall. This is, of course, still China, and things are much more tame than

---

Jamming

'Don't go to the Yufeng Disco,' the locals warned me. 'It's full of Burmese who'll mug you and steal all your money.' Having never been mugged in China, I wandered into the gloomy surroundings of the disco at around 9 pm. Within minutes I had met all the Burmese in the bar, including the band members, who invited me up for a number *(all* Westerners eat hamburgers and play guitar like ringin' a bell, right?). A few beers got me in the mood, and after much conferring we came up with *Get Back* and *Get Off My Cloud*, the former sung in Burmese because I could only remember the chorus and something about JoJo leaving his home somewhere in Alabama. We cranked up the amps and ripped through our numbers, much to the bewilderment of the audience (who weren't sure whether to foxtrot or to samba), and to the annoyance of two PSB men (who seemed to sense that this was cultural pollution of the highest order). I left the stage to find that my bar tab had been paid by a Burmese business person. ■

Bangkok or Manila. Everything closes down around 1 to 2 am, and you needn't worry about being flagged down in the street by pimps. Still, be aware if you decide to get adventurous and duck into a dark bar for a drink.

The discos are still in action, though they tend to close even earlier, around 11 pm or midnight. The Mingrui Hotel has a disco on the 2nd floor that seems to do fairly well. There is also a dance hall opposite the Burmese restaurants on Renmin Jie that has a live band playing most nights. Whether this is an improvement over what the Chinese pop DJ has to offer is up to you to decide. There is usually an entrance fee of Y20 or so, depending on where you go, but it's worth it for an insight into China's jiving nightspots.

Getting There & Away Ruili has flight connections to Kunming via Mangshi. Flights leave daily, take 50 minutes and cost Y530. Tickets can be booked at an office just outside the entrance to the Ruili Guesthouse. Minibuses leave daily at 11 am for the two-hour trip to the airport. You can also use the ticket office to reconfirm return flights.

At the time of writing flights were also available to Chengdu, for the steep price of Y1000. Whether demand will justify the continuation of this service is difficult to say – it might not be a good idea to build firm plans around it.

Buses for Kunming leave from the long-distance bus station at 6.20 am. There are also sleepers leaving at 12.30, 1.30 and 6.30 pm. Prices for the 30-hour journey range from Y120 for a 'luxury bus', (which means the seats may recline several cm if you're lucky), to Y190 for a sleeper. Give the sleeper serious consideration: although the roads are much improved, this is still a long journey. Sleeper buses to Xiaguan (Dali) take 14 hours, leave at 6.20 am and 7 pm and cost Y90. This trip can take even longer if the border guards are in one of their inspection-happy moods, in which case you can expect to be roused from sleep and ordered off the bus up to five times during the ride. They're mostly looking for drugs smuggled

in from Myanmar, but pornographic magazines and videos are also fair game. Baoshan is seven to eight hours away; there are several buses between 6.20 am and noon for Y30, and a sleeper at 8 am for Y50. This ride should become shorter as work progresses on a new primary-grade road linking Ruili and Baoshan. Buses for Tengchong leave at 7 am for Tengchong; the trip takes anywhere between five and seven hours and costs Y25. There is one direct bus to Yingjiang daily at 9.30 am. Finally, buses leave for Mangshi frequently between 8 am and 3 pm from a driveway just east of the long-distance bus station. The two-hour ride costs Y15.

Minibuses and vans leave for more local destinations from opposite the long-distance bus station. It's about an hour to Wanding (Y15). Other destinations are the border checkpoint at Jiegao (Y5), and the village of Nongdao (Y7). Buses to Zhangfeng leave from up on Xinjian Lu. The hour-plus ride costs Y10.

Getting Around Ruili itself is easily explored on foot, but all the most interesting day-trips require a bicycle. Like accommodation, in Ruili bicycles don't come cheap, or at least the deposit doesn't. The only place renting bicycles at present is the Mingrui Hotel. The charge is Y1 an hour or Y10 per day; the deposit is a hefty Y300 or Y200 and your passport, and no amount of arguing will change their minds about it. Make sure you get a receipt, though there have been no reports of deposits disappearing.

Around Ruili
Most of the sights around Ruili can be explored easily by bicycle. It's worth making frequent detours down the narrow paths that lead off the main roads to visit minority villages. The people are friendly, and there are lots of photo opportunities.

Nongan Golden Duck Temple (*nóngān jīnyā tǎ*) A short ride to the south-west of town, the Golden Duck Temple is an attractive stupa in a courtyard. It is said to have been established to mark the arrival of a pair of golden ducks that brought good fortune to what was previously an uninhabited marshy area.

Jiegao Border Checkpoint Continue straight ahead from the Golden Duck Temple, cross the Myanmar bridge over the Ruili River and you will come to Jiegao, a little thumb of land jutting into Myanmar that serves as the main checkpoint for a steady stream of cross-border traffic. This is where to come if you want to try to cross into Myanmar, whether for onward travel or a day-trip to the village of Muse. See the Myanmar Border Crossing section earlier for more details. If you're not making the trip across, there's not a lot to see. But you can still marvel at how laid-back everything seems on both sides of the fence and indulge the perennial fascination with illicit borders. Jiegao is about seven km from the Ruili long-distance bus station and minivans will take you there for Y5.

Temples Just after the Golden Duck Temple is a crossroads. The road to the right leads to the villages of Jiexiang and Nongdao, and on the way are a number of small temples, villages and stupas worth a look. Most of them are not particularly noteworthy and the village life nearby is more interesting – there are often small market areas near the temples.

The first major temple is the **Hansha Temple** (*hánshāzhuāng sì*), a fine wooden structure with a few resident monks. It's set a little off the road but easy to find. Another 15 minutes or so down the road, look out for a white stupa on the hillside to the right. This is **Leizhuangxiang** (*léizhuāngxiāng*), Ruili's oldest stupa, dating back to the middle of the Tang Dynasty. There's a nunnery in the grounds of the stupa and fantastic views of the Ruili area. Once the stupa comes into view, take the next path to the right that cuts through the fields. There are signs in Chinese and Dai pointing the way, which leads through a couple of Dai villages. You'll need to get off your bicycle and push for the last ascent up to the stupa.

A few km past the town of Jiexiang is the

Denghannong Temple (*děnghánnóngzhuāng sì*), a wooden Dai temple with pleasant surroundings. Like the other temples in the area, the effect is spoiled somewhat by the corrugated tin roof.

Nongdao (*nóngdǎo*) Around 29 km southwest of Ruili, the small town of Nongdao is worth an overnight trip. The locals (mainly Burmese and Dai) don't get all that many foreign visitors and are a friendly lot. There's a solitary hotel in town (you can't miss it) that has cheap doubles. It would be possible to cycle here, stopping off at some of the temple sights along the way, or take a minibus from Ruili – they leave fairly frequently through the day.

Jiele Golden Pagoda (*jiělè jīntǎ*) A few km to the east of Ruili on the road to Wanding is the Jiele Golden Pagoda, a fine structure that dates back 200 years.

Wanding
(*wǎndīng*)

Many travellers don't make it to Wanding, or do it only as a day-trip. It's not as interesting as Ruili, but there's cheaper accommodation here and it's a nice laid-back place to spend a day or so. Part of the attraction is that the town is right on the Myanmar border, and the Wanding Guesthouse and the Yufeng Hotel provide good views of the hills, small township and occasional stupa over on the Myanmar side.

Information The Wanding Travel Bureau can provide you with some information on the area as well as arrange boat trips and other excursions. There's a branch of the Bank of China on the main road that comes in from Ruili. The post office, where you can make international phone calls, is next door to the Xinhua Bookstore on the same road. Staff at the foreign affairs office of the PSB, just across from the Chinese border checkpoint, seem quite easy-going, and although they won't help you sneak into Myanmar, they are otherwise quite accommodating.

Things to See & Do The new **Cooperative Border Market** is a vast multistorey affair complete with atrium and skylights, and hundreds of stalls for would-be border traders. At the time of writing, occupants numbered only several dozen, and the empty, echoing hallways seemed to be waiting for a vast surge of business that was still nowhere in sight. You might want to stop by to see if things have picked up. Two minutes' walk down from the Yufeng Hotel will see you in Myanmar. The only giveaway is the dilapidated customs office. Apparently a Belgian couple did a day-trip into Myanmar for US$20 several years ago (the proceeds were shared by those who failed to notice them crossing the bridge), but the guards were not interested in allowing a repeat performance when we were in town. Talk to the Wanding Travel Bureau for the latest on this situation.

It's worth climbing up to the north of town to take a look at the **Wanding Forest Reserve**

(*wǎndīng sēnlín gōngyuán*). There's a Y2 entry charge and some pleasant walks. Avoid the absolutely pathetic zoo, home to three psychotic monkeys, a couple of peacocks and an unidentifiable ball 'of fur that was either fast asleep or dead.

The Wanding Travel Bureau can organise river trips which include a barbecue lunch in a minority village. Prices vary depending on the number of participants, but you should be able to do it for Y40 to Y50 per person. Alternatively, it is possible to catch a lift on a boat with locals by taking a minibus in the direction of Mangshi and getting off at the bridge that connects with the main Ruili-Mangshi road. Travellers have caught boats back to the second bridge closer to Ruili and then hitched back to Ruili or Wanding. Serious haggling is required for boat trips, but hitching by road can be done with the aid of some foreign cigarettes or a few Y10 notes waved in the air.

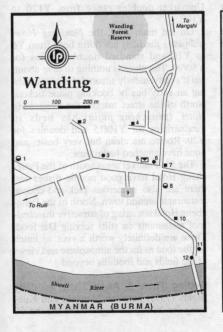

WANDING 畹町

1 New Bus Station
   新客运中心
2 Wanding Guesthouse
   畹町宾馆
3 Wanding Travel Bureau
   畹町旅游局
4 Business Hotel
   商业饭店
5 Post Office
   邮局
6 Xinhua Bookstore
   新华书店
7 Yufeng Hotel
   裕丰大楼
8 Minivans to Ruili & Mangshi
   芒市,瑞丽 小型汽车站
9 Cooperative Border Market
   中缅友谊市场
10 Zhongyin Hotel
   中银宾馆
11 PSB
   公安局
12 Myanmar Border Checkpoint
   缅甸边界

Places to Stay & Eat The cheapest place to stay is the clean and friendly *Yufeng Hotel (yùfēng dàlóu)*. Dorm beds here are Y15 and basic doubles are Y40. The *Wanding Guesthouse (wǎndīng bīnguǎn)* is in a rambling building up on the hill with good views of Myanmar. Comfortable doubles with attached bathroom and satellite TV (catch up with the latest MTV video clips on the China-Myanmar border!) are Y80. Triples are also available for Y70. Look for the alabaster statue of a frolicking maiden holding what looks to be a miniature UFO in her hand at the front entrance.

Hidden up a narrow alleyway off the road to Mangshi, the *Business Hotel (shāngyè fàndiàn)* is quite laid-back despite its name and has basic doubles for Y40. But if you stay here you may as well go for the doubles with attached bath, TV and fan for Y60. Similar triples are available for Y80. Just up the street from the border, the *Zhongyin Hotel (zhōngyín bīnguǎn)* is Wanding's most upmarket choice, with doubles from Y80.

The area around the Yufeng Hotel is best for cheap restaurants. Most of them are of the pick-and-choose variety, and all are much the same. In the mornings try the dumpling stands opposite the turn-off for the Wanding Guesthouse.

Getting There & Away Minibuses run to Ruili for Y15 and to Mangshi for Y30. They leave through the day whenever they are full. You shouldn't have to wait more than 15 minutes for a bus to Ruili; buses to Mangshi are less frequent. By the time you are reading this, the towering new long-distance bus station should be open and have daily links to Baoshan, Xiaguan and Kunming. This mammoth structure seems quite out of proportion with Wanding's modest transport needs – perhaps the architects were betting on the same business boom that inspired the ghost-like Cooperative Market.

Mangshi (Luxi)

(mángshì)

Mangshi is Dehong's air link with the outside world. If you fly in from Kunming there are minibuses running direct from the airport to Ruili and most people take this option. But Mangshi has a casual south-east Asian feel to it, and there are a few sights in and around the town that make dallying here a day or so worthwhile if you have the time.

Things to See Mangshi is not a particularly big place, and it's interesting just to take a wander round. There are a couple of markets in town and a number of **temples** in the vicinity of the Dehong Guesthouse. Around seven or eight km south of town are the **Fapa Hot Springs** *(fǎpà wēnquán)*; they get good reports from travellers who have cycled out to them. Not far from the Dehong Guesthouse is the **Mangshi Nationalities Palace** *(mínzú wénhuà gōng)*.

Places to Stay & Eat The most popular place to stay is the peaceful *Dehong State Mangshi Guesthouse (déhóng zhōu mángshì bīnguǎn)*. Doubles/triples with bath, TV and fan are Y30/Y20 per bed, an excellent deal. Upmarket doubles range from Y120 to Y180.

On the main road, the *Nanjiang Hotel (nánjiāng fàndiàn)* has dorm beds from Y6 to Y10 and standard doubles/triples for Y80/90. The place is nothing to rave about, but it's conveniently situated if you're catching an early bus or booking plane tickets. North of the street market, the *Pengcheng Hotel (péngchéng jiǔjiā)* has beds in quads/triples for Y10/15 and doubles for Y20. Rooms are clean but very basic, and none have attached bathrooms.

The food market areas south of the Pengcheng Hotel have good noodle dishes and there are also numerous pick-and-choose restaurants around town. North of the Pengcheng Hotel is a string of attractive thatched-roof restaurants on stilts serving Dai food. These are definitely worth a visit, as much for the food as for the atmosphere and views of the fields and foothills beyond.

Getting There & Away There are daily flights (737s) between Mangshi and Kunming for Y530; the flight takes around 50

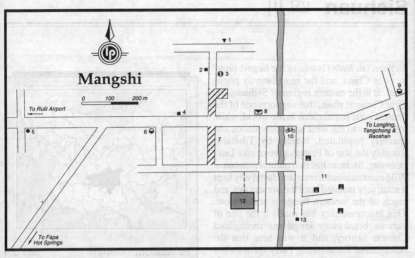

MANGSHI 芒市

1 Dai Restaurants
傣味餐厅

2 Pengcheng Hotel
鹏呈酒家

3 Bank of China
中国银行

4 Nanjiang Hotel
南疆饭店

5 CAAC
中国民航

6 South Bus Station
汽车南站

7 Market
市场

8 Post Office
邮局

9 Long-Distance Bus
Station
客运中心

10 Bicycle Rental
自行车出租

11 Temples
寺庙

12 Mangshi Nationalities
Palace
民族文化宫

13 Dehong State
Mangshi Guesthouse
德宏宾馆

minutes. Minibuses leave from the Mangshi CAAC office for the airport around an hour before flight departures. There are also flights to Chengdu several times a week: tickets cost Y1000. It is possible to book or reconfirm flights here, or you could wait until you get to Ruili, where the Ruili Guesthouse offers the same service.

Minibuses connect Mangshi with Wanding and Ruili for Y30. There are frequent departures. The long-distance bus station has scheduled daily buses to Ruili at 7, 8 and 9 am. The ride takes around two hours and costs Y15. There are several buses to Baoshan between 7 am and noon. The five-hour ride costs Y12. Buses to Tengchong leave at 7 and 10 am, take five hours and cost Y13. There is one bus daily to Xiaguan at 8 am (12 hours, Y50) and sleeper buses to Kunming at 8 and 9.30 am (22 hours, Y155).

Sichuan 四川

Sichuan *(sìchuān)* is one of the largest provinces in China, and the most heavily populated. It is the eastern region of Sichuan, the great Chuanxi plain, that supports one of the densest rural populations in the world, while the regions to the west are mountainous and sparsely populated, mainly by Tibetans. Roughly the size of France, give or take Luxembourg, Sichuan has rich natural resources. Wild mountainous terrain and fast rivers kept it relatively isolated until the present era, and much of the western fringe is still remote. This inaccessibility has made it the site of various breakaway kingdoms throughout Chinese history, and it was here that the beleaguered Kuomintang Party spent its last days before being vanquished and fleeing to Taiwan. The capital is Chengdu; the largest city is Chongqing, which is also the stepping stone for the ferry ride down the Yangzi River.

The Chinese often refer to Sichuan as *tiānfǔ zhī guó*, the 'Heavenly Kingdom', a reference to its resources, prosperity and rich cultural heritage. The province continues to get rich, having played an active role in China's labouring economic reforms over the last 18 years. Zhao Ziyang – who soared from the post of First Party Secretary of Sichuan to General Secretary of the Communist Party before falling from grace in the wake of the Tiananmen massacre – made his reputation by instituting pioneering agricultural reforms in the province. Under the so-called 'responsibility system', plots of land were let out to farmers for individual use on the condition that a portion of the crops be sold back to the government. By 1984 the reforms had spread throughout the whole of China and were later applied to the industrial sector.

There is nowhere better to see the fruits of these reforms than Chengdu, the capital of the province. It is without a doubt the most prosperous, liberal and fashionable city in the south-west. There are bustling commer-

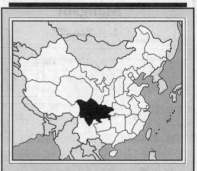

Population: 110 million
Capital: Chengdu
Highlights:

- Despite modernisation efforts, Chengdu still has some charming back streets and great places to eat
- Jiuzhaigou, a national park with gorgeous alpine scenery that authorities are keeping pristine
- Western Sichuan, with its soaring snow-capped peaks, grasslands, glaciers and a heavy Tibetan influence
- Grand Buddha – the world's largest Buddha sits in splendour across from the city of Leshan
- Emeishan, one of China's four famous Buddhist holy mountains, is great for hiking and monastery-hopping
- Relax aboard ship for a few days on a Yangzi River cruise and see the famous Three Gorges before they're submerged forevermore by a mammoth dam project

cial markets everywhere, the department stores are crowded with the latest consumer goodies, and locals dressed in Hong Kong fashions zip around town on motorbikes and multi-geared mountain bikes. Chengdu has also enjoyed an influx of foreign investors and students in recent years, and in some

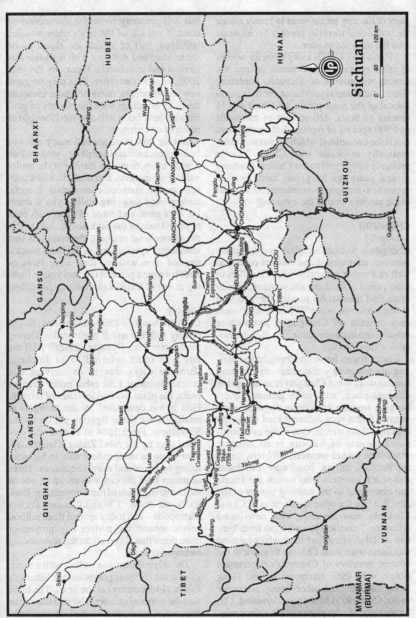

Sichuan

0   60   120 km

parts of the city locals seem to barely notice the occasional traveller passing by, let alone take the time out to stare.

Meanwhile, worlds away from the scenes of urban renewal and economic reform, the remote mountains of Sichuan, bordering Gansu and Shaanxi provinces, are the natural habitat of the giant panda. Of China's 1174 species of birds, 420 species of mammals and 500 species of reptiles and amphibians, this is the one animal which Westerners automatically associate with China. This is probably due in part to the Chinese fondness several years ago for giving them away as presents to foreign governments, but the cute black patches around the eyes help too.

CHENGDU
(chéngdū)

Chengdu is Sichuan's capital, and its administrative, educational and cultural centre, as well as a major industrial base. Travellers to most points in northern and western Sichuan often find themselves passing through here at least once or twice. While it may seem easy to write off Chengdu as just another massive urban construction site, the city warrants a closer look.

Comparisons between Chengdu and Beijing are tempting – the same city-planning hand at work – but Chengdu is an altogether different place, with more greenery, overhanging wooden housing in the older parts of town and a very different kind of energy coming off the streets. One of the most intriguing aspects of the city is its artisans: small-time basket-weavers, cobblers, itinerant dentists, tailors, houseware merchants and snack hawkers who swarm the streets and contribute to the bustling energy of the city. But like the other major cities of China, Chengdu also abounds with new-found affluence. Travellers just off a bus from Yunnan or Tibet often find themselves rubbing shoulders with rural Chinese to gawk at the opulent interiors of Chengdu's department stores, with their electronic goods, Hong Kong fashions and other trendy consumer items. Chengdu is bent on modernising. Unfortunately, if city planners have their way,

this will probably mean the destruction of most, if not all, of the city's older wooden buildings, half of which are slated to be demolished and replaced with high-rise residential and commercial blocks by the year 2000, or soon thereafter. This may be good news for residents, many of whom associate the older buildings with the poverty of generations past, but it will also rob Chengdu of much of its charm.

But for now there are still many miles of bustling backstreets to explore – strike off on a walk away from the Beijing-style boulevards. Free markets, flea markets, black markets, pedlar markets, commercial districts, underground shopping malls – you'll stumble over more and more of them with each twist and turn of the back alleys. Add to this the indoor food markets, the countless tiny restaurants specialising in Sichuan snacks, the old men walking their song birds or huddled over a game of Go, and you're looking at one of China's more intriguing cities.

History

Chengdu boasts a 2500-year history, linked closely with the arts & crafts trades. During the Eastern Han Dynasty (25-220 AD) the city was often referred to as Jincheng (Brocade City), due to its thriving silk brocade industry. Like other major Chinese cities, the place has had its share of turmoil. First it was devastated by the Mongols in retaliation for fierce fighting put up by the Sichuanese. From 1644 to 1647 it was presided over by the rebel Zhang Xiangzhong, who set up an independent state in Sichuan, ruling by terror and mass executions. Three centuries later the city was set up as one of the last strongholds of the Kuomintang. Ironically, the name 'Chengdu' means Perfect Metropolis – and today around three million people inhabit the perfect city proper, or three times that if you count the surrounding metropolitan area.

The original city was walled with a moat, gates at the compass points and the Viceroy's Palace (14th century) at the heart. The latter was the imperial quarter. The remains of the city walls were demolished in the early

1960s, and the Viceroy's Palace was blown to smithereens at the height of the Cultural Revolution. In its place was erected the Russian-style Exhibition Hall. Outside, a massive Mao statue waves merrily down Renmin Lu. The Great Helmsman's gaze also used to take in four enormous portraits of Marx, Engels, Lenin and Stalin. But the forefathers of Communism have now been removed in favour of larger-than-life advertisements for cognac and imported watches.

Orientation

Chengdu has echoes of boulevard-sweeping Beijing in its grand scale, except that here flowering shrubs and foliage line many of the expanses. As in Beijing there are ring roads right around the outer city, though Chengdu has only two to Beijing's four: the first ring road (yīhuánlù) and the second (èrhuánlù). These are divided into numbered segments (duàn). The main boulevard that sweeps through the centre of everything is Renmin Lu, in its north (běi), central (zhōng) and south (nán) manifestations. The nucleus of the city is the square that interrupts the progress of Renmin Lu, with administrative buildings, the Sichuan Exhibition Hall, a sports stadium and, at its southern extent, a colossal Mao presiding over a city long since oblivious to his presence.

The area where Renmin Nanlu crosses the Jin River, near the Jinjiang and Traffic hotels, has become the city's tourist ghetto. This is where you'll find most of the restaurants and arts & crafts shops catering for foreigners, and even nowadays a couple of pubs.

Finally, Chengdu is a true Asian city in its nonchalant disregard of systematic street numbering and naming. It's not unusual, when following street numbers in one direction, to meet another set coming the other way, often leaving the poor family in the middle with five sets of numbers over their doorway. Street names, also, seem to change every 100 metres or so. Bear this in mind when you're looking for somewhere in particular, and rely more on nearby landmarks and relative locations on maps than on street numbers and names

Information

CITS Unless you're interested in joining a tour group, there's no real point in bothering the people at CITS. Staff in the main office (☎ 667-3689) on Renmin Nanlu opposite the Jinjiang Hotel are friendly but can't book train tickets and have been trained to say 'Tibet is closed'. About the only useful thing they can do for you is book Dragonair flights to Hong Kong. For the kind of help that individual travellers need, try the small outfits in and around the Traffic Hotel.

PSB The main office is on the part of Xinhua Donglu named Wenwu Lu, east of the intersection with Renmin Zhonglu. But whether you're seeking permits to visit 'closed' areas in Sichuan, visa extensions or even reporting a theft, you'll probably do better at the Foreign Affairs section (☎ 630-1454), a single-storey brown brick building at No 40 Wenmiaohou Jie, which is off Nan Dajie to the west of the Jinjiang Hotel. Some members of the staff speak excellent English. This office is open Monday to Friday from 8 to 11 am and from 2.30 to 5 pm, and on Saturday from 8.30 to 11 am.

Money Many hotels, including the Traffic and Jinjiang, have foreign-exchange counters. There is also a new Bank of China branch on Renmin Nanlu, in front of the Jinjiang Hotel. The main branch of the Bank of China is in a huge yellow building up on Renmin Donglu. This is the place for credit card withdrawals and the like.

Post & Telecommunications The main post office is housed in what looks like a converted church on the corner of Huaxingzheng Jie and Shuwa Beijie, close to the Cultural Palace in the centre of town. Poste-restante mail is kept at the international mail department at the northern end of the building. More convenient might be the poste-restante service at the Traffic Hotel, which holds letters and parcels for 15 days at the luggage storage counter. Items should be mailed care of the Traffic Hotel, 77 Linjiang Road, Xinnanmen, Chengdu 610041.

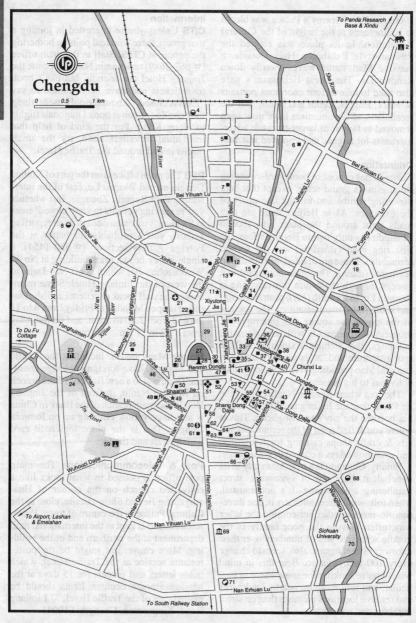

Chengdu

To Panda Research
Base & Xindu

To Du Fu
Cottage

To Airport, Leshan
& Emeishan

To South Railway Station

Sichuan
University

0   0.5   1 km

Fu River

Sha River

Bei Erhuan Lu

Jiefang Lu

Renmin Beilu

Fuqing Lu

Bei Yihuan Lu

Shihui Jie

Xian Lu

Xinhua Xilu

Renmin Zhonglu

Caoshi Jie

Xinhua Donglu

Xijiao River

Tonghuimen

Xiatongren Lu

Shangtongren Lu

Dongchenggen Jie

Xiyulong
Jie

Xunchengcheng Jie

Chunxi Lu

Huaixingzheng Jie

Dongfeng
Lu

Dong Yihuan Lu

Jinhe
Lu

Renmin Donglu

Shaanxi Jie

Wenmiaohou
Jie

Shang Dong
Dajie

Xia Dong Dajie

Hongxing Lu

Jin River

Renmin Lu

Wuhouci Dajie

Jinjiang Jie

Nan Dajie

Ximan Jie

Ximan Nanlu

Ximan Qiao Jie

Nan Yihuan Lu

Renmin Nanlu

Wangjiang Lu

Nan Erhuan Lu

CHENGDU 城都

PLACES TO STAY

5 Chengdu Grand Hotel
成都大酒店
6 Jingrong Hotel
京蓉宾馆
7 Tibet Hotel
西藏饭店
14 Jindi Hotel
金地饭店
25 Jinhe Hotel
金河宾馆
31 Zhufeng Hotel
珠峰宾馆
37 Sichuan Hotel
四川宾馆
43 Xingchuan Hotel
兴川饭店
45 Chengdu Hotel
成都饭店
48 Yuanding Hotel
园丁饭店
50 Rongcheng Hotel
蓉成饭店
61 Jinjiang Hotel
锦江宾馆
62 Minshan Hotel
岷山饭店
64 Binjiang Hotel
滨江饭店
65 Black Coffee Hotel
黑咖啡饭店
66 Traffic Hotel
交通饭店

PLACES TO EAT

13 Zhang Liangfen
Restaurant
张凉粉
15 Longyan Baozi Dump-
ling Restaurant
龙眼包子
16 Guo Soup Balls
Restaurant
郭汤元
17 Chen Mapo Doufu
Restaurant
陈麻婆豆腐
33 Dan Dan Noodle
Restaurant
担担面

39 Shimeixuan Restaurant
市美轩餐厅
53 Chengdu Restaurant
成都餐厅
54 Long Chao Shou
Special Restaurant
龙抄手餐厅
56 Yaohua Restaurant
耀华餐厅
57 Banna Restaurant
版纳酒家

OTHER

1 Chengdu Zoo
动物圆
2 Zhaojue Temple
照觉寺
3 North Railway Station
火车北站
4 North Bus Station
城北汽车客运中心
8 Ximen Bus Station
西门汽车站
9 Tomb of Wang Jian
王建墓
10 Army Surplus Store
军衣店
11 PSB
公安局
12 Wenshu Monastery
文殊院
18 Advance Rail Booking
Office
火车站售票处
19 Recreation Park
市游乐园
20 Mengzhuiwan Swimming
Pool
猛追湾游泳池
21 No 3 Hospital
三医院
22 Tape and CD Shop
音像书店
23 Qingyang Palace
(Wenhua Park)
青羊宫 (文化公园)
24 Baihuatan Park
百华潭公园
26 Sichuan Fine Arts
Exhibition Hall
四川美术展览馆

27 Sichuan Exhibition
Centre
省展览馆
28 Mao Statue
毛主席像
29 Municipal Sports
Stadium
市体育场
30 Telecommunications
Centre
电话电报大楼
32 Cultural Palace
文化宫
34 PICC Office
35 Hongqi Market
红旗商场
36 Main Post Office
市电信局
38 Jinjiang Theatre
锦江剧场
40 Sichuan Foreign
Languages Bookstore
省外文书店
41 Bank of China
银行大厦
42 Chunxi Commercial
District
春熙路商业区
44 Municipal Museum
市博物馆
46 Renmin Park
人民公园
47 People's Market
人民商场
49 PSB
省公安局外事科
51 Chengdu Department
Store
成都百货大楼
52 Advance Rail Booking
Office
火车站售票处
55 Friendship Store
友谊商店
58 China Southwest
Airlines & Pubs
中国西南航空公司
59 Wuhou Temple/
Nanxiao Park
武侯祠/南郊公园
60 Bank of China
中国银行
63 CAAC
中国民航售票处
(Continued)

The best place in town for making collect calls is in the telecommunications centre, east of the Sichuan Exhibition Centre. You can also make direct-dial overseas calls from here.

Consulates The US Consulate (☎ 558-3992) is located in a small fortress at No 4 Lingshiguan Lu, just off Renmin Nanlu between the first and second ring roads.

Bookshop The Sichuan Foreign Languages Bookstore has mildly captivating tourist literature and general data, as well as the usual collection of English-teaching materials, novels such as *Jane Eyre*, US and British short-story collections and Grimm's fairy tales. The 1st floor has gone over to music and video: disco, Chinese pop, watery versions of Western music and traditional Chinese works are all available on tape or CD, next to which are racks displaying videotapes and laser discs of Chinese and (dubbed) Western films. The store is just down the road south of the Sichuan Hotel on Dongfeng Lu.

Maps City bus maps can be found at railway and bus stations, the Traffic Hotel and Xinhua Bookstores. Three different maps in Chinese provide excellent detail for Sichuan Province, Chengdu city or its surrounding areas, and one also has a fair amount of English street and place names.

Dangers & Annoyances There have been several reports of foreigners becoming targets for rip-offs and theft in Chengdu. In particular there have been a couple of inci-

dents (one foreigner was stabbed) on the riverside pathway between the Jinjiang and Traffic hotels. Take care late at night – it's best not to walk alone.

To avoid getting ripped off by taxi and pedicab drivers and restaurants, always get the price at the start of proceedings. Pickpockets are common around bus and railway stations and post offices, and watch out for gangs who use razors to slit your bags on buses. It's a good idea to use a money belt. If you want to play it safe with train tickets, make a note of the ticket numbers. If the tickets are stolen you'll be given replacements, providing you can supply the numbers of the old ones.

Should things get out of hand, ring the Foreign Affairs section of the PSB. English is spoken and the staff usually do their best to be of assistance.

Wenshu Monastery
(wénshū yuàn)
Wenshu Monastery, which dates back to the Tang Dynasty, is Chengdu's largest and best preserved Buddhist place of worship. It was originally known as Xinxiang Temple, but was renamed after a Buddhist monk who lived there in the late 17th century. It is believed that his presence literally illuminated the monastery. Many of the buildings in the complex are carved with exquisite relief work.

Perhaps the best thing about the monastery are the bustling crowds of worshippers who flock to the place. It's a fairly active place of worship and as such is well worth the trip. The alley off Renmin Zhonglu, on which Wenshu is located, is a curiosity in itself, with joss-stick vendors, foot-callus removers, beggars, blind fortune-tellers with bamboo spills, and flower and fireworks sellers. In the monastery area, check out the teahouse and vegetarian restaurant. The monastery is open daily from 6 am to 9 pm, and there's an entry charge of Y1.

Tomb of Wang Jian
(wángjiàn mù)
In the north-west of town, the Tomb of Wang Jian was until 1942 thought to be Zhuge

JO O'BRIEN

CHRIS TAYLOR

CHRIS TAYLOR

Top: Pilgrims at the Buddhist holy mountain of Emeishan, Sichuan
Bottom Left: Carving at Dazu Grotto, Sichuan
Bottom Right: Man at prayer in Chengdu, Sichuan

CHRIS TAYLOR

The cliff carvings and statues of Dazu County, Sichuan – some of which date back to the 9th century – are among the best in China.

Liang's music pavilion (see Wuhou Temple, in the following Temple Parks section). The tomb in the central building is surrounded by statues of 24 musicians all playing different instruments, and is considered to be the best surviving record of a Tang Dynasty musical troupe.

Wang Jian (847-918 AD) was a Tang general who established the Former Shu kingdom in the aftermath of the collapse of the Tang in 907 AD. Also featured are relics taken from the tomb itself, including a jade belt, mourning books and imperial seals. The tomb is open daily from 8.30 am to 5.30 pm.

Temple Parks

There are a couple of worthwhile temple parks in the city area, all within cycling distance of the Jinjiang and Traffic hotels, and all open seven days a week.

Due west of Mao on the western section of the circular road is **Wénhua Park** (wénhuà gōngyuán), home to **Qingyang Palace** (qīngyáng gōng). It is the oldest and most extensive Taoist temple in the Chengdu area. The story goes that Laotse, the shadowy high priest of Taoism and reputed author of the *Daodejing*, *The Way and Its Power*, asked a friend to meet him there. When the friend arrived he saw only a boy leading two goats on a leash...and, in a fabulous leap of lateral thinking, realised the boy was Laotse. The goats are represented in bronze in the rear building on the temple grounds. If the one with only one horn looks slightly ungoatlike, it is because it combines features of all the Chinese zodiac animals: a mouse's ears; a cow's nose; a horse's mouth; the back of a rabbit; a snake's tail; neck of a monkey; and a pig's bum. The solitary horn was borrowed from a dragon. And if you're wondering whether the goat has any goatish qualities at all, take a look at the beard. The other goat can vanquish life's troubles and pains if you stroke its flank. The park is open from 6 am to 8 pm and costs Y2 to enter.

Qingyang Palace can be combined with a visit to the nearby **Du Fu Cottage** (dùfǔ cǎotáng), erstwhile home of the celebrated Tang Dynasty poet. Something of a rover, Du Fu (712-70 AD) was born in Henan and left his home province to see China at the tender age of 20. He was an official in Chang'an (the ancient capital on the site of modern-day Xi'an) for 10 years, was later captured by rebels after an uprising and fled to Chengdu, where he stayed for four years. He built himself a humble cottage and penned over 200 poems on simple themes around the lives of the people who lived and worked nearby.

The present grounds – 20 hectares of leafy bamboo and luxuriant vegetation – are a much enlarged version of Du Fu's original poetic retreat. It's also the centre of the Chengdu Du Fu Study Society, and several display halls house examples of the poet's work. Du Fu's statue is accompanied by statues of two lesser poets: Li You and Huang Tingjian. From the time of his death in exile (in Hunan), Du Fu acquired a cult status, and his poems have been a major source of inspiration for many Chinese artists. Du Fu Cottage is open from 7 am to 11 pm. The entry fee is Y15 for foreigners, as opposed to Y2 for Chinese, but includes the Y3 admission required to enter the cottage area proper.

To the west of the Jinjiang Hotel and next to Nanjiao Park is **Wuhou Temple** (wǔhóu cí). Wuhou might be translated as 'Minister of War', and was the title given to Zhuge Liang, a famous military strategist of the Three Kingdoms Period (220-80 AD) immortalised in one of the classics of Chinese literature, *The Tale of the Three Kingdoms*. Curiously, for the Chinese, Zhuge Liang is not the main attraction of the temple. The front shrine is dedicated to Liu Bei, Zhuge Liang's emperor. Liu's temple, the Hanzhaolie Temple, was moved here and rebuilt during the Ming Dynasty, but the Wuhou Temple name stuck all the same. Liu is a common Chinese surname and many Overseas Chinese with the surname make a point of visiting the temple while they are in Chengdu on the glorious off-chance that the emperor is a distant ancestor. One sour note here is the admission, a mere Y0.5 for Chinese, but Y15 for foreign guests!

In the south-east of town, near Sichuan

University, is **River Viewing Pavilion Park**
(wàngjiāng lóu). The pavilion itself is a four-
storey Qing wooden structure overlooking
the Jinjiang River. The park is famous for its
lush forests of bamboo, and boasts over 150
types of bamboo from China, Japan and
south-east Asia. They range from bonsai-
sized potted plants to towering giants, creating a shady retreat in the heat of summer (a
cold, damp retreat in winter). The pavilion
was built to the memory of Xue Tao, a female
Tang Dynasty poet with a great love for
bamboo. Nearby is a well, said to be the place
where she drew water to dye her writing
paper. The park is open from 6 am to 9 pm
and the entry fee is Y1.

Renmin Park
(rénmín gōngyuán)
This is one Chinese park well worth recommending. It's to the south-west of the city
centre. The teahouse here is excellent (see
the Places to Eat section) and a perfect perch
for people-watching and whiling away a lazy
afternoon. The park also holds a bonsai
rockery, a kids' playground, a few swimming
pools, and the Monument to the Martyrs of
the Railway-Protecting Movement (1911).
This obelisk, decorated with shunting manoeuvres and railway tracks, marks an uprising of the people against officers who
pocketed cash raised for the construction of
the Chengdu-Chongqing line. Since Renmin
Park was also at the time a private officer's
garden, it was a fitting place to erect the
structure.

Across the lake from the teahouse is the
entry to an underground museum/funhouse
that must count as one of Chengdu's weirder
experiences. An entry fee of Y10 buys you a
tour through a converted air raid shelter that
houses among other things: models of New
York, Sydney, Rome and the Taj Mahal (the
latter two each having a copy of Moscow's
St Basil's Cathedral thrown in for good
measure), a life-size statue of Saddam
Hussein, and a miniature subway that takes
you through 'outer space', 'the rain forest',
'undersea', 'hell' and several other choice

locales. The point of all this is anyone's
guess, but it makes for an entertaining visit.

Renmin Park opens at 6.30 am and stays
open until 2 am to allow free access to
patrons of a disco dance hall located on park
grounds. Admission is Y0.5.

Sichuan Museum
(sìchuānshěng bówùguǎn)
The Sichuan Museum is the largest provincial museum in China's south-west, with
more than 150,000 items on display. For
historians, the displays of tiled murals and
frescoes taken from tombs are of great interest in their depictions of ancient daily
activities from agriculture to dance. The
museum is open daily from 9 am to 5 pm. It's
down Renmin Nanlu in the direction of the
south railway station, but is still within
cycling distance of the Jinjiang Hotel.

Sichuan University Museum
(sìdà bówùguǎn)
Founded in 1914 by US scholar D S Dye, this
museum underwent several closings and
name changes before reopening under its
current name in 1984. The four exhibition
rooms display, on a rotating basis, a collection of over 40,000 items. The collection is
particularly strong in the fields of ethnology,
folklore and traditional arts. The ethnology
room exhibits artefacts from the Yi, Qiang,
Miao, Jingpo, Naxi and Tibetan cultures. The
Chinese painting and calligraphy room displays works from the Tang, Song, Yuan,
Ming and Qing dynasties. Some labels are in
English.

The museum is open Monday to Friday,
from 8.30 am to 11.30 am and from 2.40 to
5 pm. The university grounds are within easy
walking distance of Jiuyanqiao bus station in
the south-east of the city, next to the Nine-
Arch Bridge. From the bus station, cross the
bridge and walk south on Wangjiang Lu for
10 minutes until you reach the university's
main gate. Enter and go straight until the
road ends at a 'T' intersection. The museum
is the first building on the right.

Zoo
(*dòngwùyuán*)

Chinese zoos are always slightly depressing experiences, and it's difficult not to compare the lush expansive grounds that the humans get to stroll around in with the concrete bunkers allocated to the exhibits. Although now upstaged by the nearby Giant Panda Breeding Research Base, the Chengdu Zoo still has a respectable collection of around six pandas; during the hottest summer months, however, they're not very active.

The zoo is about six km from Chengdu city centre, and is open from 7.30 am to 8 pm daily. Admission is Y2.5. The best way to get there is by bicycle (around half an hour from the Traffic Hotel). There are also minibuses running direct to the zoo from the north railway station.

Zhaojue Temple
(*zhàojué sì*)

Next door to the zoo, Zhaojue Temple is a Tang Dynasty building dating back to the 7th century. It underwent extensive reconstruction under the supervision of Po Shan, a famous Buddhist monk, during the early Qing, with waterways and groves of trees being established around the temple. The temple itself has served as a model for many Japanese and south-east Asian Buddhist temples. Naturally, it went through hard times during the Cultural Revolution, and has only been restored over the last 10 years. It's worth combining with a trip to the zoo. There's a vegie restaurant on the grounds that serves lunch from 11 am to 2 pm, and a teahouse adjacent. The temple is open from 7 am to 7 pm, and admission is Y1.

Giant Panda Breeding Research Base

About six km north of the zoo, this research station and breeding ground for both giant and lesser pandas has been in operation since 1990, but was opened to the public only in early 1995. About 10 to 12 pandas currently reside at the base, in quarters considerably more humane than those at the zoo. There is also a breeding area where China's animal ambassadors will eventually be allowed to freely roam and, it is hoped, procreate. Just past the entrance gate, the base museum has detailed exhibits on panda evolution, habits, habitats and conservation efforts, all with English captions. The base now covers about 36 hectares, but the breeding ground area is projected to grow to over 230 hectares sometime early in the next century.

Staff at the base say the best time to visit is between 8.30 and 10 am, when the pandas are feeding; soon thereafter they return to their predominant pastime, sleeping. The entry fee of Y30 is a bit steep, but at least some of the money goes to a good cause, and you are guaranteed a look at these elusive animals, something often denied those who make the long trip up to Wolong Nature Reserve. The base is open daily from 8 am to 6 pm.

Getting There & Away Bicycling may be your best option. Follow the road north past the zoo for about 2.5 km, keeping an eye out for an overhead road sign with a panda on it. At the sign, turn right onto Panda Avenue (Xiongmao Dadao) and continue for another 3 km. The base is not served by any bus routes, so your other options are to take a taxi all the way there or to bicycle to the zoo and from there take a taxi or motor-tricycle, for which the one-way fare should be Y10. Travel outfits at the Traffic Hotel also offer tours for around Y80 per person.

Places to Stay – bottom end
The *Traffic Hotel* (☎ 555-1017) (*jiāotōng fàndiàn*), next to Xinnanmen bus station, has for a long time been the main hang-out for backpackers. Prices have been on the rise over recent years, but you get your money's worth. It's clean, comfortable, fairly quiet and close to a number of good dining spots.

A bed in a triple is Y40, with immaculate showers and toilet down the hall. Doubles/triples with satellite TV and private bathroom cost Y84/57 per bed. All prices include a decidedly uninspiring breakfast. The staff are friendly and there's a notice board with travel information just outside the foyer. Another useful service here is a baggage room where you can leave heavy backpacks for a few days while you head off to Emeishan, Jiuzhaigou or wherever. To get here from the northern railway station, take the No 16 bus across the bridge just south of the Jinjiang Hotel and walk west along the south bank of the river to the hotel.

For nearly a decade the *Black Coffee Hotel* (*hēi kāfēi fàndiàn*) offered one of China's most unique hotel options. Basically a bomb shelter converted into an underground hotel, karaoke parlour and bar, this somewhat sleazy landmark was scheduled for an 'upgrade' when we last visited. It's hard to imagine renovating the place with anything other than a wrecking ball, and staff were unsure what type of establishment would result. But it still might be worth looking into – you may find yourself in China's first three-star bomb shelter.

If the Traffic Hotel is full, or if you wish to be closer to the bustling shopping/restaurant district around Chunxi Lu, you can try the *Xingchuan Hotel* (☎ 667-1188) (*xīngchuān fàndiàn*) at 109 Dong Dajie. It has similar rates and standards to the Traffic Hotel, except instead of free breakfast it offers a Y5 coupon with each night's stay which is good for food or lobby shop purchases. Doubles and triples with attached bathroom are Y120; beds in triples without bath cost Y40.

One of the cheapest options around is the *Yuanding Hotel* (☎ 663-6522) (*yuándīng fàndiàn*), which is up an alley to the west of Renmin Nanlu. A bed in a quad with common washroom is Y20; beds in doubles/triples with attached bath are Y60/50. Not far from here is the *Rongcheng Hotel* (☎ 663-2687) (*róngchéng fàndiàn*), a slightly chaotic kind of place with doubles with bathroom for Y80. There are also triples for Y90 and 'superior doubles' that start at Y150.

Places to Stay – middle
Chengdu is pretty short of mid-range accommodation. The best choice is still probably the Traffic Hotel, which has already been mentioned in the bottom-end section. The *Binjiang Hotel*, not far from the Traffic, used

to be a popular mid-range option, but it has gone for a major face-lift, jacked up its prices and for all that still looks quite shabby.

Another option might be the *Jindi Hotel* (674-0339) (*jīndì fàndiàn*), which has standard doubles for Y190 to Y260, and is in a good location for visiting sights in northern Chengdu. Up north by the railway station, the *Jingrong Hotel* (333-7878) (*jīngróng bīnguǎn*) has doubles with all mod cons for Y298.

Places to Stay – top end
The *Jinjiang Hotel* (☎ 558-2222) (*jǐnjiāng bīnguǎn*) at 180 Renmin Nanlu was once the headquarters for all travellers who made it to Chengdu. Now it has become a four-star giant with standard doubles starting at Y1000. There are good views to be had from the rooftop Chinese restaurant here, but at a high price: beer and sodas are around Y30 each.

Opposite the Jinjiang on Renmin Nanlu is the newer, 21-storey *Minshan Hotel* (☎ 558-3333) (*mínshān fàndiàn*), which does a brisk tour-group business. Modern doubles start at Y950 and suites are Y1980. The Minshan has a couple of bars, a coffee shop and five restaurants.

Opposite the north railway station is the *Chengdu Grand Hotel* (☎ 333-3888) (*chéngdū dàjiǔdiàn*), a plush place designed to attract the roving business account. Prices vary according to demand (they often double when conferences are held in town), but you can reckon on a minimum of US$62 for a standard double.

Not far down Renmin Beilu is the *Tibet Hotel* (☎ 333-3988) (*xīzàng fàndiàn*), with similar standards to the Chengdu Grand Hotel. Just east of the Sichuan Exhibition Centre, the *Sichuan Hotel* (☎ 675-5555) (*sìchuān bīnguǎn*) has been remodelled yet again, this time fairly tastefully. Singles/doubles are Y420/540. The management is also teaming up with US hotel chain Sheraton to build a four-star hotel next door.

Places to Eat
Sichuan cuisine is world famous and in a class of its own. The Chinese claim that it

comprises more than 4000 dishes, of which over 300 are said to be famous. It's easily China's hottest and spiciest cuisine, often using *huājiāo*, literally 'flower pepper', a crunchy little item that leaves a numbing and strangely unfamiliar aftertaste – some compare it to spicy detergent. Sichuan chefs have a catch-cry that draws attention to the diversity of Sichuanese cooking styles: '*bǎicài, bǎiwèi*', literally 'a hundred dishes, a hundred flavours'.

Whether 'a hundred flavours' is a characteristic Chinese exaggeration or not it is difficult to say. There is, nevertheless, a bewildering cornucopia of Sichuanese sauces and culinary-preparation techniques; in fact, there are so many that you could spend a couple of months eating out in Chengdu and still only have scratched the surface. Some of the more famous varieties are *yúxiāng wèi*, a really tasty fish-flavoured sauce that draws heavily on vinegar, soy sauce and mashed garlic and ginger; *málà wèi*, a numbingly spicy sauce that is often prepared with bean curd; *yānxūn wèi*, a 'smoked flavour' sauce, of which the most justifiably famous is that used with smoked duck; and, perhaps most famous of all – the hot and sour sauce *(suānlà wèi)*. The hot and sour soup, *suānlà tāng*, is eaten throughout China and is great on a cold day.

There are also some well-known Sichuan dishes to look out for. The most famous is spicy chicken fried with peanuts *(gōngbǎo jīdīng)*, which is served by almost all the local restaurants. Equally well known is *mápō dòufu*, which is bean curd, pork and chopped spring onions prepared in a chilli sauce – there are a couple of restaurants specialising in this dish in Chengdu. A favourite with travellers and worth trying simply for the novelty value is *guōbā ròupiàn*. *Guōbā* refers to the crispy bits of rice, uncannily similar to Rice Krispies, that get stuck to the bottom of the rice pot – they are put on a plate, and pork and gravy added in front of the diner. Also look out for 'pocket bean curd' *(kǒudài dòufu)*, cubes of stuffed bean curd; 'strange taste chicken' *(guàiwèi jīsī)*, diced chicken prepared with a sweet yet spicy sauce; and 'smoked-tea duck' *(zhāngchá yāzi)*.

Famous Restaurants The *Chengdu Restaurant (chéngdū cāntīng)* at 134 Shangdong Dajie is one of Chengdu's most famous and authentic Sichuan restaurants – a favourite with travellers. Good atmosphere, decent food, reasonable prices – downstairs serves set courses of Sichuan appetisers, while full meals can be had upstairs. Try to assemble a party of vagabonds from the hotel before sallying forth, since tables are large, and you get to sample more with a bigger group. It's about a 20-minute walk along a side alley opposite the Jinjiang Hotel. Arrive early: the place starts shutting down around 8.30 pm.

For guoba roupian, you can't beat the *Shimeixuan Restaurant (shìměixuān cāntīng)* opposite the Jinjiang Theatre on Huaxingzheng Jie. A large plate of the crispy rice in pork and lychee sauce costs around Y10, plenty for two. The restaurant has lots of other great dishes, too, and the proprietors don't seem to mind if you walk through the kitchen and point out what you want. Large, clean dining rooms with wooden tables and ceiling fans make eating here even more enjoyable.

Another main-course restaurant in the heart of the city is the *Yaohua Restaurant (yàohuá fàndiàn)* at 22 Chunxi Lu. A visit by Mao himself in 1958 clinched the restaurant's reputation. Among Chinese, the restaurant is also renowned for its Western food – be adventurous and judge for yourself.

Riverside Restaurants The south side of the Jin River between the Jinjiang and Traffic hotels used to be home to a string of small restaurants and teahouses with outdoor tables. At the time of writing, most buildings in this area had been torn down, and all those up to the Traffic Hotel were slated for demolition. A riverside park is being planned for the area. Whether restaurants will again sprout up here is uncertain: owners were uniformly vague as to where they would finally end up after the wrecking ball visited their establishments.

Vegetarian A special treat for ailing vegetarians is to head out to the Wenshu Monastery, where there is an excellent vegetarian restaurant with an English menu. The Zhaojue Temple also serves up vegie dishes for lunch, but the menu is only in Chinese. If you're really keen, you might ride out to the *Monastery of Divine Light* in Xindu, 18 km north of Chengdu, in time for lunch (11 am to noon). For details of the bus service see the Around Chengdu section later in this chapter.

Snacks Many of Chengdu's specialities originated as *xiǎo chī*, or 'little eats'. The snack bars are great fun and will cost you next to nothing. In fact, the offerings can be outdone in no other Chinese city – and if you line up several of these places you will get yourself a banquet in stages.

Unfortunately, many of Chengdu's famous snack places are falling prey to the massive reconstruction work that is tearing down neighbourhoods and starting from scratch. This is particularly true of the Dongfeng Lu area, though a few places are still hanging in there. We can't promise that all the places marked on the map and mentioned here will still be there by the time you set out in search of them. Take a look anyway – it's worth the effort.

Pock-marked Grandma Chen's Bean Curd (chén mápó dòufu) serves mapo doufu with a vengeance. Soft bean curd is served up with a fiery meat sauce (laced with garlic, minced beef, salted soybean, chilli oil and nasty little peppercorns). As the story goes, the madame with the pock-marked face set up shop here (reputed to be the same shop as today's) a century ago, providing food and lodging for itinerant peddlers (the clientele don't seem to have changed a great deal).

Bean curd is made on the premises and costs around Y3 a bowl. Beer is served to cool the fires. Don't worry about the grotty, greasy decor – those spices should kill any lurking bugs. Also served are spicy chicken and duck, and plates of tripe. Situated at 113 Xiyulong Jie, the shop has a vertical sign out front, the outside edge of which has the name in Pinyin. Be sure to sit downstairs: the second floor has been redone to look like a typical Chinese banquet hall, and carries a Y5 'seating charge' as well.

Another place that is still going strong is *Long Chao Shou Special Restaurant (lóng-chāoshǒu cāntīng)*. The beauty of this little restaurant is that it has sampler courses that allow you to dip into the whole gamut of the Chengdu snack experience. The Y5 course gives you a range of sweet and savoury items, while the Y10 and Y15 courses are basically the same deal on a grander and more filling scale. The restaurant is on the north-east corner of Chunxi Lu and Dong Dajie.

Hotpot Although it is said to have originated in Chongqing, *huǒguō*, or hotpot, is very popular in Chengdu. You'll see lots of sidewalk hotpot operations in the older section of town near the Chunxi Lu market as well as along the river. Big woks full of hot, spiced oil (not to be confused with the mild Mongolian version, which employs simmering soup broth) invite passers-by to sit down, pick out skewers of raw ingredients and make a do-it-yourself fondue. You pay by the skewer – it's best to ask the price of a skewer before you place it in the oil. During the winter months the skewered items on offer tend to be meat or 'heavy' vegetables like potatoes. In the summer months lighter, mostly vegetarian fare is the norm.

This stuff is *very* hot, and many non-Sichuanese can't take it. If this is the case, try asking for *báiwèi*, the hotpot for wimps. Chinese (and some travellers) will turn their noses up at this, claiming that it's not the real thing – just ignore them.

Dai Minority Food Generally, eating out in Chinese cities means choosing between Chinese or diabolically prepared Western food. Chengdu has at least one alternative to both of these in the *Banna Restaurant (bǎnnà jiǔjiā)*, which serves Dai minority food. It's a little pricey (figure on Y20 per head at least) by Chinese standards, but the food is excellent.

There is an English menu, although some of the names are still beyond comprehension. Small wonder: the Chinese menu is almost indecipherable even if you have good Chinese. Try asking for *zhúzi niúròu* (curry beef cooked in bamboo) or *yézi jīròu* (curry chicken cooked in a coconut). The rice is prepared in bamboo also and is delicious. Also tasty are the crispy fish and pork spring rolls (*xiāngcǎo kǎoyú*), though watch out for the fish bones.

The restaurant decor is almost tasteful, done out in bamboo. Cross the bridge from the Traffic Hotel and walk north-east to the first big intersection. The restaurant is on the south-west corner.

Teahouses The teahouse, or *chádiàn*, has always been the equivalent of the French cafe or the British pub in China – or at least this was true of the pre-1949 era. Activities ranged from haggling over a bride's dowry to fierce political debate (and sometimes drinking tea). The latter was especially true of Sichuan, which historically has been one of the first areas to rebel and one of the last to come to heel.

Chengdu's teahouses are thus somewhat special – as in other Chinese cities, they were closed down during the Cultural Revolution because they were thought to be dangerous assembly places for 'counter-revolutionaries'. With factional battles raging in Sichuan as late as 1975, re-emergence of this part of daily life has been slow – but you can't keep an old tea addict down! Teahouses sprawl over Chengdu sidewalks (in back-alley sections), with bamboo armchairs that permit ventilation of one's back.

In the past, Chengdu teahouses also functioned as venues for Sichuan opera – the plain-clothes variety, performed by amateurs or retired workers. But the advent of VCRs and karaoke have dealt a blow to such live performances: a local may be able to direct to you any that are still ongoing. Other kinds of entertainment include storytelling and

musical performances, while some teahouses seem given over entirely to chess. Most Chinese teahouses cater for the menfolk, young and old (mostly old), who come to meet, stoke their pipes or thump cards on the table. But the women are increasing their presence and can often be found piling up winnings at the mahjong table.

The *Renmin Teahouse (rénmín cháguǎn)* in Renmin Park is a leisurely tangle of bamboo armchairs, sooty kettles and ceramics, with a great outdoor location by a lake. It's mixed, a family-type teahouse – crowded on weekends. In the late afternoon workers roll up to soothe factory-shattered nerves – and some just doze off in their armchairs. You can do the same. A most pleasant afternoon can be spent here in relative anonymity over a bottomless cup of stone-flower tea at a cost so ridiculous it's not worth quoting. When enough tea freaks appear on the terrace, the stray earpicker, with Q-tips at the ready, roves through, and paper-profile cutters with deft scissors also make the rounds.

A charming indoor family-type teahouse is also to be found in Wenshu Monastery, with a crowded and steamy ambience. Another teahouse definitely worth checking out is in the Jinjiang Theatre, not far from the post office. This place also has performances of Sichuan opera.

Entertainment

Entertainment can be fruitful hunting in Chengdu, but you will have to hunt. If you don't speak Chinese, ask around among the English-speaking staff at the Traffic Hotel or the travel outfits nearby. If something strikes your fancy, get it written down in Chinese, and get a good map location – these places are often hard to find, especially at night. If you have more time, try and get advance tickets. Offerings include teahouse entertainment, acrobatics, cinema, Sichuan opera, Beijing opera, drama, art exhibits, traditional music, storytelling and shadow plays among other things.

Chengdu is the home of Sichuan opera, which has a 200-year tradition and features slapstick dress-up, eyeglass-shattering songs, men dressed as women and occasional gymnastics. There are several opera houses scattered throughout the older sections of town. As attendances fall however, most have cut back performances to only once or twice per week.

One of the easier Sichuan opera venues to find is the *Jinjiang Theatre (jǐnjiāng jùyuàn)* on Huaxingzheng Jie, which is a combination of teahouse, opera theatre and cinema. Sichuan opera performances here are given every Sunday afternoon and are of a high standard. Some of the restaurants near the Traffic Hotel used to offer Sichuan opera tours. Check around the hotel to see if anyone still carries on this service.

Pubs Most of Chengdu's boozing options are of the karaoke variety. These places tend to be expensive and of limited interest to most Westerners. But the area near the China Southwest Airlines office on Renmin Nanlu has seen the emergence of several western-style pubs. The pioneer is called *The Pub* and still seems to be the favoured hang-out for the foreigner population as well as for young hip Chinese. There are several knock-off imitations nearby that don't seem to be generating the same amount of business. But around the corner from The Pub, the *Reggae Lounge* does a brisk trade, and although it doesn't play much reggae, the club's dance floor is packed from around 9 pm onward. Open till the wee hours, these spots can make for an entertaining evening, but can also play havoc with early morning travel plans (did I say I was catching the 7 am bus to Leshan?).

Things to Buy
Chengdu is home to a host of commercial and shopping districts: the Qingyang Palace Commercial Street; the Shudu Boulevard Commercial Street; the Chenghuang Miao Electronic Market; the Chunxi Lu Commercial Street; and even, as one locally produced English map indicates, 'Electronic Brain Street – No 1 Ring Road' (in Chinese, electronic brain means 'computer'). Let's assume, however, that you don't want to spend the rest of your life conspicuously consuming in Chengdu's commercial streets; if this is the case, the pick of the bunch for a stroll and a few purchases is Chunxi Lu.

Chunxi Lu is the main shopping artery, lined with department stores, art dealers, secondhand bookshops, stationers, spectacle shops and photo stores. At No 10 is the Arts & Crafts Service Department Store *(chéngdū měishùpǐn fúwùbù)*, dealing in most of the Sichuan specialities (lacquerware, silverwork, bamboo products).

The best advice for Chunxi Lu is just to stroll around and dive into any shop that looks interesting. You are almost bound to come up with something you couldn't possibly do without. Look out for the Derentang Chemist, the oldest and largest of all Chengdu's Chinese pharmacies, at the bottom end (south) of the road on the left. The Sichuan Antique Store that used to be on the northern end of Chunxi Lu has now moved to a huge new building opposite the Sichuan Fine Arts Exhibition Hall on Renmin Lu. It's worth a visit, and while a lot of the stuff is overpriced there are usually still a few bargains to be had.

People's Market *(rénmín shìchǎng)* is a maze of daily necessity stuff – worth poking your nose into but not of great interest for purchases. If you're interested in picking up a fur-lined sheepskin or leather jacket, or even a heavy PLA-type overcoat (not a bad idea if you're heading to Tibet or Jiuzhaigou in spring or autumn), there's a place selling army surplus stuff up on Renmin Zhonglu.

Getting There & Away
Transport connections in Chengdu are more comprehensive than in other parts of the south-west.

Air China Southwest Airlines (☎ 666-5911) is diagonally opposite the Jinjiang Hotel, and is a good place to purchase tickets for destinations all across China. The smaller Sichuan Provincial Airlines also has an office nearby. It flies to many of the same destinations as Southwest, but it's probably a good idea to only use it at a pinch. Its fleet of aircraft mainly comprises Russian hand-me-downs from CAAC.

Destinations served by China Southwest include Beijing, Chongqing, Guangzhou, Guilin, Guiyang, Kunming, Lhasa, Nanjing, Shanghai and Ürümqi. There are also several flights weekly to Hong Kong (Y2400). CAAC runs a bus every half hour between the ticket office on Renmin Nanlu and Shuangliu Airport, located 18 km west of the city. The fare is Y3. A taxi should cost around Y60.

The most frequently asked question in Chengdu must be 'Can I fly to Lhasa?' If you're on your own, the official answer is usually 'No'. To get around this, travel agents can sign you onto a 'tour', which usually includes a one-way ticket to Lhasa, the two-hour transfer from Gonggar Airport to Lhasa and your first night's accommodation there. The fact that members of the tour group have never seen each other prior to the flight, and split up immediately after, is overlooked by the authorities. These packages cost around Y2200. You can always try picking up a ticket from Southwest yourself: some travellers occasionally get lucky. Just make sure you have the cash on hand to snatch up the ticket before they change their mind. Another trick is asking for a 1st-class ticket.

Bus The main bus station, Xinnanmen bus station, next to the Traffic Hotel, sells tickets to most destinations around Sichuan but not to the north. For northern destinations you will need to head over to the Ximen bus station in the north-west of the city. A third bus station is near the north railway station.

For Emeishan, the best option is the 8.30 am bus that runs direct to Baoguo Monastery (Y19). Buy your ticket the day before to ensure a seat. There are frequent buses all morning to Leshan (Y17) and Dujiangyan (Y6.50). Buses to Chongqing leave at 9 am, and sleepers at 5.30 pm. The 10-hour ride costs Y45 by day and Y65 by night. Other buses include Dazu (7 am and 5.30 pm), Luding (6.30 am) and Kangding (6.30 am and 5.30 pm). Day buses to Kangding and

Luding cross the notoriously dangerous Erlangshan pass, which is often subject to landslides that have stretched the 10-hour trip to 18 or 20 hours. The sleeper bus to Kangding skirts Erlangshan by taking a southern route via Shimian, which although longer at 16 hours, is more likely to get you there on time.

The Ximen bus station is for travellers heading up to Jiuzhaigou or taking the overland route to Xiahe in Gansu Province by way of northern Sichuan. Unlike the Xinnanmen bus station, this place has special foreigners' prices (a surcharge of 70%) and they're quite insistent. Buses to Songpan leave at 7 am and cost Y62.20 (foreigners' price). There are buses running direct from Songpan to Jiuzhaigou. Buses to Maoxian (en route to Songpan) leave at 7.20 and 11 am and cost Y16.90 (Chinese price). Other buses include Dujiangyan every 10 minutes for Y4.70 and Qingcheng Shan every 20 minutes from 7 to 9.50 am for Y8.10. You can also catch buses from here to Leshan (7 am, 8.40 am and 2.30 pm) and Baoguo Monastery (7.20 am).

The north bus station is west of the railway station and has buses (Y14.90) and minibuses (Y17.40) every half hour to Leshan from 7 am to 5.30 pm. Buses to Baoguo Monastery leave every half hour between 6.30 am and 4.30 pm and cost Y14.90. Sleeper buses to Chongqing leave at 5, 5.30 and 6.30 pm for Y65.90.

Train Getting train tickets out of Chengdu is no easy feat. Many travellers simply give up on the idea and get locals around the Traffic Hotel to fix tickets up for them. This is fine if you don't mind paying extra for their services. Doing it yourself can be time-consuming and frustrating. Some travellers have had success at the advance booking offices around town and others have managed to buy direct from black marketeers at the railway station. Give it a try if you wish, but if it looks like you're going to be spending all your time in Chengdu chasing a ticket, spend the extra Y50 or so and get the locals to arrange it for you. You'll usually need to arrange tickets three days in advance. Don't bother with CITS.

For those wanting to go to Lijiang and Dali, there are trains to Panzhihua (also known as Jinjiang) on the Chengdu-Kunming route. The Xi'an-Kunming express (No 65) leaves at 2.15 pm and gets into Panzhihua at 6.25 am the following morning, which will allow you to hook up with a bus or minibus to either Lijiang or Dali and avoid a miserable evening in Panzhihua. The No 84 leaves at 6.15 pm, arriving in Panzhihua at 9.40 am the following day. If you can't get tickets for either of these two notoriously overcrowded trains, try No 321, which leaves at 7.15 pm and gets to Panzhihua at 11.47 am the following day. The Chengdu-Kunming express (No 67) leaves at 9.48 am and puts you into Panzhihua at just after midnight. Hard-sleeper tickets are Y144 for foreigners. Hard sleepers onward to Kunming cost Y240.

You can use any of the trains headed for Kunming or Panzhihua to get to Emei. Express trains take just under two hours, while fast trains take around three hours. A hard seat should cost Y7. Trains to Kunming take either 23 hours or 26 hours, depending on whether they are express or fast, and the cost is around Y230 for a hard sleeper. There are seven trains daily to Chongqing, most of which leave in the afternoon or evening. The trip takes around 12 hours, with the exception of one non-stop express (No 95), which leaves at 10.40 pm and does the journey in 9 hours. Hard sleeper should cost approximately Y180, again all foreigners' prices. If you're headed to Dazu, your best bet is the No 86 train, which leaves around 9 am and puts you into Youtingpu at 4 pm, where you can catch a minibus to Dazu, 30 km to the north.

Other rail options include Beijing, Guangzhou, Guiyang, Hefei, Lanzhou, Shanghai, Taiyuan, Ürümqi and Xi'an.

Getting Around

Bus The most useful bus is No 16, which runs from Chengdu north railway station to the south railway station along Renmin Nanlu.

Bus maps carry colour coding for electric and ordinary buses – bus Nos 2, 4 and 5 can also be electric buses bearing the same number. Electric bus No 5 runs from the north railway station to the Jiuyanqiao bus station. Ordinary bus No 4 runs from the Ximen bus station (north-western end of town) to the south-eastern sector, and continues service until 1 am (most others cease around 9.30 to 10.30 pm). Minibuses also carry numbers, but the routes differ from those of the big buses. Minibus No 12 circles the city along the first ring road (Yihuan Lu), starting and ending at the north railway station.

Bicycle Many of Chengdu's old bicycle hire shops have disappeared, and most travellers hire their bikes these days from the Traffic Hotel, which does a fairly good job of bicycle maintenance. You might try scouting around for other places, but if you're staying in or nearby the Traffic Hotel this is the easiest option.

The usual rules apply – check your bike before you cycle off; some of them are death traps. Also make an effort to park your bike in a designated parking area. Bicycle theft is a problem here as in most Chinese cities.

AROUND CHENGDU
Monastery of Divine Light
(bǎoguāng sì)

This monastery in the north of Xindu County is an active Buddhist temple. It comprises five halls and 16 courtyards, surrounded by bamboo. Pilgrims, monks and tourists head for Xindu, which makes for lively proceedings and attracts a fine line-up of hawkers. The temple was founded in the 9th century, was subsequently destroyed, and was reconstructed in the 17th century.

Among the monastery treasures are a white jade Buddha from Myanmar (Burma), Ming and Qing paintings and calligraphy, a stone tablet engraved with 1000 Buddhist figures (540 AD) and ceremonial musical instruments. Unfortunately, most of the more valuable items are locked away and require special permission to view them – you may be able to get this if you can find whoever's in charge around here.

The Arhat Hall, built in the 19th century, contains 500 two-metre-high clay figurines representing Buddhist saints and disciples. Well, not all of them: among this spaced-out lot are two earthlings – emperors Kangxi and Qianlong. They're distinguishable by their royal costumes, beards, boots and capes. One of the impostors, Kangxi, is shown with a pockmarked face, perhaps a whim of the sculptor. About one km from the monastery is Osmanthus Lake and its bamboo groves, lotuses and osmanthus trees. In the middle of the lake is a small memorial hall for the Ming scholar Yang Shengan.

The temple has an excellent vegetarian restaurant where a huge array of dishes is prepared by monastic chefs. The restaurant's opening hours are from 10 am to 3 pm, though it is best to be here around lunch time, when there is more available. The monastery itself is open daily between 8 am and 5.30 pm.

Getting There & Away Xindu is 18 km north of Chengdu: a round trip on a bicycle would be 40 km, or at least four hours' cycling time on a Chinese bike. Alternatively, buses to Xindu run from in front of the railway station and from the north bus station from around 6 am to 6 pm. The trip takes just under an hour.

Qingcheng Shan
(qīngchéng shān)
For those with limited time, Qingcheng Shan, a holy Taoist mountain some 65 km west of Chengdu, is a good alternative to the more rigorous climb at Emeishan. The peak is 1600 metres. There are numerous Taoist temples en route to the summit. The Jianfu Temple *(jiànfú gōng)* at the entrance to the mountain area is probably the best preserved. Of the 500 or so Taoist monks in residence on the mountain prior to Liberation, there are now thought to be around 100 left.

There's accommodation and food available at three spots on the mountain: at the

base at Jianfu Temple, about halfway up at Tianshi Cave *(tiānshī dòng)* and at the summit at Shangqing Temple *(shàngqīng gōng)*. Reckon on around Y10 to Y15 per person, Y20 to Y30 if you want your own bathroom. There are also some smaller privately run hostels along the way, but many of these seem reluctant to take foreigners. Most people ascend by way of Tianshi Cave and descend via Siwang Pavilion and Banshan Pavilion.

The climb to the top is a leisurely four-hour hike, making Qingcheng Shan a pleasant (though fairly long) day trip from Chengdu.

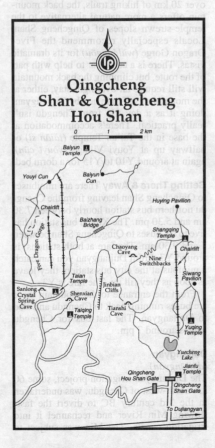

It might be more relaxing to set off around midday, stay overnight at Shangqing Temple and hike up to the summit for the sunrise. This leaves time to walk down and head over to Dujiangyan for the afternoon. There's a Y20 entry charge for the mountain area. There is a cable car that reduces the hike to Shangqing Temple to around one hour, but the Y24 one-way fare may have you sticking to the trail.

In a bid to bolster tourism, local authorities have also recently opened up the 'Qingcheng Hou Shan' (Qingcheng Back Mountain), the base of which lies about 15 km north-west of the base of Qingcheng Shan proper. With over 20 km of hiking trails, the back mountain offers a more natural alternative to the temple-strewn slopes of Qingcheng Shan. Locals especially recommend the Five-Dragon Gorge (wǔlónggōu) for its dramatic vistas. There is a cable car to help with part of the route, but climbing the back mountain will still require an overnight stay, either at the mountain itself or in nearby Dujiangyan: doing it as a day trip from Chengdu isn't really practical. There's accommodation at the base in the Tai'an Temple (tài'ān sì) or halfway up at Youyi Village (yòuyī cūn), again at around Y10 to Y15 for a dorm bed.

Getting There & Away There are minibuses to Qingcheng Shan leaving from the Chengdu northern bus station hourly between 7.30 am and 5.30 pm. The Ximen bus station has five to six buses to Qingcheng Shan between 7 and 9.30 am. The fare at both stations is around Y7. From Dujiangyan you can catch a minibus at the city bus station: they leave as soon as they fill up. The fare is Y3.

From the entrance to the mountain there are buses running back to Chengdu and also to Dujiangyan. The last bus for Chengdu leaves around 7 pm.

Dujiangyan
(dūjiāngyàn)
The Dujiangyan irrigation project, some 60 km north-west of Chengdu, was undertaken in the 3rd century BC to divert the fast-flowing Min River and rechannel it into irrigation canals. The Min was subject to

flooding at this point, yet when it subsided droughts could ensue. A weir system was built to split the force of the river, and a trunk canal was cut through a mountain to irrigate the Chengdu plain. Thus the mighty Min was tamed, and a temple was erected to commemorate the occasion in 168 AD. The temple, **Fulong Temple** (fúlóng guān), can still be seen in the Lidui Park (lídūi gōngyuán).

The project is ongoing – it originally irrigated over a million hectares of land, and since Liberation this has expanded to three million hectares. Most of the present dams, reservoirs, pumping stations, hydroelectric works, bridgework and features are modern; a good overall view of the outlay can be gained from **Two Kings Temple** (èrwáng miào), which dates back to 494 AD. The two kings are Li Bing, governor of the kingdom of Shu and father of the irrigation project, and his son, Er Lang. Inside is a statue of Li Bing, shockingly lifelike; in the rear hall is a standing figure of his son holding a dam tool. There's also a Qing Dynasty project map, and behind the temple there is a terrace saying in effect, 'Mao was here' (1958).

DUJIANGYAN 都江堰

1 Anlan Cable Bridge
   安澜索桥
2 Two Kings Temple
   二王庙
3 Chairlift
   索道
4 Fulong Temple
   伏龙观
5 South Bridge
   南桥
6 Dujiangyan Hotel
   都江堰宾馆
7 City Bus Station
   市客运站
8 County Bus Station
   县客运站
9 Post Office
   邮电大楼
10 Kuiguang Pagoda
   奎光塔

Dujiangyan gets mixed reports from travellers. Some people love the place, others find the whole idea of visiting a massive irrigation project boring. There's not a great deal of local flavour, although there are small teahouses lining the river around the **South Bridge** *(nánqiáo)*, near Lidui Park entrance, and visiting the nearby temples is not a bad way to while away an afternoon.

Dujiangyan is easy to do as a day trip. But should you decide to stay overnight, perhaps to tackle Qingcheng Shan the next day, the *Dujiangyan Hotel (dūjiāngyàn bīnguǎn)*, about 15 minutes' walk from the city bus station, has beds in triples for as low as Y24, and air-con doubles for Y100.

Don't bother with the *China Travel Service Hotel*, a shabby-looking two-star nearby. The management are under the illusion that some wayward foreigner would consider shelling out US$33 for a mouldy double.

Getting There & Away Buses run to Dujiangyan from Ximen bus station in Chengdu every 10 minutes. There are also hourly buses leaving the Chengdu northern bus station from 7.30 am to 5.30 pm. Both cost around Y5, and the trip takes 1½ hours. From the Dujiangyan city bus station it's not a bad idea to catch another bus on to the Two Kings Temple and work your way back. It's also possible to hook up with buses here going to Qingcheng Shan. Going back to Chengdu, there are frequent minibuses departing from along Taiping Jie, in the area of the city bus station. The last one leaves around 8 pm.

Wolong Nature Reserve
(wòlóng zìrán bǎohùqū)

Wolong Nature Reserve lies 140 km north-west of Chengdu, about eight hours of rough roads by bus (via Dujiangyan). It was set up in the late 1970s and is the largest of the 16

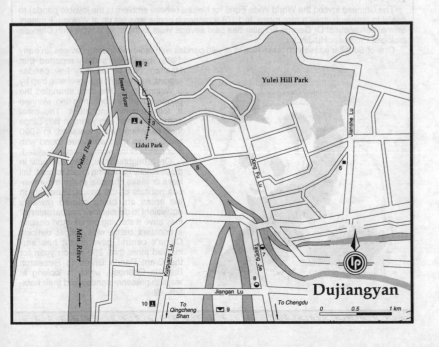

Pandas: Elusive and Endangered

Estimates place the total number of giant pandas at a round figure of 1000, separated into 30 isolated groups, most of which are distributed in 28 counties of north and north-western Sichuan (with further ranges in Gansu and Shaanxi). Other animals protected here are the golden monkey, golden langur, musk deer and snow leopard. The reserve is estimated to have some 3000 kinds of plants and covers an area of 200,000 hectares. To the north-west is Mt Siguniang (6240 metres) and to the east it drops as low as 155 metres. Pandas like to dine in the zone from 2300 to 3200 metres, ranging lower in winter.

The earliest known remains of the panda date back 600,000 years. It's stoutly built, rather clumsy, and has a thick pelt of fine hair, a short tail and a round white face with eyes set in black-rimmed sockets. Though it staggers when it walks, the panda is a good climber, and lives mostly on a vegetarian diet of bamboo and sugar-cane leaves. Mating season has proved a great disappointment to observers at the Wolong Reserve, since pandas are rather particular. Related to the bear and the raccoon, pandas – despite their human-looking shades – can be vicious in self-defence. In captivity they establish remarkable ties with their keepers after a period of time, and can be trained to do a repertoire of tricks.

Chinese literature has references to pandas going back over 3000 years. It wasn't until 1869 that the West found out about the panda, when a French missionary brought a pelt back with him to Paris. Now, in the 20th century, the giant panda is headed for extinction. Part of the problem is the gradual diminution of their food supply; in the mid-'70s more than 130 pandas starved to death when one of the bamboo species on which they feed flowered and withered in the Minshan mountains of Sichuan. Pandas consume enormous amounts of bamboo, although their digestive tracts get little value from the plant (consumption is up to 20 kg of bamboo a day in captivity). They are carnivorous, but they're slow to catch animals. Other problems are genetic defects, internal parasites and a slow reproductive rate (artificial insemination has been used at Beijing Zoo).

The Chinese invited the World Wide Fund for Nature (whose emblem is the lovable panda) to assist in research, itself a rare move. In 1978 a research centre was set up at Wolong. Eminent animal behaviourist Dr George Schaller has paid several visits to the area to work with Chinese biologist Professor Hu Jinchu.

One of Schaller's research tasks was to fit wild pandas with radio-monitoring devices. In early

1983, the *People's Daily* reported that Hanhan, one of the very few pandas tagged, was caught in a steel wire trap by a Wolong local. The man strangled the panda, cut off its monitoring ring, skinned it, took it home and ate it. The meal earned the man two years in jail. Since then penalties have increased; in 1990 two Sichuan men who were found with four panda skins were publicly executed.

On a brighter note, laws are now in place strictly forbidding locals to hunt, fell trees or make charcoal in the mountainous habitats of the panda. Peasants in the areas are being offered rewards equivalent to double their annual salary if they save a starving panda. And despite a constant battle with budget deficits, China's central government has earmarked more than 200 million yuan for the Giant Panda Breeding Research Base in Chengdu, which is looking at ways to preserve pandas and their habitats. ■

reserves set aside by the Chinese government especially for panda conservation. Of these 16 reserves, 11 are in Sichuan. The United Nations has designated Wolong as an international biosphere preserve.

Before setting out for Wolong be forewarned: there is little chance of seeing a panda in the wild. Dr George Schaller, invited by China to help with panda research and conservation efforts, spent two months trekking in the mountains before he got to see one. To see a live panda in something resembling its natural habitat, your best bet is the Giant Panda Breeding Research Base in Chengdu (see the earlier Chengdu Things to See section). If you're just out to commune with nature, Wolong is nice, but your time may be better spent making the trip up to Songpan and Jiuzhaigou.

The opening of the research base and improved access to northern Sichuan Province has dampened demand for tours of the Wolong Reserve. Though most travel outfits

at the Traffic Hotel have dropped this tour, one or two still offer packages that include transportation, entry to the reserve and one night's accommodation in Wolong town for Y400 per person, with a four-person minimum. Your other option is to catch a bus to Dujiangyan, where there is a bus to Wolong leaving at 1.30 pm from the county bus station. The latter trip takes about 4 hours and costs Y14. In Wolong, the *Wolong Hostel* (wòlóng zhāodàisuǒ) has doubles for around Y100. Entry to the nature reserve is Y50.

EMEISHAN
(éméishān)
Emeishan (Mt Emei), locked in a medieval time warp, receives a steady stream of happy pilgrims with their straw hats, makeshift baggage, walking canes and fans. The monasteries hold sombre Buddhist monks, the tinkle of bells, clouds of incense, and firewood and coal lumped in the courtyards for the winter months.

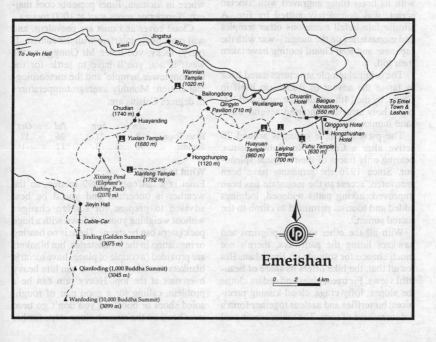

It is more or less a straight mountain climb, with your attention directed to the luxuriant scenery – and, as in *The Canterbury Tales*, to fellow pilgrims. Admirable are the hardened affiliates of Grannies Alpine Club, who slog it up there with the best of them, walking sticks at the ready lest a brazen monkey dare think them easy prey for a food-mugging. They come yearly for the assault, and burn paper money as a Buddhist offering for longevity. The climb no doubt adds to their longevity, so the two factors may be related. For the traveller itching to do something, the Emei climb is a good opportunity to air the respiratory organs, as well as to observe post-1976 religious freedoms in action, since you are obliged to stay in the rickety monasteries along the route.

One of the Middle Kingdom's four famous Buddhist mountains (the others are Putuo, Wutai and Jiuhua), Emeishan has little of its original temple-work left. The glittering Jinding (Golden Summit) Temple, with its brass tiling engraved with Tibetan script, was completely gutted by fire. A similar fate befell numerous other temples and monasteries on the mount – war with the Japanese and Red Guard looting have taken their toll.

The original temple structures dated back as far as the advent of Buddhism itself in China; by the 14th century, the estimated 100 or so holy structures housed several thousand monks.

The present temple count is around 20 active after a Cultural Revolution hiatus, bearing only traces of their original splendour. Since 1976 the remnants have been renovated, access to the mountain has been improved, hiking paths widened, lodgings added and tourists permitted to climb to the sacred summit.

With all the other tourists, pilgrims and hawkers lining the pathways, there's not much chance for solitude on Emeishan. But for all that, the hike offers its share of beautiful views. Fir trees, pines and cedars clothe the slopes; lofty crags, cloud-kissing precipices, butterflies and azaleas together form a nature reserve of sorts. The major scenic goal

of Chinese hikers is to witness a sunrise or sunset over the sea of clouds at the summit. On the rare afternoon there is a phenomenon known as Buddha's Aureole – rainbow rings, produced by refraction of water particles, attach themselves to a person's shadow in a cloud bank below the summit. Devout Buddhists, thinking this was a call from yonder, used to jump off the Cliff of Self-Sacrifice in ecstasy, so during the Ming and Qing dynasties officials set up iron poles and chain railings to prevent suicides. These days your head can be stuck in a cardboard cutout on the site, and you can be photographed in that same act of attaining nirvana.

Climate

The best season to visit is from May to October. Winter is not impossible, but will present some trekking problems – iron soles with spikes can be hired to deal with encrusted ice and snow on the trails. At the height of summer, which is scorching elsewhere in Sichuan, Emei presents cool majesty. Temperate zones start at 1000 metres.

Cloud cover and mist are prevalent, and will most likely interfere with the sunrise. If (very) lucky, you'll see Mt Gongga to the west; if not, you'll have to settle for the telecom tower 'temple' and the meteorological station. Monthly average temperatures in degrees Celsius are:

	Jan	Apr	Jul	Oct
Emei Town	7	21	26	17
Summit	-6	3	12	-1

What to Bring

Emei is a tall one at 3099 metres, so the weather is uncertain and you'd be best advised to prepare for sudden changes without weighing yourself down with a huge pack (steps can be steep). There is no heating or insulation in the monasteries, but blankets are provided (a couple of places have electric blankets nowadays), and you can hire heavy overcoats at the top. Heavy rain can be a problem, calling for a good pair of rough-soled shoes or boots, so you don't go head over heels on the smooth stone steps further up. Flimsy plastic macs are sold by enterprising vendors on the slopes – these will last about 10 minutes before you get wet.

Strange hiking equipment as it may sound, a fixed-length umbrella would be most useful – for the rain, and as a walking stick (scare the hell out of those monkeys by pressing auto-release!). These kinds of umbrellas cost from around Y30 to Y45 in China. If you want to look more authentic you can get yourself a handcrafted walking stick, very cheap – and while you're at it, get a fan and a straw hat too. A torch would be handy. Food supplies are not necessary, but a pocket of munchies wouldn't hurt. Bring toilet paper with you.

Some travellers have become sick from contaminated water supplies on the mountain, so you might consider carrying bottled water.

Ascending the Heights

You can dump your bags for a modest charge at the Chuanlin Hotel or the Hongzhushan Hotel, both of which are near the Baoguo Monastery. (It may be possible to dump them at the Baoguo Monastery or the Emei town railway station as well.)

Most people start their ascent of the mountain at Wannian Temple (*wànnián sì*) and come down through Qingyin Pavilion. From Baoguo Monastery there are minibuses running close to Wannian Temple and to Qingyin Pavilion between 7 am and 3 pm. Buses leave as soon as they fill up, so it's better to go in the early morning hours, when there are more passengers about. Fares range between Y5 and Y10, depending on the driver and your ability to bargain. Buses to Wannian Temple are more frequent. Coming back from Wannian, buses start running around 8 am and stop at 4 pm.

The bus depot near Qingyin Pavilion also has connections back to Emei town and to Leshan, but there are more running from Baoguo Monastery. If you're stuck for connections you may be able to hitch back to Baoguo, otherwise it's a 15-km hike.

For a 'softer' combination, take a minibus to Qingyin Pavilion and then walk along the more scenic route via Hongchunping and Yuxian up to Jieyin Hall, from where you can catch a chairlift (Y40) up to the Golden Summit. From there you can descend the six km back to Jieyin and take a bus back down. If you want to 'cheat' in earnest, see the Cheating section below.

One thing to watch out for: Emeishan levies a Y20 entry fee for foreigners, good for one entry only. So if, for instance, you catch a bus at Jieyin Hall, and take it down to Wannian Temple, you will be required to buy another entry ticket. Take this unpleasant little fact into account when planning your route. If you're hiking the entire way, this won't be a problem.

Routes Most people ascend Emeishan via Wannian Temple, Chu Temple, Huayan Summit, Xixiang Pond and on to the summit, and descend from the summit via Xixiang Pond, Xianfeng Temple Hongchunping and Qingyin Pavilion. The paths converge just below Xixiang Pond – there are several small restaurants where the path forks. To give you an idea of the distances involved (remember you are going uphill), the above route pans out as follows:

Baoguo Monastery – 15 km – Wannian Temple – 15 km – Xixiang Pond – 5½ km – Jieyin Hall – 3½ km – Golden Summit – 4 km – Ten Thousand Buddha Summit – 4 km – Golden Summit – 9 km – Xixiang Pond – 7 km – Xianfeng Temple – 6 km – Hongchunping – 6 km – Qingyin Pavilion – 9½ km – Leiyin Temple – 1½ km – Fuhu Temple – 1 km – Baoguo Monastery.

Duration Two to three days on site is enough. You usually need one day up and one day down. Enough time should be left for a slow-paced descent, which can be more punishing for the old trotters. A hardy Frenchman made it up and down on the same day, but he must have had unusual legs. Chinese and Western sources have some wildly misleading figures on the length and difficulty of the Emei climb. These figures can be attributed to geriatric or Chinese walking times, or discounting of the buses running to Wannian Temple.

Assuming that most people will want to start climbing from Qingyin Pavilion or Wannian Temple, buses from Baoguo Monastery run close to these points, so that knocks off the initial 15 km. Wannian Temple is at 1020 metres, and the Golden Summit is at 3075 metres. With a healthy set of lungs, at a rate of 200 metres' elevation gain per hour, the trip up from Wannian Temple could be done in 10 hours if foul weather does not develop.

Starting off early in the morning from Wannian Temple, you should be able to get to a point below the Golden Summit by nightfall, then continue to the Golden and Ten Thousand Buddha summits the next day, before descending to Baoguo Monastery. Some people prefer to spend two days up and two days down, spending more time exploring along the way. If you have time to spare, you could meander over the slopes to villages hugging the mountainsides.

On the main routes described above, in climbing time you'd be looking at:

Ascent Qingyin Pavilion (one hour), Wannian Temple (four hours), Xixiang Pond (three hours), Jieyin Hall (one hour), Golden Summit (one hour), Ten Thousand Buddha Summit

Descent Ten Thousand Buddha Summit (45 minutes), Golden Summit (45 minutes), Jieyin Hall (2½ hours), Xixiang Pond (two hours), Xianfeng Temple (3½ hours), Qingyin Pavilion

Cheating Cheating is a popular pastime on Emei. Old women are portered up on the sturdy backs of young men (likewise, healthy-looking young women as well as men are carried up). If this mode of transport isn't your cup of tea, there are also minibuses leaving from the square in front of Baoguo Monastery between 8 am and 5 pm, though the wait can get quite long once the morning rush of tourists has passed. They run along a recently surfaced road round the back of the mountain up to Jieyin Hall (2640 metres). From there, it's only 1½ hours to the top. The ride takes around two hours and costs Y15. If you don't feel up to the Jieyin Hall-Golden Summit climb, a cable car will haul you up there in about 20 minutes for Y40 one way,

Y70 return (foreigners' prices). Lines can get very long, particularly just before sunrise.

If for some reason you wish to do the whole mountain in one day, most hotels can book you on a bus leaving at 3.30 am (!). This gets you to the summit in time to see the sunrise, and is a popular option with Chinese tourists. The buses head down from Jieyin Hall around mid-morning, stopping at various temples along the way and finally bringing you back to Baoguo at around 5 pm. The round trip costs about Y40 and will probably leave your head spinning.

Places to Stay & Eat

The old monasteries offer food, shelter and sights all rolled into one, and, while Spartan, are a delightful change from the regular tourist hotels. They've got maybe as much as 1000 years of character.

You may well be asked to pay some ridiculous prices, so be prepared to bargain. Prices range from Y3 in a very large dormitory (10 beds or more) to Y40 per person in a single, double or triple room. It's very difficult to get into the dorms – the staff usually let in only the Chinese. In between are other options like a four-bed room at Y10 to Y15 per person – again, the Chinese get preference for these. Plumbing and electricity are primitive; candles are supplied. Rats can be a nuisance, particularly if you leave food lying around your room.

There are eight monastery guesthouses – at Baoguo Monastery, Qingyin Pavilion, Wannian Temple, Xixiang Pond, Xianfeng Temple, Hongchunping, Fuhu Temple and Leiyin Temple. There's also a host of smaller lodgings at Chu Temple, Jieyin Hall, Yuxian, Bailongdong, the Golden Summit and Huayuan, for instance. The smaller places will accept you if the main monasteries are overloaded. Failing those, you can kip out virtually anywhere – a teahouse, a wayside restaurant – if night is descending.

Be prepared to backtrack or advance under cover of darkness, as key points are often full of pilgrims – old women two to a bed, camped down the corridors, or camping out in the hallowed temple itself, on the floor.

Monasteries usually have halfway hygienic restaurants with monk-chefs serving up the vegetarian fare; from Y5 to Y10 should cover a meal. There is often a small retail outlet selling peanuts, biscuits, beer and canned fruit within the monastery precincts.

Hotel prices get steep once you reach the summit, except for the Golden Summit Temple (see later in this section). There are some cheap spots, but many may refuse to accept foreigners. A good rule of thumb here is to avoid any hotel which has several different time-zone clocks in the lobby unless you're willing to pay over Y100 for a double. If you are in the mood for (relative) luxury, the Woyun Hotel, located just under the cable-car station, is the summit's only hotel that can boast 24-hour hot water. Standard doubles are Y180.

Along the route are small restaurants and food stalls where you can replenish the guts and the tea mug. Food gets more expensive and less varied the higher you mount, due to cartage surcharges and difficulties. Be wary of teahouses or restaurants serving 'divine water' (shénshuǐ), or any type of tea or food said to possess mystical healing qualities. While you're very unlikely to witness a miracle, you'll definitely end up being charged Y10 for a cup of tea.

Some notes on the monasteries follow. Most of the ones mentioned are located at key walking junctions and tend to be packed out. If you don't get in, do check out the restaurant and its patrons.

Baoguo Monastery (*bàoguó sì*) This monastery was built in the 16th century, enlarged in the 17th century by Emperor Kangxi and recently renovated. Its 3½-metre porcelain buddha, made in 1415, is housed near the Sutra Library. To the left of the gate is a rockery for potted miniature trees and rare plants. There's a nice vegetarian restaurant and teahouse with solid wood tables. Prices range from Y3 for a bed in a seven-person dorm to Y25 per bed in a 'fancy' triple.

Fuhu Temple (*fúhǔ sì*) 'Crouching Tiger Monastery', as it is known in Chinese, is sunk in the forest. Inside is a seven-metre-high copper pagoda inscribed with Buddhist images and texts. The monastery has been completely renovated, with the addition of bedding for 400 and restaurant seating for 200. At Y30 to Y40 for a bed in a double, a stay here costs a bit more than at the average Emeishan monastery but is well worth it if you can get in.

Wannian Temple (*wànnián sì*) The Temple of 10,000 Years is the oldest surviving Emei monastery (reconstructed in the 9th century). It's dedicated to the man on the white elephant, the bodhisattva Puxian, who is the protector of the mountain. This statue, 8½ metres high, cast in copper and bronze, weighing an estimated 62,000 kg, is found in Brick Hall, a domed building with small stupas on it. The statue was made in 980 AD. Accommodation in the Wannian Temple area is Y20 to Y30 per person, with good vegetarian food. If it's full, go back towards Qingyin Pavilion to Bailongdong, a small guesthouse.

Qingyin Pavilion (*qīngyīn gé*) Named the Pure Sound Pavilion because of the sound effects produced by rapid waters coursing around rock formations in the area, the temple itself is built on an outcrop in the middle of a fast-flowing stream. There are small pavilions from which to observe the waterworks and appreciate the natural music. Swimming here is possible.

Xixiang Pond (*xǐxiàng chí*) According to legend, the Elephant Bathing Pool is the spot where Puxian flew his elephant in for a big scrub, but there's not much of a pool to speak of today. Being almost at the crossroads of both major trails, this is something of a hangout and beds are scarce, unless you get here in the early afternoon. New extensions to the accommodation haven't completely solved the problem of pilgrim overload, so be prepared to move on.

The monkeys have got it all figured out – Xixiang Pond is the place to be. If you come across a monkey 'tollgate', the standard procedure is to thrust open palms towards the outlaw to show you have no food. The Chinese find the monkeys an integral part of the Emei trip, and like to tease them. As an aside, monkeys form an important part of Chinese mythology – and there is a saying in Chinese, 'With one monkey in the way, not even 10,000 men can pass' – which may be deeper than you think!

Some of these chimps are big buggers, and staying cool when they look like they might make a leap at you is easier said than done. There is much debate as to whether it's better to give them something to eat or to fight them off. One thing is certain, if you do throw them something, don't do it in too much moderation. They get annoyed very quickly if they think they are being undersold.

Golden Summit Temple *(jīndǐng sì)* At 3077 metres, the magnificent Golden Summit Temple is as far as most hikers make it. It has been entirely rebuilt since being gutted by a fire several years ago. Covered with glazed tile and surrounded by white marble balustrades, it now occupies 1695 sq metres. The original temple had a bronze-coated roof, which is how it got the name Jinding (which can mean 'Gold Top' as well as 'Golden Summit'). Constantly overrun with tourists, pilgrims and monks, this is one of the noisiest places to stay on the summit, but also one of the cheapest. A bed in a large seven to 10-bed dorm is Y10, if you can get it. Otherwise there are beds in five-person dorms for Y20 and quads/doubles for Y30/50. Coming from the trail leading up to the summit, the rooms are located in a big building just before you reach the temple itself.

Xianfeng Temple *(xiānfēng sì)* The surroundings are wonderful, backed onto rugged cliffs, and the Magic Peak Monastery has loads of character. Try and get a room at the rear, where the floors give pleasant views. It's off the main track so it's not crowded. Nearby is Jiulao Cave, inhabited by big bats.

Around the Base There is also accommodation at the foot of Emeishan, in addition to the Baoguo Monastery. Five minutes' walk west of Baoguo lies the *Chuanlin Hotel (chuānlín bīnguǎn)*, a sleepy place where a bed in a basic quad will cost you Y20.

Doubles with attached bath are available for Y80 and Y120.

East of the monastery, located at an intersection, is the *Qinggong Hotel (qīnggōng bīnguǎn)*, with standard doubles/triples for Y120/ 150. Past the Qinggong, the *Hongzhushan Hotel (hóngzhūshān bīnguǎn)*, also lacks cheap accommodation. The cheapest room is Y90, and they'll probably push you toward the Y198 'villa-style' rooms.

Along the road leading to Emei Town are scattered a number of hotels, a few of which may accept foreigners depending on their mood. Prices are generally high, but you may be able to scare up some dorm rooms if the Chuanlin Hotel isn't to your liking. This area also has a slew of small restaurants lining both sides of the street. One spot on the north side of the street, the *Teddy Bear Restaurant*, caters to travellers, and has an English menu and some tasty fare. If you go there in the evening, you may bump into Zhang Guangyui, a local English teacher who is happy to give advice on places to stay and hike.

Getting There & Away
The hubs of the transport links to Emeishan are Baoguo village and Emei town. Emei town itself is best skipped, though it does have markets, some cheap hotels, restaurants and a long-distance bus station.

Emei town lies 3½ km from the railway station. Baoguo is another 6½ km from Emei town. At Emei Railway Station, buses will be waiting for train arrivals – the short trip to Baoguo is Y2 in a minibus, and Y1 in a local bus. From Baoguo there are frequent minibuses throughout the day to Emei town and on to Leshan, from where there are good bus connections to Chengdu. The ride to Leshan (Y4) takes around one hour. There are also occasional direct buses between Emei and Qingyin Pavilion.

Direct minibuses also run from Baoguo to Chengdu. Again, these depart as they fill up – there is no set timetable. The fare is around Y20 and the trip takes four to five hours.

Emei Railway Station is on the Chengdu-Kunming railway line, and the three-hour trip to Chengdu costs Y9 (hard seat, Chinese price). The train from Emei town is more comfortable than the bus, but does not offer the convenience of leaving from Baoguo (trains are also less frequent and timing may be off). Trains bound for Chengdu depart from Emei Railway Station at 8.17 am (No 68), 9.14 am (No 86), 10.42 am (No 322), 12.52 pm (No 542) and 1.28 pm (No 66).

LESHAN
(lèshān)

Once a sleepy counterpart to Emeishan, Leshan has taken off as China's newly afflu-

ent tourists flock to see the city's claim to fame, the towering Grand Buddha. Old brick and plaster homes are increasingly giving way to apartment towers, and the city centre is rife with neon signs for imported electronics, Coca-Cola and stock brokerages. But for

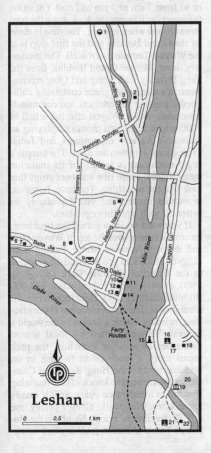

```
LESHAN 乐山

 1  Long-Distance Bus Station
    长途汽车站
 2  Leshan Education Hotel
    乐山教育宾馆
 3  Lianyun Bus Co
    联运汽车站
 4  Jiading Hotel
    嘉定饭店
 5  Dongfeng Hotel
    东风饭店
 6  The Yangs' Restaurant
    杨家餐厅
 7  Jiazhou Hotel
    嘉州宾馆
 8  Workers' Cultural Palace
    劳动人民文化宫
 9  Post Office
    邮电局
10  Provincial Bus Co.
    省汽车运输公司
11  Ferries to Chongqing, Yibin
    长途码头
12  Ferry Ticket Office
    渡轮售票处
13  Taoyuan Hotel
    桃源宾馆
14  Tour Boat Dock
    短途码头
15  Grand Buddha
    大佛
16  Grand Buddha Temple
    大佛寺
17  Nanlou Guesthouse
    南楼宾馆
18  Jiurifeng Hotel
    就日峰宾馆
19  Mahaoya Tomb Museum
    麻浩崖博物馆
20  Oriental Buddha Park
    东方佛都
21  Wuyou Temple
    乌尤寺
22  Xiandao Hotel
    仙岛宾馆
```

all that, Leshan is still on a scale you can be comfortable with. The hotel situation is pretty good, decent food can be unearthed and it's a good resting spot for those Emei-weary legs.

Things to See

The **Grand Buddha** *(dàfó)* is 71 metres high, carved into a cliff face overlooking the confluence of the Dadu and Min rivers. It qualifies as the largest Buddha in the world, with the one at Bamian, Afghanistan, as runner-up (besides, the Leshan model is sitting down!). Dafo's ears are seven metres long, insteps 8½ metres broad, and a picnic could be conducted on the nail of his big toe, which is 1½ metres long – the toe itself is 8½ metres long.

This lunatic project was begun in the year 713 AD, engineered by a Buddhist monk called Haitong who organised fund raising and hired workers; it was completed 90 years later. Below the Buddha was a hollow where boatmen used to vanish – Haitong hoped that the Buddha's presence would subdue the swift currents and protect the boatmen, and Dafo did do a lot of good, as the surplus rocks from the sculpting filled the river hollow. Haitong gouged out his own eyes in an effort to protect funding from disappearing into the hands of officers, but he died before the completion of his life's work. A building used to shelter the giant statue, but it was destroyed during a Ming Dynasty war.

Inside the body, hidden from view, is a water-drainage system to prevent weathering, although the stone statue has seen its fair share. Dafo is so old that foliage is trying to reclaim him – flowers growing on the giant hands, a bushy chest, ferns in his topknots, and weeds winding out of his earholes. He gazes down, perhaps in alarm, at the drifting pollutants in the river that presumably come from the paper mill at the industrial end of town (which started large-scale operation in 1979).

Officials are worried about the possibility of a collapse due to soil erosion; one suggestion that has not met with an enthusiastic response is to cover the Buddha with a huge transparent shell.

It's worth making several passes at big Buddha, as there are all kinds of angles on him. You can go to the top, opposite the head, and then descend a short stairway to the feet for a Lilliputian perspective. Tour boats pass by for a frontal view, which reveals two guardians in the cliff side, not visible from land.

To make a round tour that encompasses these possibilities, take a tour boat from the Leshan pier, across from the Taoyuan Hotel. Boats leave approximately every 30 minutes or so from 7 am to 5 pm and cost Y8; sit on the upper deck facing the dock, since the boat turns around when leaving. You pass in close by the Grand Buddha and the first stop is at the **Wuyou Temple** *(wūyōu sì)*. The monastery dates, like the Grand Buddha, from the Tang Dynasty with Ming and Qing renovations; it's a museum piece containing calligraphy, painting and artefacts, and commands panoramic views. Wuyou also has a hall of 1000 arhats, terracotta monks displaying an incredible variety of postures and facial expressions – no two are alike. The temple's vegie restaurant is famed for its imitation meats dishes: spare ribs and beef strips that look like the real thing. The taste, however, is another matter, and you'll probably be better off with straight vegetables.

If you want you can get off the boat here, go cross-country over the top of Wuyou Hill, and down to a small bridge linking it to Lingyun Hill. Here you will find the entrance to the **Oriental Buddha Park** *(dōngfāng fódū)*, a newly assembled collection of 3,000 Buddha statutes and figurines from all around Asia. The centrepiece is a 170-metre-long reclining Buddha, said to be the world's longest. Though touted by local tourist authorities as a major attraction, the park seems more a hasty effort to cash in on Buddha-mania – the Hong Kong and Chinese sculptors raced to knock off the reclining Buddha in a mere two years. Still it makes for an interesting walk, albeit a pricey one at Y30 (foreigners' price). Nearby is the **Mahaoya Tomb Museum** *(máhàoyámù bówù-*

guǎn), which has a modest collection of tombs and burial artefacts dating from the Eastern Han Dynasty.

Continuing past the Buddha Park and up Lingyun Hill brings you to the semi-active **Grand Buddha Temple** (*dàfó sì*), which sits near Dafo's head. From here you can catch views of Dafo's head, have a picture taken of you sticking your finger in his ear and walk down a narrow staircase to reach his feet. To get back to Leshan walk south to the small ferry going direct across the Min River.

This whole exercise can be done in less than 1½ hours from the Leshan dock; however, it's worth making a day of it. If you want to avoid the crowds, you should consider doing this route in reverse, that is, starting with the Dafo Temple and Grand Buddha in the morning and on to Wuyou Monastery in the afternoon.

It would be a mistake to think of Leshan as one big Buddha, for the area is steeped in history. North of Leshan, 2½ km west of the railway station at Jiajiang, are the **Thousand-Buddha Cliffs** (*jiājiāng qiānfóyán*). For once, the name is not an exaggeration: over 2,400 Buddhas dot the cliffs, dating back as far as the Eastern Han Dynasty (25-220 AD). The statues are said to be in fairly good shape, despite the ravages of time and the Cultural Revolution.

There are some pleasant walks to be had in Leshan itself. By the remains of the town ramparts is an older section of town where you can still find some cobbled streets and green, blue and red-shuttered buildings. The area around the ferry docks and the old town buzzes with market activity. In season, the markets yield a surprising array of fresh fruit and vegetables, so you can do more than look at them. Further out, by the Jiazhou Hotel, are teahouses with bamboo chairs spilling onto the street.

Entry Fees Be prepared to be constantly forking out money when you visit the Grand Buddha. The separate entry fees probably add up to a total of Y40. Some examples are the fees for the main entry gate (Y22), the Buddha's feet (Y5), the descent from head to feet (Y4), the Grand Buddha Temple (Y2), Wuyou Temple (Y2) and a host of little fees for footbridges and so on. Some travellers get very irate about all these hidden costs, but rules is rules!

Places to Stay & Eat
Probably the most popular place with backpackers these days is the *Leshan Education Hotel* (☎ 235661) (*lèshān jiàoyù yánjiūsuǒ*) at 156 Liren Jie, around the corner from the Lianyun bus depot in the northern section of town. Staff prowl the bus stations for arriving foreigners, so you may not have to search for the place. Beds in fairly clean doubles/triples with common bath are Y30/24. Somewhat damp and shabby doubles with bath attached are considerably more expensive at Y200: definitely not good value.

Just south of the Education Hotel, at the corner of Jiading Zhong Lu and Renmin Donglu, lurks the *Jiading Hotel* (*jiādìng fàndiàn*), which is decidedly more proletarian. Beds in doubles/triples without bath cost Y15/10, while dingy standard doubles are Y60 to Y80. The place is pretty noisy, but it should be okay for a couple of nights. The No 4 bus, which links Leshan pier with the Leshan long-distance bus station, passes near both hotels.

Other budget options are limited. The formerly decrepit *Dongfeng Hotel* (*dōngfēng fàndiàn*) was scheduled for a facelift at the time of writing, and will probably only have luxury rooms in its new guise. Down by the Leshan pier, the newly opened *Taoyuan Hotel* (*táoyuán bīnguǎn*) was tentatively pricing beds in doubles with common washroom at Y20. If they maintain this price it will be good news, as the hotel is in a convenient location and also offers great views of the Grand Buddha. Standard doubles were expected to cost around Y200.

Over on the Buddha's side of the Min River are a couple of pricey but pleasant places to stay. Near the Wuyou Temple is the friendly *Xiandao Hotel* (*xiāndǎo bīnguǎn*) (☎ 233268) with upscale doubles for Y218. Triples are a bit more affordable at Y188.

There appear to be several good restaurants here, and the hotel even has a sauna.

There are two hotels in the area above the head of the Grand Buddha, *Nanlou Guesthouse (nánlóu bīnguǎn)* and *Jiurifeng Hotel (jiǔrìfēng bīnguǎn)*. Perhaps due to the Buddha's drainage system, the cliff around here is wet, and the dampness can extend to the rooms. The Nanlou, set right next to the Grand Buddha Temple, is definitely out of budget range, only offering standard doubles for Y320. The Jiurifeng is only slightly cheaper and not quite as nice, so the former may be the better choice if you're in the mood to spend.

Top-of-the-line is the three-star *Jiazhou Hotel (jiāzhōu bīnguǎn)*, which has become rather expensive. Doubles and triples start at Y200 and suites at Y600. The hotel is in a pleasant area; to get there take the No 1 bus from near the corner of Jiading Nanlu and Dong Dajie to the terminal.

The area between the Jiazhou Hotel and the pier is good for small restaurants and street stalls. For a home-style meal and good conversation, wander over to *The Yang's Restaurant*, a tiny wooden hole-in-the-wall at 49 Baita Jie. The owner, Mr Yang, speaks English and has an interesting history. Travellers have raved about his ad hoc tours to small villages around Leshan, and he's also willing to lend a hand in making travel arrangements.

Getting There & Away

Bus There are three bus stations in Leshan, which is understandably confusing for many travellers. The main one for travellers is the Leshan long-distance bus station, somewhat inconveniently located in the northern reaches of the city. There are daily buses running every 20 minutes to Chengdu (the first at 6.10 am and the last at 6 pm). The 165-km trip takes five hours and the fare is Y15.

One thing to watch out for is the bus's Chengdu destination. Most of the buses run to the Xinnanmen bus station next to the Traffic Hotel, but several run to the north bus station or railway station, which are inconvenient for Chengdu's budget accommodation.

If you're headed to Chengdu, consider treating yourself to one of the nicest bus rides in China. The Dongguang High Speed Bus *(dōngguāng gāosù qìchē)* offers direct *nonstop* service to Chengdu's Jiuyanqiao bus station using new South Korean buses that make the trip in just over three hours. Drinks and snacks are served, the seats recline and, best of all, the bus never stops en route to pull in more passengers! For Y21.50 it's a great deal and a welcome break from the standard timetables-be-damned service you're used to. Buses leave at 3.50 pm daily.

From Emeishan to Leshan is 30 km; minibuses run every 15 minutes to Emei town and Baoguo Monastery between 6.20 am and 6 pm. The ride is one hour and costs Y4.

Buses to Chongqing leave daily at 6 am and 3 pm. The trip takes 10 hours and costs around Y55. There's also a sleeper bus (Y95) leaving at 5 pm, but bear in mind this puts you in Chongqing at around 3 am. The other bus stations around town are the Provincial Bus Co *(shěng qìchē yùnshū gōngsī)* and the Lianyun *(liányùn chēzhàn)*. Both have numerous daily departures for Chengdu, Baoguo and Emei. The former is close to the longdistance ferry dock and the latter is about 30 minutes' walk to the north of the ferry dock, near the Education Hotel. Buses departing Lianyun for Chengdu only go to the railway station, though staff may tell you they go to Xinnanmen just to get you to buy a ticket.

Boat There is a boat to Chongqing, departing Leshan every two days at 7 am. The trip takes 36 hours and a 3rd-class berth costs Y131.60. The passenger service only operates from April to October, closing down for the winter. There are also boats to Yibin which depart daily at 8.30 am and cost Y45 in 3rd class. Yibin is part-way to Chongqing and has a railway station. Tickets for both destinations can be bought at a ticket office across the street from Leshan Pier.

Getting Around

The No 1 and No 4 buses run the length of Jiading Lu and connect the pier area with the long-distance bus station, and the Jiading, Dongfeng and Education hotels. Buses runs from 6 am to 6 pm, at roughly 20-minute intervals. On foot, it's about an hour walk from one end of town to the other. A pedicab from the pier to the Educational Hotel should cost Y3 to Y5. Unfortunately, there doesn't seem to be any bicycle hire, though maybe the people at the Educational Hotel can help you arrange something. It's not a big problem if you're just visiting the Grand Buddha, since much of the walking is up and down staircases and steep hills, where bikes would be of limited use.

MEISHAN

(méishān)

Meishan, 90 km south-west of Chengdu by road or rail (it's on the Kunming-Chengdu railway line), is largely of interest to those with a knowledge of Chinese language, literature and calligraphy. It was the residence of Su Xun and his two sons, Su Shi and Su Zhe, the three noted literati of the Northern Song Dynasty (960-1126). Their residence was converted into a temple in the early Ming Dynasty, with renovations under the Qing emperor Hongwu (1875-1909). The mansion and pavilions now operate as a museum for the study of the writings of the Northern Song period. Historical documents, relics of the Su family, writings, calligraphy – some 4500 items all told – are on display at the Sansu (Three Sus) shrine.

CHONGQING

(chóngqìng)

Perched on steep hills overlooking the confluence of two rivers, Chongqing is one of China's more unusual cities. Dusty grey tenements and shining office towers cling to precipitous hillsides that make up much of the city centre. Another unique aspect is the absence of bicycles. There's barely a cyclist to be found, as the hill climbs make it coronary country for any would-be rider.

Chongqing is quite pleasant to stroll around, and even if it's not exactly brimming with 'sights' there's nevertheless a certain picturesque quality to this grey city. For Chinese tourists the 'sights' are usually connected with the Communist Revolution, most of which are linked to the city's role as the wartime capital of the Kuomintang from 1938 to 1945.

Though it plays second fiddle to Chengdu, Chongqing is hardly a backwater. It is rated as the chief industrial city of south-west China, with its production amounting to a fifth of Sichuan's total industrial output. The total metropolitan area has a population of some 14 million; around 3 million live in the city proper.

China's economic boom has infected Chongqing with a severe case of skyscraper fever: at every turn there seems to be either a tower going up or a vast hole in the ground awaiting a foundation. In ten years the city centre may look a bit like Hong Kong with its sparkling skyscrapers and mountain backdrop.

Within China, Chongqing is famous for its searing summers, when temperatures can exceed 40°C. This lovely climate has earned the city a place among the country's 'three furnaces', the other two being Wuhan and Nanjing.

History

Chongqing (known in pre-Pinyin China as 'Chungking') was opened as a treaty port in 1890, but not many foreigners made it up the river to this isolated outpost, and those who did had little impact. A programme of industrialisation got under way in 1928, but it was in the wake of the Japanese invasion that Chongqing really took off as a major centre, after the Kuomintang retreated to set up its wartime capital here. Refugees from all over China flooded in, swelling the population to over two million. The irony of this overpopulated, overstrained city with its bomb-shattered houses is that the name means something like 'double jubilation' or 'repeated good luck'. Emperor Zhao Dun of the Song Dynasty succeeded to the throne in 1190, having previously been made the

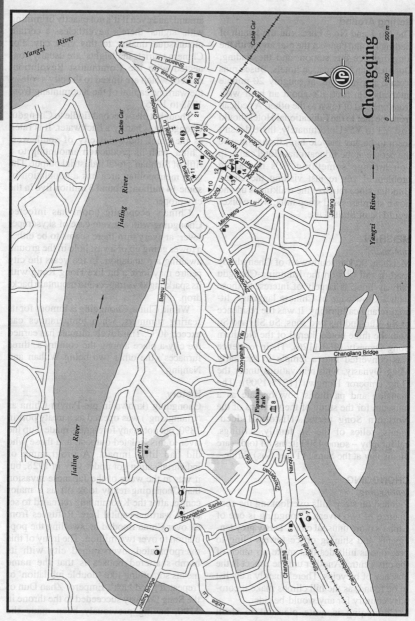

Chongqing

Yangzi River

Jialing River

Yangzi River

Jialing River

Shaanxi Lu

Xinhua Lu

Jiefang Lu

Chaoqian Lu

Cangbai Lu

Linjiang Lu

Wuyi Lu

Bayi Lu

Minsheng Lu

Mingsheng

Zhongshan Yilu

Pipashan Park

Renmin Lu

Zhongshan Sanlu

Zhongshan

Nanqu Lu

Changjiang

Shanchengzhi Lu

Lizhu Lu

Jialing Bridge

Changjiang Bridge

500 m

250

0

N

prince of the city of Gongzhou; as a celebration of these two happy events, he renamed Gongzhou Chongqing.

Edgar Snow arrived in the city in 1939 and found it:

...a place of moist heat, dirt and wide confusion, into which, between air raids, the imported central government...made an effort to introduce some technique of order and construction. Acres of buildings had been destroyed in the barbaric raids of May and June. The Japanese preferred moonlit nights for their calls, when from their base in Hankow they could follow the silver banner of the Yangzi up to its confluence with the Jialing, which identified the capital in a way no blackout could obscure. The city had no defending air force and only a few anti-aircraft guns...Spacious public shelters were being dug, but it was estimated that a third of the population still had no protection. Government officials, given advance warning, sped outside the city in their motor cars – cabinet ministers first, then vice-ministers, then minor bureaucrats. The populace soon caught on; when they saw a string of official cars racing to the west, they dropped everything and ran. A mad scramble of rickshaws, carts, animals and humanity blew up the main streets like a great wind, carrying all before it.

Living in the shadow of strutting Kuomintang military leaders, representatives of the Chinese Communist Party (including Zhou Enlai) acted as 'liaisons' between Chongqing and the Communists' headquarters at Yan'an, in Shaanxi Province. Repeated efforts to bring the two sides together in a unified front against the Japanese largely failed due to mutual distrust and Chiang Kaishek's obsession with wiping out the Communists, even at the cost of yielding Chinese territory to an invading army. The wartime offices and living quarters of the Communist officials form the bulk of Chongqing's tourist attractions, along with museums depicting atrocities committed by the Kuomintang and its US backers.

Orientation

The heart of Chongqing spreads across a hilly peninsula of land wedged between the Jialing River to the north and the Yangzi River to the south. The rivers meet at the tip of the peninsula at the eastern end of the city.

The central focus of this congested peninsula of winding streets for most visitors is the Liberation Monument, which is walking distance from most of Chongqing's accom-

CHONGQING 重庆	PLACES TO EAT	8	Chongqing Museum 博物馆
PLACES TO STAY	10 Yizhishi Restaurant 颐之时大酒店	11	PSB 公安局外事科
4 Renmin Hotel & CITS 人民宾馆, 中国国际旅行社	19 Lamb Restaurant 羊肉馆	12	Liberation Monument 解放碑
5 Shancheng Hotel 山城饭店	20 Lao Sichuan 老四川	13	Xinhua Bookstore 新华书店
6 Chongqing Guest- house 重庆宾馆	**OTHER**	14	Foreign Languages Bookstore 外文书店
15 Yudu Hotel 愉都宾馆	1 Buses to SACO Prisons 至中美合作所汽车站	16	Post Office 邮电局
17 Huixianlou Hotel 会仙楼宾馆	2 CAAC 中国民船	18	Bank of China 中国银行
22 Chongqing Shipin Mansion 食品大厦	3 Kangfulai Bus Stop 康福来汽车站	21	Luohan Temple 罗汉寺
23 Chung King Hotel 重庆饭店	Railway Station 火车站	24	Chaotianmen Dock (Booking Hall) 朝天门码头 (售票处)
	7 Long-Distance Bus Station 长途汽车站		

modation. Getting there from the railway station is a matter of taking one of the frequent minibuses that run between the station, Liberation Monument and the Chaotianmen dock area for Y1. Bus No 102 also runs between the railway station and Chaotianmen. If you're headed for the western part of town, around the Renmin Hotel, you can walk up to Zhongshan Lu; there is a tram, but it's under renovation and will be for some years to come.

Chongqing is a good city for exploring on foot. The distances are manageable, and there's always an interesting alley to duck into. Between the Liberation monument and the Chaotianmen dock area are a number of steep, laddered alleyways, usually lined with little shops. Also of interest, and within walking distance of the Liberation Monument, are the two cable cars over the Jialing and Yangzi rivers.

Information

CITS The travel service (☎ 385-0589) has its office in a building in the Renmin Hotel compound. They're friendly enough but are still oriented towards large tour groups.

PSB The office (☎ 383-1830) is on Linjiang Lu. Bus No 103 from the front of the Renmin Hotel will take you there. If it's permits for the wilds of northern Sichuan that you are after, wait until you get to Chengdu, where they are more used to dealing with this kind of thing.

Money The main Chongqing branch of Bank of China is on Minzu Lu, just up the road from the Huixianlou Hotel. The branch right next door to the Huixianlou also has a window for changing money on the 2nd floor. Most of the hotels also have foreign-exchange counters.

Post There is a branch post office on Minzu Lu within walking distance of the Chung King and Huixianlou hotels. Most of the top-end hotels offer limited postal services.

Maps Good maps in Chinese and less detailed ones in English are available from street vendors (the ones selling newspapers) around the Liberation Monument area.

Luohan Temple
(luóhàn sì)

Luohan is the Chinese rendering of the Sanskrit 'arhat', which is a Buddhist term referring to people who have released themselves from the psychological bondage of greed, hate and delusion. Built around 1000 years ago, Luohan Temple features a long entrance-way flanked by rock carvings, a hall of painted terracotta arhat sculptures (the usual 500) and a hall containing a large gold Buddha figure. Behind the Buddha altar is an Indian-style jataka mural depicting Prince Siddhartha in the process of cutting his hair to renounce the world.

At its peak, Luohan Temple was home to some 70 monks; there are around 18 in residence these days. The temple is popular with local worshippers, who burn tonnes of fragrant incense. Try and make an effort to call into this temple, even if it's just to take a quick look at the incredibly lifelike arhats.

The vegetarian restaurant here is excellent and very cheap, but it's only open for lunch (approximately 11.30 am to 1.30 pm). Admission to the temple is Y2.

Red Cliff Village
(hóngyán cūn)

During the tenuous Kuomintang-Communist alliance against the Japanese during WW II, Red Cliff Village outside Chongqing was used as the offices and living quarters of the Communist representatives to the Kuomintang. Among others, Ye Jianying, Zhou Enlai and Zhou's wife Deng Yingchao lived here. After the Japanese surrender in 1945, it was also to Chongqing that Mao Zedong – at the instigation of US ambassador Patrick Hurley – came in August of that year to join in the peace negotiations with the Kuomintang. The talks lasted 42 days and resulted in a formal agreement which Mao described as 'words on paper'.

One of China's better revolutionary history museums now stands at the site, and has a large collection of photos, though none of the captions are in English. A short walk from the museum is the building which housed the South Bureau of the Communist Party's Central Committee and the office of the representatives of the Eighth Route Army – though there's little to see except a few sparse furnishings and photographs.

To get to Red Cliff Village, the best bus to take is the No 104 from its terminal on Beiqu Lu just north of the Liberation monument. Alternatively, Chinese tour buses from the Chaotianmen dock and the railway station take in Red Cliff Village and other Communist sights around town for Y10. Red Cliff Village is open daily from 8 am to 5.30 pm and admission is Y6.

US-Chiang Kaishek Criminal Acts Exhibition Hall & SACO Prisons
(zhōngměi hézuòsuǒ jízhōngyíng jiùzhǐ)
In 1941 the USA and Chiang Kaishek signed a secret agreement to set up the Sino-American Cooperation Organisation (SACO), under which the USA helped to train and dispatch secret agents for the Kuomintang government. The chief of SACO was Tai Li, the notorious head of the Kuomintang military secret service; its deputy chief was a US Navy officer, Commodore M E Miles.

The SACO prisons were set up outside Chongqing during WW II. The Kuomintang never recognised the Communist Party as a legal political entity, although in theory it recognised its army as allies in the struggle against the Japanese invaders. Civilian Communists remained subject to the same repressive laws, and though these were not enforced at the time, they were not actually rescinded. Hundreds of political prisoners were still kept captive by the Kuomintang in these prisons and others, and according to the Communists many were executed.

Unfortunately, the absence of English captions makes this sight a fairly uninteresting one for most Western visitors. The exhibition hall has lots of photos on display; there are manacles and chains but nothing to ghoul over. The hall is open from 8 am to 7 pm and admission is Y2.

To get there take bus No 217 from the terminus on Zhongshan Sanlu, just in front of the Jialing Bridge. It's about a 45-minute ride. Make sure that the driver knows where you want to get off, as the place is not obvious. The SACO Prisons are a long hour's walk from the hall. Alternatively, if you are really keen to see these sights, there are Chinese tour buses leaving from the Chaotianmen dock and railway station areas for Y10. They take in both the hall and the prisons and throw in some other revolutionary sights as well.

Temple Parks
Chongqing's two temple parks get neglected by many visitors, but they are a pleasant enough way to while away an afternoon. **Pipashan Park** *(pípáshān gōngyuán)* at 345 metres marks the highest point on the Chongqing peninsula. The Hongxing Pavilion at the top of the park provides good views of Chongqing. The park is open from 6 am to 10 pm.

The **Eling Park** *(élíng gōngyuán)* at the neck of the peninsula is more of a hike and not really worth a special trip. You can find the Liangjiang Pavilion here.

Bridges
Worth checking out are the enormous Jialing and Yangzi bridges. The Jialing Bridge, which crosses the river north of central Chongqing, was built between 1963 and 1966. It is 150 metres long and 60 metres high and for 15 years was one of the few means of access to the rest of China. The Yangzi Bridge to the south was finished in 1981. In 1989 the new Shimen Bridge over the Yangzi River was completed.

Cable-Car Trips
There are cable cars spanning both of the rivers that cut through Chongqing: the Jialing River and the Yangzi River. The rides provide views of precipitously stacked housing and environment-unfriendly industrial estates. Both are within walking distance of the Liberation Monument. The Jialing River cable car starts from Cangbai

Lu, and the Yangzi River cable car starts from near Xinhua Lu.

Chongqing Museum
(chóngqìng bówùguǎn)

If you are really stuck for something to do you might wander over to the museum. The dinosaur skeletons on display were unearthed between 1974 and 1977 at Zigong, Yangchuan and elsewhere in Sichuan Province. It's open from 9 am to 5 pm. The museum is at the foot of Pipashan Park in the southern part of town.

Northern Hot Springs
(běi wēnquán gōngyuán)

Fifty-five km north-east of the city, overlooking the Jialing River, the Northern Hot Springs are in a large park which is the site of a 5th-century Buddhist temple. The springs have an Olympic-size swimming pool where you can bathe to an audience. There are also private rooms with hot baths – big tubs where the water comes up to your neck if you sit and up to your waist if you stand. Water temperature averages around 32°C. Swimsuits can be hired here – they're coloured red, symbolising happiness. There's another group of springs 20 km south of Chongqing with hotter waters, but the northern group is said to be better.

To get to the springs, take bus No 306 from the Liberation monument.

Places to Stay – bottom end

Chongqing has a serious shortage of budget accommodation, which means that most travellers get out of town as quickly as possible. The only dorms in town are the seven-bed rooms at the *Huixianlou Hotel* (☎ 384-5101) *(huìxiānlóu bīnguǎn)*, close to the Liberation Monument, where a bed will set you back Y50. About the best thing that can be said for this place is that it is well located. Service can be pretty frosty, the rooms noisy and less than hygienic. From the railway station, walk up to Zhongshan Lu and take bus No 405 to the Liberation Monument *(jiěfàng bēi)*.

A more pleasant option is *Chongqing*

Shipin Mansion (☎ 384-7300) *(chóngqìng shípǐn dàshà)* at 72 Shanxi Lu, near the Chaotianmen dock. This place recently got approval to take foreigners, and has pleasant, clean doubles with bath and air-con for Y130 and triples for Y150. The rate card mentions that foreigners should be charged an extra 50%, but the manager doesn't like the dual-pricing system, which means you pay what the Chinese pay. The reception staff are not yet used to dealing with non-Chinese speakers, so go easy on them. The hotel also has doubles and triples with common bath for Y60/90, but you may have to do a little persuading to get these. They'll also help you book boat and rail tickets here.

If you're really on a low budget, try the *No 2 Hostel (dì èr zhāodàisuǒ)*, a floating hotel of sorts down at Chaotianmen dock. Beds in quads are Y16, triples Y20 and doubles Y30. None of the rooms have washrooms, and facilities are generally pretty crude, but it's without doubt the cheapest spot in town. To check in, go to the Yangzi ferry booking office at the new Chaotianmen terminal. The hotel has a little counter set up there where they will check you in and then walk you to their floating flophouse.

Places to Stay – top end

Basically, most hotels in Chongqing charge ridiculous amounts of money. It's probably something to do with limited room for expansion on the crowded peninsula. If you don't mind an expensive stay, the *Renmin Hotel* (☎ 385-1421) *(rénmín bīnguǎn)* is one of the most incredible hotels in China, and if you don't stay here you have got to at least visit the place.

It's quite literally a palace, with a design that seems inspired by the Temple of Heaven and the Forbidden City in Beijing. The hotel comprises three wings (north, south and east), and these are separated by an enormous circular concert hall that is 65 metres high and seats 4000 people. The hotel was constructed in 1953.

Singles are US$48 while doubles range between US$48 and US$60. There's a presidential suite that commands a cool US$460 a night: it no doubt resembles a scene from *The Last Emperor*. From the railway station, the best way to get to the hotel is to head up to Zhongshan Lu and catch bus No 401 or 405 to the traffic circle and walk east down Renmin Lu. Alternatively, if you are spending this kind of money for a room, catch a taxi for Y15.

Better in terms of service and value is the *Chung King Hotel* (☎ 384-9301) *(chóngqìng fàndiàn)*, a joint-venture operation on Xinhua Lu near the Chaotianmen dock area. Singles cost US$42 and doubles US$60. Facilities include a small gift shop (with a few English titles), foreign exchange, post and telecommunications, taxi and clinic. The hotel has its own shuttle bus to and from the railway station and the airport.

The *Chongqing Guesthouse* (☎ 384-5888) *(chóngqìng bīnguǎn)* on Minsheng Lu has transformed itself into a four-star Chinese-style luxury hotel. Doubles in the old wing are Y270, while singles/doubles in the new VIP wing start at Y540/660, breakfast included. Close to Liberation Monument, the *Yudu Hotel (yúdū jiǔdiàn)* boasts a good location, but is probably not worth the Y383 they charge for a standard double.

Finally, on the southern side of the Yangzi, a fair trudge from all the action, is the *Yangtze Chongqing Holiday Inn* (☎ 280-3380) *(yángzǐjiāng jiàrì jiǔdiàn)*, with all the services that you would expect of a Holiday Inn Group hotel. Room rates start at US$115, though discounts are possible when the hotel isn't flooded with tour groups.

Places to Eat

The central business district in the eastern section of the city near the docks abounds with small restaurants and street vendors. For tasty noodles and baozi, check out Xinhua Lu and Shaanxi Lu towards Chaotianmen dock. There are some good night markets behind the Huixianlou Hotel, in the vicinity of Luohan Temple and near the Yudu Hotel.

Chongqing's number one speciality is *huǒguō*, or hotpot. Skewers of pre-sliced meat and vegetables are placed in boiling hot, spiced oil. Hotpot is usually priced by the skewer, and while it's usually cheap it's a good idea to check prices as you go along. Although hotpot can be found wherever there are street vendors or small restaurants, Wuyi Lu has the greatest variety and is locally known as *huǒguō jiē*, or 'hotpot street'. Wuyi Lu runs off Minzu Lu, parallel to Xinhua Lu, a couple of blocks away from the Huixianlou and Chung King hotels. Bayi Lu is also a great street for snack hunting.

Zourong Lu is a good street for larger, sit-down restaurants when you've got a group and feel like feasting on Sichuanese main courses. Among them is the well-known *Yizhishi Restaurant, (yízhīshí cāntīng)*, which serves Sichuan-style pastries in the morning and local specialities like tea-smoked duck and dry-stewed fish at lunch and dinner. The 2nd floor has full-course meals; go up to the 3rd floor and Y25 will buy you a sampler course of famous Chongqing snacks. Draft beer and special 'eight-treasure tea' do a fine job of washing it all down.

The area around Huixianlou Hotel, where many travellers stay, is teeming with restaurants. But if you're stuck for ideas you can try the *Lamb Restaurant (yángròu guǎn)* just up the road from the hotel. All the lamb dishes here are *hot*, but the kebabs aren't too punishing on the taste buds. Also not far away is the *Lao Sichuan Restaurant (lǎo sìchuān)*, which is going on 80 years old and is considered Chongqing's most famous Sichuan eatery. Prices are reasonable, but get there early: it closes at 8 pm.

Of the hotel restaurants, *Chung King Hotel* has the best food – expensive by Chinese standards but moderately priced for most foreigners. Opened shortly after Liberation, this place is another favourite with locals, who just call it 'the old restaurant'. The dishes are nicely presented and accompanied by live Chinese music at night. The hotel's coffee shop serves Western breakfasts.

Getting There & Away

Air The CAAC office (☎ 386-2970) is near the corner of Zhongshan Sanlu and Renmin Lu, and can be accessed from either street.

You can also book flights at the Chung King Hotel, and numerous ticket offices around the Liberation Monument.

Chongqing is connected by daily flights to major cities such as Beijing, Chengdu, Guangzhou, Kunming, Shanghai, Ürümqi and Xi'an. There are also five flights a week to Hong Kong (Y2270).

Chongqing's new Jiangbei Airport is located 25 km north of the city. CAAC runs shuttle buses between the airport and the ticket office, timed to coincide with flights. Buses to the airport leave 2½ hours before scheduled flight times. The fare is Y10.

Bus Bus travel in and out of Chongqing has become much more convenient with the opening of a new multi-storey long-distance bus terminal next to the railway station. With two ticket halls, two waiting halls and dozens of gates, the station can process 800 to 1000 buses daily, or so the management claims. Bus schedules will remain tentative until sometime in 1996 as passenger demand is worked out. Buses to Dazu are expected to leave every half hour between 4.30 am and 9 pm, and half-hourly to Chengdu between 6 am and 9.30 pm. Luxury express buses to

Chengdu via the Chengyu Expressway take 4 hours and leave at 7, 8.30 and 11 am and 5 pm. The fare is Y72.

Another option is a company called Kangfulai *(kāngfúlái)* (KFL), which has ticketing offices and departure points across the street from the Chongqing Guesthouse, to the west of the main entrance of the Renmin Hotel and on the northern side of the railway station, next to the Shancheng Hotel. KFL buses to Dazu leave at 7.30 am and 2.10 pm from the Chongqing Guesthouse and west of the Renmin Hotel – the latter buses pass by the railway station on their way out of town. The trip to Dazu takes 3 hours and costs Y20. KFL also has buses to Chengdu at 2.30 and 4.30 pm as well as a 6.30 am bus departing on even days only. The journey takes 5 hours and tickets are Y48.

Train From Chongqing there are direct trains to Shanghai, Xi'an, Guiyang, Nanning (every other day), Chengdu, Zhengzhou, Guangzhou, Beijing and Kunming. For trains to Dazu, there are at least three trains heading for Chengdu from Chongqing between 6.40 and 9.15 am. The 6.40 am train (No 84) gets to Dazu (Youtingpu) at around 11 am.

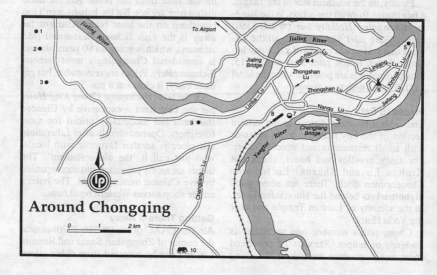

Around Chongqing

0   1   2 km

Trains to Nanning go via Guiyang and Liuzhou (five or six hours by bus from Guilin) and take around 32 hours; a hard-sleeper should cost Y145. Trains to Guiyang take around 12 hours and cost Y124 for a hard sleeper. Trains to Shanghai also take in Guiyang, before making a long haul through the sticks to Hangzhou and on to the final destination. The journey takes around 50 hours and costs Y255 for a hard sleeper. To Chengdu, it takes around 11 hours and costs Y105 for a hard sleeper. Trains to Kunming and Panzhihua (for Lijiang and Dali) go via Chengdu, and it makes a lot of sense to break your trip at this point.

If you want to get to Guilin in a hurry you will have to fly – travelling by train requires that you change in Guiyang. Alternatively, you might travel to Liuzhou by train and go on direct to Yangshuo or Guilin by bus.

Boat There are boats from Chongqing down the Yangzi River to Wuhan. The ride is a popular tourist trip, a good way of getting away from the trains and an excellent way to get to Wuhan. For details, see the following section on the Yangzi River as well as the

sections on Wuhan (Hubei chapter), Yue-yang (Hunan chapter) and Shanghai.

Another boat option, and one that very few travellers use, is the service to Leshan. Sorting out just when the boats leave is a bit of a hassle. Though the ride downstream from Leshan enjoys steady passenger demand, the longer return trip is often just used for freight, so you have to ask. Boats leave from Pier 12. Third-class tickets are Y131.

Getting Around

Buses in Chongqing can be tediously slow, and since there are no bicycles they're even more crowded than in other Chinese cities. Useful routes include: No 401, which runs between the Chaotianmen dock and the CAAC office at the intersection of Renmin Lu and Zhongshan Sanlu; No 405, running the length of Zhongshan Lu up to the Liber-ation Monument; and No 102, which con-nects the railway station and Chaotianmen dock. There are also minibuses running between the dock and the railway station for Y1.

Nowadays, as in most other Chinese cities, flagging down a taxi is no problem. Flagfall ranges between Y9 and Y12, depending on the size of the car, if you can get them to use the meter. Otherwise, expect to pay a mini-mum of Y15 for all runs on the peninsula.

DOWNRIVER ON THE YANGZI: CHONGQING TO WUHAN

The dramatic scenery and rushing waters of China's greatest river may have been inspi-rational to many of China's painters and poets, but there was little in the way of inspiration for those with the task of negoti-ating this dangerous stretch of water's twists and turns. And there was not just danger to contend with; there was also sheer hard work. A large boat pushing upstream often needed hundreds of coolies (trackers), who lined the riverbanks and hauled the boat with long ropes against the surging waters. Even today smaller boats can still be seen being pulled up the river by their crews.

The Yangzi is China's longest river and the

AROUND CHONGQING 重庆地区

1. Zhazhidong-SACO Prison
   渣滓洞
2. Baigongguan-SACO Prison
   白公馆
3. Martyrs' Cemetery
   烈士墓
4. Renmin Hotel
   人民饭店
5. Chaotianmen Dock
   朝天门码头
6. Liberation Monument
   解放纪念碑
7. Long-Distance Bus Station
   长途汽车站
8. Railway Station
   火车站
9. Red Cliff Village
   红岩村
10. Zoo
    动物园

third-longest in the world at 6300 km, emanating from the snow-covered Tanggulashan mountains in south-west Qinghai and cutting its way through Tibet and seven Chinese provinces before emptying into the East China Sea just north of Shanghai. Between the towns of Fengjie in Sichuan and Yichang in Hubei lie three great gorges, regarded as one of the great scenic attractions of China. The steamer ride from Chongqing to Wuhan is a popular tourist trip and the scenery is pleasant, but don't expect to be dwarfed by mile-high cliffs! A lot of people find the trip quite boring, possibly because of over-anticipation.

The ride downriver from Chongqing to Wuhan takes three days and two nights. Upriver the ride takes five days – see the Wuhan section in the Hubei chapter for details. One possibility is to take the boat as far as Yichang, which will let you see the gorges and the huge Gezhouba Dam, the most scenic parts. You may also be able to shave one day off the trip by taking a hydrofoil from Chongqing to Wanxian, where you can usually hook up with another ferry for the Three Gorges section. How much time you save depends on what boats are in Wanxian when you arrive, when they're leaving and whether there are any empty berths.

At Yichang you can take direct trains to Beijing, Wuhan and Xi'an. Trains also run south to Huaihua, where you can connect with trains to Changsha, Guangzhou, Guilin or Liuzhou. If you continue the boat ride you can get off at Yueyang and take the train to

Guangzhou, or you can carry on to Wuhan. There are also a few boats that go beyond Wuhan, including one all the way to Shanghai, which is 2400 km downriver – a week's journey.

Tickets

You can buy tickets for the boats from CITS in Chongqing or from the booking office at the massive new Chaotianmen terminal building. While it's good to book two or three days ahead of your intended date of departure, a rapid expansion in the number of Yangzi cruise operators means tickets are more readily available. Many people have arrived, got their tickets and left the same day (there's a direct minibus from the railway station to Chaotianmen for Y1 per person). CITS adds a service charge of Y15 to the price of the tickets. Budget travellers take note: if you book tickets with CITS, make sure you're not being put on one of the luxury liners reserved solely for foreigners: the price could inflict mortal damage on your cash reserves.

The main booking office at Chaotianmen dock is open daily from 6 am to 11 pm. Outside this main hall are several small agencies that also sell marked-up boat tickets; it's worth trying them if the main office doesn't have tickets for the day you want. Tickets for foreigners carry a 50% surcharge: some operators may waive this if you can show them a student card; it depends on how desperate they are for your business. There is a chance that this could land you in trouble once aboard, however. The ticket-takers on

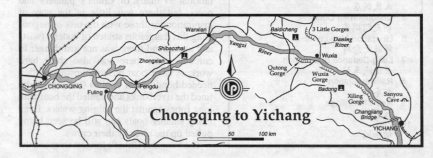

Chongqing to Yichang

the boat may ask you to show proof of residence in China as a foreign expert or student – a fake student card may not pass inspection.

First and 2nd-class cabins tend to fill up quickly, although with more than 50 companies working the Yangzi river tours, you have a lot of alternatives. This rapid growth in the industry, combined with some recent sinkings and mid-river collisions, has alarmed the central government and brought ominous threats of a crackdown on 'unqualified' operators. How serious this will be remains to be seen, but tourists will still probably have many boats from which to choose.

Classes

In a sign of the changing times in what was once egalitarian China, some boats now boast 1st-class cabins. These come with two beds, private bathrooms, television and air-con. Second class cabins have two to four berths, with soft beds, a small desk and chair, and a washbasin. Showers and toilets are private cubicles shared by the passengers.

Third class usually has from six to 12 beds depending on what boat you're on. Fourth class usually has eight to 12, but on older vessels can have over 20 beds. Toilets and showers are communal, though you should be able to use the toilets and showers in 2nd class. If they don't let you into the 2nd-class area then have a look around the boat; some boats have some toilet cubicles on the lower deck with doors and partitions. Lounges with soft seating and, you guessed it, karaoke, can normally be found adjacent to the 2nd-class cabins or on the top deck. There doesn't seem to be any problem just wandering into these places and plonking yourself down.

Some boats also have a couple of large cabins the entire width of the boat that accommodate about 40 people on tripletiered bunks. Foreigners are not often given tickets for this class. If you get one, remember that this part of China is very cold in winter and very hot in summer. Petty thieves have been reported in the dorms, so keep valuable items safe – particularly at night.

In addition to the Chinese tour boats

described above, there are also several 'foreigner only' vessels plying the waters of the Yangzi. These are mostly reserved for large tour groups who can afford the hundreds of US dollars that these trips cost. CITS and some of the independent booking agents around the Chaotianmen dock area can arrange tickets for these luxury liners.

Fares

Tickets for foreigners at the main booking hall at Chaotianmen dock carry a 50% surcharge. One of the ticket windows will have a sheet with foreign prices, but likely as not it will be in Chinese! Following are foreign ticket prices posted at the Chaotianmen booking office for the major destinations on the river. Prices will be higher if you book through CITS or one of the independent operators around the dock area, though it's possible to bargain with the latter if there are several of you.

Destination	2nd Class (Y)	3rd Class (Y)	4th Class (Y)
Yichang	535	235	160
Wuhan (Hankou)	790	381	237
Nanjing	1032	532	381
Shanghai	1210	607	438

The Chaotianmen terminal booking office does not sell tickets for boats with 1st-class cabins: for these you have to go to the independents, some of whom may eventually move into the new terminal building. First class to Yichang was quoted at around Y950; to Wuhan, Y1350. At the time of writing, there were no 1st-class cabins all the way to Shanghai on Chinese boats.

There are lots of other intermediate destinations, including Jiujiang and Wuhu (potential jumping-off points for Lushan and Huangshan) and Nanjing (Jiangsu) on the Shanghai route. Between Nanjing and Wuhan (Hubei) a hydrofoil service cuts travelling time down from 40 hours to just 10 – see the Wuhan section for details.

Departure Times

Boats that terminate in Yichang (Hubei) generally depart Chongqing at 6 pm. Those that go beyond to Shashi and Wuhan usually depart between 8 and 11 am, though there are evening sailings as well. Boats to Shanghai generally leave at 8 am and 9 am. These times can change from season to season depending on the river level, so check at the signboards at the main ticket hall to be sure. On the signboards, Wuhan is listed as Hankou, since this is the district of Wuhan where the boat docks.

You can sleep on the boat the night before departure for Y24 in 2nd class and Y17 in 3rd class. It's cheaper than the Huixianlou Hotel and easier than getting up early and hoofing it down to the pier. Your ticket should give the number of the pier where your boat will be waiting the night before.

Once you've boarded, a steward will exchange your ticket for a numbered, colour-coded tag that denotes your bed assignment. Hang onto the tag, since it must be exchanged for your ticket at the end of the voyage – without it they may not let you off the boat.

Food

There are usually a couple of restaurants on the boat. Those on the lower decks cater for the masses and can be pretty terrible. If there's a restaurant on the upper deck chances are it's a bit better, but how much you're charged seems to vary from boat to boat. It's a good idea to bring some of your own food with you. When the boat stops at a town for any length of time, passengers may disembark and eat at little restaurants near the pier.

The Route

Boats stop frequently during the cruise to visit cities, towns and a slew of tourist sights. What you will see during daylight hours depends on what time your boat sets sail from Chongqing. Boats leaving in the evening tend to spend the first night docked at Fengdu, then continue on to tie up for the second night in Fengjie. The following

morning they enter the Three Gorges, and then proceed to Yichang and Wuhan.

Morning boats usually end their first day at Wanxian, leave before dawn the following day and pass through the Three Gorges around midday or later before heading to Yichang and Wuhan.

Most boats stop between the first and second gorge for six hours for tours of the 'Little Three Gorges' (see the Wanxian to Yichang section below). For travellers who want to avoid this, there are some boats that pass directly through, but you'll have to ask around.

Chongqing to Wanxian

For the first few hours the river is lined with factories, though this gives way to some pretty, green terraced countryside with the occasional small town.

One of the first stops is usually the town of **Fuling**. The town overlooks the mouth of the Wu River, which runs southward into Guizhou; it controls the river traffic between Guizhou and eastern Sichuan. Near Fuling in the middle of the Yangzi River is a huge rock called Baihe Ridge. On one side of the rock are three carvings known as 'stone fish' which date back to ancient times and are thought to have served as watermarks – the rock can be seen only when the river is at its very lowest. In addition to the carvings, there is a large number of inscriptions describing the culture, art and technology of these ancient times.

The next major town is **Fengdu** (*fēngdū*). Nearby Pingdushan mountain is said to be the abode of devils. The story goes that during the Han Dynasty two men, Yin Changsheng and Wang Fangping, lived on the mountain, and when their family names were joined together they were mistakenly thought to be the Yinwang, the King of Hell. Numerous temples containing sculptures of demons and devils have been built on the mountain since the Tang Dynasty, with heartening names like 'Between the Living and the Dead', 'Bridge of Helplessness' and 'Palace of the King of Hell'. Travellers have given mixed reviews to this little 'Hell

World' exhibit: some love the campy fire and brimstone while others find it hardly merits the entry fee, which at last count was Y20.

The boat then passes through **Zhongxian County**. North-east of the county seat of Zhongzhou is the **Qian Jinggou** site, where primitive stone artefacts, including axes, hoes and stone weights attached to fishing nets, were unearthed.

Soon after comes the **Shibaozhai** (Stone Treasure Stronghold) on the northern bank of the river. Shibaozhai is a 30-metre-high rock which is supposed to look something like a stone seal. During the early years of Emperor Qianlong's reign (1736-97) an impressive red wooden temple, the Lanruodian, shaped like a pagoda and 11 storeys high, was built on the rock. It houses a statue of Buddha and inscriptions which commemorate its construction.

Next is the large town of **Wanxian**, where most morning boats tie up for the night. Wanxian is the hub of transportation and communications along the river between eastern Sichuan and western Hubei and has traditionally been known as the gateway to Sichuan. It was opened to foreign trade in 1917. It's a neat, hilly town and a great place to wander around for a few hours while the boat is in port. There's a pleasant park around the tower in the centre of town. A long flight of steps leads from the pier up the riverbank to a bustling night market where you can get something to eat or buy very cheap wickerwork baskets, chairs and stools.

Wanxian to Yichang

Boats overnighting at Wanxian generally depart before dawn. Before entering the gorges the boat passes by (and may stop at) the town of **Fengjie**. This ancient town was the capital of the state of Kui during the Spring and Autumn and Warring States periods from 722 to 221 BC. The town overlooks the Qutang Gorge, the first of the three Yangzi gorges. Just east of Fengjie is a one-km-long shoal where the remains of stone piles could be seen when the water level was low. These piles were erected in the Stone

and Bronze ages, possibly for commemorative and sacrificial purposes, but their remains were removed in 1964 since they were considered a danger to navigation. Another set of similar structures can be found east of Fengjie outside a place called Baidicheng.

At the entrance to the Qutang Gorge is **Baidicheng**, or White King Town, on the river's northern bank, 7½ km from Fengjie. The story goes that a high official proclaimed himself king during the Western Han Dynasty, and moved his capital to this town. A well was discovered which emitted a fragrant white vapour; this struck him as such an auspicious omen that he renamed himself the White King and his capital 'White King Town'.

The spectacular **Sanxia** (Three Gorges), Qutang, Wu and Xiling, start just after Fengjie and end near Yichang, a stretch of about 200 km. The gorges vary from 300 metres at their widest to less than 100 metres at their narrowest. The seasonal difference in water level can be as much as 50 metres.

Qutang Gorge *(qūtáng xiá)* is the smallest and shortest gorge (only eight km long), though the water flows most rapidly here. High on the north bank, at a place called Fengxiang (Bellows) Gorge, are a series of crevices. There is said to have been an ancient tribe in this area whose custom was to place the coffins of their dead in high mountain caves. Nine coffins were discovered in these crevices, some containing bronze swords, armour and other artefacts, but they are believed to date back only as far as the Warring States Period.

Wu Gorge *(wū xiá)* is about 40 km in length and the cliffs on either side rise to just over 900 metres. The gorge is noted for the Kong Ming tablet, a large slab of rock at the foot of the Peak of the Immortals. Kong Ming was prime minister of the state of Shu during the period of the Three Kingdoms (220-280 AD). On the tablet is a description of his stance upholding the alliance between the states of Shu and Wu against the state of Wei. **Badong** is a town on the southern bank of the river within the gorge. The town is a communications centre from which roads span out into western Hubei Province.

In between the Qutang and Wu Gorges, most boats will stop for five to six hours so passengers can shift to smaller boats for tours of the 'Little Three Gorges'. Flanking the Daning River, these gorges are much narrower than their larger counterparts and, some travellers say, more dramatic. The tour usually costs Y50 to Y60, with a foreigners' surcharge of 25% to 50% often tacked on as well. Though some travellers have complained of the cost, many enjoy the chance to get out and view the rock formations up close. You may even get some exercise: when the river is low passengers often have to abandon the boats and walk upriver. On the way to the Little Three Gorges the boats usually stop at several gratuitous tourist traps, most of which are not worth the entry fee. For example, one stop promises views of a mysterious mountain cave coffin on high, which turns out to mean a brief look through a pair of binoculars.

Xiling Gorge (*xīlíng xiá*) is the longest of the three gorges at 80 km. At the end of the gorge everyone crowds out onto the deck to watch the boat pass through the locks of the huge **Gezhouba Dam**.

The next stop is the industrial town of **Yichang**. From here you can take a train to Xiangfan and points north, east and west, or to Huaihua, where you can catch trains to southern destinations. Yichang is regarded as the gateway to the Upper Yangzi and was once a walled city dating back at least as far as the Sui Dynasty. The town was opened to foreign trade in 1877 by a treaty between Britain and China, and a foreign concession area was set up along the river front to the south-east of the walled city.

Near the Yichang Railway Station you can take bus No 10 to **White Horse Cave** (*báimǎ dòng*), where for a fee you can boat and walk through caverns with impressive stalactites and stalagmites. Five minutes' walk from the other end is an equally impressive place – **Three Visitors Cave** (*sānyǒu dòng*), along with a cliff trail that overlooks the Yangzi River.

Yichang to Wuhan

After leaving Yichang, the boat passes under the immense **Changjiang Bridge** at the town of **Zhicheng**. The bridge is 1700 metres long and supports a double-track railway with roads for trucks and cars on either side. It came into operation in 1971.

The next major town is **Shashi**, a light industrial town. As early as the Tang Dynasty Shashi was a trading centre of some importance, enjoying great prosperity during the Taiping Rebellion when trade lower down the Yangzi was largely at a standstill. It was opened up to foreign trade in 1896 by the Treaty of Shimonoseki between China and Japan, and though an area outside the town was assigned as a Japanese concession it was never developed. About 7½ km from Shashi is the ancient town of **Jingzhou**, to which you can catch a bus.

After Shashi there's not much to look at: you're out on the flat plains of eastern China, the river widens immensely and you can see little of the shore. The boat continues down the river to pass by (and possibly stop at) the town of **Chenglingji**, which lies at the confluence of Lake Dongting and the Yangzi River. East of Lake Dongting is the town of **Yueyang**, from where you can catch trains heading either toward Changsha, Guilin and Guangzhou, or toward Wuhan and points north. Another nine hours will bring you to Wuhan, at which point most travellers are quite ready to part ways with their boat. (For details on Yueyang and Wuhan and the Yangzi River between Wuhan and Shanghai, see the separate sections in this book.)

DAZU
(*dàzú*)

The grotto art of Dazu County, 160 km northwest of Chongqing, is rated alongside China's other great Buddhist cave sculpture at Dunhuang, Luoyang and Datong. Historical records for Dazu are sketchy. The cliff carvings and statues (with Buddhist, Taoist and Confucian influences) amount to thousands of pieces, large and small, scattered over the county in some 40-odd places. The main groupings are at Beishan (North Hill) and the more interesting Baoding. They date from the Tang Dynasty (9th century) to the Song (13th century).

The town of Dazu is a small, unhurried place. It's also been relatively unvisited by Westerners – though this is gradually changing – and the surrounding countryside is superb. One of the only problems is the low-end accommodation: there isn't any.

Beishan
(běi shān)

Beishan is about a 30-minute hike from Dazu town – aim straight for the pagoda visible from the bus station. There are good overall views from the top of the hill. The dark niches hold small statues, many in poor condition; only one or two really stand out.

Niche No 136 depicts Puxian, the patron saint (male) of Emeishan, riding a white elephant. The same niche has the androgynous Sun and Moon Guanyin. Niche 155 holds a bit more talent, the Peacock King. According to inscriptions, the Beishan site was originally a military camp, with the earliest carvings commissioned by a general.

At Beishan there's a Y5 entry fee for the park area and a further Y20 entry fee for the sculptures. The park is open from 8 am to 5 pm.

Baoding
(bǎodǐng shān)

Fifteen km north-east of Dazu town, the Baoding sculptures are definitely more interesting than those at Beishan. The founding work is attributed to Zhao Zhifeng, a monk from an obscure Yoga sect of Tantric Buddhism. There's a monastery with nice woodwork and throngs of pilgrims. On the lower section of the hill on which the monastery sits is a horseshoe-shaped cliff sculptured with coloured figures, some of them up to eight metres high. The centrepiece is a 31-metre-long, five-metre-high reclining buddha, depicted in the state of entering nirvana, the torso sunk into the cliff face – most peaceful.

Statues around the rest of the 125-metre horseshoe vary considerably: Buddhist

preachers and sages, historical figures, realistic scenes (on the rear of a postcard one is described as 'Pastureland – Cowboy at Rest') and delicate sculptures a few cm in height. Some of them have been eroded by wind and rain, some have lost layers of paint, but generally there is a remarkable survival rate (fanatical Red Guards did descend on the Dazu area bent on defacing the sculptures, but were stopped – so the story goes – by an urgent order from Zhou Enlai).

Baoding differs from other grottoes in that it was based on a preconceived plan which incorporated some of the area's natural features – a sculpture next to the reclining buddha, for example, makes use of an underground spring. Completion of the sculptures is believed to have taken 70 years, between 1179 and 1249 AD. It's easy to spend a few hours wandering around this area. Showpieces are the enormous reclining buddha and, inside a small temple on the carved cliff, the goddess of mercy, with a spectacular gilt forest of fingers (1007 hands if you care to check). Each hand has an eye, the symbol of wisdom. But besides the major attractions there are countless minor details that will capture your attention.

Minibuses to Baoding leave the Dazu bus station every 30 minutes or so (or as soon as they fill up) through the day, though they start to thin out by about 4 pm; the fare is Y1.50, but the locals will probably try to charge you Y5. The last bus departs Baoding for Dazu at around 6 pm. The sites are open from 8 am to 5 pm, and there's a Y45 foreigners' price entry charge. As you pass by in the bus, keep an eye on the cliff faces for solo sculptures that may occasionally pop up.

Places to Stay & Eat

The local PSB appears to have done a good job of cowing most hotels into refusing foreigners, leaving you with only two options in Dazu, neither or which are cheap.

The *Beishan Hotel (běishān bīnguǎn)*, located near the base of Beishan, is a pleasant though somewhat unkempt place aimed at the less-affluent tour-group traveller. Standard doubles cost Y300, but they also have doubles with attached bath for Y100 that are perfectly fine, and triples for Y150. They won't volunteer this information, and you may have to do some persuading to get these prices, especially if the hotel is crowded. To get there, turn left out of the bus station, cross the bridge and proceed past the roundabout straight up the main road through town. After about 500 metres the road ends in a three-way intersection. Turn right; the hotel is on the left-hand side of the street. One good point about the Beishan is that it's close to the Beishan stone carvings. Facing the hotel, the road up to the statues is on the left, just next to the indoor sports arena.

The *Dazu Guesthouse (dàzú bīnguǎn)*, like so many other hotels in Chinese tourist towns, has been reborn as a three-star hotel, which means you won't be able to get a room for under US$50. Should the urge for luxury grab you, turn left out of the bus station, cross over the bridge and bear right at the roundabout. The hotel is about 500 metres up the road on the left.

Finding a bite to eat in Dazu is no problem. At night the main road, from the bus station all the way to the Beishan Hotel, comes alive with dozens of street stalls serving noodles, dumplings, hotpot and wok-fried dishes. There are also a few point-and-choose restaurants along the way. You might try wandering down the first street on the right up from the roundabout. You have to walk around 500 metres before the restaurants start appearing, but along the way are street vendors selling everything from raw hand-made noodles to fresh spices to black lace lingerie. The restaurant at the Beishan Hotel is best left to its own devices.

Getting There & Away

Bus There are several options by bus. The first is the direct bus to Dazu from Chongqing's new long-distance bus station. Times were not yet set at the time of writing, but buses were expected to run every half-hour between 8 am and 9 pm. Fares should be around Y20. The trip takes a quick 3 to 4 hours, thanks to the new Chengdu-Chongqing expressway.

The second option in Chongqing is the Kangfulai (KFL) bus company, which has three ticket offices and pickup points: next to the Chongqing Guesthouse, the railway station and the Renmin Hotel. Tickets cost Y20 and buses depart at 7.30 am and 2.40 pm.

Buses from Chengdu to Dazu leave from the Xinnanmen bus station next to the Traffic Hotel at 7 am. The journey takes around 10 hours, travelling on back roads, and the fare is Y27. At the time of writing a direct bus to Dazu via the expressway was being planned. Check at the north bus station, as this could cut travel time to around 5 hours.

From Dazu there are onward buses to Chongqing and Chengdu. Buses to Chongqing from the bus station leave every hour between 8 am to 10.30 pm and cost Y15. KFL has air-con coaches leaving at 8 am and 2.30 pm. The trip takes 3 hours and costs Y20. Across from KFL, another private operator has buses leaving at 6 and 9.30 am and 1.30 pm for Y18. For Chengdu there is a daily 7 am bus leaving from the bus station. There is also a night bus, but it is best avoided. It arrives in Chengdu at around 3 am and terminates at the north railway station, not the greatest place to be in the dead of night.

Train To get to Dazu by train, you should get off the Chengdu-Chongqing railway line at Youtingpu town (five hours from Chongqing, seven hours from Chengdu), which is the nearest stop to Dazu. Despite the fact that the town is around 30 km from Dazu, train timetables refer to it as Dazu station. See the Train sections of the Chongqing and Chengdu Getting There & Away sections for more information on trains to Dazu. There are frequent minibuses running from the railway station to Dazu.

WESTERN SICHUAN & THE ROAD TO TIBET

Literally the next best thing to Tibet are the Sichuan mountains to the north and west of Chengdu – heaps of whipped cream that rise above 5000 metres, with deep valleys and rapid rivers. Tibetans and Tibetan-related peoples (Qiang) live by herding yaks, sheep and goats on the high-altitude Kangba Plateau Grasslands to the far north-west. Another zone, the Zöigê Grassland (north of Chengdu, towards the Gansu border) is over 3000 metres above sea level. Closer to Chengdu, the Tibetans have been assimilated, speak Chinese and are less bound by tradition, although they're regarded as a separate minority and are exempt from birth control quotas. Further out, however, Tibetan customs and clothing are much more in evidence.

Towns on the Kangba Plateau experience cold temperatures, with up to 200 freezing days per year; summers are blistering by day and the high altitude invites particularly bad sunburn. Lightning storms are frequent from May to October; cloud cover can shroud the scenic peaks. On a more pleasant note, there appear to be sufficient hot springs in these areas to have a solid bath along the route.

Ancient Chinese poetry has it that the road to Sichuan is harder to travel than the road to heaven. In the present era, with the province more accessible by road, we can shift the poetry to Tibet and the highway connecting it with western Sichuan.

The Sichuan-Tibet Highway, begun in 1950 and finished in 1954, is one of the world's highest, roughest, most dangerous and most beautiful roads. The highway has been split into northern and southern routes; it forks 70 km west of Kangding. The northern route (2412 km) runs via Kangding, Ganzi and Dêgê before crossing the boundary into Tibet. The southern route (2140 km) runs via Kangding, Litang and Batang before entering Tibet (see the Ganzi and Litang sections further on).

Whether you are able to actually enter Tibet is an open question. The land route between Chengdu and Lhasa is still for all intents closed to foreigners for reasons of safety and political security. Some palefaces have succeeded and arrived intact in Lhasa, usually by hitching rides on trucks. The PSB has cracked down on this now, however, and it's reportedly getting harder to find rides.

It is possible to do the trip by local buses, but foreigners will likely encounter problems near the Tibetan border, and may even have trouble buying tickets for Batang or Dêgê. A few travellers have reportedly managed to bribe their way across, but at a cost that makes flying from Chengdu to Lhasa more economical.

Years ago there was a legendary crate, the Chengdu-Lhasa bus, which suffered countless breakdowns and took weeks to arrive. In 1985 a monumental mudslip on the southern route took out the road for dozens of km and the service was discontinued. Trucks are the only transport travelling consistently long hauls on this highway. The major truck depots are in Chengdu, Chamdo and Lhasa. Trucks usually run from Lhasa or from Chengdu only as far as Chamdo, where you have to find another lift. But police keep an eye out for truckers giving lifts to foreigners and it's not likely you'll slip past the checkpoints at Dêgê or Batang. If drivers are caught, they could lose their licences or receive massive fines. Foreigners caught arriving from Chengdu are sometimes fined and always sent back. However, if you're arriving from Tibet nobody gives a damn.

In sum, the odds are stacked much higher against you when travelling into, rather than out of, Tibet. Whatever you do, bear in mind the risk and equip yourself properly with food and warm clothing. And remember, accidents can happen. Some years back a group of Americans and Australians were on the back of a truck which overturned close to Dêgê; one member of the group lost half an arm and another member sustained multiple injuries to her back. It took several days for medical help to be sent and even longer before the injured could be brought back to Chengdu. For information on Tibet and Qinghai see the separate chapters in this book. The Sichuan-Tibet Highway is given in-depth coverage in Lonely Planet's *Tibet* guidebook.

Bus service on the Sichuan-Tibet Highway will take you all the way to the border, and at the time of writing it was not difficult to buy tickets to Batang, Ganzi and Dêgê and other towns in the Ganzi (Garzê) Autonomous Prefecture. Having said that, the Exit-Entry Administration Office of Chengdu's PSB does not seem keen to give out permits to these places, so clampdowns are always a possibility.

Kangding (Dardo)
(kāngdìng)

Kangding (2560 metres) is a fairly large town nestled in a steep river valley. Swift currents from the rapids of the Zhepuo River give Kangding hydroelectric power, the source of heating and electricity for the town. The town itself is nothing special, but you must stop here en route to anywhere in western Sichuan. The surrounding scenery is beautiful, and there are a few sights worth walking to in the area.

Towering above Kangding is the mighty peak of Mt Gongga (7556 metres) – to behold it is worth 10 years of meditation, says an inscription in a ruined monastery by the base. The mountain is apparently often covered with cloud so patience is required for the beholding. It sits in a mountain range, with a sister peak just below it towering to 5200 metres. Pilgrims used to circle the two for several hundred km to pay homage.

Mt Gongga is on the open list for foreign mountaineers – in 1981 it buried eight Japanese climbers in an avalanche. Known conquests of this awesome 'goddess' are those by two Americans in 1939, and by six Chinese in 1957.

Things to See There are several lamaseries in and around Kangding. About half a km from the bus station, the **Anjue Monastery** *(ānjuésì)* is fairly quiet, with several monks and a few prayer wheels. To get there, walk uphill from the bus station along the main road to where the town is divided by the Zhepuo River. Cross the third bridge: the monastery is on the right.

With 70 to 80 lamas, the **Nanwu Monastery** *(nánwù sì)* is the most active lamasery in the area. Set in the western part of the town on the northern bank of the river, it affords good views of Kangding and the valley.

Walk uphill along the main road for two km, cross the bridge at the end of town and go another 300 metres. Next to a walled Han Chinese cemetery you will find a dirt path leading uphill alongside a stream which leads right to the lamasery.

For great views of Kangding and (if the weather obliges) nearby snow-capped mountains, try the 500-metre hike to the top of **Mt Paoma** *(pǎomǎshān)*. The ascent takes you past several Buddhist temples and up to a white stupa. From there, if you're lucky, you may even catch a glimpse of Mt Gongga. Take the fork in the road just uphill from the bus station and walk about 10 minutes until you reach a concrete stairway on the left side of the road. From there it's another 30 to 40 minutes to the top.

Places to Stay & Eat The first option you will be confronted with is the *Bus Station Hotel (chēzhàn jiāotōng lǚshè)*. The place is a noisy, filthy dump, but it's cheap. Beds in a triple are Y9, in a double Y12. Up next to the Anjue Monastery the *Gongga Shan Hostel (gònggàshān lǚshè)* is more expensive with doubles/triples for Y20/15 per bed. It's also quieter, cleaner and a hell of a lot more pleasant. There's no English sign: look for the balcony that looks out over the river. The doorway to the hotel office is next to a small teahouse/noodle shop.

The *Traffic Hotel (jiāotōng fàndiàn)*, while decidedly inferior to its namesake in Chengdu, is still okay, with rooms looking out over the river. Beds are Y10 in a triple, Y15 in a double, while singles are Y30. The only drawback is the location: the hotel is more than 1 km uphill from the bus station.

For more upscale rooms, try the *Paoma Guesthouse (pǎomǎ bīnguǎn)*. Their cheapest option is a bed in a triple with attached bath for Y80. Doubles are Y200, which is amazingly expensive for this part of the world. Just up the street, the *Kangding Guesthouse (kāngdìng bīnguǎn)* has slightly shabbier accommodation for slightly less money.

For a rousing cup of yak butter tea, try the teahouse adjacent to the Gonggashan Hostel. Their noodles are also quite tasty. Otherwise, there are numerous point-and-choose restaurants along Kangding's main drag. Food can't compare to Chengdu in most cases, but you should get by without too much problem.

Getting There & Away There are daily buses to Kangding departing Chengdu's Xinnanmen bus station at 6.30 and 7.30 am (Y57). There is also a sleeper at 5.30 pm (Y86). For a spectacular, hair-raising ride, you can try the day buses, which strain their way over the hazardous Erlangshan pass. The ride is supposed to take 12 hours, but is often longer due to traffic and all-too-frequent landslides. The sleeper bus to Kangding skirts Erlangshan by taking a southern route via Shimian, which although longer at 16 hours, offers you a better chance of arriving on time and in one piece.

Back to Chengdu, there are fairly frequent buses between 6 am and 6 pm, including several sleepers.

Buses to Luding leave every two hours between 9 am and 4 pm and cost Y7. There is one bus daily to Moxi at 1 pm. If you're headed to Hailuogou Glacier, this bus will save you having to spend the night in Luding.

Going west from Kangding, there are buses daily to Litang (Y47, 12 hours), Batang (Y80, two days) and Ganzi (14 hours, Y62). There is also a bus to Xiangcheng, which departs at 7 am on odd days of the month, and overnights in Litang en route. For more information see the Northern and Southern Route sections later in this chapter.

Around Kangding About 110 km northwest of Kangding lies the **Tagong Grasslands** (*tǎgōng cǎoyuán*), a vast expanse of green meadow surrounded by snow-capped peaks, and dotted with Tibetan herdsmen and tents. Nearby is the Tagong Lamasery, which blends Han Chinese and Tibetan styles and dates back to the Qing Dynasty. Both areas are being promoted by local tourism authorities, but are still said to be largely unspoiled despite the increase in visitors. There are daily buses from Kangding at 6 and 7 am, which return in the afternoon.

There are also several mountain lakes and

hot springs in the vicinity of Kangding. Lying 21 km to the north of town, **Mugecuo Lake** (*mùgécuò*) is one of the highest lakes in north-west Sichuan at 3700 metres. Locals also boast it's one of the most beautiful, though there are likely many such spots in this superb part of China.

There is no bus service to Mugecuo, so you pretty much have to hire a vehicle. About 300 metres uphill from the bus station is a small tourism office (note the large map of the region above the shop) that can help you arrange a van and also suggest other wilderness outings. Idle van drivers seem to while away their hours in front of the shop as well, so hiring a vehicle shouldn't be too difficult. Getting to Mugecuo and back should cost around Y100 to Y150.

Moxi
(*móxī*)
Nestled in the mountains around 50 km south-west of Luding, this peaceful one-street town is the gateway to the **Hailuogou Glacier Park**.

There's a reception office for Hailuogou Glacier Park several doors up the road from the Catholic church (you can't miss it – it has a steeple with a cross on the top). This place has ponies and guides for hire at around Y30 to Y35 per day, and sells tickets for the glacier. As for the church, its principal claim to fame is that Mao slept in it during the Long March.

Places to Stay There are several very basic hotels, two of which flank the main bus stop. To the left, bearing an English sign which says 'Reception Center' is the *Luyou Hotel* (*lǚyóu fàndiàn*), which has beds in quiet, all-wood rooms for Y10. To the right is a hotel which, despite lacking any sort of sign, has beds for Y5, though the rooms are bit grimy and face the main street. About 500 metres up the road, near the entrance to Hailuogou, is the *Hailin Guesthouse (hǎilín bīnguǎn)*, a grey concrete hulk that in addition to marring the scenery, offers beds in a double with attached bath for Y40.

Getting There & Away There is one bus daily from Kangding to Moxi which leaves at 1 pm and costs Y13. From Luding there are three to four buses daily between 7.30 am and 2.30 pm. The 54-km trip takes nearly three hours and costs Y7. It should also get your pulse racing: there are several cliffside sections where the road seems to disappear from under your bus, which will almost certainly be bulging with passengers, just to add to the excitement. From Moxi there are buses at 7 and 8 am which go to Luding and then on to Kangding, and an 11.30 am bus that terminates at Luding. The early morning bus is usually jam-packed with locals heading down to Luding, so if you want a seat you should walk up to where the bus starts, near the Hailin Guesthouse, around 6.45 am.

Many travellers who come up here to visit Hailuogou set out by way of Kangding, and return via Luding, which has direct buses to Chengdu at 7 am, and a sleeper bus which leaves at 3 pm. Another option is to continue south and loop around to Emeishan and Leshan. Take the 7 am bus to Luding, but tell the driver to let you off at Maoziping (*māozǐpíng*). Cross the suspension bridge to the other side of the river and the main road linking Luding with Shimian. From here you can flag down a (crowded) bus to Wusihe, which is on the Chengdu-Kunming railway line. For more details, see the Luding – Wusihe – Leshan section below.

Hailuogou Glacier Park
(*hǎiluógōu bīngchuān gōngyuán*)
Hailuogou Glacier Park is part of Mt Gongga and is the lowest glacier in Asia. The main glacier (No 1 Glacier) is 14 km in length and covers an area of 16 sq km. It's relatively young as glaciers go: around 1600 years. Guides from the town of Moxi lead inexpensive three to seven-day pony treks along glacier trails. The top of Hailuogou can offer incredible vistas of Mt Gongga, but how much you actually see is entirely up to Mother Nature. If you are after spectacular views it will probably pay to build a couple of extra days into your schedule. The rainy season for this area spans July and August,

and some travellers have found heavy cloud cover and drizzle take a lot of fun out of the trip. Locals say the best time to visit is during late September and October, when skies are generally clear.

The trek has become much more accessible over recent years, but it's still a good idea to come prepared. Bring warm clothing and good sunglasses with you as a minimum. There is food and drink available en route, but it's still worth bringing some high-calorie food with you.

If you are on a pony you can do the entire trip through to the No 3 Camp in around seven to eight hours. On foot you would be better off doing the trip over two days, though it's probably possible to make it to the No 3 Camp in one day if you keep up a brisk pace. The guides will likely push you toward the three-day two-night trek. This usually consists of spending the first night at No 1 camp, riding up to No 3 camp the next day for lunch and glacier viewing, and then heading back down to spend the second night at the No 2 camp. Pony rental is Y30 to Y35 per day.

Most of the pony ride follows a dirt road and is fairly straightforward. Some travellers have had problems on the way back down when some of the younger guides tend to pick up the pace.

If you opt to hike, you can also rent a pack horse for Y30 per day which can carry up to three bags. You can even rent ponies for just the ride up (Y15 to No 1 camp, Y35 to No 3), and then walk back on your own. Maps with English are available at the park reception office in Moxi.

From Moxi the path follows the Yanzigou River. Just after Moxi you'll be stopped at the park gate, where you will be charged a Y47 entry fee. From here it's a straightforward walk or ride (if you are on a pony) around 11 km to the **No 1 Camp** (*yīhào yíngdì*), which is at 1940 metres. En route you'll cross a rickety bridge over the river. The distance to the next camp is around six km.

At the **No 2 Camp** (*èrhào yíngdì*) (2620 metres) the path leaves the river valley and passes through lush rainforest for around five km. At the **No 3 Camp** (*sānhào yíngdì*) (2940 meters) there is a sign notifying visitors that you should take a guide to the glacier itself. Pony guides from Moxi do not qualify, but the hire of a glacier guide is included in the park entry fee, so you shouldn't have to pay any extra. From the No 3 camp the first stop is the **Glacier Viewing Platform** (*bīngchuān guānjǐngtái*) at 3000 metres. From here you can see the **Glacier Tongue** to the left and to the right the **No 2 Glacier**. From the platform it is possible to continue 2½ km on a path that runs alongside the glacier to the **Glacier Waterfall Viewing Platform** (*bīngchuān pùbù guānjǐngtái*).There is also an ice cave another half-hour's walk beyond that. Just how far you get from the No 3 Camp will depend entirely on weather conditions.

Places to Stay & Eat Accommodation in damp and dirty lodges runs around Y20 per bed at each of the camps en route to the glacier, and service can be glacial as well. On the brighter side, both the No 1 and No 2 camps have hot springs if you are in need of a soak. Some people do the walk slowly (three or four hours a day), overnighting at each of the camps. But it is possible to head straight up to the No 3 Camp, where there is chalet-style accommodation, albeit a bit run down. The park authorities seem to frown on camping, and there isn't a great deal in the way of flat ground on the way up in any case. Naturally you can't expect any showering facilities up here – save your dirt for the hot springs lower down.

The camps all sell some food and drinks. Mineral water, soft drinks and beer are all usually available. Food is uniformly miserable – a steady diet of cabbage soup and green peppers fried with pork fat. Better bring some of your own munchies along.

Getting There & Away Hailuogou is accessible via the town of Moxi, which in turn can be reached by bus from Kangding and Luding. See the previous entry on Moxi for details.

Luding
(*lùdìng*)

Luding is around halfway between Kangding and Moxi, and is possibly worth a brief stop en route to either destination, or if you're heading back to Chengdu. Luding is famous throughout China as the site of what is commonly regarded as the most glorious moment of the Great March. The key element in this is the Luding Bridge, a chain suspension affair high over the Dadu River.

In May 1935 the Communist troops were approaching the Luding Bridge, only to discover that Kuomintang troops had beat them to it, removed the planks from the bridge and had it covered with firepower. In response, 20 Communist troops crossed the bridge hand by hand armed with grenades and then proceeded to overcome the Kuomintang troops on the other side. This action allowed the Long March to continue before the main body of the Kuomintang forces could catch up with them.

The **Luding Bridge** (*lùdìng qiáo*) is in the south of town. The original bridge was first constructed in 1705 and was an important link in the Sichuan-Tibet road. On the main street in town you might want to look out for the **Luding Bridge Revolutionary Artefacts Museum** (*lùdìng qiáo gémìng wénwù chénlièguǎn*), which houses a collection of some 150 items left behind by members of the Long March.

Places to Stay There are a few hotels in Luding. Off the main road down south of the bus station, the *Luding County Government Guesthouse* (*xiàn zhǎodàisuǒ*) has beds in triples for Y17, and beds in acceptable doubles with bath for Y40. Confusingly, the Guesthouse is also referred to as the *Luding Hotel* (*lùdìng bīnguǎn*) – there's a small English sign, but you can't see it from the main road.

The *Bus Station Hotel* (*chēzhàn lǚguǎn*), has beds in triples for Y12, while the *Comfortable Inn* (*shūshì lǚshè*), near the southern bus station, sports an English sign and has dorm beds for Y7.

Getting There & Away For some strange reason, Luding has two bus stations. The major bus station is on the main road from Kangding, at the northern edge of town. From here you can get buses to Moxi (Y10), Kangding (Y7) and direct to Chengdu (Y50). Buses to Chengdu leave at 7 am and take 12 hours barring landslides. There are also sleeper buses leaving at 3 pm which go via Shimian, skirting Erlangshan pass. Buses to Kangding run frequently between 7.30 am and 2.30 pm. There are only a few buses to Moxi, at 7.30 am, and at 1.30 and 2.30 pm. There are several buses each morning departing for Shimian, where you can switch to a bus bound for Wusihe, which is on the Chengdu-Kunming railway line.

At the southern part of town, one street uphill from the main road, is the southern bus station. There's not much need to come here, as the main station has all the routes covered. But you may get dropped off here, especially if you're on a bus from Kangding. This station also has buses running to Chengdu, Kangding and Shimian.

Luding-Wusihe-Leshan

If you're headed to Leshan, Emeishan or even Kunming, and don't feel like doubling back to Chengdu, you can try heading down to the railhead at Wusihe. There are usually one or two buses daily from Luding to Wusihe, but if you miss these, just jump on a bus to Shimian, where there are frequent onward buses. Buses from Shimian to Wusihe stop for an hour or so at Hanyuan for some bizarre reason, one of many such halts you're likely to encounter en route. Altogether the 210 km journey requires most of the day, but it does take you through some impressive gorge and river scenery.

As most trains from Wusihe to Emei and Leshan leave between 7.50 and 10.30 am, you will probably have to overnight in Wusihe – there are several hotels clustered around the railway station, all with beds for Y7 to Y10. The one just off the road leading into the station is not bad. There is a 12.26 am train to Leshan, which arrives at 3.47 am, but locals don't recommend it. A hard-seat

ticket to either Emei or Leshan should cost around Y8. The ride is about 3½ hours on most trains.

If you're headed south to Panzhihua (where you connect with buses to Lijiang in Yunnan Province) or Kunming, be advised that you can only buy hard-seat tickets at the Wusihe Railway Station. The notoriously crowded No 66 express to Kunming stops in Wusihe at 7.50 pm, and the No 321 to Panzhihua at 1.27 am.

Sichuan-Tibet Highway – Northern Route

Of the two routes, this is the less heavily travelled, probably because it's nearly 300 km longer than the southern route. One added advantage for travellers is that if you are turned back at the Tibet border, you may be able to work your way up to Qinghai Province via Sêrxu (shíqǔ). However, even getting this far could be a problem: at the time of writing the PSB was doing a good job of closing this route off to foreigners, and the Kangding bus station wouldn't even sell tickets to Ganzi. If you do make it up here, remember that bus service is sparse and erratic: this is no place to be if you're in a hurry.

Ganzi
(gānzī)

The capital of the Ganzi (Garzê) Autonomous Prefecture sits at 3800 metres in Cholashan mountain valley 385 km northwest of Kangding, and is populated by mostly Tibetans and Khampas. Very few Westerners have sojourned here, in part because the PSB, suspecting you are Tibetbound, will do their best to stop you from doing so. As the Xining-Chengdu route between Qinghai and Sichuan becomes more popular it may yet get its due, and it's easier to get here if you're headed toward Chengdu. For now it's little more than an intermediate stop between Sêrxu and Kangding for travellers in a hurry to reach 'civilisation' after the rigours of the Xining-Sêrxu road.

The **Ganzi Lamasery** *(gānzī sì)* just north of the town's Tibetan quarter is worth a visit for views of the Ganzi valley, although it's not a particularly spectacular structure.

The *Ganzixian Hotel (gānzǐxiàn zhāodàisuǒ)* has beds for Y10 to Y20, a decent dining room, friendly staff and plenty of hot water.

For details on the trip north to Xining via Sêrxu, see the Xining section in the Qinghai chapter.

Getting There & Away Buses to Ganzi leave Kangding daily at 6 am, take 14 hours and cost Y62. From Ganzi, there is also one bus daily to Kangding, leaving around daybreak. There are buses every third day onward to Dêgê which originate in Kangding, overnight in Luhuo and pass through Ganzi around 10 am. Under ideal conditions the 200-km ride from Ganzi to Dêgê takes eight hours. Similarly, buses to Sêrxu originate in Kangding every third day or so, overnight in Daofu and stop over in Ganzi around 1 pm before resuming their drive.

Dêgê
(dégé)

This is the last town on the northern route before it enters Tibet proper. As such, it's reportedly well patrolled and it may be difficult to slip past the checkpoint. Guards are said to keep a sharp lookout for foreigners trying to sneak through on the backs of trucks, and a fair number of travellers have been turned back at this point.

Dêgê is home to the 250-year-old **Bakong Scripture Printing Lamasery**, housing an extensive collection of Tibetan scriptures of the five Lamaist sects which are revered by followers the world over. Under the direction of the abbot are some 300 workers; housed within the monastery are over 200,000 hardwood printing plates. Texts include ancient works on astronomy, geography, music, medicine and Buddhist classics. A history of Indian Buddhism, comprising 555 woodblock plates, is the only surviving copy in the world (written in Hindi, Sanskrit and Tibetan). Protecting the monastery from fire and earthquake is a guardian goddess, a green Avalokitesvara.

Accommodation in Dêgê is very basic: no showers and hard wooden beds at the bus station hotel for Y5 to Y10.

Getting There & Away There is a direct bus to Dêgê from Kangding. At the time of writing departures were every three days starting on the third of the month (3, 6, 9 etc.) but this schedule is 'flexible' to say the least. The bus leaves Kangding at 7 am, overnights in Luhuo, passes through Ganzi around 10 am and arrives in Dêgê that same evening, barring any inevitable delays. Buses to Ganzi and on to Kangding leave Dêgê every third day starting on the second of the month (2, 5, 8 etc).

Sichuan-Tibet Highway – Southern Route

This route sees considerably more travellers, though many of these only go as far as Litang before heading down to Xiangcheng and the back route into Yunnan. Between Kangding and the border town of Batang lie more than 500 km of dirt roads, 4000-metre mountain passes, stunning scenery and occasional landslides. A few travellers have made it out to Batang recently, only to be politely turned around. But if this happens, at least you have the option of making your way down to Zhongdian in Yunnan, rather than slogging it all the way back to Chengdu, a four-day journey. For more details, see the Litang to Zhongdian section below.

Litang
(lǐtáng)

At over 4000 metres Litang is one of the highest towns in China, and even a short hike around here may have you wondering where the oxygen went. The town rests at the edge of a vast grassland and is the watering hole for neighbouring Tibetan herdsmen, who can be seen kicking up a trail of dust through town at dusk. Some travellers have found great bargains here on yak skin boots, cloaks and other Tibetan clothing. A trading fair and festival lasting 10 days is held here annually beginning on the 13th day of the sixth lunar month; it's sponsored by the Panchen Lama.

Litang also has a lamasery that is said to have been built by the Third Dalai Lama and contains a buddha statue that locals claim was brought over from Lhasa by foot. Friendly monks are apparently happy to pull in any wandering foreigners for extensive tours of the lamasery.

Places to Stay The hotel at the bus station, located in the southern part of town, has dorm beds for Y8. Like many of these charming places, you share the bathroom with any and all bus passengers. Up the road about 150 metres on the right-hand side is another small guesthouse that has cleaner, quieter dorm beds for Y11. Neither place has showers, but around 15 minutes' walk from the bus station is a public bath where you can get all the hot water your heart desires for Y4. The people at the bus station can point you in the right direction.

Getting There & Away There is one bus daily from Kangding to Litang, leaving at 6 am. The fare is Y47 and the 284-km journey, which crosses several high passes, takes at least 12 hours. Even in summer months it would be best to have some warm clothing to fend off the arctic blasts that live above 4000 metres. From Litang, there are buses to Kangding at 6.30 am, though if the bus that day originates from Batang, then you may not leave until later in the morning. There is a mad scramble for seats, so get there early (or before the bus arrives) if don't wish to stand for 12 hours of bone-jarring dirt road travel. Buses for Batang leave daily in the morning: how early depends on whether the bus, which originates in Kangding, overnights in Litang itself or Yajiang, 136 km east of Litang. There are also buses from here to Xiangcheng, leaving around 10 am on even days of the month.

Batang
(bātáng)
Lying 32 km from the Tibet border, Batang is not much more than a glorified truck park and bus station. But this one-street town is reportedly quite friendly and populated almost completely by Tibetans. Most of the activity centres around the steady stream of truck traffic heading into Tibet. Several Tibetan truckers separately offered one traveller here a ride to Lhasa for Y500, so it may be possible to sneak across here. Just don't pay in advance, in case you're dragged out of your hiding place at the border and sent back to Chengdu. Most travellers who have made it out to Batang have been fined and asked to turn back within 24 hours. One traveller reports:

I heard a knock on my door, and opened it to find two PSB officers there. They were really quite polite, and said they were sorry but I was not supposed to be here, and could I please leave the next day. They then reluctantly fined me Y130, but when I showed them a student card, they gave me a discount of Y95!

Places to Stay Coming from Litang, the bus station hotel is halfway into town on the right-hand side and has beds for Y5. Coming out of the bus station, about 50 metres up the street to the right is a small two-storey white building with yellow trim. There's no sign or reception area, but the place is a hotel all the same, with friendly staff and beds in fairly clean, quiet rooms for Y8.

Getting There & Away There is one bus leaving Batang for Litang daily in the early morning. The trip takes 12 to 14 hours and crosses the 4675-metre Haizishan Pass. For more details on getting to Batang, see the Litang Getting There & Away section above.

Litang to Zhongdian: The Back Door to Yunnan
This has become an increasingly popular route for travellers with time on their hands and Tibet on the brain. The 400-km journey takes you over several breathtaking passes and past fields of Tibetan nomads, semi-submerged Tibetan cabins and endless mountain vistas. Like the rest of western Sichuan, bus service is limited to one run daily at most, and in many cases buses only leave every other day. But if you're taking this route this shouldn't matter too much: it's a fascinating

region that deserves a closer look. And if you can't get to Tibet, this is undoubtedly the next best thing.

Buses leave Litang for Xiangcheng in the morning on even days of the month. The exact departure time varies, as the bus originates in Kangding and may have overnighted in Yajiang. The ride is 200 km of rough gravel, single-lane track, takes 10 hours and costs Y36.

If you're headed in the opposite direction, north to Litang, buses leave Xiangcheng on odd days of the month at 6.30 am.

Xiangcheng is a pretty riverside village of square stone houses with wooden roofs, Tibetan monasteries and the occasional nomad passing through. Monks at the monasteries have welcomed foreign visitors and given them guided tours of the premises. The bus station hotel has beds in quads for Y5. There's a chance that the local PSB will only let you stay one night or two nights here, depending on which day your bus is leaving.

Heading to Zhongdian, buses leave daily at 6 am. The vehicles used are reportedly some of the most haggard in China, so don't expect much. The ride takes 12 hours and costs Y36. Coming the other way, buses leave Zhongdian for Xiangcheng daily at 7.30 am. For details on Zhongdian, see the Yunnan chapter.

NORTHERN SICHUAN

The Aba (Tibet & Qiang) Autonomous Prefecture of northern Sichuan is one of the most Tibetan areas of the province and doesn't require any special permits from the Chengdu PSB. With dense alpine forests and wide grasslands, it's also a great place to get out and commune with nature. Pony treks around Songpan and hiking in the nature preserve of Jiuzhaigou have made this area increasingly popular with travellers, many of whom pass through here on their way up to Langmusi, Xiahe and other destinations in Gansu Province.

Most of northern Sichuan is between 2000 and 3000 metres in altitude, so make sure you take warm clothing: even in summer temperatures can dip to 15°C at night. The rainy season lasts from June to August. While you're getting prepared, also bear in mind that there are few places to change money in this region, so bring sufficient cash.

Roads in these regions are dangerous so don't expect more than minimum standards of vehicle, driver or road maintenance. Roads are particularly hazardous in summer when heavy rains prompt frequent landslides, and you might want to think about planning this trip for the spring or autumn, when the weather is better anyway. Several foreigners were killed in the summer of 1995 when their bus got caught in a landslip and plunged into a river.

Songpan
(sōngpān)

Though largely viewed as a stopover point on the road to Jiuzhaigou, this bustling, friendly town merits a visit of its own. A fair number of its old wooden buildings are still intact, as are the ancient gates that date back from when Songpan was a walled city. Farmers and Tibetan cattle herders clop down the cobblestone streets on horseback, street artisans peddle their wares in the market area, and several km out of town lie idyllic mountain forests and emerald-green lakes.

Horse Treks Though Songpan is nice, the surrounding mountain scenery is better still. One of the best ways to experience it is by joining up with a horse trek. Guides take you out for anywhere from two to seven days, bringing you through valleys and forests so pristine and peaceful that you may not believe you're still in China.

There are several horse trek operators in Songpan. By far the best choice is Shun Jiang Horse Treks (shùnjiāng lǚyóu mǎdùi), run out of a little office across from the bus station. Don't worry about finding the place: their staff will probably track you down before you even get off the bus. Though facing a sales pitch is not the perfect way to cap off the hellish 14-hour ride up from Chengdu, try not to be put off. What they're selling is well worth it. For Y70 per day, you get a horse, three meals a day, tents, bedding and even warm jackets in case you get chilly. The guides take care of everything: you won't touch a tent pole or a cooking pot unless you want to.

The basic three-day trip takes you to a series of mountain lakes and a hot spring at Erdao Hai, and then on the next day to the Zhaga Waterfall. There are entry fees of Y32 at both areas: the money goes directly to park maintenance. Food consists mainly of potatoes, some green vegetables and bread (someone told the owner that foreigners love potatoes). Bring some extra snacks along if you want more variety. Also, if you want beer, you'll have to supply that yourself too. If you've been itching to really get out and enjoy China's beautiful scenery, this is a great opportunity to view it up close.

Places to Stay & Eat The *Bus Station Hotel* (*chēzhàn zhāodàisuǒ*) is about as basic as it comes. Beds in draughty two and three-bed

rooms are Y10 to Y15. The main gripe with this place has to be the bathrooms, which are located across the bus parking lot and shared

SONGPAN 松潘

PLACES TO STAY

1　Guesthouse
　　旅社
5　Lin Ye Hotel
　　林业宾馆
7　Songzhou Hotel
　　松州宾馆
8　Songpan County Government Hostel
　　县政府招待所
11　Huanglong Hotel
　　黄龙宾馆
17　Songpan Hotel
　　松潘宾馆

PLACES TO EAT

6　Xin Xin Restaurant
　　忻忻饭店
10　The Happiest Restaurant
　　福餐厅
15　Muslim Restaurant
　　穆斯林餐厅

OTHER

2　Shun Jiang Horse Treks
　　顺江旅游马队
3　Main Bus Station
　　汽车北站
4　North Gate
　　北门
9　Post Office
　　邮局
12　Cinema
　　电影院
13　East Gate
　　东门
14　East Bus Station
　　汽车东站
16　Covered Bridge
　　古松桥
18　Hospital
　　医院
19　South Gate
　　南门

Songpan

with all bus passengers passing through. Try not to use them after eating. The hotel does offer hot showers, which are marginally cleaner than the toilets.

Turning left out of the bus station just up the street is a little no-name guesthouse with beds in quad dorm rooms for Y5. No showers and one stinking toilet constitute the amenities. A better option may be the *Lin Ye Hotel* (*línyè bīnguǎn*), which is relatively clean and quiet, and sits next to the Min River. Dorm beds are Y15, doubles Y60.

On the main street, the *Songpan County Government Guesthouse (xiànzhèngfǔ zhāodàisuǒ)* has a well-earned reputation as a place to avoid. Dorm beds in filthy rooms are outrageously priced at Y30, the bathrooms are disgusting and the service frigid. Across the street, the *Songzhou Hotel (sōngzhōu bīnguǎn)* has similar prices, but is considerably more pleasant. They even have rooms with attached bath, though the Y180 price tag is a bit steep. A bit further down the street, the *Huanglong Hotel (huánglóng bīnguǎn)*, is a bit run-down, but has dorm beds for Y12 and singles/doubles with common washroom for Y50/80.

The top spot in town is probably the *Songpan Hotel (sōngpān bīnguǎn)*, which has newly finished standard doubles/triples for Y160/150. Beds in triples with common bathroom are Y25. Its main drawback is location, being about 15 minutes' walk from the town centre. The Songpan Hotel may have competition when a new hotel going up next to the main bus station is finished.

Songpan is gradually coming to grips with foreign visitors, and there are a fair number of small restaurants with English signs and menus. The *Happiest Restaurant (fúcāntīng)* and the *Xin Xin Restaurant (xīnxīn fàndiàn)* both have decent fare. Down near the covered bridge and market area, the *Muslim Restaurant (mùsīlín fàndiàn)* is clean and has great food. Prices are a bit higher, especially for chicken and fish, and there's no English menu, but you can easily go pick out what you want in the kitchen. In the morning, check out the dumplings at some of the little breakfast spots along the main street.

Getting There & Away Though a fairly small town, Songpan has two bus stations. There are usually three buses leaving Chengdu's Ximen bus station daily at 7 am for Songpan: two of these usually go to the main bus station, at the northern end of town, while one may end up at the east bus station. Going back to Chengdu, each station has a bus leaving daily at 5 am, and the north station sometimes has another bus departing at 6 am on even days of the month. The Chengdu-Songpan route's 335 km includes some of the worst roads in Sichuan Province, so be prepared for 12 to 14 hours of heavy-duty shock absorption. The road is slated for improvement so that tourists can be whisked to Jiuzhaigou in one day, but completion looks to be far off.

From Songpan, there are buses to Jiuzhaigou at 6 am which continue on to Nanping. Buses to Zöigê leave the main bus station on even days at 6.30 am, and the east bus station on odd days at the same time. The ride takes six to seven hours and costs Y36 (foreigners' price).

Warning Travellers may be required to purchase insurance from the People's Insurance Company of China (PICC) for bus travel in northern Sichuan and Gansu provinces. The ticket office at the Ximen bus station in Chengdu used to require that foreigners present a PICC card, but now say they factor insurance into the cost of foreigners' double-priced bus tickets (isn't that nice of them?). However, travellers in Zöigê and towns in Gansu have been sent to PICC branch offices to pick up insurance cards before being allowed to board their bus, which often leaves without them anyway. Don't bother telling them you have travel insurance already: non-PICC coverage is not recognised. This policy apparently follows from a lawsuit brought upon the Chinese government by the family of a Japanese tourist who was killed in a bus crash in the Jiuzhaigou area. If you're just headed to Jiuzhaigou and back you probably won't have any problem, but for travel further north it may be wise to pick up a card in Chengdu. The card costs

Y30 for one month's cover and is available from the PICC office (zhōngguó rénmín bǎoxiǎn gōngsī) on Shudu Dadao (Renmin Donglu), just down the road from the Hongqi Market in Chengdu.

Huanglong
(huánglóng)

This valley, studded with terraced, coloured ponds (blue, yellow, white and green) and waterfalls, is about 56 km from Songpan, on the main road to Jiuzhaigou. The Yellow Dragon Temple (huánglóng sì) and the surrounding area were designated a national park in 1983. The most spectacular terraced ponds are behind the temple, about a two-hour walk from the main road. Huanglong is almost always included on the itinerary for one of the seven-day Jiuzhaigou tours run out of Chengdu, but some people find it disappointing and prefer an extra day at Jiuzhaigou. An annual Miao Hui (Temple Fair) held here around the middle of the sixth lunar month (roughly mid-August) attracts large numbers of traders from the Qiang minority.

In the national park are several small guesthouses with beds for Y5 to Y10 or less – no frills, just hard beds and maybe a coal burner in the winter. The Huanglong Hotel (huánglóng zhāodàisuǒ) has slightly more upmarket accommodation, with beds in triples with attached bath for Y30, and standard doubles for Y80. It's down at the entrance to the park.

There is no public bus service to Huanglong, and it will be difficult to get here unless you've signed up with a tour. You might be able to jump on a tour bus setting out from either Songpan or Jiuzhaigou early in the morning, but drivers are often reluctant to take foreigners, citing the risk of insurance liability.

Jiuzhaigou
(jiǔzhàigōu)

In northern Sichuan, close to the Gansu border, is Jiuzhaigou (literally: Nine Stockade Gully), which was 'discovered' in the '70s and is now being groomed for an annual influx of 300,000 visitors. In 1984 Zhao Ziyang made the famous comment which all Sichuanese tourism officials love to quote: 'Guilin's scenery ranks top in the world, but Jiuzhaigou's scenery even tops Guilin's'.

Jiuzhaigou, which has several Tibetan settlements, offers a number of dazzling features – it is a nature reserve area (with some panda conservation zones) with North-American-type alpine scenes (peaks, clear lakes, forests). Scattered throughout the region are Tibetan prayer wheels and chortens, Tibetan stupas. The remoteness of the region and the chaotic transport connections have kept it clean and relatively untouristed.

Despite the good intentions of the authorities, all this looks certain to change fast. A helicopter landing pad is under construction even though the mountain ranges between Chengdu and Jiuzhaigou are not ideal terrain for helicopters. And Chinese resort-style hotels, though as yet largely empty, line the road leading to the park entrance.

You should calculate between a week and 10 days for the round trip by road. It takes from two to three days to get there and you can easily spend three or four days, or even weeks, doing superb hikes along trails which cross spectacular scenery of waterfalls, ponds, lakes and forests – just the place to rejuvenate polluted urban senses. In a bid to prevent the forest from being trampled by hordes of tourists, park authorities have stationed locals on some of the off-road trails to turn back wandering hikers. If you run into one, it's best to be friendly and head back to the road.

The entrance to Jiuzhaigou National Park is close to the Yangdong Hotel, where the bus will likely drop you off. Here lies probably the most painful part of the trip: a park entry fee of Y158. This is really high for China (even locals must pay Y67), and there's no real way around it: student cards don't work, unless you can back it up with a legitimate residence or work certificate. At least the money goes toward a national park, rather than into the pockets of some shady hotel or tour operator. The entry fee includes one night's stay at the Nuorilang Hotel in a three-bed dormitory.

From the park entrance to the first hotels within the park it's about 5 km along a surfaced road, and 14 km to the Nuorilang Hotel. You can arrange rides from local drivers hanging around the entrance gate. Up to Nuorilang should cost Y10 to Y12 per person, though they'll likely try to charge more. Bargain hard with these guys.

At the Nuorilang Hotel the road splits: branch right for Swan Lake; branch left for Long Lake. Nuorilang to Long Lake is 18 km, Nuorilang to Rize is nine km and Rize to Swan Lake is eight km. Long Lake generally sees fewer tourists, as there is no surfaced road leading to it.

Places to Stay & Eat Unless you're catching an early bus the next day, you're better off staying inside the park. Just above Nuorilang Falls, the *Nuorilang Hotel (nuòrìláng bīnguǎn)* is where you're likely to spend your first night, since your entry fee includes one night's stay there. It features the standard concrete block decor, but the rooms are large and the beds comfortable enough. If you decide to stay past the first night, beds in a triple with common bathroom are Y25. There are even hot showers (Y5), though the plumbing doesn't always cooperate.

If you take a left fork in the road and walk about 100 metres past the Nuorilang Hotel, you'll come to a cluster of Tibetan-style wooden hotels. Facilities are basic: no showers and some places don't even have electricity. But they have considerably more personality than the Nuorilang Hotel and are cheaper at Y15 to Y20 per bed. The owners are also quite friendly, though this may mean sitting through several cups of yak-butter tea, without doubt an acquired taste.

There are no longer any hotels along the road to Swan Lake – local authorities ordered them closed to preserve the natural environment. Your other options within the park are some Tibetan-style hotels in the villages of Heye and Shuzheng, located 4 km and 9 km from the park entrance respectively. Again, amenities are limited to the basics,

and beds run around Y20, though you can bargain down if you stay several days.

About 500 metres west of the park entrance, next to the river, the *Shangye Hotel (shāngyè bīnguǎn)* has standard Chinese-style accommodation at Y25 per bed in double or triple dorm rooms.

Just outside the park entrance, the *Yangdong Hotel (yángdóng bīnguǎn)* offers a more upmarket stay, with standard doubles with attached bath and TV for Y80.

Cheaper Tibetan-style hotels can be found in Jiuzhaigou Town, located about 1 km west along the road to Songpan. There are several

such places, with beds in comfortable wooden rooms for around Y15.

In the park, the dining hall next to the Nuorilang Hotel is the only large restaurant in the park. Food is mediocre, service abysmal. Across the street is a small noodle shop with outstanding vegie noodle soup for Y5. Further up the road, toward the Tibetan hotels, is another restaurant with a menu similar to the hotel dining hall, but with better food and friendlier staff. Otherwise, dining options are limited, so it would be wise to bring some of your own food. Chengdu would be a good place to stock up.

Getting There & Away Until local authorities get desperate, level a mountain or two and build an airport, the local bus remains the best means of transport. It can be taken in one dose or as part of a bus/train combination.

The most direct way is to take the bus from Chengdu to Songpan, then catch a Nanping bus, which passes Jiuzhaigou, the following day at 6 am. For more details, see the Getting There & Away section for Songpan. If you're coming down from Gansu via Zöigê, you'll also have to go through Songpan. From Songpan to Jiuzhaigou takes around 3 hours and costs Y20.

Alternatively, it is possible to travel direct to Jiuzhaigou by taking a Chengdu-Nanping bus and getting off at Jiuzhaigou. The bus leaves from the Ximen bus station at 7.20 am and, depending on the road and the sanity of the driver, sometimes does the 18-hour trip in one day. If conditions are bad you will probably overnight in Maowen or Songpan. Next to the bus station in Maowen is the *Renmin Hotel*, with inexpensive three-bed dorms. If you nod off and miss the entrance to Jiuzhaigou, you will have to overnight in Nanping and backtrack the next day. Buses to Nanping cost around Y80 for foreigners.

Bus/train combinations are more troublesome, but can be done. The most popular option is to travel north on the Chengdu-Baoji railway line as far as Zhaohua, where you will have to stay overnight. From Zhao-

hua there are usually tour buses to both Jiuzhaigou and Huanglong in the height of the tourist season, but if this isn't the case you can either bus to Nanping and overnight there before doing the final 41 km the next morning or take a Chengdu-bound bus to Jiuzhaigou. Buses for Chengdu go via Nanping and Jiuzhaigou (check to be certain). It's a good idea to book your onward bus ticket as soon as you get into Zhaohua. The road between Zhaohua and Nanping is notoriously dangerous – this is not a trip for those with no stomach for adventurous travel.

Another train/bus option is to take a train or bus to either Mianyang or Jiangyou, both north of Chengdu. Then take a bus to Pingwu, where you can change for a bus to Jiuzhaigou. This road is reportedly superior to the one between Zhaohua and Nanping.

Between October and April snow often cuts off access to Jiuzhaigou for weeks on end. But even at the best of times, transport is not plentiful – if you board en route rather than catching a bus at its originating point, be prepared for some tough competition for seats. To maximise your chances of a seat on a bus out of Jiuzhaigou, it's best to book your ticket three days in advance at the entrance to the reserve. Hitching has been known to work, though tour buses will be less likely to pick you up.

During the summer, various companies in Chengdu operate tours to Jiuzhaigou. Some include side trips in the general region. These tours take a lot of the hassle out of travelling in a region where roads and transport links are quite poor. Of course, they also dictate your schedule, which could be a problem if you decide you want to spend some more time in Jiuzhaigou or Songpan, for example.

Most of the trips are advertised for a certain day, but the bus will only go if full. If you are unlucky you may spend days waiting. Find out exactly how many days the trip lasts and which places are to be visited. If you're not sure about the tour company, avoid paying in advance. If there's a booking list, have a look and see how many people have registered. You can register first and pay before departure.

A standard tour includes Huanglong and Jiuzhaigou, lasts seven days and costs an average of Y200 to Y300 per person. Hotels, food and entry fees are not included. There are longer tours which include visits to the Tibetan grassland areas of Barkam and Zöigê. Prices vary according to the colour of your skin and the scruples of the companies involved. Travel agencies in the Traffic Hotel, the Ximen bus station, the Jinjiang Hotel and CITS all offer tours. The latter two are the most expensive. Check around and compare prices.

A word of warning. Several tour operators in Chengdu have been blacklisted by travellers for lousy service, rip-offs and rudeness. Ask around among travellers to pinpoint a reliable agency.

Chengdu to Xiahe

This journey has emerged as a popular backdoor route into Gansu Province for many travellers. Those who have done this route in the winter months don't recommend it. The roads often become impassable and temperatures plummet way past the tolerance levels of most mere mortals. Even in good weather, you need to give yourself at least five days to do the trip, more if you want to poke around some monasteries or make a side trip to Jiuzhaigou.

The first leg is from Chengdu to Songpan (see Getting There & Away in the Songpan section earlier in this chapter). Most travellers take a side trip from Songpan to Jiuzhaigou at this point. From Songpan you can travel 168 km north-west to your next overnight stop in Zöigê *(ruòěrgài)*, a dusty little town surrounding by sweeping grasslands. There is some confusion as to the status of Zöigê for individual travellers. There is a 'Foreigners' Registration Office' near the main bus station. Some travellers have successfully ignored it, while others have had to pay for a travel permit. Don't worry about it too much – the PSB will find you if they think it's important. From the cinema in town it is possible to walk up the hills and visit a couple of monasteries. There are superb views from up here.

There are a couple of hotels which take foreigners in Zöigê. The *Grain Bureau Guest House (liángjú bīnguǎn)* is probably the best choice, with beds in very clean triples for Y11 (Y22 if you want TV). Doubles are Y46. There are common showers and toilets on each floor. To get there, turn right out of the main bus station, and take the first left. You'll come to a three-way intersection. Turn right: the hotel is on the left-hand side of the street.

Further down the street, also on the left, the *Zöigê County Government Hostel (ruòěrgài xiànzhèngfǔ zhāodàisuǒ)* is a bit cheaper at Y5 per bed in a triple, but the rooms are filthy and the toilets putrid. Doubles at the back of the building for Y30 are a bit cleaner. There are a few restaurants and lots of cheap noodle places near the Grain Bureau Guest House.

Zöigê has two bus stations at either end of town with buses back to Songpan and on to Langmusi and Hezuo on alternating days. If you can't get an onward ticket for the next day at one bus station, try the other. Buses to Langmusi leave at 6.40 am, take from two to 3½ hours and cost Y24 for foreigners. Direct buses to Hezuo leave at 6.20 am. The eight-hour ride costs Y43.

Langmusi is probably worth a stopover. It's an attractive Tibetan village nestled in the mountains, and travellers have had great visits with the monks at the local lamasery.

From Langmusi it's easy to catch a bus to Hezuo. Hezuo is by all accounts a dump, but is only a few hours from Xiahe, so you may not have to overnight there. From Xiahe you have the option of travelling on to Lanzhou or taking the more unusual option of travelling on to Xining in Qinghai Province via Tongren.

Xinjiang 新疆

A land of vast mountains and deserts, Xinjiang *(xīnjiāng)* is China's largest province. Xinjiang is inhabited by something like 13 of China's official total of 56 national minorities. The Turkish-speaking Muslim Uighurs *(wéiwúěr)* are the most numerous in this interesting population of ethnic groups. To the west of Ürümqi, where the Tianshan range divides in two, is the Ili Valley. The population in the valley consists of Kyrgyz, Kazaks and Han Chinese, and even includes a colony of Sibo (the descendants of the Manchu garrison that was stationed here after the conquests of the 18th century). Another peculiar army to hit Xinjiang was that of the refugee White Russian troops who fled Russia after their defeat in the Russian Civil War. Some settled here and founded scattered colonies.

In 1955 the province of Xinjiang was renamed the Uighur Autonomous Region. At that time more than 90% of the population was non-Chinese. With the building of the railway from Lanzhou to Ürümqi and the development of industry in the region, there was a large influx of Han Chinese people who now form a majority in the northern area while the Uighurs continue to predominate in the south. Xinjiang's population now exceeds 15 million with the Han making up slightly over half the total.

A dominant feature of Xinjiang is the Tarim Basin, a huge, barely inhabited depression whose centre is the sands of the Taklamakan Desert. Streams flowing into the basin lose themselves and evaporate, never reaching the sea. Here you'll find the large salt lake of Lop Nur where the Chinese have been testing nuclear bombs since 1964.

Xinjiang is several time zones removed from Beijing, which prefers to ignore the fact. Officially, Beijing time applies; in practice, Xinjiang time is used haphazardly for meal times in hotels, bus departures etc. Xinjiang time is one hour behind Beijing time. Try and straighten out any confusion

Population: 15 million
Capital: Ürümqi
Highlights:

- Tianchi, a chunk of alpine scenery that looks like a Swiss postcard
- Turpan, a desert oasis, the lowest and hottest spot in China, bedecked with grape vines, mosques and abandoned ancient cities
- Kashgar, a fabled Muslim city on the Silk Road that astonished Marco Polo when he passed through in the 13th century
- The Karakoram Highway, one of the most beautiful road journeys in the world, crosses the China-Pakistan border

by asking whether the stated time is Beijing time *(běijīng shíjiān)*, Beijing daylight-saving time *(xiàlìng shíjiān)* or Xinjiang time *(xīnjiāng shíjiān)*. Kashgar time *(kāshí shíjiān)* is one hour behind Xinjiang time and two hours behind Beijing.

See Lonely Planet's *Pakistan, Tibet, Central Asia* and *Karakoram Highway* guides for more information on this area.

History

The history of this desolate north-western region has largely been one of continuing wars and conflicts between the native populations,

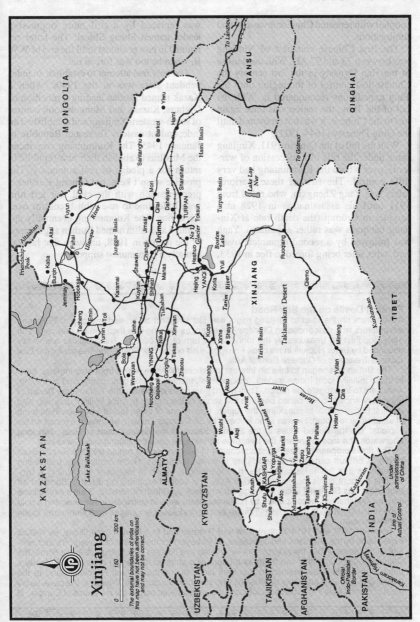

Xinjiang

0   150   300 km

The external boundaries of India on
this map have not been authenticated
and may not be correct.

coupled with repeated Chinese invasions and subjugations.

The first Chinese conquest of Xinjiang was between 73 and 97 AD. With the demise of the Han Dynasty in the 3rd century the Chinese lost control of the region until the Tang expeditions reconquered it. With the fall of the Tang, the region was once again lost to the Chinese; it was not recovered until the Qing Dynasty (1644-1911).

With the fall of the Qing in 1911, Xinjiang came under the rule of a succession of warlords, over whom the Kuomintang had very little control. The first of these warlord-rulers was Yang Zhengxin, who ruled from 1911 until his assassination in 1928 at a banquet in Ürümqi (the death rate at Xinjiang banquets was rather appalling). Yang was followed by a second tyrannical overlord, who, after being forced to flee in 1933,

was replaced by a still more oppressive leader named Sheng Shicai. The latter remained in power almost until the end of WW II, when he too was forced out.

The only real attempt to establish an independent state was in the 1940s, when a Kazak named Osman leading a rebellion of Uighurs, Kazaks and Mongols took control of south-western Xinjiang and established an independent eastern Turkestan Republic in January 1945. The Kuomintang convinced the Muslims to abolish their new republic in return for a pledge of real autonomy. The promise wasn't kept, but Chiang Kaishek's preoccupation with the civil war left him with little time to re-establish control over the region. The Kuomintang eventually appointed a Muslim named Burhan as governor of the region in 1948, unaware that he was actually a Communist supporter.

Foreign Devils on the Silk Road

Adventurers on the road to Xinjiang might well like to reflect on an earlier group of European adventurers who descended on Chinese Turkestan, as Xinjiang was then known, and carted off early Buddhist art treasures by the tonne at the turn of the century. Their exploits are vividly described by Peter Hopkirk in his book *Foreign Devils on the Silk Road – the Search for the Lost Cities & Treasures of Chinese Central Asia.*

The British first began to take an interest in the central Asian region from their imperial base in India. Initially, local Indian traders, 'moonshees', trained in basic cartography and surveying, were sent to investigate the region. They heard from oasis dwellers in the Taklamakan Desert of legendary ancient cities buried beneath the sands of the desert. In 1864 William Johnson was the first British official to sneak into the region, visiting one of these fabled lost cities in its tomb of sand close to Hotan. He was soon followed by Sir Douglas Forsyth, who made a report on his exploits: 'On the Buried Cities in the Shifting Sands of the Great Desert of Gobi'. Not long afterwards, the race to unearth the treasures beneath the desert's 'shifting sands' was on.

The first European archaeologist/adventurer to descend on the region was the Swede Sven Hedin. A brilliant cartographer and fluent in seven languages, Hedin made three trailblazing expeditions into the Taklamakan Desert, unearthing a wealth of treasures and writing a two-volume account of his journeys: *Through Asia.* The second explorer, in pursuit of Buddhist art treasures, was Sir Auriel Stein, a Hungarian who took up British citizenship. Stein's expeditions into the Taklamakan, accompanied by his terrier Dash, were to culminate in his removing a gold mine of Buddhist texts in Chinese, Tibetan and central Asian languages from Dunhuang to the British Museum.

Between 1902 and 1914 Xinjiang saw four German and four French expeditions, as well as expeditions by the Russians and Japanese, all jockeying for their share of the region's archaeological treasures. While these explorers were feted and lionised by adoring publics at home, the Chinese today commonly see them as robbers who stripped the region of its past. Defenders point to the wide-scale destruction that took place during the Cultural Revolution and to the defacing of Buddhist art works by Muslims who stumbled across them. Whatever the case, today most of central Asia's finest archaeological finds are scattered across the museums of Europe. ■

A Muslim league opposed to Chinese rule was formed in Xinjiang, but in August 1949 a number of its most prominent leaders died in a mysterious plane crash on their way to Beijing to hold talks with the new Communist leaders. Muslim opposition to Chinese rule collapsed, though the Kazak Osman continued to fight until he was captured and executed by the Chinese Communists in early 1951.

Since 1949 Beijing's main goal has been to keep a lid on minority separatism while flooding the region with Han settlers.

ÜRÜMQI
(wūlǔmùqí)

The capital of Xinjiang, Ürümqi has little to distinguish itself other than the claim to being the farthest city in the world from the ocean. Pretty much located in the middle of nowhere, Ürümqi's economic fortunes improved after the Communists built the railway line from Lanzhou across the desert. About one million people live here now, 80% of them Han Chinese. The inspired concrete-block architecture has been imported lock, stock and barrel from socialist eastern China, and Ürümqi essentially looks little different from the smokestack cities 2000 km east. There are few 'sights' as such, but it's an important crossroad and perhaps an intrinsically interesting place to visit.

Orientation

One of the difficulties of finding your way around is that the streets have a notorious habit of changing names every few blocks – a nightmare for map makers. Most of the sights, tourist facilities and hotels are scattered across the city, though they're all easily reached on local buses.

The railway and long-distance bus stations are in the south-western corner of the city. There are two candidates for the title of 'city centre': the first is the area around the large Hongshan Department Store, where some of the major arteries intersect; the other is in the eastern part of the city, where you'll find the main shopping district, the PSB and the Bank of China.

Information

Travel Agencies CYTS (☎ 281-6017; fax 281-7078) has a branch on the 1st floor of the Hongshan Hotel, and seems relatively efficient and cheap for organising tickets and tours. The little-used main branch of CYTS (☎ 283-4969) is at 9 Jianshe Lu.

The Lüyou Hotel (just behind Holiday Inn) is home to several travel agencies. Up on the 5th floor is the Xinjiang Overseas Tourist Corporation (☎ 281-4490; fax 282-1445), a friendly place with Uighur management. The *real* CITS (☎ 282-6719; fax 281-0689) is on the ground floor of the same building. The 'CITS' in the Hongshan Hotel is a fake.

PSB This is a 10-minute walk from the CITS office, in a large government building just to the north-west of Renmin Square.

Money The Bank of China is at 343 Jiefang Nanlu, close to Renmin Square. There is another Bank of China opposite the main post office. There are also money-changing facilities inside the CAAC office, Lüyou Hotel and Holiday Inn.

Post The main post office is a big Corinthian-colonnaded building directly across the traffic circle from the Hongshan Department Store. The foreign section is efficient and has a packing service.

Xinjiang Autonomous Region Museum
(xīnjiāng wéiwúér zìzhìqū bówùguǎn)

Xinjiang covers 16% of China's total land surface. It is inhabited not only by the Han Chinese but also by 13 of China's ethnic minorities. One wing of the museum contains an interesting exhibition relating to some of the Xinjiang minority groups and it's well worth a look.

Notable among the exhibits are the Daur hats (made from animal heads) with large fur rims – there are about 103,000 Daur people spread across Xinjiang, Inner Mongolia and Heilongjiang. The Tajik exhibition features silver and coral beads supporting silver pendants – the people number about 29,000 and are found only in Xinjiang. There are about

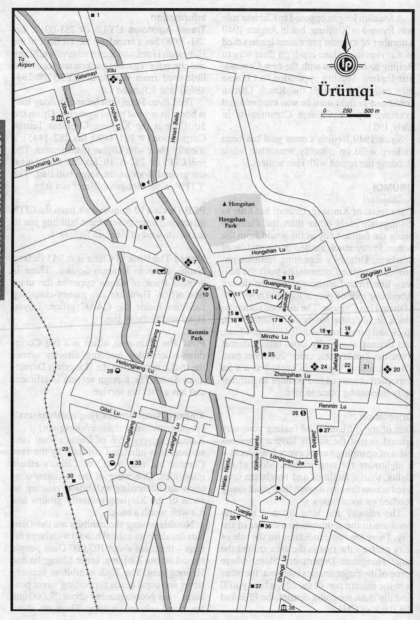

Ürümqi

0   250   500 m

▲ Hongshan

Hongshan Park

ÜRÜMQI 乌鲁木齐

PLACES TO STAY

1　Kunlun Guesthouse
　　昆仑宾馆
6　Pea Fowl Hotel
　　孔雀大厦
12　Hongshan Hotel &
　　CYTS
　　红山宾馆，
　　中国青年旅行社
13　Bogda Hotel
　　博格达宾馆
15　Holiday Inn
　　假日大酒店
16　Lüyou Hotel & CITS
　　旅游宾馆，
　　中国国际旅行社
17　Laiyuan Hotel
　　徕远宾馆
22　Grand Islam Hotel
　　伊斯兰大酒店
23　Dianli Hotel
　　电力宾馆
29　Jinyinchuan Hotel
　　金银川大厦
30　Ya'ou Hotel
　　亚欧宾馆
33　Xinjiang Hotel
　　新疆饭店
36　Shancheng Hotel
　　山城大酒店
37　Overseas Chinese
　　Hotel
　　华侨宾馆

PLACES TO EAT

11　John's Information
　　& Cafe
　　约翰中西餐厅
14　Restaurant Alley
　　建设路
18　Hongchunyuan
　　Restaurants
　　鸿春园饭店
35　Guangdong Jiujia
　　(Restaurant)
　　广东酒家

OTHER

2　Youhao Department
　　Store
　　友好商场
3　Xinjiang Autonomous
　　Region Museum
　　新疆维吾尔自治区
　　博物馆
4　Xinhua Bookstore
　　新华书店
5　CAAC
　　中国民航
7　Hongshan Department
　　Store
　　红山商场
8　Main Post Office
　　总邮局
9　Bank of China
　　中国银行

10　Buses to Tianchi &
　　Baiyanggou
　　往天池/白扬沟汽车站
19　PSB
　　公安局外事科
20　Tianbai Department
　　Store
　　天百商场
21　Renmin Square
　　人民广场
24　Xinbai Department
　　Store
　　新百商场
25　Foreign Languages
　　Bookstore
　　外文书店
26　Bank of China
　　中国银行
27　Xinhua Bookstore
　　新华书店
28　Long-Distance Bus
　　Station
　　长途汽车站
31　Railway Station
　　火车站
32　Kashgar Bus Station
　　喀什办事处
34　Erdaoqiao Market
　　(Buses to Turpan)
　　二道桥 (吐鲁番汽车站)
38　Eighth Route Army
　　Office Museum
　　八路军办事处

one million Kazaks living in Xinjiang and their exhibition in the museum features a heavily furnished yurt. The Mongol exhibit includes particularly ornate silver bridles and saddles studded with semi-precious stones, stringed musical instruments and decorated riding boots.

Another wing of the museum has a fascinating section devoted to history. Prime exhibits are the preserved bodies of two men and two women discovered in tombs in Xinjiang, similar to those in the museum at Hangzhou. Also interesting is the collection of multicoloured clay figurines unearthed from Turpan, dating back to the Tang Dynas-

ty. Note the collection of silk fragments with various patterns from different dynasties.

The distinctive Soviet-style building with a green dome is on Xibei Lu, about 20 minutes' walk from the Kunlun Guesthouse. From Hongshan Department Store take bus No 7 for four stops and ask to get off at the museum *(bówùguǎn)*.

Renmin Park
(rénmín gōngyuán)
This beautiful, tree-shaded park is about one km in length and can be entered from either the north or south gates. The best time to visit is early in the morning when the Chinese are

out here doing their exercises. There are plenty of birds in the park and a few pavilions. Near the north end is a lake where you can hire rowing boats – a pleasant way to relax after dinner. Try to avoid the park on Sunday, when the locals descend on the place in force.

Hongshan Park & Pagoda
(hóngshān gōngyuán)
It's not exactly one of the world's eight wonders, but the pagoda sits on top of a big hill just to the north of Renmin Park and affords sweeping views of the city.

Eighth Route Army Office Museum
(bālù jūn bànshìchù)
This small museum occupies a high rung in the ladder of Xinjiang's Communist mythology. In the war of resistance against Japan, the Communist Eighth Route Army had its headquarters here between 1937 and 1942.

The reason why the office was closed in 1942 is perhaps the most interesting part of the story. Sheng Shicai, a Xinjiang warlord who had initially followed a pro-Communist policy, suddenly embarked on an anti-Communist purge in 1942. Among those executed was Mao Zemin, a younger brother of Mao Zedong, who had been sent by the Party to Xinjiang in 1938 to work as Sheng's financial adviser. The museum has a display telling of the life and times of little Mao, along with 10 other revolutionary martyrs who got the axe in 1942.

The office served as a crash pad for senior Communist officials and military figures who happened to be passing through. Zhou Enlai slept here. Another well-known backpacker who took advantage of the budget accommodation was Chen Yun, later to become Deng Xiaoping's anti-reform nemesis to the bitter end (Chen died in May 1995 while Deng was on his deathbed).

The museum is in a courtyard off Lane 2 on Shengli Lu in the south-east part of town.

Places to Stay – bottom end
The *Hongshan Hotel* (☎ 284-761) *(hóngshān bīnguǎn)* is a good base in the centre of town

and is very popular with budget travellers. Dorm beds cost Y40 in a three-bed room without private bath. The communal showers invariably have long queues. For Y150 there are doubles with private bath; these rooms are small but comfortable enough.

The Hongshan often becomes full in summer, and much of the overflow traffic goes to the two-star *Bogda Hotel (bógédá bīnguǎn)*. Here three-bed dormitories come in at Y45 per person. Double rooms cost Y250.

In the vicinity of the railway station, the best option for budget travellers is the *Xinjiang Hotel* (☎ 585-2511) *(xīnjiāng fàndiàn)* at 107 Changjiang Lu. Dorm beds cost Y30 to Y60. Doubles with attached bath cost Y360 and Y400. A suite costs Y1000 and a 'magnificent room' costs Y2000.

One of the best deals around is the *Pea Fowl Hotel* (☎ 484-2988) *(kǒngquè dàshà)* directly opposite the CAAC booking office. Plush doubles cost Y168 and Y238, or you can get a suite for Y358.

The *Overseas Chinese Hotel* (☎ 286-0793; fax 286-2279) *(huáqiáo bīnguǎn)* is a drab concrete block at 51 Xinhua Nanlu. It's far from the town centre but you can get there on overloaded bus No 7. Doubles in the old building cost Y174. In the new building rooms cost Y304 and Y404.

The *Lüyou Hotel* (☎ 282-1788) *(lǚyóu bīnguǎn)* at 51 Xinhua Beilu is an 11-storey building behind Holiday Inn. There are 36 double rooms here priced at Y210, but there are plans to renovate soon and prices will no doubt rise.

Places to Stay – middle
The fancy *Ya'ou Hotel* (☎ 585-6699) *(yǎ'ōu bīnguǎn)* is adjacent to the railway station. The hotel itself is fine; it's a pity that the railway station area is such a dump. Beds in a triple cost Y75 per person, or you can get a clean double for Y225. The nearby *Jinyinchuan Hotel (jīnyínchuān dàshà)* looks OK from the outside, but was not yet open for business during our visit.

The *Shancheng Hotel* (☎ 287-3888; fax 286-0958) *(shānchéng dà jiǔdiàn)* at 8 Tuanjie

CHRIS TAYLOR

CHRIS BEALL

CHRIS BEALL

CHRIS TAYLOR

Top Left: Spices and beans at Kashgar market, Xinjiang
Top Right: Shoe repair in Xinjiang
Bottom Left: Tribeswoman from Xinjiang, home to a large number of minority nationalities
Bottom Right: Taking care of business, Kashgar

Top: The Bezeklik Thousand Buddha Caves near Turpan, Xinjiang
Middle: A market in the desert oasis of Turpan, the lowest and hottest place in China
Bottom: A camel rests near the ruins of Gaochang, the former capital of the Uighurs and a staging post on the Silk Road, Xinjiang.

Lu is very fancy and worth the price. Doubles cost Y280, Y320 and Y388.

The *Dianli Hotel* (☎ 282-2911) on Minzhu Lu belongs to the power company, so at least the electricity supply should be reliable. Rooms cost Y288, Y338 and Y580, plus 15% surcharge.

The *Grand Islam Hotel* (☎ 282-8360) (*yīsīlán dà fàndiàn*) at 22 Zhongshan Lu looks a bit shaky, literally. We couldn't help noticing that several more storeys were being added onto the roof, a practice which has caused a number of buildings in China to collapse. If you have confidence in this building technique, you can get a room here for Y378, Y408 or Y645.

The *Kunlun Guesthouse* (☎ 484-0411; fax 484-0213) (*kūnlún bīnguǎn*) at 38 Youhao Beilu stretches the definition of 'mid-range' with rooms starting at Y450.

Places to Stay – top end

Holiday Inn (☎ 281-8788; fax 281-7422) (*xīnjiāng jiàrì dàjiǔdiàn*) has 383 cushy rooms at 168 Xinhua Beilu. Even if you can't afford to stay here, they have great coffee, an excellent breakfast buffet and the wildest disco in western China. Standard/superior rooms cost Y713/830 and suites cost Y1535 to Y3735. Significant discounts can be negotiated during the quieter winter months.

The *Laiyuan Hotel* (☎ 282-8368; fax 282-5109) (*láiyuàn bīnguǎn*) on Jianshe Lu likes to pretend it's on a par with Holiday Inn, even though it isn't. Doubles begin at Y700 and are not really worth it.

Places to Eat

Ürümqi is a good place to try Uighur foods such as shish kebab (*kǎoròu*) with flat-bread (*náng*). Another local speciality is noodles (*lāmiàn*) with spicy vegetables, beef or lamb. Just on the south side of the Hongshan Hotel is a food stall that specialises in these foods.

Just opposite the Hongshan Hotel is *John's Cafe*, which has three branches in Xinjiang. This place serves Western and Chinese food at backpacker prices.

During the summer, the markets are packed with delicious fruit, both fresh and dried. Try the *Erdaoqiao Market* (*èrdàoqiáo shìchǎng*) near the Turpan bus station.

The *Hongchunyuan Restaurant* (*hóngchūnyuán fàndiàn*), close to the PSB, is actually a Chinese-only hotel with two restaurants. One serves Chinese food (*zhōng cān*) and the other, called the *Pumpkin Restaurant*, serves Western food (*xī cān*). The Western restaurant has an English menu; the Chinese restaurant doesn't. Prices are cheap.

Near the Overseas Chinese Hotel is a good Cantonese restaurant called *Guangdong Jiujia*. In the morning they serve dim sum, and Hong Kongers flock to this place. From the Overseas Chinese Hotel, go one block north and turn left – the restaurant is on the left side.

The Holiday Inn has a few restaurants with extremely high standards and prices to match. *Kashgari's* serves up Muslim dishes, while the *Xi Wang Mu* has everything Chinese from Sichuan to Cantonese dim sum. If you've been starved of creature comforts for a while, call in in the morning for the breakfast buffet.

Entertainment

On the 2nd floor of the Holiday Inn is *Silks*, a disco that's open until 2 am – the cover charge is a steep Y55 if you're not a guest. The bar in the hotel lobby has a Filipino band.

Things to Buy

Ürümqi is not particularly good for Uighur handicrafts – look for this stuff in Kashgar and Turpan.

Han handicrafts are another matter. Good places for general shopping include the department stores – try the Hongshan, Tianbai, Xinbai and Youhao.

The Foreign Languages Bookstore has no English sign. Look for Luchinos, an Italian fashion store on Xinhua Beilu – the bookstore is on the 2nd and 3rd floors of the same building.

Getting There & Away

Air CAAC does international flights to Almaty (Kazakstan), Hong Kong, Islamabad (Pakistan), Moscow, Novosibirsk (Russia) and Tashkent (Uzbekistan). Aeroflot has a booking office in the Overseas Chinese Hotel and offers flights to Moscow for US$260.

Domestic flights connect Ürümqi with Beijing, Changchun, Changsha, Chengdu, Chongqing, Dalian, Guangzhou, Guilin, Haikou, Hangzhou, Harbin, Kunming, Lanzhou, Qingdao, Shanghai, Shenyang, Shenzhen, Tianjin, Wuhan, Xiamen, Xi'an, Xining and Zhengzhou.

There are also flights from Ürümqi to the following places in Xinjiang: Aksu (Akesu), Altai (Aletai), Fuyun, Hotan (Hetian), Karamai (Kelamayi), Kashgar (Kashi), Korla (Kuerle), Qiemo (Jumo), Tacheng and Yining.

The CAAC office (☎ 281-7942) is on Youhao Lu, just up the road from the post office; it's open from 10 am to 1.30 pm and from 4 to 8 pm. There's a special foreigners' counter, where the staff speak English and issue tickets with a minimum of fuss. Bus Nos 1 and 2 go past the office.

Bus The long-distance bus station is on Heilongjiang Lu. The departure time given on your ticket is normally Beijing time; check if you're not sure. There are buses for most cities in Xinjiang. Here, a 100% foreigners' surcharge is added to the price of tickets, which is a complete scam – you'll still be sitting on the same crowded, ramshackle contraption as the locals.

An interesting option is the Almaty (ālāmùtú) bus service. The 1052-km trip takes 24 hours straight through with three stops for meals, and costs US$60. A visa for Kazakstan is needed and the Chinese government might require that you get an exit permit at the PSB. Check at window No 8 in the bus station for the latest on this service.

The most popular destinations within Xinjiang are Turpan, Korla, Kuqa and Kashgar. For both Turpan and Kashgar, there are alternative bus stations. Large public buses and more comfortable minibuses to Turpan also run from the Erdaoqiao Market. If you're heading to Kashgar, you can get a sleeper bus from the Kashgar bus station, which is just east of the railway station.

It is possible to travel all the way to Dunhuang by bus, but not easily and not comfortably. Travel first to Hami, and from there to Liuyuan. From Liuyuan you can take another bus to Dunhuang.

Train From Ürümqi there are eastbound express trains six times daily. All of these trains run on the same line until Lanzhou, after which they take different routes to their various destinations.

Destination	Train No	Departure Time
Shanghai	54	4.53 pm
Beijing	70	2.50 pm
Zhengzhou	98	8.24 pm
Chengdu	114	12.45 pm
Xi'an	144	10.08 pm
Lanzhou	244	6.26 pm

There is intense competition for tickets at the railway station, where the market has been cornered by a variety of touts both inside and outside the system. Try to book as far in advance as possible and join the queue before 8 am. If all else fails, head down to CYTS in the Hongshan Hotel.

There is a rail link between Ürümqi and Korla via Daheyan (Turpan Railway Station). At present, only 500-series trains (hard seat only) run on this route, which may be scenic but is hardly worth 16 hours of hard-seat travel. See the Korla section later in this chapter for the schedule.

See the Getting There & Away chapter in the front of the book for information about the train between Ürümqi and Kazakstan. You will, of course, need a visa for Kazakstan, and these cannot be arranged in Xinjiang. Lonely Planet also publishes a *Central Asia* guide.

Getting Around

To/From the Airport Minibuses depart from the CAAC office about two hours before flight time and cost Y8. Public bus No 51 goes to the airport – this is the cheapest but slowest way.

The airport is 20 km from the CAAC office. Taxis congregate at the CAAC office and ask about Y60 for the trip. Minibuses greet all incoming flights and cost Y6.

Bus Ürümqi's public buses are packed to the roof and beyond. It's much wiser to spend a big Y1 for a minibus. If you resort to the public buses, be warned that there have been numerous reports of pickpocketing and bag slashing.

AROUND ÜRÜMQI

Tianchi
(tiānchí)

Tianchi (Lake of Heaven) is a sight you'll never forget. Halfway up a mountain in the middle of a desert, it looks like a chunk of Switzerland or Canada that's been exiled to western China. The small, deep-blue lake is surrounded by hills covered with fir trees and grazed by horses. Scattered around are the yurts of the Kazak people who inhabit the mountains; in the distance are the snow-covered peaks of the Tianshan range, and you can climb the hills right up to the snow line.

The lake is 115 km east of Ürümqi at an elevation of 1980 metres. Nearby is the 5445-metre-high Bogda Feng, the Peak of God – it can be climbed by well-equipped mountaineers with permits (ask CITS). The lake freezes over in Xinjiang's bitter winter and the roads up here are open only in the summer months – a pity, since it would make an excellent place for ice-skating.

There are boat cruises on the lake. The other possibility, of course, is to hike into the hills and go camping – it's a great opportunity, and a rare one in China. The surrounding countryside is absolutely stunning. Follow the track skirting the lake for about four km to the far end and walk up the valley. During the summer, Kazaks set up yurts in this area for tourist accommodation at Y20 per person. Horses are also offered (at Y100 per day) for a trek to the snow line. The return trek takes 10 hours. Water is best taken from the spring gushing straight out of the mountain at the edge of the lake rather than further up the valley where humans and livestock have contributed to the liquid.

The *Heavenly Lake Hotel (tiānchí zhāo-dàisuǒ)* on the banks of the lake is a garish building utterly out of place compared with the blues and greens of the surroundings. There are dorm beds for Y60.

The first buses to Tianchi leave Ürümqi at around 9 am from both the north and south gates of Renmin Park – the north side is more convenient if you're staying at the Hongshan Hotel. Departures are from where the sign says (in English) 'Taxi Service'. Buy your ticket about 30 minutes ahead of time to ensure getting a seat, though you can buy advance tickets from CYTS in the Hongshan Hotel. There are about 10 buses daily and the trip takes over three hours. The bus will probably drop you off at the end of the lake – from there it's a 20-minute walk to the hotel on the banks. The last bus back to Ürümqi leaves at around 4 pm from a bus park just over a low ridge at the back of the hotel.

If you stay overnight you'll have the place pretty much to yourself in the morning and after 4 pm, since most people only come here on day-trips. Some people have hitched on trucks to the lake.

A one-way ticket costs Y15 or Y20 depending on which class of bus.

No 1 Glacier
(yīhào bīngchuān)

Aside from Tianchi, the Tianshan Mountains dish up a few other scenic surprises, including the No 1 Glacier. The translucent bluish ice is the main source of the Ürümqi River. A visit to the glacier is good fun, but is only feasible in summer.

The No 1 Glacier is 120 km east of Ürümqi. There is no regular bus service, so some sort of minibus rental will be required. You should be able to round up some enthusiastic travellers at the Hongshan Hotel and also book a minibus there.

Baiyanggou
(báiyánggōu)

Baiyanggou, also known as the Southern Mountains *(nánshān)*, is a vast expanse of grazing land set in a valley surrounded by snow-capped peaks. The valley is 2100 metres above sea level and 75 km south of Ürümqi. The land is inhabited by Kazak herdsmen who graze sheep, cattle and horses here during the summer months.

Though not quite as stunning as Tianchi, it's nevertheless a beautiful place. The upper end of the valley is most impressive – surrounded by spruce trees is a waterfall with a drop of 40 metres.

Curious stories have been told of the gangs of Hong Kong Chinese who come here by the minibusload. Unused to vast open spaces or to the sight of animals almost in the wild, they leap from the bus and charge at the unsuspecting creatures, who scatter in all directions. A distraught Kazak herdsman usually rides up waving his arms in the air and shouting abuse, and must be placated by the tour guide with apologies and cigarettes.

It's a 1½-hour ride from Ürümqi. The directions for getting a bus are the same as for Tianchi – at the north and south gates of Renmin Park in Ürümqi there are buses departing at approximately 9 am from where the sign says 'Taxi Service'.

It is possible to stay up in the pasturelands at some of the Kazak yurts.

HAMI
(hāmì)

The town of Hami is a small oasis at the remotest end of China. Known in the past as Kumul, it was once an important caravan stop on the northern route of the Silk Road. Hami's most famous product is the delicious Hami melon *(hāmì guā)*, highly prized by thirsty train passengers who scramble to buy them during the short stop at Hami Railway Station. You can also buy these melons in Turpan.

There are reportedly buses running from Hami to Liuyuan in Gansu Province, making this an interesting alternative route to Dunhuang.

DAHEYAN
(dàhéyán)

The jumping-off point for Turpan is a place on the railway line signposted 'Turpan

Zhan' *(tǔlǔfān zhàn)*. In fact, you are actually in Daheyan, and the Turpan oasis is a 58-km drive south across the desert. Daheyan is not a place you'll want to hang around, so spare a thought for the locals, who have to eke out a sane living here.

The bus station is a five-minute walk from the railway station. Walk up the road leading from the railway station and turn right at the first main intersection; the bus station is a few minutes' walk ahead on the left-hand side of the road. Minibuses run from here to Turpan about once every 30 minutes throughout the day. The fare is Y10 for the trip, which takes 1½ hours.

Although Daheyan Railway Station is never crowded, buying a ticket to anywhere can be a slow process here. The sleepy staff need about 10 minutes to sell each ticket. If six persons are in line ahead of you, it's going to take an hour – bring a Walkman or something to read.

Most travellers are interested in the trains heading east, since people going westward from Turpan usually travel direct by bus to Ürümqi. All express trains going east go as far as Lanzhou, from where they then diverge to other destinations in China. Avoid train No 404, which is a slow local and will only get you as far as Yumen (east of Dunhuang). The schedule of eastbound trains from Daheyan is as follows:

Destination	Train No	Departure Time
Shanghai	54	7.57 pm
Beijing	70	5.57 pm
Zhengzhou	98	11.22 pm
Chengdu	114	4.09 pm
Xi'an	144	1.24 am
Lanzhou	244	10.07 pm
Yumen	404	2.12 am

The train from Daheyan to Ürümqi takes three hours, to Liuyuan takes 13 hours, to Jiayuguan takes 19 hours and to Lanzhou takes 37 hours.

Some (not many) travellers are interested in the train from Daheyan to Korla. It departs from Daheyan once daily at 10.57 pm and it's hard-seat only.

TURPAN
(tǔlǔfān)

East of Ürümqi the Taishan mountains split into a southern and a northern range; between the two lie the Hami and Turpan basins. Both are below sea level and receive practically no rain; summers are searingly hot. Part of the Turpan Basin is 154 metres below sea level – the lowest spot in China and the second-lowest depression in the world (after the Dead Sea).

Turpan County is inhabited by about 170,000 people: about 120,000 are Uighurs and the rest mostly Chinese. The centre of the county is the large Turpan oasis. It's little more than a few main streets set in a vast tract of grain fields, and more importantly it's been spared the architectural horrors that have been inflicted on Ürümqi. Most of the streets are planted with trees and are lined with mud-brick walls enclosing mud houses. Open channels with flowing water run down the sides of the streets; the inhabitants draw water from these and use them to wash their clothes, dishes and themselves in.

Of the major towns in Xinjiang visited by foreigners, Turpan and Kashgar remain closest to traditional Uighur culture; Ürümqi and Shihezi are Chinese settlements. Turpan also holds a special place in Uighur history, since nearby Gaochang was once the capital of the Uighurs. It was an important staging post on the Silk Road and was a centre of Buddhism before being converted to Islam in the 8th century. During the Chinese occupation it served as a garrison town.

Turpan is a quiet place (one of the few in China) and some guesthouses provide good spots to sit underneath the vine trellises and contemplate the moon and stars. The living is cheap, the food is good and the people are friendly, and there are numerous interesting sights scattered around to keep you occupied. It's one of the increasingly rare places in China where you can relax and withdraw a bit from the tensions of crowded trains, buses and noisy cities.

Turpan is the hottest spot in China – the highest recorded temperature here was 49.6°C. Fortunately, the humidity is low – so low that your laundry is practically dry by the time you get it hung up!

Orientation

The centre of the Turpan oasis is little more than a few main roads and a couple of side streets. You'll find the shops, market, long-distance bus station, tourist hotels and a couple of plodding donkey carts all within easy walking distance of each other. The centre is called 'Old City' *(lǎochéng)* and the western part is called 'New City' *(xīnchéng)*. Most of the sights are scattered on the outskirts of the oasis or in the surrounding desert.

Information

CITS (☎ 522-768) has a branch in the Oasis Hotel. The PSB is on Gaochang Lu, north of the Gaochang Hotel.

The most convenient place to change money is at the Oasis Hotel. There is also a Bank of China about 10 minutes' walk from the hotel. The post office is right near the bus station and the bazaar. More convenient is the post office inside the Oasis Hotel – they can handle parcels.

Bazaar
(nóngmào shìchǎng)

This is one of the most fascinating markets in China – only Kashgar's can match it. You'll find lots of exotica on sale, including brightly decorated knives, Muslim clothing, delicious flat-bread, goats (both living and cooked) and unusual fruits. Bargaining is expected, but it's mostly good-natured, not the usual tug of war experienced elsewhere in China.

The market is across from the bus station, within walking distance of all the hotels. Most travellers visit here the day before heading out on the minibus tours. It's a good place for stocking up on munchies – raisins and peanuts mixed together make good travelling food.

City Mosque
(qīngzhēn sì)

There are several mosques in town. The City Mosque, the most active of them, is on the

THE NORTH & NORTH-WEST

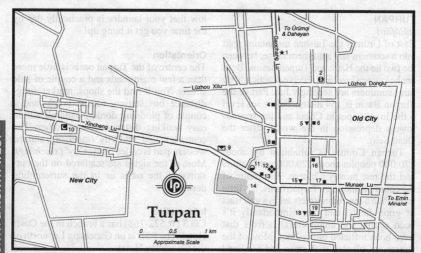

To Ürümqi & Daheyan

Gaochang Lu

Lůzhou Xilu

Lůzhou Donglu

Old City

Xincheng Lu

New City

Munaer Lu

To Emin Minaret

Turpan

0   0.5   1 km

Approximate Scale

western outskirts about three km from the town centre. Take care not to disturb the worshippers. You can get here by bicycle.

Emin Minaret
(émǐn tǎ)

Also known as Sugongta, this tower and adjoining mosque is just three km from Turpan on the eastern outskirts of town. It's designed in a simple Afghani style and was built in the late 1770s by a local ruler. The minaret is circular, 44 metres high and tapers towards the top. The temple is bare inside, but services are held every Friday and on holidays.

You could possibly walk or bicycle here from the Turpan Guesthouse, but most people stop here on a minibus tour. Turn left out of the guesthouse and left again at the first crossroad; this road leads straight down to the mosque. There is a hole in the wall at the side of the mosque so you can get into the main building. If you want to climb the minaret you'll have to ask the keeper to unlock the door to the stairway; he lives in the small whitewashed building beside the mosque.

Places to Stay

The *Turpan Guesthouse* (☎ 522-301; fax 523262) *(tǔlǔfān bīnguǎn)* gets the nod for sumptuous surroundings. However, the staff seem to take great pleasure in fining foreigners who pick the grapes (Y50 a time!) – it doesn't stop them grabbing handfuls for themselves. The shade of the vine trellises is a good place to sit while saturating yourself with beer or cold drinks (try the watermelon juice). Rates are Y50 for a dormitory bed and Y100 to Y240 for a double.

The *Gaochang Hotel* (☎ 523229) *(gāochāng bīnguǎn)* is currently the best deal in town. A double with attached bath and air-con costs a mere Y42. There are two problems – these low prices will probably not last, and also there are not enough rooms to accommodate the large numbers of tourists during the summer.

The *Oasis Hotel* (☎ 522-478) *(lǜzhōu bīnguǎn)* is the main tourist hotel in Turpan. Dorm beds cost Y21, while doubles go for Y260.

The *Grain Trade Hotel* (☎ 522-448) *(liángmào bīnguǎn)* only opened in 1994 and is already falling apart. It must be made out of cornflakes. If you don't mind that, dorms

TURPAN 吐鲁番

PLACES TO STAY

4 Gaochang Hotel & Turpan Museum
高昌宾馆，吐鲁番博物馆
6 Oasis Hotel & CITS
绿洲宾馆，中国国际旅行社
7 Tulufan Hotel
吐鲁番饭店
8 Olympic Hotel
奥林匹克大酒店
13 Jiaotong Hotel
交通宾馆
16 Yiyuan Hotel
颐园宾馆
17 Grain Trade Hotel
粮贸宾馆
19 Turpan Guesthouse
吐鲁番宾馆

PLACES TO EAT

5 Silk Road Restaurant
丝路酒家
15 Chuanbei & Lanxin Restaurants
川北餐厅，兰新餐厅
18 John's Information & Cafe
约翰中西餐厅

OTHER

1 PSB
公安馆
2 Bank of China
中国银行
3 Night Market
夜市
9 Post Office
邮局
10 City Mosque
清真寺
11 Long-Distance Bus Station
长途汽车站
12 Department Store
百货商店
14 Bazaar
农贸市场

without attached bath are Y20, or Y40 to Y60 with bath. Doubles with private bath are Y120.

Just around the corner is the *Yiyuan Hotel* (☎ 522-170) (*yíyuán bīnguǎn*). It's a small but friendly place. Beds in a double with attached bath cost Y40.

The *Tulufan Hotel* (☎ 522-336) (*tǔlǔfān fàndiàn*) is large but not terribly attractive. Dorm beds cost Y22 to Y44, doubles cost Y80 to Y120 and suites cost Y260 to Y360.

The *Olympic Hotel* (☎ 521680) (*àolínpīkè dà jiǔdiàn*) is low standard but friendly and offers the cheapest dorms in town. The price per bed is Y11 to Y16. All rooms have shared bath.

The *Jiaotong Hotel* (☎ 523-238) (*jiāotōng bīnguǎn*) is right next to the bus station and market – a busy, noisy place. Doubles with attached bath cost Y60 or Y80.

Places to Eat

The night market opposite the Gaochang Hotel is worth a look in the evening for kebabs. The *Muslim Restaurant* inside the Gaochang Hotel itself is also not bad.

Opposite the Turpan Hotel is *John's Information & Cafe* (☎ 524237). This is the only place in town that does good Western food, but there are Chinese meals available too. The menu is in English, prices are reasonable and you can even get cold drinks with ice (much appreciated in Turpan's heat!).

Opposite the Oasis Hotel is the *Silk Road Restaurant* with a menu made up mainly of Chinese dishes with the occasional Muslim dish thrown in for good measure. The *Chuanbei Restaurant*, the neighbouring *Lanxin Restaurant* and other nearby restaurants are also good places to eat. A couple of the restaurants here have English menus and the staff are all very friendly.

Entertainment

A traditional Uighur music, song and dance show is staged in the courtyard of the *Turpan Guesthouse* under the trellises almost nightly in the tourist season (summer). Most of the singers and dancers are women, but there is usually at least one man. During the summer, the shows are held almost every night from around 10 pm. They're fun nights that usually end up with the front row of the audience being dragged out to dance with the performers. Admission to the performance costs Y20.

Things to Buy

The market has a good selection of Uighur handicrafts – the ornate knives are particularly well crafted. The tourist souvenir shops in Turpan are an absurd rip-off – you pay 10 times the going rate. The large number of Japanese tour groups has helped to ramp up prices.

Getting There & Away

Bus The bus station is near the market. Make sure you get to the station an hour before departure, because there is invariably a long queue for tickets. The Uighurs are even worse than the Chinese about standing in line, but Turpan employs an 'enforcer' to keep order – if only more stations would do this! There are buses from here to Ürümqi and to Daheyan.

There are at least four large buses daily to Ürümqi plus private minibuses about once every hour. Foreigners are charged double, though you can often manage to pay less with a student card or some other ID with your photograph (try a driver's licence).

It's great scenery along the route to Ürümqi – immense grey sand dunes, and snow-capped mountains visible in the distance. The 180-km trip takes four hours.

Minibuses to Daheyan run approximately once every 30 minutes throughout the day and take 1½ hours for the trip.

Train The nearest railway station is at Daheyan, 58 km north of Turpan. There are trains going east and west, but most travellers will only want to use the eastbound ones since direct buses to Ürümqi are faster and more convenient than the train. See the previous Daheyan section for the train schedule.

Getting Around

Public transport around Turpan is by minibus, bicycle or donkey cart. Bicycles are most convenient for the town itself. The only place hiring bicycles is the Turpan Guesthouse. Bikes here cost Y15 per day. Minibus

drivers usually hang around the hotel gates – negotiate the fare in advance. Donkey carts can be found around the market, but this mode of transport is gradually fading.

AROUND TURPAN

There are many sights in the countryside around Turpan, and it requires at least a day to see everything of importance.

The only way to see the sights is to hire a minibus for a full day (about 10 hours). You won't have to look for them – the drivers will come looking for you. It's easy to find other travellers to share the expense. Figure on spending Y300 to Y500 (depending on bargaining) for the whole group. The minibuses normally hold six passengers; any more than eight would be uncomfortable. Make sure it's clearly understood which places you want to see. A typical trip should include the Atsana Graves, Gaochang Ruins, Bezeklik Caves, Grape Valley, Emin Minaret, Karez underground irrigation channels and Jiaohe Ruins (usually in that order).

Practically no drivers speak English, but many speak fluent Japanese – they know which side of the bread is buttered. Be forewarned that some drivers are bad news – they may try to rush you or skip some of the places you want to see – but most are OK. The driver we had last time was great, and we wound up buying him lunch, cold drinks and a large watermelon as a parting gift.

Don't underestimate the weather. The desert sun is hot – damn hot – and it can bake your brain in less time than it takes to make fried rice. Essential survival gear includes a water bottle, sunglasses and straw hat. Some UV lotion and Vaseline (or Chapstick) for your lips will prove useful.

There are admission fees to a few of the sites – most cost less than Y20.

Atsana Graves

(āsītǎnà gǔmùqū)

These graves, where the dead of Gaochang are buried, lie north-west of the ancient city. Only three of the tombs are open to tourists, and each of these is approached by a short flight of steps which leads down to the burial

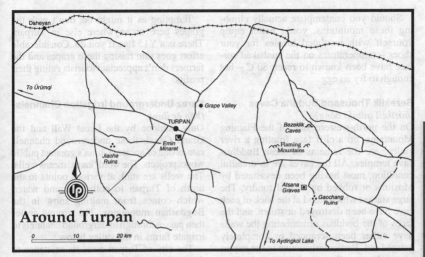

Around Turpan

0   10   20 km

chamber about six metres below ground level.

One tomb contains portraits of the deceased painted on the walls, while another has paintings of birds. The third tomb holds two well-preserved corpses (one mummy from the original trio seems to have been removed to Turpan's museum) like those in the museums at Ürümqi and Hangzhou. Some of the artefacts date back as far as the Jin Dynasty, from the 3rd to 5th centuries AD. The finds include silks, brocades, embroideries and many funerary objects, such as shoes, hats and sashes made of recycled paper. The last turned out to be quite special for archaeologists, since the paper included deeds, records of slave purchases, orders for silk and other everyday transactions.

Gaochang Ruins
(gāochāng gùchéng)

About 46 km east of Turpan are the ruins of Gaochang, the capital of the Uighurs when they moved into the Xinjiang region from Mongolia in the 9th century. The town was originally founded in the 7th century during the Tang Dynasty and became a major staging post on the Silk Road.

The walls of the city are clearly visible. They stood as much as 12 metres thick, formed a rough square with a perimeter of six km, and were surrounded by a moat. Gaochang was divided into an outer city, an inner city within the walls, and a palace and government compound. A large monastery in the south-western part of the city is in reasonable condition, with some of its rooms, corridors and doorways still preserved.

Flaming Mountains
(huǒyànshān)

North of Gaochang lie the aptly named Flaming Mountains – they look like they're on fire in the midday sun. Purplish-brown in colour, they are 100 km long and 10 km wide. The minibus tours don't usually include a stop here, but they drive through on the way to Bezeklik Caves.

The Flaming Mountains were made famous in Chinese literature by the classic novel *Journey to the West*. The story is about the monk Xuan Zang and his followers who travelled west in search of the Buddhist sutra. The mountains were a formidable barrier which they had to cross.

Should you contemplate actually climbing these mountains, you'd better equip yourself with insulated insoles for your shoes – temperatures on the sunbaked surface have been known to reach 80°C – hot enough to fry an egg.

Bezeklik Thousand Buddha Caves
(bózīkèlǐ qiānfó dòng)

On the north-western side of the Flaming Mountains, on a cliff face fronting a river valley, are the remains of these Buddhist cave temples. All the caves are in dreadful condition, most having been devastated by Muslims or robbed by all and sundry. The large statues which stood at the back of each cave have been destroyed or stolen, and the faces of the buddhas ornamenting the walls have either been scrapped or completely gouged out. Particularly active in the export of murals was a German, Albert von Le Coq, who removed whole frescoes from the stone walls and transported them back to the Berlin Museum – where Allied bombing wiped most of them out during WW II. Today the caves reveal little more than a hint of what these works of art were like in their heyday.

Photography is forbidden inside the caves, but there isn't much reason to bother. Fortunately, the scenery just outside the caves is fine.

Grape Valley
(pútáo gōu)

In this small paradise – a thick maze of vines and grape trellises – stark desert surrounds you. Most of the minibus tours stop here for lunch – the food isn't bad, and there are plenty of grapes in season (early September is best). The children here are remarkably friendly and like to pose for photos – they don't ask any money for this so please don't turn them into beggars by offering anything.

There is a winery *(guǒjiǔchǎng)* near the valley and lots of well-ventilated brick buildings for drying grapes – wine and raisins are major exports of Turpan. CITS is trying to organise an annual 'grape festival' which they expect to hold during the third week of August.

Tempting as it might be, don't pick the grapes here or anywhere else in Turpan. There is a Y15 fine if you do. Considerable effort goes into raising these grapes and the farmers don't appreciate tourists eating their profits.

Karez Underground Irrigation Channels
(kǎn ěr jǐng)

Only outdone by the Great Wall and the Grand Canal, these underground channels rate as one of ancient China's greatest public works projects. The word 'karez' means wells. The wells are sunk at various points to the north of Turpan to collect ground water, which comes from melting snow in the Bogdashan mountains. The ground water then passes through underground channels to irrigate farms in the valley below.

The city of Turpan owes its existence to these vital wells and channels, some of which were constructed over 2000 years ago. Part of the channel system is on the surface, but putting them underground greatly reduces water loss from evaporation. They are fed entirely by gravity, thus eliminating the need for pumps. There are over a thousand wells, and the total length of the channels exceeds 3000 km. It's remarkable to think that this extensive irrigation system was all constructed by hand and without modern machinery or building materials.

There are a number of places to view the channels, but most of the minibus tours stop at one particular spot on the west side of Turpan. Unfortunately, there are a few children here who ask foreigners for money.

Jiaohe Ruins
(jiāohé gùchéng)

During the Han Dynasty, Jiaohe was established by the Chinese as a garrison town to defend the borderlands. The city was decimated by Genghis Khan's 'travelling road show' but you'd be forgiven if you thought it had been struck by an A-bomb. The buildings are rather more obvious than the ruins of Gaochang though, and you can walk through the old streets and along the roads. A main road cuts through the city, and at the end is a large monastery with figures of Buddha still visible.

The ruins are around seven to eight km west of Turpan and stand on an island bound by two small rivers – thus the name Jiaohe, which means 'confluence of two rivers'. During the cooler months it is possible to cycle out here without any problem.

Sand Therapy Clinic
(shā liáo zhàn)

Over 5000 people a year – mostly Kazaks – come to Turpan to get buried up to their necks in the sand. It is believed that the hot sand can greatly relieve the aches of rheumatism. The Sand Therapy Clinic is pretty much an outdoor sandbox, and it only operates from June to August. There's not much to see here and the minibuses usually don't include this as part of your tour except by special request. If you're plagued by rheumatism, you might want to give this therapy a try.

Aydingkol Salt Lake
(àidīng hú)

At the very bottom of the Turpan depression is Aydingkol Lake, 154 metres below sea level. The 'lake' usually has little water – it's a huge, muddy evaporating pond with a surface of crystallised salt, but technically it's the second-lowest lake in the world, surpassed only by the Dead Sea in Israel and Jordan.

Most of the tours do not stop here. If you want to see Aydingkol Lake, tell your driver and expect to pay extra for the additional distance.

SHIHEZI
(shíhézi)

A couple of hours' drive north-west of Ürümqi is the town of Shihezi, or Stony Creek. It's a Chinese outpost and almost all the inhabitants are Han. The town is officially open to foreigners, but it looks so boring that even a statue would pack up and leave town. The bus between Ürümqi and Yining passes through here.

KORLA
(kùěrlè)

Korla was an important junction on the old Silk Road. The famous travelling monk Xuan Zang paid an obligatory visit in the 7th century. These days it's most used by travellers as a transit point, though there are a couple of things to see in the vicinity.

The town of Yanqi, 52 km north of Korla (reachable by rail or bus), has some nearby Buddhist caves. However, the prime attraction is Bosten Lake (bósīténg hú), the largest lake in Xinjiang. From Yanqi to the lakeside centre of Bohu is about 12 km. Access to the lake from Bohu could involve a mud-wading expedition, but the fishing villages can be worth visiting.

Bosten Lake receives most of its water from the Peacock River (kǒngquè hé), which passes through a gap between two mountains known as the Iron Door (tiě mén).

Prices charged for transport can be as high as Y150 per day for a motorised three-wheeler – bargaining is advised.

Places to Stay

The Loulan Hotel (lóulán bīnguǎn) is a one-star hotel and the favourite of backpackers. Dorms begin at Y20 per bed.

The Bosten Hotel (bósīténg bīnguǎn) and Bayinguoleng Hotel (bayinguoleng bīnguǎn) both fall in the two-star range.

Getting There & Away

Air There are five flights weekly between Ürümqi and Korla. A flight you are very unlikely to use runs between Korla and the outpost of Qiemo (Jumo) in the southern end of Xinjiang. There are occasional (summer only) flights between Korla and Kuqa.

Bus Korla is 470 km from Ürümqi and the bus ride takes a full day. There are sleeper buses between Korla and Ürümqi, making an overnight trip feasible and comfortable.

There are also bus connections with Daheyan (Turpan Railway Station) and Yining.

Train A rail line links Korla with Ürümqi via Daheyan (Turpan Railway Station), but there

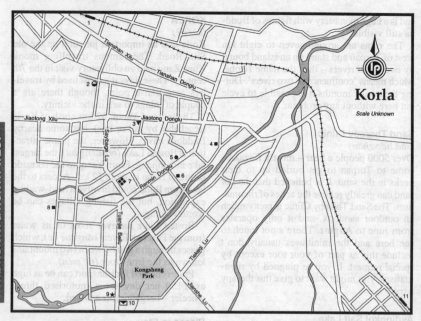

Korla

Scale Unknown

is only one train daily in each direction. Train No 512 departs Ürümqi at 7.18 pm, stops in Daheyan at 10.57 pm and arrives in Korla the following day at 11.23 am. Train No 511 departs Korla at 6.14 pm and arrives in Ürümqi the following morning at 10.30 am.

Now for the bad news – it's hard-seat only on this train. Unless you want to endure 16 hours of hard-seat hell, consider taking the bus.

KUQA
(kùchē)

On the Silk Road between Turpan and Kashgar lies Kuqa. Scattered around the Kuqa region are at least seven Thousand Buddha Caves (qiānfó dòng) which rival those of Dunhuang, Datong and Luoyang. There are also at least four ancient ruined cities in the area.

Modern-day Kuqa can be sectioned into an old city and a much newer Chinese part of town. The Buddhist cave paintings and ruined cities in the area are remains of a pre-Islamic Buddhist civilisation. When the

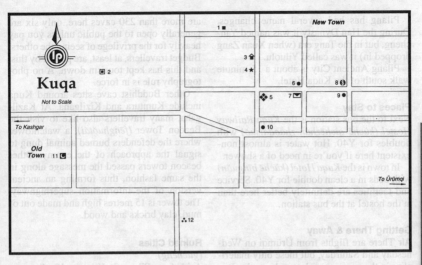

KUQA 库车

1 Kuqa Hotel
库车宾馆
2 Molana Eshding Tomb
默拉纳额什丁麻扎
3 Old Cadre Hostel
旧干部招待所
4 PSB
公安局

5 Xinhua Department Store
新华商行
6 City Hall
市政府
7 Post & Telephone Office
邮电局
8 Industrial Commercial Bank
工商银行

9 Xinhua Bookstore
新华书店
10 Market
市场
11 Grand Mosque
清真大寺
12 Pilang Ancient City
皮朗古城

7th century Chinese monk Xuan Zang passed through Kuqa he recorded that the city's western gate was flanked by two enormous 30-metre-high Buddha statues and that there were numerous monasteries decorated with beautiful Buddhist frescoes in the area. Twelve hundred years later, the German archaeologist-adventurers Grünwedel and Le Coq removed many of these paintings and sculptures and took them to Berlin.

Molana Eshding Tomb
(mòlānà éshídīng mázā)
Sandwiched between the old town and new town of Kuqa, this place is also known as the

Molana Hoja Tomb. Eshding is credited with being the first Islamic missionary from the Middle East to visit Kuqa. The name 'Molana' means 'the sage's descendants'.

Eshding died in Kuqa from unknown causes, and his tomb is a fairly nice work of art. The four large Chinese characters on the tomb mean 'the Arabian sages'.

Pilang Ancient City
(pílǎng gǔchéng)
These ruins are all that is left of the ancient capital of Qiuci. Qiuci was one of several ancient feudal states in what was once loosely called the Western Region of China.

Pilang has had several name changes. During the Han Dynasty it was named Yancheng, but in the Tang era (when Xuan Zang dropped in) it was called Yiluolu.

Pilang Ancient City is about a 15-minute walk south of the Kuqa Hotel.

Places to Stay

Next to the bus station is the *Kuqa Railway Hostel (kùchē qìchēzhàn zhāodàisuǒ)* with doubles for Y40. Hot water is almost non-existent here if you're in need of a shower.

In town is the *Kuqa Hotel (kùchē bīnguǎn)* with beds in a clean double for Y40. Service and facilities are definitely better here than at the hostel at the bus station.

Getting There & Away

Air There are flights from Ürümqi on Wednesday and Saturday, but these only materialise in the summer peak travel months. It is not possible to fly onwards from Kuqa to Kashgar, so you'll have to backtrack to Ürümqi for this.

Bus Buses from Ürümqi to Kuqa require around 1½ days' travel, though only one day from Korla. There are sleeper buses between Ürümqi and Kuqa, the preferred way to go. From Kuqa it's another 1½ days on to Kashgar by bus. There are also buses to Yining.

Getting Around

Kuqa's sights are scattered around the surrounding countryside, and the only way to get to see them is to hire a vehicle. The 3rd floor of the Government Building *(zhèngfǔ dàlóu)* in the centre of town has a branch of CITS, where you can hire a car for the day. Local private entrepreneurs are cheaper.

AROUND KUQA

Kizil Thousand Buddha Caves
(kèzīěr qiānfó dòng)

There are quite a lot of Thousand Buddha Caves around Kuqa, but the most important site is this one, around 70 km to the west of Kuqa in Baicheng County. The caves date back to the 3rd century AD. Although there

are more than 230 caves here, only six are generally open to the public unless you pay heavily for the privilege of seeing the others. Budget travellers, at least, are put off by this, and this has kept tourism down. A no photography rule is in force.

Other Buddhist cave sites around Kuqa include Kumtura and Kizilgaha. At Kizilgaha, many travellers also like to visit the Beacon Tower *(fēnghuǒtái)*, a watchtower where the defenders burned animal dung to signal the approach of the enemy. Other beacon towers passed the message along in the same fashion, thus forming an ancient version of the information superhighway. The tower is 15 metres high and made out of mud, clay bricks and wood.

Ruined Cities
(gùchéng)

Aside from Pilang (in Kuqa itself), there are several other ruined cities in the area. Around 23 km to the north-east of Kuqa is the ancient city of Subashi. About 20 km to the south of Kuqa is the ancient city of Wushkat. About 60 km south-west of Kuqa is Tonggusibashi, one of the largest and best preserved of the ruined cities.

KASHGAR
(kāshí)

Kashgar is a giant oasis near the westernmost tip of China. It experiences blistering hot summers, though at 1290 metres above sea level it's cooler than Turpan. A thousand years ago Kashgar was a key centre on the Silk Road, and when Marco Polo passed through he commented that:

The inhabitants live by trade and industry. They have fine orchards and vineyards and flourishing estates. Cotton grows here in plenty, besides flax and hemp. The soil is fruitful and productive of all the means of life. The country is the starting-point from which many merchants set out to market their wares all over the world.

History

In the early part of this century, Kashgar was a relatively major town on the edge of a vast

THE NORTH & NORTH-WEST

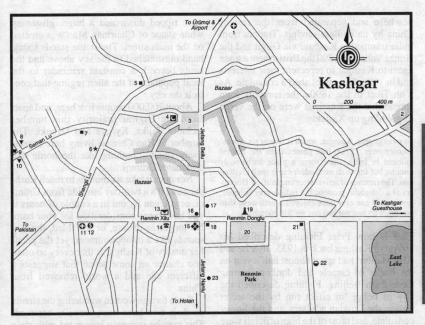

nowhere and separated from the rest of China by an endless sandpit. Traders from India tramped to Kashgar via Gilgit and the Hunza Valley; in 1890 the British sent a trade agent to Kashgar to represent their interests and in 1908 they established a consulate. As with Tibet in the 1890s, the rumours soon spread that the Russians were on the verge of gobbling up Xinjiang.

To most people, Kashgar, which is five or six weeks' journey over 15,000-foot passes from the nearest railhead in India, must seem a place barbarously remote; but for us its outlandish name spelt civilisation. The raptures of arrival were unqualified. Discovery is a delightful process, but rediscovery is better; few people can ever have enjoyed a bath more than we did, who had not had one for 5½ months.

That is how Peter Fleming described his arrival in Kashgar back in 1935, after he and Kini Maillart had spent almost half a year on the backs of camels and donkeys getting there from Beijing. Fleming described the city as being 'in effect run by the secret police, the Russian advisers, and the Soviet consulate, and most of the high officials were only figureheads'. The rest of the foreign community consisted of the British Consul and his wife, their 15 Hunza guards from the north of Pakistan and a couple of Swedish missionaries.

Rumours, and also banquets, seemed to be at their most eccentric in Kashgar. Fleming describes his last night there at a banquet given by the city officials:

...half in their honour and half in ours...You never know what may happen at a banquet in Kashgar and each of our official hosts had prudently brought his own bodyguard. Turkic and Chinese soldiers lounged everywhere; automatic rifles and executioner's swords were much in evidence, and the Mauser pistols of the waiters knocked ominously against the back of your chair as they leant over you with the dishes. Speeches made by just about everyone were feverishly translated into English, Russian, Chinese and Turkish, and no-one was assassinated.

The Kashgar of today has lost much of the 'romantic' value that made eating there in the '30s a slightly nervous experience. When the Communists came to power the city walls were ripped down and a huge, glistening white statue of Chairman Mao was erected on the main street. The statue stands today, hand outstretched to the sky above and the lands beyond, a constant reminder to the local populace of the alien regime that controls the city.

About 200,000 people live here, and apart from the Uighur majority this number includes Tajiks, Kyrgyz and Uzbeks. The number of Han Chinese living here is relatively small – nothing like the horde that dominates Ürümqi.

Nor does it take six months to reach Kashgar now; it's a two-day bus ride from Ürümqi, or you can fly out in a couple of hours if you have more consideration for your bum. No longer as remote, or as fabled, the city sounds like a disappointment, yet the peculiar quality of Kashgar is that every so often you chance on some scene that suggests a different age and a world removed from China.

Some foreign women wandering the streets on their own have been sexually harassed. This may be remotely connected with style of dress or even the town's diet of bawdy films. Whatever the reason, it's best for women travellers to dress as would be appropriate in any Muslim country.

Information

CITS has an office in the Chini Bagh Hotel (☎ 225390), but the staff seem to have little understanding of the needs of individual travellers.

The PSB is on Shengli Lu.

Sunday Market

(xīngqīrì shìchǎng)

You should not miss the bumper market that takes place every Sunday on the eastern fringe of town. Hundreds of donkey carts, horse riders, pedestrians and animals thunder into town for a bargaining extravaganza.

Be especially careful of pickpockets and bag slashers here. Many travellers have lost passports and travellers' cheques here to razorblade artists.

Bazaar
(nóngmào shìchǎng)
Sundays excepted, the bazaar is the focus of activity in Kashgar. The main market street can be reached from the lanes opposite the Id Kah Square which run off the main north-south road. Kashgar is noted for the ornate knives sold in the bazaar and by hawkers in the streets. It's also a hat-making centre, and the northern end of the street is devoted entirely to stalls selling embroidered caps and fur-lined headgear. Blacksmiths pound away on anvils, colourful painted wooden saddles can be bought, and you can pick your dinner from a choice line-up of goats' heads and hoofs. Boots are a good buy at around Y35 per pair. The price varies with the size, shape and quality of the soles, and you should allow three days for them to be finished.

Old Asian men with long thick beards, fur overcoats and high leather boots swelter in the sun. The Muslim Uighur women here dress in skirts and stockings like the Uighur women in Ürümqi and Turpan, but there's a much greater prevalence of faces hidden behind veils of brown gauze. In the evening the Id Kah Square is a bustling marketplace, and numerous market streets lead off from the square.

Some of the best areas for walking are east of the main bazaar and north-west of the Id Kah Mosque. To the south of the centre is a large cluster of mud-brick houses covering a sort of plateau – it's worth a wander round.

Id Kah Mosque
(ài tí gǎ ér qīngzhēn sì)
The Id Kah Mosque is a stark contrast to the Chinese-style mosques in eastern cities like Xi'an. The Id Kah looks like it's been lifted out of Pakistan or Afghanistan, and has the central dome and flanking minarets which Westerners usually associate with a mosque. Prayer time is around 10 pm, though that may vary throughout the year. During the festival of Korban Bairam, usually held in September and October, pilgrims gather in front of the mosque and gradually twirl themselves into a frenzy of dancing which is

driven by wailing music from a small band perched on the mosque's portal.

Smaller mosques are scattered among the houses on the streets around the town centre.

Abakh Hoja Tomb
(xiāngfēi mù)
This strange construction is in the eastern part of the oasis. It looks something like a stubby, multicoloured miniature of the Taj Mahal, with green tiles on the walls and dome. To one side of the mosque is a large cemetery, with a rectangular base surmounted by fat, conical mud structures. The tomb is the burial place of Hidajetulla Hoja, a Muslim missionary and saint, and his 72 descendants. It's an hour's walk from the Kashgar Guesthouse but a reasonable trip by bicycle. The tomb lies on a side street off a long east-west road.

The Chinese call this place the Fragrant Concubine's Tomb *(xiāngfēi mù)* in honour of one daughter of the Hoja clan who was married to the emperor Qianlong. However, her body was later moved to Hebei Province and is not actually entombed here. It's said that she was forced to commit suicide in 1761 by Qianlong's mother, the empress dowager.

Renmin Park & Zoo
(rénmín gōngyuán, dòngwùyuán)
The park is a pleasant place in which to sit, but the zoo is depressing. The kindest thing you could do for some of the animals would be to shoot them. In front of the entrance to the park is Renmin Square and on the opposite side of the road is the massive white statue of Mao Zedong.

Places to Stay
The *Seman Hotel* (☎ 222-129) *(sèmǎn bīnguǎn)* is probably the best place to base yourself in Kashgar. It's in the former Soviet consulate on the western edge of town. A double with bath costs Y120 to Y180. A bed in the dormitory costs Y25 (only available during the summer months). Take a look at the sign outside which modestly points out that the 'Seman Hotel was appraised to be one of the 10 hotels famed for their best

service in the world in 1988'. The thing is that the locals actually believe it: 'Staying at the Seman Hotel? Yes, one of the best hotels in the world'.

The *People's Hotel* (☎ 223-373) *(rénmín fàndiàn)* has a central location and not much else going for it. Dorm beds are Y24, while doubles are Y146.

The other place in backpacker class is the *Tiannan Hotel* (☎ 222-211) *(tiānnán fàndiàn)* near the bus station. It's a bit of a dive, but it has bicycle hire, a laundry service and reasonably priced rooms. Dorms cost from Y10 to Y30 per bed. Doubles cost from Y60 to Y200.

The *Silk Road Hotel (sīlù fàndiàn)* on Seman Lu only operates during the summer months. Prices were not available because it was closed during the time of research, but it should be similar to the Seman Hotel.

The *Chini Bagh Hotel* (☎ 222103) *(qínībāhé bīnguǎn)* is probably the next best place to stay, though it gets very noisy in the summer months when it fills up with Pakistani traders. Dorms cost Y32 to Y52 per bed. Doubles with bathroom cost from Y164 to Y200. Western visitors, both male and female, have complained of sexual harassment from Pakistani guests at this hotel.

The *Kashgar Guesthouse* (☎ 222-363, 224-679; fax 224-954) *(kāshí gě'ěr bīnguǎn)* is the top-rated hotel in town and is up to the same good standard of any other basic Chinese tourist hotel further east. The problem with this place is that it's too far from the town centre – the main intersection is a good hour's walk away, and there's no bus. Now that donkey carts have been driven off the streets of Kashgar, it's not even possible to resort to this mode of transport. Doubles go for Y220.

Places to Eat

Opposite the Seman Hotel is *John's Information & Cafe* (☎ 224-186; fax 222-861), one of the best places to eat and also to get the lowdown on travelling around Kashgar and to Pakistan. John himself is a mine of information and offers competitive rates for minibus and 4WD hire.

There are plenty of other small restaurants around the Seman Hotel area – quality varies.

The *Oasis Cafe* in the Silk Road Hotel is another option, though it's gradually getting more expensive.

For a wide variety of Uighur foods, pop into the food market close to the Id Kah Mosque. There you can try shish kebab, rice with mutton, fried fish, samosa and fruit. To the left of the mosque is a teahouse with a balcony above the bustling crowds. Flatbread and shish kebab are sold at the huddle of stalls on the main road, just west of Renmin Square opposite the Mao statue. There are a couple of excellent ice-cream stalls here, too – selling very cold and very vanilla ice-cream. There are more ice-cream stalls in the Id Kah Square, and you should find eggs and roast chicken being sold near the main intersection at night.

Entertainment

There is an excellent traditional Uighur song and dance show performed nightly at the *Seman Hotel*; admission costs Y15. You can also entertain yourself at the Seman Hotel's swimming pool, which is open only during summer.

Things to Buy

Kashgar is the best place in Xinjiang to buy Uighur handicrafts – check out the bazaar for knives, hats and other local products. The souvenir shops in the hotels are rapacious – you have to engage in vociferous bargaining even for the postcards and maps!

Getting There & Away

Air There are daily flights from Kashgar to Ürümqi, but competition for seats can be keen. It seems more difficult to get a flight out of Kashgar than to get one from Ürümqi to Kashgar. The flight takes slightly under two hours.

The CAAC office (☎ 222-113) is on Jiefang Nanlu south of the Id Kah Mosque.

Bus There are buses from the Kashgar long-distance bus station to Aksu, Daheyan, Hotan, Kargilik, Makit, Maralbixi, Payziwat,

Ürümqi, Yakam, Yengisar and Yopuria. The Kashgar bus station, like its counterpart in Ürümqi, charges a 100% surcharge for foreigners' tickets. Oddly, their prices are even more expensive than Ürümqi's.

The daily bus to Ürümqi travels via Aksu, Korla and Toksun. Tickets can only be bought one day before departure and the bus is scheduled to depart Kashgar at 8 am. The trip takes two days on a sleeper bus, or three on the slower buses, which stop off for the night en route. The bus seat costs Y200 for foreigners, or pay Y365 for the more comfortable sleeper.

The bus to Turpan is an old rattletrap and not recommended. The trip takes three days and the bus actually dumps you in Daheyan, a small railway town 58 km from Turpan.

You won't have access to baggage stored on the roof of the bus during the trip, so take a small bag of essentials on board with you. Be warned that buses don't always run on schedule.

The road between Xinjiang and Tibet, one of the roughest in the world, passes through the disputed territory of Aksai Chin. This route is not officially open to foreigners; some have hitched unofficially from Lhasa to Kashgar in as little as 16 days, others have taken months. Plenty of foreigners have been fined travelling towards Lhasa from Kashgar, and the PSB's worries about safety are understandable in this instance. Lonely Planet's *Tibet* guide contains more details on this route, which should not be attempted without full preparations for high-altitude travel. At least two foreigners have died on this 'road': one was thrown from the back of a truck when it hit a pothole; the other died of a combination of hypothermia and altitude sickness, also while riding on the back of a truck.

The road connection between China and Pakistan via the Karakoram Highway is described later in this chapter.

Getting Around

To/From the Airport A CAAC bus meets incoming flights. Tell the conductor where you will be staying and the driver will drop you at the front door of your hotel, though you will be charged an extra Y2 for this service. Taxis want Y50 for the 11 km trip between the airport and the centre.

Other The city buses are of no use; to get around you have to walk or hire a bike. The most common transport in Kashgar is the bicycle. Donkey carts have been banned from the streets.

The Tiannan Hotel has bike hire, and John's Information & Cafe has some bikes. Check also at the Seman Hotel.

For jeep and minibus hire, the best place to inquire is John's Information & Cafe.

AROUND KASHGAR
Hanoi
(hànnuòyī gùchéng)

No, Xinjiang does not have a common border with Vietnam. The ruins of the ancient city of Hanoi lie about 30 km north-east of Kashgar. The town had its start about 1500 years ago, reached its zenith during the Tang and Song dynasties but was abandoned after the 11th century.

Several km north of Hanoi is the Mor Pagoda, a Buddhist structure that has all but crumbled into dust.

To get to Hanoi you'll have to hire a jeep. It's a rough ride to see mediocre rubble.

Three Immortals Buddhist Caves
(sānxiān dòng)

These Buddhist caves are on a sheer cliff on the south bank of the Qiakmakh River about 20 km north of Kashgar. There are three caves, one with frescos which are still discernible. Going to the caves makes a pleasant excursion, but it's not worth it just for the art.

KARAKORAM HIGHWAY
(zhōngbā gōnglù)

This highway over Khunjerab Pass (4800 metres) is the gateway to Pakistan. For centuries this route was used by caravans plodding down the Silk Road. Khunjerab means 'valley of blood', a reference to local bandits who took advantage of the terrain to plunder caravans and slaughter the merchants.

Nearly 20 years were required to plan, push, blast and level the present road between Islamabad and Kashgar; over 400 road-builders died. Facilities en route are being steadily improved, but take warm clothing, food and drink on board with you – once stowed on the roof of the bus your baggage will not be easily accessible.

Even if you don't wish to go to Pakistan, it's worth doing the trip up to Tashkurgan from Kashgar – there's plenty to see. From Kashgar, you first cross the Pamir Plateau (3000 metres), passing the foothills of Kongurshan (*gōnggé'ér shān*), which is 7719 metres high, and nearby Muztag-Atashan (*mùshìtǎgé shān*) at 7546 metres. The journey continues through stunning scenery: high mountain pastures with grazing camels and yaks tended by Tajiks who live in yurts. Some travellers have stayed in yurts beside Karakuri Lake (*kǎlākùlì hú*) at 3800 metres, close to both these mountains.

The last town on the Chinese side is Tashkurgan (*tǎshíkù ěrgān*) at 3600 metres. If you don't continue to Pakistan, you can spend the night here. Tashkurgan is a predominantly Tajik town which could be used as a base to explore the nearby ruined fort, local cemeteries and surrounding high country.

In Kashgar, you can rent jeeps to take you to Tashkurgan and bring you back the following day. John's Information & Cafe in Kashgar charges Y700 for a jeep that can carry four passengers. CITS also rents jeeps, but at twice the price.

Officially, the border is open on 15 April and closes on 31 October. However, the border can open late or close early depending on conditions at Khunjerab Pass. Travel formalities are performed at Sust, on the Pakistan border; the Chinese border post is at Tashkurgan. There are two police checkpoints between Tashkurgan and Kashgar.

In Tashkurgan, most travellers stay at the *Seman Hotel* (*sèmǎn bīnguǎn*), which charges Y31 per person in the dorm or Y90 for a single. The hotel is dirty, has no water and

food is expensive. The other main guesthouse is the *Ice Mountain Hotel* (*bīngshān bīnguǎn*), which is much the same. There is a third hotel in Tashkurgan with a Chinese name only – *Shiping Gongsi Lüshe*; it's a dump but has good food.

For further information, see the Getting There & Away chapter at the front of this book. Lonely Planet also publishes a separate guide, *Karakoram Highway*.

HOTAN
(hétián)

At a distance of around 1980 km south-west of Ürümqi by road (via Kashgar), Hotan is one of the remotest parts of Xinjiang. It is also in real desert country at the southern boundary of the Taklamakan Desert. Despite this, it is renowned for its temperate climate (by Xinjiang standards at least), not being subject to such extremes of seasonal temperatures as Turpan or Ürümqi.

Like Kuqa, the sights are spread around the surrounding countryside and are of the ruined city variety. Ten km to the west of town are the **Yurturgan Ruins** (*yuètègān yízhǐ*), the ancient capital of a pre-Islamic kingdom dating from the 3rd to 8th centuries AD. The **Malikurwatur Ruins** (*málìkèwǎtè gùchéng*) are 12 km south of town, and there are some temples and pagoda-like buildings a further 10 km to the south.

Hotan is renowned for its precious stones. Hotan jade is considered the finest in China. You can even see deposits of white jade along the Jade Dragon Kashgar River (*yùlóng kāshì hé*), which runs close to town.

Other local products include walnuts, silk and carpets. **Jiyaxiang** (*jíyǎxiāng*), a small town 11 km north-east of Hotan, still produces hand-woven carpets using looms. Most of the houses in town are tiny, family-run factories. In town itself, on the eastern bank of the Jade Dragon Kashgar River, just north of the road to Qiemo, is a carpet factory.

Places to Stay & Eat
The *Hotan No 1 Guesthouse* (*hétián dìqū dìyī zhāodàisuǒ*) has basic accommodation, as

well as few more-upmarket rooms. The CAAC office is here also. The other option is the *Hotan Guesthouse (hétián bīnguǎn)*, which is newer and probably more expensive than the No 1.

Visitors to Hotan are advised to take care with the local food. The meals available at both the hotels are reported to be fairly safe, but it's easy to get sick from eating the street food.

Getting There & Away
There are three flights weekly between Hotan and Ürümqi. Buses from Ürümqi to Hotan generally travel by way of Kashgar and can take as long as five days. It makes more sense to visit Hotan from Kashgar, which is a distance of 509 km. The trip takes one to two days, and buses from Kashgar depart at 8 am. One possibility might be to take a bus from Kashgar to Hotan and then fly back to Ürümqi.

Getting Around
Hiring a vehicle is the only way to get around Hotan's sights. There should be locals with vehicles for hire on the lookout for visiting foreigners. Failing this, try the bus station or the No 7 Bus Company *(dìqī yùnshū gōngsī)*.

YINING
(yíníng)
Also known as Gulja, Yining lies close to the border, about 700 km west of Ürümqi. It is the centre of the Ili Kazak Autonomous Prefecture.

On the death of Genghis Khan in 1227, his four sons inherited responsibility for the Mongol empire. Chaghatai, the second-eldest, took over a huge area which included Turkestan, Xinjiang and, further south, most of Khorasan. Chaghatai is said to have made his capital at Almalik, close to Yining in the valley of the Ili River.

The Ili Valley became an easy access point for invaders and later for the northern route of the Silk Road. Yining was occupied by the tsar's troops in 1876 during Yakub Beg's independent rule of Kashgaria. Five years

later, the Chinese cracked down on Yakub Beg and Yining was handed back by the Russians. In 1962 there were major Sino-Soviet clashes along the Ili River. In late 1986 the Chinese claimed to have shot six Soviet infiltrators.

Chinese appear uneasy here and warn against staying out after dark, when knives are fast and streets unsafe. The local Kazaks and Uzbeks can be a rough bunch (regularly drunk in the evenings and occasionally involved in street fights) but are very friendly towards foreigners, whom they put in a different category from those in authority.

In particular, now that there are direct bus and train services between Ürümqi and Almaty, there is no real overpowering reason to visit Yining itself. Unless, of course, you're the kind of traveller who revels in far-flung places where nothing seems to work – planes don't arrive, banks run out of money, telephones are perpetually out of order, government workers don't show up for work and much of the population is drunk. Indeed, it seems more like Russia than China.

Information
The PSB is two blocks from the Ili Hotel, near a big radio tower. The Bank of China is one block south of the Ili Hotel and the post office is right on the big traffic circle in the centre of town.

Architecture & Markets
Yining is a grubby place that has a few faded remnants of Russian architecture, but overall there's not much to the town itself. The Uighur Market near the Huacheng Hotel is mildly interesting. The street markets are famous for fruit (especially in August), carpets and leather (boots). The main attraction here is the local Uighur, Kazak and Uzbek culture.

It's worthwhile leaving the main streets to follow alleys which pass the occasional Russian-style house with carved window-frames, painted shutters and plaster peeling from ornate designs.

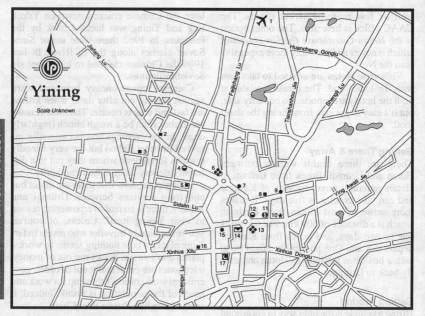

Yining

Scale Unknown

Places to Stay

Most budget travellers stay in the *Ili Hotel* (☎ 22794) *(yīlí bīnguǎn)* close to the bus station and the CAAC. The hotel features lovely, tree-shaded grounds, but the staff are incredibly lethargic. Dorms cost Y10 and doubles range from Y40 to Y80. Showers are available sometime in the evening and are turned off at 10 pm; buy shower tickets at the front desk for Y0.50.

The only other place worth considering is the *Friendship Hotel* (☎ 24631) *(yǒuyì bīnguǎn)*. It doesn't have all the nice trees of the Ili Hotel, but the rooms are very clean and the staff are not only conscious, but actually friendly! The dorms cost Y18 – there are two beds in each room and an attached bathroom. The main problem with the Friendship Hotel is that it's hard to find – it's down an obscure side street and the only sign pointing the way is in Chinese.

One other place accepts foreigners – the *Huacheng Hotel* (☎ 2911 ext 296) *(huāchéng*

bīnguǎn). Doubles are Y60 and the rooms look decent, but it's too far from everything and there are no cheap dorms.

Places to Eat

The *Ili Hotel* serves filling but unexciting set meals. Buy your meal ticket from the staff at the front desk. Lunch is served around 2 pm.

Go out the main gate of the Ili Hotel, turn right and walk for half a block – there's a small, unnamed restaurant on the left. There's good and cheap food, but lots of hot peppers. If you don't want it hot, say *'búyào làjiāo'*.

Food markets can be interesting places to eat. There's one about 10 minutes' walk south-east of the bus station. Apart from the usual kebabs and flat-bread *(náng)*, there's another type of kebab which is dipped in batter before roasting. When you try it, make sure that they use meat and not mutton fat or it will taste revolting.

On the main street close to the cinema are two food markets on opposite sides of the

YINING 伊宁

1 Airport
  飞机场
2 Huamingyuan Hotel
  花明园饭店
3 Huacheng Hotel
  花城宾馆
4 Bus Station
  长途汽车站
5 Friendship Hotel
  友谊宾馆
6 Department Store
  民贸商场
7 CAAC
  中国民航
8 Ili Hotel
  伊犁宾馆
9 Horse Carriages
  马车
10 PSB
  公安局外事科
11 Bank of China
  中国银行
12 Bus Station
  长途汽车站
13 Yining Department Store
  伊宁商场
14 Post Office
  邮局
15 CITS
  中国国际旅行社
16 Hulejia Hotel
  呼勒佳宾馆
17 Mosque
  清真寺

street, one catering for Chinese tastes, the other for the wild minority population. The Chinese sector does the usual meat and vegetable dishes. The wild side is almost medieval, with restaurant proprietors yelling at you over steaming cauldrons, while drunken customers roll around on benches and tables set outside. The staple foods seem to be mutton stew, kebab and flat-bread.

Getting There & Away

Air It's relatively easy to buy an air ticket from Ürümqi to Yining, but difficult or impossible to get a flight back. The one-way fare is Y176 and the flight takes 1½ hours.

Flights run six days a week. If you're determined to fly back to Ürümqi, your best bet is to buy tickets through the hotels. You could also try CITS or go directly to the airport.

The CAAC office is one block west of the Ili Hotel in Yining, but the office is often closed. A lot of foreigners have complained, so perhaps things will change – someday.

Figure on spending at least three to four working days to buy an air ticket in Yining. Cancelled and delayed flights are the norm.

Bus Buses leave daily from Ürümqi at 9 am (Beijing summer time) and take two days to get to Yining. Departures from Yining are at 8 am during summer, and at 7 am the rest of the year. It's best to purchase tickets a day in advance. There are two bus stations in Yining – buses from one station do not stop at the other, so you must buy your ticket at the place from which you want to depart.

Buses run daily to Kashgar via Korla, Kuqa and Aksu. The full trip to Kashgar takes three days and the ticket costs Y93.

It is possible to travel by bus from Yining to Almaty in Kazakstan. For full details, see the Getting There & Away chapter at the front of the book.

AROUND YINING

Ili Valley
(yīlí gǔ)

About six km south of the town centre is a bridge over the Ili River. The Ili Valley is pretty – the roads are lined with tall birch trees and there are farms everywhere. The best way to get out and see the countryside is to take a horse carriage (mǎ chē). These cost about Y30 for a 1½-hour tour. Most of the carriage drivers congregate in an area about one block east of the Ili Hotel. Communication can be a real problem – the drivers are Kazaks and few speak Chinese – the only English they know is 'change money'.

Sayram Lake
(sàilìmù hú)

The large and beautiful Sayram Lake is to the north of Yining. The bus between Ürümqi and Yining makes a 30-minute rest stop here. The bus from Yining to Sayram Lake takes slightly more than three hours.

If you would like to explore this alpine lake, it's possible to spend the night here, though very few travellers do this. The best place to stay is the *Guozigou Hostel (guǒzigōu zhāodàisuǒ)*, where rooms are just Y3. There is one other hotel, the *Sayram Hostel (sàilǐmù zhāodàisuǒ)*, a terrible place that looks like it might collapse soon. There is food up here, but the selection is limited, so bring what you need.

It is possible to hire horses at the lake and go riding with the Kazak shepherds. It costs about Y40 for a whole day, but be sure to bargain. The area presents some good hiking opportunities. The water from the lake is considered drinkable, but be careful about contamination (from sheep) around the shoreline.

ALTAI
(ā'lètài)
Near the northernmost tip of Xinjiang is Altai, 922 metres above sea level. It's in a much colder region than Ürümqi – even summer can be chilly. The lowest temperature recorded here was a nippy - 49.8°C. The population is a mere 170,000, 63% of whom are Han Chinese and the rest mostly Kazaks.

Altai is close to the border with three nations – Kazakstan, Russia and Mongolia. For this reason, the Chinese are paranoid about the place and hard-to-obtain permits are needed to visit the region to the north of town, though Altai itself is open.

Places to Stay
The only place for foreigners is the *Altai Hotel (☎ 223-804) (ā'lètài fàndiàn)* at 37 Gongyuan Lu. It's on the far side of the Kelan River (cross the bridge) just opposite the town centre. Dorm beds start at Y25 while cushier doubles cost Y120.

Getting There & Away
Without the requisite permits for the nature reserve, there seems little point in visiting Altai. But if you want to go, CAAC has flights from Ürümqi three times weekly. Two days on a rattletrap bus from Ürümqi will also get you to Altai.

AROUND ALTAI
The area north of Altai is positively stunning, perhaps the most spectacular scenery in Xinjiang. It's a land of thick evergreen forests, rushing rivers and lakes. The Ertrix River, which drains the area, is the only river in China to flow into the Arctic Ocean. This area is officially labelled the Hanas Nature Reserve and you will need a permit to visit.

Hanas Lake
(kānàsī hú)
The most splendid sight in the Altai region is Hanas Lake, an alpine lagoon surrounded by pines, boulders and mountains. In the autumn, the aspen and maple trees do their thing and provide a scenic backdrop of riotous colours. There's an excellent hotel here, a plush A-frame that looks like a ski lodge in the Swiss Alps. However, it's hard to understand why the Chinese bothered to build it – obtaining the coveted travel permit requires a month of bureaucratic paper-shuffling. Access is also impeded by bad roads – the lake is a 100-km bone-jarring journey from Altai and you'll need to hire a jeep.

Friendship Peak
(yǒuyí fēng)
Mountain climbers are enthralled with the Altai region. The highest summit in the area is Friendship Peak at 4374 metres. Standing on the glacier-covered summit allows you to be in three nations at once. Presumably, you won't need a visa for each one, but you will need a climbing permit, guide, ice axe, crampons and other mountaineering paraphernalia.

Gansu 甘肃

A rugged and barren province consisting mostly of mountains and deserts, Gansu (*gānsù*) has long been a poor and forgotten backwater only loosely controlled by Beijing. However, Gansu's role in Chinese history should not be understated. The famed Silk Road, the ancient highway along which camel caravans carried goods in and out of China, threaded its way through Gansu. The most common export was the highly prized Chinese silk, from which the road took its name. Travellers and merchants from as far away as the Roman Empire entered the Middle Kingdom via this route, using the string of oasis towns as stepping-stones through the barren wastes. Buddhism was also carried into China along the Silk Road, and the Buddhist cave temples found all the way from Xinjiang through Gansu and up through northern China are reminders of the influx of ideas the road made possible.

The Great Wall snaked its way across northern China and into Gansu, finishing up not far past the town of Jiayuguan. All was not peaceful within the wall, however. The Muslim rebellion of 1862-78 was put down with incredible savagery by the Chinese; untold numbers of people, probably millions, were killed and the destruction of cities and property brought the province to ruin and finally established Chinese control. The century was topped off by a massive famine.

Traditionally the towns of Gansu have been established in the oases along the major caravan route where agriculture is possible. With the coming of modern methods of transport, some industrial development and mining has taken place. The 1892-km Lanzhou-Ürümqi railway line, completed in 1963, was one of the great achievements of the early Communist regime; it's done much to relieve the isolation and backwardness of this region. Tourism is now an important cash cow, especially in Lanzhou, Dunhuang and Jiayuguan.

Twenty-three million people now inhabit

Population: 23 million
Capital: Lanzhou
Highlights:
- Bingling Si, Buddhist grottoes carved into a splendid area of cliffs towering over a branch of the Yellow River
- The incredible Tibetan monastery town of Xiahe, a magnet for pilgrims dressed in their finest
- Jiayuguan, where the Great Wall ends and the desert begins
- Dunhuang, home of China's most stunning Buddhist grottoes, set amid the towering sand dunes

Gansu. The province has a considerable variety of minority peoples, among them the Hui, Mongols, Tibetans and Kazaks. The Han Chinese are now, of course, in the vast majority.

LANZHOU
(lánzhōu)

The capital of Gansu, Lanzhou has been an important garrison town and transport centre since ancient times.

The development of Lanzhou as an industrial centre began after the Communist victory and the city's subsequent integration into China's expanding national rail network.

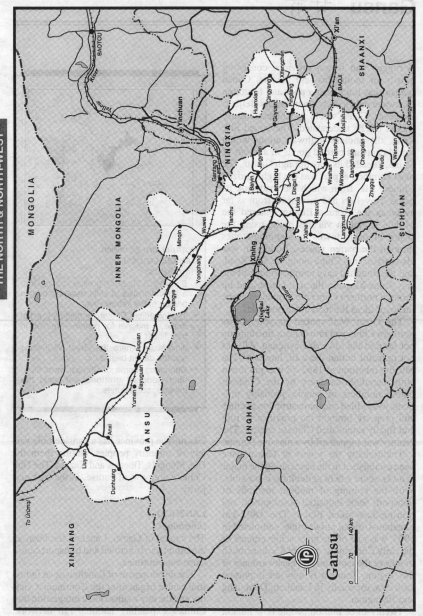

Gansu

0   70   140 km

The city's population increased more than tenfold within little more than a generation.

Although Lanzhou is not a major tourist drawcard in itself, there are some very interesting sights in the surrounding area. Furthermore, Lanzhou's strategic location makes it an important transport hub for travellers heading into the vast oblivion of western China.

Orientation

Geography has conspired to make Lanzhou a city of poor design. At 1600 metres above sea level, the city is crammed into a narrow valley walled in by steep mountains. The mountains have forced the city to develop westwards in a long urban corridor extending for over 20 km along the southern banks of the Yellow River. The valley is a perfect trap for exhaust fumes emanating from motor vehicles and chimneys, burying Lanzhou in a perpetual haze of pollution. Nevertheless, the rugged topography does give the city a certain unique charm.

Information

Heaps of travel agencies cater to the foreign market, offering one-day and overnight tours to scenic spots in the Lanzhou vicinity. Most popular with budget travellers seems to be Western Travel Service (☎ 841-6321; fax 841-8608), 204 Donggang Xilu, within the grounds of the Lanzhou Hotel. CITS (☎ 841-6638 ext 761) is on Nongmin Xiang, the lane running behind the Jincheng Hotel. Almost next door is Tianma Travel, which offers similar services.

Two offices of the PSB have entry-exit offices issuing visa extensions and alien travel permits. The 'provincial' office is at 38 Qingyang Lu on The East Is Red Square. From the main old green-and-white-tiled building at the front, walk left to a separate wing; the office is on the 3rd floor, left of the stairs. The PSB's smaller 'city' office is at 132 Wudu Lu on the right as you enter the compound.

The Bank of China has its main branch (☎ 841-8957) just north of The East Is Red Square on Pingliang Lu.

There are post offices across from Lanzhou (main) Railway Station and at the west bus station. The main post and telephone office is on the corner of Minzhu Lu and Pingliang Lu. A good place to make international collect calls is the telephone and telegram office on the corner of Qingyang Lu and Jinchang Lu.

Gansu Provincial Museum
(gānsù shěng bówùguǎn)

The Provincial Museum is directly across the street from the Huayi Hotel, and is among the best of China's smaller provincial museums.

On the 2nd floor is a newly refurbished exhibition, 'Cultural Relics of the Silk Road'. It starts with Neolithic painted pottery taken from a site 300 km south-east of here at Dadiwan. The Dadiwan culture existed at least 7000 years ago, and is thought by some archaeologists to predate the better-known Yangshuo culture. Some of the Dadiwan pieces bear painted black signs, which are believed to be early forms of pictographic characters. Later Han Dynasty exhibits include a 70-cm-long piece of fine embroidered lace and inscribed wooden tablets used to relay messages along the Silk Road. Outstanding is a 1½-metre-high Tang Dynasty warrior made from glaze-coloured earthenware, the largest such piece found yet in China.

Also interesting is a 2nd-century BC gilded silver plate depicting Bacchus, the Greek god of wine, from the Eastern Roman Empire. It was unearthed at Jingyuan, 120 km north-east of Lanzhou, in 1989 and is evidence of significant contact between the two distant ancient civilisations.

There is also a bronze replica of a galloping horse with numerous accompanying chariots and mounted horsemen, excavated from the Leitai Han Tomb in Wuwei; the original is now housed in Beijing. Among the Yuan Dynasty relics is a pocket edition of a Chinese-Tibetan bilingual Buddhist scripture, and a handwritten copy of the Koran with Persian annotations.

On the ground floor are some rather mundane exhibits of Gansu's flora, fauna and

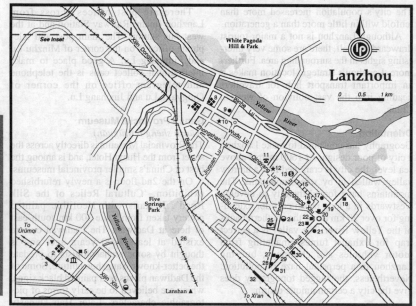

geology. Much more interesting is a fossilised skeleton of a giant mammoth unearthed in 1973. There are also fragments of skeletons, teeth and tusks from other extinct members of the pachyderm family.

The museum is open from 9 to 11.30 am and from 2.30 to 5 pm; it's closed on Sunday.

White Pagoda Hill
(báitǎ shān)
This pleasant, well-managed park is on the north bank of the Yellow River near the old Zhongshan Bridge. The steep slopes are terraced, with lots of small walkways leading through the forest to pavilions, teahouses and a plant nursery on a secluded hillside. On top of the hill is the White Pagoda Temple, originally built during the Yuan Dynasty, from where you get a good view across the city. There are several mosques on the park periphery. In summer it's open from 6.30 am to 10 pm. Bus No 7 from the railway station goes there.

Lanshan
(lánshān gōngyuán)
This mountain range rises steeply to the south of Lanzhou, reaching over 2000 metres. The temperature on top is normally a good 5°C cooler than in the valley, so it's a good retreat in summer. The quickest and easiest way up is by chairlift from behind Five Springs Park. The chairlift takes about 20 minutes to make the diagonal climb to the upper terminal. On the summit you'll find the Santai Pavilion *(sāntái gé)*, refreshment stands and a fun park. You can plonk yourself down in a deck chair, sip some tea and observe the chaos of city life rolling on below you. A paved trail zigzags its way back down to Five Springs Park.

Places to Stay
Several mid-range places in close proximity to the main railway station accept foreigners. Best of these is the *Yingbin Hotel* (☎ 888-652) *(yíngbīn fàndiàn)* on Tianshui Lu,

LANZHOU 兰州

PLACES TO STAY

5 Huayi Hotel
华谊大酒店
18 Ningwozhuang Guest-
house
宁卧庄宾馆
19 Jincheng Hotel
金城饭店
20 Lanzhou Hotel &
Western Travel Service
兰州饭店, 西方旅行社
22 Lanzhou Legend Hotel
兰州飞天大酒店
23 Dongfang Hotel
东方宾馆
27 Nongken Hotel
农垦宾馆
28 Lanzhou Mansions
兰州大厦
29 Yingbin Hotel
迎宾饭店
30 Heping Hotel
和平饭店
31 Lanshan Hotel
兰山宾馆

PLACES TO EAT

1 Star Moon Restaurant
星月楼酒家
15 Food Alley
农民巷

OTHER

2 Huangjin Shopping
Centre
黄金大厦
3 West Railway Station
火车西站
4 Provincial Museum
甘肃省博物馆
6 West Bus Station
汽车西站
7 Jinda Shopping Centre
金达商厦
8 Asia-Europe Shopping
Centre
亚欧商厦
9 Foreign Languages
Bookstore
外文书店
10 PSB (City Office)
市公安局

11 Telephone & Telegram
Office
电信大楼
12 PSB (Provincial Office)
省公安局
13 Bank of China
中国银行
14 The East Is Red
Square
东方红广场
16 CAAC
中国民航
17 CITS
中国国际旅行社
21 Lanzhou University
兰州大学
24 East Bus Station
汽车东站
25 Post & Telephone
Office
邮电局
26 Chairlift to Lanshan
兰山索道
32 Main Railway Station
火车总站

which charges Y80 for a basic triple or Y150 to Y200 for a double. *Lanzhou Mansions* (☎ 841-7210) *(lánzhōu dàshà)*, the big tower immediately left as you exit the railway station, charges Y50 for a room with shared bath or Y176 to Y516 for rooms with private bath. Just behind Lanzhou Mansions in a small alley is enormous *Nongken Hotel* (☎ 841-7878) *(nóngkěn bīnguǎn)*, which has doubles for Y180 to Y210. The big yellow building opposite the station is the *Lanshan Hotel* (☎ 882-7211) *(lánshān bīnguǎn)* with doubles for Y80 to Y210.

A 10-minute walk down Tianshui Lu brings you to the *Heping Hotel (hépíng fàndiàn)*. It's an old place that's been heavily renovated and offers reasonable double rooms with private bath for Y120.

The *Lanzhou Hotel* (☎ 841-6321) *(lánzhōu fàndiàn)* is another of those over-dimensional Sino-Stalinist edifices put up back in the

1950s, but the interior has been fully re-modelled and it's a popular place to stay. Budget travellers are stashed in the old wing where dorm beds cost Y30 a crack in a triple room. Otherwise, you're looking at private rooms priced from Y420 to Y500. The hotel is a 20-minute walk from the main railway station or you can take bus No 1 or No 7 for two stops.

The *Jincheng Hotel* (☎ 841-6638; fax 841-8438) *(jīnchéng fàndiàn)* is a plush tourist playground adjacent to the Lanzhou Hotel. The dorms are behind the main hotel building, on the 4th floor of a separate wing best reached from the rear gate next to the CITS office. At Y40 per bed, these depressing concrete-floor rooms are poor value. Over in the cushy main tower, room rates are from Y456 to Y1162.

Opposite the Lanzhou Hotel on the same traffic circle is the glittering *Lanzhou Legend*

Hotel (☎ 888-2876; fax 888-7876) *(lánzhōu fēitiān dà jiǔdiàn)*. The service is legendary, and so are the prices – rooms cost Y664, Y1245 and Y4980. This is the most up-market hotel in town. Next door is the *Dongfang Hotel (dōngfāng bīnguǎn)*, a towering pleasure palace which was still under construction at the time of writing.

The *Huayi Hotel* (☎ 233-3051) *(huáyí dà jiǔdiàn)* at 14 Xijin Xilu is distinguished by being far to the western side of town. It's a useful staging point if you're catching the early-morning bus to Xiahe from the west bus station; otherwise don't bother. While it's very near Lanzhou's west railway station, most express trains *don't* stop here. Dorm beds in the old building cost Y90 each, but rooms in the new building are priced at Y518.

The spacious and sleepily quiet *Ningwozhuang Guesthouse* (☎ 841-6221) *(níngwòzhuāng bīnguǎn)* has doubles from Y400 upwards. Once an exclusive residence for visiting cadres, this place has some of the most extensive and well-kept gardens you'll see in any Chinese hotel. The reception area is decorated with photos of distinguished former hotel guests (no backpackers) including the president of Mali, a Singapore cabinet minister and a Thai princess.

Places to Eat

Almost all hotels in Lanzhou have excellent restaurants and prices are generally reasonable (but ask first). The restaurant in *Lanzhou Mansions* offers a choice of set meals at various prices – the Y15 meal is more than most people can finish. The *Huayi Hotel* in the western part of town has a good restaurant, though you may want to check out the nearby *Star Moon Restaurant (xīngyuè lóu jiǔjiā)*.

Probably the best place for street food is the food alley *Nongmin Xiang*, the lane running behind the Jincheng Hotel.

Several typical Lanzhou specialities are sold on the streets. One is called *ròujiābǐng*, which is lamb or pork fried with onion, capsicum and a dash of paprika, served inside a 'pocket' of flat-bread.

Lanzhou is famous for its noodles. The beef noodles *(niúròu miàn)* are served in spicy soup – if you can't handle chillies, say '*bùyào làjiāo*'. Some travellers prefer the fried noodles *(chǎo miàn)*.

For dessert there is the local Muslim dish, *tiánpéizi*. It's made by lightly boiling highland barley kernels, then leaving the soaked grains for several days until a mild fermentation occurs. It's served with a sour-sweet milky-white sauce and has a delicious, aromatic flavour.

Getting There & Away

Air CAAC's office is at 46 Donggang Xilu at the corner of a small lane, a five-minute walk north-west of the Lanzhou Hotel. It's open from 8.30 to 11.30 am and from 3 to 6 pm.

There are two direct flights weekly between Lanzhou and Hong Kong. Lanzhou also has air connections to:

Beijing, Changsha, Chengdu, Chongqing, Dunhuang, Fuzhou, Guangzhou, Guilin, Haikou, Hangzhou, Jiayuguan, Kunming, Ningbo, Qingdao, Shanghai, Shenyang, Shenzhen, Ürümqi, Wuhan, Xiamen and Xi'an.

Bus The west bus station *(qìchē xīzhàn)* handles departures to Linxia, Xiahe and Hezuo. Foreigner-price bus fares out of Lanzhou are relatively expensive, but it's difficult to get them at Chinese prices. There are seven buses per day to Linxia (3½ hours), but only one daily direct bus to Xiahe (eight hours) leaving at 7.30 am. Linxia is on the way to Xiahe and all buses call in there, so if you can't get on a direct bus to Xiahe take an early bus to Linxia and change there. There are also buses to Wuwei (seven hours), Zhangye (11 hours) and Jiayuguan (15 hours). Most of the overnight buses to Jiayuguan are sleeper coaches *(wòpù qì chē)*, easily worth their slightly higher cost.

The east bus station on Pingliang Lu has departures mainly for eastern destinations such as Xi'an, Yinchuan and Guyuan (in Ningxia).

Travel Insurance A regulation requires foreigners who travel by public bus in Gansu to be insured with the People's Insurance Company of China (PICC), regardless of whether they have taken out their own travel insurance or not. Apparently, this follows a successful lawsuit against the Gansu provincial government by the parents of a Japanese tourist who was killed in a bus accident here in 1991. Depending on how you view this matter, the insurance requirement is either an act of collective punishment aimed at all foreigners, or merely a prudent means of covering any future liability claims (or simply another cash cow for the government). In any case, some long-distance bus stations may refuse to sell you a ticket unless you can show them your PICC insurance, or else they will charge you an 'insurance fee' on the spot (no receipt issued though). The requirement is currently being enforced mainly on routes in and out of Lanzhou and in north-western Gansu. It is doubtful that you could actually collect anything from this insurance policy if you were involved in an accident – it merely insures the government bus company against lawsuits.

Travellers have managed to avoid paying insurance by showing someone else's papers when they buy their bus ticket or getting a Chinese person to buy it for them. Some buy the ticket on the bus itself, but drivers often demand a generous 'tip' for their compliance. Frankly, it's less hassle to just buy insurance and forget the whole thing. Private long-distance minibuses pay little heed to the insurance 'requirement' – basically, it's a government operation.

In Lanzhou you can buy insurance at the PICC office (☎ 841-6422 ext 114) at 150 Qingyang Lu, the CITS office, other travel agencies and most of the tourist hotels. It costs Y20 for seven days and Y40 for 15 days, plus Y2 for each additional day. CITS and some of the hotels charge an additional Y10 commission.

Train Trains run to Ürümqi, to Beijing via Hohhot and Datong, to Golmud via Xining, to Shanghai via Xi'an and Zhengzhou, and to Beijing via Xi'an and Zhengzhou, or you can go south to Chengdu. Heading west, it takes 18 hours to reach Jiayuguan, 24 hours to Liuyuan, 37 hours to Turpan, and 40 hours to Ürümqi.

The main railway station has a separate window for foreigners (currently No 12, but it's been moved around), but it's difficult to get anything other than a hard seat. Travel agencies and hotels can get you sleeper tickets at one day's notice.

Getting Around
To/From the Airport The airport is at Zhongchuan, 87 km north of the city. Airport buses leave from the CAAC office three to four times a day. Our experience has been that you should be prepared to board the bus about 20 minutes before the time printed on your bus ticket; the buses will often depart early! The fare is Y25. Buses can and do fill up, so buy your ticket as soon as you've decided on a departure time. Upmarket hotels also run buses out to the airport.

Be very wary of the taxi drivers who hang around the CAAC office and offer to take you to the airport for Y100. There is no way that they are going to carry you 87 km so cheaply; you can expect them to ask for double fare once you are 10 km out of the city, and if you refuse then you get dumped in the middle of nowhere!

CAAC has several airport hotels for people catching early-morning flights. The newer *Zhongchuan Hotel* (☎ 841-5926) *(zhōngchuān bīnguǎn)* charges Y415 for a standard double. The cheapest beds are Y80 in doubles with attached bath.

Bus The most useful bus routes are No 1 and trolley-bus No 31 running from the main railway station to the west bus station and the Huayi Hotel. Public buses cost Y0.30.

AROUND LANZHOU
Bingling Si
(bǐnglíng sì)
This set of Buddhist grottoes carved into the cliffs of a 60-metre-high gorge is one of the most unusual sights in Gansu. Isolated by the

Maitreya Buddha, in the spectacular Bingling Si caves, near Lanzhou.

waters of the Liujiaxia Reservoir on the Yellow River, the grottoes were spared the vandalism of the Cultural Revolution. The reservoir itself at one time actually threatened to inundate the caves, but a levy now protects the area from flooding during high-water periods.

Bingling Si is also called the Thousand Buddha Caves *(qiān fódòng)*, though in fact the total number of caves is only 183. The setting is spectacular. The cliffs are composed of an eroded and porous rock with numerous natural cavities, giving the area an appearance reminiscent of southern Utah (in the USA) or Australia's Bungle Bungle country. The creators of these grottoes dangled from ropes while carving their masterpieces into the face of the cliffs – one has to wonder how many artisans fell to their deaths.

The oldest caves have been repaired and added to on numerous occasions since they were built during the Western Qin Dynasty. They contain 694 statues, 82 clay sculptures and a number of frescoes. Cave 169, contain-

ing one buddha and two bodhisattvas, is one of the oldest and best preserved in China. Most of the other caves were completed during the prosperous Tang period. The star of the caves is the 27-metre-high seated statue of Maitreya, the future Buddha.

Depending on which caves you want to see, entry costs Y5 to Y200. The cheaper tickets are for the unlocked caves, while the Y200 ticket gives you a complete guided tour including the magnificent Caves 169 and 172.

Places to Stay In Yongjing you can stay at the *Lidian Hotel (lìdiàn bīnguǎn)* for Y80 for a good double with bathroom, or the *Huanghe Hotel (huánghé bīnguǎn)* for Y50 a room.

Getting There & Away From Lanzhou to the caves is a 12-hour round trip, half of that time on a bus and half on a boat. The caves are inaccessible in winter because the water level in the river is too low and ice may also block the boats. Western Travel Service (in the Lanzhou Hotel), CITS and Tianma Travel all run tours to the caves whenever they have enough people (the minimum is six unless you're prepared to pay more); the usual tour price is Y130 (excluding entry tickets), which is quite reasonable.

Unless you take a tour or charter a vehicle, it's not really possible to get to the Bingling Si and back in one day. If you organise the trip yourself, you'll probably have to stay overnight in Yongjing, because the boat normally gets back from the caves after the last bus has left for Lanzhou. You can take a 7.30 am bus to Yongjing from the west bus station. The 7.30 bus often arrives just in time for you to catch one of the boats to Bingling Si. The railway line to Yongjing does not carry passenger services.

All boats depart from Liujiaxia, a tiny port half an hour's walk uphill from Yongjing. The trip costs Y50 for foreigners (no student discounts) and takes three hours each way; boats only stay at the caves for one hour, so don't mess about! Food and drink are not available on the boat, so bring some with

The Potala Palace in Lhasa dominates the city's skyline, Tibet. The palace has thousands of rooms and is the burial place of previous Dalai Lamas.

CHRIS BEALL

CHRIS TAYLOR

CHRIS TAYLOR

Top: Monk with human thighbone trumpet, Lhasa, Tibet
Bottom Left: Prayer flags in the snow, on the road to Nepal, Tibet
Bottom Right: Prayer flags, Tibet

you. You can also charter a speed boat across the reservoir for Y170 return.

If you're going on to Linxia or Xiahe, you can avoid backtracking to Lanzhou by taking a direct bus to Linxia from the main street of Yongjing (4½ hours). The bus takes an interesting high route east of the Yellow River through areas settled by the Dongxiang ethnic minority.

Xinglongshan
(xīnglóngshān)

The name means Flourishing Mountain, though it's more romantically known as Xiyunshan (Perch Cloud Mountain). The elevation at the summit is 2400 metres and the peak is decorated by more than 40 temples and pavilions which date back to the Han Dynasty. The history of this scenic spot extends back some 2000 years, though it has only recently made it into the tourist circuit.

The mountain is 60 km east of Lanzhou in Yuzhong County. Buses from Lanzhou's east bus station offer the cheapest transport for individual travellers. Not surprisingly, travel agents in Lanzhou are keen to book tours. These cost around Y80 per person based on a minimum group size of six persons and the full round-trip journey can be done in one day if you start out early.

MAIJISHAN & TIANSHUI
(màijīshān / tiānshu)

Maijishan, a mountain famed for its grottoes, lies south of Tianshui town in south-eastern Gansu Province. The mountain bears some resemblance to a corn rick, hence the name Maijishan (Corn Rick Mountain).

Orientation

Tianshui has two sections: the railhead, known as Beidao, and the main city area 20 km to the east, known as Qincheng. Minibuses and public buses run very frequently between the two districts (Y2, 30 minutes each way), but unless you're staying there or have some business with CITS there's no real reason to go to Qincheng.

Maijishan is about 35 km south of Beidao. There are no direct public buses to Maijishan,

only public buses from the railway station to Qincheng (bus No 1), and from Qincheng to Maijishan (bus No 5), but you can easily change buses at the turn-off three km south of the station (near the Longlin Hotel). There are also many private minibuses that pick up arriving tourists and ferry them straight out to the caves. The trip takes over an hour one way, and on weekends the whole operation can be pretty crowded.

Information

CITS (☎ 214-463) has its main office in Qincheng at 1 Huancheng Donglu on the 3rd floor, and another branch in the Tianshui Hotel.

Maijishan Grottoes
(màijīshān shíkū)

The Maijishan grottoes are one of China's four largest temple groups; the others are at Datong, Luoyang and Dunhuang. The caves date back to the Northern Wei and Song dynasties and contain clay figures and wall paintings. It's not certain just how the artists managed to clamber so high; one theory is that they piled up blocks of wood to the top of the mountain before moving down, gradually removing blocks of wood as they descended. Stone sculptures were evidently brought in from elsewhere, since the local rock is too soft for carving, as at Dunhuang.

Earthquakes have demolished many of the caves in the central section, while murals have tended to drop off due to damp or rain; fire has destroyed a large number of the wooden structures. Parts of the rock wall have now been stabilised with sprayed-on liquid cement.

Catwalks and steep spiral stairs have been built across the cliff face. It's scary to look down, but perfectly safe. Most of the remaining 194 caves can only be seen through wire netting or barred doors – take a torch. Apart from the Qifo Pavilion and the huge buddha statues which are easily accessible, it's hard to get a rewarding peek into many of the caves unless you take a guide. If you want a guide, you had best contact CITS in Tianshui; there are guides available at Maijishan (at the main office uphill from the bus station)

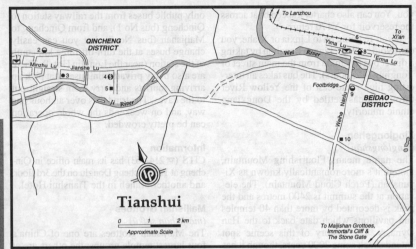

Tianshui

0   1   2 km

Approximate Scale

To Maijishan Grottoes,
Immortal's Cliff &
The Stone Gate

for a fee, but getting an English-speaking one at short notice is not always possible.

Visitors often pause above the statue of Buddha and attempt to throw coins or even cigarettes onto his head. If the objects stay there, so the story goes, the thrower's mind is pure. The visitor may be pure, but Buddha certainly cops a load of rubbish.

The ticket office is about a 15-minute walk uphill from where the bus lets you off. Cameras and bags may not be taken into the caves area; the ticket office has a cheap left-luggage section for this purpose. The caves are open from 9 am to 5 pm.

To reach the high ridge rising behind the ticket office, follow the road up towards the ticket office, but when you get to the sharp bend to the left, take the forest track to the right. Continue uphill along this trail for about 15 minutes and then look for a path climbing off to the left. If you follow this, you'll find yourself on a dizzying, knife-edge route with fine views of the grottoes on the cliff face.

Places to Stay & Eat

The *Government Hostel* (*zhèngfǔ zhāodàisuǒ*) in the green-tiled building slightly left

of the railway station will accept foreigners and is very cheap. The most expensive beds in the hotel are in doubles with attached bath (Y30).

The *Longlin Hotel* (☎ 235-594) (*lónglín fàndiàn*) is south of the railway station where the Maijishan and Qincheng roads diverge. The hotel entrance is just left (east) around the corner. A reasonable double with private bathroom costs Y200, or you can take just one bed for exactly half the price. The dining hall on the ground floor is quite all right, and there are a few good restaurants outside as well.

The *Tianshui Hotel* (☎ 212-410) (*tiānshuǐ bīnguǎn*) at 5 Yingbin Lu is still the only luxury hotel in the city. Its location on the Qincheng side of town is somewhat inconvenient, since the Maijishan caves are in the opposite direction from the railway station. Minibuses from the railway station can drop you off at the corner just up from the hotel. The rate for a standard double room with a private bathroom is Y300. There is a restaurant in the hotel itself and also an eatery next door.

There are food stalls and cheap restaurants at Maijishan.

TIANSHUI
天水

1 Post & Telephone Office
  邮电大楼
2 Long-Distance Bus Station
  长途汽车站
3 CITS
  中国国际旅行社
4 Bank of China
  中国银行
5 Tianshui Hotel
  天水宾馆
6 Railway Station
  火车站
7 Post & Telephone Office
  邮电局
8 Government Hostel
  政府招待所
9 Long-Distance Bus Station
  长途汽车站
10 Longlin Hotel
  陇林饭店

Getting There & Away

Tianshui is on the Xi'an-Lanzhou railway line; there are dozens of daily trains in either direction, and all stop here. If you arrive early you can visit Maijishan as a day trip, avoiding the need to stay overnight in Tianshui. From the long-distance bus station in Qincheng, there are buses to Lanzhou, Gangu, Guyuan (in Ningxia) and Hanzhong (in south-eastern Shaanxi). Tianshui has a noisy military airport, but apart from occasional charter aircraft there are no CAAC flights here.

GANGU
(gāngǔ)

At Gangu, on the railway line 45 km west of Tianshui, is a massive 23-metre-tall buddha, high on a cliff overlooking the Wei River. The statue is evidently of Tang Dynasty origin and sports a twirled moustache. A path along a steep ridge leads up past several small temples to a platform below the statue, from where you get an excellent view of the valley and town below. The *Nanling Guesthouse (nánlǐng bīnguǎn)* near the bus station

has basic doubles with bathroom for Y50. There are regular buses to Gangu from Tianshui and Wushan, but express trains don't stop here.

LUOMEN
(luòmén)

In the Wushan ranges outside Luomen, a small town 250 km south-east of Lanzhou, are the Buddhist Lashao Caves and Water Curtain Temple. Carved onto a rock face is a remarkable 31-metre-high figure of Sakyamuni, made during the Northern Wei period. The temple is a quaint old building nestled in a shallow cave on the nearby forested mountainside. Also nearby is the Ten Thousand Buddha Cave which, sadly, is in a state of poor repair. The Water Curtain Caves and Temple are in a remote and spectacular gorge, accessible only in good weather via a 17-km makeshift road up the dry river bed. You can charter a minibus from Luomen and back for around Y80. The *Government Hostel (zhèngfǔ zhāodàisuǒ)* in Luomen has rooms from Y32.

LINXIA
(línxià)

Linxia was once an important stop on the Silk Road between Lanzhou and Yangguan. Today the town has a decidedly Muslim Hui character, with a large mosque in the centre of town; old men with long stringy beards and white caps shuffle about the streets. In the markets you'll also see carved gourds, daggers, saddlery, carpets, and wrought iron goods. Linxia does a thriving trade in spectacles made with ground crystal lenses and metal frames.

Linxia is also a regional centre for the Dongxiang minority. The Dongxiang minority speak their own Altaic language and are believed to be descendants of 13th-century immigrants from central Asia who were moved forcibly to China after Kublai Khan's conquest of the Middle East. Some have greenish-blue eyes, high cheekbones and large noses.

The Yugur minority, numbering only 8000, live around the town of Jishishan near the Yellow River about 75 km from Linxia. The

THE NORTH & NORTH-WEST

Yugur speak a language derived partly from Uighur and are followers of Tibetan Buddhism.

Places to Stay & Eat

The cheerful *Shuiquan Hotel (shuǐquán bīnguǎn)* is 50 metres along to the right as you leave the south long-distance bus station. It offers beds in three-person dorms for Y30, and various doubles with bathroom for Y80, Y90 and Y150.

The Islamic restaurant in the *Minzu Hotel* has simple Hui dishes. It's north of the south bus station near the large traffic circle.

Getting There & Away

You can get buses to Linxia from Lanzhou's west bus station; there are seven departures between 7.30 am and 4 pm. The trip takes 3½ hours and costs Y22. From Linxia there are eight buses to Xiahe. The trip up takes four hours and the last bus leaves around 2.30 pm. The final bus back to Lanzhou departs at 5 pm. Other useful departures go to Hezuo (four daily), Xining (several daily, eight hours) and Tongren (in Qinghai, one daily).

There are two long-distance bus stations in Linxia: a newer, larger south bus station and the old north bus station about three km away. The south bus station has most connections to and from Lanzhou, Xiahe and Hezuo. However, direct buses between Lanzhou and Xiahe generally call in for a lunch stop at the north bus station.

XIAHE
(xiàhé)

Xiahe is one of the most enchanting places to visit in China, especially if you can't get to Tibet. Outside of Lhasa, it's the leading Tibetan monastery town. Indeed, in some ways it's better than Tibet – many Tibetans come here on pilgrimage dressed in their finest, most colourful clothing. The pilgrims, the monks, the monastery, the mountain scenery – when you enter Xiahe, you feel like you've entered another world.

The religious activity is focused on the Labrang Monastery, one of the six major Tibetan monasteries of the Gelukpa (Yellow Hat sect of Tibetan Buddhism). The others are Ganden, Sera and Drepung monasteries in the Lhasa area; Tashilhunpo Monastery in Shigatse; and Ta'er Monastery in Huangzhong, Qinghai Province.

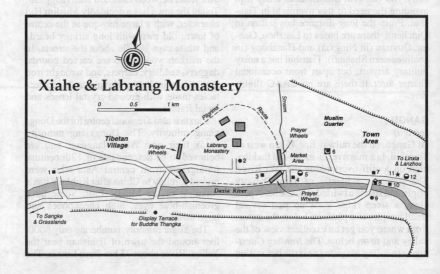

Xiahe & Labrang Monastery

0   0.5   1 km

- Tibetan Village
- Prayer Wheels
- Labrang Monastery
- Pilgrims Route
- Stream
- Prayer Wheels
- Muslim Quarter
- Town Area
- Market Area
- Daxia River
- Prayer Wheels
- 1 ■
- ● 2
- 3 ■
- ● 5
- ■ 4
- © 6
- ■ 7   11 ★ © 12
- ■ 8 ● 10
- ● 9
- To Linxia & Lanzhou
- To Sangke & Grasslands
- Display Terrace for Buddha Thangka

Today Xiahe is a microcosm of south-western Gansu, with the area's three main ethnic groups represented; roughly speaking, Xiahe's population is 45% Tibetan, 45% Han and 10% Muslim.

Orientation

At 2920 metres above sea level, Xiahe stretches for several km east-to-west along the valley of the Daxia River. The Labrang Monastery is roughly halfway along, and marks a division between Xiahe's mainly Han and Hui Chinese eastern quarter and the overwhelmingly Tibetan village to the west. The Muslim quarter is also to the east of the monastery.

A three-km pilgrims' way with long rows of prayer wheels and Buddhist shrines encompasses the monastery. The route crosses the road just up from the upper bus station and continues along the river, back across the road and around the slopes above

XIAHE & LABRANG MONASTERY
夏河，拉卜楞寺

1 Labrang Hotel & CITS
  拉卜楞宾馆，中国国际旅行社
2 Monastery Ticket Office
  售票处
3 Labrang Monastery Guesthouse
  拉卜楞寺招待所
4 Waterworks Hostel
  自来水招待所
5 Upper Bus Station
  上汽车站
6 Mosque
  清真寺
7 Dasha Hotel
  大厦宾馆
8 Xinhua Hostel
  新华招待所
9 PICC
  中国人民保险公司
10 Minzu (Nation) Hotel
  民族饭店
11 PSB
  公安局
12 Lower Bus Station
  下汽车站

Labrang. From here you can see the small gold-painted dagobas on the rooftops glistening magnificently in the afternoon sun. It's a good introduction to Xiahe.

There are some 40 smaller monasteries affiliated with Labrang in the surrounding mountains (as well as many others scattered across Tibet and China) and the area is a great place for hiking in clean, peaceful surroundings. Take warm clothing and rain gear. You can follow the river up to Sangke or head up into the surrounding valleys, but carry a stick or a pocket full of rocks (or crossbow?), as wild dogs are a serious threat.

Information

CITS is at the Labrang Hotel. There are several banks in Xiahe but no Bank of China, and it is very difficult to change travellers' cheques here. However, some of the small antique shops along the main street will give you a reasonable rate for US$ cash. There is a small post office a short way up from the Minzu (Nation) Hotel. The PSB is directly opposite the hotel. If you need to buy insurance for bus travel, there is a PICC office in a compound just across the first bridge. You can rent bikes at several of the restaurants along the main road for about Y15 a day.

Labrang Monastery
(lābǔlèng sì)

The monastery was built in 1709 by E'ang-zongzhe, the first-generation Jiamuyang ('living buddha'), who came from the nearby town of Ganjia. It houses six institutes (Institute of Esoteric Buddhism, Higher & Lower Institutes of Theology, Institute of Medicine, Institute of Astrology and Institute of Law). There are also numerous temple halls, 'living buddha' residences and living quarters for the monks.

At its peak the monastery housed nearly 4000 monks, but their ranks were decimated during the Cultural Revolution, when monks and buildings took a heavy beating. The numbers are gradually recovering, and there are about 1700 monks today, drawn from Qinghai, Gansu, Sichuan and Inner Mongolia.

THE NORTH & NORTH-WEST

In April 1985 the main Prayer Hall of the Institute of Esoteric Buddhism was razed in a fire caused by faulty electrical wiring. The fire is said to have burnt for a week and destroyed some priceless relics. The hall's reconstruction was completed at great cost in mid-1990, but the monks remain reluctant to allow the use of electricity in most parts of the monastery.

At noon every day senior monks participate in scholarly debates in the large grassy compound on the main road; these debates are something of a spectacle for locals and visitors alike. Later in the afternoon, monks sit on the grass beside the river preparing ritual music for the religious ceremonies that take place at various times of the year. Their musical instruments include horns and trumpets made from human bones.

Entry to the monastery is by tour only (no student discounts). One of the monks (some speak English well) will show you around. The ticket office and souvenir shop are on the right side of the monastery car park. To get there walk 500 metres west (up the valley) from the upper bus station and take a right turn. The office closes from noon to 2 pm, and the last tours end before 4 pm.

Tours generally include the Institute of Medicine, the Ser Kung Golden Temple, the Prayer Hall and the museum. Its collection includes ancient Buddhist pieces rescued from the fire, and some amazingly detailed yak-butter sculptures made for the annual winter festivities. In temperatures of around minus 20°C, the sculptures are delicately moulded in a tub of freezing water to prevent the butter being melted by the warmth of the hands.

Festivals

These are important not only for the monks but also for the nomads, who stream into town from the grasslands in multicoloured splendour. Since the Tibetans use a lunar calendar, dates for individual festivals vary from year to year.

The Monlam (Great Prayer) Festival starts three days after the Tibetan New Year, which is usually in February or early March. On the

13th, 14th, 15th and 16th days of this month there are some spectacular ceremonies.

On the morning of the 13th a *thangka* (sacred painting on cloth) of Buddha measuring over 30 metres by 20 metres is unfurled on the other side of the Daxia River from the hillside facing the monastery. This event is accompanied by processions and prayer assemblies. On the 14th there is an all-day session of Cham dances performed by 35 masked dancers, with Yama, the lord of death, playing the leading role. On the 15th there is an evening display of butter lanterns and sculptures. On the 16th the Maitreya statue is paraded around the monastery all day.

During the second month (usually starting in March or early April) there are several interesting festivals, especially those held on the seventh and eighth days. Scriptural debates, lighting of butter lamps, collective prayers and blessings take place at other times during the year to commemorate Sakyamuni, Tsong Khapa or individual generations of the 'living buddhas'.

Places to Stay

The *Dasha Hotel (dàshà bīnguǎn)* near the bridge charges Y30 in quads or Y25 in triples; average doubles with bathroom are Y120. There's hot water for showering at night. Opposite is the *Xinhua Hostel (xīnhuá zhāodàisuǒ)*, where beds in doubles/triples are Y30/15. The place has a spartan orderliness; there are no showers and only a solitary toilet.

The next place up is the *Waterworks Hostel (zìláishuǐ zhāodàisuǒ)*, with beds from Y20. (They also have an ultra-basic dorm with beds for just Y10, but it's only intended as a crash pad for Tibetans). The showers are disgusting and there's no hot water anyway, but you can get yourself clean for Y5 at the public bathhouse a few doors up. They do have a few better doubles for Y50 and Y70. To get there from the upper bus station, head a short way west to the small bridge where a dirt lane leads left down to the hostel.

The *Labrang Monastery Guesthouse (lābǔlèng sì zhāodàisuǒ)* has beds for Y30 in double and triple rooms. It's run by old monks who potter around and smile a lot. It doesn't have showers, but there's always plenty of hot water from the boiler.

The nicest accommodation in Xiahe is the *Labrang Hotel* (☎ 21849) *(lābǔlèng bīnguǎn)* by the river a few km up the valley from the village. Originally the head lama's summer residence, it was knocked down by rampaging Red Guards and – a sore point with locals – rebuilt as a tourist hotel during the early 1980s. Nevertheless, it's a very friendly and tranquil place, and one of the few hotels in China where you can wake to the gentle sound of a rushing stream.

A double suite with nice bathroom is Y350; other doubles with bathroom cost Y200 and Y150. Beds in ornately painted triples are Y30, and Y20 in an eight-person dorm with communal showers. All rooms are heated in winter and there's hot water in the morning and evening. It's excellent value and recommended if you don't mind staying a bit out of the village. You can get there by motor-tricycle for about Y10, or walk there in 45 minutes. The hotel rents out good bicycles for Y5 per hour or Y20 a day.

The *Minzu (Nation) Hotel* near the lower bus station has been renovated recently. Prices for doubles have climbed to Y150 for doubles, or Y40 in the dorms.

Places to Eat

The *Labrang Hotel* has a restaurant, which serves good food. The restaurant downstairs in the *Dasha Hotel* also has some great dishes and a detailed English/Chinese menu. There are a number of simple and cheap Sichuan restaurants along the main street, north of the monastery.

The *Tibet Restaurant (zàng cāntīng)* is on the 2nd floor on the left a few minutes' walk up from the Dasha. It was started by a local Tibetan, but has recently been taken over by a Han Chinese newcomer, so it's lost some of its authenticity. On the menu are Tibetan staples such as yak-milk yoghurt with honey and tsampa. Tsampa is made from yak butter, coarse milk powder and highland-barley flour mixed into a dough with the fingers and eaten uncooked – just the thing to see you

through a Himalayan winter. Don't expect to see only vegetarian dishes – as the Dalai Lama himself has said, if the highland Tibetans didn't eat meat they would have starved to death long ago.

Things to Buy

The shops along Xiahe's main street are good places to pick up Tibetan handicrafts. Prices are highly negotiable. On sale are yak-butter pots, daggers, fur-lined boots, colourful Tibetan shawls, tiny silver teapots, amber products and Tibetan *laba* trumpets. If you're heading off into the hills, consider buying a *gǒubàng*, a heavy tapered metal rod attached to a leather cord and used as a defence against wild dogs.

Also on sale are a disturbingly large number of otter, lynx and even endangered snow-leopard hides, poached from the wilds of Qinghai and Tibet. Needless to say, carrying any of this stuff across an international border could land you in trouble with customs.

Getting There & Away

Xiahe is accessible only by bus. Most travellers arrive from Lanzhou, but some visit Xiahe as a stop en route between Gansu and Sichuan. From Lanzhou, there is only one direct daily bus departing from the west bus station at 7.30 am (Y40). It's a nine-hour ride, including a stop for lunch at Linxia. If you can't get a direct ticket from Lanzhou to Xiahe, then take a morning bus to Linxia and change there. The road between Linxia and Xiahe is being upgraded, with the eventual aim of enabling return day trips by tourist coach from Lanzhou.

All buses out of Xiahe pass through the lower bus station, so it's most convenient to board there. The direct bus to Lanzhou departs at 6.30 am, so if you need to load your luggage onto the roof, turn up a bit earlier. In summer there are eight scheduled daily buses to Linxia between 6 am and 4 pm (3½ hours), and seven daily buses to Hezuo between 6.30 am and 3.40 pm (including two buses running via Hezuo en route to Maqu). A few private minibuses also leave irregularly for Hezuo and Linxia from along the main street. There's also one bus a day to Tongren (in Qinghai) at 6.30 am.

AROUND XIAHE
Sangke Grasslands
(sāngkē cǎoyuán)

Around and beyond the village of Sangke, 14 km up the valley from Xiahe, is a small lake surrounded by large expanses of open grassland where the Tibetans graze their yak herds. In summer these rolling pastures are at their greenest and have numerous wildflowers. It's a lovely place for walking. The Labrang Hotel has nomad-style tents up on the grasslands where you can stay overnight for around Y30 per bed. The road from Xiahe rises gradually and you can bicycle up in about one hour. You can also get up there by motor-tricycle for about Y50 return.

GANSU-SICHUAN ROUTE

This scenic route goes via rough dirt roads along the eastern edge of the Tibetan mountains. Although a few buses go all the way from Lanzhou to Chengdu in Sichuan Province, it's best to do it in several stages, stopping at Linxia, Xiahe, Hezuo, Langmusi or Zoigê, a trip taking at least four days. For travel through this area you're supposed to have a travel permit and PICC insurance.

All buses pass through Hezuo (*hézuò*), an ugly town, of interest only as a transit point. In summer there are six or seven daily buses to Hezuo from Xiahe (2½ hours) and Linxia (Y11, three hours). There is only one direct bus a day from Hezuo and Zoigê (eight hours), but more frequent connections to Luqu (*lùqǔ*), a predominantly Tibetan-speaking village several hours south of Hezuo on the Tao River. Other buses go to Maqu (*mǎqǔ*), which is off the route and closed to foreigners, but on the way Maqu buses pass near to Langmusi (*lángmùsì*), just inside Gansu Province.

Langmusi has two very large Tibetan Buddhist monasteries, each with around 600 monks. Unlike other monastic centres it's not surrounded by a large town, just a small village and many active temples. There's

mountainous scenery on all sides and the local people still get around on the back of yaks. It's the most Tibetan place travellers are likely to get to outside of Tibet. Langmusi has two simple guesthouses with beds for around Y20.

On a highland plateau two hours further south in Sichuan is Zoigê (*ruòěrgài*), from where it's possible to make a side trip to Jiuzhaigou National Park. From Zoigê it's a full day's journey by bus south to Chengdu.

TIANZHU
(tiānzhù)

Tianzhu, a predominantly Tibetan-speaking town on the railway line between Lanzhou and Wuwei, is still very much closed to foreigners. To go there you must have a travel permit, issued specifically for Tianzhu by the Lanzhou PSB, otherwise you'll be detained while the authorities decide how heavy your fine should be. It's highly unlikely they'll give you a permit anyway, but even if they do you won't necessarily be welcome with the PSB in Tianzhu itself.

WUWEI
(wǔwēi)

Wuwei is the next town on the long Gansu rail corridor. The famous galloping horse (now at the Museum of Chinese History in Beijing) was recovered in 1969 from a tomb at the Leitai Temple on the northern edge of the city. The local museum is housed in the Wenmiao Temple; its collection includes Han porcelain pieces, millstones, bronze utensils, tiny clay stoves, Northern Wei armour and carved stone tablets. The old Bell Tower in a backstreet behind Dong Dajie can be climbed; at the top is a massive cast-iron bell still in occasional use. The Luoshen Pagoda on Bei Dajie is also worth a look.

Places to Stay & Eat

The *Liangzhou Hotel* (*liángzhōu bīnguǎn*) has beds in simple doubles for Y40, and very nice double rooms with bathroom for Y150. The *Tianma Hotel* (*tiānmǎ bīnguǎn*) charges Y200 for standard doubles. It has a CITS office, a money-changing service and a large

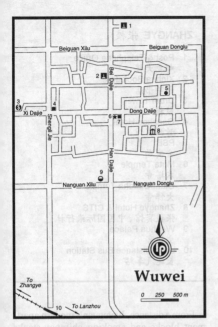

Wuwei

WUWEI 武威

1 Leitai Temple
雷台寺
2 Luoshen Pagoda
罗什塔
3 Bank of China
中国银行
4 Tianma Hotel & CITS
天马宾馆，中国国际旅行社
5 Bell Tower
钟楼
6 PSB
公安局外事科
7 Liangzhou Hotel
凉州宾馆
8 Museum (Wenmiao Temple)
博物馆
9 Long-Distance Bus Station
长途汽车站
10 Railway Station
火车站

dining hall downstairs. In the evening a diverse range of street food is available from stalls near the park on Xi Dajie.

Getting There & Away

Wuwei is on the main Lanzhou-Ürümqi railway line. There is also a direct line east from Wuwei via Gantang to Zhongwei in Ningxia roughly 300 km shorter than journeying via Lanzhou, but only infrequent and slow regional trains run this route. There are also daily buses to Zhongwei (six hours), Zhangye (five hours) and Jiayuguan (10 hours), as well as some 15 bus departures a day to Lanzhou (7½ hours). They'll probably want to see your PICC insurance at the ticket office.

ZHANGYE
(zhāngyè)

Zhangye is the biggest town in Gansu north of Wuwei. It was once an important garrison town and a stop on the Silk Road (Marco Polo supposedly spent a year here). Photographs taken at the turn of the century show a still largely intact old city with high defensive walls, but little remains of the original Zhangye today. Definitely worth a visit is the Giant Buddha Temple (dàfó sì), which houses an impressive 34-metre-long sleeping buddha. This clay statue is the largest indoor reclining buddha in China and was built during the Western Xia period.

At Mati (mǎtí), a beautiful Tibetan village 135 km south of Zhangye in the foothills of the Qilianshan, is the Horse's Hoof Temple (mǎtí sì), built within a high cliff face and accessible only via an amazing passageway through the caves. Just outside Mati are the Thousand Buddha Caves (qiānfó dòng). Mati is still little visited by foreigners, and to visit the area you need a travel permit issued by the PSB in Zhangye or Lanzhou. Visitors have to stay overnight in Mati, since there's only one bus there each day.

Places to Stay

The Ganzhou Hotel (gānzhōu bīnguǎn) on Nan Jie charges Y120 for a standard double and Y30 per bed in quads. The only other

ZHANGYE 张掖

1   Post & Telephone Office
    邮电大楼
2   Xinhua Bookstore
    新华书店
3   Drum Tower
    鼓楼
4   Ganzhou Hotel
    甘州宾馆
5   PSB
    公安局
6   Muta Temple
    木塔寺
7   Giant Buddha Temple
    大佛寺
8   Zhangye Hotel & CITS
    张掖宾馆，中国国际旅行社
9   Wenhua Palace
    文化宫
10 Long-Distance Bus Station
    长途汽车站

foreigners' hotel is the *Zhangye Hotel (zhāng-yè bīnguǎn)* at 65 Xianfu Nanjie, which has beds in small dorms for Y35 and doubles for Y180; this hotel also has a CITS office.

Getting There & Away

All trains running between Lanzhou and Ürümqi stop at Zhangye. The bus to Mati departs from the main long-distance bus station at 2.20 pm and returns to Zhangye the next day at 6.20 am; the trip takes three hours. There are also a number of daily buses from Zhangye south to Wuwei and north to Jiayuguan. However, foreigners are not supposed to travel the latter route by road, apparently due to sensitivity regarding the Long March rocket-launching site near Jiuquan.

JIAYUGUAN
(jiāyùguān)

Jiayuguan (Jiayu Pass) is an ancient Han Chinese outpost. The Great Wall once extended beyond here, but in 1372, during the first few years of the Ming Dynasty, a fortress was built. From then on Jiayuguan was considered both the western tip of the wall and the western boundary of the empire.

From a distance, Jiayuguan's modern apartment blocks and smoking chimney-stacks stand out like an industrial oasis in the desert. The snow-capped mountains form a dramatic backdrop when the weather is clear.

Not far out of Jiayuguan is the Jiuquan Satellite Centre, where Long March rockets are tested and launched. It was from here that China sent its first satellite into space in 1970, broadcasting 'The East Is Red' back to a startled audience on earth. The satellite centre is still in use, but is not open to tourists.

Information

CITS (☎ 226-598) is in the Changcheng Hotel. Xiongguan Travel Service is in the Jiayuguan Hotel.

The PSB is inside the grounds of the Jiayuguan Hotel.

There is a post and telephone office diagonally opposite the Jiayuguan Hotel. It's open from 8.30 am to 7 pm.

The Bank of China is on Xinhua Nanlu south of the Traffic Hotel and is open from 9 am to noon and from 2.30 to 7.30 pm.

Jiayuguan Fort
(jiāyùguān chénglóu)

This is Jiayuguan's main tourist drawcard, and has taken on a sort of carnival atmosphere. The fort guards the pass which lies between the snow-capped Qilianshan peaks and Black Mountain *(hēishān)* of the Mazong range. During the Ming Dynasty this was considered the terminus of the Great Wall, though crumbling fragments can be seen to the west.

The fort was dubbed the 'Impregnable Defile Under Heaven'. Although the Chinese often controlled territory far beyond

Jiayuguan, this was the last major stronghold of the empire to the west.

The fort was built in 1372, with additional towers and battlements added later. The outer wall is about 733 metres in circumference and almost 10 metres high. At the eastern end of the fort is the Gate of Enlightenment *(guānghuà mén)* and in the west is the Gate of Conciliation *(róuyuǎn mén)*. Over each gate stand 17-metre-high towers with upturned flying eaves. On the inside of each gate are horse lanes leading up to the top of the wall. At the fort's four corners are blockhouses, bowmen's turrets and watchtowers. Outside the Gate of Enlightenment but inside the outer wall are three interesting buildings: the Wenchang Pavilion, Guandi Temple and the open-air theatre stage *(zhàntái)*.

The fort is five km west of Jiayuguan. You can cycle out there in about half an hour, or

Jiayuguan

0   150   300 m

To Jiayuguan Fort (5 km)

Xiangguan Donglu
Xiangguan Xilu
Xinhua Nanlu
Xinhua Nanlu

To Jiuquan

Jianshe Xilu

To Railway Station

JIAYUGUAN 嘉峪关

1 Jiayuguan Hotel, Xiongguan Travel Service & PSB
嘉峪关宾馆,雄关旅行社,公安局
2 Post & Telephone Office
邮电局
3 CAAC
中国民航
4 Xinhua Bookstore
新华书店
5 Yingbin Hotel & Linyuan Restaurant
迎宾大厦,林苑酒家
6 Wumao Hotel
物贸宾馆
7 Long-Distance Bus Station
长途汽车站
8 Xiongguan Hotel
雄关宾馆
9 Traffic Hotel
交通宾馆
10 Bank of China
中国银行
11 Youth Hotel
青年宾馆
12 Changcheng Hotel & CITS
长城宾馆,中国国际旅行社
13 Great Wall Museum
长城博物馆

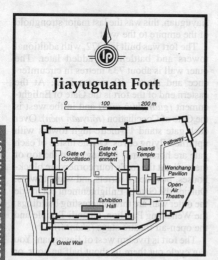

Jiayuguan Fort

0   100   200 m

Gate of Conciliation

Gate of Enlightenment

Guandi Temple

Pathway

Wenchang Pavilion

Open-Air Theatre

Exhibition Hall

Great Wall

pick up a motorbike, taxi or minibus outside the Jiayuguan Hotel; for a small taxi, bargain for around Y50 there and back. The fort is open from 8 am to 12.30 pm, and from 2.30 to 6 pm. A sign at the entrance says that video cameras are prohibited! Foreigners' entry tickets cost Y20, plus another Y3 to go up into the main viewing tower. For an additional fee you can have your photo taken while sitting on a camel, or dressed like Robin Hood while practising archery. Horseback riding and cotton candy also costs extra.

Overhanging Great Wall
(xuánbì chángchéng)

The Overhanging Great Wall is seven km north-west of Jiayuguan and in some respects more interesting than the fort. Linking Jiayuguan with Black Mountain, the wall is believed to have been constructed in 1540. It had since pretty much crumbled to dust but was reconstructed in 1987. Students were brought in to do the reconstruction work and were paid one fen for each brick laid. From the upper tower high on a ridge (quite a steep climb!) you get a sweeping view of the desert, the oasis of Jiayuguan and the glittering snow-capped peaks in the distance.

The wall is roughly six km north of Jiayuguan Fort via the shortest route (a rough dirt road leading north towards the mountains) or 10 km on the surfaced road (the route preferred by taxi drivers). Admission to the site costs Y5.

Xincheng Wei-Jin Art Gallery
(xīnchéng wèijìn mù)

If you're interested in Chinese art, you should find this place fascinating. It's not really an art gallery, but ancient tombs with original wall paintings. There are literally thousands of tombs in the desert 20 km east of Jiayuguan, but only one is currently open to visitors. The tombs date from approximately 220 to 420 AD (the Wei and Jin periods).

Very few tourists come here, so there are no regular buses. You can hire a minibus for around Y50. The gallery is open each day from 8 am to 7 pm.

Black Mountain Rock Paintings
(hēishān yánhuà)

About nine km to the north-west of Jiayuguan are some rock paintings dating back to the Warring States Period (453-221 BC). While they are not as bright or interesting as those in the Xincheng gallery, they are considerably older – a good place for the true art historian.

There's no public transport out there, so you'll have to make your own way by bicycle, taxi or minibus.

First Beacon Tower
(dìyī dūn)

This is the crumbling remains of a tower built on top of a cliff in 1539 at what was once the westernmost edge of the Great Wall. There isn't much to this place now, but you could include it with a taxi trip to Jiayuguan Fort. It's six km south-west of Jiayuguan.

July 1st Glacier
(qīyī bīngchuān)

CITS calls this place the 'Magical Glacier', a name which mystifies the locals. The glacier lies at 4300 metres, high up in the

Qilianshan mountains. Hikers can walk a five-km-long trail alongside the glacier, but at that elevation it gets cold even in summer, so come prepared. The area looks as if it would present a serious challenge even for experienced mountaineers – just getting through the inevitable red tape could be more exhausting than the actual climb!

The glacier is 120 km south-west of Jiayuguan and reached via a rotten road. To charter a small minibus with three passengers to the glacier costs about Y450 return (CITS asks Y950). If you've got a strong posterior you might choose to get there on the back of a motorbike for Y150.

Places to Stay

The *Wumao Hotel* (☎ 227-514) *(wùmào bīnguǎn)* is opposite the bus station. This new place has beds in three-bed dorms for Y20 each, or Y35 in a two-bed dorm. Doubles with attached bath are Y70 to Y120.

The *Xiongguan Hotel* (☎ 225-115) *(xióngguān bīnguǎn)* on Xinhua Nanlu has doubles with private bath for Y128 and Y200 (dorms half that price), or dorm beds without bath for Y32. It's a lacklustre affair, though the staff do their best.

The all-new *Yingbin Hotel* *(yíngbīn dàshà)* is opposite the bus station. It was not yet ready for the grand opening during our visit, so we can't give definite prices. Most likely, it will be low to mid-range.

The situation was much the same at the *Traffic Hotel* *(jiāotōng bīnguǎn)* opposite the Xiongguan Hotel. We were told that the ribbon-cutting ceremony was just weeks away, but no-one knew the prices.

The *Youth Hotel* (☎ 225-833) *(qīngnián bīnguǎn)* is built in an incongruous European 'castle style' complete with flags and turrets – all that's needed is a moat and drawbridge. Nevertheless, it's a fine place to stay. Rates in the dorm are from Y30 to Y50, or pay Y100 for a double. The hotel is on Jianshe Xilu, at the southern end of town.

On the traffic circle at the centre of town is the *Jiayuguan Hotel* (☎ 226-983; fax 227-174) *(jiāyùguāan bīnguǎn)*. The charge for a double ranges from Y220 to Y320. The dorm

rooms have no attached bath and are not such good value by Jiayuguan standards – rates per bed are Y25 to Y35.

Jiayuguan's three-star luxury accommodation is the *Changcheng Hotel* (☎ 225-213; fax 226-016) *(chángchéng bīnguǎn)* at 6 Jianshe Xilu. The 'dorms' (actually triples with a private bath) cost Y85 per bed. Double rooms are Y300 and suites are Y450 to Y750. It might be worth staying for the swimming pool out the back.

The *Railway Guesthouse (tiědào bīnguǎn)* is next to the railway station, four km south of central Jiayuguan. A dorm bed in a room with no bath is Y35. Dorms with attached bath cost Y70. Doubles are Y120 to Y350.

Places to Eat

The local food is certainly nothing to get excited about, but you didn't come to the deserts of western China to eat anyway – face it, you're a long way from Guangzhou! Hotels do acceptable cuisine, the best (and priciest) offerings are served at the restaurant of the *Changcheng Hotel*.

Just opposite the bus station is a collection of competing restaurants – the mid-range ones have fine food and pleasant decor. A good one in this league is the *Linyuan Restaurant (línyuàn jiǔjiā)*, which does spicy Sichuan food, but there is no English sign or English menu.

Getting There & Away

Air There are flights to Dunhuang (twice weekly), Lanzhou (five times weekly) and Xi'an (twice weekly), though the flight schedule tends to expand in summer and shrink in winter. The CAAC office (☎ 226-237) is on Xinhua Nanlu, a stone's throw south of the Jiayuguan Hotel.

Bus There are five direct daily buses between Dunhuang and Jiayuguan – the 380km trip takes seven hours. There are also sleeper coaches to Lanzhou. Although the town of Jiuquan has little worth seeing, the half-hour trip only costs Y3 and buses leave frequently.

THE NORTH & NORTH-WEST

Train Jiayuguan lies on the Lanzhou-Ürümqi railway line. There are three expresses and three rapid trains each way daily; it's six hours to Liuyuan and 18 hours to Lanzhou. The railway station is four km south of the centre.

The train schedule is as follows:

Destination	Train No	Departure Time
Beijing	70	1.54 pm
Chengdu	114	12.57 pm
Lanzhou	244	9.07 pm
Shanghai	54	4.04 pm
Ürümqi	53	5.28 pm
Ürümqi	69	8.17 pm
Ürümqi	97	1.15 pm
Ürümqi	113	7.23 pm
Ürümqi	143	8.02 am
Ürümqi	243	6.25 am
Xi'an	144	11.04 pm
Zhengzhou	98	7.08 pm

Getting Around

To/From the Airport The airport is 13 km north-east of the city and taxis can be had for Y50 or so. An airport bus from the CAAC office meets all flights.

Bus Infrequent minibuses and public buses to the railway station run down Xinhua Nanlu then past the Changcheng Hotel.

Taxi & Tours Taxis, motorbikes and minibuses congregate outside the Jiayuguan Hotel and around the bus station – be prepared for some bargaining. As a general rule, taxi drivers want Y50 for each tourist site they take you to, though the fee includes their waiting time while you do your exploring.

CITS and other travel agencies are ever ready to sell you a day tour for a higher price than one you could arrange yourself. Apart from the July 1st Glacier, all the sights can be visited in a single day's tour. Getting together a group of travellers brings down the cost.

Bicycle The Jiayuguan Hotel and the Youth Hotel have bicycles for rent at Y1 per hour. Bikes are excellent for getting around town, to the fort and (if you don't mind the occasional gulp of dust) to the Overhanging Great

Wall too. However, you'll need motorised transport for the other sights.

LIUYUAN
(liŭyuán)

Liuyuan, on the Lanzhou-Ürümqi railway line, is the jumping-off point for Dunhuang. It's a forlorn-looking one-horse town – without the horse. You may want to visit the local karaoke to see if you can cheer up the Chinese.

The town's two hotels are both near the bus station and have the same name in English, *Liuyuan Hotel*. The Chinese names differ (*liŭyuán bīnguǎn* and *liŭyuán fàndiàn*). Both are on the main street by the bus station; dorm beds are Y30 and doubles cost Y130.

There are six trains daily in each direction. Going east, it takes six hours to reach Jiayuguan and 18 hours to reach Lanzhou. Heading west, it's 13 hours to Turpan and 16 hours to Ürümqi.

Minibuses depart for Dunhuang on average every 30 minutes (though several depart at once when a train arrives). The bus station is one block south of the railway station. Buy your ticket inside the bus station for Y10, or buy it on the bus for Y20!

Though subject to change, the all-important railway schedule for Liuyuan is as follows:

Destination	Train No	Departure Time
Beijing	70	9.09 am
Chengdu	114	7.08 am
Lanzhou	244	11.33 am
Shanghai	54	10.48 am
Ürümqi	53	11.16 pm
Ürümqi	69	1.58 am
Ürümqi	97	7.08 pm
Ürümqi	113	1.07 am
Ürümqi	143	2.49 pm
Ürümqi	243	12.45 pm
Xi'an	144	4.23 pm
Zhengzhou	98	2.05 pm

DUNHUANG
(dūnhuáng)

Dunhuang is a large oasis in one of China's most arid regions. After travelling for hours towards Dunhuang, the flat, barren desert landscape suddenly gives way to lush green cultivated fields with mountainous rolling sand dunes as a backdrop. The area has a certain haunting beauty, especially at night under a star-studded sky.

However, it's not so much the desert dunes and romantic nights that attract tourists to Dunhuang, but the superb Buddhist art at the nearby Mogao Caves. During the Han and Tang dynasties, Dunhuang was a major point of interchange between China and the outside world, a stopping-off post for both incoming and outgoing trading caravans. These days, Dunhuang's economic fortunes have been revived by tourism – it's one of the leading travel destinations in the country.

Orientation

Dunhuang radiates from the main traffic circle by the post office; all life-support systems are within walking distance of this point. The long-distance bus station is a 15-minute walk away on Dingzi Lu.

Information

The main CITS office is in the International Hotel, but there is a branch inside the Dunhuang Hotel (Binguan). There are other travel agents scattered about town, sequestered in various hotels. Since you can't buy train tickets in Dunhuang, there isn't a whole lot they can do for you other than arrange tours to remote sights such as Yumen Pass.

The PSB is on Xi Dajie, near the Bank of China. The Bank of China is open from 9 am to noon, and from 2.30 to 5.30 pm.

The post and telephone office is on the north-western side of the main traffic circle.

There is a left-luggage room in the long-distance bus station.

Dunhuang County Museum

(dūnhuáng xiàn bówùguǎn)

The museum is on Dong Dajie east of the main traffic circle. It's divided into three sections. The first section displays some of the Tibetan and Chinese scriptures unearthed from Cave No 17 at Mogao. The second section shows sacrificial objects from the Han to the Tang dynasties. The third section includes relics such as silks, brocades,

bamboo slips and reed torches (for the beacons) from the Yangguan and Yumen passes. A pleasant museum for a browse.

Places to Stay

Most hotels in Dunhuang vary the rates by season. Basically, the tourist season is from June to September, and hotel rates rise about 30% or more at that time. The rates quoted in this section are the off-season rates.

The *Western Region Hotel* (☎ 23017) *(xīyù bīnguǎn)* is a white-tiled building a few doors south of the long-distance bus station. Dorms with shared bath cost Y12 to Y18 per person. More spiffy doubles with private bath cost Y70 to Y200, though you can also rent these by the bed and pay half. This hotel is popular with backpackers for its low prices and convenient location.

Almost directly opposite the long-distance bus station is the two-star *Feitian Hotel* (☎ 22337) *(fēitiān bīnguǎn)*. Their multi-bed dorms cost Y15, and doubles/suites are Y100/150.

The *Mogao Hotel* (☎ 23009) *(mògāo bīnguǎn)* is a new place with a fresh feel and reasonable prices. Dorms are priced at Y15 to Y80 per bed, and doubles are Y90 to Y160.

The *Xuanquan Hotel* (☎ 23251) *(xuánquán bīnguǎn)* is also new and nice with low prices. Dorms are Y20 to Y30, doubles with attached bath are Y60 per bed, or book the whole room for Y120. Suites cost Y300.

The *Nation Guesthouse* (☎ 22690) *(mínzú bīnguǎn)* is certainly cheap, though its location on a 'wild west street' may leave you nonplussed. There's plenty of dust and tumbleweeds – all that's missing is a corral to tie up the horses. Dorm beds are Y10 to Y20 with shared bath, or Y40 to Y60 per bed in doubles with private bath.

Over on the eastern end of town is the plush *Silk Road Hotel* (☎ 23807; fax 22371). If you can afford the tariff (which is reasonable), this is *the* place to stay thanks to the super-courteous staff. A triple room with shared bath is Y90, but doubles with private bath are Y300 to Y350. The clerks at the front desk serve iced tea and present you with a

THE NORTH & NORTH-WEST

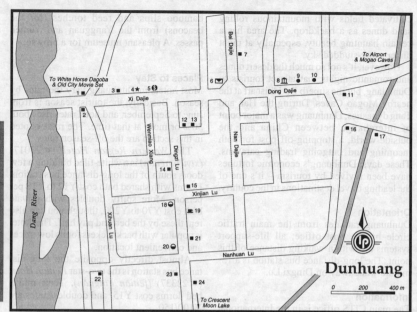

To White Horse Dagoba
& Old City Movie Set

Xi Dajie

Dong Dajie

Bei Dajie

Wenmiao Xiang

Dingzi Lu

Nan Dajie

Xihuan Lu

Xinjian Lu

Nanhuan Lu

Dang River

To Crescent
Moon Lake

To Airport
& Mogao Caves

Dunhuang

0   200   400 m

DUNHUANG 敦煌	15 Dunhuang Hotel (Fandian) 敦煌饭店	OTHER
PLACES TO STAY	16 Silk Road Hotel 丝路宾馆	4 PSB 公安局
1 Jinlong Hotel 金龙大酒店	17 Liyuan Hotel 丽园宾馆	5 Bank of China 中国银行
2 Jinshan Hotel 金山宾馆	21 Feitian Hotel 飞天宾馆	6 Post & Telephone Office 邮电局
3 Xuanquan Hotel 悬泉宾馆	22 Nation Guesthouse 民族宾馆	8 Dunhuang County Museum 敦煌县博物馆
7 Solar Energy Hotel 太阳能宾馆	23 Western Region Hotel & Shirley's Cafe 西域宾馆，风味餐馆	9 Xinhua Bookstore 新华书店
11 Dunhuang Hotel (Binguan) 敦煌宾馆	24 International Hotel & CITS 国际大酒店，中国国际旅行社	10 CAAC 中国民航
12 Mingshan Hotel 鸣山宾馆		18 Minibus Stop 小公共汽车站
13 Yangguan Hotel 阳关宾馆	**PLACES TO EAT**	20 Long-Distance Bus Station 长途汽车站
14 Mogao Hotel 莫高宾馆	19 Charlie Johng's Cafe 风味餐馆	

damp cloth to wipe your face while you're checking in.

Just across the irrigation canal from the Silk Road Hotel is the *Liyuan Hotel* (☎ 22047; fax 22070). Prices for doubles go from Y120 to Y340.

There are two places in town calling themselves the 'Dunhuang Hotel' in English, but they have different Chinese names. The smaller of the two is the *Dunhuang Hotel (Fandian)* (☎ 22413) *(dūnhuáng fàndiàn)* and is near the bus station. This place is actually ridiculously expensive for the grotty rooms you get – a dorm bed in a room without bath costs Y25 to Y70 per person. A dorm bed in a double with attached bath and leaking plumbing costs Y120 per person. This hotel only seems to get business because it's located right opposite the minibus stop, but you can do much better elsewhere.

The larger *Dunhuang Hotel (Binguan)* (☎ 22773) *(dūnhuáng bīnguǎn)* is at 1 Dong Dajie on the eastern side of town. This is a three-star place that packs in the tour groups. Doubles are Y425, suites cost Y510 and the 'super-suites' are Y680. The hotel boasts its own Friendship Store by the main gate.

The *Mingshan Hotel* (☎ 22132) *(míngshān bīnguǎn)* is an old-style place with a 'seen better days' feel. Hard, solid dorm beds cost Y24 to Y30. A double room with shared bath costs Y100, or pay Y160 if you want the bathroom attached.

The *Yangguan Hotel* (☎ 22459) *(yángguān bīnguǎn)* is a friendly place with pleasant rooms. Rates for clean doubles with air-conditioning and attached bath are Y120 to Y360.

The curiously named *Solar Energy Hotel* (☎ 22306) *(tàiyángnéng bīnguǎn)* is at 14 Bei Dajie, north of the central traffic circle. There are just a few rooms with shared bath costing Y83, but most rooms are doubles with private bath priced between Y370 and Y580.

The *Jinlong Hotel* (☎ 23202) *(jīnlóng dà jiǔdiàn)* seems pricey. Doubles are Y290 to Y415.

One of the most expensive places in town (and really not worth it) is the *Jinshan Hotel* (☎ 21077) *(jīnshān bīnguǎn)*. Twin rooms are Y1100 to Y1800.

The *International Hotel (guójì dà jiǔdiàn)* is the new upmarket place in town. It was not yet open at the time of writing, but certainly will be by the time you read this.

Places to Eat
First prize goes to *Charlie Johng's Cafe* just north of the Feitian Hotel. Good Western and Chinese food at cheap prices, plus an English menu and nice background music, all contribute to the atmosphere. Charlie's sister operates *Shirley's Cafe* near the Western Region Hotel, which is also excellent.

The *Dunhuang Hotel (Binguan)* has a more upmarket restaurant with an English menu, whose contents include 'camels paw' and 'dates in honey sauce'.

Getting There & Away
Air In the summer peak season there are daily flights to/from Lanzhou and Xi'an, and less frequent air services to/from Beijing and Jiayuguan. The number of flights is reduced during the winter months. Seats can be booked at the CAAC office (☎ 22389) on Dong Dajie or at the Dunhuang Hotel (Binguan).

Bus Minibuses to Liuyuan (130 km) depart when full, from the minibus stop opposite the Dunhuang Hotel (Fandian). The fare is Y10 though the drivers may attempt to charge foreigners double. The trip takes about 2½ hours on an excellent surfaced road.

All other buses depart from the long-distance bus station. There are scheduled public buses to Jiayuguan (seven hours) at 7.30, 9 and 11.30 am, and at 1, 4.30, 6 and 10.30 pm. Most buses actually go to Jiuquan (a rather boring place), stopping only briefly in Jiayuguan. Foreigners must pay Y48, Y20 of which is 'insurance'.

There's one early-morning bus to Golmud (13 hours) via a rugged but scenic route that crosses the snow-capped Altunshan. Arrive early enough to store your luggage on the roof. It's chilly up in the mountains, so keep some warm clothing handy regardless of how hot it may be in Dunhuang itself.

Train Liuyuan is on the Lanzhou-Ürümqi railway line (see the Liuyuan section for the train schedule).

Getting Around

To/From the Airport Dunhuang's airport is 13 km east of town. In addition to the CAAC bus, you can hire a minibus for about Y30.

Minibus Dunhuang has no taxis as such, but minibuses can easily be chartered. The minibus stop opposite the Dunhuang Hotel (Fandian) is the place to go to start the negotiations.

Bicycle Dunhuang is one of the easiest places in China to hire bicycles. The Feitian Hotel has the most modern and best-maintained bikes, and charges a reasonable Y1 per hour. Doing a bit of exploratory pedalling around the oasis is fine, but getting to most outlying sights is not feasible by bike.

AROUND DUNHUANG

Highlights around Dunhuang include the Mogao Caves, the Old City Movie Set, White Horse Dagoba and Crescent Moon Lake. To charter a small minibus to all these places should cost around Y150.

Crescent Moon Lake
(yuèyáquán)

The lake is four km south of the centre of Dunhuang at the Singing Sand Mountains *(míngshāshān)*, where the oasis meets the desert. Spring water trickles up into a depression between huge sand dunes, forming a small, crescent-shaped pond (not to be confused with the concrete storage pool nearby). The climb to the top of the dunes is sweaty work, but the dramatic view back across the rolling desert sands towards the oasis makes the effort worthwhile.

Out here the recreational activities include the predictable camel rides, more novel 'dune surfing' (sand sliding) and paragliding (jumping off the top of high dunes with a chute on your back). Novices may find the idea of sailing high above the evening desert landscape a bit unnerving, but – the Chinese-made gliding gear notwithstanding – soft, loose sand makes even a crash-landing relatively unhazardous. Even so, it might be prudent to look at your insurance policy before you leap! Paragliding costs Y30 a go – that's for one successful flight.

The admission fee to the lake and dunes area is Y15 for foreigners – a Chinese student card should earn you a discount.

If you go walking off into the dunes in the heat of the day (not recommended), be sure to carry water and wear a hat (or you'll fry your brains). A compass would come in handy; getting lost in the sea of sand could have serious consequences.

Most tourists head out to the dunes in the evening around 5 pm when the weather starts to cool down. You can ride a bike out there, but minibuses cost Y2 and make the run whenever full. You can, of course, book the whole minibus for around Y20.

White Horse Dagoba
(báimǎ tǎ)

Something of an anticlimax, the dagoba is four km west of town and is easily combined with the trip out to the Old City Movie Set. It makes a good place for a short bicycle excursion.

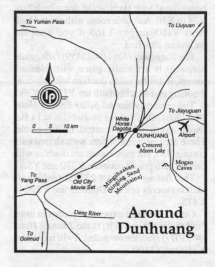

Old City Movie Set
(diànyǐng gǔchéng)

This reconstructed Song-Dynasty town, complete with five-metre-high city walls, was built in 1987 as a movie set for a Sino-Japanese co-production titled *Dunhuang*. Standing isolated out in the desert some 20 km south-west of Dunhuang, from a distance the Old City has a dramatic and strikingly realistic appearance. Close up, though, the place is starting to look a bit shabby; the mud-brick walls are crumbling and the bare yards behind the makeshift façades are scattered with litter. It's vaguely reminiscent of a 'wild west' ghost town. Nevertheless, it's a reasonably interesting place for a short visit.

Chinese minibuses to the Old City leave from the side street one block north of Dunhuang's long-distance bus station; they charge only Y10, but generally stay far too long. You can get there by bicycle, and will arrive fit and thirsty. Entry costs Y15 (Y7 for students).

Mogao Caves
(mògāo kū)

The Mogao Caves are the most impressive and best-preserved examples of Buddhist cave art anywhere in China, and are the highlight of a visit to Dunhuang. According to legend, in 366 AD the vision of a thousand buddhas inspired a wandering monk to cut the first of hundreds of caves into the sandstone cliff face. Over the next 10 centuries Dunhuang became a flourishing centre of Buddhist culture on the Silk Road.

The grottoes were then abandoned and eventually forgotten. At the turn of the 20th century a Taoist monk by the name of Wang Yuan stumbled across a cave filled with a treasure trove of documents and paintings. The cave had been bricked up to stop the contents falling into the hands of invaders and the dry desert air had preserved much of the material.

In 1907, the British explorer Sir Aurel Stein heard a rumour of the hoard, tracked down the monk and was allowed to inspect the contents of the cave. It was an archaeological gold mine of Buddhist texts in Chinese, Tibetan and many other central Asian languages, some known and some long forgotten. There were paintings on silk and linen, and what may be the oldest printed book in existence (dating from 868 AD).

The sacking of the caves began in earnest. Stein convinced Wang to part with a large section of the library in return for a donation towards the restoration of some of the grottoes. He carted away 24 packing cases of manuscripts and five of paintings, embroideries and art relics, all of which were deposited in the British Museum. The following year a French explorer, Pelliot, passed through Dunhuang and bought more of the manuscripts from the monk.

He was followed by others from the USA, Japan and Russia, who all carted off their booty. News of the find filtered through to Beijing, and the imperial court ordered the remainder of the collection to be transported to the capital. Many items were pilfered while they sat in the Dunhuang government offices, and Stein reported in 1914 when he returned to the area that fine Buddhist manuscripts were brought to him for sale. He also said that Wang had regretted not taking up his original offer to buy the entire collection.

For the Chinese, it's another example of the plundering of the country by foreigners in the 19th and early 20th centuries. Half the world seems to have ended up in the British Museum – the Greeks want their Parthenon frieze back and the Chinese want the Dunhuang manuscripts back. Of course, one hates to think what would have happened to the collection if Stein had left it where it was – most likely the Red Guards would have used it for a road base during the Cultural Revolution.

The Mogao Caves are set into desert cliffs above a river valley about 25 km south-east of Dunhuang. Unfortunately, the area is highly exposed to the elements and the erosion of wind and water have severely damaged quite a few of the caves. Today, 492 grottoes are still standing. The grottoes honeycomb the 1600-metre-long cliff face which sits on a north-south axis. Altogether they contain over 2000 statues and over

45,000 separate murals. Cave 17 is where Wang Yuan discovered the hoard of manuscripts and artworks.

Most of the Dunhuang art dates from the Northern and Western Wei, Northern Zhou, Sui and Tang dynasties, though examples from the Five Dynasties, Northern Song, Western Xia and Yuan can also be found. The Northern Wei, Western Wei, Northern Zhou and Tang caves are in the best state of preservation.

The caves tend to be rectangular or square with recessed, decorated ceilings. The focal point of each is the group of brightly painted statues representing Buddha and the Bodhisattvas, or Buddha's disciples. The smaller statues are made of terracotta, coated with a kind of plaster surface so that intricate details could be etched into the surface. The walls and ceilings were also plastered with layers of cement and clay and then painted with watercolour. Large sections of the mural are made up of decorative patterns using motifs from nature, architecture, or textiles.

Northern Wei, Western Wei & Northern Zhou Caves The Turkic-speaking Tobas who inhabited the region north of China invaded and conquered the country in the 4th century and founded the Northern Wei Dynasty around 386 AD. They deliberately adopted a policy of copying Chinese customs and lifestyle. But friction between groups who wanted to maintain the traditional Toba lifestyle and those who wanted to assimilate with the Chinese eventually split the Toba empire in two in the middle of the 6th century. The eastern part adopted the Chinese way of life and the rulers took the dynasty name of Northern Qi. The western part took the dynasty name of Northern Zhou and tried to revert to Toba customs, without success. By 567 AD, however, they had defeated the Qi and taken control of all of northern China.

The fall of the Han Dynasty in 220 AD had sent Confucianism into decline. With the turmoil produced by the Toba invasions, Buddhism's teachings of nirvana and personal salvation became highly appealing.

The religion spread rapidly under the patronage of the new rulers, and made a new and decisive impact on Chinese art which can be seen in the Buddhist statues at Mogao.

The art of this period is characterised by its attempt to depict the spirituality of those who had achieved enlightenment and transcended the material world through their asceticism. The Wei statues are slim, ethereal figures with finely chiselled features and comparatively large heads.

The Wei and Zhou paintings at Mogao are some of the most interesting in the grottoes. The figures are simple, almost cartoon-like, with round heads, elongated ears and puppet-like, segmented bodies which are boldly outlined. The female figures are all naked to the waist, with large breasts; these characteristics suggest an Indian influence.

Sui Caves The throne of the Northern Zhou Dynasty was usurped by a general of Chinese or mixed Chinese-Toba origin. Prudently putting to death all the sons of the former emperor, he embarked on a series of wars which by 589 AD had reunited northern and southern China for the first time in 360 years. The Tobas simply disappeared from history, either mixing with other Turkish tribes from central Asia or assimilating with the Chinese.

The Sui Dynasty was short-lived, and very much a transition between the Wei and Tang periods. It did not leave any great masterpieces. Again, the best Sui art was of Buddhist origin. What separates the Sui style from that of the Wei is the rigidity of its sculpture. The figures of the Buddha and Bodhisattvas are stiff and immobile; their heads are curiously oversized and their torsos elongated. They wear Chinese robes and show none of the Indian-inspired softness and grace of the Wei figures.

Tang Caves The reign of the last Sui emperor, Yang Ti, was characterised by imperial extravagance, cruelty and social injustice. Taking advantage of the inevitable peasant revolts which had arisen in eastern China, a noble family of Chinese-Turkish descent assassinated the emperor, took control of the capital, Chang'an (present-day Xi'an), and assumed the throne, taking the dynasty name of Tang.

During the Tang period, China pushed its borders forcefully westward as far as Lake Balkhash in today's Kazakstan. Outside trade expanded and foreign merchants and people of diverse religions streamed into the Tang capital of Chang'an. Buddhism became prominent and Buddhist art reached its peak; the proud bearing of the Buddhist figures in the Mogao Caves reflects the feelings of the times, the prevailing image of the brave Tang warrior, and the strength and steadfastness of the empire.

The portraits of Tang nobles are considerably larger than those of the Wei and Sui dynasties, and the figures tend to occupy important positions within the murals. In some cases the patrons are portrayed in the same scene as the Buddha.

Unlike the figures of the Wei, Zhou and Sui periods, the Tang figures are realistic with a range of very human expressions.

Later Caves The Tang period marked the ultimate development of the cave paintings. During later dynasties, the economy around Dunhuang went into decline and the luxuriousness and vigour typical of Tang painting began to be replaced by simpler drawing techniques and flatter figures. However, during the Northern Song period a number of important breakthroughs were made in landscape painting.

Admission Foreigners have the choice of buying a ticket for Y25 or for Y65; the Y25 ticket lets you see 10 caves, while the Y65 ticket is for 30 caves (give or take a few). Unless you're on a particularly tight budget or have limited interest in Buddhist cave art, the Y65 ticket is worth the extra money.

All visitors must be accompanied by a local guide (included in the admission fee). Even if there are only a few of you, foreigners are generally put into a separate tour group with a guide who speaks English. Otherwise you could round up any foreigners

present into a single group and ask to have an English-speaking guide assigned to you.

The caves are open from 8.30 to 11.30 am and from 2 to 3.45 pm. More people tend to turn up for the morning session, but it's longer so you have more time to look around; the afternoon session can be a bit rushed.

Except for the small niches (most of them in very bad condition or bare of statues and paintings), all the caves have locked gates. Many of the locked caves are in such poor condition that they are simply not worth opening to the general public. Some, like Cave 462, the Mizong Cave, contain Tantric art whose explicit sexual portrayals have been deemed too corrupting for the public to view. A few caves are in the process of being restored.

Photography is strictly prohibited everywhere within the fenced-off caves area, though photos are sometimes permitted after payment of an appropriately large sum of money; cameras and all hand luggage must be deposited at an office near the entrance gate. Shops at the caves and in Dunhuang itself sell comprehensive sets of slides, postcards and books. Most caves are lit only by indirect sunlight from outside, often making it hard to see detail, particularly in the niches. Heavy but low-powered torches (flashlights) can be hired at the ticket office; if you have your own, bring it.

Getting There & Away The Mogao Caves are 25 km and 30 minutes by bus from Dunhuang. There are no scheduled public buses, but minibuses make the run regularly. You can either book the whole bus for yourself (thus making it into a taxi) or hang around the minibus stand and wait until there are sufficient passengers to split the tariff. The minibus stand is opposite the Dunhuang Hotel (Fandian).

Depending on your bargaining skills, you should be able to hire a minibus out there for around Y50 return, including the driver's waiting time.

Some people ride out to the caves on a bicycle, but be warned that half the ride is through total desert – hot work in summer.

The Mogao Hostel (*mògāokū zhāodàisuǒ*) is the only accommodation at the caves; it has rooms for Y50 and does good set meals in the tourist season.

Yang & Yumen Passes
(*yángguān, yùménguān*)

Some 76 km south-west of Dunhuang is the Yang (South) Pass. Here, Han Dynasty beacon towers marked the caravan route westwards and warned of advancing invaders, but what remains has now largely disappeared under the shifting sands. Nearby are the ruins of the ancient Han town of Shouchang. The Yumen (Jade Gate) Pass, 98 km north-west of Dunhuang, is also known for its ancient ruins.

Caravans heading out of China would travel up the Gansu corridor to Dunhuang; the Yumen Pass was the starting point of the road which ran across the north of what is now Xinjiang Province, and the Yang Pass was the start of the route which cut through the south of the region.

The trip out to either Yang Pass or Yumen Pass takes a whole day. There are irregular tours to the passes sometimes including a few other sights such as the Old City Movie Set on the way mainly during the tourist season; inquire at the main CITS or at the Dunhuang Hotel (Binguan). The only other way to get there is by chartered vehicle; count on paying around Y250 all-inclusive for a small minibus.

Ningxia 宁夏

Ningxia *(níngxià)* was carved out as a separate administrative region in 1928 and remained a province until 1954, when it was absorbed into Gansu Province. In 1958 Ningxia re-emerged, this time as an autonomous region with a large Hui population. The boundaries of the region have ebbed and flowed since then – Inner Mongolia was included at one time, but the borders are now somewhat reduced.

Part of the arid north-west of China, much of Ningxia is populated by a few hardy nomads who make their living grazing sheep and goats. Winters are hard and cold, with plummeting temperatures; blistering summers make irrigation a necessity. In fact, the province would be virtually uninhabitable if it were not for the Yellow River, Ningxia's lifeline. Most of the population lives near the river or the irrigation channels which run off it. These channels were created in the Han Dynasty, when the area was first settled by the Han Chinese in the 1st century BC.

Only about a third of Ningxia's people are Hui, living mostly in the south of the province. The rest are Han Chinese. The Hui minority are descended from Arab and Iranian traders who travelled to China during the Tang Dynasty. Their numbers were later increased during the Yuan Dynasty by immigrants from central Asia. Apart from their continued adherence to Islam, the Hui have been assimilated into Han culture.

The completion of the Baotou-Lanzhou railway in 1958 helped to relieve the area's isolation and develop some industry in this otherwise almost exclusively agricultural region.

YINCHUAN
(yínchuān)

Sheltered from the deserts of Mongolia by the high ranges of the Helanshan to its west and abundantly supplied with water from the nearby Yellow River, Yinchuan occupies a favoured geographical position in otherwise

Population: five million
Capital: Yinchuan
Highlights:
* Yinchuan, the laid-back capital city of this remote province and the launchpad for trips to Helanshan
* The unusual 108 Dagobas near Qingtongxia, which pop out of the desert landscape
* Zhongwei, where the eerie beauty of the sand dunes are enhanced by water wheels on the Yellow River

harsh surroundings. This city was once the capital of the Western Xia, a mysterious kingdom founded during the 11th century.

Orientation
Yinchuan is divided into two parts. The new industrialised section is close to the railway station and is simply called 'New City' *(xīn chéng)*. The 'Old City' *(lǎo chéng)* is about five km away and has most of the town's sights, as well as the long-distance bus station. The Old City is a lively commercial shopping and eating district and also has most of Yinchuan's tourist hotels.

Information
The main CITS (☎ 543-720) and CTS (☎ 544-485) offices are both upstairs at 150 Jiefang

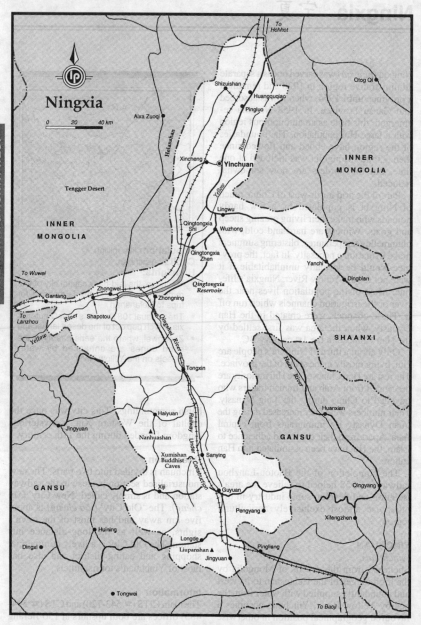

Ningxia

0   20   40 km

To Hohhot

Otog Qi

Shizuishan

Huangquqiao

Pingluo

Aixa Zuoqi

Helanshan

INNER MONGOLIA

Xincheng   Yinchuan

Yellow River

Tengger Desert

Lingwu

INNER MONGOLIA

Qingtongxia Shi   Wuzhong

Qingtongxia Zhen

Yanchi

Dingbian

To Wuwei   Gantang   Zhongwei   Zhongning   Qingtongxia Reservoir

Shapotou   Qingshui River

To Lanzhou   Yellow River

SHAANXI

Huan River

Tongxin

Haiyuan   Railway Under Construction   Huanxian

Nanhuashan   Jingyuan

GANSU

Xumishan Buddhist Caves   Sanying

Xiji   Guyuan   Qingyang

Huining   Pengyang   Xifengzhen

GANSU

Dingxi   Longde   Pingliang

Liupanshan   Jingyuan

Tongwei

To Baoji

Xijie. There is also a small CITS office inside the Ningxia Hotel. The PSB is in a white building on Jiefang Xijie.

The main branch of the Bank of China (☎ 543-307) is at 102 Jiefang Jie in a white-tiled building near the Ningxia Hotel. The post and telephone office is right in the centre of town at the corner of Minzu Jie and Jiefang Xijie.

Haibao Pagoda
(hǎibǎo tǎ)

Haibao Pagoda, also called North Pagoda *(běi tǎ)*, stands out prominently in the north of the city. Records of the structure date from the 5th century. In 1739 an earthquake toppled the lot, but it was rebuilt in 1771 in the original style. It's part of a monastery which has also been spruced up as a tourist attraction.

There is no public transport out here. Other than walking, you can reach the pagoda by bicycle or taxi. It's 2½ km from the Oasis Hotel.

Ningxia Museum
(níngxià bówùguǎn)

The museum is on Jinning Jie, three blocks south of Jiefang Xijie, in the old Chengtian Monastery. Its collection includes Western Xia and Northern Zhou historical relics as well as material covering the Hui culture. Within the leafy courtyard is the Chengtian Monastery Pagoda, also known as the West Pagoda *(xī tǎ)*. The museum is open from 8.30 am to 6.30 pm; it's closed on Monday.

Drum Tower
(gǔlóu)

The Drum Tower stands in the middle of a small intersection several blocks east of the post office. It's a classical Chinese-style building and is worth climbing for a quick look.

Yuhuang Pavilion
(yùhuáng gé)

This restored 400-year-old building is on Jiefang Jie, one block east of the Drum Tower. The pavilion has a tiny museum whose collection includes two fascinating mummified bodies taken from tombs outside Yinchuan.

South Gate
(nánmén lóu)

This is in the south-east of the city near the long-distance bus station. It's been likened to a scaled-down version of Beijing's Tiananmen, complete with Mao portrait. Despite its lack of grandeur, the South Gate is popular with Chinese tourists as a backdrop for their own portrait shots of Mao.

Nanguan Mosque
(nánguān qīngzhēn sì)

The mosque is a modern Middle Eastern-style structure showing little Chinese architectural influence, with Islamic arches and dome roofs covered in green tiles. This is Yinchuan's main mosque, and an active place of worship, so don't just stroll in without first asking permission. It's within easy walking distance of the South Gate.

Places to Stay

New City The most convenient place for making a quick getaway is the *Railway Hotel* (☎ 366-361, 369-119) *(tiělù bīnguǎn)*, just a short walk from the station. Double rooms here cost Y80 with shared bath, or Y140 to Y360 with private bath.

Behind the railway station and reachable by bus No 1 is the *Taoyuan Hotel* (☎ 368-470) *(táoyuán bīnguǎn)*. Doubles are priced at Y136, Y144 and Y172.

Old City At the railway station, hop on bus No 1 to reach the *Oasis Hotel* (☎ 532-951) *(lǜzhōu fàndiàn)*. It's on Jiefang Xijie and is easily distinguished by the 'rocket ship' on the roof. Rooms here cost Y96 to Y440.

The newest place in town is the *Yindu Hotel* (☎ 531-888) *(yíndū dà jiǔdiàn)* at 59 Jiefang Xijie. Room rates are Y88 to Y368.

The *Ningxia Hotel* (☎ 545-131) *(níngxià bīnguǎn)*, at 3 Gongyuan Jie near Zhongshan Park, is a classy establishment with prices from Y198 to Y462. Pleasant gardens cover the compound.

The *Ningfeng Hotel* (☎ 628-898) *(níngfēng bīnguǎn)*, diagonally opposite the post office, is another upmarket place. Doubles are Y330, Y396 and Y616.

Places to Eat

Good for street food are the stalls in the back-streets around the long-distance bus station or those on Xinhua Xijie near the museum. On offer are beef and lamb dishes, noodles, fried dumplings and Islamic pastries.

A local Hui sweet called 'eight treasures rice' (*bābǎo fàn*) is made from jujubes and rice, which are pressed together and steam-cooked to form an enormous loaf. Street vendors sell slices with a topping of honey for about Y1.

The *Huanying Islamic Restaurant (huān-yíng qīngzhēn fànzhuāng)*, at 23 Jiefang Jie (next to the Yinchuan Hotel), has some tasty dishes in the section upstairs.

Yinchuan is known for its special blend of tea, called by a variety of names: three bubbles platform (*sānpào tái*), eight treasures tea (*bābǎo chá*) and lid bowl tea (*gàiwǎn chá*). It's based on a mixture of dried ingredients including persimmons, longans, grapes, walnuts, sesame seeds and green tea, and is served in a small porcelain bowl with a lid. A generous chunk of rock sugar is thrown in so the brew sweetens gradually. Virtually all restaurants in town can brew you a cup, and you can even buy it in packets to take home.

THE NORTH & NORTH-WEST

YINCHUAN 银川	6	Haibao Pagoda	18	Yinchuan Depart-
		海宝塔		ment Store
PLACES TO STAY	7	Yinchuan Recreation		银川百货大楼
		Park	20	Ningxia Museum &
3 Railway Hotel		银川游乐园		Chengtian Monas-
铁路宾馆	8	CITS		tery Pagoda
4 Taoyuan Hotel		中国国际旅行社		宁夏博物馆,
桃园宾馆	9	Xinhua Bookstore		承天寺塔
11 Ningxia Hotel		新华书店	21	Drum Tower
宁夏宾馆	10	Bank of China		鼓楼
12 Oasis & Yindu Hotels		中国银行	22	Yuhuang Pavilion
绿洲饭店, 银都大酒店	13	PSB		玉皇阁
19 Ningfeng Hotel		公安局	23	Shopping Street
宁丰宾馆	14	Foreign Languages		商城
		Bookstore	24	Nanguan Mosque
OTHER		外文书店		南关清真寺
	15	Huanying Islamic	25	South Gate
1 Yinchuan Airport		Restaurant		南门楼
银川飞机场		欢迎清真饭店	26	Long-Distance Bus
2 Railway Station	16	CAAC		Station
火车站		中国民航		银川汽车站
5 Xihu Recreation Park	17	Post & Telephone Office		
西湖游乐园		邮电大楼		

Things to Buy

The Foreign Languages Bookstore (☎ 624-353) at 46 Jiefang Xijie has a decent collection of classic novels in English on the ground floor. Go upstairs to find the music tape and CD collection – there's a surprisingly good assortment of Western rock and classical music.

Gulou Jie (south of Jiefang Dongjie) is the place to look for everything else, from clothing to electronics.

Getting There & Away

Air The main CAAC ticket office (☎ 622-143) is at 14 Minzu Beijie. There are flights connecting Yinchuan with Beijing, Guangzhou, Shanghai and Xi'an.

Bus The long-distance bus station is in the south-eastern part of town on the square near the South Gate. Regular buses connect Yinchuan with Qingtongxia Shi, Zhongwei, Tongxin, Guyuan and, alongside the Great Wall, Dingbian in Shaanxi Province. There are also four standard buses each day to Xi'an (via Guyuan) and one sleeper bus. There is also one daily bus to Lanzhou.

Train Yinchuan lies on the Lanzhou-Beijing railway line, which also runs through Zhongwei, Hohhot and Datong. Express trains from Yinchuan take 10 hours to Lanzhou and 12 hours to Hohhot.

Destination	Train No	Departure Time
Beijing	44	7.41 pm
Beijing	78	11.20 am
Hohhot	202	6.50 am
Lanzhou	43	11.10 am
Lanzhou	201	11.17 pm
Lanzhou	93	8.38 pm

Getting Around

To/From the Airport A CAAC bus meets incoming and departing flights. The airport is some 13 km out of town.

Bus Yinchuan's traffic is light, making getting around town fast and pleasant. You might even find a vacant seat on the bus! Bus No 1 runs back and forth along Jiefang Jie, connecting the railway station to the Old City. The fare is just Y0.70. Minibuses cover the same route faster but charge Y3.

Taxi Taxis between the railway station and the Old City want Y30.

AROUND YINCHUAN
Helanshan
(hèlánshān)

The mountains of the Helanshan range are clearly visible from Yinchuan. The range forms an important natural barrier against desert winds and invaders alike, with the highest peak reaching 3556 metres. Along the foothills of the Helanshan lie some interesting sights.

About 17 km north-west of Yinchuan is the historic pass village of **Gunzhongkou**, where there are walking trails up into the surrounding hills. There are scheduled buses to Gunzhongkou only in July and August, when people from the city come up here to escape the summer heat.

Not far to the north of the resort are the Twin **Pagodas of Baisikou** (báisìkǒu shuāngtǎ), 13 and 14 storeys high and decorated with statuettes of Buddha.

South of Gunzhongkou is the **Western Xia Mausoleum** (xīxià wánglíng), the main tourist destination in this area. According to legend, the founder of the Western Xia kingdom, Li Yuanhao, built 72 tombs. One was for himself, others held relatives or were left empty. The Western Xia Kingdom lasted for 190 years and 10 successive emperors, but was wiped out by Genghis Khan. For some reason, the kingdom was not included in *The 24 Histories*, the standard Chinese work on the history of that era. Numerous Chinese scholars have joined the hunt to solve this mystery.

To visit the Twin Pagodas and the mausoleum (or Gunzhongkou out of season) you will have to either join one of the occasional CITS tours or hire a taxi. Because of the area's poor roads, a trip including all three sights would take a full day.

Qingtongxia
(qīngtóngxiá)

Two places go by the name of Qingtongxia: the 'city' (Qingtongxia *Shi*) on the main highway 54 km south of Yinchuan, and the smaller 'town' (Qingtongxia *Zhen*) 29 km further south at the dam built across the Yellow River in 1962.

Near Qingtongxia Zhen is the famous group known as the 108 Dagobas (yìbǎi líng bā tǎ). The 12 rows of brick pagodas are arranged in a large triangular constellation, standing defiantly above a great artificial lake. Their white vase-like shape contrasts strikingly with the arid slopes above them. Dating from the Yuan Dynasty, it's still not known why they were erected here.

Getting There & Away The 108 Dagobas are best seen as a day-trip from Yinchuan. There are many daily buses and minibuses to Qingtongxia Shi, but only two direct buses (at 9 am and 12.30 pm) to the 108 Dagobas. If you take the 12.30 pm bus there, on the way back you will have to change buses in Qingtongxia Zhen. Alternatively, take a slow train to the nearby Qingtongxia Railway Station, then walk or catch a bus to the dam site. At Qingtongxia Zhen, you can either walk over the dam bridge and then follow paths along the lake shore (1½ hours return), or take a speedboat across (10 minutes).

ZHONGWEI
(zhōngwèi)

Zhongwei lies 167 km south-west of Yinchuan on the Lanzhou-Baotou railway line. It's sandwiched between the sand dunes of the Tengger Desert to the north and the Yellow River to the south. This is a market town with a plodding, peaceful pace, a complete change from the hurly-burly of most Chinese cities.

Gao Temple
(gāo miào)

The main attraction in town is the Gao Temple, an eclectic, multipurpose temple which serves Buddhism, Confucianism and Taoism. Built during the 15th century and flattened by an earthquake during the 18th century, it was later rebuilt and expanded several times until being virtually razed again by fire in 1942. Extensive repairs have been made to the present wooden structure,

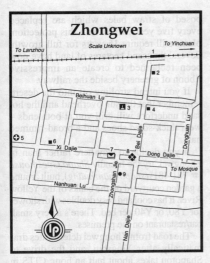

Zhongwei

Scale Unknown

To Lanzhou — To Yinchuan

Beihuan Lu

Xi Dajie

Nanhuan Lu

Bei Dajie

Dong Dajie

Donghuan

Zhongshan Jie

Nan Dajie

To Mosque

ZHONGWEI 中卫

1 Railway Station
   火车站
2 Railway Hotel
   铁路宾馆
3 Gao Temple
   高庙
4 Zhongwei Hotel
   中卫饭店
5 Hospital
   医院
6 Yellow River Guesthouse
   黄河宾馆
7 Post Office
   邮局
8 Department Store
   百货商店
9 Market
   市场

whose dozens of towers and pavilions look like parts of a jagged wedding cake. The temple includes a hotchpotch of statues from all three religions, so you can see Gautama Buddha, bodhisattvas, the Jade Emperor and the Holy Mother under one roof.

Places to Stay

The *Railway Hotel (tiělù bīnguǎn)*, directly opposite the station, has beds in triples for Y30 and doubles with bathroom for Y100.

The *Yellow River Guesthouse* (☎ 712-941) *(huánghé bīnguǎn)*, a short way west of the Drum Tower, is Zhongwei's only tourist hotel. Standard doubles go for Y150. CITS (☎ 712-620) has an office on the 4th floor of the 'government wing'. The hotel rents bikes for Y1 per hour.

The decrepit *Zhongwei Hotel* (☎ 712-219) *(zhōngwèi fàndiàn)* on Bei Dajie is another option.

There's a guesthouse at Shapotou (16 km from Zhongwei) that's nicer than anything in town (see the Shapotou section for details).

Getting There & Away

From Zhongwei there is one daily express and two slower trains to Yinchuan or Lan-

zhou, and infrequent services to Wuwei in Gansu Province via a direct line west. Zhongwei also has bus connections with Yinchuan and Guyuan.

Destination	Train No	Departure Time
Beijing	44	4.37 pm
Yinchuan	94	5.41 am
Hohhot	202	3.21 am
Lanzhou	43	2.22 pm
Lanzhou	93	11.50 pm
Lanzhou	201	2.32 am

AROUND ZHONGWEI
Water Wheels
(shuǐchē)

Since the Han Dynasty, water wheels have been a common sight in Ningxia Province and in other regions crossed by the Yellow River. Mechanical pumps have now taken over, though water wheels are occasionally used to pump water from the river down a complicated system of ducts and canals to the fields.

To see some old idle water wheels, ride or bus your way to Yingshui, a village west of Zhongwei on the Shapotou road. From here a dirt road goes seven km to the Yellow River, where a ferry will take you across to

Xiaheye. On the other side, walk east (left) for about two km to the water wheels near the river.

Leather Rafts
(*yángpí fázi*)

Leather rafts have been a traditional mode of transport on the Yellow River for centuries. They usually served for short crossings, although thousands of rafts were used during the 1950s to freight huge loads of tobacco, herbs or people on a two-week trip covering nearly 2000 km between Lanzhou and Baotou. The largest raft then in use was made from 600 sheepskins, measured 12 metres by seven metres and could carry loads of up to 30 tonnes.

The raft-making process begins with careful skinning of sheep (or sometimes cattle) carcasses. The skins are then soaked for several days in oil and brine before being taken out and inflated. An average of 14 hides are tied together under a wooden framework to make a strong raft capable of carrying four people and four bikes. Single-skin rafts are also used in parts of Gansu and Qinghai, where you either lie on top of your raft or crawl inside while the rafter lies on top to direct your passage across the river. There is usually enough air inside a large cowhide to last for 15 minutes which, reportedly, is about twice the time needed for an average crossing.

Skin rafts are still used quite a bit in western China. You can see them in action on the Yellow River at Shapotou; you could even have a go yourself.

Shapotou Desert Research Centre
(*shāpōtóu shāmò yánjiūsuǒ*)

Shapotou lies about 16 km west of Zhongwei on the fringe of the Tengger Desert. The Desert Research Centre was founded in 1956 with the task of researching methods to fix or hold back the moving sand dunes from the railway. From 1962 onwards, the researchers have been using the 'chequerboard method' for sand blockage and fixation introduced in the 1950s by a Soviet adviser. Plants are protected inside small chequerboards composed of straw bales which are replaced every five years. Even with this protection, plants still require 15 years for full growth. Several thousand hectares of land have now been reclaimed to create an impressive ribbon of greenery beside the railway.

If you intend strolling off into the desert, remember that the sun overhead and the hot sand underfoot will grill you at both ends – wear thick-soled shoes and a broad-rimmed hat.

If you decide to stay here rather than in Zhongwei, try the friendly *Shapo Guesthouse* (☎ 781-481) (*shāpō shānzhuāng*), built around a garden courtyard on the banks of the Yellow River. It has cool and cosy doubles with shower for Y80, or Y40 per bed. There's a very small bar/restaurant on the premises.

The road from Zhongwei deteriorates dramatically after Yingshui, and the drive to Shapotou takes about half an hour. CITS in Zhongwei often organises tours out here. Otherwise you can charter your own three-wheeler and perhaps include a side trip to see the water wheels too.

TONGXIN
(*tóngxīn*)

Tongxin, on the road between Zhongning and Guyuan, has an overwhelmingly Hui population. The main attraction is the Great Mosque (*qīngzhēn dàsì*), a few km south of the bus station, that was built during the Ming Dynasty. One of the largest mosques in Ningxia Province, this is a traditional Chinese wooden structure with Islamic woodcuts and decorations of carved brick.

GUYUAN
(*gùyuán*)

Guyuan is in the south of Ningxia Province, 460 km from Yinchuan. There is a fine set of Buddhist grottoes at Xumishan (*xūmíshān shíkū*) about 50 km north-west of Guyuan. Xumi is the Chinese version of the Sanskrit word *sumeru*, which means 'treasure mountain'.

Cut into five adjacent peaks are 132 caves containing over 300 Buddhist statues dating back 1400 years, from the Northern Wei to

---

Save the Trees

Straddling the Great Wall is the world's most ambitious reafforestation and afforestation programme – a shelter belt creeping toward its ultimate length of 6000 km. Known as the 'Green Wall', the belt is designed to protect precious farmland from the sands of the Gobi Desert when the winter winds blow. It will eventually stretch from Xinjiang to Heilongjiang (China's last great timber preserve). This huge tree-planting programme is only a small part of the PRC's schedule – there's a similar belt along the south-east coast to break the force of summer typhoons. It's an attempt to reverse the effects of centuries of careless tree cutting, which, combined with slash-and-burn farming, has contributed to disastrous flooding and other ecological catastrophes.

Tree planting is the duty of every able-bodied person in China. In the early years of the PRC forest cover was reduced to about 9%, but the goal for the year 2000 is 20% cover. This will require tree planting on a total of 70 million hectares. Planting in the northern frontier zones is done in one-km-wide strips; millions of hectares have already been reafforested, with a survival rate of 55%. Wasteland and barren hills are allocated to rural households for planting and farming (also done on a contract basis), and the government provides seeds, saplings and know-how. ■

THE NORTH & NORTH-WEST

the Sui and Tang dynasties. The finest Buddhist statues are found in Caves 14, 45, 46, 51, 67 and 70. Cave 5 contains the most famous statue on Xumishan: a colossal Maitreya Buddha, 19 metres high. It remains remarkably well preserved even though the protective tower has long since collapsed and left it exposed to the elements.

Over 60 miniature Buddhist statues and tombs dating from the Han Dynasty have been found in Xiji County, about 60 km west of Guyuan.

There is no regular transport to the caves; to reach the site you'll have to charter a vehicle (minibus or motor-tricycle), either directly from Guyuan or from Sanying (*sānyíng*). Sanying is on the main road 40 km north of town near the Xumishan turn-off.

Places to Stay

The *Jiaotong Hotel (jiāotōng fàndiàn)*, upstairs in the enormous long-distance bus station,

has dorm beds in clean triples for Y30 and doubles with bath for Y90. The *Guyuan Guesthouse (gùyuán bīnguǎn)* on Zhengfu Jie south-east of the bus station has rather better doubles for Y120.

Getting There & Away

A Zhongwei-Baoji (Shaanxi Province) railway line routed through Guyuan has been under construction for some years now. When completed it will make travelling here much less uncomfortable. At the moment, however, the only way to and from Guyuan is by bus. There are buses from Lanzhou (via Xiji, nine hours), Tianshui (in Gansu, eight hours), Xi'an (11 hours), Baoji (in Shaanxi, eight hours) and Yinchuan (nine hours). The hill country of southern Ningxia has some lovely scenery, the green well-watered valleys contrast starkly with the region's arid north.

Inner Mongolia 内蒙古

For most foreigners, the big attraction of Inner Mongolia is the chance to view the grasslands, perhaps ride horses and see the Mongolian way of life. But just how much of the Mongolian way of life you can see in China is debatable. As for horses, the grasslands are indeed perfect horse country, and horse-drawn carts seem to be a common form of transport on the communes (a Hohhot tourist leaflet shows foreigners riding in a decorated camel cart with suspension and truck tyres). However, the small Mongolian horse is being phased out – herders can now purchase motorcycles (preferred over bicycles because of substantial wind force), and helicopters and light aircraft are used to round up steers and spot grazing herds.

It's important to distinguish between Inner Mongolia (the Chinese province) and Mongolia, the independent country to the north, formerly called Outer Mongolia. For more information on the country of Mongolia, see Lonely Planet's *Mongolia* guide.

HISTORY

The nomadic tribes to the north of China had always been a problem for China's rulers. The first emperor of the Qin Dynasty, Qin Shihuang, had the Great Wall built simply to keep them out.

Inner Mongolia *(nèi ménggǔ)* is only one part of what was originally the Mongol homeland, a vast area that also encompasses all of Outer Mongolia and a large slice of Siberia. In the grasslands beyond the Great Wall and the Gobi Desert, the Mongols endured a rough life as shepherds and horse-breeders. They moved with the seasons in search of pastures for their animals, living in tents known as *yurts* (a Russian word) or *gers* (a Mongolian word). The yurts were made of animal hide usually supported by wooden rods, and could be taken apart quickly to pack onto wagons.

At the mercy of their environment, the Mongols based their religion on the forces of

Population: 22 million
Capital: Hohhot
Highlights:
- The Grasslands, where it is still possible to get a glimpse of the vanishing traditional lifestyle of the Mongolians
- Dongsheng, the staging post for visiting Genghis Khan's Mausoleum
- Manzhouli, the bordertown with Russia and gateway to splendid Dalai Lake

nature: moon, sun and stars were all revered, as were the rivers. The gods were virtually infinite in number, signifying a universal supernatural presence; the Mongol priests could speak to the gods and communicate their orders to the tribal chief, the Khan. The story goes that Genghis Khan overcame the power of the priests by allowing one to be killed for alleging the disloyalty of the Khan's brother – a calculated act of sacrilege which proclaimed the Khan's absolute power.

Mongol Empire

The Mongols were united by Genghis Khan after 20 years of warfare; by the year 1206 all opposition to his rule among the tribes had surrendered or been wiped out and the Mongol armies stood ready to invade China. Not

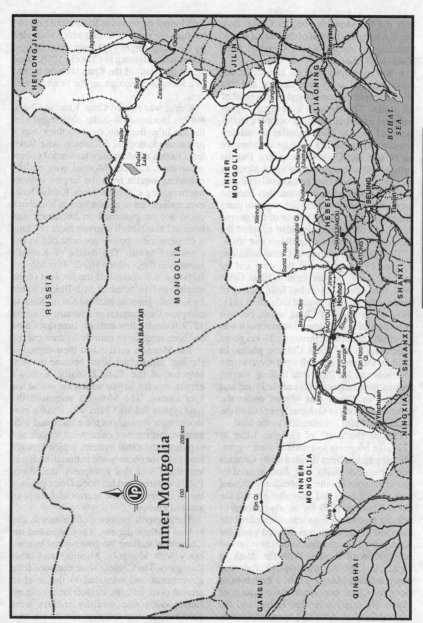

Inner Mongolia

only did the Mongols conquer China, they went on to conquer most of the known world, founding an empire which stretched from Vietnam to Hungary.

It was an empire won on horseback; the entire Mongol army was cavalry and this allowed rapid movement and deployment of the armies. The Mongols were highly organised and expert at planning complex strategies and tactics. They excelled in military science and were quick to adopt and improve on Persian and Chinese weaponry. But the cultural and scientific legacy of the Mongols was meagre. Once they abandoned their policies of terror and destruction, they became patrons of science and art, although not practitioners. Under the influence of the people they had conquered, they also adopted the local religions – mainly Buddhism and Islam.

The Mongol conquest of China was slow, delayed by campaigns in the west and by internal strife. Secure behind their Great Wall, the Chinese rulers had little inkling of the fury the Mongols would unleash in 1211, when the invasion of China began. For two years the Great Wall deterred them, but it was eventually penetrated through a 27-km gorge which led to the north Chinese plains. In 1215 a Chinese general went over to the Mongols and led them into Beijing. Nevertheless, the Chinese stubbornly held out, and the war in China was placed under the command of one of Genghis' generals so the Khan could turn his attention to the west.

Despite the death of Genghis Khan in 1227, the Mongols lost none of their vigour. The empire had been divided up by Genghis into separate domains, each domain ruled by one of his sons or other descendants. Ogadai was given China and was also elected the Great Khan in 1229 by an assemblage of princes. Northern China was subdued but the conquest of the south was delayed while the Khan turned his attention to the invasion and subjugation of Russia. With the death of Ogadai in 1241, the invasion of Europe was cancelled and Mangu Khan, a grandson of Genghis Khan, continued the conquest of China. He sent his brother Kublai and the general Subotai (who had been responsible for Mongol successes in Russia and Europe) to attack the south of China, which was ruled by the Song emperors. Mangu died of dysentery while fighting in China in 1259. Once again, the death of the Khan brought an end to a Mongol campaign on the brink of success.

Kublai was elected Great Khan in China, but his brother Arik-Boko challenged him for the title. Between the two there was a profound ideological difference. Arik-Boko led a faction of Mongols who wanted to preserve the traditional Mongol way of life, extracting wealth from the empire without intermingling with other races. Kublai, however, realised that an empire won on horseback could not be governed on horseback and intended to establish a government in China with permanent power concentrated in the cities and towns. The deaths of Kublai's enemies in the 'Golden Horde' (the Mongol faction which controlled the far west of the empire) and the defeat of Arik-Boko's forces by Kublai's generals enabled Kublai Khan to complete the conquest of southern China by 1279. It was the first and only time that China has been ruled in its entirety by foreigners.

The Mongols established their capital at Beijing, and Kublai Khan became the first emperor of the Yuan Dynasty. Kublai's empire was the largest nation the world has ever known. The Mongols improved the road system linking China with Russia, promoted trade throughout the empire and with Europe, instituted a famine relief scheme and expanded the canal system, which brought food from the countryside to the cities. It was into this China that foreigners like Marco Polo wandered, and his book *Description of the World* revealed the secrets of Asia to an amazed Europe.

The Mongols' conquest of China was also to lead to their demise. They alienated the Chinese by staffing the government bureaucracy with Mongols, Muslims and other foreigners. The Chinese were excluded from government and relegated to the level of second-class citizens in their own country. Landowners and wealthy traders were favoured, taxation was high and the prosperity of the empire did little to improve the lot of the peasant. Even though the Mongols did not mix with their Chinese subjects, they did succumb to Chinese civilisation: the warriors grew soft. Kublai died in 1294, the last Khan to rule over a united Mongol empire. He was followed by a series of weak and incompetent rulers who were unable to contain the revolts that spread all over China. In 1368 Chinese rebels converged on Beijing and the Mongols were driven out by an army led by Zhu Yuanzhang, who then founded the Ming Dynasty.

The entire Mongol empire had disintegrated by the end of the 14th century, and the Mongol homeland returned to the way of life it knew before Genghis Khan. Once again the Mongols became a collection of disorganised roaming tribes, warring among themselves and occasionally raiding China, until the Qing emperors finally gained control over them in the 18th century.

Divided Mongolia

The eastern expansion of the Russian empire placed the Mongols in the middle of the border struggles between the Russians and the Chinese, and the Russian empire set up a 'protectorate' over the northern part of Mongolia. The rest of Mongolia was governed by the Chinese until 1911, when the Qing fell. For eight years Mongolia remained an independent state until the Chinese returned. Then in 1924 during the Soviet civil war, the Soviet Communist Army pursued White Russian leaders to Urga (now Ulaan Baatar), where they helped create the Mongolian People's Republic by ousting the lama priesthood and the Mongol princes. The new republic remained very much under Soviet domination.

During the war between China and Japan in the 1930s and '40s, parts of what is now Inner Mongolia were occupied by the Japanese, and Communist guerrillas also operated there. In 1936 Mao Zedong told Edgar Snow in Yan'an:

As for Inner Mongolia, which is populated by both Chinese and Mongolians, we will struggle to drive Japan from there and help Inner Mongolia to establish an autonomous state...when the people's revolution has been victorious in China, the Outer Mongolian republic will automatically become part of the Chinese federation, at its own will.

But that was not to be. In 1945 Stalin extracted full recognition of the independence of Outer Mongolia from Chiang Kaishek when the two signed an anti-Japanese Sino-Soviet alliance. Two years later, with the resumption of the civil war in China, the Chinese Communists designated what was left to China of the Mongol territories as the 'Autonomous Region of Inner Mongolia'. With the Communist victory in 1949, Outer Mongolia did not join the People's Republic as Mao had said it would. The region remained firmly under Soviet control, though it was relatively benign until the 1960s when China and the USSR suddenly became enemies. Mongolia found itself the meat in the sandwich – more than 100,000 Soviet soldiers poured into Mongolia, effectively turning it into a huge military base.

It was not until 1962 that the border with Outer Mongolia was finally settled, though parts of the far north-east were disputed by the Soviet Union. Then in 1969 the Chinese carved up Inner Mongolia and donated bits of it to other provinces – they were reinstated in 1979. The Chinese seem sufficiently confident about the assimilation of the Mongols to talk about historical absurdities like 'Genghis Khan's Chinese armies' or the 'minority assistance in building the Great Wall'.

Mongolia Today

The Mongolians only make up about 15% of the total population of Inner Mongolia – the other 85% are basically Han Chinese. However, there are a smattering of minority Huis, Manchus, Daurs and Ewenkis.

Since 1949 the Chinese have done their best to assimilate the Mongols, but to be fair the Mongolians have been permitted to keep their written and spoken language. Tibetan Buddhism, the traditional religion of the Mongols, has not fared so well.

The Mongolians are scattered throughout China's north-eastern provinces, as well as through Qinghai and Xinjiang. In total, there are some 3½ million Mongolians living in China, and another half a million in Russia.

The 'Inner Mongolia Autonomous Region' enjoys little or no autonomy at all. Since the break-up of the Soviet Union in 1991, Outer Mongolia has been free of Soviet control and is reasserting its nationalism. This has the Chinese worried – nationalistic movements like those in Tibet and Xinjiang do not exactly please Beijing. As a result, the PSB keeps a tight lid on potential real or imagined independence activists.

Much of the Inner Mongolia region comprises vast areas of natural grazing land. However, the far north is forested – the Greater Hinggan range makes up about one-sixth of the country's forests and is an important source of timber and paper pulp. Inner Mongolia is also rich in minerals such as coal and iron ore, as you will clearly see if you visit Baotou.

The Mongolian climate tends towards extremes. Siberian blizzards and cold currents rake the plains in winter (from December to March) – forget it! In winter you'll even witness the phenomenon of snow on the desert sand dunes. Summer (from June to August) brings pleasant temperatures, but daytime can get scorching hot in the western areas. Visiting from May to September is recommended, but pack warm clothing for the Inner Mongolian spring or autumn.

HOHHOT
(hūhéhàotè)
Hohhot became the capital of Inner Mongolia in 1952, when it served as the administrative and educational centre. It was founded in the 16th century and, like the other towns, grew around its temples and lamaseries, which are now in ruins. Hide and wool industries are the mainstay, backed up by machine-building, a sugar refinery, fertiliser plants, a diesel-engine factory and iron and steel production. The population is just under one million if the outlying areas are included.

Hohhot means Blue City in Mongolian, though many Chinese-speaking locals mistakenly claim it means 'green city'. Perhaps the name refers to the crisp blue skies – this is one of the sunniest parts of China outside of the western deserts. Hohhot is certainly one of China's more pleasant cities and the main entrance point for tours of the grasslands.

Both CITS and CTS turn on the culture in Hohhot, from the grasslands tour to the equestrian displays at the horse-racing ground. Horse racing, polo and stunt riding are put on for large tour groups, if you latch onto one somehow; otherwise, they take place only on rare festive occasions. Likewise with song and dance soirees.

Information
The CITS office (☎ 624-494) is in the lobby of the Inner Mongolia Hotel. CTS (☎ 626-774) is on the 3rd floor of the rear building of the Inner Mongolia Hotel, and we've found them to be more knowledgeable. Another

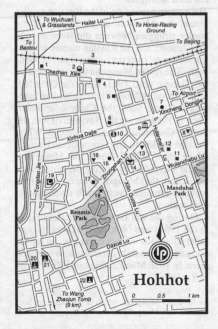

Hohhot

travel agency plugging grassland tours is China Merchants Travel Service (☎ 668-613) on the 4th floor of the Tongda Hotel.

The PSB is in the vicinity of Renmin Park, near the corner of Zhongshan Lu and Xilin Guole Lu.

Most convenient for changing money are the Bank of China branches inside the Inner Mongolia and Zhaojun hotels. The main branch is on Xinhua Dajie.

Inner Mongolia Museum
(nèi ménggǔ bówùguǎn)
Well presented and definitely worth a visit, this is the biggest attraction in town. The museum includes a large mammoth skeleton dug out of a coal mine, a yurt and a fantastic array of Mongolian costumery, artefacts, archery equipment and saddles. The top floors of the museum are sometimes closed. The flying horse on top of the building is meant to symbolise the forward spirit of the Mongolian people. The museum is at 1 Xinhua Dajie.

Five Pagoda Temple
(wǔtǎ sì)
This miniaturised structure dating back to 1740 is now bereft of its temple, leaving the Five Pagodas standing on a rectangular block. The pagodas are built with glazed bricks and are inscribed in Mongolian, Sanskrit and Tibetan. Cut into niches are small Buddhist figures; around the back is a screen wall with an astronomical chart inscribed in Mongolian. The Five Pagodas are on the bus No 1 route.

Dazhao Temple
(dàzhào)
The old part of town directly north of the tomb of Wang Zhaojun has some interesting sights. Down some alleys off a main street is the Dazhao Temple, which has almost fallen apart. The temple is incidental; the main action is on the streets. Around the area of the Dazhao Temple are some fascinating adobe houses, low and squat with decorated glass windows.

Xiletuzhao Temple
(xílètúzhào)
Not far from the Dazhao Temple is the Xiletuzhao Temple. It's the stomping ground of the 11th Grand Living Buddha, who dresses in civvies and is apparently active. There's nothing special to see though. The original

---

HOHHOT 呼和浩特

PLACES TO STAY

1 Jindi Hotel 金帝大酒店
4 Tongda Hotel & China Merchants Travel Service 通达饭店
5 Hohhot Hotel 呼和浩特宾馆
6 Zhaojun Hotel 昭君大酒店
11 Inner Mongolia Hotel & CITS 内蒙古饭店 中国国际旅行社
12 Xincheng Hotel 新城宾馆

17 Yunzhong Hotel & Minzu Department Store 云中大酒店,民族商场

PLACES TO EAT

8 Malaqin Restaurant 马拉沁饭店
13 Yikesai Restaurant 伊克赛酒楼
16 Balingxiang Restaurant 百灵香餐厅

OTHER

2 Long-Distance Bus Station 长途汽车站
3 Railway Station 火车站

7 Bailing Market 百灵商场
9 Inner Mongolia Museum 内蒙古博物馆
10 Bank of China 中国银行
14 Post Office 邮局
15 CAAC 中国民航
18 PSB 公安局外事科
19 Grand Mosque 清真大寺
20 Dazhao Temple 大召
21 Xiletuzhao Temple 席勒图召
22 Five Pagoda Temple 五塔寺

temple burned down and the present one was built in the 19th century; the Chinese-style building has a few Tibetan touches. The reverse swastika symbols on the exterior have long been used in Persian, Indian, Greek and Jewish cultures – they symbolise truth and eternity (no relation to its mirror image, the Nazi swastika).

Great Mosque
(qīngzhēn dà sì)

North of Xiletuzhao on Tongdao Jie is the Great Mosque, which is not so great – in fact, it's in sad shape. It dates from the Qing Dynasty, with later expansions.

Wang Zhaojun Tomb
(zhāojūn mù)

The tomb of this Han Dynasty concubine to Emperor Yuandi (1st century BC) is a bit of a bore, although it does permit some countryside viewing at the edge of town. It would be more interesting if the tomb were in better condition. Presently, it's in rather pathetic shape, though perhaps some renovation work will be considered when CITS recognises the hard currency potential. The tomb is nine km from the city on the bus No 14 route.

Naadam
(nādámù)

The summer festival known as Naadam features traditional Mongolian sports such as competition archery, horse racing, wrestling and camel racing. Prizes vary from a goat to a fully equipped horse. The fair has its origins in the ancient Obo-Worshipping Festival (an *obo* is a pile of stones with a hollow space for offerings – a kind of shaman shrine). The Mongolian clans make a beeline for the fairs on any form of transport they can muster, and create an impromptu yurt city. For foreigners, Hohhot is a good place to see the Naadam festivities. The exact date of Naadam varies in China, but is usually around mid-August. It's worth knowing that Naadam is celebrated at a different time in Outer Mongolia – always 11 to 13 July, which corresponds to the date of Mongolia's 1921

revolution. To find out just when and where Naadam events are being staged, contact the Hohhot CITS or CTS – other branches of CITS in China know very little about Naadam, so don't even bother asking in Beijing or Guangzhou.

Places to Stay

The *Tongda Hotel* (☎ 668-731) *(tōngdá fàndiàn)* at 10 Chezhan Dongjie is opposite the railway station. Basic rooms go for Y54.

The *Hohhot Hotel* (☎ 662-200) *(hūhéhàotè bīnguǎn)* is within walking distance of the railway station and has rooms for Y320.

Xincheng Hotel (☎ 663-322) *(xīnchéng bīnguǎn)* draws in a sizable portion of the backpacker trade. With large rooms and tree-shaded spacious grounds, it's rather like living in a park. It's two km from the railway station. No bus runs from the railway station to the hotel – bus No 20 stops near the hotel, but to catch this bus you must turn left as you exit the railway station and walk a long block to Hulunbei'er Lu. Otherwise, take a taxi. Doubles are priced at Y140, Y160, Y200, Y300 and Y700. Bicycle rentals are available.

Just around the corner from the Xincheng Hotel is the *Inner Mongolia Hotel* (☎ 664-233; fax 661-479) *(nèi ménggǔ fàndiàn)*, a 14-storey high-rise on Wulanchabu Xilu. This is the home of CITS and CTS, and though the standard is three-star, the plumbing is falling apart. Dorms with three beds cost Y50 per person, doubles are Y420 and Y520.

The *Yunzhong Hotel* (☎ 668-822) *(yúnzhōng dàjiūdiàn)* is a new place on Zhongshan Lu, hidden behind the Minzu Department Store. Doubles cost Y180, Y200 and Y260.

The *Jindi Hotel* (☎ 653-300; fax 658-565) *(jīndì dà jiǔdiàn)* is at 35 Chezhan Xijie, a 10-minute walk west of the railway station. This is the newest hotel in town and offers doubles for Y360 and Y480.

The *Zhaojun Hotel* (☎ 662-211; fax 668-825) *(zhāojūn dàjiūdiàn)*, 11 Xinhua Dajie, is a fancy Hong Kong joint venture. Everything here works well – the heat, the plumbing – and the staff are very friendly. The luxury is something you pay for: doubles cost Y280, Y480 and Y620.

Places to Eat
Budget cuisine is, as always, available from stalls all around the railway station.

The Chinese restaurant in the *Inner Mongolia Hotel* plays a dirty trick on foreigners – the English menu has higher prices than the Chinese menu and none of the inexpensive dishes appear on the English menu. Unless your Chinese reading ability is keen, it's better to eat elsewhere. Cheap local restaurants are in the alley just across the street from the hotel.

The *Malaqin Restaurant (malaqin* means 'horseman') is recommended for both Chinese and Mongolian food. Try the Mongolian hotpot, roasted lamb and kebab. Prices are moderate even though this place caters to foreign tour groups, and the friendly staff speak some English.

Yikesai (yīkèsài jiŭlóu) and *Bailingxiang (băilíngxiāng cāntīng)* restaurants also serve good Mongolian food.

Entertainment
Just east of the intersection of Xinhua Dajie and Hulunbei'er Lu is the Bailing Market *(băilíng shāngchǎng)*. As you face the market, on the right side of the building is a theatre where you can see brilliant Mongolian singing and dancing performances at night. When we went there, we found just four people watching the show – all foreigners! This is despite the fact that the performance was outstanding. It could be that performances are not held every night – we assume that someone actually has to buy a ticket or the show will be cancelled. Tickets are sold at all the big hotels. If the front desk staff at your hotel seem to know nothing about this, ask CITS or CTS.

Things to Buy
The Minority Handicraft Factory on the southern side of town on the bus No 1 route has a retail shop for tourists. There is a limited selection, but wares include inlaid knife and chopstick sets, daggers, boots, embroidered shoes, costumes, brassware, blankets and curios.

You'll actually find a better selection and lower prices at the Minzu Department Store *(mínzú shāngchǎng)*. It's on Zhongshan Lu where the stairs cross the road. This is also where you'll find the Friendship Store.

Getting There & Away
Air CAAC's office (☎ 664-103) is on Xilin Guole Lu. There are flights connecting Hohhot to Beijing, Chifeng, Guangzhou, Hailar, Shanghai, Shenzhen, Shijiazhuang, Tongliao, Ulanhot, Wuhan and Xilinhot. There is also a seasonal (summer only) international flight to Ulaan Baatar in Outer Mongolia which costs US$150.

Air tickets between Hohhot and Beijing are harder to buy than the Holy Grail. Try the CTS office – sometimes you get lucky. Otherwise, go directly to CAAC.

Bus There are sporadic bus connections between Hohhot and Datong. Buses to Baotou go once every half hour or so. The most useful bus for travellers is the one to Dongsheng, which departs at 7.40 am.

Train Hohhot is on the Beijing-Lanzhou railway line that cuts a long loop through Inner Mongolia; about 2½ hours out of Beijing you'll pass the crumbled remains of the Great Wall (it looks like little more than a dirt embankment). On the fastest trains, Beijing to Hohhot is a 12-hour trip, Datong to Hohhot takes five hours, Baotou to Hohhot takes three hours, and Yinchuan to Hohhot takes 12 hours. Trains are most frequent between Hohhot and Beijing, less so between Yinchuan and Hohhot, and run only twice a day between Lanzhou and Yinchuan. There are twice-daily connections between Taiyuan and Datong, where a connection to Hohhot can be made.

Unless you have a relative on the inside, getting a sleeper is nearly impossible if you go to the station on your own – even getting hard-seat tickets seems to take connections! All tickets are sold through the back door – the back door for foreigners is CTS at the

THE NORTH & NORTH-WEST

Inner Mongolia Hotel (CITS also does it but they seem more bureaucratic).

Getting Around

To/From the Airport Hohhot Airport is about 35 km east of the city. There is a bus from the CAAC booking office. Taxi drivers ask around Y120 for the journey.

Bus You can get a detailed bus map (in Chinese only), which includes surrounding regions, from the hotel gift shops and bookstalls around town. Check with hotel staff for your proposed route. Bus No 1 runs from the railway station to the old part of the city in the south-western corner.

Taxi These are available from the hotels and railway station area. The taxis have no meters, but drivers charge around Y15 between the railway station and the Inner Mongolia Hotel.

Bicycle Hohhot is reasonably small and, weather permitting, you can go a long way on a pair of self-propelled wheels. Bikes can be hired at both the Xincheng and Inner Mongolia hotels, and there are numerous bike stalls along the main road to the left of the station.

AROUND HOHHOT

About 15 km west of Hohhot, the Sino-Tibetan monastery **Wusutuzhao** is hardly worth looking at, but the surrounding arid landscape is impressive.

About 20 km east of Hohhot, along the airport road, is the **White Pagoda** (*báitǎ*), a seven-storey octagonal tower. The pagoda can be reached by a half-hour suburban train ride, or drop in by taxi if you're on the way to the airport.

THE GRASSLANDS
(*cǎoyuán*)

This is what most travellers come to see in Inner Mongolia. If you want to get further out into the grasslands, consider a trip to Hailar or Manzhouli.

Organised Tours

Cashing in on the magic draw of 'Mongolia' is the name of the game here. As for visions of the descendants of the mighty Khan riding the endless plains, the herds of wild horses and the remnants of Xanadu, remember that this is China and most of the population is now Han Chinese. Nevertheless, CTS and CITS are only too happy to organise tours to give you a glimpse of the traditional Mongolian lifestyle, which now seems to be an anachronism in Inner Mongolia.

The real country for seeing Mongolians in their native habitat is Outer Mongolia, but getting there is both expensive and difficult. Grasslands and yurt dwellings can be seen in other parts of China – in Xinjiang for example. Remember that grass is only green in summer – the verdant pasturelands can turn a shrivelled shade of frost-coated brown from November to April. Take warm, windproof clothing – there's a considerable windchill factor even in the middle of summer.

There are three grasslands targeted for CITS and CTS tours: Xilamuren (80 km from Hohhot), Gegentala (170 km away in Siziwang Qi) and Huitengxile (120 km from Hohhot), which is the most beautiful but least visited.

There are some fledgling private travel agents who try to solicit business in the lobbies of the tourist hotels – you can talk to them and discuss prices. There are also individual taxi drivers around the railway station who do self-styled grasslands tours for around Y250 per person, which includes an overnight stay in a yurt belonging to the driver's family. The name of the game is 'bargain'. Be aware that these unofficial tours get mixed reviews. One traveller was served a wretched meal in a yurt – cooked over a cow-dung fire – and got food poisoning. As you'll discover if you explore the Mongolian hinterland, sanitation is not a strong point, so watch what you eat and drink.

The following prices for tours are quoted by CTS:

To Xilamuren

No of People	Cost per person (Y)		
	1 Day	2 Days	3 Days
1	748	904	1126
2-3	412	508	664
4-6	270	369	453
7-10	216	277	351
11-20	174	232	322
over 20	154	225	309

To Gegentala

No of people	Cost per person (Y)	
	2 Days	3 Days
1	1246	1477
2-3	693	840
4-6	435	505
7-10	330	420
11-20	312	390
over 20	291	363

To Huitengxile

No of people	Cost per person (Y)	
	2 Days	3 Days
1	1036	1258
2-3	582	729
4-6	372	447
7-10	304	381
11-20	262	345
over 20	240	322

For pure theatre, nothing beats the CITS Grasslands Tour. Here's a two-day itinerary to give you some idea of the picnics, outings and carnivals in Inner Mongolia.

Day 1 At 2.30 pm, we discover the first day is half over – the tour is by calendar days. After a three-hour drive over the mountains to the grasslands plateau we arrive at Wulantuge commune. The major industry here seems to be shepherding tourists. It's the first commune from Hohhot, so lots of groups are processed through this meatworks. On our arrival, a woman in Mongolian costume (still, however, wearing slacks underneath and a tell-tale pair of tennis shoes) pops out of a door to greet us. Dinner is very good – baozi (steamed meat buns) and meat dishes. The guide motions toward the yurt compound at the edge of town. These are on fixed brick and concrete foundations with 75-watt light bulbs dangling from each yurt-hole. The yurts are only for tourists – the

natives live in sensibly thick-walled brick structures. The outhouse is primitive – I'm wondering if the joke is on us, and whether the locals are sitting on porcelain models with flushers. A clammy, damp cold permeates the yurts, sufficient to send an arthritic into spasms.

Day 2 Breakfast is at 8.30 am, a decidedly Western hour. We take advantage of the lull to poke around – post office, school, souvenir shop. There's a large temple structure with Sino-Tibetan features, probably 18th century, with colonnade, intricate windows and doorways, devilish frescoes – but entry is barred. Part of the complex around it has been turned into a dining hall for receiving the likes of us. At breakfast I ask the guide (who sits at a separate table with the driver) a few questions in relation to the tourist industry, which he either ignores, evades, or pretends not to understand. Back at the yurts are two ruddy-cheeked gentlemen waiting with two moth-eaten animals. The ruddy complexion comes from wind chill – the animals have not weathered it so well. One is, I guess you might call it, yes, a horse. The other is the worst-looking excuse for a camel I've seen. I mean, camels are ugly, but this one had just about fallen apart. It's strictly a mounted picture-taking session; the attendants keep these pathetic specimens on leashes, explaining that they're too dangerous to be ridden solo.

At 9.30 am the driver whips over the grasslands – very nice, peaceful, dirt paths. It's reassuring to see some real grass in China. Hong Kongers get most enthralled about this; there isn't too much of the stuff around Kowloon. We stop to observe a flock of sheep – the shepherd poses for photos. Then, the highlight of the tour, a visit to a typical Mongolian family. They live in a three-room brick dwelling, and there, smack on the wall as you enter, is a giant poster of a koala (New South Wales Tourist Authority). The typical family is wearing standard Han ration clothing (did we catch them with their pants down?) but they bring out Mongolian garb for dress-up photo-sessions – for us to dress up, that is. They've obviously given up. Parked out the back is their form of transport – bicycles.

Motoring off again, we visit an obo, a pile of stones in the middle of nowhere. When nomads used to gather for mid-May festivals, each would bring a stone and lay it here. We go back to Wulantuge for a banquet-style lunch; a sheep is slaughtered and barbecued, for a surcharge. After lunch, the guide announces that it's time for xiūxi – the rest period will be 2½ hours. We wave goodbye to the woman near the yurt compound (she struggles to get into her Mongolian robes in time), and head back for Hohhot. We arrive around 4.30 that afternoon; the tour is supposed to last until 6 pm and there is a filler of sights around town.

In sum, depending on what you've negotiated, your real time on the grasslands amounts to about two hours, plus the drive there and back. You spend a lot of time sleeping, eating, waiting and taking pictures of each other. The three-day itineraries may be better, with archery or song and dance routines thrown in. The best part of the trip was, unexpectedly, the food – the meals were banquet-size and tasty.

BAOTOU
(bāotóu)

The largest city in Inner Mongolia (and certainly the ugliest), Baotou lies on the bleak northernmost reaches of the Yellow River, to the west of Hohhot. The name means 'land with deer' in Mongolian, and though there is still a deer farm outside of Baotou, you are only likely to encounter these creatures on the dinner plate in some of the upmarket restaurants around town.

Previously set in an area of undeveloped semi-desert inhabited by Mongol herders, Baotou underwent a radical change when the Communists came to power in 1949. In the next decade, a 1923 railway line linking the town with Beijing was extended south-east to Yinchuan, and roads were constructed to facilitate access to the region's iron, coal and other mineral deposits.

Today, Baotou is an industrial community of about one million people; despite the showcase Mongolian street signs, nearly the entire population is Han Chinese. The city is not blessed with scenic sights, though for some reason Japanese tour groups continue to throng here and pay high prices for the privilege. Baotou is definitely a city of specialised interests – a couple of nearby monasteries, a steel mill, steam locomotive museum, small sand dunes and a mausoleum dedicated to Genghis Khan. Most of these sights are not in the city itself, but a couple of hours outside the town. Overall, Baotou is a useful transit point and you can keep yourself amused here for a day or so, but if you miss it, don't lose any sleep. The best thing we can say for the place is that the people are friendly.

Orientation

Baotou is a huge town – 20 km of urban sprawl separate the eastern and western parts of the city. It's the eastern area that most travellers visit because it's useful as a transit hub – the western area has the steel mill and locomotive museum.

The station for the western area is Baotou Railway Station *(bāotóu zhàn)*; for the eastern area it's Baotou East Railway Station *(bāotóu dōng zhàn)*. The eastern district is called

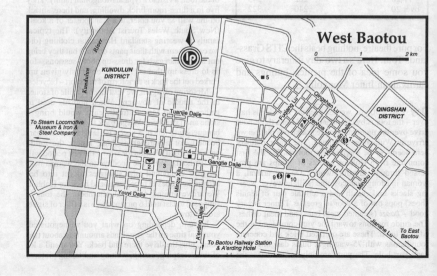

West Baotou

KUNDULUN DISTRICT

QINGSHAN DISTRICT

To Steam Locomotive Museum & Iron & Steel Company

Tuanjie Dajie

Qingshan Lu

Wenhua Lu

Ershan Lu

Hudenglin Dajie

Kexue Lu

Gangtie Dajie

Minzu Xilu

A'erding Dajie

Youyi Dajie

Jianshe Lu

Minzhu Lu

To Baotou Railway Station & A'erding Hotel

To East Baotou

0   1   2 km

Donghe; the western area is subdivided into two adjacent districts, Qingshan and Kundulun.

Information

CITS (☎ 554-615; fax 554-615) is in the Baotou Guesthouse. Ditto for the PSB.

None of the hotels have a money-changing desk, but there are four branches of the Bank of China which handle foreign exchange. In western Baotou, one is on Gangtie Dajie near the TV tower and another on Wenhua Lu. In eastern Baotou, there is one up the street from the Donghe Hotel and another next to the entrance of Renmin Park.

Baotou Iron & Steel Company
(bāotóu gāngtiě gōngsī)

A purple cloud hangs over the western horizon of the city. The source of these colourful sunsets is the Baotou Iron & Steel Company, which was supervised by the Soviets until their abrupt exit in 1960. The original plan foresaw use of ore from Bayan Obo (about 140 km further north). Unfortunately, the

---

local ore couldn't make the grade and the company now imports the stuff. Foreigners can only get inside the steelworks via a CITS tour. Besides the cost of your CITS guide, there is a Y10 per person admission fee.

Steam Locomotive Museum
(zhēngqì huǒchē bówùguǎn)

The museum is fairly small but there is talk of expanding it. CITS offers tours but you can easily visit on your own.

Places to Stay

East Baotou The *Donghe Hotel* (☎ 472-541) (dōnghé bīnguǎn), 14 Nanmenwai, is about 15 minutes' walk (or take bus No 5) from Baotou East Railway Station. Doubles range from Y80 to Y120. This place is the most popular with budget travellers.

The *Guanghua Hotel* (guānghuá fàndiàn) is hesitant to take foreigners, but will do so if you smile. Rooms cost Y54 and Y88.

The *North Pacific Hotel* (☎ 475-656) (běiyáng fàndiàn) is the upmarket tourist place in eastern Baotou. Doubles are Y160 and Y360.

West Baotou Your only option for budget accommodation is a little dump, the *A'erding Hotel* (ā'ěrdīng fàndiàn), next to Baotou Railway Station. Doubles are Y50. It's just to your right as you exit the station. The area around the western station is pretty bleak – a couple of shops, foodstalls and not much else. But if you're only staying in Baotou to catch some sleep before heading elsewhere, this hotel will do.

The *Baotou Guesthouse* (☎ 556-655) (bāotóu bīnguǎn) on Gangtie Dajie in the Kundulun District has become ridiculously overpriced. Doubles start at Y380. If arriving by train, get off at Baotou Railway Station. The station is seven km from the hotel – take bus No 1, a taxi or a motor-tricycle. If arriving by bus from Hohhot, you can ask the driver to drop you off right in front of the hotel.

Qingshan Guesthouse (☎ 334-091) (qīngshān bīnguǎn) is the plushest place in the western part of Baotou. Doubles are Y160, Y300, Y350 and Y1200. Adjacent to the

---

WEST BAOTOU 包头西部

1 Xinhua Bookstore
   新华书店
2 Post Office
   邮局
3 Bayi Park
   八一公园
4 Baotou Guesthouse, CITS, PSB
   & CAAC
   包头宾馆, 中国国际旅行社,
   公安局, 中国民航
5 Qingshan Guesthouse
   青山宾馆
6 Dafulin Restaurant
   大福林饭庄
7 Bank of China (Qingshan Branch)
   中国银行 (青山商业大厦)
8 Laodong Park
   劳动公园
9 Bank of China
   中国银行
10 TV Tower
   电视塔

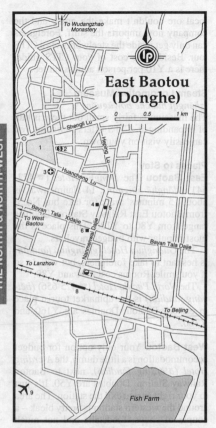

East Baotou (Donghe)

To Wudangzhao Monastery

Shengli Lu

Heping Lu

Huancheng Lu

Bayan Tala Xidajie

To West Baotou

Nanmenwai Dajie

Bayan Tala Dajie

To Lanzhou

To Beijing

Fish Farm

0   0.5   1 km

EAST BAOTOU (DONGHE)
包头东河区

1   Renmin Park
    人民公园
2   Bank of China
    中国银行
3   No 2 Hospital
    第二医院
4   Donghe Hotel & CAAC
    东河宾馆，中国民航
5   Guanghua Hotel & Asian Fastfood
    光华饭店，亚州快餐
6   North Pacific Hotel
    北洋饭店
7   Long-Distance Bus Station
    长途汽车站
8   Baotou East Railway Station
    包头东站
9   Airport
    飞机场

hotel is a Friendship Store. There is no public transport, though bus No 10 runs within one km of the hotel. Access is usually by taxi.

Places to Eat
If you're staying at the Donghe Hotel, don't eat there unless you've brought along 10 friends; this place caters to banquets and doesn't know how to deal with individuals who just want to order one plateful of food. It's much better to go across the street to the *Asia Fast Food Restaurant (yàzhōu kuài cāntīng)*, which offers meals for around Y7. Or you can walk down to the Baotou East

Railway Station, where the abundant food-stalls all seem to offer the exact same menu.

Over in the western part of town, the big famous place is the *Dafulin Restaurant (dàfúlín fànzhuāng)* about one km from the Qingshan Guesthouse.

Things to Buy
The hotel gift shops offer a small selection of tourist-oriented minority handicrafts, but Hohhot is a better place to buy this stuff. As China's mineral capital, Baotou would be a good place to find bargains on iron ore, cobalt and lignite, in case you need to stock up.

Getting There & Away
Air CAAC has two ticket offices – one inside the Baotou Guesthouse and another at the Donghe Hotel. There are flights connecting Baotou to Guangzhou and Wuhan.

Bus A bus from Baotou East Railway Station to Hohhot is Y20 for the three-hour trip, or an extra Y3 from Baotou Railway Station. Buy your ticket on the bus.

Getting Around

To/From the Airport The airport is two km south of Baotou East Railway Station. Despite the short distance, taxis ask around Y25 for the one-way journey.

Bus Bus Nos 5 and 10 stop close to the Baotou Guesthouse and shuttle between the western and eastern sections of Baotou in 45 minutes. Much more comfortable are the minibuses *(zhōngbā)*, which cost Y3 to Y4 – you board these at the regular bus stops.

Taxi Taxis and motor-tricycles congregate at the railway stations and tourist hotels. No meters exist, so the fare is negotiable.

AROUND BAOTOU
Wudangzhao Monastery
(wūdāngzhào)

The main tourist attraction near Baotou is the large Wudangzhao Monastery, about 2½ hours from the city by bus. This monastery of the Gelukpa (Yellow Hat sect of Tibetan Buddhism) was built around 1749 in typical Tibetan style with flat-roofed buildings. It once housed 1200 monks. The ashes of seven reincarnations of the monastery's 'living buddha' are kept in a special hall. Today all religious activity is restricted to a handful of pilgrims and doorkeeper-monks who collect the admission fee.

For the crowds of day-tripping, camera-clicking tourists this is no place for religion. The surrounding hillsides are carpeted with hundreds of smashed bottles and piles of garbage. Try to walk into the hills away from the pandemonium; the site has a peculiar strength in its secretive, brooding atmosphere.

There's a basic dorm next to the monastery. CITS organises tours, but you can easily manage on your own. Take a torch if you want to see anything inside the monastery.

Getting There & Away The monastery is 70 km north-east of Baotou. Bus No 7 goes to Shiguai – halfway to the monastery – and from Shiguai there are minibuses which do the second leg of the journey.

At 7 am there is a bus direct from the long-distance bus station (eastern Baotou) to the monastery – no need to change buses. For the return trip, at 4 pm you can catch this same bus from the same place you were dropped off (check with the driver when you arrive). Otherwise, do the minibus shuffle again.

Perhaps the best option is the minibuses which leave from in front of the Baotou East Railway Station and go directly to the monastery for Y10.

Meidaizhao Monastery
(měidàizhào)

This monastery is much smaller than Wudangzhao and consequently little visited, although it's more accessible. Meidaizhao is halfway between Baotou and Hohhot, less than half a km north of the main highway (a 10-minute walk). Buses on the Baotou-Hohhot route can drop you off here. Like Wudangzhao, the monastery is devoted to the Gelukpa.

Resonant Sand Gorge
(yīméng xiǎng shāwān)

The Gobi Desert starts just to the south of Baotou. Some 60 km south of Baotou and a few km west of the Baotou-Dongsheng highway is a gorge filled to the brim with sand dunes. Although the gorge has long been known to locals as a barren place to be avoided (no grass for the sheep), it has recently been turned into a money spinner by CITS. Japanese tour groups in particular come here to frolic in the sand. To spice up the romance of such frolicking, the area has been named Resonant Sand Gorge, a reference to the swooshing sound made by loose sand when you step on it.

The highest dunes are about 40 metres above their own base. But you can find much more spectacular sand dunes in other parts of China – in particular, check out Dunhuang in Gansu Province. This is not to say you shouldn't visit Baotou's Resonant Sand Gorge, but getting to the gorge might be problematic unless you are on a tour or charter a taxi.

DONGSHENG
(dōngshèng)

Dongsheng lies south-west of Baotou and serves as a staging post for the site of Genghis Khan's Mausoleum. The main language spoken in Dongsheng is Mongolian, though most of the locals can speak Chinese. Street names are also Mongolian, though the street signs have been rendered into Chinese characters.

Dongsheng itself is not blessed with copious scenic attractions, though the place looks a bit like a wild west town, with wind, dust, sand and donkeys.

A plan to dress up the town for tourism gave birth to the **Jinyuan Ancient City** *(jīn-yuán chéng)* – the 'ancient city' consists of a single street of reconstructed buildings which looks much like a movie set. Probably more interesting is the **Minsheng Indoor Market** *(mínshēng shìchǎng)*, where you can buy practical things such as clothing (not Mongolian style).

If you get an early start, it's possible to reach Dongsheng in the morning, visit Genghis Khan's Mausoleum, then return to Dongsheng to spend the night, or possibly travel all the way back to Baotou the same day (this

would be exhausting though). Actually, Dongsheng is not a bad place to spend the night – accommodation is cheap and of good standard. Furthermore, the locals are extremely friendly, and it's certainly a more attractive place to hang out than Baotou.

Information

The Ordos Travel Agency (☎ 321-501 ext 2427) is on the 4th floor of the Ih Ju League Hotel. The CITS office (☎ 26301) is in the remote Ordos Hotel – English is spoken and the staff are overjoyed to find a real live foreigner to practise with.

Places to Stay

No matter where you stay, take your evening shower early. Dongsheng is plagued by water shortages and the water is always turned off by midnight, often earlier. It usually comes on again at 6 am, but that is not guaranteed.

The *Dongsheng Hotel* (☎ 321-961) *(dōng-shèng dà jiǔdiàn)* is good value, with plush double rooms for Y100.

Just opposite the foregoing is the *Minzu Hotel* (☎ 323-699) *(mínzú fàndiàn)*. Dorms/doubles are Y60/120. It's not a particularly nice spot – you can do better.

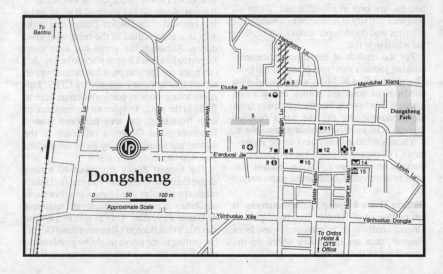

The *Ih Ju League Hotel* (☎ 321-292) (*yīkè zhāoméng bīnguǎn*), usually just called the *Yimeng Binguan*, is a very popular place with travellers. Triples can cost as little as Y30 per person. Other rooms cost Y90, Y160 and Y600. The hotel is on E'erduosi Jie.

The *Continental Grand Hotel* (☎ 328-171, 328-274) (*wǔzhōu jiǔdiàn*) sounds more impressive than it really is. Doubles are Y160 and Y240.

The most upmarket and remote place in town is the *Ordos Hotel* (☎ 26301) (*è'erduō-sī fàndiàn*), which has doubles for Y200. It's a stiff 40-minute walk from the bus station, but you might want to drop in here just to cheer up the CITS staff.

DONGSHENG 东胜

1 Railway Station
 火车站
2 Jinyuan Ancient City
 金元城
3 PSB
 市公安局
4 Bus Station
 长途汽车站
5 Minsheng Indoor Market
 民生市场
6 Meng Hospital
 盟医院
7 Dongsheng Hotel
 东胜大酒店
8 Bank of China
 中国银行
9 Minzu Hotel
 民族饭店
10 Continental Grand Hotel
 五洲酒店
11 Xinhua Bookstore
 新华书店
12 Ih Ju League Hotel
 & Ordos Travel Agency
 伊克昭盟宾馆
13 Dongsheng Department Store
 东胜市百货大楼
14 Post & Telephone Office
 邮电大楼
15 Museum
 博物馆

Getting There & Away

Bus Most travellers take the bus directly from Hohhot. It departs at 7.40 am, takes 5½ hours and costs Y35. This bus is amazingly comfortable, with videos included. Sit on the right side of the bus for mountain views along the way (or left side on the way back). The bus goes via Baotou but doesn't stop there. Just to the south of Baotou, the bus crosses the Yellow River. There are two express buses daily departing Dongsheng for Hohhot, one at 6 am and another at noon.

Another route is to go from Baotou. Catch buses to Dongsheng from the long-distance bus station (eastern Baotou). Buses runs about twice hourly, beginning at 6.30 am. The journey from Baotou to Dongsheng takes about 2½ hours.

Train The train was mostly built to haul coal and is little used by passengers because it's slow, infrequent and unreliable. Nevertheless, you can go this way if you're really determined. At least in theory, it runs twice daily. Official departure times from Baotou are at 8 and 11 am. The train leaves Dongsheng at 4 and 7 pm.

AROUND DONGSHENG
Genghis Khan's Mausoleum
(*chéngjí sīhàn língyuán*)
The mausoleum is a bus trip away from Dongsheng, in the middle of nowhere.

In 1954, what are said to be the ashes of the Khan were brought back from Qinghai (where they had been taken to prevent them from falling into the hands of the Japanese) and a large Mongolian-style mausoleum was built near Ejin Horo Qi. As for why the Japanese should want the Khan's ashes, it had to do with Japan's attempted invasion of Mongolia – Japanese propagandists, citing legends that Genghis Khan came from across the sea, claimed that the Mongolian people originated in Japan. This was to assure the Mongolians that reuniting with the Japanese motherland was just like getting together with family. As it turned out, a joint Russian-Mongolian (mostly Russian) force overwhelmingly defeated the Japanese attack on Outer Mongolia in 1939, though the Japanese successfully occupied Inner Mongolia and held it until the war's end in 1945.

The Cultural Revolution did enough damage to the mausoleum to keep the renovators busy for eight years and the result looks new. With the collapse of Soviet domination in 1991, Mongolia has been whipping itself up into a nationalistic fervour and Genghis Khan has been elevated to god-like status. As a result, holy pilgrimages to the mausoleum have become the sacred duty of both Inner and Outer Mongolians. If you want to meet any true Mongolians, this is probably one of the best places in China to do it.

Ceremonies are held four times a year at the mausoleum to honour his memory. Butter lamps are lit, *khatas* (ritual scarves) presented and whole cooked sheep piled high before the Khan's stone statue while chanting is performed by Mongolian monks and specially chosen elders from the Daur nationality.

Photographers outside the mausoleum have robes so you can dress up and have your photo taken posing as the Great Khan. Inside are displays of Genghis Khan's martial gear and statue. Various yurts contain the biers of Genghis and his close relatives. The huge frescoes around the walls are done in cartoon style to depict important stages in the Khan's rise – all that's missing is bubble captions with 'pow' or 'zap'.

The mausoleum gets good reviews from travellers. One traveller wrote to Lonely Planet and said 'I wouldn't have missed it for the world'. Even if you're not a mausoleum buff, the scenery along the way is intriguing.

At the end of the dirt road to the right of the mausoleum's entrance, go one km to reach the temporary residence of the Khan. You can get into this residence on the same ticket you bought for the mausoleum. Nearby is a compound (open only in summer) with nice grasslands, horses, sheep, goats and cows, plus some interesting buildings with traditional clothing, warrior outfits and riding equipment inside – all ready for the Naadam tourist carnival.

Places to Stay

There is a tourist yurt camping ground *(ménggūbāo)* near the mausoleum, where you can stay for Y40.

The other place is a hostel *(chéngjí sīhàn líng zhāodàisuŏ)* with no English name. However, most visitors elect to stay in Dongsheng and commute to the mausoleum for a day trip.

Getting There & Away

Two buses daily depart Dongsheng for the mausoleum, one at 6 am and the other at noon. The journey from Dongsheng to the mausoleum takes 1½ hours.

Another strategy is to take a bus from Dongsheng to Ejin Horo Qi *(yījīn huòluò qí)*, which is 25 km from the mausoleum, and then switch to a minibus which takes 30 minutes to complete the journey.

HAILAR
(hăilāěr)

The northernmost major town in Inner Mongolia, Hailar has very little to offer visitors beyond being a useful transit point. Nearby Manzhouli (see next section) does not yet have an airport – when it gets one, there will be little need to visit Hailar.

Information

CITS (☎ 221-728) is on the 2nd floor of the post office building *(jiànfā dàshà)*.

Places to Stay

The rather dilapidated *Minzu Hotel* (☎ 332-211) *(minzu fàndiàn)* has a very central location at Qiaotou Dajie and Caoshi Jie. Beds cost Y30 each in a double room with attached bath.

The *Friendship Hotel* (☎ 331-040) *(youyi dà jiŭdiàn)* on Qiaotou Dajie is a fine place to stay. Doubles/triples with attached bath cost Y122/150. The reception desk is hidden on the 2nd floor.

The *Beier Hotel* (☎ 332-511) *(beier jiŭdiàn)* on Zhongyang Dajie offers very comfortable doubles for Y120.

Across the street from the foregoing is the disappointing *Xisi Hotel* (☎ 332-911) *(xīsì fàndiàn)*. It costs Y35 per person for a double with bath, but the rooms look pretty bleak.

The *Laodong Hotel* (☎ 338-111) *(laodong dàshà)* is a luxurious place where doubles cost Y100. Check out the magnificent suites, which are actually quite a bargain at Y288.

The *Meng Hotel* (☎ 222-212) *(meng bīnguǎn)* is an enormous Stalinesque sort of place charging absurdly high prices. Standard doubles cost Y297.

Getting There & Away
There are direct flights between Hailar and Beijing four times weekly, and less frequent flights to Hohhot. You can also reach Hailar by doing a long train ride from Harbin.

Getting Around
The short ride to the airport costs Y2 on the CAAC bus or Y20 by taxi. Motor-tricycles and taxis are abundant, but you can get around the town easily on foot.

MANZHOULI
(mǎnzhōulǐ)
The border town where the Trans-Siberian Railway crosses from China to Russia, Manzhouli has some of the greenest grasslands in China. It's also another option for pursuing the topic of the disappearing Mongols. It's possible to arrange taxi or jeep excursions to the grasslands with overnight stops in yurts, tea-tasting and campfires. Should you strike a Mongol living traditionally, you might get a cup of their milk tea. It's made of horse's milk and salt, and tastes revolting; it's also most impolite to refuse.

The main attraction outside Manzhouli is Hulun Lake *(hūlún hú)*, also known as Dalai Lake *(dàlài hú)*. One of the largest lakes in China, it unexpectedly pops out of the Mongolian grasslands like an enormous inland sea. It's a prime venue for fishing, bird-watching and minority-watching. Slightly further south is Beier Lake *(běiěr hú)*, which straddles the border with Outer Mongolia.

The other big feature is for train buffs – the steam locomotive storage and repair yards in Manzhouli are some of the more impressive in China.

CITS has established a Manzhouli branch at 121 Erdaojie, but you can often do better

by either joining a Chinese tour through one of the hotels or simply hiring a taxi and heading out on your own.

You can access Manzhouli by train from either Harbin (28 hours) or from Hailar (3½ hours). If you're doing the Trans-Siberian, you can either enter or leave the train at Manzhouli. There are also buses connecting Manzhouli to Hailar. See the Hailar section for details about flights.

XANADU
(yuánshàngdū)
About 320 km north of Beijing, tucked away near Duolun in Inner Mongolia, are the remains of Xanadu, the great Kublai Khan's palace of legendary splendour. Marco Polo visited the Khan in the 13th century and recorded his impressions of the palace:

There is at this place a very fine marble palace, the rooms of which are all gilt and painted with figures of men and beasts and birds, and with a variety of trees and flowers, all executed with such exquisite art that you regard them with delight and astonishment.

Round this palace a wall is built enclosing a compass of 16 miles, and inside the Park there are fountains and rivers and brooks, and beautiful meadows, with all kinds of wild animals (excluding such as are of ferocious nature), which the Emperor has procured and placed there to supply food for his gerfalcons and hawks. Moreover (at a spot in the Park where there is a charming wood) he has another Palace built of cane. It is gilt all over, and most elaborately finished inside. The Lord abides at this Park of his, dwelling sometimes in the Marble Palace and sometimes in the Cane Palace for three months of the year, to wit, June, July and August; preferring this residence because it is by no means hot; in fact it is a very cool place. When the 28th day of August arrives, he takes his departure, and the Cane Palace is taken to pieces.

In the 19th century, Samuel Taylor Coleridge (who never went near the place) stoked his imagination with some opium and composed *Kubla Khan*, a glowing poem about Xanadu that has been on the set menu for students of English literature ever since.

Over the centuries the deserted palace has crumbled back to dust and the site has been visited by very few foreigners. Hardly anything remains of Xanadu.

TIBET & QINGHAI

Tibet 西藏

Locked away in its mountain fortress of the Himalaya, Tibet *(xīzàng)* has long exercised a unique hold on the imagination of the West: 'Shangri-La', 'the Land of Snows', 'the Rooftop of the World', Tibet is mysterious in a way that few other places are.

Until recently, not many outsiders had laid eyes on the holy city of Lhasa and the other secrets of Tibet. It's more the pity that when Tibet finally opened to tourism in the mid-1980s, it was no longer the magical Buddhist kingdom that had so intoxicated early Western travellers. In 1950, the newly established People's Republic of China (PRC) decided to make good a long-held Chinese claim on the strategically important high plateau that straddled the Himalaya between China and the subcontinent. It made no difference that the Chinese claim was made on highly dubious historical grounds: between 1950 and 1970, the Chinese 'liberated' the Tibetans of their independence, drove their spiritual leader and 100,000 of Tibet's finest into exile, caused 1.2 million Tibetan deaths and destroyed most of the Tibetan cultural heritage.

Tibetans have never had it easy. Theirs is a harsh environment, and human habitation has always been a precarious proposition here. By necessity, Tibetans have become a tough and resilient people. Yet despite what seems like a continuous grim struggle against nature and misfortunes, Tibetans have not only survived, but have managed to retain a remarkably cheerful outlook on life.

Most of Tibet is too arid and cold to support human life and the place is still very thinly populated. With a geographical area more than twice the size of France, Tibet manages a total population of only 2.3 million. However, there are thought to be some four million Tibetans spread out over Tibet, Qinghai, Sichuan, Gansu and Yunnan.

Most of Tibet is an immense plateau which lies at an altitude from 4000 to 5000 metres. The Qamdo region in the east is a somewhat

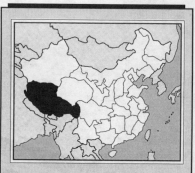

Population: 2.3 million
Capital: Lhasa
Highlights:
- Lhasa, home of the Potala Palace, Jokhang Temple and the Barkhor
- Shigatse, Tibet's second city, where you'll find Tashilhunpo Monastery, the traditional home of the Panchen Lama
- Mt Kailash, a beautiful range of peaks, is a trekker's delight and the source of the Ganges River

lower section of plateau, drained by the headwaters of the Salween, Mekong and Upper Yangzi rivers. It's an area of considerably greater rainfall than the rest of Tibet and the climate is less extreme. Most of the Tibetan population lives in the valleys of this area. On the uplands surrounding these valleys, the inhabitants are mainly pastoralists who raise sheep, yaks and horses.

Since full-scale treatment of Tibetan regions would take a whole book, Lonely Planet has published a separate *Tibet* guide.

HISTORY

Recorded Tibetan history begins in the 7th century AD when the Tibetan armies were considered as great a scourge to their neighbours as the Huns were to Europe. Under

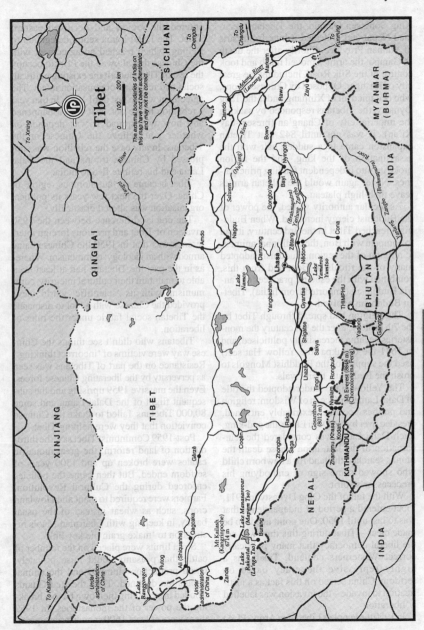

King Songtsen Gampo, the Tibetans occupied Nepal and collected tribute from parts of Yunnan Province. Shortly after the death of Gampo, the armies moved north and took control of the Silk Road, including the great city of Kashgar. Opposed by Chinese troops, who occupied all of Xinjiang under the Tang Dynasty, the Tibetans responded by sacking the imperial city of Chang'an (present-day Xi'an). It was not until 842 that Tibetan expansion came to a sudden halt with the assassination of the king, and the region broke up into independent feuding principalities. Never again would the Tibetan armies leave their high plateau.

As secular authority waned, the power of the Buddhist clergy increased. When Buddhism reached Tibet in the 3rd century, it had to compete with Bon, the traditional animistic religion of the region. Buddhism adopted many of the rituals of Bon, and from this, combined with the esoteric practices of Tantric Buddhism (imported from India), Tibetan Buddhism evolved.

The religion had spread through Tibet by the 7th century; after the 9th century the monasteries became increasingly politicised, and in 1641 the Gelukpa (the Yellow Hat sect) used the support of the Buddhist Mongols to crush the Red Hats, their rivals.

The Yellow Hats' leader adopted the title of Dalai Lama, or Ocean of Wisdom; religion and politics became inextricably entwined, presided over by the Dalai Lama, the god-king. Each Dalai Lama was considered the reincarnation of the last, upon whose death the monks searched the land for a newborn child who showed some sign of embodying his predecessor's spirit.

With the fall of the Qing Dynasty in 1911, Tibet entered a period of independence that was to last until 1950. One point needs to be made clear – Tibet during this time was not the liberal democracy that many politically correct Westerners contend. Tibet was a highly repressive theocracy based on serfdom. China seized on this fact as a justification to invade – the invasion was labelled a 'liberation'.

In 1950 the People's Liberation Army (PLA)

entered the region and occupied eastern Tibet. The Dalai Lama sent a delegation to Beijing, which reached an agreement with the Chinese that allowed the PLA to occupy the rest of Tibet but left the existing political, social and religious organisation intact. The agreement was to last until 1959. In that year a rebellion broke out. Just why it happened and how widespread it was depends on whether you believe the Chinese or the Tibetans. In any case the rebellion was suppressed by Chinese troops and the Dalai Lama and his retinue fled to India.

Tibet became an 'autonomous region' of China. Over the next few years its political organisation was altered drastically.

The crucial difference between the 1950 invasion of Tibet and previous foreign interference was that in 1950 the Chinese came armed with an ideology: communism. Whereas in the past the Tibetans had at least been able to maintain their cultural integrity, communism, with its 'scientific' world view, provided the Chinese with a tool to dismantle the Tibetan social fabric under the rules of liberation.

Tibetans who didn't see things the Chinese way were victims of 'incorrect thinking.' Resistance on the part of Tibetans was seen as perversity by the liberating Chinese forces. Even the massive 1959 uprising and the subsequent flight of the Dalai Lama and some 80,000 Tibetans failed to shake the Chinese conviction that they were helping Tibet.

Post-1959 Communist Tibet saw the introduction of land reform: the great monastic estates were broken up and 1300 years of serfdom ended. But then came the policies enforced during the Cultural Revolution. Farmers were required to plant alien lowland crops, such as wheat instead of the usual barley, in keeping with Chairman Mao's instruction to 'make grain the key link'.

Strict limits were placed on the number of cattle that peasants could raise privately. Grain production slumped and the animal population declined. Then the Red Guards flooded in, wreaking their own havoc, breaking the power of the monasteries. In 1959 there were at least 1600 monasteries operat-

The 14th Dalai Lama, now exiled in Dharamsala, India.

ing in Tibet; by 1979 there were just 10. Most monasteries were used for artillery practice, and monks were either executed or sent to work in fields and labour camps.

The Chinese basically made a mess of Tibet's economy. Of course, it wasn't just Tibet; the Cultural Revolution was a disaster for all of China. Grudgingly, the Chinese have admitted to making 'mistakes' in Tibet.

The Maoist Communist Party chief in Tibet, General Ren Rong, was sacked in 1979. Most of the rural communes were disbanded and the land was returned to private farmers who were allowed to grow or graze whatever they wanted and to sell their produce in free markets. Taxes were reduced and state subsidies to the region increased. Some of the monasteries have reopened, and the Chinese are wooing the Dalai Lama in the hope that he will return to Tibet. But as his status in the outside world continues to improve, it is becoming increasingly unlikely that he will return to accept what would most likely be an office job in Beijing with the effect of legitimising Chinese rule.

In 1985 the 'celebrations' marking the 20th anniversary of the Tibetan Autonomous Region (TAR) went off like a damp squib. Apart from banning the Western press from the event, the Chinese provided Lhasa with a tight military blanket, including sharp shooters on the roof of the Potala Palace. The general picture looked more like a nervous show of strength than anything else.

Despite Chinese efforts to paint a rosy picture of life on the roof of the world, the general picture is of a country under occupation. The Dalai Lama continues to be worshipped by his people, and his acceptance in late 1989 of the Nobel Peace Prize marked a greater sympathy on the part of the Western world for the plight of the Tibetan people.

The Dalai Lama himself has referred to China's policies as 'cultural genocide' for the Tibetan people. Unfortunately, China's great potential as a trading nation and as a market for Western goods makes many world leaders wary of raising the Tibet issue with China. Those who believe that pressure from Western governments will eventually force China to grant Tibet independence or true autonomy are probably being unduly optimistic.

For their part, the Chinese can't understand the ingratitude of the Tibetans. As they see it, China has built roads, schools, hospitals, an airport, factories and a budding tourist industry. The Chinese honestly believe that they saved the Tibetans from feudalism and that their continued occupation is a mission of mercy.

The Tibetans, who cannot forgive the destruction of their monasteries and attacks on their religion and culture, see it differently. Nor do the Tibetans get much joy from the continuous heavy-handed presence of the Chinese police and military. Certainly the Chinese are not winning any friends in Tibet with their policy of stealthy resettlement: a massive influx of Han settlers from surrounding provinces threatens to make Tibetans a minority in their own 'autonomous region' and swamp the Tibetan culture with that of the Han Chinese.

Nevertheless, the Chinese grew so confident in their ability to control Tibet that they decided to open the area to foreign tourism in late 1984. The situation changed quite dramatically in 1987 when Tibetans in Lhasa gave vent to their rage about the Chinese and

TIBET & QINGHAI

their policies. A series of demonstrations virtually became an uprising. Chinese security forces reportedly opened fire on the demonstrators, many of whom were monks from the monasteries around Lhasa. Both sides suffered casualties and at least one police station was reduced to a smoking pile of rubble. The response of the Chinese authorities was swift; Lhasa was swamped with plain-clothes police and uniformed security, who put an abrupt end to the uprising. The embarrassment of foreign press coverage was neatly solved when all members of the foreign media covering events in Lhasa were unceremoniously booted out. Within a few weeks, it was the turn of individual travellers to be similarly ejected.

Tibet basically remained closed to individual travellers for five years – the only way to get in was with a carefully controlled tour group. In 1992, the authorities surprised everyone by opening Tibet again to individuals, though with some ludicrous permit requirements. The present Chinese policy on individual tourism in Tibet basically seems to be one of extorting as much cash as possible from foreigners, but not so much as to scare them off completely.

CLIMATE
See the Climate section in the Facts about the Country chapter.

TREKKING
Trekking is not officially approved in Tibet; the local PSB will advise about the legalities and any permits required. It is feasible for the experienced walker, providing you are prepared to be self-sufficient in food, fuel and shelter. Bring equipment suitable for sub-zero temperatures, such as a high-quality down sleeping bag, thermal underwear, ground mat, four-season tent, stove and fuel. Remember that gas canisters and bottles of flammable liquids may not be welcome on planes. Check with CAAC.

LANGUAGE
Lonely Planet produces the *Tibetan phrasebook*, which should prove useful.

Although many Tibetans in the cities have a rudimentary command of Chinese, you'll have to use Tibetan out on the desolate plateau. The following are some phrases that you might find useful:

Hello.
   Tashi delag.
Thank you.
   Thuk ji chay.
How are you?
   Kuzak de po yinpe?
How much?
   Di gatse ray?
It's very good.
   Shidak yak po dhuk.
Cheers!
   Tamdil!

TRAVEL RESTRICTIONS
The current regulations (which could change tomorrow) say that all foreigners wanting to visit Tibet must book a three-day tour around the Lhasa area. The cost of the tour is added on to the price of your ticket to Tibet. The good news is that the cost of these tours has been reduced to something affordable (approximately Y750 to Y900). You are not actually required to attend the tour, and many foreigners just skip it even though they've already paid.

On the other hand, many popular places beyond Lhasa (the Everest Base Camp, Mt Kailash etc) require you to procure a travel permit. In fact, three permits are needed – one from the PSB, one from the military and another from some shadow organisation called the Tibet Tourist & Culture Bureau. The cost of these permits varies, but expect to pay around Y100 per permit. Getting the permits yourself is a nonstarter – the PSB insists you go through an authorised travel agency and that you be a member of a tour group. Not surprisingly, Lhasa has a large number of travel agencies catering to this market, organising 'groups' which quickly disband after the permits are issued.

Travellers have reasonable freedom of movement within Tibet, but this doesn't mean that they are not watched. If you just go about your business of visiting monasteries and buying jars of yoghurt at the market, there should be no problems. Visitors who go in with a political agenda are another matter. It's worth bearing in mind that Tibet (much more than the rest of China) is effectively a police state, and political discussions with local Tibetans can have serious consequences. Incidentally, many of the secret police are ethnic Tibetans.

WHAT TO BRING

Figuring out what type of clothing to bring is tricky, due to the extremes of the climate. Department stores in Xining, Golmud and Lhasa have a wide selection of warm clothing. The PLA military overcoats are a cheap alternative to down jackets. Also keep the cold at bay with a woollen sweater, long underwear, woollen socks, gloves and woolly hat. Protect yourself against the sun with lip salve, sunscreen, sunglasses and something to cover your head.

Food is no problem in Lhasa, but remote areas offer little to eat beyond lichens, dust and rocks. If entering from Nepal, it's wise to bring food for the overland journey.

There are several medications which are particularly useful in Tibet, and you should bring them from abroad rather than rely on local supplies. Drugs to consider carrying include Diomox, Tiniba and Flagyl – see the following Health section for an explanation.

HEALTH
Acute Mountain Sickness

Most visitors to Tibet and Qinghai – both high-altitude regions with thin air – will suffer some symptoms of acute mountain sickness (AMS), often just called 'altitude sickness'. Until your body has become acclimatised to the lack of oxygen, you may experience temporary symptoms such as headaches, sleeping difficulties, dizziness, nausea and vomiting. Travelling by bus into Lhasa requires ascending several mountain passes over 5000 metres high – this is where you are most likely to suffer. By the time you arrive in Lhasa itself, you should be feeling better. If not, and if you start feeling much

worse, it's time to check with one of the hospitals there and consider a flight to Chengdu. The drug Diomox is not a panacea, but it's known to help reduce the symptoms of AMS – bring some. Oxygen is available at all Lhasa tourist hotels; make use of it if you feel rotten.

More serious than AMS is pulmonary oedema. Unlike AMS, which merely makes you feel rotten, pulmonary oedema can rapidly prove fatal. What happens is that the small blood vessels in the lungs start to rupture and the victim then begins to cough up blood. Pulmonary oedema usually takes a few days to develop, so you aren't likely to perish on the aforementioned mountain passes if you are just driving through. Bicyclists and mountaineers, on the other hand, cannot move as quickly as a bus – some have indeed perished from pulmonary oedema.

Pulmonary oedema is rare in Lhasa itself, but over 4000 metres, the danger increases dramatically. Again, becoming acclimatised gradually is your best defence.

To prepare yourself for higher altitudes, spend the first few days taking your exercise slowly. Drink plenty of liquids (keep your urine a nice pale colour!) to avoid dehydration. Alcohol, tobacco and sedatives are best avoided.

Giardiasis

A nasty amoeba called *Giardia* has travelled from Nepal to Lhasa, where it treks the intestinal paths of unfortunate foreigners – the locals seem immune. The symptoms include stomach cramps, diarrhoea and a general feeling of doom. After a few weeks of misery, the symptoms tend to subside, but then you can look forward to repeated relapses unless you get cured. Fortunately, there are a number of highly effective anti-giardiasis drugs on the market which will rid you of the bug in a few days. Brand names to look for include Tiniba and Flagyl, but take these drugs as a cure only, not as a preventive. Never consume even a drop of alcohol when taking anti-amoebic drugs – the resulting reaction is said to feel like imminent death.

Read the labels inside the drug bottles

about possible side effects – anti-amoebic drugs have come in for some criticism by the medical establishment. It would be wise to bring your own supply of these drugs. Some of the most poignant notices in Lhasa are those by foreigners urgently seeking these magical medicines – two such foreigners in constant search of relief received the nickname of 'flagylantes'.

DANGERS & ANNOYANCES
Not Shangri-La
Tibetans are among the friendliest, most hospitable people in the world. At the same time, however, there is little point in pretending that visiting the Land of Snows is a Disneyland holiday. Most Tibetans are exceedingly friendly and only too happy to have foreign visitors in their country, but do not expect smiles all the way. Travellers who have poked their noses into Tibetan funerals and other personal matters have rightly received a very hostile reception. Stories abound of surly monks, of aggressive Tibetans at checkpoints (in particular in the Everest region) and of rip-offs. Tibetan tour operators can be just as rapacious as their Chinese counterparts. Some foreigners have a few bad experiences and come away disillusioned.

Dogs
Tibetan dogs are even more xenophobic than the PSB. They (the dogs) roam in packs around monasteries and towns, and seem to have a particular antipathy to foreigners who look and smell different from the locals. Several foreign visitors have been badly bitten. Keep your distance during the day, and watch your step in the dark. Getting yourself vaccinated for rabies is not a bad idea either.

GETTING AROUND
Transport can be a major hurdle if you want to explore the backwaters. The four main types of vehicle are bus, minibus, truck and 4WD. On some routes there are modern Japanese buses; other routes are covered by battered wrecks which gasp over each high pass as if it's their last. Trucks are often more comfortable, more fun and faster than the

bus. Landcruisers are pricey, but not impossible for middle-class travellers willing to split the cost among several people.

Bus prices in Tibet have been doubled, or in some cases trebled, for foreigners. This price hike could be considered acceptable for deluxe buses, but not for the old bangers. Trucks tend to charge the same as buses, but the Chinese government has moved to stop foreigners from hitching rides on trucks by threatening the drivers with fines or confiscation of their vehicles.

In Tibet, 'road safety' is just a slogan. Potential hazards include bad roads, vehicle breakdowns, icy weather and reckless drivers (not necessarily your driver, but the other maniacs on the road). Tibetans take their minds off these variables by praying, and you'd be wise to follow their example unless you want to end up a gibbering bag of nerves. Road accidents are frequent and foreigners have been injured or killed in the past.

Be prepared for the cold, which can easily go below zero at night even during summer. All buses have heaters, though these are sometimes broken. More seriously, a mechanical breakdown could have fatal consequences if you have no warm clothing.

As for bicycling – yes – it's possible, but not without its hazards. Aside from hassles with the PSB, cyclists in Tibet have died from road accidents, hypothermia and pulmonary oedema. Tibet is not the place to learn the ins and outs of long-distance cycling – do your training elsewhere.

ORGANISED TOURS
Several agencies in Kathmandu and Chengdu (in Sichuan) arrange organised tours to Lhasa and Shigatse only. There are no minimum numbers required for the tours, but naturally the more of you there are, the cheaper it ends up per head. You can easily book tours to Tibet's remote hinterland after you've arrived in Lhasa.

LHASA
(lāsà)
Lhasa, the heart and soul of Tibet, abode of the Dalai Lamas, an object of devout pil-

grimage, is still, despite the large-scale encroachments of Chinese influence, a city of wonders. As you enter the Kyi Chu Valley, either on the long haul from Golmud or from Gonggar Airport, your first hint that Lhasa is close at hand is the sight of the Potala, a vast white and ochre fortress soaring over one of the world's highest cities. It is a sight that has heralded the marvels of the holy city to travellers for three centuries.

The Potala dominates the Lhasa skyline. The location of the tombs of previous Dalai Lamas, it was once the seat of Tibetan government and the winter residence of the Dalai Lama. While it serves as a symbolic focus for Tibetan hopes of self-government, it is the Jokhang, some two km to the east of the Potala, that is the spiritual heart of the city. The Jokhang, a curious mix of sombre darkness, wafting incense and prostrating pilgrims, is the most sacred and active of Tibet's temples. Encircling it is the Barkhor, the holiest of Lhasa's devotional circumambulation circuits. And it is here that most visitors first fall in love with Tibet. The medieval push and shove of crowds from another time and place, the street performers, the stalls hawking everything from prayer flags to jewel-encrusted yak skulls, and the devout tapping their foreheads to the ground at every step is an exotic brew that few newcomers can resist.

Modern Lhasa divides clearly into a western, Chinese, section and an eastern, Tibetan, section. For travellers who have arrived from other parts of China, the Chinese part of town harbours few surprises. Nestled at the foot of the Potala and extending a couple of km westward is an uninspired muddle of restaurants, karaoke bars, administrative blocks and department stores. The Tibetan part of town, which begins not far west of the Jokhang, is altogether more colourful and is the best area to be based in.

Information

The best place for the latest on Tibetan individual travel these days is one of the popular Tibetan hotels, or a table in Tashi's Restaurant.

Travel Agencies If you want to do any trekking or visit remote areas, you need to visit a travel agency in order to secure a permit, motorised transport (usually a jeep) and (possibly) a guide. CITS has an unhelpful head office opposite the Holiday Inn. Another office calling itself 'CITS Shigatse' (☎ 32234; fax 32345) is just next to the Yak Hotel and offers better service, but their prices are still high. Inside the Yak Hotel itself, you can make contact with Potala Folk Travel Service (☎ 23496), though their main office (☎ 24822, 33551) is located elsewhere in an obscure alley. Tibet Traffic Travel (☎ 33931; fax 32837), inside the Banak Shol Hotel, is another possibility. By no means is it certain that the foregoing travel agencies are the cheapest or best in town; you need to talk to other travellers and shop around. There has been a recent proliferation of travel services in Lhasa, many of them inexperienced, expensive and incompetent; proceed with caution.

PSB There are two PSB offices in Lhasa, though it's doubtful that either will prove to be of much use. The one on the eastern end of Beijing Donglu issues travel permits, but they are unwilling to issue these to individual travellers and will instead refer you to a travel agency.

The other PSB office on Linkuo Beilu theoretically does visa extensions, but at the time of writing they were being exceedingly uncooperative. Basically, they were telling travellers that visa extensions could only be issued if you had a travel permit valid for the number of days you wanted to extend. (Meanwhile, the other PSB office was refusing to issue travel permits unless you had a visa extension!).

Money The main Bank of China is behind the Potala – turn at the yak statues and look for it on the left. Opening hours are 9.30 am to 12.30 pm and 2 to 5.30 pm weekdays, 9.30 am to 12.30 pm Saturday, closed Sunday. Travellers' cheques and cash in most major currencies can be exchanged with a minimum of fuss.

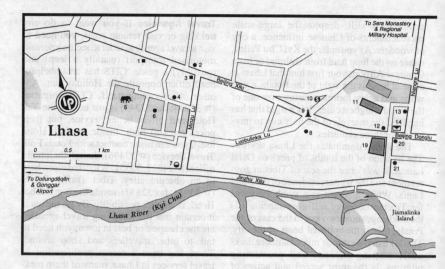

Lhasa 拉薩

0   0.5   1 km

To Sera Monastery & Regional Military Hospital

Beijing Xilu

Luobulinka Lu

Beijing Donglu

Jinzhu Xilu

Lhasa River (Kyi Chu)

Jiamalinka Island

To Doilungdêqên & Gonggar Airport

There is a black market for US dollars in Lhasa but, given that rates are slightly lower than those given at the bank, the risks involved (there are a lot of counterfeit Y100 notes floating about) make such transactions rather silly unless you are caught cashless after hours.

You can also change money at the Tibet

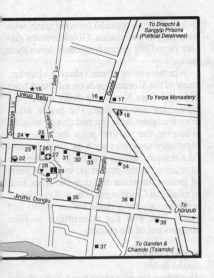

To Drapchi & Sangyip Prisons (Political Detainees)

Linkuo Beilu

To Yerpa Monastery

To Lhünzub

To Ganden & Chamdo (Tsiamdo)

15	PSB (Visa Extensions)
	公安局外事科
18	Bank of China
	中国银行
19	Workers' Cultural Palace
	劳动人民文化宫
20	Photo Shops
	照相馆
21	Xinhua Bookstore
	新华书店
22	Minibus Stand
	小型车站
27	Tibetan Autonomous Region
	People's Hospital
	西藏自治区人民医院
29	Jokhang Temple
	大昭寺
30	Ganden Bus Tickets
	汽车售票处
34	PSB Headquarters (Travel Permits)
	公安局总部
38	Tibet University
	西藏大学

Hotel or Yingqiao Hotel by paying a 2% commission. The Holiday Inn is unobliging about serving those who are not staying at the hotel.

Nepalese Consulate-General The Nepalese consulate (☎ 22880) is on a side street just south of the Holiday Inn and north of the Norbu Lingka. Visa-application hours are Monday to Saturday, from 9.30 am to 12.30 pm. Visas are issued the following day. At the time of writing, the visa fee had changed three times in the previous year and was hovering precariously at US$15 for a 15-day visa and US$25 for a 30-day visa. It is possible to pay in RMB and you should remember to bring along one visa photo.

It is also possible to obtain visas for the same costs as above at Kodari, the Nepalese bordertown, though it would be sensible to check first that this has not been changed.

Medical Services Several hospitals in Lhasa treat foreigners. The Tibetan Autonomous Region People's Hospital and the Regional Military Hospital have been recommended.

Potala Palace
(bùdǎlā gōng)
The most imposing attraction of Lhasa is the Potala, once the centre of the Tibetan government and the winter residence of the Dalai Lama. One of the architectural wonders of the world, this immense construction has thousands of rooms, shrines and statues. It dates from the 17th century but is on the site of a former structure built a thousand years earlier. Each day a stream of pilgrims files through this religious maze while chanting, prostrating themselves and offering *khata* (ceremonial scarves) or yak butter.

The general layout of the Potala includes a Red Palace for religious functions and a White Palace for the living quarters of the Dalai Lama. The Red Palace contains many halls and chapels – the most stunning chapels house the jewel-bedecked tombs of previous Dalai Lamas. The apartments of the 13th and 14th Dalai Lamas in the White Palace offer an insight into the high life. You will find that the roof has marvellous views, if the monks will let you go there.

The Potala is open Monday and Thursday from 9 am to noon only. Foreigners pay a hefty Y45 admission or engage in a lengthy

TIBET & QINGHAI

discussion with the door-keepers about how they misplaced their student card and should only be paying Y15 – it rarely works. The long climb to the entrance is not recommended on your first day in town; do something relaxing at ground level. Remember, photography is not officially allowed.

Jokhang Temple
(dàzhāo sì)

The golden-roofed Jokhang is 1300 years old and one of Tibet's holiest shrines. It was built to commemorate the marriage of the Tang princess Wen Cheng to King Songtsen Gampo, and houses a pure gold statue of the Buddha Sakyamuni brought to Tibet by the princess. Here, too, pilgrims in their hundreds prostrate themselves in front of the temple entrance before continuing on their circuit. Follow the pilgrims through a labyrinth of shrines, halls and galleries containing some of the finest and oldest treasures of Tibetan art. Some were destroyed during the Cultural Revolution and have been replaced with duplicates. Take a torch if you want a closer look, and to avoid getting lost copy the nomad kids and hang onto the tresses of the pilgrim in front.

The Jokhang is best visited early in the morning; you may not be allowed to enter after 11 am. Whatever you do, be considerate to the pilgrims and respect the sacred nature of the place.

Barkhor
(bākuò)

The Barkhor is essentially a pilgrim circuit which is followed clockwise round the periphery of the Jokhang. It is also a hive of market activity, an astounding jamboree, a Tibetan-style stock exchange. All round the circuit are shops, stalls, teahouses and hawkers. There's a wide variety of items to gladden a Tibetan heart – prayer flags, block prints of the holy scriptures, earrings, Tibetan boots, Nepalese biscuits, puffed rice, yak butter and incense.

People who roll up from remote parts of Tibet include Khambas from eastern Tibet, who braid their hair with red yarn and stride around with ornate swords or daggers, and Goloks (Tibetan nomads) from the north, who wear ragged sheepskins. Golok women display incredibly ornate hairbands down their backs.

Whether you buy from a shop or a hawker, many of the Tibetan goods on sale have been imported from Nepal and many of the 'antiques' are not genuine. The prices asked from foreigners have reached absurd heights. Whatever the starting price for any item, especially souvenirs such as turquoise and fake antiques, expect to halve it. Much of the 'turquoise' in the market is, in fact, a paste of ground turquoise and cement. Also, bear in mind that Chinese customs will confiscate antiques (anything made before 1959) and could fine you for attempting to take antiques out of the country.

Norbu Lingka
(luóbù línkǎ)

About three km west of the Potala is the Norbu Lingka, which used to be the summer residence of the Dalai Lama. The pleasant park contains small palaces, chapels and a zoo.

Yak Statue
(máoniú xiàng)

This is not a sight to seek out, but you'll probably wander past the pair of bronze yaks set in the middle of the road just down from the Potala and wonder how they came to be there. They were actually erected in 'celebration' of the 1991 anniversary of the Chinese takeover ('liberation' in China-speak). They have slightly more appeal than your average Mao statue, and that's about the most that can be said for them.

Places to Stay – bottom end

The *Yak Hotel (yàkè lǚshè)* is a travellers' institution. With its Tibetan flavour, low prices and location near the Barkhor, it's not hard to see why. The hotel has dorm beds from Y25 to Y35. Check out the beautiful Tibetan-style Y180 doubles (with attached bath) if you've got an extra few yuan in your wallet. Hot water is intermittent – keep an ear to the ground. The Yak has a good information board and provides bicycles for hire.

Snowlands Hotel (☎ 23687) *(xuěyù lǚguǎn)*, close to the Jokhang Temple, is a friendly place with rooms arranged around a courtyard. Beds cost Y25 in a quad, Y30 in a triple and Y60 to Y70 in a double. Only rooms with shared bath are available. Ask at reception about luggage storage and bike hire.

The *Banak Shol Hotel* (☎ 23829) *(bālángxuě lǚguǎn)* at 43 Beijing Donglu has a charming Tibetan-style courtyard and a free laundry service. Dorms cost Y26 per bed, singles without bath are Y35 and a plush double with attached bathroom costs Y120.

The *Kirey Hotel* *(jírì lǚguǎn)*, close to the Banak Shol, charges from Y25 and Y30 for dorm beds. It has great showers and superfriendly staff – all it lacks is atmosphere, and this is no doubt what keeps the crowds at bay.

Also lacking charm is the *Plateau Hotel* *(gāoyuán lǚguǎn)* on Linkuo Beilu. At least it's cheap; a bed costs Y30 in a triple and Y80 in a double, but all rooms have shared bath.

The *Khada Hotel (hādá lǚguǎn)* on Jinzhu Donglu is unique in being an *unfriendly* Tibetan hotel. Grotty doubles with shared bath are overpriced at Y120. This place is unpopular for good reason; give it a miss.

Places to Stay – middle

Most of Lhasa's mid-range places are recently constructed in the Chinese-style that you've become accustomed to elsewhere on your trip – but that's not what people come all the way to Tibet for, is it? Still, if the Tibetan-style hotels are full (as they sometimes are during the peak season), a mid-range Chinese hotel might be worth considering.

One of the older Chinese-style places that at least tries to look Tibetan is the one-star *Himalaya Hotel* (☎ 208271; fax 34855) *(xīmǎlāyǎ fàndiàn)*. Its location south of Jinzhu Donglu is rather inconvenient, but a lot of tour groups put up here. Doubles with attached bath cost Y250.

The *Sunlight Hotel* (☎ 22943) *(rìguāng bīnguǎn)* is a fancy Chinese-style place also popular with the tour groups. Doubles are Y280 and Y300.

The *Yingqiao Hotel* (☎ 30663) *(yínqiáo fàndiàn)* is a sparkling new place on Linkuo

Beilu. There are 42 double rooms with attached bath, priced between Y230 and Y280.

The *Gangjian Hotel* (☎ 35365) *(gāngjiān fàndiàn)* at 196 Beijing Xilu is a new two-star Chinese-style place. Prices had not been established at the time of writing.

Places to Stay – top end

The *Lhasa Holiday Inn* (☎ 32221; fax 35796) *(lāsà fàndiàn)* at 1 Minzu Lu boasts 468 luxurious rooms. Economy/superior rooms are Y600/992. Suites and Tibetan-style rooms are also available, priced from Y1470 to Y1931. Rates are raised by 20% for the busy month of August. During the quieter winter months from 1 November to 31 March there are substantial discounts available. A free shuttle service using minibuses operates between the hotel and the Barkhor. The transport desk arranges day trips to Drepung, Sera or Ganden monasteries. Inquire at the transport desk about hiring a bicycle, taxi, jeep or minibus.

The *Tibet Hotel* (☎ 36784; fax 36787) *(xīzàng bīnguǎn)* is at 221 Beijing Xilu, a few hundred metres up the road from the Lhasa Holiday Inn. Built in mock-Tibetan-style, it offers comfortable, if pricey, rooms. Doubles/suites cost Y420/1900. Like the management at the Holiday Inn, the management here is open to a little haggling during the low-occupancy winter months.

Places to Eat

Food can be mighty scarce out on the high plateau, but Lhasa offers Chinese, Western, Tibetan and even some Nepalese cuisine. The staple diet in Tibet consists of tsampa (roasted barley meal) and butter tea. Momo (dumplings filled with meat) and thukpa (noodles with meat) are usually available at small restaurants. Tibetans consume large quantities of chang, a tangy alcoholic drink made from fermented barley.

Tashi's Restaurant on the Barkhor deserves a plug – the service is very friendly, prices are cheap and everything on the menu is good. Special praise is reserved for the bobis (chapatti-like unleavened bread), which most people order with seasoned cream cheese and fried vegetables or meat. Tashi's apple momos and cheesecakes are also a hit. *Tashi's II*, which has opened inside the grounds of the Kirey Hotel, is not as good as the first, but is much less crowded.

The *Kailash Restaurant* on the 2nd floor of the Banak Shol Hotel is also excellent. With dishes such as vegetarian lasagne and yak burgers (as good as those at the Holiday Inn and much cheaper) on the menu, the Kailash is a great alternative to the Chinese and Tibetan fare in the old part of town.

Other recent competitors on the backpacker dining circuit include the *Crazy Yak Saloon Restaurant* (next to the Yak Hotel) and the *Lost Horizons Cafe* (just west of the Yak Hotel).

The *Barkhor Cafe* overlooks the Barkhor. This place has great ambience, but the food is nothing to write home about.

For the truly famished and financially solvent, there's a smorgasbord of gastronomical delights at the *Holiday Inn*. The *Tibet Hotel* chips in with all-you-can-eat buffets – Y68 for breakfast, Y85 for lunch and dinner.

Getting There & Away

Air Chengdu is Lhasa's window on the world. Flights to Lhasa depart Chengdu twice daily at 7 and 7.10 am (figure that one out). Going the other way, the same aircraft depart Lhasa at 9.50 and 10 am.

There is a once-weekly (Sunday) flight between Lhasa and Beijing, which also goes via Chengdu. The only other domestic flight is the twice-weekly Lhasa-Chongqing run.

Lhasa-Kathmandu flights operate on Tuesday and Saturday – they depart Lhasa at 10.30 am and leave Kathmandu at 12.30 pm.

No matter if you fly in from Chengdu, Beijing, Chongqing or Kathmandu, an additional Y750 minimum is tacked onto the price of your ticket for the mandatory three-day 'Lhasa tour'.

The CAAC office (☎ 22417) at 88 Niangre Lu has helpful and friendly staff, but they are currently not authorised to sell tickets to foreigners. They will direct you to Tibet Air Travel Service in the Tibet Hotel, which is well organised – getting flights at short notice is usually no problem. Tibet Air Travel is open on weekdays from 9 am until 12.30 pm, and from 2 to 4 pm; on Sundays from 10 am to 12.30 pm.

Bus The bus station is a deserted monstrosity three km from the post office, near the Norbu Lingka. Foreigners are charged from two to five times the local price. Buy your tickets several days in advance and roll up early. Alternatively, buy your tickets from any number of travel agencies around town.

From Lhasa to Golmud, prices are Y414 for a Chinese-made 'Japanese' bus or Y391 for a genuine Chinese bus (a wreck on wheels). In Golmud, foreigners pay Y1077 for a ticket to Lhasa on the Chinese bus – the justification is that you are paying for the three-day Lhasa tour. The fare should include transport from your hotel to the bus station.

There are daily departures in the early morning to Shigatse (Y70), Tsetang and Golmud. The schedule for buses to Zhangmu is a bit hit or miss. There should be a weekly service on Saturday; failing this, buses run every 10 days.

Very few foreigners use the bus station's Shigatse service, as there are now minibuses departing from in front of the Kirey Hotel starting from 7 am. They do the trip quicker than the public buses and cost only Y30. Since the completion of the new Lhasa-Shigatse highway, there is no public transport direct to Gyantse. It is necessary to travel to Shigatse first and then change to a private minibus or a public bus.

The tickets sold to foreigners at the bus station are foreigners' tickets, and if that's what you paid for then check that you have actually been issued a foreigners' ticket. There have been reports of bus station staff pocketing cash and issuing a Chinese ticket. This can create problems when you board the bus, and to top it off you can get fined at police road blocks.

Road Routes Although there are five major road routes to Lhasa, foreigners are officially allowed to use only the Nepal and Qinghai routes.

Nepal Route The road connecting Lhasa with Nepal is officially called the Friendship Highway and runs from Lhasa to Zhangmu (the Chinese border post) via Gyantse and Shigatse. It's a spectacular trip over high passes and across the plateau, the highest point being La Lungla Pass (5200 metres). If the weather's good, you'll get a fine view of Mt Everest from the Tibetan village of Tingri. From Zhangmu, it's 11 km to the Nepalese border post at Kodari, which has transport connections to Kathmandu.

Accommodation en route is generally fairly basic, but prices are usually reasonable, and there's no great hardship involved, as long as you don't mind doing without luxuries (such as a shower) for the duration of your trip. The food situation has also improved greatly in recent years.

Very few people do the Nepal trip by local bus nowadays, mainly because you have no control over your itinerary this way. By far the most popular option is renting a 4WD through a hotel or travel agency, and sorting out a private itinerary with the driver.

Travelling from Nepal to Lhasa, the only transport for foreigners is arranged through tour agencies. If you already have a Chinese visa, you can try turning up at the border. The occasional traveller slips through (even a couple on bicycles). At Zhangmu (Khasa) you can hunt around for buses, minibuses, 4WDs or trucks heading towards Lhasa.

Qinghai Route An asphalt road connects Xining with Lhasa via Golmud; it crosses the desolate, barren and virtually uninhabited Tibetan Plateau. The highest point is Tangula Pass (5180 metres), but despite the altitude the scenery is not really very interesting.

Theoretically, local Chinese buses and decidedly more comfortable 'Japanese' buses (made in China) do the run. However, the 'Japanese' buses are often not available, so you get to ride budget class at five-star prices. Whatever you do, do not succumb to the blandishments of CITS in Golmud and hire one of their minibuses for the trip. These invariably break down, and if this happens you're likely to be stranded in the middle of

nowhere, a far worse scenario than 30-odd hours on a Chinese bus. CITS are not in the habit of recompensing inconvenienced (or dead) travellers either.

Reckon on around 35 hours from Golmud to Lhasa by bus. Chinese buses cost Y470 (three times the local price!) and Japanese buses, when they're available, cost Y520.

Take warm clothing, food and water on the bus, since baggage is not accessible during the trip.

Other Routes Between Lhasa and Sichuan, Yunnan or Xinjiang provinces are some of the wildest, highest and most dangerous routes in the world; these are not open to foreigners.

The lack of public transport on these routes makes it necessary to hitch, but that is also prohibited. There are very few people hitching into or out of Lhasa these days. The authorities have come down very heavily on truck drivers giving lifts to foreigners, particularly on the Yunnan and Sichuan routes in or out of Tibet. On either of these routes, very few drivers would be willing to risk the very high fines exacted for carrying foreign cargo. Some foreigners who look Chinese have gotten away with it, but you shouldn't underestimate the physical dangers.

Rented Vehicles Rented vehicles have emerged as the most popular way to get away from Lhasa in recent years. The most popular route is a leisurely and slightly circuitous journey down to Zhangmu on the Tibetan-Nepalese border, taking in Yamdrok-tso lake, Gyantse, Shigatse, Sakya, Everest Base Camp and Tingri on the way. A six to seven-day trip of this sort in a jeep costs around Y6000. At the time of writing, only the Everest Base Camp required a permit for the above itinerary. Other popular trips included Mt Kailash and Nam-tso lake, but these also require permits.

The Yak Hotel operation is a reliable option for vehicles and you can generally trust your driver to hold to a spoken agreement. If you go for one of the other operators in town, it would probably be a good idea to get everything down in writing. Check with the driver about the latest on permit requirements.

Getting Around

To/From the Airport Gonggar Airport is 90 km (a good two hours by bus) from Lhasa, and all flights leave early in the morning. This forces most travellers to take an afternoon bus out to the airport and stay overnight. Buses leave from the car park behind the CAAC office every 20 minutes or so between 2.30 and 4.30 pm and cost Y25. Tickets are sold on the bus, not in advance – buses leave when full, so show up early to guarantee yourself a seat.

The only alternative to this is to hire a car, jeep or minibus in advance. You'll have to head out between 5 and 6 am in order to catch your flight. Chartering a car to the airport typically costs Y400 to Y500, and the vehicles typically can carry from four to seven passengers, who can split the cost. Places to look for vehicles include the hotels (even budget hotels) and travel agencies.

The airport bus will drop you off at the derelict CAAC Hotel, which costs Y60 for a bed in a basic triple or Y80 in a double. The hotel is a disgrace – the cold water goes off for several hours at a time, the hot water doesn't function at all, power failures are frequent (bring a flashlight, candles and matches), some beds and chairs have legs missing, the wallpaper is peeling off the walls etc. The hotel restaurant functions between 6 and 8 pm; don't show up later than 7 pm if you expect anything to eat.

CAAC buses greet incoming flights, so getting into town from the airport is no problem.

Minibus Privately run minibuses are frequent on Beijing Lu, and run from just east of the main post office up past the Holiday Inn. There is a flat Y1 charge. This is the quickest and cheapest way to get across town.

From the intersection of Beijing Donglu and Jiefang Beilu there are also jeeps and minibuses running up to Sera Monastery.

Pedicab There is no shortage of pedicabs

plying the streets of Lhasa, but as they are slow and relatively expensive there is little incentive to use them. A trip between the Banak Shol Hotel and the post office, for example, costs around Y5 (after much haggling). All things considered, you are better off hiring a bicycle and peddling yourself around.

AROUND LHASA
Monasteries

Prior to 1959, Lhasa had three monasteries which functioned as 'pillars of the Tibetan state'. As part of a concerted effort to smash the influence of these, the Cultural Revolution wiped out the monastic population, which once numbered thousands. The buildings of Ganden Monastery were shelled and demolished. Today, buildings are being reconstructed, and even if Chinese motives in all this are centred more on the tourist dollar than on any notions of religious freedom and making amends for past wrongs, it is still gratifying to see that the monasteries are starting to come to life again, although nowhere near the scale on which they once operated.

Drepung (*zhébàng sì*) The Drepung dates back to the early 15th century and lies about seven km west of Lhasa. In its time it was the largest of Tibet's monastic towns and, some maintain, the largest monastery in the world. Today, the total number of monks in residence here has dwindled from 7000 to around 400. Around 40% of the monastery's structures have been destroyed.

While exploring the monastery grounds maintain a watchful eye for packs of vicious dogs. A walking stick for beating them off might be a good idea. Bites are not uncommon.

Drepung is easily reached by bike, though most people take a minibus from the stand down the road from the Jokhang. The fare is Y1 to the turn-off and Y2 if you take a minibus up the hill to the monastery itself.

Sera (*sèlā sì*) About four km north of Lhasa, this monastery was founded in 1419 by a disciple of Tsong Khapa. About 300 monks are now in residence, well down from an original population of around 5000. Debating takes place from 3 pm in a garden next to the central assembly hall (Jepa Duchen) in the centre of the monastery.

At the base of a mountain just east of the monastery is a Tibetan 'sky burial' site, where the deceased are chopped up and then served to vultures. Tourism has reduced this admittedly grisly event to an almost daily confrontation between *domden* (undertakers) and scores of photo-hungry visitors. The reactions of the domden have become very violent. Our advice is to leave the place alone.

An hour's walk will get you up to the monastery, but most people hitch a ride with a tractor for Y3.

Ganden (*gāndān sì*) About 45 km east of Lhasa, this monastery was founded in 1409 by Tsong Khapa. During the Cultural Revolution the monastery was subjected to intense shelling, and monks were made to dismantle the remains. Some 400 monks have returned now, but the reconstruction work awaiting them is huge. For all this, the monastery is still well worth visiting and remains an important pilgrimage site.

Pilgrim buses leave for Ganden from the south-western corner of the Jokhang, early in the morning. The ticket office is a small tin structure on the Barkhor circuit and they are not keen on selling tickets to foreigners. Persistence pays off, however. Buy tickets the day before you intend to travel.

YARLUNG VALLEY
(*yálǔ liúyù*)
About 170 km south-east of Lhasa, this valley is considered to be the birthplace of Tibetan culture. Near the town of Tsetang, which forms the administrative centre of the region, are several sites of religious importance.

Samye Monastery
This lies about 30 km west of Tsetang, on the opposite bank of the Yarlung Zangbo (Brahmaputra River). It was founded in 775 AD

A young monk from one of the newly reconstructed monasteries outside Lhasa.

by King Trisong Detsen and was the first monastery in Tibet. Getting there is complicated, but the monastery commands a beautiful, secluded position.

To reach Samye, catch a bus from Lhasa to Tsetang. Buses leave at 7.30 am from the bus station. Buses from the small bus station south of the Barkhor square are much cheaper at around Y25 and also leave at around 7.30 am. You will be dropped off close to a ferry which functions sporadically and will take you across the river. From there, a tractor, truck or horse and cart will carry you the five km to Samye. There's inexpensive accommodation at the monastery and also in Tsetang.

Yumbulagang
About 12 km south-west of Tsetang, Yumbulagang is the legendary first building in Tibet. Although small in scale, it soars in recently renovated splendour above the valley. Get there by hiring a bike or 4WD in Tsetang, or hitch on a tractor.

Tombs of the Kings
At Chongye, about 26 km west of Tsetang, these tombs are less of a visual treat than

Yumbulagang; their importance is essentially historical. To get there, hire a 4WD or spend half the day pedalling there and back on a bike.

Places to Stay & Eat

About 10 minutes' walk south of the Tsetang traffic circle is the *Tsetang Guesthouse*, a drab Chinese-style establishment with dorm beds for Y15. There is a reasonably good restaurant (though no better than the ones out on the street) and a well-stocked shop. Practically on the traffic circle is the *Himalayan Tibetan Restaurant & Hotel*. It's noisy and not particularly clean, but at Y15 per bed the price is right.

Tsetang's premier lodging is the *Tsetang Hotel*, just down the road from the guesthouse. Economy doubles are Y110 per person. This is one of the few hotels in Tibet with a 24-hour hot-water supply and the Cantonese-style restaurant is excellent.

Getting There & Away

Buses for Tsetang leave Lhasa two or three times a day. The first leaves at 7.30 am from the Lhasa bus station. Buses heading back to Lhasa leave from the traffic circle in Tsetang every morning.

SHIGATSE
(rìkèzé)

The second-largest urban centre in Tibet is Shigatse. This is the seat of the Panchen Lama, a reincarnation of Amitabha (Buddha of Infinite Light), who ranks close to the Dalai Lama. The 10th Panchen Lama, who died in 1989, was taken to Beijing during the '60s and lived a largely puppet existence there, visiting Tibet only occasionally. The search for his successor has led to verbal conflict between the Dalai Lama and the Chinese government, as the Dalai Lama got in first and nominated a new Panchen Lama. The Chinese subsequently placed the Dalai Lama's nominee, Gedhun Choekyi Nyima, under house arrest in Beijing and nominated their own candidate.

Like everywhere else in Tibet, once you get off the main streets of Shigatse for some

exploring, you should maintain a vigilant eye for packs of dogs. The pilgrim circuit is particularly bad.

Tashilhunpo Monastery
(zhāshílúnbù sì)

The main attraction in Shigatse is the seat of the Panchen Lama – Tashilhunpo Monastery. Built in 1447 by a nephew of Tsong Khapa, the monastery once housed over 4000 monks, but now there are only 600. Apart from a giant statue of the Maitreya Buddha (nearly 27 metres high) in the Temple of the Maitreya, the monastery is also famed for its Grand Hall with its opulent tomb (containing 85 kg of gold and masses of jewels) of the fourth Panchen Lama. The monastery is open from 9.30 am to 5.30 pm, but is closed on Sunday.

Shigatse Fortress
(rìkèzé zōng)

Very little remains of the old Shigatse Fortress, but the ruins on the skyline are imposing all the same. It's possible to hike up to the fortress from the pilgrim circuit for good views of the town.

Shigatse

Market

(nóngmaò shìchǎng)

Shigatse's market is a great place if you enjoy participating in wrestling matches, otherwise beware. The vendors smile, but some of them grab your arm and won't let go until you buy something. This has caused a few scuffles, and it might just be best to avoid wandering into the market altogether.

Places to Stay & Eat

Everybody, even elderly tour groups coming in from Kathmandu, seems to stay at the Tibetan-run *Tenzin Hotel*. It has a roof terrace and is opposite the market in the Tibetan part of town. Beds cost Y15 in the dorm rooms, Y20 in the doubles or Y40 in the Dalai Lama suite. Check out the latter even if you don't stay there.

Just down the road and around the corner from the Tenzin is the mock Tibetan-style *Sanzhuzi Hotel*. Dorm beds are cheap at Y12 to Y16 and doubles are available for Y30 per bed. The hot showers are more reliable than those at the Tenzin.

The Chinese-style *Orchard Hotel*, oppo-site the entrance to Tashilhunpo Monastery, also sees a fair number of foreign guests. Dorm beds cost Y15.

The *Transport Hotel* near the bus station is a complete dump, but costs only Y10 for dorm beds. Opposite the bus station is another cheap, Chinese-style hotel – only for the desperate.

The *Shigatse Hotel* (☎ 22519) is Shigatse's attempt at top-end accommodation. The problem is that it's inconveniently located in the far south of town next to the Bank of China, and has a sort of amusement-park decor. Standard doubles with attached bath-rooms (24-hour hot water!) cost Y280, and economy triples are available for Y270. High-fliers might like the Tibetan suites, which cost from Y480 to Y600.

The most popular place to eat is the *Yuanfu Restaurant*, which offers an English menu. The house speciality is the fish-tasting egg-plant – an amazing dish that some travellers order twice a day. Also popular is the no-name place around the corner from the Sanzhuzi Hotel. Look out for the curtain outside – we've named the place *Curtain Restaurant*.

SHIGATSE 日喀则

PLACES TO STAY

3 Tenzin Hotel & CITS 天新旅馆，中国国际旅行社
9 Sanzhuzi Hotel 三珠子旅馆
13 Orchard Hotel 果园旅馆
19 Transport Hotel 运输旅馆
21 Cheap Hotel 招待所
23 Shigatse Hotel 日喀则宾馆

PLACES TO EAT

5 Yuanfu Restaurant 远富餐厅
8 Curtain Restaurant 帘餐厅
22 Restaurants 餐厅

OTHER

1 Shigatse Fortress 日喀则宗
2 Market 农贸市场
4 Shops 商场
6 Skating Rink 滑冰场
7 PSB 公安局外事科
10 Medical Clinic 诊所
11 Tashilhunpo Monastery 扎十伦布寺
12 Monastery Entrance 扎十伦布寺入口
14 Tibet-Shigatse Regional People's Hospital 西藏日喀则人民医院
15 Xinhua Bookstore 新华书店
16 Red Cross 红十字会
17 Post Office 邮局
18 Department Store 商场
20 Main Bus Station & Minibus Stand 长途汽车站
24 Bank of China 中国银行

TIBET & QINGHAI

Getting There & Away

Between Lhasa and Shigatse most travellers use the minibus service that costs Y30. This is a big saving on the slower and less comfortable public bus service which runs from the main Lhasa bus station for Y95. In Shigatse, the main bus station and minibus stand are located together.

From the main bus station there are also three buses a week for Sakya. Buses go to Lhatse once a week for around Y50. The Lhasa-Zhangmu bus should pass through Shigatse three times a month, but it is often full and rarely arrives when it is supposed to.

Those heading out to the Nepal border or Tingri have very few options. One possibility is to inquire at the Shigatse Hotel for minibuses or landcruisers heading out to the border to pick up tour groups. The cost for hooking up with one of these is around Y200, but service is unreliable.

Renting vehicles in Shigatse is more difficult than in Lhasa and prices are not as competitive. The few agencies operating in town all have a reputation for flakiness – surprisingly, CITS seems to be better than the Tenzin Hotel in this regard.

GYANTSE

(jiāngzī)

Gyantse is one of the least Chinese-influenced towns in Tibet and is worth a visit for this reason alone. It's also one of southern Tibet's chief centres, although it's more like a small village. Keep a respectful distance from the dogs here.

Things to See

The **Palkhor Monastery**, built in 1427, is notable for its superb Kumbum (10,000 images) stupa, which has nine tiers and, according to Buddhist tradition, 108 chapels. The monks may not allow you to complete the pilgrim circuit to the top, but the lower tiers contain excellent murals. Take a torch.

The **Dzong** (old fort), which towers above Gyantse, offers a fine view over the valley. The entrance is usually locked, but you may be able to get the key (for a small fee) from a little house at the foot of the steps leading up the hill; it's close to the tiny bridge on the main road.

Places to Stay & Eat

Just to confuse things, there are two guesthouses called the Gyantse Hotel in town (some travellers have reported a third on the outskirts of town). One of them is to the east of the main intersection and is a Chinese place; the other is to the west and is Tibetan. Most travellers stay at the latter.

The Tibetan-style *Gyantse Hotel* has dorm accommodation for Y10. There are no showers available and toilet facilities are very primitive.

The Chinese-style *Gyantse Hotel* attempts to offer a bit more comfort, but falls short. Doubles and triples with attached bathrooms cost Y25 and Y20 respectively, but the plumbing is perpetually broken. Cheaper five-bed dorms are also available for Y15.

On the southern corner of the main intersection is the *Tibetan Guesthouse*, a Third World nightmare with dorm beds for Y10.

Getting There & Away

All public transport to Gyantse is by way of Shigatse. There are usually minibuses running from the minibus stand in front of the Shigatse bus station until around 4 pm. The trip takes from three to four hours. Minibuses from Gyantse back to Shigatse leave on an irregular basis through the day from the main intersection.

Most travellers with hired vehicles heading to the Nepal border pass through Gyantse.

SAKYA

(sàjiā)

Sakya is 152 km west of Shigatse and about 25 km south of the main road. The huge, brooding monastery at Sakya was Tibet's most powerful 700 years ago, and was once the centre for the Sakyapa sect founded in the 11th century. The monastery probably contains the finest collection of Tibetan religious relics remaining in Tibet, although the monks may restrict you to viewing only a couple of halls.

Places to Stay & Eat

If you come into Sakya by bus or rented transport, you will inevitably be dropped off at the *Sakya County Guesthouse (sàjiāxiàn zhāodàisuǒ)*, a Chinese-style hotel notable for sneering staff. Dorm beds are Y10 to Y16.

Just around the corner is the much friendlier *Tibetan Hotel* – look out for the sign next door saying 'Sofia's Soda & Cigs'. Tibetan-style rooms cost Y10.

Getting There & Away

Most people arrange to see Sakya as an overnight stop when they hire a 4WD to the border or to the Everest Base Camp. It's possible to do it by public transport, but it will take time.

There's a bus (somewhat unreliable) from Shigatse to Sakya in the morning on Monday and Thursday; buses returning to Shigatse do so on Tuesday and Friday. Buy your ticket the day before.

TINGRI

(dìngrì)

There are in fact two Tingris: new Tingri (Xêgar) and old Tingri (Tingri). New Tingri has a checkpoint and a tourist hotel, and not much else. Old Tingri is a Tibetan town. There's not much to do here except look for Everest on the skyline, but most travellers use Tingri as a final stopover before heading on to Zhangmu on the Nepalese border.

The best place to stay in town is the *Everest View Hotel* with beds for Y15. Meals are available here.

From Tingri it's three or four spectacular hours to the border, up, up and then down, down, down.

RONGBUK MONASTERY & EVEREST BASE CAMP

Before heading down to the border, many travellers doing the Lhasa-Kodari trip take in Rongbuk and the Everest Base Camp (also known as Mt Qomolangma Base Camp). Some people have had problems with their 4WD drivers refusing to drive up to Rongbuk or the base camp because of the condition of the trail. It would make sense to check

on this situation in Lhasa before you set off, and make sure that your driver is aware that you expect him to drive up there.

There is dorm accommodation at Rongbuk Monastery, which is about three hours' walk from the base camp. Beds cost Y15, and it's a good idea to bring your own food. Monks at the monastery are sometimes willing to sell food, much of it stuff that has been left behind by previous expeditions, but it's probably best not to count on this.

If you are hiking up to the base camp from Rongbuk, you'll know you've reached your destination when you come across a toilet block. For those thinking of hiking the whole way from Xêgar or Tingri, refer to Lonely Planet's *Tibet* guide for detailed hiking information. It's a four-day walk up to Rongbuk.

ZHANGMU

(zhāngmù)

The last Chinese town you'll see before hitting Nepal has plenty of places to stay and eat, and in some ways represents a better place to spend your last night than Tingri – it's lower (around 2000 metres) and warmer at least.

The main hotel is the *Zhangmu Guesthouse*, right down in the south of town next to customs. It's expensive and apathetically run. Standard doubles cost Y80 per bed, triples are Y50 per bed. There is no hot water in the showers.

Most travellers prefer the *Himalaya Lodge*, a great little hotel up the road south of the bank and near a small stupa. Chinese, Tibetan and Nepalese food is available here until late at night and at very reasonable prices. This is also the place to change Chinese yuan and Nepalese rupees – very good rates are available. Comfortable doubles here cost Y10 per bed.

There are several other accommodation options in Zhangmu. Back down the road towards the Zhangmu Guesthouse, look out for a Chinese-style hotel on the right. This place has beds for Y25. There is another hotel further up the hill past the bank if all of these are full.

TIBET & QINGHAI

ZHANGMU TO KODARI

Access to Nepal is via the Friendship Bridge and Kodari, around 10 km below Zhangmu. Traffic on the stretch of no-man's land between the two countries has increased over the last couple of years and it has now become quite easy to hitch a lift, though you will probably have to pay. Around Y15 should do the trick. If you decide to walk, it will take you a couple of hours down to the bridge. There are porters at both customs points who will carry your pack for a few rupees or Chinese yuan. Look out for short cuts down between the hairpin bends of the road. They save quite a bit of time if you find them, though they put a real strain on the knees.

For those looking at continuing straight on to Kathmandu, there are a couple of buses a day from Kodari that leave whenever they are full. The other option is to hire a vehicle. There are touts for vehicles to Kathmandu up at Chinese customs. The cost is around R1500 to R2000.

Qinghai 青海

Qinghai *(qīnghǎi)* lies on the north-east border of Tibet and is one of the great cartographical constructions of our time. For centuries this was part of the Tibetan world, and today it's separated from the Tibetan Autonomous Region by nothing more than the colours on a Chinese-made map.

With the exception of the eastern area around the capital Xining, Qinghai (formerly known as Amdo) was not incorporated into the Chinese empire until the early 18th century. And since 1949, the province has served as a sort of Chinese Siberia where common criminals as well as political prisoners are incarcerated. These prisoners have included former Kuomintang army and police officers, 'rightists' arrested in the late 1950s harvesting of the Hundred Flowers, victims of the Cultural Revolution, former Red Guards arrested for their activities during the Cultural Revolution, supporters of the Gang of Four and opponents of the present regime.

Eastern Qinghai is a high grassy plateau rising between 2500 and 3000 metres above sea level, and is slashed by a series of mountain ranges whose peaks rise to 5000 metres. It's the source of the Yellow River.

Most of the agricultural regions are concentrated in the east around the Xining area, but the surrounding uplands and the regions west of Qinghai Lake have good pasturelands for sheep, horses and cattle.

North-west Qinghai is a great basin surrounded by mountains. It's littered with salt marshes and saline lakes and afflicted with harsh, cold winters. Parts of it are barren desert, but it's also rich in mineral deposits, particularly oil.

Southern Qinghai is a high plateau 3500 metres above sea level. It's separated from Tibet by the Tanggula range, whose peaks rise to over 6500 metres, and the Yangzi and the Mekong rivers have their source here. Most of the region is grassland and the population is composed almost entirely of

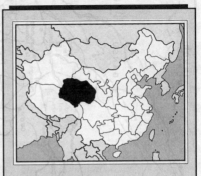

Population: 4.5 million
Capital: Xining
Highlights:
- Ta'er Monastery, one of the six great monasteries of the Yellow Hat sect of Tibetan Buddhism
- Qinghai Lake, China's largest lake, known for breathtaking scenery and abundant wildlife
- Bird Island, a special place for bird lovers

TIBET & QINGHAI

semi-nomadic Tibetan herders rearing goats, sheep and yaks.

The population of Qinghai is a mixture of minorities including the Kazaks, Mongols and Hui. Tibetans are found throughout the province and the Han settlers are concentrated around the area of Xining, the provincial capital.

XINING
(xīníng)

Xining is the only large city in Qinghai and is the capital of the province. It's a long-established Chinese city, and has been a military garrison and trading centre since the 16th century.

Nowadays, it's a stopover for foreigners following the route between Qinghai and

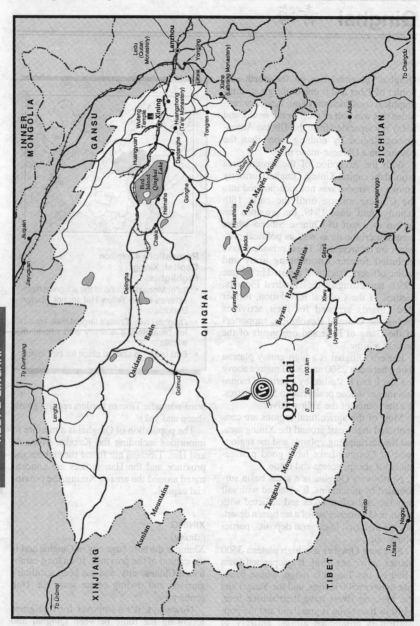

TIBET & QINGHAI

Tibet. Perched at 2200 metres elevation on the edge of the Tibetan Plateau, you can pause to consider the direction of your plunge.

Xining has nothing exceptional to see, but it is a convenient staging post for visiting Ta'er Monastery and Qinghai Lake.

Information

CITS (☎ 42721) and its competitor Kunlun Travel are both ensconced in the front building of the Xining Hotel. The new upstart Qinghai International Sport Travel Service is inside the Youzheng Gongyu Hotel.

You'll find the PSB on Bei Dajie.

The Bank of China's location off Dongguan Dajie is a little inconvenient if you're walking. The Qinghai Hotel has a money exchange service.

Beishan Temple
(běishàn sì)

The temple is about a 45-minute walk up the mountainside north-west of the Xining Hotel. The hike is pleasant and you'll be rewarded with a good view over Xining.

Great Mosque
(qīngzhēn dà sì)

The mosque is on Dongguan Dajie. Built during the late 14th century, this mosque is one of the largest in China's north-west and attracts large crowds of worshippers, particularly on Friday.

Shuijing Xiang Market
(shuǐjǐng xiàng shāngchǎng)

The Shuijing Xiang Market (Water Well Alley) is the most colourful market in town, although even the wells have long since gone dry. Stock up on munchies here, especially if you're heading to Golmud, Qinghai Lake or over the mountains to Chengdu. The market is near the West Gate *(xīmén)*.

Places to Stay

The *Yongfu Hotel* (☎ 814-0236) *(yǒngfù bīnguǎn)* gets the nod from budget travellers. The hotel is just across the bridge to the south of the railway station. The staff are friendly and the rooms all have attached bath. Dorm

beds cost Y35 while singles/doubles are Y60/70. The coffee shop here is a pleasant place to hang out.

Youzheng Gongyu Hotel (☎ 814-9484) *(yóuzhèng gōngyù bīnguǎn)* at 138 Huzhu Lu, the continuation of Qilian Lu, is just east of the railway station. This friendly little place charges Y76 for a double.

Xining Mansions (☎ 409-991) *(xīníng dàshà)* is a gloomy place, but it has the advantage of being the cheapest in town. Rock-bottom dorms are Y15 per bed. A depressing double room without bath costs Y23, or Y34 to Y48 with an attached shower. From the railway station it's a 10-minute walk to the hotel, or take bus No 1 and get off at the second stop.

The *Xining Hotel* (☎ 308-701) *(xīníng bīnguǎn)* is probably better avoided. There are no longer any dorms here, and the rooms that are available are overpriced. Rates are from Y166 to Y375. If you're still interested, reception is in the building at the rear. Take bus No 9 from opposite the railway station – it's five km.

The *Qinghai Hotel* (☎ 404-888; fax 44145) *(qīnghǎi bīnguǎn)* is Xining's interpretation of a high-class international hotel – they got the room rates right at least. Doubles start at Y415, while the best room in the house fetches a staggering Y12,450. The hotel is almost nine km from the railway station, ridiculously inconvenient if you've got an early-morning train to catch.

Places to Eat

The area around the Xining Mansions has good kebab stalls during the evening. Also look into the *kebab tents* opposite the railway station.

If you're staying at the *Yongfu Hotel*, check out the hotel's restaurant. It has excellent noodle dishes at reasonable prices. Turn left out of the hotel towards the station and it's a few doors down. Just up the road from the hotel are a number of popular Muslim restaurants.

Out near the Shuijing Xiang Market are a number of fine places. If you like dumplings, try the *Dumpling Restaurant (jiǎozi guǎn)*.

TIBET & QINGHAI

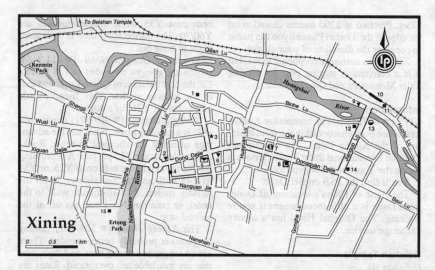

Xining

0   0.5   1 km

The most upmarket eatery in town for Chinese food is the *Peace Restaurant* (☎ 48069) (*hépíng cāntīng*) on Dong Dajie.

The *Qinghai Hotel* has an excellent Chinese restaurant on its 2nd floor if you don't mind travelling so far for a meal. The menu is only in Chinese, but there should be an English speaker on the staff. Considering the quality of the food, it's good value.

Getting There & Away
Air The CAAC office is on the 1st floor of the Qinghai Hotel. After more than seven years of planning, the proposed flights to Golmud have yet to materialise. At present the only options are Beijing (twice weekly), Chengdu (once weekly), Guangzhou (twice weekly) and Ürümqi (twice weekly).

Bus The main bus station, opposite the railway station, has daily departures in the morning for Heimahe (near Qinghai Lake), Golmud and the Ta'er Monastery. Between 8.30 am and noon there are three buses running to Tongren. From Tongren it is possible to take onward buses to Xiahe in Gansu Province. There are buses to Lanzhou at 7.30 am. An interesting option might be the bus service to Lenghu (*lěnghú*), in the north, close to the border with Xinjiang. Theoretically it is possible to continue on to Ürümqi or *somewhere* in Xinjiang from Lenghu. Locals weren't sure about this but agreed it *might* be possible.

Some travellers looking for an offbeat Tibetan experience have made the journey from Xining to Chengdu (Sichuan) by bus. The scenery is stunning and very Tibetan, but it's a rough trip requiring nearly a week. Accidents occur frequently. Don't bother to ask CITS for information about this journey – they told us 'if I were going there, I wouldn't start from here'.

The route to Chengdu is as follows: by bus from Xining to Madoi (*mǎdūo*) (two days); Madoi to Xiwu (*xiēwǔ*); by bus or truck to Sêrxu (*shíqú*) in Sichuan Province; then from Sêrxu to Kangding (*kāngdìng*) (two days); and Kangding to Chengdu (two days). All along the way there are cheap places to stay – the bus company will either put you up at its own hostels or direct you to another hotel.

Train Xining has frequent rail connections to Lanzhou (4½ hours). Other train connec-

XINING 西宁

PLACES TO STAY

1 Xining Hotel, CITS & Kunlun Travel
   西宁宾馆，中国国际旅行社，
   昆仑旅行社
11 Youzheng Gongyu Hotel &
   Qinghai Int'l Sport Travel Service
   邮政公寓宾馆，青海国际体育旅行社
12 Yongfu Hotel
   永富宾馆
14 Xining Mansions
   西宁大厦
15 Qinghai Hotel & CAAC
   青海宾馆，中国民航

PLACES TO EAT

2 Dumpling Restaurant
   饺子馆
6 Peace Restaurant
   和平酒家
9 Kebab Tents
   帐蓬餐厅

OTHER

3 PSB
   公安局
4 Shuijing Xiang Market
   水井巷商场
5 Post Office
   邮政大楼
7 Bank of China
   中国银行
8 Grand Mosque
   清真寺
10 Railway Station
   火车站
13 Long-Distance Bus Station
   长途汽车站

tions include Beijing, Shanghai, Qingdao, Xi'an and Golmud. There are two trains to Golmud (see the Golmud section in this chapter for the schedule).

AROUND XINING
Ta'er Monastery
(tǎ'ěr sì)

One of the six great monasteries of the Yellow Hat sect of Tibetan Buddhism, Ta'er

Monastery is found in the town of Huangzhong, a mere 26 km south-east of Xining. It was built in 1577 on sacred ground – the birthplace of Tsong Khapa, founder of the Yellow Hat sect.

The monastery is noted for its extraordinary sculptures of human figures, animals and landscapes carved out of yak butter. The art of butter sculpture probably dates back 1300 years in Tibet and was taken up by the Ta'er Monastery in the last years of the 16th century. At the time of writing, the monastery was undergoing a major renovation.

It's a pretty place and very popular with the local tourists. Go hiking in the surrounding area or follow the pilgrims clockwise on a scenic circuit round the monastery. Six temples are open; buy admission tickets from the window close to the row of stupas.

Photography is prohibited inside the temples, and they mean it! Outside the house with the butter statues, the monks have nailed to the wall all the film they have ripped out of cameras.

Places to Stay & Eat Ask about the possibility of staying inside the monastery itself. In the past this was possible, but we aren't sure what the policy will be once the present renovation is completed. At the time of writing, it was definitely *not* possible due to the construction work.

The *Ta'er Hotel (tǎ'ěr sì bīnguǎn)* is just opposite the Tibetan hospital (near the monastery) and charges Y100 for a double.

The food at the monastery is good. For some variety, take a stroll down the hill towards town and try some noodles in a Muslim restaurant. Stalls on the approach road to the monastery sell great yoghurt and peaches.

Getting There & Away Many travellers visit the monastery as a stopover on the way to Qinghai Lake. This can easily be arranged if you've booked a tour (see the Qinghai Lake section for details).

Buses to Huangzhong leave from the Xining long-distance bus station about every 10 minutes between 7 am and 6.30 pm. The trip takes 45 minutes on a public bus, but minibuses do the trip faster. Catch your return bus or minibus to Xining from the square in Huangzhong.

QINGHAI LAKE
(qīnghǎi hú)

Qinghai Lake (Koko Nor), known as the Western Sea in ancient times, is a somewhat surreal-looking saline lake lying 300 km west of Xining and 3200 metres above sea level. It's the largest lake in China and contains huge numbers of fish.

The main attraction is Bird Island, a breeding ground for thousands of wild geese, gulls, cormorants, sandpipers, extremely rare black-necked cranes and many other bird species. Perhaps most interesting are the bar-headed geese. These hardy birds migrate high over the Himalaya to spend winter on the Indian plains, and have been spotted flying at 10,000 metres.

You will see birds in quantity only during the breeding season – between March and early June.

It gets chilly at night so bring warm clothing. The lake water is too salty to drink, so be sure to carry a sufficient supply if you intend to do any hiking. There are nomads around the lake – most are friendly and may invite you in for a cup of tea in their tents.

Organised Tours

Probably the best deals going are the tours offered through the Yongfu Hotel in Xining. The minibus costs Y700 for the entire 620-km round trip, which can be completed in 12 hours. For an additional Y100, the driver will make the 60-km detour to Ta'er Monastery, which requires an additional hour of your time. There is also a brief stop at Sun Moon Mountain Pass *(rìyuè shānkǒu)* for some photo opportunities.

CITS charges Y1600 for a vehicle to Bird Island, but you can do much better than this on the free market.

Places to Stay & Eat

If you're not content with a day-trip, you can stay overnight at the *Bird Island Hotel (niǎo*

dǎo bīnguǎn) for Y80. The hotel's restaurant is surprisingly good. You must register at the hotel and pay Y10 admission before being shepherded to the island (16 km).

Getting There & Away

Bus Most travellers head for Bird Island *(niǎo dǎo)*, 310 km from Xining on the south shore of the lake. It's difficult to reach Bird Island on public transport. The small settlement of Heimahe *(hēimǎhé)*, 50 km from Bird Island, is the closest town that has a regular bus service to Xining.

Train The northern shore of the lake is readily accessible by train. Unfortunately, this is not the part of the lake that has many birds and you might be disappointed if this is all you get to see. Ha'ergai Railway Station is the jumping-off point and the lake is an hour's walk away. If you are going to Golmud, you'll get good views of the whole northern shoreline from the train's windows.

GOLMUD
(géérmù)

Golmud is a pioneering outpost in the oblivion end of China – the residents will be the first to tell you that from here to hell is a local call. The town owes its existence to mining and oil drilling. It's mostly a Chinese city, but there are a few Tibetans around. For travellers, Golmud is important as a staging post for onward travel to Tibet.

The eerie moonscape of the Tibetan Plateau can be an inhospitable place – come prepared! At 2800 metres elevation, summer days can be very warm but the nights are always cool. The daytime sun is incredibly bright – sunglasses and sunblock lotion are *de rigueur*. Winters are brutally cold.

The city itself is devoid of scenic spots. It's not unpleasant to walk around, but it doesn't take long to cover the whole town on foot.

You might be able to find a taxi to take you to the pasturelands *(cǎoyuán)* on the edge of town. Here the nomads live in yurts and the area has a nice backdrop of snow-capped

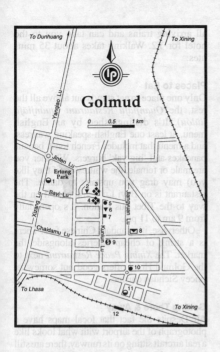

peaks to the south, but exploring them requires hard-to-obtain permits.

Information

CITS (☎ 412-764; fax 413-003) has an office in the Golmud Hotel. The best advice we can give is to avoid the place, but this is difficult to do if you plan to head overland to Tibet. Many travellers have gone directly to the Tibet bus station in the hopes of purchasing a bus ticket to Lhasa – the staff at the station politely tell them to go to CITS.

At the time of this writing, CITS has the monopoly on these coveted bus tickets. That could change in the future, so inquire in Golmud. If you do go to CITS, don't be tempted by their offer to book one of their private minibuses to Lhasa. Breakdowns are frequent – the minibuses are just not up to the kind of terrain that separates Golmud from Lhasa. There will be no compensation and you'll either have to wait a couple of days for help or hitch onwards – neither is

much fun and the latter is technically illegal. A traveller reports:

There were eight of us in Golmud, and the CITS minibus (just US$20 more than the public bus) sounded like such an easy option that we decided to go with it. There were problems, of course (the bus was being repaired), but Mr Hou suggested that if we went out for drinks with him he'd be able to let us know by the end of the evening.

One drink led to another and before we knew it we were in the Golmud Hotel karaoke bar. Mr Hou wheezed incoherently through a couple of numbers and then danced with each of the girls in our group one by one. Protests cut no ice with Mr Hou – you *do* want to get to Tibet, don't you?

The next day we didn't leave until noon. The driver had apparently spent two hours supplying the minibus with petrol and another two hours washing it down as a result of the mess incurred in the filling up process. Well, that was the story anyway. The first few hours of the trip were great (the girls agreed it was almost worth dancing with Mr Hou for). Seven hours and a snapped chassis later we were standing around in a blizzard.

It's not easy for eight foreigners with huge back-

TIBET & QINGHAI

packs to hitch a ride to Lhasa. Big bribes are required. A bit of hysterical screaming doesn't go astray either. If you do manage to get onto a bus, don't expect a seat. The interior of the bus we hooked up with looked like a rugby scrum. 'Mind you give a seat to the foreign guests', shouted the driver into the melee. We spent the next 30 hours standing up. The only stop was at noon the next day for a bowl of noodles.

The Golmud Hotel is where you can buy a simple map of the city, and is also the location of the PSB. The Bank of China is on the corner of Kunlun Lu and Chaidamu Lu. You'll find the post office on the corner of Chaidamu Lu and Jiangyuan Lu.

Qinghai Potash Plant
(*qīnghǎi jiáfēichǎng*)
The pride and joy of Golmud, the Qinghai Potash Plant is also the town's No 1 employer. The plant itself is 60 km from Golmud, though the mining company operates a number of businesses and employee apartment blocks in town.

The potash plant is not exactly a scenic area, but it's different. Only three such plants exist in the world – the other two are at Salt Lake City in the USA and Israel's Dead Sea. China's plant was built with US technical assistance. Potash is harvested from three reservoirs six metres deep and three sq km in area.

Tours of the plant are free. To arrange a visit, drop in at the potash company office – the tall, modern building with a steeple, near the railway station – in Golmud. Inside the building, the place you need to find is called the General Engineering Office (*zǒnggōng-bàn*). As you approach the plant, the scenery becomes incredibly desolate – not a blade of grass grows in this salty soil.

Places to Stay
There's only one place accepting foreigners, the *Golmud Hotel* (☎ 412-817) (*géěrmù bīn-guǎn*) at 160 Kunlun Lu. Dorms in the old building cost Y17 to Y30, and doubles with private bath are Y160 to Y180. The staff are notably surly and the hot water supply is erratic. The new wing is more expensive, with rooms priced at Y240. Minibuses meet all arriving trains and can take you to the hotel for Y2. Walking takes about 35 minutes.

Places to Eat
Only one place to eat stands out above all the rest, the *Quanjiafu Restaurant* (*quánjiāfú jiǔlóu*). It's distinguished by an English menu, at least one English-speaking waitress, and a menu that includes French toast, banana pancakes and 'big yak' burgers. Whether you are male or female, the waitresses (if they like you) may drag you upstairs to dance. The restaurant is on Bayi Lu – you pass it on the way to the Tibet bus station. It's open daily from 9 am to 11 pm.

Otherwise, it's standard Chinese fare. There is a string of cheap eateries alongside the market. The *Xining Peace Restaurant* next to the Golmud Hotel offers good but somewhat pricey Sichuan cuisine.

Getting There & Away
Air Despite the fact that local maps have a photograph of the airport with what looks like a real aircraft sitting on its runway, there are still no flights. No-one knows when or if the much-touted plans to establish a service connecting Golmud and Lhasa will ever come to anything. The CAAC office in the Golmud Hotel is a deserted dust-trap full of stacked-up chairs and mattresses. Check in Xining or Lhasa for the latest developments.

Bus The Golmud bus station is just opposite the railway station. The journey from Golmud to Dunhuang is 524 km (13 hours). The bus departs at 6.30 am. Foreigners are charged double, and it's highly advisable to buy your ticket a day in advance. The bus leaves from behind the station, not in front – nobody will bother to tell you this and you could easily miss it. Luggage must be stored on the roof. Be sure to keep a jacket with you – it gets cold in those mountain passes. It's a rough, corrugated road and the screeching music on board will batter your eardrums until your brain turns to cottage cheese.

There are also daily buses to Xining, but it

makes little sense to go this way, as the train is faster and smoother.

Buses for Lhasa leave from the Tibet bus station on Xizang Lu. There's a special foreigners' section inside with English-speaking staff – they will politely inform you that you must go to CITS to make the booking. Prices for the decrepit 'Chinese bus' (that's what they call it) are Y140 for Chinese, Y1077 for foreigners! The so-called 'Japanese bus' (which is in fact made in China) costs about Y50 more, but is easily worth it for the roomier seats. Of course, there is a reason for the high price (besides cheating you) – you are paying for a three-day tour in Lhasa, whether you want it or not.

Most of the buses are piloted by two drivers who take turns sleeping – they do the trip straight through with only a couple of meal stops. The journey takes from 28 to 35 hours and would have to rate as one of the world's worst bus rides. After five or six hours you'll probably start to lose interest in the scenery, and after 20 hours you'll be grappling with an unhealthy desire to throw yourself off the nearest precipice.

Golmud is a good place to stock up on a few necessities for the bus journey to Tibet. Toasty-warm PLA overcoats are available from the department stores for around Y110 – consider getting one even if you wind up giving it away in Lhasa. It can easily get down to minus 10°C or lower in those mountain passes at night; though the buses are heated, you could be in serious trouble if you are unequipped and there is a breakdown.

Train Express trains (Nos 303 & 304) on the Xining-Golmud route take 17 hours, while the locals (Nos 507 & 508) chug along for 23 hours. The schedule is as follows:

Train No	From	To	Departs	Arrives	
303	Xining	Golmud	5.35 pm	12.54 pm	(every 2 days)
507	Xining	Golmud	7.40 am	7.06 am	(daily)
304	Golmud	Xining	3.20 pm	11.14 am	(every 2 days)
508	Golmud	Xining	8.15 pm	7.24 pm	(daily)

An attempt to build a railway from Golmud to Lhasa was abandoned after it was discovered that it would be necessary to bore a tunnel through an ice-filled mountain. The Chinese consulted the Swiss (the world's best tunnel builders), who concluded that it was impossible.

Glossary

Place Names with Chinese Characters
(provinces in bold)

Altai	阿勒泰	Dehong	德宏
Anhui	安徽	Dingshu	丁蜀
Anshun	安顺	Dongning	东宁
Anyang	安阳	Dongsheng	东胜
		Dujiangyan	都江堰
Badaling	八达岭	Dunhuang	敦煌
Baisha	白沙		
Baiyanggou	白扬沟	Emeishan	峨眉山
Banpo	半坡		
Baoding	宝顶山	Foshan	佛山
Baoshan	保山	**Fujian**	福建
Baotou	包头	Fuyuan	抚远
Beidaihe	北戴河	Fuzhou	福州
Beihai	北海		
Beijing	北京	Gangu	甘谷
Beishan	北山	Ganlanba (Menghan)	橄榄坝
Benxi	本溪	**Gansu**	甘肃
Bozhou	亳州	Ganzi	甘孜
		Golmud	格尔木
Cangyanshan	苍岩山	Grand Canal	大运河
Changchun	长春	Great Wall	长城
Changsha	长沙	**Guangdong**	广东
Chaozhou	潮州	**Guangxi**	广西
Chengde	承德	Guangzhou	广州
Chengdu	成都	Guichi	贵池
Chong'an	重安	Guilin	桂林
Chongqing	重庆	Guiyang	贵阳
Conghua	从化	**Guizhou**	贵州
		Guyuan	固原
Daheyan	大河沿	Gyantse	江孜
Dali	大理		
Dalian	大连	Haikou	海口
Damenglong	大勐龙	Hailar	海拉尔
Dandong	丹东	**Hainan Island**	海南岛
Daqing	大庆	Hami	哈密
Datong	大同	Hangzhou	杭州
Dazu	大足	Hanoi	河内
Dege	德格	Harbin	哈尔滨
		Hebei	河北
		Hefei	合肥
		Heihe	黑河

Heilongjiang	黑龙江	Lanzhou	兰州
Helanshan	贺兰山	Leshan	乐山
Henan	河南	Lhasa	拉萨
Hengyang	衡阳	Lianyungang	连云港
Heqing	鹤庆	**Liaoning**	辽宁
Hong Kong	香港	Lijiang	丽江
Hohhot	呼和浩特	Linxia	临夏
Hotan	和田	Liping	黎平
Huaihua	怀化	Litang	理塘
Huangguoshu	黄果树	Liuyuan	柳园
Huangling	皇陵	Liuzhou	柳州
Huanglong	黄龙	Longsheng	龙胜
Huangpu River	黄浦	Luding	泸定
Huangshan	黄山	Lunan	路南
Huashan	华山	Luomen	洛门
Hubei	湖北	Luoyang	洛阳
Humen	虎门	Lushan	庐山
Hunan	湖南		
Hunchun	珲春	Macau	澳门
		Maijishan	麦积山
Jagdaqi	加格达奇	Mangshi	芒市
Ji'nan	济南	Manzhouli	满洲里
Jiamusi	佳木斯	Mayu Island	妈屿
Jianchuan	剑川	Meishan	眉山
Jiangsu	江苏	Meizhou	湄州
Jiangxi	江西	Menghai	勐海
Jiayuguan	嘉峪关	Menghun	勐混
Jilin	吉林	Mohe	漠河
Jingbo Lake	镜泊湖	**Mongolia** (Inner)	内蒙古
Jingdezhen	景德镇	Moxixiang	磨西乡
Jinggangshan	井岗山	Mudanjiang	牡丹江
Jinghong	景洪	Mutianyu	慕田峪
Jinjiang	金江		
Jingzhen	景真	Nanchang	南昌
Jinshan	金山	Nanjing	南京
Jiuhuashan	九华山	Nanluoshan	南罗山
Jiujiang	九江	Nanning	南宁
Jiuzhaigou	九寨沟	Ningbo	宁波
		Ningxia	宁夏
Kaifeng	开封		
Kaili	凯里	Panshan	盘山
Kangding (Dardo)	康定	Pearl River	珠江
Kashgar	喀什	Penglai	蓬莱
Kunming	昆明	Pingxiang	凭祥
Kuqa	库车	Putuoshan	普陀山

Qianshan	千山		Tengchong	腾冲
Qingdao	青岛		Tianchi	天池
Qinghai	青海		**Tianjin**	天津
Qingtongxia	青铜峡		Tianshui	天水
Qinhuangdao	秦皇岛		Tiantaishan	天台山
Qiongzhong	琼中		Tianzhu	天祝
Qiqihar	齐齐哈尔		**Tibet**	西藏
Quanzhou	泉州		Tingri	定日
Qufu	曲阜		Tongjiang	同江
			Tongxin	同心
Ruili	瑞丽		Tongzha	通什
			Tumen	图门
Sakya	萨迦		Tunxi	屯溪
Sanjiang	三江		Turpan	吐鲁番
Sanya	三亚			
Shaanxi	陕西		Ürümqi	乌鲁木齐
Shandong	山东			
Shanghai	上海		Wanding	畹町
Shanhaiguan	山海关		Weihai	威海
Shantou	汕头		Wenchang	文昌
Shanxi	山西		Wenzhou	温州
Shaoshan	韶山		Wolong Reserve	卧龙自然保护区
Shaoxing	绍兴		Wudalianchi	五大连池
Shekou	蛇口		Wudangshan	武当山
Shennongjia	神农架		Wuhan	武汉
Shenyang	沈阳		Wuhu	芜湖
Shenzhen	深圳		Wulingyuan	武陵源
Shibing	施秉		Wutaishan	五台山
Shidu	十渡		Wuwei	武威
Shigu	石鼓		Wuxi	无锡
Shigatse	日喀则		Wuyishan	武夷山
Shihezi	石河子		Wuzhou	梧州
Shijiazhuang	石家庄			
Shiwan	石湾		Xanadu	上都
Sichuan	四川		Xi'an	西安
Simao	思茅		Xiahe	夏河
Simatai	司马台		Xiamen	厦门
Suifenhe	绥芬河		Xiangtan	湘潭
Suzhou	苏州		Xianyang	咸阳
			Xibaipo	西柏坡
Tai'an	泰安		Xikou	西口
Taishan	泰山		Xilinhot	锡林浩特
Taiyuan	太原		Xincun	新村
Tanggu	塘沽		Xinglong	兴隆
Tangkou	汤口		Xingyi	兴义
Tangshan	塘山		Xining	西宁

Index

Abbreviations

Maps

Text

Map references are in **bold** type

ABA Autonomous Prefecture
    (Sic) 849
accommodation 133-5
acrobatics (S'hai) 365, 366
acupuncture 107
air travel **168**
    to/from China 149-54
    within China 166-7
Altai (Xin) 888
Ancestor Temple (G'dong) 636-7
Anhui 332-42, **333**
Anshun (Gui) 708-10, **709**
Antu (Jil) 435
Anyang (Hen) 500-1
architecture 49-50
area codes 95
arts 47-57
Aydingkol Salt Lake (Xin) 875

Azure Clouds Temple (Bei) 229

Badachu (Bei) 230
Badong (Sic) 837
Bai (people) (Hun) 545, (Yunn)
    717, 744
Baidicheng (Sic) 837
Baihe (Jil) 435
Baihuashan Waterfall (HI) 669
Baisha (Yunn) 759
Baishui Tai (Yunn) 763
Baiyanggou (Xin) 867-8
bamboo 41
Bamboo Temple (Yunn) 734-5
Banpo Neolithic Village (Shaa)
    478-80
Baoding (Sic) 839
Baoshan (Yunn) 777-80, **778**
Baotou (In Mon) 938-41
bargaining 86-7

Batang (Sic) 848
Batik (Gui) 711
Beidahu Ski Resort (Jil) 433
Beidaihe (Heb) 261-6, **261,
    262-3**
Beier Lake (In Mon) 945
Beihai (G'xi) 678-9
Beihai Park (Bei) 203
Beijing 184-232, **185, 188-9,
    196-7**
    entertainment 215-7
    getting around 222-5
    getting there & away 219-22
    information 186-90
    places to eat 212-5
    places to stay 209-12
    shopping 217-8
    subway **223**
    things to see 195-209
Beijing Massacre 33-4, 42

Continued from page 4

From the Authors

Chris Taylor Travelling the east coast of China was for the most part a lonely, thankless task, but I managed to accumulate a few debts all the same. In Taiwan, thanks as always to my wife, Wen-ying, who ungrudgingly checked maps and Chinese script and occasionally delved into Chinese sources for me. In Hong Kong, Christine Jones took care of my travel arrangements, and along with Rob Walker put me up on their Lama fold-up bed. Ron Gluckman, as ever, was generous with his contacts. Thanks too to Patrick Hogan for the last-minute use of his Happy Valley flat.

In China a big thanks to Brian Grossman in Shanghai, who put me up in his flat and gave me an extended break from Chinese hotels – much appreciated, Brian, and thanks for the late-night tours of Shanghai. In Guangzhou Chris Oakey found me nursing a beer alone, took me under his wing, gave me a place to stay, introduced me to JJs and provided countless G&Ts. In Beijing, thanks to Mure Dickie, rising Reuters star, who provided an entertaining evening *en famille*. Rob Timmermans of the Holiday Inn Crowne Plaza was generous with his time and gave me a flying introduction to Beijing after-hours.

As usual, chance encounters along the way, provided useful information and lifted my spirits. Eugene Leong turned a potentially dull visit to Fuzhou into an eventful couple of days. John Fisher joined me in a trip around Shandong province and up Taishan. Cliff, grimly incarcerated in Tai'an, joined me on a pub crawl of Nanjing and later proved to be a welcoming host when I finally made it to Tai'an.

Finally, thanks to Linda Suttie for keeping the editorial queries to minimum, to Nicko for last minute Shanghai tips and to Robert for picking up the pieces of my failed Shijiazhuang trip.

Robert Storey Robert would like to give special thanks to Chiu Miaoling (Taiwan), Maria Pia Baroncelli (Italy), Akemi Shirasaki (Japan), Ron Gluckman (USA), Louise Armstrong (UK), Liam Winston (UK), Carl Pryce (UK), Rosie Hickey (NZ) and Roy Grundy (UK).

Nicko Goncharoff Believe it or not, China is not all that easy a place to work in. Fortunately, I met up with some excellent people who helped smooth the way a bit. In Yangshuo, Huang Gao Feng was a wonderful host and guide. Piers Leveroni was kind enough to share his expertise on Guizhou province and Liuzhou, and made a fine drinking partner besides. Dave Watts deserves a hand for his exhaustive reporting on various lovely bus rides through southeastern Guizhou.

Thanks also to Robert Van der Hoop and Emmie Leenen for ducking into hotels in Huaihua (I made it there eventually). Special appreciation to Keith Su and other rockers at the Ocean-Side Music Bar in Changsha: keep up the good work gentlemen! Kym Hogan did a great job of keeping my mind off the crumbling cliffs on the way to Songpan, and sent back an excellent account of Zoigê and beyond. Ben Wiehe and Jeff Hille came through with the ziplocs and the white rabbits, for which they won't be forgotten.

Many thanks to Fiona McCallum and Chris Bailey for letting me peek at their amazing notes on the journey from Zhongdian to Litang, and to Dave Woodberry for info on Batang and other less earthly topics. Alan Richardson of Balmain, Oz, filled me in on the situation in Hekou before disappearing by truck back into the wilds of South-East Asia. The intrepid Dutch trio of Boris Dongelmans, Tom Hooymans and Adriaan Bakker braved the dreaded switch at Jinjiang and lived to write about it later. Special thanks to Rob Dean, who made my stay in Dali that much more fun, and to Mike Kline, who did the same in Ruili.

Chris Meech did a fine job of introducing me to Mugua Jiu, and had some helpful tips on Jizu Shan as well. Rick and Talya Raburn were among the finest travellers one could hope to meet. Lijiang wouldn't have been the same without He Yong (long live rock!) and Yu Yu, who also took the trouble to share their experiences at Lugu Lake, as did several other fine folks who wish to remain anonymous. Marc Buchmueller and Lisa Musiol helped take the edge off my frantic scrambling in Kunming. Marion and Pierre brought a smile to my face every time we crossed paths.

To all of you, and to those others who have escaped mention, thanks a million. May the road lie before you and wind be at your back.

Thanks

Thanks to the many travellers who wrote in with helpful hints, useful advice and interesting and funny stories about China:

Jorgen Aabenhus (Dk), Marcus Adams (UK), Florence Akst (UK), David Allison (Aus), Terry Anderson (USA), Alessandro Arduino (I), Lambert Arno (B), Constantin Arnocouros (G), K Askham (UK), Alexander Atepolikhin, Robyn Atkins (NZ), Mojca Aupic (Cz)

Jens Baier (D), Jonathan Baker (USA), Scott A Baker (USA), Paul Bakker (Aus), Wim Bals (Nl), Phil Barlow (UK), Buck Barnes (USA), Paul Barrett (UK), Marie-Louise Barte (Nl), Richard Bartlett, Andrew Bartram (UK), Richard Beal (USA), Andrew Beale (Aus), Stephen Beale, Max Beer (C), Jo Inge Bekkevold, Bert Bemer (Nl), Diana Benedetto (F), Andrew Bennett (Aus), Brenda Berck (C), David Bercovich (Isr), Patrice Berman (USA), Mary Berry (USA), Alain & Channe Bertrand (F), Chris Biggs (USA), Liz & Mike Bissett (UK), N Blasco (B), Anne Bloom (USA), Rainer Boit (D), Brandon Booth (USA), Wietske Bouma (Nl), Jason Boyd (USA), Ute Braml (D), Gail & Robert Breines (USA), M Breuer (D), C Brittenden (Aus), Joe Brock (USA), Eli Brollo (I), Louise Brooks (Aus), Abe Brouwer (Nl), Emma Brown (UK), James Brown (UK), Ray Brunsberg (USA), Peter Buechel (CH), Marshall Burgess (C), Lorie Burnett (USA)

Christine Campbell (Aus), David Campbell (USA), Richard Cann (UK), K C Carlson, Patricia Carmel (Isr), Juliet Chamberlain (UK), Wing Cheong Chan (Sin), Craig Chapin (USA), Ken Chen, Joe Chew (Sin), Lawrence Chi, Steve Chiu, Ori Choshen (Isr), Melinda Choy (USA), Sebastian Christians, J K & M G Clark (NZ), Kay Clarke (Chi), Lou & Janet Clarke (Aus), Rod Clarke & Family, Stuart Cohen (USA), Alan Cole (Aus), Jane Colstrom (USA), Allison Comp (Nl), Joan Cooper (UK), Sarah Corby (UK), Emma Cowie (UK), Steven Coxhead, Brian Coxon (SA), Cristina Cramerotti (F), Anna Cumming (UK), David Cummings (USA), John Currie (Aus), Graham Currie (Aus)

Romana & Jan Danser (Nl), Vincent Dautry (UK), M Scott Davis (USA), Minzu Daxue, Bennett Dean (UK), Christine Dee (USA), Alexander Des Forges (USA), Anne Dethlefsen (HK), M Dewbaelle (Nl), Jan Dixon (UK), Helen Dixon (UK), C Docherty (UK), K Donnelly (USA), John Donovan, James Doschur (USA), Thom S Downing, Denise Drurry (UK), G Dudink (Nl), M Duffy (UK), L G Duijzer (Nl), Jackie Dumpis, Barbra Duncan (UK), Angela Durose (UK), Sandra Dykstra (Nl)

Christof Ebert (D), Victor Edlenbosch (Nl), Robert Eidschun (USA), Ebihara Eiko (Jap), Simon Eisinger (USA), Keith Eldridge (USA), Tim Elliott (UK), John Eriksen (Dk), David Erskine (Aus), S Eskildsen (Dk), Jonathon F B Evans (Aus), Dr David Evans (UK), S Evans (UK), J Everall (UK)

P Faase (Nl), Michael Fackler (D), Zoya Fansler (USA), Beth Farber, Tim Farlam (UK), Anne Farrar (USA), Rebecca Faulkner (UK), Ann Fehle (UK), Kasi Fellman (CH), Sebastian Ferenczi (F), Laramie Ferreira (SA), Dan Finch (USA), Mary Finch (USA), Mette Finle (Dk), I Fleten (N), Gillian Foo (Sin), Josep Albeniz Fornells, Carol Forsett (USA), Benny Forsman (S), Janne-Kristin Fossum (N), Sharifa Foum, Paul Francis (UK), David Fregona (I), Tanya Frymersum (USA), Joseph Fullop

Kim Gage (USA), Judy Galiher (USA), Bernd Gammerl (D), Rob Gardner (NZ), Derek Garrison, Adam Gault (USA), J Geddes (UK), Alison Gee (UK), Beny Gefen (Isr), Shawn Geise, Andrea Gentili (I), Fotini Georgakopoulou (G), Lucy Gibbs (UK), A Gibert (Sp), Tim Gibson (UK), Elfi Gilissen (D), F. Gingras (C), James Godwin (USA), R Goldberg (USA), Paul Goodwin (C), John Grace (Aus), Rene Granacher (D), Camilla Granlaund (Dk), Erwin Grimm (D), Edward Grulich (USA), Henrik Gudme (D), Zhu Guihua (Chi), M Gunton (UK)

Kim Dong Ha (Chi), Oliver Hagemann (D), Paul Hague (UK), Mr J B Hak (Nl), Liz Halsey (USA), V Halsmingar (S), Ute Hanisch (D), Jakob Lage Hansen (Dk), Geoff Harman (UK), Richard Harrold (UK), Kieren Haskell (Aus), Francoise Hauser (D), Lukas Havlicek, M Helmbrecht (USA), Tom Hendrix (USA), Klaus Henke (D), Jill Henry (USA), Melissa Henwood (Aus), Gera Heuvelsland (Nl), Steve Hicks (Aus), Paul Hider (Chi), Michael Hill (C), J Hinterleitner (A), Meiling Ho (Aus), Don Hoard (USA), Pettina Hodgson (Aus), Blaine Hollinger (USA), Paul Hollis (Aus), Vanessa Hoppe (USA), S Horn (D), Patrick Hosford (C), Mark Hunnebell (UK), Paul Hunter (UK), Eija Huovila (S), V Ingemann (D)

Miki Jablkowska (UK), Michael Jacobson (USA), I Jacquemin (B), Ludo Jambrich, Bridgett James (UK), Jock Janice (UK), Joy Jarman (USA), Robert Jaszewski (CH), Lisa Jensen (C), Anna E Jessen (Dk),

Yang Jing (Chi), Tine Elgaard Joensen (D), Carol Johnson (USA), M Jollands (Aus), Dean Jones (Aus), Mrs D J Jones (UK), Mandy Jones (UK), Nena Joy (C), Laura Joyce (UK), Elaine & Robert Juhre (USA), Liu Jun (Chi)

Jenn Kahn (USA), A Katlo (N), Zane Katsikis (F), Simon Kay (UK), Sam Kebby (Aus), Kate Kelly (Aus), Stuart Kelly (Chi), Susan Kennedy (UK), Katherine Keynes (Aus), Geoff Kingsmill (Aus), Mathias Kirschner (D), Bart Kleijer (Nl), O S Knowles (UK), Sofie Koch (Dk), Frederick Koppl (D), Arik Korman (USA), Peter Kornberg (USA), Wim Kranendonk, Ties Kroezen (Nl), Wolfgang Krones (D), Frank Kruger (D), Rami Kunitcher (Isr), Mr & Mrs H Kuwada (USA), Jasper Kyndi (Dk)

Barbara Laine (UK), Sisko Laine (Fin), Paule & Gwenael Lamargue (F), Suzanne Lamb (Aus), Jeffrey Langer, Eric Langhammer (Ire), Thomas Klarskov Larson (Dk), Nina Laskowski (Aus), Arthur Lathrop (USA), Jean Laurent (Aus), Mark Lawton (UK), Jean Pierre Le Lagadec (F), Marcus Lee (Sin), Susanne Wah Lee (USA), Janya Leelamanothum, Cressida Lennox (USA), F & B Leplingard (USA), Andrew Levy (USA), Sarah Lewis, Gwen Liang (USA), Lisa Libassi (USA), Kenneth Lim (USA), Jukka Lindell (Fin), Goran Lindgren (S), Wallace Lo (UK), Jeannette Loakman (C), HH Long (Sin), Deanne Lowe (USA), John Lumley-Holmes (HK)

Calum Macleod (Aus), Elizabeth MacRae (C), Alexander McBean (Aus), Lisa & Pat McCarthy (UK), Ian McKay (Jap), John McKenna (Aus), John McKenna (NZ), John McKimmy (USA), Susan McLaney (UK), S McNutt (Ire), Ian McVittie (UK), Yung Yu Ma (HK), Charlene Makley (Chi), Maureen Maloney (Aus), Carol Mansfield (USA), E Marchetti (B), L Marconi (B), Allison Margolies (USA), Ruth Marper, Bob & Chris Marshall (UK), Nina Martins (UK), William & Susan Martorano (USA), Chris Marulf (CH), Ken Mathers (Aus), Yoshihiko Matsuyama (Jap), Cecilia Mau (UK), Shiela Mavinang, Konrad Maziarz, Simon Medelko (Aus), Jorgen Mejer (D), Mark Micallef (Aus), Riikka Miettinen (Fin), Csaba Mikusi (H), Burkhard Militzer (D), Joanne Miller (USA), Teddy Milne (USA), Amin Mirabdolbaghi (CH), Claudia Monson (Aus), Marti Morthorst (D), David Mountain (USA), Martha Muck (A), B J Murphy-Bridge (USA), Bryan Myer (UK)

Paul & Mabel Nash (C), Jim Needell (UK), Monica Neubauer (USA), Caroline Newhouse (UK), Kerryn Newton (Aus), Geoff Nichols (USA), J P Niestern (NI), Eric Noble (C), Bert Nuss (Aus), William O'Donnell, Brent Ohlund (C), Henri Olink (Nl), James Oliver (UK), Rudi Ongena (B), HF Oostergo (Aus), Andrew Oppenheim (UK), Mary Oppenheimer (USA), C A Osborne (UK), Marsha Oshima (USA), Pam Oxley (UK)

R G Palim (B), Paco Panconcelli (D), Claude Payen (F), Janet Penny (C), Marsha B Pereira, Karen Petersen (Aus), Debbie Petleung, Con Piercy (C),

Shai Pinto (Isr), Klemen Pogacnik (Slov), Dan Pool (USA), Mike Poulard (UK), Sally Price (UK), Ethan Pride (USA), M B Priemus-Noach (NI), Marc Proksch, Beatrice Quevedo (F)

Talya & Rick Rabern, Robel Rainer (D), Andrea Rantenberg (D), Christian Reinholdt (D), Adrienne Reynolds (USA), Douglas Reynolds (USA), Pauline Richards (UK), Sabine Ritter (D), Alexandra Robak (UK), Arthur Robb (USA), Rainer Robel (D), Mr G Roberts (UK), Mrs N Roderick (UK), Karen Rosenberg (USA), Mike Roussakis (C), Teresa Rubnikowicz (UK), Julia Rudden (USA), Jose Ruiz (USA), Herman Rutten (Nl), Patrick Ryden (USA)

Katie Saemann (USA), Bridget Sandover (UK), Clara & Marco Sandrin (I), Hans Sauseng (D), Andi Scheef (Nl), Stefan Scheel (D), Bernd & Elke Scheffler (D), Tim Scheur (USA), Lambertus Schreuder (Nl), Jon Schuetz (USA), Graziano Scotto (I), Joann Scurlock (USA), Tamzin Seaton-Hogg (UK), John Sehn (USA), Jose Serra Vega, Jill Sherdan (UK), C Emma Short (Aus), Richard Shuntoff (USA), Susan Simerly (UK), Deborah Sinay (USA), Brett Sinclair (Aus), Lisbeth Sjemann (Dk), Mrs P Skinn (UK), Tarjei Skirbekk (N), Chris Smart (UK), Ide Smit (Nl), Andrea Smith (UK), Ashley Smith (UK), M Smith (Aus), Sanya Reid Smith (Aus), Jane Smith (Aus), Andrew & Marnie Smith (C), Kim Sonnack (USA), Kasper Sonne (Dk), C Spiller (Aus), Mr & Mrs A Spilman (UK), D Stamboulis, Dr Richard Stanzel (D), Ran Stavsky (Isr), Diana Stent (UK), Tia Stephens (C), David Stokes (USA), Alexander & Agnes Studel (CH), H Sumita, Mr & Mrs Sureshbabu (Kor), Michael Sutherland (USA), Peter Swainger, K J Swinburn (D)

P Hua Tan (HK), Paul Tanner (UK), David Taylor (UK), Joanne Taylor, Miriam Taylor (Aus), Ian & Jo Taylor (HK), Mary Temignani (USA), Frank Theissen (D), Paul Thissen (USA), Dr Axel Thomas (D), M. Thomas (B), Felix Thommen (CH), Bernard Thompson (USA), I Timmerman (Nl), Brian Wong Ting (HK), Ryland Tippett, Jim Tomlinson (UK), Renmans Toon (B), Martin Trueman (C), Denise Tsang (Aus), Leonard Turnball, Ethel & Bob Turner (UK), Julie Tuulianinen (Fin), Joe Twinn (UK), Oren Tzadok (Isr)

Heinrich M Umbach (D), Eric Upton (Aus), J Ustes (Sp), Christopher Vadot (B), M van Vlerken (NI), R van der Molen (UK), Frans van Eijk (Nl), Niels van Erck (Nl), R Veldhuijsen (NI), Giovanni Venosta (I), W Verschueren (B), Christine Veulemans (F), Amanda Vincent (UK), Ton Vink (Nl), Ron & Cindy Voskuijl (Nl)

Amir Wachs (Isr), Stefanie Wachter (USA), Caroline Wagenaar (Nl), E O Wagner (USA), Sylvia Wagner (UK), Adam Wake (UK), Ann Walgraeve (B), Jennifer Wallace (UK), Deborah Wallach (USA), Ute Wallenboeck (A), Thomas Du Jin Wan (Chi), Simon Ward (UK), L J Warren (USA), Amy Weedman (USA), Michael Wehner (D), Robert Weins (D),

Sascha Wentzlaff (D), Les Whelan (Aus), Pam Whitfield, Madine Wilburn (USA), Sue Wilkinson (UK), Paul Willen (USA), N Williams (C), Greg Willson (Aus), Jean-Phillipe Wispelaere (Aus), Sophy Wong (USA), Brad Wong, Wing Sing Woo (HK), Steve Wood (Aus), Mike Woodhead (NZ), Michael Woodhead (UK), George & Caroline Woodruff, Tim Woodward (HK), Simon Woolrych (UK), Judy Wormwell (Aus), Hannie Wouters (Nl), Stephen Wrage (USA), Stephanie Wu (Chi), Thomas Wulff (Dk), Cynthia Wuu (USA)

Tsao Yang (Chi), Dan Yao (USA), Madeline Yap (Aus), Emilt Yeh (USA), Belinda Yeo (NZ), Heather Young (USA), Julie Young (UK), Rodger Young (USA), Zhang Guang Yui (Chi), D Jvan Zeist (Nl), Martina Zettergren (S), He Zhanting (Chi), Monica Ziezulewicz (USA), Stav Zotalis (Aus), Martine & Lycke (Dk), Yabbe & Charlotte (Dk)

A = Austria, Aus = Australia, B = Belgium, C = Canada, CH = Switzerland, Chi = China, Cz = Czech Republic, D = Germany, Dk = Denmark, F = France, Fin = Finland, G = Greece, H = Hungary, HK = Hong Kong, Ire = Ireland, Isr = Israel, I = Italy, Jap = Japan, Kor = Korea, N = Norway, Nl = The Netherlands, NZ = New Zealand, Sin = Singapore, SA = South Africa, Slov = Slovak Republic, Sp = Spain, S = Sweden, UK = United Kingdom, USA = United States of America

Update – December 1996

After more than a decade of double-digit growth in its gross domestic product, China's economy grew at a rate of 9.8% in 1995 and an estimated 8% in 1996. According to official government statistics the inflation rate so far in 1996 is 8% but the real rate is probably significantly higher.

The boy named by the Dalai Lama as the reincarnation of the Panchen Lama (and thus the second-highest monk in Tibetan Buddhism) has been missing for eighteen months, along with his family. The Chinese had denounced the appointment and appointed their own.

VISAS

Chinese visas in Vienna, Austria, are not available from the embassy but the consulate (☎ 712 55 270) at Reisnerstr. 55-57, 1030 Vienna.

MONEY

The official exchange rate is now US$1 to Y8.30.

DANGERS & ANNOYANCES

Lonely Planet has had several reports that the Chinese border guards at the Alashakou train border post (at the China/Kazakstan border) are demanding fines for expired visas which are still in fact valid. The asking price is US$1000 but some travellers have bargained the fine to several hundred dollars. Travellers who refuse to pay are threatened with imprisonment. On the Kazakstan side of the border at Dostyq, the Kazak customs officials are apparently also notoriously corrupt.

GETTING THERE & AWAY
Land

To/From Hong Kong A high speed rail link between Beijing and Hong Kong will open later this year. In Beijing it departs from the huge new Beijing West railway station. Lo Wu border crossing now has a moneychanging facility.

Dear traveller

Prices go up, good places go bad, bad places go bankrupt...and every guidebook is inevitably outdated in places. Fortunately, many travellers write to us about their experiences, telling us when things have changed. If we reprint a book between editions, we try to include the best of this information in an Update section. We also make travellers' tips immediately available on our award-winning World Wide Web Internet site (http://www.lonelyplanet.com) and in a free quarterly newsletter, *Planet Talk*.

Although much of this information has not been verified by our own first-hand research, we believe it can be very useful. We cannot vouch for its accuracy, however, so bear in mind that it could be wrong.

We really enjoy hearing from people out on the road, and apart from guaranteeing that others will benefit from your good and bad experiences, we're prepared to bribe you with an offer of a free book for sending us substantial useful information.

I hope you do find this book useful – and that you let us know when it isn't. Thank you to everyone who has written.

Tony Wheeler

To/From Pakistan The situation on the overland trip from Pakistan to China has changed. The bus can now be taken only from Sust to Tashkurgan. Both the tourist and local buses cost US$23. The Tourist Bureau bus is more convenient as the only passengers are tourists, which makes customs processing in Sust and Tashkurgan much faster. The bus can also pick up passengers at their hotel.

To/From Kazakstan Visas for Kazakstan are no longer available at the China-Kazakstan border. You must get your visa from the embassy in Beijing. The weekly train runs between Ürümqi and Alma Ata (going as far as Tashkent), takes three days and costs US$65, or US$52 with an ISIC card. The train stops for eight hours at the China-Kazakstan border. At the Chinese side there is an HIV control centre, but apparently only the Russians get asked for their HIV-free certificates. Some Russians proved negativity with US$5! The result of the HIV test was surprisingly known in about one minute!

Alternatively, there is a direct fortnightly bus between Ürümqi and Alma Ata that costs US$52, no discounts. There is also a network of local buses and taxis that cross the border and do the same journey in stages, but we have no detailed information on these. There is reportedly a US$10 border tax.

To/From Kyrgyzstan The overland route between Kashgar (China) and Bishkek (Kyrgyzstan) is open to independent travellers and theoretically possible (though still problematic) for hitch-hikers. There is one Chinese bus with a Russian driver between the towns, but there is no fixed timetable. It just turns around and goes back when it has enough passengers, perhaps three or four times a month in summer, less at other times. The 1½-day trip includes one overnight stop and is perfectly legal, though passengers must see to their own visas. Tickets cost US$60 to US$70 in Bishkek or Y800 in Kashgar. The Bishkek office (☎ 22-3670) is at Razzakov (formerly Pervomayskaya) 7, near the railway station, and is open from 9 am to 5 pm. In Kashgar it's at the Wuzi Binguan (Wuzi Hotel), half a block south of the post office. Tickets are sold in the lobby but no English is spoken.

Visas for Kyrgyzstan and the other Central Asian republics must be obtained in advance; the closest point in China is Beijing. Visas for China can be obtained in Bishkek, but only with an invitation – usually with a telex sent to the Chinese embassy from some officially licensed Chinese agency confirming that they are meeting you on the China side. Otherwise, you should get one at home, preferably including written permission to cross at the Torugart Pass.

To/From Vietnam China has restored its rail link with Vietnam. Two trains a week run between Beijing and Hanoi. The new train

No 5 is an express luxury service between the two cities.

Tickets for this journey in Beijing are available from BRITS United Ticket Centre, in the Beijing West station's east supplementary building. The office is in the lobby of the railway branch of the Construction Bank. A soft sleeper ticket is Y1502, which includes a booking fee of Y50. The trains now go all the way to Dong Dang in Vietnam, where a change of train to Hanoi is required. Customs is cleared on the Chinese side of the border at Ping Xiang and on the Vietnamese side at Dong Dang.

To/From Laos Several travellers have reported that to get to the China/Laos border crossing at Mohan/Boten, it is possible to take a direct bus from Kunming to Mengla (about 28 hours), so there is really no need to go to Jinghong. From Mengla the buses still run to Mohan, taking one hour and 40 minutes. In Kunming you have to ask around for the Mengla bus and be persistent, as most ticket sellers are very eager to put you onto the more frequent Jinghong buses, which they are always anxious to fill up.

Once you clear Chinese border control, it is a five minute tuk-tuk ride through no-man's-land road to the Lao border post (Y3). The Lao side is called Boten. It is best to get to Boten early in the day, as pick-up trucks to Namtha and Muang Xai (Udomxai) are intermittent. To Namtha it takes about three hours, and the fare is now 2000 kip.

Marcus Lee – UK

BEIJING
There have also been reports in the Chinese media of 18 former communist party members involved in corruption. Apparently, something around the US$2.2 billion mark is missing from municipal funds, which was the reason for the resignation of the Beijing Communist Party leader Chen Xitong and the suicide of his deputy Wang Baosen.

The Bank of China (☎ 5199114, fax 51993 68, cable CITYCHUNG, telex 210245 BO-CCB CN) in Beijing has moved to a new location at 8 Yabaolu, Chaoyang District.

Interesting Chinese books can be found at the Sanwei Bookshop, just across Fuxingmennei Dajie from the Minzu Hotel and Nationalities Cultural Palace (it actually opens onto the side street). It is a trendy bookstore for intellectuals with a tea shop upstairs. They have a good selection of contemporary Chinese literature.

At the entrance to the Forbidden City unscrupulous characters approach visitors pretending to be official guides and insisting that the place can be visited only with a guide. This is not true.

From 15 May 1996 smoking was banned in public places and in the streets. The on-the-spot fine for foreigners and locals is apparently Y10.

Beijing has joined the web café mania that is the latest craze in many other cities around the globe. *Time* magazine reports that in November 1996, Unicom-Sparkice Co, opened the first multimedia cybercafé, which has large TV monitors and the MTV channel. There are 15 computer terminals and it costs about US$3 to use one for an hour. The cybercafé can be checked out at
www.sparkice.co.cn/cafe/cafe.htm.

Airport Transport

There are many unmetered taxis at Beijing airport, and they will charge you as much as they think you are willing to pay. However, the increasing competition among taxis has ensured that this is one area which has not suffered price increases. Beijing taxis still cost from Y1 to Y2 per km after the flagfall, and Beijing airport is only 25 km out, so by the meter the fare into town should not be more than Y100. Don't listen to any demands over Y150, but if the taxi is unmetered it is best to agree on a flat fare in advance.

Taxi drivers will deny the existence of the airport bus. However, its ticket counter is to the right after you pass through customs. It is not easy to buy the Y12 ticket, as the ticket seller ignores customers. If you wish to buy the ticket you need to be forceful. Hold on to your ticket, as it is collected at the end of your journey. The same scenario with taxi drivers

will be played out at the Aviation Building in Beijing, where taxi drivers will take tourists to their hotels at double or triple the normal fare. This can be avoided by getting off the bus when it stops at one of the metro stations along the way from the airport and taking the metro the rest of the way to your hotel.

One trick used by a taxi driver in Beijing to get away with more money from a traveller was to start shouting, 'Police! Police!', immediately after giving the traveller his change. The taxi driver seemed very disturbed and urged the traveller to leave the taxi. The traveller kept his cool and when he counted his change, he found that instead of yuan, he was given jiao notes.

SHANGHAI

The *Far Eastern Economic Review* magazine has reported a 63% increase in the number of counterfeit renminbi notes in circulation and a 22% increase in confiscated money during the first half of 1996. Another report that is of concern was a three-fold increase in the number of cases of corruption and bribe-taking among many Shanghai bank depart- ment chiefs.

GUANGDONG
Guangzhou

From June 1996, all Guangzhou telephone numbers changed from seven to eight digits. Add the number 8 before telephone numbers beginning with 2, 3, 4, 5, 6 or 7. Telephone numbers beginning with an 8 get 1 after the 8 (in other words make the second digit 1).

There are now many nonstop, long-distance, air-con buses between Shenzhen and Guangzhou along the new motorway.

GUANGXI
Guilin

The No 21 bus can be caught just across the road from the railway station and goes to the Yangshuo bus terminal for 50 jiao. From here it is a Y5 minibus ride to Yangshuo, although more may be demanded for backpacks.

Harry & Heather Pearman – UK

Wuzhou

The ferry dock for boats between Guangzhou and Wuzhou has been relocated further east along Xijiang Lu and is now across the street from the Xinxi Hotel.

SICHUAN
Chongqing
Lonely Planet has had reports of touts in Chongqing trying to sell tickets for the trip to Yichang for up to 100% more than the regular boat price. The major complaint was they were shown a photo of a luxury boat, but the boat that they boarded was run-down and dirty.

GANSU
Xiahe
The lower bus station does not exist any more. Buses to Lanzhou and Tongren leave from the bus station next to the market area, not the upper bus station which is opposite the market.

TIBET & QINGHAI
Many of the high passes are frequently closed not only because of the monsoon landslides, but because some are temporarily closed due to higher than usual snow falls (between November and April). Try and find out what the conditions are at the passes before setting out in a hired vehicle, as there are no refunds for an abandoned journey due to blocked passes.

Visas & Permits
There are no separate visa or permit regulations for Tibet. A Chinese visa is sufficient. The visa application asks a number of questions, including places in China you plan to visit and entry/exit points. You can deviate from these without any problems – the most important point is not to write anything about planning to visit Tibet.

Dangers & Annoyances
The Chinese authorities are clamping down on westerners who distribute photos and tapes of the Dalai Lama. Several travellers have been caught and deported from China for this 'crime'.

INTERNET INFO
For the latest travel information, check out the Lonely Planet web site:
   http://www.lonelyplanet.com
This award-winning site contains updates, recent travellers' letters and a useful travellers' bulletin board.

Two other useful web sites that include Chinese news, culture, travel and other information are: China Multi List at
   http://china.ml.org/
   or China Home Page at
   http://solar.rtd.utk.edu/china/china.html.

ACKNOWLEDGMENTS
The information in this Update was compiled by Richard Nebesky from various sources, with help from one of the authors of this guide, Nicko Goncharoff, and reports by the following travellers: Thomas Apfel (D), Andrew Beale (Aus), Ing Uwe Hanke & Ina Mende (D), Susanne Kob (A), Erik Ling (S), Barrie McCormick (UK), Roger Michael Phillips, Noam Urbach (Isr) & Robert Walker (USA).

LONELY PLANET JOURNEYS

JOURNEYS is a unique collection of travel writing – published by the company that understands travel better than anyone else. It is a series for anyone who has ever experienced – or dreamed of – the magical moment when they encountered a strange culture or saw a place for the first time. They are tales to read while you're planning a trip, while you're on the road or while you're in an armchair, in front of a fire.

JOURNEYS books catch the spirit of a place, illuminate a culture, recount a crazy adventure, or introduce a fascinating way of life. They always entertain, and always enrich the experience of travel.

'Idiosyncratic, entertainingly diverse and unexpected . . . from an international writership'
– The Australian

'Books which offer a closer look at the people and culture of a destination, and enrich travel experiences'
– American Bookseller

LOST JAPAN
Alex Kerr

Originally written in Japanese, this passionate, vividly personal book draws on the author's experiences in Japan over thirty years. Alex Kerr takes us on a backstage tour, as he explores the ritualised world of Kabuki, retraces his initiation into Tokyo's boardrooms during the heady Bubble Years, tells how he stumbled on a hidden valley that became his home . . . and exposes the environmental and cultural destruction that is the other face of contemporary Japan.

Alex Kerr is an American who lives in Japan. He majored in Japanese studies at Yale, collects Japanese art and has founded his own art-dealing business. Simultaneously 'a foreigner' and 'an insider', Alex Kerr brings a unique perspective to writing about contemporary Japan.

Winner of Japan's 1994 Shincho Gakugei Literature Prize.

'This deeply personal witness to Japan's wilful loss of its traditional culture is at the same time an immensely valuable evaluation of just what that culture was' **– Donald Ritchie, Japan Times**

'Brilliantly combines essays and autobiography, chronicling Kerr's love affair with Japan' **– The Times**

LONELY PLANET TRAVEL ATLASES

Lonely Planet has long been famous for the number and quality of its guidebook maps. Now we've gone one step further and in conjunction with Steinhart Katzir Publishers produced a handy companion series: Lonely Planet travel atlases – maps of a country produced in book form.

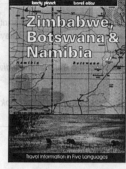

Unlike other maps, which look good but lead travellers astray, our travel atlases have been researched on the road by Lonely Planet's experienced team of writers. All details are carefully checked to ensure the atlas corresponds with the equivalent Lonely Planet guidebook.

The handy atlas format means no holes, wrinkles, torn sections or constant folding and unfolding. These atlases can survive long periods on the road, unlike cumbersome fold-out maps. The comprehensive index ensures easy reference.

- full-colour throughout
- maps researched and checked by Lonely Planet authors
- place names correspond with Lonely Planet guidebooks
  – no confusing spelling differences
- legend and travelling information in English, French, German, Japanese and Spanish
- size: 230 x 160 mm

Available now:
Chile; Egypt; India & Bangladesh; Israel & the Palestinian Territories; Jordan, Syria & Lebanon; Laos; Thailand; Vietnam; Zimbabwe, Botswana & Namibia

---

LONELY PLANET TV SERIES & VIDEOS

Lonely Planet travel guides have been brought to life on television screens around the world. Like our guides, the programmes are based on the joy of independent travel, and look honestly at some of the most exciting, picturesque and frustrating places in the world. Each show is presented by one of three travellers from Australia, England or the USA and combines an innovative mixture of video, Super-8 film, atmospheric soundscapes and original music.

Videos of each episode – containing additional footage not shown on television – are available from good book and video shops, but the availability of individual videos varies with regional screening schedules.

Video destinations include: Alaska; Australia (Southeast); Brazil; Ecuador & the Galápagos Islands; Indonesia; Israel & the Sinai Desert; Japan; La Ruta Maya (Yucatán, Guatemala & Belize); Morocco; North India (Varanasi to the Himalaya); Pacific Islands; Vietnam; Zimbabwe, Botswana & Namibia.

Coming soon: The Arctic (Norway & Finland); Baja California; Chile & Easter Island; China (Southeast); Costa Rica; East Africa (Tanzania & Zanzibar); Great Barrier Reef (Australia); Jamaica; Papua New Guinea; the Rockies (USA); Syria & Jordan; Turkey.

The Lonely Planet TV series is produced by:
Pilot Productions
Duke of Sussex Studios
44 Uxbridge St
London W8 7TG UK

Lonely Planet videos are distributed by:
IVN Communications Inc
2246 Camino Ramon
California 94583, USA

107 Power Road, Chiswick
London W4 5PL UK

Music from the TV series is available on CD & cassette.
For ordering information contact your nearest Lonely Planet office.

PLANET TALK

Lonely Planet's FREE quarterly newsletter

We love hearing from you and think you'd like to hear from us.

*When...*is the right time to see reindeer in Finland?
*Where...*can you hear the best palm-wine music in Ghana?
*How...*do you get from Asunción to Areguá by steam train?
*What...*is the best way to see India?

For the answer to these and many other questions read PLANET TALK.

Every issue is packed with up-to-date travel news and advice including:

- a letter from Lonely Planet co-founders Tony and Maureen Wheeler
- go behind the scenes on the road with a Lonely Planet author
- feature article on an important and topical travel issue
- a selection of recent letters from travellers
- details on forthcoming Lonely Planet promotions
- complete list of Lonely Planet products

To join our mailing list contact any Lonely Planet office.

Also available: Lonely Planet T-shirts. 100% heavyweight cotton..

LONELY PLANET ONLINE

Get the latest travel information before you leave or while you're on the road

Whether you've just begun planning your next trip, or you're chasing down specific info on currency regulations or visa requirements, check out the Lonely Planet World Wide Web site for up-to-the-minute travel information.

As well as travel profiles of your favourite destinations (including interactive maps and full-colour photos), you'll find current reports from our army of researchers and other travellers, updates on health and visas, travel advisories, and the ecological and political issues you need to be aware of as you travel.

There's an online travellers' forum (the Thorn Tree) where you can share your experiences of life on the road, meet travel companions and ask other travellers for their recommendations and advice. We also have plenty of links to other Web sites useful to independent travellers.

With tens of thousands of visitors a month, the Lonely Planet Web site is one of the most popular on the Internet and has won a number of awards including GNN's Best of the Net travel award.

http://www.lonelyplanet.com

LONELY PLANET PRODUCTS

Lonely Planet is known worldwide for publishing practical, reliable and no-nonsense travel information in our guides and on our web site. The Lonely Planet list covers just about every accessible part of the world. Currently there are eight series: *travel guides, shoestring guides, walking guides, city guides, phrasebooks, audio packs, travel atlases* and *Journeys* – a unique collection of travellers' tales.

EUROPE

Austria • Baltic States & Kaliningrad • Baltic States phrasebook • Britain • Central Europe on a shoestring • Central Europe phrasebook • Czech & Slovak Republics • Denmark • Dublin city guide • Eastern Europe on a shoestring • Eastern Europe phrasebook • Finland • France • Greece • Greek phrasebook • Hungary • Iceland, Greenland & the Faroe Islands • Ireland • Italy • Mediterranean Europe on a shoestring • Mediterranean Europe phrasebook • Paris city guide • Poland • Prague city guide • Russia, Ukraine & Belarus • Russian phrasebook • Scandinavian & Baltic Europe on a shoestring • Scandinavian Europe phrasebook • Slovenia • St Petersburg city guide • Switzerland • Trekking in Greece • Trekking in Spain • Ukrainian phrasebook • Vienna city guide • Walking in Switzerland • Western Europe on a shoestring • Western Europe phrasebook

NORTH AMERICA

Alaska • Backpacking in Alaska • Baja California • California & Nevada • Canada • Florida • Hawaii • Honolulu city guide • Los Angeles city guide • Mexico • Miami city guide • New England • New Orleans city guide • Pacific Northwest USA • Rocky Mountain States • San Francisco city guide • Southwest USA • USA phrasebook

CENTRAL AMERICA & THE CARIBBEAN

Bermuda • Central America on a shoestring • Costa Rica • Cuba • Eastern Caribbean • Guatemala, Belize & Yucatán: La Ruta Maya • Jamaica

SOUTH AMERICA

Argentina, Uruguay & Paraguay • Bolivia • Brazil • Brazilian phrasebook • Buenos Aires city guide • Chile & Easter Island • Chile & Easter Island travel atlas • Colombia • Ecuador & the Galápagos Islands • Latin American Spanish phrasebook • Peru • Quechua phrasebook • Rio de Janeiro city guide • South America on a shoestring • Trekking in the Patagonian Andes • Venezuela

Travel Literature: Full Circle: A South American Journey

ANTARCTICA

Antarctica

ISLANDS OF THE INDIAN OCEAN

Madagascar & Comoros • Maldives & Islands of the East Indian Ocean • Mauritius, Réunion & Seychelles

AFRICA

Arabic (Moroccan) phrasebook • Africa on a shoestring • Cape Town city guide • Central Africa • East Africa • Egypt • Egypt travel atlas • Ethiopian (Amharic) phrasebook • Kenya • Morocco • North Africa • South Africa, Lesotho & Swaziland • Swahili phrasebook • Trekking in East Africa • West Africa • Zimbabwe, Botswana & Namibia • Zimbabwe, Botswana & Namibia travel atlas

ALSO AVAILABLE:

Travel with Children • Traveller's Tales

MAIL ORDER

Lonely Planet products are distributed worldwide. They are also available by mail order from Lonely Planet, so if you have difficulty finding a title please write to us. North American and South American residents should write to Embarcadero West, 155 Filbert St, Suite 251, Oakland CA 94607, USA; European and African residents should write to 10 Barley Mow Passage, Chiswick, London W4 4PH; and residents of other countries to PO Box 617, Hawthorn, Victoria 3122, Australia.

NORTH-EAST ASIA

Beijing city guide • Cantonese phrasebook • China • Hong Kong, Macau & Guangzhou • Hong Kong city guide • Japan • Japanese phrasebook • Japanese audio pack • Korea • Korean phrasebook • Mandarin phrasebook • Mongolia • Mongolian phrasebook • North-East Asia on a shoestring • Seoul city guide • Taiwan • Tibet • Tibet phrasebook • Tokyo city guide

Travel Literature: Lost Japan

INDIAN SUBCONTINENT

Bangladesh • Bengali phrasebook • Delhi city guide • Hindi/Urdu phrasebook • India • India & Bangladesh travel atlas • Indian Himalaya • Karakoram Highway • Nepal • Nepali phrasebook • Pakistan • Rajasthan • Sri Lanka • Sri Lanka phrasebook • Trekking in the Indian Himalaya • Trekking in the Karakoram & Hindukush • Trekking in the Nepal Himalaya

Travel Literature: In Rajasthan • Shopping for Buddhas

SOUTH-EAST ASIA

Bali & Lombok • Bangkok city guide • Burmese phrasebook • Cambodia • Ho Chi Minh city guide • Indonesia • Indonesian phrasebook • Indonesian audio pack • Jakarta city guide • Java • Laos • Lao phrasebook • Laos travel atlas • Malay phrasebook • Malaysia, Singapore & Brunei • Myanmar (Burma) • Philippines • Pilipino phrasebook • Singapore city guide • South-East Asia on a shoestring • South-East Asia phrasebook • Thailand • Thailand travel atlas • Thai phrasebook • Thai audio pack • Thai Hill Tribes phrasebook • Vietnam • Vietnamese phrasebook • Vietnam travel atlas

AUSTRALIA & THE PACIFIC

Australia • Australian phrasebook • Bushwalking in Australia • Bushwalking in Papua New Guinea • Fiji • Fijian phrasebook • Islands of Australia's Great Barrier Reef • Melbourne city guide • Micronesia • New Caledonia • New South Wales & the ACT • New Zealand • Northern Territory • Outback Australia • Papua New Guinea • Papua New Guinea phrasebook • Queensland • Rarotonga & the Cook Islands • Samoa • Solomon Islands • South Australia • Sydney city guide • Tahiti & French Polynesia • Tasmania • Tonga • Tramping in New Zealand • Vanuatu • Victoria • Western Australia

Travel Literature: Islands in the Clouds • Sean & David's Long Drive

MIDDLE EAST & CENTRAL ASIA

Arab Gulf States • Arabic (Egyptian) phrasebook • Central Asia • Iran • Israel & the Palestinian Territories • Israel & the Palestinian Territories travel atlas • Istanbul city guide • Jerusalem city guide • Jordan & Syria • Jordan, Syria & Lebanon travel atlas • Middle East • Turkey • Turkish phrasebook • Trekking in Turkey • Yemen

Travel Literature: The Gates of Damascus • Kingdom of the Film Stars: Journey into Jordan

THE LONELY PLANET STORY

Lonely Planet published its first book in 1973 in response to the numerous 'How did you do it?' questions Maureen and Tony Wheeler were asked after driving, bussing, hitching, sailing and railing their way from England to Australia.

Written at a kitchen table and hand collated, trimmed and stapled, *Across Asia on the Cheap* became an instant local bestseller, inspiring thoughts of another book.

Eighteen months in South-East Asia resulted in their second guide, *South-East Asia on a shoestring*, which they put together in a backstreet Chinese hotel in Singapore in 1975. The 'yellow bible', as it quickly became known to backpackers around the world, soon became *the* guide to the region. It has sold well over half a million copies and is now in its 8th edition, still retaining its familiar yellow cover.

Today there are over 180 titles, including travel guides, walking guides, language kits & phrasebooks, travel atlases and travel literature. The company is one of the largest travel publishers in the world. Although Lonely Planet initially specialised in guides to Asia, we now cover most regions of the world, including the Pacific, North America, South America, Africa, the Middle East and Europe.

The emphasis continues to be on travel for independent travellers. Tony and Maureen still travel for several months of each year and play an active part in the writing, updating and quality control of Lonely Planet's guides.

They have been joined by over 70 authors and 170 staff at our offices in Melbourne (Australia), Oakland (USA), London (UK) and Paris (France). Travellers themselves also make a valuable contribution to the guides through the feedback we receive in thousands of letters each year.

The people at Lonely Planet strongly believe that travellers can make a positive contribution to the countries they visit, both through their appreciation of the countries' culture, wildlife and natural features, and through the money they spend. In addition, the company makes a direct contribution to the countries and regions it covers. Since 1986 a percentage of the income from each book has been donated to ventures such as famine relief in Africa; aid projects in India; agricultural projects in Central America; Greenpeace's efforts to halt French nuclear testing in the Pacific; and Amnesty International.

'I hope we send the people out with the right attitude about travel. You realise when you travel that there are so many different perspectives about the world, so we hope these books will make people more interested in what they see. These are guidebooks, but you can't really guide people. All you can do is point them in the right direction.'

– Tony Wheeler

LONELY PLANET PUBLICATIONS

Australia
PO Box 617, Hawthorn 3122, Victoria
tel: (03) 9819 1877 fax: (03) 9819 6459
e-mail: talk2us@lonelyplanet.com.au

USA
Embarcadero West, 155 Filbert St, Suite 251,
Oakland, CA 94607
tel: (510) 893 8555 TOLL FREE: 800 275-8555
fax: (510) 893 8563
e-mail: info@lonelyplanet.com

UK
10 Barley Mow Passage, Chiswick,
London W4 4PH
tel: (0181) 742 3161 fax: (0181) 742 2772
e-mail: 100413.3551@compuserve.com

France:
71 bis rue du Cardinal Lemoine, 75005 Paris
tel: 1 44 32 06 20 fax: 1 46 34 72 55
e-mail: 100560.415@compuserve.com

World Wide Web: http://www.lonelyplanet.com